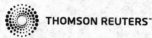

West's
MINNESOTA
PROBATE LAW

SELECTED MINNESOTA STATUTES
AND COURT RULES RELATING
TO PROBATE LAW

Combined Index

As amended through the 2008 Regular Session

THOMSON
™
WEST

Mat#40616480

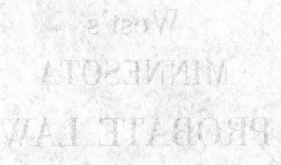

© 2008 Thomson Reuters/West

ISBN 978–0–314–98300–8

PREFACE

This pamphlet contains selected Minnesota statutes and court rules relating to probate law. The chapters and rules included are:

The text of all statutes is complete through the 2008 Regular Session of the 85th Legislature. The text of the court rules is complete with changes received through November 1, 2008.

A detailed descriptive word Index covering all statutes and rules included in this pamphlet is provided for convenient reference.

Comprehensive coverage of the judicial constructions and interpretations of the statutes and rules relating to family law, together with cross references, references to law review commentaries discussing particular provisions, and other editorial features, is provided in the volumes of Minnesota Statutes Annotated or on Westlaw in MN–ST–ANN.

THE PUBLISHER

December, 2008

*

RELATED PRODUCTS FROM WEST

MINNESOTA PRACTICE SERIES™

Civil Rules Annotated
David F. Herr and Roger S. Haydock

Civil Practice Forms
Roger S. Haydock, David F. Herr and Sonja Dunnwald Peterson

Appellate Rules Annotated
Eric J. Magnuson and David F. Herr

General Rules of Practice Annotated
David F. Herr

Jury Instruction Guides—Civil
Minnesota District Judges Association
Committee on Jury Instruction Guides—Civil

Methods of Practice: Civil Advocacy
Roger S. Haydock and Peter B. Knapp

Methods of Practice
Steven J. Kirsch

Criminal Law and Procedure
Henry W. McCarr and Jack S. Nordby

Jury Instruction Guides—Criminal
Minnesota District Judges Association
Committee on Jury Instruction Guides—Criminal

Evidence
Peter N. Thompson

Courtroom Handbook of Minnesota Evidence
Peter N. Thompson and David F. Herr

Juvenile Law and Practice
Robert Scott and John O. Sonsteng

Family Law
Martin L. Swaden and Linda A. Olup

Employment Law and Practice
Stephen F. Befort

Minnesota Employment Laws
Karen G. Schanfield

Corporation Law and Practice
John H. Matheson and Phillip S. Garon

Business Law Deskbook—Formation and Operation of Businesses and Advanced Topics in Business Law
Brent A. Olson

RELATED PRODUCTS

Business Regulation in Minnesota—State and Federal
Brent A. Olson

Administrative Practice and Procedure
William J. Keppel

Insurance Law and Practice
Britton D. Weimer, Clarence E. Hagglund and Andrew F. Whitman

Insurance Statutes
Britton D. Weimer, Clarence E. Hagglund and Andrew F. Whitman

Trial Handbook for Minnesota Lawyers
Ronald I. Meshbesher

Minnesota Probate Deskbook
Susan J. Link and John W. Provo

Real Estate Law
Eileen M. Roberts

Minnesota Real Estate Laws
Eileen M. Roberts

Collections Handbook
Allan Zlimen

Products Liability Law
Michael K. Steenson, J. David Prince and Sarah L. Brew

Elements of an Action
David F. Herr

Motions in Limine
Lisa McGuire and David N. Finley

OTHER WEST PRODUCTS

Minnesota Statutes Annotated

Minnesota Rules of Court—State and Federal

Minnesota Reporter

Minnesota Digest

Westlaw

WestCheck.com™

West CD–ROM Libraries™

VI

RELATED PRODUCTS

ANNUAL PAMPHLETS

Minnesota Civil Procedure Law

Minnesota Corporation, Limited Liability Company, and Partnership Laws

Minnesota Criminal Law Handbook

Minnesota Family Law

Minnesota Probate Law

Rules Governing Workers' Compensation Practice & Procedure

To order any of these Minnesota practice tools, call
your West Representative or **1–800–328–9352.**

NEED RESEARCH HELP?

You can get quality research results with free help—call the West Reference
Attorneys when you have questions concerning Westlaw or West
Publications at **1–800–REF–ATTY (1–800–733–2889).**

INTERNET ACCESS

Contact the West Editorial Department directly with your questions
and suggestions by e-mail at west.editor@thomson.com. Visit
West's home page at west.thomson.com.

*

WESTLAW ELECTRONIC RESEARCH GUIDE

Westlaw—Expanding the Reach of Your Library

Westlaw is West's online legal research service. With Westlaw, you experience the same quality and integrity that you have come to expect from West books, plus quick, easy access to West's vast collection of statutes, case law materials, public records, and other legal resources, in addition to current news articles and business information. For the most current and comprehensive legal research, combine the strengths of West books and Westlaw.

When you research with westlaw.com you get the convenience of the Internet combined with comprehensive and accurate Westlaw content, including exclusive editorial enhancements, plus features found only in westlaw.com such as Results Plus™ or StatutesPlus.™

Accessing Databases Using the Westlaw Directory

The Westlaw Directory lists all databases on Westlaw and contains links to detailed information relating to the content of each database. Click Directory on the westlaw.com toolbar. There are several ways to access a database even when you don't know the database identifier. Browse a directory view. Scan the directory. Type all or part of a database name in the Search these Databases box. The Find a Database Wizard can help you select relevant databases for your search. You can access up to ten databases at one time for user-defined multibase searching.

Retrieving a Specific Document

To retrieve a specific document by citation or title on westlaw.com click **Find&Print** on the toolbar to display the Find a Document page. If you are unsure of the correct citation format, type the publication abbreviation, e.g., **xx-st** (where xx is a state's two-letter postal abbreviation), in the Find this document by citation box and click **Go** to display a fill-in-the-blank template. To retrieve a specific case when you know one or more parties' names, click **Find a Case by Party Name**.

KeyCite®

KeyCite, the citation research service on Westlaw, makes it easy to trace the history of your case, statute, administrative decision or regulation to determine if there are recent updates, and to find other documents that cite your document. KeyCite will also find pending legislation relating to federal or state statutes. Access the powerful features of KeyCite from the westlaw.com toolbar, the **Links** tab, or KeyCite flags in a document display. KeyCite's red and yellow warning flags tell you at a glance whether your document has negative history. Depth-of-treatment stars help you focus on the most important citing references.

WESTLAW GUIDE

KeyCite Alert allows you to monitor the status of your case, statute or rule, and automatically sends you updates at the frequency you specify.

ResultsPlus™

ResultsPlus is a Westlaw technology that automatically suggests additional information related to your search. The suggested materials are accessible by a set of links that appear to the right of your westlaw.com search results:

- Go directly to relevant ALR® articles and Am Jur® annotations.

- Find on-point resources by key number.

- See information from related treatises and law reviews.

StatutesPlus™

When you access a statutes database in westlaw.com you are brought to a powerful Search Center which collects, on one toolbar, the tools that are most useful for fast, efficient retrieval of statutes documents:

- Have a few key terms? Click **Statutes Index**.

- Know the common name? Click **Popular Name Table**.

- Familiar with the subject matter? Click **Table of Contents**.

- Have a citation or section number? Click **Find by Citation**.

- Interested in topical surveys providing citations across
  multiple state statutes? Click **50 State Surveys**.

- Or, simply search with **Natural Language** or **Terms and
  Connectors.**

When you access a statutes section, click on the **Links** tab for all relevant links for the current document that will also include a KeyCite section with a description of the KeyCite status flag. Depending on your document, links may also include administrative, bill text, and other sources that were previously only available by accessing and searching other databases.

Additional Information

Westlaw is available on the Web at www.westlaw.com.

For search assistance, call the West Reference Attorneys at
1–800–REF–ATTY (1–800–733–2889).

For technical assistance, call West Customer Technical Support at
1–800–WESTLAW (1–800–937–8529).

TABLE OF CONTENTS

Combined Index
(Page I–1)
*

Chapter 55

SAFE DEPOSIT COMPANIES

For complete statutory history see Minnesota Statutes Annotated.

55.01. Definitions

Subdivision 1. Scope. Unless the language or context clearly indicates that a different meaning is intended, the following words, terms, and phrases shall, for the purposes of the laws of this state, be given the meanings subjoined to them.

Subd. 2. Safe deposit box. The words "safe deposit box" mean any box, safe, safe deposit box, receptacle, or any part or parts thereof, and any space in a vault, which may be used for the safekeeping and storage of valuable personal property.

Subd. 3. Valuable personal property. The words "valuable personal property" mean jewelry, plate, money, specie, bullion, stocks, bonds, valuable papers, or other personal property of value.

Subd. 4. Person. "Person" means an individual, partnership, unincorporated association or a corporation. "It" includes "he," "she," and "they."

Subd. 5. Safe deposit company. "Safe deposit company" means any person who lets out or rents, as lessor, for hire, safe deposit boxes, or space therein.

Amended by Laws 1945, c. 114, § 1; Laws 1986, c. 444.

1

55.02. Powers

Any safe deposit company which complies with the provisions of this chapter shall have power:

(1) to let out or rent as lessor, for hire, safe deposit boxes, upon such terms and for such compensation as may be agreed upon by such safe deposit company and the lessee; and

(2) to take and receive valuable personal property for safekeeping and storage, as bailee, for hire, upon such terms and for such compensation as may be agreed upon by such safe deposit company and the bailor. No such safe deposit company shall make any loans or advances upon any valuable personal property so left with it for safekeeping and storage.

Amended by Laws 1945, c. 114, § 2.

55.03. License required

Except as in this chapter otherwise provided, no person shall exercise the powers granted safe deposit companies by section 55.02 unless licensed so to do.

Amended by Laws 1945, c. 114, § 3.

55.04. Licenses

Subdivision 1. Place of business. The commissioner of commerce may license any person to engage in the business of a safe deposit company and to exercise the powers set forth in section 55.02, which license shall designate the place of business of the safe deposit company, which place of business shall be located upon the premises in which the safe deposit boxes are located.

Subd. 2. Application for license. Application for license shall be in writing, under oath, and in the form prescribed by the commissioner of commerce, and contain the name and address, both of the residence and place of business, of the applicant, and if the applicant is a partnership or unincorporated association, of every member thereof, and if a corporation, of each officer and director thereof; also the county and municipality, with street and number, if any, where the business is to be conducted; and further information the commissioner of commerce requires. The applicant at the time of making application shall pay to the commissioner the sum of $250 as a fee for investigating the application, and the additional sum of $150 as an annual license fee for a period terminating on the last day of the current calendar year.

Subd. 3. Business at stated place only. It shall be unlawful for any safe deposit company holding such license to engage in this business upon any premises or in any building other than that designated in the license.

Amended by Laws 1945, c. 114, § 4; Laws 1982, c. 473, § 22, eff. March 19, 1982; Laws 1983, c. 289, § 114, subd. 1, eff. July 1, 1983; Laws 1984, c. 655, art. 1, § 92; Laws 1999, c. 151, § 31, eff. July 1, 1999.

55.041. Annual license fee

Every licensee shall, on or before the 20th day of each December, pay to the commissioner the sum of $150 as an annual license fee for the next succeeding calendar year.

Laws 1982, c. 473, § 23, eff. March 19, 1982.

55.05. Bonds

Before a license is issued, the applicant shall execute and file with the commissioner of commerce a bond to the state of Minnesota in the penal sum of not less than $5,000 nor more than $1,000,000, as fixed by the commissioner of commerce. The bond must be issued by a corporate surety in good standing authorized to do business in this state and must secure the faithful performance of the safe deposit company's contracts of rental or deposit and protect persons doing business with it from the results of its negligence. The bond must enure to the benefit of any one damaged by a breach of a rental or deposit contract or negligence. Each bond, or a substitute like bond, approved by the commissioner of commerce shall be kept on file and maintained in effect by the safe deposit company so long as that company continues to do business. Failure to maintain the bond shall be grounds for revocation of the safe deposit company's license by the commissioner of commerce. No safe deposit company shall lease a safe deposit box or receive valuable personal property for safekeeping or storage until the bond is on file and in force.

Amended by Laws 1945, c. 114, § 5; Laws 1982, c. 473, § 24, eff. March 19, 1982; Laws 1983, c. 289, § 114, subd. 1, eff. July 1, 1983; Laws 1984, c. 655, art. 1, § 92.

55.06. Business not to be conducted without license

Subdivision 1. Prohibition. No person except a bank, a savings bank, a credit union, a savings association, industrial loan and thrift company issuing investment certificates of indebtedness, or a trust company may let out or rent as lessor, for hire, safe deposit boxes or take or receive valuable personal property for safekeeping and storage, as bailee, for hire, without procuring a license and giving a bond, as required by this chapter, except as otherwise authorized by law so to do.

Subd. 2. Civil penalty. Every person who shall violate the provisions of subdivision 1 or any other provision of this chapter shall forfeit to the state the sum of not to exceed $100 for each day the violation shall continue, after written notice by the commissioner of commerce to discontinue such violation, to be recovered in a civil action brought by the attorney general in the name of the state at the request of the commissioner of commerce, and may be enjoined by any court having jurisdiction from any further violation, in an equitable action brought by the attorney general in the name of the state for that purpose.

Amended by Laws 1945, c. 114, § 6; Laws 1977, c. 84, § 2, eff. May 12, 1977; Laws 1980, c. 524, § 6, eff. April 8, 1980; Laws 1983, c. 289, § 114, subd. 1, eff. July 1, 1983; Laws 1984, c. 655, art. 1, § 92; Laws 1997, c. 157, § 47, eff. May 17, 1997.

55.07. Deposits, how kept; accounts kept

Subdivision 1. Vault approved by commissioner. No person shall carry on the business of a safe deposit company as authorized by section 55.02 unless the safe deposit boxes let out or rented by it and the valuable personal property taken and received by it for safekeeping and storage are kept in a fireproof vault approved by the commissioner of commerce.

Subd. 2. Accounts. Every licensed safe deposit company shall keep books in which shall be entered an account of all its transactions relative to the letting, renting, or leasing of its safe deposit boxes, and to the receipt of valuable personal property for safekeeping or storage.

Amended by Laws 1945, c. 114, § 7; Laws 1983, c. 289, § 114, subd. 1, eff. July 1, 1983; Laws 1984, c. 655, art. 1, § 92.

55.08. License posted

Immediately upon the receipt of the license issued by the commissioner of commerce, pursuant to the provisions of this chapter, the licensee named therein shall cause the license to be posted and conspicuously displayed in the place of business for which it is issued, so that all persons visiting the place of business may readily see the same. It shall be unlawful for any safe deposit company holding a license to post the license, or permit the license to be posted, upon premises other than that designated therein, or knowingly deface or destroy any such license.

Amended by Laws 1945, c. 114, § 8; Laws 1983, c. 289, § 114, subd. 1, eff. July 1, 1983; Laws 1984, c. 655, art. 1, § 92.

55.09. Repealed by Laws 1984, c. 543, § 69

Historical and Statutory Notes

Laws 1984, c. 543, § 70, provided that this section was repealed effective January 1, 1985, except as the section applied to independent school districts, with respect to which it was repealed effective July 1, 1985.

55.095. Duties of commissioner of commerce

Every safe deposit company is at all times under the supervision and subject to the control of the commissioner of commerce. The commissioner may at any time examine a licensed safe deposit company to ascertain whether the safe deposit company is complying with the provisions of this chapter and whether its methods and systems are in accordance with law and designed to protect the property of persons doing business with it. For each examination the commissioner shall charge the actual expenses of examination. If the commissioner of commerce determines that the safe deposit company is violating the provisions of this chapter, any law of the state, or has engaged or the commissioner has reason to believe that a licensee is about to engage in an unlawful, unsafe, or unsound practice in the conduct of its business, the commissioner may proceed pursuant to sections 46.24 to 46.33 or serve notice on the safe deposit company of intention to revoke the license, stating in general the grounds therefor and giving reasonable opportunity to be heard. If for a period of 15 days after the notice, the violation continues, the commissioner of commerce may revoke the license and take possession of the business and property of the safe deposit company and maintain possession until the time the commissioner permits it to continue business, or its affairs are finally liquidated. The liquidation must proceed pursuant to sections 49.04 to 49.32.

Laws 1945, c. 114, § 10. Amended by Laws 1977, c. 347, § 14; Laws 1980, c. 524, § 7, eff. April 8, 1980; Laws 1983, c. 289, § 114, subd. 1, eff. July 1, 1983; Laws 1984, c. 655, art. 1, § 92; Laws 1985, 1st Sp., c. 13, § 190; Laws 1986, c. 444; Laws 1987, c. 349, art. 2, § 1, eff. July 1, 1987.

55.10. Liability; exemptions

Subdivision 1. Permitting access, removal, or delivery. When a safe deposit box shall have been hired from any licensed safe deposit company in the name of two or more persons, including husband and wife, with the right of access being given to either, or with access to either or the survivor or survivors of the person, or property is held for safekeeping by any licensed safe deposit company for two or more persons, including husband and wife, with the right of delivery being given to either, or with the right of delivery to either of the survivor or survivors of these persons, any one or more of these persons, whether the other or others be living or not, shall have the right of access to the safe deposit box and the right to remove all, or any part, of the contents thereof, or to have delivered to all or any one of them, or any part of the valuable personal property so held for safekeeping; and, in case of this access, removal, or delivery, the safe deposit company shall be exempt from any liability for permitting the access, removal, or delivery.

Subd. 2. Repealed by Laws 1985, 1st Sp., c. 14, art. 13, § 14.

Subd. 3. Access granted to agents, government officers. No safe deposit company shall be liable to any person by reason of having permitted access to a safe deposit box to an authorized agent of the tenant of such box, after the death of such tenant, until actual notice of such death has been received by the safe deposit company, nor shall any such company be liable to any person because of having granted access to any safe deposit box to any state or federal officer acting under authority of an order of any court of general jurisdiction.

Subd. 4. Will searches, burial documents procurement, and inventory of contents. (a) Upon being furnished with satisfactory proof of death of a sole lessee or the last surviving co-lessee of a safe deposit box, an employee of the safe deposit company shall open the box and examine the contents in the presence of an individual who appears in person and furnishes an affidavit stating that the individual believes:

(1) the box may contain the will or deed to a burial lot or a document containing instructions for the burial of the lessee or that the box may contain property belonging to the estate of the lessee; and

(2) the individual is an interested person as defined in this section and wishes to open the box for any one or more of the following purposes:

(i) to conduct a will search;

(ii) to obtain a document required to facilitate the lessee's wishes regarding body, funeral, or burial arrangements; or

(iii) to obtain an inventory of the contents of the box.

(b) The safe deposit company may not open the box under this section if it has received a copy of letters of office of the representative of the deceased lessee's estate or other applicable court order.

(c) The safe deposit company need not open the box if:

(1) the box has previously been opened under this section for the same purpose;

(2) the safe deposit company has received notice of a written or oral objection from any person or has reason to believe that there would be an objection; or

(3) the lessee's key or combination is not available.

(d) For purposes of this section, the term "interested person" means any of the following:

(1) a person named as personal representative in a purported will of the lessee;

(2) a person who immediately prior to the death of the lessee had the right of access to the box as a deputy;

(3) the surviving spouse of the lessee;

(4) a devisee of the lessee;

(5) an heir of the lessee;

(6) a person designated by the lessee in a writing acceptable to the safe deposit company which is filed with the safe deposit company before death; or

(7) a state or county agency with a claim authorized by section 256B.15.

(e) For purposes of this section, the term "will" includes a will or a codicil.

(f) If the box is opened for the purpose of conducting a will search, the safe deposit company shall remove any document that appears to be a will and make a true and correct machine copy thereof, replace the copy in the box, and then deliver the original thereof to the clerk of court for the county in which the lessee resided immediately before the lessee's death, if known to the safe deposit company, otherwise to the clerk of the court for the county in which the safe deposit box is located. The will must be personally delivered or sent by registered mail. If the interested person so requests, any deed to burial lot or document containing instructions for the burial of the lessee may be copied by the safe deposit box company and the copy or copies thereof delivered to the interested person.

(g) If the box is opened for the purpose of obtaining a document required to facilitate the lessee's wishes regarding the body, funeral, or burial arrangements, any such document may be removed from the box and delivered to the interested person with a true and correct machine copy retained in the box. If the safe deposit box company discovers a document that appears to be a will, the safe deposit company shall act in accordance with paragraph (f).

(h) If the box is opened for the purpose of obtaining an inventory of the contents of the box, the employee of the safe deposit company shall make, or cause to be made, an inventory of the contents of the box, to which the employee and the interested person shall attest under penalty of perjury to be correct and complete. Within ten days of opening the box pursuant to this subdivision, the safe deposit company shall deliver the original inventory of the contents to the court administrator for the county in which the lessee resided immediately before the lessee's death, if known to the safe deposit company, otherwise to the court administrator for the county in which the safe deposit box is located. The inventory must be personally delivered or sent by registered mail. If the interested person so requests, the safe deposit company shall make a true and correct copy of any document in the box, and of the completed inventory form, and deliver that copy to the interested person. If the contents of the box include a document that appears to be a will, the safe deposit company shall act in accordance with paragraph (f).

(i) If a box opened for the purpose of conducting an inventory, will search, or burial document search is completely empty, the safe deposit company need not follow the procedures above. Instead, the employee of the safe deposit company can complete an inventory of the box contents indicating the fact that the box contained nothing. The form must be signed by the employee and the interested person. If the interested person so requests, the safe deposit company may provide a copy of the completed inventory form to the interested person. The interested person shall then complete the documentation needed by the safe deposit company to surrender the empty box. If another interested person inquires about the box after it has been surrendered, the safe deposit company may state that the deceased renter had previously rented the box and that the box was surrendered because it was empty.

(j) The safe deposit company need not ascertain the truth of any statement in the affidavit required to be furnished under this subdivision and when acting in reliance upon an affidavit, it is discharged as if it dealt with the personal representative of the lessee. The safe deposit company is not responsible for the adequacy of the description of any property included in an inventory of the contents of a safe deposit box, nor for conversion of the property in connection with actions performed under this subdivision, except for conversion by intentional acts of the company or its employees, directors, officers, or agents. If the safe deposit company is not satisfied that the requirements of this subdivision have been met, it may decline to open the box.

(k) No contents of a box other than a will and a document required to facilitate the lessee's wishes regarding body, funeral, or burial arrangements may be removed pursuant to this subdivision. The entire contents of the box, however, may be removed pursuant to section 524.3–1201.

Amended by Laws 1945, c. 114, § 11; Laws 1986, c. 444; Laws 1986, 1st Sp., c. 3, art. 1, § 82; Laws 1988, c. 581, § 1, eff. April 22, 1988; Laws 1995, c. 130, § 1; Laws 1996, c. 414, art. 1, § 26, eff. April 3, 1996; Laws 1997, c. 217, art. 2, § 1; Laws 2005, c. 118, § 7.

Historical and Statutory Notes

Laws 1985, 1st Sp., c. 14, art. 13, § 15, provides that the repeal of subd. 2 is effective for estates of persons dying after December 31, 1985.

Laws 1995, c. 130, § 22, provides in part that chapter 130, in part amending subd. 4 of this section, is effective January 1, 1996, and that §§ 1, 14, 17, 18, 19, and 20 apply to all decedents' estates, whenever the decedent died.

55.11. Not charged with notice of fiduciary relation

No such safe deposit company shall be obliged to ascertain or take notice of any trust or fiduciary relationship which the tenant of a safe deposit box may bear to the contents thereof, but shall be presumed to deal with the tenant of a box in an individual and not in a representative capacity, and shall be protected if it grants access to a box to the lessee thereof, according to the terms of the contract of rental.

Amended by Laws 1945, c. 114, § 12; Laws 1986, c. 444.

55.12. Liability may be limited

Any licensed safe deposit company may, in any lease or contract governing or regulating the use of any safe deposit box to or by any customer or customers, limit its liability as such lessor or bailee in the following respects:

(1) limit its total liability for any loss by negligence to such maximum amount as may be stipulated; and

(2) stipulate that it shall in no event be liable for loss of such valuable property as may be excepted against in such lease or contract.

Amended by Laws 1945, c. 114, § 13.

55.13. Repealed by Laws 1987, c. 349, art. 1, § 40

55.14. Repealed by Laws 1977, c. 137, § 13, eff. July 1, 1977

55.15. Application

This chapter shall not be held or construed as limiting, restricting, or in any way affecting the operation or management of safe deposit boxes or vaults, or a safe deposit business, by any savings bank, bank, credit union, or trust company. If any bank, savings bank, credit union, or trust company elects to transact the business of a safe deposit company under the provisions of this chapter, it shall so notify the commissioner of commerce and thereafter the provisions of sections 55.02 and 55.10 to 55.12 shall apply to such safe deposit business and said bank, savings bank, credit union, or trust company shall have the benefit thereof. The provisions of sections 55.03 to 55.08 and the provisions of section 55.095 shall not apply to a bank, savings bank, credit union, or trust company carrying on the business of a safe deposit company.

Amended by Laws 1945, c. 114, § 16; Laws 1981, 1st Sp., c. 4, art. 1, § 48; Laws 1983, c. 289, § 114, subd. 1, eff. July 1, 1983; Laws 1984, c. 655, art. 1, § 92; Laws 1987, c. 349, art. 1, § 35; Laws 2004, c. 174, § 1.

Chapter 144

DEPARTMENT OF HEALTH

Section
144.221. Death registration.

For complete statutory history see Minnesota Statutes Annotated.

144.221. Death registration

Subdivision 1. When and where to file. A death record for each death which occurs in the state shall be filed with the state registrar within five days after death and prior to final disposition.

Subd. 2. Rules governing death registration. The commissioner of health shall establish in rule an orderly mechanism for the registration of deaths including at least a designation for who must file the death record, a procedure for the registration of deaths in moving conveyances, and provision to include cause and certification of death and assurance of registration prior to final disposition.

Subd. 3. When no body is found. When circumstances suggest that a death has occurred although a dead body cannot be produced to confirm the fact of death, a death record shall not be registered until a court has adjudicated the fact of death.

Laws 1978, c. 699, § 10, eff. March 29, 1978. Amended by Laws 2001, 1st Sp., c. 9, art. 15, §§ 18, 19, 32; Laws 2005, c. 106, § 56.

Historical and Statutory Notes

Laws 2002, c. 379, art. 1, § 113, provides:

"2001 First Special Session Senate File No. 4, as passed by the senate and the house of representatives on Friday, June 29, 2001, and subsequently published as Laws 2001, First Special Session chapter 9, is reenacted. Its provisions are effective on the dates originally provided in the bill."

Chapter 145B

LIVING WILL

For complete statutory history see Minnesota Statutes Annotated.

145B.01. Citation

This chapter may be cited as the "Minnesota Living Will Act."

Laws 1989, c. 3, § 1. Amended by Laws 1991, c. 148, § 1.

145B.011. Application of chapter

This chapter applies only to living wills executed before August 1, 1998. If a document purporting to be a living will is executed on or after August 1, 1998, its legal sufficiency, interpretation, and enforcement must be determined under the provisions of chapter 145C in effect on the date of its execution.

Laws 1998, c. 399, § 2, eff. Aug. 1, 1998.

Historical and Statutory Notes

Laws 1998, c. 399, § 38, provides:

"A document executed prior to August 1, 1998, that purports to be a living will under Minnesota Statutes, chapter 145B, a durable power of attorney for health care under Minnesota Statutes, chapter 145C, or a declaration regarding intrusive mental health treatment un-

der Minnesota Statutes, section 253B.03, subdivision 6a, is valid if the document:

"(1) complied with the law in effect on the date it was executed; or

"(2) complies with the requirements of Minnesota Statutes, section 145C.03.

"If the document complied with the law in effect on the date it was executed but does not also comply with the requirements of Minnesota Statutes, section 145C.03, it shall be given effect in accordance with the laws in effect on the date it was executed, unless the document provides otherwise.

"Nothing in sections 1 to 38 impairs the evidentiary effect under common law or reasonable medical practice with respect to other written or oral expressions of an individual's desires regarding health care."

145B.02. Definitions

Subdivision 1. Applicability. The definitions in this section apply to this chapter.

Subd. 2. Living will. "Living will" means a writing made according to section 145B.03.

Subd. 3. Health care. "Health care" means care, treatment, services, or procedures to maintain, diagnose, or treat an individual's physical condition when the individual is in a terminal condition.

Subd. 4. Health care decision. "Health care decision" means a decision to begin, continue, increase, limit, discontinue, or not begin any health care.

Subd. 5. Health care facility. "Health care facility" means a hospital or other entity licensed under sections 144.50 to 144.58; a nursing home licensed to serve adults under section 144A.02; or a home care provider licensed under sections 144A.43 to 144A.47.

Subd. 6. Health care provider. "Health care provider" means a person, health care facility, organization, or corporation licensed, certified, or otherwise authorized or permitted by the laws of this state to administer health care directly or through an arrangement with other health care providers.

Subd. 7. HMO. "HMO" means an organization licensed under sections 62D.01 to 62D.30.

Subd. 8. Terminal condition. "Terminal condition" means an incurable or irreversible condition for which the administration of medical treatment will serve only to prolong the dying process.

Laws 1989, c. 3, § 2. Amended by Laws 1991, c. 148, § 6; Laws 2008, c. 277, art. 1, § 17, eff. July 1, 2008.

145B.03. Living will

Subdivision 1. Scope. A competent adult may make a living will of preferences or instructions regarding health care. These preferences or instructions may include, but are not limited to, consent to or refusal of any health care, treatment, service, procedure, or placement. A living will may include preferences or instructions regarding health care, the designation of a proxy to make health care decisions on behalf of the declarant, or both.

Subd. 2. Requirements for executing a living will. (a) A living will is effective only if it is signed by the declarant and two witnesses or a notary public.

(b) A living will must state:

(1) the declarant's preferences regarding whether the declarant wishes to receive or not receive artificial administration of nutrition and hydration; or

(2) that the declarant wishes the proxy, if any, to make decisions regarding the administering of artificially administered nutrition and hydration for the declarant if the declarant is unable to make health care decisions and the living will becomes operative. If the living will does not state the declarant's preferences regarding artificial administration of nutrition and hydration, the living will shall be enforceable as to all other preferences or instructions regarding health care, and a decision to administer, withhold, or withdraw nutrition and hydration artificially shall be made pursuant to section 145B.13. However, the mere existence of a living will or appointment of a proxy does not, by itself, create a presumption that the declarant wanted the withholding or withdrawing of artificially administered nutrition or hydration.

(c) The living will may be communicated to and then transcribed by one of the witnesses. If the declarant is physically unable to sign the document, one of the witnesses shall sign the document at the declarant's direction.

(d) Neither of the witnesses can be someone who is entitled to any part of the estate of the declarant under a will then existing or by operation of law. Neither of the witnesses nor the notary may be named as a proxy in the living will. Each witness shall substantially make the following declaration on the document:

"I certify that the declarant voluntarily signed this living will in my presence and that the declarant is personally known to me. I am not named as a proxy by the living will."

Subd. 3. Guardian. Except as otherwise provided in the living will, designation of a proxy is considered a nomination of a guardian for purposes of sections 524.5–101 to 524.5–502.

Laws 1989, c. 3, § 3. Amended by Laws 1991, c. 148, § 6; Laws 2004, c. 146, art. 3, § 2.

145B.04. Suggested form

A living will executed after August 1, 1989, under this chapter must be substantially in the form in this section. Forms printed for public distribution must be substantially in the form in this section.

"Health Care Living Will

Notice:

This is an important legal document. Before signing this document, you should know these important facts:

(a) This document gives your health care providers or your designated proxy the power and guidance to make health care decisions according to your wishes when you are in a terminal condition and cannot do so. This document may include what kind of treatment you want or do not want and under what circumstances you want these decisions to be made. You may state where you want or do not want to receive any treatment.

(b) If you name a proxy in this document and that person agrees to serve as your proxy, that person has a duty to act consistently with your wishes. If the proxy does not know your wishes, the proxy has the duty to act in your best interests. If you do not name a proxy, your health care providers have a duty to act consistently with your instructions or tell you that they are unwilling to do so.

(c) This document will remain valid and in effect until and unless you amend or revoke it. Review this document periodically to make sure it continues to reflect your preferences. You may amend or revoke the living will at any time by notifying your health care providers.

(d) Your named proxy has the same right as you have to examine your medical records and to consent to their disclosure for purposes related to your health care or insurance unless you limit this right in this document.

(e) If there is anything in this document that you do not understand, you should ask for professional help to have it explained to you.

TO MY FAMILY, DOCTORS, AND ALL THOSE CONCERNED WITH MY CARE:

I, ..., born on .... (birthdate), being an adult of sound mind, willfully and voluntarily make this statement as a directive to be followed if I am in a terminal condition and become unable to participate in decisions regarding my health care. I understand that my health care providers are legally bound to act consistently with my wishes, within the limits of reasonable medical practice and other applicable law. I also understand that I have the right to make medical and health care decisions for myself as long as I am able to do so and to revoke this living will at any time.

(1) The following are my feelings and wishes regarding my health care (you may state the circumstances under which this living will applies):

....
....
....
....

(2) I particularly want to have all appropriate health care that will help in the following ways (you may give instructions for care you do want):

....
....
....
....

(3) I particularly do not want the following (you may list specific treatment you do not want in certain circumstances):

. . . .
. . . .

(4) I particularly want to have the following kinds of life-sustaining treatment if I am diagnosed to have a terminal condition (you may list the specific types of life-sustaining treatment that you do want if you have a terminal condition):

. . . .
. . . .
. . . .
. . . .

(5) I particularly do not want the following kinds of life-sustaining treatment if I am diagnosed to have a terminal condition (you may list the specific types of life-sustaining treatment that you do not want if you have a terminal condition):

. . . .
. . . .
. . . .
. . . .

(6) I recognize that if I reject artificially administered sustenance, then I may die of dehydration or malnutrition rather than from my illness or injury. The following are my feelings and wishes regarding artificially administered sustenance should I have a terminal condition (you may indicate whether you wish to receive food and fluids given to you in some other way than by mouth if you have a terminal condition):

. . . .
. . . .
. . . .
. . . .

(7) Thoughts I feel are relevant to my instructions. (You may, but need not, give your religious beliefs, philosophy, or other personal values that you feel are important. You may also state preferences concerning the location of your care.)

. . . .
. . . .
. . . .
. . . .

(8) Proxy Designation. (If you wish, you may name someone to see that your wishes are carried out, but you do not have to do this. You may also name a proxy without including specific instructions regarding your care. If you name a proxy, you should discuss your wishes with that person.)

If I become unable to communicate my instructions, I designate the following person(s) to act on my behalf consistently with my instructions, if any, as stated in this document. Unless I write instructions that limit my proxy's authority, my proxy has full power and authority to make health care decisions for me. If a guardian is to be appointed for me, I nominate my proxy named in this document to act as my guardian.

Name: ....

Address: ....

Phone Number: ....

Relationship: (If any) ....

If the person I have named above refuses or is unable or unavailable to act on my behalf, or if I revoke that person's authority to act as my proxy, I authorize the following person to do so:

Name: ....

Address: ....

Phone Number: ....

Relationship: (If any) ....

I understand that I have the right to revoke the appointment of the persons named above to act on my behalf at any time by communicating that decision to the proxy or my health care provider.

(9) Organ Donation After Death. (If you wish, you may indicate whether you want to be an organ donor upon your death.) Initial the statement which expresses your wish:

..... In the event of my death, I would like to donate my organs. I understand that to become an organ donor, I must be declared brain dead. My organ function may be maintained artificially on a breathing machine, (i.e., artificial ventilation), so that my organs can be removed.

Limitations or special wishes: (If any) ....
....
....

I understand that, upon my death, my next of kin may be asked permission for donation. Therefore, it is in my best interests to inform my next of kin about my decision ahead of time and ask them to honor my request.

I (have) (have not) agreed in another document or on another form to donate some or all of my organs when I die.

..... I do not wish to become an organ donor upon my death.

DATE: ....

SIGNED: ....

STATE OF ....

....

COUNTY OF ....

Subscribed, sworn to, and acknowledged before me by .... on this
..... day of ...., ...

....

NOTARY PUBLIC

OR

(Sign and date here in the presence of two adult witnesses, neither of whom
is entitled to any part of your estate under a will or by operation of law, and
neither of whom is your proxy.)

I certify that the declarant voluntarily signed this living will in my presence
and that the declarant is personally known to me. I am not named as a proxy
by the living will, and to the best of my knowledge, I am not entitled to any part
of the estate of the declarant under a will or by operation of law.

Witness .... Address ....

Witness .... Address ....

Reminder: Keep the signed original with your personal papers.

Give signed copies to your doctors, family, and proxy."

Laws 1989, c. 3, § 4. Amended by Laws 1991, c. 148. § 6; Laws 1992, c. 535, § 1;
Laws 1995, c. 211, § 1; Laws 1998, c. 254, art. 1, § 107; Laws 2005, c. 10, art. 4, § 2.

Historical and Statutory Notes

Laws 1992, c. 535, § 2, provides that § 1 (amending this section) does not affect the validity of a declaration that does not contain the provisions of § 1, if the declaration is otherwise substantially in the form in § 145B.04.

Laws 1995, c. 211, § 3 provides that § 1, inserting cl. (9) of this section, does not affect the validity of a living will not containing these provisions, and that nothing in this act affects or overrides the provisions of the uniform anatomical gift act in §§ 525.921 to 525.9224.

145B.05. When operative

A living will becomes operative when it is delivered to the declarant's
physician or other health care provider. The physician or provider must
comply with it to the fullest extent possible, consistent with reasonable medical
practice and other applicable law, or comply with the notice and transfer
provisions of sections 145B.06 and 145B.07. The physician or health care
provider shall continue to obtain the declarant's informed consent to all health
care decisions if the declarant is capable of informed consent.

Laws 1989, c. 3, § 5. Amended by Laws 1991, c. 148, § 6.

145B.06.   Compliance with living will

Subdivision 1.   By health care provider.   (a) A physician or other health care provider shall make the living will a part of the declarant's medical record. If the physician or other health care provider is unwilling at any time to comply with the living will, the physician or health care provider must promptly notify the declarant and document the notification in the declarant's medical record. After notification, if a competent declarant fails to transfer to a different physician or provider, the physician or provider has no duty to transfer the patient.

(b) If a physician or other health care provider receives a living will from a competent declarant and does not advise the declarant of unwillingness to comply, and if the declarant then becomes incompetent or otherwise unable to seek transfer to a different physician or provider, the physician or other care provider who is unwilling to comply with the living will shall promptly take all reasonable steps to transfer care of the declarant to a physician or other health care provider who is willing to comply with the living will.

Subd. 2.   By proxy. A proxy designated to make health care decisions and who agrees to serve as proxy may make health care decisions on behalf of a declarant to the same extent that the declarant could make the decision, subject to limitations or conditions stated in the living will.   In exercising this authority, the proxy shall act consistently with any desires the declarant expresses in the living will or otherwise makes known to the proxy.   If the declarant's desires are unknown, the proxy shall act in the best interests of the declarant.

Laws 1989, c. 3, § 6. Amended by Laws 1991, c. 148, § 6.

145B.07.   Transfer of care

If a living will is delivered to a physician or other health care provider who transfers care of patients to other health care providers, or if a living will is delivered to a health care provider, including a health care facility or HMO that delivers patient care through an arrangement with individual providers, the physician or other health care provider receiving a living will shall make reasonable efforts:

(1) to ensure that an agreement with the patient to comply with the living will will be honored by others who provide health care to that patient; or

(2) to identify and deliver the living will to the individual providers and facilitate the declarant's discussion with those individuals whose agreement to comply with the living will is required.

Laws 1989, c. 3, § 7. Amended by Laws 1991, c. 148, § 6.

145B.08.   Access to medical information by proxy

Unless a living will under this chapter provides otherwise, a proxy has the same rights as the declarant to receive information regarding proposed health care, to receive and review medical records, and to consent to the disclosure of medical records for purposes related to the declarant's health care or insurance.

Laws 1989, c. 3, § 8. Amended by Laws 1991, c. 148, § 6.

145B.09. Revocation

Subdivision 1. General. A living will under this chapter may be revoked in whole or in part at any time and in any manner by the declarant, without regard to the declarant's physical or mental condition. A revocation is effective when the declarant communicates it to the attending physician or other health care provider. The attending physician or other health care provider shall note the revocation as part of the declarant's medical record.

Subd. 2. Effect of marriage dissolution or annulment on designation of proxy. Unless a living will under this chapter expressly provides otherwise, if after executing a living will the declarant's marriage is dissolved or annulled, the dissolution or annulment revokes any designation of the former spouse as a proxy to make health care decisions for the declarant.

Laws 1989, c. 3, § 9. Amended by Laws 1991, c. 148, § 6.

145B.10. Repealed by Laws 1993, c. 312, § 17

145B.105. Penalties

Subdivision 1. Gross misdemeanor offenses. Whoever commits any of the following acts is guilty of a gross misdemeanor:

(1) willfully conceals, cancels, defaces, or obliterates a living will of a declarant without the consent of the declarant;

(2) willfully conceals or withholds personal knowledge of a revocation of a living will;

(3) falsifies or forges a living will or a revocation of a living will;

(4) coerces or fraudulently induces another to execute a living will; or

(5) requires or prohibits the execution of a living will as a condition for being insured for or receiving all or some health care services.

Subd. 2. Felony offenses. Whoever commits an act prohibited under subdivision 1 is guilty of a felony if the act results in bodily harm to the declarant or to the person who would have been a declarant but for the unlawful act.

Laws 1993, c. 312, § 1.

Historical and Statutory Notes

Laws 1993, c. 312, § 18, provides in part that § 1 (enacting this section) is effective August 1, 1993, and applies to offenses committed on or after that date.

145B.11. Effect on insurance

The making or effectuation of a living will under this chapter does not affect the sale, procurement, issuance, or validity of a policy of life insurance or annuity, nor does it affect, impair, or modify the terms of an existing policy of life insurance or annuity or the liability of the party issuing the policy or annuity contract.

Laws 1989, c. 3, § 11. Amended by Laws 1991, c. 148, § 6.

145B.12. What if there is no living will or proxy?

Subdivision 1. No presumption created. If an individual has not executed or has revoked a living will under this chapter, a presumption is not created with respect to:

(1) the individual's intentions concerning the provision of health care; or

(2) the appropriate health care to be provided.

Subd. 2. Nutrition or hydration. Nothing in this chapter shall be construed to authorize or justify the withholding or withdrawal of artificially administered nutrition or hydration from any person who has not issued a living will or designated a proxy under this chapter.

Laws 1989, c. 3, § 12. Amended by Laws 1991, c. 148, § 6.

145B.13. Reasonable medical practice required

In reliance on a patient's living will, a decision to administer, withhold, or withdraw medical treatment after the patient has been diagnosed by the attending physician to be in a terminal condition must always be based on reasonable medical practice, including:

(1) continuation of appropriate care to maintain the patient's comfort, hygiene, and human dignity and to alleviate pain;

(2) oral administration of food or water to a patient who accepts it, except for clearly documented medical reasons; and

(3) in the case of a living will of a patient that the attending physician knows is pregnant, the living will must not be given effect as long as it is possible that the fetus could develop to the point of live birth with continued application of life-sustaining treatment.

Laws 1989, c. 3, § 13. Amended by Laws 1991, c. 148, § 6.

145B.14. Certain practices not condoned

Nothing in this chapter may be construed to condone, authorize, or approve mercy killing, euthanasia, suicide, or assisted suicide.

Laws 1989, c. 3, § 14.

145B.15.   Recognition of previously executed living will

A living will that substantially complies with section 145B.03, but is made before August 1, 1989, is an effective living will under this chapter.

Laws 1989, c. 3, § 15.   Amended by Laws 1991, c. 148, § 6.

145B.16.   Recognition of document executed in another state

A living will executed in another state is effective if it substantially complies with this chapter.

Laws 1989, c. 3, § 16.   Amended by Laws 1991, c. 148, § 6.

145B.17.   Existing rights

Nothing in this chapter impairs or supersedes the existing rights of any patient or any other legal right or legal responsibility a person may have to begin, continue, withhold, or withdraw health care. Nothing in this chapter prohibits lawful treatment by spiritual means through prayer in lieu of medical or surgical treatment when treatment by spiritual means has been authorized by the declarant.

Laws 1989, c. 3, § 17.

Chapter 145C

HEALTH CARE DIRECTIVES

For complete statutory history see Minnesota Statutes Annotated.

145C.01. Definitions

Subdivision 1. Applicability. The definitions in this section apply to this chapter.

Subd. 1a. Act in good faith. "Act in good faith" means to act consistently with a legally sufficient health care directive of the principal, a living will executed under chapter 145B, a declaration regarding intrusive mental health treatment executed under section 253B.03, subdivision 6d, or information otherwise made known by the principal, unless the actor has actual knowledge of the modification or revocation of the information expressed. If these sources of information do not provide adequate guidance to the actor, "act in good faith" means acting in the best interests of the principal, considering the principal's overall general health condition and prognosis and the principal's personal values to the extent known. Notwithstanding any instruction of the principal, a health care agent, health care provider, or any other person is not acting in good faith if the person violates the provisions of section 609.215 prohibiting assisted suicide.

Subd. 1b. Decision–making capacity. "Decision–making capacity" means the ability to understand the significant benefits, risks, and alternatives to proposed health care and to make and communicate a health care decision.

Subd. 2. Health care agent. "Health care agent" means an individual age 18 or older who is appointed by a principal in a health care power of attorney to make health care decisions on behalf of the principal. "Health care agent" may also be referred to as "agent."

Subd. 3. Health care power of attorney. "Health care power of attorney" means an instrument appointing one or more health care agents to make health care decisions for the principal.

Subd. 4. Health care. "Health care" means any care, treatment, service, or procedure to maintain, diagnose, or otherwise affect a person's physical or mental condition. "Health care" includes the provision of nutrition or hydration parenterally or through intubation but does not include any treatment, service, or procedure that violates the provisions of section 609.215 prohibiting assisted suicide. "Health care" also includes the establishment of a person's abode within or without the state and personal security safeguards for a person, to the extent decisions on these matters relate to the health care needs of the person.

Subd. 5. Health care decision. "Health care decision" means the consent, refusal of consent, or withdrawal of consent to health care.

Subd. 5a. Health care directive. "Health care directive" means a written instrument that complies with section 145C.03 and includes one or more health care instructions, a health care power of attorney, or both; or a durable power of attorney for health care executed under this chapter before August 1, 1998.

Subd. 6. Health care provider. "Health care provider" means a person, health care facility, organization, or corporation licensed, certified, or otherwise authorized or permitted by the laws of this state to administer health care directly or through an arrangement with other health care providers, including health maintenance organizations licensed under chapter 62D.

Subd. 7. Health care facility. "Health care facility" means a hospital or other entity licensed under sections 144.50 to 144.58, a nursing home licensed to serve adults under section 144A.02, a home care provider licensed under sections 144A.43 to 144A.47, an adult foster care provider licensed under chapter 245A and Minnesota Rules, parts 9555.5105 to 9555.6265, or a hospice provider licensed under sections 144A.75 to 144A.755.

Subd. 7a. Health care instruction. "Health care instruction" means a written statement of the principal's values, preferences, guidelines, or directions regarding health care.

Subd. 8. Principal. "Principal" means an individual age 18 or older who has executed a health care directive.

Subd. 9. Reasonably available. "Reasonably available" means able to be contacted and willing and able to act in a timely manner considering the urgency of the principal's health care needs.

Laws 1993, c. 312, § 2. Amended by Laws 1998, c. 254, art. 1, § 36; Laws 1998, c. 399, §§ 3 to 11, eff. Aug. 1, 1998; Laws 2002, c. 252, § 20; Laws 2004, c. 288, art. 6, § 16.

Historical and Statutory Notes

Laws 1993, c. 312, § 18, provides in part that § 2 (enacting this section) is effective August 1, 1993, and applies to offenses committed on or after that date.

Laws 2002, c. 252, § 24, par. (b), provides:

"(b) Sections 1 to 23, except section 15, subdivision 1, are effective upon adoption of licensure rules. Minnesota Rules, chapters 4668 and 4669, govern the licensure of hospices until new rules are adopted. With enactment of Minnesota Statutes, sections 144A.75 to 144A.756, licensure orders issued to licensed hospices under Minnesota Statutes, section 144A.45, and Minnesota Rules, chapters 4668 and 4669, shall remain valid and shall be subject to the issuance of a penalty assessment for failure to correct, under Minnesota Statutes, section 144A.752 (section 15)." [Publisher's note: New rules relating to hospices were adopted as Minnesota Rules, chapter 4664, in 2004.]

145C.02. Health care directive

A principal with the capacity to do so may execute a health care directive. A health care directive may include one or more health care instructions to direct health care providers, others assisting with health care, family members, and a health care agent. A health care directive may include a health care power of attorney to appoint a health care agent to make health care decisions for the principal when the principal, in the judgment of the principal's attending physician, lacks decision-making capacity, unless otherwise specified in the health care directive.

Laws 1993, c. 312, § 3. Amended by Laws 1998, c. 399, § 12, eff. Aug. 1, 1998.

Historical and Statutory Notes

Laws 1993, c. 312, § 18, provides in part that § 3 (enacting this section) is effective August 1, 1993, and applies to offenses committed on or after that date.

145C.03. Requirements

Subdivision 1. Legal sufficiency. To be legally sufficient in this state, a health care directive must:

(1) be in writing;

(2) be dated;

(3) state the principal's name;

(4) be executed by a principal with capacity to do so with the signature of the principal or with the signature of another person authorized by the principal to sign on behalf of the principal;

(5) contain verification of the principal's signature or the signature of the person authorized by the principal to sign on behalf of the principal, either by a notary public or by witnesses as provided under this chapter; and

(6) include a health care instruction, a health care power of attorney, or both.

Subd. 2. Individuals ineligible to act as health care agent. (a) An individual appointed by the principal under section 145C.05, subdivision 2, paragraph (b), to make the determination of the principal's decision-making capacity is not eligible to act as the health care agent.

(b) The following individuals are not eligible to act as the health care agent, unless the individual appointed is related to the principal by blood, marriage, registered domestic partnership, or adoption, or unless the principal has otherwise specified in the health care directive:

(1) a health care provider attending the principal on the date of execution of the health care directive or on the date the health care agent must make decisions for the principal; or

(2) an employee of a health care provider attending the principal on the date of execution of the health care directive or on the date the health care agent must make decisions for the principal.

Subd. 3. Individuals ineligible to act as witnesses or notary public. (a) A health care agent or alternate health care agent appointed in a health care power of attorney may not act as a witness or notary public for the execution of the health care directive that includes the health care power of attorney.

(b) At least one witness to the execution of the health care directive must not be a health care provider providing direct care to the principal or an employee of a health care provider providing direct care to the principal on the date of execution. A person notarizing a health care directive may be an employee of a health care provider providing direct care to the principal.

Laws 1993, c. 312, § 4. Amended by Laws 1998, c. 399, § 13, eff. Aug. 1, 1998.

Historical and Statutory Notes

Laws 1993, c. 312, § 18, provides in part that § 4 (enacting this section) is effective August 1, 1993, and applies to offenses committed on or after that date.

Laws 1998, c. 399, § 38, provides:

"A document executed prior to August 1, 1998, that purports to be a living will under Minnesota Statutes, chapter 145B, a durable power of attorney for health care under Minnesota Statutes, chapter 145C, or a declaration regarding intrusive mental health treatment under Minnesota Statutes, section 253B.03, subdivision 6a, is valid if the document:

"(1) complied with the law in effect on the date it was executed; or

"(2) complies with the requirements of Minnesota Statutes, section 145C.03.

"If the document complied with the law in effect on the date it was executed but does not also comply with the requirements of Minnesota Statutes, section 145C.03, it shall be given effect in accordance with the laws in effect on the date it was executed, unless the document provides otherwise.

"Nothing in sections 1 to 38 impairs the evidentiary effect under common law or reasonable medical practice with respect to other written or oral expressions of an individual's desires regarding health care."

145C.04. Executed in another state

(a) A health care directive or similar document executed in another state or jurisdiction is legally sufficient under this chapter if it:

(1) complies with the law of the state or jurisdiction in which it was executed; or

(2) complies with section 145C.03.

(b) Nothing in this section shall be interpreted to authorize a directive or similar document to override the provisions of section 609.215 prohibiting assisted suicide.

Laws 1993, c. 312, § 5. Amended by Laws 1998, c. 399, § 14, eff. Aug. 1, 1998.

Historical and Statutory Notes

Laws 1993, c. 312, § 18, provides in part that § 5 (enacting this section) is effective August 1, 1993, and applies to offenses committed on or after that date.

145C.05. Suggested form; provisions that may be included

Subdivision 1. Content. A health care directive executed pursuant to this chapter may, but need not, be in the form contained in section 145C.16.

Subd. 2. Provisions that may be included. (a) A health care directive may include provisions consistent with this chapter, including, but not limited to:

(1) the designation of one or more alternate health care agents to act if the named health care agent is not reasonably available to serve;

(2) directions to joint health care agents regarding the process or standards by which the health care agents are to reach a health care decision for the principal, and a statement whether joint health care agents may act independently of one another;

(3) limitations, if any, on the right of the health care agent or any alternate health care agents to receive, review, obtain copies of, and consent to the disclosure of the principal's medical records or to visit the principal when the principal is a patient in a health care facility;

(4) limitations, if any, on the nomination of the health care agent as guardian for purposes of sections 524.5-202, 524.5-211, 524.5-302, and 524.5-303;

(5) a document of gift for the purpose of making an anatomical gift, as set forth in chapter 525A, or an amendment to, revocation of, or refusal to make an anatomical gift;

(6) a declaration regarding intrusive mental health treatment under section 253B.03, subdivision 6d, or a statement that the health care agent is authorized to give consent for the principal under section 253B.04, subdivision 1a;

(7) a funeral directive as provided in section 149A.80, subdivision 2;

(8) limitations, if any, to the effect of dissolution or annulment of marriage or termination of domestic partnership on the appointment of a health care agent under section 145C.09, subdivision 2;

(9) specific reasons why a principal wants a health care provider or an employee of a health care provider attending the principal to be eligible to act as the principal's health care agent;

(10) health care instructions by a woman of child bearing age regarding how she would like her pregnancy, if any, to affect health care decisions made on her behalf; and

26

(11) health care instructions regarding artificially administered nutrition or hydration.

(b) A health care directive may include a statement of the circumstances under which the directive becomes effective other than upon the judgment of the principal's attending physician in the following situations:

(1) a principal who in good faith generally selects and depends upon spiritual means or prayer for the treatment or care of disease or remedial care and does not have an attending physician, may include a statement appointing an individual who may determine the principal's decision-making capacity; and

(2) a principal who in good faith does not generally select a physician or a health care facility for the principal's health care needs may include a statement appointing an individual who may determine the principal's decision-making capacity, provided that if the need to determine the principal's capacity arises when the principal is receiving care under the direction of an attending physician in a health care facility, the determination must be made by an attending physician after consultation with the appointed individual.

If a person appointed under clause (1) or (2) is not reasonably available and the principal is receiving care under the direction of an attending physician in a health care facility, an attending physician shall determine the principal's decision-making capacity.

(c) A health care directive may authorize a health care agent to make health care decisions for a principal even though the principal retains decision-making capacity.

Laws 1993, c. 312, § 6. Amended by Laws 1995, c. 211, § 2; Laws 1998, c. 399, §§ 15, 16, eff. Aug. 1, 1998; Laws 2004, c. 146, art. 3, § 3; Laws 2007, c. 147, art. 9, § 22, eff. July 1, 2007.

Historical and Statutory Notes

Laws 1993, c. 312, § 18, provides in part that § 6 (enacting this section) is effective August 1, 1993, and applies to offenses committed on or after that date.

145C.06. When effective

A health care directive is effective for a health care decision when:

(1) it meets the requirements of section 145C.03, subdivision 1; and

(2) the principal, in the determination of the attending physician of the principal, lacks decision-making capacity to make the health care decision; or if other conditions for effectiveness otherwise specified by the principal have been met.

A health care directive is not effective for a health care decision when the principal, in the determination of the attending physician of the principal, recovers decision–making capacity; or if other conditions for effectiveness otherwise specified by the principal have been met.

Laws 1993, c. 312, § 7. Amended by Laws 1998, c. 399, § 17, eff. Aug. 1, 1998.

Historical and Statutory Notes

Laws 1993, c. 312, § 18, provides in part that   1993, and applies to offenses committed on or
§ 7 (enacting this section) is effective August 1,   after that date.

145C.07.   Authority and duties of health care agent

Subdivision 1.   Authority. The health care agent has authority to make any particular health care decision only if the principal lacks decision-making capacity, in the determination of the attending physician, to make or communicate that health care decision; or if other conditions for effectiveness otherwise specified by the principal have been met. The physician or other health care provider shall continue to obtain the principal's informed consent to all health care decisions for which the principal has decision–making capacity, unless other conditions for effectiveness otherwise specified by the principal have been met. An alternate health care agent has authority to act if the primary health care agent is not reasonably available to act.

Subd. 2.   Health care agent as guardian. Unless the principal has otherwise specified in the health care directive, the appointment of the health care agent in a health care directive is considered a nomination of a guardian for purposes of sections 524.5–101 to 524.5–502.

Subd. 3.   Duties. In exercising authority under a health care directive, a health care agent has a duty to act in good faith. A health care agent or any alternate health care agent has a personal obligation to the principal to make health care decisions authorized by the health care power of attorney, but this obligation does not constitute a legal duty to act.

Subd. 4.   Inconsistencies among documents. In the event of inconsistency between the appointment of a proxy under chapter 145B or section 253B.03, subdivision 6d, or of a health care agent under this chapter, the most recent appointment takes precedence. In the event of other inconsistencies among documents executed under this chapter, under chapter 145B, or under sections 253B.03, subdivision 6d, or 524.5–101 to 524.5–502, or other legally sufficient documents, the provisions of the most recently executed document take precedence only to the extent of the inconsistency.

Subd. 5.   Visitation. A health care agent may visit the principal when the principal is a patient in a health care facility regardless of whether the principal retains decision-making capacity, unless:

(1) the principal has otherwise specified in the health care directive;

(2) a principal who retains decision-making capacity indicates otherwise; or

(3) a health care provider reasonably determines that the principal must be isolated from all visitors or that the presence of the health care agent would endanger the health or safety of the principal, other patients, or the facility in which the care is being provided.

Laws 1993, c. 312, § 8. Amended by Laws 1998, c. 399, § 18, eff. Aug. 1, 1998; Laws 2004, c. 146, art. 3, §§ 4, 5; Laws 2007, c. 147, art. 9, § 23, eff. July 1, 2007.

Historical and Statutory Notes

Laws 1993, c. 312, § 18, provides in part that § 8 (enacting this section) is effective August 1, 1993, and applies to offenses committed on or after that date.

145C.08. Authority to review medical records

A health care agent acting pursuant to a health care directive has the same right as the principal to receive, review, and obtain copies of medical records of the principal, and to consent to the disclosure of medical records of the principal, unless the principal has otherwise specified in the health care directive.

Laws 1993, c. 312, § 9. Amended by Laws 1998, c. 399, § 19, eff. Aug. 1, 1998.

Historical and Statutory Notes

Laws 1993, c. 312, § 18, provides in part that § 9 (enacting this section) is effective August 1, 1993, and applies to offenses committed on or after that date.

145C.09. Revocation of health care directive

Subdivision 1. Revocation. A principal with the capacity to do so may revoke a health care directive in whole or in part at any time by doing any of the following:

(1) canceling, defacing, obliterating, burning, tearing, or otherwise destroying the health care directive instrument or directing another in the presence of the principal to destroy the health care directive instrument, with the intent to revoke the health care directive in whole or in part;

(2) executing a statement, in writing and dated, expressing the principal's intent to revoke the health care directive in whole or in part;

(3) verbally expressing the principal's intent to revoke the health care directive in whole or in part in the presence of two witnesses who do not have to be present at the same time; or

(4) executing a subsequent health care directive, to the extent the subsequent instrument is inconsistent with any prior instrument.

Subd. 2. Effect of dissolution, annulment, or termination of domestic partnership. Unless the principal has otherwise specified in the health care directive, the appointment by the principal of the principal's spouse or registered domestic partner as health care agent under a health care power of attorney is revoked by the commencement of proceedings for dissolution, annulment, or termination of the principal's marriage or commencement of proceedings for termination of the principal's registered domestic partnership.

Subd. 3. Power of a guardian. The powers of a guardian to revoke the appointment of a health care agent in a health care directive of which the ward is the principal or to revoke the health care directive itself are specified in section 524.5–315.

Laws 1993, c. 312, § 10. Amended by Laws 1998, c. 399, § 20, eff. Aug. 1, 1998; Laws 2003, c. 12, art. 2, § 1.

Historical and Statutory Notes

Laws 1993, c. 312, § 18, provides in part that § 10 (enacting this section) is effective August 1, 1993, and applies to offenses committed on or after that date.

Laws 2003, c. 12, art. 2, § 9, provided:

"(a) Articles 1 and 2 apply to each guardianship or conservatorship proceeding and each appointment of guardian or conservator commenced on or after the effective date of articles 1 and 2. Except as otherwise provided in this section, articles 1 and 2 apply to each guardianship or conservatorship approved by the court prior to the effective date of articles 1 and 2, and to any guardianship or conservatorship proceeding pending in court on the effective date of articles 1 and 2, unless the court finds for good cause or in the interests of judicial economy that the proceeding should be completed under the provisions of Minnesota Statutes, chapter 525, as it existed prior to the effective date of articles 1 and 2.

"(b) A guardian or conservator who is not discharged prior to the effective date of articles 1 and 2 shall continue to hold the appointment but shall have only the powers specified in the order of appointment and in Minnesota Statutes, chapter 525, as it existed prior to the effective date of articles 1 and 2. Each guardian or conservator holding an appointment on the effective date of articles 1 and 2 shall continue to be bound by the duties imposed by the order of appointment; by Minnesota Statutes, chapter 525, as it existed prior to the effective date of articles 1 and 2; and by article 1, section 50; and shall be bound by any additional duties imposed by articles 1 and 2 starting on the first day of the next month starting after the effective date of articles 1 and 2 or on the next anniversary date of the appointment, whichever occurs later.

"(c) Any act done prior to the effective date of articles 1 and 2 in any proceeding and any right accrued under Minnesota Statutes, chapter 525, prior to the effective date of articles 1 and 2 shall not be impaired by articles 1 and 2. If a right is acquired, extinguished, or barred upon the expiration of a prescribed period of time which has commenced to run in accordance with the provisions of any statute before the effective date of articles 1 and 2, the provisions of the prior statute shall remain in force with respect to that right notwithstanding the statute's amendment or repeal by articles 1 and 2.

"(d) An order of the court or letters of guardianship or conservatorship issued by the court prior to the effective date of articles 1 and 2 shall remain in full force and effect in accordance with its terms and conditions and in accordance with the provisions of prior law until the court modifies the order or letters in accordance with the provisions of articles 1 and 2. Upon request for a certified copy of an order or letters which remains in full force and effect under this paragraph, the court administrator shall certify that the order or letters remains in full force and effect pursuant to this paragraph.

"(e) The court, without hearing or notice to any person, may issue new letters of guardianship or conservatorship under articles 1 and 2 to replace similar letters issued prior to the effective date of articles 1 and 2. The new letters shall be effective under articles 1 and 2 with the same force and effect as the prior letters and shall remain in full force and effect until modified by the court in accordance with the provisions of articles 1 and 2.

"(f) A power of attorney executed in accordance with Minnesota Statutes, section 524.5–505, prior to the effective date of articles 1 and 2, or any surety bond, deed, or other instrument, report, or other undertaking executed in accordance with Minnesota Statutes, chapter 525, prior to the effective date of articles 1 and 2, shall remain in full force and effect for all purposes in accordance with its terms and conditions and the provisions of the applicable statutes under which the power of attorney, surety bond, deed, or other instrument, report, or other undertaking was executed, until the power of attorney, surety bond, deed, or other instrument, report, or other undertaking expires according to its terms or pursuant to the statutes governing its execution, or is modified, terminated, or superseded by a new power of attorney, surety bond, deed, or other instrument, report, or other undertaking executed in accordance with the provisions of articles 1 and 2."

145C.10. Presumptions

(a) The principal is presumed to have the capacity to execute a health care directive and to revoke a health care directive, absent clear and convincing evidence to the contrary.

(b) A health care provider or health care agent may presume that a health care directive is legally sufficient absent actual knowledge to the contrary. A health care directive is presumed to be properly executed, absent clear and convincing evidence to the contrary.

(c) A health care agent, and a health care provider acting pursuant to the direction of a health care agent, are presumed to be acting in good faith, absent clear and convincing evidence to the contrary.

(d) A health care directive is presumed to remain in effect until the principal modifies or revokes it, absent clear and convincing evidence to the contrary.

(e) This chapter does not create a presumption concerning the intention of an individual who has not executed a health care directive and, except as otherwise provided by section 145C.15, does not impair or supersede any right or responsibility of an individual to consent, refuse to consent, or withdraw consent to health care on behalf of another in the absence of a health care directive.

(f) A copy of a health care directive is presumed to be a true and accurate copy of the executed original, absent clear and convincing evidence to the contrary, and must be given the same effect as an original.

(g) When a patient lacks decision-making capacity and is pregnant, and in reasonable medical judgment there is a real possibility that if health care to sustain her life and the life of the fetus is provided the fetus could survive to the point of live birth, the health care provider shall presume that the patient would have wanted such health care to be provided, even if the withholding or withdrawal of such health care would be authorized were she not pregnant. This presumption is negated by health care directive provisions described in section 145C.05, subdivision 2, paragraph (a), clause (10), that are to the contrary, or, in the absence of such provisions, by clear and convincing evidence that the patient's wishes, while competent, were to the contrary.

Laws 1993, c. 312, § 11. Amended by Laws 1998, c. 399, § 21, eff. Aug. 1, 1998.

Historical and Statutory Notes

Laws 1993, c. 312, § 18, provides in part that § 11 (enacting this section) is effective August 1, 1993, and applies to offenses committed on or after that date.

145C.11. Immunities

Subdivision 1. Health care agent. A health care agent is not subject to criminal prosecution or civil liability if the health care agent acts in good faith.

Subd. 2. Health care provider. (a) With respect to health care provided to a patient with a health care directive, a health care provider is not subject to criminal prosecution, civil liability, or professional disciplinary action if the health care provider acts in good faith and in accordance with applicable standards of care.

(b) A health care provider is not subject to criminal prosecution, civil liability, or professional disciplinary action if the health care provider relies on a health care decision made by the health care agent and the following requirements are satisfied:

(1) the health care provider believes in good faith that the decision was made by a health care agent appointed to make the decision and has no actual knowledge that the health care directive has been revoked; and

(2) the health care provider believes in good faith that the health care agent is acting in good faith.

(c) A health care provider who administers health care necessary to keep the principal alive, despite a health care decision of the health care agent to withhold or withdraw that treatment, is not subject to criminal prosecution, civil liability, or professional disciplinary action if that health care provider promptly took all reasonable steps to:

(1) notify the health care agent of the health care provider's unwillingness to comply;

(2) document the notification in the principal's medical record; and

(3) permit the health care agent to arrange to transfer care of the principal to another health care provider willing to comply with the decision of the health care agent.

Laws 1993, c. 312, § 12. Amended by Laws 1998, c. 399, § 22, eff. Aug. 1, 1998.

Historical and Statutory Notes

Laws 1993, c. 312, § 18, provides in part that § 12 (enacting this section) is effective August 1, 1993, and applies to offenses committed on or after that date.

145C.12. Prohibited practices

Subdivision 1. Health care provider. A health care provider, health care service plan, insurer, self-insured employee welfare benefit plan, or nonprofit hospital plan may not condition admission to a facility, or the providing of treatment or insurance, on the requirement that an individual execute a health care directive.

Subd. 2. Insurance. A policy of life insurance is not legally impaired or invalidated in any manner by the withholding or withdrawing of health care pursuant to the direction of a health care agent appointed pursuant to this chapter, or pursuant to the implementation of health care instructions under this chapter.

Laws 1993, c. 312, § 13. Amended by Laws 1998, c. 399, § 23, eff. Aug. 1, 1998.

Historical and Statutory Notes

Laws 1993, c. 312, § 18, provides in part that § 13 (enacting this section) is effective August 1, 1993, and applies to offenses committed on or after that date.

145C.13. Penalties

Subdivision 1. Gross misdemeanor offenses. Whoever commits any of the following acts is guilty of a gross misdemeanor:

(1) willfully conceals, cancels, defaces, or obliterates a health care directive of a principal without the consent of the principal;

(2) willfully conceals or withholds personal knowledge of a revocation of a health care directive;

(3) falsifies or forges a health care directive or a revocation of the instrument;

(4) coerces or fraudulently induces another to execute a health care directive; or

(5) requires or prohibits the execution of a health care directive as a condition for being insured for or receiving all or some health care services.

Subd. 2. Felony offenses. Whoever commits an act prohibited under subdivision 1 is guilty of a felony if the act results in bodily harm to the principal or to the person who would have been a principal but for the unlawful act.

Laws 1993, c. 312, § 14. Amended by Laws 1998, c. 399, § 25, eff. Aug. 1, 1998.

Historical and Statutory Notes

Laws 1993, c. 312, § 18, provides in part that § 14 (enacting this section) is effective August 1, 1993, and applies to offenses committed on or after that date.

145C.14. Certain practices not condoned

Nothing in this chapter may be construed to condone, authorize, or approve mercy killing or euthanasia.

Laws 1993, c. 312, § 15.

145C.15. Duty to provide life-sustaining health care

(a) If a proxy acting under chapter 145B or a health care agent acting under this chapter directs the provision of health care, nutrition, or hydration that, in reasonable medical judgment, has a significant possibility of sustaining the life of the principal or declarant, a health care provider shall take all reasonable steps to ensure the provision of the directed health care, nutrition, or hydration if the provider has the legal and actual capability of providing the health care either itself or by transferring the principal or declarant to a health care provider who has that capability. Any transfer of a principal or declarant under this paragraph must be done promptly and, if necessary to preserve the life of the principal or declarant, by emergency means. This paragraph does not apply if a living will under chapter 145B or a health care directive indicates an intention to the contrary.

(b) A health care provider who is unwilling to provide directed health care under paragraph (a) that the provider has the legal and actual capability of providing may transfer the principal or declarant to another health care provider willing to provide the directed health care but the provider shall take all reasonable steps to ensure provision of the directed health care until the principal or declarant is transferred.

(c) Nothing in this section alters any legal obligation or lack of legal obligation of a health care provider to provide health care to a principal or declarant who refuses, has refused, or is unable to pay for the health care.

Laws 1993, c. 312, § 16. Amended by Laws 1998, c. 399, § 26, eff. Aug. 1, 1998.

145C.16. Suggested form

The following is a suggested form of a health care directive and is not a required form.

HEALTH CARE DIRECTIVE

I, ..., understand this document allows me to do ONE OR BOTH of the following:

PART I: Name another person (called the health care agent) to make health care decisions for me if I am unable to decide or speak for myself. My health care agent must make health care decisions for me based on the instructions I provide in this document (Part II), if any, the wishes I have made known to him or her, or must act in my best interest if I have not made my health care wishes known.

AND/OR

PART II: Give health care instructions to guide others making health care decisions for me. If I have named a health care agent, these instructions are to be used by the agent. These instructions may also be used by my health care providers, others assisting with my health care and my family, in the event I cannot make decisions for myself.

PART I: APPOINTMENT OF HEALTH CARE AGENT

THIS IS WHO I WANT TO MAKE HEALTH CARE DECISIONS

FOR ME IF I AM UNABLE TO DECIDE OR SPEAK FOR MYSELF

(I know I can change my agent or alternate agent at any time and I know I do not have to appoint an agent or an alternate agent)

NOTE: If you appoint an agent, you should discuss this health care directive with your agent and give your agent a copy. If you do not wish to appoint an agent, you may leave Part I blank and go to Part II.

When I am unable to decide or speak for myself, I trust and appoint .... to make health care decisions for me. This person is called my health care agent.

Relationship of my health care agent to me: ....

Telephone number of my health care agent: ....

Address of my health care agent: ....

(OPTIONAL) APPOINTMENT OF ALTERNATE HEALTH CARE AGENT: If my health care agent is not reasonably available, I trust and appoint .... to be my health care agent instead.

Relationship of my alternate health care agent to me: ....

Telephone number of my alternate health care agent: ....

Address of my alternate health care agent: ....

THIS IS WHAT I WANT MY HEALTH CARE AGENT TO BE ABLE TO DO IF I AM UNABLE TO DECIDE OR SPEAK FOR MYSELF

(I know I can change these choices)

My health care agent is automatically given the powers listed below in (A) through (D). My health care agent must follow my health care instructions in this document or any other instructions I have given to my agent. If I have not given health care instructions, then my agent must act in my best interest.

Whenever I am unable to decide or speak for myself, my health care agent has the power to:

(A) Make any health care decision for me. This includes the power to give, refuse, or withdraw consent to any care, treatment, service, or procedures. This includes deciding whether to stop or not start health care that is keeping me or might keep me alive, and deciding about intrusive mental health treatment.

(B) Choose my health care providers.

(C) Choose where I live and receive care and support when those choices relate to my health care needs.

(D) Review my medical records and have the same rights that I would have to give my medical records to other people.

If I DO NOT want my health care agent to have a power listed above in (A) through (D) OR if I want to LIMIT any power in (A) through (D), I MUST say that here:

....
....
....

My health care agent is NOT automatically given the powers listed below in (1) and (2). If I WANT my agent to have any of the powers in (1) and (2), I must INITIAL the line in front of the power; then my agent WILL HAVE that power.

... (1) To decide whether to donate any parts of my body, including organs, tissues, and eyes, when I die.
... (2) To decide what will happen with my body when I die (burial, cremation).

If I want to say anything more about my health care agent's powers or limits on the powers, I can say it here:

. . . .
. . . .
. . . .

PART II: HEALTH CARE INSTRUCTIONS

NOTE: Complete this Part II if you wish to give health care instructions. If you appointed an agent in Part I, completing this Part II is optional but would be very helpful to your agent. However, if you chose not to appoint an agent in Part I, you MUST complete some or all of this Part II if you wish to make a valid health care directive.

These are instructions for my health care when I am unable to decide or speak for myself. These instructions must be followed (so long as they address my needs).

THESE ARE MY BELIEFS AND VALUES ABOUT MY HEALTH CARE
(I know I can change these choices or leave any of them blank)

I want you to know these things about me to help you make decisions about my health care:

My goals for my health care: . . . .
. . . .
. . . .

My fears about my health care: . . . .
. . . .
. . . .

My spiritual or religious beliefs and traditions: . . . .
. . . .
. . . .

My beliefs about when life would be no longer worth living: . . . .
. . . .
. . . .

My thoughts about how my medical condition might affect my family: . . . .
. . . .
. . . .

THIS IS WHAT I WANT AND DO NOT WANT FOR MY HEALTH CARE
(I know I can change these choices or leave any of them blank)

Many medical treatments may be used to try to improve my medical condition or to prolong my life. Examples include artificial breathing by a machine connected to a tube in the lungs, artificial feeding or fluids through tubes, attempts to start a stopped heart, surgeries, dialysis, antibiotics, and blood transfusions. Most medical treatments can be tried for a while and then stopped if they do not help.

I have these views about my health care in these situations:

(Note: You can discuss general feelings, specific treatments, or leave any of them blank)

If I had a reasonable chance of recovery, and were temporarily unable to decide or speak for myself, I would want: ....

....

....

If I were dying and unable to decide or speak for myself, I would want: ..

....

....

If I were permanently unconscious and unable to decide or speak for myself, I would want: ....

....

....

If I were completely dependent on others for my care and unable to decide or speak for myself, I would want: ....

....

....

In all circumstances, my doctors will try to keep me comfortable and reduce my pain. This is how I feel about pain relief if it would affect my alertness or if it could shorten my life: ....

....

....

There are other things that I want or do not want for my health care, if possible:

Who I would like to be my doctor: ....

....

....

Where I would like to live to receive health care: ....

....

....

Where I would like to die and other wishes I have about dying: ....

....

....

My wishes about donating parts of my body when I die: ....

....

....

My wishes about what happens to my body when I die (cremation, burial):

....

....

....

Any other things: ....
....
....

PART III: MAKING THE DOCUMENT LEGAL

This document must be signed by me. It also must either be verified by a notary public (Option 1) OR witnessed by two witnesses (Option 2). It must be dated when it is verified or witnessed.

I am thinking clearly, I agree with everything that is written in this document, and I have made this document willingly.

....
My Signature
   Date signed: ....
   Date of birth: ....
   Address: ....
            ....

If I cannot sign my name, I can ask someone to sign this document for me.

....
Signature of the person who I asked to sign this document for me.

....
Printed name of the person who I asked to sign this document for me.

Option 1: Notary Public

In my presence on .... (date), ... (name) acknowledged his/her signature on this document or acknowledged that he/she authorized the person signing this document to sign on his/her behalf. I am not named as a health care agent or alternate health care agent in this document.

....
(Signature of Notary)   (Notary Stamp)

Option 2: Two Witnesses

Two witnesses must sign. Only one of the two witnesses can be a health care provider or an employee of a health care provider giving direct care to me on the day I sign this document.

Witness One:

(i) In my presence on .... (date), ... (name) acknowledged his/her signature on this document or acknowledged that he/she authorized the person signing this document to sign on his/her behalf.

(ii) I am at least 18 years of age.

(iii) I am not named as a health care agent or an alternate health care agent in this document.

(iv) If I am a health care provider or an employee of a health care provider giving direct care to the person listed above in (A), I must initial this box: [ ]

I certify that the information in (i) through (iv) is true and correct.

....
(Signature of Witness One)
Address: ....
....

Witness Two:

(i) In my presence on .... (date), ... (name) acknowledged his/her signature on this document or acknowledged that he/she authorized the person signing this document to sign on his/her behalf.

(ii) I am at least 18 years of age.

(iii) I am not named as a health care agent or an alternate health care agent in this document.

(iv) If I am a health care provider or an employee of a health care provider giving direct care to the person listed above in (A), I must initial this box: [ ]

I certify that the information in (i) through (iv) is true and correct.

....
(Signature of Witness Two)
Address: ....
....

REMINDER: Keep this document with your personal papers in a safe place (not in a safe deposit box). Give signed copies to your doctors, family, close friends, health care agent, and alternate health care agent. Make sure your doctor is willing to follow your wishes. This document should be part of your medical record at your physician's office and at the hospital, home care agency, hospice, or nursing facility where you receive your care.

Laws 1998, c. 399, § 24, eff. Aug. 1, 1998. Amended by Laws 1999, c. 14, § 1.

Chapter 289A

ADMINISTRATION AND COMPLIANCE

For complete statutory history see Minnesota Statutes Annotated.

GENERAL PROVISIONS

289A.01. Application of chapter

This chapter applies to laws administered by the commissioner under chapters 290, 290A, 291, and 297A, and sections 298.01 and 298.015.

Laws 1990, c. 480, art. 1, § 1, eff. April 25, 1990. Amended by Laws 1991, c. 291, art. 11, § 1; Laws 1997, c. 31, art. 1, § 2, eff. April 16, 1997.

Historical and Statutory Notes

Laws 1991, c. 291, art. 11, § 21 provides in part that § 1 (amending this section) is effective for ores mined after December 31, 1990.

289A.02. Definitions

Subdivision 1. Applicability. Unless the context clearly requires otherwise, the following terms used in this chapter have the following meanings.

Subd. 2. Commissioner. "Commissioner" means the commissioner of revenue of the state of Minnesota or a person to whom the commissioner has delegated functions.

Subd. 3. Taxpayer. "Taxpayer" means a person subject to, or liable for, a state tax; a person required to file a return with respect to, or to pay, or withhold or collect and remit, a state tax; or a person required to obtain a license or a permit or to keep records under a law imposing a state tax.

Subd. 4. Person. "Person" means an individual, partnership, corporation, association, governmental unit or agency, or public or private organization of any kind, under a duty to comply with state tax laws because of its character or position.

Subd. 5. Other words. Unless specifically defined in this chapter, or unless the context clearly indicates otherwise, the words used in this chapter have the same meanings as they are defined in chapters 290, 290A, 291, and 297A.

Subd. 6. Mining company. "Mining company" means a person engaged in the business of mining or producing ores in Minnesota subject to the taxes imposed by section 298.01 or 298.015.

Subd. 7. Internal Revenue Code. Unless specifically defined otherwise, "Internal Revenue Code" means the Internal Revenue Code of 1986, as amended through February 13, 2008 [1].

Subd. 8. Electronic means. "Electronic means" refers to a method that is electronic, as defined in section 325L.02, paragraph (e), and that is prescribed by the commissioner.

Laws 1990, c. 480, art. 1, § 2, eff. April 25, 1990. Amended by Laws 1991, c. 291, art. 11, § 2; Laws 1994, c. 587, art. 1, § 3; Laws 1995, c. 264, art. 1, § 4; Laws 1996, c. 471, art. 4, § 1; Laws 1997, c. 231, art. 6, § 1; Laws 1998, c. 389, art. 7, § 1; Laws 1999, c. 243, art. 3, § 1; Laws 2000, c. 490, art. 12, § 1, eff. May 16, 2000; Laws 2001, 1st Sp., c. 5, art. 10, § 1, eff. July 1, 2001; Laws 2001, 1st. Sp., c. 5, art. 17, § 7, eff. July 1, 2001; Laws 2002, c. 377, art. 2, § 1; Laws 2003, c. 127, art. 4, § 1, eff. May 26, 2003; Laws 2003, 1st Sp., c. 21, art. 3, § 1; Laws 2005, 1st Sp., c. 3, art. 4, § 1, eff. July 14, 2005; Laws 2006, c. 259, art. 2, § 1, eff. June 2, 2006; Laws 2008, c. 154, art. 4, § 1, eff. March 8, 2008.

[1] 26 U.S.C.A. § 1 et seq.

Historical and Statutory Notes

Laws 1991, c. 291, art. 11, § 21 provides in part that § 2 (adding subd. 6 of this section) is effective for ores mined after December 31, 1990.

Laws 1996, c. 471, art. 4, § 6, provides in part that § 1 (amending subd. 7) is effective at the same time section 1 of Public Law Number 104–117 is effective.

Public Law Number 104–117 (109 Stat. 827), approved March 20, 1996, was generally effective November 21, 1995, although the effective date of some of the withholding provisions was dependent upon the date of enactment. See, 26 U.S.C.A. § 2, note.

Laws 1997, c. 231, art. 6, § 25, provides in part that § 1 (amending subd. 7) is effective at the same time and for the same years as the federal changes made in 1996 were effective for federal purposes.

Laws 1998, c. 389, art. 7, § 13, provides in part that the amendment to subd. 7 is effective for tax years beginning after December 31, 1997.

Laws 1999, c. 243, art. 3, § 7, provides in part that § 1, amending subd. 7, is effective at the same time federal changes made by the

Internal Revenue Service Restructuring and Reform Act of 1998, Public Law Number 105–206 and the Omnibus Consolidation and Emergency Supplemental Appropriations Act, 1999, Public Law Number 105–277 which are incorporated into Minnesota Statutes, chapters 289A, 290, 290A, and 291 by these sections become effective for federal tax purposes.

Laws 2002, c. 377, art. 2, § 1, amending subd. 7, also provides that the amendment is effective the day following final enactment. Laws 2002, c. 377, was filed without signature of the governor May 18, 2002. See §§ 645.01 and 645.02.

Laws 2003, 1st. Sp., c. 21, art. 3, § 1, amending subd. 7, also provided that the amendment was effective June 9, 2003, and was intended to adopt the provisions of H.R. 2, the Jobs and Growth Tax Relief Reconciliation Act of 2003, if enacted into law.

Laws 2003, 1st Sp., c. 21, art. 3, § 5, provides:

"This article is effective only after the state makes a certification to the Secretary of the Treasury of the United States that satisfies the requirements of section 601(e) of the Jobs and

Growth Tax Relief and Reconciliation Act of 2003, H.R. 2. The commissioner of finance shall certify to the commissioner of revenue when the requirements of this section have been met."

289A.07. Repealed by Laws 2005, c. 151, art. 1, § 117, eff. Aug. 1, 2005

Historical and Statutory Notes

Laws 2005, c. 151, art. 1, § 115, provided:

"Subdivision 1. Purpose. It is the intent of the legislature to simplify Minnesota's tax laws by consolidating and recodifying tax administration and compliance provisions now contained in Minnesota Statutes, chapter 270, and several other chapters of Minnesota Statutes. The provisions of this act may not be used to determine the law in effect prior to the effective dates in this act.

"Subd. 2. Effect. Due to the complexity of the recodification, prior provisions are repealed on the effective date of the new provisions. The repealed provisions, however, continue to remain in effect until superseded by the analogous provision in the new law."

FILING, REPORTING, REGISTRATION REQUIREMENTS

289A.08. Filing requirements for individual income, fiduciary income, corporate franchise, mining company, and entertainment taxes

Subdivision 1. Generally; individuals. (a) A taxpayer must file a return for each taxable year the taxpayer is required to file a return under section 6012 of the Internal Revenue Code,[1] except that:

(1) an individual who is not a Minnesota resident for any part of the year is not required to file a Minnesota income tax return if the individual's gross income derived from Minnesota sources as determined under sections 290.081, paragraph (a), and 290.17, is less than the filing requirements for a single individual who is a full year resident of Minnesota; and

(2) an individual who is a Minnesota resident is not required to file a Minnesota income tax return if the individual's gross income derived from Minnesota sources as determined under section 290.17, less the amount of the individual's gross income that consists of compensation paid to members of the armed forces of the United States or United Nations for active duty performed outside Minnesota, is less than the filing requirements for a single individual who is a full-year resident of Minnesota.

(b) The decedent's final income tax return, and other income tax returns for prior years where the decedent had gross income in excess of the minimum amount at which an individual is required to file and did not file, must be filed by the decedent's personal representative, if any. If there is no personal representative, the return or returns must be filed by the transferees, as defined in section 270C.58, subdivision 3, who receive property of the decedent.

(c) The term "gross income," as it is used in this section, has the same meaning given it in section 290.01, subdivision 20.

Subd. 2. Returns filed by fiduciaries. (a) The trustee or other fiduciary of property held in trust must file a return with respect to the taxable net income of the trust or estate if it exceeds an amount determined by the commissioner and if the trust belongs to the class of taxable persons.

(b) The receivers, trustees in bankruptcy, or assignees operating the business or property of a taxpayer must file a return with respect to the taxable net income of the taxpayer if a return is required.

Subd. 3. Corporations. A corporation that is subject to the state's jurisdiction to tax under section 290.014, subdivision 5, must file a return, except that a foreign operating corporation as defined in section 290.01, subdivision 6b, is not required to file a return. The commissioner shall adopt rules for the filing of one return on behalf of the members of an affiliated group of corporations that are required to file a combined report. All members of an affiliated group that are required to file a combined report must file one return on behalf of the members of the group under rules adopted by the commissioner. If a corporation claims on a return that it has paid tax in excess of the amount of taxes lawfully due, that corporation must include on that return information necessary for payment of the tax in excess of the amount lawfully due by electronic means.

Subd. 4. Exempt organizations; unrelated business income. An exempt organization that is subject to tax on unrelated business income under section 290.05, subdivision 3, must file a return for each taxable year in which the organization is required to file a return under section 6012 of the Internal Revenue Code because of the receipt of unrelated business income. If an organization is required to file a return under federal law but has no federal tax liability for the taxable year, the commissioner may provide that the filing requirement under this paragraph is satisfied by filing a copy of the taxpayer's federal return.

Subd. 5. Annual return; exceptions. A return under this section must cover a 12-month period, except in the following cases:

(1) A return made by or for a taxpayer in existence for less than the whole of a taxable year must cover the part of the taxable year the taxpayer was in existence;

(2) A taxpayer who, in keeping books, regularly computes income on the basis of an annual period that varies from 52 to 53 weeks and ends always on the same day of the week, and ends always (i) on the date that day of the week last occurs in a calendar month or (ii) on the date that day of the week falls that is nearest to the last day of a calendar month, may compute the taxpayer's net income and taxable net income on the basis of that annual period in accordance with rules prescribed by the commissioner. If the effective date or the applicability of a provision of this chapter or chapter 290 is expressed in terms of taxable years beginning or ending with reference to a named date that is the first or last day of a month, a taxable year must be treated as beginning with the first day of the calendar month beginning nearest to the first day of that

taxable year, or as ending with the last day of the calendar month ending nearest to the last day of that taxable year, as the case may be;

(3) A taxpayer who changes from one taxable year to another must make a return for the fractional parts of the year, under section 290.32.

Subd. 6. Returns of married persons. A husband and wife must file a joint Minnesota income tax return if they filed a joint federal income tax return. If the husband and wife have elected to file separate federal income tax returns, they must file separate Minnesota income tax returns. This election to file a joint or separate return must be changed if they change their election for federal purposes. In the event taxpayers desire to change their election, the change must be done in the manner and on the form prescribed by the commissioner.

The determination of whether an individual is married shall be made under the provisions of section 7703 of the Internal Revenue Code.

Subd. 7. Composite income tax returns for nonresident partners, shareholders, and beneficiaries. (a) The commissioner may allow a partnership with nonresident partners to file a composite return and to pay the tax on behalf of nonresident partners who have no other Minnesota source income. This composite return must include the names, addresses, Social Security numbers, income allocation, and tax liability for the nonresident partners electing to be covered by the composite return.

(b) The computation of a partner's tax liability must be determined by multiplying the income allocated to that partner by the highest rate used to determine the tax liability for individuals under section 290.06, subdivision 2c. Nonbusiness deductions, standard deductions, or personal exemptions are not allowed.

(c) The partnership must submit a request to use this composite return filing method for nonresident partners. The requesting partnership must file a composite return in the form prescribed by the commissioner of revenue. The filing of a composite return is considered a request to use the composite return filing method.

(d) The electing partner must not have any Minnesota source income other than the income from the partnership and other electing partnerships. If it is determined that the electing partner has other Minnesota source income, the inclusion of the income and tax liability for that partner under this provision will not constitute a return to satisfy the requirements of subdivision 1. The tax paid for the individual as part of the composite return is allowed as a payment of the tax by the individual on the date on which the composite return payment was made. If the electing nonresident partner has no other Minnesota source income, filing of the composite return is a return for purposes of subdivision 1.

(e) This subdivision does not negate the requirement that an individual pay estimated tax if the individual's liability would exceed the requirements set forth in section 289A.25. A composite estimate may, however, be filed in a manner similar to and containing the information required under paragraph (a).

(f) If an electing partner's share of the partnership's gross income from Minnesota sources is less than the filing requirements for a nonresident under this subdivision, the tax liability is zero. However, a statement showing the partner's share of gross income must be included as part of the composite return.

(g) The election provided in this subdivision is only available to a partner who has no other Minnesota source income and who is either (1) a full-year nonresident individual or (2) a trust or estate that does not claim a deduction under either section 651 or 661 of the Internal Revenue Code.

(h) A corporation defined in section 290.9725 and its nonresident shareholders may make an election under this paragraph. The provisions covering the partnership apply to the corporation and the provisions applying to the partner apply to the shareholder.

(i) Estates and trusts distributing current income only and the nonresident individual beneficiaries of the estates or trusts may make an election under this paragraph. The provisions covering the partnership apply to the estate or trust. The provisions applying to the partner apply to the beneficiary.

(j) For the purposes of this subdivision, "income" means the partner's share of federal adjusted gross income from the partnership modified by the additions provided in section 290.01, subdivision 19a, clauses (6) to (10), and the subtractions provided in: (i) section 290.01, subdivision 19b, clause (9), to the extent the amount is assignable or allocable to Minnesota under section 290.17; and (ii) section 290.01, subdivision 19b, clause (14). The subtraction allowed under section 290.01, subdivision 19b, clause (9), is only allowed on the composite tax computation to the extent the electing partner would have been allowed the subtraction.

Subd. 8. Returns of entertainment entities. An entertainment entity subject to the tax imposed by section 290.9201 shall file an annual return for the calendar year with the commissioner.

Subd. 9. Repealed by Laws 1993, c. 375, art. 2, § 36, eff. May 25, 1993.

Subd. 10. Filing of proper return. The return must specifically set forth the items of gross income, deductions, credits against the tax, and any other data necessary for computing the amount of any item required for determining the amount of the net income tax liability. The return must be filed in the form and manner the commissioner prescribes. The filing of a return required under this section is considered an assessment. The return must be signed by the taxpayer in the case of an individual's return, by both spouses in the case of a joint return, by someone designated by the corporation, partnership, entertainment entity, or mining company in the case of a corporate, composite income, entertainment, or occupation tax return, and by the trustee, receiver, or other fiduciary in the case of a fiduciary's return.

Subd. 11. Information included in income tax return. (a) The return must state:

(1) the name of the taxpayer, or taxpayers, if the return is a joint return, and the address of the taxpayer in the same name or names and same address as the taxpayer has used in making the taxpayer's income tax return to the United States;

(2) the date or dates of birth of the taxpayer or taxpayers;

(3) the Social Security number of the taxpayer, or taxpayers, if a Social Security number has been issued by the United States with respect to the taxpayers; and

(4) the amount of the taxable income of the taxpayer as it appears on the federal return for the taxable year to which the Minnesota state return applies.

(b) The taxpayer must attach to the taxpayer's Minnesota state income tax return a copy of the federal income tax return that the taxpayer has filed or is about to file for the period, unless the taxpayer is eligible to telefile the federal return and does file the Minnesota return by telefiling.

Subd. 12. Repealed by Laws 1993, c. 375, art. 2, § 36, eff. May 25, 1993.

Subd. 13. Long and short forms; local use tax instructions. The commissioner shall provide a long form individual income tax return and may provide a short form individual income tax return. The returns shall be in a form that is consistent with the provisions of chapter 290, notwithstanding any other law to the contrary. The nongame wildlife checkoff provided in section 290.431 and the dependent care credit provided in section 290.067 must be included on the short form. The commissioner must provide information on local use taxes in the individual income tax instruction booklet. The commissioner must provide this information in the same section of the booklet that provides information on the state use tax.

Subd. 14. Voter registration form. The commissioner shall insert securely in the individual income tax return form or instruction booklet distributed for an odd-numbered year a voter registration form, returnable to the secretary of state. The form shall be designed according to rules adopted by the secretary of state. This requirement applies to forms and booklets supplied to post offices, banks, and other outlets, as well as to those mailed directly to taxpayers.

Subd. 15. Mining companies. A mining company must file an annual return.

Subd. 16. Tax refund or return preparers; electronic filing; paper filing fee imposed. (a) A "tax refund or return preparer," as defined in section 289A.60, subdivision 13, paragraph (h), who prepared more than 100 Minnesota individual income tax returns for the prior calendar year must file all Minnesota individual income tax returns prepared for the current calendar year by electronic means.

(b) Paragraph (a) does not apply to a return if the taxpayer has indicated on the return that the taxpayer did not want the return filed by electronic means.

(c) For each return that is not filed electronically by a tax refund or return preparer under this subdivision, including returns filed under paragraph (b), a paper filing fee of $5 is imposed upon the preparer. The fee is collected from the preparer in the same manner as income tax. The fee does not apply to returns that the commissioner requires to be filed in paper form.

Laws 1990, c. 480, art. 1, §§ 3, 46. Amended by Laws 1990, c. 480, art. 5, §§ 4, 5; Laws 1990, c. 604, art. 10, § 23; Laws 1991, c. 291, art. 6, § 46; Laws 1991, c. 291, art. 11, § 3; Laws 1992, c. 511, art. 6, § 19; Laws 1993, c. 375, art. 2, §§ 3 to 5, eff. May 25, 1993; Laws 1993, c. 375, art. 8, § 14; Laws 1994, c. 416, art. 2, § 1; Laws 1994, c. 587, art. 1, § 24; Laws 1997, c. 31, art. 1, § 3; Laws 1997, c. 84, art. 2, § 1; Laws 2000, c. 490, art. 4, § 1; Laws 2003, 1st Sp., c. 1, art. 2, § 81; Laws 2003, 1st Sp., c. 21, art. 11, § 12; Laws 2005, c. 151, art. 2, § 17; Laws 2005, c. 151, art. 6, § 1; Laws 2005, c. 151, art. 9, § 15; Laws 2005, 1st Sp., c. 3, art. 3, §§ 1 to 3; Laws 2008, c. 154, art. 11, § 2, eff. Jan. 1, 2008; Laws 2008, c. 277, art. 1, § 61, eff. July 1, 2008.

[1] All text references to Internal Revenue Code sections are to Title 26 of U.S.C.A.

Historical and Statutory Notes

Laws 1990, c. 480, art. 1, § 46(a) provides that if a provision of a section of Minnesota Statutes repealed or amended by this article is amended by the 1990 regular session, the revisor shall codify the amendment consistent with the recodification of the affected section by this act, notwithstanding any law to the contrary.

Laws 1990, c. 480, art. 5, § 16 provides in part that § 5 (amending § 290.39, subd. 5 and incorporated in subd. 7, par. (c) of this section) is effective for taxable years beginning after December 31, 1989.

Laws 1994, c. 416, art. 2, § 7 provides in part that § 1 (amending subd. 7) is effective for taxable years beginning after December 31, 1993.

Laws 1997, c. 31, art. 1, § 19, provides in part that § 3 (amending subd. 11) is effective for taxable years beginning after December 31, 1995.

Laws 1997, c. 84, art. 2, § 7, provides in part that § 1 (amending subd. 3) is effective for tax years beginning after December 31, 1997.

Laws 2000, c. 490, art. 4, § 1, adding subd. 16, also provides in part that subd. 16 is effective for tax returns prepared for taxable years beginning after December 31, 1999.

Laws 2003, 1st Sp., c. 1, art. 2, § 81, amending subd. 16, also provided that the amendment was effective for returns filed for tax years beginning after December 31, 2002.

Laws 2003, 1st Sp., c. 21, art. 11, § 12, amending subd. 16, also provided that the amendment was effective for returns filed for tax years beginning after December 31, 2002.

Laws 2005, c. 151, art. 6, § 1, amending subd. 3, also provided:

"This section is effective for returns filed after December 31, 2005."

Laws 2005, 1st Sp., c. 3, art. 3, §§ 1 and 3, amending subds. 1 and 13, respectively, each also provided:

"This section is effective for taxable years beginning after December 31, 2004."

Laws 2005, 1st Sp., c. 3, art. 3, § 2, amending subd. 7, also provided:

"This section is effective for tax years ending after December 31, 2004."

Laws 2008, c. 154, art. 11, § 2, amending subd. 11, also provided:

"This section is effective for taxable years beginning after December 31, 2007."

**289A.09. Filing requirements for taxes withheld from wages, from compen-
            sation of entertainers, and from payments to out-of-state con-
            tractors; and taxes withheld by partnerships and small business
            corporations**

   Subdivision 1. Returns. (a) An employer who is required to deduct and
withhold tax under section 290.92, subdivision 2a or 3, and a person required
to deduct and withhold tax under section 290.923, subdivision 2, must file a
return with the commissioner for each quarterly period unless otherwise
prescribed by the commissioner.

   (b) A person or corporation required to make deposits under section
290.9201, subdivision 8, must file an entertainer withholding tax return with
the commissioner.

   (c) A person required to withhold an amount under section 290.9705, subdivision 1, must file a return.

   (d) A partnership required to deduct and withhold tax under section 290.92,
subdivision 4b, must file a return.

   (e) An S corporation required to deduct and withhold tax under section
290.92, subdivision 4c, must also file a return.

   (f) Returns must be filed in the form and manner, and contain the information prescribed by the commissioner. Every return for taxes withheld must be
signed by the employer, entertainment entity, contract payor, partnership, or S
corporation, or a designee.

   Subd. 2. Withholding statement.   (a) A person required to deduct and
withhold from an employee a tax under section 290.92, subdivision 2a or 3, or
290.923, subdivision 2, or who would have been required to deduct and
withhold a tax under section 290.92, subdivision 2a or 3, or persons required to
withhold tax under section 290.923, subdivision 2, determined without regard
to section 290.92, subdivision 19, if the employee or payee had claimed no
more than one withholding exemption, or who paid wages or made payments
not subject to withholding under section 290.92, subdivision 2a or 3, or
290.923, subdivision 2, to an employee or person receiving royalty payments in
excess of $600, or who has entered into a voluntary withholding agreement
with a payee under section 290.92, subdivision 20, must give every employee or
person receiving royalty payments in respect to the remuneration paid by the
person to the employee or person receiving royalty payments during the
calendar year, on or before January 31 of the succeeding year, or, if employment is terminated before the close of the calendar year, within 30 days after
the date of receipt of a written request from the employee if the 30–day period
ends before January 31, a written statement showing the following:

   (1) name of the person;

(2) the name of the employee or payee and the employee's or payee's Social Security account number;

(3) the total amount of wages as that term is defined in section 290.92, subdivision 1, paragraph (1); the total amount of remuneration subject to withholding under section 290.92, subdivision 20; the amount of sick pay as required under section 6051(f) of the Internal Revenue Code;[1] and the amount of royalties subject to withholding under section 290.923, subdivision 2; and

(4) the total amount deducted and withheld as tax under section 290.92, subdivision 2a or 3, or 290.923, subdivision 2.

(b) The statement required to be furnished by paragraph (a) with respect to any remuneration must be furnished at those times, must contain the information required, and must be in the form the commissioner prescribes.

(c) The commissioner may prescribe rules providing for reasonable extensions of time, not in excess of 30 days, to employers or payers required to give the statements to their employees or payees under this subdivision.

(d) A duplicate of any statement made under this subdivision and in accordance with rules prescribed by the commissioner, along with a reconciliation in the form the commissioner prescribes of the statements for the calendar year, including a reconciliation of the quarterly returns required to be filed under subdivision 1, must be filed with the commissioner on or before February 28 of the year after the payments were made.

(e) If an employer cancels the employer's Minnesota withholding account number required by section 290.92, subdivision 24, the information required by paragraph (d), must be filed with the commissioner within 30 days of the end of the quarter in which the employer cancels its account number.

(f) The employer must submit the statements required to be sent to the commissioner in the same manner required to satisfy the federal reporting requirements of section 6011(e) of the Internal Revenue Code and the regulations issued under it. For wages paid in calendar year 2008, an employer must submit statements to the commissioner required by this section by electronic means if the employer is required to send more than 100 statements to the commissioner, even though the employer is not required to submit the returns federally by electronic means. For calendar year 2009, the 100 statements threshold is reduced to 50, and for calendar year 2010, the threshold is reduced to 25, and for 2011 and after, the threshold is reduced to ten.

(g) A "third-party bulk filer" as defined in section 290.92, subdivision 30, paragraph (a), clause (2), must submit the returns required by this subdivision and subdivision 1, paragraph (a), with the commissioner by electronic means.

Subd. 3. Federal annuities; tax withholding request. The commissioner of revenue shall participate with the United States Office of Personnel Management in a program of voluntary state income tax withholding on the federal annuities of retired federal employees. Upon the request of the taxpayer to the commissioner of revenue, and only on request of the taxpayer, the commissioner shall provide for state income tax withholding on federal annuities paid to the taxpayer.

Laws 1990, c. 480, art. 1, § 4. Amended by Laws 1991, c. 291, art. 6, § 46; Laws 1992, c. 511, art. 6, § 19; Laws 1993, c. 375, art. 2, § 6, eff. May 25, 1993; Laws 1993, c. 375, art. 8, §§ 1, 14; Laws 1994, c. 587, art. 1, § 24; Laws 1997, c. 31, art. 1, § 4; Laws 1997, c. 84, art. 6, § 19; Laws 1998, c. 300, art. 1, § 1; Laws 2008, c. 154, art. 11, § 3, eff. Jan. 1, 2008.

[1] All text references to Internal Revenue Code sections are to Title 26 of U.S.C.A.

Historical and Statutory Notes

Laws 1990, c. 480, art. 1, § 47, provides in part that §§ 3 to 14 and 25 [enacting §§ 289A.08 to 289A.31 and 289A.56] are effective for returns, reports, taxes or other payments first becoming due on or after August 1, 1990, except that the exclusion for foreign operating corporations from the filing requirements in § 289A.08 is effective on the effective date of § 290.01, subd. 6b.

Laws 1997, c. 84, art. 6, § 29, provides in part that § 19 (amending subd. 2) is effective for returns for amounts withheld for periods after December 31, 1997.

Laws 1998, c. 300, art. 1, § 9, provides:

"Sections 1, 2, and 8 are effective for withholding on wages paid after December 31, 1997. Sections 3 and 4 are effective for federal extensions granted and final determinations made after the date of final enactment [March 18, 1998]. Sections 5 to 7 are effective for certificates issued after December 31, 1996, and used in taxable years beginning after July 31, 1997."

Laws 2008, c. 154, art. 11, § 3, amending subd. 2, also provided:

"This section is effective for wages paid after December 31, 2007."

289A.10. Filing requirements for estate tax returns

Subdivision 1. Return required. In the case of a decedent who has an interest in property with a situs in Minnesota, the personal representative must submit a Minnesota estate tax return to the commissioner, on a form prescribed by the commissioner, if:

(1) a federal estate tax return is required to be filed; or

(2) the federal gross estate exceeds $700,000 for estates of decedents dying after December 31, 2001, and before January 1, 2004; $850,000 for estates of decedents dying after December 31, 2003, and before January 1, 2005; $950,000 for estates of decedents dying after December 31, 2004, and before January 1, 2006; and $1,000,000 for estates of decedents dying after December 31, 2005.

The return must contain a computation of the Minnesota estate tax due. The return must be signed by the personal representative.

Subd. 2. Documents required. The commissioner may designate on the return the documents that are required to be filed together with the return to determine the computation of tax.

Subd. 3. Definitions. For purposes of this section, the definitions contained in section 291.005 apply.

Laws 1990, c. 480, art. 1, § 5. Amended by Laws 1997, c. 31, art. 1, § 5; Laws 2002, c. 377, art. 12, § 10; Laws 2003, c. 127, art. 3, § 1.

Historical and Statutory Notes

Laws 1990, c. 480, art. 1, § 47, provides in part that §§ 3 to 14 and 25 [enacting §§ 289A.08 to 289A.31 and 289A.56] are effective for returns, reports, taxes or other payments first becoming due on or after August 1, 1990, except that the exclusion for foreign operating corporations from the filing requirements in § 289A.08 is effective on the effective date of § 290.01, subd. 6b.

Laws 1997, c. 31, art. 1, § 19, provides in part that § 5 (amending subd. 1) is effective for

estates of decedents dying after the date of final enactment (April 15, 1997).

Laws 2002, c. 377, art. 12, § 10, amending subd. 1, also provides that the amendment is effective for estates and decedents dying after December 31, 2001.

Laws 2003, c. 127, art. 3, § 1, in the effective date portion, provided that art. 3, § 1, amending subd. 1, was effective for estates of decedents dying after December 31, 2002.

289A.11. Filing requirements for sales and use tax returns

Subdivision 1. Return required. Except as provided in section 289A.18, subdivision 4, for the month in which taxes imposed by chapter 297A are payable, or for which a return is due, a return for the preceding reporting period must be filed with the commissioner in the form and manner the commissioner prescribes. A person making sales at retail at two or more places of business may file a consolidated return subject to rules prescribed by the commissioner. In computing the dollar amount of items on the return, the amounts are rounded off to the nearest whole dollar, disregarding amounts less than 50 cents and increasing amounts of 50 cents to 99 cents to the next highest dollar.

Notwithstanding this subdivision, a person who is not required to hold a sales tax permit under chapter 297A and who makes annual purchases, for use in a trade or business, of less than $18,500, or a person who is not required to hold a sales tax permit and who makes purchases for personal use, that are subject to the use tax imposed by section 297A.63, may file an annual use tax return on a form prescribed by the commissioner. If a person who qualifies for an annual use tax reporting period is required to obtain a sales tax permit or makes use tax purchases, for use in a trade or business, in excess of $18,500 during the calendar year, the reporting period must be considered ended at the end of the month in which the permit is applied for or the purchase in excess of $18,500 is made and a return must be filed for the preceding reporting period.

Subd. 2. Repealed by Laws 2008, c. 277, art. 1, § 98, subd. 5, eff. July 1, 2008.

Subd. 3. Who must file return. For purposes of the sales tax, a return must be filed by a retailer who is required to hold a permit. For the purposes of the use tax, a return must be filed by a retailer required to collect the tax and by a person buying any items, the storage, use or other consumption of which is subject to the use tax, who has not paid the use tax to a retailer required to collect the tax. The returns must be signed by the person filing the return or by the person's agent duly authorized in writing.

Laws 1990, c. 480, art. 1, § 6. Amended by Laws 1991, c. 249, § 31; Laws 1991, c. 291, art. 8, § 3; Laws 1992, c. 511, art. 8, § 2, eff. April 25, 1992; Laws 1993, c. 375, art. 2, §§ 7, 8, eff. May 25, 1993; Laws 1994, c. 587, art. 2, § 1, eff. May 6, 1994; Laws 1997, c. 31, art. 2, § 4, eff. July 1, 1997; Laws 2000, c. 418, art. 1, § 44, subd. 2, eff. July 1, 2001; Laws 2005, 1st Sp., c. 3, art. 5, § 2.

Historical and Statutory Notes

Laws 1990, c. 480, art. 1, § 47, provides in part that §§ 3 to 14 and 25 [enacting §§ 289A.08 to 289A.31 and 289A.56] are effective for returns, reports, taxes or other payments first becoming due on or after August 1, 1990, except that the exclusion for foreign operating corporations from the filing requirements in § 289A.08 is effective on the effective date of § 290.01, subd. 6b.

Laws 1991, c. 291, art. 8, § 31 provides in part that § 3 (amending subd. 1 of this section) is effective for purchases made after June 30, 1991.

Laws 2005, 1st Sp., c. 3, art. 5, § 2, amending subd. 1, also provided:

"This section is effective for returns filed after December 31, 2005."

289A.12. Filing requirements for information returns and reports

Subdivision 1. Repealed by Laws 1992, c. 511, art. 7, § 26, eff. April 25, 1992.

Subd. 2. Returns required of banks; common trust funds. The commissioner may by notice and demand require a bank maintaining a common trust fund to file with the commissioner a return for a taxable year, stating specifically with respect to the fund, the items of gross income and deductions provided by section 290.281, subdivision 1. The return must include the names and addresses of the participants entitled to share the net income if distributed and the amount of the proportionate share of each participant.

Subd. 3. Returns or reports by partnerships, fiduciaries, and S corporations. (a) Partnerships must file a return with the commissioner for each taxable year. The return must conform to the requirements of section 290.311, and must include the names and addresses of the partners entitled to a distributive share in their taxable net income, gain, loss, or credit, and the amount of the distributive share to which each is entitled. A partnership required to file a return for a partnership taxable year must furnish a copy of the information required to be shown on the return to a person who is a partner at any time during the taxable year, on or before the day on which the return for the taxable year was filed.

(b) The fiduciary of an estate or trust making the return required to be filed under section 289A.08, subdivision 2, for a taxable year must give a beneficiary who receives a distribution from the estate or trust with respect to the taxable year or to whom any item with respect to the taxable year is allocated, a statement containing the information required to be shown on the return, on or before the date on which the return was filed.

(c) An S corporation must file a return with the commissioner for a taxable year during which an election under section 290.9725 is in effect, stating specifically the names and addresses of the persons owning stock in the corporation at any time during the taxable year, the number of shares of stock owned by a shareholder at all times during the taxable year, the shareholder's pro rata share of each item of the corporation for the taxable year, and other information the commissioner requires. An S corporation required to file a return under this paragraph for any taxable year must furnish a copy of the information shown on the return to the person who is a shareholder at any time during the taxable year, on or before the day on which the return for the taxable year was filed.

(d) The partnership or S corporation return must be signed by someone designated by the partnership or S corporation.

*Text of subd. 4 effective for forms required to be filed
by federal law on or before December 31, 2009.*

Subd. 4. Returns by persons, corporations, cooperatives, governmental entities, or school districts. The commissioner may by notice and demand require to the extent required by section 6041 of the Internal Revenue Code,[1] a person, corporation, or cooperative, the state of Minnesota and its political subdivisions, and a city, county, and school district in Minnesota, making payments in the regular course of a trade or business during the taxable year to any person or corporation of $600 or more on account of rents or royalties, or of $10 or more on account of interest, or $10 or more on account of dividends or patronage dividends, or $600 or more on account of either wages, salaries, commissions, fees, prizes, awards, pensions, annuities, or any other fixed or determinable gains, profits or income, not otherwise reportable under section 289A.09, subdivision 2, or on account of earnings of $10 or more distributed to its members by savings associations or credit unions chartered under the laws of this state or the United States, (1) to file with the commissioner a return (except in cases where a valid agreement to participate in the combined federal and state information reporting system has been entered into, and the return is filed only with the commissioner of internal revenue under the applicable filing and informational reporting requirements of the Internal Revenue Code) with respect to the payments in excess of the amounts named, giving the names and addresses of the persons to whom the payments were made, the amounts paid to each, and (2) to make a return with respect to the total number of payments and total amount of payments, for each category of income named, which were in excess of the amounts named. This subdivision does not apply to the payment of interest or dividends to a person who was a nonresident of Minnesota for the entire year.

A person, corporation, or cooperative required to file returns under this subdivision must file the returns on magnetic media if magnetic media was used to satisfy the federal reporting requirement under section 6011(e) of the Internal Revenue Code, unless the person establishes to the satisfaction of the commissioner that compliance with this requirement would be an undue hardship.

Text of subd. 4 effective for forms required to be filed
by federal law after December 31, 2009.

Subd. 4. Returns by persons, corporations, cooperatives, governmental entities, or school districts. (a) The commissioner may by notice and demand require to the extent required by section 6041 of the Internal Revenue Code, [1] a person, corporation, or cooperative, the state of Minnesota and its political subdivisions, and a city, county, and school district in Minnesota, making payments in the regular course of a trade or business during the taxable year to any person or corporation of $600 or more on account of rents or royalties, or of $10 or more on account of interest, or $10 or more on account of dividends or patronage dividends, or $600 or more on account of either wages, salaries, commissions, fees, prizes, awards, pensions, annuities, or any other fixed or determinable gains, profits or income, not otherwise reportable under section 289A.09, subdivision 2, or on account of earnings of $10 or more distributed to its members by savings associations or credit unions chartered under the laws of this state or the United States, (1) to file with the commissioner a return (except in cases where a valid agreement to participate in the combined federal and state information reporting system has been entered into, and the return is filed only with the commissioner of internal revenue under the applicable filing and informational reporting requirements of the Internal Revenue Code) with respect to the payments in excess of the amounts named, giving the names and addresses of the persons to whom the payments were made, the amounts paid to each, and (2) to make a return with respect to the total number of payments and total amount of payments, for each category of income named, which were in excess of the amounts named. This subdivision does not apply to the payment of interest or dividends to a person who was a nonresident of Minnesota for the entire year.

(b) For payments for which a return is covered by paragraph (a), regardless of whether the commissioner has required filing under paragraph (a), the payor must file a copy of the return with the commissioner if:

(i) the return is for a payment made to a Minnesota resident, to a recipient with a Minnesota address, or for activity occurring in the state of Minnesota; and

(ii) the payment is for wages, salaries, or other compensation for services provided. The commissioner may require this information to be filed in electronic or another form that the commissioner determines is appropriate, notwithstanding the provisions of paragraph (c).

(c) A person, corporation, or cooperative required to file returns under this subdivision must file the returns on magnetic media if magnetic media was used to satisfy the federal reporting requirement under section 6011(e) of the Internal Revenue Code, unless the person establishes to the satisfaction of the commissioner that compliance with this requirement would be an undue hardship.

Subd. 5.   Returns by brokers. The commissioner may, within 30 days after notice and demand, require a person doing business as a broker to give the commissioner the names and addresses of customers for whom they have transacted business, and the details regarding gross proceeds and other information concerning the transactions as will enable the commissioner to determine whether the income tax due on profits or gains of those customers has been paid. The provisions of section 6045 of the Internal Revenue Code which define terms and require that a statement be furnished to the customer apply.

Subd. 6.   Returns by agents. The commissioner may, within 30 days after notice and demand, require a person acting as agent for another to make a return furnishing the information reasonably necessary to properly assess and collect the tax imposed by chapter 290 upon the person for whom the agent acts.

Subd. 7.   Returns for real property holdings of aliens. The commissioner may by notice and demand require a person or corporation required to make a return under section 6039C (relating to information return on a foreign person holding a United States real property interest) of the Internal Revenue Code to make a similar return for the commissioner for foreign persons holding a Minnesota real property interest.

Subd. 8.   Returns for unemployment benefits. The commissioner may by notice and demand require a person who makes payments of unemployment benefits totaling $10 or more to any individual during a calendar year and who is required to make and file a return under section 6050B of the Internal Revenue Code to file a copy of the return with the commissioner.

Subd. 9.   Returns for payments of remuneration for services and direct sales. The commissioner may by notice and demand require a person who is required to make a return under section 6041A (relating to information returns regarding payments of remuneration for services and direct sales) of the Internal Revenue Code to file a copy of the return containing the information required under that section with the commissioner. The provisions of that section govern the requirements of a statement that must be given to persons with respect to whom information is required to be given.

Subd. 10.   Returns relating to Social Security benefits. The commissioner may by notice and demand require the appropriate federal official who is required to make a return under section 6050F (relating to Social Security benefits) of the Internal Revenue Code, to file a copy of the return containing the information required under that section with the commissioner.

Subd. 11.   Returns by trustees. The commissioner may by notice and demand require the trustee of an individual retirement account and the issuer of an endowment contract or an individual retirement annuity who is required to make a report under section 408(i) of the Internal Revenue Code, to file with the commissioner a copy of that report containing the information required under that subsection. The provisions of that subsection govern when the reports are to be filed and the requirements of a statement that must be given to persons with respect to whom information must be given.

Subd. 12. Statements to payees. A person who can be required to file a return with the commissioner under subdivisions 4 to 10 must furnish to a person whose name is set forth in the return a written statement showing the name and address of the person making the return, and the aggregate amount of payments to the person shown on the return.

This written statement must be given to the person on or before January 31 of the year following the calendar year for which the return was made.

Subd. 13. Supplying of Social Security number. An individual with respect to whom a return, statement, or other document is required under this section to be made by another person must furnish to that person the individual's Social Security account number. A person required under this section to make a return, statement, or other document with respect to another person who is an individual must request from that individual and must include in the return, statement, or other document the individual's Social Security account number. A return of an estate or trust with respect to its liability for tax, and any statement or other document in its support, is considered a return, statement, or other document with respect to the individual beneficiary of the estate or trust; otherwise, a return of an individual with respect to the individual's liability for tax, or any statement or other document in its support, is not considered a return, statement, or other document with respect to another person.

Subd. 14. Regulated investment companies; reporting exempt-interest dividends. (a) A regulated investment company paying $10 or more in exempt-interest dividends to an individual who is a resident of Minnesota must make a return indicating the amount of the exempt-interest dividends, the name, address, and Social Security number of the recipient, and any other information that the commissioner specifies. The return must be provided to the shareholder no later than 30 days after the close of the taxable year. The return provided to the shareholder must include a clear statement, in the form prescribed by the commissioner, that the exempt-interest dividends must be included in the computation of Minnesota taxable income. The regulated investment company is required in a manner prescribed by the commissioner to file a copy of the return with the commissioner.

(b) This subdivision applies to regulated investment companies required to register under chapter 80A.

(c) For purposes of this subdivision, the following definitions apply.

(1) "Exempt-interest dividends" mean exempt-interest dividends as defined in section 852(b)(5) of the Internal Revenue Code, but does not include the

portion of exempt-interest dividends that are not required to be added to federal taxable income under section 290.01, subdivision 19a, clause (1)(ii).

(2) "Regulated investment company" means regulated investment company as defined in section 851(a) of the Internal Revenue Code or a fund of the regulated investment company as defined in section 851(g) of the Internal Revenue Code.

Subd. 15. Report of job opportunity zone benefits; penalty for failure to file report. (a) By October 15 of each year, every qualified business, as defined under section 469.310, subdivision 11, must file with the commissioner, on a form prescribed by the commissioner, a report listing the tax benefits under section 469.315 received by the business for the previous year.

(b) The commissioner shall send notice to each business that fails to timely submit the report required under paragraph (a). The notice shall demand that the business submit the report within 60 days. Where good cause exists, the commissioner may extend the period for submitting the report as long as a request for extension is filed by the business before the expiration of the 60–day period. The commissioner shall notify the commissioner of employment and economic development and the appropriate job opportunity subzone administrator whenever notice is sent to a business under this paragraph.

(c) A business that fails to submit the report as required under paragraph (b) is no longer a qualified business under section 469.310, subdivision 11, and is subject to the repayment provisions of section 469.319.

Laws 1990, c. 480, art. 1, § 7. Amended by Laws 1991, c. 291, art. 6, §§ 7, 46; Laws 1992, c. 511, art. 6, § 19; Laws 1993, c. 375, art. 2, § 9; Laws 1993, c. 375, art. 2, § 10, eff. May 25, 1993; Laws 1993, c. 375, art. 2, §§ 11 to 18; Laws 1993, c. 375, art. 8, § 14; Laws 1994, c. 488, § 8; Laws 1994, c. 587, art. 1, § 24; Laws 1995, c. 202, art. 1, § 25, eff. May 25, 1995; Laws 1998, c. 389, art. 7, § 12; Laws 1999, c. 107, § 66; Laws 2000, c. 343, § 4, eff. April 7, 2000; Laws 2001, 1st Sp., c. 5, art. 7, § 32; Laws 2008, c. 154, art. 3, § 1, eff. Jan. 1, 2010; Laws 2008, c. 154, art. 11, § 4, eff. Jan. 1, 2008; Laws 2008, c. 366, art. 5, § 8, eff. Oct. 15, 2008.

[1] All text references to Internal Revenue Code sections are to Title 26 of U.S.C.A.

Historical and Statutory Notes

Laws 1990, c. 480, art. 1, § 47, provides in part that §§ 3 to 14 and 25 [enacting §§ 289A.08 to 289A.31 and 289A.56] are effective for returns, reports, taxes or other payments first becoming due on or after August 1, 1990, except that the exclusion for foreign operating corporations from the filing requirements in § 289A.08 is effective on the effective date of § 290.01, subd. 6b.

Laws 1991, c. 291, art. 6, § 48 provides in part that except where otherwise specifically provided, this article is effective for taxable years beginning after December 31, 1990. There were no specified effective date provisions listed in Laws 1991, c. 291, art. 6 for §§ 7 to 12, 14, 16, 18 to 23, 26 to 29, and 32 to 40.

Laws 1993, c. 375, art. 2, §§ 37, provides in part that §§ 9 and 11 to 18 (amending subds. 2, 4, 7, 8, 9, 10, 11, 12, and 14 of this section) are

effective for tax returns due after December 31, 1992.

Laws 1993, c. 375, art. 8, § 15, provides in part that § 14 is effective for tax years beginning after December 31, 1992.

Laws 2001, 1st Sp., c. 5, art. 7, § 32, also provided that the amendment of this section was effective for tax years beginning after December 31, 2000.

Laws 2008, c. 154, art. 3, § 1, amending subd. 4, also provided:

"This section is effective for forms required to be filed by federal law after December 31, 2009."

Laws 2008, c. 154, art. 11, § 4, amending subd. 14, also provided:

"This section is effective for taxable years beginning after December 31, 2007."

Laws 2008, c. 366, art. 5, § 8, adding subd. 15, also provided: "This section is effective beginning with reports required to be filed October 15, 2008."

289A.121. Tax shelters; special rules

Subdivision 1. Scope. The provisions of this section apply to a tax shelter that:

(1) is organized in this state;

(2) is doing business in this state;

(3) is deriving income from sources in this state; or

(4) has one or more investors that are Minnesota taxpayers under chapter 290.

Subd. 2. Definitions. (a) For purposes of this section, the definitions under sections 6111, 6112, and 6707A of the Internal Revenue Code, [1] including the regulations under those sections, apply.

(b) The term "tax shelter" means any reportable transaction as defined under section 6707A(c)(1) of the Internal Revenue Code.

Subd. 3. Registration. (a) Any material advisor required to register a tax shelter under section 6111 of the Internal Revenue Code must register the shelter with the commissioner.

(b) A material advisor subject to this subdivision must send a duplicate of the federal registration information, along with any other information the commissioner requires, to the commissioner not later than the day on which interests in that tax shelter are first offered for sale to Minnesota taxpayers.

(c) In addition to the requirements under paragraph (b), any listed transaction must be registered with the commissioner by the latest of:

(1) 60 days after entering into the transaction;

(2) 60 days after the transaction becomes a listed transaction; or

(3) October 15, 2005.

Subd. 4. Registration number. (a) Any person required to register under section 6111 of the Internal Revenue Code who receives a tax registration number from the Secretary of the Treasury must file, within 30 days after requested by the commissioner, a statement of the registration number with the commissioner.

(b) Any person who sells or otherwise transfers an interest in a tax shelter must, in the same time and manner required under section 6111(b) of the Internal Revenue Code, furnish to each investor who purchases or otherwise acquires an interest in the tax shelter the identification number assigned under federal law to the tax shelter.

(c) Any person claiming any deduction, credit, or other tax benefit by reason of a tax shelter must include on the return on which the deduction, credit, or other benefit is claimed the identification number assigned under federal law to the tax shelter.

Subd. 5. Reportable transactions. (a) For each taxable year in which a taxpayer must make a return or a statement under Code of Federal Regulations, title 26, section 1.6011-4, for a reportable transaction, including a listed transaction, in which the taxpayer participated in a taxable year for which a return is required under chapter 290, the taxpayer must file a copy of the disclosure with the commissioner.

(b) Any taxpayer that is a member of a unitary business group that includes any person that must make a disclosure statement under Code of Federal Regulations, title 26, section 1.6011-4, must file a disclosure under this subdivision.

(c) Disclosure under this subdivision is required for any transaction entered into after December 31, 2001, that the Internal Revenue Service determines is a listed transaction at any time, and must be made in the manner prescribed by the commissioner. For transactions in which the taxpayer participated for taxable years ending before December 31, 2005, disclosure must be made by the extended due date of the first return required under chapter 290 that occurs 60 days or more after July 14, 2005. With respect to transactions in which the taxpayer participated for taxable years ending on and after December 31, 2005, disclosure must be made in the time and manner prescribed in Code of Federal Regulations, title 26, section 1.6011-4(e).

(d) Notwithstanding paragraphs (a) to (c), no disclosure is required for transactions entered into after December 31, 2001, and before January 1, 2006, if (1) the taxpayer has filed an amended income tax return which reverses the tax benefits of the tax shelter transaction, or (2) as a result of a federal audit the Internal Revenue Service has determined the tax treatment of the transaction and an amended return has been filed to reflect the federal treatment.

Subd. 6. Lists of investors. (a) Any person required to maintain a list under section 6112 of the Internal Revenue Code with respect to any reportable transaction must furnish the list to the commissioner no later than when required under federal law. The list required under this subdivision must include the same information required with respect to a reportable transaction under section 6112 of the Internal Revenue Code, and any other information the commissioner requires.

(b) For transactions entered into on or after December 31, 2001, that become listed transactions at any time, the list must be furnished to the commissioner by the latest of:

(1) 60 days after entering into the transaction;

(2) 60 days after the transaction becomes a listed transaction; or

(3) October 15, 2005.

Laws 2005, 1st Sp., c. 3, art. 8, § 2, eff. July 14, 2005. Amended by Laws 2006, c. 259, art. 8, § 8.

[1] All text references to Internal Revenue Code sections are to Title 26 of U.S.C.A.

Historical and Statutory Notes

Laws 2006, c. 259, art. 8, § 8, amending subd. 5, also provided:

"This section is effective for disclosures of reportable transactions in which the taxpayer participated for taxable years ending before December 31, 2005."

289A.13. Repealed by Laws 2005, c. 151, art. 1, § 117, eff. Aug. 1, 2005

Historical and Statutory Notes

Laws 2005, c. 151, art. 1, § 115, provided:

"Subdivision 1. Purpose. It is the intent of the legislature to simplify Minnesota's tax laws by consolidating and recodifying tax administration and compliance provisions now contained in Minnesota Statutes, chapter 270, and several other chapters of Minnesota Statutes. The provisions of this act may not be used to determine the law in effect prior to the effective dates in this act.

"Subd. 2. Effect. Due to the complexity of the recodification, prior provisions are repealed on the effective date of the new provisions. The repealed provisions, however, continue to remain in effect until superseded by the analogous provision in the new law."

DUE DATES AND FILING EXTENSIONS

289A.18. Due dates for filing of returns

Subdivision 1. Individual income, fiduciary income, corporate franchise, and entertainment taxes; partnership and S corporation returns; information returns; mining company returns. The returns required to be made under sections 289A.08 and 289A.12 must be filed at the following times:

(1) returns made on the basis of the calendar year must be filed on April 15 following the close of the calendar year, except that returns of corporations must be filed on March 15 following the close of the calendar year;

(2) returns made on the basis of the fiscal year must be filed on the 15th day of the fourth month following the close of the fiscal year, except that returns of corporations must be filed on the 15th day of the third month following the close of the fiscal year;

(3) returns for a fractional part of a year must be filed on the 15th day of the fourth month following the end of the month in which falls the last day of the period for which the return is made, except that the returns of corporations must be filed on the 15th day of the third month following the end of the tax year; or, in the case of a corporation which is a member of a unitary group, the return of the corporation must be filed on the 15th day of the third month following the end of the tax year of the unitary group in which falls the last day of the period for which the return is made;

(4) in the case of a final return of a decedent for a fractional part of a year, the return must be filed on the 15th day of the fourth month following the close of the 12–month period that began with the first day of that fractional part of a year;

(5) in the case of the return of a cooperative association, returns must be filed on or before the 15th day of the ninth month following the close of the taxable year;

(6) if a corporation has been divested from a unitary group and files a return for a fractional part of a year in which it was a member of a unitary business that files a combined report under section 290.17, subdivision 4, the divested corporation's return must be filed on the 15th day of the third month following the close of the common accounting period that includes the fractional year;

(7) returns of entertainment entities must be filed on April 15 following the close of the calendar year;

(8) returns required to be filed under section 289A.08, subdivision 4, must be filed on the 15th day of the fifth month following the close of the taxable year;

(9) returns of mining companies must be filed on May 1 following the close of the calendar year; and

(10) returns required to be filed with the commissioner under section 289A.12, subdivision 2 or 4 to 10, must be filed within 30 days after being demanded by the commissioner.

Subd. 2.   Withholding returns, entertainer withholding returns, returns for withholding from payments to out–of–state contractors, and withholding returns from partnerships and S corporations.   Withholding returns for the first, second, and third quarters are due on or before the last day of the month following the close of the quarterly period.   However, if the return shows timely deposits in full payment of the taxes due for that period, the returns for the first, second, and third quarters may be filed on or before the tenth day of the second calendar month following the period.   The return for the fourth quarter must be filed on or before the 28th day of the second calendar month following the period.   An employer, in preparing a quarterly return, may take credit for deposits previously made for that quarter.   Entertainer withholding tax returns are due within 30 days after each performance.   Returns for withholding from payments to out-of-state contractors are due within 30 days after the payment to the contractor.   Returns for withholding by partnerships are due on or before the due date specified for filing partnership returns.   Returns for withholding by S corporations are due on or before the due date specified for filing corporate franchise tax returns.

Subd. 3.   Estate tax returns.   An estate tax return must be filed with the commissioner within nine months after the decedent's death.

Subd. 4.   Sales and use tax returns.   (a) Sales and use tax returns must be filed on or before the 20th day of the month following the close of the preceding reporting period, except that annual use tax returns provided for under section 289A.11, subdivision 1, must be filed by April 15 following the close of the calendar year, in the case of individuals. Annual use tax returns of businesses, including sole proprietorships, and annual sales tax returns must be filed by February 5 following the close of the calendar year.

(b) Returns for the June reporting period filed by retailers required to remit their June liability under section 289A.20, subdivision 4, paragraph (b), are due on or before August 20.

(c) If a retailer has an average sales and use tax liability, including local sales and use taxes administered by the commissioner, equal to or less than $500 per month in any quarter of a calendar year, and has substantially complied with the tax laws during the preceding four calendar quarters, the retailer may request authorization to file and pay the taxes quarterly in subsequent calendar quarters. The authorization remains in effect during the period in which the retailer's quarterly returns reflect sales and use tax liabilities of less than $1,500 and there is continued compliance with state tax laws.

(d) If a retailer has an average sales and use tax liability, including local sales and use taxes administered by the commissioner, equal to or less than $100 per month during a calendar year, and has substantially complied with the tax laws during that period, the retailer may request authorization to file and pay the taxes annually in subsequent years. The authorization remains in effect during the period in which the retailer's annual returns reflect sales and use tax liabilities of less than $1,200 and there is continued compliance with state tax laws.

(e) The commissioner may also grant quarterly or annual filing and payment authorizations to retailers if the commissioner concludes that the retailers' future tax liabilities will be less than the monthly totals identified in paragraphs (c) and (d). An authorization granted under this paragraph is subject to the same conditions as an authorization granted under paragraphs (c) and (d).

(f) A taxpayer who is a materials supplier may report gross receipts either on:

(1) the cash basis as the consideration is received; or

(2) the accrual basis as sales are made.

As used in this paragraph, "materials supplier" means a person who provides materials for the improvement of real property; who is primarily engaged in the sale of lumber and building materials-related products to owners, contractors, subcontractors, repairers, or consumers; who is authorized to file a mechanics lien upon real property and improvements under chapter 514; and who files with the commissioner an election to file sales and use tax returns on the basis of this paragraph.

(g) Notwithstanding paragraphs (a) to (f), a seller that is not a Model 1, 2, or 3 seller, as those terms are used in the Streamlined Sales and Use Tax

Agreement, that does not have a legal requirement to register in Minnesota, and that is registered under the agreement, must file a return by February 5 following the close of the calendar year in which the seller initially registers, and must file subsequent returns on February 5 on an annual basis in succeeding years. Additionally, a return must be submitted on or before the 20th day of the month following any month by which sellers have accumulated state and local tax funds for the state in the amount of $1,000 or more.

Subd. 5. Property tax refund claims. A claim for a refund based on property taxes payable must be filed with the commissioner on or before August 15 of the year in which the property taxes are due and payable. Any claim for refund based on rent paid must be filed on or before August 15 of the year following the year in which the rent was paid.

Laws 1990, c. 480, art. 1, § 8. Amended by Laws 1991, c. 291, art. 6, § 8; Laws 1991, c. 291, art. 7, § 1; Laws 1991, c. 291, art. 8, § 4; Laws 1991, c. 291, art. 11, § 4; Laws 1992, c. 511, art. 8, § 3; Laws 1993, c. 375, art. 2, §§ 20, 21; Laws 1993, c. 375, art. 10, § 13; Laws 1994, c. 510, art. 3, § 7; Laws 1995, c. 264, art. 10, § 1; Laws 1995, c. 264, art. 17, § 1; Laws 1997, c. 31, art. 1, § 6; Laws 1999, c. 243, art. 4, § 1; Laws 2001, c. 7, § 56; Laws 2001, 1st Sp., c. 5, art. 17, § 8; Laws 2003, c. 127, art. 1, § 3; Laws 2005, c. 151, art. 6, § 2; Laws 2008, c. 154, art. 11, § 5, eff. Jan. 1, 2008; Laws 2008, c. 366, art. 12, § 1.

Historical and Statutory Notes

Laws 1990, c. 480, art. 1, § 47, provides in part that §§ 3 to 14 and 25 [enacting §§ 289A.08 to 289A.31 and 289A.56] are effective for returns, reports, taxes or other payments first becoming due on or after August 1, 1990, except that the exclusion for foreign operating corporations from the filing requirements in § 289A.08 is effective on the effective date of § 290.01, subd. 6b.

Laws 1991, c. 291, art. 6, § 48 provides in part that except where otherwise specifically provided, this article is effective for taxable years beginning after December 31, 1990. There were no specified effective date provisions listed in Laws 1991, c. 291, art. 6 for §§ 7 to 12, 14, 16, 18 to 23, 26 to 29, and 32 to 40.

Laws 1991, c. 291, art. 7, § 27 provides:

"Sections 2 [amending § 289A.26, subd. 1], 9 [amending § 290.05, subd. 3], 15 to 19 [amending §§ 290.0922, subd. 1, 290.17, subd. 5, 290.191, subds. 6, 8, and 11], 21 to 24 [in § 290.9727, amending subds. 1 and 3 and adding subds. 1a and 5], and 26 [repealing §§ 290.068, subd. 6, 290.069, subds. 2a, 4a, and 4b, 290.17, subd. 7, and 290.191, subd. 7] are effective for taxable years beginning after December 31, 1990, provided that the carryover for the credit provided under Minnesota Statutes, section 290.068, subdivision 6, that is repealed by section 26, remains in effect for taxable years beginning before 2003. Sections 10 [amending § 290.06, subd. 21] and 14 [amending § 290.0921, subd. 8] are effective the day following final enactment. Sections 1 [amending § 289A.18, subd. 1], 3 [amending § 289A.26, subd. 6], 20 [amending § 290.35, subd. 3], and 25 are effective for taxable years beginning after December 31, 1989."

Laws 1991, c. 291, art. 8, § 31 provides in part that § 4 (amending subd. 4 of this section) is effective for purchases made after June 30, 1991.

Laws 1991, c. 291, art. 11, § 21, provides in part that § 4 (amending subd. 1 of this section) is effective for ores mined after December 31, 1990.

Laws 1992, c. 511, art. 8, § 39, provides in part that § 3 is effective for tax payments due for sales made after September 30, 1992.

Laws 1993, c. 375, art. 2, § 37, provides in part that § 20 (amending subd. 1) is effective for tax returns due after December 31, 1992, and that § 21 (amending subd. 4) is effective for tax returns due for the calendar year 1993, and thereafter.

Laws 1993, c. 375, art. 10, § 52, provides in part that § 13 (amending subd. 4) is effective for payments due in the calendar year 1994, and thereafter, based upon payments made in the fiscal year ending June 30, 1993, and thereafter; provided that § 13 (amending subd. 4), as it relates to quarterly and annual sales and use tax returns, is effective for returns due for calendar quarters beginning with the first quarter of 1994, and for calendar years beginning with 1994.

Laws 1994, c. 510, art. 3, § 14, provides in part that § 7 (amending subd. 4) is effective for returns due after December 31, 1994.

Laws 1995, c. 264, art. 10, § 15, provides in part that § 1 (amending subd. 2) is effective for returns due after December 31, 1995.

Laws 1995, c. 264, art. 17, § 12, provides in part that § 1 (amending subd. 4) is effective for returns due in 1996 and thereafter.

Laws 1997, c. 31, art. 1, § 19, provides in part that § 6 (amending subd. 2) is effective for returns due after December 31, 1996.

Laws 1999, c. 243, art. 4, § 19, provides in part that § 1, amending subd. 4, is effective for sales and purchases made after June 30, 1999.

Laws 2001, 1st Sp., c. 5, art. 17, § 8, also provides that the amendment of subd. 4 is effective for returns due on or after July 1, 2001.

Laws 2003, c. 127, art. 1, § 3, amending subd. 4 by adding par. (g), also provided that the amendment was effective for sales and purchases made on or after January 1, 2004.

Laws 2005, c. 151, art. 6, § 2, amending subd. 1, also provided:

"This section is effective for fractional years closing after December 31, 2004."

Laws 2008, c. 154, art. 11, § 5, amending subd. 1, also provided:

"This section is effective for taxable years beginning after December 31, 2007."

Laws 2008, c. 366, art. 12, § 1, amending subd. 1, also provided:

"This section is effective [May 30, 2008] except that the change in clause (6) is effective for taxable years beginning after December 31, 2007."

289A.19. Extensions for filing returns

Subdivision 1. Fiduciary income, entertainment tax, and information returns. When, in the commissioner's judgment, good cause exists, the commissioner may extend the time for filing entertainment tax returns for not more than six months. The commissioner shall grant an automatic extension of six months to file a partnership, "S" corporation, or fiduciary income tax return if all of the taxes imposed on the entity for the year by chapter 290 and section 289A.08, subdivision 7, have been paid by the date prescribed by section 289A.18, subdivision 1.

Subd. 2. Corporate franchise and mining company taxes. Corporations or mining companies shall receive an extension of seven months or the amount of time granted by the Internal Revenue Service, whichever is longer, for filing the return of a corporation subject to tax under chapter 290 or for filing the return of a mining company subject to tax under sections 298.01 and 298.015. Interest on any balance of tax not paid when the regularly required return is due must be paid at the rate specified in section 270C.40, from the date such payment should have been made if no extension was granted, until the date of payment of such tax.

If a corporation or mining company does not:

(1) pay at least 90 percent of the amount of tax shown on the return on or before the regular due date of the return, the penalty prescribed by section 289A.60, subdivision 1, shall be imposed on the unpaid balance of tax; or

(2) pay the balance due shown on the regularly required return on or before the extended due date of the return, the penalty prescribed by section 289A.60,

subdivision 1, shall be imposed on the unpaid balance of tax from the original due date of the return.

Subd. 3. Withholding returns. The commissioner shall grant an automatic extension of 60 days to file a withholding tax return with the commissioner provided all the withholding taxes have been paid by the date prescribed by section 289A.20, subdivision 2. In any case where good cause exists, the commissioner may grant an extension of time of not more than 60 days for filing a withholding return.

Subd. 4. Estate tax returns. When an extension to file the federal estate tax return has been granted under section 6081 of the Internal Revenue Code, the time for filing the estate tax return is extended for that period. If the estate requests an extension to file an estate tax return within the time provided in section 289A.18, subdivision 3, the commissioner shall extend the time for filing the estate tax return for six months.

Subd. 5. Sales and use tax returns. Where good cause exists, the commissioner may extend the time for filing sales and use tax returns for not more than 60 days.

Subd. 6. Repealed by Laws 1991, c. 291, art. 6, § 47.

Subd. 7. Federal extensions. When an extension of time to file a partnership or S corporation tax return is granted by the Internal Revenue Service, the commissioner shall grant an automatic extension to file the comparable Minnesota return for that period. An extension granted under this subdivision does not affect the due date for making payments of tax.

Laws 1990, c. 480, art. 1, § 9. Amended by Laws 1991, c. 291, art. 6, § 9; Laws 1991, c. 291, art. 11, § 5; Laws 1992, c. 511, art. 6, § 19; Laws 1993, c. 375, art. 8, § 14; Laws 1994, c. 587, art. 1, § 24; Laws 1997, c. 31, art. 1, §§ 7 to 10; Laws 1998, c. 389, art. 6, § 1; Laws 2002, c. 377, art. 9, § 6; Laws 2003, c. 127, art. 3, § 2; Laws 2005, c. 151, art. 2, § 17; Laws 2005, c. 151, art. 6, § 3; Laws 2008, c. 366, art. 4, §§ 1, 2, eff. May 30, 2008.

Historical and Statutory Notes

Laws 1990, c. 480, art. 1, § 47, provides in part that §§ 3 to 14 and 25 [enacting §§ 289A.08 to 289A.31 and 289A.56] are effective for returns, reports, taxes or other payments first becoming due on or after August 1, 1990, except that the exclusion for foreign operating corporations from the filing requirements in § 289A.08 is effective on the effective date of § 290.01, subd. 6b.

Laws 1991, c. 291, art. 6, § 48 provides in part that except where otherwise specifically provided, this article is effective for taxable years beginning after December 31, 1990. There were no specified effective date provisions listed in Laws 1991, c. 291, art 6 for §§ 7 to 12, 14, 16, 18 to 23, 26 to 29, and 32 to 40.

Laws 1991, c. 291, art. 6, § 48 provides in part that § 47 (repealing subd. 6 of this section) is effective beginning for refunds based on property taxes payable in 1991 and for refunds based on rent constituting property taxes paid in 1990.

Laws 1991, c. 291, art. 11, § 21, provides in part that § 5 (amending subd. 2 of this section) is effective for ores mined after December 31, 1990.

Laws 1993, c. 375, art. 8, § 15, provides in part that § 14 is effective for tax years beginning after December 31, 1992.

Laws 1997, c. 31, art. 1, § 19, provides in part that § 7 (amending subd. 1) is effective for returns due after December 31, 1996, § 9 (amending subd. 3) is effective for returns due after July 30, 1997, and § 10 (amending subd. 4) is effective for estates of decedents dying after the date of final enactment (April 15, 1997).

Laws 1998, c. 389, art. 6, § 21, provides in part that the amendment to subd. 2 is effective for extensions received under subd. 2 for tax years beginning after December 31, 1996.

Laws 2002, c. 377, art. 9, § 6, amending subd. 1, also provides that the amendment is effective for returns due after December 31, 2002.

Laws 2003, c. 127, art. 3, § 2, in the effective date portion, provided that art. 3, § 2, amend-

ing subd. 4, was effective for estates of decedents dying after December 31, 2001.

Laws 2005, c. 151, art. 6, § 3, amending subd. 4, also provided:

"This section is effective for estates of decedents dying after December 31, 2004."

Laws 2008, c. 366, art. 4, §§ 1 and 2, amending subd. 2 and adding subd. 7, both also provided:

"This section is effective [May 30, 2008] and applies to any federal extension that allows filing after that date."

289A.20. Due dates for making payments of tax

Subdivision 1. Individual income, fiduciary income, mining company, corporate franchise, and entertainment taxes. (a) Individual income, fiduciary, mining company, and corporate franchise taxes must be paid to the commissioner on or before the date the return must be filed under section 289A.18, subdivision 1, or the extended due date as provided in section 289A.19, unless an earlier date for payment is provided.

Notwithstanding any other law, a taxpayer whose unpaid liability for income or corporate franchise taxes, as reflected upon the return, is $1 or less need not pay the tax.

(b) Entertainment taxes must be paid on or before the date the return must be filed under section 289A.18, subdivision 1.

(c) If a fiduciary administers 100 or more trusts, fiduciary income taxes for all trusts administered by the fiduciary must be paid by electronic means.

Subd. 2. Withholding from wages, entertainer withholding, withholding from payments to out–of–state contractors, and withholding by partnerships, small business corporations, trusts. (a) A tax required to be deducted and withheld during the quarterly period must be paid on or before the last day of the month following the close of the quarterly period, unless an earlier time for payment is provided. A tax required to be deducted and withheld from compensation of an entertainer and from a payment to an out-of-state contractor must be paid on or before the date the return for such tax must be filed under section 289A.18, subdivision 2. Taxes required to be deducted and withheld by partnerships, S corporations, and trusts must be paid on a quarterly basis as estimated taxes under section 289A.25 for partnerships and trusts and under section 289A.26 for S corporations.

(b) An employer who, during the previous quarter, withheld more than $1,500 of tax under section 290.92, subdivision 2a or 3, or 290.923, subdivision 2, must deposit tax withheld under those sections with the commissioner within the time allowed to deposit the employer's federal withheld employment taxes under Code of Federal Regulations, title 26, section 31.6302–1, as amended through December 31, 2001, without regard to the safe harbor or de minimis rules in subparagraph (f) or the one-day rule in subsection (c), clause (3). Taxpayers must submit a copy of their federal notice of deposit status to the commissioner upon request by the commissioner.

(c) The commissioner may prescribe by rule other return periods or deposit requirements. In prescribing the reporting period, the commissioner may classify payors according to the amount of their tax liability and may adopt an appropriate reporting period for the class that the commissioner judges to be consistent with efficient tax collection. In no event will the duration of the reporting period be more than one year.

(d) If less than the correct amount of tax is paid to the commissioner, proper adjustments with respect to both the tax and the amount to be deducted must be made, without interest, in the manner and at the times the commissioner prescribes. If the underpayment cannot be adjusted, the amount of the underpayment will be assessed and collected in the manner and at the times the commissioner prescribes.

(e) If the aggregate amount of the tax withheld is:

(1) $20,000 or more in the fiscal year ending June 30, 2005; or

(2) $10,000 or more in the fiscal year ending June 30, 2006, and fiscal years thereafter,

the employer must remit each required deposit for wages paid in the subsequent calendar year by electronic means.

(f) A third-party bulk filer as defined in section 290.92, subdivision 30, paragraph (a), clause (2), who remits withholding deposits must remit all deposits by electronic means as provided in paragraph (e), regardless of the aggregate amount of tax withheld during a fiscal year for all of the employers.

Subd. 3. Estate tax. Taxes imposed by chapter 291 take effect at and upon the death of the person whose estate is subject to taxation and are due and payable on or before the expiration of nine months from that death.

Text of subd. 4 effective for tax liabilities before June 2009.

Subd. 4. Sales and use tax. (a) The taxes imposed by chapter 297A are due and payable to the commissioner monthly on or before the 20th day of the month following the month in which the taxable event occurred, or following another reporting period as the commissioner prescribes or as allowed under section 289A.18, subdivision 4, paragraph (f) or (g), except that use taxes due on an annual use tax return as provided under section 289A.11, subdivision 1, are payable by April 15 following the close of the calendar year.

(b) A vendor having a liability of $120,000 or more during a fiscal year ending June 30 must remit the June liability for the next year in the following manner:

(1) Two business days before June 30 of the year, the vendor must remit 78 percent of the estimated June liability to the commissioner.

(2) On or before August 20 of the year, the vendor must pay any additional amount of tax not remitted in June.

(c) A vendor having a liability of:

(1) $20,000 or more in the fiscal year ending June 30, 2005; or

(2) $10,000 or more in the fiscal year ending June 30, 2006, and fiscal years thereafter,

must remit all liabilities on returns due for periods beginning in the subsequent calendar year by electronic means on or before the 20th day of the month following the month in which the taxable event occurred, or on or before the 20th day of the month following the month in which the sale is reported under section 289A.18, subdivision 4, except for 78 percent of the estimated June liability, which is due two business days before June 30. The remaining amount of the June liability is due on August 20.

Text of subd. 4 effective beginning with June 2009 tax liabilities.

Subd. 4. Sales and use tax. (a) The taxes imposed by chapter 297A are due and payable to the commissioner monthly on or before the 20th day of the month following the month in which the taxable event occurred, or following another reporting period as the commissioner prescribes or as allowed under section 289A.18, subdivision 4, paragraph (f) or (g), except that use taxes due on an annual use tax return as provided under section 289A.11, subdivision 1, are payable by April 15 following the close of the calendar year.

(b) A vendor having a liability of $120,000 or more during a fiscal year ending June 30 must remit the June liability for the next year in the following manner:

(1) Two business days before June 30 of the year, the vendor must remit 90 percent of the estimated June liability to the commissioner.

(2) On or before August 20 of the year, the vendor must pay any additional amount of tax not remitted in June.

(c) A vendor having a liability of:

(1) $20,000 or more in the fiscal year ending June 30, 2005; or

(2) $10,000 or more in the fiscal year ending June 30, 2006, and fiscal years thereafter,

must remit all liabilities on returns due for periods beginning in the subsequent calendar year by electronic means on or before the 20th day of the month following the month in which the taxable event occurred, or on or before the 20th day of the month following the month in which the sale is reported under section 289A.18, subdivision 4, except for 90 percent of the estimated June liability, which is due two business days before June 30. The remaining amount of the June liability is due on August 20.

Subd. 5. Payment of franchise tax on LIFO recapture. If a corporation is subject to LIFO recapture under section 1363(d) of the Internal Revenue Code,[1] any increase in the tax imposed by section 290.06, subdivision 1, by reason of the inclusion of the LIFO recapture amount in its income is payable in four equal installments.

The first installment must be paid on or before the due date, determined without regard to extensions, for filing the return for the first taxable year for which the corporation was subject to the LIFO recapture. The three succeeding installments must be paid on or before the due date, determined without regard to extensions, for filing the corporation's return for the three succeeding taxable years.

For purposes of computing interest on underpayments, the last three installments must not be considered underpayments until after the payment due date specified in this subdivision.

Laws 1990, c. 480, art. 1, § 10. Amended by Laws 1991, c. 291, art. 6, § 10; Laws 1991, c. 291, art. 8, § 5; Laws 1991, c. 291, art. 11, § 6; Laws 1991, c. 291, art. 17, §§ 2 to 4; Laws 1992, c. 511, art. 6, § 19; Laws 1992, c. 511, art. 7, § 10; Laws 1992, c. 511, art. 8, § 4; Laws 1993, c. 13, art. 1, § 34; Laws 1993, c. 375, art. 1, § 3, eff. May 25, 1993; Laws 1993, c. 375, art. 8, §§ 2, 14; Laws 1993, c. 375, art. 10, §§ 14, 15; Laws 1994, c. 510, art. 3, § 8, eff. April 26, 1994; Laws 1994, c. 587, art. 1, § 24; Laws 1995, c. 264, art. 10, § 2; Laws 1997, c. 84, art. 6, §§ 20, 21; Laws 1998, c. 300, art. 1, § 2; Laws 1999, c. 243, art. 4, § 2; Laws 2000, c. 490, art. 4, § 2; Laws 2000, c. 490, art. 8, § 1; Laws 2001, 1st Sp., c. 5, art. 12, § 1; Laws 2001, 1st Sp., c. 5, art. 17, §§ 9, 10, eff. July 1, 2001; Laws 2001, 1st Sp., c. 5, art. 17, § 11; Laws 2002, c. 377, art. 2, § 2; Laws 2002, c. 377, art. 3, § 2; Laws 2003, 1st Sp., c. 21, art. 8, § 2; Laws 2005, 1st Sp., c. 3, art. 3, § 4; Laws 2005, 1st Sp., c. 3, art. 9, §§ 1, 2; Laws 2006, c. 259, art. 13, § 2; Laws 2008, c. 154, art. 6, § 1, eff. June 1, 2009; Laws 2008, c. 366, art. 8, § 1, eff. June 1, 2009.

[1] 26 U.S.C.A. § 1363(d).

Historical and Statutory Notes

Laws 1990, c. 480, art. 1, § 47, provides in part that §§ 3 to 14 and 25 [enacting §§ 289A.08 to 289A.31 and 289A.56] are effective for returns, reports, taxes or other payments first becoming due on or after August 1, 1990, except that the exclusion for foreign operating corporations from the filing requirements in § 289A.08 is effective on the effective date of § 290.01, subd. 6b.

Laws 1991, c. 291, art. 6, § 48 provides in part that except where otherwise specifically provided, this article is effective for taxable years beginning after December 31, 1990. There were no specified effective date provisions listed in Laws 1991, c. 291, art. 6 for §§ 7 to 12, 14, 16, 18 to 23, 26 to 29, and 32 to 40.

Laws 1991, c. 291, art. 8, § 31 provides in part that § 5 (amending subd. 4 of this section) is effective for purchases made after June 30, 1991.

Laws 1991, c. 291, art. 11, § 21 provides in part that § 6 (amending subd. 1 of this section) is effective for ores mined after December 31, 1990.

Laws 1991, c. 291 art. 17, provides in part that §§ 2 to 4 (amending subds. 1, 2, and 4 of this section) are effective for payments due in the calendar year beginning January 1, 1992, based upon payments made in the fiscal year ending June 30, 1991.

Laws 1992, c. 511, art. 7, § 27, provides in part that § 10 (amending subd. 1) is effective for payments with corporate franchise tax returns due on or after January 1, 1992.

Laws 1992, c. 511, art. 8, § 39, provides in part that § 4 is effective for tax payments due for sales made after September 30, 1992.

Laws 1993, c. 375, art. 8, § 15, provides that art. 8, § 2, is effective for payments received after December 31, 1993, and that art. 8, § 14, is effective for tax years beginning after December 31, 1992.

Laws 1993, c. 375, art. 10, § 52, provides in part that art. 10, §§ 14 and 15, are effective for payments due in the calendar year 1994, and thereafter, based upon payments made in the fiscal year ending June 30, 1993.

Laws 1995, c. 264, art. 10, § 15, provides in part that § 2 (amending subd. 2) as it relates to quarterly withholding deposits is effective for withholding done after December 31, 1995, and the remainder of § 2 is effective for payments due after December 31, 1995.

Laws 1997, c. 84, art. 6, § 29, provides in part that § 20 (amending subd. 1) is effective for tax payments for the taxable years beginning after December 31, 1997, and § 21 (amending subd. 2) is effective for withholding on wages after December 31, 1997.

Laws 1998, c. 300, art. 1, § 9, provides:

"Sections 1, 2, and 8 are effective for withholding on wages paid after December 31, 1997. Sections 3 and 4 are effective for federal extensions granted and final determinations made after the date of final enactment [March 18, 1998]. Sections 5 to 7 are effective for certificates issued after December 31, 1996, and used in taxable years beginning after July 31, 1997."

Laws 1999, c. 243, art. 4, § 19, provides in part that § 2, amending subd. 4, is effective for sales and purchases made after June 30, 1999.

Laws 2000, c. 490, art. 4, § 2, amending subd. 2, also provides in part that the amendment is effective for wages paid after December 31, 1999.

Laws 2000, c. 490, art. 8, § 1, amending subd. 4, also provides in part that the portion of the amendment of subd. 4 relating to the percentage of the June liability that must be filed by two business days before the end of June is

effective beginning with the June 2002 liability, and that the remainder of the amendment of subd. 4 is effective May 16, 2000.

Laws 2001, 1st Sp., c. 5, art. 17, § 11, also provides that the amendment of subd. 4 is effective for payments due on or after July 1, 2001.

Laws 2002, c. 377, art. 2, § 2, amending subd. 2, also provides that the amendment is effective the day following final enactment. Laws 2002, c. 377, was filed without signature of the governor May 18, 2002. See §§ 645.01 and 645.02.

Laws 2002, c. 377, art. 3, § 2, amending subd. 4, also provides that the amendment is effective for June 2002 and June 2003 tax liabilities.

Laws 2003, 1st Sp., c. 21, art. 8, § 2, amending subd. 4a, also provided that the amendment of subd. 4a, par. (a), was effective for sales and purchases made on or after January 1, 2004, and the rest of the amendment of subd. 4 was effective for payments made after December 31, 2003.

Laws 2005, 1st Sp., c. 3, art. 3, § 4, amending subd. 2, also provided:

"This section is effective for tax years beginning after December 31, 2005."

Laws 2005, 1st Sp., c. 3, art. 9, § 5, provided:

"This article is effective for payments due in calendar year 2006, and in calendar years thereafter, based upon liabilities incurred in the fiscal year ending June 30, 2005, and in fiscal years thereafter."

Laws 2006, c. 259, art. 13, § 2, amending subd. 4, also provided:

"This section is effective for sales tax payments in June 2007 and thereafter."

Laws 2008, c. 154, art. 6, § 1, amending subd. 4, also provided:

"This section is effective beginning with June 2009 tax liabilities."

Laws 2008, c. 366, art. 8, § 1, amending subd. 4, also provided:

"This section is effective beginning with June 2009 tax liabilities."

PAYMENT OF ESTIMATED TAX

289A.25. Payment of estimated tax by individuals, trusts, or partnerships

Subdivision 1. Requirements to pay. An individual, trust, or partnership must, when prescribed in subdivision 3, paragraph (b), make payments of estimated tax. The term "estimated tax" means the amount the taxpayer estimates is the sum of the taxes imposed by chapter 290 for the taxable year. If the individual is an infant or incompetent person, the payments must be made by the individual's guardian. If joint payments on estimated tax are made but a joint return is not made for the taxable year, the estimated tax for that year may be treated as the estimated tax of either the husband or the wife or may be divided between them.

Notwithstanding the provisions of this section, no payments of estimated tax are required if the estimated tax, as defined in this subdivision, less the credits allowed against the tax, is less than $500.

Subd. 2. Additions to tax for underpayment. (a) In the case of any underpayment of estimated tax by a taxpayer, except as provided in subdivision 6 or 7, there must be added to and become a part of the taxes imposed by chapter 290, for the taxable year an amount determined at the rate specified in section 270C.40 upon the amount of the underpayment for the period of the underpayment.

(b) For purposes of paragraph (a), the amount of underpayment shall be the excess of

(1) the amount of the installment required to be paid, over

(2) the amount, if any, of the installment paid on or before the last day prescribed for the payment.

Subd. 3. Period of underpayment. (a) The period of the underpayment shall run from the date the installment was required to be paid to the earlier of the following dates:

(1) The 15th day of the fourth month following the close of the taxable year.

(2) With respect to any part of the underpayment, the date on which that part is paid. For purposes of this clause, a payment of estimated tax on any installment date is considered a payment of any unpaid required installments in the order in which the installments are required to be paid.

(b) For purposes of this subdivision, there shall be four required installments for a taxable year. The times for payment of installments shall be:

For the following required installments:	The due date is:
1st	April 15
2nd	June 15
3rd	September 15
4th	January 15 of the following taxable year

Subd. 4. No addition to tax where tax is small. No addition to tax is imposed under subdivision 2 for a taxable year if the tax shown on the return for the taxable year (or, if no return is filed, the tax) reduced by the credits allowable is less than $500.

Subd. 5.   Amount of required installment.   The amount of any installment required to be paid shall be 25 percent of the required annual payment except as provided in clause (3).   The term "required annual payment" means the lesser of

(1) 90 percent of the tax shown on the return for the taxable year or 90 percent of the tax for the year if no return is filed; or

(2) the total tax liability shown on the return of the taxpayer for the preceding taxable year, if a return showing a liability for the taxes was filed by the taxpayer for the preceding taxable year of 12 months.   If the adjusted gross income shown on the return of the taxpayer for the preceding taxable year exceeds $150,000, this clause shall be applied by substituting "110 percent of the total tax liability" for "the total tax liability"

(i) for an individual who is not a Minnesota resident for the entire year, the term "adjusted gross income" means the Minnesota share of that income apportioned to Minnesota under section 290.06, subdivision 2c, paragraph (e), or

(ii) for a trust the term "adjusted gross income" means the income assigned to Minnesota under section 290.17; or

(3) an amount equal to the applicable percentage of the tax for the taxable year computed by placing on an annualized basis the taxable income and alternative minimum taxable income for the months in the taxable year ending before the month in which the installment is required to be paid.   The applicable percentage of the tax is 22.5 percent in the case of the first installment, 45 percent for the second installment, 67.5 percent for the third installment, and 90 percent for the fourth installment.   For purposes of this clause, the taxable income and alternative minimum taxable income shall be placed on an annualized basis by

(i) multiplying by 12 (or in the case of a taxable year of less than 12 months, the number of months in the taxable year) the taxable income and alternative minimum taxable income computed for the months in the taxable year ending before the month in which the installment is required to be paid; and

(ii) dividing the resulting amount by the number of months in the taxable year ending before the month in which the installment date falls.

A reduction in an installment under clause (3) must be recaptured by increasing the amount of the next required installment by the amount of the reduction.

Subd. 5a.   Repealed by Laws 1994, c. 587, art. 1, § 25, par. (b).

Subd. 6.   Exception to addition to tax.   No addition to the tax shall be imposed under this section for any taxable year if:

(1) the taxpayer did not have liability for tax for the preceding taxable year,

(2) the preceding taxable year was a taxable year of 12 months, and

(3) the individual or trust was a resident of Minnesota throughout the preceding taxable year.

Subd. 7. Waiver of addition to tax. No addition to the tax is imposed under this section with respect to an underpayment to the extent the commissioner determines that the provisions of section 6654(e)(3) of the Internal Revenue Code,[1] apply.

Subd. 8. Application of section; tax withheld on wages. For purposes of this section, the estimated tax must be computed without reduction for the amount that the taxpayer estimates as the taxpayer's credit under section 290.92, subdivision 12 (relating to tax withheld at source on wages), and any other refundable credits allowed against income tax liability, and the amount of those credits for the taxable year is considered a payment of estimated tax, and an equal part of those amounts is considered paid on the installment date, determined under subdivision 3, paragraph (b), for that taxable year, unless the taxpayer establishes the dates on which the amounts were actually withheld, in which case the amounts so withheld are considered payments of estimated tax on the dates on which the amounts were actually withheld.

Subd. 9. Special rule for return filed on or before January 31. If, on or before January 31 of the following taxable year, the taxpayer files a return for the taxable year and pays in full the amount computed on the return as payable, then no addition to tax is imposed under subdivision 2 with respect to any underpayment of the fourth required installment for the taxable year.

Subd. 10. Special rule for farmers and fishermen. For purposes of this section, if an individual is a farmer or fisherman as defined in section 6654(i)(2) of the Internal Revenue Code for a taxable year, only one installment is required for the taxable year, the due date of which is January 15 of the following taxable year, the amount of which is equal to the required annual payment determined under subdivision 5 by substituting "66–2/3 percent" for "90 percent," and subdivision 9 shall be applied by substituting "March 1" for "January 31," and by treating the required installment described as the fourth required installment.

Subd. 11. Fiscal year taxpayer. The application of this section to taxable years beginning other than January 1 must be made by substituting, for the months named in this section, the months that correspond. This section must be applied to taxable years of less than 12 months, under rules issued by the commissioner.

Subd. 12. Estates. The provisions of this section do not apply to an estate.

Subd. 13. Overpayment of estimated tax installment. If an installment payment of estimated tax exceeds the correct amount of the installment payment, the overpayment must be credited against the unpaid installments, if any.

Laws 1990, c. 480, art. 1, § 11. Amended by Laws 1991, c. 291, art. 6, § 46; Laws 1992, c. 511, art. 6, §§ 3, 19; Laws 1993, c. 375, art. 2, §§ 22 to 26; Laws 1993 c. 375, art. 2, § 27, eff. May 25, 1993; Laws 1993, c. 375, art. 2, § 28; Laws 1993, c. 375, art. 8, § 14; Laws 1994, c. 416, art. 2, § 2; Laws 1994, c. 587, art. 1, §§ 4, 24; Laws 2005, c. 151, art. 2, § 17.

[1] All text references to Internal Revenue Code sections are to Title 26 of U.S.C.A.

Historical and Statutory Notes

Laws 1990, c. 480, art. 1, § 47, provides in part that §§ 3 to 14 and 25 [enacting §§ 289A.08 to 289A.31 and 289A.56] are effective for returns, reports, taxes or other payments first becoming due on or after August 1, 1990, except that the exclusion for foreign operating corporations from the filing requirements in § 289A.08 is effective on the effective date of § 290.01, subd. 6b.

Laws 1992, c. 511, art. 6, § 21, provides in part that § 3, adding subd. 5a, is effective for taxable years beginning after December 31, 1992.

Laws 1993, c. 375, art. 2, § 37, provides in part that §§ 22 to 26 and 28 (amending subds. 1, 2, 5a, 6, 8, and 12) are effective for tax years beginning after December 31, 1992.

Laws 1993, c. 375, art. 8, § 15, provides in part that § 14 is effective for tax years beginning after December 31, 1992.

Laws 1994, c. 416, art. 2, § 7, provides in part that § 2 (amending subd. 5) is effective for taxable years beginning after December 31, 1993.

Laws 1994, c. 587, art. 1, § 27, provides in part that §§ 4 and 25, par. (b), (amending subd. 5 and repealing subd. 5a, respectively) are effective for installments of estimated taxes due after May 6, 1994.

289A.26. Payment of estimated tax by corporations

Subdivision 1. Minimum liability. A corporation subject to taxation under chapter 290 (excluding section 290.92) or an entity subject to taxation under section 290.05, subdivision 3, must make payment of estimated tax for the taxable year if its tax liability so computed can reasonably be expected to exceed $500, or in accordance with rules prescribed by the commissioner for an affiliated group of corporations filing one return under section 289A.08, subdivision 3.

Subd. 2. Amount and time for payment of installments. The estimated tax payment required under subdivision 1 must be paid in four equal installments on or before the 15th day of the third, sixth, ninth, and 12th month of the taxable year.

Subd. 2a. Electronic payments. If the aggregate amount of estimated tax payments made is:

(1) $20,000 or more in the fiscal year ending June 30, 2005; or

(2) $10,000 or more in the fiscal year ending June 30, 2006, and fiscal years thereafter,

all estimated tax payments in the subsequent calendar year must be paid by electronic means.

Subd. 3. Short taxable year. (a) An entity with a short taxable year of less than 12 months, but at least four months, must pay estimated tax in equal installments on or before the 15th day of the third, sixth, ninth, and final month of the short taxable year, to the extent applicable based on the number of months in the short taxable year.

(b) An entity is not required to make estimated tax payments for a short taxable year unless its tax liability before the first day of the last month of the taxable year can reasonably be expected to exceed $500.

(c) No payment is required for a short taxable year of less than four months.

Subd. 4. Underpayment of estimated tax. If there is an underpayment of estimated tax by a corporation, there shall be added to the tax for the taxable year an amount determined at the rate in section 270C.40 on the amount of the underpayment, determined under subdivision 5, for the period of the underpayment determined under subdivision 6. This subdivision does not apply in the first taxable year that a corporation is subject to the tax imposed under section 290.02.

Subd. 5. Amount of underpayment. For purposes of subdivision 4, the amount of the underpayment is the excess of

(1) the required installment, over

(2) the amount, if any, of the installment paid on or before the last date prescribed for payment.

Subd. 6. Period of underpayment. The period of the underpayment runs from the date the installment was required to be paid to the earlier of the following dates:

(1) the 15th day of the third month following the close of the taxable year for corporations, and the 15th day of the fifth month following the close of the taxable year for entities subject to tax under section 290.05, subdivision 3; or

(2) with respect to any part of the underpayment, the date on which that part is paid. For purposes of this clause, a payment of estimated tax shall be credited against unpaid required installments in the order in which those installments are required to be paid.

Subd. 7. Required installments. (a) Except as otherwise provided in this subdivision, the amount of a required installment is 25 percent of the required annual payment.'

(b) Except as otherwise provided in this subdivision, the term "required annual payment" means the lesser of:

(1) 100 percent of the tax shown on the return for the taxable year, or, if no return is filed, 100 percent of the tax for that year; or

(2) 100 percent of the tax shown on the return of the entity for the preceding taxable year provided the return was for a full 12-month period, showed a liability, and was filed by the entity.

(c) Except for determining the first required installment for any taxable year, paragraph (b), clause (2), does not apply in the case of a large corporation. The term "large corporation" means a corporation or any predecessor corporation that had taxable net income of $1,000,000 or more for any taxable year during the testing period. The term "testing period" means the three taxable years immediately preceding the taxable year involved. A reduction allowed to a large corporation for the first installment that is allowed by applying paragraph (b), clause (2), must be recaptured by increasing the next required installment by the amount of the reduction.

(d) In the case of a required installment, if the corporation establishes that the annualized income installment is less than the amount determined in paragraph (a), the amount of the required installment is the annualized income installment and the recapture of previous quarters' reductions allowed by this paragraph must be recovered by increasing later required installments to the extent the reductions have not previously been recovered.

(e) The "annualized income installment" is the excess, if any, of:

(1) an amount equal to the applicable percentage of the tax for the taxable year computed by placing on an annualized basis the taxable income:

(i) for the first two months of the taxable year, in the case of the first required installment;

(ii) for the first two months or for the first five months of the taxable year, in the case of the second required installment;

(iii) for the first six months or for the first eight months of the taxable year, in the case of the third required installment; and

(iv) for the first nine months or for the first 11 months of the taxable year, in the case of the fourth required installment, over

(2) the aggregate amount of any prior required installments for the taxable year.

(3) For the purpose of this paragraph, the annualized income shall be computed by placing on an annualized basis the taxable income for the year up to the end of the month preceding the due date for the quarterly payment multiplied by 12 and dividing the resulting amount by the number of months in the taxable year (2, 5, 6, 8, 9, or 11 as the case may be) referred to in clause (1).

(4) The "applicable percentage" used in clause (1) is:

For the following required installments:	The applicable percentage is:
1st	25
2nd	50
3rd	75
4th	100

(f) (1) If this paragraph applies, the amount determined for any installment must be determined in the following manner:

(i) take the taxable income for the months during the taxable year preceding the filing month;

(ii) divide that amount by the base period percentage for the months during the taxable year preceding the filing month;

(iii) determine the tax on the amount determined under item (ii); and

(iv) multiply the tax computed under item (iii) by the base period percentage for the filing month and the months during the taxable year preceding the filing month.

(2) For purposes of this paragraph:

(i) the "base period percentage" for a period of months is the average percent that the taxable income for the corresponding months in each of the three preceding taxable years bears to the taxable income for the three preceding taxable years;

(ii) the term "filing month" means the month in which the installment is required to be paid;

(iii) this paragraph only applies if the base period percentage for any six consecutive months of the taxable year equals or exceeds 70 percent; and

(iv) the commissioner may provide by rule for the determination of the base period percentage in the case of reorganizations, new corporations, and other similar circumstances.

(3) In the case of a required installment determined under this paragraph, if the entity determines that the installment is less than the amount determined in paragraph (a), the amount of the required installment is the amount determined under this paragraph and the recapture of previous quarters' reductions allowed by this paragraph must be recovered by increasing later required installments to the extent the reductions have not previously been recovered.

Subd. 8. Definition of tax. The term "tax" as used in this section means the tax imposed by chapter 290.

Subd. 9. Failure to file an estimate. In the case of an entity that fails to file an estimated tax for a taxable year when one is required, the period of the underpayment runs from the four installment dates in subdivision 2 or 3, whichever applies, to the earlier of the periods in subdivision 6, clauses (1) and (2).

Subd. 10. Payment on account. Payment of the estimated tax or any installment of it shall be considered payment on account of the taxes imposed by chapter 290, for the taxable year.

Subd. 11. Overpayment of estimated tax installment. If the amount of an installment payment of estimated tax exceeds the amount determined to be the correct amount of the installment payment, the overpayment must be credited against the unpaid installments, if any.

Laws 1990, c. 480, art. 1, § 12. Amended by Laws 1991, c. 291, art. 7, §§ 2, 3; Laws 1991, c. 291, art. 17, § 5; Laws 1992, c. 511, art. 6, §§ 4 to 9; Laws 1993, c. 375, art. 2, §§ 29 to 31; Laws 1993, c. 375, art. 8, § 3; Laws 1994, c. 587, art. 1, § 5; Laws 1995, c. 264, art. 13, § 10; Laws 2000, c. 490, art. 4, § 3, eff. May 16, 2000; Laws 2001, 1st. Sp., c. 5, art. 17, § 12, eff. July 1, 2001; Laws 2005, c. 151, art. 2, § 17; Laws 2005, 1st Sp., c. 3, art. 9, § 3.

Historical and Statutory Notes

Laws 1990, c. 480, art. 1, § 47, provides in part that §§ 3 to 14 and 25 [enacting §§ 289A.08 to 289A.31 and 289A.56] are effective for returns, reports, taxes or other payments first becoming due on or after August 1, 1990, except that the exclusion for foreign operating corporations from the filing requirements in § 289A.08 is effective on the effective date of § 290.01, subd. 6b.

Laws 1991, c. 291, art. 7, § 27 provides:

"Sections 2 [amending § 289A.26, subd. 1], 9 [amending § 290.05, subd. 3], 15 to 19 [amending §§ 290.0922, subd. 1, 290.17, subd. 5, 290.191, subds. 6, 8, and 11], 21 to 24 [in § 290.9727, amending subds. 1 and 3 and adding subds. 1a and 5], and 26 [repealing §§ 290.068, subd. 6, 290.069, subds. 2a, 4a, and 4b, 290.17, subd. 7, and 290.191, subd. 7] are effective for taxable years beginning after December 31, 1990, provided that the carryover for the credit provided under Minnesota Statutes, section 290.068, subdivision 6, that is repealed by section 26, remains in effect for taxable years beginning before 2003. Sections 10 [amending § 290.06, subd. 21] and 14 [amending § 290.0921, subd. 8] are effective the day following final enactment. Sections 1 [amending § 289A.18, subd. 1], 3 [amending § 289A.26, subd. 6], 20 [amending § 290.35, subd. 3], and 25 are effective for taxable years beginning after December 31, 1989."

Laws 1991, c. 291, art. 17, § 13 provides in part that § 5 (adding subd. 2a to this section) is effective for payments due in the calendar year beginning January 1, 1992, based upon payments made in the fiscal year ending June 30, 1991.

Laws 1992, c. 511, art. 6, § 18, made effective for estimated tax payments for tax years beginning after December 31, 1991 by Laws 1992, c. 511, art. 6, § 21, provides:

"Transition relief for change in corporate estimated tax.

"For the purposes of computing the amount of underpayment of corporate estimated tax on installment payments due before June 1, 1992, 90 percent shall be substituted for 93 percent in Minnesota Statutes, section 289A.26, subdivision 7, paragraph (b), clause (1), and 22.5 percent shall be substituted for 23.25 percent in paragraph (e), clause (4), if there is not an underpayment of estimated tax for the second installment due in calendar year 1992."

Laws 1992, c. 511, art. 6, § 21, provides in part that §§ 4 to 7, and 9 (amending subds. 1, 3, 4, 6, and 9 of this section, respectively), are effective for taxable years beginning after June 1, 1992, and that § 8 (amending subd. 7 of this section), is effective for estimated tax payments for tax years beginning after December 31, 1991, except that the amendments changing the words "corporation" to "entity" are effective for taxable years beginning after June 1, 1992.

Laws 1993, c. 375, art. 2, § 37, provides in part that §§ 29 to 31 (amending subds. 1, 4, and 6) are effective for tax years beginning after December 31, 1992.

Laws 1993, c. 375, art. 8, § 15, provides in part that § 3 (amending subd. 7) is effective for tax years beginning after December 31, 1993.

Laws 1994, c. 587, art. 1, § 27, provides in part that § 5 (amending subd. 7) is effective for taxable years beginning after December 31, 1994.

Laws 1995, c. 264, art. 13, § 24, provides in part that § 10 (amending subd. 2a) is effective for payments due for tax years beginning after December 31, 1995.

Laws 2005, 1st Sp., c. 3, art. 9, §5, provided:

"This article is effective for payments due in calendar year 2006, and in calendar years thereafter, based upon liabilities incurred in the fiscal year ending June 30, 2005, and in fiscal years thereafter."

PAYMENT EXTENSIONS AND LIABILITY

289A.30. Extensions for paying tax

Subdivision 1. Fiduciary income, corporate franchise tax. Where good cause exists, the commissioner may extend the time for payment of the amount determined as a fiduciary income tax or corporate franchise tax by the taxpayer, or an amount determined as a deficiency, for a period of not more than six months from the date prescribed for the payment of the tax.

Subd. 2. Estate tax. Where good cause exists, the commissioner may extend the time for payment of estate tax for a period of not more than six months. If an extension to pay the federal estate tax has been granted under section 6161 of the Internal Revenue Code,[1] the time for payment of the estate tax without penalty is extended for that period. A taxpayer who owes at least $5,000 in taxes and who, under section 6161 or 6166 of the Internal Revenue Code, has been granted an extension for payment of the tax shown on the return, may elect to pay the tax due to the commissioner in equal amounts at the same time as required for federal purposes. A taxpayer electing to pay the tax in installments must notify the commissioner in writing no later than nine months after the death of the person whose estate is subject to taxation. If the taxpayer fails to pay an installment on time, unless it is shown that the failure is due to reasonable cause, the election is revoked and the entire amount of unpaid tax plus accrued interest is due and payable 90 days after the date on which the installment was payable.

Laws 1990, c. 480, art. 1, § 13. Amended by Laws 1991, c. 291, art. 6, § 11, 46; Laws 1992, c. 511, art. 6, § 19; Laws 1993, c. 375, art. 8, § 14; Laws 1994, c. 587, art. 1, § 24.

[1] All text references to Internal Revenue Code sections are to Title 26 of U.S.C.A.

Historical and Statutory Notes

Laws 1990, c. 480, art. 1, § 47, provides in part that §§ 3 to 14 and 25 [enacting §§ 289A.08 to 289A.31 and 289A.56] are effective for returns, reports, taxes or other payments first becoming due on or after August 1, 1990, except that the exclusion for foreign operating corporations from the filing requirements in § 289A.08 is effective on the effective date of § 290.01, subd. 6b.

Laws 1991, c. 291, art. 6, § 48 provides in part that except where otherwise specifically provided, this article is effective for taxable years beginning after December 31, 1990. There were no specified effective date provisions listed in Laws 1991, c. 291, art. 6 for §§ 7 to 12, 14, 16, 18 to 23, 26 to 29, and 32 to 40.

Laws 1993, c. 375, art. 8, § 15, provides in part that § 14 is effective for tax years beginning after December 31, 1992.

289A.31. Liability for payment of tax

Subdivision 1. Individual income, fiduciary income, mining company, corporate franchise, and entertainment taxes. (a) Individual income, fiduciary income, mining company, and corporate franchise taxes, and interest and penalties, must be paid by the taxpayer upon whom the tax is imposed, except in the following cases:

(1) The tax due from a decedent for that part of the taxable year in which the decedent died during which the decedent was alive and the taxes, interest, and penalty due for the prior years must be paid by the decedent's personal representative, if any. If there is no personal representative, the taxes, interest, and penalty must be paid by the transferees, as defined in section 270C.58, subdivision 3, to the extent they receive property from the decedent;

(2) The tax due from an infant or other incompetent person must be paid by the person's guardian or other person authorized or permitted by law to act for the person;

(3) The tax due from the estate of a decedent must be paid by the estate's personal representative;

(4) The tax due from a trust, including those within the definition of a corporation, as defined in section 290.01, subdivision 4, must be paid by a trustee; and

(5) The tax due from a taxpayer whose business or property is in charge of a receiver, trustee in bankruptcy, assignee, or other conservator, must be paid by the person in charge of the business or property so far as the tax is due to the income from the business or property.

(b) Entertainment taxes are the joint and several liability of the entertainer and the entertainment entity. The payor is liable to the state for the payment of the tax required to be deducted and withheld under section 290.9201, subdivision 7, and is not liable to the entertainer for the amount of the payment.

(c) The tax imposed under section 290.0922 on partnerships is the joint and several liability of the partnership and the general partners.

Subd. 2. Joint income tax returns. (a) If a joint income tax return is made by a husband and wife, the liability for the tax is joint and several. A spouse who qualifies for relief from a liability attributable to an underpayment under section 6015(b) of the Internal Revenue Code [1] is relieved of the state income tax liability on the underpayment.

(b) In the case of individuals who were a husband and wife prior to the dissolution of their marriage or their legal separation, or prior to the death of one of the individuals, for tax liabilities reported on a joint or combined return, the liability of each person is limited to the proportion of the tax due on the return that equals that person's proportion of the total tax due if the husband and wife filed separate returns for the taxable year. This provision is effective only when the commissioner receives written notice of the marriage dissolution, legal separation, or death of a spouse from the husband or wife. No refund may be claimed by an ex-spouse, legally separated or widowed spouse for any taxes paid more than 60 days before receipt by the commissioner of the written notice.

(c) A request for calculation of separate liability pursuant to paragraph (b) for taxes reported on a return must be made within six years after the due date of the return. For calculation of separate liability for taxes assessed by the commissioner under section 289A.35 or 289A.37, the request must be made within six years after the date of assessment. The commissioner is not required to calculate separate liability if the remaining unpaid liability for which recalculation is requested is $100 or less.

Subds. 3, 4. Repealed by Laws 2005, c. 151, art. 1, § 117, eff. Aug. 1, 2005.

Subd. 5. Withholding tax, withholding from payments to out-of-state contractors, and withholding by partnerships and small business corporations. (a) Except as provided in paragraph (b), an employer or person withholding tax under section 290.92 or 290.923, subdivision 2, who fails to pay to or deposit with the commissioner a sum or sums required by those sections to be deducted, withheld, and paid, is personally and individually liable to the state for the sum or sums, and added penalties and interest, and is not liable to another person for that payment or payments. The sum or sums deducted and withheld under section 290.92, subdivision 2a or 3, or 290.923, subdivision 2, must be held as a special fund in trust for the state of Minnesota.

(b) If the employer or person withholding tax under section 290.92 or 290.923, subdivision 2, fails to deduct and withhold the tax in violation of those sections, and later the taxes against which the tax may be credited are paid, the tax required to be deducted and withheld will not be collected from the employer. This does not, however, relieve the employer from liability for any penalties and interest otherwise applicable for failure to deduct and withhold.

(c) Liability for payment of withholding taxes includes a responsible person or entity described in the personal liability provisions of section 270C.56.

(d) Liability for payment of withholding taxes includes a third party lender or surety described in section 270C.59.

(e) A partnership or S corporation required to withhold and remit tax under section 290.92, subdivisions 4b and 4c, is liable for payment of the tax to the commissioner, and a person having control of or responsibility for the withholding of the tax or the filing of returns due in connection with the tax is personally liable for the tax due.

(f) A payor of sums required to be withheld under section 290.9705, subdivision 1, is liable to the state for the amount required to be deducted, and is not liable to an out-of-state contractor for the amount of the payment.

Subd. 6. Repealed by Laws 2005, c. 151, art. 1, § 117, eff. Aug. 1, 2005.

Subd. 7. Sales and use tax. (a) The sales and use tax required to be collected by the retailer under chapter 297A constitutes a debt owed by the retailer to Minnesota, and the sums collected must be held as a special fund in trust for the state of Minnesota.

A retailer who does not maintain a place of business within this state as defined by section 297A.66, subdivision 1, shall not be indebted to Minnesota for amounts of tax that it was required to collect but did not collect unless the retailer knew or had been advised by the commissioner of its obligation to collect the tax.

(b) The use tax required to be paid by a purchaser is a debt owed by the purchaser to Minnesota.

(c) The tax imposed by chapter 297A, and interest and penalties, is a personal debt of the individual required to file a return from the time the liability arises, irrespective of when the time for payment of that liability occurs. The debt is, in the case of the executor or administrator of the estate of a decedent and in the case of a fiduciary, that of the individual in an official or fiduciary capacity unless the individual has voluntarily distributed the assets held in that capacity without reserving sufficient assets to pay the tax, interest, and penalties, in which case the individual is personally liable for the deficiency.

(d) Liability for payment of sales and use taxes includes any responsible person or entity described in the personal liability provisions of section 270C.56.

(e) Any amounts collected, even if erroneously or illegally collected, from a purchaser under a representation that they are taxes imposed under chapter 297A are state funds from the time of collection and must be reported on a return filed with the commissioner.

Subd. 8. Liability of vendor for repayment of refund. If an individual income tax refund resulting from claiming an education credit under section 290.0674 is paid by means of directly depositing the proceeds of the refund into a bank account controlled by the vendor of the product or service upon which the education credit is based, and the commissioner subsequently disallows the credit, the commissioner may seek repayment of the refund from the vendor. The amount of the repayment must be assessed and collected in the same time and manner as an erroneous refund under section 289A.37, subdivision 2.

Laws 1990, c. 480, art. 1, § 14. Amended by Laws 1991, c. 291, art. 6, § 46; Laws 1991, c. 291, art. 11, § 7; Laws 1992, c. 511, art. 6, § 19; Laws 1993, c. 375, art. 8, § 14; Laws 1994, c. 587, art. 1, § 24; Laws 1997, c. 84, art. 6, § 22 eff. May 3, 1997; Laws 1999, c. 243, art. 16, § 14; Laws 2000, c. 418, art. 1, § 3; Laws 2001, 1st Sp., c. 5, art. 12, § 2; Laws 2003, c. 127, art. 3, § 3; Laws 2003, c. 127, art. 8, §§ 7, 8; Laws 2003, 1st Sp., c. 21, art. 8, § 3; Laws 2005, c. 151, art. 2, § 17; Laws 2005, c. 151, art. 6, § 4.

[1] 26 U.S.C.A. § 6015(b).

Historical and Statutory Notes

Laws 1990, c. 480, art. 1, § 47, provides in part that §§ 3 to 14 and 25 [enacting §§ 289A.08 to 289A.31 and 289A.56] are effective for returns, reports, taxes or other payments first becoming due on or after August 1, 1990, except that the exclusion for foreign operating corporations from the filing requirements in § 289A.08 is effective on the effective date of § 290.01, subd. 6b.

Laws 1991, c. 291, art. 11, § 21 provides in part that § 7 (amending subd. 1 of this section) is effective for ores mined after December 31, 1990.

Laws 1999, c. 243, art. 16, § 40, provides in part that § 14, par. (a) (amending subd. 2, par. (a), of this section), is effective at the same time that section 6015(b) of the Internal Revenue Code is effective for federal tax purposes, and that § 14, par. (b) (amending subd. 2, par. (b), of this section), is effective for claims for inno-

cent spouse relief, requests for allocation of joint income tax liability, and taxes filed or paid on or after May 26, 1999.

Laws 2000, c. 418, art. 1, § 46, provides in part that § 3, par. (e), adding subd. 7, par. (e), is effective for amounts collected after June 30, 2001, and that § 3, par. (f), adding subd. 7, par. (f), is effective for sales taxes retained after June 30, 2001.

Laws 2001, 1st Sp., c. 5, art. 12, § 2, also provides that the amendment of subd. 7 is effective for amounts collected after June 30, 2001.

Laws 2003, c. 127, art. 3, § 3, adding subd. 8, also provided that subd. 8 was effective for refunds paid to accounts controlled by a vendor on or after May 26, 2003.

Laws 2003, c. 127, art. 8, §§ 7 and 8, amending subds. 3 and 4, also provided that the amendment of subd. 3 was effective for refunds paid on or after May 26, 2003, and that the amendment of subd. 4 was effective for taxes imposed and property tax refunds claimed on or after May 26, 2003.

Laws 2003, 1st Sp., c. 21, art. 8, § 3, amending subd. 7, also provided that the amendment was effective for sales taxes collected on sales occurring after June 30, 2003.

Laws 2005, c. 151, art. 1, § 115, provided:

"Subdivision 1. Purpose. It is the intent of the legislature to simplify Minnesota's tax laws by consolidating and recodifying tax administration and compliance provisions now contained in Minnesota Statutes, chapter 270, and several other chapters of Minnesota Statutes. The pro-

visions of this act may not be used to determine the law in effect prior to the effective dates in this act.

"Subd. 2. Effect. Due to the complexity of the recodification, prior provisions are repealed on the effective date of the new provisions. The repealed provisions, however, continue to remain in effect until superseded by the analogous provision in the new law."

Laws 2005, c. 151, art. 6, § 4, amending subd. 2, also provided:

"This section is effective for requests for relief made on or after the day following final enactment."

ASSESSMENTS, EXAMINATIONS, AND STATUTES OF LIMITATIONS

289A.35. Assessments on returns

The commissioner may audit and adjust the taxpayer's computation of federal taxable income, items of federal tax preferences, or federal credit amounts to make them conform with the provisions of chapter 290 or section 298.01. If a return has been filed, the commissioner shall enter the liability reported on the return and may make any audit or investigation that is considered necessary.

Laws 1990, c. 480, art. 1, § 15. Amended by Laws 1991, c. 291, art. 11, § 8; Laws 1997, c. 31, art. 2, § 5, eff. July 1, 1997; Laws 2000, c. 490, art. 13, § 11, eff. May 16, 2000; Laws 2005, c. 151, art. 2, § 8, eff. Aug. 1, 2005.

Historical and Statutory Notes

Laws 1990, c. 480, art. 1, § 47, provides in part that § 15 [enacting this section] is effective for audits or investigations initiated on or after August 1, 1990.

Laws 1991, c. 291, art. 11, § 21 provides in part that § 8 (amending this section) is effective for ores mined after December 31, 1990.

289A.36. Repealed by Laws 2005, c. 151, art. 1, § 117, eff. Aug. 1, 2005

Historical and Statutory Notes

Laws 2005, c. 151, art. 1, § 115, provided:

"Subdivision 1. Purpose. It is the intent of the legislature to simplify Minnesota's tax laws by consolidating and recodifying tax administration and compliance provisions now contained in Minnesota Statutes, chapter 270, and several other chapters of Minnesota Statutes. The provisions of this act may not be used to determine

the law in effect prior to the effective dates in this act.

"Subd. 2. Effect. Due to the complexity of the recodification, prior provisions are repealed on the effective date of the new provisions. The repealed provisions, however, continue to remain in effect until superseded by the analogous provision in the new law."

289A.37. Assessments; erroneous refunds; joint income tax returns

Subdivision 1. Repealed by Laws 2005, c. 151, art. 1, § 117, eff. Aug. 1, 2005.

Subd. 2. Erroneous refunds. An erroneous refund is considered an underpayment of tax on the date made. An assessment of a deficiency arising out of an erroneous refund may be made at any time within two years from the making of the refund. If part of the refund was induced by fraud or misrepresentation of a material fact, the assessment may be made at any time.

Subds. 3 to 5. Repealed by Laws 2005, c. 151, art. 1, § 117, eff. Aug. 1, 2005.

Subd. 6. Order of assessment if joint income tax return. If a joint income tax return is filed by a husband and wife, an order of assessment may be a single joint notice. If the commissioner has been notified by either spouse that that spouse's address has changed and if that spouse requests it, then, instead of the single joint notice mailed to the last known address of the husband and wife, a duplicate or original of the joint notice must be sent to the requesting spouse at the address designated by the requesting spouse. The other joint notice must be mailed to the other spouse at that spouse's last known address. An assessment is not invalid for failure to send it to a spouse if the spouse actually receives the notice in the same period as if it had been mailed to that spouse at the correct address or if the spouse has failed to provide an address to the commissioner other than the last known address.

Laws 1990, c. 480, art. 1, § 17. Amended by Laws 1991, c. 291, art. 16, § 8, eff. June 1, 1991; Laws 1992, c. 511, art. 6, § 10, eff. April 25, 1992; Laws 1994, c. 510, art. 4, § 9, eff. April 26, 1994; Laws 1997, c. 84, art. 6, § 23.

Historical and Statutory Notes

Laws 1990, c. 480, art. 1, § 47, provides in part that § 17 [enacting this section] is effective for assessments or other determinations made on or after August 1, 1990.

Laws 1997, c. 84, art. 6, § 29, provides in part that § 23 (amending subd. 1) is effective for orders of assessment issued on or after May 3, 1997.

Laws 2005, c. 151, art. 1, § 115, provided:

"Subdivision 1. Purpose. It is the intent of the legislature to simplify Minnesota's tax laws by consolidating and recodifying tax administration and compliance provisions now contained in Minnesota Statutes, chapter 270, and several other chapters of Minnesota Statutes. The provisions of this act may not be used to determine the law in effect prior to the effective dates in this act.

"Subd. 2. Effect. Due to the complexity of the recodification, prior provisions are repealed on the effective date of the new provisions. The repealed provisions, however, continue to remain in effect until superseded by the analogous provision in the new law."

289A.38. Limitations on time for assessment of tax

Subdivision 1. General rule. Except as otherwise provided in this section, the amount of taxes assessable must be assessed within 3-1/2 years after the date the return is filed.

Subd. 2. Filing date. For purposes of this section, a tax return filed before the last day prescribed by law for filing is considered to be filed on the last day.

Subd. 3. Estate taxes. Estate taxes must be assessed within 180 days after the return and the documents required under section 289A.10, subdivision 2, have been filed.

Subd. 4. Property tax refund. For purposes of computing the limitation under this section, the due date of the property tax refund return as provided for in chapter 290A is the due date for an income tax return covering the year in which the rent was paid or the year preceding the year in which the property taxes are payable.

Subd. 5. False or fraudulent return; no return. Notwithstanding the limitations under subdivisions 1 and 3, the tax may be assessed at any time if a false or fraudulent return is filed or when a taxpayer fails to file a return.

Subd. 6. Omission in excess of 25 percent. Additional taxes may be assessed within 6-½ years after the due date of the return or the date the return was filed, whichever is later, if:

(1) the taxpayer omits from gross income an amount properly includable in it that is in excess of 25 percent of the amount of gross income stated in the return;

(2) the taxpayer omits from a sales, use, or withholding tax return an amount of taxes in excess of 25 percent of the taxes reported in the return; or

(3) the taxpayer omits from the gross estate assets in excess of 25 percent of the gross estate reported in the return.

Subd. 7. Federal tax changes. If the amount of income, items of tax preference, deductions, or credits for any year of a taxpayer as reported to the Internal Revenue Service is changed or corrected by the commissioner of Internal Revenue or other officer of the United States or other competent authority, or where a renegotiation of a contract or subcontract with the United States results in a change in income, items of tax preference, deductions, credits, or withholding tax, or, in the case of estate tax, where there are adjustments to the taxable estate, the taxpayer shall report the change or correction or renegotiation results in writing to the commissioner. The report must be submitted within 180 days after the final determination and must be in the form of either an amended Minnesota estate, withholding tax, corporate franchise tax, or income tax return conceding the accuracy of the federal determination or a letter detailing how the federal determination is incorrect or does not change the Minnesota tax. An amended Minnesota income tax return must be accompanied by an amended property tax refund return, if necessary. A taxpayer filing an amended federal tax return must also file a copy of the amended return with the commissioner of revenue within 180 days after filing the amended return.

Subd. 8. Failure to report change or correction of federal return. If a taxpayer fails to make a report as required by subdivision 7, the commissioner may recompute the tax, including a refund, based on information available to the commissioner. The tax may be recomputed within six years after the report should have been filed, notwithstanding any period of limitations to the contrary.

Subd. 9. Report made of change or correction of federal return. If a taxpayer is required to make a report under subdivision 7, and does report the change or files a copy of the amended return, the commissioner may recompute and reassess the tax due, including a refund (1) within one year after the report or amended return is filed with the commissioner, notwithstanding any period of limitations to the contrary, or (2) within any other applicable period stated in this section, whichever period is longer. The period provided for the carryback of any amount of loss or credit is also extended as provided in this subdivision, notwithstanding any law to the contrary. If the commissioner has completed a field audit of the taxpayer, and, but for this subdivision, the commissioner's time period to adjust the tax has expired, the additional tax due or refund is limited to only those changes that are required to be made to the return which relate to the changes made on the federal return. This subdivision does not apply to sales and use tax.

For purposes of this subdivision and section 289A.42, subdivision 2, a "field audit" is the physical presence of examiners in the taxpayer's or taxpayer's representative's office conducting an examination of the taxpayer with the intention of issuing an assessment or notice of change in tax or which results in the issuing of an assessment or notice of change in tax. The examination may include inspecting a taxpayer's place of business, tangible personal property, equipment, computer systems and facilities, pertinent books, records, papers, vouchers, computer printouts, accounts, and documents.

Subd. 10. Incorrect determination of federal adjusted gross income. Notwithstanding any other provision of this chapter, if a taxpayer whose net income is determined under section 290.01, subdivision 19, omits from income an amount that will under the Internal Revenue Code,[1] extend the statute of limitations for the assessment of federal income taxes, or otherwise incorrectly determines the taxpayer's federal adjusted gross income resulting in adjustments by the Internal Revenue Service, then the period of assessment and determination of tax will be that under the Internal Revenue Code. When a change is made to federal income during the extended time provided under this subdivision, the provisions under subdivisions 7 to 9 regarding additional extensions apply.

Subd. 11. Net operating loss carryback. If a deficiency of tax is attributable to a net operating loss carryback that has been disallowed in whole or in part, the deficiency may be assessed at any time that a deficiency for the taxable year of the loss may be assessed.

Subd. 12. Request for early audit for individual income, fiduciary income, mining company, and corporate franchise taxes. (a) Tax must be assessed within 18 months after written request for an assessment has been made in the case of income received (1) during the lifetime of a decedent, (2) by the decedent's estate during the period of administration, (3) by a trustee of a terminating trust or other fiduciary who, because of custody of assets, would be liable for the payment of tax under section 270C.58, subdivision 2, or (4) by a mining company or a corporation. A proceeding in court for the collection of the tax must begin within two years after written request for the assessment (filed after the return is made and in the form the commissioner prescribes) by the personal representative or other fiduciary representing the estate of the decedent, or by the trustee of a terminating trust or other fiduciary who, because of custody of assets, would be liable for the payment of tax under section 270C.58, subdivision 2, or by the corporation. Except as provided in section 289A.42, subdivision 1, an assessment must not be made after the expiration of 3-1/2 years after the return was filed, and an action must not be brought after the expiration of four years after the return was filed.

(b) Paragraph (a) only applies in the case of a mining company or a corporation if:

(1) the written request notifies the commissioner that the corporation contemplates dissolution at or before the expiration of the 18-month period;

(2) the dissolution is begun in good faith before the expiration of the 18-month period; and

(3) the dissolution is completed within the 18-month period.

Subd. 13. Repealed by Laws 2005, c. 151, art. 1, § 117, eff. Aug. 1, 2005.

Subd. 14. Failure to timely file withholding reconciliation. If an employer fails to timely file the reconciliation required by section 289A.09, subdivision 2, paragraph (d), withholding taxes may be assessed within the period prescribed in subdivision 1, or within one year from the date the reconciliation is filed with the commissioner, whichever is later.

Subd. 15. Purchaser filed refund claims. If a purchaser refund claim is filed under section 289A.50, subdivision 2a, and the basis for the claim is that the purchaser was improperly charged tax on an improvement to real property or on the purchase of nontaxable services, sales or use tax may be assessed for the cost of materials used to make the real property improvement or to perform the nontaxable service. The assessment may be made against the person making the improvement to real property or the sale of nontaxable services, within the period prescribed in subdivision 1, or within one year after the date of the refund order, whichever is later.

Subd. 16. Reportable transactions. (a) If a taxpayer fails to include on any return or statement for any taxable year any information with respect to a reportable transaction, as required by federal law and under section 289A.121, the commissioner may recompute the tax, including a refund, within the later of:

(1) six years after the return is filed with respect to the taxable year in which the taxpayer participated in the reportable transaction; or

(2) for a listed transaction, as defined in section 289A.121, for which the taxpayer fails to include on any return or statement for any taxable year any

information that is required under section 289A.121, one year after the earlier of:

(i) the date the taxpayer furnishes the required information to the commissioner; or

(ii) the date that a material advisor, as defined in section 289A.121, meets the requirements of section 289A.121, relating to the transaction with respect to the taxpayer.

(b) If tax is assessable solely because of this section, the assessable deficiency is limited to the items that were not disclosed as required under section 289A.121.

Laws 1990, c. 480, art. 1, § 18. Amended by Laws 1991, c. 291, art. 6, § 12; Laws 1991, c. 291, art. 6, § 13, eff. July 1, 1991; Laws 1991, c. 291, art. 6, § 46; Laws 1991, c. 291, art. 11, § 9; Laws 1992, c. 511, art. 6, § 19; Laws 1993, c. 375, art. 8, § 14; Laws 1994, c. 587, art. 1, § 24; Laws 1995, c. 264, art. 10, § 3; Laws 1997, c. 31, art. 1, § 11; Laws 1998, c. 300, art. 1, § 3; Laws 2005, c. 151, art. 2, § 17; Laws 2005, c. 151, art. 6, § 5, eff. June 3, 2005; Laws 2005, c. 151, art. 7, § 1, eff. June 3, 2005; Laws 2005, c. 151, art. 7, § 2; Laws 2005, 1st Sp., c. 3, art. 8, § 3, eff. July 14, 2005; Laws 2008, c. 154, art. 11, § 6, eff. March 8, 2008.

[1] 26 U.S.C.A. § 1 et seq.

Historical and Statutory Notes

Laws 1990, c. 480, art. 1, § 47, provides in part that § 18 [enacting this section] is effective for returns becoming due on or after August 1, 1990.

Laws 1991, c. 291, art. 6, § 48 provides in part that § 13 (amending subd. 10 of this section) is effective July 1, 1991. There was no specified effective date provision for § 12 (amending subd. 9 of this section). Laws 1991, c. 291, art. 6, § 48 also provided that except where otherwise specifically provided, the rest of this article is effective for taxable years beginning after December 31, 1990.

Laws 1991, c. 291, art. 11, § 21 provides in part that § 9 (amending subd. 12 of this section) is effective for ores mined after December 31, 1990.

Laws 1993, c. 375, art. 8, § 15, provides in part that § 14 is effective for tax years beginning after December 31, 1992.

Laws 1995, c. 264, art. 10, § 14, provides:

"Effective for decedents dying before August 1, 1990, the provisions of Minnesota Statutes, section 289A.38, subdivision 6, apply to assets omitted from an inheritance tax return or estate tax return rather than the provisions of Minnesota Statutes 1988, section 291.11, subdivision 1, clause (2)(c)."

Laws 1995, c. 264, art. 10, §15, provides in part that § 3 (amending subd. 7) is effective for federal determinations after December 31, 1995.

Laws 1997, c. 31, art. 1, § 19, provides in part that § 11 (amending subd. 11) is effective for federal changes beginning after the date of final enactment (April 15, 1997).

Laws 1998, c. 300, art. 1, § 9, provides:

"Sections 1, 2, and 8 are effective for withholding on wages paid after December 31, 1997. Sections 3 and 4 are effective for federal extensions granted and final determinations made after the date of final enactment [March 19, 1998]. Sections 5 to 7 are effective for certificates issued after December 31, 1996, and used in taxable years beginning after July 31, 1997."

Laws 2005, c. 151, art. 1, § 115, provided:

"Subdivision 1. Purpose. It is the intent of the legislature to simplify Minnesota's tax laws by consolidating and recodifying tax administration and compliance provisions now contained in Minnesota Statutes, chapter 270, and several other chapters of Minnesota Statutes. The provisions of this act may not be used to determine the law in effect prior to the effective dates in this act.

"Subd. 2. Effect. Due to the complexity of the recodification, prior provisions are repealed on the effective date of the new provisions. The repealed provisions, however, continue to remain in effect until superseded by the analogous provision in the new law."

Laws 2005, c. 151, art. 7, § 2, adding subd. 15, also provided:

This section is effective for purchaser refund claims filed on or after July 1, 2005."

289A.39. Limitations; armed services

Subdivision 1. Extensions for service members. (a) The limitations of time provided by this chapter, chapter 290 relating to income taxes, chapter 271 relating to the Tax Court for filing returns, paying taxes, claiming refunds, commencing action thereon, appealing to the Tax Court from orders relating to income taxes, and the filing of petitions under chapter 278 that would otherwise be due prior to May 1 of the year in which the taxes are payable, and appealing to the Supreme Court from decisions of the Tax Court relating to income taxes are extended, as provided in section 7508 of the Internal Revenue Code.[1]

(b) If a member of the National Guard or reserves is called to active duty in the armed forces, the limitations of time provided by this chapter and chapters 290 and 290A relating to income taxes and claims for property tax refunds are extended by the following period of time:

(1) in the case of an individual whose active service is in the United States, six months; or

(2) in the case of an individual whose active service includes service abroad, the period of initial service plus six months.

Nothing in this paragraph reduces the time within which an act is required or permitted under paragraph (a).

(c) If an individual entitled to the benefit of paragraph (a) files a return during the period disregarded under paragraph (a), interest must be paid on an overpayment or refundable credit from the due date of the return, notwithstanding section 289A.56, subdivision 2.

(d) The provisions of this subdivision apply to the spouse of an individual entitled to the benefits of this subdivision with respect to a joint return filed by the spouses.

Subd. 2. Interest and penalties. Interest on income tax must not be assessed or collected from an individual, and interest must not be paid upon an income tax refund to any individual, with respect to whom, and for the period during which, the limitations or time are extended as provided in subdivision 1. A penalty will not be assessed or collected from an individual for failure during that period to perform an act required by the laws described in subdivision 1.

Subd. 3. Assessments; actions. The time limitations provided for the assessment of a tax, penalty, or interest, are extended, with respect to those individuals and for the period provided in subdivision 1 and for a further period of six months; and the time limitations for the commencement of action to collect a tax, penalty, or interest from those individuals are extended for a period ending six months after the expiration of the time for assessment as provided in this section.

Subd. 4. Applicability. Nothing in this section reduces the time within which an act is required or permitted under this chapter.

Subd. 5. Extension limitations. This section does not extend the time for performing any of the acts set forth in this chapter beyond the expiration of three months after the appointment of a personal representative or guardian, in this state, for any individual described in this section, except as provided in subdivision 6.

Subd. 6. Death while serving in armed forces. If an individual dies while in active service as a member of the military or naval forces of the United States or of any of the United Nations, an income tax imposed under chapter 290 will not be imposed for the taxable year in which the individual dies. Income tax imposed for a prior taxable year that is unpaid at the date of death (including additions to the tax, penalties) must not be assessed, and if assessed, the assessment must be abated. In addition, upon the filing of a claim for refund within seven years from the date the return was filed, the tax paid or collected with respect to any taxable year beginning after December 31, 1949, during which the decedent was in active service must be refunded.

Subd. 7. Death of civilian while outside United States. If an individual dies while a civilian employee of the United States as a result of wounds or injuries incurred while the individual was a civilian employee of the United States, and which were incurred outside the United States in a terroristic or military action, a tax imposed by chapter 290 does not apply with respect to the taxable year in which the death falls and with respect to any prior taxable years in the period beginning with the last taxable year ending before the taxable year in which the wounds or injury were incurred. Terroristic or military action has the meaning given it in section 692(c)(2) of the Internal Revenue Code.

Laws 1990, c. 480, art. 1, § 19, eff. Aug. 1, 1990. Amended by Laws 1991, c. 18, § 2; Laws 1991, c. 291, art. 6, § 46; Laws 1991, c. 291, art. 21, § 12, eff. June 1, 1991; Laws 1992, c. 511, art. 6, § 19; Laws 1993, c. 375, art. 8, § 14; Laws 1994, c. 587, art. 1, § 24; Laws 1996, c. 471, art. 4, § 2; Laws 2005, c. 151, art. 6, § 6.

1 All text references to Internal Revenue Code sections are to Title 26 of U.S.C.A.

Historical and Statutory Notes

Laws 1991, c. 18, § 3 provides in part that this amendment is effective for taxable years beginning after December 31, 1989, and for claims for property tax refunds filed after August 15, 1990.

Laws 1993, c. 375, art. 8, § 15, provides in part that § 14 is effective for tax years beginning after December 31, 1992.

Laws 1996, c. 471, art. 4, § 6, provides in part that § 2 (amending subd. 1) is effective for taxable years beginning after December 31, 1994, and claims for property tax refunds filed after April 12, 1996.

Laws 2005, c. 151, art. 6, § 6, amending subd. 1, also provided:

"This section is effective for taxable years beginning after December 31, 2002, and for property taxes payable after 2003."

289A.40. Limitations on claims for refund

Subdivision 1. Time limit; generally. Unless otherwise provided in this chapter, a claim for a refund of an overpayment of state tax must be filed within 3–½ years from the date prescribed for filing the return, plus any extension of time granted for filing the return, but only if filed within the extended time, or one year from the date of an order assessing tax under section 270C.33 or an order determining an appeal under section 270C.35, subdivision 8, or one year from the date of a return made by the commissioner under section 270C.33, subdivision 3, upon payment in full of the tax, penalties, and interest shown on the order or return made by the commissioner, whichever period expires later. Claims for refund, except for taxes under chapter 297A, filed after the 3–½ year period but within the one-year period are limited to the amount of the tax, penalties, and interest on the order or return made by the commissioner and to issues determined by the order or return made by the commissioner.

In the case of assessments under section 289A.38, subdivision 5 or 6, claims for refund under chapter 297A filed after the 3–½ year period but within the one-year period are limited to the amount of the tax, penalties, and interest on the order or return made by the commissioner that are due for the period before the 3–½ year period.

Subd. 1a. Individual income taxes; suspension during period of disability. If the taxpayer meets the requirements for suspending the running of the time period to file a claim for refund under section 6511(h) of the Internal Revenue Code,[1] the time period in subdivision 1 for the taxpayer to file a claim for an individual income tax refund is suspended.

Subd. 2. Bad debt loss. If a claim relates to an overpayment because of a failure to deduct a loss due to a bad debt or to a security becoming worthless, the claim is considered timely if filed within seven years from the date prescribed for the filing of the return. A claim relating to an overpayment of taxes under chapter 297A must be filed within 3–½ years from the date when the bad debt was (1) written off as uncollectible in the taxpayer's books and records, and (2) either eligible to be deducted for federal income tax purposes or would have been eligible for a bad debt deduction for federal income tax purposes if the taxpayer were required to file a federal income tax return, or within one year from the date the taxpayer's federal income tax return is timely filed claiming the bad debt deduction, whichever period is later. The refund or credit is limited to the amount of overpayment attributable to the loss. "Bad debt" for purposes of this subdivision, has the same meaning as that term is used in United States Code, title 26, section 166, except that for a claim relating to an overpayment of taxes under chapter 297A the following are excluded from the calculation of bad debt: financing charges or interest; sales or use taxes charged on the purchase price; uncollectible amounts on property that remain in the possession of the seller until the full purchase price is paid; expenses incurred in attempting to collect any debt; and repossessed property. For purposes of reporting a payment received on previously claimed bad debt under chapter 297A, any payments made on a debt or account are applied first proportionally to the taxable price of the property or service and the sales tax on it, and secondly to interest, service charges, and any other charges.

Subd. 3. Net operating loss; individuals. A refund or credit must be allowed for a net operating loss carryback to any taxable year authorized by section 290.095, or section 172 of the Internal Revenue Code, but the refund or credit is limited to the amount of overpayment arising from the carryback.

Subd. 4. Property tax refund claims. A property tax refund claim under chapter 290A is not allowed if the initial claim is filed more than one year after the original due date for filing the claim.

Subd. 5. Purchaser filed refund claims. A claim for refund of taxes paid on a transaction not subject to tax under chapter 297A, where the purchaser may apply directly to the commissioner under section 289A.50, subdivision 2a, must be filed within 3–½ years from the 20th day of the month following the month of the invoice date for the purchase.

Subd. 6. Capital equipment refund claims. A claim for refund for taxes paid under chapter 297A on capital equipment must be filed within 3–½ years from the 20th day of the month following the month of the invoice date for the purchase of the capital equipment. A claim for refund for taxes imposed on capital equipment under section 297A.63 must be filed within 3–½ years from the date prescribed for filing the return, or one year from the date of an order assessing tax under section 289A.37, subdivision 1, upon payment in full of the tax, penalties, and interest shown on the order, whichever period expires later.

Laws 1990, c. 480, art. 1, § 20. Amended by Laws 1991, c. 291, art. 6, § 46; Laws 1992, c. 511, art. 6, § 19; Laws 1993, c. 375, art. 8, § 14; Laws 1993, c. 375, art. 10, § 18; Laws 1994, c. 587, art. 1, § 24; Laws 1995, c. 264, art. 13, § 11; Laws 1996, c. 471, art. 2, § 7, eff. April 13, 1996; Laws 1997, c. 84, art. 3, § 1; Laws 1997, c. 84, art. 6, § 24; Laws 1999, c. 243, art. 16, §§ 15, 16; Laws 2001, c. 7, § 57; Laws 2003, c. 127, art. 1, § 4; Laws 2005, c. 151, art. 2, § 17; Laws 2005, c. 151, art. 7, §§ 3 to 5; Laws 2008, c. 154, art. 12, § 1, eff. March 8, 2008.

[1] All text references to Internal Revenue Code sections are to Title 26 U.S.C.A.

Historical and Statutory Notes

Laws 1990, c. 480, art. 1, § 47, provides in part that § 20 [enacting this section] is effective for overpayments of taxes or other payments first becoming due on or after August 1, 1990.

Laws 1993, c. 375, art. 8, § 15, provides in part that § 14 is effective for tax years beginning after December 31, 1992.

Laws 1993, c. 375, art. 10, § 52, provides in part that § 18 (adding subd. 1a) is effective for returns due for taxable years beginning after December 31, 1982.

Laws 1995, c. 264, art. 13, § 24, provides in part that § 11 (amending subd. 1) is effective for claims for refund which have not been filed as of June 2, 1995, and in which the time period for filing the claim has not expired under the provisions in effect prior to June 2, 1995. The time period for filing such claims is the time period prescribed in the enacted sections, or one year after June 2, 1995, whichever is greater.

Laws 1997, c. 84, art. 3, § 9, provides in part that § 1 (amending subd. 2) is effective for refund claims filed for bad debts recognized for federal income tax purposes after June 30, 1997.

Laws 1997, c. 84, art. 6, § 29, provides in part that § 24 (amending subd. 1) is effective for claims for refunds filed on or after May 3, 1997.

Laws 1999, c. 243, art. 16, § 40, provides in part that § 15 (amending subd. 1 of this section) is effective for orders issued on or after May 26, 1999, and that § 16 (amending subd. 1a of this section) is effective for disabilities existing on or after May 25, 1999, for which claims for refund have not expired under the time limit in § 289A.40, subd. 1. Claims based upon reasonable cause must be filed prior to the expiration of the repealed ten-year period or within one year after May 25, 1999, whichever is earlier.

Laws 2003, c. 127, art. 1, § 4, amending subd. 2, also provided that the amendment was effective for sales or purchases made on or after January 1, 2004.

Laws 2005, c. 151, art. 7, § 3, amending subd. 2, also provided:

"For claims relating to an overpayment of taxes under chapter 297A, this section is effective for sales and purchases made on or after January 1, 2004; for all other bad debts or claims, this section is effective on or after July 1, 2003."

Laws 2005, c. 151, art. 7, §§ 4 and 5, adding subds. 5 and 6, also provided that subds. 5 and 6 were effective for claims filed on or after June 3, 2005.

289A.41. Bankruptcy; suspension of time

The running of the period during which a tax must be assessed or collection proceedings commenced is suspended during the period from the date of a filing of a petition in bankruptcy until 30 days after either notice to the commissioner of revenue that the bankruptcy proceedings have been closed or dismissed, or the automatic stay has been terminated or has expired, whichever occurs first.

The suspension of the statute of limitations under this section applies to the person the petition in bankruptcy is filed against and other persons who may also be wholly or partially liable for the tax.

Laws 1990, c. 480, art. 1, § 21, eff. Aug. 1, 1990.

289A.42. Consent to extend statute

Subdivision 1. Extension agreement. If before the expiration of time prescribed in sections 289A.38 and 289A.40 for the assessment of tax or the filing of a claim for refund, both the commissioner and the taxpayer have consented in writing to the assessment or filing of a claim for refund after that time, the tax may be assessed or the claim for refund filed at any time before the expiration of the agreed upon period. The period may be extended by later agreements in writing before the expiration of the period previously agreed upon. The taxpayer and the commissioner may also agree to extend the period for collection of the tax.

Subd. 2. Federal extensions. When a taxpayer consents to an extension of time for the assessment of federal withholding or income taxes, the period in which the commissioner may recompute the tax is also extended, notwithstanding any period of limitations to the contrary, as follows:

(1) for the periods provided in section 289A.38, subdivisions 8 and 9;

(2) for six months following the expiration of the extended federal period of limitations when no change is made by the federal authority. If no change is made by the federal authority, and, but for this subdivision, the commissioner's time period to adjust the tax has expired, and if the commissioner has completed a field audit of the taxpayer, no additional changes resulting in additional tax due or a refund may be made. For purposes of this subdivision, "field audit" has the meaning given it in section 289A.38, subdivision 9.

Laws 1990, c. 480, art. 1, § 22, eff. Aug. 1, 1990. Amended by Laws 1991, c. 291, art. 6, § 14; Laws 1991, c. 291, art. 16, § 9, eff. June 1, 1991; Laws 1998, c. 300, art. 1, § 4; Laws 2005, c. 151, art. 2, § 9; Laws 2006, c. 212, art. 3, § 25; Laws 2007, c. 13, art. 3, § 16, eff. Aug. 1, 2007.

Historical and Statutory Notes

Laws 1991, c. 291, art. 6, § 48 provides in part that except where otherwise specifically provided, this article is effective for taxable years beginning after December 31, 1990. There were no specified effective date provisions listed in Laws 1991, c. 291, art. 6 for §§ 7 to 12, 14, 16, 18 to 23, 26 to 29, and 32 to 40.

Laws 1998, c. 300, art. 1, § 9, provides:

"Sections 1, 2, and 8 are effective for withholding on wages paid after December 31, 1997. Sections 3 and 4 are effective for federal extensions granted and final determinations made after the date of final enactment [March 19, 1998]. Sections 5 to 7 are effective for certificates issued after December 31, 1996, and used in taxable years beginning after July 31, 1997."

289A.43. Repealed by Laws 2005, c. 151, art. 1, § 117, eff. Aug. 1, 2005

Historical and Statutory Notes

Laws 2005, c. 151, art. 1, § 115, provided:

"Subdivision 1. Purpose. It is the intent of the legislature to simplify Minnesota's tax laws by consolidating and recodifying tax administration and compliance provisions now contained in Minnesota Statutes, chapter 270, and several other chapters of Minnesota Statutes. The provisions of this act may not be used to determine

the law in effect prior to the effective dates in this act.

"Subd. 2. Effect. Due to the complexity of the recodification, prior provisions are repealed on the effective date of the new provisions. The repealed provisions, however, continue to remain in effect until superseded by the analogous provision in the new law."

REFUNDS

289A.50. Claims for refunds

Subdivision 1. General right to refund. (a) Subject to the requirements of this section and section 289A.40, a taxpayer who has paid a tax in excess of the taxes lawfully due and who files a written claim for refund will be refunded or credited the overpayment of the tax determined by the commissioner to be erroneously paid.

(b) The claim must specify the name of the taxpayer, the date when and the period for which the tax was paid, the kind of tax paid, the amount of the tax that the taxpayer claims was erroneously paid, the grounds on which a refund is claimed, and other information relative to the payment and in the form required by the commissioner. An income tax, estate tax, or corporate franchise tax return, or amended return claiming an overpayment constitutes a claim for refund.

(c) When, in the course of an examination, and within the time for requesting a refund, the commissioner determines that there has been an overpayment of tax, the commissioner shall refund or credit the overpayment to the taxpayer and no demand is necessary. If the overpayment exceeds $1, the amount of the overpayment must be refunded to the taxpayer. If the amount of the overpayment is less than $1, the commissioner is not required to refund. In these situations, the commissioner does not have to make written findings or serve notice by mail to the taxpayer.

(d) If the amount allowable as a credit for withholding, estimated taxes, or dependent care exceeds the tax against which the credit is allowable, the amount of the excess is considered an overpayment. The refund allowed by section 290.06, subdivision 23, is also considered an overpayment. The requirements of section 270C.33 do not apply to the refunding of such an overpayment shown on the original return filed by a taxpayer.

(e) If the entertainment tax withheld at the source exceeds by $1 or more the taxes, penalties, and interest reported in the return of the entertainment entity or imposed by section 290.9201, the excess must be refunded to the entertainment entity. If the excess is less than $1, the commissioner need not refund that amount.

(f) If the surety deposit required for a construction contract exceeds the liability of the out-of-state contractor, the commissioner shall refund the difference to the contractor.

(g) An action of the commissioner in refunding the amount of the overpayment does not constitute a determination of the correctness of the return of the taxpayer.

(h) There is appropriated from the general fund to the commissioner of revenue the amount necessary to pay refunds allowed under this section.

Subd. 1a. Refund form. On or before January 1, 2000, the commissioner of revenue shall prepare and make available to taxpayers a form for filing claims for refund of taxes paid in excess of the amount due. The commissioner may require corporate franchise taxpayers claiming a refund of corporate franchise taxes paid in excess of the amount lawfully due to include on the claim for refund or amended return information necessary for payment of the taxes paid in excess of taxes lawfully due by electronic means.

Subd. 2. Refund of sales tax to vendors; limitation. If a vendor has collected from a purchaser and remitted to the state a tax on a transaction that is not subject to the tax imposed by chapter 297A, the tax is refundable to the vendor only if and to the extent that the tax and any interest earned on the tax is credited to amounts due to the vendor by the purchaser or returned to the purchaser by the vendor. In addition to the requirements of subdivision 1, a claim for refund under this subdivision must state in writing that the tax and interest earned on the tax has been or will be refunded or credited to the purchaser by the vendor.

Subd. 2a. Refund of sales tax to purchasers. (a) If a vendor has collected from a purchaser a tax on a transaction that is not subject to the tax imposed by chapter 297A, the purchaser may apply directly to the commissioner for a refund under this section if:

(1) the purchaser is currently registered or was registered during the period of the claim, to collect and remit the sales tax or to remit the use tax; and

(2) either

(i) the amount of the refund to be applied for exceeds $500, or

(ii) the amount of the refund to be applied for does not exceed $500, but the purchaser also applies for a capital equipment claim at the same time, and the total of the two refunds exceeds $500.

(b) The purchaser may not file more than two applications for refund under this subdivision in a calendar year.

Subd. 2b. Certified service provider; bad debt claim. A certified service provider, as defined in section 297A.995, subdivision 2, may claim on behalf of a taxpayer that is its client any bad debt allowance provided by section 297A.81. The certified service provider must credit or refund to its client the full amount of any bad debt allowance or refund received.

Subd. 2c. Notice from purchaser to vendor requesting refund. (a) If a vendor has collected from a purchaser a tax on a transaction that is not subject to the tax imposed by chapter 297A, the purchaser may seek from the vendor a return of over-collected sales or use taxes as follows:

(1) the purchaser must provide written notice to the vendor;

(2) the notice to the vendor must contain the information necessary to determine the validity of the request; and

(3) no cause of action against the vendor accrues until the vendor has had 60 days to respond to the written notice.

(b) In connection with a purchaser's request from a vendor of over-collected sales or use taxes, a vendor is presumed to have a reasonable business practice, if in the collection of such sales or use taxes, the vendor: (1) uses a certified service provider as defined in section 297A.995, a certified automated system, as defined in section 297A.995, or a proprietary system that is certified by the state; and (2) has remitted to the state all taxes collected less any deductions, credits, or collection allowances.

Subd. 3. Withholding tax and entertainer withholding tax refunds. When there is an overpayment of withholding tax by an employer or a person making royalty payments, or an overpayment of entertainer withholding tax by the payor, a refund allowable under this section is limited to the amount of the overpayment that was not deducted and withheld from employee wages or from the royalty payments, or from the compensation of an entertainer.

Subd. 4. Notice of refund. The commissioner shall determine the amount of refund, if any, that is due, and notify the taxpayer of the determination as soon as practicable after a claim has been filed.

Subd. 5. Withholding of refunds from child support and maintenance debtors. (a) If a court of this state finds that a person obligated to pay child support or maintenance is delinquent in making payments, the amount of child support or maintenance unpaid and owing, including attorney fees and costs incurred in ascertaining or collecting child support or maintenance, must be withheld from a refund due the person under chapter 290. The public agency responsible for child support enforcement or the parent or guardian of a child for whom the support, attorney fees, and costs are owed or the party to whom maintenance, attorney fees, and costs are owed may petition the district court for an order providing for the withholding of the amount of child support, maintenance, attorney fees, and costs unpaid and owing as determined by court order. The person from whom the refund may be withheld must be notified of the petition under the Rules of Civil Procedure before the issuance of an order under this subdivision. The order may be granted on a showing to the court that required support or maintenance payments, attorney fees, and costs have not been paid when they were due.

(b) On order of the court, the commissioner shall withhold the money from the refund due to the person obligated to pay the child support or maintenance. The amount withheld shall be remitted to the public agency responsible for child support enforcement, the parent or guardian petitioning on behalf of the child, or the party to whom maintenance is owed, after any delinquent tax obligations of the taxpayer owed to the revenue department have been satisfied and after deduction of the fee prescribed in section 270A.07, subdivision 1. An amount received by the responsible public agency, or the petitioning parent or guardian, or the party to whom maintenance is owed, in excess of the amount of public assistance spent for the benefit of the child to be supported, or the amount of any support, maintenance, attorney fees, and costs that had been the subject of the claim under this subdivision that has been paid by the taxpayer before the diversion of the refund, must be paid to the person entitled to the money. If the refund is based on a joint return, the part of the refund that must be paid to the petitioner is the proportion of the total refund that equals the proportion of the total federal adjusted gross income of the spouses that is the federal adjusted gross income of the spouse who is delinquent in making the child support or maintenance payments.

(c) A petition filed under this subdivision remains in effect with respect to any refunds due under this section until the support or maintenance, attorney fees, and costs have been paid in full or the court orders the commissioner to discontinue withholding the money from the refund due the person obligated to pay the support or maintenance, attorney fees, and costs. If a petition is filed under this subdivision concerning child support and a claim is made under chapter 270A with respect to the individual's refund and notices of both are received before the time when payment of the refund is made on either claim, the claim relating to the liability that accrued first in time must be paid first. The amount of the refund remaining must then be applied to the other claim.

Subd. 6. Repealed by Laws 1998, c. 389, art. 6, § 20.

Subd. 7. Remedies. (a) If the taxpayer is notified by the commissioner that the refund claim is denied in whole or in part, the taxpayer may:

(1) file an administrative appeal as provided in section 270C.35, or an appeal with the Tax Court, within 60 days after issuance of the commissioner's notice of denial; or

(2) file an action in the district court to recover the refund.

(b) An action in the district court on a denied claim for refund must be brought within 18 months of the date of the denial of the claim by the commissioner.

(c) No action in the district court or the Tax Court shall be brought within six months of the filing of the refund claim unless the commissioner denies the claim within that period.

(d) If a taxpayer files a claim for refund and the commissioner has not issued a denial of the claim, the taxpayer may bring an action in the district court or the Tax Court at any time after the expiration of six months from the time the claim was filed.

(e) The commissioner and the taxpayer may agree to extend the period for bringing an action in the district court.

(f) An action for refund of tax by the taxpayer must be brought in the district court of the district in which lies the county of the taxpayer's residence or principal place of business. In the case of an estate or trust, the action must be brought at the principal place of its administration. Any action may be brought in the district court for Ramsey County.

Subd. 8. Mistake discovered by commissioner. If money has been erroneously collected from a taxpayer or other person, the commissioner shall, within the period named in section 289A.40 for filing a claim for refund, and, subject to the provisions of chapter 270A, section 270C.64, and this section, grant a refund to that taxpayer or other person.

Subd. 9. Petition in Tax Court; refund of interest. Notwithstanding any other law, within one year after a decision of the Tax Court upholding an assessment of the commissioner of revenue becomes final, if the taxpayer has paid the assessment in full, plus interest calculated by the commissioner, the taxpayer may petition the Tax Court to reopen the case solely for a determination that the interest paid exceeds the interest legally due, and if so, the amount of the overpayment. A determination of overpayment of interest under this subdivision is a determination of overpayment of tax under section 271.12, and is reviewable in the same manner as any other decision of the Tax Court.

Subd. 10. Limitation on refund. If an addition to federal taxable income under section 290.01, subdivision 19a, clause (1), is judicially determined to discriminate against interstate commerce, the legislature intends that the discrimination be remedied by adding interest on obligations of Minnesota governmental units and Indian tribes to federal taxable income. This subdivision applies beginning with the taxable years that begin during the calendar year in which the court's decision is final. Other remedies apply for previous taxable years.

Laws 1990, c. 480, art. 1, § 23. Amended by Laws 1990, c. 604, art. 1, § 21; Laws 1991, c. 291, art. 6, § 15, eff. July 1, 1991; Laws 1992, c. 511, art. 7, § 12; Laws 1993, c. 322, § 6; Laws 1993, c. 375, art. 8, § 4; Laws 1995, c. 264, art. 1, § 1, eff. June 2, 1995; Laws 1995, c. 264, art. 19, § 5, eff. June 2, 1995; Laws 1996, c. 471, art. 2, § 8; Laws 1999, c. 243, art. 16, §§ 17, 18; Laws 2001, c. 7, § 58; Laws 2001, 1st Sp., c. 5, art. 7, § 33, eff. July 1, 2001; Laws 2001, 1st Sp., c. 5, art. 12, § 3; Laws 2003, c. 127, art. 1, §§ 5, 6; Laws 2003, c. 127, art. 6, § 1, eff. May 26, 2003; Laws 2005, c. 151, art. 2, § 17; Laws 2005, c. 151, art. 6, § 7.

Historical and Statutory Notes

Laws 1990, c. 480, art. 1, § 47, provides in part that § 23 [enacting this section] is effective for overpayments of taxes or other payments first becoming due on or after August 1, 1990.

Laws 1990, c. 604, art. 1, § 23, provides in part that § 21 [adding subd. 9] is effective for interest payments made on or after August 1, 1990.

Laws 1992, c. 511, art. 7, § 27, provides in part that the 1992 amendment is effective for refund offsets made on or after July 1, 1992.

Laws 1995, c. 264, art. 19, § 5, in subd. 1, par. (d), provides that § 270.10, subd. 1, does not apply to refunds of overpayments shown on the original return.

Laws 1996, c. 471, art. 2, § 31, provides in part that § 8 (adding subd. 2a) is effective for refunds applied for after December 31, 1996.

Laws 1998, c. 389, art. 6, § 21, provides in part that the repeal of subd. 6 is effective for tax years beginning after December 31, 1997.

Laws 1999, c. 243, art. 16, § 40, provides in part that § 18, amending subd. 7, is effective for refund claims filed on or after May 26, 1999.

Laws 2001, 1st Sp., c. 5, art. 12, § 3, also provides that the amendment of subd. 2 is effective for claims for refunds after June 30, 2001.

Laws 2003, c. 127, art. 1, §§ 5 and 6, the effective date portions, provided that the addition of subds. 2b and 2c by art. 1, §§ 5 and 6, were effective for sales or purchases made on or after January 1, 2004.

Laws 2003, c. 127, art. 6, § 1, amending subd. 2a, also provided that the amendment was effective for claims filed on or after May 26, 2003.

Laws 2005, c. 151, art. 6, § 7, amending subd. 1a, also provided:

"This section is effective for claims for refund filed after December 31, 2005."

INTEREST

289A.55.   Interest payable to commissioner

Subdivision 1.   Interest rate. When interest is required under this section, interest is computed at the rate specified in section 270C.40.

Subd. 2.   Late payment. If a tax is not paid within the time named by law for payment, the unpaid tax bears interest from the date the tax should have been paid until the date the tax is paid.

100

Subd. 3. Extensions. When an extension of time for payment has been granted, interest must be paid from the date the payment should have been made, if no extension had been granted, until the date the tax is paid.

Subd. 4. Additional assessments. When a taxpayer is liable for additional taxes because of a redetermination by the commissioner, or for any other reason, the additional taxes bear interest from the time the tax should have been paid, without regard to an extension allowed, until the date the tax is paid.

Subd. 5. Excessive claims for refunds under chapter 290A. When it is determined that a claim for a property tax refund was excessive, the amount that the taxpayer must repay bears interest from the date the claim was paid until the date of repayment.

Subd. 6. Erroneous refunds. In the case of an erroneous refund, interest begins to accrue from the date the refund was paid unless the erroneous refund results from a mistake of the department, in which case no interest or penalty will be imposed, unless the deficiency assessment is not satisfied within 60 days of the order.

Subd. 7. Installment payments; estate tax. Interest must be paid on unpaid installment payments of the tax authorized under section 289A.30, subdivision 2, beginning on the date the tax was due without regard to extensions allowed or extensions elected, at the rate given in section 270C.40.

Subd. 8. Interest on judgments. Notwithstanding section 549.09, if judgment is entered in favor of the commissioner with regard to any tax, the judgment bears interest at the rate given in section 270C.40 from the date the judgment is entered until the date of payment.

Subd. 9. Interest on penalties. (a) A penalty imposed under section 289A.60, subdivision 1, 2, 2a, 4, 5, 6, or 21 bears interest from the date the return or payment was required to be filed or paid, including any extensions, to the date of payment of the penalty.

(b) A penalty not included in paragraph (a) bears interest only if it is not paid within 60 days from the date of notice. In that case interest is imposed from the date of notice to the date of payment.

Subd. 10. Relief for purchasers. A purchaser that meets the requirements of section 297A.995, subdivision 11, is relieved from the imposition of interest on tax and penalty.

Laws 1990, c. 480, art. 1, § 24. Amended by Laws 1995, c. 264, art. 10, § 4; Laws 1999, c. 243, art. 16, § 19; Laws 2000, c. 490, art. 13, § 12; Laws 2001, 1st Sp., c. 5, art. 11, § 1; Laws 2005, c. 151, art. 2, § 17; Laws 2008, c. 366, art. 13, § 1, eff. Jan. 1, 2009.

Historical and Statutory Notes

Laws 1990, c. 480, art. 1, § 47, provides in part that § 24 [enacting this section] is effective   for interest on amounts first becoming due to the commissioner on or after August 1, 1990.

Laws 1995, c. 264, art. 10, § 15, provides in part that § 4 (amending subd. 7) is effective for estates of decedents dying after June 1, 1995.

Laws 1999, c. 243, art. 16, § 40, provides in part that § 19, amending subd. 9 of this section, is effective for payments due on or after May 26, 1999.

Laws 2000, c. 490, art. 13, § 12, amending subd. 9, also provides that the amendment is effective for penalties assessed after May 15, 2000.

Laws 2001, 1st Sp., c. 5, art. 11, § 1, also provides that the amendment of subd. 9 is effective for tax years beginning after December 31, 2000, and for estate tax returns due after January 1, 2002.

Laws 2008, c. 366, art. 13, § 1, adding subd. 10, also provided:

"This section is effective for sales and purchases made after December 31, 2008."

289A.56. Interest on overpayments

Subdivision 1. Interest rate. When interest is due on an overpayment under this section, it must be computed at the rate specified in section 270C.405.

Subd. 2. Corporate franchise, mining company, individual and fiduciary income, and entertainer tax overpayments. Interest must be paid on an overpayment refunded or credited to the taxpayer from the date of payment of the tax until the date the refund is paid or credited. For purposes of this subdivision, the prepayment of tax made by withholding of tax at the source or payment of estimated tax before the due date is considered paid on the last day prescribed by law for the payment of the tax by the taxpayer. A return filed before the due date is considered as filed on the due date.

When the amount of tax withheld at the source or paid as estimated tax or allowable as other refundable credits, or withheld from compensation of entertainers, exceeds the tax shown on the original return by $10, the amount refunded bears interest from 90 days after (1) the due date of the return of the taxpayer, or (2) the date on which the original return is filed, whichever is later, until the date the refund is paid to the taxpayer. Where the amount to be refunded is less than $10, no interest is paid. However, to the extent that the basis for the refund is a net operating loss carryback, interest is computed only from the end of the taxable year in which the loss occurs.

Subd. 3. Withholding tax, entertainer withholding tax, withholding from payments to out–of–state contractors, estate tax, and sales tax overpayments. When a refund is due for overpayments of withholding tax, entertainer withholding tax, or withholding from payments to out-of-state contractors, interest is computed from the date of payment to the date the refund is paid or credited. For purposes of this subdivision, the date of payment is the later of the date the tax was finally due or was paid.

For the purposes of computing interest on estate tax refunds, interest is paid from the later of the date of overpayment, the date the estate tax return is due, or the date the original estate tax return is filed to the date the refund is paid.

For purposes of computing interest on sales and use tax refunds, interest is paid from the date of payment to the date the refund is paid or credited, if the refund claim includes a detailed schedule reflecting the tax periods covered in the claim. If the refund claim submitted does not include a detailed schedule reflecting the tax periods covered in the claim, interest is computed from the date the claim was filed.

Subd. 4. Capital equipment and certain building materials refunds; refunds to purchasers. Notwithstanding subdivision 3, for refunds payable under sections 297A.75, subdivision 1, and 289A.50, subdivision 2a, interest is computed from 90 days after the refund claim is filed with the commissioner.

Subd. 5. Sales tax or sales tax on motor vehicles; retailers. In the case of a refund allowed under section 297A.90, subdivision 3, interest is allowed only from the date on which the person has both registered as a retailer and filed a claim for refund.

Subd. 6. Property tax refunds under chapter 290A. (a) When a renter is owed a property tax refund, an unpaid refund bears interest after August 14, or 60 days after the refund claim was made, whichever is later, until the date the refund is paid.

(b) When any other claimant is owed a property tax refund, the unpaid refund bears interest after September 29, or 60 days after the refund claim was made, whichever is later, until the date the refund is paid.

Subd. 7. Biotechnology and health sciences industry zone refunds. Notwithstanding subdivision 3, for refunds payable under section 297A.68, subdivision 38, interest is computed from 90 days after the refund claim is filed with the commissioner.

Subd. 8. Border city zone refunds. Notwithstanding subdivision 3, for refunds payable under section 469.1734, subdivision 6, interest is computed from 90 days after the refund claim is filed with the commissioner.

Laws 1990, c. 480, art. 1, § 25. Amended by Laws 1991, c. 291, art. 11, § 10; Laws 1993, c. 375, art. 9, § 15; Laws 1994, c. 587, art. 2, § 21; Laws 1996, c. 471, art. 2, § 9; Laws 1997, c. 231, art. 7, § 1; Laws 1999, c. 243, art. 4, § 3; Laws 2000, c. 418, art. 1, § 44, subd. 2, eff. July 1, 2001; Laws 2003, c. 127, art. 1, § 7; Laws 2003, c. 127, art. 3, § 4; Laws 2005, c. 151, art. 2, § 17; Laws 2005, 1st Sp., c. 3, art. 7, § 7; Laws 2008, c. 154, art. 12, § 2, eff. July 1, 2008.

Historical and Statutory Notes

Laws 1990, c. 480, art. 1, § 47, provides in part that §§ 3 to 14 and 25 [enacting §§ 289A.08 to 289A.31 and 289A.56] are effective for returns, reports, taxes or other payments first becoming due on or after August 1, 1990, except that the exclusion for foreign operating corporations from the filing requirements in § 289A.08 is effective on the effective date of § 290.01, subd. 6b.

Laws 1991, c. 291, art. 11, § 21 provides in part that § 10 (amending subd. 2 of this section) is effective for ores mined after December 31, 1990.

Laws 1993, c. 375, art. 9, § 51, provides in part that § 15 (amending subd. 3) is effective for refund claims submitted on or after July 1, 1993.

Laws 1996, c. 471, art. 2, § 31, provides in part that § 9 (amending subd. 4) is effective for refunds applied for after December 31, 1996.

Laws 1997, c. 231, art. 7, § 47, provides in part that § 1 (amending subd. 4) is effective for refund claims filed after June 30, 1997.

Laws 1999, c. 243, art. 4, § 19, provides in part that § 3, amending subd. 4, is effective for amended returns and refund claims filed on or after July 1, 1999.

Laws 2003, c. 127, art. 1, § 7, amending subd. 4, also provided that the amendment of subd. 4 was effective for refund claims filed on or after April 1, 2003.

Laws 2003, c. 127, art. 3, § 4, amending subd. 3, also provided that the amendment was effective for estates of decedents dying after December 31, 2003.

Laws 2005, 1st Sp., c. 3, art. 7, § 7, adding subd. 7, also provided:

"This section is effective for refund claims filed on or after August 1, 2005."

Laws 2008, c. 154, art. 12, § 2, adding subd. 8, also provided:

"This section is effective for refund claims filed after June 30, 2008."

CIVIL PENALTIES

289A.60. Civil penalties

Subdivision 1. Penalty for failure to pay tax. (a) If a corporate franchise, fiduciary income, mining company, estate, partnership, S corporation, or nonresident entertainer tax is not paid within the time specified for payment, a penalty of six percent is added to the unpaid tax, except that if a corporation or mining company meets the requirements of section 289A.19, subdivision 2, the penalty is not imposed.

(b) For the taxes listed in paragraph (a), in addition to the penalty in that paragraph, whether imposed or not, if a return or amended return is filed after the due date, without regard to extensions, and any tax reported as remaining due is not remitted with the return or amended return, a penalty of five percent of the tax not paid is added to the tax. If the commissioner issues an order assessing additional tax for a tax listed in paragraph (a), and the tax is not paid within 60 days after the mailing of the order or, if appealed, within 60 days after final resolution of the appeal, a penalty of five percent of the unpaid tax is added to the tax.

(c) If an individual income tax is not paid within the time specified for payment, a penalty of four percent is added to the unpaid tax. There is a presumption of reasonable cause for the late payment if the individual: (i) pays by the due date of the return at least 90 percent of the amount of tax, after credits other than withholding and estimated payments, shown owing on the return; (ii) files the return within six months after the due date; and (iii) pays the remaining balance of the reported tax when the return is filed.

(d) If the commissioner issues an order assessing additional individual income tax, and the tax is not paid within 60 days after the mailing of the order or, if appealed, within 60 days after final resolution of the appeal, a penalty of four percent of the unpaid tax is added to the tax.

(e) If a withholding or sales or use tax is not paid within the time specified for payment, a penalty must be added to the amount required to be shown as tax. The penalty is five percent of the tax not paid on or before the date specified for payment of the tax if the failure is for not more than 30 days, with an additional penalty of five percent of the amount of tax remaining unpaid during each additional 30 days or fraction of 30 days during which the failure continues, not exceeding 15 percent in the aggregate.

Subd. 2. Penalty for failure to make and file return. If a taxpayer fails to make and file a tax return within the time prescribed, including an extension, or fails to file an individual income tax return within six months after the due date, a penalty of five percent of the amount of tax not paid by the end of that period is added to the tax.

Subd. 2a. Penalties for extended delinquency. (a) If an individual income tax is not paid within 180 days after the date of filing of a return or, in the case of taxes assessed by the commissioner, within 180 days after the assessment date or, if appealed, within 180 days after final resolution of the appeal, an extended delinquency penalty of five percent of the tax remaining unpaid is added to the amount due.

(b) If a tax return is not filed within 30 days after written demand for the filing of a delinquent return, an extended delinquency penalty of five percent of the tax not paid prior to the demand or $100 is imposed, whichever amount is greater.

Subd. 3. Repealed by Laws 2001, 1st Sp., c. 5, art. 11, § 8.

Subd. 4. Substantial understatement of liability; penalty. (a) The commissioner of revenue shall impose a penalty for substantial understatement of any tax payable to the commissioner, except a tax imposed under chapter 297A.

(b) There must be added to the tax an amount equal to 20 percent of the amount of any underpayment attributable to the understatement. There is a substantial understatement of tax for the period if the amount of the understatement for the period exceeds the greater of:

(1) ten percent of the tax required to be shown on the return for the period; or

(2)(i) $10,000 in the case of a mining company or a corporation, other than an S corporation as defined in section 290.9725, when the tax is imposed by chapter 290 or section 298.01 or 298.015, or

(ii) $5,000 in the case of any other taxpayer, and in the case of a mining company or a corporation any tax not imposed by chapter 290 or section 298.01 or 298.015.

(c) For a corporation, other than an S corporation, there is also a substantial understatement of tax for any taxable year if the amount of the understatement for the taxable year exceeds the lesser of:

(1) ten percent of the tax required to be shown on the return for the taxable year (or, if greater, $10,000); or

(2) $10,000,000.

(d) The term "understatement" means the excess of the amount of the tax required to be shown on the return for the period, over the amount of the tax imposed that is shown on the return. The excess must be determined without regard to items to which subdivision 27 applies. The amount of the understatement shall be reduced by that part of the understatement that is attributable to the tax treatment of any item by the taxpayer if (1) there is or was substantial authority for the treatment, or (2)(i) any item with respect to which the relevant facts affecting the item's tax treatment are adequately disclosed in the return or in a statement attached to the return and (ii) there is a reasonable basis for the tax treatment of the item. The exception for substantial authority under clause (1) does not apply to positions listed by the Secretary of the Treasury under section 6662(d)(3) of the Internal Revenue Code. [1] A corporation does not have a reasonable basis for its tax treatment of an item attributable to a multiple–party financing transaction if the treatment does not clearly reflect the income of the corporation within the meaning of section 6662(d)(2)(B) of the Internal Revenue Code. The special rules in cases involving tax shelters provided in section 6662(d)(2)(C) of the Internal Revenue Code shall apply and shall apply to a tax shelter the principal purpose of which is the avoidance or evasion of state taxes.

(e) The commissioner may abate all or any part of the addition to the tax provided by this section on a showing by the taxpayer that there was reasonable cause for the understatement, or part of it, and that the taxpayer acted in good faith. The additional tax and penalty shall bear interest at the rate specified in section 270C.40 from the time the tax should have been paid until paid.

Subd. 5. Penalty for intentional disregard of law or rules. If part of an additional assessment is due to negligence or intentional disregard of the provisions of the applicable tax laws or rules of the commissioner, but without intent to defraud, there must be added to the tax an amount equal to ten percent of the additional assessment.

Subd. 5a. Penalty for repeated failures to file returns or pay taxes. If there is a pattern by a person of repeated failures to timely file withholding or sales or use tax returns or timely pay withholding or sales or use taxes, and written notice is given that a penalty will be imposed if such failures continue, a penalty of 25 percent of the amount of tax not timely paid as a result of each such subsequent failure is added to the tax. The penalty can be abated under the abatement authority in section 270C.34.

Subd. 6. Penalty for failure to file, false or fraudulent return, evasion. (a) If a person, with intent to evade or defeat a tax or payment of tax, fails to file a return, files a false or fraudulent return, or attempts in any other manner to evade or defeat a tax or payment of tax, there is imposed on the person a penalty equal to 50 percent of the tax, less amounts paid by the person on the basis of the false or fraudulent return, if any, due for the period to which the return related.

(b) If a person files a false or fraudulent return that includes a claim for refund, there is imposed on the person a penalty equal to 50 percent of the portion of any refund claimed that is attributable to fraud. The penalty under this paragraph is in addition to any penalty imposed under paragraph (a).

Subd. 7. Penalty for frivolous return. If a taxpayer files what purports to be a tax return or a claim for refund but which does not contain information on which the substantial correctness of the purported return or claim for refund may be judged or contains information that on its face shows that the purported return or claim for refund is substantially incorrect and the conduct is due to a position that is frivolous or a desire that appears on the purported return or claim for refund to delay or impede the administration of Minnesota tax laws, then the individual shall pay a penalty of the greater of $1,000 or 25 percent of the amount of tax required to be shown on the return. In a proceeding involving the issue of whether or not a person is liable for this penalty, the burden of proof is on the commissioner.

Subd. 8. Penalties; failure to file informational return; incorrect taxpayer identification number. (a) In the case of a failure to file an informational return required by section 289A.12 with the commissioner on the date prescribed (determined with regard to any extension of time for filing), the person failing to file the return shall pay a penalty of $50 for each failure or in the case of a partnership, S corporation, or fiduciary return, $50 for each partner, shareholder, or beneficiary; but the total amount imposed on the delinquent person for all failures during any calendar year must not exceed $25,000. If a failure to file a return is due to intentional disregard of the filing requirement, then the penalty imposed under the preceding sentence must not be less than an amount equal to:

(1) in the case of a return not described in clause (2) or (3), ten percent of the aggregate amount of the items required to be reported;

(2) in the case of a return required to be filed under section 289A.12, subdivision 5, five percent of the gross proceeds required to be reported; and

(3) in the case of a return required to be filed under section 289A.12, subdivision 9, relating to direct sales, $100 for each failure; however, the total amount imposed on the delinquent person for intentional failures during a calendar year must not exceed $50,000. The penalty must be collected in the same manner as a delinquent income tax.

(b) If a partnership or S corporation files a partnership or S corporation return with an incorrect tax identification number used for a partner or shareholder after being notified by the commissioner that the identification number is incorrect, the partnership or S corporation must pay a penalty of $50 for each such incorrect number.

Subd. 9. Repealed by Laws 1996, c. 305, art. 1, § 64.

Subd. 10. Penalty for failure to provide Social Security number as required. A person who is required by law to: (1) give the person's Social Security account number to another person; or (2) include in a return, statement, or other document made with respect to another person that individual's Social Security account number, who fails to comply with the requirement when prescribed, must pay a penalty of $50 for each failure. The total amount imposed on a person for failures during a calendar year must not exceed $25,000.

Subd. 11. Penalties relating to information reports, withholding. (a) When a person required under section 289A.09, subdivision 2, to give a statement to an employee or payee and a duplicate statement to the commissioner, or to give a reconciliation of the statements and quarterly returns to the commissioner, gives a false or fraudulent statement to an employee or payee or a false or fraudulent duplicate statement or reconciliation of statements and quarterly returns to the commissioner, or fails to give a statement or the reconciliation in the manner, when due, and showing the information required by section 289A.09, subdivision 2, or rules prescribed by the commissioner under that section, that person is liable for a penalty of $50 for an act or failure to act. The total amount imposed on the delinquent person for failures during a calendar year must not exceed $25,000.

(b) In addition to any other penalty provided by law, an employee who gives a withholding exemption certificate or a residency affidavit to an employer that decreases the amount withheld under section 290.92 and as of the time the certificate or affidavit was given to the employer there was no reasonable basis for the statements in the certificate or affidavit is liable to the commissioner of revenue for a penalty of $500 for each instance.

(c) In addition to any other penalty provided by law, an employer who fails to submit a copy of a withholding exemption certificate or a residency affidavit required by section 290.92, subdivision 5a, clause (1)(a), (1)(b), or (2) is liable to the commissioner of revenue for a penalty of $50 for each instance.

(d) An employer or payor who fails to file an application for a withholding account number, as required by section 290.92, subdivision 24, is liable to the commissioner for a penalty of $100.

Subd. 12. Penalties relating to property tax refunds. (a) If it is determined that a property tax refund claim is excessive and was negligently prepared, a claimant is liable for a penalty of ten percent of the disallowed claim. If the claim has been paid, the amount disallowed must be recovered by assessment and collection.

(b) An owner who without reasonable cause fails to give a certificate of rent constituting property tax to a renter, as required by section 290A.19, paragraph (a), is liable to the commissioner for a penalty of $100 for each failure.

(c) If the owner or managing agent knowingly gives rent certificates that report total rent constituting property taxes in excess of the amount of actual rent constituting property taxes paid on the rented part of a property, the owner or managing agent is liable for a penalty equal to the greater of (1) $100 or (2) 50 percent of the excess that is reported. An overstatement of rent constituting property taxes is presumed to be knowingly made if it exceeds by ten percent or more the actual rent constituting property taxes.

Subd. 13. Penalties for tax return preparers. (a) If an understatement of liability with respect to a return or claim for refund is due to a reckless disregard of laws and rules or willful attempt in any manner to understate the liability for a tax by a person who is a tax return preparer with respect to the return or claim, the person shall pay to the commissioner a penalty of $500. If a part of a property tax refund claim is excessive due to a reckless disregard or willful attempt in any manner to overstate the claim for relief allowed under chapter 290A by a person who is a tax refund or return preparer, the person shall pay to the commissioner a penalty of $500 with respect to the claim. These penalties may not be assessed against the employer of a tax return preparer unless the employer was actively involved in the reckless disregard or willful attempt to understate the liability for a tax or to overstate the claim for refund. These penalties are income tax liabilities and may be assessed at any time as provided in section 289A.38, subdivision 5.

(b) A civil action in the name of the state of Minnesota may be commenced to enjoin any person who is a tax return preparer doing business in this state as provided in section 270C.447.

(c) The commissioner may terminate or suspend a tax preparer's authority to transmit returns electronically to the state, if the commissioner determines that the tax preparer has engaged in a pattern and practice of conduct in violation of paragraph (a) of this subdivision or has been convicted under section 289A.63.

(d) For purposes of this subdivision, the term "understatement of liability" means an understatement of the net amount payable with respect to a tax imposed by state tax law, or an overstatement of the net amount creditable or refundable with respect to a tax. The determination of whether or not there is an understatement of liability must be made without regard to any administrative or judicial action involving the taxpayer. For purposes of this subdivision, the amount determined for underpayment of estimated tax under either section 289A.25 or 289A.26 is not considered an understatement of liability.

(e) For purposes of this subdivision, the term "overstatement of claim" means an overstatement of the net amount refundable with respect to a claim for property tax relief provided by chapter 290A. The determination of whether or not there is an overstatement of a claim must be made without regard to administrative or judicial action involving the claimant.

(f) For purposes of this section, the term "tax refund or return preparer" means an individual who prepares for compensation, or who employs one or more individuals to prepare for compensation, a return of tax, or a claim for refund of tax. The preparation of a substantial part of a return or claim for refund is treated as if it were the preparation of the entire return or claim for refund. An individual is not considered a tax return preparer merely because the individual:

(1) gives typing, reproducing, or other mechanical assistance;

(2) prepares a return or claim for refund of the employer, or an officer or employee of the employer, by whom the individual is regularly and continuously employed;

(3) prepares a return or claim for refund of any person as a fiduciary for that person; or

(4) prepares a claim for refund for a taxpayer in response to a tax order issued to the taxpayer.

Subd. 14. Penalty for use of sales tax exemption certificates to evade tax. A person who uses an exemption certificate to buy property or purchase services that will be used for purposes other than the exemption claimed, with the intent to evade payment of sales tax to the seller, is subject to a penalty of $100 for each transaction where that use of an exemption certificate has occurred.

Text of subd. 15 effective until June 2009 tax liabilities.

Subd. 15. Accelerated payment of June sales tax liability; penalty for underpayment. For payments made after December 31, 2006, if a vendor is required by law to submit an estimation of June sales tax liabilities and 78 percent payment by a certain date, the vendor shall pay a penalty equal to ten percent of the amount of actual June liability required to be paid in June less the amount remitted in June. The penalty must not be imposed, however, if the amount remitted in June equals the lesser of 78 percent of the preceding May's liability or 78 percent of the average monthly liability for the previous calendar year.

Text of subd. 15 effective beginning with June 2009 tax liabilities.

Subd. 15. Accelerated payment of June sales tax liability; penalty for underpayment. For payments made after December 31, 2006, if a vendor is required by law to submit an estimation of June sales tax liabilities and 90 percent payment by a certain date, the vendor shall pay a penalty equal to ten percent of the amount of actual June liability required to be paid in June less the amount remitted in June. The penalty must not be imposed, however, if the amount remitted in June equals the lesser of 90 percent of the preceding May's liability or 90 percent of the average monthly liability for the previous calendar year.

Subd. 16. Penalty for sales after revocation. A person who engages in the business of making retail sales after revocation of a permit under section 270C.722 is liable for a penalty of $100 for each day the person continues to make taxable sales.

Subd. 17. Operator of flea markets; penalty. A person who fails to comply with the provisions of section 297A.87 is subject to a penalty of $100 for each day of each selling event that the operator fails to obtain evidence that a seller is the holder of a valid seller's permit issued under section 297A.83.

Subd. 18. Payment of penalties. The penalties imposed by this section are collected and paid in the same manner as taxes.

Subd. 19. Penalties are additional. The civil penalties imposed by this section are in addition to the criminal penalties imposed by this chapter.

Subd. 20. Penalty for promoting abusive tax shelters. (a) Any person who:

(1) (i) organizes or assists in the organization of a partnership or other entity, an investment plan or arrangement, or any other plan or arrangement, or (ii) participates in the sale of any interest in an entity or plan or arrangement referred to in clause (i); and

(2) makes or furnishes in connection with the organization or sale a statement with respect to the allowability of a deduction or credit, the excludability of income, or the securing of any other tax benefit by reason of holding an interest in the entity or participating in the plan or arrangement that the person knows or has reason to know is false or fraudulent concerning any material matter, shall pay a penalty equal to the greater of $1,000 or 20 percent of the gross income derived or to be derived by the person from the activity.

The penalty imposed by this subdivision is in addition to any other penalty provided by this section. The penalty must be collected in the same manner as any delinquent income tax. In a proceeding involving the issue of whether or not any person is liable for this penalty, the burden of proof is upon the commissioner.

(b) If an activity for which a penalty imposed under this subdivision involves a statement that a material advisor, as defined in section 289A.121, has reason to know is false or fraudulent as to any material matter, the amount of the penalty equals the greater of:

(1) the amount determined under paragraph (a); or

(2) 50 percent of the gross income derived or to be derived from the activity.

Subd. 20a. Aiding and abetting understating of tax liability. (a) A penalty in the amount specified under paragraph (b) for each document is imposed on each person who:

(1) aids or assists in, procures, or advises with respect to, the preparation or presentation of any portion of a return, affidavit, claim, or other document;

(2) knows or has reason to believe that the portion of a return, affidavit, claim, or other document will be used in connection with any material matter arising under the Minnesota individual income or corporate franchise tax; and

(3) knows that the portion, if so used, would result in an understatement of the liability for tax of another person.

(b)(1) Except as provided in clause (2), the amount of the penalty imposed by this subdivision is $1,000.

(2) If the return, affidavit, claim, or other document relates to the tax liability of a corporation, the amount of the penalty imposed by paragraph (a) is $10,000.

(3) If any person is subject to a penalty under paragraph (a) for any document relating to any taxpayer for any taxable period or taxable event, the person is not subject to a penalty under paragraph (a) for any other document relating to the taxpayer for the taxable period or event.

(c) For purposes of this subdivision, "procures" includes (1) ordering or otherwise causing any other person to do an act, and (2) knowing of, and not attempting to prevent, participation by any other person in an act.

(d) In a proceeding involving the issue of whether or not any person is liable for this penalty, the burden of proof is upon the commissioner. The penalty applies whether or not the understatement is with the knowledge or consent of the persons authorized or required to present the return, affidavit, claim, or other document.

(e) For purposes of paragraph (a), clause (1), a person furnishing typing, reproducing, or other mechanical assistance with respect to a document is not treated as having aided or assisted in the preparation of the document by reason of the assistance.

(f)(1) Except as provided by clause (2), the penalty imposed by this section is in addition to any other penalty provided by law.

(2) No penalty applies under subdivision 20 to any person for any document for which a penalty is assessed on the person under this subdivision.

Subd. 21. Penalty for failure to make payment by electronic means. In addition to other applicable penalties imposed by this section, after notification from the commissioner to the taxpayer that payments are required to be made by electronic means under section 289A.20, subdivision 2, paragraph (e), or 4, paragraph (c), or 289A.26, subdivision 2a, and the payments are remitted by some other means, there is a penalty in the amount of five percent of each payment that should have been remitted electronically. After the commissioner's initial notification to the taxpayer that payments are required to be made by electronic means, the commissioner is not required to notify the taxpayer in subsequent periods if the initial notification specified the amount of tax liability at which a taxpayer is required to remit payments by electronic means. The penalty can be abated under the abatement procedures prescribed in section 270C.34, subdivision 2, if the failure to remit the payment electronically is due to reasonable cause.

Subd. 22. Composite returns. For the purposes of the penalties imposed by subdivisions 1 and 2, the payment of a composite tax or filing of a composite return pursuant to section 289A.08, subdivision 7, is considered the payment and filing of a corporate tax.

Subd. 23. Withholding for nonresident partners or shareholders. For the purposes of the penalties imposed by subdivisions 1, 2, and 5a, the filing of returns required by section 289A.09, subdivision 1, paragraphs (d) and (e), and the payment of amounts withheld under section 290.92, subdivisions 4b and 4c, are considered filing and payment corporate tax rather than withholding tax.

Subd. 24. Penalty for failure to notify of federal change. If a person fails to report to the commissioner a change or correction of the person's federal return in the manner and time prescribed in section 289A.38, subdivision 7, there must be added to the tax an amount equal to ten percent of the amount of any underpayment of Minnesota tax attributable to the federal change.

Subd. 25. Penalty for failure to properly complete sales and use tax return. A person who fails to report local taxes required to be reported on a sales and use tax return or who fails to report local taxes on separate tax lines on the sales and use tax return is subject to a penalty of five percent of the amount of tax not properly reported on the return. A person who files a consolidated tax return but fails to report location information is subject to a $500 penalty for each return not containing location information. In addition, the commissioner may revoke the privilege for a taxpayer to file consolidated returns and may require the taxpayer to separately register each location and to file a tax return for each location.

Subd. 26. Tax shelter penalties; registration and listing. (a) For purposes of this subdivision, "material advisor" has the meaning given it under section 6111(b)(1) of the Internal Revenue Code.

(b) The penalties in this subdivision apply in connection with the use of tax shelters, as defined under section 289A.121, and the definitions under that section apply for the purposes of this subdivision.

(c) A material advisor who fails to register a tax shelter, including providing all of the required information under section 289A.121, on or before the date prescribed or who files false or incomplete information with respect to the transaction is subject to a penalty of $50,000. If the tax shelter is a listed transaction, a penalty applies equal to the greater of:

(1) $200,000;

(2) 50 percent of the gross income that the material advisor derived from that activity; or

(3) 75 percent of the gross income that the material advisor derived from that activity if the material advisor intentionally failed to act.

(d)(1) Any person who fails to include on a return or statement any information with respect to a reportable transaction as required under section 289A.121 is subject to a penalty equal to:

(i) $10,000 in the case of an individual and $50,000 in any other case; or

(ii) with respect to a listed transaction, $100,000 in the case of an individual and $200,000 in any other case.

(2) For a unitary business in which more than one member fails to include information on its return or statement for the same reportable transaction, the

penalty under clause (1) for each additional member that fails to include the required information on its return or statement for the reportable transaction is limited to the following amount:

(i) $500 for each member, subject to a maximum additional penalty of $25,000; and

(ii) with respect to a listed transaction, $1,000 for each member, subject to a maximum additional penalty of $100,000.

(e) A material advisor required to maintain or provide a list under section 289A.121, subdivision 6, is subject to a penalty equal to $10,000 for each day after the 20th day that the material advisor failed to make the list available to the commissioner after written request for that list was made. No penalty applies for a failure on any day if the failure is due to reasonable cause.

(f) The penalty imposed by this subdivision is in addition to any other penalty imposed under this section.

(g) Notwithstanding section 270C.34, the commissioner may abate all or any portion of any penalty imposed by paragraphs (c) and (d) for any violation, only if all of the following apply:

(1) the violation is for a reportable transaction, other than a listed transaction; and

(2) abating the penalty would promote compliance with the requirements of chapter 290.

(h) Notwithstanding any other law or rule, a determination under paragraph (g) may not be reviewed in any judicial proceeding.

Subd. 27. Reportable transaction understatement. (a) If a taxpayer has a reportable transaction understatement for any taxable year, an amount equal to 20 percent of the amount of the reportable transaction understatement must be added to the tax.

(b)(1) For purposes of this subdivision, "reportable transaction understatement" means the product of:

(i) the amount of the increase, if any, in taxable income that results from a difference between the proper tax treatment of an item to which this section applies and the taxpayer's treatment of that item as shown on the taxpayer's tax return; and

(ii) the highest rate of tax imposed on the taxpayer under section 290.06 determined without regard to the understatement.

(2) For purposes of clause (1)(i), any reduction of the excess of deductions allowed for the taxable year over gross income for that year, and any reduction in the amount of capital losses which would, without regard to section 1211 of the Internal Revenue Code, be allowed for that year, must be treated as an increase in taxable income.

(c) This subdivision applies to any item that is attributable to:

(1) any listed transaction under section 289A.121; and

(2) any reportable transaction, other than a listed transaction, if a significant purpose of that transaction is the avoidance or evasion of federal income tax liability.

(d) Paragraph (a) applies by substituting "30 percent" for "20 percent" with respect to the portion of any reportable transaction understatement with respect to which the disclosure requirements of section 289A.121, subdivision 5, and section 6664(d)(2)(A) of the Internal Revenue Code are not met.

(e)(1) No penalty applies under this subdivision with respect to any portion of a reportable transaction understatement if the taxpayer shows that there was reasonable cause for the portion and that the taxpayer acted in good faith with respect to the portion. This paragraph applies only if:

(i) the relevant facts affecting the tax treatment of the item are adequately disclosed as required under section 289A.121;

(ii) there is or was substantial authority for the treatment; and

(iii) the taxpayer reasonably believed that the treatment was more likely than not the proper treatment.

(2) A taxpayer who did not adequately disclose under section 289A.121 meets the requirements of clause (1)(i), if the commissioner abates the penalty imposed by subdivision 26, paragraph (d), under subdivision 26, paragraph (g).

(3) For purposes of clause (1)(iii), a taxpayer is treated as having a reasonable belief with respect to the tax treatment of an item only if the belief:

(i) is based on the facts and law that exist when the return of tax which includes the tax treatment is filed; and

(ii) relates solely to the taxpayer's chances of success on the merits of the treatment and does not take into account the possibility that a return will not be audited, the treatment will not be raised on audit, or the treatment will be resolved through settlement if it is raised.

(4) An opinion of a tax advisor may not be relied upon to establish the reasonable belief of a taxpayer if:

(i) the tax advisor:

(A) is a material advisor, as defined in section 289A.121, and participates in the organization, management, promotion, or sale of the transaction or is related (within the meaning of section 267(b) or 707(b)(1) of the Internal Revenue Code) to any person who so participates;

(B) is compensated directly or indirectly by a material advisor with respect to the transaction;

(C) has a fee arrangement with respect to the transaction which is contingent on all or part of the intended tax benefits from the transaction being sustained; or

(D) has a disqualifying financial interest with respect to the transaction, as determined under United States Treasury regulations prescribed to implement the provisions of section 6664(d)(3)(B)(ii)(IV) of the Internal Revenue Code; or

(ii) the opinion:

(A) is based on unreasonable factual or legal assumptions, including assumptions as to future events;

(B) unreasonably relies on representations, statements, findings, or agreements of the taxpayer or any other person;

(C) does not identify and consider all relevant facts; or

(D) fails to meet any other requirement as the Secretary of the Treasury may prescribe under federal law.

(f) The penalty imposed by this subdivision applies in lieu of the penalty imposed under subdivision 4.

Subd. 28. Preparer identification number. Any Minnesota individual income tax return or claim for refund prepared by a "tax refund or return preparer" as defined in subdivision 13, paragraph (f), shall bear the identification number the preparer is required to use federally under section 6109(a)(4) of the Internal Revenue Code. A tax refund or return preparer who prepares a Minnesota individual income tax return or claim for refund and fails to include the required number on the return or claim is subject to a penalty of $50 for each failure.

Subd. 29. Penalty for failure to report liquor sales. In the case of a failure to file an informational report required by section 297A.8155 with the commissioner on or before the date prescribed, the person failing to file the report shall pay a penalty of $500 for each failure. If a failure to file a report is intentional, the penalty shall be $1,000 for each failure.

Subd. 30. Relief for purchasers. A purchaser that meets the requirements of section 297A.995, subdivision 11, is relieved from the imposition of penalty.

Laws 1990, c. 480, art. 1, § 26. Amended by Laws 1991, c. 291, art. 6, §§ 16, 17, 46; Laws 1991, c. 291, art. 8, § 6; Laws 1991, c. 291, art. 11, § 11; Laws 1991, c. 291, art. 16, § 10, eff. June 1, 1991; Laws 1992, c. 511, art. 6, § 19; Laws 1993, c. 375, art. 8, § 14; Laws 1993, c. 375, art. 10, §§ 19 to 23; Laws 1994, c. 510, art. 2, §§ 2, 3; Laws 1994, c. 587, art. 1, § 24; Laws 1994, c. 587, art. 12, § 6; Laws 1995, c. 264, art. 4, § 9; Laws 1995, c. 264, art. 10, § 5; Laws 1995, c. 264, art. 11, § 8; Laws 1995, c. 264, art. 13, § 12, eff. June 2, 1995; Laws 1997, c. 84, art. 3, § 2; Laws 1999, c. 243, art. 16, § 20; Laws 1999, c. 243, art. 16, § 21, eff. May 26, 1999; Laws 2000, c. 418, § 44, subd. 2, eff. July 1, 2001; Laws 2000, c. 490, art. 4, § 4; Laws 2000, c. 490, art. 8, §§ 2, 3; Laws 2001, c. 7, §§ 59, 60; Laws 2001, 1st Sp., c. 5, art. 11, §§ 2 to 5; Laws 2001, 1st Sp., c. 5, art. 17, § 13, eff. July 1, 2001; Laws 2002, c. 377, art. 10, § 10; Laws 2003, c. 127, art. 3, § 5; Laws 2003, c. 127, art. 6, §§ 2, 3; Laws 2003, 1st Sp., c. 21, art. 8, § 4; Laws 2005, c. 151, art. 2, § 10, eff. Aug. 1, 2005; Laws 2005, c. 151, art. 2, § 17; Laws 2005, c. 151, art. 6, §§ 8 to 10; Laws 2005, c. 151, art. 9, §§ 17 to 19; Laws 2005, 1st Sp., c. 3, art. 8, §§ 4 to 8; Laws 2005, 1st Sp., c. 3, art. 11, § 5, eff. July 14, 2005; Laws 2006, c. 259, art. 13, § 3; Laws 2008, c. 154, art. 6, § 2, eff. June 1, 2009; Laws 2008, c. 154, art. 11, § 7, eff. Jan. 1, 2009; Laws 2008, c. 154, art. 11, § 8, eff. July 1, 2008; Laws 2008, c. 154, art. 11, § 9, eff. March 8, 2008; Laws 2008, c. 154, art. 11, § 10, eff. Jan. 1, 2008; Laws 2008, c. 154, art. 12, § 3, eff. July 1, 2008; Laws 2008, c. 154, art. 12, § 4, eff. Jan. 1, 2009; Laws 2008, c. 366, art. 8, § 2, eff. June 1, 2009; Laws 2008, c. 366, art. 13, § 2, eff. Jan. 1, 2009.

[1] All text references to Internal Revenue Code sections are to Title 26 of U.S.C.A.

Historical and Statutory Notes

Laws 1990, c. 480, art. 1, § 47, provides in part that § 26 [enacting this section] is effective for payments, returns, reports, or other documents first becoming due, or acts committed, on or after August 1, 1990.

Laws 1991, c. 291, art. 6, § 48 provides in part that § 17 (amending subd. 12 of this section) except par. (e) is effective July 1, 1991, and that par. (e) is effective beginning for refunds based on property taxes payable in 1991 and for refunds based on rent constituting property taxes paid in 1990.

Laws 1991, c. 291, art. 6, § 48 provided no specific effective date provision for § 16 (amending subd. 2 of this section). Laws 1991, c. 291, art. 6, § 48 also provided that except where otherwise specifically provided, the rest of this article is effective for taxable years beginning after December 31, 1990.

Laws 1991, c. 291, art. 8, § 31, provides in part that § 6 (amending subd. 15 of this section) is effective for the June 1992 payment and thereafter.

Laws 1991, c. 291, art. 11, § 21 provides in part that § 11 (amending subd. 4 of this section) is effective for ores mined after December 31, 1990.

Laws 1993, c. 375, art. 8, § 15, provides in part that § 14 is effective for tax years beginning after December 31, 1992.

Laws 1993, c. 375, art. 10, § 51, provides:

"Before imposing a penalty under section 3, 6, 21, 26, 35, 41, 45, or 49 [adding sections 60A.15, subd. 9e, 60A.199, subd. 6a, 289A.60, subd. 5a, 294.03, subd. 4, 297.43, subd. 4a, 297C.14, subd. 9, 299F.23, subd. 5, and 349.217, subd. 5a, respectively] the commissioner of revenue shall promulgate rules under Minnesota Statutes, chapter 14, that prescribe what constitutes 'repeated failures to timely file returns or timely pay taxes' for purposes of the penalty under each section and any other matters the commissioner determines appropriate."

Laws 1993, c. 375, art. 10, § 52, provides in part:

"Sections [19 to 21]... [amending subds. 1 and 2 and adding subd. 5a] are effective for taxes and returns due on or after January 1, 1994.

"For purposes of imposing the penalties under sections 3, 6, 21, 26, 35, 41, 45, and 49 [adding sections 60A.15, subd. 9e, 60A.199, subd. 6a, 289A.60, subd. 5a, 294.03, subd. 4, 297.43, subd. 4a, 297C.14, subd. 9, 299F.23, subd. 5, and 349.217, subd. 5a, respectively], violations for late filing of returns or late payment of taxes can occur before or after January 1, 1994, but no penalty may be imposed under those sections until final rules promulgated under the administrative procedures act satisfying requirements of section 51 take effect."

Laws 1993, c. 375, art. 10, § 52, also provides in part that § 22 (amending subd. 15) is effective for payments due in the calendar year 1994, and thereafter, based upon payments made in the fiscal year ending June 30, 1993, and thereafter, and that § 23 (adding subd. 21) is effective for taxes due on or after October 1, 1993.

Laws 1994, c. 510, art. 2, § 6, provides in part that §§ 2 and 3 (adding subds. 22 and 23) are effective for tax returns due for tax years beginning after December 31, 1993.

Laws 1994, c. 587, art. 12, § 24, provides in part that § 6 (amending subd. 21) is effective for payments due after May 5, 1994.

Laws 1995, c. 264, art. 1, § 3, provides:

"The changes made by sections 721, 722, 723, and 744 of Legislation to Implement Uruguay Round of General Agreement on Tariffs and Trade, Public Law Number 103–465 and section 4 of the Self-Employed Health Insurance Act of 1995, Public Law Number 104–7, which affect the computation of the Minnesota working family credit under Minnesota Statutes, section 290.0671, subdivision 1, and the computation of the substantial understatement of liability penalty of Minnesota Statutes, section 289A.60, subdivision 4, shall become effective at the same time the changes become effective for federal purposes."

Laws 1995, c. 264, art. 4, § 20, provides in part that § 9 (amending subd. 12) is effective for property tax refunds payable as deductions on property tax statements in 1998 and thereafter.

Laws 1995, c. 264, art. 10, §15, provides in part that § 5 (adding subd. 24) is effective for federal determinations after December 31, 1995.

Laws 1995, c. 264, art. 11, § 9, provides in part that § 8 (amending subd. 12) is effective for certificates of rent paid required after June 1, 1995.

Laws 1996, c. 471, art. 3, § 52, provides:

"The dates contained in Laws 1995, chapter 264, article 4, sections 16, 17, 18, 19, and 20 are delayed for a period of one year from the dates contained in those sections."

Laws 1997, c. 84, art. 3, § 9, provides in part that § 2 (amending subd. 15) is effective for returns filed after January 1, 1998.

Laws 1999, c. 243, art. 16, § 40, provides in part that § 20, amending subd. 3, is effective for tax years ending on or after May 26, 1999.

Laws 2000, c. 490, art. 4, § 4, amending subd. 1, also provides that the amendment of subd. 1 is effective for taxable years beginning after December 31, 1999.

Laws 2000, c. 490, art. 8, §§ 2 and 3, amending subds. 14 and 15, respectively, also provide that the amendment of subd. 14 is effective for exemption certificates used on or after July 1, 2000, and that the amendment of subd. 15 is effective beginning with the June 2002 liability.

Laws 2001, 1st Sp., c. 5, art. 11, §§ 2 to 5 and 8, also provide that the amendments of subds. 1 and 2, the addition of subd. 2a, and the repeal of subd. 3 are effective for tax years beginning after December 31, 2000, and for estate tax returns due after January 1, 2002, and that the amendment of subd. 7 is effective for returns or claims for refunds filed on or after July 1, 2001.

Laws 2002, c. 377, art. 3, § 24, amended Laws 2001, 1st Sp., c. 5, art. 12, § 95, par. (d), by making the repeal of subd. 15 effective for liabilities after January 1, 2004, rather than for liabilities after January 1, 2003.

Laws 2002, c. 377, art. 3, § 24, also provided in part that Laws 2001, 1st Sp., c. 5, art. 12, § 95, par. (d), repealing subd. 15, was effective the day after final enactment. Laws 2002, c. 377, was filed without signature of the governor May 18, 2002. See §§ 645.01 and 645.02.

Laws 2002, c. 377, art. 10, § 10, amending subd. 2, also provides that the amendment is effective the day following final enactment. Laws 2002, c. 377, was filed without signature of the governor May 18, 2002. See §§ 645.01 and 645.02.

Laws 2003, c. 127, art. 3, § 5, amending subd. 7, also provided that the amendment was effective for estates of decedents dying after December 31, 2003.

Laws 2003, c. 127, art. 6, §§ 2 and 3, amending subd. 15 and adding subd. 25, also provided that the amendment of subd. 15 was effective for payments due after December 31, 2002, and that the addition of subd. 25 was effective for returns filed after June 30, 2003.

Laws 2003, 1st Sp., c. 21, art. 8, § 4, amending subd. 15, as amended by Laws 2003, c. 127, art. 6, § 2, also provided that in subd. 15, par. (a) was effective for payments made after De-

cember 31, 2002, and before January 1, 2004, and par. (b) was effective for payments made after December 31, 2003.

Laws 2003, 1st Sp., c. 21, art. 8, § 15, amended Laws 2001, 1st Sp., c. 5, art. 12, § 95, as amended by Laws 2002, c. 377, art. 3, § 24, by deleting par. (d), which, as amended, repealed subd. 15 effective for liabilities after January 1, 2004.

Laws 2005, c. 151, art. 6, §§ 8 to 10, amending subds. 6, 12, and 13, respectively, each also provided:

"This section is effective for returns filed after December 31, 2005."

Laws 2005, c. 151, art. 9, § 17, amending subd. 2a, also provided:

"This section is effective for returns originally due on or after August 1, 2005."

Laws 2005, c. 151, art. 9, § 18, amending subd. 11, also provided:

"This section is effective for certificates and affidavits given to employers after December 31, 2005."

Laws 2005, 1st Sp., c. 3, art. 8, § 4, amending subd. 4, also provided:

"This section is effective for taxable years beginning after December 31, 2004."

Laws 2005, 1st Sp., c. 3, art. 8, § 5, amending subd. 20, also provided that the amendment is effective for transactions entered into after July 14. 2005.

Laws 2005, 1st Sp., c. 3, art. 8, § 6, adding subd. 20a, also provided that the amendment is effective for documents prepared after July 14, 2005, that relate to taxable years beginning after December 31, 2004, or to returns filed after July 14, 2005.

Laws 2005, 1st Sp., c. 3, art. 8, § 7, adding subd. 26, also provided:

"This section is effective for taxable years beginning after December 31, 2000. For taxable years beginning before January 1, 2005, paragraphs (c) and (d) apply only if disclosure or registration was not made by October 15, 2005."

Laws 2005, 1st Sp., c. 3, art. 8, § 8, adding subd. 27, also provided:

"This section is effective for taxable years beginning after December 31, 2000. For taxable years beginning before January 1, 2005, it applies only if disclosure was not made by October 15, 2005, as required by Minnesota Statutes, section 289A.121."

Laws 2006, c. 259, art. 4, § 21, provided:

"Notwithstanding Minnesota Statutes, section 289A.60, subdivision 12, or any other law to the contrary, the commissioner of revenue shall not disallow any part of a claim for a property tax refund filed in 2005 or an earlier year to the extent that the claim was excessive because it did not include in the claimant's income as determined under Minnesota Statutes, section 290A.03, subdivision 3, the cash value of a tuition discount provided by a postsecondary education institution. If a claimant was required to repay any part of a property tax refund based on inclusion of this discount in the claimant's income on a claim filed in 2005 or an earlier year, the commissioner must refund that amount to the claimant."

Laws 2006, c. 259, art. 13, § 3, amending subd. 15, also provided:

"This section is effective for sales tax payments in June 2007 and thereafter."

Laws 2008, c. 154, art. 6, § 2, amending subd. 15, also provided:

"This section is effective beginning with June 2009 tax liabilities."

Laws 2008, c. 154, art. 11, § 7, amending subd. 8, also provided:

"This section is effective for returns filed after December 31, 2008."

Laws 2008, c. 154, art. 11, § 8, amending subd. 12, also provided:

"This section is effective for property tax refund claims filed after June 30, 2008."

Laws 2008, c. 154, art. 11, § 10, adding subd. 28, also provided:

"This section is effective for returns prepared for taxable years beginning after December 31, 2007."

Laws 2008, c. 154, art. 12, § 3, amending subd. 25, also provided:

"This section is effective for returns filed after June 30, 2008."

Laws 2008, c. 154, art. 12, § 4, adding subd. 29, also provided:

"This section is effective for reports filed after December 31, 2008."

Laws 2008, c. 366, art. 8, § 2, amending subd. 15, also provided:

"This section is effective beginning with June 2009 tax liabilities."

Laws 2008, c. 366, art. 13, § 2, adding subd. 30, also provided:

"This section is effective for sales and purchases made after December 31, 2008."

CRIMINAL PENALTIES

289A.63. Criminal penalties

Subdivision 1. Penalties for knowing failure to file or pay; willful evasion. (a) A person required to file a return, report, or other document with the commissioner, who knowingly, rather than accidentally, inadvertently, or negligently, fails to file it when required, is guilty of a gross misdemeanor. A person required to file a return, report, or other document who willfully attempts in any manner to evade or defeat a tax by failing to file it when required, is guilty of a felony.

(b) A person required to pay or to collect and remit a tax, who knowingly, rather than accidentally, inadvertently, or negligently, fails to do so when required, is guilty of a gross misdemeanor. A person required to pay or to collect and remit a tax, who willfully attempts to evade or defeat a tax law by failing to do so when required, is guilty of a felony.

Subd. 2. False or fraudulent returns; penalties. (a) A person who files with the commissioner a return, report, or other document, known by the person to be fraudulent or false concerning a material matter, is guilty of a felony.

(b) A person who knowingly aids or assists in, or advises in the preparation or presentation of a return, report, or other document that is fraudulent or false concerning a material matter, whether or not the falsity or fraud committed is with the knowledge or consent of the person authorized or required to present the return, report, or other document, is guilty of a felony.

Subd. 3. Sales without permit; violations. (a) A person who engages in the business of making retail sales in Minnesota without the permit required under chapter 297A, or a responsible officer of a corporation who so engages in business, is guilty of a gross misdemeanor.

(b) A person who engages in the business of making retail sales in Minnesota after revocation of a permit under section 270C.722, when the commissioner has not issued a new permit, is guilty of a felony.

Subd. 4. Advertising no sales or use tax; violation. It is a misdemeanor for a person to broadcast or publish, or arrange to have broadcast or published, an advertisement in a publication or broadcast media, printed, distributed, broadcast, or intended to be received in this state, that states that no sales or use tax is due, when the person knows the advertisement is false.

Subd. 5. Employee giving employer false information. An employee required to supply information to an employer under section 290.92, subdivisions 4a and 5, who knowingly fails to supply information or who knowingly supplies false or fraudulent information to an employer, is guilty of a gross misdemeanor.

Subd. 6. Collection of tax; penalty. An agent, canvasser, or employee of a retailer, who is not authorized by permit from the commissioner, may not collect the sales tax as imposed by chapter 297A, nor sell, solicit orders for, nor deliver, any tangible personal property in this state. An agent, canvasser, or employee violating the provisions of section 297A.63; 297A.66 to 297A.71; 297A.75; 297A.76, subdivision 1; 297A.77; 297A.78; 297A.80; 297A.82, subdivision 4; 297A.83; 297A.89; 297A.90; 297A.91; or 297A.96 is guilty of a misdemeanor.

Subd. 7. Renumbered 270B.18, subd. 4, in St.2006

Subd. 8. Criminal penalties. Criminal penalties imposed by section 270B.18, subdivision 4, and this section are in addition to any civil penalties imposed by this chapter.

Subd. 9. Statute of limitations. Notwithstanding section 628.26, or any other provision of the criminal laws of this state, an indictment may be found and filed, or a complaint filed, upon a criminal offense named in section 270B.18, subdivision 4, and this section, in the proper court within six years after the offense is committed.

Subd. 10. Person defined. The term "person" as used in section 270B.18, subdivision 4, and this section includes any officer or employee of a corporation or a member or employee of a partnership who as an officer, member, or employee is under a duty to perform the act in respect to which the violation occurs.

Subd. 11. Consolidation of venue. If two or more offenses in section 270B.18, subdivision 4, and this section are committed by the same person in more than one county, the accused may be prosecuted for all the offenses in any county in which one of the offenses was committed.

Laws 1990, c. 480, art. 1, § 27. Amended by Laws 1993, c. 326, art. 4, § 7; Laws 1993, c. 375, art. 9, § 16, eff. July 1, 1993; Laws 2000, c. 418, art. 1, § 44, subd. 2, eff. July 1, 2001; Laws 2005, c. 151, art. 2, § 17; Laws 2008, c. 277, art. 1, § 62, eff. July 1, 2008.

Historical and Statutory Notes

Laws 1990, c. 480, art. 1, § 47, provides in part that § 27 [enacting this section] is effective for crimes committed on or after August 1, 1990.

Laws 1993, c. 326, art. 4, § 41, provides in part that § 7 (enacting subd. 11) is effective August 1, 1993, and applies to crimes committed on or after that date.

289A.65. Repealed by Laws 2005, c. 151, art. 1, § 117, eff. Aug. 1, 2005

Historical and Statutory Notes

Laws 2005, c. 151, art. 1, § 115, provided:

"Subdivision 1. Purpose. It is the intent of the legislature to simplify Minnesota's tax laws by consolidating and recodifying tax administration and compliance provisions now contained in Minnesota Statutes, chapter 270, and several other chapters of Minnesota Statutes. The provisions of this act may not be used to determine

the law in effect prior to the effective dates in this act.

"Subd. 2. Effect. Due to the complexity of the recodification, prior provisions are repealed on the effective date of the new provisions. The repealed provisions, however, continue to remain in effect until superseded by the analogous provision in the new law."

Chapter 291

ESTATE TAX

For complete statutory history see Minnesota Statutes Annotated.

291.005. Definitions

Subdivision 1. Scope. Unless the context otherwise clearly requires, the following terms used in this chapter shall have the following meanings:

(1) "Federal gross estate" means the gross estate of a decedent as valued and otherwise determined for federal estate tax purposes by federal taxing authorities pursuant to the provisions of the Internal Revenue Code.

(2) "Minnesota gross estate" means the federal gross estate of a decedent after (a) excluding therefrom any property included therein which has its situs outside Minnesota, and (b) including therein any property omitted from the federal gross estate which is includable therein, has its situs in Minnesota, and was not disclosed to federal taxing authorities.

(3) "Personal representative" means the executor, administrator or other person appointed by the court to administer and dispose of the property of the decedent. If there is no executor, administrator or other person appointed, qualified, and acting within this state, then any person in actual or constructive possession of any property having a situs in this state which is included in the federal gross estate of the decedent shall be deemed to be a personal representative to the extent of the property and the Minnesota estate tax due with respect to the property.

(4) "Resident decedent" means an individual whose domicile at the time of death was in Minnesota.

(5) "Nonresident decedent" means an individual whose domicile at the time of death was not in Minnesota.

(6) "Situs of property" means, with respect to real property, the state or country in which it is located; with respect to tangible personal property, the state or country in which it was normally kept or located at the time of the decedent's death; and with respect to intangible personal property, the state or country in which the decedent was domiciled at death.

(7) "Commissioner" means the commissioner of revenue or any person to whom the commissioner has delegated functions under this chapter.

(8) "Internal Revenue Code" means the United States Internal Revenue Code of 1986, as amended through February 13, 2008.[1]

(9) "Minnesota adjusted taxable estate" means federal adjusted taxable estate as defined by section 2011(b)(3) of the Internal Revenue Code, increased by the amount of deduction for state death taxes allowed under section 2058 of the Internal Revenue Code.

Subd. 2. Incorporation by reference of Uniform Probate Code definitions. The definitions set forth in section 524.1–201, wherever appropriate to the administration of the provisions of this chapter are incorporated by reference.

Laws 1963, c. 740, § 26. Amended by Laws 1973, c. 185, § 1; Laws 1973, c. 582, § 3; Laws 1975, c. 347, § 2, eff. Jan. 1, 1976; Laws 1979, c. 303, art. 3, § 1; Laws 1980, c. 439, § 4; Laws 1981, c. 49, § 2; Laws 1981, 3rd Sp., c. 2, art. 6, § 1; Laws 1983, c. 222, § 22; Laws 1985, 1st Sp., c. 14, art. 13, § 2; Laws 1986, c. 444; Laws 1989, c. 28, § 23; Laws 1990, c. 604, art. 2, § 16; Laws 1991, c. 291, art. 6, § 46; Laws 1992, c. 511, art. 6, § 19; Laws 1993, c. 375, art. 8, § 14; Laws 1994, c. 587, art. 1, § 24; Laws 1995, c. 264, art. 1, § 4; Laws 1996, c. 471, art. 4, § 5; Laws 1997, c. 231, art. 6, § 22; Laws 1998, c. 389, art. 7, § 11; Laws 1999, c. 243, art. 3, § 6; Laws 2000, c. 490, art. 12, § 5, eff. May 16, 2000; Laws 2001, 1st Sp., c. 5, art. 10, § 10, eff. July 1, 2001; Laws 2002, c. 377, art. 12, § 11; Laws 2003, c. 127, art. 3, § 16; Laws 2005, c. 151, art. 6, § 19; Laws 2006, c. 259, art. 2, § 8; Laws 2008, c. 154, art. 4, § 9, eff. March 8, 2008.

[1] All text references to Internal Revenue Code sections are to Title 26 of U.S.C.A.

Historical and Statutory Notes

Section 7 of Laws 1973, c. 185, provided:

"This act shall be effective for all gifts made on or after January 1, 1973."

Laws 1979, c. 303, art. 3, § 43 provided in part that this amendment was effective for estates of decedents dying after December 31, 1979.

Laws 1980, c. 439, § 36 provided in part that this amendment was effective for estates of decedents dying after December 31, 1979.

Laws 1981, c. 49, § 12 provides in part that this amendment is effective for estates of decedents dying after December 31, 1980.

Laws 1981, 3rd Sp., c. 2, art. 6, § 8, as amended by Laws 1982, c. 523, art. 26, § 8 provides:

"Sections 1 to 7 are effective for estates of decedents dying after December 31, 1981, provided that the provisions of PL 97–34 that are made retroactive pursuant to section 421(k)(5) shall be effective for estates of decedents dying after December 31, 1979."

Laws 1983, c. 222, § 46 provides in part that this amendment is effective for estates of decedents dying after December 31, 1982.

Laws 1985, 1st Sp., c. 14, art. 13, § 15, provides that the amendment to this section by art.

13, § 2, is effective for estates of persons dying after Dec. 31, 1985, except that the update of the Internal Revenue Code is effective for estates of persons dying after Dec. 31, 1984.

Laws 1989, c. 28, § 27 provides in part that § 23 (amending subd. 1) is effective for dates of death after December 31, 1988.

Laws 1990, c. 604, art. 2, § 22 provides in part that § 16 is effective for taxable years beginning after December 31, 1989, except as otherwise provided.

Laws 1991, c. 291, art. 6, § 44 provides:

"The changes made by sections 11301, 11302, 11303, 11304, 11305, 11343, 11344, 11531, 11601, 11602, 11701, 11702, 11703, and 11704 of the Revenue Reconciliation Act of 1990, Public Law Number 101–508, which affect the definition of net income of insurance companies as defined in Minnesota Statutes, section 290.35, the definition of alternative minimum taxable income as defined in Minnesota Statutes, sections 290.091, subdivision 2, and 290.0921, subdivision 3, grantor as defined in Minnesota Statutes, section 290.25, federal gross estate as defined in Minnesota Statutes, section 291.005, gross income as defined in Minnesota Statutes, section 290.01, subdivision 20, and the definition of wages as defined in

Minnesota Statutes, section 290.92, subdivision 1, shall be effective at the same time they become effective for federal tax purposes.

"The waiver of estimated tax penalties provided by section 11307 of the Revenue Reconciliation Act of 1990 shall also apply to Minnesota to the extent the underpayment was created or increased by the changes made by sections 11301, 11302, 11303, and 11305."

Laws 1991, c. 291, art. 6, § 48, an effective date section, gave no specific effective date for §§ 44 and 46. Laws 1991, c. 291, art. 6, § 48, provided in part that "(e)xcept where otherwise specifically provided, the rest of this article is effective for taxable years beginning after December 31, 1990".

Laws 1993, c. 375, art. 8, § 15, provides in part that § 14 is effective for tax years beginning after December 31, 1992.

Laws 1996, c. 471, art. 4, § 6, provides in part that § 5 (amending subd. 1) is effective at the same time section 1 of Public Law Number 104–117 is effective.

Public Law Number 104–117 (109 Stat. 827), approved March 20, 1996, was generally effective November 21, 1995, although the effective date of some of the withholding provisions was dependent upon the date of enactment. See, 26 U.S.C.A. § 2, note.

Laws 1997, c. 231, art. 6, § 25, provides in part that § 22 (amending subd. 1) is effective at the same time and for the same years as the federal changes made in 1996 were effective for federal purposes.

Laws 1998, c. 389 art. 7, § 13, provides:

"Sections 1, 3, 4, and 6 to 9 are effective for tax years beginning after December 31, 1997.

Sections 5, 10, and 11 are effective at the same time federal changes made by the Taxpayer Relief Act of 1997, Public Law Number 105–34, which are incorporated into Minnesota Statutes, chapters 290, 290A, and 291 by these sections, become effective for federal tax purposes."

Laws 1999, c. 243, art. 3, § 7, provides in part that § 6, amending subd. 1 by substituting "1998" for "1997" at the end of cl. (8), is effective at the same time federal changes made by the Internal Revenue Service Restructuring and Reform Act of 1998, Public Law Number 105–206 and the Omnibus Consolidation and Emergency Supplemental Appropriations Act, 1999, Public Law Number 105–277 which are incorporated into Minnesota Statutes, chapters 289A, 290, 290A, and 291 by these sections become effective for federal tax purposes.

Laws 2002, c. 377, art. 12, § 11, amending subd. 1, also provides that the amendment is effective for estates of decedents dying after December 31, 2001.

Laws 2003, c. 127, art. 3, § 16, in the effective date portion, provided that art. 3, § 16, amending subd. 1, was effective for estates of decedents dying after December 31, 2002.

Laws 2005, c. 151, art. 6, § 19, amending subd. 1, also provided:

"The change to clause (8) is effective for estates of decedents dying after January 31, 2003, and the new clause (9) is effective for estates of decedents dying after December 31, 2004."

Laws 2006, c. 259, art. 2, § 8, amending subd. 1, also provided:

"This section is effective for estates of decedents dying after December 31, 2005."

291.01. Tax imposed

A tax is hereby imposed upon the transfer of estates of decedents as prescribed by this chapter.

Amended by Laws 1949, c. 735, § 1; Laws 1953, c. 629, § 1; Laws 1955, c. 552, § 1; Laws 1961, c. 442, § 1; Laws 1963, c. 182, § 1; Laws 1963, c. 218, § 1; Laws 1963, c. 740, §§ 1, 2; Laws 1965, c. 89, § 1, eff. March 17, 1965; Laws 1965, c. 555, § 1, eff. May 22, 1965; Laws 1967, c. 850, § 1, eff. May 25, 1967; Laws 1978, c. 741, § 1; Laws 1979, c. 303, art. 3, § 2; Laws 1980, c. 439, § 5.

Historical and Statutory Notes

Laws 1979, c. 303, art. 3, § 43, provided in part that this amendment was effective for estates of decedents dying after December 31, 1979.

291.015. Repealed by Laws 1985, 1st Sp., c. 14, art. 13, § 14

Historical and Statutory Notes

Laws 1985, 1st Sp., c. 14, art. 13, § 15, provides that this repeal is effective for estates of persons dying after Dec. 31, 1985.

291.02. Repealed by Laws 1979, c. 303, art. 3, § 41

Historical and Statutory Notes

Laws 1979, c. 303, art. 3, § 41 provides in part that this repeal is effective for estates of decedents dying after December 31, 1979.

291.03. Rates

Subdivision 1. Tax amount. (a) The tax imposed shall be an amount equal to the proportion of the maximum credit for state death taxes computed under section 2011 of the Internal Revenue Code,[1] but using Minnesota adjusted taxable estate instead of federal adjusted taxable estate, as the Minnesota gross estate bears to the value of the federal gross estate.

(b) The tax determined under this subdivision must not be greater than the sum of the following amounts multiplied by a fraction, the numerator of which is the Minnesota gross estate and the denominator of which is the federal gross estate:

(1) the rates and brackets under section 2001(c) of the Internal Revenue Code multiplied by the sum of:

(i) the taxable estate, as defined under section 2051 of the Internal Revenue Code; plus

(ii) adjusted taxable gifts, as defined in section 2001(b) of the Internal Revenue Code; less

(2) the amount of tax allowed under section 2001(b)(2) of the Internal Revenue Code; and less

(3) the federal credit allowed under section 2010 of the Internal Revenue Code.

(c) For purposes of this subdivision, "Internal Revenue Code" means the Internal Revenue Code of 1986, as amended through December 31, 2000.

Subd. 1a. Expenses disallowed. For the purposes of this section, expenses which are deducted for federal income tax purposes under section 642(g) of the Internal Revenue Code are not allowable in computing the tax under this chapter.

Subd. 2. Repealed by Laws 2002, c. 377, art. 12, § 18.

Subds. 3 to 7.   Repealed by Laws 1985, 1st Sp., c. 14, art. 13, § 14.

Amended by Laws 1959, Ex.Sess., c. 70, art. 4, § 1; Laws 1963, c. 107, § 1; Laws 1973, c. 185, § 2; Laws 1976, c. 320, § 1; Laws 1979, c. 303, art. 3, § 4; Laws 1980, c. 439, § 7; Laws 1981, c. 49, § 3; Laws 1981, 3rd Sp., c. 2, art. 6, § 3; Laws 1982, c. 523, art. 26, § 3; Laws 1983, c. 222, § 23; Laws 1985, 1st Sp., c. 14, art. 13, § 3; Laws 2002, c. 377, art. 12, § 12; Laws 2002, c. 400, § 11; Laws 2003, c. 127, art. 3, § 17; Laws 2005, c. 151, art. 6, § 20; Laws 2008, c. 366, art. 4, §§ 15, 16, eff. Jan. 1, 2006.

[1] All text references to Internal Revenue Code sections are to Title 26 of U.S.C.A.

Historical and Statutory Notes

Laws 1959, Ex.Sess., c. 70, art. 4, § 4 provides:

"The provisions of this article [amendment of §§ 291.03 and 291.05 and repeal of § 291.04] shall become effective and apply in all cases where death occurs on or after July 1, 1959.

"The rates and exemptions in effect at the date of death shall apply in all cases where death occurs prior to July 1, 1959."

Laws 1973, c. 185, § 7 provides in part that this amendment is effective for all gifts made on or after January 1, 1973.

Laws 1976, c. 320, § 12, provides: "Section 9 of this act is effective January 1, 1976. The remainder of this act is effective for estates of decedents dying after June 30, 1976."

Laws 1979, c. 303, art. 3, § 43 provided in part that this amendment was effective for decedents dying after December 31, 1979.

Laws 1980, c. 439, § 36 provided in part that this amendment was effective for estates of decedents dying after December 31, 1979.

The effective date of Laws 1981, 3rd Sp., c. 2, art. 6, as specified in section 8 thereof, was amended by Laws 1982, c. 523, art. 26, § 8 to read:

"Sections 1 to 7 are effective for estates of decedents dying after December 31, 1981, provided that the provisions of PL 97–34 that are made retroactive pursuant to section 421(k)(5) shall be effective for estates of decedents dying after December 31, 1979."

Laws 1985, 1st Sp., c. 14, art. 13, § 15, provides that the amendment of subd. 1 and the repeal of subds. 3 to 7 by c. 14, is effective for estates of persons dying after Dec. 31, 1985.

Laws 1990, c. 604, art. 2, § 17, provides in part that the changes made by §§ 7841, 7304(a), 7817, 7110, 7815, 7816, and 7811(d) of the

Omnibus Budget Reconciliation Act of 1989, Public Law No. 101–239, and §§ 202, 203, and 204 of Public Law No. 101–140 that affect the computation of the credit for state death taxes allowable as defined in subd. 1 of this section shall be in effect at the same time they become effective for federal income and estate tax purposes.

Laws 2002, c. 377, art. 12, § 12, amending subd. 1, also provides that the amendment is effective for the estates of decedents dying after December 31, 2001.

Laws 2002, c. 377, art. 12. § 18, repealing subd. 2, also provides that the repeal of subd. 2 is effective for estates of decedents dying after December 31, 2001.

Laws 2002, c. 400, § 14, provides that, unless provided otherwise, each section of Laws 2002, c. 400, takes effect at the time the provision being corrected takes effect. Laws 2002, c. 377, art. 12, § 12, whose amendment of subd. 1 was in turn amended by Laws 2002, c. 400, § 11, also provides in part that the amendment of subd. 1 is effective for estates of decedents dying after December 31, 2001.

Laws 2003, c. 127, art. 3, § 17, in the effective date portion, provided that art. 3, § 17, amending subd. 1, was effective for estates of decedents dying after December 31, 2002.

Laws 2005, c. 151, art. 6, § 20, amending subd. 1, also provided:

"This section is effective for estates of decedents dying after December 31, 2004."

Laws 2008, c. 366, art. 4, §§ 15 and 16, amending subd. 1 and adding subd. 1a, both also provided:

"This section is effective for estates of decedents dying after December 31, 2005."

291.04. Repealed by Laws 1959, Ex.Sess., c. 70, art. 4, § 2

Historical and Statutory Notes

Laws 1959, Ex.Sess., c. 70, art. 4, § 4, provided:

"The provisions of this article [amendment of §§ 291.03 and 291.05 and repeal of § 291.04] shall become effective and apply in all cases where death occurs on or after July 1, 1959.

"The rates and exemptions in effect at the date of death shall apply in all cases where death occurs prior to July 1, 1959."

291.05. Repealed by Laws 1985, 1st Sp., c. 14, art. 13, § 14

291.051. Repealed by Laws 1981, 3rd Sp., c. 2, art. 6, § 7; Laws 1985, 1st Sp., c. 14, art. 13, § 14

291.06, 291.065. Repealed by Laws 1985, 1st Sp., c. 14, art. 13, § 14

Historical and Statutory Notes

Laws 1985, 1st Sp., c. 14, art. 13, § 15, provides that this repeal is effective for estates of persons dying after Dec. 31, 1985.

291.07. Repealed by Laws 1979, c. 303, art. 3, § 41; Laws 1983, c. 222, § 45; Laws 1985, 1st Sp., c. 14, art. 13, § 14

Historical and Statutory Notes

Laws 1985, 1st Sp., c. 14, art. 13, § 15, provides that this repeal is effective for estates of persons dying after Dec. 31, 1985.

291.075. Special use valuation of qualified property

If, after the final determination of the tax imposed by this chapter, the property valued pursuant to section 2032A of the Internal Revenue Code[1] is disposed of or fails to qualify and an additional tax is imposed pursuant to section 2032A(c), any increase in the credit for state death taxes shall be reported to the commissioner within 90 days after final determination of the increased credit. Upon notification the commissioner may assess an additional tax in accordance with section 291.03, subdivision 1.

Laws 1979, c. 303, art. 3, § 10. Amended by Laws 1980, c. 439, § 13; Laws 1985, 1st Sp., c. 14, art. 13, § 4.

[1] 26 U.S.C.A. § 2032A.

Historical and Statutory Notes

Laws 1980, c. 439, § 36 provided in part that this amendment was effective for estates of decedents dying after December 31, 1979.

Laws 1985, 1st Sp., c. 14, art. 13, § 15, provides that this amendment is effective for estates of persons dying after Dec. 31, 1985.

291.08. Repealed by Laws 1985, 1st Sp., c. 14, art. 13, § 14

Historical and Statutory Notes

Laws 1985, 1st Sp., c. 14, art. 13, § 15, provides that this repeal is effective for estates of persons dying after Dec. 31, 1985.

291.09. Repealed by Laws 1990, c. 480, art. 1, § 45, eff. Aug. 1, 1990

291.10. Repealed by Laws 1979, c. 303, art. 3, § 41

Historical and Statutory Notes

Laws 1979, c. 303, art. 3, § 43 provides in part that this section is repealed effective for estates of decedents dying after December 31, 1979.

291.11. Repealed by Laws 1990, c. 480, art. 1, § 45, eff. Aug. 1, 1990

Historical and Statutory Notes

Laws 1990, c. 480, art. 1, § 44, provides:

"It is the intent of the legislature to simplify Minnesota's tax laws by consolidating and recodifying tax administration and compliance provisions now contained in several chapters of Minnesota Statutes. Due to the complexity of the recodification, prior provisions are repealed on the effective date of the new provisions. The repealed provisions, however, continue to remain in effect until superseded by the analogous provision in the new law."

Laws 1995, c. 264, art. 10, § 14, provides:

"Effective for decedents dying before August 1, 1990, the provisions of Minnesota Statutes, section 289A.38, subdivision 6, apply to assets omitted from an inheritance tax return or estate tax return rather than the provisions of Minnesota Statutes 1988, section 291.11, subdivision 1, clause (2)(c)."

See, now, M.S.A. §§ 289A.18, subd. 3, 289A.20, subd. 3, 289A.30, subd. 2, 289A.38.

291.111. Repealed by Laws 1980, c. 439, § 35; Laws 1985, 1st Sp., c. 14, art. 13, § 14

Historical and Statutory Notes

Laws 1985, 1st Sp., c. 14, art. 13, § 15, provides that this repeal is effective for estates of persons dying after Dec. 31, 1985.

291.12. Collection of tax by representative or trustee

Subdivision 1. Requirement. Any representative or trustee who has in possession or under control, property, the transfer of which is subject to any tax imposed by this chapter and from which such tax may lawfully be paid by the representative or trustee, shall either deduct the amount of tax due or shall collect from the person entitled to such property, the amount of tax due, together with any accrued interest thereon, before completing the transfer of such property or making delivery thereof and shall pay to the commissioner all taxes and interest so deducted or collected.

Subd. 2. Liability. Any representative or trustee having in possession or under control any property to which a person, from whom a tax is known by such representative or trustee to be due under the provisions of this chapter, is entitled, shall be personally liable for the payment of such tax and any interest accrued, to the extent of the value of such property; provided, however, that there shall be no such liability if such property cannot be lawfully used by the representative or trustee for the payment of such taxes or interest.

Subd. 3. Effect on duty to transfer or deliver property. No representative or trustee shall be required to transfer or deliver any property in possession or under control unless all taxes and interest due from the person entitled thereto under the provisions of this chapter have either been deducted or collected by the representative or trustee or paid by the transferee to the commissioner.

Subd. 4. Repealed by Laws 1979, c. 303, art. 3, § 41.

Amended by Laws 1953, c. 628, § 1; Laws 1963, c. 740, § 6; Laws 1986, c. 444.

Historical and Statutory Notes

Laws 1963, c. 740, § 27 provides that the provisions of this act shall become effective on January 1, 1964.

291.13. Taxes to be paid to commissioner of revenue

Subdivision 1. Requirement. All taxes imposed by this chapter shall be paid to the commissioner.

Subd. 2. Repealed by Laws 1978, c. 766, § 20, eff. July 1, 1978.

Subd. 3. Deposit in general fund. All taxes paid under the provisions of this chapter shall be deposited by the commissioner in the state treasury, and shall belong to and be a part of the general fund of the state.

Amended by Laws 1953, c. 630, § 1; Laws 1963, c. 740, § 7; Laws 1969, c. 399, § 49.

Historical and Statutory Notes

Laws 1963, c. 740, § 27 provides that the provisions of this act shall become effective on January 1, 1964.

291.131. Repealed by Laws 1990, c. 480, art. 1, § 45, eff. Aug. 1, 1990

Historical and Statutory Notes

Laws 1990, c. 480, art. 1, § 44, provides:

"It is the intent of the legislature to simplify Minnesota's tax laws by consolidating and recodifying tax administration and compliance provisions now contained in several chapters of Minnesota Statutes. Due to the complexity of the recodification, prior provisions are repealed on the effective date of the new provisions. The repealed provisions, however, continue to remain in effect until superseded by the analogous provision in the new law."

291.132. Repealed by Laws 1985, 1st Sp., c. 14, art. 13, § 14

Historical and Statutory Notes

Laws 1985, 1st Sp., c. 14, art. 13, § 15, provides that this repeal is effective for estates of persons dying after Dec. 31, 1985.

291.14.   Repealed by Laws 1990, c. 480, art. 1, § 45, eff. Aug. 1, 1990

Historical and Statutory Notes

Laws 1990, c. 480, art. 1, § 44, provides:

"It is the intent of the legislature to simplify Minnesota's tax laws by consolidating and recodifying tax administration and compliance provisions now contained in several chapters of

Minnesota Statutes. Due to the complexity of the recodification, prior provisions are repealed on the effective date of the new provisions. The repealed provisions, however, continue to remain in effect until superseded by the analogous provision in the new law."

291.15.   Interest

Subdivision 1.   Repealed by Laws 1990, c. 480, art. 1, § 45, eff. Aug. 1, 1990.

Subd. 2.   Repealed by Laws 1985, 1st Sp., c. 14, art. 13, § 14.

Subd. 3.   Repealed by Laws 1990, c. 480, art. 1, § 45, eff. Aug. 1, 1990.

Historical and Statutory Notes

Laws 1990, c. 480, art. 1, § 44, provides:

"It is the intent of the legislature to simplify Minnesota's tax laws by consolidating and recodifying tax administration and compliance provisions now contained in several chapters of

Minnesota Statutes. Due to the complexity of the recodification, prior provisions are repealed on the effective date of the new provisions. The repealed provisions, however, continue to remain in effect until superseded by the analogous provision in the new law."

291.16.   Power of sale

Every executor, administrator, or trustee shall have full power to sell the property embraced in any inheritance, devise, bequest, or legacy to pay the tax imposed by this chapter, in the same manner as entitled by law to do for the payment of the debts of a testator or intestate.

Amended by Laws 1986, c. 444.

291.17.   Repealed by Laws 1980, c. 439, § 35

Historical and Statutory Notes

Laws 1980, c. 439 made technical adjustments and clarified certain provisions relating to estate tax, effective for estates of decedents dying after December 31, 1979.

291.18.   Repealed by Laws 1985, 1st Sp., c. 14, art. 13, § 14

Historical and Statutory Notes

Laws 1985, 1st Sp., c. 14, art. 13, § 15, provides that this repeal is effective for estates of persons dying after Dec. 31, 1985.

291.19.   Personal property of nonresident decedent, transfer

Subds. 1 to 4.   Repealed by Laws 1980, c. 439, § 35.

Subd. 5.   Repealed by Laws 1979, c. 303, art. 3, § 41.

Subds. 6, 7.   Repealed by Laws 1947, c. 556, § 3.

291.20. Repealed by Laws 1979, c. 303, art. 3, § 41; Laws 1980, c. 439, § 35; Laws 1985, 1st Sp., c. 14, art. 13, § 14

Historical and Statutory Notes

Laws 1985, 1st Sp., c. 14, art. 13, § 15, provides that the repeal by § 14 is effective for estates of persons dying after Dec. 31, 1985.

291.21. Letters of administration

Subdivision 1. Rights of commissioner. The commissioner shall have the same rights to apply for letters of administration as are conferred upon creditors by law.

Subd. 2. Repealed by Laws 1979, c. 303, art. 3, § 41.

Amended by Laws 1963, c. 740, § 10.

Historical and Statutory Notes

Laws 1963, c. 740, § 27 provides that the provisions of this act shall become effective on January 1, 1964.

291.215. Valuation of estate

Subdivision 1. Determination. All property includable in the Minnesota gross estate of a decedent shall be valued in accordance with the provisions of sections 2031 or 2032 and, if applicable, 2032A, of the Internal Revenue Code [1] and any elections made in valuing the federal gross estate shall be applicable in valuing the Minnesota gross estate. The value of all property includable in the Minnesota gross estate of a decedent may be independently determined under those sections for Minnesota estate tax purposes except:

(1) as otherwise provided in section 291.075; or

(2) if the Internal Revenue Service, after receiving the estate's federal estate tax return, either conducts a separate appraisal of an asset reported on the return or proposes a change in the reported valuation of an asset in the estate, in which case the federal final determination of the value controls.

Subds. 2, 3. Repealed by Laws 1990, c. 480, art. 1, § 45, eff. Aug. 1, 1990.

Laws 1979, c. 303, art. 3, § 24. Amended by Laws 1980, c. 439, § 22; Laws 1983, c. 222, § 28; Laws 1985, 1st Sp., c. 14, art. 13, § 11; Laws 1986, c. 444; Laws 2008, c. 154, art. 7, § 1, eff. Jan. 1, 2007.

[1] 26 U.S.C.A. §§ 2031, 2032, 2032A.

Historical and Statutory Notes

Laws 1980, c. 439 made technical adjustments and clarified certain provisions relating to estate tax, effective for estates of decedents dying after December 31, 1979. This effective date of the 1980 amendment of subd. 1 is the same as the 1979 enactment.

Laws 1985, 1st Sp., c. 14, art. 13, § 15, provides that this amendment is effective for estates of persons dying after Dec. 31, 1985.

Laws 1990, c. 480, art. 1, § 44, provides:

"It is the intent of the legislature to simplify Minnesota's tax laws by consolidating and recodifying tax administration and compliance provisions now contained in several chapters of Minnesota Statutes. Due to the complexity of the recodification, prior provisions are repealed on the effective date of the new provisions. The repealed provisions, however, continue to remain in effect until superseded by the analogous provision in the new law."

Laws 2008, c. 154, art. 7, § 1, amending subd. 1, also provided:

"This section is effective retroactively for estates of decedents dying after December 31, 2006."

291.22. Repealed by Laws 1979, c. 303, art. 3, § 41

291.23. Repealed by Laws 1979, c. 303, art. 3, § 41

291.24. Repealed by Laws 1979, c. 303, art. 3, § 41

291.25. Repealed by Laws 1979, c. 303, art. 3, § 41

291.26. Repealed by Laws 1979, c. 303, art. 3, § 41

291.27. Unpaid tax; omitted property

Any tax due and unpaid under the provisions of this chapter may be enforced and collected from any transferee of property included in the Minnesota estate by action in the court of administration of the estate of the decedent or in a court of general jurisdiction by the personal representative of any estate, the attorney general, or the commissioner in the name of the state.

Any property which for any cause is omitted from the Minnesota estate tax return so that its value is not taken into consideration in the determination of the estate tax, may be subsequently taxed against the persons receiving the same, or any part thereof, to the same effect as if included in the estate tax return, except that any personal representative of an estate discharged in the meantime shall not be liable for the payment of such tax. When any property has been omitted in the determination of an estate tax, the tax thereon may be determined and recovered in a civil action brought by the attorney general or the commissioner, in the name of the state, in any court of general jurisdiction.

Amended by Laws 1947, c. 519, § 1; Laws 1963, c. 740, § 15; Laws 1979, c. 303, art. 3, § 25; Laws 1986, c. 444.

Historical and Statutory Notes

Laws 1963, c. 740, § 27 provides that the provisions of this act shall become effective on January 1, 1964.

291.28. Omitted as unnecessary in St.1945

291.29. Report of county recorder

Subds. 1 to 4. Repealed by Laws 1979, c. 303, art. 3, § 41.

Subd. 5. Repealed by Laws 1985, 1st Sp., c. 14, art. 13, § 14, eff. June 29, 1985.

291.30. Repealed by Laws 1979, c. 303, art. 3, § 41

291.31. Repealed by Laws 1990, c. 480, art. 1, § 45; Laws 1990, c. 480, art. 2, § 18

Historical and Statutory Notes

Laws 1990, c. 480, art. 1, § 44, provided:

"It is the intent of the legislature to simplify Minnesota's tax laws by consolidating and recodifying tax administration and compliance provisions now contained in several chapters of

Minnesota Statutes. Due to the complexity of the recodification, prior provisions are repealed on the effective date of the new provisions. The repealed provisions, however, continue to remain in effect until superseded by the analogous provision in the new law."

291.32. Repealed by Laws 1990, c. 480, art. 1, § 45, eff. Aug. 1, 1990

Historical and Statutory Notes

Laws 1990, c. 480, art. 1, § 44, provides:

"It is the intent of the legislature to simplify Minnesota's tax laws by consolidating and recodifying tax administration and compliance provisions now contained in several chapters of

Minnesota Statutes. Due to the complexity of the recodification, prior provisions are repealed on the effective date of the new provisions. The repealed provisions, however, continue to remain in effect until superseded by the analogous provision in the new law."

291.33. Repealed by Laws 1981, 1st Sp., c. 1, art. 3, § 4

291.34. Repealed by Laws 1979, c. 303, art. 3, § 41

291.35. Repealed by Laws 1979, c. 303, art. 3, § 41

291.36. Repealed by Laws 1979, c. 303, art. 3, § 41

291.37. Repealed by Laws 1979, c. 303, art. 3, § 41

291.38. Repealed by Laws 1979, c. 303, art. 3, § 41

291.39. Repealed by Laws 1979, c. 303, art. 3, § 41

291.40. Repealed by Laws 1979, c. 303, art. 3, § 41

291.41. Definitions

Subdivision 1. Scope. For the purposes of sections 291.41 to 291.47 the terms defined in this section shall have the meanings ascribed to them.

Subd. 2. Executor. "Executor" means an executor of the will or administrator of the estate of the decedent, but does not include an ancillary administrator.

Subd. 3. Taxing official. "Taxing official" means the commissioner of revenue of this state and the officer or body designated as such in the statute of a reciprocal state substantially similar to sections 291.41 to 291.47.

Subd. 4. Death tax. "Death tax" means any tax levied by a state on account of the transfer or shifting of economic benefits in property at death, or in contemplation thereof, or intended to take effect in possession or enjoyment at or after death, whether denominated an "inheritance tax," "transfer tax," "succession tax," "estate tax," "death duty," "death dues," or otherwise.

Subd. 5. Interested person. "Interested person" means any person who may be entitled to receive, or who has received any property or interest which may be required to be considered in computing the death tax of any state involved.

Laws 1951, c. 247, § 1. Amended by Laws 1973, c. 582, § 3.

UNIFORM INTERSTATE ARBITRATION OF DEATH TAXES ACT

Table of Jurisdictions Wherein Act Has Been Adopted

For text of Uniform Act, and variation notes and annotation materials for adopting jurisdictions, see Uniform Laws Annotated, Master Edition, Volume 8A.

Jurisdiction	Laws	Effective Date	Statutory Citation
California	1949, p. 588	10–1–1949	West's Ann.Cal.Rev. & T.Code, §§ 13820 to 13824.
Colorado	1953, c. 132	3–19–1953	West's C.R.S.A. §§ 39–24–101 to 39–24–114.
Connecticut	1949 Rev., § 2048	6–1–1949	C.G.S.A. §§ 12–372 to 12–374.
Delaware	43 Del. Laws c. 5		30 Del.C. §§ 1701 to 1706.
Maine...............	1949, c. 33	8–6–1949	36 M.R.S.A. §§ 3911 to 3924.
Maryland	1945, c. 982	6–1–1945	Code, Tax-General §§ 7–104 to 7–115.
Massachusetts	1943, c. 428	6–4–1943	M.G.L.A. c. 65B, §§ 1 to 7.
Michigan	1956, No. 173	8–11–1956	M.C.L.A. §§ 205.601 to 205.607.
Minnesota	1951, c. 247	4–7–1951	M.S.A. §§ 291.41 to 291.47.
Nebraska	1976, LB 584	7–10–1976	R.R.S.1943, §§ 77–3301 to 77–3316.
Nevada.............	1987, p. 2105		N.R.S. 375A.450 to 375A.510.
Oregon	1959, c. 573		ORS 118.855 to 118.880.
Pennsylvania	1949, p. 1726	5–23–1949	72 P.S. §§ 9156 to 9163.
Rhode Island	1950, c. 2508		Gen.Laws 1956, §§ 44–23–27 to 44–23–32.
South Carolina	1987, No. 70	5–16–1987	Code 1976, §§ 12–16–210 to 12–16–320.
Tennessee...........	1951, c. 183	3–15–1951	T.C.A. §§ 67–8–501 to 67–8–506.
Vermont.............	1947, No. 22	7–1–1947	32 V.S.A. §§ 7101 to 7111.
Virginia	1948, c. 432		Code 1950, §§ 58.1–920 to 58.1–930.
West Virginia	1959, c. 163	2–19–1959	Code, 11–11B–1 to 11–11B–14.
Wisconsin	1971, c. 310	5–14–1972	W.S.A. 72.35.

UNIFORM INTERSTATE COMPROMISE OF DEATH TAXES ACT

Table of Jurisdictions Wherein Act Has Been Adopted

For text of Uniform Act, and variation notes and annotation materials for adopting jurisdictions, see Uniform Laws Annotated, Master Edition, Volume 8A.

Jurisdiction	Laws	Effective Date	Statutory Citation
California	1949, p. 587	10–1–1949	West's Ann.Cal.Rev. & T.Code, §§ 13801 to 13810.4.

Jurisdiction	Laws	Effective Date	Statutory Citation
Colorado	1953, c. 132	3–19–1953	West's C.R.S.A. §§ 39–24–101 to 39–24–114.
Connecticut	1947, Supp.	6–1–1947	C.G.S.A. §§ 12–372 to 12–374.
Delaware	43 Del. Laws c. 5		30 Del.C. §§ 1701 to 1706.
Kentucky	1960, c. 186	6–16–1960	KRS 140.285.
Maine	1949, c. 34	8–6–1949	36 M.R.S.A. §§ 3981 to 3985.
Maryland	1945, c. 983	6–1–1945	Code, Tax-General §§ 7–118 to 7–122.
Massachusetts	1943, c. 428	6–4–1943	M.G.L.A. c. 65B, §§ 1 to 7.
Michigan	1956, No. 173	8–11–1956	M.C.L.A. §§ 205.601 to 205.607.
Minnesota	1951, c. 247	4–7–1951	M.S.A. §§ 291.41 to 291.47.
Nebraska	1976, LB 584	7–10–1976	R.R.S.1943, §§ 77–3301 to 3316.
Nevada	1987, p. 2105		N.R.S. 375A.400 to 375A.420.
New Jersey	1944, c. 220	4–21–1944	N.J.S.A. 54:38A–1, 54:38A–2.
New York	1941, c. 280	4–12–1941	McKinney's Tax Law § 978.
Ohio	1967, 132 v S 326	7–1–1968	R.C. § 5731.35.
Oregon	1959, c. 573		ORS 118.855 to 118.880.
Pennsylvania	1949, p. 1726	5–23–1949	72 P.S. §§ 9156 to 9163.
Rhode Island	1950, c. 2508		Gen.Laws 1956, §§ 44–23–27 to 44–23–32.
South Carolina	1987, No. 70	5–16–1987	Code 1976, §§ 12–16–210 to 12–16–320.
Tennessee	1951, c. 183	3–15–1951	T.C.A. §§ 67–8–501 to 67–8–506.
Vermont	1947, No. 23	7–1–1947	32 V.S.A. §§ 7201 to 7203.
Virginia	1948, c. 432		Code 1950, §§ 58.1–920 to 58.1–930.
West Virginia	1959, c. 162	2–19–1959	Code, 11–11A–1 to 11–11A–5.

291.42. Election to invoke

In any case in which this state and one or more other states each claims that it was the domicile of a decedent at the time of death, at any time prior to the commencement of legal action for determination of domicile within this state or within 60 days thereafter, any executor, or the taxing official of any such state, may elect to invoke the provisions of sections 291.41 to 291.47. Such executor or taxing official shall send a notice of such election by certified mail, receipt requested, to the taxing official of each such state and to each executor, ancillary administrator, and interested person. Within 40 days after the receipt of such notice of election any executor may reject such election by sending a notice, by certified mail, receipt requested, to the taxing officials involved and to all other executors and to all interested parties. When an election has been rejected no further proceedings shall be had under sections 291.41 to 291.47. If such election is not rejected within the 40-day period, the dispute as to death taxes shall be determined solely in accordance with the provisions of sections 291.41 to 291.47. No other proceedings to determine or assess such death taxes shall thereafter be instituted in any court of this state or otherwise.

Laws 1951, c. 247, § 2. Amended by Laws 1978, c. 674, § 60; Laws 1986, c. 444.

291.43. Agreements as to death tax

In any case in which an election is made and not rejected the commissioner of revenue of this state may enter into a written agreement with the other taxing officials involved and with the executors to accept a certain sum in full payment of any death taxes, together with interest and penalties, that may be due this state, provided this agreement fixes the amount to be paid the other states involved in the dispute.

Laws 1951, c. 247, § 3. Amended by Laws 1973, c. 582, § 3.

291.44. Determination of domicile

If in any such case it appears that an agreement cannot be reached, as provided in section 291.43, or if one year shall have elapsed from the date of the election without such an agreement having been reached, the domicile of the decedent at the time of death shall be determined solely for death tax purposes as follows:

(1) Where only this state and one other state are involved, the commissioner of revenue and the taxing official of the other state shall each appoint a member of a board of arbitration, and these members shall appoint the third member of the board. If this state and more than one other state are involved, the taxing officials thereof shall agree upon the authorities charged with the duty of administering death tax laws in three states not involved in the dispute and each of these authorities shall appoint a member of the board of arbitration. The board shall select one of its members as chair.

(2) Such board shall hold hearing at such places as are deemed necessary, upon reasonable notice to the executors, ancillary administrators, all other interested persons, and to the taxing officials of the states involved, all of whom are entitled to be heard.

(3) Such board may administer oaths, take testimony, subpoena witnesses and require their attendance, require the production of books, papers, and documents, issue commissions to take testimony. Subpoenas may be issued by any member of the board. Failure to obey a subpoena may be punished by any court of record in the same manner as if the subpoena had been issued by such court.

(4) Whenever practicable such board shall apply the Rules of Evidence then prevailing in the federal courts under the federal Rules of Civil Procedure.

(5) Such board shall determine the domicile of the decedent at the time of death. This determination is final and conclusive and binds this state, and all of its judicial and administrative officials on all questions concerning the domicile of the decedent for death tax purpose.

(6) The reasonable compensation and expenses of the members of the board and its employees shall be agreed upon among such members, the taxing officials involved, and the executors. If an agreement cannot be reached, such compensation and expenses shall be determined by such taxing officials; and, if they cannot agree, by the appropriate court having probate jurisdiction of the state determined to be the domicile. Such amount shall be borne by the estate and shall be deemed an administration expense.

(7) The determination of such board and the record of its proceeding shall be filed with the authority having jurisdiction to assess the death tax in the state determined to be the domicile of the decedent and with the authorities which would have had jurisdiction to assess the death tax in each of the other states involved if the decedent had been found to be domiciled therein.

Laws 1951, c. 247, § 4. Amended by Laws 1973, c. 582, § 3; Laws 1986, c. 444; Laws 1995, c. 189, § 8; Laws 1996, c. 277, § 1.

291.45. Acceptance of agreed sum in full payment

Notwithstanding the commencement of a legal action for determination of domicile within this state or the commencement of an arbitration proceeding, as provided in section 291.44, the commissioner of revenue of this state may in any case enter into a written agreement with the other taxing officials involved and with the executors to accept a certain sum in full payment of any death tax, together with interest and penalties, that may be due this state, provided this agreement fixes the amount to be paid the other states involved in the dispute, at any time before such proceeding is concluded. Upon the filing of this agreement with the authority which would have jurisdiction to assess the death tax of this state, if the decedent died domiciled in this state, an assessment shall be made as provided in such agreement, and this assessment finally and conclusively fixes the amount of death tax due this state. If the aggregate amount payable under such agreement or under an agreement made in accordance with the provisions of section 291.43 to the states involved is less than the minimum credit allowable to the estate against the United States estate tax imposed with respect thereto, the executor forthwith shall also pay to the commissioner of revenue of this state the same percentage of the difference between such aggregate amount of such credit as the amount payable to such commissioner under such agreement bears to such aggregate amount.

Laws 1951, c. 247, § 5. Amended by Laws 1973, c. 582, § 3.

291.46. Penalties, interest; limitation

When in any case the board of arbitration determines that a decedent died domiciled in this state, the total amount of interest and penalties for nonpayment of the tax, between the date of the election and the final determination of the board, shall not exceed ten percent of the amount of the taxes per annum.

Laws 1951, c. 247, § 6. Amended by Laws 1975, c. 377, § 26.

Historical and Statutory Notes

Laws 1975, c. 377, § 42, provides in part that the section of the session law relating to this section is effective for taxes becoming due after July 1, 1975.

291.47. Application

Sections 291.41 to 291.47 apply only to cases in which each of the states involved in the dispute has in effect therein a law substantially similar to sections 291.41 to 291.47.

Laws 1951, c. 247, § 7.

291.48. Repealed by Laws 1989, c. 184, art. 1, § 20, eff. July 1, 1989

Historical and Statutory Notes

Laws 1989, c. 184, art. 1, § 21 provides that the repeal of this section is effective July 1, 1989, and applies to all department of revenue data created, collected, or maintained on, before, or after that date.

Chapter 500

ESTATES IN REAL PROPERTY

For complete statutory history see Minnesota Statutes Annotated.

500.01. Division as to quantity

Estates in lands are divided into estates of inheritance, estates for life, estates for years, and estates at will and by sufferance.

500.02. Estates of inheritance

Every estate of inheritance shall continue to be termed a fee simple, or fee; and every such estate, when not defeasible or conditional, shall be a fee simple absolute or an absolute fee.

500.03. Effect of conveyance to grantee in fee tail

In all cases where any person, if this chapter had not been passed, would at any time hereafter become seized in fee tail of any lands, tenements, or hereditaments by virtue of any devise, gift, grant, or other conveyance heretofore made, or hereafter to be made, or by any other means, such person, instead of becoming seized thereof in fee tail, shall be deemed and adjudged to be seized thereof as in fee simple.

500.04. Conveyance by owner of fee tail estate

Where lands, tenements, or hereditaments heretofore have been devised, granted, or otherwise conveyed by a tenant in tail, and the person to whom such devise, grant, or other conveyance has been made, or that person's heirs or assigns, have from the time such devise took effect, or from the time such grant or conveyance was made, to the day of passing this chapter, been in the uninterrupted possession of such lands, tenements, or hereditaments, and claiming and holding the same under or by virtue of such devise, grant, or other conveyance, they shall be deemed as good and legal to all intents and purposes as if such tenant in tail had, at the time of making such devise, grant, or other conveyance, been seized in fee simple of such lands, tenements, or hereditaments, any law to the contrary notwithstanding.

Amended by Laws 1986, c. 444.

500.05. Division of realty or personalty

Estates of inheritance and for life shall be denominated estates of freehold; estates for years shall be denominated chattels real; and estates at will or by sufferance shall be chattel interests, but shall not be liable as such to sale on execution.

An estate for the life of a third person, whether limited to heirs or otherwise, shall be deemed a freehold only during the life of the grantee or devisee, but after the death of the grantee or devisee it shall be deemed a chattel real.

Amended by Laws 1986, c. 444.

500.06. Division as to time

Estates, as respects the time of their enjoyment, are divided into estates in possession and estates in expectancy.

500.07. Estates in possession

An estate in possession is where the owner has an immediate right to the possession of the land; an estate in expectancy is where the right to the possession is postponed to a future period.

500.08. Estates in expectancy

Estates in expectancy are divided into, (1) reversions, and (2) estates commencing at a future day, denominated future estates. All expectant estates, except such as are enumerated and defined in this chapter, are abolished.

500.09. Reversions

A reversion is the residue of an estate left in the grantor, or the grantor's heirs, or in the heirs of a testator, commencing in possession on the determination of a particular estate granted or devised.

Amended by Laws 1986, c. 444.

500.10. Future estate; statutory remainders

A future estate is an estate limited to commence in possession at a future day, either without the intervention of a precedent estate, or on the determination, by lapse of time or otherwise, of a precedent estate created at the same time.

500.11. Future estates; inclusiveness

Subdivision 1. Common law remainders. When a future estate is dependent upon a precedent estate, it may be termed a remainder, and may be created and transferred by that name.

When a remainder on an estate for life or for years is not limited on a contingency defeating or avoiding such precedent estate, it shall be construed as intended to take effect only on the death of the first taker, or at the expiration, by lapse of time, of such term of years.

Subd. 2. Conditional limitations; shifting interests. A remainder may be limited on a contingency which, in case it should happen, will operate to abridge or determine the precedent estate; and every such remainder shall be construed a conditional limitation, and have the same effect as such limitation would have by law.

Subd. 3. Springing interests. Subject to the rules established in this chapter, a freehold estate, as well as a chattel real, may be created to commence at a future day; an estate for life may be created in a term of years, and a remainder limited thereon.

500.12. Future estates; contingent

Future estates are either vested or contingent. They are contingent while the person to whom, or the event upon which, they are limited to take effect remains uncertain.

500.13.   Repealed by Laws 1987, c. 60, § 6; Laws 1988, c. 482, § 2; Laws 1989, c. 340, art. 1, § 77, eff. Jan. 1, 1990

Historical and Statutory Notes

Laws 1989, c. 340, art. 1, § 76, in part provides:

"Except as required by section 645.35 or as otherwise provided in sections 47 [section 501B.55], 60 [section 501B.71], 62 [section 501B.73], 70 [section 501B.86], subdivision 9, and 72 [section 501B.88], this article is effective January 1, 1990, and applies to trusts, property interests, and powers of appointment whenever created to the extent permitted under the United States Constitution and the Minnesota Constitution."

500.14.   Future estates construed; validity; creating instruments

Subdivision 1.   Failure of heirs or issue.   Unless a different intent is effectively manifested, whenever property is limited upon the death of any person without "heirs" or "heirs of the body" or "issue" general or special, or "descendants" or "offspring" or "children" or any such relative described by other terms, the limitation is to take effect only when that person dies not having such relative living at the time of the person's death, or in gestation and born alive thereafter, and is not a limitation to take effect upon the indefinite failure of such relatives; nor, unless a different intent is effectively manifested, does the limitation mean that death without such relative is restricted in time to the lifetime of the creator of the interest.

Subd. 2.   Alternative future estates.   Two or more future estates may also be created, to take effect in the alternative, so that if the first in order fails to vest the next in succession shall be substituted for it, and take effect accordingly.

Subd. 3.   Probability of contingency.   No future estate, otherwise valid, shall be void on the ground of the probability or improbability of the contingency on which it is limited to take effect.

Subd. 4.   Certain remainders vest by purchase.   When a remainder is limited to the heirs, or heirs of the body, of a person to whom a life estate in the same premises is given, the persons who, on the termination of the life estate, are the heirs or heirs of the body of such tenant for life shall be entitled to take as purchasers, by virtue of the remainder so limited to them.   No conveyance, transfer, devise, or bequest of an interest, legal or equitable, in real or personal property, shall fail to take effect by purchase because limited to a person or persons, howsoever described, who would take the same interest by descent or distribution.

Subd. 5.   Posthumous children as remainderpersons.   When a future estate is limited to heirs, or issue, or children, posthumous children shall be entitled to take in the same manner as if living at the death of their parent.

Subd. 6.   Posthumous birth averts "death without issue."   A future estate, depending on the contingency of the death of any person without heirs or issue or children, shall be defeated by the birth of a posthumous child of such person capable of taking by descent.

Amended by Laws 1986, c. 444.

500.15.   Future estates; protection from destructibility rules

Subdivision 1.   Owner's destruction of precedent estate.   No expectant estate can be defeated or barred by any alienation or other act of the owner of the intermediate or precedent estate, nor by any destruction of such precedent estate, by disseisin, forfeiture, surrender, merger, or otherwise.

Subd. 2.   Exception.   Subdivision 1 shall not be construed to prevent an expectant estate from being defeated in any manner, or by any act or means, which the party creating such estate has, in the creation thereof, provided or authorized; nor shall an expectant estate thus liable to be defeated be on that ground adjudged void in its creation.

Subd. 3.   Premature determination of precedent estate.   No remainder, valid in its creation, shall be defeated by the determination of the precedent estate before the happening of the contingency on which the remainder is limited to take effect; but, should such contingency afterward happen, the remainder shall take effect in the same manner and to the same extent as if the precedent estate had continued to the same period.

500.16.   Expectant estates: descendible, devisable, alienable

Expectant estates are descendible, devisable, and alienable in the same manner as estates in possession; and hereafter contingent rights of reentry for breach of conditions subsequent, and rights to possession for breach of conditions subsequent after breach but before entry made, and possibilities of reverter, shall be descendible, devisable, and alienable in the same manner as estate in possession.

500.17.   Future estates; rents and profits

Subdivision 1.   Disposal; rules governing.   Dispositions of the rents and profits of lands, to accrue and be received at any time subsequent to the execution of the instrument creating such disposition, shall be governed by the rules established in this chapter in relation to future estates in lands.

Subd. 2.   Accumulation.   Where the controlling will or other written instrument permits accumulation, either expressly or by necessary implication, income from personal property and rents and profits from real estate may be accumulated for the period during which the power of alienation may be suspended by future interests in real or personal property not held in trust under section 501B.09, subdivision 3.   Where any will or other instrument authorizes accumulation beyond the period permissible under this section, such authorization shall be void only as to the excess period.

Reasonable sums set aside for depreciation and depletion shall not be deemed an accumulation within the meaning of this section.

Subd. 3. Repealed by Laws 1965, c. 682, § 2.

Subd. 4. Support of minor beneficiaries. When such rents and profits are directed to be accumulated for the benefit of infants entitled to the expectant estate, and such infants are destitute of other sufficient means of support and education, the district court, upon the application of their guardian, may direct a suitable sum, out of such rents and profits, to be applied to their maintenance and education.

Subd. 5. Ownership if alienation suspended. When, in consequence of a valid limitation of an expectant estate, there is a suspension of the power of alienation, or of ownership, during the continuance of which the rents and profits are undisposed of, and no valid direction for their accumulation is given, such rents and profits shall belong to the person presumptively entitled to the next eventual estate.

Subd. 6. Trustee's accumulation of rents, profits of realty. The provisions of this section shall not apply to the accumulations of rents and profits of real estate held or owned by a trustee or trustees of a trust forming a part of a stock bonus, pension, retirement or profit-sharing plan or fund exempt from tax under the provisions of the Internal Revenue Code of the United States, and rents and profits of real estate held or owned by any such trustee or trustees may be accumulated without restriction as to time.

Laws 1953, c. 424, § 1. Amended by Laws 1965, c. 682, § 1; Laws 1987, c. 60, § 9, eff. Jan. 1, 1990; Laws 1989, c. 340, art. 1, § 73.

Historical and Statutory Notes

Laws 1987, c. 60, § 10 provides that this amendment takes effect August 1, 1988. But see 1988 and 1989 legislation notes, post.

Laws 1988, c. 482, § 2 amended Laws 1987, c. 60, § 10 to provide that the 1987 amendment of subd. 2 takes effect January 1, 1990. But see 1989 legislation note, post.

Laws 1989, c. 340, art. 1, § 76 provides: "Except as required by section 645.35 or as otherwise provided in sections 47 [section 501B.55], 60 [section 501B.71], 62 [section 501B.73], 70 [section 501B.86], subdivision 9, and 72 [section 501B.88]; this article is effective January 1, 1990, and applies to trusts, property interests, and powers of appointment whenever created to the extent permitted under the United States Constitution and the Minnesota Constitution."

Laws 1989, c. 340, art. 3, § 2 amended Laws 1987, c. 60, § 10 as amended by Laws 1988, c. 482 § 2 to provide that the 1987 amendment to subd. 2 takes effect January 1, 1991.

500.18. Commencement of expectant estates

The delivery of the grant, where an expectant estate is created by grant, and, where it is created by devise, the death of the testator, shall be deemed the time of the creation of the estate.

500.19. Division

Subdivision 1. According to number. Estates, in respect to the number and connection of their owners, are divided into estates in severalty, in joint tenancy, and in common; the nature and properties of which, respectively, shall continue to be such as are now established by law, except so far as the same may be modified by the provisions of this chapter.

Subd. 2. Construction of grants and devises. All grants and devises of lands, made to two or more persons, shall be construed to create estates in common, and not in joint tenancy, unless expressly declared to be in joint tenancy. This subdivision shall not apply to mortgages, nor to devises or grants made in trust, or to executors.

Subd. 3. Joint tenancy requirements abolished. The common law requirement for unity of time, title, interest, and possession in the creation of a joint tenancy is abolished.

Subd. 4. Conveying interest directly. (a) Subject to section 507.02 specifying when both spouses must join in a conveyance of their homestead, one or more owners of an interest in real estate may convey all or part of the interest directly to one or more other persons or to one or more of themselves, or to any combination of one or more of themselves and other persons.

(b) Subject to section 507.02 specifying when both spouses must join in a conveyance of their homestead, conveyances between spouses are allowed under paragraph (a) to the same extent as those between unmarried persons.

Subd. 5. Severance of estates in joint tenancy. A severance of a joint tenancy interest in real estate by a joint tenant shall be legally effective only if (1) the instrument of severance is recorded in the office of the county recorder or the registrar of titles in the county where the real estate is situated; or (2) the instrument of severance is executed by all of the joint tenants; or (3) the severance is ordered by a court of competent jurisdiction; or (4) a severance is effected pursuant to bankruptcy of a joint tenant.

A decree of dissolution of a marriage severs all joint tenancy interests in real estate between the parties to the marriage, except to the extent the decree declares that the parties continue to hold an interest in real estate as joint tenants.

Amended by Laws 1979, c. 123, §§ 1 to 4; Laws 1986, c. 444; Laws 1987, c. 26, § 2; Laws 1990, c. 575, § 4; Laws 1994, c. 388, art. 1, § 3.

500.20. Defeasible estates

Subdivision 1. Nominal conditions and limitations. When any covenants, conditions, restrictions or extensions thereof annexed to a grant, devise or conveyance of land are, or shall become, merely nominal, and of no actual and substantial benefit to the party or parties to whom or in whose favor they are to be performed, they may be wholly disregarded; and a failure to perform the same shall in no case operate as a basis of forfeiture of the lands subject thereto.

Subd. 2. Repealed by Laws 1982, c. 500, § 5.

Subd. 2a. Restriction of duration of condition. Except for any right to reenter or to repossess as provided in subdivision 3, all private covenants, conditions, or restrictions created by which the title or use of real property is affected, cease to be valid and operative 30 years after the date of the deed, or other instrument, or the date of the probate of the will, creating them, and may be disregarded.

This subdivision does not apply to covenants, conditions, or restrictions:

(1) that were created before August 1, 1959, under which a person who owns or has an interest in real property against which the covenants, conditions, or restrictions have been filed claims a benefit of the covenant, condition, or restriction if the person records in the office of the county recorder or files in the office of the registrar of titles in the county in which the real estate affected is located, on or before March 30, 1989, a notice sworn to by the claimant or the claimant's agent or attorney: setting forth the name of the claimant; describing the real estate affected; describing the deed, instrument, or will creating the covenant, condition, or restriction; and stating that the covenant, condition, or restriction is not nominal and may not be disregarded under subdivision 1;

(2) that are created by the declaration, bylaws, floor plans, or condominium plat of a condominium created before August 1, 1980, under chapter 515, or created on or after August 1, 1980, under chapter 515A or 515B, or by any amendments of the declaration, bylaws, floor plans, or condominium plat;

(3) that are created by the articles of incorporation, bylaws, or proprietary leases of a cooperative association formed under chapter 308A;

(4) that are created by a declaration or other instrument that authorizes and empowers a corporation of which the qualification for being a stockholder or member is ownership of certain parcels of real estate, to hold title to common real estate for the benefit of the parcels;

(5) that are created by a deed, declaration, reservation, or other instrument by which one or more portions of a building, set of connecting or adjacent buildings, or complex or project of related buildings and structures share support, structural components, ingress and egress, or utility access with another portion or portions;

(6) that were created after July 31, 1959, under which a person who owns or has an interest in real estate against which covenants, conditions, or restrictions have been filed claims a benefit of the covenants, conditions, or restrictions if the person records in the office of the county recorder or files in the office of the registrar of titles in the county in which the real estate affected is located during the period commencing on the 28th anniversary of the date of the deed or instrument, or the date of the probate of the will, creating them and ending on the 30th anniversary, a notice as described in clause (1); or

(7) that are created by a declaration or bylaws of a common interest community created under or governed by chapter 515B, or by any amendments thereto.

A notice filed in accordance with clause (1) or (6) delays application of this subdivision to the covenants, conditions, or restrictions for a period ending on the later of seven years after the date of filing of the notice, or until final judgment is entered in an action to determine the validity of the covenants, conditions, or restrictions, provided in the case of an action the summons and complaint must be served and a notice of lis pendens must be recorded in the office of the county recorder or filed in the office of the registrar of titles in each county in which the real estate affected is located within seven years after the date of recording or filing of the notice under clause (1) or (6).

County recorders and registrars of titles shall accept for recording or filing a notice conforming with this subdivision and charge a fee corresponding with the fee charged for filing a notice of lis pendens of similar length. The notice may be discharged in the same manner as a notice of lis pendens and when discharged, together with the information included with it, ceases to constitute either actual or constructive notice.

Subd. 3. Time to assert power of termination. Hereafter any right to reenter or to repossess land on account of breach made in a condition subsequent shall be barred unless such right is asserted by entry or action within six years after the happening of the breach upon which such right is predicated.

Amended by Laws 1982, c. 500, § 1; Laws 1988, c. 477, § 1; Laws 1989, c. 144, art. 2, § 9; Laws 1993, c. 222, art. 5, § 2, eff. June 1, 1994; Laws 1999, c. 11, art. 3, § 18; Laws 2005, c. 119, § 1.

Historical and Statutory Notes

Laws 1988, c. 477, § 2 provides that section 1 (adding subd. 2a) does not apply to real property in the city of North Oaks.

Laws 1988, c. 477, § 3 provides that section 2 (see above) is effective the day after compliance with Minnesota Statutes, section 645.021, subd. 3, by the governing body of the city of North Oaks.

500.21. Application to ground lease

The provisions of sections 500.16 and 500.20 shall not apply to so-called ground leases providing for the construction by the lessee of buildings or other structures upon the lands of the lessor.

500.215. Limits on certain residential property rights prohibited; flag display

Subdivision 1. General rule. (a) Any provision of any deed restriction, subdivision regulation, restrictive covenant, local ordinance, contract, rental agreement or regulation, or homeowners association document that limits the right of an owner or tenant of residential property to display the flag of the United States and the flag of the State of Minnesota is void and unenforceable.

(b) "Homeowners association document" includes the declaration, articles of incorporation, bylaws, and rules and regulations of:

(1) a common interest community, as defined in section 515B.1–103(C)(10), regardless of whether the common interest community is subject to chapter 515B; and

(2) a residential community that is not a common interest community, as defined in section 515B.1–103(C)(10).

Subd. 2. Exceptions. (a) This section does not prohibit limitations narrowly tailored to protect health or safety.

(b) This section does not prohibit limitations that restrict:

(1) the size of the flag to be displayed to a size customarily used on residential property;

(2) the installation and display of the flag to a portion of the residential property to which the person who displays the flag has exclusive use; or

(3) illuminating the flag.

(c) This section does not prohibit a requirement that the flag be displayed in a legal manner under Minnesota law, that the flag be in good condition and not altered or defaced, or that the flag not be affixed in a permanent manner to that portion of property to be maintained by others or in a way that causes more than inconsequential damage to others' property. A person who causes damage is liable for the repair costs.

Subd. 3. Applicability. This section applies to all limitations described in subdivision 1 and not excepted in subdivision 2, regardless of whether adopted before, on, or after August 1, 2005.

Subd. 4. Recovery of attorney fees. If an owner or tenant of residential property is denied the right provided by this section, the owner or tenant is entitled to recover, from the party who denied the right, reasonable attorney fees and expenses if the owner or tenant prevails in enforcing the right. If a flag is installed or displayed in violation of enforceable restrictions or limitations, the party enforcing the restrictions or limitations is entitled to recover, from the party displaying the flag, reasonable attorney fees and expenses if the enforcing party prevails in enforcing the restrictions or limitations.

Laws 2005, c. 168, § 1.

500.22. Repealed by Laws 1977, c. 269, § 2, eff. May 27, 1977

500.221. Restrictions on acquisition of title

Subdivision 1. Definitions. For purposes of this section, "agricultural land" means land capable of use in the production of agricultural crops, livestock or livestock products, poultry or poultry products, milk or dairy products, or fruit and other horticultural products but does not include any land zoned by a local governmental unit for a use other than and nonconforming with agricultural use. For the purposes of this section, "interest in agricultural land" includes any leasehold interest. For the purposes of this section, a "permanent resident alien of the United States" is a natural person who:

(1) has been lawfully admitted to the United States for permanent residence; or

(2) is a holder of a nonimmigrant treaty investment visa pursuant to United States Code, title 8, section 1101(a)15(E)(ii).

A person who qualifies as a permanent resident alien of the United States under clause (1) must also maintain that person's principal, actual dwelling place within the United States for at least six months out of every consecutive 12–month period without regard to intent. A person who qualifies as a permanent resident alien of the United States under clause (2) must also maintain that person's principal actual dwelling place in Minnesota for at least ten months out of every 12–month period, and is limited to dairy farming and up to 1,500 acres of agricultural land. The eligibility of a person under clause (2) is limited to three years, unless the commissioner waives the three–year limitation upon finding that the person is actively pursuing the status under clause (1) or United States citizenship. For the purposes of this section, "commissioner" means the commissioner of agriculture.

Subd. 1a. Determination of alien status. An alien who qualifies under subdivision 1, clause (1), and has been physically absent from the United States for more than six months out of any 12–month period shall be presumed not to be a permanent resident alien. An alien who qualifies under subdivision 1, clause (2), and has been physically absent from Minnesota for more than two months out of any 12–month period shall be presumed not to be a permanent resident alien. Every permanent resident alien of the United States who purchases property subject to this section must:

(1) file a report with the commissioner within 30 days of the date of purchase; and

(2) annually, at some time during the month of January, file with the commissioner a statement setting forth the dates and places of that person's residence in the United States during the prior calendar year.

The statement required under clause (2) must include an explanation of absences totaling more than two months during the prior calendar year and any facts which support the continuation of permanent resident alien status. Upon receipt of the statement, the commissioner shall have 30 days to review the statement and notify the resident alien whether the facts support continuation of the permanent resident alien status.

Subd. 2. Aliens and non–American corporations. Except as hereinafter provided, no natural person shall acquire directly or indirectly any interest in agricultural land unless the person is a citizen of the United States or a permanent resident alien of the United States. In addition to the restrictions in section 500.24, no corporation, partnership, limited partnership, trustee, or other business entity shall directly or indirectly, acquire or otherwise obtain any interest, whether legal, beneficial or otherwise, in any title to agricultural land unless at least 80 percent of each class of stock issued and outstanding or 80 percent of the ultimate beneficial interest of the entity is held directly or indirectly by citizens of the United States or permanent resident aliens. This section shall not apply:

(1) to agricultural land that may be acquired by devise, inheritance, as security for indebtedness, by process of law in the collection of debts, or by any procedure for the enforcement of a lien or claim thereon, whether created by mortgage or otherwise. All agricultural land acquired in the collection of debts or by the enforcement of a lien or claim shall be disposed of within three years after acquiring ownership;

(2) to citizens or subjects of a foreign country whose rights to hold land are secured by treaty;

(3) to lands used for transportation purposes by a common carrier, as defined in section 218.011, subdivision 10;

(4) to lands or interests in lands acquired for use in connection with (i) the production of timber and forestry products by a corporation organized under the laws of Minnesota, or (ii) mining and mineral processing operations. Pending the development of agricultural land for the production of timber and forestry products or mining purposes the land may not be used for farming except under lease to a family farm, a family farm corporation or an authorized farm corporation;

(5) to agricultural land operated for research or experimental purposes if the ownership of the agricultural land is incidental to the research or experimental objectives of the person or business entity and the total acreage owned by the person or business entity does not exceed the acreage owned on May 27, 1977;

(6) to the purchase of any tract of 40 acres or less for facilities incidental to pipeline operation by a company operating a pipeline as defined in section 216G.01, subdivision 3;

(7) to agricultural land and land capable of being used as farmland in vegetable processing operations that is reasonably necessary to meet the requirements of pollution control law or rules; or

(8) to an interest in agricultural land held on the August 1, 2003, by a natural person with a nonimmigrant treaty investment visa, pursuant to United States Code, title 8, section 1101(a)15(E)(ii), if, within five years after August 1, 2003, the person:

(i) disposes of all agricultural land held; or

(ii) becomes a permanent resident alien of the United States or a United States citizen.

Subd. 2a. Loss of exempt status. If any person or business entity acquires an interest in agricultural land as permitted by subdivision 2 and thereafter ceases to be a person or entity qualified to acquire an interest in agricultural land as permitted by subdivision 2 by reason of the loss of citizenship or permanent residence status or the loss of citizenship or permanent residence status of its shareholders or the holders of ultimate beneficial interests, the person or entity shall:

(a) Notify the commissioner within 30 days of the loss of qualification and file a report with the commissioner of agriculture giving a description of all agricultural land owned by the person or entity within the state, the date upon which the land was acquired, the date upon which the person or entity ceased to be qualified, and other information reasonably required by the commissioner;

(b) Divest itself of any agricultural land acquired after May 27, 1981 within one year of the date upon which the person or entity ceased to be qualified;

(c) Report the divestiture to the commissioner of agriculture within 90 days after it occurs;

(d) Make other reports as the commissioner may reasonably require; and

(e) Continue to file periodic reports as required by subdivision 4 with respect to any land acquired on or before May 27, 1977.

Subd. 2b. Investigation by commissioner. The commissioner, upon the request of any person or upon receipt of any information which leads the commissioner to believe that a violation of this section may exist, may issue subpoenas requiring the appearance of witnesses, the production of relevant records and the giving of relevant testimony. On concluding, as a result of the investigation, that a violation of this section may have occurred, the commissioner shall provide the landowner or the landowner's designee with the opportunity to meet with the commissioner or the commissioner's designee in the county where the land is located to exchange information relating to the compliance with this section and any necessity for divestiture. The commissioner shall have the power to issue additional subpoenas for the meeting. The landowner and any person subpoenaed by the commissioner may be represented by counsel. Notwithstanding the provisions of chapter 14, the preliminary investigation and the meeting do not constitute a contested case hearing.

Subd. 3. Enforcement. With reason to believe, after investigation, that any person is violating this section, the commissioner shall commence an action in the district court in which any agricultural land relative to the violation is situated, or if situated in two or more counties, in any county in which a substantial part of the land is situated. The commissioner shall file for record with the county recorder or the registrar of titles of each county in which any portion of the land is located a notice of the pendency of the action as provided in section 557.02. If the court finds that the land in question is being held in violation of subdivision 2, it shall enter an order so declaring. The commissioner shall file for record any order with the county recorder or the registrar of titles of each county in which any portion of the land is located. Thereafter, the natural person, corporation, partnership, limited partnership, trustee or other business entity, shall have a period of one year from the date of the order to divest itself of the lands. The aforementioned one year limitation period shall be deemed a covenant running with the title to the land against any grantee or assignee or successor corporation or any noncorporation entity acting as agent, assignee, or successor on behalf of a corporation. Any land not so divested within the time prescribed shall be sold at public sale in the manner prescribed by law for the foreclosure of a mortgage by action. No title to land shall be invalid or subject to forfeiture by reason of the alienage of any former owner or person having a former interest therein.

Subd. 3a. Injunction. The commissioner may seek injunctive relief whenever a violation of this section is threatened.

Subd. 3b. Agreement. The commissioner is authorized to enter into a written agreement in settlement of any alleged violation, whether or not a hearing is held on the violation. An agreement may provide for an extension of the time period for divestiture but shall not include a waiver of a divestiture required by this section. The agreement shall be construed as a "No Contest" pleading and may include any sanctions, penalties, or affirmative actions which are mutually satisfactory and are consistent with this section. The agreement shall be final and conclusive with respect to the action, except upon a showing of fraud, malfeasance, or misrepresentation of a material fact. The matter agreed upon shall not be reopened or modified by an officer, employee, or agent of the state. The agreement shall be filed in Ramsey County District Court and shall be enforceable by it or the district court of the county in which the person resides or principally does business. Any violator of an agreement may, after notice is given to the alleged violator and a hearing is held, be punished by the district court as for contempt, in addition to other remedies in this section.

Subd. 4. Reports. Any natural person, corporation, partnership, limited partnership, trustee, or other business entity prohibited from future acquisition of agricultural land may retain title to any agricultural land lawfully acquired within this state prior to June 1, 1981, but shall file a report with the commissioner of agriculture annually before January 31 containing a description of all agricultural land held within this state, the purchase price and market value of the land, the use to which it is put, the date of acquisition and any other reasonable information required by the commissioner. The commissioner shall make the information available to the public. All required annual reports shall include a filing fee of $50 plus $10 for each additional quarter section of land.

Subd. 5. Penalty. Willful failure to properly file a report required under subdivision 1a or to properly register any parcel of land as required by subdivision 4 is a gross misdemeanor.

Laws 1977, c. 269, § 1, eff. May 27, 1977. Amended by Laws 1981, c. 337, § 1; Laws 1982, c. 424, § 130; Laws 1983, c. 240, § 1; Laws 1983, c. 293, § 107; Laws 1986, c. 444; Laws 1989, c. 353, § 10, eff. July 1, 1989; Laws 1989, c. 356, § 66; Laws 1996, c. 315, § 1, eff. March 16, 1996; Laws 2003, c. 107, § 31, eff. May 28, 2003; Laws 2004, c. 254, §§ 38 to 40, eff. May 22, 2004.

Historical and Statutory Notes

Laws 1989, c. 356, § 68 provides:

"Unless provided otherwise, the sections of this act that amend other 1989 enactments take effect on the same dates as the enactments that they amend."

500.222. Exempt acreage in land exchange

A local unit of government may exchange a parcel of land owned by it or acquired for it by a qualified intermediary, for a parcel of agricultural real estate that is owned by an individual exempt under section 500.221 based on ownership being lawfully acquired prior to June 1, 1981. The agricultural land being exchanged for the parcel that is currently exempt shall also be exempt under section 500.221 as if it had been purchased by the owner prior to June 1, 1981. The exchanged parcel shall have exactly the same status under section 500.221 as the parcel to be exchanged and the status may be stated on the deeds used to effectuate the transaction.

Laws 2001, c. 206, § 14. Amended by Laws 2002, c. 373, § 32, eff. May 18, 2002.

USE OF AGRICULTURAL LAND BY BUSINESS ORGANIZATIONS

500.23. Repealed by Laws 1973, c. 427, § 2, eff. May 20, 1973

500.24. Farming by business organizations

Subdivision 1. Purpose. The legislature finds that it is in the interests of the state to encourage and protect the family farm as a basic economic unit, to insure it as the most socially desirable mode of agricultural production, and to enhance and promote the stability and well-being of rural society in Minnesota and the nuclear family.

Subd. 2. Definitions. The definitions in this subdivision apply to this section.

(a) "Farming" means the production of (1) agricultural products; (2) livestock or livestock products; (3) milk or milk products; or (4) fruit or other horticultural products. It does not include the processing, refining, or packaging of said products, nor the provision of spraying or harvesting services by a processor or distributor of farm products. It does not include the production of timber or forest products, the production of poultry or poultry products, or the feeding and caring for livestock that are delivered to a corporation for slaughter or processing for up to 20 days before slaughter or processing.

(b) "Family farm" means an unincorporated farming unit owned by one or more persons residing on the farm or actively engaging in farming.

(c) "Family farm corporation" means a corporation founded for the purpose of farming and the ownership of agricultural land in which the majority of the stock is held by and the majority of the stockholders are persons, the spouses of persons, or current beneficiaries of one or more family farm trusts in which the trustee holds stock in a family farm corporation, related to each other within the third degree of kindred according to the rules of the civil law, and at least one of the related persons is residing on or actively operating the farm, and none of whose stockholders are corporations; provided that a family farm corporation shall not cease to qualify as such hereunder by reason of any:

(1) transfer of shares of stock to a person or the spouse of a person related within the third degree of kindred according to the rules of civil law to the person making the transfer, or to a family farm trust of which the shareholder, spouse, or related person is a current beneficiary; or

(2) distribution from a family farm trust of shares of stock to a beneficiary related within the third degree of kindred according to the rules of civil law to a majority of the current beneficiaries of the trust, or to a family farm trust of which the shareholder, spouse, or related person is a current beneficiary.

For the purposes of this section, a transfer may be made with or without consideration, either directly or indirectly, during life or at death, whether or not in trust, of the shares in the family farm corporation, and stock owned by a family farm trust are considered to be owned in equal shares by the current beneficiaries.

(d) "Family farm trust" means:

(1) a trust in which:

(i) a majority of the current beneficiaries are persons or spouses of persons who are related to each other within the third degree of kindred according to the rules of civil law;

(ii) all of the current beneficiaries are natural persons or nonprofit corporations or trusts described in the Internal Revenue Code, section 170(c), as amended,[1] and the regulations under that section; and

(iii) one of the family member current beneficiaries is residing on or actively operating the farm; or the trust leases the agricultural land to a family farm unit, a family farm corporation, an authorized farm corporation, an authorized livestock farm corporation, a family farm limited liability company, a family farm trust, an authorized farm limited liability company, a family farm partnership, or an authorized farm partnership; or

(2) a charitable remainder trust as defined in the Internal Revenue Code, section 664, as amended, and the regulations under that section, and a charitable lead trust as set forth in the Internal Revenue Code, section 170(f), and the regulations under that section.

(e) "Authorized farm corporation" means a corporation meeting the following standards:

(1) it has no more than five shareholders, provided that for the purposes of this section, a husband and wife are considered one shareholder;

(2) all its shareholders, other than any estate, are natural persons or a family farm trust;

(3) it does not have more than one class of shares;

(4) its revenue from rent, royalties, dividends, interest, and annuities does not exceed 20 percent of its gross receipts;

(5) shareholders holding 51 percent or more of the interest in the corporation reside on the farm or are actively engaging in farming;

(6) it does not, directly or indirectly, own or otherwise have an interest in any title to more than 1,500 acres of agricultural land; and

(7) none of its shareholders are shareholders in other authorized farm corporations that directly or indirectly in combination with the corporation own more than 1,500 acres of agricultural land.

(f) "Authorized livestock farm corporation" means a corporation formed for the production of livestock and meeting the following standards:

(1) it is engaged in the production of livestock other than dairy cattle;

(2) all its shareholders, other than any estate, are natural persons, family farm trusts, or family farm corporations;

(3) it does not have more than one class of shares;

(4) its revenue from rent, royalties, dividends, interest, and annuities does not exceed 20 percent of its gross receipts;

(5) shareholders holding 75 percent or more of the control, financial, and capital investment in the corporation are farmers, and at least 51 percent of the required percentage of farmers are actively engaged in livestock production;

(6) it does not, directly or indirectly, own or otherwise have an interest in any title to more than 1,500 acres of agricultural land; and

(7) none of its shareholders are shareholders in other authorized farm corporations that directly or indirectly in combination with the corporation own more than 1,500 acres of agricultural land.

(g) "Agricultural land" means real estate used for farming or capable of being used for farming in this state.

(h) "Pension or investment fund" means a pension or employee welfare benefit fund, however organized, a mutual fund, a life insurance company separate account, a common trust of a bank or other trustee established for the investment and reinvestment of money contributed to it, a real estate investment trust, or an investment company as defined in United States Code, title 15, section 80a–3.

(i) "Farm homestead" means a house including adjoining buildings that has been used as part of a farming operation or is part of the agricultural land used for a farming operation.

(j) "Family farm partnership" means a limited partnership formed for the purpose of farming and the ownership of agricultural land in which the majority of the interests in the partnership is held by and the majority of the partners are natural persons or current beneficiaries of one or more family farm trusts in which the trustee holds an interest in a family farm partnership related to each other within the third degree of kindred according to the rules of the civil law, and at least one of the related persons is residing on the farm, actively operating the farm, or the agricultural land was owned by one or more of the related persons for a period of five years before its transfer to the limited partnership, and none of the partners is a corporation. A family farm partnership does not cease to qualify as a family farm partnership because of a:

(1) transfer of a partnership interest to a person or spouse of a person related within the third degree of kindred according to the rules of civil law to the person making the transfer or to a family farm trust of which the partner, spouse, or related person is a current beneficiary; or

(2) distribution from a family farm trust of a partnership interest to a beneficiary related within the third degree of kindred according to the rules of civil law to a majority of the current beneficiaries of the trust, or to a family farm trust of which the partner, spouse, or related person is a current beneficiary.

For the purposes of this section, a transfer may be made with or without consideration, either directly or indirectly, during life or at death, whether or not in trust, of a partnership interest in the family farm partnership, and interest owned by a family farm trust is considered to be owned in equal shares by the current beneficiaries.

(k) "Authorized farm partnership" means a limited partnership meeting the following standards:

(1) it has been issued a certificate from the secretary of state or is registered with the county recorder and farming and ownership of agricultural land is stated as a purpose or character of the business;

(2) it has no more than five partners;

(3) all its partners, other than any estate, are natural persons or family farm trusts;

(4) its revenue from rent, royalties, dividends, interest, and annuities does not exceed 20 percent of its gross receipts;

(5) its general partners hold at least 51 percent of the interest in the land assets of the partnership and reside on the farm or are actively engaging in farming not more than 1,500 acres as a general partner in an authorized limited partnership;

(6) its limited partners do not participate in the business of the limited partnership including operating, managing, or directing management of farming operations;

(7) it does not, directly or indirectly, own or otherwise have an interest in any title to more than 1,500 acres of agricultural land; and

(8) none of its limited partners are limited partners in other authorized farm partnerships that directly or indirectly in combination with the partnership own more than 1,500 acres of agricultural land.

(*l*) "Family farm limited liability company" means a limited liability company founded for the purpose of farming and the ownership of agricultural land in which the majority of the membership interests is held by and the majority of the members are natural persons, or current beneficiaries of one or more family farm trusts in which the trustee holds an interest in a family farm limited liability company related to each other within the third degree of kindred according to the rules of the civil law, and at least one of the related persons is residing on the farm, actively operating the farm, or the agricultural land was owned by one or more of the related persons for a period of five years before its transfer to the limited liability company, and none of the members is a corporation or a limited liability company. A family farm limited liability company does not cease to qualify as a family farm limited liability company because of:

(1) a transfer of a membership interest to a person or spouse of a person related within the third degree of kindred according to the rules of civil law to the person making the transfer or to a family farm trust of which the member, spouse, or related person is a current beneficiary; or

(2) distribution from a family farm trust of a membership interest to a beneficiary related within the third degree of kindred according to the rules of civil law to a majority of the current beneficiaries of the trust, or to a family farm trust of which the member, spouse, or related person is a current beneficiary.

For the purposes of this section, a transfer may be made with or without consideration, either directly or indirectly, during life or at death, whether or not in trust, of a membership interest in the family farm limited liability company, and interest owned by a family farm trust is considered to be owned in equal shares by the current beneficiaries. Except for a state or federally chartered financial institution acquiring an encumbrance for the purpose of security or an interest under paragraph (x), a member of a family farm limited liability company may not transfer a membership interest, including a financial interest, to a person who is not otherwise eligible to be a member under this paragraph.

(m) "Authorized farm limited liability company" means a limited liability company meeting the following standards:

(1) it has no more than five members;

(2) all its members, other than any estate, are natural persons or family farm trusts;

(3) it does not have more than one class of membership interests;

(4) its revenue from rent, royalties, dividends, interest, and annuities does not exceed 20 percent of its gross receipts;

(5) members holding 51 percent or more of both the governance rights and financial rights in the limited liability company reside on the farm or are actively engaged in farming;

(6) it does not, directly or indirectly, own or otherwise have an interest in any title to more than 1,500 acres of agricultural land; and

(7) none of its members are members in other authorized farm limited liability companies that directly or indirectly in combination with the authorized farm limited liability company own more than 1,500 acres of agricultural land.

Except for a state or federally chartered financial institution acquiring an encumbrance for the purpose of security or an interest under paragraph (x), a member of an authorized farm limited liability company may not transfer a membership interest, including a financial interest, to a person who is not otherwise eligible to be a member under this paragraph.

(n) "Farmer" means a natural person who regularly participates in physical labor or operations management in the person's farming operation and files "Schedule F" as part of the person's annual Form 1040 filing with the United States Internal Revenue Service.

(o) "Actively engaged in livestock production" means performing day-to-day physical labor or day-to-day operations management that significantly contributes to livestock production and the functioning of a livestock operation.

(p) "Research or experimental farm" means a corporation, limited partnership, pension, investment fund, or limited liability company that owns or operates agricultural land for research or experimental purposes, provided that any commercial sales from the operation are incidental to the research or experimental objectives of the corporation. A corporation, limited partnership, limited liability company, or pension or investment fund seeking initial approval by the commissioner to operate agricultural land for research or experimental purposes must first submit to the commissioner a prospectus or proposal of the intended method of operation containing information required by the commissioner including a copy of any operational contract with individual participants.

(q) "Breeding stock farm" means a corporation, limited partnership, or limited liability company, that owns or operates agricultural land for the purpose of raising breeding stock, including embryos, for resale to farmers or for the purpose of growing seed, wild rice, nursery plants, or sod. An entity that is organized to raise livestock other than dairy cattle under this paragraph that does not qualify as an authorized farm corporation must:

(1) sell all castrated animals to be fed out or finished to farming operations that are neither directly nor indirectly owned by the business entity operating the breeding stock operation; and

(2) report its total production and sales annually to the commissioner.

(r) "Aquatic farm" means a corporation, limited partnership, or limited liability company, that owns or leases agricultural land as a necessary part of an aquatic farm as defined in section 17.47, subdivision 3.

(s) "Religious farm" means a corporation formed primarily for religious purposes whose sole income is derived from agriculture.

(t) "Utility corporation" means a corporation regulated under Minnesota Statutes 1974, chapter 216B, that owns agricultural land for purposes described in that chapter, or an electric generation or transmission cooperative that owns agricultural land for use in its business if the land is not used for farming except under lease to a family farm unit, a family farm corporation, a family farm trust, a family farm partnership, or a family farm limited liability company.

(u) "Development organization" means a corporation, limited partnership, limited liability company, or pension or investment fund that has an interest in agricultural land for which the corporation, limited partnership, limited liability company, or pension or investment fund has documented plans to use and subsequently uses the land within six years from the date of purchase for a specific nonfarming purpose, or if the land is zoned nonagricultural, or if the land is located within an incorporated area. A corporation, limited partnership, limited liability company, or pension or investment fund may hold agricultural land in the amount necessary for its nonfarm business operation; provided, however, that pending the development of agricultural land for nonfarm purposes, the land may not be used for farming except under lease to a family farm unit, a family farm corporation, a family farm trust, an authorized farm corporation, an authorized livestock farm corporation, a family farm partnership, an authorized farm partnership, a family farm limited liability company, or an authorized farm limited liability company, or except when controlled through ownership, options, leaseholds, or other agreements by a corporation that has entered into an agreement with the United States under the New Community Act of 1968 (Title IV of the Housing and Urban Development Act of 1968, United States Code, title 42, sections 3901 to 3914) as amended, or a subsidiary or assign of such a corporation.

(v) "Exempt land" means agricultural land owned or leased by a corporation as of May 20, 1973, agricultural land owned or leased by a pension or investment fund as of May 12, 1981, agricultural land owned or leased by a limited partnership as of May 1, 1988, or agricultural land owned or leased by a trust as of the effective date of Laws 2000, chapter 477, including the normal expansion of that ownership at a rate not to exceed 20 percent of the amount of land owned as of May 20, 1973, for a corporation; May 12, 1981, for a pension or investment fund; May 1, 1988, for a limited partnership, or the effective date of Laws 2000, chapter 477, for a trust, measured in acres, in any five-year period, and including additional ownership reasonably necessary to meet the requirements of pollution control rules. A corporation, limited partnership, or pension or investment fund that is eligible to own or lease agricultural land under this section prior to May 1997, or a corporation that is eligible to own or lease agricultural land as a benevolent trust under this section prior to the effective date of Laws 2000, chapter 477, may continue to own or lease agricultural land subject to the same conditions and limitations as previously allowed.

(w) "Gifted land" means agricultural land acquired as a gift, either by grant or devise, by an educational, religious, or charitable nonprofit corporation, limited partnership, limited liability company, or pension or investment fund if all land so acquired is disposed of within ten years after acquiring the title.

(x) "Repossessed land" means agricultural land acquired by a corporation, limited partnership, limited liability company, or pension or investment fund by process of law in the collection of debts, or by any procedure for the enforcement of a lien or claim on the land, whether created by mortgage or otherwise if all land so acquired is disposed of within five years after acquiring the title. The five-year limitation is a covenant running with the title to the land against any grantee, assignee, or successor of the pension or investment fund, corporation, limited partnership, or limited liability company. The land so acquired must not be used for farming during the five-year period, except under a lease to a family farm unit, a family farm corporation, a family farm trust, an authorized farm corporation, an authorized livestock farm corporation, a family farm partnership, an authorized farm partnership, a family farm limited liability company, or an authorized farm limited liability company. Notwithstanding the five-year divestiture requirement under this paragraph, a financial institution may continue to own the agricultural land if the agricultural land is leased to the immediately preceding former owner, but must dispose of the agricultural land within ten years of acquiring the title. Livestock acquired by a pension or investment fund, corporation, limited partnership, or limited liability company in the collection of debts, or by a procedure for the enforcement of lien or claim on the livestock whether created by security agreement or otherwise after August 1, 1994, must be sold or disposed of within one full production cycle for the type of livestock acquired or 18 months after the livestock is acquired, whichever is earlier.

(y) "Commissioner" means the commissioner of agriculture.

(z) "Nonprofit corporation" means a nonprofit corporation organized under state nonprofit corporation or trust law or qualified for tax-exempt status under federal tax law that uses the land for a specific nonfarming purpose or leases the agricultural land to a family farm unit, a family farm corporation, an authorized farm corporation, an authorized livestock farm corporation, a family farm limited liability company, a family farm trust, an authorized farm limited liability company, a family farm partnership, or an authorized farm partnership.

(aa) "Current beneficiary" means a person who at any time during a year is entitled to, or at the discretion of any person may, receive a distribution from the income or principal of the trust. It does not include a distributee trust, other than a trust described in section 170(c) of the Internal Revenue Code, as amended, but does include the current beneficiaries of the distributee trust. It does not include a person in whose favor a power of appointment could be exercised until the holder of the power of appointment actually exercises the power of appointment in that person's favor. It does not include a person who is entitled to receive a distribution only after a specified time or upon the occurrence of a specified event until the time or occurrence of the event. For the purposes of this section, a distributee trust is a current beneficiary of a family farm trust.

(bb) "De minimis" means that any corporation, pension or investment fund, limited liability company, or limited partnership that directly or indirectly owns, acquires, or otherwise obtains any interest in 40 acres or less of agricultural land and annually receives less than $150 per acre in gross revenue from rental or agricultural production.

Subd. 3. Farming and ownership of agricultural land by corporations restricted. (a) No corporation, limited liability company, pension or investment fund, trust, or limited partnership shall engage in farming; nor shall any corporation, limited liability company, pension or investment fund, trust, or limited partnership, directly or indirectly, own, acquire, or otherwise obtain any interest, in agricultural land other than a bona fide encumbrance taken for purposes of security. This subdivision does not apply to general partnerships. This subdivision does not apply to any agricultural land, corporation, limited partnership, trust, limited liability company, or pension or investment fund that meet any of the definitions in subdivision 2, paragraphs (b) to (f), (j) to (m), (p) to (x), (z), and (bb), has a conservation plan prepared for the agricultural land, and reports as required under subdivision 4.

(b) A corporation, pension or investment fund, trust, limited liability company, or limited partnership that cannot meet any of the definitions in subdivision 2, paragraphs (b) to (f), (j) to (m), (p) to (x), (z), and (bb), may petition the commissioner for an exemption from this subdivision. The commissioner may issue an exemption if the entity meets the following criteria:

(1) the exemption would not contradict the purpose of this section; and

(2) the petitioning entity would not have a significant impact upon the agriculture industry and the economy.

The commissioner shall review annually each entity that is issued an exemption under this paragraph to ensure that the entity continues to meet the criteria in clauses (1) and (2). If an entity fails to meet the criteria, the commissioner shall withdraw the exemption and the entity is subject to enforcement proceedings under subdivision 5. The commissioner shall submit a report with a list of each entity that is issued an exemption under this paragraph to the chairs of the senate and house of representatives agricultural policy committees by October 1 of each year.

Subd. 3a. Lease agreement; conservation practice protection clause. A corporation, pension or investment fund, limited partnership, or limited liability company other than those meeting any of the definitions in subdivision 2, paragraphs (c) to (f) or (j) to (m), when leasing farm land to a family farm unit, a family farm corporation, a family farm trust, an authorized farm corporation, an authorized livestock farm corporation, a family farm partnership, an authorized farm partnership, a family farm limited liability company, or an authorized farm limited liability company, under provisions of subdivision 2, paragraph (x), must include within the lease agreement a provision prohibiting intentional damage or destruction to a conservation practice on the agricultural land.

Subd. 3b. Protection of conservation practices. A corporation, pension or investment fund, or limited partnership, or limited liability company other than those meeting any of the definitions in subdivision 2, paragraphs (c) to (f) or (j) to (m), which, during the period of time it holds agricultural land under subdivision 2, paragraph (x), intentionally destroys a conservation practice as defined in section 103F.401, subdivision 3, to which the state has made a financial contribution, must pay the commissioner, for deposit in the general fund, an amount equal to the state's total contributions to that conservation practice plus interest from the time of investment in the conservation practice. Interest must be calculated at an annual percentage rate of 12 percent.

Subd. 4. Reports. (a) The chief executive officer of every pension or investment fund, corporation, limited partnership, limited liability company, or entity that is seeking to qualify for an exemption from the commissioner, and the trustee of a family farm trust that holds any interest in agricultural land or land used for the breeding, feeding, pasturing, growing, or raising of livestock, dairy or poultry, or products thereof, or land used for the production of agricultural crops or fruit or other horticultural products, other than a bona fide encumbrance taken for purposes of security, or which is engaged in farming or proposing to commence farming in this state after May 20, 1973,

163

shall file with the commissioner a report containing the following information and documents:

(1) the name of the pension or investment fund, corporation, limited partnership, or limited liability company and its place of incorporation, certification, or registration;

(2) the address of the pension or investment plan headquarters or of the registered office of the corporation in this state, the name and address of its registered agent in this state and, in the case of a foreign corporation, limited partnership, or limited liability company, the address of its principal office in its place of incorporation, certification, or registration;

(3) the acreage and location listed by quarter-quarter section, township, and county of each lot or parcel of agricultural land or land used for the keeping or feeding of poultry in this state owned or leased by the pension or investment fund, limited partnership, corporation, or limited liability company;

(4) the names and addresses of the officers, administrators, directors, or trustees of the pension or investment fund, or of the officers, shareholders owning more than ten percent of the stock, including the percent of stock owned by each such shareholder, the members of the board of directors of the corporation, and the members of the limited liability company, and the general and limited partners and the percentage of interest in the partnership by each partner;

(5) the farm products which the pension or investment fund, limited partnership, corporation, or limited liability company produces or intends to produce on its agricultural land;

(6) with the first report, a copy of the title to the property where the farming operations are or will occur indicating the particular exception claimed under subdivision 3; and

(7) with the first or second report, a copy of the conservation plan proposed by the soil and water conservation district, and with subsequent reports a statement of whether the conservation plan was implemented.

The report of a corporation, trust, limited liability company, or partnership seeking to qualify hereunder as a family farm corporation, an authorized farm corporation, an authorized livestock farm corporation, a family farm partnership, an authorized farm partnership, a family farm limited liability company, an authorized farm limited liability company, or a family farm trust or under an exemption from the commissioner shall contain the following additional information: the number of shares, partnership interests, or governance and financial rights owned by persons or current beneficiaries of a family farm trust residing on the farm or actively engaged in farming, or their relatives within the third degree of kindred according to the rules of the civil law or their spouses; the name, address, and number of shares owned by each shareholder, partnership interests owned by each partner or governance and financial rights owned by each member, and a statement as to percentage of gross receipts of the corporation derived from rent, royalties, dividends, interest, and annuities. No pension or investment fund, limited partnership, corporation, or limited liability company shall commence farming in this state until the commissioner has inspected the report and certified that its proposed operations comply with the provisions of this section.

(b) Every pension or investment fund, limited partnership, trust, corporation, or limited liability company as described in paragraph (a) shall, prior to April 15 of each year, file with the commissioner a report containing the information required in paragraph (a), based on its operations in the preceding calendar year and its status at the end of the year. A pension or investment fund, limited partnership, corporation, or limited liability company that does not file the report by April 15 must pay a $500 civil penalty. The penalty is a lien on the land being farmed under subdivision 3 until the penalty is paid.

(c) The commissioner may, for good cause shown, issue a written waiver or reduction of the civil penalty for failure to make a timely filing of the annual report required by this subdivision. The waiver or reduction is final and conclusive with respect to the civil penalty, and may not be reopened or modified by an officer, employee, or agent of the state, except upon a showing of fraud or malfeasance or misrepresentation of a material fact. The report required under paragraph (b) must be completed prior to a reduction or waiver under this paragraph. The commissioner may enter into an agreement under this paragraph only once for each corporation or partnership.

(d) Failure to file a required report or the willful filing of false information is a gross misdemeanor.

Subd. 5. Enforcement. With reason to believe that a corporation, limited partnership, limited liability company, trust, or pension or investment fund is violating subdivision 3, the attorney general shall commence an action in the district court in which any agricultural lands relative to such violation are situated, or if situated in two or more counties, in any county in which a substantial part of the lands are situated. The attorney general shall file for record with the county recorder or the registrar of titles of each county in which any portion of said lands are located a notice of the pendency of the action as provided in section 557.02. If the court finds that the lands in question are being held in violation of subdivision 3, it shall enter an order so declaring. The attorney general shall file for record any such order with the county recorder or the registrar of titles of each county in which any portion of said lands are located. Thereafter, the pension or investment fund, limited partnership, or corporation owning such land shall have a period of five years from the date of such order to divest itself of such lands. The aforementioned five-year limitation period shall be deemed a covenant running with the title to the land against any pension or investment fund, limited partnership, or corporate grantee or assignee or the successor of such pension or investment fund, limited partnership, or corporation. Any lands not so divested within the time prescribed shall be sold at public sale in the manner prescribed by law for the foreclosure of a mortgage by action. In addition, any prospective or threatened violation may be enjoined by an action brought by the attorney general in the manner provided by law.

Subds. 6 to 8.   Renumbered § 500.245, subds. 1 to 3 in St.1997 Supp.

Laws 1973, c. 427, § 1, eff. May 20, 1973. Amended by Laws 1975, c. 324, § 1; Laws 1976, c. 181, § 2; Laws 1976, c. 239, § 123; Laws 1978, c. 722, § 1; Laws 1980, c. 497, § 3; Laws 1981, c. 173, §§ 1 to 4, eff. May 12, 1981; Laws 1985, c. 80, § 1, eff. May 7, 1985; Laws 1985, c. 248, § 70; Laws 1985, 1st Sp., c. 10, § 116, eff. June 28, 1985; Laws 1986, c. 398, art. 7, §§ 2, 3, eff. April 1, 1986; Laws 1986, c. 398, art. 20, § 1, eff. March 22, 1986; Laws 1986, c. 444; Laws 1986, 1st Sp., c. 2, art. 2, § 13, eff. April 12, 1986; Laws 1987, c. 396, art. 2, §§ 1 to 3, eff. July 1, 1987; Laws 1988, c. 610, §§ 2 to 9, eff. May 1, 1988; Laws 1988, c. 700, §§ 1, 2; Laws 1989, c. 350, art. 16, § 1; Laws 1990, c. 391, art. 8, § 55; Laws 1990, c. 561, § 13, eff. Jan. 1, 1991; Laws 1990, c. 580, § 1; Laws 1990, c. 604, art. 10, § 22; Laws 1991, c. 263, § 1; Laws 1991, c. 309, § 16, eff. June 4, 1991; Laws 1992, c. 517, art. 1, § 36, eff. Jan. 1, 1993; Laws 1993, c. 123, §§ 1, 2; Laws 1994, c. 622, §§ 2, 3; Laws 1997, c. 7, art. 1, § 163; Laws 1997, c. 126, §§ 1 to 5, eff. May 10, 1997; Laws 1999, c. 231, §§ 187, 188; Laws 2000, c. 477, §§ 67 to 72, eff. May 16, 2000; Laws 2004, c. 254, §§ 41, 42.

[1] All text references to Internal Revenue Code sections are to Title 26 of U.S.C.A.

Historical and Statutory Notes

Section 4 of Laws 1987, c. 396, art. 2 provides that the art. is eff. July 1, 1987, and applies to property with initial offers made under § 500.24, subd. 6, after July 1, 1987.

Laws 1988, c. 700, § 13, provided in part that the amendment of subd. 6 (by Laws 1988, c. 700, § 1), is effective April 29, 1988, except that notice that the agricultural land or the farm homestead will be offered for sale under section 500.24, subd. 6(a), must be as follows:

"(1) for property that has been offered for sale before the eighth day after final enactment, but not sold, and the immediately preceding former owner has not received written notice that the property will be offered for sale, written notice must be provided to the preceding former owner before the eighth day after final enactment; and

"(2) section 500.24, subdivision 6, paragraph (n), does not apply to a sale relating to an offer made to an immediately preceding former owner before final enactment.

"Section 2 applies to notices given after the 14th day after final enactment."

Laws 1988, c. 700, § 13, provides in part that the amendment of subd. 7 applies to notices given after the 14th day after final enactment (final enactment was April 28, 1988).

500.245.   Right of first refusal for agricultural land

Subdivision 1. Disposal of land.   (a) A state or federal agency, limited partnership, corporation, or limited liability company may not lease or sell agricultural land or a farm homestead before offering or making a good faith effort to offer the land for sale or lease to the immediately preceding former owner at a price no higher than the highest price offered by a third party that is acceptable to the seller or lessor. The offer must be made on the notice to offer form under subdivision 2. The requirements of this subdivision do not apply to a sale or lease by a corporation that is a family farm corporation or an authorized farm corporation or to a sale or lease by the commissioner of agriculture of property acquired by the state under the family farm security program under chapter 41. This subdivision applies only to a sale or lease when the seller or lessor acquired the property by enforcing a debt against the agricultural land or farm homestead, including foreclosure of a mortgage, accepting a deed in lieu of foreclosure, terminating a contract for deed, or accepting a deed in lieu of terminating a contract for deed. Selling or leasing property to a third party at a price is prima facie evidence that the price is acceptable to the seller or lessor. The seller must provide written notice to the immediately preceding former owner that the agricultural land or farm homestead will be offered for sale at least 14 days before the agricultural land or farm homestead is offered for sale.

(b) An immediately preceding former owner is the entity with record legal title to the agricultural land or farm homestead before acquisition by the state or federal agency or corporation except: if the immediately preceding former owner is a bankruptcy estate, the debtor in bankruptcy is the immediately preceding former owner; and if the agricultural land or farm homestead was acquired by termination of a contract for deed or deed in lieu of termination of a contract for deed, the immediately preceding former owner is the purchaser under the contract for deed. For purposes of this subdivision, only a family farm, family farm corporation, family farm partnership or family farm limited liability company can be an immediately preceding former owner.

(c) An immediately preceding former owner may elect to purchase or lease the entire property or an agreed to portion of the property. If the immediately preceding former owner elects to purchase or lease a portion of the property, the election must be reported in writing to the seller or lessor prior to the time the property is first offered for sale or lease. If election is made to purchase or lease a portion of the property, the portion must be contiguous and compact so that it does not unreasonably reduce access to or the value of the remaining property.

(d) For purposes of this subdivision, the term "a price no higher than the highest price offered by a third party" means the acceptable cash price offered by a third party or the acceptable time-price offer made by a third party. A cash price offer is one that involves simultaneous transfer of title for payment of the entire amount of the offer. If the acceptable offer made by a third party is a time-price offer, the seller or lessor must make the same time-price offer or an equivalent cash offer to the immediately preceding former owner. An equivalent cash offer is equal to the total of the payments made over a period of the time-price offer discounted by yield curve of the United States treasury notes and bonds of similar maturity on the first business day of the month in which the offer is personally delivered or mailed for time periods similar to the time period covered by the time-price offer, plus 2.0 percent. A time-price offer is an offer that is financed entirely or partially by the seller and includes an offer to purchase under a contract for deed or mortgage. An equivalent cash offer is not required to be made if the state participates in an offer to a third party through the Rural Finance Authority.

(e) This subdivision applies to a seller when the property is sold and to a lessor each time the property is leased, for the time period specified in section 500.24, subdivision 2, paragraph (v), after the agricultural land is acquired except:

(1) an offer to lease to the immediately preceding former owner is required only until the immediately preceding owner fails to accept an offer to lease the property or the property is sold;

(2) an offer to sell to the immediately preceding former owner is required until the property is sold; and

(3) if the immediately preceding former owner elects to lease or purchase a portion of the property, this subdivision does not apply to the seller with regard to the balance of the property after the election is made under paragraph (c).

(f) The notice of an offer under subdivision 2 that is personally delivered with a signed receipt or sent by certified mail with a receipt of mailing to the immediately preceding former owner's last known address is a good faith offer.

(g) This subdivision does not apply to a sale or lease that occurs after the seller or lessor has held the property for the time period specified in section 500.24, subdivision 2, paragraph (x).

(h) For purposes of this subdivision, if the immediately preceding former owner is a bankruptcy estate the debtor in the bankruptcy is the immediately preceding owner.

(i) The immediately preceding former owner must exercise the right to lease all or a portion of the agricultural land or a homestead located on agricultural land in writing within 15 days after an offer to lease under this subdivision is mailed with a receipt of mailing or personally delivered. If election is made to lease only the homestead or a portion of the agricultural land, the portion to be leased must be clearly identified in writing. The immediately preceding former owner must exercise the right to buy the agricultural land, a portion of the agricultural land, or a farm homestead located on agricultural land, in writing, within 65 days after an offer to buy under this subdivision is mailed with a receipt of mailing or is personally delivered. Within ten days after exercising the right to lease or buy by accepting the offer, the immediately preceding owner must fully perform according to the terms of the offer including paying the amounts due. A seller may sell and a lessor may lease the agricultural land or farm homestead subject to this subdivision to the third party in accordance with their lease or purchase agreement if:

(1) the immediately preceding former owner does not accept an offer to lease or buy before the offer terminates; or

(2) the immediately preceding former owner does not perform the obligations of the offer, including paying the amounts due, within ten days after accepting the offer.

(j) A certificate indicating whether or not the property contains agricultural land or a farm homestead that is signed by the county assessor where the property is located and recorded in the office of the county recorder or the registrar of titles where the property is located is prima facie evidence of whether the property is agricultural land or a farm homestead.

(k) As prima facie evidence that an offer to sell or lease agricultural land or a farm homestead has terminated, a receipt of mailing the notice under subdivision 2 and an affidavit, signed by a person authorized to act on behalf of a state, federal agency, or corporation selling or leasing the agricultural land or a farm homestead may be filed in the office of the county recorder or registrar of titles of the county where the agricultural land or farm homestead is located. The affidavit must state that:

(1) notice of an offer to buy or lease the agricultural land or farm homestead was provided to the immediately preceding former owner at a price not higher than the highest price offered by a third party that is acceptable;

(2) the time during which the immediately preceding former owner is required to exercise the right to buy or lease the agricultural land or farm homestead has expired;

(3) the immediately preceding former owner has not exercised the right to buy or lease the agricultural land or farm homestead as provided in this subdivision or has accepted an offer and has not fully performed according to the terms of the offer; and

(4) the offer to the immediately preceding former owner has terminated.

(*l*) The right of an immediately preceding former owner to receive an offer to lease or purchase agricultural land under this subdivision or to lease or purchase at a price no higher than the highest price offered by a third party that is acceptable to the seller or lessor may be extinguished or limited by an express statement signed by the immediately preceding owner that complies with the plain language requirements of section 325G.31. The right may not be extinguished or limited except by:

(1) an express statement in a deed in lieu of foreclosure of the agricultural land;

(2) an express statement in a deed in lieu of a termination of a contract for deed for the agricultural land;

(3) an express statement conveying the right to the state or federal agency or corporation owning the agricultural land that is required to make an offer under this subdivision; however, the preceding former owner may rescind the conveyance by notifying the state or federal agency or corporation in writing within 20 calendar days after signing the express statement;

(4) to cure a title defect, an express statement conveying the right may be made to a person to whom the agricultural land has been transferred by the state or federal agency or corporation; or

(5) an express statement conveying the right to a contract for deed vendee to whom the agricultural land or farm homestead was sold under a contract for deed by the immediately preceding former owner if the express statement and the contract for deed are recorded.

(m) The right of an immediately preceding former owner to receive an offer to lease or purchase agricultural land under this subdivision may not be assigned or transferred except as provided in paragraph (*l*), but may be inherited.

(n) An immediately preceding former owner, except a former owner who is actively engaged in farming as defined in section 500.24, subdivision 2, paragraph (a), and who agrees to remain actively engaged in farming on a portion of the agricultural land or farm homestead for at least one year after accepting an offer under this subdivision, may not sell agricultural land acquired by accepting an offer under this subdivision if the arrangement of the sale was negotiated or agreed to prior to the former owner accepting the offer under this subdivision. A person who sells property in violation of this paragraph is liable for damages plus reasonable attorney fees to a person who is damaged by a sale in violation of this paragraph. There is a rebuttable presumption that a sale by an immediately preceding former owner is in violation of this paragraph if the sale takes place within 270 days of the former owner accepting the offer under this subdivision. This paragraph does not apply to a sale by an immediately preceding former owner to the owner's spouse, the owner's parents, the owner's sisters and brothers, the owner's spouse's sisters and brothers, or the owner's children.

Subd. 2. Notice of offer. (a) The state, a federal agency, limited partnership, corporation, or limited liability company subject to subdivision 1 must provide a notice of an offer to sell or lease agricultural land substantially as follows, after inserting the appropriate terms within the parentheses:

"NOTICE OF OFFER TO (LEASE, BUY) AGRICULTURAL LAND

TO: (...Immediately preceding former owner...)
FROM: (...The state, federal agency, limited partnership, corporation, or limited
          liability company subject to subdivision 1...)
DATE: (...date notice is mailed or personally delivered...)

(...The state, federal agency, limited partnership, corporation, or limited liability company...) HAS ACQUIRED THE AGRICULTURAL LAND DESCRIBED BELOW AND HAS RECEIVED AN ACCEPTABLE OFFER TO (LEASE, SELL) THE AGRICULTURAL LAND FROM ANOTHER PARTY. UNDER MINNESOTA STATUTES, SECTION 500.245, SUBDIVISION 1, AN OFFER FROM (...the state, federal agency, limited partnership, corporation, or limited liability company...) MUST BE MADE TO YOU AT A PRICE NO HIGHER THAN THE HIGHEST OFFER MADE BY ANOTHER PARTY.

THE AGRICULTURAL LAND BEING OFFERED CONTAINS APPROXIMATELY (...approximate number of acres...) ACRES AND IS INFORMALLY DESCRIBED AS FOLLOWS:

(Informal description of the agricultural land being offered that reasonably describes the land. This description does not need to be a legal description.)

(...The state, federal agency, limited partnership, corporation, or limited liability company...) OFFERS TO (SELL, LEASE) THE AGRICULTURAL LAND DESCRIBED ABOVE FOR A CASH PRICE OF $(...cash price or equivalent cash price for lease and lease period, or cash price or equivalent cash price for sale of land...), WHICH IS NOT HIGHER THAN THE PRICE OFFERED BY ANOTHER PARTY. THE PRICE IS OFFERED ON THE FOLLOWING TERMS:

(Terms, if any, of acceptable offer)

IF YOU WANT TO ACCEPT THIS OFFER YOU MUST NOTIFY (...the state, federal agency, limited partnership, corporation, or limited liability company...) IN WRITING THAT YOU ACCEPT THE OFFER OR SIGN UNDERNEATH THE FOLLOWING PARAGRAPH AND RETURN A COPY OF THIS NOTICE BY (15 for a lease, 65 for a sale) DAYS AFTER THIS NOTICE IS PERSONAL-LY DELIVERED OR MAILED TO YOU. THE OFFER IN THIS NOTICE TERMINATES ON (...date of termination – 15 days for lease and 65 days for sale after date of mailing or personal delivery...)

ACCEPTANCE OF OFFER

I ACCEPT THE OFFER TO (BUY, LEASE) THE AGRICULTURAL LAND DESCRIBED ABOVE AT THE PRICE OFFERED TO ME IN THIS NOTICE. AS PART OF ACCEPTING THIS OFFER I WILL PERFORM ACCORDING TO THE TERMS OF THE OFFER, INCLUDING MAKING PAYMENTS DUE UNDER THE OFFER, WITHIN TEN DAYS AFTER THE DATE I ACCEPT THIS OFFER. I UNDERSTAND THAT NEGOTIATING OR AGREEING TO AN ARRANGEMENT TO SELL THE AGRICULTURAL LAND TO ANOTHER PER-SON PRIOR TO ACCEPTING THIS OFFER MAY BE A VIOLATION OF LAW AND I MAY BE LIABLE TO A PERSON DAMAGED BY THE SALE.

....
Signature of Former Owner Accepting Offer
....
Date"

IMPORTANT NOTICE

ANY ACTION FOR THE RECOVERY OF THE AGRICULTURAL LAND DESCRIBED ABOVE OR ANY ACTION FOR DAMAGES, EXCEPT FOR DAM-AGES FOR FRAUD, REGARDING THIS OFFER MUST BE COMMENCED BY A LAWSUIT BEFORE THE EXPIRATION OF THREE YEARS AFTER THIS LAND IS SOLD TO ANOTHER PARTY. UPON FILING A LAWSUIT, YOU MUST ALSO FILE A NOTICE OF LIS PENDENS WITH THE COUNTY RECORDER OR REGISTRAR OF TITLES IN THE COUNTY WHERE THE LAND IS LOCATED.

(b) For an offer to sell, a copy of the purchase agreement containing the price and terms of the highest offer made by a third party that is acceptable to the seller and a signed affidavit by the seller affirming that the purchase agreement is true, accurate, and made in good faith must be included with the notice under this subdivision. At the seller's discretion, reference to the third party's identity may be deleted from the copy of the purchase agreement.

(c) For an offer to lease, a copy of the lease containing the price and terms of the highest offer made by a third party that is acceptable to the lessor and a signed affidavit by the lessor affirming that the lease is true, accurate, and made in good faith must be included with the notice under this subdivision. At the lessor's discretion, reference to the third party's identity may be deleted from the copy of the lease agreement.

(d) The affidavit under paragraphs (b) and (c) is subject to section 609.48.

Subd. 3. Failure to bring action. An action for the recovery of title to or possession of real property or any right in the property or any action for damages, except for damages for fraud, based upon a failure to comply with the requirements of subdivision 1 or 2 must be commenced, and a notice of lis pendens filed with the county recorder or registrar of titles in the county where the real property is located, within three years after the conveyance on which the action is based was recorded with the county recorder or registrar of titles.

Amended by Laws 1999, c. 86, art. 1, § 75; Laws 2000, c. 477, §§ 73, 74, eff. May 16, 2000.

500.25. Rights of farm tenants on termination of life estates

Subdivision 1. Definition. For the purposes of this section, "farm tenancy" is a tenancy involving 40 or more acres of tillable land or crop land rented for agricultural purposes.

Subd. 2. Continuation of tenancy. Upon the death of a life tenant between March 2 and the following October 31, a farm tenancy granted by the life tenant shall continue until the earlier of the following March 1, the completion of harvest, or the expiration of the lease by its terms. If a life tenant dies between November 1 and the following March 1, the farm tenancy shall continue for the following crop year and shall terminate on the earlier of the March 1 following that crop year, the completion of harvest, or the expiration of the lease by its terms. However, if the lease is binding upon the remainderperson by specific commitment of the remainderperson, the lease shall terminate as provided by that commitment.

Subd. 3. Rental value. A remainderperson who is required by subdivision 2 to continue a tenancy shall be entitled to a rental amount equal to the prevailing fair market rental amount in the area. If the parties cannot agree on a rental amount, either party may petition the district court for a declaratory judgment setting the rental amount. The costs of the action shall be apportioned between the parties by the court.

Laws 1981, c. 370, § 1. Amended by Laws 1986, c. 444.

Historical and Statutory Notes

Section 2 of Laws 1981, c. 370 provides that this act is effective for leases entered into after November 1, 1982.

500.30. Solar or wind easements

Section effective until June 1, 2010. See, also, section effective June 1, 2010.

Subdivision 1. Solar easement. "Solar easement" means a right, whether or not stated in the form of a restriction, easement, covenant, or condition, in any deed, will, or other instrument executed by or on behalf of any owner of land or solar skyspace for the purpose of ensuring adequate exposure of a solar energy system as defined in section 216C.06, subdivision 17, to solar energy.

Subd. 1a. Wind easement. "Wind easement" means a right, whether or not stated in the form of a restriction, easement, covenant, or condition, in any deed, will, or other instrument executed by or on behalf of any owner of land or air space for the purpose of ensuring adequate exposure of a wind power system to the winds.

Text of subdivision 2 effective until June 1, 2010.

Subd. 2. Like any conveyance. Any property owner may grant a solar or wind easement in the same manner and with the same effect as a conveyance of an interest in real property. The easements shall be created in writing and shall be filed, duly recorded, and indexed in the office of the recorder of the county in which the easement is granted. No duly recorded easement shall be unenforceable on account of lack of privity of estate or privity of contract; such easements shall run with the land or lands benefited and burdened and shall constitute a perpetual easement, except that an easement may terminate upon the conditions stated therein or pursuant to the provisions of section 500.20. A wind easement, easement to install wind turbines on real property, option, or lease of wind rights shall also terminate after seven years from the date the easement is created or lease is entered into, if a wind energy project on the property to which the easement or lease applies does not begin commercial operation within the seven-year period.

Text of subdivision 2 effective June 1, 2010.

Subd. 2. Like any conveyance. Any property owner may grant a solar or wind easement in the same manner and with the same effect as a conveyance of an interest in real property. The easements shall be created in writing and shall be filed, duly recorded, and indexed in the office of the recorder of the county in which the easement is granted. No duly recorded easement shall be unenforceable on account of lack of privity of estate or privity of contract; such easements shall run with the land or lands benefited and burdened and shall constitute a perpetual easement, except that an easement may terminate upon the conditions stated therein or pursuant to the provisions of section 500.20.

Subd. 3. Required contents. Any deed, will, or other instrument that creates a solar or wind easement shall include, but the contents are not limited to:

(a) a description of the real property subject to the easement and a description of the real property benefiting from the solar or wind easement; and

(b) for solar easements, a description of the vertical and horizontal angles, expressed in degrees and measured from the site of the solar energy system, at which the solar easement extends over the real property subject to the easement, or any other description which defines the three dimensional space, or the place and times of day in which an obstruction to direct sunlight is prohibited or limited;

(c) a description of the vertical and horizontal angles, expressed in degrees, and distances from the site of the wind power system in which an obstruction to the winds is prohibited or limited;

(d) any terms or conditions under which the easement is granted or may be terminated;

(e) any provisions for compensation of the owner of the real property benefiting from the easement in the event of interference with the enjoyment of the easement, or compensation of the owner of the real property subject to the easement for maintaining the easement;

(f) any other provisions necessary or desirable to execute the instrument.

Subd. 4. Enforcement. A solar or wind easement may be enforced by injunction or proceedings in equity or other civil action.

Subd. 5. Depreciation, not appreciation counted for taxes. Any depreciation caused by any solar or wind easement which is imposed upon designated property, but not any appreciation caused by any easement which benefits designated property, shall be included in the net tax capacity of the property for property tax purposes.

Laws 1978, c. 786, § 21, eff. April 6, 1978. Amended by Laws 1981, c. 356, § 248; Laws 1982, c. 563, § 16; Laws 1988, c. 719, art. 5, § 84; Laws 1989, c. 329, art. 13, § 20, eff. June 2, 1989; Laws 2007, c. 136, art. 4, § 15, eff. May 26, 2007; Laws 2008, c. 296, art. 1, § 25, eff. June 1, 2010.

Historical and Statutory Notes

Laws 2007, c. 136, art. 4, § 15, the effective date portion, provides that the amendment of subd. 2 is effective May 26, 2007, and applies to wind easements created and wind rights leases entered into on and after May 26, 2007.

Chapter 501A

STATUTORY RULE AGAINST PERPETUITIES

For complete statutory history see Minnesota Statutes Annotated.

501A.01. When nonvested interest, powers of appointment are invalid; exceptions

(a) A nonvested property interest is invalid unless:

(1) when the interest is created, it is certain to vest or terminate no later than 21 years after the death of an individual then alive; or

(2) the interest either vests or terminates within 90 years after its creation.

(b) A general power of appointment not presently exercisable because of a condition precedent is invalid unless:

(1) when the power is created, the condition precedent is certain to be satisfied or become impossible to satisfy no later than 21 years after the death of an individual then alive; or

(2) the condition precedent either is satisfied or becomes impossible to satisfy within 90 years after its creation.

(c) A nongeneral power of appointment or a general testamentary power of appointment is invalid unless:

(1) when the power is created, it is certain to be irrevocably exercised or otherwise to terminate no later than 21 years after the death of an individual then alive; or

(2) the power is irrevocably exercised or otherwise terminates within 90 years after its creation.

(d) In determining whether a nonvested property interest or a power of appointment is valid under paragraph (a), clause (1), paragraph (b), clause (1), or paragraph (c), clause (1), the possibility that a child will be born to an individual after the individual's death is disregarded.

(e) If, in measuring a period from the creation of a trust or other property arrangement, language in a governing instrument seeks to:

(1) disallow the vesting or termination of any interest trust beyond;

(2) postpone the vesting or termination of any interest or trust until; or

(3) operate in effect in any similar fashion upon,

the later of the expiration of a period of time not exceeding 21 years after the death of the survivor of specified lives in being at the creation of the trust or other property arrangement, or the expiration of a period of time that exceeds or might exceed 21 years after the death of the survivor of lives in being at the creation of the trust or other property arrangement;

that language is inoperative to the extent it produces a period of time that exceeds 21 years after the death of the survivor of the specified lives.

Laws 1987, c. 60, § 1. Amended by Laws 2002, c. 347, § 1.

UNIFORM STATUTORY RULE AGAINST PERPETUITIES

Table of Jurisdictions Wherein Act Has Been Adopted

For text of Uniform Act, and variation notes and annotation materials for adopting jurisdictions, see Uniform Laws Annotated, Master Edition, Volume 8B.

Jurisdiction	Laws	Effective Date	Statutory Citation
Alaska	1994, c. 82	1–1–1996	AS 34.27.050 to 34.27.100.
Arizona	1994, c. 290	After 12–31–1994	A.R.S. §§ 14–2901 to 14–2906.
Arkansas	2007, c. 240	3–9–2007	A.C.A. §§ 18–3–101 to 18–3–109.
California	1991, c. 156	7–22–1991 *	West's Ann.Cal.Probate Code, §§ 21200 to 21231.
Colorado	1991, c. 315	5–31–1991	West's C.R.S.A. §§ 15–11–1101 to 15–11–1107.
Connecticut	1989, P.A. No. 89–44	5–2–1989 *	C.G.S.A. §§ 45a–490 to 45a–496.
District of Columbia	2001, D.C. Law 13–292	4–27–2001	D.C. Official Code, 2001 Ed. §§ 19–901 to 19–907.
Florida	1988, c. 88–40	10–1–1988	West's F.S.A. § 689.225.
Georgia	1990, p. 1837	5–1–1990	O.C.G.A. §§ 44–6–200 to 44–6–206.
Hawaii	1992, Act 262	6–18–1992	HRS §§ 525–1 to 525–6.
Indiana	2002, P.L. 2–2002	7–1–2002	West's A.I.C. 32–17–8–1 to 32–17–8–6.
Kansas	1992, c. 302	5–22–1992 *	K.S.A. 59–3401 to 59–3408.
Massachusetts	1989, c. 668	6–30–1990	M.G.L.A. c. 184A, §§ 1 to 11.
Michigan	1988, P.A. 418	12–24–1988	M.C.L.A. §§ 554.71 to 554.78.
Minnesota	1987, c. 60	1–1–1991	M.S.A. §§ 501A.01 to 501A.07.
Montana	1989, c. 250	10–1–1989	MCA 72–2–1001 to 72–2–1007.
Nebraska	1989, LB377	8–25–1989	R.R.S. 1943, §§ 76–2001 to 76–2008.
Nevada	1987, c. 25	3–17–1987 *	N.R.S. 111.103 to 111.1039.
New Jersey	1999, c. 159	7–8–1999 *	N.J.S.A. 46:2F–9 to 46:2F–11.
New Mexico	1992, c. 66	7–1–1992	NMSA 1978, §§ 45–2–901 to 45–2–906.
North Carolina	1995, c. 190	10–1–1995	G.S. §§ 41–15 to 41–23.
North Dakota	1991, c. 484	7–1–1991	NDCC 47–02–27.1 to 47–02–27.5.
Oregon	1989, c. 208	1–1–1990	ORS 105.950 to 105.975.

Jurisdiction	Laws	Effective Date	Statutory Citation
South Carolina	1987, No. 12	3–12–1987	Code 1976, §§ 27–6–10 to 27–6–80.
Tennessee............	1994, c. 654	7–1–1994	T.C.A. §§ 66–1–201 to 66–1–208.
Virginia	2000, c. 714	7-1-2000	Code 1950, §§ 55–12.1 to 55–12.6.
West Virginia	1992, c. 74	90 days from 2–10–1992	Code, 36–1A–1 to 36–1A–8.

* Date of approval.

Historical and Statutory Notes

Laws 1987, c. 60, § 10 provides that this section takes effect August 1, 1988. But see 1988 and 1989 legislation notes, post.

Laws 1988, c. 482, § 2 amended Laws 1987, c. 60, § 10 to provide that this section takes effect January 1, 1990. But see 1989 legislation note, post.

Laws 1989, c. 340, art. 3, § 2 amended Laws 1987, c. 60, § 10 as amended by Laws 1988, c. 482, § 2 to provide that this section takes effect January 1, 1991.

501A.02. When nonvested property interest or power of appointment created

(a) Except as provided in subsections (b) and (c) and in section 501A.05, subsection (a), the time of creation of a nonvested property interest or a power of appointment is determined under general principles of property law.

(b) For purposes of sections 501A.01 to 501A.07, if there is a person who alone can exercise a power created by a governing instrument to become the unqualified beneficial owner of (i) a nonvested property interest or (ii) a property interest subject to a power of appointment described in section 501A.01, subsection (b) or (c), the nonvested property interest or power of appointment is created when the power to become the unqualified beneficial owner terminates.

(c) For purposes of sections 501A.01 to 501A.07, a nonvested property interest or a power of appointment arising from a transfer of property to a previously funded trust or other existing property arrangement is created when the nonvested property interest or power of appointment in the original contribution was created.

Laws 1987, c. 60, § 2.

Historical and Statutory Notes

Laws 1987, c. 60, § 10 provides that this section takes effect August 1, 1988. But see 1988 and 1989 legislation notes, post.

Laws 1988, c. 482, § 2 amended Laws 1987, c. 60, § 10 to provide that this section takes effect January 1, 1990. But see 1989 legislation note, post.

Laws 1989, c. 340, art. 3, § 2 amended Laws 1987, c. 60, § 10 as amended by Laws 1988, c. 482, § 2 to provide that this section takes effect January 1, 1991.

501A.03. Reformation

Upon the petition of an interested person, a court shall reform a disposition in the manner that most closely approximates the transferor's manifested plan of distribution and is within the 90 years allowed by section 501A.01, subsection (a)(2), (b)(2), or (c)(2) if:

(1) a nonvested property interest or a power of appointment becomes invalid under section 501A.01 (statutory rule against perpetuities);

(2) a class gift is not but might become invalid under section 501A.01 (statutory rule against perpetuities) and the time has arrived when the share of any class member is to take effect in possession or enjoyment; or

(3) a nonvested property interest that is not validated by section 501A.01, subsection (a)(1) can vest but not within 90 years after its creation.

Laws 1987, c. 60, § 3.

Historical and Statutory Notes

Laws 1987, c. 60, § 10 provides that this section takes effect August 1, 1988. But see 1988 and 1989 legislation notes, post.

Laws 1988, c. 482, § 2 amended Laws 1987, c. 60, § 10 to provide that this section takes effect January 1, 1990. But see 1989 legislation note, post.

Laws 1989, c. 340, art. 3, § 2 amended Laws 1987, c. 60, § 10 as amended by Laws 1988, c. 482, § 2 to provide that this section takes effect January 1, 1991.

501A.04. Exclusions from statutory rule

Section 501A.01 (statutory rule against perpetuities) does not apply to:

(1) a nonvested property interest or a power of appointment arising out of a nondonative transfer, except a nonvested property interest or a power of appointment arising out of (i) a premarital or postmarital agreement, (ii) a separation or divorce settlement, (iii) a spouse's election, (iv) a similar arrangement arising out of a prospective, existing, or previous marital relationship between the parties, (v) a contract to make or not to revoke a will or trust, (vi) a contract to exercise or not to exercise a power of appointment, (vii) a transfer in satisfaction of a duty of support, or (viii) a reciprocal transfer;

(2) a fiduciary's power relating to the administration or management of assets, including the power of a fiduciary to sell, lease, or mortgage property, and the power of a fiduciary to determine principal and income;

(3) a power to appoint a fiduciary;

(4) a discretionary power of a trustee to distribute principal before termination of a trust to a beneficiary having an indefeasibly vested interest in the income and principal;

(5) a nonvested property interest held by a charity, government, or governmental agency or subdivision, if the nonvested property interest is preceded by an interest held by another charity, government, or governmental agency or subdivision;

(6) a nonvested property interest in or a power of appointment with respect to a trust or other property arrangement forming part of a pension, profit sharing, stock bonus, health, disability, death benefit, income deferral, or other

178

current or deferred benefit plan for one or more employees, independent contractors, or their beneficiaries or spouses, to which contributions are made for the purpose of distributing to or for the benefit of the participants or their beneficiaries or spouses the property, income, or principal in the trust or other property arrangement, except a nonvested property interest or a power of appointment that is created by an election of a participant or a beneficiary or spouse; or

(7) a property interest, power of appointment, or arrangement that was not subject to the common law rule against perpetuities or is excluded by another statute of this state.

Laws 1987, c. 60, § 4.

Historical and Statutory Notes

Laws 1987, c. 60, § 10 provides that this section takes effect August 1, 1988. But see 1988 and 1989 legislation notes, post.

Laws 1988, c. 482, § 2 amended Laws 1987, c. 60, § 10 to provide that this section takes effect January 1, 1990. But see 1989 legislation note, post.

Laws 1989, c. 340, art. 3, § 2 amended Laws 1987, c. 60, § 10 as amended by Laws 1988, c. 482, § 2 to provide that this section takes effect January 1, 1991.

501A.05. Prospective application

(a) Except as extended by subsection (b), sections 501A.01 to 501A.07 apply to a nonvested property interest or a power of appointment that is created after December 31, 1991. For purposes of this section, a nonvested property interest or a power of appointment created by the exercise of a power of appointment is created when the power is irrevocably exercised or when a revocable exercise becomes irrevocable.

(b) If a nonvested property interest or a power of appointment was created before January 1, 1992, and is determined in a judicial proceeding, commenced after December 31, 1991, to violate this state's rule against perpetuities as that rule existed before January 1, 1992, a court upon the petition of an interested person may reform the disposition in the manner that most closely approximates the transferor's manifested plan of distribution and is within the limits of the rule against perpetuities applicable when the nonvested property interest or power of appointment was created.

Laws 1987, c. 60, § 5. Amended by Laws 1988, c. 482, § 1; Laws 1989, c. 340, art. 3, § 1; Laws 1990, c. 581, § 1.

Historical and Statutory Notes

Laws 1987, c. 60, § 8 provides:

"Where used in sections 1 to 7 [enacting §§ 501A.01 to 501A.07] the term 'this act' refers to sections 1 to 7."

Laws 1987, c. 60, § 10 provides that this section takes effect August 1, 1988. But see 1988 and 1989 legislation notes, post.

Laws 1988, c. 482, § 2 amended Laws 1987, c. 60, § 10 to provide that this section takes effect January 1, 1990. But see 1989 legislation note, post.

Laws 1989, c. 340, art. 3, § 2 amended Laws 1987, c. 60, § 10 as amended by Laws 1988, c.

482, § 2 to provide that this section takes effect January 1, 1991.

Laws 1990, c. 581, § 9, provides in part that, except as otherwise provided, this act is effective January 1, 1990, and applies to trusts, property interests, and powers of appointment whenever created to the extent permitted under the United States Constitution and the Minnesota Constitution.

501A.06. Supersedes common law rule

Sections 501A.01 to 501A.07 supersede the rule of the common law known as the rule against perpetuities.

Laws 1987, c. 60, § 6. Amended by Laws 1989, c. 340, art. 2, § 2, eff. Jan. 1, 1990.

Historical and Statutory Notes

Laws 1987, c. 60, § 10 provides that this section takes effect August 1, 1988. But see 1988 and 1989 legislation notes, post.

Laws 1988, c. 482, § 2 amended Laws 1987, c. 60, § 10 to provide that this section takes effect January 1, 1990. But see 1989 legislation note, post.

Laws 1989, c. 340, art. 2, § 2 provides that this amendment is effective January 1, 1990.

501A.07. Short title

Sections 501A.01 to 501A.07 may be cited as the Uniform Statutory Rule Against Perpetuities.

Laws 1987, c. 60, § 7.

Historical and Statutory Notes

Laws 1987, c. 60, § 10 provides that this section takes effect August 1, 1988. But see 1988 and 1989 legislation notes, post.

Laws 1988, c. 482, § 2 amended Laws 1987, c. 60, § 10 to provide that this section takes effect January 1, 1990. But see 1989 legislation note, post.

Laws 1989, c. 340, art. 3, § 2 amended Laws 1987, c. 60, § 10 as amended by Laws 1988, c. 482, § 2 to provide that this section takes effect January 1, 1991.

Chapter 501B

TRUSTS

GENERAL PROVISIONS

182

For complete statutory history see Minnesota Statutes Annotated.

GENERAL PROVISIONS

501B.01. Purposes for which express trusts may be created

An active express trust may be created for any lawful purpose.

Laws 1989, c. 340, art. 1, § 1.

Historical and Statutory Notes

Laws 1989, c. 340, art. 1, § 76 provides:

"Except as required by section 645.35 or as otherwise provided in sections 47 [section 501B.55], 60 [section 501B.71], 62 [section 501B.73], 70 [section 501B.86], subdivision 9, and 72 [section 501B.88], this article is effective January 1, 1990, and applies to trusts, property interests, and powers of appointment whenever created to the extent permitted under the United States Constitution and the Minnesota Constitution."

501B.012. Memorial fund

Subdivision 1. Establishment. A trust may be created for the purpose of establishing a fund for the benefit of one or more individuals with a single transfer under the Minnesota Uniform Custodial Trust Act in the manner and form provided by section 529.17. A trust authorized under this section must be created and administered and is subject to the Minnesota Uniform Custodial Trust Act.

Subd. 2. Additional funds. Notwithstanding subdivision 1, after a fund has been created, additional funds may be transferred to the fund without the formalities required by chapter 529 if the transferor manifests a reasonable expression of intent to make the transfer, together with a reasonable form of delivery of the property including, but not limited to, the following:

(1) a check payable to the name of the fund and delivered to the trustee or the trustee's custodial agent;

(2) delivery of cash or tangible personal property to the trustee or to the trustee's custodial agent;

(3) delivery and recording of title of stock or other registered security in the name of the fund;

(4) delivery of a deed and acceptance of the deed by the trustee of the fund, or the recording of a deed in the name of the trustee of the fund with the applicable county recorder or registrar of titles for real property; and

(5) any other means of transfer and delivery so that a reasonable person would conclude that the transferor intended the property be titled in the name of, and used for the benefit of the beneficiaries of, the fund.

Laws 2004, c. 146, art. 1, § 1.

501B.02. Passive trusts abolished

Passive express trusts of real or personal property are abolished. An attempt to create a passive trust vests the entire estate granted in the beneficiary.

Laws 1989, c. 340, art. 1, § 2.

Historical and Statutory Notes

Laws 1989, c. 340, art. 1, § 76 provides:

"Except as required by section 645.35 or as otherwise provided in sections 47 [section 501B.55], 60 [section 501B.71], 62 [section 501B.73], 70 [section 501B.86], subdivision 9, and 72 [section 501B.88], this article is effective January 1, 1990, and applies to trusts, property interests, and powers of appointment whenever created to the extent permitted under the United States Constitution and the Minnesota Constitution."

501B.03. Termination of trust purposes

If the purposes for which an active express trust is created have been accomplished, or become impossible of accomplishment or illegal, the trust will be terminated.

Laws 1989, c. 340, art. 1, § 3.

Historical and Statutory Notes

Laws 1989, c. 340, art. 1, § 76 provides:

"Except as required by section 645.35 or as otherwise provided in sections 47 [section 501B.55], 60 [section 501B.71], 62 [section 501B.73], 70 [section 501B.86], subdivision 9, and 72 [section 501B.88], this article is effective January 1, 1990, and applies to trusts, property interests, and powers of appointment whenever created to the extent permitted under the United States Constitution and the Minnesota Constitution."

501B.04. Reversion in grantor

Every legal estate and interest not embraced in an express trust and not otherwise disposed of remains in the grantor.

Laws 1989, c. 340, art. 1, § 4.

Historical and Statutory Notes

Laws 1989, c. 340, art. 1, § 76 provides:

"Except as required by section 645.35 or as otherwise provided in sections 47 [section 501B.55], 60 [section 501B.71], 62 [section 501B.73], 70 [section 501B.86], subdivision 9, and 72 [section 501B.88], this article is effective January 1, 1990, and applies to trusts, property interests, and powers of appointment whenever created to the extent permitted under the United States Constitution and the Minnesota Constitution."

501B.05. Bona fide purchasers protected

An express trust not declared in the disposition to the trustee or a constructive or resulting trust does not defeat the title of a purchaser from the trustee for value and without notice of the trust, or the rights of a creditor who extended credit to the trustee in reliance upon the trustee's apparent ownership of the trust property.

Laws 1989, c. 340, art. 1, § 5.

Historical and Statutory Notes

Laws 1989, c. 340, art. 1, § 76 provides:

"Except as required by section 645.35 or as otherwise provided in sections 47 [section 501B.55], 60 [section 501B.71], 62 [section 501B.73], 70 [section 501B.86], subdivision 9, and 72 [section 501B.88], this article is effective January 1, 1990, and applies to trusts, property interests, and powers of appointment whenever created to the extent permitted under the United States Constitution and the Minnesota Constitution."

501B.06. Misapplication of payment to trustee

A person who actually and in good faith makes a payment to a trustee that the trustee, as such, is authorized to receive, is not responsible for the proper application of the payment according to the trust. No right or title derived by the person from the trustee, in consideration of the payment, may be impeached or called in question because of a misapplication of the payment by the trustee.

Laws 1989, c. 340, art. 1, § 6.

Historical and Statutory Notes

Laws 1989, c. 340, art. 1, § 76 provides:

"Except as required by section 645.35 or as otherwise provided in sections 47 [section 501B.55], 60 [section 501B.71], 62 [section 501B.73], 70 [section 501B.86], subdivision 9, and 72 [section 501B.88], this article is effective January 1, 1990, and applies to trusts, property interests, and powers of appointment whenever created to the extent permitted under the United States Constitution and the Minnesota Constitution."

501B.07. Purchase money resulting trusts

If a transfer of property is made to one person and the purchase price is paid by another, a resulting trust is presumed to arise in favor of the person by whom the purchase price is paid, except:

(1) if the person by whom the purchase price is paid manifests a contrary intention, no resulting trust is presumed to arise;

(2) if the transferee is a spouse, child, or other natural object of bounty of the payor, a gift in favor of the transferee is presumed and no resulting trust is presumed to arise; and

(3) if the transfer is made to accomplish an illegal purpose, no resulting trust is presumed to arise unless it is needed to prevent unjust enrichment of the transferee.

Laws 1989, c. 340, art. 1, § 7.

Historical and Statutory Notes

Laws 1989, c. 340, art. 1, § 76 provides:

"Except as required by section 645.35 or as otherwise provided in sections 47 [section 501B.55], 60 [section 501B.71], 62 [section 501B.73], 70 [section 501B.86], subdivision 9, and 72 [section 501B.88], this article is effective January 1, 1990, and applies to trusts, property interests, and powers of appointment whenever created to the extent permitted under the United States Constitution and the Minnesota Constitution."

501B.08. Appointment of and acquisition of title by successor trustees and confirmation of acts performed during vacancies in trusteeship

If the terms of a trust provide for the appointment of a successor trustee and direct how the successor is to qualify, title to the trust assets vests in the successor trustee upon qualification, unless the terms of the trust expressly provide otherwise.

If the terms of a trust do not effectively provide for the appointment of a successor trustee and appointment of a successor is required, or if title to the trust assets does not vest in a successor trustee, the district court may appoint a successor trustee or vest title in a successor trustee.

Whenever the district court appoints a successor trustee, it is presumed that a corporate trustee must be replaced by another corporate trustee unless the court finds it would best serve the interests of all the beneficiaries and is not inconsistent with a material purpose of the trust to not appoint a corporate trustee.

The district court may confirm an act performed by a person in execution of the trust while there was no acting trustee.

Laws 1989, c. 340, art. 1, § 8. Amended by Laws 2004, c. 146, art. 1, § 2.

Historical and Statutory Notes

Laws 1989, c. 340, art. 1, § 76 provides:

"Except as required by section 645.35 or as otherwise provided in sections 47 [section 501B.55], 60 [section 501B.71], 62 [section 501B.73], 70 [section 501B.86], subdivision 9, and 72 [section 501B.88], this article is effective January 1, 1990, and applies to trusts, property interests, and powers of appointment whenever created to the extent permitted under the United States Constitution and the Minnesota Constitution."

501B.09. Suspension of the power of alienation

Subdivision 1. Suspension; exceptions. The power of alienation is suspended if there are no persons in being who, alone or in conjunction with others, can convey an absolute fee in possession or absolute ownership of real property or absolute ownership of personal property.

(a) There is no suspension of the power of alienation by the terms of a trust or by interests in property held in trust if there is an unlimited power in one or more persons then in being to terminate the trust, by revocation or otherwise, and to acquire an absolute fee in possession or absolute ownership of the trust property.

(b) There is no suspension of the power of alienation by the terms of a trust or by interests in property held in trust if the trustee has power to sell an absolute fee in possession or absolute ownership of the trust property.

Subd. 2. Suspension for 21 years. The power of alienation of property held in trust may be suspended, by the terms of the trust, for a period of not more than 21 years. During any period of suspension of the power of alienation of real property, section 501B.46 applies. Notwithstanding any contrary term of a trust, suspension of the power of alienation by the terms of a trust ceases after a period of 21 years, after which the trustee has the power to convey an absolute fee in possession or absolute ownership of the trust property, and to mortgage, pledge, and lease the same. A provision in the terms of a trust for forfeiture of the interest of a trustee or beneficiary if the trustee or beneficiary participates in or seeks to convey, mortgage, pledge, or lease trust property after the expiration of a 21-year period of suspension is void.

Subd. 2a. Inapplicable to certain trusts. Subdivision 2 does not apply to a trust if the beneficial interests in the trust are evidenced by or constitute securities within the meaning of section 2(1) of the Securities Act of 1933, title 15, United States Code, section 77(b)(1).

Subd. 3. Void future interests. Every future interest in real or personal property not held in trust is void in its creation if it might suspend the power of alienation for a period longer than a life or lives in being plus 21 years.

Laws 1989, c. 340, art. 1, § 9. Amended by Laws 1990, c. 581, § 2.

Historical and Statutory Notes

Laws 1989, c. 340, art. 1, § 76 provides:

"Except as required by section 645.35 or as otherwise provided in sections 47 [section 501B.55], 60 [section 501B.71], 62 [section 501B.73], 70 [section 501B.86], subdivision 9, and 72 [section 501B.88], this article is effective January 1, 1990, and applies to trusts, property interests, and powers of appointment whenever created to the extent permitted under the United States Constitution and the Minnesota Constitution."

Laws 1990, c. 581, § 9, provides in part that, except as otherwise provided, this act is effective January 1, 1990, and applies to trusts, property interests, and powers of appointment whenever created to the extent permitted under the United States Constitution and the Minnesota Constitution.

501B.10, 501B.11.   Repealed by Laws 1996, c. 314, § 8, eff. Jan. 1, 1997

Historical and Statutory Notes

See, now, M.S.A. §§ 501B.151, 501B.152.

501B.12.   Grantor and agents of grantor

If a trust instrument reserves to the grantor, in a nonfiduciary capacity, the control over any or all investment decisions, the trustee is not responsible for the investment decisions made by the grantor or an agent of the grantor.

Laws 1989, c. 340, art. 1, § 12.

Historical and Statutory Notes

Laws 1989, c. 340, art. 1, § 76 provides:

"Except as required by section 645.35 or as otherwise provided in sections 47 [section 501B.55], 60 [section 501B.71], 62 [section 501B.73], 70 [section 501B.86], subdivision 9, and 72 [section 501B.88], this article is effective January 1, 1990, and applies to trusts, property interests, and powers of appointment whenever created to the extent permitted under the United States Constitution and the Minnesota Constitution."

501B.13. Nonmerger of trusts

Subdivision 1. Same trustee and beneficiary. No trust is invalid or terminated, and title to trust assets is not merged, because the trustee or trustees are the same person or persons as the beneficiaries of the trust.

Subd. 2. Applicability. Subdivision 1 applies to all trusts whenever executed or created.

Laws 1992, c. 548, § 1.

501B.14. Prohibition against exercise of powers by trustee

Subdivision 1. Prohibition. No trustee may exercise or participate in the exercise of any of the following powers:

(1) any power of the trustee to make discretionary distributions of either principal or income to or for the benefit of the trustee as beneficiary, unless by the terms of the will or other written instrument those discretionary distributions are limited by an ascertainable standard relating to that trustee's health, education, maintenance, or support as described in sections 2041 and 2514 of the Internal Revenue Code of 1986, as amended through December 31, 1992; [1] or

(2) any power to make discretionary distributions of either principal or income to discharge any legal support or other obligations of the trustee to any person.

Subd. 2. Exercise of affected powers. Any power described in subdivision 1 that is conferred upon two or more trustees may be exercised by the trustee or trustees who are not disqualified under subdivision 1. If there is no trustee qualified to exercise the power, any trustee or other person interested in the trust may petition the district court pursuant to section 501B.16 to appoint an additional trustee. The district court may limit the powers of an additional trustee appointed under this subdivision to exercise the power to make discretionary distributions when no other trustee may exercise that power.

Subd. 3. Application. (a) Except as provided in paragraph (b), this section applies to any exercise of any powers of the trustee after May 14, 1993, under any trust created before, on, or after May 14, 1993, unless the terms of the trust refer specifically to this section and provide that this section does not apply.

(b) This section does not apply to a trustee:

(1) who retains or is granted an unlimited lifetime or testamentary power, exercisable in a capacity other than as trustee, to revoke the trust, or to

withdraw all of the income and principal of the trust, or to appoint all of the income and principal of the trust to the trustee individually or the trustee's estate;

(2) of a trust created on or before May 14, 1993, if the entire principal of the trust would be included in the gross estate of the trustee for federal estate tax purposes if the trustee had died on May 14, 1993, without regard to any power described in subdivision 1;

(3) of a trust created on or before May 14, 1993, if no part of the principal of the trust would be included in the gross estate of the trustee for federal estate tax purposes if the trustee had died on May 14, 1993, without exercising the power; or

(4) of a trust created on or before May 14, 1993, if (i) the trust is not exempt from generation-skipping transfer tax under chapter 13 of the Internal Revenue Code of 1986, as amended through December 31, 1992, because of Public Law 99–514, section 1433(b) to (d) [2]; (ii) there would be a taxable termination with respect to the assets held in the trust if the trustee and all beneficiaries of the trust who are assigned to the trustee's generation or a higher generation had died on May 14, 1993; and (iii) the trust would have an inclusion ratio, as defined in section 2642(c) of the Internal Revenue Code of 1986, as amended through December 31, 1992, of one with respect to the taxable termination.

(c) This section has no effect on an action taken by a trustee on or before May 14, 1993.

Laws 1993, c. 169, § 1, eff. May 15, 1993. Amended by Laws 2004, c. 146, art. 1, § 3.

[1] All text references to Internal Revenue Code sections are to Title 26 of U.S.C.A.

[2] 26 U.S.C.A. § 2601, note.

501B.15. Division and merger of trusts

Subdivision 1. Division. A trustee may, without the approval of any court, divide a trust, before or after it is funded, into two or more separate trusts if the trustee determines that dividing the trust is in the best interests of all persons interested in the trust and will not substantially impair the accomplishment of the purposes of the trust.

Subd. 2. Merger. A trustee may, without the approval of any court, merge two or more trusts having substantially similar terms and identical beneficiaries into a single trust if the trustee determines that merging the trusts is in the best interests of all persons interested in the trusts and will not substantially impair the accomplishment of the purposes of the trusts.

Subd. 3. Application. Subdivisions 1 and 2 apply to all trusts whenever executed or created.

Laws 1995, c. 130, § 2.

Historical and Statutory Notes

Laws 1989, c. 340, art. 1, § 76 provides:

"Except as required by section 645.35 or as otherwise provided in sections 47 [section 501B.55], 60 [section 501B.71], 62 [section 501B.73], 70 [section 501B.86], subdivision 9, and 72 [section 501B.88], this article is effective January 1, 1990, and applies to trusts, property interests, and powers of appointment whenever created to the extent permitted under the United States Constitution and the Minnesota Constitution."

501B.151. Investment and management of trust assets

Subdivision 1. Prudent investor rule. (a) Except as otherwise provided in paragraph (b), a trustee who invests and manages trust assets shall comply with the prudent investor rule set forth in this section.

(b) The prudent investor rule, a default rule, may be expanded, restricted, eliminated, or otherwise altered by the provisions of a trust. A trustee is not liable to a beneficiary to the extent that the trustee acted in reasonable reliance on the provisions of the trust.

Subd. 2. Standard of care; portfolio strategy; risk and return objectives. (a) A trustee shall invest and manage trust assets as a prudent investor would, by considering the purposes, terms, distribution requirements, and other circumstances of the trust. In satisfying this standard, the trustee shall exercise reasonable care, skill, and caution.

(b) A trustee's investment and management decisions respecting individual assets must be evaluated not in isolation but in the context of the trust portfolio as a whole and as a part of an overall investment strategy having risk and return objectives reasonably suited to the trust.

(c) The circumstances that a trustee may consider in making investment decisions include, without limitation, the following:

(1) general economic conditions;

(2) the possible effect of inflation;

(3) the expected tax consequences of investment decisions or strategies;

(4) the role that each investment or course of action plays within the overall trust portfolio;

(5) the expected total return from income and the appreciation of capital;

(6) other resources of the beneficiaries known to the trustee, including earning capacity;

(7) needs for liquidity, regularity of income, and preservation or appreciation of capital; and

(8) an asset's special relationship or special value, if any, to the purposes of the trust or to one or more of the beneficiaries if consistent with the trustee's duty of impartiality.

(d) A trustee may invest in any kind of property or type of investment consistent with the standards of this section.

(e) A trustee who has special skills or expertise, or is named trustee in reliance upon the trustee's representation that the trustee has special skills or expertise, has a duty to use those special skills or expertise.

Subd. 3. Diversification. A trustee shall diversify the investments of the trust unless the trustee reasonably determines that, because of special circumstances, the purposes of the trust are better served without diversifying.

Subd. 4. Duties at inception of trusteeship. Within a reasonable time after accepting a trusteeship or receiving trust assets, a trustee shall review the trust assets and make and implement decisions concerning the retention and disposition of assets, in order to bring the trust portfolio into compliance with the purposes, terms, distribution requirements, and other circumstances of the trust, and with the requirements of this section.

Subd. 5. Investment costs. In investing and managing trust assets, a trustee may only incur costs that are appropriate and reasonable in relation to the assets, the purposes of the trust, and the skills of the trustee.

Subd. 6. Reviewing compliance. Compliance with the prudent investor rule is determined in light of the facts and circumstances existing at the time of a trustee's decision or action and not by hindsight. The prudent investor rule is a test of conduct and not of resulting performance.

Subd. 7. Language invoking standard. The following terms or comparable language in the provisions of a trust, unless otherwise limited or modified, authorizes any investment or strategy permitted under this section: "investments permissible by law for investment of trust funds," "legal investments," "authorized investments," "using the judgment and care under the circumstances then prevailing that persons of prudence, discretion, and intelligence exercise in the management of their own affairs, not in regard to speculation but in regard to the permanent disposition of their funds, considering the probable income as well as the probable safety of their capital," "prudent man rule," "prudent trustee rule," "prudent person rule," and "prudent investor rule."

Subd. 8. Disposal of property. Unless the trust instrument or a court order specifically directs otherwise, a trustee need not dispose of any property, real, personal, or mixed, or any kind of investment, in the trust, however acquired, until the trustee determines in the exercise of a sound discretion that it is advisable to dispose of the property. Nothing in this subdivision excuses the trustee from the duty to exercise discretion at reasonable intervals and to determine at those intervals the advisability of retaining or disposing of property.

Subd. 9. No limitation on powers of court. This section does not restrict the power of a court of proper jurisdiction to permit a trustee to deviate from the terms of a will, agreement, court order, or other instrument relating to the acquisition, investment, reinvestment, exchange, retention, sale, or management of trust property.

Subd. 10. Trustees defined. As used in this section, "trustee" means individual trustees and corporations having trust powers acting under wills, agreements, court orders, and other instruments, whether existing on January 1, 1997, or made at a later time.

Subd. 11. Investment companies. (a) In the absence of an express prohibition in the trust instrument, the trustee may acquire and retain securities of any open-end or closed-end management type investment company or investment trust registered under the Federal Investment Company Act of 1940. The fact that a trustee which is a banking institution, as defined in section 48.01, subdivision 2, or any affiliate of a trustee which is a banking institution, is providing services to the investment company or trust as investment advisor, sponsor, broker, distributor, custodian, transfer agent, registrar, or otherwise, and receiving compensation for the services shall not preclude the trustee from investing in the securities of that investment company or trust. A trustee which is a banking institution shall disclose to all current income beneficiaries of the trust the rate, formula, and method of the compensation.

(b) This subdivision does not alter the degree of care and judgment required of trustees under this section.

Subd. 12. Application to existing trusts. This section applies to trusts existing on and created after January 1, 1997. As applied to trusts existing on January 1, 1997, this section governs only decisions or actions occurring after that date.

Subd. 13. Short title. This section may be cited as the "Minnesota Prudent Investor Act."

Laws 1996, c. 314, § 4.

UNIFORM PRUDENT INVESTOR ACT

Table of Jurisdictions Wherein Act Has Been Adopted

For text of Uniform Act, and variation notes and annotation materials for adopting jurisdictions, see Uniform Laws Annotated, Master Edition, Volume 7B.

Jurisdiction	Laws	Effective Date	Statutory Citation
Alabama	2006, c. 216	1–1–2007	Code 1975, §§ 19–3B–901 to 19–3B–906.
Alaska	1998, c. 43	5–23–1998	AS §§ 13.36.225 to 13.36.290.
Arizona	1996, c. 107	4–9–1996 *	A.R.S. §§ 14–7601 to 14–7611.
Arkansas	2001, Act 151	2–8–2001	A.C.A. §§ 24–2–610 to 24–2–619.
California	1995, c. 63	1–1–1996	West's Ann. Cal. Probate Code, §§ 16045 to 16054.
Colorado	1995, S.B. 95–121	7–1–1995	West's C.R.S.A. §§ 15–1.1–101 to 15–1.1–115.
Connecticut	1997, P.A. 97–140	6–13–1997*	C.G.S.A. §§ 45a–541 to 45a–541l.
District of Columbia	2004, c. 15–104	3–10–2004	D.C. Official Code, 2001 Ed. §§ 19–1309.01 to 19–1309.06.

Jurisdiction	Laws	Effective Date	Statutory Citation
Florida	1993, c. 93–257	10–1–1993	West's F.S.A. §§ 518.11, 518.112.
Hawaii	1997, c. 26	4–14–1997	H.R.S. §§ 554C–1 to 554C–12.
Idaho	1997, c. 14	7–1–1997	I.C. §§ 68–501 to 68–514.
Illinois	1992, P.A. 87–715	1–1–1992	S.H.A. 760 ILCS 5/5, 5/5.1.
Indiana	1999, P.L. 137–1999	7–1–1999	West's A.I.C. §§ 30–4–3.5–1 to 30–4–3.5–13.
Iowa	1999, H.F. 663	7–1–2000	I.C.A. §§ 633A.4301 to 633A.4309.
Kansas	2000, c. 80	7–1–2000	K.S.A. 58–24a01 to 58–24a19.
Maine	2004, c. 618	7–1–2005	18–B M.R.S.A. §§ 901 to 908.
Massachusetts	1998, c. 398	12–4–1998*	M.G.L.A. c. 203C, §§ 1 to 11.
Michigan	1998, P.A. 386	4–1–2000	M.C.L.A. §§ 700.1501 to 700.1512.
Minnesota	1996, c. 314	1–1–1997	M.S.A. §§ 501B.151, 501B.152.
Mississippi	2006, c. 474	7–1–2006	Code 1972, §§ 91–9–601 to 91–9–627.
Missouri	2004, H.B. No. 1511	1–1–2005	V.A.M.S. §§ 469.900 to 469.913.
Montana	2003, c. 484	10–1–2003	M.C.A. 72–34–601 to 72–34–610.
Nebraska	2003, LB 130	1–1–2005	R.R.S. 1943, §§ 30–3883 to 30–3889.
Nevada	2003, c. 355	10–1–2003	NRS 164.700 to 164.775.
New Hampshire	2004, c. 130	10–1–2004	RSA 564–B:9–901 to 564–B:9–906.
New Jersey	1997, c. 26	3–7–1997	N.J.S.A. 3B:20–11.1 to 3B:20–11.12.
New Mexico	1995, c. 210	7–1–1995	NMSA 1978, §§ 45–7–601 to 45–7–612.
New York	1994, c. 609	1–1–1995	McKinney's EPTL 11–2.3.
North Carolina	2005, c. 192	1–1–2006	G.S. §§ 36C–9–901 to 36C–9–907.
North Dakota	2007, c. 549	8–1–2007	NDCC 59–17–01 to 59–17–06.
Ohio	2006, H.B. 416	1–1–2007	R.C. §§ 5809.01 to 5809.08.
Oklahoma	1995, c. 351	11–1–1995	60 Okl.St.Ann. §§ 175.60 to 175.72.
Oregon	2005, c. 348	6–29–2005 *	ORS 130.750 to 130.775.
Pennsylvania	1999, c. 1999–28	6–25–1999*	20 Pa. C.S.A. §§ 7201 to 7214.
Rhode Island	1996, c. 276	8–6–1996*	Gen. Laws 1956, §§ 18–15–1 to 18–15–13.
South Carolina	2005, c. 66	1–1–2006	Code 1976, § 62–7–933.
Tennessee	2002, c. 696	7–1–2002	T.C.A. §§ 35–14–101 to 35–14–114.
Texas	2003, c. 1103	1–1–2004	V.T.C.A. Property Code §§ 117.001 to 117.012.
Utah	2004, c. 89	7–1–2004	U.C.A. 1953, 75–7–901 to 75–7–907.
Vermont	1998, P.A. 67	7–1–1998	9 V.S.A. §§ 4651 to 4662.
Virgin Islands	2004, No. 6678	8–12–2004 *	9 V.I.C. §§ 701 to 714.
Virginia	1999, c. 772	1–1–2000	Code 1950, § 26–45.3 to 26–45.14.
Washington	1995, S.S.B. 5333	7–23–1995	West's RCWA 11.100.010 to 11.100.140.
West Virginia	1996, S.B. 294	7–1–1996	Code, 44–6C–1 to 44–6C–15.
Wisconsin	2004, c. 283	4–30–2004	W.S.A. 881.01.
Wyoming	2003, c. 124	7–1–2003	Wyo.Stat.Ann. §§ 4–10–901 to 4–10–913.

* Date of approval.

Historical and Statutory Notes

Laws 1989, c. 340, art. 1, § 76 provides:

"Except as required by section 645.35 or as otherwise provided in sections 47 [section 501B.55], 60 [section 501B.71], 62 [section 501B.73], 70 [section 501B.86], subdivision 9, and 72 [section 501B.88], this article is effective January 1, 1990, and applies to trusts, property interests, and powers of appointment whenever created to the extent permitted under the United States Constitution and the Minnesota Constitution."

501B.152. Agents of trustee

(a) Unless prohibited or otherwise restricted by the terms of the trust instrument, a trustee may delegate to any person, even if the person is associated with the trustee, any trust function that a prudent person of comparable skills could properly delegate under the circumstances. The trustee shall exercise reasonable care, skill, and caution in:

(1) selecting an agent;

(2) establishing the scope and terms of the delegation, consistent with the purposes and terms of the trust; and

(3) periodically reviewing the agent's actions in order to monitor the agent's performance and compliance with the terms of the delegation.

(b) In performing a delegated trust function, an agent owes a duty to the trust to comply with the terms of the delegation and to act in a manner consistent with the purposes and terms of the trust. This duty shall be enforced by the trustee.

(c) A trustee who complies with the requirements of paragraph (a) is not liable to the beneficiaries or to the trust for the decisions or actions of the agent to whom the trust function was delegated.

(d) By accepting the delegation of a trust function from the trustee of a trust that is subject to the laws of this state, an agent submits to the jurisdiction of the courts of this state.

Laws 1996, c. 314, § 5.

Historical and Statutory Notes

Laws 1989, c. 340, art. 1, § 76 provides:

"Except as required by section 645.35 or as otherwise provided in sections 47 [section 501B.55], 60 [section 501B.71], 62 [section 501B.73], 70 [section 501B.86], subdivision 9, and 72 [section 501B.88], this article is effective January 1, 1990, and applies to trusts, property interests, and powers of appointment whenever created to the extent permitted under the United States Constitution and the Minnesota Constitution."

501B.154. Nonjudicial settlement agreements

(a) The trustee and all beneficiaries of a trust not under court supervision may enter into a binding nonjudicial settlement agreement with respect to the matters listed in paragraph (c).

(b) A nonjudicial settlement agreement is valid only to the extent it does not violate a material purpose of the trust, subject to paragraph (c), clause (5), and includes terms and conditions that could be properly approved by the court under applicable law.

(c) Matters that may be resolved by nonjudicial settlement agreement are:

(1) the approval of a trustee's accounting;

(2) the resignation of a trustee;

(3) the determination of a trustee's compensation;

(4) the transfer of the trust's situs; and

(5) the termination of a noncharitable trust and distribution of the trust property if the fair market value of the trust is less than $50,000, as determined on the date of the nonjudicial settlement agreement, and it has been determined that relative to the costs of administering the trust, continuance pursuant to its existing terms will defeat or substantially impair the accomplishment of its purposes. The trust property must be distributed in a manner which conforms as nearly as possible to the intention of the grantor. The existence of a spendthrift or similar protective provision in the trust does not conclusively make this clause inapplicable.

Laws 2004, c. 146, art. 1, § 4.

501B.155. Representation; pleadings; when parties are bound by others; notice

Subdivision 1. Applicability. Subdivisions 2 to 4 apply in judicial proceedings involving trusts and in nonjudicial settlement agreements under section 501B.154.

Subd. 2. Description to give reasonable notice. Interests to be affected must be described in the agreement or pleadings which give reasonable information to owners by name or class, by reference to the instrument creating the interests, or in another appropriate manner.

Subd. 3. Binding effect of orders and agreements. (a) Persons are bound by orders and nonjudicial settlement agreements binding others in the cases in paragraphs (b) to (d).

(b) Orders and agreements binding the sole holder or all coholders of a power of revocation or a presently exercisable general power of appointment, including one in the form of a power of amendment, bind all persons to the extent that their interests, as objects, takers in default, or otherwise are subject to the power.

(c) To the extent there is no conflict of interest between them or among persons represented:

(1) orders and agreements binding a conservator of the property bind the protected person;

(2) orders and agreements binding a guardian bind the ward if no conservator of the estate has been appointed; and

(3) orders imposed upon and agreements entered into by an agent having authority to represent and act on behalf of the principal with respect to a particular question or dispute bind the principal.

(d) An unborn or unascertained person, a person whose identity or location is unknown and not reasonably ascertainable, a minor, or any other person under a legal disability who is not otherwise represented is bound by an order or nonjudicial settlement agreement to the extent that the person's interest is represented by another party having a substantially identical interest, but only to the extent there is no conflict of interest between them or among persons represented. A person's identity or location is not reasonably ascertainable if the identity or location is unable to be determined or ascertained after a diligent search is made.

Subd. 4. Required notice. In judicial proceedings involving trusts, notice is required as follows:

(1) notice as prescribed by section 501B.18 must be given to every interested person or to one who can bind an interested person as described in subdivision 3, paragraph (c), clause (1), (2), or (3), and may be given both to a person and to another who may bind the person;

(2) notice is given to unborn or unascertained persons, who are not represented under subdivision 3, paragraph (c), clause (1), (2), or (3), by giving notice to all known persons whose interests in the proceedings are substantially identical to those of the unborn or unascertained persons.

Laws 2004, c. 146, art. 1, § 5.

COURT PROCEEDINGS

501B.16. Petition for court order

A trustee of an express trust by will or other written instrument or a person interested in the trust may petition the district court for an order:

(1) to confirm an action taken by a trustee;

(2) upon filing of an account, to settle and allow the account;

(3) to determine the persons having an interest in the income or principal of the trust and the nature and extent of their interests;

(4) to construe, interpret, or reform the terms of a trust, or authorize a deviation from the terms of a trust, including a proceeding involving section 501B.31;

(5) to approve payment of the trustee's fees, attorneys' fees, accountants' fees, or any other fees to be charged against the trust;

(6) to confirm the appointment of a trustee;

(7) to accept a trustee's resignation and discharge the trustee from the trust;

(8) to require a trustee to account;

(9) to remove a trustee for cause; or if the court finds that removal of the trustee best serves the interests of all of the beneficiaries, is not inconsistent with a material purpose of the trust, and one or more of the following elements is found:

(i) the trustee has committed a serious breach of trust;

(ii) lack of cooperation among cotrustees substantially impairs the administration of the trust;

(iii) the unfitness, unwillingness, or persistent failure of the trustee to administer the trust effectively;

(iv) there has been a substantial change of circumstances; or

(v) removal is requested by all of the beneficiaries not under disability who, on the date the petition is signed, either are current permissible distributees of trust income or principal, or would be permissible distributees of trust income or principal if the trust terminated on that date;

(10) to appoint a successor trustee when required by the terms of the trust instrument or when by reason of death, resignation, removal, or other cause there is no acting trustee;

(11) to confirm an act performed in execution of the trust by a person while there was no acting trustee;

(12) to subject a trust to continuing court supervision under section 501B.23;

(13) to remove a trust from continuing court supervision under section 501B.23;

(14) to mortgage, lease, sell, or otherwise dispose of real property held by the trustee notwithstanding any contrary provision of the trust instrument;

(15) to suspend the powers and duties of a trustee in military service or war service in accordance with section 525.95 and to order further action authorized in that section;

(16) to secure compliance with the provisions of sections 501B.33 to 501B.45, in accordance with section 501B.41;

(17) to determine the validity of a disclaimer filed under section 501B.86;

(18) to change the situs of a trust;

(19) to redress a breach of trust;

(20) to terminate a trust;

(21) to divide a trust under section 501B.15;

(22) to merge two or more trusts under section 501B.15; or

(23) to instruct the trustee, beneficiaries, and any other interested parties in any matter relating to the administration of the trust and the discharge of the trustee's duties.

Laws 1989, c. 340, art. 1, § 13. Amended by Laws 1995, c. 130, § 3; Laws 2004, c. 146, art. 1, § 6.

Historical and Statutory Notes

Laws 1989, c. 340, art. 1, § 76 provides:

"Except as required by section 645.35 or as otherwise provided in sections 47 [section 501B.55], 60 [section 501B.71], 62 [section 501B.73], 70 [section 501B.86], subdivision 9, and 72 [section 501B.88], this article is effective January 1, 1990, and applies to trusts, property interests, and powers of appointment whenever created to the extent permitted under the United States Constitution and the Minnesota Constitution."

Laws 1995, c. 130, § 22, provides in part that chapter 130 is effective January 1, 1996.

501B.17. Venue

Subdivision 1. Filing of petition. A petition under section 501B.16 or 501B.22 may be filed:

(1) in the case of a trust created by will, in the district court for (i) the county where the will was probated, (ii) the county where a trustee having custody of part or all of the trust assets resides or has a trust office, or (iii) the county in which the trust is administered;

(2) in the case of a nontestamentary trust, in the district court for (i) the county where a trustee having custody of part or all of the trust assets resides or has a trust office or (ii) the county in which the trust is administered; or

(3) in the case of a trust holding real property, in the district court for any county in which the real estate is situated.

Subd. 2. Prior court proceedings. In the case of a trust with respect to which there have been prior court proceedings in this state, a petition under section 501B.16 or 501B.22 must be filed in the court in which the prior proceedings were held.

Laws 1989, c. 340, art. 1, § 14. Amended by Laws 2005, c. 26, § 1.

Historical and Statutory Notes

Laws 1989, c. 340, art. 1, § 76 provides:

"Except as required by section 645.35 or as otherwise provided in sections 47 [section 501B.55], 60 [section 501B.71], 62 [section 501B.73], 70 [section 501B.86], subdivision 9, and 72 [section 501B.88], this article is effective January 1, 1990, and applies to trusts, property interests, and powers of appointment whenever created to the extent permitted under the United States Constitution and the Minnesota Constitution."

501B.18. Order for hearing

Upon the filing of a petition under section 501B.16, the court shall, by order, fix a time and place for a hearing, unless notice and hearing have been waived in writing by the beneficiaries of the trust then in being. Unless waived, notice of the hearing must be given as follows: (1) by publishing, at least 20 days before the date of the hearing, a copy of the order for hearing one time in a legal newspaper for the county in which the petition is filed; and (2) by mailing, at least 15 days before the date of the hearing, a copy of the order for hearing to those beneficiaries of the trust who are known to or reasonably ascertainable by the petitioner. In the case of a beneficiary who is a minor or an incapacitated person as defined in section 524.5–102 and for whom a conservator, guardian, or guardian ad litem known to the petitioner has been appointed, notice must be mailed to that fiduciary. Notice may be given in any other manner the court orders.

Laws 1989, c. 340, art. 1, § 15. Amended by Laws 2005, c. 10, art. 4, § 21.

Historical and Statutory Notes

Laws 1989, c. 340, art. 1, § 76 provides:

"Except as required by section 645.35 or as otherwise provided in sections 47 [section 501B.55], 60 [section 501B.71], 62 [section 501B.73], 70 [section 501B.86], subdivision 9, and 72 [section 501B.88], this article is effective January 1, 1990, and applies to trusts, property interests, and powers of appointment whenever created to the extent permitted under the United States Constitution and the Minnesota Constitution."

501B.19. Representation of persons who are unborn, unascertained, unknown, or minors or incapacitated persons

If an interested person is a minor or an incapacitated person as defined in section 524.5–102 and has no guardian or conservator within the state, or if an interested person is unborn, unascertained, or a person whose identity or address is unknown to the petitioner, the court shall represent that person, unless the court, upon the application of the trustee or any other interested person, appoints a guardian ad litem to represent the person.

Laws 1989, c. 340, art. 1, § 16. Amended by Laws 2005, c. 10, art. 4, § 22.

Historical and Statutory Notes

Laws 1989, c. 340, art. 1, § 76 provides:

"Except as required by section 645.35 or as otherwise provided in sections 47 [section 501B.55], 60 [section 501B.71], 62 [section 501B.73], 70 [section 501B.86], subdivision 9, and 72 [section 501B.88], this article is effective January 1, 1990, and applies to trusts, property interests, and powers of appointment whenever created to the extent permitted under the United States Constitution and the Minnesota Constitution."

501B.20. Holder of a general power

For purposes of giving notice, waiving notice, initiating a proceeding, granting consent or approval, or objecting with regard to any proceedings under this chapter, the sole holder or all coholders of a presently exercisable or testamentary general power of appointment, power of revocation, or unlimited power of withdrawal are deemed to represent and act for beneficiaries to the extent that their interests as objects, takers in default, or otherwise are subject to the power.

Laws 1989, c. 340, art. 1, § 17. Amended by Laws 1989, 1st Sp., c. 2, § 1.

Historical and Statutory Notes

Laws 1989, c. 340, art. 1, § 76 provides:

"Except as required by section 645.35 or as otherwise provided in sections 47 [section 501B.55], 60 [section 501B.71], 62 [section 501B.73], 70 [section 501B.86], subdivision 9, and 72 [section 501B.88], this article is effective January 1, 1990, and applies to trusts, property interests, and powers of appointment whenever created to the extent permitted under the United States Constitution and the Minnesota Constitution."

501B.21. Order and appeal

Upon hearing a petition filed under section 501B.16, the court shall make an order it considers appropriate. The order is final as to all matters determined by it and binding in rem upon the trust estate and upon the interests of all beneficiaries, vested or contingent, even though unascertained or not in being. An appeal from the order may be taken by any party after service by any party of written notice of its filing under the Rules of Appellate Procedure or, if no notice is served, within six months after the filing of the order.

Laws 1989, c. 340, art. 1, § 18. Amended by Laws 2000, c. 362, § 1.

Historical and Statutory Notes

Laws 1989, c. 340, art. 1, § 76 provides:

"Except as required by section 645.35 or as otherwise provided in sections 47 [section 501B.55], 60 [section 501B.71], 62 [section 501B.73], 70 [section 501B.86], subdivision 9, and 72 [section 501B.88], this article is effective January 1, 1990, and applies to trusts, property interests, and powers of appointment whenever created to the extent permitted under the United States Constitution and the Minnesota Constitution."

501B.22. Confirmation of appointment of trustee

A person appointed as trustee of an express trust by a will or other written instrument or any interested person may file in the district court an ex parte petition to confirm the appointment of the trustee and specify the manner in which the trustee must qualify. Upon consideration of the petition, the court shall make an order it considers appropriate. A trustee whose appointment is confirmed under this section is subject to section 501B.23.

Laws 1989, c. 340, art. 1, § 19.

Historical and Statutory Notes

Laws 1989, c. 340, art. 1, § 76 provides:

"Except as required by section 645.35 or as otherwise provided in sections 47 [section 501B.55], 60 [section 501B.71], 62 [section 501B.73], 70 [section 501B.86], subdivision 9, and 72 [section 501B.88], this article is effective January 1, 1990, and applies to trusts, property interests, and powers of appointment whenever created to the extent permitted under the United States Constitution and the Minnesota Constitution."

501B.23. Inventory; annual account; continuing court supervision

A trustee whose appointment has been confirmed by court order under section 501B.22 or a trustee otherwise subject to continuing court supervision by court order shall file with the court administrator of the district court an inventory containing a list of all property then belonging to the trust. The trustee shall then render to the court at least annually a verified account containing a complete inventory of the trust assets and itemized principal and income accounts. This section does not apply to trusts established in connection with bonds issued under chapter 474.

Laws 1989, c. 340, art. 1, § 20.

Historical and Statutory Notes

Laws 1989, c. 340, art. 1, § 76 provides:

"Except as required by section 645.35 or as otherwise provided in sections 47 [section 501B.55], 60 [section 501B.71], 62 [section 501B.73], 70 [section 501B.86], subdivision 9, and 72 [section 501B.88], this article is effective January 1, 1990, and applies to trusts, property interests, and powers of appointment whenever created to the extent permitted under the United States Constitution and the Minnesota Constitution."

501B.24. Jurisdiction

Once a district court has assumed jurisdiction of a trust, the district court has jurisdiction as a proceeding in rem, until jurisdiction is transferred to another court or terminated by court order. This chapter does not limit or abridge the power or jurisdiction of the district court over trusts and trustees.

Laws 1989, c. 340, art. 1, § 21.

Historical and Statutory Notes

Laws 1989, c. 340, art. 1, § 76 provides:

"Except as required by section 645.35 or as otherwise provided in sections 47 [section 501B.55], 60 [section 501B.71], 62 [section 501B.73], 70 [section 501B.86], subdivision 9, and 72 [section 501B.88], this article is effective January 1, 1990, and applies to trusts, property interests, and powers of appointment whenever created to the extent permitted under the United States Constitution and the Minnesota Constitution."

501B.25. Application

Sections 501B.16 to 501B.23 do not apply to trusts in the nature of mortgages or to trusts commonly known as voting trusts. Sections 501B.16 to 501B.23 apply, however, unless otherwise provided in the trust instrument, to trusts established in connection with bonds issued under chapter 469, and, at the sole election of the issuer of bonds issued under chapter 469, without a trust indenture, to the pledges and other bond covenants made by the issuer in one or more resolutions with respect to the bonds. If the issuer so elects to apply sections 501B.16 to 501B.23, for such purposes only, the pledges and other bond covenants shall be deemed the "trust," the resolution or resolutions shall be deemed the "trust instrument," and the issuer shall be deemed the "trustee" notwithstanding the absence of any fiduciary responsibility owed by the "issuer" toward the bondholders. Nothing in this section shall preclude the issuer from seeking approval under sections 501B.16 to 501B.23 of the creation of any express trust under a trust indenture and the appointment of a trustee thereunder to act as a fiduciary for the benefit of the bondholders. As used in sections 501B.16 to 501B.23, "person" includes an artificial as well as a natural person, and "beneficiary" includes a bondholder.

Laws 1989, c. 340, art. 1, § 22. Amended by Laws 1993, c. 271, § 8, eff. May 20, 1993.

Historical and Statutory Notes

Laws 1989, c. 340, art. 1, § 76 provides:

"Except as required by section 645.35 or as otherwise provided in sections 47 [section 501B.55], 60 [section 501B.71], 62 [section 501B.73], 70 [section 501B.86], subdivision 9, and 72 [section 501B.88], this article is effective January 1, 1990, and applies to trusts, property interests, and powers of appointment whenever created to the extent permitted under the United States Constitution and the Minnesota Constitution."

CHARITABLE TRUSTS AND THEIR SUPERVISION

501B.31.   Charitable trusts

Subdivision 1.   Validity and construction. No charitable trust is invalid because of indefiniteness or uncertainty of the object of the trust or of its beneficiaries designated in the instrument creating the trust or because the trust violates a statute or rule against perpetuities. No charitable trust may prevent or limit the free alienation of the title to any of the trust estate by the trustee in the administration of the trust, except as may be permitted under existing or subsequent statutes.

Subd. 2.   Liberal interpretation; administration. A charitable trust must be liberally construed by the courts so that the intentions of the donor are carried out when possible, and the trust must not fail solely because the donor has imperfectly outlined the purpose and object of the charity or the method of administration. If the district court of the proper county determines that the purpose and object of the donor's charity are imperfectly expressed, the method of administration is incomplete or imperfect, or circumstances have so changed since the execution of the instrument creating the trust as to render impracticable, inexpedient, or impossible a literal compliance with the terms of the instrument, the court may, upon the petition of the trustee under section 501B.16, make an order directing that the trust must be administered or expended in a manner the court determines will, as nearly as possible, accomplish the general purposes of the instrument and the object and intention of the donor without regard to, and free from any specific restriction, limitation, or direction it contains.

Subd. 3.   Laws not affected. Nothing in this section impairs, limits, or abridges the operation and efficacy of the whole or any part of a statute that authorizes the creation of a corporation for charitable purposes or that permits a municipal corporation to act as trustee for a public or charitable purpose. Nothing in subdivisions 1 to 3 of this section applies to a gift, bequest, devise, or trust made, created, or arising by or under the provisions of the will of a person who died before April 15, 1927.

Subd. 4.   Determination of trust, gift, bequest, devise. (a) This subdivision applies to a gift or trust made or created by a living person before April 15, 1927, or a gift, bequest, devise, or trust made or created by or under the will of a person who died before April 15, 1927.

(b) If a gift, trust, or devise has been made for a charitable, benevolent, educational, religious, or other public use or trust, or upon a condition, limitation, or restriction of any kind, the property given, entrusted, or devised may be used only for that use or trust and in accordance with the condition, limitation, or restriction. The grantee, devisee, trustee, or other holder of property may petition the court under section 501B.16 for determination of the legal rights and relationship of the holder, the public, the grantor, and the grantor's heirs, representatives, or assigns in and to the property.

(c) If the court determines that circumstances have so changed since the execution of the instrument as to render impracticable, inexpedient, or impossible a literal compliance with the terms or conditions of the instrument, but the terms and purposes of the instrument may be substantially performed, the court may order that the terms of the instrument be performed and the property be administered or expended in a manner that will, in the judgment of the court, as nearly as possible, accomplish the general purposes of the instrument and the intention of the grantor without regard to, and free from any, specific restriction, limitation, condition, or direction contained in the instrument.

Subd. 5. Attorney general. In cases arising under this section, the attorney general must be given notice of any court proceedings pursuant to section 501B.18. The attorney general shall represent the beneficial interests in those cases and shall enforce affected trusts.

Laws 1989, c. 340, art. 1, § 23.

Historical and Statutory Notes

Laws 1989, c. 340, art. 1, § 76 provides:

"Except as required by section 645.35 or as otherwise provided in sections 47 [section 501B.55], 60 [section 501B.71], 62 [section 501B.73], 70 [section 501B.86], subdivision 9, and 72 [section 501B.88], this article is effective January 1, 1990, and applies to trusts, property interests, and powers of appointment whenever created to the extent permitted under the United States Constitution and the Minnesota Constitution."

501B.32. Private foundations; charitable trusts; split-interest trusts

Subdivision 1. Incorporated provisions. A will or trust instrument that creates a trust that is: (1) a "private foundation," as defined in section 501(a) of the Internal Revenue Code of 1986;[1] or (2) a "charitable trust," as defined in section 4947(a)(1) of the Internal Revenue Code of 1986; or (3) a "split-interest trust," as defined in section 4947(a)(2) of the Internal Revenue Code of 1986, and any other instrument governing the trustee of one of those trusts or the use, retention, or disposition of any of the income or property of one of those trusts, must be considered to have incorporated within it the provisions in paragraphs (a) to (e) with respect to the trust and its trustee. Except as provided in subdivision 2, paragraphs (a) to (e) govern the administration and distribution of the trust notwithstanding provisions of the governing instrument, statute, or law of this state to the contrary.

(a) The trustee shall distribute for each taxable year of the trust amounts at least sufficient to avoid liability for the tax imposed by section 4942(a) of the Internal Revenue Code of 1986.

(b) The trustee shall not engage in an act of "self-dealing," as defined in section 4941(d) of the Internal Revenue Code of 1986, which would give rise to liability for the tax imposed by section 4941(a) of the Internal Revenue Code of 1986.

(c) The trustee shall not keep "excess business holdings," as defined in section 4943(c) of the Internal Revenue Code of 1986, that would give rise to liability for the tax imposed by section 4943(a) of the Internal Revenue Code of 1986.

(d) The trustee shall not make investments that would jeopardize the carrying out of any of the exempt purposes of the trust, within the meaning of section 4944 of the Internal Revenue Code of 1986, so as to give rise to liability for the tax imposed by section 4944(a) of the Internal Revenue Code of 1986.

(e) The trustee shall not make a "taxable expenditure," as defined in section 4945(d) of the Internal Revenue Code of 1986, that would give rise to liability for the tax imposed by section 4945(a) of the Internal Revenue Code of 1986.

Subd. 2. Exception. Subdivision 1 does not apply to the extent that a court of competent jurisdiction determines that application would be contrary to the terms of the will, trust instrument, or other governing instrument described in subdivision 1 and that the will, trust instrument, or other governing instrument may not be changed to conform to subdivision 1.

Subd. 3. Rights and powers of courts, attorney general. Nothing in this section impairs the rights and powers of the attorney general or the courts of this state with respect to a trust.

Laws 1989, c. 340, art. 1, § 24.

[1] All text references to Internal Revenue Code sections are to Title 26 of U.S.C.A.

Historical and Statutory Notes

Laws 1989, c. 340, art. 1, § 76 provides:

"Except as required by section 645.35 or as otherwise provided in sections 47 [section 501B.55], 60 [section 501B.71], 62 [section 501B.73], 70 [section 501B.86], subdivision 9, and 72 [section 501B.88], this article is effective January 1, 1990, and applies to trusts, property interests, and powers of appointment whenever created to the extent permitted under the United States Constitution and the Minnesota Constitution."

SUPERVISION OF CHARITABLE TRUSTS AND TRUSTEES ACT

501B.33. Citation

Sections 501B.33 to 501B.45 may be cited as the "Supervision of Charitable Trusts and Trustees Act."

Laws 1989, c. 340, art. 1, § 25.

Historical and Statutory Notes

Laws 1989, c. 340, art. 1, § 76 provides:

"Except as required by section 645.35 or as otherwise provided in sections 47 [section 501B.55], 60 [section 501B.71], 62 [section 501B.73], 70 [section 501B.86], subdivision 9, and 72 [section 501B.88], this article is effective January 1, 1990, and applies to trusts, property interests, and powers of appointment whenever created to the extent permitted under the United States Constitution and the Minnesota Constitution."

501B.34. Charitable trusts; supervision by attorney general

Sections 501B.33 to 501B.45 apply to trustees holding property for charitable purposes. In connection with the supervision, administration, and enforcement of charitable trusts, the attorney general has the rights, duties, and powers in sections 501B.33 to 501B.45, and common law and statutory rights, duties, and powers.

Laws 1989, c. 340, art. 1, § 26.

Historical and Statutory Notes

Laws 1989, c. 340, art. 1, § 76 provides:

"Except as required by section 645.35 or as otherwise provided in sections 47 [section 501B.55], 60 [section 501B.71], 62 [section 501B.73], 70 [section 501B.86], subdivision 9, and 72 [section 501B.88], this article is effective January 1, 1990, and applies to trusts, property interests, and powers of appointment whenever created to the extent permitted under the United States Constitution and the Minnesota Constitution."

501B.35. Definitions

Subdivision 1. Scope. The definitions in this section apply to sections 501B.31 to 501B.45 and do not modify or abridge any law or rule respecting the nature of a charitable trust or the nature and extent of the duties of a trustee except duties imposed by sections 501B.31 to 501B.45.

Subd. 2. Charitable purpose. "Charitable purpose" means an actual or purported charitable, philanthropic, religious, social service, educational, eleemosynary, or other public use or purpose.

Subd. 3. Charitable trust. "Charitable trust" means a fiduciary relationship with respect to property that arises as a result of a manifestation of an intention to create it, and that subjects the person by whom the property is held to equitable duties to deal with the property for a charitable purpose. As used in this definition, property includes all income derived from fees for services.

Subd. 4. Trustee. "Trustee" means a person or group of persons either in an individual or a joint capacity, or a director, officer, or other agent of an association, foundation, trustee corporation, corporation, or other legal entity who is vested with the control or responsibility of administering property held for a charitable purpose.

Laws 1989, c. 340, art. 1, § 27. Amended by Laws 1997, c. 222, § 57, eff. May 31, 1997.

Historical and Statutory Notes

Laws 1989, c. 340, art. 1, § 76 provides:

"Except as required by section 645.35 or as otherwise provided in sections 47 [section 501B.55], 60 [section 501B.71], 62 [section 501B.73], 70 [section 501B.86], subdivision 9, and 72 [section 501B.88], this article is effective January 1, 1990, and applies to trusts, property interests, and powers of appointment whenever created to the extent permitted under the United States Constitution and the Minnesota Constitution."

501B.36. Registration and reporting

The registration and reporting provisions of sections 501B.37 and 501B.38 apply to a charitable trust, including an organization with a charitable purpose, that has gross assets of $25,000 or more at any time during the year, except that the provisions do not apply to:

(1) a charitable trust administered by the United States or a state, territory, or possession of the United States, the District of Columbia, the Commonwealth of Puerto Rico, or any of their agencies or subdivisions;

(2) a religious association organized under chapter 315 or chapter 317A;

(3) a charitable trust organized and operated exclusively for religious purposes and administered by a religious association organized under chapter 315 or 317A;

(4) an organization described in section 509(a)(3) of the Internal Revenue Code of 1986 [1] and operated, supervised, or controlled by or in connection with one or more organizations described in clauses (2) to (5); a pooled income fund as defined in section 642(c)(5) of the Internal Revenue Code of 1986 maintained by an organization described in clauses (2) to (5); or a charitable remainder annuity trust or unitrust, as defined in section 664 of the Internal Revenue Code of 1986;

(5) a trust in which the only charitable interest is a contingent interest for which no charitable deduction has been allowed for Minnesota income, inheritance, or gift tax purposes or a trust in which not all of the unexpired interests are devoted to one or more charitable purposes and in which the only charitable interest is an annuity or an income interest with respect to which a charitable deduction is allowed the trust under applicable Minnesota income tax laws;

(6) an organization registered with the attorney general pursuant to sections 309.52 and 309.53;

(7) a trust for individual and charitable beneficiaries that is described in section 4947(a)(2) of the Internal Revenue Code of 1986, also known as a split-interest trust; or

(8) a charitable gift, bequest, or devise not held and continued by a private express trust or corporation even though the gift, bequest, or devise creates a fiduciary relationship, unless there is no named charitable beneficiary in existence or unless a named charitable beneficiary elects in a writing filed with the attorney general and with the fiduciary to come within the provisions of sections 501B.37 and 501B.38.

Laws 1989, c. 340, art. 1, § 28. Amended by Laws 1989, c. 340, art. 2, § 6, eff. Jan. 1, 1990; Laws 1995, c. 235, § 12.

[1] All text references to Internal Revenue Code sections are to Title 26 of U.S.C.A.

Historical and Statutory Notes

Laws 1989, c. 340, art. 1, § 76 provides:

"Except as required by section 645.35 or as otherwise provided in sections 47 [section 501B.55], 60 [section 501B.71], 62 [section 501B.73], 70 [section 501B.86], subdivision 9, and 72 [section 501B.88], this article is effective January 1, 1990, and applies to trusts, property interests, and powers of appointment whenever created to the extent permitted under the United States Constitution and the Minnesota Constitution."

501B.37. Register of trusts and trustees

Subdivision 1. Establishment of register; transfer to attorney general. The attorney general shall establish and maintain a register of charitable trusts and trustees subject to sections 501B.33 to 501B.45.

Subd. 2. Filing of instruments. Except as otherwise provided in section 501B.36, a charitable trust shall register and file with the attorney general a copy of its articles of incorporation or the instrument that created the charitable trust, including any amendments, within three months after the charitable trust first receives possession or control of property authorized or required to be applied, either at present or in the future, for charitable purposes.

Subd. 3. Registration fee. A $25 registration fee shall be paid by every charitable trust filing the information required by this section.

Laws 1989, c. 340, art. 1, § 29. Amended by Laws 1995, c. 235, §§ 13, 14.

Historical and Statutory Notes

Laws 1989, c. 340, art. 1, § 76 provides:

"Except as required by section 645.35 or as otherwise provided in sections 47 [section 501B.55], 60 [section 501B.71], 62 [section 501B.73], 70 [section 501B.86], subdivision 9, and 72 [section 501B.88], this article is effective January 1, 1990, and applies to trusts, property interests, and powers of appointment whenever created to the extent permitted under the United States Constitution and the Minnesota Constitution."

501B.38. Information filing

Subdivision 1. Deadlines; extensions. A charitable trust subject to sections 501B.33 to 501B.45 must file with the attorney general a copy of its federal tax or information return, including all schedules and amendments, submitted by the charitable trust to the Internal Revenue Service for the period covered in the trust's accounting year last completed. If the charitable trust does not file a federal tax or information return, it shall file a balance sheet and a statement of income and expenses for the accounting year last completed.

Subd. 1a. Extensions. The information required by this section must be filed annually on or before the 15th day of the fifth month following the close of the charitable trust's taxable year as established for federal tax purposes. The time for filing may be extended by application to the attorney general, for up to six months, provided the applicant has requested an extension to file its federal tax return under section 6081 of the Internal Revenue Code of 1986.[1] A charitable trust that files the information required under this subdivision with the attorney general is not required to file the same information with the commissioner of revenue.

Subd. 2. Suspension of filing. The attorney general may suspend the filing requirements under subdivision 1 for a particular charitable trust for a reasonable, specifically designated time on written application of the trustee filed with the attorney general. If the filing requirements are suspended, the attorney general shall file in the register of charitable trusts a written statement that the interests of the beneficiaries will not be prejudiced by the suspension and that the information required by this section is not required for proper supervision by the attorney general's office.

Subd. 3. Filing fee. A $25 filing fee shall be paid by every charitable trust filing the information required by this section.

Laws 1989, c. 340, art. 1, § 30. Amended by Laws 1995, c. 235, § 15; Laws 1996, c. 471, art. 13, § 22.

¹ 26 U.S.C.A. § 6081.

Historical and Statutory Notes

Laws 1989, c. 340, art. 1, § 76 provides:

"Except as required by section 645.35 or as otherwise provided in sections 47 [section 501B.55], 60 [section 501B.71], 62 [section 501B.73], 70 [section 501B.86], subdivision 9, and 72 [section 501B.88], this article is effective January 1, 1990, and applies to trusts, property interests, and powers of appointment whenever created to the extent permitted under the United States Constitution and the Minnesota Constitution."

501B.39. Public inspection of records

The register, copies of instruments, and the reports filed with the attorney general must be open to public inspection.

Laws 1989, c. 340, art. 1, § 31.

Historical and Statutory Notes

Laws 1989, c. 340, art. 1, § 76 provides:

"Except as required by section 645.35 or as otherwise provided in sections 47 [section 501B.55], 60 [section 501B.71], 62 [section 501B.73], 70 [section 501B.86], subdivision 9, and 72 [section 501B.88], this article is effective January 1, 1990, and applies to trusts, property interests, and powers of appointment whenever created to the extent permitted under the United States Constitution and the Minnesota Constitution."

501B.40. Investigatory powers of the attorney general; custodians to furnish copies of records

Subdivision 1. Discovery. The attorney general may conduct investigations that are reasonably necessary for: (1) the administration of sections 501B.33 to 501B.45; or (2) determining whether property held for charitable purposes is properly administered. In connection with an investigation under this section, the attorney general may obtain discovery from an agent, trustee, fiduciary, beneficiary, institution, association, corporation, or other person regarding a matter, fact, or circumstance, not privileged, that is relevant to the subject matter involved in the investigation. The discovery may be obtained without commencement of a civil action and without leave of court, except as expressly required by subdivision 2. The applicable protective provisions of rules 26.02, 30.02, and 30.04, of the Rules of Civil Procedure for the District Court apply to discovery procedures instituted under this section. The attorney general or a person to whom discovery is directed may apply to and obtain leave of the district court in order to reduce or extend the time requirements of this subdivision, and, upon a showing of good cause, the district court shall order a reduction or extension. In order to obtain discovery, the attorney general may:

(1) serve written interrogatories on a person. Within 20 days after service of interrogatories, separate written answers and objections to each interrogatory must be mailed to the attorney general;

(2) upon reasonable written notice of no less than 15 days, require a person to produce for inspection and copying documents, papers, books, accounts, letters, photographs, objects, or tangible things in the person's possession, custody, or control; and

(3) upon reasonable written notice of no less than 15 days, take the testimony of a person by deposition as to a fact or opinion relevant to the subject matter involved in the pending investigation.

Subd. 2. Order by court. If a person fails or refuses to answer interrogatories, produce materials, or be examined under oath, the attorney general may, upon notice to the person, apply to the district court in the county where the person resides or is found, for an order to compel compliance. On a showing of cause by the attorney general, the court may issue an order to compel compliance with the discovery procedures authorized by this section.

Subd. 3. Public records. A custodian of records of a court having jurisdiction of probate matters or of charitable trusts, and a custodian of records of a department, agency, or political subdivision of this state shall, upon request, furnish to the attorney general, free of charge, copies of records relating to the subject of sections 501B.33 to 501B.45.

Subd. 4. Report of applications for tax exemption. Every officer, agency, board, or commission of this state that receives an application for exemption from taxation from a charitable trust subject to sections 501B.33 to 501B.45 shall annually file with the attorney general a list of all applications received during the year and shall notify the attorney general of the suspension or revocation of a tax exempt status previously granted.

Laws 1989, c. 340, art. 1, § 32.

Historical and Statutory Notes

Laws 1989, c. 340, art. 1, § 76 provides:

"Except as required by section 645.35 or as otherwise provided in sections 47 [section 501B.55], 60 [section 501B.71], 62 [section 501B.73], 70 [section 501B.86], subdivision 9, and 72 [section 501B.88], this article is effective January 1, 1990, and applies to trusts, property interests, and powers of appointment whenever created to the extent permitted under the United States Constitution and the Minnesota Constitution."

501B.41. Breach of trust; proceedings to secure compliance

Subdivision 1. Enforcement powers. The attorney general may institute appropriate proceedings to obtain compliance with sections 501B.33 to 501B.45 and the proper administration of a charitable trust. The powers and duties of the attorney general in this section are in addition to all other powers and duties.

Subd. 2. Participation by attorney general. The attorney general must be notified of, and has the right to participate as a party in, all court proceedings:

(1) to terminate a charitable trust or to liquidate or distribute its assets;

(2) to modify or depart from the objects or purposes of a charitable trust as contained in the instrument governing the trust, including a proceeding for the application of the doctrine of cy pres;

(3) to construe the provisions of an instrument with respect to a charitable trust;

(4) to review an accounting of a charitable trust submitted by a trustee; or

(5) involving a charitable trust when the interests of the uncertain or indefinite charitable beneficiaries may be affected.

Subd. 3. Exemption from notice requirement. The attorney general need not be provided with notice under subdivision 2 of a charitable gift, devise, or bequest (1) for which the donor or testator has named as a charitable beneficiary an organization that is then in existence; or (2) that is not held and continued by a private express trust or corporation, whether or not the gift, devise, or bequest creates a fiduciary relationship.

This subdivision does not affect any other notice to the attorney general required by this chapter.

Subd. 4. Failure to give notice. If proceedings are commenced without service of process and service of the pleadings upon the attorney general, a judgment or order rendered in the proceedings is voidable, unenforceable, and, upon the attorney general's motion seeking relief, may be set aside. With respect to the proceedings, no compromise, settlement agreement, contract, or judgment agreed to by any or all of the parties having or claiming to have an interest in a charitable trust is valid unless the attorney general was made a party to the proceedings and joined any agreement or the attorney general, in writing, waived the right to participate. The attorney general may enter into a compromise, settlement agreement, contract, or judgment that the attorney general believes is in the best interests of the people of the state and the uncertain or indefinite beneficiaries.

Subd. 5. Wills. The personal representative shall send to the attorney general a copy of the petition or application for probate together with a copy of the will and any codicils that are being offered for probate:

(1) when a will provides for a bequest or devise for a charitable purpose for which there is no named charitable beneficiary or for which there is then in existence no named charitable beneficiary;

(2) when a will provides for bequests or devises for charitable purposes in excess of $150,000;

(3) when a will provides for a bequest or devise to a named charitable beneficiary that is in receivership; or

(4) upon a written request served on the personal representative by a named charitable beneficiary prior to the order allowing the final account or, in unsupervised proceedings, within 30 days after service of the final account on the charitable beneficiary.

The personal representative shall serve the documents on the attorney general and file with the appropriate court a copy of the affidavit of service on the attorney general. If the personal representative was requested to notify the attorney general of the probate proceedings according to clause (4), the requesting party shall file with the court a copy of the request and the affidavit of service on the personal representative.

If objections are filed to a will or codicil containing any bequest or devise to a charitable trust, the person filing the objections, at least 14 days before the hearing, shall send to the attorney general a copy of the objections, a copy of the petition or application for probate, a copy of the will, and any codicil that has been offered for probate.

Any service upon the attorney general under this section must be made personally or by registered or certified mail, return receipt requested. The attorney general may become a party in the estate proceedings.

Subd. 6. Breach of trust. The failure of a trustee to register under section 501B.37, to file annual reports under section 501B.38, or to administer and manage property held for charitable purposes in accordance with law or consistent with fiduciary obligations constitutes a breach of trust.

Subd. 7. Civil actions. The attorney general may begin a civil action in order to remedy and redress a breach of trust, as described in subdivision 6 or as otherwise provided by law, committed by a trustee subject to sections 501B.33 to 501B.45. If it appears to the attorney general that a breach of trust has been committed, the attorney general may sue for and obtain:

(1) injunctive relief against the breach of trust or threatened breach of trust;

(2) the removal of a trustee who has committed or is committing a breach of trust;

(3) the recovery of damages; and

(4) another appropriate remedy.

Laws 1989, c. 340, art. 1, § 33.

Historical and Statutory Notes

Laws 1989, c. 340, art. 1, § 76 provides:

"Except as required by section 645.35 or as otherwise provided in sections 47 [section 501B.55], 60 [section 501B.71], 62 [section 501B.73], 70 [section 501B.86], subdivision 9, and 72 [section 501B.88], this article is effective January 1, 1990, and applies to trusts, property interests, and powers of appointment whenever created to the extent permitted under the United States Constitution and the Minnesota Constitution."

501B.42. Contrary provisions of instrument invalid

Sections 501B.33 to 501B.45 apply regardless of contrary provisions of an instrument.

Laws 1989, c. 340, art. 1, § 34.

Historical and Statutory Notes

Laws 1989, c. 340, art. 1, § 76 provides:

"Except as required by section 645.35 or as otherwise provided in sections 47 [section 501B.55], 60 [section 501B.71], 62 [section 501B.73], 70 [section 501B.86], subdivision 9, and 72 [section 501B.88], this article is effective January 1, 1990, and applies to trusts, property interests, and powers of appointment whenever created to the extent permitted under the United States Constitution and the Minnesota Constitution."

501B.43. Cost of investigations and proceedings; registration and filing fees

Subdivision 1. Expenses payable. In a proceeding brought by the attorney general or in which the attorney general intervenes under sections 501B.33 to 501B.45, the judgment or order may provide that the trustee must pay the reasonable expenses necessarily incurred by the attorney general in the investigation and prosecution of the action, including attorneys' fees, if it is determined in the proceeding that the trustee has been guilty of an intentional or grossly negligent breach of trust.

Subd. 2. Disposition of money. All money received by the attorney general under this section must be deposited in the state treasury and credited to the general fund.

Laws 1989, c. 340, art. 1, § 35.

Historical and Statutory Notes

Laws 1989, c. 340, art. 1, § 76 provides:

"Except as required by section 645.35 or as otherwise provided in sections 47 [section 501B.55], 60 [section 501B.71], 62 [section 501B.73], 70 [section 501B.86], subdivision 9, and 72 [section 501B.88], this article is effective January 1, 1990, and applies to trusts, property interests, and powers of appointment whenever created to the extent permitted under the United States Constitution and the Minnesota Constitution."

501B.44. Immunity of charitable trusts

A charitable trust is an "organization" for purposes of section 317A.257, and that section applies to charitable trusts.

Laws 1989, c. 340, art. 1, § 36. Amended by Laws 1989, c. 340, art. 2, § 7, eff. Jan. 1, 1990.

Historical and Statutory Notes

Laws 1989, c. 340, art. 1, § 76 provides:

"Except as required by section 645.35 or as otherwise provided in sections 47 [section 501B.55], 60 [section 501B.71], 62 [section 501B.73], 70 [section 501B.86], subdivision 9, and 72 [section 501B.88], this article is effective January 1, 1990, and applies to trusts, property interests, and powers of appointment whenever created to the extent permitted under the United States Constitution and the Minnesota Constitution."

Laws 1989, c. 340, art. 2, § 13 provides that § 7 (amending this section) is effective January 1, 1990.

501B.45. Sale of banks owned by charitable trusts

Subdivision 1. Definitions. For the purpose of this section, "charitable trust" means a charitable trust subject to supervision by the attorney general under the Supervision of Charitable Trusts and Trustees Act, sections 501B.33 to 501B.45, that is required to divest excess business holdings by section 4943 of the Internal Revenue Code of 1986 [1] and that owned 100 percent of a bank holding company on May 26, 1969, the date of enactment of section 4943 of the Internal Revenue Code of 1954.

Subd. 2. Authorization. The stock or assets of one or more banks or a bank holding company owned directly or indirectly by a charitable trust may be sold, assigned, merged, or transferred by the charitable trust under the procedures in section 48.93 to a bank holding company, bank, or other qualified entity as permitted by applicable banking laws without regard to whether the entity acquiring the stock or assets is located in a reciprocating state.

Subd. 3. Legislative intent. It is the express intention of the Minnesota legislature to act pursuant to United States Code, title 12, section 1842(d), to permit certain charitable trusts to sell, assign, or transfer certain financial institutions' assets without regard to whether the entity acquiring the assets of the charitable trust is located outside of this state.

Subd. 4. Additional acquisitions. A bank holding company, other than a reciprocating state bank holding company as defined in section 48.92, subdivision 8, that directly or indirectly acquires control of a bank located in this state under the provisions of this section may acquire additional bank assets through the expenditure of an annual amount not to exceed five percent of the Minnesota assets of the acquired bank holding company as of December 31 of the preceding year. The restrictions within this subdivision apply only until the bank holding company making an acquisition under this section becomes a reciprocating state bank holding company. This section does not prohibit the bank holding company from being granted a charter for a de novo bank or from establishing de novo detached facilities pursuant to Minnesota law.

Laws 1989, c. 340, art. 1, § 37.

[1] 26 U.S.C.A. § 4943.

Historical and Statutory Notes

Laws 1989, c. 340, art. 1, § 76 provides:

"Except as required by section 645.35 or as otherwise provided in sections 47 [section

501B.55], 60 [section 501B.71], 62 [section 501B.73], 70 [section 501B.86], subdivision 9, and 72 [section 501B.88], this article is effective January 1, 1990, and applies to trusts, property

interests, and powers of appointment whenever created to the extent permitted under the United States Constitution and the Minnesota Constitution."

SALES AND LEASES OF REAL PROPERTY

501B.46. Petition for court order to sell, mortgage, or lease real property held in trust

(a) Except as provided in paragraph (c), if the assets of an express trust by will or other written instrument include real property in this state that the trustee is not, under the terms of the trust, then permitted to sell, mortgage, or lease, and if section 501B.23 is applicable to the trust, the trustee or a beneficiary of the trust may petition the court then having jurisdiction of the trust for an order directing the trustee to sell, mortgage, or lease the real property or a part of the real property.

(b) Except as provided in paragraph (c), if the assets of an express trust by will or other written instrument include real property in this state that the trustee is not, under the terms of the trust, then permitted to sell, mortgage, or lease, and if section 501B.23 is not applicable to the trust, the trustee or a beneficiary of the trust may petition an appropriate district court under section 501B.16 for an order directing the trustee to sell, mortgage, or lease the real property or a part of the real property.

(c) If a trust is of the kind described in section 501B.09, subdivision 2a, no order described in paragraph (a) or (b) may be entered upon a petition filed by a person other than the trustee.

Laws 1989, c. 340, art. 1, § 38. Amended by Laws 1990, c. 581, § 3.

Historical and Statutory Notes

Laws 1989, c. 340, art. 1, § 76 provides:

"Except as required by section 645.35 or as otherwise provided in sections 47 [section 501B.55], 60 [section 501B.71], 62 [section 501B.73], 70 [section 501B.86], subdivision 9, and 72 [section 501B.88], this article is effective January 1, 1990, and applies to trusts, property interests, and powers of appointment whenever

created to the extent permitted under the United States Constitution and the Minnesota Constitution."

Laws 1990, c. 581, § 9, provides in part that § 3 [amending § 501B.46] applies to proceedings initiated after January 1, 1990, with respect to interests created before, on, or after January 1, 1990.

501B.47. Petition by owner of present or future interest for court order to sell, mortgage, or lease interests in real property

Notwithstanding a contrary provision in the instrument creating the interests, when the ownership of real property situated in this state is divided into one or more possessory interests and one or more future interests, the owner of an interest may petition the district court for the county in which any of the real property is situated for an order directing that the real property or part of the real property be sold, mortgaged, or leased. If an owner is a minor or incapacitated person as defined in section 524.5–102, subdivision 6 or 10, or otherwise under conservatorship, the petition may be made on behalf of the owner by a custodian, conservator, or guardian.

Laws 1989, c. 340, art. 1, § 39. Amended by Laws 2004, c. 146, art. 3, § 33.

Historical and Statutory Notes

Laws 1989, c. 340, art. 1, § 76 provides:

"Except as required by section 645.35 or as otherwise provided in sections 47 [section 501B.55], 60 [section 501B.71], 62 [section 501B.73], 70 [section 501B.86], subdivision 9, and 72 [section 501B.88], this article is effective January 1, 1990, and applies to trusts, property interests, and powers of appointment whenever created to the extent permitted under the United States Constitution and the Minnesota Constitution."

501B.48. When petition may be granted

Subdivision 1. Petition under section 501B.46. The court to which a petition to sell, mortgage, or lease has been made under section 501B.46 may grant the petition, on terms it considers appropriate, if the court determines that:

(1) if the interest in real property were owned in fee simple or absolute ownership by a single individual, a sale or mortgage of the interest would be desirable because total investment returns, including appreciation and the value of any use of the real property by trust beneficiaries, were inadequate; or

(2) an order directing a sale or mortgage would be economically advantageous to the trust beneficiaries to whom trust income is distributable or may be distributed and would not be seriously disadvantageous to any trust beneficiary.

The court to which a petition to lease has been made under section 501B.46 may grant the petition on terms it considers appropriate, even though the term of the lease may extend beyond the term of the trust, if the court determines that an order directing a lease would be economically advantageous to the trust beneficiaries to whom trust income is distributable or may be distributed and would not be seriously disadvantageous to any trust beneficiary.

Subd. 2. Petition under section 501B.47. The court to which a petition to sell or mortgage has been made under section 501B.47 may grant the petition on terms it considers appropriate if the court determines that:

(1) were the real property held in trust for the owners of the possessory and future interests in the property, retention of the real property by the trustee without the sale or mortgage would be inconsistent with a trustee's common law duty to administer the trust impartially as between the holders of successive interests in income and principal;

(2) if the interest in real property were owned in fee simple or absolute ownership by a single individual, a sale or mortgage of the interest would be desirable because total investment returns, including appreciation and the value of any use of the real property by possessory owners, were inadequate; or

(3) an order directing a sale or mortgage would be economically advantageous to the owners of possessory interests in the real property and would not be seriously disadvantageous to the owner of any interest in the property.

The court to which a petition to lease has been made under section 501B.47 may grant the petition on terms it considers appropriate, even though the term of the lease may extend beyond the duration of the possessory interests in the real property, if the court determines that an order directing a lease would be economically advantageous to the owners of possessory interests in the real property and would not be seriously disadvantageous to the owner of any interest in the property.

Laws 1989, c. 340, art. 1, § 40.

Historical and Statutory Notes

Laws 1989, c. 340, art. 1, § 76 provides:

"Except as required by section 645.35 or as otherwise provided in sections 47 [section 501B.55], 60 [section 501B.71], 62 [section 501B.73], 70 [section 501B.86], subdivision 9, and 72 [section 501B.88], this article is effective January 1, 1990, and applies to trusts, property interests, and powers of appointment whenever created to the extent permitted under the United States Constitution and the Minnesota Constitution."

501B.49. Notice of hearing

Subdivision 1. Hearing required. On the filing of a petition under section 501B.46 or 501B.47, the court shall, by order, fix a time and place for a hearing on the petition unless a hearing has been waived in writing. In the case of a petition under section 501B.46, each beneficiary of the trust then in being must join in the waiver. In the case of a petition under section 501B.47, each person in being who owns an interest in the real property must join in the waiver.

Subd. 2. Notice. Notice of hearing must be given by publishing a copy of the order for hearing one time in a legal newspaper for the county in which the petition is filed at least 20 days before the date of the hearing, and by mailing copies of the order for hearing in the manner specified in this subdivision or in another manner ordered by the court. In the case of a petition under section 501B.46, mailed notice must be given by mailing a copy of the order for hearing to those beneficiaries of the trust then in being who are known to or reasonably ascertainable by the petitioner and, in the case of a beneficiary who is a minor or an incapacitated person as defined in section 524.5–102, subdivision 6 or 10, or otherwise under conservatorship, to the conservator or guardian, or if none is acting within the state, to the guardian ad litem of the beneficiary, at least 15 days before the date of the hearing. In the case of a petition under section 501B.47, mailed notice must be given by mailing a copy of the order for hearing to those persons owning an interest in the real property then in being who are known to or reasonably ascertainable by the petitioner and, in the case of a person who is a minor or an incapacitated person as defined in section 524.5–102, subdivision 6 or 10, or otherwise under conservatorship, to the conservator or guardian, or if none is acting within the state, to the guardian ad litem of the person, at least 15 days before the date of the hearing.

Laws 1989, c. 340, art. 1, § 41. Amended by Laws 2004, c. 146, art. 3, § 34.

Historical and Statutory Notes

Laws 1989, c. 340, art. 1, § 76 provides:

"Except as required by section 645.35 or as otherwise provided in sections 47 [section 501B.55], 60 [section 501B.71], 62 [section 501B.73], 70 [section 501B.86], subdivision 9, and 72 [section 501B.88], this article is effective January 1, 1990, and applies to trusts, property interests, and powers of appointment whenever created to the extent permitted under the United States Constitution and the Minnesota Constitution."

501B.50. Representation of persons who are unborn, unascertained, unknown, or minors or incapacitated persons

If an interested person is a minor or an incapacitated person as defined in section 524.5–102, subdivision 6 or 10, or otherwise under conservatorship, and does not have a guardian or conservator within the state, the court shall appoint a guardian ad litem for the person. If an interested person is unborn, unascertained, or a person whose identity or address is unknown to the petitioner, the court shall represent the person, but the court may, upon the application of the petitioner or another interested person or on its own motion, appoint a guardian ad litem to represent the person.

Laws 1989, c. 340, art. 1, § 42. Amended by Laws 2004, c. 146, art. 3, § 35.

Historical and Statutory Notes

Laws 1989, c. 340, art. 1, § 76 provides:

"Except as required by section 645.35 or as otherwise provided in sections 47 [section 501B.55], 60 [section 501B.71], 62 [section 501B.73], 70 [section 501B.86], subdivision 9, and 72 [section 501B.88], this article is effective January 1, 1990, and applies to trusts, property interests, and powers of appointment whenever created to the extent permitted under the United States Constitution and the Minnesota Constitution."

501B.51. Order upon petition; execution of transaction

Subdivision 1. Form of order; conclusiveness. At a hearing under section 501B.49, the court shall make an order it considers appropriate. If the petition is granted in whole or in part, the order must specify the real property to be sold, mortgaged, or leased and the terms and conditions on which the transaction is to be consummated. The order is final and conclusive as to all matters determined by it and binding in rem on all persons interested in the real property, whether their interests are vested or contingent, even though the person is a minor, incapacitated as defined in section 524.5–102, subdivision 6 or 10, or otherwise subject to conservatorship, unascertained, or not in being, except that appeal may be taken in the manner provided in the Rules of Appellate Procedure.

Subd. 2. Execution of order. (a) In the case of a petition under section 501B.46, all transactions required by the order must be executed by the trustee.

(b) In the case of a petition under section 501B.47, the court shall appoint a suitable person as receiver to act for the court in executing each transaction required by the order. Each required transaction must be executed by the receiver.

Laws 1989, c. 340, art. 1, § 43. Amended by Laws 2004, c. 146, art. 3, § 36.

Historical and Statutory Notes

Laws 1989, c. 340, art. 1, § 76 provides:

"Except as required by section 645.35 or as otherwise provided in sections 47 [section 501B.55], 60 [section 501B.71], 62 [section 501B.73], 70 [section 501B.86], subdivision 9, and 72 [section 501B.88], this article is effective January 1, 1990, and applies to trusts, property interests, and powers of appointment whenever created to the extent permitted under the United States Constitution and the Minnesota Constitution."

501B.52. Report of agreement for confirmation

Before a sale, mortgage, or lease is made under an order described in section 501B.51, the trustee or receiver shall enter into an agreement for the sale, mortgage, or lease, subject to the approval of the court, and must report the agreement to the court under oath. At least 15 days before the hearing on the confirmation of the agreement, the trustee or receiver shall mail a copy of the agreement to each interested party to whom mailed notice was given under section 501B.49 and to any interested party who did not receive notice but appeared at the hearing on the petition.

Laws 1989, c. 340, art. 1, § 44.

Historical and Statutory Notes

Laws 1989, c. 340, art. 1, § 76 provides:

"Except as required by section 645.35 or as otherwise provided in sections 47 [section 501B.55], 60 [section 501B.71], 62 [section 501B.73], 70 [section 501B.86], subdivision 9, and 72 [section 501B.88], this article is effective January 1, 1990, and applies to trusts, property interests, and powers of appointment whenever created to the extent permitted under the United States Constitution and the Minnesota Constitution."

501B.53. Order of confirmation; contents and subsequent procedures; distribution of assets

Subdivision 1. Order to execute agreement. If an agreement reported to the court under section 501B.52 is found by the court to conform to the order described in section 501B.51, the court shall make an order approving and confirming the agreement and directing the trustee or receiver to execute and deliver the deed, mortgage, or lease of real property required by the agreement.

Subd. 2. Costs; allowances. The order of confirmation may direct that each participant in the proceeding be paid reasonable costs of the proceeding incurred by the participant. The order of confirmation may make appropriate allowances to persons who have served in the proceeding as receiver, guardian ad litem, or counsel, and may direct the manner of payment of these allowances.

Subd. 3. Safekeeping, management, and distribution of assets. The order of confirmation must include appropriate provisions for the safekeeping, management, and distribution of assets derived from the ordered transaction. In the case of assets derived from a transaction executed by a trustee under section 501B.51, subdivision 2, paragraph (a), distribution must be made to the trustee for administration as trust assets. In the case of assets derived from a transaction executed by a receiver under section 501B.51, subdivision 2, paragraph (b), distribution must be made to the owners, at the time of the sale or mortgage, of present possessory interests in the real property that was sold or mortgaged, and to the owners of leased real property who would be entitled to possession on the present termination of the lease. Notwithstanding any contrary provision in the terms of the instrument creating the interests in real property sold, mortgaged, or leased under this subdivision, the same possessory and future interests exist in the assets distributed as existed in the real property, and any provision in the creating instrument for forfeiture of an interest in real property upon a sale or other assignment must be disregarded by the court in directing distribution or other assignment of interests in the proceeds of a sale.

Subd. 4. Hearing on confirmation order. The trustee or receiver shall obtain from the court a time and place for the court's hearing on the confirmation of the agreement and shall give mailed notice of the time and place of the hearing to the interested parties described in section 501B.51 at least 15 days before the date of that hearing. The order of confirmation is final and conclusive as to all matters determined by it and binding in rem on all persons interested in the real property, whether their interests are vested or contingent, even though a person is a minor or incapacitated, as defined in section 524.5–102, subdivision 6 or 10, or otherwise under conservatorship, unascertained, or not in being, except that appeal may be taken in the manner provided in the Rules of Appellate Procedure.

Subd. 5. Combined proceedings. In appropriate circumstances, proceedings under this section and section 501B.52 may be combined with proceedings under sections 501B.46 to 501B.51.

Laws 1989, c. 340, art. 1, § 45. Amended by Laws 2004, c. 146, art. 3, § 37.

501B.54. Legal effect of deed, mortgage, or lease made under section 501B.53

A deed, mortgage, or lease executed and delivered in accordance with an order of confirmation under section 501B.53 binds the interests of the applicant for the order and of all other persons interested in the real property sold, mortgaged, or leased.

Laws 1989, c. 340, art. 1, § 46.

Historical and Statutory Notes

Laws 1989, c. 340, art. 1, § 76 provides:

"Except as required by section 645.35 or as otherwise provided in sections 47 [section 501B.55], 60 [section 501B.71], 62 [section 501B.73], 70 [section 501B.86], subdivision 9, and 72 [section 501B.88], this article is effective January 1, 1990, and applies to trusts, property interests, and powers of appointment whenever created to the extent permitted under the United States Constitution and the Minnesota Constitution."

501B.55. Date of creation of interests affected by the procedures in sections 501B.46 to 501B.54

The procedures in sections 501B.46 to 501B.54 apply to proceedings initiated after January 1, 1990, with respect to interests created before, on, or after January 1, 1990.

Laws 1989, c. 340, art. 1, § 47.

Historical and Statutory Notes

Laws 1989, c. 340, art. 1, § 76 provides:

"Except as required by section 645.35 or as otherwise provided in sections 47 [section 501B.55], 60 [section 501B.71], 62 [section 501B.73], 70 [section 501B.86], subdivision 9, and 72 [section 501B.88], this article is effective January 1, 1990, and applies to trusts, property interests, and powers of appointment whenever created to the extent permitted under the United States Constitution and the Minnesota Constitution."

501B.56. Certificate of trust

Subdivision 1. Contents of certificate. The grantor or a trustee of a trust, at any time after execution or creation of a trust, may execute a certificate of trust that sets forth less than all of the provisions of a trust instrument and any amendments to the instrument. The certificate of trust may be used for purposes of selling, conveying, pledging, mortgaging, leasing, or transferring title to any interest in real or personal property. The certificate of trust must include:

(1) the name of the trust, if one is given;

(2) the date of the trust instrument;

(3) the name of each grantor;

(4) the name of each original trustee;

(5) the name and address of each trustee empowered to act under the trust instrument at the time of execution of the certificate;

(6) the following statement: "The trustees are authorized by the instrument to sell, convey, pledge, mortgage, lease, or transfer title to any interest in real or personal property, except as limited by the following: (if none, so indicate)";

(7) any other trust provisions the grantors or trustees include; and

(8) a statement as to whether the trust instrument has terminated or been revoked.

The certificate of trust must be upon the representation of the grantors or trustees that the statements contained in the certificate of trust are true and correct and that there are no other provisions in the trust instrument or amendments to it that limit the powers of the trustees to sell, convey, pledge, mortgage, lease, or transfer title to interests in real or personal property. The signature of the grantors or trustees must be under oath before a notary public or other official authorized to administer oaths.

Subd. 2. Effect. A certificate of trust executed under subdivision 1 may be recorded in the office of the county recorder for any county or filed with the office of the registrar of titles with respect to registered land described in the certificate of trust or any attachment to it. When it is recorded or filed in a county where real property is situated, or in the case of personal property, when it is presented to a third party, the certificate of trust serves to document the existence of the trust, the identity of the trustees, the powers of the trustees and any limitations on those powers, and other matters the certificate of trust sets out, as though the full trust instrument had been recorded, filed, or presented. Until amended or revoked under subdivision 3, or until the full trust instrument is recorded, filed, or presented, a certificate of trust is prima facie proof as to the matters contained in it and any party may rely upon the continued effectiveness of the certificate.

Subd. 3. Amendment or revocation. Amendment or revocation of a certificate of trust may be made only by a written instrument executed by the grantor or a trustee of a trust. Amendment or revocation of a certificate of trust is not effective as to a party unless that party has actual notice of the amendment or revocation.

For purposes of this subdivision, "actual notice" means that a written instrument of amendment or revocation has been received by the party or, in the case of real property, that either a written instrument of amendment or revocation has been received by the party or that a written instrument of amendment or revocation containing the legal description of the real property has been recorded in the office of the county recorder or filed in the office of the registrar of titles where the real property is situated.

Subd. 4. Application. Subdivisions 1 to 3 are effective August 1, 1992, but apply to trust instruments whenever created or executed.

Laws 1992, c. 548, § 2.

501B.561. Certificate of custodianship

Subdivision 1. Contents of certificate. (a) A custodian or the owner of property held in a custodianship, at any time after execution or creation of a custodianship instrument, may execute a certificate of custodianship that sets forth less than all of the provisions of the custodial instrument and any amendments to the instrument. The certificate of custodianship may be used for purposes of selling, conveying, pledging, mortgaging, leasing, or transferring title to any interest in real or personal property. The certificate of custodianship must include:

(1) the name of the custodianship, if one is given;

(2) the date of the custodianship instrument;

(3) the name of each owner of property held in the custodianship;

(4) the name of each original custodian;

(5) the name and address of each custodian empowered to act under the custodianship instrument at the time of execution of the certificate;

(6) the following statement: "The custodians are authorized by the instrument to sell, convey, pledge, mortgage, lease, or transfer title to any interest in real or personal property, except as limited by the following: (if none, so indicate)";

(7) any other custodianship provisions the custodians or owners of property held in the custodianship include; and

(8) a statement as to whether the custodianship instrument has terminated or been revoked.

(b) The certificate of custodianship must be upon the representation of the custodians or the owners of property held in the custodianship that the statements contained in the certificate of custodianship are true and correct and that there are no other provisions in the custodianship instrument or amendments to it that limit the powers of the custodianship to sell, convey, pledge, mortgage, lease, or transfer title to interests in real or personal property. The signature of the custodians or the owners of property held in the custodianship must be under oath before a notary public or other official authorized to administer oaths.

Subd. 2. Effect. A certificate of custodianship executed under subdivision 1 may be recorded in the office of the county recorder for any county, or filed with the office of the registrar of titles with respect to registered land described in the certificate of custodianship or any attachment to it. When it is recorded or filed in a county where real property is situated, or in the case of personal property, when it is presented to a third party, the certificate of custodianship serves to document the existence of the custodianship, the identity of the custodians, the powers of the custodians and any limitations on those powers, and other matters the certificate of custodianship sets out, as though the full custodianship instrument had been recorded, filed, or presented. Until amended or revoked under subdivision 3, or until the full custodianship instrument is recorded, filed, or presented, a certificate of custodianship is prima facie proof as to the matters contained in it, and any party may rely upon the continued effectiveness of the certificate.

Subd. 3. Amendment or revocation. (a) Amendment or revocation of a certificate of custodianship may be made only by a written instrument executed by a custodian or an owner of property held in the custodianship. Amendment or revocation of a certificate of custodianship is not effective as to a party unless that party has actual notice of the amendment or revocation.

(b) For purposes of this subdivision, "actual notice" means that a written instrument of amendment or revocation has been received by the party or, in the case of real property, that either a written instrument of amendment or revocation has been received by the party or that a written instrument of amendment or revocation containing the legal description of the real property has been recorded in the office of the county recorder or filed in the office of the registrar of titles where the real property is situated.

Subd. 4. Application. (a) Subdivisions 1 to 3 are effective August 1, 2006, but apply to custodianship instruments whenever created or executed.

(b) Subdivisions 1 to 3 apply only to custodianships established under a federal law or under a statute of this or any other state. Subdivisions 1 to 3 do not apply to custodianships governed by chapter 527 or by the similar laws of another state.

Laws 2006, c. 221, § 4.

501B.57. Affidavit of trustee in real property transactions

Subdivision 1. Form of affidavit for inter vivos trust. An affidavit of a trustee or of trustees of an inter vivos trust in support of a real property transaction may be substantially in the following form:

STATE OF MINNESOTA)   AFFIDAVIT OF TRUSTEE
) ss.
COUNTY OF   )

.........., being first duly sworn on oath says that:

1. Affiant is the trustee (one of the trustees) named in that certain Certificate of Trust (or Trust Instrument)

    filed for record ...., ..., as Document No. ... (or in Book ... of .... Page ....) in the Office of the (County Recorder/Registrar of Titles) of .... County, Minnesota,

    OR

    to which this Affidavit is attached,

executed by Affiant or another trustee or the grantor of the trust described in the Certificate of Trust (or set forth in the Trust Instrument), and which relates to real property in .... County, Minnesota legally described as follows:

....

....

....

(If more space is needed, continue on back or on attachment.)

2. The name(s) and address(es) of the trustee(s) empowered by the Trust Instrument to act at the time of the execution of this Affidavit are as follows:

....

....

....

3. The trustee(s) who have executed that certain instrument relating to the real property described above between ...., as trustee(s) and ...., dated ...., ...:

(a) are empowered by the provisions of the trust to sell, convey, pledge, mortgage, lease, or transfer title to any interest in real property held in trust; and

(b) are the requisite number of trustees required by the provisions of the trust to execute and deliver such an instrument.

4. The trust has not terminated and has not been revoked.

– OR –

4. The trust has terminated (or has been revoked). The execution and delivery of the instrument described in paragraph 3 has been made pursuant to the provisions of the trust.

5. There has been no amendment to the trust which limits the power of trustee(s) to execute and deliver the instrument described in paragraph 3.

6. The trust is not supervised by any court.

– OR –

6. The trust is supervised by the .... Court of .... County, ... All necessary approval has been obtained from the court for the trustee(s) to execute and deliver the instrument described in paragraph 3.

7. Affiant does not have actual knowledge of any facts indicating that the trust is invalid.

_____

....
, Affiant

Subscribed and sworn to before me
this ..... day of ...., ...

Notary Stamp or Seal

....
Signature of Notary Public or
Other Official

This instrument was drafted by:
....
....

Subd. 1a. Form of affidavit for testamentary trust. An affidavit of a trustee or of trustees of a testamentary trust in support of a real property transaction may be substantially in the following form:

STATE OF MINNESOTA   )   AFFIDAVIT OF TRUSTEE
) ss.
COUNTY OF   )

.........., being first duly sworn on oath says that:

1. The .... Trust was created by the Last Will and Testament of ...., Decedent, dated ...., ... Decedent died on ...., ... Affiant, as trustee of the Trust, acquired by instrument or decree dated ...., ..., filed in the office of the County Recorder/Registrar of Titles, ... County, Minnesota, as Document No. ...., an interest in real property in .... County, Minnesota, legally described as follows:

....

....

....

....

(If more space is needed, continue on back or on an attachment.)

2. The name(s) and address(es) of the trustee(s) empowered by the terms of decedent's will to act at the time of the execution of this Affidavit are as follows:

....

....

....

3. The trustee(s) who have executed that certain instrument relating to the real property described above between ...., as trustee(s) and ...., dated ...., ...:

(a) are empowered by the provisions of the trust under decedent's will to sell, convey, pledge, mortgage, lease, or transfer title to any interest in real property held in trust; and

(b) are the requisite number of trustees required by the provisions of the will to execute and deliver such an instrument.

4. The Trust has not terminated and has not been revoked.

– OR –

4. The Trust has terminated (or has been revoked). The execution and delivery of the instrument described in paragraph 3 has been made pursuant to the provisions of the Trust.

5. There has been no amendment to the Trust which limits the powers of the trustee(s) to execute and deliver the instrument described in paragraph 3.

6. The Trust is not supervised by any court.

– OR –

6. The Trust is supervised by the .... Court of .... County. .... All necessary approval has been obtained from the court for the trustee(s) to execute and deliver the instrument described in paragraph 3.

7. Affiant does not have actual knowledge of any facts indicating that the Trust is invalid.

                              ....
                                                              , Affiant

Subscribed and sworn to before me
this .... day of ...., ...

                              ....
                              Signature of Notary Public or
                              Other Official

Notary Stamp or Seal
This instrument was drafted by:
....
....
....

Subd. 2. Effect. An affidavit by the trustee or trustees under subdivision 1 or 1a is proof that:

(i) the trust described in the affidavit is a valid trust;

(ii) either the trust has not terminated or been revoked or, if the trust has terminated or been revoked, the conveyance described in the affidavit is made pursuant to the provisions of the trust;

(iii) the powers granted the trustee or trustees extend to the real property described in the affidavit or attachment to the affidavit;

(iv) no amendment to the trust has been made limiting the power of the trustee or trustees to sell, convey, pledge, mortgage, lease, or transfer title to the real property described in the affidavit or attachment to the affidavit, if any;

(v) the requisite number of trustees have executed and delivered the instrument of conveyance described in the affidavit; and

(vi) any necessary court approval of the transaction has been obtained.

The proof is conclusive as to any party relying on the affidavit, except a party dealing directly with the trustee or trustees who has actual knowledge of facts to the contrary.

Subd. 3. Recording or filing. An Affidavit of Trustee or Trustees under subdivisions 1 and 1a may be recorded in the office of the county recorder for any county, or filed with the office of the registrar of titles for any county with respect to registered land described in the affidavit, or in the Certificate of Trust or Trust Instrument referred to in the affidavit, and may be recorded or filed as a separate document or combined with or attached to an original or certified copy of a Certificate of Trust or Trust Instrument, and recorded or filed as one document.

Laws 1992, c. 548, § 3. Amended by Laws 1996, c. 338, art. 2, § 1; Laws 1998, c. 254. art. 1, § 107; Laws 1998, c. 262, §§ 5, 6.

501B.571. Affidavit of custodian in real property transactions

Subdivision 1. Form of affidavit for custodianship. An affidavit of a custodian or of custodians of a custodianship in support of a real property transaction may be substantially in the following form:

```
STATE OF MINNESOTA          )   AFFIDAVIT OF CUSTODIAN
                            )   ss.
COUNTY OF                   )
```

.........................., being first duly sworn on oath says that:

1. Affiant is the custodian (one of the custodians) named in that certain Certificate of Custodianship (or Custodianship Instrument)

filed for record ...., ..., as Document No. ..... (or in Book ..... of ...., Page ......) in the Office of the (County Recorder/ Registrar of Titles) of .... County, Minnesota,

OR

to which this Affidavit is attached,

executed by Affiant or another custodian or by the owner of the property that is held in the custodianship described in the Certificate of Custodianship (or set forth in the Custodianship Instrument), and which relates to real property in .... County, Minnesota, legally described as follows:

_____ _____

_____ _____

(If more space is needed, continue on back or on attachment.)

2. The name(s) and address(es) of the custodian(s) empowered by the Custodian Instrument to act at the time of the execution of this Affidavit are as follows:

_____ _____

_____

3. The custodian(s) who have executed that certain instrument relating to the real property described above between ...., as custodian(s) and ...., dated ...., ...:

(i) are empowered by the provisions of the custodianship to sell, convey, pledge, mortgage, lease, or transfer title to any interest in real property held in custodianship; and

(ii) are the requisite number of custodians required by the provisions of the custodianship to execute and deliver such an instrument.

4. The custodianship has not terminated and has not been revoked.

– OR –

4. The custodianship has terminated (or has been revoked). The execution and delivery of the instrument described in paragraph 3 has been made pursuant to the provisions of the custodianship.

5. There has been no amendment to the custodianship which limits the power of custodian(s) to execute and deliver the instrument described in paragraph 3.

6. The custodianship is not supervised by any court.

– OR –

6. The custodianship is supervised by the .... Court of .... County, ... All necessary approval has been obtained from the court for the custodian(s) to execute and deliver the instrument described in paragraph 3.

7. Affiant does not have actual knowledge of any facts indicating that the custodianship is invalid.

....

Subscribed and sworn to before me   , Affiant

this .... day of ...., ...

....

Notary Stamp or Seal   Signature of Notary Public or

                                                            Other Official

This instrument was drafted by:

....
....

Subd. 2. Effect. An affidavit by the custodian or custodians under subdivision 1 is proof that:

(1) the custodianship described in the affidavit is a valid custodianship;

(2) either the custodianship has not terminated or been revoked or, if the custodianship has terminated or been revoked, the conveyance described in the affidavit is made pursuant to the provisions of the custodianship;

(3) the powers granted the custodian or custodians extend to the real property described in the affidavit or attachment to the affidavit;

(4) no amendment to the custodianship has been made limiting the power of the custodian or custodians to sell, convey, pledge, mortgage, lease, or transfer title to the real property described in the affidavit or attachment to the affidavit, if any;

(5) the requisite number of custodians have executed and delivered the instrument of conveyance described in the affidavit; and

(6) any necessary court approval of the transaction has been obtained.

The proof is conclusive as to any party relying on the affidavit, except a party dealing directly with the custodian or custodians who has actual knowledge of facts to the contrary.

Subd. 3. Recording or filing. An Affidavit of Custodian or Custodians under subdivision 1 may be recorded in the office of the county recorder for any county, or filed with the office of the registrar of titles for any county with respect to registered land described in the affidavit, or in the Certificate of Custodianship or Custodianship Instrument referred to in the affidavit, and may be recorded or filed as a separate document or combined with or attached to an original or certified copy of a Certificate of Custodianship or Custodianship Instrument, and recorded or filed as one document.

Subd. 4. Application. (a) Subdivisions 1 to 3 are effective August 1, 2006, but apply to custodianship instruments whenever created or executed.

(b) Subdivisions 1 to 3 apply only to custodianships established under a federal law or under a statute of this or any other state. Subdivisions 1 to 3 do not apply to custodianships governed by chapter 527 or by the similar laws of another state.

Laws 2006, c. 221, § 5.

UNIFORM PRINCIPAL AND INCOME ACT

501B.59. Definitions

Subdivision 1. Scope. The definitions in this section apply to sections 501B.59 to 501B.76.

Subd. 1a. Accounting period. "Accounting period" means a calendar year unless another 12–month period is selected by the trustee. Accounting period includes a portion of a calendar year or other 12–month period that begins when an income interest begins or ends when an income interest ends.

Subd. 2. Income beneficiary. "Income beneficiary" means the person to whom income is presently payable or for whom it is accumulated for distribution as income.

Subd. 3. Inventory value. "Inventory value" means the cost of property purchased by the trustee and the market value of other property at the time it became subject to the trust, but in the case of a testamentary trust the trustee may use any value finally determined for the purposes of an estate or inheritance tax.

Subd. 4. Remainderperson. "Remainderperson" means the person entitled to principal, including income accumulated and added to principal.

Subd. 5. Trustee. "Trustee" means an original trustee and any successor or added trustee.

Laws 1989, c. 340, art. 1, § 48. Amended by Laws 2001, c. 15, § 2.

UNIFORM PRINCIPAL AND INCOME ACT (1997)

Table of Jurisdictions Wherein 1997 Act Has Been Adopted

For text of Uniform Act, and variation notes and annotation materials for adopting jurisdictions, see Uniform Laws Annotated, Master Edition, Volume 7B.

Jurisdiction	Laws	Effective Date	Statutory Citation
Alabama	2000, Act 675	1–1–2001	Code 1975, §§ 19–3A–101 to 19–3A–606.
Alaska	2003, c. 145	9–1–2003	AS §§ 13.38.200 to 13.38.990.
Arizona	2001, c. 176	1–1–2002	A.R.S. §§ 14–7401 to 14–7431.
Arkansas	1999, Act 647	1–1–2000	A.C.A. §§ 28–70–101 to 28–70–605.
California	1999, c. 145	1–1–2000	West's Ann.Cal.Probate Code §§ 16320 to 16375.
Colorado	2000, c. 257	7–1–2001	West's C.R.S.A. §§ 15–1–401 to 15–1–434.
Connecticut	1999, P.A. 99–164	1–1–2000	C.G.S.A. §§ 45a–542 to 45a–542ff.
District of Columbia	2001, D.C. Law 13–292	4–27–2001	D.C. Official Code, 2001 Ed. §§ 28–4801.01 to 28–4806.02.
Florida	2002, c. 42	1–1–2003	West's F.S.A. §§ 738.101 to 738.804.
Hawaii	2000, c. 191	7–1–2000	HRS §§ 557A–101 to 557A–506.
Idaho	2001, c. 261	7–1–2001	I.C. §§ 68–10–101 to 68–10–605.
Indiana	2002, c. 84	1–1–2003	West's A.I.C. §§ 30–2–14–1 to 30–2–14–44.
Iowa	1999, H.F. 584	7–1–1999	I.C.A. §§ 637.101 to 637.701.
Kansas	2000, c. 61	7–1–2000	K.S.A. §§ 58–9–101 to 58–9–603.
Kentucky	2004, c. 158	1–1–2005	KRS 386.450 to 386.504.
Maine	2002, c. 544	1–1–2003	18–A M.R.S.A. §§ 7–701 to 7–773.
Maryland	2000, c. 292	10–1–2000	Code, Estates and Trusts, §§ 15–501 to 15–530.
Massachusetts	2005, c. 129	1–1–2006	M.G.L.A. c. 203D, §§ 1 to 29.
Michigan	2004, c. 159	9–1–2004	M.C.L.A. §§ 555.501 to 555.1005.
Minnesota[1]	1969, c. 1006	1–1–1970	M.S.A. §§ 501B.59 to 501B.76.
Missouri	2001, H.B. 241	7–10–2001 *	V.A.M.S. §§ 469.401 to 469.467.
Montana	2003, c. 506	4–25–2003 *	MCA §§ 72–34–421 to 72–34–453.
Nebraska	2001, LB 56	9–1–2001	R.R.S.1943, §§ 30–3116 to 30–3149.
Nevada	2003, c. 355	10–1–2003	NRS 164.780 to 164.925.
New Hampshire	2006, c. 320	1–1–2007	RSA 564–C:1–101 to 564–C:6–602.
New Jersey	2001, c. 212	1–1–2002	N.J.S.A. 3B:19B–1 to 3B:19B–31.

Jurisdiction	Laws	Effective Date	Statutory Citation
New Mexico	2001, c. 113	7–1–2001	NMSA 1978, §§ 46–3A–101 to 46–3A–603.
New York	2001, c. 243	1–1–2002	McKinney's EPTL 11–A–1.1 to 11–A–6.4.
North Carolina	2003, c. 232	1–1–2004	G.S. §§ 37A–1–101 to 37A–6–602.
North Dakota	1999, c. 532	8–1–1999	NDCC 59–04.2–01 to 59–04.2–30.
Ohio	2006, H.B. 416	1–1–2007	R.C. §§ 5812.01 to 5812.52.
Oklahoma	1998, c. 115	11–1–1998	60 Okl.St.Ann. §§ 175.101 to 175.602.
Oregon	2003, c. 279	1–1–2004	ORS 116.007, 129.200 to 129.450.
Pennsylvania	2002, c. 50	5–16–2002 *	20 Pa.C.S.A. §§ 8101 to 8191.
South Carolina	2005, c. 66	1–1–2006	Code 1976, §§ 62–7–901 to 62–7–932.
South Dakota[2].......	2007, c. 282	7–1–2007	SDCL 55–13A–101 to 55–13A–602.
Tennessee...........	2000, c. 829	7–1–2000	T.C.A. §§ 35–6–101 to 35–6–602.
Texas	2003, c. 659	1–1–2004	V.T.C.A. Property Code §§ 116.001 to 116.206.
Utah................	2004, c. 285	5–3–2004	U.C.A. 1953, 22–3–101 to 22–3–603.
Virginia	1999, c. 975	1–1–2000	Code 1950, §§ 55–277.1 to 55–277.33.
Washington	2002, c. 345	1–1–2003	West's RCWA 11.104A.001 to 11.104A.905.
West Virginia	2000, c. 273	7–1–2000	Code, 44B–1–101 to 44B–6–604.
Wisconsin	2005, c. 10	5–17–2005	W.S.A. 701.20.
Wyoming	2001, c. 11	7–1–2001	Wyo.Stat.Ann. §§ 2–3–801 to 2–3–834.

* Approval date.

[1] Minnesota's act remains a substantial adoption of the provisions of the Uniform Principal and Income Act (1962), but various amendments and newly enacted sections have adopted several provisions of the Uniform Principal and Income Act (1997). Therefore, Minnesota will be carried in the Table of Adopting Jurisdictions for both acts.

[2] Enacted the Uniform Principal and Interest Act (1997) without repealing the Uniform Principal and Interest Act (1962). See the General Statutory Note, post.

UNIFORM PRINCIPAL AND INCOME ACT

REVISED 1962 ACT

Table of Jurisdictions Wherein 1962 Act Has Been Adopted

For text of Uniform Act, and variation notes and annotation materials for adopting jurisdictions, see Uniform Laws Annotated, Master Edition, Volume 7B.

Jurisdiction	Laws	Effective Date	Statutory Citation
Georgia	Acts 1991, p. 810	7–1–1991	O.C.G.A. §§ 53–12–210 to 53–12–222.
Illinois	1981, P.A. 82–390	1–1–1982	S.H.A. 760 ILCS 15/1 to 15/17.
Minnesota[1]	1969, c. 1006	1–1–1970	M.S.A. §§ 501B.59 to 501B.76.
Mississippi	1966, c. 371	1–1–1967	Code 1972, §§ 91–17–1 to 91–17–31.
South Dakota[2] ...	1984, c. 323	7–1–1984	SDCL 55–13–1 to 55–13–18.

[1] Minnesota's act remains a substantial adoption of the provisions of the Uniform Principal and Income Act (1962), but various amendments and newly enacted sections have adopted several provisions of the Uniform Principal and Income Act (1997). Therefore, Minnesota will be carried in the Table of Adopting Jurisdictions for both acts.

[2] Enacted the Uniform Principal and Interest Act (1997) without repealing the Uniform Principal and Interest Act (1962). See the General Statutory Note, post.

Historical and Statutory Notes

Laws 1989, c. 340, art. 1, § 76 provides:

"Except as required by section 645.35 or as otherwise provided in sections 47 [section 501B.55], 60 [section 501B.71], 62 [section 501B.73], 70 [section 501B.86], subdivision 9, and 72 [section 501B.88], this article is effective January 1, 1990, and applies to trusts, property interests, and powers of appointment whenever created to the extent permitted under the United States Constitution and the Minnesota Constitution."

501B.60.   Duty of trustee as to receipts and expenditure

Subdivision 1.   General rules of administration. A trust must be administered with due regard to the respective interests of income beneficiaries and remainderpersons.   A trust is so administered with respect to the allocation of receipts and expenditures if a receipt is credited or an expenditure is charged to income or principal or partly to each:

(1) in accordance with the terms of the trust instrument, notwithstanding contrary provisions of sections 501B.59 to 501B.76;

(2) in the absence of contrary terms of the trust instrument, in accordance with sections 501B.59 to 501B.76;

(3) if neither of the preceding rules of administration is applicable, in accordance with what is reasonable and equitable in view of the interests of those entitled to income as well as of those entitled to principal, and in view of the manner in which persons of ordinary prudence, discretion, and judgment would act in the management of their own affairs.

Subd. 2.   Trustee's discretion. If a trust instrument gives the trustee discretion in crediting a receipt or charging an expenditure to income or principal or partly to each, no inference of imprudence or partiality arises from the fact that the trustee has made an allocation contrary to sections 501B.59 to 501B.76.

Subd. 3.   Standards for exercise. In exercising a power to adjust under section 501B.705 or a discretionary power of administration regarding a matter within the scope of sections 501B.59 to 501B.76, a fiduciary shall administer the trust or estate impartially, based on what is fair and reasonable to all of the beneficiaries, except to the extent that the terms of the trust or the will clearly manifest an intention that the fiduciary shall or may favor one or more of the beneficiaries.   A determination in accordance with sections 501B.59 to 501B.76 is presumed to be fair and reasonable to all of the beneficiaries.

Laws 1989, c. 340, art. 1, § 49.   Amended by Laws 2001, c. 15, § 3; Laws 2002, c. 379, art. 1, § 97.

Historical and Statutory Notes

Laws 1989, c. 340, art. 1, § 76 provides:

"Except as required by section 645.35 or as otherwise provided in sections 47 [section 501B.55], 60 [section 501B.71], 62 [section 501B.73], 70 [section 501B.86], subdivision 9, and 72 [section 501B.88], this article is effective January 1, 1990, and applies to trusts, property interests, and powers of appointment whenever created to the extent permitted under the United States Constitution and the Minnesota Constitution."

501B.61. Income; principal; charges

Subdivision 1. Income defined. "Income" means the return in money or property derived from the use of principal, including return received as:

(1) rent of real or personal property, including sums received for cancellation or renewal of a lease;

(2) interest on money lent, including sums received as consideration for the privilege of prepayment of principal, except as provided in section 501B.65 on bond premium and bond discount;

(3) income earned during administration of a decedent's estate as provided in section 501B.63;

(4) corporate distributions as provided in section 501B.64;

(5) accrued increment on bonds or other obligations issued at discount as provided in section 501B.65;

(6) receipts from business and farming operations as provided in section 501B.665;

(7) receipts from disposition of natural resources as provided in sections 501B.67 and 501B.68; and

(8) receipts from other principal subject to depletion as provided in section 501B.69.

Subd. 2. Principal defined. "Principal" means the property set aside by the owner or the person legally empowered so that it is held in trust eventually to be delivered to a remainderperson while the return or use of the principal is in the meantime taken or received by or held for accumulation for an income beneficiary. Principal includes:

(1) consideration received by the trustee on the sale or other transfer of principal, on repayment of a loan, or as a refund, replacement, or change in the form of principal;

(2) proceeds of property taken on eminent domain proceedings;

(3) proceeds of insurance on property forming part of the principal, except proceeds of insurance on a separate interest of an income beneficiary;

(4) stock dividends, receipts on liquidation of a corporation, and other corporate distributions as provided in section 501B.64;

(5) receipts from the disposition of corporate securities as provided in section 501B.65;

(6) royalties and other receipts from disposition of natural resources as provided in sections 501B.67 and 501B.68;

(7) receipts from other principal subject to depletion as provided in section 501B.69;

(8) profit resulting from a change in the form of principal;

(9) allowances for depreciation established under sections 501B.665 and 501B.71, subdivision 1, clause (2); and

(10) gain or loss, including the purchase premium, if any, from the grant of an option to buy or sell property of the trust, whether or not the trust owns the property when the option is granted.

Subd. 3. Charges. After determining income and principal in accordance with the terms of the trust instrument or of sections 501B.59 to 501B.76, the trustee shall charge to income or principal expenses and other charges as provided in section 501B.71.

Laws 1989, c. 340, art. 1, § 50. Amended by Laws 1990, c. 426, art. 1, § 52; Laws 2001, c. 15, § 4; Laws 2002, c. 379, art. 1, § 98.

Historical and Statutory Notes

Laws 1989, c. 340, art. 1, § 76 provides:

"Except as required by section 645.35 or as otherwise provided in sections 47 [section 501B.55], 60 [section 501B.71], 62 [section 501B.73], 70 [section 501B.86], subdivision 9, and 72 [section 501B.88], this article is effective January 1, 1990, and applies to trusts, property interests, and powers of appointment whenever created to the extent permitted under the United States Constitution and the Minnesota Constitution."

501B.62. When right to income arises; apportionment of income

Subdivision 1. General rule. An income beneficiary is entitled to income from the date specified in the trust instrument or, if none is specified, from the date an asset becomes subject to the trust. In the case of an asset that becomes subject to a trust because of the death of any person, it becomes subject to the trust as of the date of the death of the person or, if later, the date the estate or trust becomes entitled to the asset if acquired after the death of the person, even though there is an intervening period of administration of an estate or trust during which the beneficiary may have no right to a distribution of the income.

Subd. 2. Receipts due but not paid; periodic payments. In the administration of a decedent's estate or an asset that becomes subject to a trust by reason of a will:

(1) receipts due but not paid at the date of death of the testator are principal;

(2) receipts in the form of periodic payments, other than corporate distributions to stockholders, including rent, interest, or annuities, not due at the date of the death of the testator must be treated as accruing from day to day. That portion of the receipt that accrues before the date of death is principal, and the balance is income.

Subd. 3. Other receipts. In all other cases, any receipt from an income-producing asset is income even though the receipt was earned or accrued in whole or in part before the date when the asset became subject to the trust.

Subd. 4. Termination of income interest. On termination of an income interest, the income beneficiary whose interest is terminated, or the income beneficiary's estate, is entitled to:

(1) income undistributed on the date of termination;

(2) income due but not paid to the trustee on the date of termination; and

(3) income in the form of periodic payments, other than corporate distributions to stockholders, including rent, interest, or annuities, not due on the date of termination, accrued from day to day.

Subd. 5. Corporate distributions to stockholders. Corporate distributions to stockholders must be treated as due on the day fixed by the corporation for determination of stockholders of record entitled to distribution or, if no date is fixed, on the date of declaration of the distribution by the corporation.

Laws 1989, c. 340, art. 1, § 51. Amended by Laws 2001, c. 15, § 5.

Historical and Statutory Notes

Laws 1989, c. 340, art. 1, § 76 provides:

"Except as required by section 645.35 or as otherwise provided in sections 47 [section 501B.55], 60 [section 501B.71], 62 [section 501B.73], 70 [section 501B.86], subdivision 9, and 72 [section 501B.88], this article is effective January 1, 1990, and applies to trusts, property interests, and powers of appointment whenever created to the extent permitted under the United States Constitution and the Minnesota Constitution."

501B.63. Income earned during administration of a decedent's estate

Subdivision 1. Expenses. Unless a will provides otherwise and subject to subdivision 2, all expenses incurred in connection with the settlement of a decedent's estate, including debts, funeral expenses, estate taxes, interest and penalties concerning taxes, family allowances, fees of attorneys and personal representatives, and court costs must be charged against the principal of the estate.

Subd. 2. Income. Unless the will or trust instrument provides otherwise, income from the assets of a decedent's estate after the death of the testator and before distribution and income from the assets of a trust after an income interest in a trust terminates, including income from property used to discharge liabilities, must be determined in accordance with the rules applicable to a trustee and distributed as follows:

(1) to specific devisees or to any beneficiary who is to receive specific property from a trust, the income from the property devised or distributed to them respectively, less property taxes, ordinary repairs, interest, and other expenses of management and operation of the property, and less an appropriate portion of taxes imposed on income, excluding taxes on capital gains, that accrue during the period of administration or after an income interest in a trust terminates;

(2) to a devisee or to any beneficiary who receives a pecuniary amount outright, the interest or any other amount provided by the will, the terms of the

trust instrument or applicable law from income determined in accordance with the rules applicable to a trustee or, to the extent income is insufficient, from principal. If a beneficiary is to receive a pecuniary amount outright from a trust after an income interest ends and no interest or other amount is provided for by the terms of the trust instrument or applicable law, the trustee shall distribute the interest or other amount to which the beneficiary would be entitled under applicable law if the pecuniary amount were required to be paid under a will;

(3) to all other devisees or beneficiaries, the balance of the income determined in accordance with the rules applicable to a trustee, less the balance of property taxes, ordinary repairs, interest, and other expenses of management and operation of all property from which the estate or trust is entitled to income, and taxes imposed on income, excluding taxes on capital gains, that accrue during the period of administration or after an income interest terminates, in proportion to their respective interests in the undistributed assets of the estate or trust computed at times of distribution on the basis of inventory value.

For purposes of this subdivision, an income interest in a trust terminates upon the occurrence of any event which causes the right of a person to receive mandatory or discretionary distributions of income from the trust to end.

Subd. 3. Income received by trustee. Income received by a trustee under subdivision 2 must be treated as income of the trust.

Laws 1989, c. 340, art. 1, § 52. Amended by Laws 2001, c. 15, § 6.

Historical and Statutory Notes

Laws 1989, c. 340, art. 1, § 76 provides:

"Except as required by section 645.35 or as otherwise provided in sections 47 [section 501B.55], 60 [section 501B.71], 62 [section 501B.73], 70 [section 501B.86], subdivision 9, and 72 [section 501B.88], this article is effective January 1, 1990, and applies to trusts, property interests, and powers of appointment whenever created to the extent permitted under the United States Constitution and the Minnesota Constitution."

501B.64. Entity distributions

Subdivision 1. Distribution of ownership interests; shares; stock splits; stock dividends; subscription rights. Distributions of shares of a distributing corporation or similar equity ownership interests in noncorporate entities, including distributions in the form of or equivalent to a stock split or stock dividend, are principal. An entity owner's right to subscribe to shares, ownership interests, or other securities of the distributing entity and the proceeds of any sale of that right are principal.

Subd. 2. Redemption; merger; reorganization; liquidation. Subject to subdivisions 3 and 4, and except to the extent that the entity indicates that some part of an entity distribution is a settlement of preferred or guaranteed corporate dividends or distribution preferences based upon a return on invested capital accrued under the governing instrument since the trustee acquired the related ownership interest or is in lieu of an ordinary cash dividend or similar distribution from current earnings of the entity, an entity distribution is principal if the distribution is pursuant to:

(1) redemption of the ownership interest or a call of shares;

(2) a merger, consolidation, reorganization, or other plan by which assets of the entity are acquired by another entity; or

(3) a total or partial liquidation of the entity, including a distribution the entity indicates is a distribution in total or partial liquidation or distribution of assets, other than cash, pursuant to a court decree or final administrative order by a government agency ordering distribution of the particular assets.

Subd. 3. Regulated investment company; real estate investment trust. Distributions made from ordinary income by a regulated investment company or by a trust qualifying and electing to be taxed under federal law as a real estate investment trust are income. All other distributions made by the company or trust, including distributions from capital gains, depreciation, or depletion, whether in the form of cash or an option to take new stock or cash or an option to purchase additional shares, are principal.

Subd. 4. Distributions from pass–through entities. Distributions from pass-through entities must be allocated between income and principal as reasonably and equitably determined by the trustee. This subdivision applies for any accounting period during which an entity is a pass–through entity for any portion of the accounting period. In making its determination, the trustee may consider the following:

(1) characterization of income, distributions, and transactions in financial or other information received from the entity, including financial statements and tax information;

(2) whether the entity completed a significant capital transaction outside of the ordinary course of business that the trustee believes has resulted in a distribution to the owners of the entity in the nature of a partial liquidating distribution;

(3) the extent to which the burden for income tax with respect to the income of the entity is to be paid by the trustee out of trust assets or by the beneficiaries of the trust;

(4) the net amount of distributions from the entity available to the trustee after estimating or accounting for tax payments by the trustee or distributions to beneficiaries for the purpose of paying taxes on income earned by the entity;

(5) whether distributions appear to be made out of or contributed to by income earned by the entity and subjected to income taxes in a prior accounting period which may include accounting periods prior to the date the trustee acquired the related ownership interest;

(6) whether the entity is consistently a pass–through entity during multiple accounting periods or a change to or from being a pass-through entity has or

will occur in accounting periods preceding or subsequent to the current accounting period;

(7) if the trust owns a controlling interest or total interest in an entity, the trustee may reasonably allocate distributions between income and principal and not necessarily as if that business interest were owned by the trust as a proprietorship; and

(8) other facts and circumstances as the trustee reasonably considers relevant to its determination.

Subd. 5. Other distributions. Except as provided in subdivisions 1, 2, 3, and 4, all distributions from entities are income. "Entity distributions" includes cash dividends, distributions of or rights to subscribe to shares or securities or obligations of entities other than the distributing entity, and the proceeds of the rights or property distributions. Except as provided in subdivisions 1, 2, 3, and 4, if the distributing entity gives the owner of an ownership interest an option to receive a distribution either in cash or in an ownership interest in the entity, the distribution chosen is income.

Subd. 6. Reliance on statements. The trustee may rely on a statement of the distributing entity as to a fact relevant under a provision of sections 501B.59 to 501B.76 concerning the source or character of dividends or distributions of corporate assets.

Subd. 7. Definitions. The definitions in this subdivision apply to this section.

(a) Entity. "Entity" means a corporation, partnership, limited liability company, regulated investment company, real estate investment trust, common or collective trust fund, or any other organization in which a trustee has an interest other than a trust or estate governed by any other provision of sections 501B.59 to 501B.76.

(b) Pass–through entity. "Pass–through entity" means any entity that passes through income, loss, deductions, credits, and other tax attributes to the owners of an interest in the entity under the Internal Revenue Code in such manner that the owner is directly subject to income taxation on all or any part of the income of the entity (whether or not the pass-through of the tax attributes is related to distributions from the entity), including, but not limited to, S corporations, partnerships, limited liability companies, or limited liability partnerships.

Laws 1989, c. 340, art. 1, § 53. Amended by Laws 2001, c. 15, § 7.

Historical and Statutory Notes

Laws 1989, c. 340, art. 1, § 76 provides:

"Except as required by section 645.35 or as otherwise provided in sections 47 [section 501B.55], 60 [section 501B.71], 62 [section 501B.73], 70 [section 501B.86], subdivision 9, and 72 [section 501B.88], this article is effective January 1, 1990, and applies to trusts, property interests, and powers of appointment whenever created to the extent permitted under the United States Constitution and the Minnesota Constitution."

501B.65. Bond premium and discount

Subdivision 1. Principal. Bonds or other obligations for the payment of money are principal at their inventory value, except as provided in subdivision 2 for discount bonds. No provision may be made for amortization of bond premiums or for accumulation for discount. The proceeds of sale, redemption, or other disposition of the bonds or obligations are principal.

Subd. 2. Income. The increment in value realized upon sale, redemption, or other disposition of a bond or other obligation for the payment of money bearing no stated interest but payable or redeemable at maturity or at a future time at an amount in excess of the amount in consideration of which it was issued or in accordance with a fixed schedule of appreciation, is distributable as income. The increment in value is distributable to the beneficiary who was the income beneficiary at the time of increment from the first principal cash available or, if none is available, when realized by sale, redemption, or other disposition. Whenever unrealized increment is distributed as income but out of principal, the principal must be reimbursed for the increment when realized.

Laws 1989, c. 340, art. 1, § 54. Amended by Laws 1990, c. 581, § 4.

Historical and Statutory Notes

Laws 1989, c. 340, art. 1, § 76 provides:

"Except as required by section 645.35 or as otherwise provided in sections 47 [section 501B.55], 60 [section 501B.71], 62 [section 501B.73], 70 [section 501B.86], subdivision 9, and 72 [section 501B.88], this article is effective January 1, 1990, and applies to trusts, property interests, and powers of appointment whenever created to the extent permitted under the United States Constitution and the Minnesota Constitution."

Laws 1990, c. 581, § 9, provides in part that §§ 4, 5, 6, and 7 [amending, respectively, § 501B.65, subd. 2, § 501B.67, § 501B.68 and § 501B.69] applied to a receipt received after December 31, 1989, by a trust, decedent's estate, or legal estate whether established before, on or after January 1, 1990, and whether the asset involved or legal estate was acquired by the trustee, personal representative, legal life tenant, or remainderperson before, on, or after January 1, 1990. Except as otherwise provided this act is effective January 1, 1990, and applies to trusts, property interests, and powers of appointment whenever created to the extent permitted under the United States Constitution and the Minnesota Constitution.

501B.66. Repealed by Laws 2001, c. 15, § 14

501B.665. Sole proprietorships

Subdivision 1. Separate account. A trustee who conducts a business or other activity as a sole proprietor may establish and maintain a separate account for the transactions of the business or other activity, whether or not its assets are segregated from other trust assets, if the trustee determines that it is in the best interest of all the beneficiaries to establish a separate account instead of accounting for the business or other activity as part of the trust's general accounting records.

(a) A trustee who establishes a separate account for a business or other activity shall determine the extent to which its net cash receipts will be retained in the separate account for working capital, the acquisition or replacement of fixed assets, and other reasonably foreseeable needs of the business or activity or will be transferred out of the separate account and accounted for as principal or income in the trust's general accounting records as the trustee reasonably and equitably determines. If a trustee sells assets of the business or other activity, other than in the ordinary course of the business or activity, and determines that any portion of the amount received is no longer required in the conduct of the business the trustee shall transfer that portion out of the separate account and shall account for that portion as principal in the trust's general accounting records.

(b) A trustee may not account separately for a traditional securities portfolio to avoid the provisions of sections 501B.59 to 501B.76 that otherwise apply to securities.

Subd. 2. Other income or losses. If a trustee does not maintain a separate account for a business or other activity conducted as a sole proprietorship, the net profits of the sole proprietorship in any fiscal or calendar year, as reasonably and equitably determined by the trustee, must be allocated to income while any net loss in that year must be charged to principal and must not be carried into any other fiscal or calendar year for purposes of calculating net income.

Laws 2001, c. 15, § 8.

501B.67. Disposition of natural resources

Subdivision 1. Allocation of receipts. If a part of the principal consists of a right to receive royalties, overriding or limited royalties, working interests, production payments, net profit interests, or other interests in minerals or other natural resources in, on, or under land, the receipts from taking the natural resources from the land must be allocated under paragraphs (a) to (c).

(a) If received as rent on a lease or extension payments on a lease, the receipts are income.

(b) If received from a production payment carved out of a mineral property, the receipts are income to the extent of a factor for interest or its equivalent provided in the governing instrument or a greater amount determined by the trustee to be reasonable and equitable in view of the interests of those entitled to income as well as those entitled to principal. The receipts not allocated to income are principal.

(c) If received as a royalty, overriding or limited royalty, or bonus or from a working, net profit, or other interest in minerals or other natural resources, receipts not provided for in paragraph (a) or (b) must be apportioned on a yearly basis in accordance with this paragraph whether or not any natural resource was being taken from the land at the time the trust was established. The receipts from these properties must be allocated in accordance with what is reasonable and equitable in view of the interests of those entitled to income as well as of those entitled to principal. The amount allocated to principal must be presumed to be reasonable and equitable if it is neither substantially more nor less than the amount allowable as a deduction for depletion, amortization, depreciation, or similar costs under the Internal Revenue Code of 1986.[1] Any allocated amount must be added to principal as an allowance for depletion of the asset. The balance of the gross receipts, after payment from the receipts of all direct and indirect expenses, is income.

Subd. 2. Timber excepted. This section does not apply to timber.

Laws 1989, c. 340, art. 1, § 56. Amended by Laws 1990, c. 581, § 5.

[1] 26 U.S.C.A. § 1 et seq.

Historical and Statutory Notes

Laws 1989, c. 340, art. 1, § 76 provides:

"Except as required by section 645.35 or as otherwise provided in sections 47 [section 501B.55], 60 [section 501B.71], 62 [section 501B.73], 70 [section 501B.86], subdivision 9, and 72 [section 501B.88], this article is effective January 1, 1990, and applies to trusts, property interests, and powers of appointment whenever created to the extent permitted under the United States Constitution and the Minnesota Constitution."

Laws 1990, c. 581, § 9, provides in part that §§ 4, 5, 6, and 7 [amending, respectively,

§ 501B.65, subd. 2, § 501B.67, § 501B.68 and § 501B.69] applied to a receipt received after December 31, 1989, by a trust, decedent's estate, or legal estate whether established before, on or after January 1, 1990, and whether the asset involved or legal estate was acquired by the trustee, personal representative, legal life tenant, or remainderperson before, on, or after January 1, 1990. Except as otherwise provided this act is effective January 1, 1990, and applies to trusts, property interests, and powers of appointment whenever created to the extent permitted under the United States Constitution and the Minnesota Constitution.

501B.68. Timber

Subdivision 1. Net receipts. If a part of the principal consists of land from which merchantable timber may be removed, the net receipts from taking the timber from the land must be allocated as follows:

(1) to income to the extent that the amount of timber removed from the land during the accounting period does not exceed the rate of growth of the timber;

(2) to principal to the extent that the amount of timber removed from the land during the accounting period exceeds the rate of growth of the timber or the net receipts are from the sale of standing timber;

(3) to or between income and principal if the net receipts are from the lease of timberland or from a contract to cut timber from land owned by a trust, by determining the amount of timber removed from the land under the lease or contract and applying the rules in clause (1) or (2); or

(4) to principal to the extent that advance payments, bonuses, and other payments are not allocated pursuant to clause (1), (2), or (3).

Subd. 2. Depletion. In determining net receipts to be allocated pursuant to subdivision 1, a trustee shall deduct and transfer to principal a reasonable amount for depletion.

Subd. 3. Scope. This section applies whether or not timber was harvested from the property before it became subject to the trust.

Laws 1989, c. 340, art. 1, § 57. Amended by Laws 1990, c. 581, § 6; Laws 2001, c. 15, § 9.

Historical and Statutory Notes

Laws 1989, c. 340, art. 1, § 76 provides:

"Except as required by section 645.35 or as otherwise provided in sections 47 [section 501B.55], 60 [section 501B.71], 62 [section 501B.73], 70 [section 501B.86], subdivision 9, and 72 [section 501B.88], this article is effective January 1, 1990, and applies to trusts, property interests, and powers of appointment whenever created to the extent permitted under the United States Constitution and the Minnesota Constitution."

Laws 1990, c. 581, § 9, provides in part that §§ 4, 5, 6, and 7 [amending, respectively,

§ 501B.65, subd. 2, § 501B.67, § 501B.68 and § 501B.69] applied to a receipt received after December 31, 1989, by a trust, decedent's estate, or legal estate whether established before, on or after January 1, 1990, and whether the asset involved or legal estate was acquired by the trustee, personal representative, legal life tenant, or remainderperson before, on, or after January 1, 1990. Except as otherwise provided this act is effective January 1, 1990, and applies to trusts, property interests, and powers of appointment whenever created to the extent permitted under the United States Constitution and the Minnesota Constitution.

501B.69. Annuities, qualified and nonqualified employee compensation, retirement plans and other property subject to depletion

Except as provided in sections 501B.67 and 501B.68, if part of the principal consists of property subject to depletion, including leaseholds, patents, copyrights, royalty rights, rights to receive payments on a contract for deferred compensation, qualified and nonqualified employer retirement plans, individual retirement accounts, and annuities, the receipts from the property must be allocated in accordance with what is reasonable and equitable in view of the interests of those entitled to income as well as of those entitled to principal. The trustee may determine the allocation based on a fixed percentage of each payment, an amortization of the inventory value of the series of payments, or, if the individual retirement account, pension, profit-sharing, stock-bonus, or stock–ownership plan consists of segregated and identifiable assets, the trustee may apply the provisions of sections 501B.59 to 501B.76 to the receipts in the account or plan in order to characterize the payments received during a trust accounting period. To the extent that a payment is characterized by the payer as interest or a dividend or a payment made in lieu of interest or a dividend, a trustee shall allocate it to income. The amount allocated to principal is presumed to be reasonable and equitable if it is neither substantially more nor less than the amount allowable as a deduction for depletion, amortization, depreciation, or similar costs under the Internal Revenue Code of 1986.[1]

Laws 1989, c. 340, art. 1, § 58. Amended by Laws 1990, c. 581, § 7; Laws 2001, c. 15, § 10.

[1] 26 U.S.C.A. § 1 et seq.

Historical and Statutory Notes

Laws 1989, c. 340, art. 1, § 76 provides:

"Except as required by section 645.35 or as otherwise provided in sections 47 [section 501B.55], 60 [section 501B.71], 62 [section 501B.73], 70 [section 501B.86], subdivision 9, and 72 [section 501B.88], this article is effective January 1, 1990, and applies to trusts, property interests, and powers of appointment whenever created to the extent permitted under the United States Constitution and the Minnesota Constitution."

Laws 1990, c. 581, § 9, provides in part that §§ 4, 5, 6, and 7 [amending, respectively, § 501B.65, subd. 2, § 501B.67, § 501B.68 and § 501B.69] applied to a receipt received after December 31, 1989, by a trust, decedent's estate, or legal estate whether established before, on or after January 1, 1990, and whether the asset involved or legal estate was acquired by the trustee, personal representative, legal life tenant, or remainderperson before, on, or after January 1, 1990. Except as otherwise provided this act is effective January 1, 1990, and applies to trusts, property interests, and powers of appointment whenever created to the extent permitted under the United States Constitution and the Minnesota Constitution.

501B.70.   Repealed by Laws 2001, c. 15, § 14

501B.705.   Trustee's power to adjust

Subdivision 1.   Power to adjust. A trustee may adjust between principal and income to the extent the trustee considers necessary to comply with section 501B.60, subdivision 3, after applying section 501B.60, subdivisions 1 and 2, if the trustee invests and manages the trust assets as a prudent investor and the terms of the trust describe the amount that may or must be distributed to a beneficiary by referring to the trust's income.

Subd. 2.   Factors to consider. In deciding whether and to what extent to exercise the power conferred by subdivision 1, a trustee shall consider all factors relevant to the trust and its beneficiaries, including, but not limited to, the following factors:

(1) the nature, purpose, and expected duration of the trust;

(2) the intent of the settlor;

(3) the identity and circumstances of the beneficiaries;

(4) the needs for liquidity, regularity of income, and preservation and appreciation of capital;

(5) the assets held in the trust; the extent to which they consist of financial assets, interests in closely held enterprises, tangible and intangible personal property, or real property; the extent to which an asset is used by a beneficiary; and whether an asset was purchased by the trustee or received from the settlor;

(6) the net amount allocated to income under the other provisions of sections 501B.59 to 501B.76 and the increase or decrease in the value of the principal assets, which the trustee may estimate as to assets for which market values are not readily available;

(7) whether and to what extent the terms of the trust give the trustee the power to invade principal or accumulate income or prohibit the trustee from invading principal or accumulating income, and the extent to which the trustee

has exercised a power from time to time to invade principal or accumulate income;

(8) the actual and anticipated effect of economic conditions on principal and income and effects of inflation and deflation;

(9) the anticipated tax consequences of an adjustment; and

(10) the investment return under current economic conditions from other portfolios meeting fiduciary requirements.

Subd. 3. Limitation on trustee's power. A trustee may not make an adjustment:

(1) that reduces the actuarial value of the income interest in a trust to which a person transfers property with the intent to qualify for a gift tax exclusion;

(2) that changes the amount payable to a beneficiary as fixed annuity or a fixed fraction of the value of the trust assets;

(3) from any amount that is permanently set aside for charitable purposes under a will or the terms of a trust unless both income and principal are so set aside; provided, however, that this limitation does not apply to any trust created prior to August 1, 2001, to the extent the trustee receives amounts during the accounting period which would, under the provisions of Minnesota Statutes 2000, section 501B.70, in effect prior to August 1, 2001, have been allocated to income;

(4) if possessing or exercising the power to make an adjustment causes an individual to be treated as owner of all or part of the trust for income tax purposes and the individual would not be treated as the owner if the trustee did not possess the power to make adjustment;

(5) if possessing or exercising the power to make an adjustment causes all or part of the trust assets to be included for estate tax purposes in the estate of an individual who has the power to remove or appoint the trustee, or both, and the assets would not be included in the estate of the individual if the trustee did not possess the power to make an adjustment;

(6) if the trustee is a beneficiary of the trust; or

(7) if the trustee is not a beneficiary, but the adjustment would benefit the trustee directly or indirectly.

Subd. 4. Cotrustee may exercise power. If the provisions of subdivision 3, clause (4), (5), (6), or (7), apply to a trustee and there is more than one trustee, a cotrustee to whom the provision does not apply may make the adjustment unless the exercise of the power by the remaining trustee or trustees is not permitted by the terms of the trust.

Subd. 5. Release of power. A trustee may release the entire power conferred by subdivision 1 or may release only the power to adjust from income to principal or to adjust from principal to income if the trustee is uncertain about whether possessing or exercising the power will cause a result described in subdivision 3, clause (1), (2), (3), (4), (5), or (7), or if the trustee determines that possessing or exercising the power will or may deprive the trust of a tax benefit or impose a tax burden not described in subdivision 3. The release may be permanent or for a specified period, including a period measured by the life of an individual.

Subd. 6. Power may be negated by specific reference. Terms of a trust that limit the power of a trustee to make an adjustment between principal and income do not affect the application of this section unless it is clear from the terms of the trust that the terms are intended to deny the trustee the power of adjustment conferred by subdivision 1.

Subd. 7. No duty to adjust; remedy. Nothing in this section is intended to create or imply a duty to make an adjustment, and a trustee is not liable for not considering whether to make an adjustment or for choosing not to make an adjustment. In a proceeding with respect to the trustee's nonexercise of the power to make an adjustment from principal to income (or with respect to the trustee's failure to make a greater adjustment from principal to income), the sole remedy is to direct or deny an adjustment (or greater adjustment) from principal to income.

Subd. 8. Notice of determination. A trustee may give notice of a proposed action regarding a matter governed by this section as provided in this subdivision. For purposes of this subdivision, a proposed action includes a course of action and a determination not to take action.

(a) The trustee shall mail notice of the proposed action to all adult beneficiaries who are receiving, or are entitled to receive, income under the trust or to receive a distribution of principal if the trust were terminated at the time the notice is given. Notice may be given to any other beneficiary.

(b) The notice of proposed action must state that it is given pursuant to this subdivision and must state the following:

(1) the name and mailing address of the trustee;

(2) the name and telephone number of a person who may be contacted for additional information;

(3) a description of the action proposed to be taken and an explanation of the reasons for the action;

(4) the time within which objections to the proposed action can be made, which must be at least 30 days from the mailing of the notice of proposed action; and

(5) the date on or after which the proposed action may be taken or is effective.

(c) A beneficiary may object to the proposed action by mailing a written objection to the trustee at the address stated in the notice of proposed action within the time period specified in the notice of proposed action.

(d) If a trustee does not receive a written objection to the proposed action from the beneficiary within the applicable period, the trustee is not liable for an action regarding a matter governed by this chapter to a beneficiary if:

(1) the beneficiary is an adult (or is a minor with a duly appointed conservator of the estate) and the notice is mailed to the adult beneficiary or conservator at the address determined by the trustee after reasonable diligence;

(2) the beneficiary is an adult (or is a minor with a duly appointed conservator of the estate) and the adult beneficiary or conservator receives actual notice;

(3) the beneficiary is not an adult and has no duly appointed conservator of the estate and an adult having a substantially identical interest and having no conflicting interest receives actual notice;

(4) the beneficiary (or the conservator of the estate of a minor beneficiary) consents in writing to the proposed action either before or after the action is taken; or

(5) the beneficiary is not an adult and has no duly appointed conservator of the estate and an adult having a substantially identical interest and having no conflicting interest consents in writing to the proposed action either before or after the action is taken.

(e) If the trustee receives a written objection within the applicable time period, either the trustee or a beneficiary may petition the court to have the proposed action performed as proposed, performed with modifications, or denied. In the proceeding, a beneficiary objecting to the proposed action has the burden of proof as to whether the trustee's proposed action should not be performed. A beneficiary who has not objected is not estopped from opposing the proposed action in the proceeding. If the trustee decides not to implement the proposed action, the trustee shall notify the beneficiaries of the decision not to take the action and the reasons for the decision, and the trustee's decision not to implement the proposed action does not itself give rise to liability to any current or future beneficiary. A beneficiary may petition the court to have the action performed and has the burden of proof as to whether it should be performed.

(f) Nothing in this subdivision limits the right of a trustee or beneficiary to petition the court pursuant to section 501B.16 for instructions as to any action, failure to act, or determination not to act regarding a matter governed by this section in the absence of notice as provided in this subdivision. In any such proceeding, any beneficiary filing such a petition or objecting to a petition of the trustee has the burden of proof as to any action taken, any failure to act, or determination not to act, by the trustee.

Laws 2001, c. 15, § 11. Amended by Laws 2005, c. 26, §§ 2 to 5.

501B.71. Charges against income and principal

Subdivision 1. Income. The following charges must be made against income:

(1) ordinary expenses incurred in connection with the administration, management, or preservation of the trust property, including regularly recurring taxes assessed against a portion of the principal, water rates, premiums on insurance taken upon the interests of the income beneficiary, remainderperson, or trustee, interest paid by the trustee, and ordinary repairs;

(2) a reasonable allowance for depreciation on property subject to depreciation under generally accepted accounting principles, but no allowance may be made for depreciation of that portion of real property used by a beneficiary as a residence or for depreciation of property held by the trustee on January 1, 1970, for which the trustee is not then making an allowance for depreciation;

(3) one-half of the court costs, attorneys' fees, and other fees on periodic accountings or judicial proceedings, unless the court directs otherwise;

(4) court costs, attorneys' fees, and other fees on other accountings or judicial proceedings if the matter primarily concerns the income interest, unless the court directs otherwise;

(5) one-half of the trustee's regular compensation for services performed for the income beneficiary or in the production of income whether based on a percentage of principal or income, and all expenses reasonably incurred for current management of principal and application of income; and

(6) any tax levied on receipts defined as income under sections 501B.59 to 501B.76 or the trust instrument and payable by the trustee.

Subd. 2. Unusual charges. If charges against income are of an unusual amount, the trustee may charge them over a reasonable period of time or, by means of reserves or other reasonable means, withhold from distribution sufficient sums to regularize distributions.

Subd. 3. Principal. The following charges must be made against principal:

(1) trustee's compensation not chargeable to income under subdivision 1, clause (5), special compensation of the trustee, expenses reasonably incurred in connection with principal, court costs and attorneys' fees primarily concerning matters of principal, and trustee's compensation computed on principal as an acceptance, distribution, or termination fee;

(2) charges not provided for in subdivision 1, including the cost of investing and reinvesting principal, the payments on principal of an indebtedness, including a mortgage amortized by periodic payments of principal, expenses for preparation of property for rental or sale, and, unless the court directs otherwise, expenses incurred in maintaining or defending any action to construe the trust or protect it or the property or assure the title of any trust property;

(3) extraordinary repairs or expenses incurred in making a capital improvement to principal, including special assessments, but a trustee may establish an allowance for depreciation out of income to the extent permitted by subdivision 1, clause (2), and by section 501B.63;

(4) any tax levied on profit, gain, or other receipts allocated to principal, even if the taxing authority calls the tax an income tax;

(5) any amount apportioned to a trust, including interest and penalties, if an estate or inheritance tax is levied in respect of a trust in which both an income beneficiary and a remainderperson have an interest.

Subd. 4. Regular charges payable from income. Regularly recurring charges payable from income must be apportioned to the same extent and in the same manner that income is apportioned under section 501B.62.

Subd. 5. Exceptions. Paragraphs (a) to (c) are exceptions to the requirements of subdivisions 1 to 4.

(a) With respect to a revocable living trust, during the lifetime of the grantor, all of the trustee's regular compensation for services performed must be charged against income, unless directed otherwise by the grantor.

(b) If charging a part or all of the trustee's regular compensation to principal, in the judgment of the trustee, is impracticable, because of the lack of sufficient cash and readily marketable assets, or inadvisable, because of the nature of the principal assets, the trustee may determine to pay part or all of the compensation out of income. The decision of the trustee to pay a larger portion or all of the trustee's regular compensation out of income is conclusive, and the income of the trust is not entitled to reimbursement from principal at any subsequent time or times.

(c) If charging a part or all of the trustee's regular compensation to income, in the judgment of the trustee, is impracticable, because of the lack of sufficient income, or inadvisable, because of a desire to provide maximum income to the beneficiary, the trustee may determine to pay part or all of such compensation out of principal. The decision of the trustee to pay a larger portion or all of the trustee's regular compensation out of the principal is conclusive.

Laws 1989, c. 340, art. 1, § 60. Amended by Laws 1995, c. 130, § 4.

Historical and Statutory Notes

Laws 1989, c. 340, art. 1, § 76 provides:

"Except as required by section 645.35 or as otherwise provided in sections 47 [section 501B.55], 60 [section 501B.71], 62 [section 501B.73], 70 [section 501B.86], subdivision 9, and 72 [section 501B.88], this article is effective January 1, 1990, and applies to trusts, property interests, and powers of appointment whenever created to the extent permitted under the United States Constitution and the Minnesota Constitution."

Laws 1995, c. 130, § 22, provides in part that chapter 130 is effective January 1, 1996, and that § 4 (adding subd. 5 of this section) applies to all trusts, whenever executed or created.

501B.72. Nontrust estates

Subdivision 1. Limitations. Sections 501B.59 to 501B.76 apply to nontrust estates, subject to:

(1) agreement of the parties;

(2) specific direction in the instrument creating the nontrust estates;

(3) subdivision 2; and

(4) other applicable statutes.

References in sections 501B.59 to 501B.76 to trusts and trustees must be read as applying to nontrust estates and to tenants and remainderpersons as the context requires.

Subd. 2. Application. In applying sections 501B.59 to 501B.76 to nontrust estates, the rules in paragraphs (a) to (d) must be followed.

(a) A legal life tenant or a remainderperson who has incurred a charge for the tenant's or remainderperson's benefit without the consent or agreement of the other, shall pay the charge in full.

(b) Costs of an improvement, including special taxes or assessments representing an addition to value of property forming part of the principal that cannot reasonably be expected to outlast the legal life estate, must be paid by the legal life tenant.

(c) If the improvement can reasonably be expected to outlast the legal life estate, only a portion of the costs must be paid by the legal life tenant and the balance by the remainderperson.

(1) The portion payable by the legal life tenant is that fraction of the total found by dividing the present value of the legal life estate by the present value of an estate of the same form as that of the legal life estate but limited to a period corresponding to the reasonably expected duration of the improvement.

(2) The present value of the legal life estate must be computed by applying the federal estate tax regulations for the calculation of the value of life estates under section 2031 of the Internal Revenue Code of 1986.[1] The federal estate tax regulations applied must be those in force on the date when the costs of the improvement are initially determined by assessment, agreement, or otherwise. No other evidence of duration or expectancy may be considered.

(d) No allowance may be made for depreciation of property held by a legal life tenant on January 1, 1990, if the life tenant was not making the allowance with respect to the property prior to January 1, 1990.

Laws 1989, c. 340, art. 1, § 61. Amended by Laws 1990, c. 581, § 8.

[1] 26 U.S.C.A. § 2031.

Historical and Statutory Notes

Laws 1989, c. 340, art. 1, § 76 provides:

"Except as required by section 645.35 or as otherwise provided in sections 47 [section 501B.55], 60 [section 501B.71], 62 [section 501B.73], 70 [section 501B.86], subdivision 9, and 72 [section 501B.88], this article is effective January 1, 1990, and applies to trusts, property interests, and powers of appointment whenever created to the extent permitted under the United States Constitution and the Minnesota Constitution."

Laws 1990, c. 581, § 9, provides in part that, except as otherwise provided, this act is effective January 1, 1990, and applies to trusts, property interests, and powers of appointment whenever created to the extent permitted under the United States Constitution and the Minnesota Constitution.

501B.73. Application

Except as specifically provided in the governing instrument, Minnesota Statutes 1988, sections 501.48 to 501.63, apply to a receipt or expense received or incurred after January 1, 1970, and before January 1, 1990, by any trust or decedent's estate whether established before or after January 1, 1970, and whether the asset involved was acquired by the trustee before or after January 1, 1970.

Except as specifically provided in the governing instrument, sections 501B.59 to 501B.76 apply to a receipt or expense received or incurred after December 31, 1989, by a trust or decedent's estate whether established before, on, or after January 1, 1990, and whether the asset involved or legal estate was acquired by the trustee, personal representative, legal life tenant, or remainderperson before, on, or after January 1, 1990.

Laws 1989, c. 340, art. 1, § 62.

Historical and Statutory Notes

Laws 1989, c. 340, art. 1, § 76 provides:

"Except as required by section 645.35 or as otherwise provided in sections 47 [section 501B.55], 60 [section 501B.71], 62 [section 501B.73], 70 [section 501B.86], subdivision 9, and 72 [section 501B.88], this article is effective January 1, 1990, and applies to trusts, property interests, and powers of appointment whenever created to the extent permitted under the United States Constitution and the Minnesota Constitution."

501B.74. Ascertainment of income or principal

Sections 501B.59 to 501B.76 do not govern the ascertainment of what constitutes the receipt of income or principal by the estate or trust for income tax purposes.

Laws 1989, c. 340, art. 1, § 63.

Historical and Statutory Notes

Laws 1989, c. 340, art. 1, § 76 provides:

"Except as required by section 645.35 or as otherwise provided in sections 47 [section 501B.55], 60 [section 501B.71], 62 [section 501B.73], 70 [section 501B.86], subdivision 9, and 72 [section 501B.88], this article is effective January 1, 1990, and applies to trusts, property interests, and powers of appointment whenever created to the extent permitted under the United States Constitution and the Minnesota Constitution."

501B.75. Uniformity of interpretation

Sections 501B.59 to 501B.76 must be so construed as to effectuate their general purpose to make uniform the law of those states that enact them.

Laws 1989, c. 340, art. 1, § 64.

Historical and Statutory Notes

Laws 1989, c. 340, art. 1, § 76 provides:

"Except as required by section 645.35 or as otherwise provided in sections 47 [section 501B.55], 60 [section 501B.71], 62 [section 501B.73], 70 [section 501B.86], subdivision 9, and 72 [section 501B.88], this article is effective January 1, 1990, and applies to trusts, property interests, and powers of appointment whenever created to the extent permitted under the United States Constitution and the Minnesota Constitution."

501B.76. Short title

Sections 501B.59 to 501B.76 may be cited as the Uniform Principal and Income Act.

Laws 1989, c. 340, art. 1, § 65.

Historical and Statutory Notes

Laws 1989, c. 340, art. 1, § 76 provides:

"Except as required by section 645.35 or as otherwise provided in sections 47 [section 501B.55], 60 [section 501B.71], 62 [section 501B.73], 70 [section 501B.86], subdivision 9, and 72 [section 501B.88], this article is effective January 1, 1990, and applies to trusts, property interests, and powers of appointment whenever created to the extent permitted under the United States Constitution and the Minnesota Constitution."

MINNESOTA TRUSTEES' POWERS ACT

501B.79. Trustee defined

As used in sections 501B.79 to 501B.82, "trustee" means a corporation, individual, or other legal entity acting as an original, added, or successor trustee of a trust created under a written instrument, whichever in a particular case is appropriate.

Laws 1989, c. 340, art. 1, § 66.

Historical and Statutory Notes

Laws 1989, c. 340, art. 1, § 76 provides:

"Except as required by section 645.35 or as otherwise provided in sections 47 [section 501B.55], 60 [section 501B.71], 62 [section 501B.73], 70 [section 501B.86], subdivision 9, and 72 [section 501B.88], this article is effective January 1, 1990, and applies to trusts, property interests, and powers of appointment whenever created to the extent permitted under the United States Constitution and the Minnesota Constitution."

501B.80. Incorporation by reference

By a clear expression in a written instrument of the intention of the grantor, one or more of the powers in section 501B.81, as they exist at the time of the signing of the written instrument, may be incorporated by reference as though that language were set forth verbatim in the instrument.

Laws 1989, c. 340, art. 1, § 67.

Historical and Statutory Notes

Laws 1989, c. 340, art. 1, § 76 provides:

"Except as required by section 645.35 or as otherwise provided in sections 47 [section 501B.55], 60 [section 501B.71], 62 [section 501B.73], 70 [section 501B.86], subdivision 9, and 72 [section 501B.88], this article is effective January 1, 1990, and applies to trusts, property interests, and powers of appointment whenever created to the extent permitted under the United States Constitution and the Minnesota Constitution."

501B.81.   Enumerated powers of trustee

Subdivision 1.   Trust assets. The trustee may retain trust assets until, in the judgment of the trustee, disposition of the assets should be made, without regard to any effect retention may have on the diversification of the assets of the trust. The property may be retained even though it includes an asset in which the trustee is personally interested.

Subd. 2.   Additions to trust assets. The trustee may receive from any source additions to the assets of the trust.

Subd. 3.   Business or enterprise. The trustee may continue or participate in the operation of a business or other enterprise, and to effect incorporation, dissolution, or other change in the form of the organization of the business or enterprise.

Subd. 4.   Undivided interest in trust asset. The trustee may acquire an undivided interest in a trust asset in which the trustee, in a trust capacity, holds an undivided interest.

Subd. 5.   Investment of trust assets. The trustee may invest and reinvest trust assets in any property or any undivided interest in the property. These investments include but are not limited to bonds, debentures, secured or unsecured notes, preferred or common stocks of corporations, mutual funds, real estate or real estate improvements or interests, wherever located, oil and mineral leases, royalty or similar interests, and interests in trusts, including investment trusts and common trust funds maintained by a corporate trustee, and insurance upon the life of a person who is or may become a trust beneficiary. These investments may be made without regard to diversification.

Subd. 6.   Deposits. The trustee may deposit trust funds in a bank, including a bank operated by the trustee, or in a state or federal savings association.

Subd. 7.   Purchase and sale. The trustee may acquire, sell, or otherwise dispose of an asset, at public or private sale, for cash or on credit, with or without security as the trustee deems advisable, and manage, develop, exchange, partition, change the character of, or abandon a trust asset or any interest in it.

Subd. 8.   Options. The trustee may grant an option for the sale or other disposition of a trust asset, or take an option for the acquisition of an asset.

Subd. 9.   Leases. The trustee may enter into a lease as lessor or lessee, with or without option to purchase or renew, though the term of the lease, renewal, or option extends beyond the terms of the trust.

Subd. 10.   Repairs; improvements; alterations. The trustee may make ordinary or extraordinary repairs, improvements, or alterations in buildings or other structures or in other trust assets, and remove or demolish improvements.

Subd. 11.   Buildings; party walls. The trustee may raze existing or erect new party walls or buildings, alone or jointly with owners of adjacent property.

Subd. 12.   Subdivision; development; dedication to public use. The trustee may subdivide, develop, or dedicate land to public use; make or obtain the vacation of plats and adjust boundaries; on exchange or partition, adjust differences in valuation by giving or receiving consideration; and dedicate easements to public use without consideration.

Subd. 13.   Exploration and removal of natural resources. The trustee may enter into a lease or arrangement for exploration for and removal of oil, gas, and other minerals or natural resources, and may enter into pooling and unitization agreements.

Subd. 14.   Insurance. The trustee may insure the assets of the trust against damage or loss and the trustee against liability with respect to third persons.

Subd. 15.   Voting stock or securities. The trustee may vote shares of stock or other securities held by the trustee, in person or by general or limited proxy, and enter into voting trust agreements on terms and for periods the trustee considers advisable.

Subd. 16.   Securities calls, assessments, and charges. The trustee may pay calls, assessments, and any other sums chargeable or accruing against or on account of shares of stock, bonds, debentures, or other corporate securities in the hands of the trustee.

Subd. 17.   Stock rights. The trustee may sell or exercise stock subscription or conversion rights, participate in foreclosures, reorganizations, consolidations, mergers, or liquidations, and consent, directly or through a committee or other agent, to corporate sales, leases, and encumbrances. In the exercise of these powers the trustee may, if the trustee considers it expedient, deposit stocks, bonds, or other securities with a protective or other similar committee, on terms and conditions respecting the deposit that the trustee approves.

Subd. 18.   Ownership in other name. The trustee may hold any asset in the name of a nominee or nominees, without disclosure of a fiduciary relationship, but the trustee is liable for acts and omissions of the nominee relating to those assets.

Subd. 19.   Borrowing; mortgages. The trustee may borrow money and mortgage or otherwise encumber or pledge trust assets for a term within or extending beyond the term of the trust, in connection with the exercise of a power vested in the trustee.

Subd. 20.   Contracts. The trustee may enter into contracts binding on the trust that are reasonably incident to the administration of the trust and that the trustee believes to be for the best interests of the trust.

Subd. 21.   Settlement of claims. The trustee may pay, compromise, contest, submit to arbitration, or otherwise settle claims in favor of or against the trust or the trustee.

Subd. 22.   Release of claims. The trustee may release, in whole or in part, a claim or lien belonging to the trust.

Subd. 23. Trust expenses. The trustee may pay taxes, assessments, compensation of the trustee, and other expenses incurred in the collection, care, administration, and protection of the trust.

Subd. 24. Reserves. The trustee may create reserves out of income for depreciation, obsolescence, or amortization, or for depletion in mineral or timber properties.

Subd. 25. Payments to minors and those under legal disability. The trustee may pay a sum distributable to a minor or other beneficiary under legal disability, without liability to the trustee, in one or more of the following ways:

(1) directly to the beneficiary;

(2) to the legal guardian or conservator of the beneficiary;

(3) directly for the maintenance, education, and general welfare of the beneficiary;

(4) to a parent of the beneficiary;

(5) to a person who has custody and care of the person of the beneficiary; or

(6) to a custodian under a uniform transfers to minors statute.

Subd. 26. Distribution of interests. The trustee may distribute property and money in divided or undivided interests and adjust resulting differences in valuation.

Subd. 27. Employment of advisors, assistants. The trustee may employ attorneys, accountants, investment advisors, agents, or other persons, even if they are associated with the trustee, to advise or assist the trustee in the performance of duties. The trustee may act without independent investigation upon their recommendations, and instead of acting personally, may employ one or more agents to perform any act of administration whether or not discretionary.

Subd. 28. Legal actions. The trustee may prosecute or defend actions, claims, or proceedings for the protection of trust assets and of the trustee in the performance of duties.

Subd. 29. Advances to beneficiaries. The trustee may advance income to or for the use of a beneficiary, for which advance the trustee has a lien on the future benefits of that beneficiary.

Subd. 30. Advances by trustee; repayment. The trustee may advance money for the protection of the trust or its assets, for all expenses and liabilities sustained or incurred in or about the administration or protection of the trust, or because of the holding or ownership of any trust assets, for which advances the trustee has a lien on the trust assets, and may be reimbursed out of the trust assets with interest.

Subd. 31. Execution and delivery of instruments. The trustee may execute and deliver instruments that will accomplish or facilitate the exercise of the powers vested in the trustee.

Subd. 32. Multiple trusts. The trustee may hold two or more trusts or parts of trusts created by the same instrument, as an undivided whole, without separation between the trusts or parts of trusts, if the separate trusts or parts of trusts have undivided interests and if no holding defers the vesting of an estate in possession or otherwise.

Laws 1989, c. 340, art. 1, § 68. Amended by Laws 1995, c. 202, art. 1, § 25, eff. May 25, 1995.

Historical and Statutory Notes

Laws 1989, c. 340, art. 1, § 76 provides:

"Except as required by section 645.35 or as otherwise provided in sections 47 [section 501B.55], 60 [section 501B.71], 62 [section 501B.73], 70 [section 501B.86], subdivision 9, and 72 [section 501B.88], this article is effective January 1, 1990, and applies to trusts, property interests, and powers of appointment whenever created to the extent permitted under the United States Constitution and the Minnesota Constitution."

501B.82. Citation

Sections 501B.79 to 501B.82 may be cited or referred to as the "Minnesota Trustees' Powers Act."

Laws 1989, c. 340, art. 1, § 69.

Historical and Statutory Notes

Laws 1989, c. 340, art. 1, § 76 provides:

"Except as required by section 645.35 or as otherwise provided in sections 47 [section 501B.55], 60 [section 501B.71], 62 [section 501B.73], 70 [section 501B.86], subdivision 9, and 72 [section 501B.88], this article is effective January 1, 1990, and applies to trusts, property interests, and powers of appointment whenever created to the extent permitted under the United States Constitution and the Minnesota Constitution."

MISCELLANEOUS

501B.86. Disclaimer of interests passing by deed, assignment, under certain nontestamentary instruments, or under certain powers of appointment

Subdivision 1. Definitions. As used in this section, unless otherwise clearly required by the context:

(a) "beneficiary" means a person entitled, but for the person's disclaimer, to take an interest:

(1) as grantee;

(2) as donee;

(3) under an assignment or instrument of conveyance or transfer;

(4) by succession to a disclaimed interest, other than by will, intestate succession, or through the exercise or nonexercise of a testamentary power of appointment;

(5) as beneficiary of an inter vivos trust or insurance contract;

(6) pursuant to the exercise or nonexercise of a nontestamentary power of appointment;

(7) as donee of a power of appointment created by a nontestamentary instrument; or

(8) otherwise under a nontestamentary instrument;

(b) "interest" means:

(1) the whole of any property, real or personal, legal or equitable;

(2) a fractional part, share, particular portion, or specific assets of property;

(3) an estate in property;

(4) a power to appoint, consume, apply, or expend property; or

(5) any other right, power, privilege, or immunity relating to property; and

(c) "disclaimer" means a written instrument that declines, refuses, releases, or disclaims an interest that would otherwise be succeeded to by a beneficiary, if the instrument defines the nature and extent of the interest disclaimed and is signed, witnessed, and acknowledged by the disclaimant in the manner provided for deeds of real estate.

Subd. 2.   Who may disclaim.   A beneficiary may disclaim an interest in whole or in part, or with reference to specific parts, shares, portions, or assets, by filing a disclaimer in court in the manner provided in this section.   A guardian or conservator of the estate of a minor or an incapacitated person under sections 524.5–101 to 524.5–502, the Uniform Guardianship and Protective Proceedings Act, or the personal representative of the estate of a deceased beneficiary may execute and file a disclaimer on behalf of the beneficiary if that representative considers it not detrimental to the best interests of the beneficiary and in the best interests of those interested in the beneficiary's estate and of those who take the beneficiary's interest by virtue of the disclaimer.   The representative may file the disclaimer with or without a court order within the time specified in subdivision 3.   A beneficiary may file a disclaimer by an attorney or attorney-in-fact.

Subd. 3.   Filing deadline.   A disclaimer under subdivision 2 may be filed at any time after the creation of the interest, but it must be filed within nine months after the effective date of the nontestamentary instrument creating the interest, or, if the disclaimant is not then finally ascertained as a beneficiary or the disclaimant's interest has not then become indefeasibly fixed both in quality and in quantity, the disclaimer must be filed not later than nine months after the event that would cause the disclaimant to become finally ascertained and the interest to become indefeasibly fixed both in quality and quantity.

Subd. 4.   Effective date.   (a) A disclaimer under subdivision 2 is effective on being filed in a district court of the state of Minnesota.   A copy of the disclaimer must be delivered or mailed to the trustee of a trust in which the interest disclaimed exists or to any other person who has legal title to, or possession of, the property in which the interest disclaimed exists. The trustee or person is not liable for any otherwise proper distribution or other disposition made without actual notice of the disclaimer.

(b) If an interest in or relating to real estate is disclaimed, the original of the disclaimer, or a copy of the disclaimer certified as true and complete by the court administrator of the district court where the disclaimer has been filed, must also be filed with the county recorder or with the registrar of titles, as appropriate, in the county or counties where the real estate is situated. The filed disclaimer is notice to all persons after the time of filing. If title to the real estate has not been registered under chapter 508, the disclaimer or certified copy must be filed with the county recorder. If title to the real estate has been registered under chapter 508, the disclaimer or certified copy must be filed with the registrar of titles.

Subd. 5. Distribution of disclaimed property. Unless otherwise provided in the nontestamentary instrument creating the interest with reference to the possibility of a disclaimer by the beneficiary, the interest disclaimed must be distributed or otherwise disposed of in the same manner as if the disclaimant had died immediately preceding the death or other event that causes the disclaimant to become finally ascertained as a beneficiary and the interest to become indefeasibly fixed both in quality and quantity. The disclaimer relates for all purposes to that date, whether filed before or after the death or other event. Unless the disclaimer provides otherwise, a person disclaiming an interest in a nonresiduary gift under a trust instrument or otherwise is not excluded from sharing in a gift of the residue even though, through lapse, the residue includes the assets disclaimed.

Subd. 6. Bars to right to disclaim. The right to disclaim is barred if the beneficiary: (1) is insolvent; (2) assigns or transfers, or contracts to assign or transfer, an interest in the property to be disclaimed; (3) in writing, waives the right to disclaim the succession to an interest in the property; or (4) sells or otherwise disposes of an interest in the property.

Subd. 7. Effect of restrictions. The right to disclaim granted by this section exists despite a limitation imposed on the interest of the disclaimant in the nature of an express or implied spendthrift provision or similar restriction. A disclaimer, when filed under this section, or a written waiver of the right to disclaim, is binding on the disclaimant or waiving beneficiary and all parties later claiming by, through, or under the disclaimant or waiving beneficiary, except that a waiving beneficiary may later transfer, assign, or release the waiving beneficiary's interest if it is not prohibited by an express or implied spendthrift provision. If an interest in real estate is disclaimed and the disclaimer is filed in accordance with subdivision 4, the spouse of the disclaimant, if spouse has consented to the disclaimer in writing, is automatically debarred from the spouse's statutory or common law right or estate by curtesy or in dower or otherwise in the real estate to which the spouse, except for the disclaimer, would have been entitled.

Subd. 8. Other law. This section does not abridge the right of a person, apart from this section, under an existing or future statute or rule of law, to disclaim an interest or to assign, convey, release, renounce, or otherwise dispose of an interest.

Subd. 9. Interests in existence on May 22, 1965. If an interest existed on May 22, 1965, it may be disclaimed under this section if it had not then become indefeasibly fixed both in quality and quantity or if its taker had not then become finally ascertained.

Subd. 10. Bank deposits. The survivor or survivors of a bank deposit held in the names of the decedent and the survivor or survivors may at any time disclaim that interest by authorizing the inclusion of the proceeds of the bank deposit in the inventory and appraisal required by law to be filed by the representative or executor of the estate of the decedent. For purposes of this subdivision, "bank deposit" includes a checking or savings account or time deposit in any financial institution authorized to accept deposits.

Laws 1989, c. 340, art. 1, § 70. Amended by Laws 2008, c. 277, art. 1, § 89, eff. July 1, 2008.

Historical and Statutory Notes

Laws 1989, c. 340, art. 1, § 76 provides:

"Except as required by section 645.35 or as otherwise provided in sections 47 [section 501B.55], 60 [section 501B.71], 62 [section 501B.73], 70 [section 501B.86], subdivision 9, and 72 [section 501B.88], this article is effective January 1, 1990, and applies to trusts, property interests, and powers of appointment whenever created to the extent permitted under the United States Constitution and the Minnesota Constitution."

501B.87. Trusts forming part of retirement plans for participating members

If a trust forms part of a retirement plan created by and for the benefit of self-employed persons for the purpose of receiving their contributions and investing, accumulating, and distributing to the persons or their beneficiaries the corpus, profits, and earnings of the trust in accordance with the plan, the power of a person beneficially interested in the trust to sell, assign, or transfer that beneficial interest, to anticipate payments under the plan, or to terminate the trust, may be limited or withheld in accordance with the provisions of the plan, whether or not the person furnished consideration for the creation of the trust.

Laws 1989, c. 340, art. 1, § 71.

Historical and Statutory Notes

Laws 1989, c. 340, art. 1, § 76 provides:

"Except as required by section 645.35 or as otherwise provided in sections 47 [section 501B.55], 60 [section 501B.71], 62 [section 501B.73], 70 [section 501B.86], subdivision 9, and 72 [section 501B.88], this article is effective January 1, 1990, and applies to trusts, property interests, and powers of appointment whenever created to the extent permitted under the United States Constitution and the Minnesota Constitution."

501B.88. Trusts not affected

Notwithstanding other law to the contrary, a trust created before June 1, 1973, relating to one's "minority" or "majority" or other related terms is governed by the definitions of those terms existing at the time of the creation of the trust.

Laws 1989, c. 340, art. 1, § 72.

Historical and Statutory Notes

Laws 1989, c. 340, art. 1, § 76 provides:

"Except as required by section 645.35 or as otherwise provided in sections 47 [section 501B.55], 60 [section 501B.71], 62 [section 501B.73], 70 [section 501B.86], subdivision 9, and 72 [section 501B.88], this article is effective January 1, 1990, and applies to trusts, property interests, and powers of appointment whenever created to the extent permitted under the United States Constitution and the Minnesota Constitution."

501B.89. Trust provisions linked to public assistance eligibility; supplemental needs trusts

Subdivision 1. Trusts containing limitations linked to eligibility for public assistance. (a) Except as allowed by subdivision 2 or 3, a provision in a trust that provides for the suspension, termination, limitation, or diversion of the principal, income, or beneficial interest of a beneficiary if the beneficiary applies for, is determined eligible for, or receives public assistance or benefits under a public health care program is unenforceable as against the public policy of this state, without regard to the irrevocability of the trust or the purpose for which the trust was created.

(b) This subdivision applies to trust provisions created after July 1, 1992. For purposes of this section, a trust provision is created on the date of execution of the first instrument that contains the provision, even though the trust provision is later amended or reformed or the trust is not funded until a later date.

Subd. 2. Supplemental trusts for persons with disabilities. (a) It is the public policy of this state to enforce supplemental needs trusts as provided in this subdivision.

(b) For purposes of this subdivision, a "supplemental needs trust" is a trust created for the benefit of a person with a disability and funded by someone other than the trust beneficiary, the beneficiary's spouse, or anyone obligated to pay any sum for damages or any other purpose to or for the benefit of the trust beneficiary under the terms of a settlement agreement or judgment.

(c) For purposes of this subdivision, a "person with a disability" means a person who, prior to creation of a trust which otherwise qualifies as a supplemental needs trust for the person's benefit:

(1) is considered to be a person with a disability under the disability criteria specified in Title II [1] or Title XVI [2] of the Social Security Act; or

(2) has a physical or mental illness or condition which, in the expected natural course of the illness or condition, either prior to or following creation of the trust, to a reasonable degree of medical certainty, is expected to:

(i) last for a continuous period of 12 months or more; and

(ii) substantially impair the person's ability to provide for the person's care or custody.

Disability may be established conclusively for purposes of this subdivision by the written opinion of a licensed professional who is qualified to diagnose the illness or condition, confirmed by the written opinion of a second licensed professional who is qualified to diagnose the illness or condition.

(d) The general purpose of a supplemental needs trust must be to provide for the reasonable living expenses and other basic needs of a person with a disability when benefits from publicly funded benefit programs are not sufficient to provide adequately for those needs. Subject to the restrictions contained in this paragraph, a supplemental needs trust may authorize distributions to provide for all or any portion of the reasonable living expenses of the beneficiary. A supplemental needs trust may allow or require distributions only in ways and for purposes that supplement or complement the benefits available under medical assistance, Minnesota supplemental aid, and other publicly funded benefit programs for disabled persons. A supplemental needs trust must contain provisions that prohibit disbursements that would have the effect of replacing, reducing, or substituting for publicly funded benefits otherwise available to the beneficiary or rendering the beneficiary ineligible for publicly funded benefits.

(e) A supplemental needs trust is not enforceable if the trust beneficiary becomes a patient or resident after age 64 in a state institution or nursing facility for six months or more and, due to the beneficiary's medical need for care in an institutional setting, there is no reasonable expectation that the beneficiary will ever be discharged from the institution or facility. For purposes of this paragraph "reasonable expectation" means that the beneficiary's attending physician has certified that the expectation is reasonable. For purposes of this paragraph, a beneficiary participating in a group residential program is not deemed to be a patient or resident in a state institution or nursing facility.

(f) The trust income and assets of a supplemental needs trust are considered available to the beneficiary for medical assistance purposes to the extent they are considered available to the beneficiary under medical assistance, supplemental security income, or Minnesota family investment program methodology, whichever is used to determine the beneficiary's eligibility for medical assistance. For other public assistance programs established or administered under state law, assets and income will be considered available to the beneficiary in accordance with the methodology applicable to the program.

(g) Nothing in this subdivision requires submission of a supplemental needs trust to a court for interpretation or enforcement.

(h) Paragraphs (a) to (g) apply to supplemental needs trusts whenever created, but the limitations and restrictions in paragraphs (c) to (g) apply only to trusts created after June 30, 1993.

Subd. 3. Supplemental needs trusts under federal law. A trust created on or after August 11, 1993, which qualifies as a supplemental needs trust for a person with a disability under United States Code, title 42, section 1396p(c)(2)(B)(iv) or 1396p(d), as amended by section 13611(b) of the Omnibus Budget Reconciliation Act of 1993, Public Law 103–66, commonly known as OBRA 1993, is enforceable, and the courts of this state may authorize creation and funding of a trust which so qualifies.

Laws 1992, c. 513, art. 7, § 129. Amended by Laws 1993, c. 108, § 1; Laws 1995, c. 207, art. 6, §§ 108, 109; Laws 1999, c. 159, § 134.

[1] 42 U.S.C.A. § 401 et seq.

[2] 42 U.S.C.A. § 1381 et seq.

Historical and Statutory Notes

Laws 1993, c. 108, § 2, provides that § 1 (amending this section) is effective retroactive to July 1, 1992, and further provides:

"Notwithstanding the provisions of section 1, [section 501B.89] subdivision 2, providing that a supplemental needs trust may not be funded by the beneficiary or a person obligated to pay the beneficiary under a settlement agreement or judgment, a supplemental needs trust may be established with the proceeds of payments made by the social security administration pursuant to the United States Supreme Court decision in Sullivan v. Zebley, 110 S.Ct. 885 (1990)."

Laws 1995, c. 207, art. 6, § 125, subd. 3, provides in part that §§ 108 and 109 (amending subd. 1 and adding subd. 3, respectively) are effective retroactive to August 11, 1993.

501B.895. Public health care programs and certain trusts

(a) It is the public policy of this state that individuals use all available resources to pay for the cost of long–term care services, as defined in section 256B.0595, before turning to Minnesota health care program funds, and that trust instruments should not be permitted to shield available resources of an individual or an individual's spouse from such use.

(b) When a state or local agency makes a determination on an application by the individual or the individual's spouse for payment of long-term care services through a Minnesota public health care program pursuant to chapter 256B, any irrevocable inter–vivos trust or any legal instrument, device, or arrangement similar to an irrevocable inter-vivos trust created on or after July 1, 2005, containing assets or income of an individual or an individual's spouse, including those created by a person, court, or administrative body with legal authority to act in place of, at the direction of, upon the request of, or on behalf of the individual or individual's spouse, becomes revocable for the sole purpose of that determination. For purposes of this section, any inter-vivos trust and any legal instrument, device, or arrangement similar to an inter–vivos trust:

(1) shall be deemed to be located in and subject to the laws of this state; and

(2) is created as of the date it is fully executed by or on behalf of all of the settlors or others.

(c) For purposes of this section, a legal instrument, device, or arrangement similar to an irrevocable inter–vivos trust means any instrument, device, or arrangement which involves a grantor who transfers or whose property is transferred by another including, but not limited to, any court, administrative body, or anyone else with authority to act on their behalf or at their direction, to an individual or entity with fiduciary, contractual, or legal obligations to the grantor or others to be held, managed, or administered by the individual or entity for the benefit of the grantor or others. These legal instruments, devices, or other arrangements are irrevocable inter–vivos trusts for purposes of this section.

(d) In the event of a conflict between this section and the provisions of an irrevocable trust created on or after July 1, 2005, this section shall control.

(e) This section does not apply to trusts that qualify as supplemental needs trusts under section 501B.89 or to trusts meeting the criteria of United States Code, title 42, section 1396p (d)(4)(a) and (c) for purposes of eligibility for medical assistance.

(f) This section applies to all trusts first created on or after July 1, 2005, as permitted under United States Code, title 42, section 1396p, and to all interests in real or personal property regardless of the date on which the interest was created, reserved, or acquired.

Laws 2005, c. 155, art. 3, § 7.

Historical and Statutory Notes

Laws 2005, 1st Sp., c. 4, art. 5, § 19, repealed
Laws 2005, 1st Sp., c. 3, art. 11, § 6, effective
July 14, 2005.

501B.90. Effect of dissolution of marriage

Subdivision 1. Revocation of certain trust provisions. If after execution of a trust instrument in which a sole grantor reserves a power to alter, amend, revoke, or terminate the provisions of the trust, the grantor's marriage is dissolved or annulled, the dissolution or annulment revokes any disposition, provision for beneficial enjoyment or appointment of property made by the trust instrument to a grantor's former spouse, any provisions conferring a general or special power of appointment on the former spouse and any appointment of the former spouse as trustee, unless the trust instrument expressly provides otherwise.

Subd. 2. Passing of property. Property prevented from passing to a former spouse because of revocation by dissolution or annulment of marriage passes as if the former spouse died on the date of the entry of the judgment and decree dissolving or annulling the grantor's marriage and other provisions conferring some power or office on the former spouse are interpreted as if the former spouse died on the date of the entry of the judgment and decree dissolving or annulling the grantor's marriage.

Subd. 3. Revival of revoked provisions. If provisions are revoked solely by this section, they are revived by the grantor's remarriage to the former spouse. For purposes of this chapter, dissolution of marriage includes divorce. A decree of separation which does not terminate the status of husband and wife is not a dissolution of marriage for purposes of this section. No change of circumstances other than as described in this section revokes a trust instrument.

Laws 1997, c. 9, § 2.

Historical and Statutory Notes

Laws 1997, c. 9, § 11, provides:

"Section 2 applies to all trusts, whenever created, in which a sole grantor has a power to alter, amend, revoke, or terminate the provisions of the trust on the later of (1) the effective date of this section, and (2) the date of the entry of the judgment and decree dissolving or annulling the grantor's marriage."

Chapter 502

POWERS OF APPOINTMENT

For complete statutory history see Minnesota Statutes Annotated.

502.01 to 502.61. Repealed by Laws 1943, c. 322, § 1

502.62. Common law of powers is law of state; exceptions

The common law of powers is hereby declared to be the law in this state, except as modified by statute.

502.63. Donor may create power of appointment

A donor may create a power of appointment only by an instrument executed with the same formalities as one which would pass title to the property covered by the power.

502.64. Donee may exercise power of appointment

A donee may exercise a power of appointment only by an instrument executed with sufficient formalities to pass title to the property covered by the power. When a power of appointment is exercisable only by will, a donee may not exercise it by deed. When a power of appointment is exercisable by deed, a donee may exercise it by will.

264

502.65. Power, when not void

A power of appointment authorized to be exercised by an instrument which would not be sufficient to transfer title to the property covered by the power is not void, but its execution must conform to the provisions of this chapter. When the power of appointment directs that formalities in addition to those prescribed in this chapter be observed in the execution of the power, the direction may be disregarded.

502.66. Power of appointment, who may exercise

Any donee, except a minor, who would be capable of conveying the property covered by the power may exercise a power of appointment.

502.67. Power of appointment vested in two or more persons

When a power of appointment is vested in two or more persons, all must unite in its exercise; provided, if one or more of such persons die, become legally incapable of exercising the power, or renounce such power, the power may be exercised by the others.

502.68. Consents must be in writing

When the consent of the donor, or of any other person is required by the donor for the exercise of a power of appointment, this consent must be in writing. To entitle the instrument exercising the power to be recorded, the signature of any person consenting must be acknowledged; and, if the consent be given in a separate instrument, that instrument must be attached to the instrument exercising the power. If any person whose consent is required dies or becomes legally incapable of consenting, the donee may exercise the power with the consent of the other persons whose consent is required. If there be no such person, the donee may exercise the power in the manner provided by section 502.64, unless the donor has manifested a contrary intent in the instrument creating the power.

502.69. Intent of power

Unless a contrary intent is manifest in the instrument creating the power, the donee may appoint all of the property to one or more of the objects to the exclusion of the others. A direction to appoint "to," "among," or "between" two or more objects is not a sufficient manifestation of a contrary intent; provided, that when the donee is prevented from excluding any object by the instrument creating the power, each object must receive an equal share, unless the instrument creating the power manifests an intent that some other division may be made.

502.70. Powers of creditor of donee

When a donee is authorized either to appoint to the donee or to appoint to the donee's estate all or part of the property covered by a power of appointment, a creditor of the donee, during the life of the donee, may subject to the creditor's claim all property which the donee could then appoint to the donee and, after the death of the donee, may subject to the creditor's claim all property which the donee could at death have appointed to the donee's estate, but only to the extent that other property available for the payment of the creditor's claim is insufficient for such payment. When a donee has exercised such a power by deed, the rules relating to fraudulent conveyances shall apply as if the property transferred to the appointee had been owned by the donee. When a donee has exercised such a power by will in favor of a taker without value or in favor of a creditor, a creditor of the donee or a creditor of the donee's estate may subject such property to the payment of the creditor's claim, but only to the extent that other property available for the payment of the claim is insufficient for such payment.

Amended by Laws 1947, c. 206, § 1; Laws 1986, c. 444.

502.71. Effect of deed

When the donee of a power of appointment makes a deed purporting to transfer all of the donee's property, the property covered by the power is included in such transfer unless it be shown that the donee did not so intend.

Amended by Laws 1975, c. 347, § 8, eff. Jan. 1, 1976; Laws 1986, c. 444.

502.72. Conveyance

A deed either creating or exercising a power of appointment over real property is a conveyance within the meaning of section 507.01. A will appointing real property is a devise within section 524.1–201.

Amended by Laws 1987, c. 384, art. 2, § 1.

502.73. Right of alienation suspended, when

The period during which the power of alienation, within the meaning of section 501B.09, may be suspended by any instrument in execution of a power is to be computed from the time of the creation of the power and not from the date of the instrument, except that in the case of a general power presently exercisable, the period is to be computed from the date of the instrument.

Amended by Laws 1989, c. 340, art. 1, § 74.

Historical and Statutory Notes

Laws 1989, c. 340, art. 1, § 76 provides:

"Except as required by section 645.35 or as otherwise provided in sections 47 [section 501B.55], 60 [section 501B.71], 62 [section 501B.73], 70 [section 501B.86], subdivision 9, and 72 [section 501B.88], this article is effective January 1, 1990, and applies to trusts, property interests, and powers of appointment whenever created to the extent permitted under the United States Constitution and the Minnesota Constitution."

502.74. Advancements

Every estate or interest given to a descendant of the donee by the exercise of a power is an advancement to such descendant to the same extent that a gift of property owned by the donee would be an advancement.

502.75. Power passes to assignee

Under a general assignment for the benefit of creditors, a power of appointment in the assignor by which the assignor is authorized to appoint the property to the assignor passes to the assignee.

Amended by Laws 1986, c. 444.

502.76. Power of revocation

When the grantor in a conveyance personally reserves, for the grantor's own benefit, an absolute power of revocation, such grantor is still the absolute owner of the estate conveyed, so far as the rights of creditors and purchasers are concerned.

Amended by Laws 1986, c. 444.

502.77. Power if part of security

When a power to sell lands is given to the grantee in a mortgage, or other conveyance intended to secure the payment of money, the power is a part of the security and vests in, and may be executed by, any person who becomes entitled to the money so secured to be paid.

502.78. Absolute power of disposition

Where an absolute power of disposition is given to a grantee or devisee of real or personal property and no reversion, remainder, or gift in default of the property undisposed of by the grantee or devisee is expressed in the instrument creating the power, the grantee or devisee is the absolute owner of the property.

502.79. Release of powers of property held in trust

Subdivision 1. Releasable powers. A power of appointment over property held in trust, whether or not coupled with an interest, and whether or not existing on the effective date of Laws 1949, Chapter 607, and whether the power is held by the donee in an individual or in a fiduciary capacity, may be released, wholly or partially, by the donee thereof, unless otherwise expressly provided in the instrument creating the power; provided, however, that a power of appointment held by a person by reason of being a trustee of an express trust shall not be releasable hereunder unless (1) the release is approved by a court of competent jurisdiction on the ground that it is for the best interests of the trust estate and of the beneficiaries thereof as a whole, or (2) the trustee or trustees having the power could exercise it only in their own favor at the time the power was released. As used in this section, the term "power of appointment" shall include all powers in respect of any kind of property, real or personal, held in trust which are in substance and effect powers of appointment, all powers to alter, amend, revoke or terminate an express trust, and all powers by the exercise of which the possession or enjoyment of property held in trust may be changed, regardless of the language used in creating them.

Subd. 2. Delivery of release. A power releasable according to subdivision 1 may hereafter be released, wholly or partially, only by the delivery to the trustee of a written release executed by the donee of the power.

Subd. 3. Extent of release. A release executed by the donee of a power releasable according to subdivision 1 and delivered in accordance with subdivision 2, whether heretofore or hereafter executed, shall be, and if heretofore executed and delivered shall be deemed to have been effective to release the power to the extent provided in such release.

Subd. 4. Release by one of several persons. If a power of appointment releasable according to subdivision 1 is or may be exercisable by two or more persons in conjunction with one another or successively, a release or disclaimer of the power, in whole or in part, executed and delivered in accordance with subdivision 2 by any one of the donees of the power shall, subject to the provisions of subdivision 2, be effective to release or disclaim, to the extent therein provided, all right of such persons to exercise, or to participate in the exercise of, the power, but, unless the instrument creating the power otherwise provides, shall not prevent or limit the exercise or participation in the exercise thereof by the other donee or donees thereof.

Subd. 5. Release defined. The word "release" as used in subdivisions 2 to 5 shall include (a) an instrument wherein the person who executes it in substance states that that person wholly releases, or agrees in no respect to exercise or participate in the exercise of, a power of appointment; and (b) an instrument wherein the person who executes it in substance states that that person releases all right to exercise, or participate in the exercise of, a power of appointment otherwise than within the limits therein defined, or agrees not to exercise, or participate in the exercise of, a power of appointment otherwise than within the limits there defined.

Subd. 6. Effect of section. This section shall not impair the validity of any releases heretofore made, and shall not create any implication that powers other than those specified herein are not releasable.

Laws 1949, c. 607, §§ 1 to 6. Amended by Laws 1986, c. 444.

Chapter 520

UNIFORM FIDUCIARIES ACT

For complete statutory history see Minnesota Statutes Annotated.

520.01. Definitions

Subdivision 1. Applicability. Unless the language or context clearly indicates that different meaning is intended, the following words, terms, and phrases, for the purposes of sections 520.01 to 520.13, shall be given the meanings subjoined to them.

Subd. 2. Bank. "Bank" includes any person or association of persons, whether incorporated or not, carrying on the business of banking.

Subd. 3. Fiduciary. "Fiduciary" includes a trustee under any trust, expressed, implied, resulting or constructive, executor, administrator, guardian, conservator, curator, receiver, trustee in bankruptcy, assignee for the benefit of creditors, partner, agent, officer of any corporation public or private, public officer, or any other person acting in a fiduciary capacity for any person, trust, or estate.

Subd. 4. Person. "Person" includes a corporation, partnership, or other association, or two or more persons having a joint or common interest.

Subd. 5. Principal. "Principal" includes any person to whom a fiduciary as such owes an obligation.

Subd. 6. In good faith. A thing is done "in good faith" when it is done honestly, whether it be done negligently or not.

Laws 1945, c. 202, § 1.

520.02. Application of payments made to fiduciaries

A person who in good faith pays or transfers to a fiduciary any money or other property which the fiduciary as such is authorized to receive, is not responsible for the proper application thereof by the fiduciary; and any right or title acquired from the fiduciary in consideration of such payment or transfer is not invalid in consequence of a misapplication by the fiduciary.

Laws 1945, c. 202, § 2.

520.03. Repealed by Laws 1961, c. 462, § 12

520.04 to 520.06. Repealed by Laws 1965, c. 811, § 336.10–102, eff. July 1, 1966

Historical and Statutory Notes

Laws 1965, c. 811 enacted the Uniform Commercial Code and repealed §§ 520.04 to 520.06. Laws 1965, c. 811, was effective July 1, 1966, except as to transactions validly entered into before the effective date (see § 336.10–102(2)).

520.07. Deposit in name of fiduciary as such

If a deposit is made in a bank to the credit of a fiduciary as such, the bank is authorized to pay the amount of the deposit or any part thereof upon the check of the fiduciary, signed with the name in which such deposit is entered, without being liable to the principal, unless the bank pays the check with actual knowledge that the fiduciary is committing a breach of an obligation as fiduciary in drawing the check or with knowledge of such facts that its action in paying the check amounts to bad faith. If such a check is payable to the drawee bank and is delivered to it in payment of or as security for a personal debt of the fiduciary to it, the bank is liable to the principal if the fiduciary in fact commits a breach of an obligation as fiduciary in drawing or delivering the check.

Laws 1945, c. 202, § 7. Amended by Laws 1986, c. 444.

520.08. Deposit in name of principal

If a check is drawn upon the account of the principal in a bank by a fiduciary who is empowered to draw checks upon the principal's account, the bank is authorized to pay such check without being liable to the principal, unless the bank pays the check with actual knowledge that the fiduciary is committing a breach of an obligation as fiduciary in drawing such check, or with knowledge of such facts that its action in paying the check amounts to bad faith. If such a check is payable to the drawee bank and is delivered to it in payment of or as security for a personal debt of the fiduciary to it, the bank is liable to the principal if the fiduciary in fact commits a breach of an obligation as fiduciary in drawing or delivering the check.

Laws 1945, c. 202, § 8. Amended by Laws 1986, c. 444.

520.09. Deposit in fiduciary's personal account

If a person who is a fiduciary makes a deposit in a bank to the person's personal credit of checks drawn by the person upon an account in the person's name as fiduciary, or of checks payable to the person as fiduciary, or of checks drawn by the person upon an account in the name of the principal if the person is empowered to draw checks thereon, or of checks payable to the principal and endorsed by the person, if empowered to endorse such checks, or if the person otherwise makes a deposit of funds held as fiduciary, the bank receiving such deposit is not bound to inquire whether the fiduciary is committing thereby a breach of an obligation as fiduciary; and the bank is authorized to pay the amount of the deposit or any part thereof upon the personal check of the fiduciary without being liable to the principal, unless the bank receives the deposit or pays the check with actual knowledge that the fiduciary is committing a breach of an obligation as fiduciary in making such deposit or in drawing such check, or with knowledge of such facts that its action in receiving the deposit or paying the check amounts to bad faith.

Laws 1945, c. 202, § 9. Amended by Laws 1986, c. 444.

520.10. Deposit in names of two or more trustees

When a deposit is made in a bank in the name of two or more persons as trustees and a check is drawn upon the trust account by any trustee or trustees authorized by the other trustee or trustees to draw checks upon the trust account, neither the payee nor other holder nor the bank is bound to inquire whether it is a breach of trust to authorize such trustee or trustees to draw checks upon the trust account, and is not liable unless the circumstances be such that the action of the payee or other holder or the bank amounts to bad faith.

Laws 1945, c. 202, § 10.

520.11. Application

The provisions of sections 520.01 to 520.13 shall not apply to transactions taking place prior to the time when Laws 1945, chapter 202,[1] takes effect.

Laws 1945, c. 202, § 11.

[1] Sections 520.01 to 520.13.

520.12. Cases not provided for in sections 520.01 to 520.13

In any case not provided for in sections 520.01 to 520.13 the rules of law and equity including the law merchant and those rules of law and equity relating to trusts, agency, negotiable instruments, and banking, shall continue to apply.

Laws 1945, c. 202, § 12.

520.13. Citation, Uniform Fiduciaries Act

Sections 520.01 to 520.13 may be cited as the Uniform Fiduciaries Act.

Laws 1945, c. 202, § 13.

UNIFORM FIDUCIARIES ACT

Table of Jurisdictions Wherein Act Has Been Adopted

For text of Uniform Act, and variation notes and annotation materials for adopting jurisdictions, see Uniform Laws Annotated, Master Edition, Volume 7A, Pt. I.

Jurisdiction	Laws	Effective Date	Statutory Citation
Alabama	1943, p. 544	7–7–1943	Code 1975, §§ 19–1–1 to 19–1–13.
Arizona	1951, c. 139	3–29–1951	A.R.S. §§ 14–7501 to 14–7512.
Colorado	1923, c. 65	4–16–1923	West's C.R.S.A. §§ 15–1–101 to 15–1–113.
District of Columbia	1928, 45 Stat. 509	5–14–1928	D.C. Official Code, 2001 Ed. §§ 21–1701 to 21–1712.
Hawaii	1945, c. 197	5–17–1945	HRS §§ 556–1 to 556–10.
Idaho	1925, c. 217	3–17–1925	I.C. §§ 68–301 to 68–315.
Illinois	1931, p. 676	7–7–1931	S.H.A. 760 ILCS 65/1 to 65/12.
Indiana	1927, c. 17	5–16–1927	West's A.I.C. 30–2–4–1 to 30–2–4–14.
Louisiana	1924, No. 226	1–1–1925	LSA–R.S. 9:3801 to 9:3814.
Maryland	1929, c. 572	4–11–1929	Code, Estates and Trusts, §§ 15–201 to 15–211.
Minnesota	1945, c. 202	3–31–1945	M.S.A. §§ 520.01 to 520.13.
Missouri	2004, H.B. No. 1511	1–1–2005	V.A.M.S. §§ 469.240 to 469.350.
Nevada	1923, c. 44	3–1–1923	N.R.S. 162.010 to 162.140.
New Jersey	1927, c. 30	7–4–1927	N.J.S.A. 3B:14–52 to 3B:14–61.
New Mexico	1923, c. 26		NMSA 1978, §§ 46–1–1 to 46–1–11.
New York	1948, c. 866	4–6–1948	McKinney's General Business Law §§ 359–i, 359–l.
North Carolina	1923, c. 85	2–27–1923	G.S. §§ 32–1 to 32–13.
Ohio	2006, H.B. 416	1–1–2007	R.C. §§ 5815.01 to 5815.11.
Pennsylvania	L.1923	5–31–1923	7 P.S. §§ 6351 to 6404.
Rhode Island	1961, c. 147	1–2–1962	Gen.Laws 1956, §§ 18–4–15 to 18–4–21.
South Dakota	1943, c. 19	2–6–1943	SDCL 55–7–2 to 55–7–15.
Tennessee	1953, c. 82	4–6–1953	T.C.A. §§ 35–2–101 to 35–2–112.
Utah	1925, c. 86	5–12–1925	U.C.A.1953, 22–1–1 to 22–1–11.
Virgin Islands	1957, Act No. 160	9–1–1957	15 V.I.C. §§ 1041 to 1053.
Wisconsin	1925, c. 227	6–1–1925	W.S.A. 112.01(1 to 16).
Wyoming	1929, c. 90	2–21–1929	Wyo.Stat.Ann. §§ 2–3–201 to 2–3–211.

520.21. Definitions

In sections 520.21 to 520.31, unless the context otherwise requires:

(a) "Assignment" includes any written stock power, bond power, bill of sale, deed, declaration of trust, or other instrument of transfer.

(b) "Claim of beneficial interest" includes a claim of any interest by a decedent's legatee, distributee, heir, or creditor, a beneficiary under a trust, a ward, a beneficial owner of a security registered in the name of a nominee, or a minor owner of a security registered in the name of a custodian, or a claim of any similar interest, whether the claim is asserted by the claimant or by a fiduciary or by any other authorized person on the claimant's behalf, and includes a claim that the transfer would be in breach of fiduciary duties.

(c) "Corporation" means a private or public corporation, association or trust issuing a security.

(d) "Fiduciary" means an executor, administrator, trustee, guardian, committee, conservator, curator, tutor, custodian, or nominee.

(e) "Person" includes an individual, a corporation, government or governmental subdivision or agency, business trust, estate, trust, partnership or association, two or more persons having a joint or common interest, or any other legal or commercial entity.

(f) "Security" includes any share of stock, bond, debenture, note, or other security issued by a corporation which is registered as to ownership on the books of the corporation.

(g) "Transfer" means a change on the books of a corporation in the registered ownership of a security.

(h) "Transfer agent" means a person employed or authorized by a corporation to transfer securities issued by the corporation.

Laws 1961, c. 462, § 1. Amended by Laws 1986, c. 444.

520.22. Registration in the name of a fiduciary

A corporation or transfer agent registering a security in the name of a person who is a fiduciary or who is described as a fiduciary is not bound to inquire into the existence, extent, or correct description of the fiduciary relationship; and thereafter the corporation and its transfer agent may assume without inquiry that the newly registered owner continues to be the fiduciary until the corporation or transfer agent receives written notice that the fiduciary is not longer acting as such with respect to the particular security.

Laws 1961, c. 462, § 2.

520.23. Assignment by a fiduciary

Except as otherwise provided in sections 520.21 to 520.31, a corporation or transfer agent making a transfer of a security pursuant to an assignment by a fiduciary:

(a) May assume without inquiry that the assignment, even though to the fiduciary personally or to a nominee, is within the fiduciary's authority and capacity and is not in breach of fiduciary duties;

(b) May assume without inquiry that the fiduciary has complied with any controlling instrument and with the law of the jurisdiction governing the fiduciary relationship, including any law requiring the fiduciary to obtain court approval of the transfer; and

(c) Is not charged with notice of and is not bound to obtain or examine any court record or any recorded or unrecorded document relating to the fiduciary relationship or the assignment, even though the record or document is in its possession.

Laws 1961, c. 462, § 3. Amended by Laws 1986, c. 444.

520.24. Evidence of appointment or incumbency

A corporation or transfer agent making a transfer pursuant to an assignment by a fiduciary who is not the registered owner shall obtain the following evidence of appointment or incumbency:

(a) In the case of a fiduciary appointed or qualified by a court, a certificate issued by or under the direction or supervision of that court or an officer thereof and dated within 60 days before the transfer; or

(b) In any other case, a copy of a document showing the appointment or a certificate issued by or on behalf of a person reasonably believed by the corporation or transfer agent to be responsible or, in the absence of such a document or certificate, other evidence reasonably deemed by the corporation or transfer agent to be appropriate. Corporations and transfer agents may adopt standards with respect to evidence of appointment or incumbency under this subsection provided such standards are not manifestly unreasonable. Neither the corporation nor transfer agent is charged with notice of the contents of any document obtained pursuant to this paragraph (b) except to the extent that the contents relate directly to the appointment or incumbency.

Laws 1961, c. 462, § 4.

520.25. Adverse claims

(a) A person asserting a claim of beneficial interest adverse to the transfer of a security pursuant to an assignment by a fiduciary may give the corporation or transfer agent written notice of the claim. The corporation or transfer agent is not put on notice unless the written notice identifies the claimant, the registered owner, and the issue of which the security is a part, provides an address for communications directed to the claimant and is received before the transfer. Nothing in sections 520.21 to 520.31 relieves the corporation or transfer agent of any liability for making or refusing to make the transfer after it is so put on notice, unless it proceeds in the manner authorized in subsection (b).

(b) As soon as practicable after the presentation of a security for transfer pursuant to an assignment by a fiduciary, a corporation or transfer agent which has received notice of a claim of beneficial interest adverse to the transfer may send notice of the presentation by registered or certified mail to the claimant at the address given by the claimant. If the corporation or transfer agent so mails such a notice it shall withhold the transfer for 30 days after the mailing and shall then make the transfer unless restrained by a court order.

Laws 1961, c. 462, § 5. Amended by Laws 1986, c. 444.

520.26. Nonliability of corporation and transfer agent

A corporation or transfer agent incurs no liability to any person by making a transfer or otherwise acting in a manner authorized by sections 520.21 to 520.31.

Laws 1961, c. 462, § 6.

520.27. Nonliability of third persons

(a) No person who participates in the acquisition, disposition, assignment or transfer of a security by or to a fiduciary, including a person who guarantees the signature of the fiduciary, is liable for participation in any breach of fiduciary duty by reason of failure to inquire whether the transaction involves a breach unless it is shown that the person acted with actual knowledge that the proceeds of the transaction were being or were to be used wrongfully for the individual benefit of the fiduciary or that the transaction was otherwise in breach of duty.

(b) If a corporation or transfer agent makes a transfer pursuant to an assignment by a fiduciary, a person who guaranteed the signature of the fiduciary is not liable on the guarantee to any person to whom the corporation or transfer agent by reason of sections 520.21 to 520.31 incurs no liability.

(c) This section does not impose any liability upon the corporation or its transfer agent.

Laws 1961, c. 462, § 7. Amended by Laws 1986, c. 444.

520.28. Territorial application

(a) The rights and duties of a corporation and its transfer agents in registering a security in the name of a fiduciary or in making a transfer of a security pursuant to an assignment by a fiduciary are governed by the law of the jurisdiction under whose laws the corporation is organized.

(b) Sections 520.21 to 520.31 apply to the rights and duties of a person other than the corporation and its transfer agents with regard to acts and omissions in this state in connection with the acquisition, disposition, assignment, or transfer of a security by or to a fiduciary and of a person who guarantees in this state the signature of a fiduciary in connection with such a transaction.

Laws 1961, c. 462, § 8.

520.29. Tax obligations

Sections 520.21 to 520.31 do not affect any obligation of a corporation or transfer agent with respect to estate, inheritance, succession, or other taxes imposed by the laws of this state.

Laws 1961, c. 462, § 9.

520.30. Uniformity of interpretation

Sections 520.21 to 520.31 shall be so construed as to effectuate its general purpose to make uniform the law of those states which enact it.

Laws 1961, c. 462, § 10.

520.31. Short title

Sections 520.21 to 520.31 may be cited as the Uniform Act for the Simplification of Fiduciary Security Transfers.

Laws 1961, c. 462, § 11.

UNIFORM SIMPLIFICATION OF FIDUCIARY SECURITY TRANSFERS ACT

Table of Jurisdictions Wherein Act Has Been Adopted

For text of Uniform Act, and variation notes and annotation materials for adopting jurisdictions, see Uniform Laws Annotated, Master Edition, Volume 7C.

Jurisdiction	Laws	Effective Date	Statutory Citation
Delaware	1963, c. 141	10–10–1963	12 Del.C. §§ 4301 to 4311.
District of Columbia	Pub.Law 86–584, 74 Stat. 322	7–5–1960	D.C. Official Code, 2001 Ed. §§ 28–2901 to 28–2909.
Idaho	1959, c. 136	3–12–1959	I.C. §§ 68–901 to 68–911.
Illinois	1957, p. 247	5–23–1957	S.H.A. 760 ILCS 70/0.01 to 70/9.
Indiana	1961, c. 124	7–6–1961	West's A.I.C. 30–2–5–1 to 30–2–5–11.
Kansas	1961, c. 123	7–1–1961	K.S.A. 17–4903 to 17–4913.
Louisiana	1960, No. 444	7–27–1960	LSA–R.S. 9:3831 to 9:3850.
Maryland	1960, c. 92	6–1–1960	Code, Estates and Trusts, §§ 15–301 to 15–311.
Michigan	1959, No. 239	3–19–1960	M.C.L.A. §§ 441.101 to 441.112.
Minnesota	1961, c. 462	4–21–1961	M.S.A. §§ 520.21 to 520.31.
Mississippi	1960, c. 266	5–11–1960	Code 1972, §§ 91–11–1 to 91–11–21.
Missouri	1959, S.B. No. 241	8–29–1959	V.A.M.S. §§ 403.250 to 403.350.

Jurisdiction	Laws	Effective Date	Statutory Citation
Nevada..............	1959, c. 394	4–2–1959	N.R.S. 162.150 to 162.250.
New Jersey	1959, c. 200	7–1–1959	N.J.S.A. 14:18–1 to 14:18–12 (14A App.).
New Mexico	1991, c. 177	7–1–1991	NMSA 1978, §§ 46–8–1 to 46–8–10.
Rhode Island	1959, c. 85	5–28–1959	Gen.Laws 1956, §§ 18–11–1 to 18–11–11.
South Dakota	1961, c. 22	7–1–1961	SDCL 55–8–1 to 55–8–18.
Utah................	1961, c. 46	5–9–1961	U.C.A.1953, 22–5–1 to 22–5–11.
West Virginia	1961, c. 16	6–6–1961	Code, 31–4D–1 to 31–4D–11.

520.32. Deposit of securities in central depository

Subdivision 1. Authorization. Notwithstanding any other provision of law, any fiduciary, as defined in sections 520.01 or 520.21, holding securities in its fiduciary capacity, any bank or trust company holding securities as a custodian or managing agent, and any bank or trust company holding securities as custodian for a fiduciary is authorized to deposit or arrange for the deposit of such securities in a clearing corporation, as defined in section 336.8–102. When such securities are so deposited, certificates representing securities of the same class of the same issuer may be merged and held in bulk in the name of the nominee of such clearing corporation with any other such securities deposited in such clearing corporation by any person regardless of the owner-ship of such securities, and certificates of small denomination may be merged into one or more certificates of larger denomination. The records of such fiduciary and the records of such bank or trust company acting as custodian, as managing agent or as custodian for a fiduciary shall at all times show the name of the party for whose account the securities are so deposited. Title to such securities may be transferred by bookkeeping entry on the books of such clearing corporation without physical delivery of certificates representing such securities. A bank or trust company so depositing securities pursuant to this section shall be subject to such rules as, in the case of state chartered institutions, the state Department of Commerce and, in the case of national banking associations, the comptroller of the currency may from time to time issue. A bank or trust company acting as custodian for a fiduciary shall, on demand by the fiduciary, certify in writing to the fiduciary the securities so deposited by such bank or trust company in such clearing corporation for the account of such fiduciary. A fiduciary shall, on demand by any party to a judicial proceeding for the settlement of such fiduciary's account or on demand by the attorney for such party, certify in writing to such party the securities deposited by such fiduciary in such clearing corporation for its account as such fiduciary.

Subd. 2. Applicability. This section shall apply to any fiduciary holding securities in its fiduciary capacity, and to any bank or trust company holding securities as a custodian, managing agent or custodian for a fiduciary, acting on February 14, 1974 or who thereafter may act regardless of the date of the agreement, instrument or court order by which it is appointed and regardless of whether or not such fiduciary, custodian, managing agent or custodian for a fiduciary owns capital stock of such clearing corporation.

Laws 1974, c. 46, § 3, eff. Feb. 14, 1974. Amended by Laws 1985, c. 248, § 70.

520.33. Deposit of United States government and agency securities with a federal reserve bank

Subdivision 1. Authorization. Notwithstanding any other provision of law, any bank or trust company, when acting as fiduciary, as defined in section 520.01 or 520.21, and any bank or trust company, when holding securities as custodian for a fiduciary, is authorized to deposit, or arrange for the deposit, with the Federal Reserve Bank in its district of any securities the principal and interest of which the United States or any department, agency or instrumentality thereof has agreed to pay, or has guaranteed payment, to be credited to one or more accounts on the books of said Federal Reserve Bank in the name of such bank or trust company, to be designated fiduciary or safekeeping accounts, to which account other similar securities may be credited. A bank or trust company so depositing securities with a Federal Reserve Bank shall be subject to such rules with respect to the making and maintenance of such deposit as, in the case of state chartered institutions, the commissioner of commerce, and, in the case of national banking associations, the comptroller of the currency, may from time to time issue. The records of such bank or trust company shall at all times show the ownership of the securities held in such account. Ownership of, and other interests in, the securities credited to such account may be transferred by entries on the books of said Federal Reserve Bank without physical delivery of any securities. A bank or trust company acting as custodian for a fiduciary shall, on demand by the fiduciary, certify in writing to the fiduciary the securities so deposited by such bank or trust company with such Federal Reserve Bank for the account of such fiduciary. A fiduciary shall, on demand by any party to its accounting or on demand by the attorney for such party, certify in writing to such party the securities deposited by such fiduciary with such Federal Reserve Bank for its account as such fiduciary.

Subd. 2. Applicability. This section shall apply to all fiduciaries, and custodians for fiduciaries, acting on May 18, 1975 or who thereafter may act regardless of the date of the instrument or court order by which they are appointed.

Laws 1975, c. 194, § 1, eff. May 18, 1975. Amended by Laws 1983, c. 289, § 114, subd. 1, eff. July 1, 1983; Laws 1984, c. 655, art. 1, § 92; Laws 1985, c. 248, § 70.

Chapter 523

POWERS OF ATTORNEY

For complete statutory history see Minnesota Statutes Annotated.

523.01. Authorization

A person who is a competent adult may, as principal, designate another person or an authorized corporation as the person's attorney-in-fact by a written power of attorney. The power of attorney is validly executed when it is dated and signed by the principal and, in the case of a signature on behalf of the principal, by another, or by a mark, acknowledged by a notary public. Only powers of attorney validly created pursuant to this section or section 523.02 are validly executed powers of attorney for the purposes of sections 523.01 to 523.24.

Laws 1984, c. 603, § 3. Amended by Laws 1993, c. 13, art. 2, § 1.

523.02. Common law, preexisting and foreign powers of attorney

A written power of attorney is a validly executed power of attorney for the purposes of sections 523.01 to 523.24, and is subject to the provisions of sections 523.01 to 523.24, if it is validly created pursuant to: (1) the law of Minnesota as it existed prior to the enactment of sections 523.01 to 523.24 if it was executed prior to August 1, 1984; (2) the common law; or (3) the law of another state or country. A power of attorney executed before August 1, 1992, in conformity with section 523.23 as that statute existed before that date is a statutory short form power of attorney. A power of attorney executed on or after August 1, 1992, in conformity with section 523.23 as it exists on or after that date is a statutory short form power of attorney. A provision in a power of attorney that would make it a durable power of attorney under section 523.07 but for its use of the term "disability" in place of "incapacity or incompetence" is nonetheless a durable power of attorney.

Laws 1984, c. 603, § 4. Amended by Laws 1992, c. 548, § 7.

523.03. Definitions

As used in this chapter:

(1) "incapacity" means cause for appointment of a guardian or conservator of an adult under sections 524.5–101 to 524.5–502;

(2) "principal" includes a guardian or conservator appointed for the principal at any time; and

(3) "power of attorney" means a validly executed power of attorney.

Laws 1984, c. 603, § 5. Amended by Laws 1992, c. 548, § 8; Laws 2004, c. 146, art. 3, § 39.

523.04. Presumption of valid execution

A written power of attorney that is dated and purports to be signed by the principal named in it is presumed to be valid. All parties may rely on this presumption except those who have actual knowledge that the power was not validly executed.

Laws 1984, c. 603, § 6.

523.05. Recording

If the exercise of the power of attorney requires execution and delivery of any instrument which is recordable, the power of attorney and any affidavit authorized under sections 523.01 to 523.24 when authenticated for record in conformity with section 507.24, are also recordable.

Laws 1984, c. 603, § 7. Amended by Laws 1993, c. 13, art. 2, § 1.

523.06. Certification

A certified copy of a power of attorney has the same force and effect as a power of attorney bearing the signature of the principal. A copy of a power of attorney may be certified by an official of a state or of a political subdivision of a state who is authorized to make certifications. The certification shall state that the certifying official has examined an original power of attorney and the copy and that the copy is a true and correct copy of the original power of attorney.

Laws 1984, c. 603, § 8.

523.07. Durable power of attorney

A power of attorney is durable if it contains language such as "This power of attorney shall not be affected by incapacity or incompetence of the principal" or "This power of attorney shall become effective upon the incapacity or incompetence of the principal," or similar words showing the intent of the principal that the authority conferred is exercisable notwithstanding the principal's later incapacity or incompetence.

Laws 1984, c. 603, § 9. Amended by Laws 1986, c. 444; Laws 1992, c. 548, § 9.

UNIFORM DURABLE POWER OF ATTORNEY ACT

Table of Jurisdictions Wherein Act Has Been Adopted

For text of Uniform Act, and variation notes and annotation materials for adopting jurisdictions, see Uniform Laws Annotated, Master Edition, Volume 8A.

Jurisdiction	Laws	Effective Date	Statutory Citation
Alabama	1981, No. 81–98 p. 117	3–4–1981	Code 1975, § 26–1–2.
Arizona	1973, c. 75	1–1–1974	A.R.S. §§ 14–5501 to 14–5503.
Arkansas	1981, No. 659		A.C.A. §§ 28–68–101, 28–68–201 to 28–68–203.
California	1981, c. 511	9–16–1981*	West's Ann.Cal.Probate Code, §§ 4124 to 4128, 4206, 4304, and 4305.
Colorado	1973, H.B. 1039	7–1–1974	West's C.R.S.A. §§ 15–14–501, 15–14–502.
Delaware	1982 [63 Del. Laws], c. 267	6–21–1982*	12 Del.C. §§ 4901 to 4905.
District of Columbia	1987, D.C. Law 6–204		D.C. Official Code, 2001 Ed. §§ 21–2081 to 21–2085.
Florida	1974, c. 74–245		West's F.S.A. § 709.08.
Hawaii	1989, c. 270	6–8–1989	HRS §§ 551D–1 to 551D–7.
Idaho	1982, c. 138		I.C. §§ 15–5–501 to 15–5–507.
Kentucky	1972, c. 168		KRS 386.093.
Maine	1979, c. 540	1–1–1981	18–A M.R.S.A. §§ 5–501 to 5–506.
Maryland	1974, c. 11		Code, Estates and Trusts, §§ 13–601 to 13–603.

Jurisdiction	Laws	Effective Date	Statutory Citation
Massachusetts	1981, c. 276	6–22–1981*	M.G.L.A. c. 201B, §§ 1 to 7.
Michigan	1998, P.A. 386	4–1–2000	M.C.L.A. §§ 700.5501 to 700.5505.
Minnesota	1984, c. 603	8–1–1984	M.S.A. §§ 523.07 to 523.08.
Mississippi	1994, c. 336	7–1–1994	Code 1972, §§ 87–3–101 to 87–3–113.
Missouri	1989, H.B.No. 145	8–28–1989	V.A.M.S. §§ 404.700 to 404.735
Montana	1985, c. 283		MCA 72–5–501, 72–5–502.
Nebraska	1985, LB 292	9–6–1985	R.R.S.1943, §§ 30–2664 to 30–2672.
New Hampshire	2001, c. 257:1	1–1–2002	RSA 506:6.
New Jersey	2000, c. 109:1	9–8–2000*	N.J.S.A. 46:2B–8.1 to 46:2B–8.14.
New Mexico	1995, c. 210	7–1–1995	NMSA 1978, §§ 45–5–501 to 45–5–505.
New York	1996, c. 499	1–1–1997	McKinney's General Obligations Law §§ 5–1501, 5–1505, 5–1506.
North Carolina	1983, c. 626		GS §§ 32A–8 to 32A–14.
North Dakota	1985, c. 370		NDCC 30.1–30–01 to 30.1–30–06.
Oklahoma	1988, c. 293	11–1–1988	58 Okl.St.Ann. §§ 1071 to 1077.
Pennsylvania	1982, P.L. 45, No. 26, § 9	2–18–1982	20 Pa.C.S.A. §§ 5604 to 5606.
South Carolina	1986, Act 539	7–1–1987	Code 1976, §§ 62–5–501 to 62–5–505.
Tennessee	1983, c. 299	7–1–1983	T.C.A. §§ 34–6–101 to 34–6–111.
Texas	1993, c. 49	9–1–1993	V.A.T.S. Probate Code §§ 481 to 506.
Utah	1975, c. 150	7–1–1977	U.C.A. 1953, 75–5–501 to 75–5–504.
Vermont	2001, No. 135	6–13–2002	14 V.S.A. § 3508.
Virgin Islands	1991, No. 5718	9–23–1991	15 V.I.C. §§ 1261 to 1267.
Washington	1985, c. 30		West's RCWA 11.94.010 to 11.94.900.
West Virginia	1986, c. 165	7–1–1986	Code, §§ 39–4–1 to 39–4–7.
Wisconsin	1981, c. 313	5–1–1982	W.S.A. 243.07.

* Date of approval.

523.075. Expiration date in a power of attorney

In a power of attorney, an expiration date, if any, must be stated in terms of a specific month, day, and year. An expiration date stated in any other way has no effect.

Laws 1992, c. 548, § 10.

523.08. Termination of a durable power

A durable power of attorney terminates on the earliest to occur of the death of the principal, the expiration of a date of termination specified in the power of attorney, or, in the case of a power of attorney to the spouse of the principal, upon the commencement of proceedings for dissolution, separation, or annulment of the principal's marriage.

Laws 1984, c. 603, § 10. Amended by Laws 1992, c. 548, § 11.

523.09. Termination of a nondurable power of attorney

A nondurable power of attorney terminates on the death of the principal, the incapacity or incompetence of the principal, the expiration of a date of termination specified in the power of attorney, or, in the case of a power of attorney to the spouse of the principal, upon the commencement of proceedings for dissolution, separation, or annulment of the principal's marriage.

Laws 1984, c. 603, § 11. Amended by Laws 1992, c. 548, § 12.

523.10. Missing persons presumed living

For purposes of this chapter, a missing person is presumed to be living until actual proof of death or legal adjudication of death occurs.

Laws 1984, c. 603, § 12.

523.11. Revocation of a power

Subdivision 1. Manner. An executed power of attorney may be revoked only by a written instrument of revocation signed by the principal and, in the case of a signature on behalf of the principal by another or a signature by a mark, acknowledged before a notary public. The conservator or guardian of the principal has the same power the principal would have if the principal were not incapacitated or incompetent to revoke, suspend, or terminate all or any part of the power of attorney.

Subd. 2. Effect; definition of actual notice of revocation. Revocation of an executed power of attorney is not effective as to any party unless that party has actual notice of the revocation.

As used in this chapter, "actual notice of revocation" means that a written instrument of revocation has been received by the party. In real property transactions only, "actual notice of revocation" means that a written instrument of revocation has been received by the party, or that a written instrument of revocation containing the legal description of the real property has been recorded in the office of the county recorder or filed in the office of the registrar of titles. Recorded or filed revocation is actual notice of revocation of a power of attorney only as to any interest in real property described in the revocation and located in the county where it is recorded.

Subd. 3. Presumptions. A written instrument of revocation that purports to be signed by the principal named in the power of attorney is presumed to be valid. Any party receiving the written instrument of revocation may rely on this presumption and is not liable for later refusing to accept the authority of the attorney-in-fact.

Subd. 4. Transferee affidavit of nonrevocation. In the case of a conveyance of an interest in property, an affidavit signed by an initial transferee of the interest of the principal stating that the initial transferee had not received, at the time of the conveyance, a written instrument of revocation of the power of attorney, constitutes conclusive proof as to all subsequent transferees that no written instrument of revocation was received by the initial transferee, except as to a subsequent transferee who commits an intentional fraud.

Laws 1984, c. 603, § 13. Amended by Laws 1992, c. 548, §§ 13, 14.

523.12. Power of attorney-in-fact to bind principal

Any action taken by the attorney-in-fact pursuant to the power of attorney binds the principal, the principal's heirs and assigns, and the representative of the estate of the principal in the same manner as though the action was taken by the principal, and, during any time while a guardian or conservator has been appointed for the principal and only the guardian or conservator has the power to take relevant action, as though the action was taken by the guardian or conservator.

Laws 1984, c. 603, § 14.

523.13. Multiple attorneys-in-fact

Unless it is provided to the contrary in a power of attorney which authorizes two or more attorneys-in-fact to act on behalf of a principal, any action taken by any one of the several attorneys-in-fact pursuant to the power of attorney, whether the other attorneys-in-fact consent or object to the action, binds the principal, the principal's heirs and assigns, and the representative of the estate of the principal in the same manner as though the action was taken by the principal, and, during any time while a guardian or conservator has been appointed for the principal and only the guardian or conservator has the power to take the relevant action, as though the action was taken by the guardian or conservator.

Laws 1984, c. 603, § 15.

523.131. Qualification of successor attorney-in-fact in statutory short form power of attorney

If two or more attorneys-in-fact are originally appointed and one dies, resigns, or is unable to serve, a successor attorney-in-fact named in a power of attorney executed in conformity with section 523.23 replaces the attorney-in-fact who dies, resigns, or is unable to serve. If the original attorneys-in-fact were required to act jointly, the attorneys-in-fact acting at any time must act jointly. If the original attorneys-in-fact were allowed to act individually, the attorneys-in-fact acting at any time may act individually. If attorneys-in-fact acting at any time are required to act jointly, and there is only one remaining attorney-in-fact because of the death, resignation, or inability to serve of all other original and successor attorneys-in-fact, the remaining attorney-in-fact may act alone.

Laws 1992, c. 548, § 15.

523.14. Successor attorney-in-fact not liable for acts of predecessor

An attorney-in-fact who is named in a power of attorney to succeed an attorney-in-fact who dies, resigns, or otherwise is unable to serve, is not liable for any action taken by the predecessor attorney-in-fact.

Laws 1984, c. 603, § 16.

284

523.15. Co-attorneys-in-fact not liable for acts of each other

When two or more attorneys-in-fact are authorized to act on behalf of a principal, an attorney-in-fact who did not join in or consent to the action of one or more co-attorneys-in-fact is not liable for that action. Failure to object to an action is not consent.

Laws 1984, c. 603, § 17.

523.16. Affidavit as proof of authority of attorney-in-fact

If the attorney-in-fact exercising a power pursuant to a power of attorney has authority to act as a result of the death, incompetency, or resignation of one or more attorneys-in-fact named in the power of attorney, an affidavit executed by the attorney-in-fact setting forth the conditions precedent to the attorney-in-fact's authority to act under the power of attorney and stating that those conditions have occurred is conclusive proof as to any party relying on the affidavit of the occurrence of those conditions.

Laws 1984, c. 603, § 18.

523.17. Affidavit of attorney-in-fact as conclusive proof of nontermination and nonrevocation in real property transactions

Subdivision 1. Form of affidavit. An affidavit of nontermination or nonrevocation in support of a real property transaction may be substantially in the following form:

AFFIDAVIT BY ATTORNEY IN FACT

STATE OF MINNESOTA)
) ss.
COUNTY OF)

.........., being first duly sworn on oath says that:

1. Affiant is the Attorney-in-Fact (or agent) named in that certain Power of Attorney dated ...., ..., and filed for record ...., ..., as Document No........... (or in Book .... of .... Page ....), in the Office of the (County Recorder) (Registrar of Titles) of .... County, Minnesota, executed by .... as Grantor and Principal, relating to real property in .... County, Minnesota, legally described as follows:

....
....
....

(If more space is needed, continue on back or on an attachment.)

2. Affiant does not have actual knowledge and has not received actual notice of the revocation or termination of the Power of Attorney by Grantor's death,

incapacity, incompetence, or otherwise, or notice of any facts indicating the same.

3. Affiant has examined the legal description(s) if any, attached to said Power of Attorney, and certifies that the description(s) has (have) not been changed, replaced, or amended subsequent to the signing of said Power of Attorney by the Principal.

_____,
Affiant

Subscribed and sworn to before me
this _____ day of _____, ____

_____

Notary Stamp or Seal   Signature of Notary Public or
                                                        Other Official

This instrument was drafted by:
_____
_____
_____

Subd. 2. Effect. An affidavit by the attorney-in-fact under subdivision 1 is conclusive proof that the power of attorney has not terminated or been revoked, and that the powers granted extended to the property described in the power of attorney or any attachment to it, as of the time of the exercise of the power, as to any party relying on the affidavit except any party dealing directly with the attorney-in-fact who has actual knowledge that the power of attorney had terminated prior to the exercise of the power or actual notice of the revocation of the power of attorney or actual knowledge that the powers do not extend to the real property legally described in the power of attorney, including any attachment.

Laws 1984, c. 603, § 19. Amended by Laws 1992, c. 548, § 16; Laws 1998, c. 254, art. 1, § 107.

523.18. Signature of attorney-in-fact as conclusive proof of nontermination

In the exercise of a power granted by a power of attorney, other than in a transaction relating to real property described in section 523.17, a signature by a person as "attorney-in-fact for (Name of the principal)" or "(Name of the principal) by (Name of the attorney-in-fact) the principal's attorney-in-fact" or any similar written disclosure of the principal and attorney-in-fact relationship constitutes an attestation by the attorney-in-fact that the attorney-in-fact did not have, at the time of signing, actual knowledge of the termination of the power of attorney by the death of the principal or, in the case of a power of attorney to the spouse of the principal, by the commencement of proceedings for dissolution, separation, or annulment of the principal's marriage, or, if the power is one which terminates upon incapacity or incompetence of the principal, actual knowledge of the principal's incapacity or incompetence, or actual notice of the revocation of the power of attorney, and is conclusive proof as to any party relying on the attestation that the power of attorney had not terminated or been revoked at the time of the signature by the attorney-in-fact on behalf of the principal except as to any party who has actual knowledge that the power of attorney had terminated prior to the signature or actual notice of the revocation of the power of attorney.

Laws 1984, c. 603, § 20. Amended by Laws 1986, c. 444; Laws 1992, c. 548, § 17.

523.19. Third parties held harmless

Any party accepting the authority of an attorney-in-fact to exercise a power granted by a power of attorney is not liable to the principal, to the heirs and assigns of the principal, or to any representative of the estate of the principal if: (1) the applicable provisions of sections 523.17 and 523.18 have been satisfied; (2) the provisions of section 523.16 have been satisfied, if applicable; (3) the party has no actual notice of the revocation of the power of attorney prior to the transaction; (4) the party has no actual knowledge of the death of the principal and, if the power of attorney is not a durable power of attorney, has not received actual notice of a judicial determination that the principal is legally incapacitated or incompetent; and (5) the duration of the power of attorney specified in the power of attorney itself, if any, has not expired. A good faith purchaser from any party who has obtained an interest in property from an attorney-in-fact is not liable to the principal, the heirs or assigns of the principal, or the representative of the estate of the principal.

Laws 1984, c. 603, § 21. Amended by Laws 1992, c. 548, § 18.

523.20. Liability of parties refusing authority of attorney-in-fact to act on principal's behalf

Any party refusing to accept the authority of an attorney-in-fact to exercise a power granted by a power of attorney which (1) is executed in conformity with section 523.23; (2) contains a specimen signature of the attorney-in-fact authorized to act; (3) with regard to the execution or delivery of any recordable instrument relating to real property, is accompanied by affidavits that satisfy the provisions of section 523.17; (4) with regard to any other transaction, is signed by the attorney-in-fact in a manner conforming to section 523.18; and (5) when applicable, is accompanied by an affidavit and any other document required by section 523.16, is liable to the principal and to the principal's heirs, assigns, and representative of the estate of the principal in the same manner as the party would be liable had the party refused to accept the authority of the principal to act on the principal's own behalf unless: (1) the party has actual notice of the revocation of the power of attorney prior to the exercise of the power; (2) the duration of the power of attorney specified in the power of attorney itself has expired; or (3) the party has actual knowledge of the death of the principal or, if the power of attorney is not a durable power of attorney, actual notice of a judicial determination that the principal is legally incompetent. This provision does not negate any liability which a party would have to the principal or to the attorney-in-fact under any other form of power of attorney under the common law or otherwise.

Laws 1984, c. 603, § 22. Amended by Laws 1986, c. 444.

523.21. Duties of an attorney-in-fact

The attorney-in-fact shall keep complete records of all transactions entered into by the attorney-in-fact on behalf of the principal. The attorney-in-fact has no duty to render an accounting of those transactions unless: (1) requested to do so at any time by the principal; (2) the instrument conferring the power of attorney requires that the attorney-in-fact render accountings and specifies to whom the accounting must be delivered; or (3) the attorney-in-fact has reimbursed the attorney-in-fact for any expenditure the attorney-in-fact has made on behalf of the principal. A written statement that gives reasonable notice of all transactions entered into by the attorney-in-fact on behalf of the principal is an adequate accounting. The persons entitled to examine and copy the records of the attorney-in-fact are the principal, a person designated by the principal in the document creating the power of attorney as the recipient of accountings required by this section, and the guardian or conservator of the estate of the principal while the principal is living and the personal representative of the estate of the principal after the death of the principal. The attorney-in-fact has no affirmative duty to exercise any power conferred upon the attorney-in-fact under the power of attorney. In exercising any power conferred by the power of attorney, the attorney-in-fact shall exercise the power in the same manner as an ordinarily prudent person of discretion and intelligence would exercise in the management of the person's own affairs and shall have the interests of the principal utmost in mind. The attorney-in-fact is personally liable to any person, including the principal, who is injured by an action taken by the attorney-in-fact in bad faith under the power of attorney or by the attorney-in-fact's failure to account when the attorney-in-fact has a duty to account under this section.

Laws 1984, c. 603, § 23. Amended by Laws 1992, c. 548, § 19.

523.22. Liability of attorney-in-fact for improper execution of affidavits and signature

Nothing in sections 523.01 to 523.24 limits any rights the principal may have against the attorney-in-fact for any fraudulent or negligent actions in executing affidavits or signing or acting on behalf of the principal as an attorney-in-fact. An attorney-in-fact who knowingly executes a false affidavit or, knowing that the conditions of section 523.18 are not satisfied, signs on behalf of the principal is liable for treble the amount of damages suffered by the principal.

Laws 1984, c. 603, § 24. Amended by Laws 1992, c. 548, § 20.

523.23. **Statutory short form of general power of attorney; formal requirements; joint agents**

Subdivision 1. Form. The following form may be used to create a power of attorney, and, when used, it must be construed in accordance with sections 523.23 and 523.24:

STATUTORY SHORT FORM POWER OF ATTORNEY
MINNESOTA STATUTES, SECTION 523.23

IMPORTANT NOTICE: The powers granted by this document are broad and sweeping. They are defined in Minnesota Statutes, section 523.24. If you have any questions about these powers, obtain competent advice. This power of attorney may be revoked by you if you wish to do so. This power of attorney is automatically terminated if it is to your spouse and proceedings are commenced for dissolution, legal separation, or annulment of your marriage. This power of attorney authorizes, but does not require, the attorney-in-fact to act for you.

PRINCIPAL   (Name and Address of Person Granting the Power)
_____
_____
_____

ATTORNEYS(S)–IN–FACT
(Name and Address)

SUCCESSOR ATTORNEY(S)–IN–FACT
(Optional) To act if any named attorney-in-fact dies, resigns, or is otherwise unable to serve.
(Name and Address)
First Successor _____
_____
Second Successor _____
_____

_____
_____
_____
_____

NOTICE: If more than one attorney-in-fact is designated, make a check or "x" on the line in front of one of the following statements:
____ Each attorney-in-fact may independently exercise the powers granted.
____ All attorneys-in-fact must jointly exercise the powers granted.

EXPIRATION DATE (Optional)
_____ ____, _____
Use Specific Month   Day   Year Only

I, (the above-named Principal) hereby appoint the above named Attorney(s)-in-Fact to act as my attorney(s)-in-fact:

FIRST: To act for me in any way that I could act with respect to the following matters, as each of them is defined in Minnesota Statutes, section 523.24:

(To grant to the attorney-in-fact any of the following powers, make a check or "x" on the line in front of each power being granted. You may, but need not, cross out each power not granted. Failure to make a check or "x" on the line in front of the power will have the effect of deleting the power unless the line in front of the power of (N) is checked or x-ed.)

Check or "x"

_____ (A)   real property transactions; I choose to limit this power to real property in _____ County, Minnesota, described as follows: (Use legal description. Do not use street address.)

_____

_____

_____

(If more space is needed, continue on the back or on an attachment.)

_____ (B)   tangible personal property transactions;
_____ (C)   bond, share, and commodity transactions;
_____ (D)   banking transactions;
_____ (E)   business operating transactions;
_____ (F)   insurance transactions;
_____ (G)   beneficiary transactions;
_____ (H)   gift transactions;
_____ (I)   fiduciary transactions;
_____ (J)   claims and litigation;
_____ (K)   family maintenance;
_____ (L)   benefits from military service;
_____ (M)   records, reports, and statements;
_____ (N)   all of the powers listed in (A) through (M) above and all other matters.

SECOND: (You must indicate below whether or not this power of attorney will be effective if you become incapacitated or incompetent. Make a check or "x" on the line in front of the statement that expresses your intent.)

_____   This power of attorney shall continue to be effective if I become incapacitated or incompetent.
_____   This power of attorney shall not be effective if I become incapacitated or incompetent.

THIRD: (You must indicate below whether or not this power of attorney authorizes the attorney-in-fact to transfer your property to the attorney-in-fact. Make a check or "x" on the line in front of the statement that expresses your intent.)

_____   This power of attorney authorizes the attorney-in-fact to transfer my property to the attorney-in-fact.
_____   This power of attorney does not authorize the attorney-in-fact to transfer my property to the attorney-in-fact.

FOURTH: (You may indicate below whether or not the attorney-in-fact is required to make an accounting. Make a check or "x" on the line in front of the statement that expresses your intent.)

290

____ My attorney-in-fact need not render an accounting unless I request it or the accounting is otherwise required by Minnesota Statutes, section 523.21.

____ My attorney-in-fact must render _____
                                                    (Monthly, Quarterly, Annual)

accountings to me or _____
                                                    (Name and Address)

during my lifetime, and a final accounting to the personal representative of my estate, if any is appointed, after my death.

In Witness Whereof I have hereunto signed my name this __ day of __, __

_____
(Signature of Principal)

(Acknowledgment of Principal)

STATE OF MINNESOTA   )
) ss.
COUNTY OF   )

The foregoing instrument was acknowledged before me this __ day of _____, ____,
by _____
        (Insert Name of Principal)

_____
(Signature of Notary Public
or other Official)

This instrument was drafted by:	Specimen Signature of Attorney(s)-in-Fact (Notarization not required)
_____	_____
_____	_____
_____	_____

Subd. 2. Failure to check or "X" a power. Any of the powers of the form in subdivision 1 which is not checked or X-ed is withheld by the principal from the attorney-in-fact unless the power of (N) of the form in subdivision 1 is checked or X-ed.

Subd. 3. Requirements. To constitute a "statutory short form power of attorney," as this phrase is used in this chapter the wording and content of the form in subdivision 1 must be duplicated exactly and with no modifications, parts First, Second, and Third must be properly completed, and the signature of the principal must be acknowledged. Failure to name a successor attorney-in-fact, to provide an expiration date, or to complete part Fourth does not invalidate the power as a statutory short form power of attorney. A power of attorney that does not satisfy the requirements of this subdivision, but purports to be a statutory short form power of attorney, may constitute a common law power of attorney that incorporates by reference the definitions of powers contained in section 523.24; however, a party refusing to accept the authority of the common law attorney-in-fact is not liable under section 523.20.

Subd. 3a. Legal description. Use of a street address instead of a legal description under the power of (A) in part First of the statutory short form power of attorney invalidates the power of (A) for all real property transactions, but does not affect the powers of (B) to (M), nor does it affect the power of (N) except with respect to real property transactions.

Subd. 4. Powers of attorney-in-fact. All powers enumerated in section 523.24 may be legally performed by an attorney-in-fact acting on behalf of a principal.

Subd. 5. Reimbursement of attorney-in-fact. The attorney-in-fact acting under a statutory short form power of attorney is authorized to reimburse the attorney-in-fact for expenditures the attorney-in-fact has made on behalf of the principal even if the principal has not authorized the attorney-in-fact to receive transfers directly under part Third. In the event a reimbursement is made, the attorney-in-fact shall render an accounting in accordance with section 523.21.

Laws 1984, c. 603, § 25. Amended by Laws 1986, c. 444; Laws 1992, c. 548, §§ 21 to 25; Laws 1995, c. 130, § 9; Laws 1998, c. 254, art. 1, § 107.

Historical and Statutory Notes

Laws 1995, c. 130, § 22, provides in part that this chapter is effective January 1, 1996.

523.24. Construction

Subdivision 1. Real property transactions. In a statutory short form power of attorney, the language conferring general authority with respect to real estate transactions, means that the principal authorizes the attorney-in-fact:

(1) to accept as a gift, or as security for a loan, to reject, to demand, to buy, to lease, to receive, or otherwise to acquire either ownership or possession of any estate or interest in real property;

(2) to sell, exchange, convey either with or without covenants, quitclaim, release, surrender, mortgage, encumber, partition or consent the partitioning, plat or consent platting, grant options concerning, lease or sublet, or otherwise to dispose of, any estate or interest in real property;

(3) to release in whole or in part, assign the whole or a part of, satisfy in whole or in part, and enforce by action, proceeding or otherwise, any mortgage, encumbrance, lien, or other claim to real property which exists, or is claimed to exist, in favor of the principal;

(4) to do any act of management or of conservation with respect to any estate or interest in real property owned, or claimed to be owned, by the principal, including by way of illustration, but not of restriction, power to insure against any casualty, liability, or loss, to obtain or regain possession or protect such estate or interest by action, proceeding or otherwise, to pay, compromise or

contest taxes or assessments, to apply for and receive refunds in connection therewith, to purchase supplies, hire assistance or labor, and make repairs or alterations in the structures or lands;

(5) to use in any way, develop, modify, alter, replace, remove, erect, or install structures or other improvements upon any real property in which the principal has, or claims to have, any estate or interest;

(6) to demand, receive, obtain by action, proceeding, or otherwise, any money, or other thing of value to which the principal is, or may become, or may claim to be entitled as the proceeds of an interest in real property or of one or more of the transactions enumerated in this subdivision, to conserve, invest, disburse, or utilize anything so received for purposes enumerated in this subdivision, and to reimburse the attorney-in-fact for any expenditures properly made by the attorney-in-fact in the execution of the powers conferred on the attorney-in-fact by the statutory short form power of attorney;

(7) to participate in any reorganization with respect to real property and receive and hold any shares of stock or instrument of similar character received in accordance with a plan of reorganization, and to act with respect to the shares, including, by way of illustration but not of restriction, power to sell or otherwise to dispose of the shares, or any of them, to exercise or sell any option, conversion or similar right with respect to the shares, and to vote on the shares in person or by the granting of a proxy;

(8) to agree and contract, in any manner, and with any person and on any terms, which the attorney-in-fact may select, for the accomplishment of any of the purposes enumerated in this subdivision, and to perform, rescind, reform, release, or modify such an agreement or contract or any other similar agreement or contract made by or on behalf of the principal;

(9) to execute, acknowledge, seal, and deliver any deed, revocation, mortgage, lease, notice, check, or other instrument which the attorney-in-fact deems useful for the accomplishment of any of the purposes enumerated in this subdivision;

(10) to prosecute, defend, submit to arbitration, settle, and propose or accept a compromise with respect to, any claim existing in favor of, or against, the principal based on or involving any real estate transaction or to intervene in any action or proceeding relating to the claim;

(11) to hire, discharge, and compensate any attorney, accountant, expert witness, or other assistant or assistants when the attorney-in-fact deems that action to be desirable for the proper execution of any of the powers described in this subdivision, and for the keeping of needed records; and

(12) in general, and in addition to all the specific acts in this subdivision, to do any other act with respect to any estate or interest in real property.

All powers described in this subdivision are exercisable equally with respect to any estate or interest in real property owned by the principal at the giving of the power of attorney or acquired after that time, and whether located in the state of Minnesota or elsewhere except when a legal description of certain real property is included in the statutory short form power of attorney, in which case the powers described in this subdivision are exercisable only with respect to the estate or interest owned by the principal in the property described in the form.

Subd. 2. Tangible personal property transactions. In a statutory short form power of attorney, the language conferring general authority with respect to tangible personal property transactions, means that the principal authorizes the attorney-in-fact:

(1) to accept as a gift, or as security for a loan, reject, demand, buy, receive, or otherwise to acquire either ownership or possession of any tangible personal property or any interest in tangible personal property;

(2) to sell, exchange, convey either with or without covenants, release, surrender, mortgage, encumber, pledge, hypothecate, pawn, grant options concerning, lease or sublet to others, or otherwise to dispose of any tangible personal property or any interest in any tangible personal property;

(3) to release in whole or in part, assign the whole or a part of, satisfy in whole or in part, and enforce by action, proceeding or otherwise, any mortgage, encumbrance, lien, or other claim, which exists, or is claimed to exist, in favor of the principal, with respect to any tangible personal property or any interest in tangible personal property;

(4) to do any act of management or of conservation, with respect to any tangible personal property or to any interest in any tangible personal property owned, or claimed to be owned, by the principal, including by way of illustration, but not of restriction, power to insure against any casualty, liability, or loss, to obtain or regain possession, or protect the tangible personal property or interest in any tangible personal property, by action, proceeding, or otherwise, to pay, compromise, or contest taxes or assessments, to apply for and receive refunds in connection with taxes or assessments, move from place to place, store for hire or on a gratuitous bailment, use, alter, and make repairs or alterations of any tangible personal property, or interest in any tangible personal property;

(5) to demand, receive, or obtain by action, proceeding, or otherwise any money or other thing of value to which the principal is, or may become, or may claim to be entitled as the proceeds of any tangible personal property or of any interest in any tangible personal property, or of one or more of the transactions enumerated in this subdivision, to conserve, invest, disburse or utilize anything so received for purposes enumerated in this subdivision, and to reimburse the attorney-in-fact for any expenditures properly made by the attorney-in-fact in the execution of the powers conferred on the attorney-in-fact by the statutory short form power of attorney;

(6) to agree and contract in any manner and with any person and on any terms which the attorney-in-fact may select, for the accomplishment of any of the purposes enumerated in this subdivision, and to perform, rescind, reform, release, or modify any agreement or contract or any other similar agreement or contract made by or on behalf of the principal;

(7) to execute, acknowledge, seal, and deliver any conveyance, mortgage, lease, notice, check, or other instrument which the attorney-in-fact deems useful for the accomplishment of any of the purposes enumerated in this subdivision;

(8) to prosecute, defend, submit to arbitration, settle, and propose or accept a compromise with respect to any claim existing in favor of or against the principal based on or involving any tangible personal property transaction or to intervene in any action or proceeding relating to such a claim;

(9) to hire, discharge, and compensate any attorney, accountant, expert witness, or other assistant when the attorney-in-fact deems that action to be desirable for the proper execution by the attorney-in-fact of any of the powers described in this subdivision, and for the keeping of needed records; and

(10) in general, and in addition to all the specific acts listed in this subdivision, to do any other acts with respect to any tangible personal property or interest in any tangible personal property.

All powers described in this subdivision are exercisable equally with respect to any tangible personal property or interest in any tangible personal property owned by the principal at the giving of the power of attorney or acquired after that time, and whether located in the state of Minnesota or elsewhere.

Subd. 3. Bond, share, and commodity transactions. In a statutory short form power of attorney, the language conferring general authority with respect to bond, share, and commodity transactions means that the principal authorizes the attorney-in-fact:

(1) to accept as a gift or as security for a loan, reject, demand, buy, receive, or otherwise to acquire either ownership or possession of any bond, share, instrument of similar character, commodity interest, or any instrument with respect to the bond, share, or interest, together with the interest, dividends, proceeds, or other distributions connected with any of those instruments;

(2) to sell or sell short and to exchange, transfer either with or without a guaranty, release, surrender, hypothecate, pledge, grant options concerning, loan, trade in, or otherwise to dispose of any bond, share, instrument of similar character, commodity interest, or any instrument with respect to the bond, share, or interest;

(3) to release in whole or in part, assign the whole or a part of, satisfy in whole or in part, and enforce by action, proceeding or otherwise, any pledge, encumbrance, lien, or other claim as to any bond, share, instrument of similar character, commodity interest or any interest with respect to the bond, share,

or interest, when the pledge, encumbrance, lien, or other claim is owned, or claimed to be owned, by the principal;

(4) to do any act of management or of conservation with respect to any bond, share, instrument of similar character, commodity interest or any instrument with respect thereto, owned or claimed to be owned by the principal or in which the principal has or claims to have an interest, including by way of illustration but not of restriction, power to insure against any casualty, liability, or loss, to obtain or regain possession or protect the principal's interest therein by action, proceeding or otherwise, to pay, compromise or contest taxes or assessments, to apply for and receive refunds in connection with taxes or assessments, to consent to and participate in any reorganization, recapitalization, liquidation, merger, consolidation, sale or lease, or other change in or revival of a corporation or other association, or in the financial structure of any corporation or other association, or in the priorities, voting rights, or other special rights with respect to the corporation or association, to become a depositor with any protective, reorganization, or similar committee of the bond, share, other instrument of similar character, commodity interest, or any instrument with respect to the bond, share, or interest, belonging to the principal, to make any payments reasonably incident to the foregoing, to exercise or sell any option, conversion, or similar right, to vote in person or by the granting of a proxy with or without the power of substitution, either discretionary, general or otherwise, for the accomplishment of any of the purposes enumerated in this subdivision;

(5) to carry in the name of a nominee selected by the attorney-in-fact any evidence of the ownership of any bond, share, other instrument of similar character, commodity interest, or instrument with respect to the bond, share, or interest, belonging to the principal;

(6) to employ, in any way believed to be desirable by the attorney-in-fact, any bond, share, other instrument of similar character, commodity interest, or any instrument with respect to the bond, share, or interest, in which the principal has or claims to have any interest, for the protection or continued operation of any speculative or margin transaction personally begun or personally guaranteed, in whole or in part, by the principal;

(7) to demand, receive, or obtain by action, proceeding or otherwise, any money or other thing of value to which the principal is, or may become, or may claim to be entitled as the proceeds of any interest in a bond, share, other instrument of similar character, commodity interest, or any instrument with respect to the bond, share, or interest, or of one or more of the transactions enumerated in this subdivision, to conserve, invest, disburse, or utilize anything so received for purposes enumerated in this subdivision, and to reimburse the attorney-in-fact for any expenditures properly made by the attorney-in-fact in the execution of the powers conferred on the attorney-in-fact by the statutory short form power of attorney;

(8) to agree and contract, in any manner, with any broker or other person, and on any terms which the attorney-in-fact selects, for the accomplishment of any of the purposes enumerated in this subdivision, and to perform, rescind, reform, release, or modify the agreement or contract or any other similar agreement made by or on behalf of the principal;

(9) to execute, acknowledge, seal, and deliver any consent, agreement, authorization, assignment, revocation, notice, waiver of notice, check, or other instrument which the attorney-in-fact deems useful for the accomplishment of any of the purposes enumerated in this subdivision;

(10) to execute, acknowledge, and file any report or certificate required by law or governmental regulation;

(11) to prosecute, defend, submit to arbitration, settle, and propose or accept a compromise with respect to, any claim existing in favor of or against the principal based on or involving any bond, share, or commodity transaction or to intervene in any related action or proceeding;

(12) to hire, discharge, and compensate any attorney, accountant, expert witness or other assistant or assistants when the attorney-in-fact deems that action to be desirable for the proper execution of any of the powers described in this subdivision, and for the keeping of needed records; and

(13) in general, and in addition to all the specific acts listed in this subdivision, to do any other acts with respect to any interest in any bond, share, other instrument of similar character, commodity, or instrument with respect to a commodity.

All powers described in this subdivision are exercisable equally with respect to any interest in any bond, share or other instrument of similar character, commodity, or instrument with respect to a commodity owned by the principal at the giving of the power of attorney or acquired after that time, whether located in the state of Minnesota or elsewhere.

Subd. 4. Banking transactions. In a statutory short form power of attorney, the language conferring general authority with respect to banking transactions, means that the principal authorizes the attorney-in-fact:

(1) to continue, modify, and terminate any deposit account or other banking arrangement made by or on behalf of the principal prior to the execution of the power of attorney;

(2) to open in the name of the principal alone, or in a way that clearly evidences the principal and attorney-in-fact relationship, a deposit account of any type with any bank, trust company, savings association, credit union, thrift company, brokerage firm, or other institution which serves as a depository for funds selected by the attorney-in-fact, to hire safe deposit box or vault space and to make other contracts for the procuring of other services made available by the banking institution as the attorney-in-fact deems desirable;

(3) to make, sign, and deliver checks or drafts for any purpose, to withdraw by check, order, or otherwise any funds or property of the principal deposited with or left in the custody of any banking institution, wherever located, either before or after the execution of the power of attorney;

(4) to prepare any necessary financial statements of the assets and liabilities or income and expenses of the principal for submission to any banking institution;

(5) to receive statements, vouchers, notices, or other documents from any banking institution and to act with respect to them;

(6) to enter at any time any safe deposit box or vault which the principal could enter if personally present;

(7) to borrow money at any interest rate the attorney-in-fact selects, to pledge as security any assets of the principal the attorney-in-fact deems desirable or necessary for borrowing, to pay, renew, or extend the time of payment of any debt of the principal;

(8) to make, assign, draw, endorse, discount, guarantee, and negotiate, all promissory notes, bills of exchange, checks, drafts, or other negotiable or nonnegotiable paper of the principal, or payable to the principal or the principal's order, to receive the cash or other proceeds of any of those transactions, to accept any bill of exchange or draft drawn by any person upon the principal, and to pay it when due;

(9) to receive for the principal and to deal in and to deal with any sight draft, warehouse receipt, or other negotiable or nonnegotiable instrument in which the principal has or claims to have an interest;

(10) to apply for and to receive letters of credit from any banking institution selected by the attorney-in-fact, giving indemnity or other agreement in connection with the letters of credit which the attorney-in-fact deems desirable or necessary;

(11) to consent to an extension in the time of payment with respect to any commercial paper or any banking transaction in which the principal has an interest or by which the principal is, or might be, affected in any way;

(12) to demand, receive, obtain by action, proceeding, or otherwise any money or other thing of value to which the principal is, or may become, or may claim to be entitled as the proceeds of any banking transaction, and to reimburse the attorney-in-fact for any expenditures properly made in the execution of the powers conferred upon the attorney-in-fact by the statutory short form power of attorney;

(13) to execute, acknowledge, and deliver any instrument of any kind, in the name of the principal or otherwise, which the attorney-in-fact deems useful for the accomplishment of any of the purposes enumerated in this subdivision;

(14) to prosecute, defend, submit to arbitration, settle, and propose or accept a compromise with respect to any claim existing in favor of or against the

principal based on or involving any banking transaction or to intervene in any related action or proceeding;

(15) to hire, discharge, and compensate any attorney, accountant, expert witness, or other assistant when the attorney-in-fact deems that action to be desirable for the proper execution of any of the powers described in this subdivision, and for the keeping of needed records; and

(16) in general, and in addition to all the specific acts listed in this subdivision, to do any other acts in connection with any banking transaction which does or might in any way affect the financial or other interests of the principal.

All powers described in this subdivision are exercisable equally with respect to any banking transaction engaged in by the principal at the giving of the power of attorney or engaged in after that time, and whether conducted in the state of Minnesota or elsewhere.

Subd. 5. Business operating transactions. In a statutory short form power of attorney, the language conferring general authority with respect to business operating transactions, means that the principal authorizes the attorney-in-fact:

(1) to discharge and perform any duty or liability and also to exercise any right, power, privilege, or option which the principal has, or claims to have, under any partnership agreement whether the principal is a general or limited partner, to enforce the terms of a partnership agreement for the protection of the principal, by action, proceeding, or otherwise, as the attorney-in-fact deems desirable or necessary, and to defend, submit to arbitration, settle, or compromise any action or other legal proceeding to which the principal is a party because of membership in the partnership;

(2) to exercise in person or by proxy or to enforce by action, proceeding, or otherwise, any right, power, privilege, or option which the principal has as the holder of any bond, share, or other instrument of similar character and to defend, submit to arbitration, settle or compromise any action or other legal proceeding to which the principal is a party because of a bond, share, or other instrument of similar character;

(3) with respect to any business enterprise which is owned solely by the principal:

(a) to continue, modify, renegotiate, extend, and terminate any contractual arrangements made with any person or entity, firm, association, or corporation by or on behalf of the principal with respect to the business enterprise prior to the granting of the power of attorney;

(b) to determine the policy of the business enterprise as to the location of the site or sites to be used for its operation, the nature and extent of the business to be undertaken by it, the methods of manufacturing, selling, merchandising, financing, accounting, and advertising to be employed in its operation, the amount and types of insurance to be carried, the mode of securing, compensating, and dealing with accountants, attorneys, servants, and other agents and employees required for its operation, and to agree and to contract in any manner, with any person, and on any terms which the attorney-in-fact deems desirable or necessary for effectuating any or all of the decisions of the attorney-in-fact as to policy, and to perform, rescind, reform, release, or modify the agreement or contract or any other similar agreement or contract made by or on behalf of the principal;

(c) to change the name or form of organization under which the business enterprise is operated and to enter into a partnership agreement with other persons or to organize a corporation to take over the operation of the business or any part of the business, as the attorney-in-fact deems desirable or necessary;

(d) to demand and receive all money which is or may become due to the principal or which may be claimed by or for the principal in the operation of the business enterprise, and to control and disburse the funds in the operation of the enterprise in any way which the attorney-in-fact deems desirable or necessary, and to engage in any banking transactions which the attorney-in-fact deems desirable or necessary for effectuating the execution of any of the powers of the attorney-in-fact described in clauses (a) to (d);

(4) to prepare, sign, file, and deliver all reports, compilations of information, returns, or other papers with respect to any business operating transaction of the principal, which are required by any governmental agency, department, or instrumentality or which the attorney-in-fact deems desirable or necessary for any purpose, and to make any related payments;

(5) to pay, compromise, or contest taxes or assessments and to do any act or acts which the attorney-in-fact deems desirable or necessary to protect the principal from illegal or unnecessary taxation, fines, penalties, or assessments in connection with the principal's business operations, including power to attempt to recover, in any manner permitted by law, sums paid before or after the execution of the power of attorney as taxes, fines, penalties, or assessments;

(6) to demand, receive, obtain by action, proceeding, or otherwise, any money or other thing of value to which the principal is, may become, or may claim to be entitled as the proceeds of any business operation of the principal, to conserve, to invest, to disburse, or to use anything so received for purposes enumerated in this subdivision, and to reimburse the attorney-in-fact for any expenditures properly made by the attorney-in-fact in the execution of the powers conferred upon the attorney-in-fact by the statutory short form power of attorney;

(7) to execute, acknowledge, seal, and deliver any deed, assignment, mortgage, lease, notice, consent, agreement, authorization, check, or other instrument which the attorney-in-fact deems useful for the accomplishment of any of the purposes enumerated in this subdivision;

(8) to prosecute, defend, submit to arbitration, settle, and propose or accept a compromise with respect to, any claim existing in favor of, or against, the

300

principal based on or involving any business operating transaction or to intervene in any related action or proceeding;

(9) to hire, discharge, and compensate any attorney, accountant, expert witness, or other assistant when the attorney-in-fact deems that action to be desirable for the proper execution by the attorney-in-fact of any of the powers described in this subdivision, and for the keeping of needed records; and

(10) in general, and in addition to all the specific acts listed in this subdivision, to do any other act which the attorney-in-fact deems desirable or necessary for the furtherance or protection of the interests of the principal in any business.

All powers described in this subdivision are exercisable equally with respect to any business in which the principal is interested at the time of giving of the power of attorney or in which the principal becomes interested after that time, and whether operated in the state of Minnesota or elsewhere.

Subd. 6. Insurance transactions. In a statutory short form power of attorney, the language conferring general authority with respect to insurance transactions, means that the principal authorizes the attorney-in-fact:

(1) to continue, pay the premium or assessment on, modify, rescind, release, or terminate any contract of life, accident, health, or disability insurance or for the provision of health care services, or any combination of these contracts procured by or on behalf of the principal prior to the granting of the power of attorney which insures either the principal or any other person, without regard to whether the principal is or is not a beneficiary under the contract;

(2) to procure new, different, or additional contracts of life, accident, health, or disability insurance for the principal or for provision of health care services for the principal, to select the amount, the type of insurance and the mode of payment under each contract, to pay the premium or assessment on, modify, rescind, release or terminate, any contract so procured by the attorney-in-fact, and to designate the beneficiary of the contract, provided, however, that the attorney-in-fact cannot be named a beneficiary except, if permitted under subdivision 8, the attorney-in-fact can be named the beneficiary of death benefit proceeds under an insurance contract, or, if the attorney-in-fact was named as a beneficiary under the contract which was procured by the principal prior to the granting of the power of attorney, then the attorney-in-fact can continue to be named as the beneficiary under the contract or under any extension or renewal of or substitute for the contract;

(3) to apply for and receive any available loan on the security of the contract of insurance, whether for the payment of a premium or for the procuring of cash, to surrender and then to receive the cash surrender value, to exercise any election as to beneficiary or mode of payment, to change the manner of paying premiums, to change or convert the type of insurance contract, with respect to any contract of life, accident, health, disability, or liability insurance as to which the principal has, or claims to have, any one or more of the powers

described in this subdivision and to change the beneficiary of the contract of insurance, provided, however, that the attorney-in-fact cannot be a new beneficiary except, if permitted under subdivision 8, the attorney-in-fact can be the beneficiary of death benefit proceeds under an insurance contract, or, if the attorney-in-fact was named as a beneficiary under the contract which was procured by the principal prior to the granting of the power of attorney, then the attorney-in-fact can continue to be named as the beneficiary under the contract or under any extension or renewal of or substitute for the contract;

(4) to demand, receive, obtain by action, proceeding, or otherwise, any money, dividend, or other thing of value to which the principal is, or may become, or may claim to be entitled as the proceeds of any contract of insurance or of one or more of the transactions enumerated in this subdivision, to conserve, invest, disburse, or utilize anything so received for purposes enumerated in this subdivision, and to reimburse the attorney-in-fact for any expenditures properly made by the attorney-in-fact in the execution of the powers conferred on the attorney-in-fact by the statutory short form power of attorney;

(5) to apply for and procure any available governmental aid in the guaranteeing or paying of premiums of any contract of insurance on the life of the principal;

(6) to sell, assign, hypothecate, borrow upon, or pledge the interest of the principal in any contract of insurance;

(7) to pay from any proceeds or otherwise, compromise, or contest, and to apply for refunds in connection with, any tax or assessment levied by a taxing authority with respect to any contract of insurance or the proceeds of the refunds or liability accruing by reason of the tax or assessment;

(8) to agree and contract in any manner, with any person, and on any terms which the attorney-in-fact selects for the accomplishment of any of the purposes enumerated in this subdivision, and to perform, rescind, reform, release, or modify the agreement or contract;

(9) to execute, acknowledge, seal, and deliver any consent, demand, request, application, agreement, indemnity, authorization, assignment, pledge, notice, check, receipt, waiver, or other instrument which the attorney-in-fact deems useful for the accomplishment of any of the purposes enumerated in this subdivision;

(10) to continue, procure, pay the premium or assessment on, modify, rescind, release, terminate, or otherwise deal with any contract of insurance, other than those enumerated in clause (1) or (2), whether fire, marine, burglary, compensation, liability, hurricane, casualty, or other type, or any combination of insurance, to do any act or acts with respect to the contract or with respect to its proceeds or enforcement which the attorney-in-fact deems desirable or necessary for the promotion or protection of the interests of the principal;

(11) to prosecute, defend, submit to arbitration, settle, and propose or accept a compromise with respect to any claim existing in favor of or against the principal based on or involving any insurance transaction or to intervene in any related action or proceeding;

(12) to hire, discharge, and compensate any attorney, accountant, expert witness, or other assistants when the attorney-in-fact deems the action to be desirable for the proper execution by the attorney-in-fact of any of the powers described in this subdivision and for the keeping of needed records; and

(13) in general, and in addition to all the specific acts listed in this subdivision, to do any other acts in connection with procuring, supervising, managing, modifying, enforcing, and terminating contracts of insurance or for the provisions of health care services in which the principal is the insured or is otherwise in any way interested.

All powers described in this subdivision are exercisable with respect to any contract of insurance or for the provision of health care service in which the principal is in any way interested, whether made in the state of Minnesota or elsewhere.

Subd. 7. Beneficiary transactions. In the statutory short form power of attorney, the language conferring general authority with respect to beneficiary transactions, means that the principal authorizes the attorney-in-fact:

(1) to represent and act for the principal in all ways and in all matters affecting any trust, probate estate, guardianship, conservatorship, escrow, custodianship, qualified benefit plan, nonqualified benefit plan, individual retirement asset, or other fund out of which the principal is entitled, or claims to be entitled, as a beneficiary or participant, to some share or payment, including, but not limited to the following:

(a) to accept, reject, disclaim, receive, receipt for, sell, assign, release, pledge, exchange, or consent to a reduction in or modification of any share in or payment from the fund;

(b) to demand or obtain by action, proceeding, or otherwise any money or other thing of value to which the principal is, may become, or may claim to be entitled by reason of the fund, to initiate, to participate in, and to oppose any proceeding, judicial, or otherwise, for the ascertainment of the meaning, validity, or effect of any deed, declaration of trust, or other transaction affecting in any way the interest of the principal, to initiate, participate in, and oppose any proceeding, judicial or otherwise, for the removal, substitution, or surcharge of a fiduciary, to conserve, invest, disburse, or use anything so received for purposes listed in this subdivision, and to reimburse the attorney-in-fact for any expenditures properly made by the attorney-in-fact in the execution of the powers conferred on the attorney-in-fact by the statutory short form power of attorney;

(c) to prepare, sign, file, and deliver all reports, compilations of information, returns, or papers with respect to any interest had or claimed by or on behalf of the principal in the fund, to pay, compromise, or contest, and apply for and receive refunds in connection with, any tax or assessment, with respect to any interest had or claimed by or on behalf of the principal in the fund or with respect to any property in which an interest is had or claimed;

(d) to agree and contract in any manner, with any person, and on any terms the attorney-in-fact selects, for the accomplishment of the purposes listed in this subdivision, and to perform, rescind, reform, release, or modify the agreement or contract or any other similar agreement or contract made by or on behalf of the principal;

(e) to execute, acknowledge, verify, seal, file, and deliver any deed, assignment, mortgage, lease, consent, designation, pleading, notice, demand, election, conveyance, release, assignment, check, pledge, waiver, admission of service, notice of appearance, or other instrument which the attorney-in-fact deems useful for the accomplishment of any of the purposes enumerated in this subdivision;

(f) to submit to arbitration or settle and propose or accept a compromise with respect to any controversy or claim which affects the administration of the fund, in any one of which the principal has, or claims to have, an interest, and to do any and all acts which the attorney-in-fact deems to be desirable or necessary in effectuating the compromise;

(g) to hire, discharge, and compensate any attorney, accountant, expert witness, or other assistant, when the attorney-in-fact deems that action to be desirable for the proper execution by the attorney-in-fact of any of the powers described in this subdivision, and for the keeping of needed records;

(h) to transfer any part or all of any interest which the principal may have in any interests in real estate, stocks, bonds, bank accounts, insurance, and any other assets of any kind and nature, to the trustee of any revocable trust created by the principal as grantor.

For the purposes of clauses (a) to (h), "the fund" means any trust, probate estate, guardianship, conservatorship, escrow, custodianship, qualified benefit plan, nonqualified benefit plan, individual retirement asset, or other fund in which the principal has or claims to have an interest.

(2) in general, and in addition to all the specific acts listed in this subdivision, to do any other acts with respect to the administration of a trust, probate estate, guardianship, conservatorship, escrow, custodianship, qualified benefit plan, nonqualified benefit plan, individual retirement asset, or other fund, in which the principal has, or claims to have, an interest as a beneficiary or participant.

All powers described in this subdivision are exercisable equally with respect to the administration or disposition of any trust, probate estate, guardianship, conservatorship, escrow, custodianship, qualified benefit plan, nonqualified benefit plan, individual retirement asset, or other fund in which the principal is interested at the giving of the power of attorney or becomes interested after that time, as a beneficiary or participant, and whether located in the state of Minnesota or elsewhere.

Subd. 8. Gift transactions. In the statutory short form power of attorney, the language conferring general authority with respect to gift transactions, means that the principal authorizes the attorney-in-fact:

(1) to make gifts to organizations, whether charitable or otherwise, to which the principal has made gifts, and to satisfy pledges made to organizations by the principal;

(2) to make gifts on behalf of the principal to the principal's spouse, children, and other descendants or the spouse of any child or other descendant, and, if authorized by the principal in part Third, to the attorney-in-fact, either outright or in trust, for purposes which the attorney-in-fact deems to be in the best interest of the principal, specifically including minimization of income, estate, inheritance, or gift taxes, provided that, notwithstanding that the principal in part Third may have authorized the attorney-in-fact to transfer the principal's property to the attorney-in-fact, no attorney-in-fact nor anyone the attorney-in-fact has a legal obligation to support may be the recipient of any gifts in any one calendar year which, in the aggregate, exceed $10,000 in value to each recipient;

(3) to prepare, execute, consent to on behalf of the principal, and file any return, report, declaration, or other document required by the laws of the United States, any state or subdivision of a state, or any foreign government, which the attorney-in-fact deems to be desirable or necessary with respect to any gift made under the authority of this subdivision;

(4) to execute, acknowledge, seal, and deliver any deed, assignment, agreement, authorization, check, or other instrument which the attorney-in-fact deems useful for the accomplishment of any of the purposes enumerated in this subdivision;

(5) to prosecute, defend, submit to arbitration, settle, and propose or accept a compromise with respect to any claim existing in favor of or against the principal based on or involving any gift transaction or to intervene in any related action or proceeding;

(6) to hire, discharge, and compensate any attorney, accountant, expert witness, or other assistant when the attorney-in-fact deems that action to be desirable for the proper execution by the attorney-in-fact of any of the powers described in this subdivision, and for the keeping of needed records; and

(7) in general, and in addition to but not in contravention of all the specific acts listed in this subdivision, to do any other acts which the attorney-in-fact deems desirable or necessary to complete any gift on behalf of the principal.

All powers described in this subdivision are exercisable equally with respect to a gift of any property in which the principal is interested at the giving of the power of attorney or becomes interested after that time, and whether located in the state of Minnesota or elsewhere.

Subd. 9. Fiduciary transactions. In a statutory short form power of attorney, the language conferring general authority with respect to fiduciary transactions, means that the principal authorizes the agent:

(1) to represent and act for the principal in all ways and in all matters affecting any fund with respect to which the principal is a fiduciary;

(2) to initiate, participate in, and oppose any proceeding, judicial or otherwise, for the removal, substitution, or surcharge of a fiduciary, to conserve, to invest or to disburse anything received for the purposes of the fund for which it is received, and to reimburse the attorney-in-fact for any expenditures properly made by the attorney-in-fact in the execution of the powers conferred on the attorney-in-fact by the statutory short form power of attorney;

(3) to agree and contract, in any manner, with any person, and on any terms which the attorney-in-fact selects for the accomplishment of the purposes enumerated in this subdivision, and to perform, rescind, reform, release, or modify the agreement or contract or any other similar agreement or contract made by or on behalf of the principal;

(4) to execute, acknowledge, verify, seal, file, and deliver any consent, designation, pleading, notice, demand, election, conveyance, release, assignment, check, pledge, waiver, admission of service, notice of appearance, or other instrument which the attorney-in-fact deems useful for the accomplishment of any of the purposes enumerated in this subdivision;

(5) to hire, discharge, and compensate any attorney, accountant, expert witness, or other assistants, when the attorney-in-fact deems that action to be desirable for the proper execution by the attorney-in-fact of any of the powers described in this subdivision, and for the keeping of needed records; and

(6) in general, and in addition to all the specific acts listed in this subdivision, to do any other acts with respect to a fund of which the principal is a fiduciary.

Nothing in this subdivision authorizes delegation of any power of a fiduciary unless the power is one the fiduciary is authorized to delegate under the terms of the instrument governing the exercise of the power or under local law.

For the purposes of clauses (1) to (6), "fund" means any trust, probate estate, guardianship, conservatorship, escrow, custodianship, or any other fund in which the principal has, or claims to have, an interest as a fiduciary.

All powers described in this subdivision are exercisable equally with respect to any fund of which the principal is a fiduciary prior to the giving of the power of attorney or becomes a fiduciary after that time, and whether located in the state of Minnesota or elsewhere.

Subd. 10. Claims and litigation. In a statutory short form power of attorney, the language conferring general authority with respect to claims and litigation, means that the principal authorizes the attorney-in-fact:

(1) to assert and prosecute before any court, administrative board, department, commissioner, or other tribunal, any cause of action, claim, counterclaim, offset, or defense, which the principal has, or claims to have, against any individual, partnership, association, corporation, government, or other person or instrumentality, including, by way of illustration and not of restriction, power to sue for the recovery of land or of any other thing of value, for the recovery of damages sustained by the principal in any manner, for the elimination or modification of tax liability, for an injunction, for specific performance, or for any other relief;

(2) to bring an action of interpleader or other action to determine adverse claims, to intervene or interplead in any action or proceeding, and to act in any litigation as amicus curiae;

(3) in connection with any action or proceeding or controversy at law or otherwise, to apply for and, if possible, procure a libel, an attachment, a garnishment, an order of arrest, or other preliminary, provisional, or intermediate relief and to resort to and to utilize in all ways permitted by law any available procedure for the effectuation or satisfaction of the judgment, order, or decree obtained;

(4) in connection with any action or proceeding, at law or otherwise, to perform any act which the principal might perform, including by way of illustration and not of restriction, acceptance of tender, offer of judgment, admission of any facts, submission of any controversy on an agreed statement of facts, consent to examination before trial, and generally to bind the principal in the conduct of any litigation or controversy as seems desirable to the attorney-in-fact;

(5) to submit to arbitration, settle, and propose or accept a compromise with respect to any claim existing in favor of or against the principal or any litigation to which the principal is, may become, or may be designated a party;

(6) to waive the issuance and service of a summons, citation, or other process upon the principal, accept service of process, appear for the principal, designate persons upon whom process directed to the principal may be served, execute and file or deliver stipulations on the principal's behalf, verify pleadings, appeal to appellate tribunals, procure and give surety and indemnity bonds at the times and to the extent the attorney-in-fact deems desirable or necessary, contract and pay for the preparation and printing of records and briefs, receive and execute and file or deliver any consent, waiver, release, confession of judgment, satisfaction of judgment, notice, agreement, or other instrument which the attorney-in-fact deems desirable or necessary in connection with the prosecution, settlement, or defense of any claim by or against the

principal or of any litigation to which the principal is or may become or be designated a party;

(7) to appear for, represent, and act for the principal with respect to bankruptcy or insolvency proceedings, whether voluntary or involuntary, whether of the principal or of some other person, with respect to any reorganization proceeding, or with respect to any receivership or application for the appointment of a receiver or trustee which, in any way, affects any interest of the principal in any real property, bond, share, commodity interest, tangible personal property, or other thing of value;

(8) to hire, discharge, and compensate any attorney, accountant, expert witness or other assistant when the attorney-in-fact deems that action to be desirable for the proper execution of any of the powers described in this subdivision;

(9) to pay, from funds in the control of the attorney-in-fact or for the account of the principal, any judgment against the principal or any settlement which may be made in connection with any transaction enumerated in this subdivision, and to receive and conserve any money or other things of value paid in settlement of or as proceeds of one or more of the transactions enumerated in this subdivision, and to receive, endorse, and deposit checks; and

(10) in general, and in addition to all the specific acts listed in this subdivision, to do any other acts in connection with any claim by or against the principal or with litigation to which the principal is or may become or be designated a party.

All powers described in this subdivision are exercisable equally with respect to any claim or litigation existing at the giving of the power of attorney or arising after that time, and whether arising in the state of Minnesota or elsewhere.

Subd. 11. Family maintenance. In a statutory short form power of attorney, the language conferring general authority with respect to family maintenance, means that the principal authorizes the attorney-in-fact:

(1) to do all acts necessary for maintaining the customary standard of living of the spouse and children, and other persons customarily supported by the principal, including by way of illustration and not by way of restriction, power to provide living quarters by purchase, lease, or other contract, or by payment of the operating costs, including interest, amortization payments, repairs, and taxes of premises owned by the principal and occupied by the principal's family or dependents, to provide normal domestic help for the operation of the household, to provide usual vacations and usual travel expenses, to provide usual educational facilities, and to provide funds for all the current living costs of the spouse, children, and other dependents, including, among other things, shelter, clothing, food, and incidentals;

(2) to pay for necessary medical, dental, and surgical care, hospitalization, and custodial care for the spouse, children, and other dependents of the principal;

(3) to continue whatever provision has been made by the principal, either prior to or after the execution of the power of attorney, for the principal's spouse and other persons customarily supported by the principal, with respect to automobiles, or other means of transportation, including by way of illustration but not by way of restriction, power to license, insure, and replace any automobiles owned by the principal and customarily used by the spouse, children, or other persons customarily supported by the principal;

(4) to continue whatever charge accounts have been operated by the principal prior to the execution of the power of attorney or thereafter for the convenience of the principal's spouse, children, or other persons customarily supported by the principal, to open new accounts the attorney-in-fact deems to be desirable for the accomplishment of any of the purposes enumerated in this subdivision, and to pay the items charged on those accounts by any person authorized or permitted by the principal to make charges prior to the execution of the power of attorney;

(5) to continue payments incidental to the membership or affiliation of the principal in any church, club, society, order, or other organization or to continue contributions to those organizations;

(6) to demand, receive, obtain by action, proceeding, or otherwise any money or other thing of value to which the principal is or may become or may claim to be entitled as salary, wages, commission, or other remuneration for services performed, or as a dividend or distribution upon any stock, or as interest or principal upon any indebtedness, or any periodic distribution of profits from any partnership or business in which the principal has or claims an interest, and to endorse, collect, or otherwise realize upon any instrument for the payment received;

(7) to use any asset of the principal for the performance of the powers enumerated in this subdivision, including by way of illustration and not by way of restriction, power to draw money by check or otherwise from any bank deposit of the principal, to sell any interest in real property, bond, share, commodity interest, tangible personal property, or other asset of the principal, to borrow money and pledge as security for a loan, any asset, including insurance, which belongs to the principal;

(8) to execute, acknowledge, verify, seal, file, and deliver any application, consent, petition, notice, release, waiver, agreement, or other instrument which the attorney-in-fact deems useful for the accomplishment of any of the purposes enumerated in this subdivision;

(9) to hire, discharge, and compensate any attorney, accountant, or other assistant when the attorney-in-fact deems that action to be desirable for the

proper execution by any of the powers described in this subdivision, and for the keeping of needed records; and

(10) in general, and in addition to all the specific acts listed in this subdivision, to do any other acts for the welfare of the spouse, children, or other persons customarily supported by the principal or for the preservation and maintenance of the other personal relationships of the principal to parents, relatives, friends, and organizations as are appropriate.

All powers described in this subdivision are exercisable equally whether the acts required for their execution relate to real or personal property owned by the principal at the giving of the power of attorney or acquired after that time and whether those acts are performable in the state of Minnesota or elsewhere.

Subd. 12. Benefits from military service. In a statutory short form power of attorney, the language conferring general authority with respect to benefits from military service, means that the principal authorizes the attorney-in-fact:

(1) to execute vouchers in the name of the principal for any and all allowances and reimbursements payable by the United States or by any state or subdivision of a state to the principal, including, by way of illustration and not of restriction, all allowances and reimbursements for transportation of the principal and of the principal's dependents, and for shipment of household effects, to receive, endorse, and collect the proceeds of any check payable to the order of the principal drawn on the treasurer or other fiscal officer or depository of the United States or of any state or subdivision of a state;

(2) to take possession and order the removal and shipment of any property of the principal from any post, warehouse, depot, dock, or other place of storage or safekeeping, either governmental or private, to execute and deliver any release, voucher, receipt, bill of lading, shipping ticket, certificate, or other instrument which the attorney-in-fact deems desirable or necessary for that purpose;

(3) to prepare, file, and prosecute the claim of the principal to any benefit or assistance, financial or otherwise, to which the principal is, or claims to be, entitled, under the provisions of any statute or regulation existing at the execution of the power of attorney or enacted after that time by the United States or by any state or by any subdivision of a state, or by any foreign government, which benefit or assistance arises from or is based upon military service performed prior to or after the execution of the power of attorney by the principal or by any person related by blood or marriage to the principal, to execute any receipt or other instrument which the attorney-in-fact deems desirable or necessary for the enforcement or for the collection of that claim;

(4) to receive the financial proceeds of any claim of the type described in this subdivision, to conserve, invest, disburse, or use anything so received for purposes enumerated in this subdivision, and to reimburse the attorney-in-fact for any expenditures properly made in the execution of the powers conferred on the attorney-in-fact by the statutory short form power of attorney;

(5) to prosecute, defend, submit to arbitration, settle, and propose or accept a compromise with respect to any claim existing in favor of or against the principal based on or involving any benefits from military service or to intervene in any related action or proceeding;

(6) to hire, discharge, and compensate any attorney, accountant, expert witness, or other assistant when the attorney-in-fact deems that action to be desirable for the proper execution by the attorney-in-fact of any of the powers described in this subdivision; and

(7) in general, and in addition to all the specific acts listed in this subdivision, to do any other acts which the attorney-in-fact deems desirable or necessary, to assure to the principal, and to the dependents of the principal, the maximum possible benefit from the military service performed prior to or after the execution of the power of attorney by the principal or by any person related by blood or marriage to the principal.

All powers described in this subdivision are exercisable equally with respect to any benefits from military service existing at the giving of the power of attorney or accruing after that time, and whether accruing in the state of Minnesota or elsewhere.

Subd. 13. Records, reports, and statements. In a statutory short form power of attorney, the language conferring general authority with respect to records, reports, and statements means that the principal authorizes the attorney-in-fact:

(1) to keep records of all cash received and disbursed for or on account of the principal, of all credits and debits to the account of the principal, and of all transactions affecting in any way the assets and liabilities of the principal;

(2) to prepare, execute, and file all tax and tax information returns, for all periods, required by the laws of the United States, any state or any subdivision of a state, or any foreign government, to prepare, execute, and file all other tax-related documents for all tax periods, including requests for extension of time, offers, waivers, consents, powers of attorney, closing agreements, and petitions to any Tax Court regarding tax matters, and to prepare, execute, and file all other instruments which the attorney-in-fact deems desirable or necessary for the safeguarding of the principal against excessive or illegal taxation or against penalties imposed for claimed violation of any law or other governmental regulation, it being the intent of this provision that it is sufficiently definite to permit the attorney-in-fact to represent the principal respecting all taxes that the principal has paid and all tax returns that the principal has filed, either personally or through an agent, with the Internal Revenue Service or any other agency of the United States government, any state department of revenue, any political subdivision of a state, and any foreign country or political subdivision of a foreign country;

(3) to prepare, execute, and file any return, report, declaration, or other document required by the laws of the United States, any state, subdivision of a

state, or any foreign government, including, by way of illustration and not as a limitation, any report or declaration required by the Social Security Administration, the commissioner of employment and economic development or other, similar, governmental agency, which the attorney-in-fact deems to be desirable or necessary for the safeguarding or maintenance of the principal's interest;

(4) to prepare, execute, and file any record, report, or statement which the attorney-in-fact deems desirable or necessary for the safeguarding or maintenance of the principal's interest, with respect to price, rent, wage, or rationing control, or other governmental activity;

(5) to hire, discharge, and compensate any attorney, accountant, or other assistant when the attorney-in-fact deems that action to be desirable for the proper execution of any of the powers described in this subdivision; and

(6) in general, and in addition to all the specific acts listed in this subdivision, to do any other acts in connection with the preparation, execution, filing, storage, or other use of any records, reports, or statements of or concerning the principal's affairs.

All powers described in this subdivision are exercisable equally with respect to any records, reports, or statements of or concerning the affairs of the principal existing at the giving of the power of attorney or arising after that time, and whether arising in the state of Minnesota or elsewhere.

Subd. 14. All other matters. In a statutory short form power of attorney, the language conferring general authority with respect to all other matters, means that the principal authorizes the attorney-in-fact to act as an alter ego of the principal with respect to any and all possible matters and affairs affecting property owned by the principal which are not enumerated in subdivisions 1 to 13, and which the principal can do through an agent.

Laws 1984, c. 603, § 26. Amended by Laws 1985, 1st Sp., c. 14, art. 9, § 75; Laws 1986, c. 444; Laws 1992, c. 548, §§ 26 to 29; Laws 1994, c. 483, § 1, eff. April 22, 1994; Laws 1995, c. 130, § 10; Laws 1995, c. 202, art. 1, § 25, eff. May 25, 1995; Laws 2004, c. 206, § 52, par. (a), eff. May 19, 2004; Laws 2007, c. 13, art. 1, § 16, eff. Aug. 1, 2007.

Historical and Statutory Notes

Laws 1995, c. 130, § 22, provides in part that chapter 130 is effective January 1, 1996, and that §§ 6 and 10 (amending § 519.06 and subd. 1 of this section, respectively) apply to powers of attorney executed on or after January 1, 1996.

523.25. Repealed by Laws 1992, c. 548, § 30

Chapter 524

UNIFORM PROBATE CODE

UNIFORM PROBATE CODE

Section

Section
524.8–103.   Early effective date.

For complete statutory history see Minnesota Statutes Annotated.

ARTICLE 1

GENERAL PROVISIONS, DEFINITIONS AND PROBATE JURISDICTION OF COURT

PART 1

CITATION, CONSTRUCTION, GENERAL PROVISIONS

524.1–100.   Renumbered 15.001 in St.2008

524.1–101.   Citation and numbering system

This chapter shall be known and may be cited as the "Uniform Probate Code." It is arranged and numbered, subject however to the provisions of section 3C.10, subdivision 1, so that the enacted chapter may be compiled in the next published edition of Minnesota Statutes without change and in conformity with the official numbering of the Uniform Probate Code. The articles of Laws 1974, Chapter 442 are numbered out of sequence to facilitate the possible inclusion of other articles of the probate code in one chapter.

Laws 1974, c. 442, art. 1, § 524.1–101, eff. Jan. 1, 1976. Amended by Laws 1984, c. 480, § 19; Laws 1984, c. 655, art. 2, § 19, subd. 7, eff. Aug. 1, 1984.

524.1–102. Purposes; rule of construction

(a) This chapter and chapter 525 shall be liberally construed and applied to promote the underlying purposes and policies.

(b) The underlying purposes and policies of this chapter and chapter 525 are:

(1) to simplify and clarify the law concerning the affairs of decedents, missing persons, protected persons, minors and incapacitated persons;

(2) to discover and make effective the intent of a decedent in distribution of property;

(3) to promote a speedy and efficient system for liquidating the estate of the decedent and making distribution to successors;

(4) to make uniform the law among the various jurisdictions.

Laws 1974, c. 442, art. 1, § 524.1–102. Amended by Laws 1975, c. 347, § 12, eff. Jan. 1, 1976; Laws 1986, c. 444.

524.1–103. Supplementary general principles of law applicable

Unless displaced by the particular provisions of this chapter, the principles of law and equity supplement its provisions.

Laws 1974, c. 442, art. 1, § 524.1–103, eff. Jan. 1, 1976.

524.1–104. Severability

If any provision of this chapter or the application thereof to any person or circumstances is held invalid, the invalidity shall not affect other provisions or applications of the chapter which can be given effect without the invalid provision or application, and to this end the provisions of this chapter are declared to be severable.

Laws 1974, c. 442, art. 1, § 524.1–104, eff. Jan. 1, 1976.

524.1–105. Repealed by Laws 1975, c. 347, § 144, eff. Jan. 1, 1976

524.1–106. Effect of fraud and evasion

Whenever fraud has been perpetrated in connection with any proceeding or in any statement filed under this chapter or if fraud is used to avoid or circumvent the provisions or purposes of this chapter, any person injured thereby may obtain appropriate relief against the perpetrator of the fraud or restitution from any person, other than a bona fide purchaser, benefiting from the fraud, whether innocent or not. Any proceeding must be commenced within two years after the discovery of the fraud, but no proceeding may be brought against one not a perpetrator of the fraud later than five years after the time of commission of the fraud. This section has no bearing on remedies relating to fraud practiced on a decedent while living which affects the succession of the estate.

Laws 1974, c. 442, art. 1, § 524.1–106, eff. Jan. 1, 1976. Amended by Laws 1986, c. 444.

524.1–107. Evidence as to death or status

In proceedings under chapter 524 the Rules of Evidence in courts of general jurisdiction including any relating to simultaneous deaths, are applicable unless specifically displaced by this chapter. In addition, the following rules relating to determination of death and status are applicable:

(1) a certified or authenticated copy of a death record purporting to be issued by an official or agency of the place where the death purportedly occurred is prima facie proof of the fact, place, date and time of death and the identity of the decedent;

(2) a certified or authenticated copy of any record or report of a governmental agency, domestic or foreign, that a person is missing, detained, dead, or alive is prima facie evidence of the status and of the dates, circumstances and places disclosed by the record or report;

(3) the provisions of section 576.141 shall govern the presumption of death of a person whose absence is not satisfactorily explained.

Laws 1974, c. 442, art. 1, § 524.1–107. Amended by Laws 1975, c. 347, § 13, eff. Jan. 1, 1976; Laws 2001, 1st Sp., c. 9, art. 15, § 32.

Historical and Statutory Notes

Laws 2002, c. 379, art. 1, § 113, provides:

"2001 First Special Session Senate File No. 4, as passed by the senate and the house of representatives on Friday, June 29, 2001, and subsequently published as Laws 2001, First Special Session chapter 9, is reenacted. Its provisions are effective on the dates originally provided in the bill."

524.1–108. Acts by holder of general power

For the purpose of granting consent or approval with regard to the acts or accounts of a personal representative or trustee, including relief from liability or penalty for failure to post bond or to perform other duties, and for purposes of consenting to modification or termination of a trust or to deviation from its terms, the sole holder or all coholders of a presently exercisable general power of appointment, including one in the form of a power of amendment or revocation, are deemed to act for beneficiaries to the extent their interests as objects, takers in default, or otherwise, are subject to the power.

Laws 1974, c. 442, art. 1, § 524.1–108. Amended by Laws 1975, c. 347, § 14, eff. Jan. 1, 1976.

PART 2

DEFINITIONS

524.1–201. General definitions

Subject to additional definitions contained in the subsequent articles which are applicable to specific articles or parts, and unless the context otherwise requires, in chapters 524 and 525:

(1) [No par. (1) in enrolled bill.]

(2) "Application" means a written request to the registrar for an order of informal probate or appointment under article III, part 3.[1]

(3) "Beneficiary," as it relates to trust beneficiaries, includes a person who has any present or future interest, vested or contingent, and also includes the owner of an interest by assignment or other transfer and as it relates to a charitable trust, includes any person entitled to enforce the trust.

(5) "Child" includes any individual entitled to take as a child under law by intestate succession from the parent whose relationship is involved and excludes any person who is only a stepchild, a foster child, a grandchild or any more remote descendant.

(6) "Claims" includes liabilities of the decedent whether arising in contract or otherwise and liabilities of the estate which arise after the death of the decedent including funeral expenses and expenses of administration. The term does not include taxes, demands or disputes regarding title of a decedent to specific assets alleged to be included in the estate, tort claims, foreclosure of mechanic's liens, or to actions pursuant to section 573.02.

(7) "Court" means the court or branch having jurisdiction in matters relating to the affairs of decedents. This court in this state is known as the district court.

(8) "Conservator" means a person who is appointed by a court to manage the estate of a protected person.

(9) "Descendant" of an individual means all of the individual's descendants of all generations, with the relationship of parent and child at each generation being determined by the definition of child and parent contained in this section.

(10) "Devise," when used as a noun, means a testamentary disposition of real or personal property and when used as a verb, means to dispose of real or personal property by will.

(11) "Devisee" means any person designated in a will to receive a devise. In the case of a devise to an existing trust or trustee, or to a trustee on trust described by will, the trust or trustee is the devisee and the beneficiaries are not devisees.

(12) "Disability" means cause for appointment of a conservator as described in section 524.5–401, or a protective order as described in section 524.5–412.

(13) "Distributee" means any person who has received or who will receive property of a decedent from the decedent's personal representative other than as a creditor or purchaser. A testamentary trustee is a distributee with respect to property which the trustee has received from a personal representative only to the extent of distributed assets or their increment remaining in the trustee's hands. A beneficiary of a testamentary trust to whom the trustee has distributed property received from a personal representative is a distributee of the personal representative. For purposes of this provision, "testamentary trustee" includes a trustee to whom assets are transferred by will, to the extent of the devised assets.

(14) "Estate" includes all of the property of the decedent, trust, or other person whose affairs are subject to this chapter as originally constituted and as it exists from time to time during administration.

(16) "Fiduciary" includes personal representative, guardian, conservator and trustee.

(17) "Foreign personal representative" means a personal representative of another jurisdiction.

(18) "Formal proceedings" means those conducted before a judge with notice to interested persons.

(20) "Guardian" means a person who has qualified as a guardian of a minor or incapacitated person pursuant to testamentary or court appointment, but excludes one who is merely a guardian ad litem.

(21) "Heirs" means those persons, including the surviving spouse, who are entitled under the statutes of intestate succession to the property of a decedent.

(22) "Incapacitated person" is as described in section 524.5–102, subdivision 6, other than a minor.

(23) "Informal proceedings" means those conducted by the judge, the registrar, or the person or persons designated by the judge for probate of a will or appointment of a personal representative in accordance with sections 524.3–301 to 524.3–311.

(24) "Interested person" includes heirs, devisees, children, spouses, creditors, beneficiaries and any others having a property right in or claim against the estate of a decedent, ward or protected person which may be affected by the proceeding. It also includes persons having priority for appointment as personal representative, and other fiduciaries representing interested persons. The meaning as it relates to particular persons may vary from time to time and must be determined according to the particular purposes of, and matter involved in, any proceeding.

(27) "Lease" includes an oil, gas, or other mineral lease.

(28) "Letters" includes letters testamentary, letters of guardianship, letters of administration, and letters of conservatorship.

(30) "Mortgage" means any conveyance, agreement or arrangement in which property is used as security.

(31) "Nonresident decedent" means a decedent who was domiciled in another jurisdiction at the time of death.

(32) "Organization" includes a corporation, government or governmental subdivision or agency, business trust, estate, trust, partnership or association, two or more persons having a joint or common interest, or any other legal entity.

(35) "Person" means an individual, a corporation, an organization, or other legal entity.

(36) "Personal representative" includes executor, administrator, successor personal representative, special administrator, and persons who perform substantially the same function under the law governing their status. "General personal representative" excludes special administrator.

(37) "Petition" means a written request to the court for an order after notice.

(38) "Proceeding" includes action at law and suit in equity.

(39) "Property" includes both real and personal property or any interest therein and means anything that may be the subject of ownership.

(40) "Protected person" is as described in section 524.5–102, subdivision 14.

(42) "Registrar" refers to the judge of the court or the person designated by the court to perform the functions of registrar as provided in section 524.1–307.

(43) "Security" includes any note, stock, treasury stock, bond, debenture, evidence of indebtedness, certificate of interest or participation in an oil, gas or mining title or lease or in payments out of production under such a title or lease, collateral trust certificate, transferable share, voting trust certificate or, in general, any interest or instrument commonly known as a security, or any certificate of interest or participation, any temporary or interim certificate, receipt or certificate of deposit for, or any warrant or right to subscribe to or purchase, any of the foregoing.

(44) "Settlement," in reference to a decedent's estate, includes the full process of administration, distribution and closing.

(45) "Special administrator" means a personal representative as described by sections 524.3–614 to 524.3–618.

(46) "State" includes any state of the United States, the District of Columbia, the Commonwealth of Puerto Rico, and any territory or possession subject to the legislative authority of the United States.

(47) "Successor personal representative" means a personal representative, other than a special administrator, who is appointed to succeed a previously appointed personal representative.

(48) "Successors" means those persons, other than creditors, who are entitled to property of a decedent under the decedent's will, this chapter or chapter 525. "Successors" also means a funeral director or county government that provides the funeral and burial of the decedent, or a state or county agency with a claim authorized under section 256B.15.

(49) "Supervised administration" refers to the proceedings described in sections 524.3–501 to 524.3–505.

(51) "Testacy proceeding" means a proceeding to establish a will or determine intestacy.

(53) "Trust" includes any express trust, private or charitable, with additions thereto, wherever and however created. It also includes a trust created or determined by judgment or decree under which the trust is to be administered in the manner of an express trust. "Trust" excludes other constructive trusts, and it excludes resulting trusts, conservatorships, personal representatives, trust accounts as defined in chapter 528, custodial arrangements pursuant to sections 149A.97, 318.01 to 318.06, 527.21 to 527.44, business trusts providing for certificates to be issued to beneficiaries, common trust funds, voting trusts, security arrangements, liquidation trusts, and trusts for the primary purpose of paying debts, dividends, interest, salaries, wages, profits, pensions, or employee benefits of any kind, and any arrangement under which a person is nominee or escrowee for another.

(54) "Trustee" includes an original, additional, or successor trustee, whether or not appointed or confirmed by court.

(55) "Ward" is as described in section 524.5–102, subdivision 17.

(56) "Will" includes codicil and any testamentary instrument which merely appoints an executor or revokes or revises another will.

Laws 1974, c. 442, art. 1, § 524.1–201. Amended by Laws 1975, c. 347, § 15, eff. Jan. 1, 1976; Laws 1978, c. 525, § 1, eff. March 24, 1978; Laws 1986, c. 444; Laws 1987, c. 384, art. 2, § 1; Laws 1992, c. 423, § 2; Laws 1994, c. 472, § 1; Laws 1995, c. 130, § 11; Laws 1995, c. 186, § 119; Laws 1995, c. 189, § 8; Laws 1996, c. 277, § 1; Laws 1997, c. 215, § 45; Laws 1997, c. 217, art. 2, § 15; Laws 2004, c. 146, art. 3, § 40.

[1] Section 524.3–301 et seq.

Historical and Statutory Notes

Laws 1994, c. 472, § 65, provides:

"(a) This act takes effect on January 1, 1996.

"(b) Except as provided elsewhere in this act:

"(1) this act applies to the rights of successors of decedents dying on or after its effective date and to any wills of decedents dying on or after its effective date;

"(2) if, before the effective date of this act, a right is either acquired, extinguished, waived, or barred upon the expiration of a prescribed period of time which commenced to run by the provisions of any statute before the effective date, the provisions of this act neither revoke, revive, restore, nor remove the bar of such right; and

"(3) any rule of construction or presumption provided in this act applies to instruments executed and multiple party accounts opened before the effective date of this act unless there is a clear indication of contrary intent."

Laws 1995, c. 130, § 22, provides in part that chapter 130 is effective January 1, 1996.

PART 3

SCOPE, JURISDICTION AND COURTS

524.1–301. Territorial application

Except as otherwise provided in this chapter, this chapter and chapter 525 apply to (1) the affairs and estates of decedents, missing persons, and persons to be protected, domiciled in this state, and (2) the property of nonresident decedents located in this state or property coming into the control of a fiduciary who is subject to the laws of this state.

Laws 1974, c. 442, art. 1, § 524.1–301. Amended by Laws 1975, c. 347, § 16, eff. Jan. 1, 1976.

524.1–302. Subject matter jurisdiction

(a) To the full extent permitted by the Constitution, the court has jurisdiction over all subject matter relating to estates of decedents, including construction of wills and determination of heirs and successors of decedents.

(b) The court has full power to make orders, judgments and decrees and take all other action necessary and proper to administer justice in the matters which come before it.

Laws 1974, c. 442, art. 1, § 524.1–302. Amended by Laws 1975, c. 347, § 17, eff. Jan. 1, 1976.

524.1–303. Venue; multiple proceedings; transfer

(a) Where a proceeding under this chapter could be maintained in more than one place in this state, the court in which the proceeding is first commenced has the exclusive right to proceed.

(b) If proceedings concerning the same estate, protected person, conservatee, or ward are commenced in more than one court of this state, the court in which the proceeding was first commenced shall continue to hear the matter, and the other courts shall hold the matter in abeyance until the question of venue is decided, and if the ruling court determines that venue is properly in another court, it shall transfer the proceeding to the other court.

(c) If a court finds that in the interest of justice a proceeding or a file should be located in another court of this state, the court making the finding may transfer the proceeding or file to the other court.

Laws 1974, c. 442, art. 1, § 524.1–303. Amended by Laws 1975, c. 347, § 18, eff. Jan. 1, 1976.

524.1–304. Practice in court

Unless inconsistent with the provisions of this chapter or chapter 525, pleadings, practice, procedure and forms in all probate proceedings shall be governed insofar as practicable by Rules of Civil Procedure provided for in section 487.23 and adopted pursuant thereto.

Laws 1977, c. 157, § 1.

524.1–305. Repealed by Laws 1975, c. 347, § 144, eff. Jan. 1, 1976

524.1–306. Jury trial

(a) If duly demanded, a party is entitled to trial by jury in any proceeding in which any controverted question of fact arises as to which any party has a constitutional right to trial by jury.

(b) If there is no right to trial by jury under subsection (a) or the right is waived, the court in its discretion may call a jury to decide any issue of fact, in which case the verdict is advisory only.

Laws 1974, c. 442, art. 1, § 524.1–306, eff. Jan. 1, 1976.

524.1–307. Registrar; powers

The acts and orders which this chapter specifies as performable by the registrar shall be performed by a judge of the court or by a person, including the court administrator, designated by the court by a written order filed and recorded in the office of the court.

In addition to acts specified in this chapter to be performed by the registrar, the registrar may take acknowledgments, administer oaths, fix and approve bonds, provide information on the various methods of transferring property of decedents under the laws of this state, issue letters in informal proceedings and perform such other acts as the court may by written order authorize as necessary or incidental to the conduct of informal proceedings. Letters, orders and documents issued by the registrar may be certified, authenticated or exemplified by the registrar or in the same manner as those issued by the court. All files shall be maintained by the court administrator. The probate registrar shall not render advice calling for the exercise of such professional judgment as constitutes the practice of law.

Laws 1974, c. 442, art. 1, § 524.1–307. Amended by Laws 1975, c. 347, § 19, eff. Jan. 1, 1976; Laws 1977, c. 440, § 2; Laws 1986, 1st Sp., c. 3, art. 1, § 82.

Historical and Statutory Notes

Laws 1977, c. 440, § 4, reads: "This act is effective the day following final enactment as to all informal proceedings commenced after January 1, 1976."

524.1–310. Verification of filed documents

Every document filed with the court under this chapter or chapter 525 shall be verified except where the requirement of verification is waived by rule and except in the case of a pleading signed by an attorney in accordance with the Rules of Civil Procedure. Whenever a document is required to be verified:

(1) such verification may be made by the unsworn written declaration of the party or parties signing the document that the representations made therein are known or believed to be true and that they are made under penalties for perjury, or

(2) such verification may be made by the affidavit of the party or parties signing the document that the representations made therein are true or believed to be true.

A party who makes a false material statement not believing it to be true in a document the party verifies in accordance with the preceding sentence and files with the court under this chapter or chapter 525 shall be subject to the penalties for perjury.

Laws 1974, c. 442, art. 1, § 524.1–310, eff. Jan. 1, 1976. Amended by Laws 1976, c. 161, § 3, eff. April 4, 1976; Laws 1986, c. 444.

PART 4

NOTICE, PARTIES AND REPRESENTATION IN ESTATE
LITIGATION AND OTHER MATTERS

524.1–401. Notice; method and time of giving

(a) If notice of a hearing on any petition is required and except for specific notice requirements as otherwise provided, the petitioner shall cause notice of the time and place of hearing of any petition to be given to any interested person or the person's attorney if the person has appeared by attorney or requested that notice be sent to the attorney. Notice shall be given:

(1) by mailing a copy thereof at least 14 days before the time set for the hearing by certified, registered or ordinary first class mail addressed to the person being notified at the post office address given in the demand for notice, if any, or at the demander's office or place of residence, if known;

(2) by delivering a copy thereof to the person being notified personally at least 14 days before the time set for the hearing; or

(3) if the address, or identity of any person is not known and cannot be ascertained with reasonable diligence, by publishing once a week for two consecutive weeks, a copy thereof in a legal newspaper in the county where the hearing is to be held, the last publication of which is to be at least 10 days before the time set for the hearing.

(b) The court for good cause shown may provide for a different method or time of giving notice for any hearing.

(c) Proof of the giving of notice shall be made on or before the hearing and filed in the proceeding.

(d) No defect in any notice nor in publication or in service thereof shall limit or affect the validity of the appointment, powers, or other duties of the personal representative. Any of the notices required by this section and sections 524.3–306, 524.3–310, 524.3–403 and 524.3–801 may be combined into one notice.

Laws 1974, c. 442, art. 1, § 524.1–401. Amended by Laws 1975, c. 347, § 20, eff. Jan. 1, 1976; Laws 1986, c. 444.

524.1–402. Notice; waiver

A person, including a guardian ad litem, conservator, or other fiduciary, may waive notice by a writing signed by the person or the person's attorney and filed in the proceeding.

Laws 1974, c. 442, art. 1, § 524.1–402, eff. Jan. 1, 1976. Amended by Laws 1986, c. 444.

524.1–403. Pleadings; when parties bound by others; notice

In formal proceedings involving estates of decedents and in judicially supervised settlements, the following apply:

(1) Interests to be affected shall be described in pleadings which give reasonable information to owners by name or class, by reference to the instrument creating the interests, or in other appropriate manner.

(2) Persons are bound by orders binding others in the following cases:

(i) Orders binding the sole holder or all coholders of a power of revocation or a presently exercisable general power of appointment, including one in the form of a power of amendment, bind other persons to the extent their interests as objects, takers in default, or otherwise, are subject to the power.

(ii) To the extent there is no conflict of interest between them or among persons represented, orders binding a conservator bind the person whose estate the conservator controls; orders binding a guardian bind the ward if no conservator of the estate has been appointed; orders binding a trustee bind beneficiaries of the trust in proceedings to probate a will establishing or adding to a trust, to review the acts or accounts of a prior fiduciary and in proceedings involving creditors or other third parties; and orders binding a personal representative bind persons interested in the undistributed assets of a decedent's estate in actions or proceedings by or against the estate. If there is no conflict of interest and no conservator or guardian has been appointed, a parent may represent the parent's minor child.

(iii) An unborn or unascertained person who is not otherwise represented is bound by an order to the extent that person's interest is adequately represented by another party having a substantially identical interest in the proceeding.

(3) Notice is required as follows:

(i) Notice as prescribed by section 524.1–401 shall be given to every interested person or to one who can bind an interested person as described in (2)(i) or

333

(2)(ii). Notice may be given both to a person and to another who may bind the person.

(ii) Notice is given to unborn or unascertained persons, who are not represented under (2)(i) or (2)(ii), by giving notice to all known persons whose interests in the proceedings are substantially identical to those of the unborn or unascertained persons.

(4) At any point in a proceeding, a court may appoint a guardian ad litem to represent the interest of a minor, an incapacitated, unborn, or unascertained person, or a person whose identity or address is unknown, if the court determines that representation of the interest otherwise would be inadequate. If not precluded by conflict of interests, a guardian ad litem may be appointed to represent several persons or interests. The court shall set out its reasons for appointing a guardian ad litem as a part of the record of the proceeding.

Laws 1974, c. 442, art. 1, § 524.1–403. Amended by Laws 1975, c. 347, § 21, eff. Jan. 1, 1976; Laws 1986, c. 444.

524.1–404. Notice to charitable beneficiaries

If a will includes a gift, devise or bequest to a named charitable beneficiary, the initial written notice of the probate proceedings given to the beneficiary shall state that the beneficiary may request notice of the probate proceedings be given to the attorney general pursuant to section 501B.41, subdivision 5.

Laws 1978, c. 601, § 27, eff. March 29, 1978. Amended by Laws 1989, c. 340, art. 2, § 3, eff. Jan. 1, 1990.

ARTICLE 2

INTESTATE SUCCESSION AND WILLS

PART 1

INTESTATE SUCCESSION

524.2–101. Intestate estate

Text of section effective for estates of decedents dying after December 31, 1986, but before January 1, 1996.

Except as provided in sections 525.14 and 525.145, and subject to the allowances provided in section 525.15, and the payment of the expenses of administration, funeral expenses, expenses of last illness, taxes, and debts, any part of the estate of a decedent not effectively disposed of by the decedent's will passes to the decedent's heirs as prescribed in sections 524.2–102 to 524.2–114.

Laws 1985, c. 250, § 1.

For text of section effective January 1, 1996, applicable to the rights of successors of decedents dying on or after January 1, 1996, and to any wills of decedents dying on or after January 1, 1996, see § 524.2–101, post.

524.2–101. Intestate estate

Text of section effective January 1, 1996, applicable to the rights of successors of decedents dying on or after January 1, 1996, and to any wills of decedents dying on or after January 1, 1996.

(a) The intestate estate of the decedent consists of any part of the decedent's estate not allowed to the decedent's spouse or descendants under sections 524.2–402, 524.2–403, and 524.2–404, and not disposed of by will. The intestate estate passes by intestate succession to the decedent's heirs as prescribed in this chapter, except as modified by the decedent's will.

(b) A decedent by will may expressly exclude or limit the right of an individual or class to succeed to property of the decedent passing by intestate succession. If that individual or a member of that class survives the decedent, the share of the decedent's intestate estate to which that individual or class would have succeeded passes as if that individual or each member of that class had disclaimed an intestate share.

Laws 1985, c. 250, § 1. Amended by Laws 1994, c. 472, § 2; Laws 1999, c. 171, § 1.

For text of section effective for estates of decedents dying after December 31, 1986, but before January 1, 1996, see § 524.2–101, ante.

Historical and Statutory Notes

Laws 1985, c. 250, § 28, provides that this section is effective for estates of decedents dying after December 31, 1986. For law effective for estates of decedents dying before December 31, 1986, see § 525.13 et seq.

Continuing Effect. For continuing effect of law relating to wills or other instruments executed on or before December 31, 1986, see § 524.2–114 as quoted in the Historical and Statutory Notes under § 524.2–115.

Laws 1994, c. 472, § 65, provides:

"(a) This act takes effect on January 1, 1996.

"(b) Except as provided elsewhere in this act:

"(1) this act applies to the rights of successors of decedents dying on or after its effective date and to any wills of decedents dying on or after its effective date;

"(2) if, before the effective date of this act, a right is either acquired, extinguished, waived, or barred upon the expiration of a prescribed period of time which commenced to run by the provisions of any statute before the effective date, the provisions of this act neither revoke, revive, restore, nor remove the bar of such right; and

"(3) any rule of construction or presumption provided in this act applies to instruments executed and multiple party accounts opened before the effective date of this act unless there is a clear indication of contrary intent."

524.2–102. Share of the spouse

Text of section effective for estates of decedents dying after December 31, 1986, but before January 1, 1996.

The intestate share of the surviving spouse is:

(1) if there is no surviving issue of the decedent, the entire intestate estate;

(2) if there are surviving issue all of whom are issue of the surviving spouse also, the first $70,000, plus one-half of the balance of the intestate estate;

(3) if there are surviving issue one or more of whom are not issue of the surviving spouse, one-half of the intestate estate.

Laws 1985, c. 250, § 2.

> *For text of section effective January 1, 1996, applicable to the rights of successors of decedents dying on or after January 1, 1996, and to any wills of decedents dying on or after January 1, 1996, see § 524.2–102, post.*

524.2–102. Share of the spouse

> *Text of section effective January 1, 1996, applicable to the rights of successors of decedents dying on or after January 1, 1996, and to any wills of decedents dying on or after January 1, 1996.*

The intestate share of a decedent's surviving spouse is:

(1) the entire intestate estate if:

(i) no descendant of the decedent survives the decedent; or

(ii) all of the decedent's surviving descendants are also descendants of the surviving spouse and there is no other descendant of the surviving spouse who survives the decedent;

(2) the first $150,000, plus one-half of any balance of the intestate estate, if all of the decedent's surviving descendants are also descendants of the surviving spouse and the surviving spouse has one or more surviving descendants who are not descendants of the decedent, or if one or more of the decedent's surviving descendants are not descendants of the surviving spouse.

Laws 1985, c. 250, § 2. Amended by Laws 1994, c. 472, § 3.

> *For text of section effective for estates of decedents dying after December 31, 1986, but before January 1, 1996, see § 524.2–102, ante.*

Historical and Statutory Notes

Laws 1985, c. 250, § 28, provides that this section is effective for estates of decedents dying after December 31, 1986. For law effective for estates of decedents dying before December 31, 1986, see § 525.13 et seq.

Continuing Effect. For continuing effect of law relating to wills or other instruments executed on or before December 31, 1986, see § 524.2–114 as quoted in the Historical and Statutory Notes under § 524.2–115.

Laws 1994, c. 472, § 65, provides:

"(a) This act takes effect on January 1, 1996.

"(b) Except as provided elsewhere in this act:

"(1) this act applies to the rights of successors of decedents dying on or after its effective date and to any wills of decedents dying on or after its effective date;

"(2) if, before the effective date of this act, a right is either acquired, extinguished, waived, or barred upon the expiration of a prescribed period of time which commenced to run by the provisions of any statute before the effective date, the provisions of this act neither revoke, revive, restore, nor remove the bar of such right; and

"(3) any rule of construction or presumption provided in this act applies to instruments executed and multiple party accounts opened before the effective date of this act unless there is a clear indication of contrary intent."

524.2–103. Share of heirs other than surviving spouse

Text of section effective for estates of decedents dying after December 31, 1986, but before January 1, 1996.

The part of the intestate estate not passing to the surviving spouse under section 524.2–102, or the entire intestate estate if there is no surviving spouse, passes as follows:

(1) to the issue of the decedent; any who are children of the decedent take equally and others by representation;

(2) if there is no surviving issue, to the parent or parents equally;

(3) if there is no surviving issue or parent, to the issue of the parents or either of them by representation;

(4) if there is no surviving issue, parent, or issue of a parent, to the next of kin in equal degree, except that when there are two or more collateral kindred in equal degree claiming through different ancestors, those who claim through the nearest ancestor shall take to the exclusion of those claiming through an ancestor more remote.

Laws 1985, c. 250, § 3.

For text of section effective January 1, 1996, applicable to the rights of successors of decedents dying on or after January 1, 1996, and to any wills of decedents dying on or after January 1, 1996, see § 524.2–103, post.

524.2–103. Share of heirs other than surviving spouse

Text of section effective January 1, 1996, applicable to the rights of successors of decedents dying on or after January 1, 1996, and to any wills of decedents dying on or after January 1, 1996.

Any part of the intestate estate not passing to the decedent's surviving spouse under section 524.2–102, or the entire intestate estate if there is no surviving spouse, passes in the following order to the individuals designated below who survive the decedent:

(1) to the decedent's descendants by representation;

(2) if there is no surviving descendant, to the decedent's parents equally if both survive, or to the surviving parent;

(3) if there is no surviving descendant or parent, to the descendants of the decedent's parents or either of them by representation;

(4) if there is no surviving descendant, parent, or descendant of a parent, but the decedent is survived by one or more grandparents or descendants of grandparents, half of the estate passes to the decedent's paternal grandparents equally if both survive, or to the surviving paternal grandparent, or to the

descendants of the decedent's paternal grandparents or either of them if both are deceased, the descendants taking by representation; and the other half passes to the decedent's maternal relatives in the same manner; but if there is no surviving grandparent or descendant of a grandparent on either the paternal or the maternal side, the entire estate passes to the decedent's relatives on the other side in the same manner as the half;

(5) if there is no surviving descendant, parent, descendant of a parent, grandparent, or descendant of a grandparent, to the next of kin in equal degree, except that when there are two or more collateral kindred in equal degree claiming through different ancestors, those who claim through the nearest ancestor shall take to the exclusion of those claiming through an ancestor more remote.

Laws 1985, c. 250, § 3. Amended by Laws 1994, c. 472, § 4.

For text of section effective for estates of decedents dying after December 31, 1986, but before January 1, 1996, see § 524.2–103, ante.

Historical and Statutory Notes

Laws 1985, c. 250, § 28, provides that this section is effective for estates of decedents dying after December 31, 1986. For law effective for estates of decedents dying before December 31, 1986, see § 525.13 et seq.

Continuing Effect. For continuing effect of law relating to wills or other instruments executed on or before December 31, 1986, see § 524.2–114 as quoted in the Historical and Statutory Notes under § 524.2–115.

Laws 1994, c. 472, § 65, provides:

"(a) This act takes effect on January 1, 1996.

"(b) Except as provided elsewhere in this act:

"(1) this act applies to the rights of successors of decedents dying on or after its effective

date and to any wills of decedents dying on or after its effective date;

"(2) if, before the effective date of this act, a right is either acquired, extinguished, waived, or barred upon the expiration of a prescribed period of time which commenced to run by the provisions of any statute before the effective date, the provisions of this act neither revoke, revive, restore, nor remove the bar of such right; and

"(3) any rule of construction or presumption provided in this act applies to instruments executed and multiple party accounts opened before the effective date of this act unless there is a clear indication of contrary intent."

524.2–104. Requirement that heir survive decedent for 120 hours

Text of section effective for estates of decedents dying after December 31, 1986, but before January 1, 1996.

A person who fails to survive the decedent by 120 hours is deemed to have predeceased the decedent for purposes of descent of the homestead, exempt property and intestate succession, and the decedent's heirs are determined accordingly. If the time of death of the decedent or of the person who would otherwise be an heir, or the times of death of both, cannot be determined, and it cannot be established that the person who would otherwise be an heir has survived the decedent by 120 hours, it is deemed that the person failed to survive for the required period. This section is not to be applied where its application would result in a taking of intestate estate by the state under section 524.2–105.

Laws 1985, c. 250, § 4.

For text of section effective January 1, 1996, applicable to the rights of successors of decedents dying on or after January 1, 1996, and to any wills of decedents dying on or after January 1, 1996, see § 524.2–104, post.

524.2–104. Requirement that heir survive decedent for 120 hours

Text of section effective January 1, 1996, applicable to the rights of successors of decedents dying on or after January 1, 1996, and to any wills of decedents dying on or after January 1, 1996.

An individual who fails to survive the decedent by 120 hours is deemed to have predeceased the decedent for purposes of homestead, exempt property, and intestate succession, and the decedent's heirs are determined accordingly. If it is not established that an individual who would otherwise be an heir survived the decedent by 120 hours, it is deemed that the individual failed to survive for the required period. This section is not to be applied if its application would result in a taking of intestate estate by the state under section 524.2–105.

Laws 1985, c. 250, § 4. Amended by Laws 1994, c. 472, § 5.

For text of section effective for estates of decedents dying after December 31, 1986, but before January 1, 1996, see § 524.2–104, ante.

Historical and Statutory Notes

Laws 1985, c. 250, § 28, provides that this section is effective for estates of decedents dying after December 31, 1986. For law effective for estates of decedents dying before December 31, 1986, see § 525.13 et seq.

Continuing Effect. For continuing effect of law relating to wills or other instruments executed on or before December 31, 1986, see § 524.2–114 as quoted in the Historical and Statutory Notes under § 524.2–115.

Laws 1994, c. 472, § 65, provides:

"(a) This act takes effect on January 1, 1996.

"(b) Except as provided elsewhere in this act:

"(1) this act applies to the rights of successors of decedents dying on or after its effective date and to any wills of decedents dying on or after its effective date;

"(2) if, before the effective date of this act, a right is either acquired, extinguished, waived, or barred upon the expiration of a prescribed period of time which commenced to run by the provisions of any statute before the effective date, the provisions of this act neither revoke, revive, restore, nor remove the bar of such right; and

"(3) any rule of construction or presumption provided in this act applies to instruments executed and multiple party accounts opened before the effective date of this act unless there is a clear indication of contrary intent."

524.2–105. No taker

Text of section effective for estates of decedents dying after December 31, 1986, but before January 1, 1996.

339

If there is no taker under the provisions of sections 524.2–102 to 524.2–114, the intestate estate passes to the state.

Laws 1985, c. 250, § 5.

> *For text of section effective January 1, 1996, applicable to the rights of successors of decedents dying on or after January 1, 1996, and to any wills of decedents dying on or after January 1, 1996, see § 524.2–105, post.*

524.2–105. No taker

> *Text of section effective January 1, 1996, applicable to the rights of successors of decedents dying on or after January 1, 1996, and to any wills of decedents dying on or after January 1, 1996.*

If there is no taker under the provisions of this article, the intestate estate passes to the state.

Laws 1985, c. 250, § 5. Amended by Laws 1994, c. 472, § 6.

> *For text of section effective for estates of decedents dying after December 31, 1986, but before January 1, 1996, see § 524.2–105, ante.*

Historical and Statutory Notes

Laws 1985, c. 250, § 28, provides that this section is effective for estates of decedents dying after December 31, 1986. For law effective for estates of decedents dying before December 31, 1986, see § 525.13 et seq.

Continuing Effect. For continuing effect of law relating to wills or other instruments executed on or before December 31, 1986, see § 524.2–114 as quoted in the Historical and Statutory Notes under § 524.2–115.

Laws 1994, c. 472, § 65, provides:

"(a) This act takes effect on January 1, 1996.

"(b) Except as provided elsewhere in this act:

"(1) this act applies to the rights of successors of decedents dying on or after its effective date and to any wills of decedents dying on or after its effective date;

"(2) if, before the effective date of this act, a right is either acquired, extinguished, waived, or barred upon the expiration of a prescribed period of time which commenced to run by the provisions of any statute before the effective date, the provisions of this act neither revoke, revive, restore, nor remove the bar of such right; and

"(3) any rule of construction or presumption provided in this act applies to instruments executed and multiple party accounts opened before the effective date of this act unless there is a clear indication of contrary intent."

524.2–106. Representation

> *Text of section effective for estates of decedents dying after December 31, 1986, but before January 1, 1996.*

If representation is called for by sections 524.2–102 to 524.2–114:

(1) In the case of issue of the decedent, the estate is divided into as many shares as there are surviving children of the decedent and deceased children who left issue who survive the decedent, each surviving child receiving one share and the share of each deceased child being divided among its issue in the same manner.

(2) In the case of issue of the parents of the decedent (other than issue of the decedent) the estate is divided into as many shares as there are surviving heirs in the nearest degree of kinship and deceased persons in the same degree who left issue who survived the decedent, each surviving heir in the nearest degree receiving one share and the share of each deceased person in the same degree being divided among the deceased person's children, and the descendants of deceased children of that deceased person, in the same manner as specified in clause (1).

Laws 1985, c. 250, § 6.   Amended by Laws 1986, c. 444.

> *For text of section effective January 1, 1996, applicable to the rights of successors of decedents dying on or after January 1, 1996, and to any wills of decedents dying on or after January 1, 1996, see § 524.2–106, post.*

524.2–106. Representation

> *Text of section effective January 1, 1996, applicable to the rights of successors of decedents dying on or after January 1, 1996, and to any wills of decedents dying on or after January 1, 1996.*

(a) Application.   If representation is called for by this article, paragraphs (b) and (c) apply.

(b) Decedent's descendants.   In the case of descendants of the decedent, the estate is divided into as many shares as there are surviving children of the decedent and deceased children who left descendants who survive the decedent, each surviving child receiving one share and the share of each deceased child being divided among its descendants in the same manner.

(c) Descendants of parents or grandparents.   If, under section 524.2–103, clause (3) or (4), a decedent's intestate estate or a part thereof passes by "representation" to the descendants of the decedent's deceased parents or either of them or to the descendants of the decedent's deceased paternal or maternal grandparents or either of them, the estate or part thereof is divided in the following manner:

(1) In the case of descendants of the decedent's deceased parents or either of them, the estate or part thereof is divided into as many equal shares as there are (i) surviving descendants in the generation nearest the deceased parents or either of them, and (ii) deceased descendants in the same generation who left surviving descendants, if any.   Each surviving descendant in the nearest generation is allocated one share, and the surviving descendants of each deceased descendant in the same generation are allocated one share, to be divided in the same manner as specified in paragraph (b).

(2) In the case of descendants of the decedent's deceased paternal or maternal grandparents or either of them, the estate or part thereof is divided into as many equal shares as there are surviving descendants in the generation nearest

the deceased grandparents or either of them that contains one or more surviving descendants. Each surviving descendant in the nearest generation is allocated one share.

Laws 1985, c. 250, § 6. Amended by Laws 1986, c. 444; Laws 1994, c. 472, § 7.

For text of section effective for estates of decedents dying after December 31, 1986, but before January 1, 1996, see § 524.2–106, ante.

Historical and Statutory Notes

Laws 1985, c. 250, § 28, provides that this section is effective for estates of decedents dying after December 31, 1986. For law effective for estates of decedents dying before December 31, 1986, see § 525.13 et seq.

Continuing Effect. For continuing effect of law relating to wills or other instruments executed on or before December 31, 1986, see § 524.2–114 as quoted in the Historical and Statutory Notes under § 524.2–115.

Laws 1994, c. 472, § 65, provides:

"(a) This act takes effect on January 1, 1996.

"(b) Except as provided elsewhere in this act:

"(1) this act applies to the rights of successors of decedents dying on or after its effective date and to any wills of decedents dying on or after its effective date;

"(2) if, before the effective date of this act, a right is either acquired, extinguished, waived, or barred upon the expiration of a prescribed period of time which commenced to run by the provisions of any statute before the effective date, the provisions of this act neither revoke, revive, restore, nor remove the bar of such right; and

"(3) any rule of construction or presumption provided in this act applies to instruments executed and multiple party accounts opened before the effective date of this act unless there is a clear indication of contrary intent."

524.2–107. Degree of kindred and kindred of half blood

Text of section effective for estates of decedents dying after December 31, 1986

The degree of kindred shall be computed according to the rules of the civil law. Relatives of the half blood inherit the same share they would inherit if they were of the whole blood.

Laws 1985, c. 250, § 7.

Historical and Statutory Notes

Laws 1985, c. 250, § 28, provides that this section is effective for estates of decedents dying after December 31, 1986. For law effective for estates of decedents dying before December 31, 1986, see § 525.13 et seq.

Continuing Effect. For continuing effect of law relating to wills or other instruments executed on or before December 31, 1986, see § 524.2–114 as quoted in the Historical and Statutory Notes under § 524.2–115.

524.2–108. After-born heirs

Text of section effective for estates of decedents dying after December 31, 1986, but before January 1, 1996.

Relatives of the decedent conceived before death but born thereafter inherit as if they had been born in the lifetime of the decedent.

Laws 1985, c. 250, § 8. Amended by Laws 1986, c. 444.

For text of section effective January 1, 1996, applicable to the rights of successors of decedents dying on or after January 1, 1996, and to any wills of decedents dying on or after January 1, 1996, see § 524.2–108, post.

524.2–108. After-born heirs

Text of section effective January 1, 1996, applicable to the rights of successors of decedents dying on or after January 1, 1996, and to any wills of decedents dying on or after January 1, 1996.

An individual in gestation at a particular time is treated as living at that time if the individual lives 120 hours or more after birth.

Laws 1985, c. 250, § 8. Amended by Laws 1986, c. 444; Laws 1994, c. 472, § 8.

For text of section effective for estates of decedents dying after December 31, 1986, but before January 1, 1996, see § 524.2–108, ante.

Historical and Statutory Notes

Laws 1985, c. 250, § 28, provides that this section is effective for estates of decedents dying after December 31, 1986. For law effective for estates of decedents dying before December 31, 1986, see § 525.13 et seq.

Continuing Effect. For continuing effect of law relating to wills or other instruments executed on or before December 31, 1986, see § 524.2–114 as quoted in the Historical and Statutory Notes under § 524.2–115.

Laws 1994, c. 472, § 65, provides:

"(a) This act takes effect on January 1, 1996.

"(b) Except as provided elsewhere in this act:

"(1) this act applies to the rights of successors of decedents dying on or after its effective date and to any wills of decedents dying on or after its effective date;

"(2) if, before the effective date of this act, a right is either acquired, extinguished, waived, or barred upon the expiration of a prescribed period of time which commenced to run by the provisions of any statute before the effective date, the provisions of this act neither revoke, revive, restore, nor remove the bar of such right; and

"(3) any rule of construction or presumption provided in this act applies to instruments executed and multiple party accounts opened before the effective date of this act unless there is a clear indication of contrary intent."

524.2–109. Meaning of child and related terms

Text of section effective for estates of decedents dying after December 31, 1986, but before January 1, 1996.

If, for purposes of intestate succession, a relationship of parent and child must be established to determine succession by, through, or from a person:

(1) An adopted person is the child of an adopting parent and not of the birth parents except that adoption of a child by the spouse of a birth parent has no effect on the relationship between the child and that birth parent. If a parent dies and a child is subsequently adopted by a stepparent who is the spouse of a surviving parent, any rights of inheritance of the child or the child's issue from or through the deceased parent of the child which exist at the time of the death of that parent shall not be affected by the adoption.

(2) In cases not covered by clause (1), a person is the child of the person's parents regardless of the marital status of the parents and the parent and child

343

relationship may be established under the parentage act, sections 257.51 to 257.74.

Laws 1985, c. 250, § 9.   Amended by Laws 1986, 1st Sp., c. 3, art. 3, § 1.

> *For text of section effective January 1, 1996, applicable to the rights of successors of decedents dying on or after January 1, 1996, and to any wills of decedents dying on or after January 1, 1996, see § 524.2–109, post.*

524.2–109. Advancements

> *Text of section effective January 1, 1996, applicable to the rights of successors of decedents dying on or after January 1, 1996, and to any wills of decedents dying on or after January 1, 1996.*

(a) If an individual dies intestate as to all or a portion of an estate, property the decedent gave during the decedent's lifetime to an individual who, at the decedent's death, is an heir is treated as an advancement against the heir's intestate share only if:

(i) the decedent declared in a contemporaneous writing or the heir acknowledged in writing that the gift is an advancement; or

(ii) the decedent's contemporaneous writing or the heir's written acknowledgment otherwise indicates that the gift is to be taken into account in computing the division and distribution of the decedent's intestate estate.

(b) For purposes of paragraph (a), property advanced is valued as of the time the heir came into possession or enjoyment of the property or as of the time of the decedent's death, whichever first occurs.

(c) If the recipient of the property fails to survive the decedent, the property is not taken into account in computing the division and distribution of the decedent's intestate estate, unless the decedent's contemporaneous writing provides otherwise.

Amended by Laws 1994, c. 472, § 9.

> *For text of section effective for estates of decedents dying after December 31, 1986, but before January 1, 1996, see § 524.2–109, ante.*

Historical and Statutory Notes

Derivation:

St.1992, § 524.2–110.	Gen.St.1913, §§ 7404 to 7407.
Laws 1986, c. 444.	Rev.Laws 1905, §§ 3797 to 3800.
Laws 1975, c. 347, § 22.	Gen.St.1894, §§ 4645 to 4652.
St.1971, § 525.53.	Laws 1889, c. 46, §§ 232 to 239.
St.Supp.1940, §§ 8992–127, 8992–128.	Gen.St.1878, c. 56, § 17.
Laws 1935, c. 72, §§ 127, 128.	Gen.St.1878, c. 46, §§ 8 to 13.
St.1927, §§ 8895 to 8898.	Gen.St.1866, c. 56, § 17.
Gen.St.1923, §§ 8895 to 8898.	Gen.St.1866, c. 46, §§ 5 to 10.
	Pub.St.1858, c. 46, § 16.

Pub.St.1858, c. 37, §§ 5 to 10.

Rev.St. (Terr.), c. 59, § 16.

Rev.St. (Terr.), c. 50, §§ 5 to 10.

Laws 1985, c. 250, § 28, provides that § 9 (enacting § 524.2–109, the former subject matter of which is contained in § 524.2–114) is effective for estates of decedents dying after December 31, 1986. For law effective for estates of decedents dying before December 31, 1986, see § 525.13 et seq.

Continuing Effect. For continuing effect of law relating to wills or other instruments executed on or before December 31, 1986, see § 524.2–114 as quoted in the Historical and Statutory Notes under § 524.2–115.

Laws 1994, c. 472, § 65, provides:

"(a) This act takes effect on January 1, 1996.

"(b) Except as provided elsewhere in this act:

"(1) this act applies to the rights of successors of decedents dying on or after its effective date and to any wills of decedents dying on or after its effective date;

"(2) if, before the effective date of this act, a right is either acquired, extinguished, waived, or barred upon the expiration of a prescribed period of time which commenced to run by the provisions of any statute before the effective date, the provisions of this act neither revoke, revive, restore, nor remove the bar of such right; and

"(3) any rule of construction or presumption provided in this act applies to instruments executed and multiple party accounts opened before the effective date of this act unless there is a clear indication of contrary intent."

Former section: St.1992, § 524.2–109, related to the meaning of child and related terms. See, now, M.S.A. § 524.2–114.

524.2–110. Advancements

Text of section effective until January 1, 1996.

If a person dies intestate as to all the person's estate, property given while living to an heir is treated as an advancement against the latter's share of the estate only if declared in a contemporaneous writing by the decedent or acknowledged in writing by the heir to be an advancement. For this purpose the property advanced is valued as of the time the heir came into possession or enjoyment of the property or as of the time of death of the decedent, whichever first occurs. If the recipient of the property fails to survive the decedent, the property is not taken into account in computing the intestate share to be received by the recipient's issue, unless the declaration or acknowledgment provides otherwise.

Laws 1975, c. 347, § 22, eff. Jan. 1, 1976. Amended by Laws 1986, c. 444.

For text of section effective January 1, 1996, applicable to the rights of successors of decedents dying on or after January 1, 1996, and to any wills of decedents dying on or after January 1, 1996, see § 524.2–110, post.

524.2–110. Debts to decedent

Text of section effective January 1, 1996, applicable to the rights of successors of decedents dying on or after January 1, 1996, and to any wills of decedents dying on or after January 1, 1996.

A debt owed to a decedent is not charged against the intestate share of any individual except the debtor. If the debtor fails to survive the decedent, the debt is not taken into account in computing the intestate share of the debtor's descendants.

Amended by Laws 1994, c. 472, § 10.

For text of section effective until January 1, 1996, see § 524.2–110, ante.

Historical and Statutory Notes

Derivation:

St.1992, § 524.2–111.

Laws 1985, c. 250, § 10.

Laws 1985, c. 250, § 28, provides that § 10 (enacting § 524.2–111, the former subject matter of which is contained in this section) is effective for estates of decedents dying after December 31, 1986. For law effective for estates of decedents dying before December 31, 1986, see § 525.13 et seq.

Continuing Effect. For continuing effect of law relating to wills or other instruments executed on or before December 31, 1986, see § 524.2–114 as quoted in the Historical and Statutory Notes under § 524.2–115.

Laws 1994, c. 472, § 65, provides:

"(a) This act takes effect on January 1, 1996.

"(b) Except as provided elsewhere in this act:

"(1) this act applies to the rights of successors of decedents dying on or after its effective date and to any wills of decedents dying on or after its effective date;

"(2) if, before the effective date of this act, a right is either acquired, extinguished, waived, or barred upon the expiration of a prescribed period of time which commenced to run by the provisions of any statute before the effective date, the provisions of this act neither revoke, revive, restore, nor remove the bar of such right; and

"(3) any rule of construction or presumption provided in this act applies to instruments executed and multiple party accounts opened before the effective date of this act unless there is a clear indication of contrary intent."

Former section: St.1992, § 524.2–110, related to advancements. See, now, M.S.A. § 524.2–109.

524.2–111. Debts to decedent

Text of section effective for estates of decedents dying after December 31, 1986, but before January 1, 1996.

A debt owed to the decedent is not charged against the intestate share of any person except the debtor. If the debtor fails to survive the decedent, the debt is not taken into account in computing the intestate share of the debtor's issue.

Laws 1985, c. 250, § 10.

For text of section effective January 1, 1996, applicable to the rights of successors of decedents dying on or after January 1, 1996, and to any wills of decedents dying on or after January 1, 1996, see § 524.2–111, post.

524.2–111. Alienage

Text of section effective January 1, 1996, applicable to the rights of successors of decedents dying on or after January 1, 1996, and to any wills of decedents dying on or after January 1, 1996.

No individual is disqualified to take as an heir because the individual or another through whom the individual claims is or has been an alien.

Amended by Laws 1994, c. 472, § 11.

For text of section effective for estates of decedents dying after December 31, 1986, but before January 1, 1996, see § 524.2–111, ante.

Historical and Statutory Notes

Derivation:

St.1992, § 524.2–112.

Laws 1986, c. 444.

Laws 1985, c. 250, § 11.

Laws 1985, c. 250, § 28, provides that § 11 (enacting § 524.2–112, the former subject matter of which is contained in this section) is effective for estates of decedents dying after December 31, 1986. For law effective for estates of decedents dying before December 31, 1986, see § 525.13 et seq.

Continuing Effect. For continuing effect of law relating to wills or other instruments executed on or before December 31, 1986, see § 524.2–114 as quoted in the Historical and Statutory Notes under § 524.2–115.

Laws 1994, c. 472, § 65, provides:

"(a) This act takes effect on January 1, 1996.

"(b) Except as provided elsewhere in this act:

"(1) this act applies to the rights of successors of decedents dying on or after its effective date and to any wills of decedents dying on or after its effective date;

"(2) if, before the effective date of this act, a right is either acquired, extinguished, waived, or barred upon the expiration of a prescribed period of time which commenced to run by the provisions of any statute before the effective date, the provisions of this act neither revoke, revive, restore, nor remove the bar of such right; and

"(3) any rule of construction or presumption provided in this act applies to instruments executed and multiple party accounts opened before the effective date of this act unless there is a clear indication of contrary intent."

Former section: St.1992, § 524.2–111, related to debts owed a decedent. See, now, M.S.A. § 524.2–110.

524.2–112. Alienage

Text of section effective for estates of decedents dying after Dec. 31, 1986, but before January 1, 1996.

No person is disqualified to take as an heir because the person or another through whom the person claims is or has been an alien.

Laws 1985, c. 250, § 11. Amended by Laws 1986, c. 444.

Repeal

This section is repealed by Laws 1994, c. 472, § 64, effective January 1, 1996.

Historical and Statutory Notes

Laws 1985, c. 250, § 28, provides that this section is effective for estates of decedents dying after December 31, 1986. For law effective for estates of decedents dying before December 31, 1986, see § 525.13 et seq.

Continuing Effect. For continuing effect of law relating to wills or other instruments executed on or before December 31, 1986, see § 524.2–114 as quoted in the Historical and Statutory Notes under § 524.2–115.

Laws 1994, c. 472, § 65, provides:

"(a) This act takes effect on January 1, 1996.

"(b) Except as provided elsewhere in this act:

"(1) this act applies to the rights of successors of decedents dying on or after its effective date and to any wills of decedents dying on or after its effective date;

"(2) if, before the effective date of this act, a right is either acquired, extinguished, waived, or barred upon the expiration of a prescribed period of time which commenced to run by the provisions of any statute before the effective date, the provisions of this act neither revoke, revive, restore, nor remove the bar of such right; and

"(3) any rule of construction or presumption provided in this act applies to instruments executed and multiple party accounts opened before the effective date of this act unless there is a clear indication of contrary intent."

See, now, M.S.A. § 524.2–111.

524.2–113. Persons related to decedent through two lines

Text of section effective for estates of decedents dying after December 31, 1986, but before January 1, 1996.

A person who is related to the decedent through two lines of relationship is entitled to only a single share based on the relationship which would entitle such person to the larger share.

Laws 1985, c. 250, § 12.

For text of section effective January 1, 1996, applicable to the rights of successors of decedents dying on or after January 1, 1996, and to any wills of decedents dying on or after January 1, 1996, see § 524.2–113, post.

524.2–113. Individuals related to decedent through two lines

Text of section effective January 1, 1996, applicable to the rights of successors of decedents dying on or after January 1, 1996, and to any wills of decedents dying on or after January 1, 1996.

An individual who is related to the decedent through two lines of relationship is entitled to only a single share based on the relationship that would entitle the individual to the larger share.

Laws 1985, c. 250, § 12. Amended by Laws 1994, c. 472, § 12.

For text of section effective for estates of decedents dying after December 31, 1986, but before January 1, 1996, see § 524.2–113, ante.

Historical and Statutory Notes

Laws 1985, c. 250, § 28, provides that this section is effective for estates of decedents dying after December 31, 1986. For law effective for estates of decedents dying before December 31, 1986, see § 525.13 et seq.

Continuing Effect. For continuing effect of law relating to wills or other instruments executed on or before December 31, 1986, see § 524.2–114 as quoted in the Historical and Statutory Notes under § 524.2–115.

Laws 1994, c. 472, § 65, provides:

"(a) This act takes effect on January 1, 1996.

"(b) Except as provided elsewhere in this act:

"(1) this act applies to the rights of successors of decedents dying on or after its effective date and to any wills of decedents dying on or after its effective date;

"(2) if, before the effective date of this act, a right is either acquired, extinguished, waived, or barred upon the expiration of a prescribed period of time which commenced to run by the provisions of any statute before the effective date, the provisions of this act neither revoke, revive, restore, nor remove the bar of such right; and

"(3) any rule of construction or presumption provided in this act applies to instruments executed and multiple party accounts opened before the effective date of this act unless there is a clear indication of contrary intent."

524.2–114. Instruments referencing intestacy laws

Text of section effective for estates of decedents dying after December 31, 1986, but before January 1, 1996.

If a maker has executed a will or other instrument on or before December 31, 1986, which directs disposition of all or part of the estate pursuant to the intestacy laws of the state of Minnesota, the laws to be applied shall be in accordance with the laws of intestate succession in effect on or before December 31, 1986, unless the will or instrument directs otherwise.

Laws 1985, c. 250, § 13.

For text of section effective January 1, 1996, applicable to the rights of successors of decedents dying on or after January 1, 1996, and to any wills of decedents dying on or after January 1, 1996, see § 524.2–114, post.

524.2–114. Meaning of child and related terms

If, for purposes of intestate succession, a relationship of parent and child must be established to determine succession by, through, or from a person:

(1) An adopted child is the child of an adopting parent and not of the birth parents except that adoption of a child by the spouse of a birth parent has no effect on the relationship between the child and that birth parent. If a parent dies and a child is subsequently adopted by a stepparent who is the spouse of a surviving parent, any rights of inheritance of the child or the child's descendant from or through the deceased parent of the child which exist at the time of the death of that parent shall not be affected by the adoption.

(2) In cases not covered by clause (1), a person is the child of the person's parents regardless of the marital status of the parents and the parent and child relationship may be established under the Parentage Act, sections 257.51 to 257.74.

Amended by Laws 1994, c. 465, art. 1, § 62; Laws 1994, c. 472, § 13; Laws 1994, c. 631, § 31; Laws 2005, c. 10, art. 1, § 75; Laws 2008, c. 361, art. 6, § 54, eff. Aug. 1, 2008.

Historical and Statutory Notes

Derivation:

St.1992, § 524.2–109.

Laws 1986, 1st Sp., c. 3, art. 3, § 1.

Laws 1985, c. 250, § 9.

Laws 1985, c. 250, § 28, provides that § 9 (enacting § 524.2–109, the former subject matter of which is contained in this section) is effective for estates of decedents dying after December 31, 1986. For law effective for estates of decedents dying before December 31, 1986, see § 525.13 et seq.

Continuing Effect. For continuing effect of law relating to wills or other instruments executed on or before December 31, 1986, see § 524.2–114 as quoted in the Historical and Statutory Notes under § 524.2–115.

Laws 1994, c. 472, § 65, provides:

"(a) This act takes effect on January 1, 1996.

"(b) Except as provided elsewhere in this act:

"(1) this act applies to the rights of successors of decedents dying on or after its effective date and to any wills of decedents dying on or after its effective date;

"(2) if, before the effective date of this act, a right is either acquired, extinguished, waived, or barred upon the expiration of a prescribed period of time which commenced to run by the provisions of any statute before the effective date, the provisions of this act neither revoke, revive, restore, nor remove the bar of such right; and

"(3) any rule of construction or presumption provided in this act applies to instruments executed and multiple party accounts opened before the effective date of this act unless there is a clear indication of contrary intent."

Former section: St.1992, § 524.2–114, related to instruments referencing intestacy laws. See, now, M.S.A. § 524.2–115.

524.2–115. Instruments referencing intestacy laws

Text of section effective January 1, 1996, applicable to the rights of successors of decedents dying on or after January 1, 1996, and to any wills of decedents dying on or after January 1, 1996.

If a maker has executed a will or other instrument before January 1, 1996, which directs disposition of all or part of the estate pursuant to the intestacy laws of the state of Minnesota, the laws to be applied shall be in accordance with the laws of intestate succession in effect on the date of the will or other instrument, unless the will or instrument directs otherwise.

Laws 1994, c. 472, § 14.

Historical and Statutory Notes

Derivation:

St.1992, § 524.2–114.

Laws 1985, c. 250, § 13.

Laws 1985, c. 250, § 28, provides that § 13 (enacting § 524.2–114, the former subject matter of which is contained in this section) is effective for estates of decedents dying after December 31, 1986. For law effective for estates of decedents dying before December 31, 1986, see § 525.13 et seq.

Continuing Effect. For continuing effect of law relating to wills or other instruments executed on or before December 31, 1986, see § 524.2–114 as quoted in the Historical and Statutory Notes under § 524.2–115.

Laws 1994, c. 472, § 13, rewrote § 524.2–114, the subject matter of which is contained in this section. Prior to revision, § 524.2–114 read:

"If a maker has executed a will or other instrument on or before December 31, 1986, which directs disposition of all or part of the estate pursuant to the intestacy laws of the state of Minnesota, the laws to be applied shall be in accordance with the laws of intestate succession in effect on or before December 31, 1986, unless the will or instrument directs otherwise."

Laws 1994, c. 472, § 65, provides:

"(a) This act takes effect on January 1, 1996.

"(b) Except as provided elsewhere in this act:

"(1) this act applies to the rights of successors of decedents dying on or after its effective date and to any wills of decedents dying on or after its effective date;

"(2) if, before the effective date of this act, a right is either acquired, extinguished, waived, or barred upon the expiration of a prescribed period of time which commenced to run by the provisions of any statute before the effective date, the provisions of this act neither revoke, revive, restore, nor remove the bar of such right; and

"(3) any rule of construction or presumption provided in this act applies to instruments executed and multiple party accounts opened before the effective date of this act unless there is a clear indication of contrary intent."

PART 2

ELECTIVE SHARE OF SURVIVING SPOUSE

524.2–201. Right to elective share

Text of section effective for estates of decedents dying after December 31, 1986, but before January 1, 1996.

(a) If a married person domiciled in this state dies, the surviving spouse has a right of election to take an elective share of one-third of the augmented estate under the limitations and conditions hereinafter stated.

(b) If a married person not domiciled in this state dies, the right, if any, of the surviving spouse to take an elective share in property in this state is governed by the law of the decedent's domicile at death.

Laws 1985, c. 250, § 14.

> *For text of section effective January 1, 1996, applicable to the rights of successors of decedents dying on or after January 1, 1996, and to any wills of decedents dying on or after January 1, 1996, see § 524.2–201, post.*

524.2–201. Definitions

> *Text of section effective January 1, 1996, applicable to the rights of successors of decedents dying on or after January 1, 1996, and to any wills of decedents dying on or after January 1, 1996.*

In this part:

(1) As used in sections other than section 524.2–205, "decedent's nonprobate transfers to others" means the amounts that are included in the augmented estate under section 524.2–205.

(2) "Interest in property held with right of survivorship" means the severable interest owned by the person or persons whose interest is being determined in property held in joint tenancy or in other form of common ownership with a right of survivorship. The interest shall be identified and valued as of the time immediately prior to the death of the decedent or the date of the transfer which causes the property to be included in the augmented estate, as the case may be. In the case of an account described in article 6, part 2, the severable interest owned by the person is the amount which belonged to the person determined under section 524.6–203. In the case of property described in article 6, part 3, the severable interest owned by the person is the amount consistent with section 524.6–306.

(3) "Marriage," as it relates to a transfer by the decedent during marriage, means any marriage of the decedent to the decedent's surviving spouse.

(4) "Nonadverse party" means a person who does not have a substantial beneficial interest in the trust or other property arrangement that would be adversely affected by the exercise or nonexercise of the power that the person possesses respecting the trust or other property arrangement. A person having a general power of appointment over property is deemed to have a beneficial interest in the property.

(5) "Power" or "power of appointment" includes a power to designate the beneficiary of an insurance policy or other contractual arrangement.

(6) "Presently exercisable general power of appointment" means a power possessed by a person at the time in question to create a present or future interest in the person, in the person's creditors, in the person's estate, or in the creditor of the person's estate, whether or not the person then had the capacity

to exercise the power. "General power of appointment" means a power, whether or not presently exercisable, possessed by a person to create a present or future interest in the person, in the person's creditors, in the person's estate, or in creditors of the person's estate.

(7) "Probate estate" means property that would pass by intestate succession if the decedent dies without a valid will.

(8) "Property" includes values subject to a beneficiary designation.

(9) "Right to income" includes a right to payments under a commercial or private annuity, an annuity trust, a unitrust, or a similar arrangement.

(10) "Transfer" includes: (i) the exercise, release, or lapse of a general power of appointment created by the decedent alone or in conjunction with any other person, or exercisable by a nonadverse party; and (ii) the exercise or release by the decedent of a presently exercisable general power of appointment created by someone other than the decedent. "Transfer" does not include the lapse, other than a lapse at death, of a power described in clause (ii).

(11) "Bona fide purchaser" means a purchaser for value in good faith and without notice or actual knowledge of an adverse claim, or a person who receives a payment or other item of property in partial or full satisfaction of a legally enforceable obligation in good faith without notice of an adverse claim. In the case of real property located in Minnesota purchased from a successor or successors in interest of a decedent, the purchaser is without notice of an adverse claim arising under this part or, if the decedent was not domiciled in Minnesota at the time of death, arising under similar provisions of the law of the decedent's domicile, unless the decedent's surviving spouse has filed a notice in the office of the county recorder of the county in which the real property is located or, if the property is registered land, in the office of the registrar of titles of the county in which the real property is located, containing the legal description of the property, a brief statement of the nature and extent of the interest claimed, and the venue, title, and file number of the proceeding for an elective share, if any has been commenced. The registrar of titles is authorized to accept for registration any such notice which relates to registered land.

Laws 1994, c. 472, § 15. Amended by Laws 1999, c. 11, art. 1, § 71, eff. Jan. 1, 2000.

For text of section effective for estates of decedents dying after December 31, 1986, but before January 1, 1996, see § 524.2–201, ante.

Historical and Statutory Notes

Laws 1985, c. 250, § 28, provides that § 14 (enacting § 524.2–201, the former subject matter of which is contained in § 524.2–202) is effective for estates of decedents dying after December 31, 1986. For law effective for estates of decedents dying before December 31, 1986, see § 525.13 et seq.

Continuing Effect. For continuing effect of law relating to wills or other instruments executed on or before December 31, 1986, see § 524.2–114 as quoted in the Historical and Statutory Notes under § 524.2–115.

Laws 1994, c. 472, § 65, provides:

"(a) This act takes effect on January 1, 1996.

"(b) Except as provided elsewhere in this act:

"(1) this act applies to the rights of successors of decedents dying on or after its effective date and to any wills of decedents dying on or after its effective date;

"(2) if, before the effective date of this act, a right is either acquired, extinguished, waived, or barred upon the expiration of a prescribed period of time which commenced to run by the provisions of any statute before the effective date, the provisions of this act neither revoke, revive, restore, nor remove the bar of such right; and

"(3) any rule of construction or presumption provided in this act applies to instruments executed and multiple party accounts opened before the effective date of this act unless there is a clear indication of contrary intent."

524.2–202. Augmented estate

Text of section effective for estates of decedents dying after December 31, 1986, but before January 1, 1996.

The augmented estate means the estate reduced by funeral and administration expenses, the homestead, family allowances and exemptions, liens, mortgages, and enforceable claims, to which is added the sum of the following amounts:

(1) The value of property, other than the homestead, transferred by the decedent at any time during the marriage, to or for the benefit of any person other than the surviving spouse, to the extent that the decedent did not receive adequate and full consideration in money or money's worth for the transfer, if the transfer is of any of the following types:

(i) any transfer under which the decedent retained at the time of death the possession or enjoyment of, or right to income from, the property;

(ii) any transfer to the extent that the decedent retained at the time of death a power, either alone or in conjunction with any other person, to revoke or to consume, invade or dispose of the principal for personal benefit;

(iii) any transfer whereby property is held at the time of decedent's death by decedent and another with right of survivorship;

(iv) any transfer made within one year of death of the decedent to the extent that the aggregate transfers to any one donee in the year exceeds $30,000.

Any transfer is excluded if made with the written consent or joinder of the surviving spouse. Property is valued as of the decedent's death except that property given irrevocably to a donee during lifetime of the decedent is valued as of the date the donee came into possession or enjoyment if that occurs first.

Notwithstanding the provisions of (i) to (iv), the augmented estate includes the proceeds of property described in clause (3) only to the extent provided in clause (3).

(2) The value of property, other than the homestead, owned by the surviving spouse at the decedent's death, plus the value of property transferred by the spouse at any time during marriage to any person other than the decedent which would have been includable in the spouse's augmented estate if the surviving spouse had predeceased the decedent, to the extent the owned or transferred property is derived from the decedent by any means other than

testate or intestate succession or as an obligation of support without a full consideration in money or money's worth. For purposes of this clause:

(i) Property derived from the decedent includes, but is not limited to, any beneficial interest of the surviving spouse in a trust created by the decedent during the decedent's lifetime; any property appointed to the spouse by the decedent's exercise of a general or special power of appointment also exercisable in favor of others than the spouse; any proceeds of insurance, including accidental death benefits, on the life of the decedent attributable to premiums paid by the decedent; any lump sum immediately payable and the commuted value of the proceeds of annuity contracts under which the decedent was the primary annuitant attributable to premiums paid by the decedent; the commuted value of amounts payable after the decedent's death under any public or private pension, disability compensation, benefit, or retirement plan or account, excluding federal social security and tier 1 railroad retirement benefits, by reason of service performed, disabilities incurred, or deposits made by the decedent; any property held at the time of decedent's death by decedent and the surviving spouse with right of survivorship; any property held by decedent and transferred by contract to the surviving spouse by reason of the decedent's death; and the value of the share of the surviving spouse resulting from rights in community property in this or any other state formerly owned with the decedent.

(ii) Property owned by the spouse at the decedent's death is valued as of the date of death. Property transferred by the spouse is valued at the time the transfer became irrevocable, or at the decedent's death, whichever occurred first. Income earned by included property prior to the decedent's death is not treated as property derived from the decedent.

(iii) Property owned by the surviving spouse as of the decedent's death of the kind described in clause (2)(i) is presumed to have been derived from the decedent except to the extent that the surviving spouse establishes that it was derived from another source. All other property owned by the surviving spouse as of the decedent's death, or previously transferred by the surviving spouse, is presumed not to have been derived from the decedent except to the extent that an interested party establishes that it was derived from the decedent.

(3) The value of property paid to, or for the benefit of, a person other than the surviving spouse as a result of the decedent's death if the property is any of the following types:

(i) proceeds of insurance, including accidental death benefits attributable to premiums paid by the decedent during the marriage except that: (a) if an enforceable claim satisfied with proceeds of insurance on the decedent's life is not deducted in computing the augmented estate, the proceeds must not be included separately; (b) if the value of a business interest is included in the augmented estate, the proceeds of insurance on the decedent's life that are paid to the business or are applied in performance of a purchase agreement relating to the business interest must not be included separately; (c) if the decedent was required by a decree or order dissolving a prior marriage to pay premiums on insurance on the decedent's life for the benefit of specified persons, the proceeds of that insurance must not be included separately; and (d) in other similar cases the proceeds of insurance must not be included separately;

(ii) a lump sum immediately payable, or the commuted value of the proceeds of annuity contracts under which the decedent was the primary annuitant attributable to premiums paid by the decedent during the marriage; or

(iii) the commuted value of amounts payable after the decedent's death under any public or private pension, disability compensation, benefit, or retirement plan or account, excluding federal social security and tier 1 railroad retirement benefits, by reason of service performed, disabilities incurred, or deposits made by the decedent, attributable to premiums or contributions paid by the decedent during the marriage.

For purposes of this clause, premiums or contributions paid by the decedent's employer, the decedent's partner, a partnership of which the decedent was a member, or the decedent's creditors, are deemed to have been paid by the decedent, and any amounts otherwise includable in the augmented estate are excluded if made with the written consent or joinder of the surviving spouse.

Unless the payer of the property has received written notice of intention to file a petition for the elective share, the property may be paid, upon request and satisfactory proof of the decedent's death, to the designated beneficiary of the property. Payment made discharges the payer from all claims for the amounts paid. This does not extend to payments made after the payer has received written notice of intention to file a petition for the elective share. Unless the notice is withdrawn by the surviving spouse, the surviving spouse must concur in any demand for withdrawal.

For an insurer, the written notice of intention to file a petition for the elective share must be mailed to its home office by registered mail, return receipt requested, or served upon the insurer in the same manner as a summons in a civil action. Upon receipt of written notice of intention to file a petition for the elective share, an insurer may pay any amounts owed by it specified in clause (3) to the court in which the probate proceedings relating to the estate of the decedent are venued, or if no proceedings have been commenced, to the court having jurisdiction of decedents' estates located in the county of the insured's residence. The court shall hold the funds and, upon its determination under section 524.2–205, subsection (d), shall order its disbursement in accordance with the determination. If no petition is filed in the court within the specified time under section 524.2–205, subsection (a), or if filed, the demand for an elective share is withdrawn under section 524.2–205, subsection (c), the court shall order disbursement to the designated beneficiary. Payment made to the court discharges the insurer from all claims for the amounts paid.

Upon petition to the probate court by the designated beneficiary, the court may order that all or part of the property be paid to the designated beneficiary in an amount and subject to conditions consistent with this section.

Laws 1985, c. 250, § 15. Amended by Laws 1986, c. 444; Laws 1986, 1st Sp., c. 3, art. 3, § 2; Laws 1987, c. 210, § 4, eff. May 27, 1987.

> *For text of section effective January 1, 1996, applicable to the rights of successors of decedents dying on or after January 1, 1996, and to any wills of decedents dying on or after January 1, 1996, see § 524.2–202, post.*

524.2–202. Elective share

> *Text of section effective January 1, 1996, applicable to the rights of successors of decedents dying on or after January 1, 1996, and to any wills of decedents dying on or after January 1, 1996.*

(a) Elective share amount. The surviving spouse of a decedent who dies domiciled in this state has a right of election, under the limitations and conditions stated in this part, to take an elective-share amount equal to the value of the elective-share percentage of the augmented estate, determined by the length of time the spouse and the decedent were married to each other, in accordance with the following schedule:

If the decedent and the spouse were married to each other:	The elective-share percentage is:
Less than one year	Supplemental amount only
One year but less than two years	Three percent of the augmented estate
Two years but less than three years	Six percent of the augmented estate
Three years but less than four years	Nine percent of the augmented estate
Four years but less than five years	12 percent of the augmented estate
Five years but less than six years	15 percent of the augmented estate
Six years but less than seven years	18 percent of the augmented estate
Seven years but less than eight years	21 percent of the augmented estate
Eight years but less than nine years	24 percent of the augmented estate
Nine years but less than ten years	27 percent of the augmented estate
Ten years but less than 11 years	30 percent of the augmented estate
11 years but less than 12 years	34 percent of the augmented estate
12 years but less than 13 years	38 percent of the augmented estate
13 years but less than 14 years	42 percent of the augmented estate
14 years but less than 15 years	46 percent of the augmented estate
15 years or more	50 percent of the augmented estate

(b) Supplemental elective-share amount. If the sum of the amounts described in sections 524.2–207, 524.2–209, paragraph (a), clause (1), and that part of the elective-share amount payable from the decedent's probate estate and nonprobate transfers to others under section 524.2–209, paragraphs (b) and (c), is less than $50,000, the surviving spouse is entitled to a supplemental elective-share amount equal to $50,000, minus the sum of the amounts described in those sections. The supplemental elective-share amount is payable from the decedent's probate estate and from recipients of the decedent's nonprobate transfers to others in the order of priority set forth in section 524.2–209, paragraphs (b) and (c).

(c) Effect of election on statutory benefits. If the right of election is exercised by or on behalf of the surviving spouse, the surviving spouse's homestead rights and other allowances under sections 524.2–402, 524.2–403 and 524.2–404, if any, are not charged against but are in addition to the elective-share and supplemental elective-share amounts.

(d) Nondomiciliary. The right, if any, of the surviving spouse of a decedent who dies domiciled outside this state to take an elective share in property in this state is governed by the law of the decedent's domicile at death.

Laws 1994, c. 472, § 16.

For text of section effective for estates of decedents dying after December 31, 1986, but before January 1, 1996, see § 524.2–202, ante.

Historical and Statutory Notes

Derivation:

St.1992, §§ 524.2–201, 524.2–206.

Laws 1986, c. 444.

Laws 1985, c. 250, §§ 14, 19.

Laws 1985, c. 250, § 28, provides that §§ 14 and 19 (enacting §§ 524.2–201 and 524.2–206 the former subject matter of which is contained in this section) are effective for estates of decedents dying after December 31, 1986. For law effective for estates of decedents dying before December 31, 1986, see §525.13 et seq.

Continuing Effect. For continuing effect of law relating to wills or other instruments executed on or before December 31, 1986, see § 524.2–114 as quoted in the Historical and Statutory Notes under § 524.2–115.

Laws 1994, c. 472, § 65, provides:

"(a) This act takes effect on January 1, 1996.

"(b) Except as provided elsewhere in this act:

"(1) this act applies to the rights of successors of decedents dying on or after its effective date and to any wills of decedents dying on or after its effective date;

"(2) if, before the effective date of this act, a right is either acquired, extinguished, waived, or barred upon the expiration of a prescribed period of time which commenced to run by the provisions of any statute before the effective date, the provisions of this act neither revoke, revive, restore, nor remove the bar of such right; and

"(3) any rule of construction or presumption provided in this act applies to instruments executed and multiple party accounts opened before the effective date of this act unless there is a clear indication of contrary intent."

Former section: St.1992, § 524.2–202, which related to the calculation of the augmented estate, was repealed by Laws 1994, c. 472, § 64. See, now, M.S.A. §§ 524.2–203 to 524.2–207.

524.2–203. Right of election personal to surviving spouse

Text of section effective for estates of decedents dying after December 31, 1986, but before January 1, 1996.

The right of election of the surviving spouse may be exercised only during the surviving spouse's lifetime. In the case of a protected person, the right of election may be exercised only by order of the court in which protective proceedings as to the protected person's property are pending, after finding (1)

that exercise is necessary to provide adequate support for the protected person
during the protected person's probable life expectancy and (2) that the election
will be consistent with the best interests of the natural bounty of the protected
person's affection.

Laws 1985, c. 250, § 16. Amended by Laws 1986, c. 444.

> *For text of section effective January 1, 1996, applicable to the rights of
> successors of decedents dying on or after January 1, 1996, and to any
> wills of decedents dying on or after January 1, 1996, see § 524.2–203,
> post.*

524.2–203. Composition of the augmented estate

> *Text of section effective January 1, 1996, applicable to the rights of
> successors of decedents dying on or after January 1, 1996, and to any
> wills of decedents dying on or after January 1, 1996.*

Subject to section 524.2–208, the value of the augmented estate, to the extent
provided in sections 524.2–204, 524.2–205, 524.2–206, and 524.2–207, consists
of the sum of the values of all property, whether real or personal, movable or
immovable, tangible or intangible, wherever situated, that constitute the decedent's net probate estate, the decedent's nonprobate transfers to others, the
decedent's nonprobate transfers to the surviving spouse, and the surviving
spouse's property and nonprobate transfers to others.

Laws 1994, c. 472, § 17.

> *For text of section effective for estates of decedents dying after Decem-
> ber 31, 1986, but before January 1, 1996, see § 524.2–203, ante.*

Historical and Statutory Notes

Derivation:

St.1992, § 524.2–202.

Laws 1987, c. 210, § 4.

Laws 1986, 1st Sp., c. 3, art. 3, § 2.

Laws 1986, c. 444.

Laws 1985, c. 250, § 15.

Laws 1985, c. 250, § 28, provides that § 15
(enacting § 524.2–202, the former subject matter of which is contained in §§ 524.2–203 to
524.2–207) is effective for estates of decedents
dying after December 31, 1986. For law effective for estates of decedents dying before December 31, 1986, see § 525.13 et seq.

Continuing Effect. For continuing effect of
law relating to wills or other instruments executed on or before December 31, 1986, see
§ 524.2–114 as quoted in the Historical and
Statutory Notes under § 524.2–115.

Laws 1994, c. 472, § 65, provides:

"(a) This act takes effect on January 1, 1996.

"(b) Except as provided elsewhere in this act:

"(1) this act applies to the rights of successors of decedents dying on or after its effective
date and to any wills of decedents dying on or
after its effective date;

"(2) if, before the effective date of this act, a
right is either acquired, extinguished, waived,
or barred upon the expiration of a prescribed
period of time which commenced to run by the
provisions of any statute before the effective
date, the provisions of this act neither revoke,
revive, restore, nor remove the bar of such
right; and

"(3) any rule of construction or presumption
provided in this act applies to instruments executed and multiple party accounts opened before the effective date of this act unless there is
a clear indication of contrary intent."

Former section: St.1992, § 524.2–203, which
provided that the right of election was personal
to the surviving spouse, was repealed by Laws
1994, c. 472, § 64. See, now, M.S.A.
§ 524.2–212.

524.2–204. Waiver of right to elect and of other rights

Text of section effective for estates of decedents dying after December 31, 1986, but before January 1, 1996.

The right of election of a surviving spouse and the rights of the surviving spouse to the homestead, exempt property and family allowance, or any of them, may be waived, wholly or partially, after marriage, by a written contract, agreement or waiver signed by the party waiving after fair disclosure. Unless it provides to the contrary, a waiver of "all rights", or equivalent language, in the property or estate of a spouse is a waiver only of the right to elective share. Any waiver prior to marriage must be made pursuant to section 519.11.

Laws 1985, c. 250, § 17.

For text of section effective January 1, 1996, applicable to the rights of successors of decedents dying on or after January 1, 1996, and to any wills of decedents dying on or after January 1, 1996, see § 524.2–204, post.

524.2–204. Decedent's net probate estate

Text of section effective January 1, 1996, applicable to the rights of successors of decedents dying on or after January 1, 1996, and to any wills of decedents dying on or after January 1, 1996.

The value of the augmented estate includes the value of the decedent's probate estate, reduced by funeral and administration expenses, the homestead, family allowances and exemptions, liens, mortgages, and enforceable claims.

Laws 1994, c. 472, § 18.

For text of section effective for estates of decedents dying after December 31, 1986, but before January 1, 1996, see § 524.2–204, ante.

Historical and Statutory Notes

Derivation:

St.1992, § 524.2–202.

Laws 1987, c. 210, § 4.

Laws 1986, 1st Sp., c. 3, art. 3, § 2.

Laws 1986, c. 444.

Laws 1985, c. 250, § 15.

Laws 1985, c. 250, § 28, provides that § 15 (enacting § 524.2–202, the former subject matter of which is contained in §§ 524.2–203 to 524.2–207) is effective for estates of decedents dying after December 31, 1986. For law effective for estates of decedents dying before December 31, 1986, see § 525.13 et seq.

Continuing Effect. For continuing effect of law relating to wills or other instruments executed on or before December 31, 1986, see § 524.2–114 as quoted in the Historical and Statutory Notes under § 524.2–115.

Laws 1994, c. 472, § 65, provides:

"(a) This act takes effect on January 1, 1996.

"(b) Except as provided elsewhere in this act:

"(1) this act applies to the rights of successors of decedents dying on or after its effective date and to any wills of decedents dying on or after its effective date;

"(2) if, before the effective date of this act, a right is either acquired, extinguished, waived, or barred upon the expiration of a prescribed period of time which commenced to run by the provisions of any statute before the effective date, the provisions of this act neither revoke, revive, restore, nor remove the bar of such right; and

"(3) any rule of construction or presumption provided in this act applies to instruments exe-cuted and multiple party accounts opened before the effective date of this act unless there is a clear indication of contrary intent."

Former section: St.1992, § 524.2–204, which related to the waiver of the right to elect and of other rights, was repealed by Laws 1994, c. 472, § 64. See, now, M.S.A. § 524.2–213.

524.2–205. Proceeding for elective share; time limit

Text of section effective for estates of decedents dying after December 31, 1986, but before January 1, 1996.

(a) The surviving spouse may elect to take an elective share in the augmented estate by filing in the court and mailing or delivering to the personal representative, if any, a petition for the elective share within nine months after the date of death, or within six months after the probate of the decedent's will, whichever limitation last expires. However, nonprobate transfers, described in section 524.2–202, clauses (1) and (3), shall not be included within the augmented estate for the purpose of computing the elective share, if the petition is filed later than nine months after death. The court may extend the time for election as it sees fit for cause shown by the surviving spouse before the time for election has expired.

(b) The surviving spouse shall give notice of the time and place set for hearing to persons interested in the estate and to the distributees and recipients of portions of the augmented net estate whose interests will be affected by the taking of the elective share.

(c) The surviving spouse may withdraw a demand for an elective share at any time before entry of an order by the court determining the elective share.

(d) After notice and hearing, the court shall determine the amount of the elective share and shall order its payment from the assets of the augmented net estate or by contribution as appears appropriate under section 524.2–207. If it appears that a fund or property included in the augmented net estate has not come into the possession of the personal representative, or has been distributed by the personal representative, the court nevertheless shall fix the liability of any person who has any interest in the fund or property or who has possession thereof, whether as trustee or otherwise. The proceeding may be maintained against fewer than all persons against whom relief could be sought, but no person is subject to contribution in any greater amount than that person would have been if relief had been secured against all persons subject to contribution.

(e) The order or judgment of the court may be enforced as necessary in suit for contribution or payment in other courts of this state or other jurisdictions.

(f) Whether or not an election has been made under subsection (a), the surviving spouse may elect statutory rights in the homestead by filing in the manner provided in this section a petition in which the spouse asserts the rights provided in section 525.145, provided that:

(1) when the homestead is subject to a testamentary disposition, the filing must be within nine months after the date of death, or within six months after the probate of the decedent's will, whichever limitation last expires; or

(2) where the homestead is subject to other disposition, the filing must be within nine months after the date of death.

The court may extend the time for election for cause shown by the surviving spouse before the time for filing has expired.

Laws 1985, c. 250, § 18. Amended by Laws 1986, c. 444; Laws 1986, 1st Sp., c. 3, art. 3, § 3.

> For text of section effective January 1, 1996, applicable to the rights of successors of decedents dying on or after January 1, 1996, and to any wills of decedents dying on or after January 1, 1996, see § 524.2–205, post.

524.2–205. Decedent's nonprobate transfers to others

> Text of section effective January 1, 1996, applicable to the rights of successors of decedents dying on or after January 1, 1996, and to any wills of decedents dying on or after January 1, 1996.

The value of the augmented estate includes the value of the decedent's nonprobate transfers to others, other than the homestead, of any of the following types, in the amount provided respectively for each type of transfer.

(1) Property owned or owned in substance by the decedent immediately before death that passed outside probate at the decedent's death. Property included under this category consists of:

(i) Property over which the decedent alone, immediately before death, held a presently exercisable general power of appointment. The amount included is the value of the property subject to the power, to the extent the property passed at the decedent's death, by exercise, release, lapse, default, or otherwise, to or for the benefit of any person other than the decedent's estate or surviving spouse.

(ii) The decedent's interest in property held with the right of survivorship. The amount included is the value of the decedent's interest, to the extent the interest passed by right of survivorship at the decedent's death to someone other than the decedent's surviving spouse.

(iii) Proceeds of insurance, including accidental death benefits, on the life of the decedent, if the decedent owned the insurance policy immediately before death or if and to the extent the decedent alone and immediately before death held a presently exercisable general power of appointment over the policy or its proceeds. The amount included is the value of the proceeds, to the extent they were payable at the decedent's death to or for the benefit of any person other than the decedent's estate or surviving spouse.

(iv) The value payable after the decedent's death to or for the benefit of any person other than the decedent's surviving spouse of the proceeds of annuity contracts under which the decedent was the primary annuitant. The amount included is any amount over which the person has an immediate right of withdrawal after the decedent's death plus the commuted value of other amounts payable in the future.

(v) The value payable after the decedent's death to or for the benefit of any person other than the decedent's surviving spouse of amounts under any public or private pension, disability compensation, benefit, or retirement plan or account, excluding the federal Social Security system. The amount included is any amount over which the person has an immediate right of withdrawal after the decedent's death plus the commuted value of other amounts payable in the future.

(2) Property transferred in any of the following forms by the decedent during marriage, to the extent not included under paragraph (1):

(i) Any irrevocable transfer in which the decedent retained the right to the possession or enjoyment of, or to the income from, the property if and to the extent the decedent's right terminated at or continued beyond the decedent's death. The amount included is the value of the fraction of the property to which the decedent's right related, to the extent the fraction of the property passed outside probate to or for the benefit of any person other than the decedent's estate or surviving spouse.

(ii) Any transfer in which the decedent created a general power of appointment over income or property exercisable by the decedent alone or in conjunction with any other person, or exercisable by a nonadverse party. The amount included with respect to a power over property is the value of the property subject to the power, and the amount included with respect to a power over income is the value of the property that produces or produced the income, to the extent in either case that the property passed at the decedent's death to or for the benefit of any person other than the decedent's estate or surviving spouse. If the power is a power over both income and property and the preceding sentence produces different amounts, the amount included is the greater amount.

(3) Property that passed during marriage and during the two-year period next preceding the decedent's death as a result of a transfer by the decedent if the transfer was of any of the following types:

(i) Any property that passed as a result of the termination of a right or interest in, or power over, property that would have been included in the augmented estate under paragraph (1), clause (i), (ii), (iv), or (v), or under paragraph (2), if the right, interest, or power had not terminated until the decedent's death. The amount included is the value of the property that would have been included under those paragraphs if the property were valued at the time the right, interest, or power terminated, and is included only to the extent the property passed upon termination to or for the benefit of any person other than the decedent or the decedent's estate, spouse, or surviving spouse. As used in this paragraph, "termination," with respect to a right or interest in property, occurs when the power is terminated by exercise, release, default, or otherwise, but with respect to a power described in paragraph (1), clause (i), "termination" occurs when the power is terminated by exercise or release, but not otherwise.

(ii) Any transfer of or relating to an insurance policy on the life of the decedent if the proceeds would have been included in the augmented estate under paragraph (1), clause (iii), had the transfer not occurred. The amount included is the value of the insurance proceeds to the extent the proceeds were payable at the decedent's death to or for the benefit of any person other than the decedent's estate or surviving spouse.

(iii) Any transfer of property, to the extent not otherwise included in the augmented estate, made to or for the benefit of a person other than the decedent's surviving spouse. The amount included is the value of the transferred property to the extent the aggregate transfers to any one donee in either of the two years exceeded $10,000.

Laws 1994, c. 472, § 19.

For text of section effective for estates of decedents dying after December 31, 1986, but before January 1, 1996, see § 524.2–205, ante.

Historical and Statutory Notes

Derivation:

St.1992, § 524.2–202.

Laws 1987, c. 210, § 4.

Laws 1986, 1st Sp., c. 3, art. 3, § 2.

Laws 1986, c. 444.

Laws 1985, c. 250, § 15.

Laws 1985, c. 250, § 28, provides that § 15 (enacting § 524.2–202, the former subject matter of which is contained in §§ 524.2–203 to 524.2–207) is effective for estates of decedents dying after December 31, 1986. For law effective for estates of decedents dying before December 31, 1986, see § 525.13 et seq.

Continuing Effect. For continuing effect of law relating to wills or other instruments executed on or before December 31, 1986, see § 524.2–114 as quoted in the Historical and Statutory Notes under § 524.2–115.

Laws 1994, c. 472, § 65, provides:

"(a) This act takes effect on January 1, 1996.

"(b) Except as provided elsewhere in this act:

"(1) this act applies to the rights of successors of decedents dying on or after its effective date and to any wills of decedents dying on or after its effective date;

"(2) if, before the effective date of this act, a right is either acquired, extinguished, waived, or barred upon the expiration of a prescribed period of time which commenced to run by the provisions of any statute before the effective date, the provisions of this act neither revoke, revive, restore, nor remove the bar of such right; and

"(3) any rule of construction or presumption provided in this act applies to instruments executed and multiple party accounts opened before the effective date of this act unless there is a clear indication of contrary intent."

Former section: St.1992, § 524.2–205, which related to the proceeding to take an elective share, was repealed by Laws 1994, c. 472, § 64. See, now, M.S.A. § 524.2–211.

524.2–206. Effect of election on benefits by will or statute

Text of section effective for estates of decedents dying after December 31, 1986, but before January 1, 1996.

A surviving spouse is entitled to the allowances provided in section 525.15 whether or not electing to take an elective share.

Laws 1985, c. 250, § 19. Amended by Laws 1986, c. 444.

For text of section effective January 1, 1996, applicable to the rights of successors of decedents dying on or after January 1, 1996, and to any wills of decedents dying on or after January 1, 1996, see § 524.2–206, post.

524.2–206. Decedent's nonprobate transfers to the surviving spouse

Text of section effective January 1, 1996, applicable to the rights of successors of decedents dying on or after January 1, 1996, and to any wills of decedents dying on or after January 1, 1996.

Excluding the homestead and property passing to the surviving spouse under the federal Social Security system, the value of the augmented estate includes the value of the decedent's nonprobate transfers to the decedent's spouse, which consists of all property that passed outside probate at the decedent's death from the decedent to the surviving spouse by reason of the decedent's death that would have been included in the augmented estate under section 524.2–205, paragraph (1) or (2), had the property passed to or for the benefit of a person other than the decedent's spouse, the decedent, or the decedent's creditors, estate, or estate creditors.

Laws 1994, c. 472, § 20.

For text of section effective for estates of decedents dying after December 31, 1986, but before January 1, 1996, see § 524.2–206, ante.

Historical and Statutory Notes

Derivation:

St.1992, § 524.2–202.

Laws 1987, c. 210, § 4.

Laws 1986, 1st Sp., c. 3, art. 3, § 2.

Laws 1986, c. 444.

Laws 1985, c. 250, § 15.

Laws 1985, c. 250, § 28, provides that § 15 (enacting § 524.2–202, the former subject matter of which is contained in §§ 524.2–203 to 524.2–207) is effective for estates of decedents dying after December 31, 1986. For law effective for estates of decedents dying before December 31, 1986, see § 525.13 et seq.

Continuing Effect. For continuing effect of law relating to wills or other instruments executed on or before December 31, 1986, see § 524.2–114 as quoted in the Historical and Statutory Notes under § 524.2–115.

Laws 1994, c. 472, § 65, provides:

"(a) This act takes effect on January 1, 1996.

"(b) Except as provided elsewhere in this act:

"(1) this act applies to the rights of successors of decedents dying on or after its effective date and to any wills of decedents dying on or after its effective date;

"(2) if, before the effective date of this act, a right is either acquired, extinguished, waived, or barred upon the expiration of a prescribed period of time which commenced to run by the provisions of any statute before the effective date, the provisions of this act neither revoke, revive, restore, nor remove the bar of such right; and

"(3) any rule of construction or presumption provided in this act applies to instruments executed and multiple party accounts opened before the effective date of this act unless there is a clear indication of contrary intent."

Former section: St.1992, § 524.2–206, which related to the effect of an election to take an elective share on other benefits provided by will

or statute, was repealed by Laws 1994, c. 472,
§ 64. See, now, M.S.A. § 524.2–202.

524.2–207. Charging spouse with gifts received; liability of others for balance of elective share

Text of section effective for estates of decedents dying after December 31, 1986, but before January 1, 1996.

(a) In the proceeding for an elective share, values included in the augmented estate which pass or have passed to the surviving spouse, or which would have passed to the surviving spouse but were renounced, are applied first to satisfy the elective share and to reduce any contributions due from other recipients of transfers included in the augmented estate. For purposes of this paragraph, the electing spouse's beneficial interest in any life estate or in any trust shall be computed as if worth one-half of the total value of the property subject to the life estate, or of the trust estate, unless higher or lower values for these interests are established by proof.

(b) Remaining property of the augmented estate is so applied that liability for the balance of the elective share of the surviving spouse is equitably apportioned among the recipients of the augmented estate in proportion to the value of their interests therein.

(c) Only original transferees from, or appointees of, the decedent and their donees, to the extent the donees have the property or its proceeds, are subject to the contribution to make up the elective share of the surviving spouse. A person liable to contribution may choose to give up the property transferred or to pay its value as of the time it is considered in computing the augmented estate.

Laws 1985, c. 250, § 20. Amended by Laws 1986, c. 444.

For text of section effective January 1, 1996, applicable to the rights of successors of decedents dying on or after January 1, 1996, and to any wills of decedents dying on or after January 1, 1996, see § 524.2–207, post.

524.2–207. Surviving spouse's property and nonprobate transfers to others

Text of section effective January 1, 1996, applicable to the rights of successors of decedents dying on or after January 1, 1996, and to any wills of decedents dying on or after January 1, 1996.

(a) Included property. Except to the extent included in the augmented estate under section 524.2–204 or 524.2–206, the value of the augmented estate includes the value of:

(1) property, other than the homestead, that was owned by the surviving spouse at the decedent's death, including the surviving spouse's interest in property held with right of survivorship; and

365

(2) property that would have been included in the surviving spouse's nonprobate transfers to others, other than the spouse's interest in property held with right of survivorship included under clause (1), had the spouse been the decedent.

(b) Time of valuation. Property included under this section is valued at the decedent's death, taking the fact that the decedent predeceased the spouse into account, but, for purposes of the surviving spouse's interest in property held with right of survivorship included under paragraph (a), clause (1), the value of the spouse's interest is determined immediately before the decedent's death if the decedent was then a joint tenant or a co-owner of the property or accounts. For purposes of paragraph (a), clause (2), proceeds of insurance that would have been included in the spouse's nonprobate transfers to others under section 524.2–205, paragraph (1), clause (iii), are not valued as if the spouse were deceased.

(c) Reduction for enforceable claims. The value of property included under this section is reduced by mortgages, liens, and enforceable claims against the property or against the surviving spouse.

Laws 1994, c. 472, § 21.

For text of section effective for estates of decedents dying after December 31, 1986, but before January 1, 1996, see § 524.2–207, ante.

Historical and Statutory Notes

Derivation:

St.1992, § 524.2–202.

Laws 1987, c. 210, § 4.

Laws 1986, 1st Sp., c. 3, art. 3, § 2.

Laws 1986, c. 444.

Laws 1985, c. 250, § 15.

Laws 1985, c. 250, § 28, provides that § 15 (enacting § 524.2–202, the former subject matter of which is contained in §§ 524.2–203 to 524.2–207) is effective for estates of decedents dying after December 31, 1986. For law effective for estates of decedents dying before December 31, 1986, see § 525.13 et seq.

Continuing Effect. For continuing effect of law relating to wills or other instruments executed on or before December 31, 1986, see § 524.2–114 as quoted in the Historical and Statutory Notes under § 524.2–115.

Laws 1994, c. 472, § 65, provides:

"(a) This act takes effect on January 1, 1996.

"(b) Except as provided elsewhere in this act:

"(1) this act applies to the rights of successors of decedents dying on or after its effective date and to any wills of decedents dying on or after its effective date;

"(2) if, before the effective date of this act, a right is either acquired, extinguished, waived, or barred upon the expiration of a prescribed period of time which commenced to run by the provisions of any statute before the effective date, the provisions of this act neither revoke, revive, restore, nor remove the bar of such right; and

"(3) any rule of construction or presumption provided in this act applies to instruments executed and multiple party accounts opened before the effective date of this act unless there is a clear indication of contrary intent."

Former section: St.1992, § 524.2–207, which related to charging a spouse with gifts received and to the liability of others for the balance of an elective share, was repealed by Laws 1994, c. 472, § 64. See, now, M.S.A. §§ 524.2–209 and 524.2–210.

524.2–208. Exclusions, valuation, and overlapping application

Text of section effective January 1, 1996, applicable to the rights of successors of decedents dying on or after January 1, 1996, and to any wills of decedents dying on or after January 1, 1996.

(a) Exclusions. The value of any property is excluded from the decedent's nonprobate transfers to others (i) to the extent the decedent received adequate and full consideration in money or money's worth for a transfer of the property, or (ii) if the property was transferred with the written joinder of, or if the transfer was consented to in writing by, the surviving spouse.

(b) Protection of bona fide purchasers. A bona fide purchaser who purchases property from a successor or successors in interest of the decedent or from a transferee of the decedent is neither obligated under this part to return the payment, item of property, or benefit nor is liable under this part for the amount of the payment or the value of the item of property or benefit.

(c) Valuation. The value of property:

(1) included in the augmented estate under section 524.2–205, 524.2–206, or 524.2–207 is reduced in each category by mortgages, liens, and enforceable claims against the included property; and

(2) includes the commuted value of any present or future interest and the commuted value of amounts payable under any trust, life insurance settlement option, annuity contract, public or private pension, disability compensation, death benefit or retirement plan, or any similar arrangement, exclusive of the federal Social Security system. The commuted value of the surviving spouse's interest in a life estate or in any trust shall be calculated as if worth one-half of the total value of the property subject to the life estate, or of the trust estate, unless higher or lower values for these interests are established by proof.

(d) Overlapping application; no double inclusion. In case of overlapping application to the same property of portions of section 524.2–205, 524.2–206, or 524.2–207, the property is included in the augmented estate under the provision yielding the greatest value, and under only one overlapping provision if they all yield the same value.

Laws 1994, c. 472, § 22.

Historical and Statutory Notes

Laws 1994, c. 472, § 65, provides:

"(a) This act takes effect on January 1, 1996.

"(b) Except as provided elsewhere in this act:

"(1) this act applies to the rights of successors of decedents dying on or after its effective date and to any wills of decedents dying on or after its effective date;

"(2) if, before the effective date of this act, a right is either acquired, extinguished, waived, or barred upon the expiration of a prescribed period of time which commenced to run by the provisions of any statute before the effective date, the provisions of this act neither revoke, revive, restore, nor remove the bar of such right; and

"(3) any rule of construction or presumption provided in this act applies to instruments executed and multiple party accounts opened before the effective date of this act unless there is a clear indication of contrary intent."

524.2–209. Sources from which elective share payable

Text of section effective January 1, 1996, applicable to the rights of successors of decedents dying on or after January 1, 1996, and to any wills of decedents dying on or after January 1, 1996.

(a) Elective-share amount only. In a proceeding for an elective share, the following are applied first to satisfy the elective-share amount and to reduce or eliminate any contributions due from the decedent's probate estate and recipients of the decedent's nonprobate transfers to others:

(1) amounts included in the augmented estate under section 524.2–204 which pass or have passed to the surviving spouse by testate or intestate succession and amounts included in the augmented estate under section 524.2–206;

(2) amounts included in the augmented estate which would have passed to the spouse but were disclaimed; and

(3) amounts included in the augmented estate under section 524.2–207 up to the applicable percentage thereof. For the purposes of this paragraph, the "applicable percentage" is twice the elective-share percentage set forth in the schedule in section 524.2–202, paragraph (a), appropriate to the length of time the spouse and the decedent were married to each other.

(b) Unsatisfied balance of elective-share amount; supplemental elective-share amount. If, after the application of paragraph (a), the elective-share amount is not fully satisfied or the surviving spouse is entitled to a supplemental elective-share amount, amounts included in the decedent's probate estate and in the decedent's nonprobate transfers to others, other than amounts included under section 524.2–205, paragraph (3), clause (i) or (iii), are applied first to satisfy the unsatisfied balance of the elective-share amount or the supplemental elective-share amount. The decedent's probate estate and that portion of the decedent's nonprobate transfers to others are so applied that liability for the unsatisfied balance of the elective-share amount or for the supplemental elective-share amount is equitably apportioned among the recipients of the decedent's probate estate and of that portion of the decedent's nonprobate transfers to others in proportion to the value of their interests therein.

(c) Unsatisfied balance of elective-share and supplemental elective-share amounts. If, after the application of paragraphs (a) and (b), the elective-share or supplemental elective-share amount is not fully satisfied, the remaining portion of the decedent's nonprobate transfers to others is so applied that liability for the unsatisfied balance of the elective-share or supplemental elective-share amount is equitably apportioned among the recipients of the remaining portion of the decedent's nonprobate transfers to others in proportion to the value of their interests therein.

Laws 1994, c. 472, § 23.

Historical and Statutory Notes

Derivation:

St.1992, § 524.2–207.

Laws 1986, c. 444.

Laws 1985, c. 250, § 20.

Laws 1985, c. 250, § 28, provides that § 20 (enacting § 524.2–207, the former subject matter of which is contained in §§ 524.2–209 and 524.2–210) is effective for estates of decedents dying after December 31, 1986. For law effective for estates of decedents dying before December 31, 1986, see § 525.13 et seq.

Continuing Effect. For continuing effect of law relating to wills or other instruments executed on or before December 31, 1986, see § 524.2–114 as quoted in the Historical and Statutory Notes under § 524.2–115.

Laws 1994, c. 472, § 65, provides:

"(a) This act takes effect on January 1, 1996.

"(b) Except as provided elsewhere in this act:

"(1) this act applies to the rights of successors of decedents dying on or after its effective date and to any wills of decedents dying on or after its effective date;

"(2) if, before the effective date of this act, a right is either acquired, extinguished, waived, or barred upon the expiration of a prescribed period of time which commenced to run by the provisions of any statute before the effective date, the provisions of this act neither revoke, revive, restore, nor remove the bar of such right; and

"(3) any rule of construction or presumption provided in this act applies to instruments executed and multiple party accounts opened before the effective date of this act unless there is a clear indication of contrary intent."

524.2–210. Personal liability of recipients

Text of section effective January 1, 1996, applicable to the rights of successors of decedents dying on or after January 1, 1996, and to any wills of decedents dying on or after January 1, 1996.

(a) Only original recipients of the decedent's nonprobate transfers to others, and the donees of the recipients of the decedent's nonprobate transfers to others, to the extent the donees have the property or its proceeds, are liable to make a proportional contribution toward satisfaction of the surviving spouse's elective-share or supplemental elective-share amount. A person liable to make contribution may choose to give up the proportional part that has been received of the decedent's nonprobate transfers or to pay the value of the amount for which the person is liable.

(b) If any section or part of any section of this part is preempted by federal law with respect to a payment, an item of property, or any other benefit included in the decedent's nonprobate transfers to others, a person who is not a bona fide purchaser and who receives the payment, item of property, or any other benefit is obligated to return the payment, item of property, or benefit, or is personally liable for the amount of the payment or the value of that item of property or benefit, as provided in section 524.2–209, to the person who would have been entitled to it were that section or part of that section not preempted.

Laws 1994, c. 472, § 24. Amended by Laws 1995, c. 186, § 96.

Historical and Statutory Notes

Derivation:

St.1992, § 524.2–207.

Laws 1986, c. 444.

Laws 1985, c. 250, § 20.

Laws 1985, c. 250, § 28, provides that § 20 (enacting § 524.2–207, the former subject matter of which is contained in §§ 524.2–209 and 524.2–210) is effective for estates of decedents dying after December 31, 1986. For law effec-

tive for estates of decedents dying before December 31, 1986, see § 525.13 et seq.

Continuing Effect. For continuing effect of law relating to wills or other instruments executed on or before December 31, 1986, see § 524.2–114 as quoted in the Historical and Statutory Notes under § 524.2–115.

Laws 1994, c. 472, § 65, provides:

"(a) This act takes effect on January 1, 1996.

"(b) Except as provided elsewhere in this act:

"(1) this act applies to the rights of successors of decedents dying on or after its effective date and to any wills of decedents dying on or after its effective date;

"(2) if, before the effective date of this act, a right is either acquired, extinguished, waived, or barred upon the expiration of a prescribed period of time which commenced to run by the provisions of any statute before the effective date, the provisions of this act neither revoke, revive, restore, nor remove the bar of such right; and

"(3) any rule of construction or presumption provided in this act applies to instruments executed and multiple party accounts opened before the effective date of this act unless there is a clear indication of contrary intent."

524.2–211. Proceeding for elective share; time limit

Text of section effective January 1, 1996, applicable to the rights of successors of decedents dying on or after January 1, 1996, and to any wills of decedents dying on or after January 1, 1996.

(a) Except as provided in paragraph (b), the election must be made by filing in the court and mailing or delivering to the personal representative, if any, a petition for the elective share within nine months after the date of the decedent's death, or within six months after the probate of the decedent's will, whichever limitation later expires. The surviving spouse must give notice of the time and place set for hearing to persons interested in the estate and to the distributees and recipients of portions of the augmented estate whose interests will be adversely affected by the taking of the elective share. Except as provided in paragraph (b), the decedent's nonprobate transfers to others are not included within the augmented estate for the purpose of computing the elective share, if the petition is filed more than nine months after the decedent's death.

(b) Within nine months after a decedent's death, the surviving spouse may petition the court for an extension of time for making an election. If, within nine months after the decedent's death, the spouse gives notice of the petition to all persons interested in the decedent's nonprobate transfers to others, the court for cause shown by the surviving spouse may extend the time for election. If the court grants the spouse's petition for an extension, the decedent's nonprobate transfers to others are not excluded from the augmented estate for the purpose of computing the elective-share and supplemental elective-share amounts, if the spouse makes an election by filing in the court and mailing or delivering to the personal representative, if any, a petition for the elective share within the time allowed by the extension.

(c) The surviving spouse may withdraw a demand for an elective share at any time before entry of a final determination by the court.

(d) After notice and hearing, the court shall determine the elective-share and supplemental elective-share amounts, and shall order its payment from the assets of the augmented estate or by contribution as appears appropriate under sections 524.2–209 and 524.2–210. If it appears that a fund or property included in the augmented estate has not come into the possession of the personal representative, or has been distributed by the personal representative, the court nevertheless shall fix the liability of any person who has any interest in the fund or property or who has possession thereof, whether as trustee or otherwise. The proceeding may be maintained against fewer than all persons against whom relief could be sought, but no person is subject to contribution in any greater amount than would have been the case under sections 524.2–209 and 524.2–210 had relief been secured against all persons subject to contribution.

(e) An order of judgment of the court may be enforced as necessary in suit for contribution or payment in other courts of this state or other jurisdictions.

(f) Whether or not an election has been made under paragraph (a), the surviving spouse may elect statutory rights in the homestead by filing in the manner provided in this section a petition in which the spouse asserts the rights provided in section 524.2–402, provided that:

(1) when the homestead is subject to a testamentary disposition, the filing must be within nine months after the date of death, or within six months after the probate of the decedent's will, whichever limitation last expires; or

(2) where the homestead is subject to other disposition, the filing must be within nine months after the date of death.

The court may extend the time for election in the manner provided in paragraph (b).

Laws 1994, c. 472, § 25.

Historical and Statutory Notes

Derivation:

St.1992, § 524.2–205.

Laws 1986, 1st Sp., c. 3, art. 3, § 3.

Laws 1986, c. 444.

Laws 1985, c. 250, § 18.

Laws 1985, c. 250, § 28, provides that § 18 (enacting § 524.2–205, the former subject matter of which is contained in this section) is effective for estates of decedents dying after December 31, 1986. For law effective for estates of decedents dying before December 31, 1986, see § 525.13 et seq.

Continuing Effect. For continuing effect of law relating to wills or other instruments executed on or before December 31, 1986, see § 524.2–114 as quoted in the Historical and Statutory Notes under § 524.2–115.

Laws 1994, c. 472, § 65, provides:

"(a) This act takes effect on January 1, 1996.

"(b) Except as provided elsewhere in this act:

"(1) this act applies to the rights of successors of decedents dying on or after its effective date and to any wills of decedents dying on or after its effective date;

"(2) if, before the effective date of this act, a right is either acquired, extinguished, waived, or barred upon the expiration of a prescribed period of time which commenced to run by the provisions of any statute before the effective date, the provisions of this act neither revoke, revive, restore, nor remove the bar of such right; and

"(3) any rule of construction or presumption provided in this act applies to instruments executed and multiple party accounts opened before the effective date of this act unless there is a clear indication of contrary intent."

524.2–212. Right of election personal to surviving spouse

Text of section effective January 1, 1996, applicable to the rights of successors of decedents dying on or after January 1, 1996, and to any wills of decedents dying on or after January 1, 1996.

The right of election of the surviving spouse may be exercised only during the surviving spouse's lifetime. In the case of a protected person, the right of election may be exercised only by order of the court in which protective proceedings as to the protected person's property are pending, after finding (1) that exercise is necessary to provide adequate support for the protected person during the protected person's probable life expectancy and (2) that the election will be consistent with the best interests of the natural bounty of the protected person's affection.

Laws 1994, c. 472, § 26.

Historical and Statutory Notes

Derivation:

St.1992, § 524.2–203.

Laws 1986, c. 444.

Laws 1985, c. 250, § 16.

Laws 1985, c. 250, § 28, provides that § 16 (enacting § 524.2–203, the former subject matter of which is contained in this section) is effective for estates of decedents dying after December 31, 1986. For law effective for estates of decedents dying before December 31, 1986, see § 525.13 et seq.

Continuing Effect. For continuing effect of law relating to wills or other instruments executed on or before December 31, 1986, see § 524.2–114 as quoted in the Historical and Statutory Notes under § 524.2–115.

Laws 1994, c. 472, § 65, provides:

"(a) This act takes effect on January 1, 1996.

"(b) Except as provided elsewhere in this act:

"(1) this act applies to the rights of successors of decedents dying on or after its effective date and to any wills of decedents dying on or after its effective date;

"(2) if, before the effective date of this act, a right is either acquired, extinguished, waived, or barred upon the expiration of a prescribed period of time which commenced to run by the provisions of any statute before the effective date, the provisions of this act neither revoke, revive, restore, nor remove the bar of such right; and

"(3) any rule of construction or presumption provided in this act applies to instruments executed and multiple party accounts opened before the effective date of this act unless there is a clear indication of contrary intent."

524.2–213. Waiver of right to elect and of other rights

Text of section effective January 1, 1996, applicable to the rights of successors of decedents dying on or after January 1, 1996, and to any wills of decedents dying on or after January 1, 1996.

The right of election of a surviving spouse and the rights of the surviving spouse to the homestead, exempt property, and family allowance, or any of them, may be waived, wholly or partially, after marriage, by a written contract, agreement, or waiver signed by the party waiving after fair disclosure. Unless it provides to the contrary, a waiver of "all rights," or equivalent language, in the property or estate of a spouse is a waiver only of the right to the elective share. Any waiver prior to marriage must be made pursuant to section 519.11.

Laws 1994, c. 472, § 27.

Historical and Statutory Notes

Derivation:

St.1992, § 524.2–204.

Laws 1985, c. 250, § 17.

Laws 1985, c. 250, § 28, provides that § 17 (enacting § 524.2–207, the former subject matter of which is contained in this section) is effective for estates of decedents dying after December 31, 1986. For law effective for estates of decedents dying before December 31, 1986, see § 525.13 et seq.

Continuing Effect. For continuing effect of law relating to wills or other instruments executed on or before December 31, 1986, see § 524.2–114 as quoted in the Historical and Statutory Notes under § 524.2–115.

Laws 1994, c. 472, § 65, provides:

"(a) This act takes effect on January 1, 1996.

"(b) Except as provided elsewhere in this act:

"(1) this act applies to the rights of successors of decedents dying on or after its effective date and to any wills of decedents dying on or after its effective date;

"(2) if, before the effective date of this act, a right is either acquired, extinguished, waived, or barred upon the expiration of a prescribed period of time which commenced to run by the provisions of any statute before the effective date, the provisions of this act neither revoke, revive, restore, nor remove the bar of such right; and

"(3) any rule of construction or presumption provided in this act applies to instruments executed and multiple party accounts opened before the effective date of this act unless there is a clear indication of contrary intent."

524.2–214. Protection of payors and other third parties

Text of section effective January 1, 1996, applicable to the rights of successors of decedents dying on or after January 1, 1996, and to any wills of decedents dying on or after January 1, 1996.

(a) Although under section 524.2–205 a payment, item of property, or other benefit is included in the decedent's nonprobate transfers to others, a payor or other third party is not liable for having made a payment or transferred an item of property or other benefit to a beneficiary designated in a governing instrument, or for having taken any other action in good faith reliance on the validity of a governing instrument, upon request and satisfactory proof of the decedent's death, before the payor or other third party received written notice from the surviving spouse or spouse's representative of an intention to file a petition for the elective share or that a petition for the elective share has been filed. A payor or other third party is liable for payments made or other actions taken after the payor or other third party received written notice of an intention to file a petition for the elective share or that a petition for the elective share has been filed.

(b) A written notice of intention to file a petition for the elective share or that a petition for the elective share has been filed must be mailed to the payor's or other third party's main office or home by registered or certified mail, return receipt requested, or served upon the payor or other third party in the same manner as a summons in a civil action. Upon receipt of written notice of intention to file a petition for the elective share or that a petition for the elective share has been filed, a payor or other third party may pay any amount owed or transfer or deposit any item of property held by it to or with the court having jurisdiction of the probate proceedings relating to the decedent's estate or, if no proceedings have been commenced, to or with the court having jurisdiction of probate proceedings relating to decedents' estates located in the county of the decedent's residence. The court shall hold the funds or item of property and, upon its determination under section 524.2–211, paragraph (d), shall order disbursement in accordance with the determination. If no petition is filed in the court within the specified time under section 524.2–211, paragraph (a), or, if filed, the demand for an elective share is withdrawn under section 524.2–211, paragraph (c), the court shall order disbursement to the designated beneficiary. Payments or transfers to the court or deposits made into court discharge the payor or other third party from all claims for amounts so paid or the value of property so transferred or deposited.

(c) Upon petition to the court described in paragraph (b) by the beneficiary designated in the governing instrument, the court may order that all or part of the property be paid to the beneficiary in an amount and subject to conditions consistent with this part.

Laws 1994, c. 472, § 28.

Historical and Statutory Notes

Laws 1994, c. 472, § 65, provides:

"(a) This act takes effect on January 1, 1996.

"(b) Except as provided elsewhere in this act:

"(1) this act applies to the rights of successors of decedents dying on or after its effective date and to any wills of decedents dying on or after its effective date;

"(2) if, before the effective date of this act, a right is either acquired, extinguished, waived, or barred upon the expiration of a prescribed period of time which commenced to run by the provisions of any statute before the effective date, the provisions of this act neither revoke, revive, restore, nor remove the bar of such right; and

"(3) any rule of construction or presumption provided in this act applies to instruments executed and multiple party accounts opened before the effective date of this act unless there is a clear indication of contrary intent."

524.2–215. Surviving spouse receiving medical assistance

(a) Notwithstanding any law to the contrary, if a surviving spouse is receiving medical assistance under chapter 256B, or general assistance medical care under chapter 256D, when the person's spouse dies, then the provisions in paragraphs (b) to (f) apply.

(b) Any time before an order or decree is entered under section 524.3–1001 or 524.3–1002 or a closing statement is filed under section 524.3–1003 the surviving spouse may:

(1) exercise the right to take an elective share amount of the decedent's estate under section 524.2–211, in which case the decedent's nonprobate transfers to others shall be included in the augmented estate for purposes of computing the elective share and supplemental elective share amounts;

(2) petition the court for an extension of time for exercising the right to an elective share amount under section 524.2–211, in which case the decedent's nonprobate transfers to others shall be included in the augmented estate for purposes of computing the elective share and supplemental elective share amounts; or

(3) elect statutory rights in the homestead or petition the court for an extension of time to make the election as provided in section 524.2–211, paragraph (f).

(c) Notwithstanding any law or rule to the contrary, the personal representative of the estate of the surviving spouse may exercise the surviving spouse's right of election and statutory right to the homestead in the manner provided for making those elections or petition for an extension of time as provided for in this section.

(d) If choosing the elective share will result in the surviving spouse receiving a share of the decedent's estate greater in value than the share of the estate under the will or intestate succession, then the guardian or conservator for the surviving spouse shall exercise the surviving spouse's right to an elective share amount and a court order is not required.

(e) A party petitioning to establish a guardianship or conservatorship for the surviving spouse may file a certified copy of the petition in the decedent's estate proceedings and serve a copy of the petition on the personal representative or the personal representative's attorney. The filing of the petition shall toll all of the limitations provided in this section until the entry of a final order granting or denying the petition. The decedent's estate may not close until the entry of a final order granting or denying the petition.

(1) Distributees of the decedent's estate shall be personally liable to account for and turn over to the ward, the conservatee, or the estate of the ward or conservatee any and all amounts which the ward or conservatee is entitled to receive from the decedent's estate.

(2) No distributee shall be liable for an amount in excess of the value of the distributee's distribution as of the time of the distribution.

(3) The ward, conservatee, guardian, conservator, or personal representative may bring proceedings in district court to enforce the rights in this section.

(f) Notwithstanding any oral or written contract, agreement, or waiver made by the surviving spouse to waive in whole or in part the surviving spouse's right of election against the decedent's will, statutory right to the homestead, exempt property, or family allowance, the surviving spouse or the surviving spouse's guardian or conservator may exercise these rights to the full extent permitted by law. The surviving spouse's rights under this paragraph do not apply to the extent there is a valid antenuptial agreement between the surviving spouse and the decedent under which the surviving spouse has waived some or all of these rights.

Laws 2000, c. 400, § 5.

PART 3

SPOUSE AND CHILDREN UNPROVIDED FOR IN WILLS

524.2–301. Omitted spouse

Text of section effective for estates of decedents dying after December 31, 1986, but before January 1, 1996.

375

(a) If a testator fails to provide by will for a surviving spouse who married the testator after the execution of the will, the omitted spouse shall receive the same share of the estate as if the decedent left no will unless it appears from the will that the omission was intentional or the testator provided for the spouse by transfer outside the will and the intent that the transfer be in lieu of a testamentary provision is shown by statements of the testator or from the amount of the transfer or other evidence.

(b) In satisfying a share provided by this section, the devises made by the will abate as provided in section 524.3–902.

Laws 1985, c. 250, § 21.   Amended by Laws 1986, c. 444.

> *For text of section effective January 1, 1996, applicable to the rights of successors of decedents dying on or after January 1, 1996, and to any wills of decedents dying on or after January 1, 1996, see § 524.2–301, post.*

524.2–301.   Entitlement of spouse;   premarital will

(a) If a testator married after making a will and the spouse survives the testator, the surviving spouse shall receivea share of the estate of the testator equal in value to that which the surviving spouse would have received if the testator had died intestate, unless:

(1) provision has been made for, or waived by, the spouse by prenuptial or postnuptial agreement;

(2) the will discloses an intention not to make provision for the spouse;   or

(3) the spouse is provided for in the will.

(b) In satisfying the share provided by this section, devises made by the will other than a devise to a child of the testator who was born before the testator married the surviving spouse and who is not a child of the surviving spouse or a devise or substitute gift under section 524.2–603 or 524.2–604 to a descendant of such a child, abate first as otherwise provided in section 524.3–902.

Laws 1985, c. 250, § 21.   Amended by Laws 1986, c. 444;   Laws 1994, c. 472, § 29; Laws 2002, c. 379, art. 1, § 101;   Laws 2008, c. 341, art. 4, § 1, eff. Aug. 1, 2008.

Historical and Statutory Notes

Laws 1985, c. 250, § 28, provides that this section is effective for estates of decedents dying after December 31, 1986.   For law effective for estates of decedents dying before December 31, 1986, see § 525.13 et seq.

Continuing Effect.   For continuing effect of law relating to wills or other instruments executed on or before December 31, 1986, see § 524.2–114 as quoted in the Historical and Statutory Notes under § 524.2–115.

Laws 1994, c. 472, § 65, provides:

"(a) This act takes effect on January 1, 1996.

"(b) Except as provided elsewhere in this act:

"(1) this act applies to the rights of successors of decedents dying on or after its effective date and to any wills of decedents dying on or after its effective date;

"(2) if, before the effective date of this act, a right is either acquired, extinguished, waived, or barred upon the expiration of a prescribed period of time which commenced to run by the provisions of any statute before the effective date, the provisions of this act neither revoke, revive, restore, nor remove the bar of such right; and

"(3) any rule of construction or presumption provided in this act applies to instruments executed and multiple party accounts opened before the effective date of this act unless there is a clear indication of contrary intent."

524.2–302. Pretermitted children

Text of section effective for estates of decedents dying after December 31, 1986, but before January 1, 1996.

(a) If a testator fails to provide for any child born or adopted after the execution of the testator's will, the omitted child receives a share in the estate equal in value to that which that child would have received if the testator had died intestate unless:

(1) it appears from the will that the omission was intentional;

(2) when the will was executed the testator had one or more children and devised substantially all the estate to the other parent of the omitted child; or

(3) the testator provided for the child by transfer outside the will and the intent that the transfer be in lieu of a testamentary provision is shown by statements of the testator or from the amount of the transfer or other evidence.

(b) If at the time of execution of the will the testator fails to provide for a living child solely because of a belief that the child is dead, the child receives a share in the estate equal in value to that which that child would have received if the testator had died intestate.

(c) In satisfying a share provided by this section, the devises made by the will abate as provided in section 524.3–902.

Laws 1985, c. 250, § 22. Amended by Laws 1986, c. 444.

For text of section effective January 1, 1996, applicable to the rights of successors of decedents dying on or after January 1, 1996, and to any wills of decedents dying on or after January 1, 1996, see § 524.2–302, post.

524.2–302. Omitted children

Text of section effective January 1, 1996, applicable to the rights of successors of decedents dying on or after January 1, 1996, and to any wills of decedents dying on or after January 1, 1996.

(a) Except as provided in paragraph (b), if a testator's will fails to provide for any of the testator's children born or adopted after the execution of the will, the omitted after-born or after-adopted child receives a share in the estate as follows:

(1) If the testator had no child living when the will was executed, an omitted after-born or after-adopted child receives a share in the estate equal in value to that which the child would have received had the testator died intestate, unless

the will devised all or substantially all the estate to the other parent of the omitted child and that other parent survives the testator and is entitled to take under the will.

(2) If the testator had one or more children living when the will was executed, and the will devised property or an interest in property to one or more of the then-living children, an omitted after-born or after-adopted child is entitled to share in the testator's estate as follows:

(i) The portion of the testator's estate in which the omitted after-born or after-adopted child is entitled to share is limited to devises made to the testator's then-living children under the will.

(ii) The omitted after-born or after-adopted child is entitled to receive the share of the testator's estate, as limited in subclause (i), that the child would have received had the testator included all omitted after-born and after-adopted children with the children to whom devises were made under the will and had given an equal share of the estate to each child.

(iii) To the extent feasible, the interest granted an omitted after-born or after-adopted child under this section must be of the same character, whether equitable or legal, present or future, as that devised to the testator's then-living children under the will.

(iv) In satisfying a share provided by this paragraph, devises to the testator's children who were living when the will was executed abate ratably. In abating the devises of the then-living children, the court shall preserve to the maximum extent possible the character of the testamentary plan adopted by the testator.

(b) Neither paragraph (a), clause (1) or (2), nor paragraph (c), applies if:

(1) it appears from the will that the omission was intentional; or

(2) the testator provided for the omitted after-born or after-adopted child by transfer outside the will and the intent that the transfer be in lieu of a testamentary provision is shown by the testator's statements or is reasonably inferred from the amount of the transfer or other evidence.

(c) If at the time of execution of the will the testator fails to provide in the will for a living child solely because the testator believes the child to be dead, the child receives a share in the estate equal in value to that which the child would have received had the testator died intestate, unless the will devised all or substantially all of the estate to the other parent of the child the testator believes to be dead and the other parent survives the testator and is entitled to take under the will.

(d) If a deceased omitted child would have been entitled to a share under this section if the omitted child had not predeceased the testator and the deceased omitted child leaves issue who survive the testator, the issue who represent the deceased omitted child are entitled to take the deceased omitted child's share.

(e) In satisfying a share provided by paragraph (a), clause (1), or (c), devises made by the will abate under section 524.3–902.

Laws 1985, c. 250, § 22. Amended by Laws 1986, c. 444; Laws 1994, c. 472, § 30; Laws 2005, c. 26, § 6.

For text of section effective for estates of decedents dying after December 31, 1986, but before January 1, 1996, see § 524.2–302, ante.

Historical and Statutory Notes

Laws 1985, c. 250, § 28, provides that this section is effective for estates of decedents dying after December 31, 1986. For law effective for estates of decedents dying before December 31, 1986, see § 525.13 et seq.

Continuing Effect. For continuing effect of law relating to wills or other instruments executed on or before December 31, 1986, see § 524.2–114 as quoted in the Historical and Statutory Notes under § 524.2–115.

Laws 1994, c. 472, § 65, provides:

"(a) This act takes effect on January 1, 1996.

"(b) Except as provided elsewhere in this act:

"(1) this act applies to the rights of successors of decedents dying on or after its effective date and to any wills of decedents dying on or after its effective date;

"(2) if, before the effective date of this act, a right is either acquired, extinguished, waived, or barred upon the expiration of a prescribed period of time which commenced to run by the provisions of any statute before the effective date, the provisions of this act neither revoke, revive, restore, nor remove the bar of such right; and

"(3) any rule of construction or presumption provided in this act applies to instruments executed and multiple party accounts opened before the effective date of this act unless there is a clear indication of contrary intent."

PART 4

EXEMPT PROPERTY AND ALLOWANCES

524.2–401. Applicable law

Text of section effective January 1, 1996, applicable to the rights of successors of decedents dying on or after January 1, 1996, and to any wills of decedents dying on or after January 1, 1996.

This part applies to the estate of a decedent who dies domiciled in this state. Rights to homestead, exempt property, and family allowance for a decedent who dies not domiciled in this state are governed by the law of the decedent's domicile at death.

Laws 1994, c. 472, § 31.

Historical and Statutory Notes

Laws 1994, c. 472, § 65, provides:

"(a) This act takes effect on January 1, 1996.

"(b) Except as provided elsewhere in this act:

"(1) this act applies to the rights of successors of decedents dying on or after its effective date and to any wills of decedents dying on or after its effective date;

"(2) if, before the effective date of this act, a right is either acquired, extinguished, waived, or barred upon the expiration of a prescribed period of time which commenced to run by the provisions of any statute before the effective date, the provisions of this act neither revoke, revive, restore, nor remove the bar of such right; and

"(3) any rule of construction or presumption provided in this act applies to instruments executed and multiple party accounts opened be- fore the effective date of this act unless there is a clear indication of contrary intent."

524.2-402. Descent of homestead

(a) If there is a surviving spouse, the homestead, including a manufactured home which is the family residence, descends free from any testamentary or other disposition of it to which the spouse has not consented in writing or as provided by law, as follows:

(1) if there is no surviving descendant of decedent, to the spouse; or

(2) if there are surviving descendants of decedent, then to the spouse for the term of the spouse's natural life and the remainder in equal shares to the decedent's descendants by representation.

(b) If there is no surviving spouse and the homestead has not been disposed of by will it descends as other real estate.

(c) If the homestead passes by descent or will to the spouse or decedent's descendants or to a trustee of a trust of which the spouse or the decedent's descendants are the sole current beneficiaries, it is exempt from all debts which were not valid charges on it at the time of decedent's death except that the homestead is subject to a claim filed pursuant to section 246.53 for state hospital care or 256B.15 for medical assistance benefits. If the homestead passes to a person other than a spouse or decedent's descendants or to a trustee of a trust of which the spouse or the decedent's descendants are the sole current beneficiaries, it is subject to the payment of expenses of administration, funeral expenses, expenses of last illness, taxes, and debts. The claimant may seek to enforce a lien or other charge against a homestead so exempted by an appropriate action in the district court.

(d) For purposes of this section, except as provided in section 524.2-301, the surviving spouse is deemed to consent to any testamentary or other disposition of the homestead to which the spouse has not previously consented in writing unless the spouse files in the manner provided in section 524.2-211, paragraph (f), a petition that asserts the homestead rights provided to the spouse by this section.

Laws 1994, c. 472, § 32. Amended by Laws 1997, c. 7, art. 1, § 165; Laws 1997, c. 9, § 6; Laws 2008, c. 341, art. 4, § 2, eff. Aug. 1, 2008.

Historical and Statutory Notes

Derivation:
   St.1994, § 525.145.
   Laws 1986, 1st Sp., c. 3, art. 3, § 4.
   Laws 1985, c. 250, § 25.
   Laws 1982, c. 641, art. 1, § 20.
   Laws 1982, c. 621, § 3.
   Laws 1981, c. 365, § 9.
   Laws 1981, c. 105, § 1.

Laws 1943, c. 329, § 1.
St.Supp.1940, § 8992-27.
Laws 1937, c. 435, § 7.
Laws 1935, c. 72, § 27.
St.1927, § 8719.
Gen.St.1923, § 8719.
Gen.St.1913, § 7237.
Rev.Laws 1905, § 3647.

Gen.St.1894, § 4470.

Laws 1889, c. 46, § 63.

Gen.St.Supp. 1878–88, c. 47, § 2.

Laws 1887, c. 52.

Laws 1883, c. 58, § 1.

Gen.St.1878, c. 46, § 2.

Laws 1876, c. 37, § 1.

Laws 1994, c. 472, § 65, provides:

"(a) This act takes effect on January 1, 1996.

"(b) Except as provided elsewhere in this act:

"(1) this act applies to the rights of successors of decedents dying on or after its effective date and to any wills of decedents dying on or after its effective date;

"(2) if, before the effective date of this act, a right is either acquired, extinguished, waived, or barred upon the expiration of a prescribed period of time which commenced to run by the provisions of any statute before the effective date, the provisions of this act neither revoke, revive, restore, nor remove the bar of such right; and

"(3) any rule of construction or presumption provided in this act applies to instruments executed and multiple party accounts opened before the effective date of this act unless there is a clear indication of contrary intent."

524.2–403. Exempt property

Text of section effective January 1, 1996, applicable to the rights of successors of decedents dying on or after January 1, 1996, and to any wills of decedents dying on or after January 1, 1996.

(a) If there is a surviving spouse, then, in addition to the homestead and family allowance, the surviving spouse is entitled from the estate to:

(1) property not exceeding $10,000 in value in excess of any security interests therein, in household furniture, furnishings, appliances, and personal effects, subject to an award of sentimental value property under section 525.152; and

(2) one automobile, if any, without regard to value.

(b) If there is no surviving spouse, the decedent's children are entitled jointly to the same property as provided in paragraph (a), except that where it appears from the decedent's will a child was omitted intentionally, the child is not entitled to the rights conferred by this section.

(c) If encumbered chattels are selected and the value in excess of security interests, plus that of other exempt property, is less than $10,000, or if there is not $10,000 worth of exempt property in the estate, the surviving spouse or children are entitled to other personal property of the estate, if any, to the extent necessary to make up the $10,000 value.

(d) Rights to exempt property and assets needed to make up a deficiency of exempt property have priority over all claims against the estate, but the right to any assets to make up a deficiency of exempt property abates as necessary to permit earlier payment of the family allowance.

(e) The rights granted by this section are in addition to any benefit or share passing to the surviving spouse or children by the decedent's will, unless otherwise provided, by intestate succession or by way of elective share.

(f) No rights granted to a decedent's adult children under this section shall have precedence over a claim under section 246.53, 256B.15, 256D.16, 261.04, or 524.3–805, paragraph (a), clause (1), (2), or (3).

Laws 1994, c. 472, § 33. Amended by Laws 1996, c. 338, art. 2, § 2; Laws 1996, c. 451, art. 2, § 54; Laws 1997, c. 9, § 7; Laws 1998, c. 262, § 9.

Historical and Statutory Notes

Derivation:

St.1994, § 525.15.

Laws 1988, c. 417, § 1.

Laws 1981, c. 103, § 1.

Laws 1975, c. 347, § 91.

Laws 1955, c. 189, § 1.

Laws 1947, c. 45, § 1.

St.Supp.1940, § 8992–28.

Laws 1935, c. 72, § 28.

St.1927, § 8726.

Gen.St.1923, § 8726.

Laws 1923, c. 347, § 1.

Laws 1921, c. 173, § 1.

Laws 1915, c. 350, § 1.

Laws 1915, c. 331, § 1.

Gen.St.1913, § 7243.

Rev.Laws 1905, § 3653.

Laws 1903, c. 334.

Laws 1899, c. 149.

Gen.St.1894, § 4477.

Laws 1893, c. 116, § 6.

Laws 1889, c. 46, § 70.

Gen.St.1878, c. 53, § 2.

Gen.St.1878, c. 51, § 1.

Gen.St.1878, c. 47, § 26.

Gen.St.1866, c. 53, § 2.

Gen.St.1866, c. 51, § 1.

Gen.St.1866, c. 47, § 26.

Pub.St.1858, c. 42, § 1.

Rev.St. (Terr.), c. 55, § 1.

Laws 1994, c. 472, § 65, provides:

"(a) This act takes effect on January 1, 1996.

"(b) Except as provided elsewhere in this act:

"(1) this act applies to the rights of successors of decedents dying on or after its effective date and to any wills of decedents dying on or after its effective date;

"(2) if, before the effective date of this act, a right is either acquired, extinguished, waived, or barred upon the expiration of a prescribed period of time which commenced to run by the provisions of any statute before the effective date, the provisions of this act neither revoke, revive, restore, nor remove the bar of such right; and

"(3) any rule of construction or presumption provided in this act applies to instruments executed and multiple party accounts opened before the effective date of this act unless there is a clear indication of contrary intent."

Laws 1996, c. 451, art. 2, § 62, par. (c), provides in part that § 54 (amending this section) applies to estates of decedents dying on or after its effective date.

Laws 1998, c. 262, § 13, as amended by Laws 1998, c. 408, § 2, provides that the amendment of this section by Laws 1998, c. 262, § 9, is effective August 1, 1998, and applies to the estate of a person dying on or after that date.

Laws 1998, c. 408, § 27, provides that, unless provided otherwise, each section of this act takes effect at the time the provision being corrected takes effect.

524.2–404. Family allowance

Text of section effective January 1, 1996, applicable to the rights of successors of decedents dying on or after January 1, 1996, and to any wills of decedents dying on or after January 1, 1996.

(a) In addition to the right to the homestead and exempt property, the decedent's surviving spouse and minor children whom the decedent was obligated to support, and children who were in fact being supported by the decedent, shall be allowed a reasonable family allowance in money out of the estate for their maintenance as follows:

(1) for one year if the estate is inadequate to discharge allowed claims; or

(2) for 18 months if the estate is adequate to discharge allowed claims.

(b) The amount of the family allowance may be determined by the personal representative in an amount not to exceed $1,500 per month.

(c) The family allowance is payable to the surviving spouse, if living; otherwise to the children, their guardian or conservator, or persons having their care and custody.

(d) The family allowance is exempt from and has priority over all claims.

(e) The family allowance is not chargeable against any benefit or share passing to the surviving spouse or children by the will of the decedent unless otherwise provided, by intestate succession or by way of elective share. The death of any person entitled to family allowance does not terminate the right of that person to the allowance.

(f) The personal representative or an interested person aggrieved by any determination, payment, proposed payment, or failure to act under this section may petition the court for appropriate relief, which may include a family allowance other than that which the personal representative determined or could have determined.

Laws 1994, c. 472, § 34.

Historical and Statutory Notes

Derivation:

St.1994, §§ 525.15, 525.151.
Laws 1989, c. 219, § 1.
Laws 1988, c. 417, §§ 1, 2.
Laws 1986, c. 444.
Laws 1981, c. 103, § 1.
Laws 1975, c. 347, §§ 91, 92.
Laws 1955, c. 189, § 1.
Laws 1947, c. 45, § 1.
St.Supp.1940, § 8992–28.
Laws 1935, c. 72, § 28.
St.1927, § 8726.
Gen.St.1923, § 8726.
Laws 1923, c. 347, § 1.
Laws 1921, c. 173, § 1.
Laws 1915, c. 350, § 1.
Laws 1915, c. 331, § 1.
Gen.St.1913, § 7243.
Rev.Laws 1905, § 3653.
Laws 1903, c. 334.
Laws 1899, c. 149.
Gen.St.1894, § 4477.
Laws 1893, c. 116, § 6.
Laws 1889, c. 46, § 70.
Gen.St.1878, c. 53, § 2.

Gen.St.1878, c. 51, § 1.
Gen.St.1878, c. 47, § 26.
Gen.St.1866, c. 53, § 2.
Gen.St.1866, c. 51, § 1.
Gen.St.1866, c. 47, § 26.
Pub.St.1858, c. 42, § 1.
Rev.St. (Terr.), c. 55, § 1.

Laws 1994, c. 472, § 65, provides:

"(a) This act takes effect on January 1, 1996.

"(b) Except as provided elsewhere in this act:

"(1) this act applies to the rights of successors of decedents dying on or after its effective date and to any wills of decedents dying on or after its effective date;

"(2) if, before the effective date of this act, a right is either acquired, extinguished, waived, or barred upon the expiration of a prescribed period of time which commenced to run by the provisions of any statute before the effective date, the provisions of this act neither revoke, revive, restore, nor remove the bar of such right; and

"(3) any rule of construction or presumption provided in this act applies to instruments executed and multiple party accounts opened before the effective date of this act unless there is a clear indication of contrary intent."

524.2–405. Source, determination, and documentation

Text of section effective January 1, 1996, applicable to the rights of successors of decedents dying on or after January 1, 1996, and to any wills of decedents dying on or after January 1, 1996.

383

(a) If the estate is otherwise sufficient, property specifically devised may not be used to satisfy rights to exempt property. Subject to this restriction, the surviving spouse, guardians or conservators of minor children, or children who are adults may select property of the estate as exempt property. The personal representative may make those selections if the surviving spouse, the children, or the guardians of the minor children are unable or fail to do so within a reasonable time or there is no guardian of a minor child.

(b) The personal representative may execute an instrument or deed of distribution to establish the ownership of property taken as exempt property.

(c) The personal representative or an interested person aggrieved by any selection, determination, payment, proposed payment, or failure to act under this section may petition the court for appropriate relief, which may include a selection or determination under this section other than that which the surviving spouse, guardians or conservators of minor children, children who are adults, or the personal representative selected, could have selected, determined, or could have determined.

Laws 1994, c. 472, § 35.

Historical and Statutory Notes

Laws 1994, c. 472, § 65, provides:

"(a) This act takes effect on January 1, 1996.

"(b) Except as provided elsewhere in this act:

"(1) this act applies to the rights of successors of decedents dying on or after its effective date and to any wills of decedents dying on or after its effective date;

"(2) if, before the effective date of this act, a right is either acquired, extinguished, waived, or barred upon the expiration of a prescribed period of time which commenced to run by the provisions of any statute before the effective date, the provisions of this act neither revoke, revive, restore, nor remove the bar of such right; and

"(3) any rule of construction or presumption provided in this act applies to instruments executed and multiple party accounts opened before the effective date of this act unless there is a clear indication of contrary intent."

PART 5

WILLS

524.2–501. Who may make a will

Any person 18 or more years of age who is of sound mind may make a will.

Laws 1975, c. 347, § 22, eff. Jan. 1, 1976.

Minnesota Rules of Evidence

Self-authentication of documents, see Rule 902.

524.2–502. Execution

Text of section effective until January 1, 1996.

Except as provided for writings within section 524.2–513 and wills within section 524.2–506, every will shall be in writing signed by the testator or in the testator's name by some other person in the testator's presence and by the testator's direction, and shall be signed by at least two persons each of whom witnessed either the signing or the testator's acknowledgment of the signature or of the will.

Laws 1975, c. 347, § 22, eff. Jan. 1, 1976. Amended by Laws 1986, c. 444.

For text of section effective January 1, 1996, applicable to the rights of successors of decedents dying on or after January 1, 1996, and to any wills of decedents dying on or after January 1, 1996, see § 524.2–502, post.

524.2–502. Execution; witnessed wills

Text of section effective January 1, 1996, applicable to the rights of successors of decedents dying on or after January 1, 1996, and to any wills of decedents dying on or after January 1, 1996.

Except as provided in sections 524.2–506 and 524.2–513, a will must be:

(1) in writing;

(2) signed by the testator or in the testator's name by some other individual in the testator's conscious presence and by the testator's direction or signed by the testator's conservator pursuant to a court order under section 524.5–411; and

(3) signed by at least two individuals, each of whom signed within a reasonable time after witnessing either the signing of the will as described in clause (2) or the testator's acknowledgment of that signature or acknowledgment of the will.

Laws 1975, c. 347, § 22, eff. Jan. 1, 1976. Amended by Laws 1986, c. 444; Laws 1994, c. 472, § 36; Laws 2003, c. 12, art. 2, § 6.

For text of section effective until January 1, 1996, see § 524.2–502, ante.

Minnesota Rules of Evidence

Self-authentication of documents, see Rule 902.

Historical and Statutory Notes

Laws 2003, c. 12, art. 2, § 9, provided:

"(a) Articles 1 and 2 apply to each guardianship or conservatorship proceeding and each appointment of guardian or conservator commenced on or after the effective date of articles 1 and 2. Except as otherwise provided in this section, articles 1 and 2 apply to each guardianship or conservatorship approved by the court prior to the effective date of articles 1 and 2, and to any guardianship or conservatorship proceeding pending in court on the effective date of articles 1 and 2, unless the court finds for good cause or in the interests of judicial economy that the proceeding should be completed under the provisions of Minnesota Statutes, chapter 525, as it existed prior to the effective date of articles 1 and 2.

"(b) A guardian or conservator who is not discharged prior to the effective date of articles 1 and 2 shall continue to hold the appointment but shall have only the powers specified in the order of appointment and in Minnesota Statutes, chapter 525, as it existed prior to the effective date of articles 1 and 2. Each guardian or conservator holding an appointment on the effective date of articles 1 and 2 shall continue to be bound by the duties imposed by the order of appointment; by Minnesota Statutes, chapter 525, as it existed prior to the effective date of articles 1 and 2; and by article 1, section 50; and shall be bound by any additional duties imposed by articles 1 and 2 starting on the first day of the next month starting after the effective date of articles 1 and 2 or on the next anniversary date of the appointment, whichever occurs later.

"(c) Any act done prior to the effective date of articles 1 and 2 in any proceeding and any right accrued under Minnesota Statutes, chapter 525, prior to the effective date of articles 1 and 2 shall not be impaired by articles 1 and 2. If a right is acquired, extinguished, or barred upon the expiration of a prescribed period of time which has commenced to run in accordance with the provisions of any statute before the effective date of articles 1 and 2, the provisions of the prior statute shall remain in force with respect to that right notwithstanding the statute's amendment or repeal by articles 1 and 2.

"(d) An order of the court or letters of guardianship or conservatorship issued by the court prior to the effective date of articles 1 and 2 shall remain in full force and effect in accordance with its terms and conditions and in accordance with the provisions of prior law until the court modifies the order or letters in accordance with the provisions of articles 1 and 2. Upon request for a certified copy of an order or letters which remains in full force and effect under this paragraph, the court administrator shall certify that the order or letters remains in full force and effect pursuant to this paragraph.

"(e) The court, without hearing or notice to any person, may issue new letters of guardianship or conservatorship under articles 1 and 2 to replace similar letters issued prior to the effective date of articles 1 and 2. The new letters shall be effective under articles 1 and 2 with the same force and effect as the prior

letters and shall remain in full force and effect until modified by the court in accordance with the provisions of articles 1 and 2.

"(f) A power of attorney executed in accordance with Minnesota Statutes, section 524.5–505, prior to the effective date of articles 1 and 2, or any surety bond, deed, or other instrument, report, or other undertaking executed in accordance with Minnesota Statutes, chapter 525, prior to the effective date of articles 1 and 2, shall remain in full force and effect for all purposes in accordance with its terms and conditions and the provisions of the applicable statutes under which the power of attorney, surety bond, deed, or other instrument, report, or other undertaking was executed, until the power of attorney, surety bond, deed, or other instrument, report, or other undertaking expires according to its terms or pursuant to the statutes governing its execution, or is modified, terminated, or superseded by a new power of attorney, surety bond, deed, or other instrument, report, or other undertaking executed in accordance with the provisions of articles 1 and 2."

Laws 1994, c. 472, § 65, provides:

"(a) This act takes effect on January 1, 1996.

"(b) Except as provided elsewhere in this act:

"(1) this act applies to the rights of successors of decedents dying on or after its effective date and to any wills of decedents dying on or after its effective date;

"(2) if, before the effective date of this act, a right is either acquired, extinguished, waived, or barred upon the expiration of a prescribed period of time which commenced to run by the provisions of any statute before the effective date, the provisions of this act neither revoke, revive, restore, nor remove the bar of such right; and

"(3) any rule of construction or presumption provided in this act applies to instruments executed and multiple party accounts opened before the effective date of this act unless there is a clear indication of contrary intent."

524.2–504. Self-proved will

Text of section effective until January 1, 1996.

An attested will may at the time of its execution or at any subsequent date be made self-proved, by the acknowledgment thereof by the testator and the affidavits of the witnesses, each made before an officer authorized to administer oaths under the laws of this state, or under the laws of the state where execution occurs, and evidenced by the officer's certificate, under official seal, attached or annexed to the will in form and content substantially as follows:

THE STATE OF . . . .

COUNTY OF . . . .

We, ..., ..., and . . . ., the testator and the witnesses, respectively, whose names are signed to the attached or foregoing instrument, being first duly sworn, do hereby declare to the undersigned authority that the testator signed and executed the instrument as the testator's last will, that the testator signed it willingly or directed another to sign it for the testator, that it was executed as a free and voluntary act for the purposes therein expressed, and that each of the witnesses, in the presence and hearing of the testator, signed the will as witnesses, and that to the best of their knowledge the testator was at the time 18 or more years of age, of sound mind and under no constraint or undue influence.

. . . .

Testator

. . . .

Witness

. . . .

Witness

Subscribed, sworn to and acknowledged before me by . . . ., the testator, and subscribed and sworn to before me by . . . . and . . . ., witnesses, this . . . . . . day of . . . ., . . .

(SEAL) (Signed) . . . .

. . . .

(Official capacity of officer)

Laws 1975, c. 347, § 22, eff. Jan. 1, 1976. Amended by Laws 1979, c. 240, § 1; Laws 1986, c. 444.

For text of section effective January 1, 1996, applicable to the rights of successors of decedents dying on or after January 1, 1996, and to any wills of decedents dying on or after January 1, 1996, see § 524.2–504, post.

524.2–504. Self-proved will

Text of section effective January 1, 1996, applicable to the rights of successors of decedents dying on or after January 1, 1996, and to any wills of decedents dying on or after January 1, 1996.

(a) A will may be contemporaneously executed, attested, and made self-proved, by acknowledgment thereof by the testator and affidavits of the witnesses, each made before an officer authorized to administer oaths under the laws of the state in which execution occurs and evidenced by the officer's certificate, under official seal, in substantially the following form:

I, ..., the testator, sign my name to this instrument this ... day of ...., and being first duly sworn, do hereby declare to the undersigned authority that I sign and execute this instrument as my will and that I sign it willingly (or willingly direct another to sign for me), that I execute it as my free and voluntary act for the purposes therein expressed, and that I am 18 years of age or older, of sound mind, and under no constraint or undue influence.

_____
                                                                Testator

We, ..., ..., the witnesses, sign our names to this instrument, being first duly sworn, and do hereby declare to the undersigned authority that the testator signs and executes this instrument as the testator's will and that the testator signs it willingly (or willingly directs another to sign for the testator), and that each of us, in the presence and hearing of the testator, hereby signs this will as witness to the testator's signing, and that to the best of our knowledge the testator is 18 years of age or older, of sound mind, and under no constraint or undue influence.

_____
                                                                Witness
_____
                                                                Witness

State of ....

County of ....

Subscribed, sworn to, and acknowledged before me by ...., the testator, and subscribed and sworn to before me by ...., and ...., witnesses, this ... day of ...., ...

(Seal)

(Signed)_____

_____
(Official capacity of officer)

(b) An attested will may be made self-proved at any time after its execution by the acknowledgment thereof by the testator and the affidavits of the witnesses, each made before an officer authorized to administer oaths under the laws of the state in which the acknowledgment occurs and evidenced by the officer's certificate, under the official seal, attached or annexed to the will in substantially the following form:

State of ....

County of ....

We, ..., ..., and ...., the testator and the witnesses, respectively, whose names are signed to the attached or foregoing instrument, being first duly sworn, do hereby declare to the undersigned authority that the testator signed and executed the instrument as the testator's will and that the testator had signed willingly (or willingly directed another to sign for the testator), and that the testator executed it as the testator's free and voluntary act for the purposes therein expressed, and each of the witnesses, in the presence and hearing of the testator, signed the will as witness and that to the best of the witness' knowledge the testator was at the time 18 years of age or older, of sound mind, and under no constraint or undue influence.

_____
Testator

_____
Witness

_____
Witness

Subscribed, sworn to, and acknowledged before me by ...., the testator, and subscribed and sworn to before me by ...., and ...., witnesses, this ... day of ...., ...

(Seal)

(Signed)_____

(Official capacity of officer)

(c) A signature affixed to a self-proving affidavit attached to a will is considered a signature affixed to the will, if necessary to prove the will's due execution.

Laws 1975, c. 347, § 22, eff. Jan. 1, 1976. Amended by Laws 1979, c. 240, § 1; Laws 1986, c. 444; Laws 1994, c. 472, § 37.

For text of section effective until January 1, 1996, see § 524.2–504, ante.

Historical and Statutory Notes

Laws 1994, c. 472, § 65, provides:

"(a) This act takes effect on January 1, 1996.

"(b) Except as provided elsewhere in this act:

"(1) this act applies to the rights of successors of decedents dying on or after its effective date and to any wills of decedents dying on or after its effective date;

"(2) if, before the effective date of this act, a right is either acquired, extinguished, waived, or barred upon the expiration of a prescribed period of time which commenced to run by the provisions of any statute before the effective date, the provisions of this act neither revoke, revive, restore, nor remove the bar of such right; and

"(3) any rule of construction or presumption provided in this act applies to instruments executed and multiple party accounts opened before the effective date of this act unless there is a clear indication of contrary intent."

524.2–505. Who may witness

Text of section effective until January 1, 1996.

(a) Any person generally competent to be a witness may act as a witness to a will.

(b) A will is not invalid because the will is signed by an interested witness.

Laws 1975, c. 347, § 22, eff. Jan. 1, 1976.

For text of section effective January 1, 1996, applicable to the rights of successors of decedents dying on or after January 1, 1996, and to any wills of decedents dying on or after January 1, 1996, see § 524.2–505, post.

524.2–505.   Who may witness

Text of section effective January 1, 1996, applicable to the rights of successors of decedents dying on or after January 1, 1996, and to any wills of decedents dying on or after January 1, 1996.

(a) An individual generally competent to be a witness may act as a witness to a will.

(b) The signing of a will by an interested witness does not invalidate the will or any provision of it.

Laws 1975, c. 347, § 22, eff. Jan. 1, 1976. Amended by Laws 1994, c. 472, § 38.

For text of section effective until January 1, 1996, see § 524.2–505, ante.

Historical and Statutory Notes

Laws 1994, c. 472, § 65, provides:

"(a) This act takes effect on January 1, 1996.

"(b) Except as provided elsewhere in this act:

"(1) this act applies to the rights of successors of decedents dying on or after its effective date and to any wills of decedents dying on or after its effective date;

"(2) if, before the effective date of this act, a right is either acquired, extinguished, waived, or barred upon the expiration of a prescribed period of time which commenced to run by the provisions of any statute before the effective date, the provisions of this act neither revoke, revive, restore, nor remove the bar of such right; and

"(3) any rule of construction or presumption provided in this act applies to instruments executed and multiple party accounts opened before the effective date of this act unless there is a clear indication of contrary intent."

524.2–506.   Choice of law as to execution

A written will is valid if executed in compliance with section 524.2–502 or if its execution complies with the law at the time of execution of the place where the will is executed, or of the law of the place where at the time of execution or at the time of death the testator is domiciled, has a place of abode or is a national.

Laws 1975, c. 347, § 22, eff. Jan. 1, 1976.

524.2–507.   Revocation by writing or by act

Text of section effective until January 1, 1996.

A will or any part thereof is revoked

(1) by a subsequent will which revokes the prior will or part expressly or by inconsistency; or

(2) by being burned, torn, canceled, obliterated, or destroyed, with the intent and for the purpose of revoking it by the testator or by another person in the testator's presence and by the testator's direction.

Laws 1975, c. 347, § 22, eff. Jan. 1, 1976. Amended by Laws 1986, c. 444.

For text of section effective January 1, 1996, applicable to the rights of successors of decedents dying on or after January 1, 1996, and to any wills of decedents dying on or after January 1, 1996, see § 524.2-507, post.

524.2-507. Revocation by writing or by act

Text of section effective January 1, 1996, applicable to the rights of successors of decedents dying on or after January 1, 1996, and to any wills of decedents dying on or after January 1, 1996.

(a) A will or any part thereof is revoked:

(1) by executing a subsequent will that revokes the previous will or part expressly or by inconsistency; or

(2) by performing a revocatory act on the will, if the testator performed the act with the intent and for the purpose of revoking the will or part or if another individual performed the act in the testator's conscious presence and by the testator's direction. For purposes of this clause, "revocatory act on the will" includes burning, tearing, canceling, obliterating, or destroying the will or any part of it. A burning, tearing, or canceling may be a "revocatory act on the will," whether or not the burn, tear, or cancellation touched any of the words on the will.

(b) If a subsequent will does not expressly revoke a previous will, the execution of the subsequent will wholly revokes the previous will by inconsistency if the testator intended the subsequent will to replace rather than supplement the previous will.

(c) The testator is presumed to have intended a subsequent will to replace rather than supplement a previous will if the subsequent will makes a complete disposition of the testator's estate. If this presumption arises and is not rebutted by clear and convincing evidence, the previous will is revoked; only the subsequent will is operative on the testator's death.

(d) The testator is presumed to have intended a subsequent will to supplement rather than replace a previous will if the subsequent will does not make a complete disposition of the testator's estate. If this presumption arises and is not rebutted by clear and convincing evidence, the subsequent will revokes the previous will only to the extent the subsequent will is inconsistent with the previous will; each will is fully operative on the testator's death to the extent they are not inconsistent.

Laws 1975, c. 347, § 22, eff. Jan. 1, 1976. Amended by Laws 1986, c. 444; Laws 1994, c. 472, § 39.

For text of section effective until January 1, 1996, see § 524.2–507, ante.

Historical and Statutory Notes

Laws 1994, c. 472, § 65, provides:

"(a) This act takes effect on January 1, 1996.

"(b) Except as provided elsewhere in this act:

"(1) this act applies to the rights of successors of decedents dying on or after its effective date and to any wills of decedents dying on or after its effective date;

"(2) if, before the effective date of this act, a right is either acquired, extinguished, waived, or barred upon the expiration of a prescribed period of time which commenced to run by the provisions of any statute before the effective date, the provisions of this act neither revoke, revive, restore, nor remove the bar of such right; and

"(3) any rule of construction or presumption provided in this act applies to instruments executed and multiple party accounts opened before the effective date of this act unless there is a clear indication of contrary intent."

524.2–508. Revocation by changes of circumstances

Text of section effective until January 1, 1996.

If after executing a will the testator's marriage is dissolved or annulled, the dissolution or annulment revokes any disposition or appointment of property made by the will to the former spouse, any provision conferring a general or special power of appointment on the former spouse, and any nomination of the former spouse as executor, trustee, conservator, or guardian, unless the will expressly provides otherwise. Property prevented from passing to a former spouse because of revocation by dissolution of marriage or annulment passes as if the former spouse failed to survive the decedent, and other provisions conferring some power or office on the former spouse are interpreted as if the spouse failed to survive the decedent. If provisions are revoked solely by this section, they are revived by testator's remarriage to the former spouse. For purposes of chapters 524 and 525, dissolution of marriage includes divorce. A decree of separation which does not terminate the status of husband and wife is not a dissolution of marriage for purposes of this section. No change of circumstances other than as described in this section revokes a will.

Laws 1975, c. 347, § 22, eff. Jan. 1, 1976.

For text of section effective January 1, 1996, applicable to the rights of successors of decedents dying on or after January 1, 1996, and to any wills of decedents dying on or after January 1, 1996, see § 524.2–508, post.

524.2–508. Revocation by changes of circumstances

Text of section effective January 1, 1996, applicable to the rights of successors of decedents dying on or after January 1, 1996, and to any wills of decedents dying on or after January 1, 1996.

Except as provided in sections 524.2–803 and 524.2–804, a change of circumstances does not revoke a will or any part of it.

Laws 1975, c. 347, § 22, eff. Jan. 1, 1976. Amended by Laws 1994, c. 472, § 40; Laws 1995, c. 130, § 12.

For text of section effective until January 1, 1996, see § 524.2–508, ante.

Historical and Statutory Notes

Laws 1994, c. 472, § 65, provides:

"(a) This act takes effect on January 1, 1996.

"(b) Except as provided elsewhere in this act:

"(1) this act applies to the rights of successors of decedents dying on or after its effective date and to any wills of decedents dying on or after its effective date;

"(2) if, before the effective date of this act, a right is either acquired, extinguished, waived, or barred upon the expiration of a prescribed period of time which commenced to run by the provisions of any statute before the effective date, the provisions of this act neither revoke,

revive, restore, nor remove the bar of such right; and

"(3) any rule of construction or presumption provided in this act applies to instruments executed and multiple party accounts opened before the effective date of this act unless there is a clear indication of contrary intent."

Laws 1995, c. 130, § 22, provides in part that chapter 130 is effective January 1, 1996, and that §§ 12, 13, and 15 (amending § 524.2–508, enacting § 524.2–804, and amending § 524.3–916, respectively) apply to the rights of successors of decedents dying on or after January 1, 1996, and to any wills of decedents dying on or after January 1, 1996.

524.2–509. Revival of revoked will

Text of section effective until January 1, 1996.

(a) If a second will which, had it remained effective at death, would have revoked the first will in whole or in part, is thereafter revoked by acts under section 524.2–507, the first will is revoked in whole or in part unless it is evident from the circumstances of the revocation of the second will or from testator's contemporary or subsequent declarations that the testator intended the first will to take effect as executed.

(b) If a second will which, had it remained effective at death, would have revoked the first will in whole or in part, is thereafter revoked by a third will, the first will is revoked in whole or in part, except to the extent it appears from the terms of the third will that the testator intended the first will to take effect.

Laws 1975, c. 347, § 22, eff. Jan. 1, 1976. Amended by Laws 1986, c. 444.

For text of section effective January 1, 1996, applicable to the rights of successors of decedents dying on or after January 1, 1996, and to any wills of decedents dying on or after January 1, 1996, see § 524.2–509, post.

524.2–509. Revival of revoked will

Text of section effective January 1, 1996, applicable to the rights of successors of decedents dying on or after January 1, 1996, and to any wills of decedents dying on or after January 1, 1996.

(a) If a subsequent will that wholly revoked a previous will is thereafter revoked by a revocatory act under section 524.2–507, paragraph (a), clause (2), the previous will remains revoked unless it is revived. The previous will is revived if it is evident from the circumstances of the revocation of the subsequent will or from the testator's contemporary or subsequent declarations that the testator intended the previous will to take effect as executed.

(b) If a subsequent will that partly revoked a previous will is thereafter revoked by a revocatory act under section 524.2–507, paragraph (a), clause (2), a revoked part of the previous will is revived unless it is evident from the circumstances of the revocation of the subsequent will or from the testator's contemporary or subsequent declarations that the testator did not intend the revoked part to take effect as executed.

(c) If a subsequent will that revoked a previous will in whole or in part is thereafter revoked by another later will, the previous will remains revoked in whole or in part, unless it or its revoked part is revived. The previous will or its revoked part is revived to the extent it appears from the terms of the later will that the testator intended the previous will to take effect.

Laws 1975, c. 347, § 22, eff. Jan. 1, 1976. Amended by Laws 1986, c. 444; Laws 1994, c. 472, § 41.

For text of section effective until January 1, 1996, see § 524.2–509, ante.

Historical and Statutory Notes

Laws 1994, c. 472, § 65, provides:

"(a) This act takes effect on January 1, 1996.

"(b) Except as provided elsewhere in this act:

"(1) this act applies to the rights of successors of decedents dying on or after its effective date and to any wills of decedents dying on or after its effective date;

"(2) if, before the effective date of this act, a right is either acquired, extinguished, waived, or barred upon the expiration of a prescribed period of time which commenced to run by the provisions of any statute before the effective date, the provisions of this act neither revoke, revive, restore, nor remove the bar of such right; and

"(3) any rule of construction or presumption provided in this act applies to instruments executed and multiple party accounts opened before the effective date of this act unless there is a clear indication of contrary intent."

524.2–510. Incorporation by reference

Any writing in existence when a will is executed may be incorporated by reference if the language of the will manifests this intent and describes the writing sufficiently to permit its identification.

Laws 1975, c. 347, § 22, eff. Jan. 1, 1976.

524.2–511. Testamentary additions to trusts

Text of section effective January 1, 1996, applicable to the rights of successors of decedents dying on or after January 1, 1996, and to any wills of decedents dying on or after January 1, 1996.

(a) A will may validly devise property to the trustee of a trust established or to be established (i) during the testator's lifetime by the testator, by the testator and some other person, or by some other person, including a funded or unfunded life insurance trust, although the settlor has reserved any or all rights of ownership of the insurance contracts, or (ii) at the testator's death by the testator's devise to the trustee, if, in either case, the trust is identified in the testator's will and its terms are set forth in a written instrument, other than a will, executed before, concurrently with, or after the execution of the testator's will or in another individual's will if that other individual has predeceased the testator, regardless of the existence, size, or character of the corpus of the trust. The devise is not invalid because the trust is amendable or revocable, or because the trust was amended after the execution of the will or the testator's death.

(b) Unless the testator's will provides otherwise, property devised to a trust described in paragraph (a) is not held under a testamentary trust of the testator, but it becomes a part of the trust to which it is devised, and must be administered and disposed of in accordance with the provisions of the governing instrument setting forth the terms of the trust, including any amendments thereto made before or after the testator's death.

(c) Unless the testator's will provides otherwise, a revocation or termination of the trust before the testator's death causes the devise to lapse.

(d) This section does not invalidate a devise made by a will executed before February 21, 1963.

Laws 1994, c. 472, § 42.

UNIFORM TESTAMENTARY ADDITIONS TO TRUSTS ACT (1991)

Table of Jurisdictions Wherein Act Has Been Adopted

For text of Uniform Acts, and variation notes and annotation materials for adopting jurisdictions, see Uniform Laws Annotated, Master Edition, Volume 8B.

Jurisdiction	Laws	Effective Date	Statutory Citation
Alaska	1996, c. 75	1–1–1997	AS 13.12.511.
Arizona	1994, c. 290	After 12–31–1994	A.R.S. § 14–2511.
Arkansas	1995, Act 751	8–1–1995	A.C.A. §§ 28–27–101 to 28–27–106.
Colorado	1994, L.B. 94–43	7–1–1995	West's C.R.S.A. § 15–11–511.
Connecticut	P.A. 94–96	10–1–1994	C.G.S.A. § 45a–260.
Delaware	1997, c. 76	6–25–1997	12 Del.C. §§ 211, 211 note.
Hawaii	1992, Act 49	4–27–1992	HRS § 560:2–511, § 560:2–511 note.
Idaho	1999, c. 304	7–1–1999	I.C. § 15–2–511.
Kentucky	1998, c. 415	4–7–1998 *	KRS 394.076.
Minnesota	1994, c. 472	1–1–1996	M.S.A. § 524.2–511.
Montana	1993, c. 494	10–1–1993	MCA § 72–2–531.
Nebraska	1999, L.B. 18	4–28–1999 *	R.R.S. 1943, § 30–2336.
New Hampshire	1996, c. 200	1–1–1997	RSA 563–A:1 to 563–A:4.
New Mexico	L.1993, c. 174	7–1–1993	NMSA 1978 § 45–2–511.
North Carolina	2007, S.L. 2007–184	7–5–2007	G.S. § 31–47.
North Dakota	1993, c. 334	1–1–1996	NDCC 30.1–08–11.
Ohio	1992, H.B. 427	10–8–1992	R.C. § 2107.63.
Rhode Island	1994, c. 352	7–12–1994	Gen.Laws 1956, §§ 18–14–1 to 18–14–6.
South Dakota	1995, c. 167	7–1–1995	SDCL 29A–2–511.

Jurisdiction	Laws	Effective Date	Statutory Citation
Utah	1998, c. 39	7–1–1998	U.C.A.1953, § 75–2–511.
Virginia	1999, c. 252	3–18–1999 *	Code 1950, § 64.1–73.1.
West Virginia	1992, c. 215	90 days from 3–6–1992	Code, 41–3–8 to 41–3–11.

* Date of approval.

Historical and Statutory Notes

Derivation:

St.1994, § 525.223.

Laws 1975, c. 347, §§ 97, 98.

Laws 1963, c. 13, §§ 1 to 5.

Laws 1994, c. 472, § 65, provides:

"(a) This act takes effect on January 1, 1996.

"(b) Except as provided elsewhere in this act:

"(1) this act applies to the rights of successors of decedents dying on or after its effective date and to any wills of decedents dying on or after its effective date;

"(2) if, before the effective date of this act, a right is either acquired, extinguished, waived, or barred upon the expiration of a prescribed period of time which commenced to run by the provisions of any statute before the effective date, the provisions of this act neither revoke, revive, restore, nor remove the bar of such right; and

"(3) any rule of construction or presumption provided in this act applies to instruments executed and multiple party accounts opened before the effective date of this act unless there is a clear indication of contrary intent."

524.2–512. Events of independent significance

Text of section effective until January 1, 1996.

A will may dispose of property by reference to acts and events which have significance apart from their effect upon the dispositions made by the will, whether they occur before or after the execution of the will or before or after the testator's death. The execution or revocation of a will of another person is such an event.

Laws 1975, c. 347, § 22, eff. Jan. 1, 1976.

For text of section effective January 1, 1996, applicable to the rights of successors of decedents dying on or after January 1, 1996, and to any wills of decedents dying on or after January 1, 1996, see § 524.2–512, post.

524.2–512. Events of independent significance

Text of section effective January 1, 1996, applicable to the rights of successors of decedents dying on or after January 1, 1996, and to any wills of decedents dying on or after January 1, 1996.

A will may dispose of property by reference to acts and events that have significance apart from their effect upon the dispositions made by the will, whether they occur before or after the execution of the will or before or after the testator's death. The execution or revocation of another individual's will is such an event.

Laws 1975, c. 347, § 22, eff. Jan. 1, 1976. Amended by Laws 1994, c. 472, § 43.

For text of section effective until January 1, 1996, see § 524.2–512, ante.

Historical and Statutory Notes

Laws 1994, c. 472, § 65, provides:

"(a) This act takes effect on January 1, 1996.

"(b) Except as provided elsewhere in this act:

"(1) this act applies to the rights of successors of decedents dying on or after its effective date and to any wills of decedents dying on or after its effective date;

"(2) if, before the effective date of this act, a right is either acquired, extinguished, waived, or barred upon the expiration of a prescribed period of time which commenced to run by the provisions of any statute before the effective date, the provisions of this act neither revoke, revive, restore, nor remove the bar of such right; and

"(3) any rule of construction or presumption provided in this act applies to instruments executed and multiple party accounts opened before the effective date of this act unless there is a clear indication of contrary intent."

524.2–513. Separate writing identifying bequest of tangible property

A will may refer to a written statement or list to dispose of items of tangible personal property not otherwise specifically disposed of by the will, other than money and coin collections, and property used in trade or business. To be admissible under this section as evidence of the intended disposition, the writing must be referred to in the will, must be either in the handwriting of the testator or be signed by the testator, and must describe the items and the devisees with reasonable certainty. The writing may be referred to as one to be in existence at the time of the testator's death; it may be prepared before or after the execution of the will; it may be altered by the testator after its preparation; and it may be a writing which has no significance apart from its effect upon the dispositions made by the will.

A writing may include multiple writings and if an item of tangible personal property is disposed of to different persons by different writings, the most recent writing controls the disposition of the item.

Laws 1975, c. 347, § 22, eff. Jan. 1, 1976. Amended by Laws 1986, c. 444; Laws 2000, c. 362, § 2.

Historical and Statutory Notes

Laws 2000, c. 362, § 5, provides that § 2 (amending this section) is effective for wills signed on or after August 1, 2000.

524.2–514. Contracts concerning succession

Text of section effective January 1, 1996, applicable to the rights of successors of decedents dying on or after January 1, 1996, and to any wills of decedents dying on or after January 1, 1996.

A contract to make a will or devise, or not to revoke a will or devise, or to die intestate, if executed after January 1, 1976, may be established only by (i) provisions of a will stating material provisions of the contract, (ii) an express reference in a will to a contract and extrinsic evidence proving the terms of the contract, or (iii) a writing signed by the decedent evidencing the contract. The execution of a joint will or mutual wills does not create a presumption of a contract not to revoke the will or wills.

Laws 1994, c. 472, § 44.

Minnesota Rules of Evidence

Presumptions in civil actions, see Rule 301.

Historical and Statutory Notes

Laws 1994, c. 472, § 65, provides:

"(a) This act takes effect on January 1, 1996.

"(b) Except as provided elsewhere in this act:

"(1) this act applies to the rights of successors of decedents dying on or after its effective date and to any wills of decedents dying on or after its effective date;

"(2) if, before the effective date of this act, a right is either acquired, extinguished, waived, or barred upon the expiration of a prescribed period of time which commenced to run by the provisions of any statute before the effective date, the provisions of this act neither revoke, revive, restore, nor remove the bar of such right; and

"(3) any rule of construction or presumption provided in this act applies to instruments executed and multiple party accounts opened before the effective date of this act unless there is a clear indication of contrary intent."

524.2–515. Deposit of will with court in testator's lifetime

Text of section effective January 1, 1996, applicable to the rights of successors of decedents dying on or after January 1, 1996, and to any wills of decedents dying on or after January 1, 1996.

A will may be deposited by the testator or the testator's agent with any court for safekeeping, under rules of the court. The will must be sealed and kept confidential. During the testator's lifetime, a deposited will must be delivered only to the testator or to a person authorized in writing signed by the testator to receive the will. A conservator or guardian may be allowed to examine a deposited will of a protected testator under procedures designed to maintain the confidential character of the document to the extent possible, and to ensure that it will be resealed and kept on deposit after the examination. Upon being informed of the testator's death, the court may deliver the will to the appropriate court.

Laws 1994, c. 472, § 45.

Historical and Statutory Notes

Laws 1994, c. 472, § 65, provides:

"(a) This act takes effect on January 1, 1996.

"(b) Except as provided elsewhere in this act:

"(1) this act applies to the rights of successors of decedents dying on or after its effective date and to any wills of decedents dying on or after its effective date;

"(2) if, before the effective date of this act, a right is either acquired, extinguished, waived, or barred upon the expiration of a prescribed period of time which commenced to run by the provisions of any statute before the effective date, the provisions of this act neither revoke, revive, restore, nor remove the bar of such right; and

"(3) any rule of construction or presumption provided in this act applies to instruments executed and multiple party accounts opened before the effective date of this act unless there is a clear indication of contrary intent."

524.2–516. Duty of custodian of will; liability

Text of section effective January 1, 1996, applicable to the rights of successors of decedents dying on or after January 1, 1996, and to any wills of decedents dying on or after January 1, 1996.

After the death of a testator and on request of an interested person, a person having custody of a will of the testator shall deliver it with reasonable promptness to an appropriate court. A person who willfully fails to deliver a will is liable to any person aggrieved for any damages that may be sustained by the failure. A person who willfully refuses or fails to deliver a will after being ordered by the court in a proceeding brought for the purpose of compelling delivery is subject to penalty for contempt of court.

Laws 1994, c. 472, § 46.

Historical and Statutory Notes

Laws 1994, c. 472, § 65, provides:

"(a) This act takes effect on January 1, 1996.

"(b) Except as provided elsewhere in this act:

"(1) this act applies to the rights of successors of decedents dying on or after its effective date and to any wills of decedents dying on or after its effective date;

"(2) if, before the effective date of this act, a right is either acquired, extinguished, waived, or barred upon the expiration of a prescribed period of time which commenced to run by the provisions of any statute before the effective date, the provisions of this act neither revoke, revive, restore, nor remove the bar of such right; and

"(3) any rule of construction or presumption provided in this act applies to instruments executed and multiple party accounts opened before the effective date of this act unless there is a clear indication of contrary intent."

524.2–517. Penalty clause for contest

Text of section effective January 1, 1996, applicable to the rights of successors of decedents dying on or after January 1, 1996, and to any wills of decedents dying on or after January 1, 1996.

A provision in a will purporting to penalize an interested person for contesting the will or instituting other proceedings relating to the estate is unenforceable if probable cause exists for instituting proceedings.

Laws 1994, c. 472, § 47.

Historical and Statutory Notes

Laws 1994, c. 472, § 65, provides:

"(a) This act takes effect on January 1, 1996.

"(b) Except as provided elsewhere in this act:

"(1) this act applies to the rights of successors of decedents dying on or after its effective date and to any wills of decedents dying on or after its effective date;

"(2) if, before the effective date of this act, a right is either acquired, extinguished, waived, or barred upon the expiration of a prescribed period of time which commenced to run by the provisions of any statute before the effective date, the provisions of this act neither revoke, revive, restore, nor remove the bar of such right; and

"(3) any rule of construction or presumption provided in this act applies to instruments executed and multiple party accounts opened before the effective date of this act unless there is a clear indication of contrary intent."

PART 6

RULES OF CONSTRUCTION APPLICABLE ONLY TO WILLS

524.2–601. Scope

Text of section effective January 1, 1996, applicable to the rights of successors of decedents dying on or after January 1, 1996, and to any wills of decedents dying on or after January 1, 1996.

In the absence of a finding of a contrary intention, the rules of construction in this part control the construction of a will.

Laws 1994, c. 472, § 48.

Historical and Statutory Notes

Derivation:

St.1992, § 524.2–603.

Laws 1986, c. 444.

Laws 1975, c. 347, § 22.

Laws 1994, c. 472, § 65, provides:

"(a) This act takes effect on January 1, 1996.

"(b) Except as provided elsewhere in this act:

"(1) this act applies to the rights of successors of decedents dying on or after its effective date and to any wills of decedents dying on or after its effective date;

"(2) if, before the effective date of this act, a right is either acquired, extinguished, waived, or barred upon the expiration of a prescribed period of time which commenced to run by the provisions of any statute before the effective date, the provisions of this act neither revoke, revive, restore, nor remove the bar of such right; and

"(3) any rule of construction or presumption provided in this act applies to instruments executed and multiple party accounts opened before the effective date of this act unless there is a clear indication of contrary intent."

524.2–602. Choice of law as to meaning and effect of wills

Text of section effective until January 1, 1996.

The meaning and legal effect of a disposition in a will shall be determined by the local law of a particular state selected by the testator in the testator's instrument unless the application of that law is contrary to the public policy of this state otherwise applicable to the disposition.

Laws 1975, c. 347, § 22, eff. Jan. 1, 1976. Amended by Laws 1986, c. 444.

For text of section effective January 1, 1996, applicable to the rights of successors of decedents dying on or after January 1, 1996, and to any wills of decedents dying on or after January 1, 1996, see § 524.2.602, post.

524.2–602. Will may pass all property and after-acquired property

Text of section effective January 1, 1996, applicable to the rights of successors of decedents dying on or after January 1, 1996, and to any wills of decedents dying on or after January 1, 1996.

A will may provide for the passage of all property the testator owns at death and all property acquired by the estate after the testator's death.

Amended by Laws 1994, c. 472, § 49.

For text of section effective until January 1, 1996, see § 524.2–602, ante.

Historical and Statutory Notes

Derivation:

St.1992, § 524.2–604.

Laws 1986, c. 444.

Laws 1975, c. 347, § 22.

St.1971, § 525.211.

St.Supp.1940, § 8992–46.

Laws 1935, c. 72, § 46.

St.1927, § 8749.

Gen.St.1923, § 8749.

Gen.St.1913, § 7264.

Rev.Laws 1905, § 3673.

Gen.St.1894, § 4425.

Laws 1889, c. 46, § 18.

Gen.St.1878, c. 47, § 3.

Gen.St.1866, c. 47, § 3.

Pub.St.1858, c. 40, § 3.

Rev.St. (Terr.), c. 53, § 3.

Laws 1994, c. 472, § 65, provides:

"(a) This act takes effect on January 1, 1996.

"(b) Except as provided elsewhere in this act:

"(1) this act applies to the rights of successors of decedents dying on or after its effective date and to any wills of decedents dying on or after its effective date;

"(2) if, before the effective date of this act, a right is either acquired, extinguished, waived, or barred upon the expiration of a prescribed period of time which commenced to run by the provisions of any statute before the effective date, the provisions of this act neither revoke, revive, restore, nor remove the bar of such right; and

"(3) any rule of construction or presumption provided in this act applies to instruments executed and multiple party accounts opened before the effective date of this act unless there is a clear indication of contrary intent."

Former section: St.1992, § 524.2–602, related to choice of law as to the meaning and effect of wills. See, now, 524.2–703.

524.2–603. Antilapse; deceased devisee; class gifts; words of survivorship

Subdivision 1. Deceased devisee. If a devisee who is a grandparent or a lineal descendant of a grandparent of the testator is dead at the time of execution of the will, fails to survive the testator, or is treated as if the devisee predeceased the testator, the issue of the deceased devisee who survive the testator by 120 hours take in place of the deceased devisee. If they are all of the same degree of kinship to the devisee, they take equally. If they are of unequal degree, those of more remote degree take by representation. A person who would have been a devisee under a class gift if the person had survived the testator is treated as a devisee for purposes of this section, whether the death occurred before or after the execution of the will.

Subd. 2. Definition. For the purposes of section 524.2–601, words of survivorship, such as, in a devise to an individual, "if he or she survives me," or, in a class gift, to "my surviving children," are a sufficient indication of an intent contrary to the application of this section.

Historical and Statutory Notes

Derivation:

St.2000, § 524.2–603.

Laws 1994, c. 472, § 50.

St.1992, § 524.2–605.

Laws 1986, c. 444.

Laws 1975, c. 347, § 22.

St.1971, § 525.203.
St.Supp.1940, § 8992–44.
Laws 1935, c. 72, § 44.
St.1927, § 8747.
Gen.St.1923, § 8747.
Gen.St.1913, § 7262.
Rev.Laws 1905, § 3671.
Gen.St.1894, § 4449.
Laws 1889, § 42.
Gen.St.1878, c. 47, § 25.
Gen.St.1866, c. 47, § 25.

Pub.St.1858, c. 40, § 29.
Rev.St. (Terr.), c. 53, § 29.

Former section: St.1992, § 524.2–603, related to the rules of construction and intention. See, now, M.S.A. § 524.2–601.

Former section: St.2000, § 524.2–603, Minnesota's antilapse statute, was repealed by Laws 2001, c. 15, § 14, with its subject matter moving to § 524.2–6031, enacted by Laws 2001, c. 15, § 13. In St.2003 Supp., § 524.2–6031 was renumbered § 524.2–603.

524.2–6031. Renumbered 524.2–603 in St.2003 Supp.

524.2–604. Construction that will passes all property; after acquired property

Text of section effective until January 1, 1996.

A will is construed to pass all property which the testator owns at death including property acquired after the execution of the will.

Laws 1975, c. 347, § 22, eff. Jan. 1, 1976. Amended by Laws 1986, c. 444.

For text of section effective January 1, 1996, applicable to the rights of successors of decedents dying on or after January 1, 1996, and to any wills of decedents dying on or after January 1, 1996, see § 524.2–604, post.

524.2–604. Failure of testamentary provision

Text of section effective January 1, 1996, applicable to the rights of successors of decedents dying on or after January 1, 1996, and to any wills of decedents dying on or after January 1, 1996.

(a) Except as provided in section 524.2–603, a devise, other than a residuary devise, that fails for any reason becomes a part of the residue.

(b) Except as provided in section 524.2–603, if the residue is devised to two or more persons, the share of a residuary devisee that fails for any reason passes to the other residuary devisee, or to other residuary devisees in proportion to the interest of each in the remaining part of the residue.

Amended by Laws 1994, c. 472, § 51; Laws 2002, c. 379, art. 1, § 102.

For text of section effective until January 1, 1996, see § 524.2–604, ante.

Historical and Statutory Notes

Derivation:
St.1992, § 524.2–606.
Laws 1986, c. 444.
Laws 1975, c. 347, § 22.
St.1971, § 525.203.

St.Supp.1940, § 8992–44.
Laws 1935, c. 72, § 44.
St.1927, § 8747.
Gen.St.1923, § 8747.
Gen.St.1913, § 7262.

Rev.Laws 1905, § 3671.

Gen.St.1894, § 4449.

Laws 1889, § 42.

Gen.St.1878, c. 47, § 25.

Gen.St.1866, c. 47, § 25.

Pub.St.1858, c. 40, § 29.

Rev.St. (Terr.), c. 53, § 29.

Laws 1994, c. 472, § 65, provides:

"(a) This act takes effect on January 1, 1996.

"(b) Except as provided elsewhere in this act:

"(1) this act applies to the rights of successors of decedents dying on or after its effective date and to any wills of decedents dying on or after its effective date;

"(2) if, before the effective date of this act, a right is either acquired, extinguished, waived, or barred upon the expiration of a prescribed period of time which commenced to run by the provisions of any statute before the effective date, the provisions of this act neither revoke, revive, restore, nor remove the bar of such right; and

"(3) any rule of construction or presumption provided in this act applies to instruments executed and multiple party accounts opened before the effective date of this act unless there is a clear indication of contrary intent."

Former section: St.1992, § 524.2-604, related to the construction that a will passes all property. See, now, M.S.A. § 524.2-602.

524.2-605. Antilapse; deceased devisee; class gifts

Text of section effective until January 1, 1996.

If a devisee who is a grandparent or a lineal descendant of a grandparent of the testator is dead at the time of execution of the will, or fails to survive the testator, the issue of the deceased devisee who survive the testator take in place of the deceased devisee and if they are all of the same degree of kinship to the devisee they take equally, but if of unequal degree then those of more remote degree take by representation. One who is a grandparent or a lineal descendant of a grandparent of the testator and who would have been a devisee under a class gift on surviving the testator is treated as a devisee for purposes of this section whether death occurred before or after the execution of the will.

Laws 1975, c. 347, § 22, eff. Jan. 1, 1976. Amended by Laws 1986, c. 444.

For text of section effective January 1, 1996, applicable to the rights of successors of decedents dying on or after January 1, 1996, and to any wills of decedents dying on or after January 1, 1996, see § 524.2-605, post.

524.2-605. Increase in securities; accessions

Text of section effective January 1, 1996, applicable to the rights of successors of decedents dying on or after January 1, 1996, and to any wills of decedents dying on or after January 1, 1996.

(a) If a testator executes a will that devises securities and the testator then owned securities that meet the description in the will, the devise includes additional securities owned by the testator at death to the extent the additional securities were acquired by the testator after the will was executed as a result of the testator's ownership of the described securities and are securities of any of the following types:

(1) securities of the same organization acquired by reason of action initiated by the organization or any successor, related, or acquiring organization, excluding any acquired by exercise of purchase options;

(2) securities of another organization acquired as a result of a merger, consolidation, reorganization, or other distribution by the organization or any successor, related, or acquiring organization; or

(3) securities of the same organization acquired as a result of a plan of reinvestment.

(b) Distributions in cash before death with respect to a described security are not part of the devise.

Amended by Laws 1994, c. 472, § 52.

For text of section effective until January 1, 1996, see § 524.2–605, ante.

Historical and Statutory Notes

Derivation:

St.1992, § 524.2–607.

Laws 1975, c. 347, § 22.

Laws 1994, c. 472, § 65, provides:

"(a) This act takes effect on January 1, 1996.

"(b) Except as provided elsewhere in this act:

"(1) this act applies to the rights of successors of decedents dying on or after its effective date and to any wills of decedents dying on or after its effective date;

"(2) if, before the effective date of this act, a right is either acquired, extinguished, waived, or barred upon the expiration of a prescribed period of time which commenced to run by the provisions of any statute before the effective date, the provisions of this act neither revoke, revive, restore, nor remove the bar of such right; and

"(3) any rule of construction or presumption provided in this act applies to instruments executed and multiple party accounts opened before the effective date of this act unless there is a clear indication of contrary intent."

Former section: St.1992, § 524.2–605, related to anti-lapsing, deceased devisees, and class gifts. See, now, M.S.A. § 524.2–603.

524.2–606.   Failure of testamentary provision

Text of section effective until January 1, 1996.

(a) Except as provided in section 524.2–605 if a devise other than a residuary devise fails for any reason, it becomes a part of the residue.

(b) Except as provided in section 524.2–605 if the residue is devised to two or more persons and the share of one of the residuary devisees fails for any reason, that share passes to the other residuary devisee, or to other residuary devisees in proportion to their interests in the residue.

Laws 1975, c. 347, § 22, eff. Jan. 1, 1976.   Amended by Laws 1986, c. 444.

For text of section effective January 1, 1996, applicable to the rights of successors of decedents dying on or after January 1, 1996, and to any wills of decedents dying on or after January 1, 1996, see § 524.2–606, post.

524.2–606.   Nonademption of specific devises;   unpaid proceeds of sale, condemnation, or insurance;   sale by conservator or guardian

(a) A specific devisee has a right to the specifically devised property in the testator's estate at death and:

(1) any balance of the purchase price, together with any security agreement, owing from a purchaser to the testator at death by reason of sale of the property;

(2) any amount of a condemnation award for the taking of the property unpaid at death;

(3) any proceeds unpaid at death on fire or casualty insurance on or other recovery for injury to the property; and

(4) property owned by the testator at death and acquired as a result of foreclosure, or obtained in lieu of foreclosure, of the security interest for a specifically devised obligation.

(b) If specifically devised property is sold or mortgaged by a conservator or guardian or by an agent acting within the authority of a durable power of attorney for an incapacitated principal, or if a condemnation award, insurance proceeds, or recovery for injury to the property are paid to a conservator or guardian or to an agent acting within the authority of a durable power of attorney for an incapacitated principal, the specific devisee has the right to a general pecuniary devise equal to the net sale price, the amount of the unpaid loan, the condemnation award, the insurance proceeds, or the recovery.

(c) The right of a specific devisee under paragraph (b) is reduced by any right the devisee has under paragraph (a).

(d) For the purposes of the references in paragraph (b) to a conservator or guardian or an agent acting within the authority of a durable power of attorney, paragraph (b) does not apply if after the sale, mortgage, condemnation, casualty, or recovery;

(1) in the case of a conservator or guardian, it was adjudicated that the testator's incapacity ceased and the testator survived the adjudication by one year; or

(2) in the case of an agent acting within the authority of a durable power of attorney, the testator's incapacity ceased and the testator survived for one year after the incapacity ceased.

(e) For the purposes of the references in paragraph (b) to an agent acting within the authority of a durable power of attorney for an incapacitated principal, (i) "incapacitated principal" means a principal who is an incapacitated person as defined in section 524.5–102, subdivision 6, and (ii) a finding of the principal's incapacity need not occur during the principal's life.

Amended by Laws 1994, c. 472, § 53; Laws 1997, c. 9, § 8; Laws 2004, c. 146, art. 3, § 41.

Historical and Statutory Notes

Derivation:

St.1992, § 524.2–608.

Laws 1986, c. 444.

Laws 1975, c. 347, § 22.

Laws 1994, c. 472, § 65, provides:

"(a) This act takes effect on January 1, 1996.

"(b) Except as provided elsewhere in this act:

"(1) this act applies to the rights of successors of decedents dying on or after its effective date and to any wills of decedents dying on or after its effective date;

"(2) if, before the effective date of this act, a right is either acquired, extinguished, waived, or barred upon the expiration of a prescribed period of time which commenced to run by the provisions of any statute before the effective date, the provisions of this act neither revoke, revive, restore, nor remove the bar of such right; and

"(3) any rule of construction or presumption provided in this act applies to instruments executed and multiple party accounts opened before the effective date of this act unless there is a clear indication of contrary intent."

Former section: St.1992, § 524.2–606, related to the failure of a testamentary provision. See, now, M.S.A. § 524.2–604.

524.2–607. Change in securities; accessions; nonademption

Text of section effective until January 1, 1996.

(a) If the testator intended a specific devise of certain securities rather than the equivalent value thereof, the specific devisee is entitled only to:

(1) as much of the devised securities as is a part of the estate at time of the testator's death;

(2) any additional or other securities of the same entity owned by the testator by reason of action initiated by the entity excluding any acquired by exercise of purchase options;

(3) securities of another entity owned by the testator as a result of a merger, consolidation, reorganization or other similar action initiated by the entity; and

(4) any additional securities of the entity owned by the testator as a result of a plan of reinvestment if it is a regulated investment company.

(b) Distributions prior to death with respect to a specifically devised security not provided for in subsection (a) are not part of the specific devise.

Laws 1975, c. 347, § 22, eff. Jan. 1, 1976.

> *For text of section effective January 1, 1996, applicable to the rights of successors of decedents dying on or after January 1, 1996, and to any wills of decedents dying on or after January 1, 1996, see § 524.2–607, post.*

524.2–607. Nonexoneration

> *Text of section effective January 1, 1996, applicable to the rights of successors of decedents dying on or after January 1, 1996, and to any wills of decedents dying on or after January 1, 1996.*

A specific devise passes subject to any mortgage or security interest existing at the date of death, without right of exoneration, regardless of a general directive in the will to pay debts.

Amended by Laws 1994, c. 472, § 54.

> *For text of section effective until January 1, 1996, see § 524.2.607, ante.*

Historical and Statutory Notes

Derivation:

St.1992, § 524.2–609.

Laws 1975, c. 347, § 22.

Laws 1994, c. 472, § 65, provides:

"(a) This act takes effect on January 1, 1996.

"(b) Except as provided elsewhere in this act:

"(1) this act applies to the rights of successors of decedents dying on or after its effective date and to any wills of decedents dying on or after its effective date;

"(2) if, before the effective date of this act, a right is either acquired, extinguished, waived, or barred upon the expiration of a prescribed period of time which commenced to run by the provisions of any statute before the effective date, the provisions of this act neither revoke, revive, restore, nor remove the bar of such right; and

"(3) any rule of construction or presumption provided in this act applies to instruments executed and multiple party accounts opened before the effective date of this act unless there is a clear indication of contrary intent."

Former section: St.1992, § 524.2–607, related to change in the value of securities, accessions, and nonademption. See, now, M.S.A. § 524.2–605.

524.2–608. Nonademption of specific devises in certain cases; sale by conservator or guardian; unpaid proceeds of sale, condemnation or insurance

Text of section effective until January 1, 1996.

(a) If specifically devised property is sold by a conservator or guardian, or if a condemnation award or insurance proceeds are paid to a conservator or guardian as a result of condemnation, fire, or casualty, the specific devisee has the right to a general pecuniary devise equal to the net sale price, the condemnation award, or the insurance proceeds. This subsection does not apply if subsequent to the sale, condemnation, or casualty, it is adjudicated that the disability of the testator has ceased and the testator survives the adjudication by one year. The right of the specific devisee under this subsection is reduced by any right possessed under subsection (b).

(b) Any specific devisee has the right to the remaining specifically devised property and:

(1) any balance of the purchase price together with any security interest owing from a purchaser to the testator at death by reason of sale of the property;

(2) any amount of a condemnation award for the taking of the property unpaid at death;

(3) any proceeds unpaid at death on fire or casualty insurance on the property; and

(4) property owned by testator at death as a result of foreclosure, or obtained in lieu of foreclosure, of the security for a specifically devised obligation.

Laws 1975, c. 347, § 22, eff. Jan. 1, 1976. Amended by Laws 1986, c. 444.

For text of section effective January 1, 1996, applicable to the rights of successors of decedents dying on or after January 1, 1996, and to any wills of decedents dying on or after January 1, 1996, see § 524.2–608, post.

524.2–608. Exercise of power of appointment

Text of section effective January 1, 1996, applicable to the rights of successors of decedents dying on or after January 1, 1996, and to any wills of decedents dying on or after January 1, 1996.

A general residuary clause in a will, or a will making general disposition of all of the testator's property, does not exercise a power of appointment held by the testator unless the testator's will manifests an intention to include property subject to the power.

Amended by Laws 1994, c. 472, § 55.

For text of section effective until January 1, 1996, see § 524.2–608, ante.

Historical and Statutory Notes

Derivation:

St.1992, § 524.2–610.

Laws 1975, c. 347, § 22.

Laws 1994, c. 472, § 65, provides:

"(a) This act takes effect on January 1, 1996.

"(b) Except as provided elsewhere in this act:

"(1) this act applies to the rights of successors of decedents dying on or after its effective date and to any wills of decedents dying on or after its effective date;

"(2) if, before the effective date of this act, a right is either acquired, extinguished, waived, or barred upon the expiration of a prescribed period of time which commenced to run by the provisions of any statute before the effective date, the provisions of this act neither revoke, revive, restore, nor remove the bar of such right; and

"(3) any rule of construction or presumption provided in this act applies to instruments executed and multiple party accounts opened before the effective date of this act unless there is a clear indication of contrary intent."

Former section: St.1992, § 524.2–608, related to nonademption of specific devises in certain cases; sale by conservator or guardian; and unpaid proceeds of sale, condemnation or insurance. See, now, M.S.A. § 524.2–606.

524.2–609. Nonexoneration

Text of section effective until January 1, 1996.

A specific devise passes subject to any security interest existing at the date of death, without right of exoneration, regardless of a general directive in the will to pay debts.

Laws 1975, c. 347, § 22, eff. Jan. 1, 1976.

For text of section effective January 1, 1996, applicable to the rights of successors of decedents dying on or after January 1, 1996, and to any wills of decedents dying on or after January 1, 1996, see § 524.2–609, post.

524.2–609. Ademption by satisfaction

Text of section effective January 1, 1996, applicable to the rights of successors of decedents dying on or after January 1, 1996, and to any wills of decedents dying on or after January 1, 1996.

(a) Property a testator, while living, gave to a person is treated as a satisfaction of a devise in whole or in part, only if (i) the will provides for deduction of the gift, (ii) the testator declared in a contemporaneous writing that the gift is in satisfaction of the devise or that its value is to be deducted from the value of the devise, or (iii) the devisee acknowledged in writing that the gift is in satisfaction of the devise or that its value is to be deducted from the value of the devise.

(b) For purposes of partial satisfaction, property given during lifetime is valued as of the time the devisee came into possession or enjoyment of the property or at the testator's death, whichever occurs first.

(c) If the devisee fails to survive the testator, the gift is treated as a full or partial satisfaction of the devise, as appropriate, in applying sections 524.2–603 and 524.2–604, unless the testator's contemporaneous writing provides otherwise.

Amended by Laws 1994, c. 472, § 56; Laws 2002, c. 379, art. 1, § 103.

For text of section effective until January 1, 1996, see § 524.2–609, ante.

Historical and Statutory Notes

Derivation:

St.1992, § 524.2–612.

Laws 1986, c. 444.

Laws 1975, c. 347, § 22.

Laws 1994, c. 472, § 65, provides:

"(a) This act takes effect on January 1, 1996.

"(b) Except as provided elsewhere in this act:

"(1) this act applies to the rights of successors of decedents dying on or after its effective date and to any wills of decedents dying on or after its effective date;

"(2) if, before the effective date of this act, a right is either acquired, extinguished, waived, or barred upon the expiration of a prescribed period of time which commenced to run by the provisions of any statute before the effective date, the provisions of this act neither revoke, revive, restore, nor remove the bar of such right; and

"(3) any rule of construction or presumption provided in this act applies to instruments executed and multiple party accounts opened before the effective date of this act unless there is a clear indication of contrary intent."

Former section: St.1992, § 524.2–609, related to nonexoneration of any mortgage interest. See, now, M.S.A. § 524.2–607.

524.2–610, 524.2–612. Repealed by Laws 1994, c. 472, § 64, eff. January 1, 1996

Historical and Statutory Notes

See, now, M.S.A. § 524.2–608.

See, now, M.S.A. § 524.2–609.

Laws 1994, c. 472, § 65, provides:

"(a) This act takes effect on January 1, 1996.

"(b) Except as provided elsewhere in this act:

"(1) this act applies to the rights of successors of decedents dying on or after its effective date and to any wills of decedents dying on or after its effective date;

"(2) if, before the effective date of this act, a right is either acquired, extinguished, waived, or barred upon the expiration of a prescribed period of time which commenced to run by the provisions of any statute before the effective date, the provisions of this act neither revoke, revive, restore, nor remove the bar of such right; and

"(3) any rule of construction or presumption provided in this act applies to instruments executed and multiple party accounts opened before the effective date of this act unless there is a clear indication of contrary intent."

PART 7

RULES OF CONSTRUCTION APPLICABLE TO WILLS AND OTHER GOVERNING INSTRUMENTS

524.2–701. Contracts concerning succession

Text of section effective until January 1, 1996.

A contract to make a will or devise, or not to revoke a will or devise, or to die intestate, if executed after the effective date of this act, can be established only by (1) provisions of a will stating material provisions of the contract; (2) an express reference in a will to a contract and extrinsic evidence proving the terms of the contract; or (3) a writing signed by the decedent evidencing the contract. The execution of a joint will or mutual wills does not create a presumption of a contract not to revoke the will or wills.

Laws 1975, c. 347, § 22, eff. Jan. 1, 1976.

For text of section effective January 1, 1996, applicable to the rights of successors of decedents dying on or after January 1, 1996, and to any wills of decedents dying on or after January 1, 1996, see § 524.2–701, post.

524.2–701. Scope

Text of section effective January 1, 1996, applicable to the rights of successors of decedents dying on or after January 1, 1996, and to any wills of decedents dying on or after January 1, 1996.

In the absence of a finding of a contrary intention, the rules of construction in this part control the construction of a governing instrument. The rules of construction in this part apply to a governing instrument of any type, except as the application of a particular section is limited by its terms to a specific type or types of provision or governing instrument.

Laws 1994, c. 472, § 57.

For text of section effective until January 1, 1996, see § 524.2–701, ante.

Historical and Statutory Notes

Laws 1994, c. 472, § 65, provides:

"(a) This act takes effect on January 1, 1996.

"(b) Except as provided elsewhere in this act:

"(1) this act applies to the rights of successors of decedents dying on or after its effective date and to any wills of decedents dying on or after its effective date;

"(2) if, before the effective date of this act, a right is either acquired, extinguished, waived, or barred upon the expiration of a prescribed period of time which commenced to run by the provisions of any statute before the effective date, the provisions of this act neither revoke, revive, restore, nor remove the bar of such right; and

"(3) any rule of construction or presumption provided in this act applies to instruments executed and multiple party accounts opened before the effective date of this act unless there is a clear indication of contrary intent."

Former section: St.1992, § 524.2–701, related to contracts concerning succession. See, now, M.S.A. § 524.2–514.

524.2–702. **Requirement of survival for 120 hours for devisees, beneficiaries of certain trusts, and appointees of certain powers of appointment; simultaneous death act for other cases**

(a) Requirement of survival for 120 hours. A beneficiary of a trust in which the grantor has reserved a power to alter, amend, revoke, or terminate the provisions of the trust who fails to survive the grantor by 120 hours, a devisee who fails to survive the testator by 120 hours, a beneficiary named in a transfer on death deed under section 507.071 who fails to survive by 120 hours the grantor owner upon whose death the conveyance to the beneficiary becomes effective, or an appointee of a power of appointment taking effect at the death of the holder of the power who fails to survive the holder of the power by 120 hours is deemed to have predeceased the grantor, grantor owner testator, or holder of the power for purposes of determining title to property passing by the trust instrument, by the testator's will, by the transfer on death deed, or by the exercise of the power of appointment.

(b)(1) Title to property in other cases. In cases not governed by section 524.2–104 or paragraph (a), where the title to property or the devolution thereof depends upon priority of death and there is no sufficient evidence that the persons have died otherwise than simultaneously, the property of each person shall be disposed of as if the person had survived, except as provided otherwise in this paragraph.

(2) Death of multiple beneficiaries; division of property. Where two or more beneficiaries are designated to take successively by reason of survivorship under another person's disposition of property and there is no sufficient evidence that these beneficiaries have died otherwise than simultaneously the property thus disposed of shall be divided into as many equal portions as there are successive beneficiaries and these portions shall be distributed respectively to those who would have taken in the event that each designated beneficiary had survived.

(3) Death of joint tenants or tenants by the entirety; division of property. Where there is no sufficient evidence that two joint tenants or tenants by the entirety have died otherwise than simultaneously the property so held shall be distributed one-half as if one had survived and one-half as if the other had survived. If there are more than two joint tenants and all of them have so died the property thus distributed shall be in the proportion that one bears to the whole number of joint tenants.

(4) Death of insured and beneficiary; division of property. Where the insured and the beneficiary in a policy of life or accident insurance have died and there is no sufficient evidence that they have died otherwise than simulta-

neously the proceeds of the policy shall be distributed as if the insured had survived the beneficiary.

(c) Not retroactive. This section does not apply to the distribution of the property of a person who has died before it takes effect. Paragraph (a) applies only to persons who die on or after August 1, 1999.

(d) Application. This section does not apply in the case of wills, trusts, deeds, contracts of insurance, or documents exercising powers of appointment wherein provision has been made for distribution of property different from the provisions of this section. Paragraph (a) does not apply to trusts which are part of a qualified or nonqualified retirement plan or individual retirement accounts.

Amended by Laws 1999, c. 171, § 2; Laws 2008, c. 341, art. 2, § 8, eff. Aug. 1, 2008.

Minnesota Rules of Evidence

Presumptions in civil cases, see Rule 301.

UNIFORM SIMULTANEOUS DEATH ACT (1953)

Table of Jurisdictions Wherein Act Has Been Adopted

For text of Uniform Act, and variation notes and annotation materials for adopting jurisdictions, see Uniform Laws Annotated, Master Edition, Volume 8B.

Jurisdiction	Laws	Effective Date	Statutory Citation
Alabama.............	1949, p. 852	9–7–1949	Code 1975, §§ 43–7–1 to 43–7–8.
Arkansas	1941, Act 15	1–30–1941 *	A.C.A. §§ 28–10–101 to 28–10–111.
California..........	1945, p. 1885	9–15–1945	West's Ann.Cal.Prob.Code, §§ 220 to 234.
Connecticut	1943, c. 266, p. 272	10–1–1943	C.G.S.A. § 45a–440.
Delaware	1945, c. 234	4–18–1945 *	12 Del.C. §§ 701 to 707.
Florida	1941, c. 20884	6–12–1941	West's F.S.A. § 732.601.
Georgia	1996, p. 504	1–1–1998	O.C.G.A. §§ 53–10–1 to 53–10–6.
Idaho	1943, c. 83	2–23–1943 *	I.C. § 15–2–613.
Illinois	1941, vol. 1, p. 6	7–16–1941	S.H.A. 755 ILCS 5/3–1, 5/3–2.
Indiana.............	1941, c. 49	2–24–1941 *	West's A.I.C. 29–2–14–1 to 29–2–14–8.
Iowa	1963, c. 326	1–1–1964	I.C.A. §§ 633.523 to 633.528.
Maine..............	1941, c. 111	3–29–1941	18–A M.R.S.A. § 2–805.
Maryland	1941, c. 191	6–1–1941	Code, Courts and Judicial Proceedings, §§ 10–801 to 10–807.
Massachusetts	1941, c. 549	7–29–1941	M.G.L.A. c. 190A, §§ 1 to 8.
Minnesota	1943, c. 248	4–2–1943 *	M.S.A. § 524.2–702.
Mississippi	1956, c. 214	7–1–1956	Code 1972, §§ 91–3–1 to 91–3–15.
Missouri	1947, Vol. 1, p. 13	9–10–1947	V.A.M.S. §§ 471.010 to 471.080.
Nebraska	1947, c. 112	3–8–1947	R.R.S.1943, §§ 30–121 to 30–128.
Nevada.............	1949, c. 44	3–9–1949 *	N.R.S. 135.010 to 135.090.
New Jersey..........	1947, c. 384	7–3–1947	N.J.S.A. 3B:6–1 to 3B:6–7.
New York...........	1966, c. 952	9–1–1967	McKinney's EPTL 2–1.6.
North Carolina	1947, c. 1016	4–5–1947	G.S. §§ 28A–24–1 to 28A–24–7.
Oklahoma..........	1959, c. 385	10–2–1959	58 Okl.St.Ann. §§ 1001 to 1008.

Jurisdiction	Laws	Effective Date	Statutory Citation
Pennsylvania	1972, No. 164	7-1-1972	20 Pa.C.S.A. §§ 8501 to 8505.
Rhode Island	1947, c. 1871	4-28-1947	Gen.Laws 1956, §§ 33-2-1 to 33-2-9.
South Carolina	1948, p. 1753	4-3-1948	Code 1976, §§ 62-1-501 to 62-1-508.
Tennessee	1941, c. 59	2-10-1941	T.C.A. §§ 31-3-101 to 31-3-120.
Texas	1955, c. 55	1-1-1956	V.A.T.S. Probate Code, § 47.
Vermont	1941, No. 41	3-21-1941	14 V.S.A. §§ 621 to 627.
Virgin Islands	1957, c. 3	9-1-1957	15 V.I.C. § 88.
Washington	1943, c. 113	3-16-1943	West's RCWA 11.05.010 to 11.05.910.
West Virginia	1953, c. 66	2-18-1953	Code, 42-5-1 to 42-5-10.
Wyoming	1941, c. 94	2-21-1941	Wyo.Stat.Ann. §§ 2-13-101 to 2-13-107.

* Date of approval.

Historical and Statutory Notes

Derivation:

Laws 1994, c. 472, § 63.

St.1992, § 525.90.

Laws 1986, c. 444.

St.Supp.1944, §§ 8992-33c to 8992-33i

Laws 1943, c. 248, §§ 1 to 7.

Laws 2008, c. 341, art. 2, § 9, provided:

"This article is effective August 1, 2008, and applies to instruments of conveyance of real property recorded on or after that date, regardless of an instrument's date of execution."

524.2-703. Choice of law as to meaning and effect of governing instrument

Text of section effective January 1, 1996, applicable to the rights of successors of decedents dying on or after January 1, 1996, and to any wills of decedents dying on or after January 1, 1996.

The meaning and legal effect of a governing instrument is determined by the local law of the state selected in the governing instrument, unless the application of that law is contrary to the provisions relating to the elective share described in part 2, the provisions relating to exempt property and allowances described in part 4, or any other public policy of this state otherwise applicable to the disposition.

Laws 1994, c. 472, § 58.

Historical and Statutory Notes

Laws 1994, c. 472, § 65, provides:

"(a) This act takes effect on January 1, 1996.

"(b) Except as provided elsewhere in this act:

"(1) this act applies to the rights of successors of decedents dying on or after its effective date and to any wills of decedents dying on or after its effective date;

"(2) if, before the effective date of this act, a right is either acquired, extinguished, waived, or barred upon the expiration of a prescribed

period of time which commenced to run by the provisions of any statute before the effective date, the provisions of this act neither revoke, revive, restore, nor remove the bar of such right; and

"(3) any rule of construction or presumption provided in this act applies to instruments executed and multiple party accounts opened before the effective date of this act unless there is a clear indication of contrary intent."

524.2-704. Power of appointment; meaning of specific reference requirement

Text of section effective January 1, 1996, applicable to the rights of successors of decedents dying on or after January 1, 1996, and to any wills of decedents dying on or after January 1, 1996.

If a governing instrument creating a power of appointment expressly requires that the power be exercised by a reference, an express reference, or a specific reference, to the power or its source, it is presumed that the donor's intention, in requiring that the donee exercise the power by making reference to the particular power or to the creating instrument, was to prevent an inadvertent exercise of the power and an attempt to exercise the power by a donee who had knowledge of and intended to exercise the power is effective.

Laws 1994, c. 472, § 59.

Historical and Statutory Notes

Laws 1994, c. 472, § 65, provides:

"(a) This act takes effect on January 1, 1996.

"(b) Except as provided elsewhere in this act:

"(1) this act applies to the rights of successors of decedents dying on or after its effective date and to any wills of decedents dying on or after its effective date;

"(2) if, before the effective date of this act, a right is either acquired, extinguished, waived, or barred upon the expiration of a prescribed period of time which commenced to run by the provisions of any statute before the effective date, the provisions of this act neither revoke, revive, restore, nor remove the bar of such right; and

"(3) any rule of construction or presumption provided in this act applies to instruments executed and multiple party accounts opened before the effective date of this act unless there is a clear indication of contrary intent."

524.2–705. Class gifts construed to accord with intestate succession

Text of section effective January 1, 1996, applicable to the rights of successors of decedents dying on or after January 1, 1996, and to any wills of decedents dying on or after January 1, 1996.

Adopted individuals and individuals born out of wedlock, and their respective descendants if appropriate to the class, are included in class gifts and other terms of relationship in accordance with the rules for intestate succession. Terms of relationship that do not differentiate relationships by blood from those by affinity, such as "uncles," "aunts," "nieces," or "nephews," are presumed to exclude relatives by affinity. Terms of relationship that do not differentiate relationships by the half blood from those by the whole blood, such as "brothers," "sisters," "nieces," or "nephews," are presumed to include both types of relationships.

Laws 1994, c. 472, § 60.

Historical and Statutory Notes

Laws 1994, c. 472, § 65, provides:

"(a) This act takes effect on January 1, 1996.

"(b) Except as provided elsewhere in this act:

"(1) this act applies to the rights of successors of decedents dying on or after its effective date and to any wills of decedents dying on or after its effective date;

"(2) if, before the effective date of this act, a right is either acquired, extinguished, waived, or barred upon the expiration of a prescribed period of time which commenced to run by the provisions of any statute before the effective date, the provisions of this act neither revoke, revive, restore, nor remove the bar of such right; and

"(3) any rule of construction or presumption provided in this act applies to instruments executed and multiple party accounts opened before the effective date of this act unless there is a clear indication of contrary intent."

524.2–708. Class gifts to "descendants," "issue," or "heirs of the body"; form of distribution if none specified

Text of section effective January 1, 1996, applicable to the rights of successors of decedents dying on or after January 1, 1996, and to any wills of decedents dying on or after January 1, 1996.

If a class gift in favor of "descendants," "issue," or "heirs of the body" does not specify the manner in which the property is to be distributed among the class members, the property is distributed among the class members who are living when the interest is to take effect in possession or enjoyment, in such shares as they would receive, under the applicable law of intestate succession, if the designated ancestor had then died intestate owning the subject matter of the class gift.

Laws 1994, c. 472, § 61.

Historical and Statutory Notes

Laws 1994, c. 472, § 65, provides:

"(a) This act takes effect on January 1, 1996.

"(b) Except as provided elsewhere in this act:

"(1) this act applies to the rights of successors of decedents dying on or after its effective date and to any wills of decedents dying on or after its effective date;

"(2) if, before the effective date of this act, a right is either acquired, extinguished, waived, or barred upon the expiration of a prescribed period of time which commenced to run by the provisions of any statute before the effective date, the provisions of this act neither revoke, revive, restore, nor remove the bar of such right; and

"(3) any rule of construction or presumption provided in this act applies to instruments executed and multiple party accounts opened before the effective date of this act unless there is a clear indication of contrary intent."

524.2–709. Representation; per stirpes; per capita at each generation

Text of section effective January 1, 1996, applicable to the rights of successors of decedents dying on or after January 1, 1996, and to any wills of decedents dying on or after January 1, 1996.

(a) Definitions. In this section:

(1) "Deceased child" or "deceased descendant" means a child or a descendant who either predeceased the distribution date or is deemed to have predeceased the distribution date under section 524.2–702.

(2) "Distribution date," with respect to an interest, means the time when the interest is to take effect in possession or enjoyment. The distribution date need not occur at the beginning or end of a calendar day, but can occur at a time during the course of a day.

(3) "Surviving ancestor," "surviving child," or "surviving descendant" means an ancestor, a child, or a descendant who neither predeceased the distribution date nor is deemed to have predeceased the distribution date under section 524.2–702.

(b) Representation; per stirpes. If an applicable statute or governing instrument calls for property to be distributed by "representation" or "per stirpes," the property is divided into as many equal shares as there are (i) surviving children of the designated ancestor and (ii) deceased children who left surviving descendants. Each surviving child, if any, is allocated one share. The share of each deceased child with surviving descendants is divided in the same manner, with subdivision repeating at each succeeding generation until the property is fully allocated among surviving descendants.

(c) Per capita at each generation. If a governing instrument calls for property to be distributed "per capita at each generation," the property is divided into as many equal shares as there are (i) surviving descendants in the generation nearest to the designated ancestor which contains one or more surviving descendants and (ii) deceased descendants in the same generation who left surviving descendants, if any. Each surviving descendant in the nearest generation is allocated one share. The remaining shares, if any, are combined and then divided in the same manner among the surviving descendants of the deceased descendants as if the surviving descendants who were allocated a share and their surviving descendants had predeceased the distribution date.

(d) Deceased descendant with no surviving descendant disregarded. For the purposes of paragraphs (b) and (c), an individual who is deceased and left no surviving descendant is disregarded, and an individual who leaves a surviving ancestor who is a descendant of the designated ancestor is not entitled to a share.

Laws 1994, c. 472, § 62.

Historical and Statutory Notes

Laws 1994, c. 472, § 65, provides:

"(a) This act takes effect on January 1, 1996.

"(b) Except as provided elsewhere in this act:

"(1) this act applies to the rights of successors of decedents dying on or after its effective date and to any wills of decedents dying on or after its effective date;

"(2) if, before the effective date of this act, a right is either acquired, extinguished, waived, or barred upon the expiration of a prescribed period of time which commenced to run by the provisions of any statute before the effective date, the provisions of this act neither revoke, revive, restore, nor remove the bar of such right; and

"(3) any rule of construction or presumption provided in this act applies to instruments executed and multiple party accounts opened before the effective date of this act unless there is a clear indication of contrary intent."

524.2–711. Future interests in "heirs," "heirs at law," or "next of kin"

If a governing instrument calls for a future distribution to or creates a future interest in a designated individual's "heirs," "heirs at law," or "next of kin," the property passes to those persons, including the state of Minnesota under section 524.2–105, and in such shares as would succeed to the designated individual's intestate estate under the laws of intestate succession of the state of Minnesota if the designated individual died when the disposition is to take effect in possession or enjoyment. If the designated individual's surviving spouse is living at the time the disposition is to take effect in possession or enjoyment, the surviving spouse is an heir of the designated individual for the purposes of this section, whether or not the surviving spouse is remarried.

Laws 1997, c. 9, § 9.

PART 8

GENERAL PROVISIONS

524.2–802. Effect of dissolution of marriage, annulment, and decree of separation

A person whose marriage to the decedent has been dissolved or annulled is not a surviving spouse unless, by virtue of a subsequent marriage, the person is married to the decedent at the time of death. A decree of separation which does not terminate the status of husband and wife is not a dissolution of marriage for purposes of this section.

Laws 1975, c. 347, § 22, eff. Jan. 1, 1976. Amended by Laws 1986, c. 444.

524.2–803. Effect of homicide on intestate succession, wills, joint assets, life insurance and beneficiary designations

(a) A surviving spouse, heir or devisee who feloniously and intentionally kills the decedent is not entitled to any benefits under the will or under this article, including an intestate share, an elective share, an omitted spouse's or child's share, homestead, exempt property, and a family allowance, and the estate of decedent passes as if the killer had predeceased the decedent. Property appointed by the will of the decedent to or for the benefit of the killer passes as if the killer had predeceased the decedent.

(b) Any joint tenant who feloniously and intentionally kills another joint tenant thereby effects a severance of the interest of the decedent so that the share of the decedent passes as the decedent's property and the killer has no rights by survivorship. This provision applies to joint tenancies in real and personal property, joint accounts in banks, savings associations, credit unions and other institutions, and any other form of co-ownership with survivorship incidents.

(c) A named beneficiary of a bond or other contractual arrangement who feloniously and intentionally kills the principal obligee is not entitled to any benefit under the bond or other contractual arrangement and it becomes payable as though the killer had predeceased the decedent.

(d) A named beneficiary of a life insurance policy who feloniously and intentionally kills the person upon whose life the policy is issued is not entitled to any benefit under the policy and the proceeds of the policy shall be paid and distributed by order of the court as hereinafter provided. If a person who feloniously and intentionally kills a person upon whose life a life insurance policy is issued is a beneficial owner as shareholder, partner or beneficiary of a corporation, partnership, trust or association which is the named beneficiary of the life insurance policy, to the extent of the killer's beneficial ownership of the corporation, partnership, trust or association, the proceeds of the policy shall be paid and distributed by order of the court as hereinafter provided.

Upon receipt of written notice by the insurance company at its home office that the insured may have been intentionally and feloniously killed by one or more named beneficiaries or that the insured may have been intentionally and feloniously killed by one or more persons who have a beneficial ownership in a corporation, partnership, trust or association, which is the named beneficiary of the life insurance policy, the insurance company shall, pending court order, withhold payment of the policy proceeds to all beneficiaries. In the event that the notice has not been received by the insurance company before payment of the policy proceeds, the insurance company shall be fully and finally discharged and released from any and all responsibility under the policy to the extent that the policy proceeds have been paid.

The named beneficiary, the insurance company or any other party claiming an interest in the policy proceeds may commence an action in the district court to compel payment of the policy proceeds. The court may order the insurance company to pay the policy proceeds to any person equitably entitled thereto, including the deceased insured's spouse, children, issue, parents, creditors or estate, and may order the insurance company to pay the proceeds of the policy to the court pending the final determination of distribution of the proceeds by the court. The insurance company, upon receipt of a court order, judgment or decree ordering payment of the policy proceeds, shall pay the policy proceeds according to the terms of the order, and upon payment of such proceeds according to the terms of the court order, shall be fully and completely discharged and released from any and all responsibility for payment under the policy.

(e) Any other acquisition of property or interest by the killer shall be treated in accordance with the principles of this section.

(f) A final judgment of conviction of felonious and intentional killing is conclusive for purposes of this section. In the absence of a conviction of felonious and intentional killing the court may determine by a preponderance of evidence whether the killing was felonious and intentional for purposes of this section.

(g) This section does not affect the rights of any person who, before rights under this section have been adjudicated, purchases from the killer for value and without notice property which the killer would have acquired except for this section, but the killer is liable for the amount of the proceeds or the value of the property. Any insurance company, bank, or other obligor making payment according to the terms of its policy or obligation is not liable by reason of this section unless prior to payment it has received at its home office or principal address written notice of a claim under this section.

Laws 1975, c. 347, § 22, eff. Jan. 1, 1976. Amended by Laws 1981, c. 315, § 1; Laws 1986, c. 444; Laws 1995, c. 202, art. 1, § 25, eff. May 25, 1995; Laws 1996, c. 338, art. 2, § 3.

524.2–804. Revocation by dissolution of marriage; no revocation by other changes of circumstances

Subdivision 1. Revocation upon dissolution. Except as provided by the express terms of a governing instrument, other than a trust instrument under section 501B.90, executed prior to the dissolution or annulment of an individual's marriage, a court order, a contract relating to the division of the marital property made between individuals before or after their marriage, dissolution, or annulment, or a plan document governing a qualified or nonqualified retirement plan, the dissolution or annulment of a marriage revokes any revocable:

(1) disposition, beneficiary designation, or appointment of property made by an individual to the individual's former spouse in a governing instrument;

(2) provision in a governing instrument conferring a general or nongeneral power of appointment on an individual's former spouse; and

(3) nomination in a governing instrument, nominating an individual's former spouse to serve in any fiduciary or representative capacity, including a personal representative, executor, trustee, conservator, agent, or guardian.

Subd. 2. Effect of revocation. Provisions of a governing instrument are given effect as if the former spouse died immediately before the dissolution or annulment.

Subd. 3. Revival if dissolution nullified. Provisions revoked solely by this section are revived by the individual's remarriage to the former spouse or by a nullification of the dissolution or annulment.

Subd. 4. No revocation for other change of circumstances. No change of circumstances other than as described in this section and in section 524.2–803 effects a revocation.

Subd. 5. Protection of payors and other third parties. (a) A payor or other third party is not liable for having made a payment or transferred an item of property or any other benefit to a beneficiary designated in a governing instrument affected by a dissolution, annulment, or remarriage, or for having taken any other action in good faith reliance on the validity of the governing instrument, before the payor or other third party received written notice of the dissolution, annulment, or remarriage. A payor or other third party is liable for a payment made or other action taken after the payor or other third party received written notice of a claimed forfeiture or revocation under this section.

419

(b) Written notice of the dissolution, annulment, or remarriage under paragraph (a) must be delivered to the payor's or other third party's main office or home. Upon receipt of written notice of the dissolution, annulment, or remarriage, a payor or other third party may pay any amount owed or transfer or deposit any item of property held by it to or with the court having jurisdiction of the probate proceedings relating to the decedent's estate or, if no proceedings have been commenced, to or with the court having jurisdiction of probate proceedings relating to decedents' estates located in the county of the decedent's residence. The court shall hold the funds or item of property and, upon its determination under this section, shall order disbursement or transfer in accordance with the determination. Payments, transfers, or deposits made to or with the court discharge the payor or other third party from all claims for the value of amounts paid to or items of property transferred to or deposited with the court.

Laws 1995, c. 130, § 13. Amended by Laws 2002, c. 347, § 2.

Historical and Statutory Notes

Laws 2004, c. 146, art. 1, § 7, amended Laws 2002, c. 347, § 5, to provide that Laws 2002, c. 347, § 2 applies to decedents dying after July 31, 2002.

Laws 1995, c. 130, § 22, provides in part that chapter 130 is effective January 1, 1996, and that §§ 12, 13, and 15 (amending § 524.2–508, enacting § 524.2–804, and amending § 524.3–916, respectively) apply to the rights of successors of decedents dying on or after January 1, 1996, and to any wills of decedents dying on or after January 1, 1996.

PART 10

INTERNATIONAL WILL INFORMATION REGISTRATION

524.2–1001. Definitions

Subdivision 1. Scope. For the purposes of sections 524.2–1001 to 524.2–1010, the terms defined in this section have the meanings ascribed to them.

Subd. 2. International will. "International will" means a will executed in conformity with sections 524.2–1002 to 524.2–1005.

Subd. 3. Authorized person. "Authorized person" and "person authorized to act in connection with international wills" means a person who by section 524.2–1009, or by the laws of the United States including members of the diplomatic and consular service of the United States designated by Foreign Service Regulations, is empowered to supervise the execution of international wills.

Laws 1978, c. 525, § 2, eff. March 24, 1978.

524.2–1002. International will; validity

Subdivision 1. Form. A will is valid as regards form, irrespective particularly of the place where it is made, of the location of the assets and of the nationality, domicile, or residence of the testator, if it is made in the form of an international will complying with the requirements of sections 524.2–1002 to 524.2–1005.

Subd. 2. Effect of invalidity. The invalidity of the will as an international will does not affect its formal validity as a will of another kind.

Subd. 3. Multiple testators. Sections 524.2–1001 to 524.2–1010 do not apply to the form of testamentary dispositions made by two or more persons in one instrument.

Laws 1978, c. 525, § 3, eff. March 24, 1978.

524.2–1003. International will; requirements

Subdivision 1. In writing. The will must be made in writing. It need not be written by the testator personally. It may be written in any language, by hand or by any other means.

Subd. 2. Testator's declaration. The testator shall declare in the presence of two witnesses and of a person authorized to act in connection with international wills that the document is the testator's will and that the testator knows the contents thereof. The testator need not inform the witnesses or the authorized person of the contents of the will.

Subd. 3. Signature. In the presence of the witnesses and of the authorized person, the testator shall sign the will or, having previously signed it, shall acknowledge the signature.

Subd. 4. Inability to sign. If the testator is unable to sign, the absence of the signature does not affect the validity of the international will if the testator indicates the reason for the inability to sign and the authorized person makes note thereof on the will. In that case, it is permissible for any other person present, including the authorized person or one of the witnesses, at the direction of the testator, to sign the testator's name for the testator if the authorized person makes note of this on the will, but it is not required that any person sign the testator's name for the testator.

Subd. 5. Attestation. The witnesses and the authorized person shall there and then attest the will by signing in the presence of the testator.

Laws 1978, c. 525, § 4, eff. March 24, 1978. Amended by Laws 1986, c. 444.

524.2–1004. International wills; other points of form

Subdivision 1. Multiple pages. The signatures must be placed at the end of the will. If the will consists of several sheets, each sheet must be signed by the testator or, if the testator is unable to sign, by the person signing on the testator's behalf or, if there is no such person, by the authorized person. In addition, each sheet must be numbered.

Subd. 2. Date. The date of the will must be the date of its signature by the authorized person. That date must be noted at the end of the will by the authorized person.

Subd. 3. Safekeeping. The authorized person shall ask whether the testator wishes to make a declaration concerning the safekeeping of the will. If so and at the express request of the testator, the place where the testator intends to have the will kept must be mentioned in the certificate provided for in section 524.2–1005.

Subd. 4. Validity. A will executed in compliance with section 524.2–1003 is not invalid merely because it does not comply with this section.

Laws 1978, c. 525, § 5, eff. March 24, 1978. Amended by Laws 1986, c. 444.

524.2–1005. International will; certificate

The authorized person shall sign and attach to the will a certificate establishing that the requirements of sections 524.2–1002 to 524.2–1005 for valid execution of an international will have been fulfilled. The authorized person shall keep a copy of the certificate and deliver another to the testator. The certificate must be substantially in the following form:

CERTIFICATE

(Convention of October 26, 1973)

1. I, ... (name, address, and capacity), a person authorized to act in connection with international wills,

2. certify that on .... (date) at.....................(place)

3. (testator) ....(name, address, date and place of birth) in my presence and that of the witnesses

4. (a) ....(name, address, date and place of birth)

   (b) ....(name, address, date and place of birth)

has declared that the attached document is his/her will and that ....he knows the contents thereof.

5. I furthermore certify that:

6. (a) in my presence and in that of the witnesses (1) the testator has signed the will or has acknowledged his/her signature previously affixed.

[1] (2) following a declaration of the testator stating that the testator was unable to sign the will for the following reason............, I have mentioned this declaration on the will,

[1] and the signature has been affixed by....................... (name and address)

7. (b) the witnesses and I have signed the will;

8. [1] (c) each page of the will has been signed by .... and numbered;

9. (d) I have satisfied myself as to the identity of the testator and of the witnesses as designated above;

10. (e) the witnesses met the conditions requisite to act as such according to the law under which I am acting;

11. [1] (f) the testator has requested me to include the following statement concerning the safekeeping of the will: ....

12. ....PLACE OF EXECUTION

13. ....DATE

14. ....SIGNATURE and, if necessary, SEAL ....

Laws 1978, c. 525, § 6, eff. March 24, 1978. Amended by Laws 1986, c. 444.
  [1] to be completed if appropriate

524.2–1006. International will; effect of certificate

In the absence of evidence to the contrary, the certificate of the authorized person is conclusive of the formal validity of the instrument as a will under sections 524.2–1001 to 524.2–1010. The absence or irregularity of a certificate does not affect the formal validity of a will under sections 524.2–1001 to 524.2–1010.

Laws 1978, c. 525, § 7, eff. March 24, 1978.

524.2–1007. International will; revocation

An international will is subject to the ordinary rules of revocation of wills.

Laws 1978, c. 525, § 8, eff. March 24, 1978.

524.2–1008. Source and construction

Sections 524.2–1001 to 524.2–1007 derive from Annex to Convention of October 26, 1973, Providing a Uniform Law on the Form of an International Will. In interpreting and applying sections 524.2–1001 to 524.2–1007, regard shall be had to its international origin and to the need for uniformity in its interpretation.

Laws 1978, c. 525, § 9, eff. March 24, 1978.

524.2–1009. Persons authorized to act in relation to international will; eligibility; recognition by authorizing agency

Individuals who have been admitted to practice law before the courts of this state and are currently licensed so to do are authorized persons in relation to international wills.

Laws 1978, c. 525, § 10, eff. March 24, 1978.

524.2–1010. International will information registration

Subdivision 1. Registry. The secretary of state shall establish a registry system by which authorized persons may register, in a central information center, information regarding the execution of international wills. The information shall be private until the death of the testator, after which date it shall be available to any person desiring information about any will who presents a death record or other satisfactory evidence of the testator's death to the secretary of state.

Subd. 2. Transmission to other registry. The secretary of state, at the request of the authorized person, may cause the information received about execution of any international will to be transmitted to the registry system of another jurisdiction as identified by the testator, if that other system adheres to rules protecting the confidentiality of the information similar to those established in this state.

Subd. 3. Information to be registered. Only the following information may be received, preserved and reported pursuant to this section:

(a) The testator's name, Social Security number or other individual identifying number established by law;

(b) The testator's address and date and place of birth; and

(c) The intended place of deposit or safekeeping of the instrument pending the death of the testator.

Laws 1978, c. 525, § 11, eff. March 24, 1978. Amended by Laws 1986, c. 444; Laws 2001, 1st Sp., c. 9, art. 15, § 32.

Historical and Statutory Notes

Laws 2002, c. 379, art. 1, § 113, provides:

"2001 First Special Session Senate File No. 4, as passed by the senate and the house of representatives on Friday, June 29, 2001, and subsequently published as Laws 2001, First Special Session chapter 9, is reenacted. Its provisions are effective on the dates originally provided in the bill."

ARTICLE 3

PROBATE OF WILLS AND ADMINISTRATION

PART 1

GENERAL PROVISIONS

524.3–101. Devolution of estate at death; restrictions

The power of a person to leave property by will, and the rights of creditors, devisees, and heirs to the person's property are subject to the restrictions and limitations contained in chapters 524 and 525 to facilitate the prompt settlement of estates. Upon death, a person's real and personal property devolves to the persons to whom it is devised by last will or to those indicated as substitutes for them in cases involving lapse, disclaimer, renunciation, or other circumstances affecting the devolution of testate estates, or in the absence of testamentary disposition, to the decedent's heirs, or to those indicated as substitutes for them in cases involving disclaimer, renunciation or other circumstances affecting devolution of intestate estates, subject to the provisions of sections 525.14 and 524.2–402, the allowances provided for by sections 524.2–403 and 524.2–404, to the rights of creditors, elective share of the surviving spouse, and to administration.

Laws 1974, c. 442, art. 3, § 524.3–101. Amended by Laws 1975, c. 347, § 23, eff. Jan. 1, 1976; Laws 1986, c. 444; Laws 1996, c. 305, art. 1, § 111.

524.3–102. Necessity of order of probate for will

Except as provided in section 524.3–1201, to be effective to prove the transfer of any property, to nominate an executor or to exercise a power of appointment, a will must be declared to be valid by an order of informal probate by the registrar, or an adjudication of probate by the court in a formal proceeding or proceedings to determine descent, except that a duly executed and unrevoked will which has not been probated may be admitted as evidence of a devise if (1) no court proceeding concerning the succession or administration of the estate has occurred, and (2) either the devisee or the devisee's successors and assigns possessed the property devised in accordance with the provisions of the will, or the property devised was not possessed or claimed by anyone by virtue of the decedent's title during the time period for testacy proceedings.

Laws 1974, c. 442, art. 3, § 524.3–102. Amended by Laws 1975, c. 347, § 24, eff. Jan. 1, 1976; Laws 1986, c. 444.

524.3–103. Necessity of appointment for administration

Except as otherwise provided in article 4, to acquire the powers and undertake the duties and liabilities of a personal representative of a decedent, a person must be appointed by order of the court or registrar, qualify and be issued letters. Administration of an estate is commenced by the issuance of letters.

Laws 1974, c. 442, art. 3, § 524.3–103, eff. Aug. 1, 1975.

524.3–104. Claims against decedent; necessity of administration

No proceeding to enforce a claim against the estate of a decedent or the decedent's successors may be revived or commenced before the appointment of a personal representative. After the appointment and until distribution, all proceedings and actions to enforce a claim against the estate are governed by this article. After distribution a creditor whose claim has not been barred may recover from the distributees as provided in section 524.3–1004 or from a former personal representative individually liable as provided in section 524.3–1005. This section has no application to a proceeding by a secured creditor of the decedent to enforce the creditor's right to the security except as to any deficiency judgment which might be sought therein.

Laws 1974, c. 442, art. 3, § 524.3–104. Amended by Laws 1975, c. 347, § 25, eff. Jan. 1, 1976; Laws 1986, c. 444.

524.3–105. Proceedings affecting devolution and administration; jurisdiction of subject matter

Any interested person in a decedent's estate may apply to the registrar for determination in the informal proceedings provided in this article, and may petition the court for orders in formal proceedings within the court's jurisdiction including but not limited to those described in this article. Interim orders approving or directing partial distributions, sale of property or granting other relief may be issued by the court at any time during the pendency of an administration on the petition of the personal representative or any interested person. The court has exclusive jurisdiction of proceedings, to determine how decedents' estates subject to the laws of this state are to be administered, expended and distributed. The court has concurrent jurisdiction of any other action or proceeding concerning a succession or to which an estate, through a personal representative, may be a party, including actions to determine title to property alleged to belong to the estate, and of any action or proceeding in which property distributed by a personal representative or its value is sought to be subjected to rights of creditors or successors of the decedent.

The court shall not have jurisdiction of foreclosure of mechanic liens, or of any action under section 573.02.

Laws 1974, c. 442, art. 3, § 524.3–105. Amended by Laws 1975, c. 347, § 26, eff. Jan. 1, 1976; Laws 1977, c. 154, § 1; Laws 1978, c. 525, § 12, eff. March 24, 1978; Laws 1979, c. 132, § 1; Laws 1980, c. 439, § 29.

Historical and Statutory Notes

Laws 1980, c. 439, § 29, made technical adjustments and clarified certain provisions relating to estate tax, effective for estates of decedents dying after December 31, 1979.

524.3–106. Proceedings within the exclusive jurisdiction of court; service; jurisdiction over persons

In proceedings within the exclusive jurisdiction of the court where notice is required by this chapter or by rule, interested persons may be bound by the orders of the court in respect to property in or subject to the laws of this state by notice in conformity with section 524.1–401. An order is binding as to all who are given notice of the proceeding though less than all interested persons are notified.

Laws 1974, c. 442, art. 3, § 524.3–106, eff. Jan. 1, 1976.

524.3–107. Scope of proceedings; proceedings independent; exception

Unless supervised administration as described in part 5 is involved, (1) each proceeding before the court or registrar is independent of any other proceeding involving the same estate; (2) petitions for formal orders of the court may combine various requests for relief in a single proceeding if the orders sought may be finally granted without delay. Except as required for proceedings which are particularly described by other sections of this article, no petition is defective because it fails to embrace all matters which might then be the subject of a final order; (3) proceedings for probate of wills or adjudications of no will may be combined with proceedings for appointment of personal representatives; and (4) a proceeding for appointment of a personal representative is concluded by an order making or declining the appointment.

Laws 1974, c. 442, art. 3, § 524.3–107, eff. Jan. 1, 1976.

524.3–108. Probate, testacy and appointment proceedings; ultimate time limit

No informal probate or appointment proceeding or formal testacy or appointment proceeding, other than a proceeding to probate a will previously probated at the testator's domicile and appointment proceedings relating to an estate in which there has been a prior appointment, may be commenced more than three years after the decedent's death, except (1) if a previous proceeding was dismissed because of doubt about the fact of the decedent's death, appropriate probate, appointment or testacy proceedings may be maintained at any time thereafter upon a finding that the decedent's death occurred prior to the initiation of the previous proceeding and the applicant or petitioner has not delayed unduly in initiating the subsequent proceeding; (2) appropriate probate, appointment or testacy proceedings may be maintained in relation to the estate of an absentee, or disappeared or missing person, at any time within three years after the death of the absentee or disappeared or missing person is established; and (3) a proceeding to contest an informally probated will and to secure appointment of the person with legal priority for appointment in the event the contest is successful, may be commenced within the later of 12 months from the informal probate or three years from the decedent's death. These limitations do not apply to proceedings to construe probated wills, determine heirs of an intestate, or proceedings to determine descent. In cases under (1) or (2) above, the date on which a testacy or appointment proceeding is properly commenced shall be deemed to be the date of the decedent's death for purposes of other limitations provisions of this chapter which relate to the date of death. Nothing herein contained prohibits the formal appointment of a special administrator at any time for the purposes of reducing assets to possession, administering the same under direction of the court, or making distribution of any residue to the heirs or distributees determined to be entitled thereto pursuant to a descent proceeding under section 525.31 or an exempt summary proceeding under section 524.3–1203, even though the three-year period above referred to has expired.

Laws 1974, c. 442, art. 3, § 524.3–108. Amended by Laws 1975, c. 347, § 27, eff. Jan. 1, 1976; Laws 1977, c. 440, § 3; Laws 1996, c. 305, art. 1, § 112.

Historical and Statutory Notes
Laws 1977, c. 440, § 4, provides: "This act is effective the day following final
                                                     enactment as to all informal proceedings com-
                                                     menced after January 1, 1976."

524.3–109. Statutes of limitation on decedent's cause of action

No statute of limitation running on a cause of action belonging to a decedent
which had not been barred as of the date of death, shall apply to bar a cause of
action surviving the decedent's death sooner than one year after death. A
cause of action which, but for this section, would have been barred less than
one year after death, is barred after one year unless tolled.

Laws 1974, c. 442, art. 3, § 524.3–109. Amended by Laws 1975, c. 347, § 28, eff. Jan.
1, 1976; Laws 1986, c. 444.

PART 2

VENUE FOR PROBATE AND ADMINISTRATION; PRIORITY
TO ADMINISTER; DEMAND FOR NOTICE

**524.3–201. Venue for first and subsequent estate proceedings; location of
property**

(a) Venue for the first informal or formal testacy or appointment proceedings
after a decedent's death is:

(1) in the county of the decedent's domicile at the time of death; or

(2) if the decedent was not domiciled in this state, in any county where property of
the decedent was located at the time of death.

(b) Venue for all subsequent proceedings within the exclusive jurisdiction of
the court is in the place where the initial proceeding occurred, unless the initial
proceeding has been transferred as provided in section 524.1–303 or (c) of this
section.

(c) If the first proceeding was informal, on application of an interested
person and after notice to the proponent in the first proceeding, the court, upon
finding that venue is elsewhere, may transfer the proceeding and the file to the
other court.

(d) For the purpose of aiding determinations concerning location of assets
which may be relevant in cases involving nondomiciliaries, a debt, other than
one evidenced by investment or commercial paper or other instrument in favor
of a nondomiciliary, is located where the debtor resides or, if the debtor is a
person other than an individual, at the place where it has its principal office.
Commercial paper, investment paper and other instruments are located where
the instrument is. An interest in property held in trust is located where the
trustee may be sued.

Laws 1974, c. 442, art. 3, § 524.3–201, eff. Jan. 1, 1976. Amended by Laws 1986, c.
444.

524.3–202. Appointment or testacy proceedings; conflicting claim of domicile in another state

If conflicting claims as to the domicile of a decedent are made in a formal testacy or appointment proceeding commenced in this state, and in a testacy or appointment proceeding after notice pending at the same time in another state, the court of this state must stay, dismiss, or permit suitable amendment in, the proceeding here unless it is determined that the local proceeding was commenced before the proceeding elsewhere. The determination of domicile in the proceeding first commenced must be accepted as determinative in the proceeding in this state.

Laws 1974, c. 442, art. 3, § 524.3–202, eff. Jan. 1, 1976.

524.3–203. Priority among persons seeking appointment as personal representative

(a) Whether the proceedings are formal or informal, persons who are not disqualified have priority for appointment in the following order:

(1) the person with priority as determined by a probated will including a person nominated by a power conferred in a will;

(2) the surviving spouse of the decedent who is a devisee of the decedent;

(3) other devisees of the decedent;

(4) the surviving spouse of the decedent;

(5) other heirs of the decedent;

(6) 45 days after the death of the decedent, any creditor;

(7) 90 days after the death of the decedent and pursuant to section 524.5–428, paragraph (b), any conservator of the decedent who has not been discharged.

(b) An objection to an appointment can be made only in formal proceedings. In case of objection the priorities stated in (a) apply except that

(1) if the estate appears to be more than adequate to meet exemptions and costs of administration but inadequate to discharge anticipated unsecured claims, the court, on petition of creditors, may appoint any qualified person;

(2) in case of objection to appointment of a person other than one whose priority is determined by will by an heir or devisee appearing to have a substantial interest in the estate, the court may appoint a person who is acceptable to heirs and devisees whose interests in the estate appear to be worth in total more than half of the probable distributable value, or, in default of this accord any suitable person.

(c) A person entitled to letters under (2) to (5) of (a) above may nominate a qualified person to act as personal representative. Any person aged 18 and over may renounce the right to nominate or to an appointment by appropriate writing filed with the court. When two or more persons share a priority, those of them who do not renounce must concur in nominating another to act for them, or in applying for appointment.

(d) Conservators of the estates of protected persons, or if there is no conservator, any guardian except a guardian ad litem of a minor or incapacitated person, may exercise the same right to nominate, to object to another's appointment, or to participate in determining the preference of a majority in interest of the heirs and devisees that the protected person or ward would have if qualified for appointment.

(e) Appointment of one who does not have priority, including priority resulting from disclaimer, renunciation or nomination determined pursuant to this section, may be made only in formal proceedings. Before appointing one without priority, the court must determine that those having priority, although given notice of the proceedings, have failed to request appointment or to nominate another for appointment, and that administration is necessary.

(f) No person is qualified to serve as a personal representative who is:

(1) under the age of 18;

(2) a person whom the court finds unsuitable in formal proceedings;

(g) A personal representative appointed by a court of the decedent's domicile has priority over all other persons except as provided in (b)(1) or where the decedent's will nominates different persons to be personal representative in this state and in the state of domicile. The domiciliary personal representative may nominate another, who shall have the same priority as the domiciliary personal representative.

(h) This section governs priority for appointment of a successor personal representative but does not apply to the selection of a special administrator.

Laws 1974, c. 442, art. 3, § 524.3–203. Amended by Laws 1975, c. 347, § 29, eff. Jan. 1, 1976; Laws 1986, c. 444; Laws 2003, c. 12, art. 2, § 7.

Historical and Statutory Notes

Laws 2003, c. 12, art. 2, § 9, provided:

"(a) Articles 1 and 2 apply to each guardianship or conservatorship proceeding and each appointment of guardian or conservator commenced on or after the effective date of articles 1 and 2. Except as otherwise provided in this section, articles 1 and 2 apply to each guardianship or conservatorship approved by the court prior to the effective date of articles 1 and 2, and to any guardianship or conservatorship proceeding pending in court on the effective date of articles 1 and 2, unless the court finds for good cause or in the interests of judicial economy that the proceeding should be completed under the provisions of Minnesota Statutes, chapter 525, as it existed prior to the effective date of articles 1 and 2.

"(b) A guardian or conservator who is not discharged prior to the effective date of articles 1 and 2 shall continue to hold the appointment but shall have only the powers specified in the order of appointment and in Minnesota Statutes, chapter 525, as it existed prior to the effective date of articles 1 and 2. Each guardian or conservator holding an appointment on the effective date of articles 1 and 2 shall continue to be bound by the duties imposed by the order of appointment; by Minnesota Statutes, chapter 525, as it existed prior to the effective date of articles 1 and 2; and by article 1, section 50; and shall be bound by any additional duties imposed by articles 1 and 2 starting on the first day of the next month starting after the effective date of articles 1 and 2 or on the next anniversary date of the appointment, whichever occurs later.

"(c) Any act done prior to the effective date of articles 1 and 2 in any proceeding and any right accrued under Minnesota Statutes, chapter 525, prior to the effective date of articles 1 and 2 shall not be impaired by articles 1 and 2. If a right is acquired, extinguished, or barred upon the expiration of a prescribed period of time which has commenced to run in accordance with the provisions of any statute before the effective date of articles 1 and 2, the provisions of the prior statute shall remain in force with respect to that right notwithstanding the statute's amendment or repeal by articles 1 and 2.

"(d) An order of the court or letters of guardianship or conservatorship issued by the court prior to the effective date of articles 1 and 2 shall remain in full force and effect in accordance with its terms and conditions and in accordance with the provisions of prior law until the court modifies the order or letters in accordance with the provisions of articles 1 and 2. Upon request for a certified copy of an order or letters which remains in full force and effect under this paragraph, the court administrator shall certify that the order or letters remains in full force and effect pursuant to this paragraph.

"(e) The court, without hearing or notice to any person, may issue new letters of guardianship or conservatorship under articles 1 and 2 to replace similar letters issued prior to the effective date of articles 1 and 2. The new letters shall be effective under articles 1 and 2 with the same force and effect as the prior letters and shall remain in full force and effect until modified by the court in accordance with the provisions of articles 1 and 2.

"(f) A power of attorney executed in accordance with Minnesota Statutes, section 524.5–505, prior to the effective date of articles 1 and 2, or any surety bond, deed, or other instrument, report, or other undertaking executed in accordance with Minnesota Statutes, chapter 525, prior to the effective date of articles 1 and 2, shall remain in full force and effect for all purposes in accordance with its terms and conditions and the provisions of the applicable statutes under which the power of attorney, surety bond, deed, or other instrument, report, or other undertaking was executed, until the power of attorney, surety bond, deed, or other instrument, report, or other undertaking expires according to its terms or pursuant to the statutes governing its execution, or is modified, terminated, or superseded by a new power of attorney, surety bond, deed, or other instrument, report, or other undertaking executed in accordance with the provisions of articles 1 and 2."

524.3–204. Demand for notice of order or filing concerning decedent's estate

Any person desiring notice of any order or filing pertaining to a decedent's estate in which the person has a financial or property interest, may file a demand for notice with the court at any time after the death of the decedent stating the name of the decedent, the nature of the interest in the estate, and the demandant's address or that of the demandant's attorney. The court administrator shall mail a copy of the demand to the personal representative if one has been appointed. After filing of a demand, no personal representative or other person shall apply to the court for an order or filing to which the demand relates unless demandant or the demandant's attorney is given notice thereof at least 14 days before the date of such order or filing, except that this requirement shall not apply to any order entered or petition filed in any formal proceeding. Such notice shall be given by delivery of a copy thereof to the person being notified or by mailing a copy thereof by certified, registered or ordinary first class mail addressed to the person at the post office address given in the demand or at the person's office or place of residence, if known. The court for good cause shown may provide for a different method or time of giving such notice and proof thereof shall be made on or before the making or acceptance of such order or filing and filed in the proceeding. The validity of an order which is issued or filing which is accepted without compliance with this requirement shall not be affected by the error, but the petitioner receiving the order or the person making the filing may be liable for any damage caused by the absence of notice. The requirement of notice arising from a demand under this provision may be waived in writing by the demandant and shall cease upon the termination of the demandant's interest in the estate.

Laws 1974, c. 442, art. 3, § 524.3–204. Amended by Laws 1975, c. 347, § 30, eff. Jan. 1, 1976; Laws 1986, c. 444; Laws 1986, 1st Sp., c. 3, art. 1, § 82.

PART 3

INFORMAL PROBATE AND APPOINTMENT PROCEEDINGS

524.3–301. Informal probate or appointment proceedings; application; contents

An informal probate proceeding is an informal proceeding for the probate of decedent's will with or without an application for informal appointment. An informal appointment proceeding is an informal proceeding for appointment of a personal representative in testate or intestate estates. These proceedings may be combined in a single proceeding. Applications for informal probate or informal appointment shall be directed to the registrar, and verified by the applicant, in accordance with section 524.1–310, to be accurate and complete to the best of applicant's knowledge and belief as to the following information:

(1) Every application for informal probate of a will or for informal appointment of a personal representative, other than a special or successor representative, shall contain the following:

(i) a statement of the interest of the applicant;

(ii) the name, birthdate, and date of death of the decedent, and the county and state of the decedent's domicile at the time of death, and the names and addresses of the spouse, children, heirs, and devisees and the ages of any who are minors so far as known or ascertainable with reasonable diligence by the applicant;

(iii) if the decedent was not domiciled in the state at the time of death, a statement showing venue;

(iv) a statement identifying and indicating the address of any personal representative of the decedent appointed in this state or elsewhere whose appointment has not been terminated;

(v) a statement indicating whether the applicant has received a demand for notice, or is aware of any demand for notice of any probate or appointment proceeding concerning the decedent that may have been filed in this state or elsewhere.

(2) An application for informal probate of a will shall state the following in addition to the statements required by (1):

(i) that the original of the decedent's last will is in the possession of the court, or accompanies the application, or that an authenticated copy of a will probated in another jurisdiction accompanies the application;

(ii) that the applicant, to the best of the applicant's knowledge, believes the will to have been validly executed;

(iii) that after the exercise of reasonable diligence, the applicant is unaware of any instrument revoking the will, and that the applicant believes that the instrument which is the subject of the application is the decedent's last will;

(iv) that the time limit for informal probate as provided in this article has not expired either because three years or less have passed since the decedent's death, or, if more than three years from death have passed, that circumstances as described by section 524.3–108 authorizing tardy probate have occurred.

(3) An application for informal appointment of a personal representative to administer an estate under a will shall describe the will by date of execution and state the time and place of probate or the pending application or petition for probate. The application for appointment shall adopt the statements in the application or petition for probate and state the name, address and priority for appointment of the person whose appointment is sought.

(4) An application for informal appointment of an administrator in intestacy shall state in addition to the statements required by (1):

(i) that after the exercise of reasonable diligence, the applicant is unaware of any unrevoked testamentary instrument relating to property having a situs in this state under section 524.1–301, or, a statement why any such instrument of which the applicant may be aware is not being probated;

(ii) the priority of the person whose appointment is sought and the names of any other persons having a prior or equal right to the appointment under section 524.3–203.

(5) An application for appointment of a personal representative to succeed a personal representative appointed under a different testacy status shall refer to the order in the most recent testacy proceeding, state the name and address of the person whose appointment is sought and of the person whose appointment will be terminated if the application is granted, and describe the priority of the applicant.

(6) An application for appointment of a personal representative to succeed a personal representative who has tendered a resignation as provided in section 524.3–610(c), or whose appointment has been terminated by death or removal, shall adopt the statements in the application or petition which led to the appointment of the person being succeeded except as specifically changed or corrected, state the name and address of the person who seeks appointment as successor, and describe the priority of the applicant.

Laws 1974, c. 442, art. 3, § 524.3–301. Amended by Laws 1975, c. 347, § 31, eff. Jan. 1, 1976; Laws 1976, c. 161, § 4, eff. April 4, 1976; Laws 1986, c. 444; Laws 1990, c. 480, art. 10, § 11, eff. April 25, 1990; Laws 2006, c. 221, § 20.

524.3–302. Informal probate; duty of registrar; effect of informal probate

Upon receipt of an application requesting informal probate of a will, the registrar, upon making the findings required by section 524.3–303 shall issue a written statement of informal probate if at least 120 hours have elapsed since the decedent's death. Informal probate is conclusive as to all persons until superseded by an order in a formal testacy proceeding. No defect in the application or procedure relating thereto which leads to informal probate of a will renders the probate void.

Laws 1974, c. 442, art. 3, § 524.3–302, eff. Jan. 1, 1976.

524.3–303. Informal probate; proof and findings required

(a) In an informal proceeding for original probate of a will, the registrar shall determine whether:

(1) the application is complete;

(2) the applicant has made oath or affirmation that the statements contained in the application are true to the best of the applicant's knowledge and belief;

(3) the applicant appears from the application to be an interested person as defined in section 524.1–201, clause (19);

(4) on the basis of the statements in the application, venue is proper;

(5) an original, duly executed and apparently unrevoked will is in the registrar's possession;

(6) any notice required by section 524.3–204 has been given; and

(7) it appears from the application that the time limit for original probate has not expired.

(b) The application shall be denied if it indicates that a personal representative has been appointed in another county of this state or except as provided in subsection (d), if it appears that this or another will of the decedent has been the subject of a previous probate order.

(c) A will which appears to have the required signatures and which contains an attestation clause showing that requirements of execution under section 524.2–502 or 524.2–506 have been met shall be probated without further proof. In other cases, the registrar may assume execution if the will appears to have been properly executed, or the registrar may accept a sworn statement or affidavit of any person having knowledge of the circumstances of execution, whether or not the person was a witness to the will.

(d) Informal probate of a will which has been previously probated elsewhere may be granted at any time upon written application by any interested person, together with deposit of an authenticated copy of the will and of the statement probating it from the office or court where it was first probated.

(e) A will from a place which does not provide for probate of a will after death and which is not eligible for probate under subsection (a), may be probated in this state upon receipt by the registrar of a duly authenticated copy of the will and a duly authenticated certificate of its legal custodian that the copy filed is a true copy and that the will has become operative under the law of the other place.

Laws 1974, c. 442, art. 3, § 524.3–303. Amended by Laws 1975, c. 347, § 32, eff. Jan. 1, 1976; Laws 1979, c. 50, § 68; Laws 1986, c. 444; Laws 1992, c. 423, § 3.

524.3–304. Repealed by Laws 1975, c. 347, § 144, eff. Jan. 1, 1976

524.3–305. Informal probate; registrar not satisfied

If the registrar is not satisfied that a will is entitled to be probated in informal proceedings because of failure to meet the requirements of section 524.3–303 or any other reason, the registrar may decline the application. A declination of informal probate is not an adjudication and does not preclude formal probate proceedings.

Laws 1974, c. 442, art. 3, § 524.3–305. Amended by Laws 1975, c. 347, § 33, eff. Jan. 1, 1976; Laws 1986, c. 444.

524.3–306. Informal probate; notice requirements

The moving party must give notice as described by section 524.1–401 of application for informal probate (1) to any person demanding it pursuant to section 524.3–204; and (2) to any personal representative of the decedent whose appointment has not been terminated. Upon issuance of the written statement by the registrar pursuant to section 524.3–302, notice of the informal probate proceedings, in the form prescribed by court rule, shall be given under the direction of the court administrator by publication once a week for two consecutive weeks in a legal newspaper in the county where the application is filed and by mailing a copy of the notice by ordinary first class mail to all interested persons, other than creditors. Further if the decedent was born in a foreign country or left heirs or devisees in any foreign country, notice shall be given to the consul or other representative of such country, if the representative resides in this state and has filed a copy of appointment with the secretary of state. The secretary of state shall forward any notice received to the appropriate consul residing in Minnesota and on file with that office.

Laws 1974, c. 442, art. 3, § 524.3–306. Amended by Laws 1975, c. 347, § 34, eff. Jan. 1, 1976; Laws 1978, c. 525, § 13, eff. March 24, 1978; Laws 1984, c. 615, § 1; Laws 1986, c. 444; Laws 1986, 1st Sp., c. 3, art. 1, § 82.

Minnesota Rules of Evidence

Subscribing witness' testimony, see Rule 903.

524.3–307. Informal appointment proceedings; delay in order; duty of registrar; effect of appointment

(a) Upon receipt of an application for informal appointment of a personal representative other than a special administrator as provided in section 524.3–614, if at least 120 hours have elapsed since the decedent's death, the registrar, after making the findings required by section 524.3–308, shall appoint the applicant subject to qualification and acceptance; provided, that if the decedent was a nonresident, the registrar shall delay the order of appointment until 30 days have elapsed since death unless the personal representative appointed at the decedent's domicile is the applicant, or unless the decedent's will directs that the estate be subject to the laws of this state.

(b) The status of personal representative and the powers and duties pertaining to the office are fully established by informal appointment. An appointment, and the office of personal representative created thereby, is subject to termination as provided in sections 524.3–608 to 524.3–612, but is not subject to retroactive vacation.

Laws 1974, c. 442, art. 3, § 524.3–307, eff. Jan. 1, 1976. Amended by Laws 1986, c. 444.

524.3–308. Informal appointment proceedings; proof and findings required

(a) In informal appointment proceedings, the registrar must determine whether:

(1) the application for informal appointment of a personal representative is complete;

(2) the applicant has made oath or affirmation that the statements contained in the application are true to the best of the applicant's knowledge and belief;

(3) the applicant appears from the application to be an interested person as defined in section 524.1-201, clause (19);

(4) on the basis of the statements in the application, venue is proper;

(5) any will to which the requested appointment relates has been formally or informally probated; but this requirement does not apply to the appointment of a special administrator;

(6) any notice required by section 524.3-204 has been given;

(7) from the statements in the application, the person whose appointment is sought has a priority entitlement to the appointment.

(b) Unless section 524.3-612 controls, the application must be denied if it indicates that a personal representative who has not filed a written statement of resignation as provided in section 524.3-610(c) has been appointed in this or another county of this state, that, unless the applicant is the domiciliary personal representative or the representative's nominee, the decedent was not domiciled in this state and that a personal representative whose appointment has not been terminated has been appointed by a court in the state of domicile, or that other requirements of this section have not been met.

Laws 1974, c. 442, art. 3, § 524.3–308, eff. Jan. 1, 1976. Amended by Laws 1986, c. 444; Laws 1992, c. 423, § 4.

524.3–309. Informal appointment proceedings; registrar not satisfied

If the registrar is not satisfied that a requested informal appointment of a personal representative should be made because of failure to meet the requirements of sections 524.3–307 and 524.3–308, or for any other reason, the registrar may decline the application. A declination of informal appointment is not an adjudication and does not preclude appointment in formal proceedings.

Laws 1974, c. 442, art. 3, § 524.3–309, eff. Jan. 1, 1976. Amended by Laws 1986, c. 444.

524.3–310. Informal appointment proceedings; notice requirements

The moving party must give notice as described by section 524.1–401 of an intention to seek an appointment informally; (1) to any person demanding it pursuant to section 524.3–204; and (2) to any person having a prior or equal right to appointment not waived in writing and filed with the court. Notice of the appointment of the personal representative shall be given under the direction of the court administrator by publication once a week for two consecutive weeks in a legal newspaper in the county where the application is filed and by mailing a copy of the notice by ordinary first class mail to all interested persons, other than creditors. The notice, in the form prescribed by court rule, shall state that any heir, devisee or other interested person may be entitled to appointment as personal representative or may object to the appointment of the personal representative and that the personal representative is empowered to fully administer the estate including, after 30 days from the date of issuance of letters, the power to sell, encumber, lease or distribute real estate, unless objections thereto are filed with the court (pursuant to section 524.3–607) and the court otherwise orders. Further, if the decedent was born in a foreign country or left heirs or devisees in any foreign country, notice shall be given to the consul or other representative of such country, if the representative resides in this state and has filed a copy of appointment with the secretary of state. The secretary of state shall forward any notice received to the appropriate consul residing in Minnesota and on file with that office. No defect in any notice nor in publication or service thereof shall limit or affect the validity of the appointment, powers, or other duties of the personal representative.

Laws 1974, c. 442, art. 3, § 524.3–310. Amended by Laws 1975, c. 347, § 35, eff. Jan. 1, 1976; Laws 1978, c. 525, § 14, eff. March 24, 1978; Laws 1984, c. 615, § 2; Laws 1986, c. 444; Laws 1986, 1st Sp., c. 3, art. 1, § 82.

524.3–311. Informal appointment unavailable in certain cases

If an application for informal appointment indicates the existence of a possible unrevoked will or codicil which may relate to property subject to the laws of this state, and which is not filed for probate in this court, the registrar shall decline the application.

Laws 1974, c. 442, art. 3, § 524.3–311. Amended by Laws 1975, c. 347, § 36, eff. Jan. 1, 1976.

PART 4

FORMAL TESTACY AND APPOINTMENT PROCEEDINGS

524.3–401. Formal testacy proceedings; nature; when commenced

A formal testacy proceeding is one conducted with notice to interested persons before a court to establish a will or determine intestacy. A formal testacy proceeding may be commenced by an interested person or a personal representative named in the will filing a petition as described in section 524.3–402(a) in which it is requested that the court, after notice and hearing, enter an order probating a will, or a petition to set aside an informal probate of a will or to prevent informal probate of a will which is the subject of a pending application, or a petition in accordance with section 524.3–402(b) for an order that the decedent died intestate.

A petition may seek formal probate of a will without regard to whether the same or a conflicting will has been informally probated. A formal testacy proceeding may, but need not, involve a request for appointment of a personal representative.

During the pendency of a formal testacy proceeding, the registrar shall not act upon any application for informal probate of any will of the decedent or any application for informal appointment of a personal representative of the decedent.

Unless a petition in a formal testacy proceeding also requests confirmation of the previous informal appointment, a previously appointed personal representative, after receipt of notice of the commencement of a formal probate proceeding, shall refrain from exercising power to make any further distribution of the estate during the pendency of the formal proceeding. A petitioner who seeks the appointment of a different personal representative in a formal proceeding also may request an order restraining the acting personal representative from exercising any of the powers of office and requesting the appointment of a special administrator. In the absence of a request, or if the request is denied, the commencement of a formal proceeding has no effect on the powers and duties of a previously appointed personal representative other than those relating to distribution.

Laws 1974, c. 442, art. 3, § 524.3–401. Amended by Laws 1975, c. 347, § 37, eff. Jan. 1, 1976; Laws 1986, c. 444.

524.3–402. Formal testacy or appointment proceedings; petition; contents

(a) Petitions for formal probate of a will, or for adjudication of intestacy with or without request for appointment of a personal representative, shall be directed to the court, request a judicial order after notice and hearing and contain further statements as indicated in this section. A petition for formal probate of a will

(1) requests an order as to the testacy of the decedent in relation to a particular instrument which may or may not have been informally probated and determining the heirs,

(2) contains the statements required for informal applications as stated in the five subparagraphs under section 524.3–301(1), the statements required by subparagraphs (ii) and (iii) of section 524.3–301(2), and

(3) states whether the original of the last will of the decedent is in the possession of the court or accompanies the petition.

If the original will is neither in the possession of the court nor accompanies the petition and no authenticated copy of a will probated in another jurisdiction accompanies the petition, the petition also shall state the contents of the will, and indicate that it is lost, destroyed, or otherwise unavailable.

(b) A petition for adjudication of intestacy and appointment of an administrator in intestacy shall request a judicial finding and order that the decedent left no will and determining the heirs, contain the statements required by (1) and (4) of section 524.3–301 and indicate whether supervised administration is sought. A petition may request an order determining intestacy and heirs without requesting the appointment of an administrator, in which case, the statements required by subparagraph (ii) of section 524.3–301(4) may be omitted.

Laws 1974, c. 442, art. 3, § 524.3–402. Amended by Laws 1975, c. 347, § 38, eff. Jan. 1, 1976.

524.3–403. Formal testacy proceeding; notice of hearing on petition

(a) Upon commencement of a formal testacy proceeding, the court shall fix a time and place of hearing. Notice, in the form prescribed by court rule, shall be given in the manner prescribed by section 524.1–401 by the petitioner to the persons herein enumerated and to any additional person who has filed a demand for notice under section 524.3–204. The petitioner, having reason to believe that the will has been lost or destroyed, shall include a statement to that effect in the notice.

Notice shall be given to the following persons: the surviving spouse, children, and other heirs of the decedent, the devisees and personal representatives named in any will that is being or has been probated, or offered for informal or formal probate in the county, or that is known by the petitioner to have been probated, or offered for informal or formal probate elsewhere, and any personal representative of the decedent whose appointment has not been terminated. Notice of the hearing, in the form prescribed by court rule, shall also be given under the direction of the court administrator by publication once a week for two consecutive weeks in a legal newspaper in the county where the hearing is to be held, the last publication of which is to be at least ten days before the time set for hearing.

If the decedent was born in a foreign country or has heirs or devisees in a foreign country, notice of a formal testacy proceeding shall be given to the consul of that country, if the consul resides in this state and has filed a copy of the appointment with the secretary of state. Any notice received by the secretary of state shall be forwarded to the appropriate consul.

(b) If it appears by the petition or otherwise that the fact of the death of the alleged decedent may be in doubt, the court shall direct the petitioner to proceed in the manner provided in chapter 576.

Laws 1974, c. 442, art. 3, § 524.3–403. Amended by Laws 1975, c. 347, § 39, eff. Jan. 1, 1976; Laws 1981, c. 161, § 1; Laws 1984, c. 615, § 3; Laws 1986, c. 444; Laws 1986, 1st Sp., c. 3, art. 1, § 82.

524.3–404. Formal testacy proceedings; written objections to probate

Any party to a formal proceeding who opposes the probate of a will for any reason shall state in pleadings the objections to probate of the will.

Laws 1974, c. 442, art. 3, § 524.3–404, eff. Jan. 1, 1976. Amended by Laws 1986, c. 444.

524.3–405. Formal testacy proceedings; uncontested cases; hearings and proof

If a petition in a testacy proceeding is unopposed, the court may order probate or intestacy on the strength of the pleadings if satisfied that the conditions of section 524.3–409 have been met, or conduct a hearing in open court and require proof of the matters necessary to support the order sought. If evidence concerning execution of the will is necessary, the affidavit or testimony of one of any attesting witnesses to the instrument is sufficient. If the affidavit or testimony of an attesting witness is not available, execution of the will may be proved by other evidence or affidavit.

Laws 1974, c. 442, art. 3, § 524.3–405, eff. Jan. 1, 1976.

524.3–406. Formal testacy proceedings; contested cases; testimony of attesting witnesses

(a) If evidence concerning execution of an attested will which is not self-proved is necessary in contested cases, the testimony of at least one of the attesting witnesses, if within the state competent and able to testify, is required. Due execution of a will may be proved by other evidence.

(b) If the will is self-proved, compliance with signature requirements for execution is conclusively presumed and other requirements of execution are presumed subject to rebuttal without the testimony of any witness upon filing the will and the acknowledgment and affidavits annexed or attached thereto, unless there is proof of fraud or forgery affecting the acknowledgment or affidavit.

Laws 1974, c. 442, art. 3, § 524.3–406. Amended by Laws 1975, c. 347, § 40, eff. Jan. 1, 1976.

Minnesota Rules of Evidence

Presumptions in civil cases, see Rule 301.

524.3–407. Formal testacy proceedings; burdens in contested cases

In contested cases, petitioners who seek to establish intestacy have the burden of establishing prima facie proof of death, venue and heirship. Proponents of a will have the burden of establishing prima facie proof of due execution in all cases, and, if they are also petitioners, prima facie proof of death and venue. Contestants of a will have the burden of establishing lack of testamentary intent or capacity, undue influence, fraud, duress, mistake or revocation. Parties have the ultimate burden of persuasion as to matters with respect to which they have the initial burden of proof. If a will is opposed by the petition for probate of a later will revoking the former, it shall be determined first whether the later will is entitled to probate, and if a will is opposed by a petition for a declaration of intestacy, it shall be determined first whether the will is entitled to probate.

Laws 1974, c. 442, art. 3, § 524.3–407, eff. Jan. 1, 1976.

524.3–408. Formal testacy proceedings; will construction; effect of final order in another jurisdiction

A final order of a court of another state determining testacy, the validity or construction of a will, made in a proceeding involving notice to and an opportunity for contest by all interested persons must be accepted as determinative by the courts of this state if it includes, or is based upon, a finding that the decedent was domiciled at death in the state where the order was made.

Laws 1974, c. 442, art. 3, § 524.3–408, eff. Jan. 1, 1976. Amended by Laws 1986, c. 444.

524.3–409. Formal testacy proceedings; order; foreign will

After the time required for any notice has expired, upon proof of notice, and after any hearing that may be necessary, if the court finds that the testator is dead, venue is proper and that the proceeding was commenced within the limitation prescribed by section 524.3–108, it shall determine the decedent's domicile at death, and decedent's heirs and state of testacy. Any will found to be valid and unrevoked shall be formally probated. Termination of any previous informal appointment of a personal representative, which may be appropriate in view of the relief requested and findings, is governed by section 524.3–612. A will from a place which does not provide for probate of a will after death, may be proved for probate in this state by a duly authenticated certificate of its legal custodian that the copy introduced is a true copy and that the will has become effective under the law of the other place.

Laws 1974, c. 442, art. 3, § 524.3–409. Amended by Laws 1975, c. 347, § 41, eff. Jan. 1, 1976; Laws 1986, c. 444.

524.3–410. Formal testacy proceedings; probate of more than one instrument

If two or more instruments are offered for probate before a final order is entered in a formal testacy proceeding, more than one instrument may be probated if neither expressly revokes the other or contains provisions which work a total revocation by implication. If more than one instrument is probated, the order shall indicate what provisions control in respect to the nomination of an executor, if any. The order may, but need not, indicate how any provisions of a particular instrument are affected by the other instrument. After a final order in a testacy proceeding has been entered, no petition for probate of any other instrument of the decedent may be entertained, except incident to a petition to vacate or modify a previous probate order and subject to the time limits of section 524.3–412.

Laws 1974, c. 442, art. 3, § 524.3–410, eff. Jan. 1, 1976.

524.3–411. Formal testacy proceedings; partial intestacy

If it becomes evident in the course of a formal testacy proceeding that, though one or more instruments are entitled to be probated, the decedent's estate is or may be partially intestate, the court shall enter an order to that effect.

Laws 1974, c. 442, art. 3, § 524.3–411, eff. Jan. 1, 1976.

524.3–412. Formal testacy proceedings; effect of order; vacation

Subject to appeal and subject to vacation as provided herein and in section 524.3–413, a formal testacy order under sections 524.3–409 to 524.3–411, including an order that the decedent left no valid will and determining heirs, is final as to all persons with respect to all issues concerning the decedent's estate that the court considered or might have considered incident to its rendition relevant to the question of whether the decedent left a valid will, and to the determination of heirs, except that:

(1) The court shall entertain a petition for modification or vacation of its order and probate of another will of the decedent if it is shown that the proponents of the later-offered will were unaware of its existence at the time of

the earlier proceeding or were unaware of the earlier proceeding and were given no notice thereof, except by publication.

(2) If intestacy of all or part of the estate has been ordered, the determination of heirs of the decedent may be reconsidered if it is shown that one or more persons were omitted from the determination and it is also shown that the persons were unaware of their relationship to the decedent, were unaware of the death or were given no notice of any proceeding concerning the estate, except by publication.

(3) A petition for vacation under either (1) or (2) must be filed prior to the earlier of the following time limits:

(i) If a personal representative has been appointed for the estate, the time of entry of any order approving final distribution of the estate, or, if the estate is closed by statement, six months after the filing of the closing statement.

(ii) Whether or not a personal representative has been appointed for the estate of the decedent, the time prescribed by section 524.3–108 when it is no longer possible to initiate an original proceeding to probate a will of the decedent.

(iii) 12 months after the entry of the order sought to be vacated.

(4) The order originally rendered in the testacy proceeding may be modified or vacated, if appropriate under the circumstances, by the order of probate of the later-offered will or the order redetermining heirs.

Laws 1974, c. 442, art. 3, § 524.3–412. Amended by Laws 1975, c. 347, § 42, eff. Jan. 1, 1976; Laws 1986, c. 444.

524.3–413. Formal testacy proceedings; vacation of order for other cause and modification of orders, judgments, and decrees

For good cause shown, an order, judgment or decree in a formal proceeding may be modified or vacated within the time limits and upon the grounds stated in section 525.02, except that the same may be modified to include omitted property or to correct a description at any time, as hereinafter provided.

Whenever real or personal property or any interest therein has been omitted from probate proceedings, from a deed or transfer of distribution, a decree of distribution, or an order for distribution, or has been incorrectly described therein, any person interested in the estate or claiming an interest in such property may petition the probate court of the county in which such proceedings were had for a decree to determine its descent and to assign it to the persons entitled thereto, or to amend the deed or transfer of distribution, decree of distribution, or order of distribution to include such omitted property, or to correct the description, with or without notice. No order or decree of omitted property shall be entered under this section until any inheritance taxes due are paid or the court finds there are no taxes due.

Laws 1974, c. 442, art. 3, § 524.3–413. Amended by Laws 1975, c. 347, § 43, eff. Jan. 1, 1976.

524.3–414. Formal proceedings concerning appointment of personal representative

(a) A formal proceeding for adjudication regarding the priority or qualification of one who is an applicant for appointment as personal representative, or of one who previously has been appointed personal representative in informal proceedings, if an issue concerning the testacy of the decedent is or may be involved, is governed by section 524.3–402, as well as by this section. In other cases, the petition shall contain or adopt the statements required by section 524.3–301(1) and describe the question relating to priority or qualification of the personal representative which is to be resolved. If the proceeding precedes any appointment of a personal representative, it shall stay any pending informal appointment proceedings as well as any commenced thereafter. If the proceeding is commenced after appointment, the previously appointed personal representative, after receipt of notice thereof, shall refrain from exercising any power of administration except as necessary to preserve the estate or unless the court orders otherwise.

(b) After notice to interested persons, including all persons interested in the administration of the estate as successors under the applicable assumption concerning testacy, any previously appointed personal representative and any person having or claiming priority for appointment as personal representative, the court shall determine who is entitled to appointment under section 524.3–203, make a proper appointment and, if appropriate, terminate any prior appointment found to have been improper as provided in cases of removal under section 524.3–611.

Laws 1974, c. 442, art. 3, § 524.3–414, eff. Jan. 1, 1976.

PART 5

SUPERVISED ADMINISTRATION

524.3–501. Supervised administration; nature of proceeding

Supervised administration is a single in rem proceeding to secure complete administration and settlement of a decedent's estate under the continuing authority of the court which extends until entry of an order approving distribution of the estate and discharging the personal representative or other order terminating the proceeding. A supervised personal representative is responsible to the court, as well as to the interested parties, and is subject to directions concerning the estate made by the court on its own motion or on the motion of any interested party. Except as otherwise provided in this part, or as otherwise ordered by the court, a supervised personal representative has the same duties and powers as a personal representative who is not supervised.

Laws 1974, c. 442, art. 3, § 524.3–501, eff. Jan. 1, 1976.

524.3–502. Supervised administration; petition; order

A petition for supervised administration may be filed by any interested person or by an appointed personal representative or one named in the will at any time or the prayer for supervised administration may be joined with a petition in a testacy or appointment proceeding. If the testacy of the decedent and the priority and qualification of any personal representative have not been adjudicated previously, the petition for supervised administration shall include the matters required of a petition in a formal testacy proceeding and the notice requirements and procedures applicable to a formal testacy proceeding apply. If not previously adjudicated, the court shall adjudicate the testacy of the decedent and questions relating to the priority and qualifications of the personal representative in any case involving a request for supervised administration, even though the request for supervised administration may be denied. After notice to interested persons, the court shall order supervised administration of a decedent's estate: (1) if the decedent's will directs supervised administration, it shall be ordered unless the court finds that circumstances bearing on the need for supervised administration have changed since the execution of the will and that there is no necessity for supervised administration; (2) if the decedent's will directs unsupervised administration, supervised administration shall be ordered only upon a finding that it is necessary for protection of persons interested in the estate; or (3) in other cases if the court finds that supervised administration is necessary under the circumstances.

Laws 1974, c. 442, art. 3, § 524.3–502. Amended by Laws 1975, c. 347, § 44, eff. Jan. 1, 1976.

524.3–503. Supervised administration; effect on other proceedings

(a) The pendency of a proceeding for supervised administration of a decedent's estate stays action on any informal application then pending or thereafter filed.

(b) If a will has been previously probated in informal proceedings, the effect of the filing of a petition for supervised administration is as provided for formal testacy proceedings by section 524.3–401.

(c) After having received notice of the filing of a petition for supervised administration, a personal representative who has been appointed previously shall not exercise the power to distribute any estate. The filing of the petition does not affect the representative's other powers and duties unless the court restricts the exercise of any of them pending full hearing on the petition.

Laws 1974, c. 442, art. 3, § 524.3–503, eff. Jan. 1, 1976.   Amended by Laws 1986, c. 444.

524.3–504. Supervised administration; powers of personal representative

Unless restricted by the court, a supervised personal representative has, without interim orders approving exercise of a power, all powers of personal representatives under this chapter, but shall not exercise the power to make any distribution of the estate without prior order of the court.   Any other restriction on the power of a personal representative which may be ordered by the court must be endorsed on the letters of appointment and, unless so endorsed, is ineffective as to persons dealing in good faith with the personal representative.

Laws 1974, c. 442, art. 3, § 524.3–504, eff. Jan. 1, 1976.   Amended by Laws 1986, c. 444.

524.3–505. Supervised administration; interim orders; distribution and closing orders

Unless otherwise ordered by the court, supervised administration is terminated by order in accordance with time restrictions, notices and contents of orders prescribed for proceedings under section 524.3–1001.   Interim orders approving or directing partial distributions, sale of property or granting other relief may be issued by the court at any time during the pendency of a supervised administration on the application of the personal representative or any interested person.

Laws 1974, c. 442, art. 3, § 524.3–505, eff. Jan. 1, 1976.   Amended by Laws 1976, c. 161, § 5, eff. April 4, 1976; Laws 1980, c. 439, § 30.

Historical and Statutory Notes

Laws 1980, c. 439, § 36, provided that § 30, making technical adjustments and clarifying certain provisions relating to estate tax, was effective for estates of decedents dying after December 31, 1979.

PART 6

PERSONAL REPRESENTATIVE; APPOINTMENT, CONTROL AND TERMINATION OF AUTHORITY

524.3–601. Qualification

Prior to receiving letters, a personal representative shall qualify by filing with the appointing court any required bond and an oath of office or, in the case of a corporate representative, a statement of acceptance of the duties of the office.

Laws 1974, c. 442, art. 3, § 524.3–601.   Amended by Laws 1975, c. 347, § 45, eff. Jan. 1, 1976; Laws 1986, c. 444.

524.3–602. Acceptance of appointment; consent to jurisdiction

By accepting appointment, a personal representative submits personally to the jurisdiction of the court in any proceeding relating to the estate that may be instituted by any interested person. Notice of any proceeding shall be delivered to the personal representative, or mailed by ordinary first class mail the address listed in the application or petition for appointment or thereafter reported to the court and to the address as then known to the petitioner. Service of process on a nonresident personal representative appointed in Minnesota shall be made pursuant to section 524.4–303.

Laws 1974, c. 442, art. 3, § 524.3–602. Amended by Laws 1975, c. 347, § 46, eff. Jan. 1, 1976; Laws 1986, c. 444.

524.3–603. Bond not required without court order; exceptions

No bond is required of a personal representative appointed in informal proceedings, except (1) upon the appointment of a special administrator; (2) when an executor or other personal representative is appointed to administer an estate under a will containing an express requirement of bond; or (3) when bond is required under section 524.3–605. No bond shall be required of a personal representative appointed in formal proceedings (i) if the will relieves the personal representative of bond, or (ii) if all interested persons with an apparent interest in the estate in excess of $1,000, other than creditors, make a written request that no bond be required, unless in either case the court determines that bond is required for the protection of interested persons. The court may by its order dispense with the requirement of bond at the time of appointment of a personal representative appointed in formal proceedings. No bond shall be required of any personal representative who, pursuant to statute, has deposited cash or collateral with an agency of this state to secure performance of duties. If two or more persons are appointed corepresentatives and one of them has complied with the preceding sentence, no bond shall be required of any such corepresentatives.

Laws 1974, c. 442, art. 3, § 524.3–603, eff. Aug. 1, 1974. Amended by Laws 1975, c. 347, § 47, eff. Jan. 1, 1976; Laws 1976, c. 161, § 6, eff. April 4, 1976; Laws 1986, c. 444.

Historical and Statutory Notes

Laws 1975, c. 347, § 145, provides: "Except as provided in Minnesota Statutes 1974, Section 524.8–103, this act and Laws 1974, Chapter 442 are effective on January 1, 1976."

524.3–604. Bond amount; security; procedure; reduction

If bond is required then the personal representative shall file the bond with the court or give other suitable security in an amount not less than the bond. The court shall determine that the bond is duly executed by a corporate surety, or one or more individual sureties whose performance is secured by pledge of

447

personal property, mortgage on real property or other adequate security. The court may permit the amount of the bond to be reduced by the value of assets of the estate deposited with a domestic financial institution, in a manner that prevents their unauthorized disposition. The court on its own motion or on petition of the personal representative or another interested person may excuse a requirement of bond, increase or reduce the amount of the bond, release sureties, or permit the substitution of another bond with the same or different sureties.

Laws 1974, c. 442, art. 3, § 524.3–604, eff. Aug. 1, 1974. Amended by Laws 1975, c. 347, § 48, eff. Jan. 1, 1976.

Historical and Statutory Notes

Laws 1975, c. 347, § 145, provides:
"Except as provided in Minnesota Statutes 1974, Section 524.8–103, this act and Laws 1974, Chapter 442 are effective on January 1, 1976."

524.3–605. Demand for bond by interested person

Any person apparently having an interest in the estate worth in excess of $1,000, or any creditor having a claim in excess of $1,000, may make a written demand that a personal representative give bond. The demand must be filed with the court and a copy mailed to the personal representative, if appointment and qualification have occurred. Thereupon, the court may require or excuse the requirement of a bond. After having received notice and until the filing of the bond or until the requirement of bond is excused, the personal representative shall refrain from exercising any powers of office except as necessary to preserve the estate. Failure of the personal representative to meet a requirement of bond by giving suitable bond within 30 days after receipt of notice is cause for removal and appointment of a successor personal representative. An interested person who initially waived bond may demand bond under this section.

Laws 1974, c. 442, art. 3, § 524.3–605, eff. Aug. 1, 1974. Amended by Laws 1975, c. 347, § 49, eff. Jan. 1, 1976; Laws 1986, c. 444.

Historical and Statutory Notes

Laws 1975, c. 347, § 145, provides:
"Except as provided in Minnesota Statutes 1974, Section 524.8–103, this act and Laws 1974, Chapter 442 are effective on January 1, 1976."

524.3–606. Terms and conditions of bonds

(a) The following requirements and provisions apply to any bond required by this part:

(1) Bonds shall name the state as obligee for the benefit of the persons interested in the estate and shall be conditioned upon the faithful discharge by the fiduciary of all duties according to law.

(2) Unless otherwise provided by the terms of the approved bond, sureties are jointly and severally liable with the personal representative and with each other. The address of sureties shall be stated in the bond.

(3) By executing an approved bond of a personal representative, the surety consents to the jurisdiction of the probate court which issued letters to the primary obligor in any proceedings pertaining to the fiduciary duties of the personal representative and naming the surety as a party. Notice of such proceeding shall be delivered to the surety or mailed by registered or certified mail at the address listed with the court where the bond is filed and to the address then known to the petitioner.

(4) On petition of a successor personal representative, any other personal representative of the same decedent, or any interested person, a proceeding in the court may be initiated against a surety for breach of the obligation of the bond of the personal representative.

(5) The bond of the personal representative is not void after the first recovery but may be proceeded against from time to time until the whole penalty is exhausted.

(b) No action or proceeding may be commenced against the surety on any matter as to which an action or proceeding against the primary obligor is barred by adjudication or limitation.

(c) If a sole or last surviving representative is removed, is disabled or dies, the court may, upon notice and hearing, order the representative's surety to file a verified final account and petition for complete settlement and, if proper, for distribution and closing of the estate.

If in a proceeding under this clause the court determines that the representative has mismanaged the estate, misappropriated funds or committed other misconduct for which the surety is liable, the court shall settle the account and enter judgment against the representative and the surety as may be appropriate. The judgment may be filed, docketed and enforced in the same manner as any other judgment. This remedy is in addition to any other remedy for breach of the obligations of the bond.

Laws 1974, c. 442, art. 3, § 524.3–606, eff. Aug. 1, 1974. Amended by Laws 1975, c. 347, § 50, eff. Jan. 1, 1976; Laws 1977, c. 154, § 2; Laws 1986, c. 444.

Historical and Statutory Notes

Laws 1975, c. 347, § 145, provides: "Except as provided in Minnesota Statutes 1974, Section 524.8–103, this act and Laws 1974, Chapter 442 are effective on January 1, 1976."

524.3–607. Order restraining personal representative

(a) On petition of any person who appears to have an interest in the estate, the court by temporary order may restrain a personal representative from performing specified acts of administration, disbursement, or distribution, or exercise of any powers or discharge of any duties of office, or make any other order to secure proper performance of a duty, if it appears to the court that the personal representative otherwise may take some action which would jeopardize unreasonably the interest of the applicant or of some other interested person. Persons with whom the personal representative may transact business may be made parties.

(b) The matter shall be set for hearing within ten days unless the parties otherwise agree. Notice as the court directs shall be given to the personal representative and the representative's attorney of record, if any, and to any other parties named defendant in the petition.

Laws 1974, c. 442, art. 3, § 524.3–607, eff. Jan. 1, 1976. Amended by Laws 1986, c. 444.

524.3–608. Termination of appointment; general

Termination of appointment of a personal representative occurs as indicated in sections 524.3–609 to 524.3–612, inclusive. Termination ends the right and power pertaining to the office of personal representative as conferred by this chapter or any will, except that a personal representative, at any time prior to distribution or until restrained or enjoined by court order, may perform acts necessary to protect the estate and may deliver the assets to a successor representative. Termination does not discharge a personal representative from liability for transactions or omissions occurring before termination, or relieve the representative of the duty to preserve assets subject to the representative's control, to account therefor and to deliver the assets. Termination does not affect the jurisdiction of the court over the personal representative, but terminates the authority to represent the estate in any pending or future proceeding.

Laws 1974, c. 442, art. 3, § 524.3–608, eff. Jan. 1, 1976. Amended by Laws 1986, c. 444.

524.3–609. Termination of appointment; death or disability

The death of a personal representative or the appointment of a conservator or guardian for the estate of a personal representative, terminates the personal representative's appointment. Until appointment and qualification of a successor or special representative to replace the deceased or protected representative, the representative of the estate of the deceased or protected personal representative, if any, has the duty to protect the estate possessed and being administered by the deceased or protected representative at the time the appointment terminates, has the power to perform acts necessary for protection and shall account for and deliver the estate assets to a successor or special personal representative upon appointment and qualification.

Laws 1974, c. 442, art. 3, § 524.3–609. Amended by Laws 1975, c. 347, § 51, eff. Jan. 1, 1976; Laws 1986, c. 444.

524.3–610. Termination of appointment; voluntary

(a) An appointment of a personal representative terminates as provided in section 524.3–1003, one year after the filing of a closing statement.

(b) An order closing an estate as provided in section 524.3–1001 or 524.3–1002 terminates an appointment of a personal representative.

(c) A personal representative may resign the position by filing a written statement of resignation with the registrar after having given at least 15 days written notice to the persons known to be interested in the estate. If no one applies or petitions for appointment of a successor representative within the time indicated in the notice, the filed statement of resignation is ineffective as a termination of appointment and in any event is effective only upon the appointment and qualification of a successor representative and delivery of the assets to the successor.

Laws 1974, c. 442, art. 3, § 524.3–610, eff. Jan. 1, 1976. Amended by Laws 1986, c. 444.

524.3–611. Termination of appointment by removal; cause; procedure

(a) A person interested in the estate may petition for removal of a personal representative for cause at any time. Upon filing of the petition, the court shall fix a time and place for hearing. Notice shall be given by the petitioner to the personal representative, and to other persons as the court may order. Except as otherwise ordered as provided in section 524.3–607, after receipt of notice of removal proceedings, the personal representative shall not act except to account, to correct maladministration or preserve the estate. If removal is ordered, the court also shall direct by order the disposition of the assets remaining in the name of, or under the control of, the personal representative being removed.

(b) Cause for removal exists when removal is in the best interests of the estate, or if it is shown that a personal representative or the person seeking the personal representative's appointment intentionally misrepresented material facts in the proceedings leading to the appointment, or that the personal representative has disregarded an order of the court, has become incapable of discharging the duties of office, or has mismanaged the estate or failed to perform any duty pertaining to the office. In determining the best interests of the estate, the personal representative's compensation and fees, and administrative expenses, shall also be considered. Unless the decedent's will directs otherwise, a personal representative appointed at the decedent's domicile, incident to securing personal appointment or the appointment of a nominee as ancillary personal representative, may obtain removal of another who was appointed personal representative in this state to administer local assets.

Laws 1974, c. 442, art. 3, § 524.3–611, eff. Jan. 1, 1976. Amended by Laws 1979, c. 137, § 2; Laws 1986, c. 444.

524.3–612. Termination of appointment; change of testacy status

Except as otherwise ordered in formal proceedings, the probate of a will subsequent to the appointment of a personal representative in intestacy or under a will which is superseded by formal probate of another will, or the vacation of an informal probate of a will subsequent to the appointment of the personal representative thereunder, does not terminate the appointment of the personal representative although the personal representative's powers may be reduced as provided in section 524.3–401. Termination occurs upon appointment in informal or formal appointment proceedings of a person entitled to appointment under the later assumption concerning testacy. If no request for new appointment is made within 30 days after expiration of time for appeal from the order in formal testacy proceedings, or from the informal probate, changing the assumption concerning testacy, the previously appointed personal representative upon request may be appointed personal representative under the subsequently probated will, or as in intestacy as the case may be.

Laws 1974, c. 442, art. 3, § 524.3–612, eff. Jan. 1, 1976. Amended by Laws 1986, c. 444.

524.3–613. Successor personal representative

Upon notice, if any, as the court or registrar shall require, the court upon petition and the registrar upon application may appoint a personal representative to succeed one whose appointment has been terminated. After appointment and qualification, a successor personal representative may be substituted in all actions and proceedings to which the former personal representative was a party, and no notice, process or claim which was given or served upon the former personal representative need be given to or served upon the successor in order to preserve any position or right the person giving the notice or filing the claim may thereby have obtained or preserved with reference to the former personal representative. Except as otherwise ordered by the court, the successor personal representative has the powers and duties in respect to the continued administration which the former personal representative would have had if the appointment had not been terminated.

Laws 1974, c. 442, art. 3, § 524.3–613, eff. Jan. 1, 1976. Amended by Laws 1977, c. 155, § 1; Laws 1986, c. 444.

524.3–614. Special administrator; appointment

A special administrator may be appointed:

(1) informally by the registrar on the application of any interested person when necessary to protect the estate of a decedent prior to the appointment of a general personal representative or if a prior appointment has been terminated as provided in section 524.3–609;

(2) in a formal proceeding by order of the court on the petition of any interested person and finding, after notice and hearing, that appointment is necessary to preserve the estate or to secure its proper administration including its administration in circumstances where a general personal representative cannot or should not act. If

it appears to the court that an emergency exists, appointment may be ordered without notice.

Laws 1974, c. 442, art. 3, § 524.3–614, eff. Jan. 1, 1976.

524.3–615. Special administrator; who may be appointed

(a) If a special administrator is to be appointed pending the probate of a will which is the subject of a pending application or petition for probate, the person named executor in the will shall be appointed if available, and qualified.

(b) In other cases, any proper person may be appointed special administrator.

Laws 1974, c. 442, art. 3, § 524.3–615, eff. Jan. 1, 1976.

524.3–616. Special administrator; appointed informally; powers and duties

A special administrator appointed by the registrar in informal proceedings pursuant to section 524.3–614(1) has the duty to collect and manage the assets of the estate, to preserve them, to account therefor and to deliver them to the general personal representative upon qualification. The special administrator has the power of a personal representative under the chapter necessary to perform these duties.

Laws 1974, c. 442, art. 3, § 524.3–616, eff. Jan. 1, 1976. Amended by Laws 1986, c. 444.

524.3–617. Special administrator; formal proceedings; power and duties

A special administrator appointed by order of the court in any formal proceeding has the power of a general personal representative except as limited in the appointment and duties as prescribed in the order. The appointment may be for a specified time, to perform particular acts or on other terms as the court may direct.

Laws 1974, c. 442, art. 3, § 524.3–617, eff. Jan. 1, 1976.

524.3–618. Termination of appointment; special administrator

The appointment of a special administrator terminates in accordance with the provisions of the order of appointment or on the appointment of a general personal representative. In other cases, the appointment of a special administrator is subject to termination as provided in sections 524.3–608 to 524.3–611.

Laws 1974, c. 442, art. 3, § 524.3–618, eff. Jan. 1, 1976.

PART 7

DUTIES AND POWERS OF PERSONAL REPRESENTATIVES

524.3–701. Time of accrual of duties and powers

The duties and powers of a personal representative commence upon appointment. The powers of a personal representative relate back in time to give acts by the person appointed which are beneficial to the estate occurring prior to appointment the same effect as those occurring thereafter. Prior to appointment, a person named executor in a will may carry out written instructions of the decedent relating to the body, funeral and burial arrangements. A personal representative may ratify and accept acts on behalf of the estate done by others where the acts would have been proper for a personal representative.

Laws 1974, c. 442, art. 3, § 524.3–701, eff. Jan. 1, 1976. Amended by Laws 1986, c. 444.

524.3–702. Priority among different letters

A person to whom general letters are issued first has exclusive authority under the letters until the appointment is terminated or modified. If, through error, general letters are afterwards issued to another, the first appointed representative may recover any property of the estate in the hands of the representative subsequently appointed, but the acts of the latter done in good faith before notice of the first letters are not void for want of validity of appointment.

Laws 1974, c. 442, art. 3, § 524.3–702, eff. Jan. 1, 1976. Amended by Laws 1986, c. 444.

524.3–703. General duties; relation and liability to persons interested in estate; standing to sue

(a) A personal representative is a fiduciary who shall observe the standards of care in dealing with the estate assets that would be observed by a prudent person dealing with the property of another, and if the personal representative has special skills or is named personal representative on a basis of representation of special skills or expertise, the personal representative is under a duty to use those skills. A personal representative is under a duty to settle and distribute the estate of the decedent in accordance with the terms of any probated and effective will and applicable law, and as expeditiously and efficiently as is consistent with the best interests of the estate. The personal representative shall use the authority conferred by applicable law, the terms of the will, if any, and any order in proceedings to which the personal representative is party for the best interests of successors to the estate.

(b) A personal representative shall not be surcharged for acts of administration or distribution if the conduct in question was authorized at the time. Subject to other obligations of administration, an informally probated will is authority to administer and distribute the estate according to its terms. An order of appointment of a personal representative, whether issued in informal or formal proceedings, is authority to distribute apparently intestate assets to the heirs of the decedent if, at the time of distribution, the personal representative is not aware of a pending testacy proceeding, a proceeding to vacate an order entered in an earlier testacy proceeding, a formal proceeding questioning the appointment or fitness to continue, or a supervised administration proceeding. Nothing in this section affects the duty of the personal representative to administer and distribute the estate in accordance with the rights of claimants, the surviving spouse, any minor and dependent children and any pretermitted child of the decedent as described elsewhere.

(c) Except as to proceedings which do not survive the death of the decedent, a personal representative of a decedent domiciled in this state at death has the same standing to sue and be sued in the courts of this state and the courts of any other jurisdiction as the decedent had immediately prior to death.

Laws 1974, c. 442, art. 3, § 524.3-703. Amended by Laws 1975, c. 347, § 52, eff. Jan. 1, 1976; Laws 1986, c. 444.

524.3-704. Personal representative to proceed without court order; exception

A personal representative shall proceed expeditiously with the settlement and distribution of a decedent's estate and, except as otherwise specified or ordered in regard to a supervised personal representative, do so without adjudication, order, or direction of the court, but the personal representative may invoke the jurisdiction of the court, in proceedings authorized by this chapter, to resolve questions concerning the estate or its administration.

Laws 1974, c. 442, art. 3, § 524.3-704, eff. Jan. 1, 1976. Amended by Laws 1986, c. 444.

524.3-705. Repealed by Laws 1975, c. 347, § 144, eff. Jan. 1, 1976

524.3-706. Duty of personal representative; inventory and appraisement

Within six months after appointment, or nine months after the death of the decedent, whichever is later, a personal representative, who is not a special administrator or a successor to another representative who has previously discharged this duty, shall prepare and file or mail an inventory of property owned by the decedent at the time of death, listing it with reasonable detail, and indicating as to each listed item, its fair market value as of the date of the decedent's death, and the type and amount of any encumbrance that may exist with reference to any item.

The personal representative shall mail or deliver a copy of the inventory to the surviving spouse, if there be one, to all residuary distributees, and to interested persons or creditors who request a copy thereof. The personal representative need not personally receive a copy as a surviving spouse or as a residuary distributee.

Laws 1974, c. 442, art. 3, § 524.3–706. Amended by Laws 1975, c. 347, § 53, eff. Jan. 1, 1976; Laws 1979, c. 303, art. 3, § 32; Laws 1982, c. 529, § 1; Laws 1986, c. 444.

Historical and Statutory Notes

Laws 1979, c. 303, art. 3, § 32, deleted a requirement that the personal representative file an executed copy of the Minnesota inheritance tax return with the court or registrar.

524.3–707. Employment of appraisers

The personal representative may employ a qualified and disinterested appraiser to assist in ascertaining the fair market value as of the date of the decedent's death of any asset the value of which may be subject to reasonable doubt. Different persons may be employed to appraise different kinds of assets included in the estate. The names and addresses of any appraiser shall be indicated on the inventory with the item or items appraised.

Laws 1974, c. 442, art. 3, § 524.3–707, eff. Jan. 1, 1976. Amended by Laws 1986, c. 444.

524.3–708. Duty of personal representative; supplementary inventory

If any property not included in the original inventory comes to the knowledge of a personal representative or if the personal representative learns that the value or description indicated in the original inventory for any item is erroneous or misleading, the personal representative shall make a supplementary inventory or appraisement showing the market value as of the date of the decedent's death of the new item or the revised market value or descriptions, and the appraisers or other data relied upon, if any, and furnish copies thereof or information thereof to persons interested in the new information, and file it with the court if the original inventory was filed.

Laws 1974, c. 442, art. 3, § 524.3–708, eff. Jan. 1, 1976. Amended by Laws 1986, c. 444; Laws 1996, c. 338, art. 2, § 4.

524.3–709. Duty of personal representative; possession of estate

Except as otherwise provided by a decedent's will, every personal representative has a right to, and shall take possession or control of, the decedent's property, except that any real property or tangible personal property may be left with or surrendered to the person presumptively entitled thereto unless or until, in the judgment of the personal representative, possession of the property by the personal representative will be necessary for purposes of administration. The request by a personal representative for delivery of any property possessed by an heir or devisee is conclusive evidence, in any action against the heir or devisee for possession thereof, that the possession of the property by the personal representative is necessary for purposes of administration. The personal representative shall pay taxes on, and take all steps reasonably necessary for the management, protection and preservation of, the estate in possession and may maintain an action to recover possession of property or to determine the title thereto.

Laws 1974, c. 442, art. 3, § 524.3–709, eff. Jan. 1, 1976. Amended by Laws 1986, c. 444.

524.3–710. Power to avoid transfers

The property liable for the payment of unsecured debts of a decedent includes all property transferred by the decedent by any means which is in law void or voidable as against creditors, and subject to prior liens, the right to recover this property, so far as necessary for the payment of unsecured debts of the decedent, is exclusively in the personal representative.

Laws 1974, c. 442, art. 3, § 524.3–710, eff. Jan. 1, 1976. Amended by Laws 1986, c. 444.

524.3–711. Powers of personal representatives; in general

Until termination of the appointment a personal representative has the same power over the title to property of the estate that an absolute owner would have, in trust however, for the benefit of the creditors and others interested in the estate. This power may be exercised without notice, hearing, or order of court and when so exercised shall transfer good title to the transferee to the same extent that decedent had title thereto; provided, however, that a personal representative appointed in an informal proceeding shall not be empowered to sell, encumber, lease or distribute any interest in real estate owned by the decedent until 30 days have passed from the date of the issuance of the letters.

Laws 1974, c. 442, art. 3, § 524.3–711. Amended by Laws 1975, c. 347, § 54, eff. Jan. 1, 1976; Laws 1986, c. 444.

524.3–712. Improper exercise of power; breach of fiduciary duty

If the exercise of power concerning the estate is improper, the personal representative is liable to interested persons for damage or loss resulting from breach of fiduciary duty to the same extent as a trustee of an express trust. The rights of purchasers and others dealing with a personal representative shall be determined as provided in sections 524.3–713 and 524.3–714.

Laws 1974, c. 442, art. 3, § 524.3–712, eff. Jan. 1, 1976. Amended by Laws 1986, c. 444.

524.3–713. Sale, encumbrance or transaction involving conflict of interest; voidable; exceptions

Any sale or encumbrance to the personal representative, the personal representative's spouse, agent or attorney, or any corporation or trust in which the personal representative has a substantial beneficial interest, or any transaction which is affected by a substantial conflict of interest on the part of the personal representative, is voidable by any person interested in the estate except one who has consented after fair disclosure, unless

  (1) the will or a contract entered into by the decedent expressly authorized the transaction; or

  (2) the transaction is approved by the court after notice to interested persons.

Laws 1974, c. 442, art. 3, § 524.3–713, eff. Jan. 1, 1976. Amended by Laws 1986, c. 444.

524.3–714. Persons dealing with personal representative; protection

(a) A person who in good faith either assists a personal representative or deals with the personal representative for value is protected as if the personal representative properly exercised power. The fact that a person knowingly deals with a personal representative does not alone require the person to inquire into the existence of a power or the propriety of its exercise. Except for restrictions on powers of supervised personal representatives which are endorsed on letters as provided in section 524.3–504, no provision in any will or order of court purporting to limit the power of a personal representative is effective except as to persons with actual knowledge thereof. A person is not bound to see to the proper application of estate assets paid or delivered to a personal representative. The protection here expressed extends to instances in which some procedural irregularity or jurisdictional defect occurred in proceedings leading to the issuance of letters, including a case in which the alleged decedent is found to be alive. The protection here expressed is not by substitution for that provided by comparable provisions of the laws relating to commercial transactions and laws simplifying transfers of securities by fiduciaries.

(b) If property is wrongfully transferred by a person acting as a personal representative to a person who is not in good faith, a subsequent good faith purchaser is protected as if the original transferee dealt in good faith. Any purchaser in good faith is protected as if all prior transfers were made in good faith.

Laws 1974, c. 442, art. 3, § 524.3–714, eff. Jan. 1, 1976. Amended by Laws 1977, c. 156, § 1; Laws 1978, c. 525, § 15, eff. March 24, 1978; Laws 1986, c. 444.

524.3–715. Transactions authorized for personal representatives; exceptions

Except as restricted or otherwise provided by the will or by an order in a formal proceeding and subject to the priorities stated in section 524.3–902, a personal representative, acting reasonably for the benefit of the interested persons, may properly:

  (1) retain assets owned by the decedent pending distribution or liquidation including those in which the representative is personally interested or which are otherwise improper for trust investment;

(2) receive assets from fiduciaries, or other sources;

(3) perform, compromise or refuse performance of the decedent's contracts that continue as obligations of the estate, as the personal representative may determine under the circumstances. In performing enforceable contracts by the decedent to convey or lease land, the personal representative, among other possible courses of action, may:

(i) execute and deliver a deed of conveyance for cash payment of all sums remaining due or the purchaser's note for the sum remaining due secured by a mortgage or deed of trust on the land; or

(ii) deliver a deed in escrow with directions that the proceeds, when paid in accordance with the escrow agreement, be paid to the successors of the decedent, as designated in the escrow agreement;

(4) satisfy written charitable pledges of the decedent irrespective of whether the pledges constituted binding obligations of the decedent or were properly presented as claims, if in the judgment of the personal representative the decedent would have wanted the pledges completed under the circumstances;

(5) if funds are not needed to meet debts and expenses currently payable and are not immediately distributable, deposit or invest liquid assets of the estate, including moneys received from the sale of other assets, in federally insured interest–bearing accounts, readily marketable secured loan arrangements or other prudent investments which would be reasonable for use by trustees generally;

(6) acquire or dispose of an asset, including land in this or another state, for cash or on credit, at public or private sale; and manage, develop, improve, exchange, partition, change the character of, or abandon an estate asset;

(7) make ordinary or extraordinary repairs or alterations in buildings or other structures, demolish any improvements, raze existing or erect new party walls or buildings;

(8) subdivide, develop or dedicate land to public use; make or obtain the vacation of plats and adjust boundaries; or adjust differences in valuation on exchange or partition by giving or receiving considerations; or dedicate easements to public use without consideration;

(9) enter for any purpose into a lease as lessor or lessee, with or without option to purchase or renew, for a term within or extending beyond the period of administration;

(10) enter into a lease or arrangement for exploration and removal of minerals or other natural resources or enter into a pooling or unitization agreement;

(11) abandon property when, in the opinion of the personal representative, it is valueless, or is so encumbered, or is in condition that it is of no benefit to the estate;

(12) vote stocks or other securities in person or by general or limited proxy;

(13) pay calls, assessments, and other sums chargeable or accruing against or on account of securities, unless barred by the provisions relating to claims;

(14) hold a security in the name of a nominee or in other form without disclosure of the interest of the estate but the personal representative is liable for any act of the nominee in connection with the security so held;

(15) insure the assets of the estate against damage, loss and liability and the personal representative against liability as to third persons;

(16) borrow money with or without security to be repaid from the estate assets or otherwise; and advance money for the protection of the estate;

(17) effect a fair and reasonable compromise with any debtor or obligor, or extend, renew or in any manner modify the terms of any obligation owing to the estate. The personal representative on holding a mortgage, pledge or other lien upon property of another person may, in lieu of foreclosure, accept a conveyance or transfer of encumbered assets from the owner thereof in satisfaction of the indebtedness secured by lien;

(18) pay in compliance with section 524.3–805, but without the presentation of a claim, the reasonable and necessary last illness expenses of the decedent (except as provided in section 524.3–806 (a)), reasonable funeral expenses, debts and taxes with preference under federal or state law, and other taxes, assessments, compensation of the personal representative and the personal representative's attorney, and all other costs and expenses of administration although the same may be otherwise barred under section 524.3–803;

(19) sell or exercise stock subscription or conversion rights; consent, directly or through a committee or other agent, to the reorganization, consolidation, merger, dissolution, or liquidation of a corporation or other business enterprise;

(20) allocate items of income or expense to either estate income or principal, as permitted or provided by law;

(21) employ persons, including attorneys, auditors, investment advisors, or agents, even if they are associated with the personal representative, to advise or assist the personal representative in the performance of administrative duties; act without independent investigation upon their recommendations; and instead of acting personally, employ one or more agents to perform any act of administration, whether or not discretionary;

(22) prosecute or defend claims, or proceedings in any jurisdiction for the protection of the estate and of the personal representative in the performance of duties;

(23) sell, mortgage, or lease any real or personal property of the estate or any interest therein, including the homestead, exempt or otherwise, for cash, credit, or for part cash and part credit, with or without security for unpaid balances, and without the consent of any devisee or heir unless the property has been

specifically devised to a devisee or heir by decedent's will, except that the homestead of a decedent when the spouse takes any interest therein shall not be sold, mortgaged or leased unless the written consent of the spouse has been obtained;

(24) continue any unincorporated business or venture in which the decedent was engaged at the time of death (i) in the same business form for a period of not more than four months from the date of appointment of a general personal representative if continuation is a reasonable means of preserving the value of the business including good will, (ii) in the same business form for any additional period of time that may be approved by order of the court in a formal proceeding to which the persons interested in the estate are parties; or (iii) throughout the period of administration if the business is incorporated by the personal representative and if none of the probable distributees of the business who are competent adults object to its incorporation and retention in the estate;

(25) incorporate any business or venture in which the decedent was engaged at the time of death;

(26) provide for exoneration of the personal representative from personal liability in any contract entered into on behalf of the estate;

(27) satisfy and settle claims and distribute the estate as provided in this chapter;

(28) foreclose a mortgage, lien, or pledge or collect the debts secured thereby, or complete any such proceeding commenced by the decedent;

(29) exercise all powers granted to guardians and conservators by sections 524.5–101 to 524.5–502.

Laws 1974, c. 442, art. 3, § 524.3–715. Amended by Laws 1975, c. 347, § 55, eff. Jan. 1, 1976; Laws 1986, c. 444; Laws 2004, c. 146, art. 3, § 42; Laws 2006, c. 221, § 21.

Historical and Statutory Notes

Laws 2006, c. 221, § 24, provided:

"Applicability; transition provisions.

"Section 21 [amending this section] applies to every conveyance by a personal representative made before, on, or after the effective date of this section, except that it does not affect an action or proceeding that is:

"(1) pending on the effective date of section 21 involving the validity of the conveyance; or

"(2) commenced prior to February 1, 2007, if a notice of the pendency of the action or proceeding is recorded before February 1, 2007, in the office of the county recorder or registrar of titles of the county in which the real property affected by the action or proceeding is located."

524.3–716. Powers and duties of successor personal representative

A successor personal representative has the same power and duty as the original personal representative to complete the administration and distribution of the estate, as expeditiously as possible, but shall not exercise any power expressly made personal to the executor named in the will.

Laws 1974, c. 442, art. 3, § 524.3–716, eff. Jan. 1, 1976. Amended by Laws 1986, c. 444.

524.3–717. Corepresentatives; when joint action required

If two or more persons are appointed corepresentatives and unless the will or the court provides otherwise, the concurrence of all is required on all acts connected with the administration and distribution of the estate. This restriction does not apply when any corepresentative receives and receipts for property due the estate, when the concurrence of all cannot readily be obtained in the time reasonably available for emergency action necessary to preserve the estate, or when a corepresentative has been delegated to act for the others. Persons dealing with a corepresentative if actually unaware that another has been appointed to serve or if advised by the personal representative with whom they deal that the personal representative has authority to act alone for any of the reasons mentioned herein, are as fully protected as if the person with whom they dealt had been the sole personal representative.

Laws 1974, c. 442, art. 3, § 524.3–717. Amended by Laws 1975, c. 347, § 56, eff. Jan. 1, 1976; Laws 1986, c. 444.

524.3–718. Powers of surviving personal representative

Unless the terms of the will otherwise provide, every power exercisable by personal corepresentatives may be exercised by the one or more remaining after the appointment of one or more is terminated, and if one of two or more nominated as coexecutors is not appointed, those appointed may exercise all the powers incident to the office.

Laws 1974, c. 442, art. 3, § 524.3–718, eff. Jan. 1, 1976.

524.3–719. Compensation of personal representative

(a) A personal representative is entitled to reasonable compensation for services. If a will provides for compensation of the personal representative and there is no contract with the decedent regarding compensation, the personal representative may renounce the provision before qualifying and be entitled to reasonable compensation. A personal representative also may renounce the right to all or any part of the compensation. A written renunciation of fee may be filed with the court.

(b) In determining what is reasonable compensation, the court shall give consideration to the following factors:

(1) the time and labor required;

(2) the complexity and novelty of problems involved; and

(3) the extent of the responsibilities assumed and the results obtained.

Laws 1974, c. 442, art. 3, § 524.3–719, eff. Jan. 1, 1976. Amended by Laws 1979, c. 137, § 3; Laws 1986, c. 444.

524.3–720. Expenses in estate litigation

Any personal representative or person nominated as personal representative who defends or prosecutes any proceeding in good faith, whether successful or not, or any interested person who successfully opposes the allowance of a will, is entitled to receive from the estate necessary expenses and disbursements including reasonable attorneys' fees incurred. When after demand the personal representative refuses to prosecute or pursue a claim or asset of the estate or a claim is made against the personal representative on behalf of the estate and any interested person shall then by a separate attorney prosecute or pursue and recover such fund or asset for the benefit of the estate, or when, and to the extent that, the services of an attorney for any interested person contribute to the benefit of the estate, as such, as distinguished from the personal benefit of such person, such attorney shall be paid such compensation from the estate as the court shall deem just and reasonable and commensurate with the benefit to the estate from the recovery so made or from such services.

Laws 1974, c. 442, art. 3, § 524.3–720. Amended by Laws 1975, c. 347, § 57, eff. Jan. 1, 1976; Laws 1986, c. 444.

524.3–721. Proceedings for review of employment of agents and compensation of personal representatives and employees of estate

After notice to all interested persons or on petition of an interested person or on appropriate motion if administration is supervised, the propriety of employment of any person by a personal representative including any attorney, auditor, investment advisor or other specialized agent or assistant, the reasonableness of the compensation of any person so employed, or the reasonableness of the compensation determined by the personal representative for personal representative services, may be reviewed by the court. Any person who has received excessive compensation from an estate for services rendered may be ordered to make appropriate refunds.

Laws 1974, c. 442, art. 3, § 524.3–721, eff. Jan. 1, 1976. Amended by Laws 1986, c. 444.

PART 8

CREDITORS' CLAIMS

524.3–801. Notice to creditors

(a) Unless notice has already been given under this section, upon appointment of a general personal representative in informal proceedings or upon the filing of a petition for formal appointment of a general personal representative, notice thereof, in the form prescribed by court rule, shall be given under the direction of the court administrator by publication once a week for two successive weeks in a legal newspaper in the county wherein the proceedings are pending giving the name and address of the general personal representative and notifying creditors of the estate to present their claims within four months after the date of the court administrator's notice which is subsequently published or be forever barred, unless they are entitled to further service of notice under paragraph (b) or (c).

(b) The personal representative shall, within three months after the date of the first publication of the notice, serve a copy of the notice upon each then known and identified creditor in the manner provided in paragraph (c). If the decedent or a predeceased spouse of the decedent received assistance for which a claim could be filed under section 246.53, 256B.15, 256D.16, or 261.04, notice to the commissioner of human services must be given under paragraph (d) instead of under this paragraph or paragraph (c). A creditor is "known" if: (i) the personal representative knows that the creditor has asserted a claim that arose during the decedent's life against either the decedent or the decedent's estate; (ii) the creditor has asserted a claim that arose during the decedent's life and the fact is clearly disclosed in accessible financial records known and available to the personal representative; or (iii) the claim of the creditor would be revealed by a reasonably diligent search for creditors of the decedent in accessible financial records known and available to the personal representative. Under this section, a creditor is "identified" if the personal representative's knowledge of the name and address of the creditor will permit service of notice to be made under paragraph (c).

(c) Unless the claim has already been presented to the personal representative or paid, the personal representative shall serve a copy of the notice required by paragraph (b) upon each creditor of the decedent who is then known to the personal representative and identified either by delivery of a copy of the required notice to the creditor, or by mailing a copy of the notice to the creditor by certified, registered, or ordinary first class mail addressed to the creditor at the creditor's office or place of residence.

(d)(1) Effective for decedents dying on or after July 1, 1997, if the decedent or a predeceased spouse of the decedent received assistance for which a claim could be filed under section 246.53, 256B.15, 256D.16, or 261.04, the personal representative or the attorney for the personal representative shall serve the commissioner of human services with notice in the manner prescribed in paragraph (c) as soon as practicable after the appointment of the personal representative. The notice must state the decedent's full name, date of birth, and Social Security number and, to the extent then known after making a reasonably diligent inquiry, the full name, date of birth, and Social Security number for each of the decedent's predeceased spouses. The notice may also contain a statement that, after making a reasonably diligent inquiry, the personal representative has determined that the decedent did not have any predeceased spouses or that the personal representative has been unable to determine one or more of the previous items of information for a predeceased spouse of the decedent. A copy of the notice to creditors must be attached to and be a part of the notice to the commissioner.

(2) Notwithstanding a will or other instrument or law to the contrary, except as allowed in this paragraph, no property subject to administration by the estate may be distributed by the estate or the personal representative until 70 days after the date the notice is served on the commissioner as provided in paragraph (c), unless the local agency consents as provided for in clause (6). This restriction on distribution does not apply to the personal representative's sale of real or personal property, but does apply to the net proceeds the estate receives from these sales. The personal representative, or any person with personal knowledge of the facts, may provide an affidavit containing the description of any real or personal property affected by this paragraph and stating facts showing compliance with this paragraph. If the affidavit describes real property, it may be filed or recorded in the office of the county recorder or registrar of titles for the county where the real property is located. This paragraph does not apply to proceedings under sections 524.3–1203 and 525.31, or when a duly authorized agent of a county is acting as the personal representative of the estate.

(3) At any time before an order or decree is entered under section 524.3–1001 or 524.3–1002, or a closing statement is filed under section 524.3–1003, the personal representative or the attorney for the personal representative may serve an amended notice on the commissioner to add variations or other names of the decedent or a predeceased spouse named in the notice, the name of a predeceased spouse omitted from the notice, to add or correct the date of birth or Social Security number of a decedent or predeceased spouse named in the notice, or to correct any other deficiency in a prior notice. The amended notice must state the decedent's name, date of birth, and Social Security number, the case name, case number, and district court in which the estate is pending, and the date the notice being amended was served on the commissioner. If the amendment adds the name of a predeceased spouse omitted from the notice, it must also state that spouse's full name, date of birth, and Social Security number. The amended notice must be served on the commissioner in the same manner as the original notice. Upon service, the amended notice relates back to and is effective from the date the notice it amends was served, and the time for filing claims arising under section 246.53, 256B.15, 256D.16 or 261.04 is extended by 60 days from the date of service of the amended notice. Claims filed during the 60–day period are undischarged and unbarred claims, may be prosecuted by the entities entitled to file those claims in accordance with section 524.3–1004, and the limitations in section 524.3–1006 do not apply. The personal representative or any person with personal knowledge of the facts may provide and file or record an affidavit in the same manner as provided for in clause (1).

(4) Within one year after the date an order or decree is entered under section 524.3–1001 or 524.3–1002 or a closing statement is filed under section

524.3–1003, any person who has an interest in property that was subject to administration by the estate may serve an amended notice on the commissioner to add variations or other names of the decedent or a predeceased spouse named in the notice, the name of a predeceased spouse omitted from the notice, to add or correct the date of birth or Social Security number of a decedent or predeceased spouse named in the notice, or to correct any other deficiency in a prior notice. The amended notice must be served on the commissioner in the same manner as the original notice and must contain the information required for amendments under clause (3). If the amendment adds the name of a predeceased spouse omitted from the notice, it must also state that spouse's full name, date of birth, and Social Security number. Upon service, the amended notice relates back to and is effective from the date the notice it amends was served. If the amended notice adds the name of an omitted predeceased spouse or adds or corrects the Social Security number or date of birth of the decedent or a predeceased spouse already named in the notice, then, notwithstanding any other laws to the contrary, claims against the decedent's estate on account of those persons resulting from the amendment and arising under section 246.53, 256B.15, 256D.16, or 261.04 are undischarged and unbarred claims, may be prosecuted by the entities entitled to file those claims in accordance with section 524.3–1004, and the limitations in section 524.3–1006 do not apply. The person filing the amendment or any other person with personal knowledge of the facts may provide and file or record an affidavit describing affected real or personal property in the same manner as clause (1).

(5) After one year from the date an order or decree is entered under section 524.3–1001 or 524.3–1002, or a closing statement is filed under section 524.3–1003, no error, omission, or defect of any kind in the notice to the commissioner required under this paragraph or in the process of service of the notice on the commissioner, or the failure to serve the commissioner with notice as required by this paragraph, makes any distribution of property by a personal representative void or voidable. The distributee's title to the distributed property shall be free of any claims based upon a failure to comply with this paragraph.

(6) The local agency may consent to a personal representative's request to distribute property subject to administration by the estate to distributees during the 70–day period after service of notice on the commissioner. The local agency may grant or deny the request in whole or in part and may attach conditions to its consent as it deems appropriate. When the local agency consents to a distribution, it shall give the estate a written certificate evidencing its consent to the early distribution of assets at no cost. The certificate must include the name, case number, and district court in which the estate is pending, the name of the local agency, describe the specific real or personal property to which the consent applies, state that the local agency consents to the distribution of the specific property described in the consent during the 70–day period following service of the notice on the commissioner, state that the consent is unconditional or list all of the terms and conditions of the

consent, be dated, and may include other contents as may be appropriate. The certificate must be signed by the director of the local agency or the director's designees and is effective as of the date it is dated unless it provides otherwise. The signature of the director or the director's designee does not require any acknowledgment. The certificate shall be prima facie evidence of the facts it states, may be attached to or combined with a deed or any other instrument of conveyance and, when so attached or combined, shall constitute a single instrument. If the certificate describes real property, it shall be accepted for recording or filing by the county recorder or registrar of titles in the county in which the property is located. If the certificate describes real property and is not attached to or combined with a deed or other instrument of conveyance, it shall be accepted for recording or filing by the county recorder or registrar of titles in the county in which the property is located. The certificate constitutes a waiver of the 70–day period provided for in clause (2) with respect to the property it describes and is prima facie evidence of service of notice on the commissioner. The certificate is not a waiver or relinquishment of any claims arising under section 246.53, 256B.15, 256D.16, or 261.04, and does not otherwise constitute a waiver of any of the personal representative's duties under this paragraph. Distributees who receive property pursuant to a consent to an early distribution shall remain liable to creditors of the estate as provided for by law.

(7) All affidavits provided for under this paragraph:

(i) shall be provided by persons who have personal knowledge of the facts stated in the affidavit;

(ii) may be filed or recorded in the office of the county recorder or registrar of titles in the county in which the real property they describe is located for the purpose of establishing compliance with the requirements of this paragraph; and

(iii) are prima facie evidence of the facts stated in the affidavit.

(8) This paragraph applies to the estates of decedents dying on or after July 1, 1997. Clause (5) also applies with respect to all notices served on the commissioner of human services before July 1, 1997, under Laws 1996, chapter 451, article 2, section 55. All notices served on the commissioner before July 1, 1997, pursuant to Laws 1996, chapter 451, article 2, section 55, shall be deemed to be legally sufficient for the purposes for which they were intended, notwithstanding any errors, omissions or other defects.

Laws 1975, c. 347, § 58, eff. Jan. 1, 1976. Amended by Laws 1986, 1st Sp., c. 3, art. 1, § 82; Laws 1989, c. 163, § 1; Laws 1996, c. 451, art. 2, § 55; Laws 1997, c. 217, art. 2, § 16; Laws 2000, c. 400, § 6; Laws 2008, c. 341, art. 4, § 3, eff. Aug. 1, 2008.

Historical and Statutory Notes

Laws 1989, c. 163, § 5, provided: "This act is effective 30 days after final enactment [approved by the governor May 17, 1989]."

Laws 1996, c. 451, art. 2, § 62, par. (c), provides in part that § 55 (amending this section) applies to estates where the notice under § 524.3–801, par. (a), was first published on or after its effective date. Section 55 does not affect any right or duty to provide notice to known creditors, including a local agency, before its effective date.

524.3–802. Statutes of limitations

Unless an estate is insolvent the personal representative, with the consent of all successors, may waive any defense of limitations available to the estate. If the defense is not waived, no claim which was barred by any statute of limitations at the time of the decedent's death shall be allowed or paid. The running of any statute of limitations measured from some other event than death or notice given under section 524.3–801 against a decedent is suspended during the 12 months following the decedent's death but resumes thereafter as to claims not barred pursuant to the sections which follow. For purposes of any statute of limitations, the proper presentation of a claim under section 524.3–804 is equivalent to commencement of a proceeding on the claim.

Laws 1975, c. 347, § 58, eff. Jan. 1, 1976. Amended by Laws 1989, c. 163, § 2.

Historical and Statutory Notes

Laws 1989, c. 163, § 5, provided: "This act is effective 30 days after final enactment [approved by the governor May 17, 1989]."

524.3–803. Limitations on presentation of claims

(a) All claims as defined in section 524.1–201(6), against a decedent's estate which arose before the death of the decedent, including claims of the state and any subdivision thereof, whether due or to become due, absolute or contingent, liquidated or unliquidated, if not barred earlier by other statute of limitations, are barred against the estate, the personal representative, and the heirs and devisees of the decedent, unless presented as follows:

(1) in the case of a creditor who is only entitled, under the United States Constitution and under the Minnesota Constitution, to notice by publication under section 524.3–801, within four months after the date of the court administrator's notice to creditors which is subsequently published pursuant to section 524.3–801;

(2) in the case of a creditor who was served with notice under section 524.3–801(c), within the later to expire of four months after the date of the first publication of notice to creditors or one month after the service;

(3) within one year after the decedent's death, whether or not notice to creditors has been published or served under section 524.3–801. Claims authorized by section 246.53, 256B.15, or 256D.16 must not be barred after one year as provided in this clause.

(b) All claims against a decedent's estate which arise at or after the death of the decedent, including claims of the state and any subdivision thereof, whether due or to become due, absolute or contingent, liquidated or unliquidated, are barred against the estate, the personal representative, and the heirs and devisees of the decedent, unless presented as follows:

(1) a claim based on a contract with the personal representative, within four months after performance by the personal representative is due;

(2) any other claim, within four months after it arises.

(c) Nothing in this section affects or prevents:

(1) any proceeding to enforce any mortgage, pledge, or other lien upon property of the estate;

(2) any proceeding to establish liability of the decedent or the personal representative for which there is protection by liability insurance, to the limits of the insurance protection only;

(3) the presentment and payment at any time within one year after the decedent's death of any claim arising before the death of the decedent that is referred to in section 524.3–715, clause (18), although the same may be otherwise barred under this section; or

(4) the presentment and payment at any time before a petition is filed in compliance with section 524.3–1001 or 524.3–1002 or a closing statement is filed under section 524.3–1003, of:

(i) any claim arising after the death of the decedent that is referred to in section 524.3–715, clause (18), although the same may be otherwise barred hereunder;

(ii) any other claim, including claims subject to clause (3), which would otherwise be barred hereunder, upon allowance by the court upon petition of the personal representative or the claimant for cause shown on notice and hearing as the court may direct.

Laws 1975, c. 347, § 58, eff. Jan. 1, 1976. Amended by Laws 1976, c. 161, § 7, eff. April 4, 1976; Laws 1986, c. 444; Laws 1986, 1st Sp., c. 3, art. 1, § 82; Laws 1989, c. 163, § 3; Laws 2006, c. 221, § 22; Laws 2008, c. 326, art. 1, § 41, eff. July 1, 2008; Laws 2008, c. 341, art. 4, § 4, eff. Aug. 1, 2008.

Historical and Statutory Notes

Laws 1989, c. 163, § 5, provided:

"This act is effective 30 days after final enactment [approved by the governor May 17, 1989]."

524.3–804. Manner of presentation of claims

Claims against a decedent's estate may be presented as follows:

(1) The claimant may deliver or mail to the personal representative a written statement of the claim indicating its basis, the name and address of the claimant, and the amount claimed, or may file a written statement of the claim, in the form prescribed by rule, with the court administrator. The claim is deemed presented on the first to occur of receipt of the written statement of

claim by the personal representative, or the filing of the claim with the court. If a claim is not yet due, the date when it will become due shall be stated. If the claim is contingent or unliquidated, the nature of the uncertainty shall be stated. If the claim is secured, the security shall be described. Failure to describe correctly the security, the nature of any uncertainty, and the due date of a claim not yet due does not invalidate the presentation made.

(2) The claimant may commence a proceeding against the personal representative in any court where the personal representative may be subjected to jurisdiction, to obtain payment of the claim against the estate, but the commencement of the proceeding must occur within the time limited for presenting the claim. No presentation of claim is required in regard to matters claimed in proceedings against the decedent which were pending at the time of death.

(3) If a claim is presented under subsection (1), no proceeding thereon may be commenced more than two months after the personal representative has mailed a notice of disallowance; but, in the case of a claim which is not presently due or which is contingent or unliquidated, the personal representative may consent to an extension of the two month period, or in any case, to avoid injustice the court, on petition, may order an extension of the two month period, but in no event shall the extension run beyond the applicable statute of limitations.

Laws 1975, c. 347, § 58, eff. Jan. 1, 1976. Amended by Laws 1986, c. 444; Laws 1986, 1st Sp., c. 3, art. 1, § 82; Laws 1996, c. 338, art. 2, § 5.

524.3–805. Classification of claims

(a) If the applicable assets of the estate are insufficient to pay all claims in full, the personal representative shall make payment in the following order:

(1) costs and expenses of administration;

(2) reasonable funeral expenses;

(3) debts and taxes with preference under federal law;

(4) reasonable and necessary medical, hospital, or nursing home expenses of the last illness of the decedent, including compensation of persons attending the decedent, a claim filed under section 256B.15 for recovery of expenditures for alternative care for nonmedical assistance recipients under section 256B.0913, and including a claim filed pursuant to section 256B.15;

(5) reasonable and necessary medical, hospital, and nursing home expenses for the care of the decedent during the year immediately preceding death;

(6) debts with preference under other laws of this state, and state taxes;

(7) all other claims.

(b) No preference shall be given in the payment of any claim over any other claim of the same class, and a claim due and payable shall not be entitled to a preference over claims not due, except that if claims for expenses of the last illness involve only claims filed under section 256B.15 for recovery of expenditures for alternative care for nonmedical assistance recipients under section 256B.0913, section 246.53 for costs of state hospital care and claims filed under section 256B.15, claims filed to recover expenditures for alternative care for nonmedical assistance recipients under section 256B.0913 shall have preference over claims filed under both sections 246.53 and other claims filed under section 256B.15, and claims filed under section 246.53 have preference over claims filed under section 256B.15 for recovery of amounts other than those for expenditures for alternative care for nonmedical assistance recipients under section 256B.0913.

Laws 1975, c. 347, § 58, eff. Jan. 1, 1976. Amended by Laws 1982, c. 621, § 2; Laws 1982, c. 641, art. 1, § 19, eff. April 1, 1982; Laws 1983, c. 180, § 19, eff. July 1, 1983; Laws 1986, c. 444; Laws 1987, c. 325, § 2, eff. May 30, 1987; Laws 2003, 1st Sp. c. 14, art. 2, § 52.

Historical and Statutory Notes

Laws 2003, 1st Sp., c. 14, art. 2, § 52, amending this section, also provided that the amendment was effective July 1, 2003, for decedents dying on or after that date.

Laws 1982, c. 621, § 2, in par. (a), added "and including a claim filed pursuant to section 256B.15" at the end of cl. (4), effective for the estates of decedents dying after August 1, 1982.

Laws 1987, c. 325, § 3, provides:

"Section 2 is effective the day following final enactment for claims filed on or after the effective date of section 2."

524.3–806. Allowance of claims

(a) As to claims presented in the manner described in section 524.3–804 within the time limit prescribed or permitted in section 524.3–803, the personal representative may mail a notice to any claimant stating that the claim has been disallowed. If, after allowing or disallowing a claim, the personal representative changes the decision concerning the claim, the personal representative shall notify the claimant. Without order of the court for cause shown, the personal representative may not change a disallowance of a claim after the time for the claimant to file a petition for allowance or to commence a proceeding on the claim has run and the claim has been barred. Every claim which is disallowed in whole or in part by the personal representative is barred so far as not allowed unless the claimant files a petition for allowance in the court or commences a proceeding against the personal representative not later than two months after the mailing of the notice of disallowance or partial allowance if the notice warns the claimant of the impending bar. Failure of the personal representative to mail notice to a claimant of action on the claim for two months after the time for original presentation of the claim has expired has the effect of a notice of allowance, except that upon petition of the personal representative and upon notice to the claimant, the court at any time before payment of such claim may for cause shown permit the personal representative to disallow such claim. Any claim in excess of $3,000 for personal services rendered by an individual to the decedent including compensation of persons attending the decedent during a last illness, and any claim of the personal representative which arose before the death of the decedent or in which the personal representative has an interest in excess of $3,000 may be allowed only in compliance with subsection (b).

(b) Upon the petition of the personal representative or of a claimant in a proceeding for the purpose, the court may allow in whole or in part any claim or claims presented to the personal representative or filed with the court administrator in due time and not barred by subsection (a) of this section. Notice in this proceeding shall be given to the claimant, the personal representative and those other persons interested in the estate as the court may direct by order entered at the time the proceeding is commenced.

(c) A judgment in a proceeding in another court against a personal representative to enforce a claim against a decedent's estate is an allowance of the claim.

(d) Unless otherwise provided in any judgment in another court entered against the personal representative, allowed claims bear interest at the legal rate for the period commencing 60 days after the time for original presentation of the claim has expired unless based on a contract making a provision for interest, in which case they bear interest in accordance with that provision. Notwithstanding the preceding sentence, claims that have been disallowed pursuant to clause (a) and are subsequently allowed by the personal representative or reduced to judgment shall bear interest at the legal rate from the latter of the following dates:

(1) 60 days after the time for original presentation of the claim; or

(2) the date the claim is allowed or the date judgment is entered.

Laws 1975, c. 347, § 58, eff. Jan. 1, 1976. Amended by Laws 1976, c. 161, § 8, eff. April 4, 1976; Laws 1986, c. 444; Laws 1986, 1st Sp., c. 3, art. 1, § 82.

524.3–807. Payment of claims

(a) Upon the expiration of the earliest of the time limitations provided in section 524.3–803 for the presentation of claims, the personal representative shall proceed to pay the claims allowed against the estate in the order of priority prescribed, after making provision for family maintenance and statutory allowances, for claims already presented which have not yet been allowed or whose allowance has been appealed, and for unbarred claims which may yet be presented, including costs and expenses of administration. By petition to the court in a proceeding for the purpose, or by appropriate motion if the administration is supervised, a claimant whose claim has been allowed but not paid as provided herein may secure an order directing the personal representative to pay the claim to the extent that funds of the estate are available for the payment.

(b) The personal representative at any time may pay any just claim which has not been barred, with or without formal presentation, but the personal representative is personally liable to any other claimant whose claim is allowed and who is injured by such payment if

(1) the payment was made before the expiration of the time limit stated in subsection (a) and the personal representative failed to require the payee to give adequate security for the refund of any of the payment necessary to pay other claimants; or

(2) the payment was made, due to the negligence or willful fault of the personal representative, in such manner as to deprive the injured claimant of the claimant's priority.

Laws 1975, c. 347, § 58, eff. Jan. 1, 1976. Amended by Laws 1986, c. 444; Laws 1989, c. 163, § 4.

Historical and Statutory Notes

Laws 1989, c. 163, § 5, provided: "This act is effective 30 days after final enactment [approved by the governor May 17, 1989]."

524.3–808. Individual liability of personal representative

(a) Unless otherwise provided in the contract, a personal representative is not individually liable on a contract properly entered into in a fiduciary capacity in the course of administration of the estate unless the personal representative fails to reveal the representative capacity and identify the estate in the contract.

(b) A personal representative is individually liable for obligations arising from ownership or control of the estate or for torts committed in the course of administration of the estate only if the personal representative is personally at fault.

(c) Claims based on contracts entered into by a personal representative in a fiduciary capacity, on obligations arising from ownership or control of the estate or on torts committed in the course of estate administration may be asserted against the estate by proceeding against the personal representative in the fiduciary capacity, whether or not the personal representative is individually liable therefor.

(d) Issues of liability as between the estate and the personal representative individually may be determined in a proceeding for accounting, surcharge or indemnification or other appropriate proceeding.

Laws 1975, c. 347, § 58, eff. Jan. 1, 1976. Amended by Laws 1986, c. 444.

524.3–809. Secured claims

Payment of a secured claim is upon the basis of the amount allowed if the creditor surrenders the security; otherwise payment is upon the basis of one of the following:

(1) if the creditor exhausts the security before receiving payment, unless precluded by other law, upon the amount of the claim allowed less the fair value of the security; or

(2) if the creditor does not have the right to exhaust the security or has not done so, upon the amount of the claim allowed less the value of the security determined by converting it into money according to the terms of the agreement pursuant to which the security was delivered to the creditor, or by the creditor and personal representative by agreement, arbitration, compromise or litigation.

Laws 1975, c. 347, § 58, eff. Jan. 1, 1976. Amended by Laws 1986, c. 444.

524.3–810. Claims not due and contingent or unliquidated claims

(a) If a claim which will become due at a future time or a contingent or unliquidated claim becomes due or certain before the distribution of the estate, and if the claim has been allowed or established by a proceeding, it is paid in the same manner as presently due and absolute claims of the same class.

(b) In other cases the personal representative or, on petition of the personal representative or the claimant in a special proceeding for the purpose, the court may provide for payment as follows:

(1) if the claimant consents, the claimant may be paid the present or agreed value of the claim, taking any uncertainty into account;

(2) arrangement for future payment, or possible payment, on the happening of the contingency or on liquidation may be made by creating a trust, giving a mortgage, obtaining a bond or security from a distributee, or otherwise.

Laws 1975, c. 347, § 58, eff. Jan. 1, 1976. Amended by Laws 1986, c. 444.

524.3–811. Counterclaims

In allowing a claim the personal representative may deduct any counterclaim which the estate has against the claimant. In determining a claim against an estate a court shall reduce the amount allowed by the amount of any counterclaims and, if the counterclaims exceed the claim, render a judgment against the claimant in the amount of the excess. A counterclaim, liquidated or unliquidated, may arise from a transaction other than that upon which the claim is based. A counterclaim may give rise to relief exceeding in amount or different in kind from that sought in the claim.

Laws 1975, c. 347, § 58, eff. Jan. 1, 1976.

524.3–812. Execution and levies prohibited

No execution may issue upon nor may any levy be made against any property of the estate under any judgment against a decedent or a personal representative, but this section shall not be construed to prevent the enforcement of mortgages, pledges or liens upon real or personal property in an appropriate proceeding.

Laws 1975, c. 347, § 58, eff. Jan. 1, 1976.

524.3–813. Compromise of claims

When a claim against the estate has been presented in any manner, the personal representative may, if it appears for the best interest of the estate, compromise the claim, whether due or not due, absolute or contingent, liquidated or unliquidated.

Laws 1975, c. 347, § 58, eff. Jan. 1, 1976.

524.3–814. Encumbered assets

If any assets of the estate are encumbered by mortgage, pledge, lien, or other security interest, the personal representative may pay the encumbrance or any part thereof, renew or extend any obligation secured by the encumbrance or convey or transfer the assets to the creditor in satisfaction of the lien, in whole or in part, whether or not the holder of the encumbrance has filed a claim, if it appears to be for the best interest of the estate. Payment of an encumbrance does not increase the share of the distributee entitled to the encumbered assets unless the distributee is entitled to exoneration.

Laws 1975, c. 347, § 58, eff. Jan. 1, 1976. Amended by Laws 1986, c. 444.

524.3–815. Administration in more than one state; duty of personal representative

(a) All assets of estates being administered in this state are subject to all claims, allowances and charges existing or established against the personal representative wherever appointed.

(b) If the estate either in this state or as a whole is insufficient to cover all family exemptions and allowances determined by the law of the decedent's domicile, prior charges and claims, after satisfaction of the exemptions, allowances and charges, each claimant whose claim has been allowed either in this state or elsewhere in administrations of which the personal representative is aware, is entitled to receive payment of an equal proportion of the claim. If a preference or security in regard to a claim is allowed in another jurisdiction but not in this state, the creditor so benefited is to receive dividends from local assets only upon the balance of the claim after deducting the amount of the benefit.

(c) In case the family exemptions and allowances, prior charges and claims of the entire estate exceed the total value of the portions of the estate being administered separately and this state is not the state of the decedent's last domicile, the claims allowed in this state shall be paid their proportion if local assets are adequate for the purpose, and the balance of local assets shall be transferred to the domiciliary personal representative. If local assets are not sufficient to pay all claims allowed in this state the amount to which they are entitled, local assets shall be marshalled so that each claim allowed in this state is paid its proportion as far as possible, after taking into account all dividends on claims allowed in this state from assets in other jurisdictions.

Laws 1975, c. 347, § 58, eff. Jan. 1, 1976. Amended by Laws 1986, c. 444.

524.3–816. Final distribution to domiciliary representative

Real estate (excluding a vendor's interest in a contract for conveyance) located in this state with regard to which the decedent died intestate and the proceeds of the sale, mortgage or lease of any such real estate available for distribution, shall pass according to the laws of this state. All other assets included in the estate of a nonresident decedent being administered by a personal representative appointed in this state shall, if there is a personal representative of the decedent's domicile willing to receive it, be distributed to the domiciliary personal representative for the benefit of the successors of the decedent unless (1) by virtue of the decedent's will, if any, the successors are identified pursuant to the local law of this state without reference to the local law of the decedent's domicile; (2) the personal representative of this state, after reasonable inquiry, is unaware of the existence or identity of a domiciliary personal representative; or (3) the court orders otherwise in a proceeding for a closing order under section 524.3–1001 or incident to the closing of a supervised administration. In other cases, distribution of the estate of a decedent shall be made in accordance with the other parts of this article.

Laws 1975, c. 347, § 58, eff. Jan. 1, 1976.

524.3–817. Joint contract claims

When two or more persons are indebted on any joint contract or upon a judgment on a joint contract, and one of them dies, the estate shall be liable therefor, and the amount thereof may be allowed the same as though the contract had been joint and several or the judgment had been against the decedent alone, but without prejudice to right to contribution.

Laws 1975, c. 347, § 58, eff. Jan. 1, 1976. Amended by Laws 1986, c. 444.

PART 9

SPECIAL PROVISIONS RELATING TO DISTRIBUTION

524.3–901. Successors' rights if no administration

In the absence of administration, the heirs and devisees are entitled to the estate in accordance with the terms of a probated will or the laws of intestate succession. Devisees may establish title by the probated will to devised property. Persons entitled to property pursuant to sections 524.2–402,

524.2–403, 525.14 or intestacy may establish title thereto by proof of the decedent's ownership and death, and their relationship to the decedent. Successors take subject to all charges incident to administration, including the claims of creditors and allowances of surviving spouse and dependent children, and subject to the rights of others resulting from abatement, retainer, advancement, and ademption.

Laws 1974, c. 442, art. 3, § 524.3–901. Amended by Laws 1975, c. 347, § 59, eff. Jan. 1, 1976; Laws 1986, c. 444; Laws 1996, c. 305, art. 1, § 113.

524.3–902. Distribution; order in which assets appropriated; abatement

(a) Except as provided in subsection (b) and except as provided in connection with the share of the surviving spouse who elects to take an elective share, shares of distributees abate, without any preference or priority as between real and personal property, in the following order: (1) property not disposed of by the will; (2) residuary devises; (3) general devises; (4) specific devises. For purposes of abatement, a general devise charged on any specific property or fund is a specific devise to the extent of the value of the property on which it is charged, and upon the failure or insufficiency of the property on which it is charged, a general devise to the extent of the failure or insufficiency. Abatement within each classification is in proportion to the amounts of property each of the beneficiaries would have received if full distribution of the property had been made in accordance with the terms of the will.

(b) If the will expresses an order of abatement, or if the testamentary plan or the express or implied purpose of the devise would be defeated by the order of abatement stated in subsection (a), the shares of the distributees abate as may be found necessary to give effect to the intention of the testator.

(c) If the subject of a preferred devise is sold or used incident to administration, abatement shall be achieved by appropriate adjustments in, or contribution from, other interests in the remaining assets.

Laws 1974, c. 442, art. 3, § 524.3–902, eff. Aug. 1, 1975.

524.3–903. Right of retainer

The amount of a noncontingent indebtedness of a successor to the estate if due, or its present value if not due, shall be offset against the successor's interest; but the successor has the benefit of any defense which would be available to the successor in a direct proceeding for recovery of the debt.

Laws 1974, c. 442, art. 3, § 524.3–903, eff. Jan. 1, 1976. Amended by Laws 1986, c. 444.

524.3–904. Interest on general pecuniary devise

General pecuniary devises bear interest at the legal rate beginning one year after the first appointment of a personal representative until payment, unless a contrary intent is indicated by the will.

Laws 1974, c. 442, art. 3, § 524.3–904, eff. Jan. 1, 1976.

524.3–905. Repealed by Laws 1994, c. 472, § 64, eff. January 1, 1996

Historical and Statutory Notes

Laws 1994, c. 472, § 65, provides:

"(a) This act takes effect on January 1, 1996.

"(b) Except as provided elsewhere in this act:

"(1) this act applies to the rights of successors of decedents dying on or after its effective date and to any wills of decedents dying on or after its effective date;

"(2) if, before the effective date of this act, a right is either acquired, extinguished, waived, or barred upon the expiration of a prescribed period of time which commenced to run by the provisions of any statute before the effective date, the provisions of this act neither revoke, revive, restore, nor remove the bar of such right; and

"(3) any rule of construction or presumption provided in this act applies to instruments executed and multiple party accounts opened before the effective date of this act unless there is a clear indication of contrary intent."

524.3–906. Distribution in kind; valuation; method

(a) Unless a contrary intention is indicated by the will, the distributable assets of a decedent's estate shall be distributed in kind to the extent possible through application of the following provisions:

(1) A specific devisee is entitled to distribution of the thing devised, and a spouse or child who has selected particular assets of an estate shall receive the items selected.

(2) Any statutory allowances or devise payable in money may be satisfied by value in kind provided

(i) the person entitled to the payment has not demanded payment in cash;

(ii) the property distributed in kind is valued at fair market value as of the date of its distribution, and

(iii) no residuary devisee has requested that the asset in question remain a part of the residue of the estate.

(3) For the purpose of valuation under paragraph (2) securities regularly traded on recognized exchanges, if distributed in kind, are valued at the price for the last sale of like securities, traded on the business day prior to distribution, or if there was no sale on that day, at the median between amounts bid and offered at the close of that day. Assets consisting of sums owed the decedent or the estate by solvent debtors as to which there is no known dispute or defense are valued at the sum due with accrued interest or discounted to the date of distribution. For assets which do not have readily ascertainable values, a valuation as of a date not more than 30 days prior to the date of distribution, if otherwise reasonable, controls. For purposes of facilitating distribution, the personal representative may ascertain the value of the assets as of the time of the proposed distribution in any reasonable way, including the employment of qualified appraisers, even if the assets may have been previously appraised.

(4) The residuary estate shall be distributed in kind if there is no objection to the proposed distribution and it is practicable to distribute undivided interests. In other cases, residuary property may be converted into cash for distribution.

(b) After the probable charges against the estate are known, the personal representative may mail or deliver a proposal for distribution to all persons who have a right to object to the proposed distribution. The right of any distributee to object to the proposed distribution on the basis of the kind or value of asset the distributee is to receive, if not waived earlier in writing, terminates if the distributee fails to object in writing received by the personal representative within 30 days after mailing or delivery of the proposal.

Laws 1974, c. 442, art. 3, § 524.3–906. Amended by Laws 1975, c. 347, § 60, eff. Jan. 1, 1976; Laws 1986, c. 444.

524.3–907. Distribution in kind; evidence

If distribution in kind is made, the personal representative shall execute an instrument or deed of distribution assigning, transferring or releasing the assets to the distributee as evidence of the distributee's title to the property.

Laws 1974, c. 442, art. 3, § 524.3–907, eff. Jan. 1, 1976.

524.3–908. Distribution; right or title of distributee

Proof that a distributee has received an instrument or deed of distribution of assets in kind, or payment in distribution, from a personal representative, is conclusive evidence that the distributee has succeeded to the interest of the decedent and the estate in the distributed assets, as against all persons interested in the estate, except that the personal representative may recover the assets or their value if the distribution was improper.

Laws 1974, c. 442, art. 3, § 524.3–908, eff. Jan. 1, 1976. Amended by Laws 1976, c. 161, § 9, eff. April 4, 1976.

524.3–909. Improper distribution; liability of distributee

Unless the distribution or payment no longer can be questioned because of adjudication, estoppel, or limitation, a distributee of property improperly distributed or paid, or a claimant who was improperly paid, is liable to return the property improperly received and its income since distribution if the distributee or claimant has the property. A distributee or claimant who does not have the property is liable to return the value as of the date of disposition of the property improperly received and any income and gain received.

Laws 1974, c. 442, art. 3, § 524.3–909, eff. Jan. 1, 1976. Amended by Laws 1986, c. 444.

524.3–910. Purchasers from distributees protected

If property distributed in kind or a security interest therein is acquired by a purchaser, or lender, for value from a distributee who has received an instrument or deed of distribution from the personal representative, the purchaser or lender takes title free of any claims of the estate and any interested person, and incurs no personal liability to them, whether or not the distribution was proper.

To be protected under this provision, a purchaser or lender need not inquire whether a personal representative acted properly in making the distribution in kind.

Laws 1974, c. 442, art. 3, § 524.3–910. Amended by Laws 1975, c. 347, § 61, eff. Jan. 1, 1976; Laws 1976, c. 161, § 10, eff. April 4, 1976.

524.3–911. Partition for purpose of distribution

When two or more heirs or devisees are entitled to distribution of undivided interests in any real or personal property of the estate, the personal representative or one or more of the heirs or devisees may petition the court prior to the formal or informal closing of the estate, to make partition. After notice to the interested heirs or devisees, the court shall partition the property in the same manner as provided by the law for civil actions of partition. The court may direct the personal representative to sell any property which cannot be partitioned without prejudice to the owners and which cannot conveniently be allotted to any one party.

Laws 1974, c. 442, art. 3, § 524.3–911, eff. Jan. 1, 1976.

524.3–912. Private agreements among successors to decedent binding on personal representative

Subject to the rights of creditors and taxing authorities, competent successors may agree among themselves to alter the interests, shares, or amounts to which they are entitled under the will of the decedent, or under the laws of intestacy, in any way that they provide in a written contract executed by all who are affected by its provisions. The personal representative shall abide by the terms of the agreement subject to the obligation to administer the estate for the benefit of creditors, to pay all taxes and costs of administration, and to carry out the responsibilities of office for the benefit of any successors of the decedent who are not parties. Personal representatives of decedent's estates are not required to see to the performance of trusts if the trustee thereof is another person who is willing to accept the trust. Accordingly, trustees of a testamentary trust are successors for the purposes of this section. Nothing herein relieves trustees of any duties owed to beneficiaries of trusts.

Laws 1974, c. 442, art. 3, § 524.3–912, eff. Jan. 1, 1976. Amended by Laws 1986, c. 444.

524.3–913. Distributions to trustee

Qualification by a court of a testamentary trustee is not required before distributions can be made by a personal representative to the trustee, unless qualification is expressly requested by will or demanded by an interested person as follows:

(1) by written demand delivered or mailed to the personal representative, or

(2) by petition to the court having jurisdiction over the probate estate.

If demand is made, the personal representative shall require proof of qualification of the trustee in a court of competent jurisdiction and the personal representative shall not make distributions to the trustee until the trustee is qualified by the court.

This section applies to all testamentary trusts without regard to the date of execution of the will or to the date of death of the testator.

Laws 1974, c. 442, art. 3, § 524.3–913. Amended by Laws 1975, c. 347, § 62, eff. Jan. 1, 1976; Laws 1985, c. 10, § 1, eff. Aug. 1, 1985; Laws 1991, c. 4, § 2, eff. March 7, 1991.

Historical and Statutory Notes

Laws 1985, c. 10, § 2, provided that § 1 was effective August 1, 1985, and applied to wills executed or amended on or after such date.

Laws 1991, c. 4, § 2, added the last paragraph, making this section applicable to all testamentary trusts.

524.3–914. Unclaimed assets

If any asset of the estate has not been distributed because the person entitled thereto cannot be found or refuses to accept the same, or for any other good and sufficient reason the same has not been paid over, the court may direct the personal representative to deposit the same with the county treasurer, taking duplicate receipts therefor, one of which the personal representative shall file with the county auditor and the other in the court. If the money on hand exceeds the sum of $5,000, the court may direct the county treasurer to invest the funds, and the county treasurer shall collect the interest on these investments as it becomes due, and the money so collected or deposited shall be credited to the county revenue fund. Upon petition to the court within 21 years after such deposit, and upon notice to the county attorney and county treasurer, the court may direct the county auditor to issue to the person entitled thereto the county auditor's warrant for the amount of the money so on deposit including the interest collected. No interest shall be allowed or paid thereon, except as herein provided, and if not claimed within such time no recovery thereof shall be had. The county treasurer, with the approval of the court, may make necessary sales, exchanges, substitutions, and transfers of investments and may present the same for redemption and invest the proceeds.

Laws 1974, c. 442, art. 3, § 524.3–914. Amended by Laws 1975, c. 347, § 63, eff. Jan. 1, 1976; Laws 1986, c. 444; Laws 1995, c. 130, § 14; Laws 1996, c. 338, art. 2, § 6.

Historical and Statutory Notes

Laws 1995, c. 130, § 22, provides in part that chapter 130 is effective January 1, 1996, and that §§ 1, 14, 17, 18, 19, and 20 (amending, inter alia, this section) apply to all decedents' estates, whenever the decedent died.

524.3–915. Distribution to person under disability

(a) A personal representative may discharge the obligation to distribute to any person under legal disability by distributing to the person's guardian or conservator, or any other person authorized by this chapter or otherwise to give a valid receipt and discharge for the distribution.

(b) When a minor child receives or is entitled to distribution of personal property the court may order and direct the personal representative of the estate to make payment of not to exceed $2,000 thereof to the parent or parents, custodian, or the person, corporation, or institution with whom the minor child is, for the benefit, support, maintenance, and education of the minor child or may direct the investment of the whole or any part thereof in a savings account, savings certificate, or certificate of deposit in a bank, savings bank, or savings association having deposit insurance, in the name of the minor child. When so invested the savings account passbook, savings certificate, certificate of deposit, or other acknowledgment of receipt of the deposit by the depository as the case may be, is to be kept as provided by the court, and the depository shall be instructed not to allow such investment to be withdrawn, except by order of the court. The court may authorize the use of any part or all thereof to purchase United States government savings bonds in the minor's name the bonds to be kept as provided by the court and to be retained until the minor reaches majority unless otherwise authorized by an order of the court.

Laws 1974, c. 442, art. 3, § 524.3–915. Amended by Laws 1975, c. 347, § 64, eff. Jan. 1, 1976; Laws 1986, c. 444; Laws 1995, c. 202, art. 1, § 25, eff. May 25, 1995.

524.3–916. Apportionment of estate taxes and generation–skipping tax

(a) For purposes of this section:

(1) "estate" means the gross estate of a decedent as determined for the purpose of federal estate tax or the estate tax payable to this state;

(2) "decedent's generation-skipping transfers" means all generation-skipping transfers as determined for purposes of the federal generation-skipping tax which occur by reason of the decedent's death which relate to property which is included in the decedent's estate;

(3) "person" means any individual, partnership, association, joint stock company, corporation, limited liability company, government, political subdivision, governmental agency, or local governmental agency;

(4) "person interested in the estate" means any person entitled to receive, or who has received, from a decedent or by reason of the death of a decedent any property or interest therein included in the decedent's estate. It includes a personal representative, guardian, conservator, trustee, and custodian;

(5) "state" means any state, territory, or possession of the United States, the District of Columbia, and the Commonwealth of Puerto Rico;

(6) "estate tax" means the federal estate tax and the state estate tax determined by the commissioner of revenue pursuant to chapter 291 and interest and penalties imposed in addition to the tax;

(7) "decedent's generation-skipping tax" means the federal generation-skipping tax imposed on the decedent's generation-skipping transfers and interest and penalties imposed in addition to the tax;

(8) "fiduciary" means personal representative or trustee.

(b) Unless the will or other governing instrument otherwise provides:

(1) the estate tax shall be apportioned among all persons interested in the estate. The apportionment is to be made in the proportion that the value of the interest of each person interested in the estate bears to the total value of the interests of all persons interested in the estate. The values used in determining the tax are to be used for that purpose; and

(2) the decedent's generation-skipping tax shall be apportioned as provided by federal law. To the extent not provided by federal law, the decedent's generation-skipping tax shall be apportioned among all persons receiving the decedent's generation-skipping transfers whose tax apportionment is not provided by federal law in the proportion that the value of the transfer to each person bears to the total value of all such transfers.

If the decedent's will or other written instrument directs a method of apportionment of estate tax or of the decedent's generation-skipping tax different from the method described in this section, the method described in the will or other written instrument controls provided, however, that:

(i) unless the decedent's will or other written instrument specifically indicates an intent to waive any right of recovery under section 2207A of the Internal Revenue Code of 1986, as amended, [1] estate taxes must be apportioned under the method described in this section to property included in the decedent's estate under section 2044 of the Internal Revenue Code of 1986, as amended; and

(ii) unless the decedent's will or other written instrument specifically indicates an intent to waive any right of recovery under section 2207B of the Internal Revenue Code of 1986, as amended, estate taxes must be apportioned under the method described in this section to property included in the decedent's estate under section 2036 of the Internal Revenue Code of 1986, as amended.

(c)(1) The court in which venue lies for the administration of the estate of a decedent, on petition for the purpose may determine the apportionment of the estate tax or of the decedent's generation-skipping tax.

(2) If the court finds that it is inequitable to apportion interest and penalties in the manner provided in subsection (b), because of special circumstances, it may direct apportionment thereof in the manner it finds equitable.

(3) If the court finds that the assessment of penalties and interest assessed in relation to the estate tax or the decedent's generation-skipping tax is due to delay caused by the negligence of the fiduciary, the court may charge the fiduciary with the amount of the assessed penalties and interest.

(4) In any action to recover from any person interested in the estate the amount of the estate tax or of the decedent's generation-skipping tax apportioned to the person in accordance with this section the determination of the court in respect thereto shall be prima facie correct.

(d)(1) The personal representative or other person in possession of the property of the decedent required to pay the estate tax or the decedent's generation-skipping tax may withhold from any property distributable to any person interested in the estate, upon its distribution, the amount of any taxes attributable to the person's interest. If the property in possession of the personal representative or other person required to pay any taxes and distributable to any person interested in the estate is insufficient to satisfy the proportionate amount of the taxes determined to be due from the person, the personal representative or other person required to pay any taxes may recover the deficiency from the person interested in the estate. If the property is not in the possession of the personal representative or the other person required to pay any taxes, the personal representative or the other person required to pay any taxes may recover from any person interested in the estate the amount of any taxes apportioned to the person in accordance with this section.

(2) If property held by the personal representative or other person in possession of the property of the decedent required to pay the estate tax or the decedent's generation-skipping tax is distributed prior to final apportionment of the estate tax or the decedent's generation-skipping tax, the distributee shall provide a bond or other security for the apportionment liability in the form and amount prescribed by the personal representative or other person, as the case may be.

(e)(1) In making an apportionment, allowances shall be made for any exemptions granted, any classification made of persons interested in the estate and for any deductions and credits allowed by the law imposing the tax.

(2) Any exemption or deduction allowed by reason of the relationship of any person to the decedent, by reason of the purposes of the gift, or by allocation to the gift (either by election by the fiduciary or by operation of federal law), inures to the benefit of the person bearing such relationship or receiving the gift; but if an interest is subject to a prior present interest which is not allowable as a deduction, the tax apportionable against the present interest shall be paid from principal.

(3) Any deduction for property previously taxed and any credit for gift taxes or death taxes of a foreign country paid by the decedent or the decedent's estate inures to the proportionate benefit of all persons liable to apportionment.

(4) Any credit for inheritance, succession or estate taxes or taxes in the nature thereof applicable to property or interests includable in the estate, inures to the benefit of the persons or interests chargeable with the payment thereof to the extent proportionately that the credit reduces the tax.

(5) To the extent that property passing to or in trust for a surviving spouse or any charitable, public or similar gift or devise is not an allowable deduction for purposes of the estate tax solely by reason of an estate tax imposed upon and deductible from the property, the property is not included in the computation provided for in subsection (b)(1) hereof, and to that extent no apportionment is made against the property. The sentence immediately preceding does not apply to any case if the result would be to deprive the estate of a deduction otherwise allowable under section 2053(d) of the Internal Revenue Code of 1986, as amended, of the United States, relating to deduction for state death taxes on transfers for public, charitable, or religious uses.

(f) No interest in income and no estate for years or for life or other temporary interest in any property or fund is subject to apportionment as between the temporary interest and the remainder. The estate tax on the temporary interest and the estate tax, if any, on the remainder is chargeable against the corpus of the property or funds subject to the temporary interest and remainder. The decedent's generation-skipping tax is chargeable against the property which constitutes the decedent's generation-skipping transfer.

(g) Neither the personal representative nor other person required to pay the tax is under any duty to institute any action to recover from any person interested in the estate the amount of the estate tax or of the decedent's generation-skipping tax apportioned to the person until the final determination of the tax. A personal representative or other person required to pay the estate tax or decedent's generation-skipping tax who institutes the action within a reasonable time after final determination of the tax is not subject to any liability or surcharge because any portion of the tax apportioned to any person interested in the estate was collectible at a time following the death of the decedent but thereafter became uncollectible. If the personal representative or other person required to pay the estate tax or decedent's generation-skipping tax cannot collect from any person interested in the estate the amount of the tax apportioned to the person, the amount not recoverable shall be equitably apportioned among the other persons interested in the estate who are subject to apportionment of the tax involved.

(h) A personal representative acting in another state or a person required to pay the estate tax or decedent's generation-skipping tax domiciled in another state may institute an action in the courts of this state and may recover a proportionate amount of the federal estate tax, of an estate tax payable to another state or of a death duty due by a decedent's estate to another state, or of the decedent's generation-skipping tax, from a person interested in the estate who is either domiciled in this state or who owns property in this state subject to attachment or execution. For the purposes of the action the determination of apportionment by the court having jurisdiction of the administration of the decedent's estate in the other state is prima facie correct.

Laws 1975, c. 347, § 65, eff. Jan. 1, 1976. Amended by Laws 1979, c. 303, art. 3, § 33; Laws 1986, c. 444; Laws 1995, c. 130, § 15; Laws 1999, c. 171, § 3.

[1] All text references to Internal Revenue Code sections are to Title 26 of U.S.C.A.

UNIFORM ESTATE TAX APPORTIONMENT (1958 ACT)

*Table of Jurisdictions Wherein The 1958 Version
of the Uniform Act Has Been Adopted*

*For text of Uniform Acts, and variation notes and annotation materi-
als for adopting jurisdictions, see Uniform Laws Annotated, Master
Edition, Volume 8A.*

Jurisdiction	Laws	Effective Date	Statutory Citation
Alaska	1972, c. 78	1–1–1973	AS 13.16.610.
Idaho	1971, c. 111		I.C. § 15–3–916.
Minnesota	1975, c. 347	1–1–1976	M.S.A. § 524.3–916.
Montana	1974, c. 365	7–1–1975	MCA 72–16–601 to 72–16–612.
New Mexico	1975, c. 257		NMSA 1978 § 45–3–916.
North Dakota	1973, c. 257	7–1–1975	NDCC 30.1–20–16.
Oregon	1969, c. 591	7–1–1970	ORS 116.303 to 116.383.
South Dakota	1994, c. 232	7–1–1995	SDCL 29A–3–916.
Wyoming	1959, c. 171	2–27–1959	Wyo.Stat.Ann. §§ 2–10–101 to 2–10–110.

Historical and Statutory Notes

Laws 1995, c. 130, § 22, provides in part that chapter 130 is effective January 1, 1996, and that §§ 12, 13, and 15 (amending § 524.2–508, enacting § 524.2–804, and amending § 524.3–916, respectively) apply to the rights of successors of decedents dying on or after January 1, 1996, and to any wills of decedents dying on or after January 1, 1996.

PART 10

CLOSING ESTATES

**524.3–1001. Formal proceedings terminating administration; testate or
intestate; order of distribution, decree, and general protection**

(a)(1) A personal representative or any interested person may petition for an order of complete settlement of the estate. The personal representative may petition at any time, and any other interested person may petition after one year from the appointment of the original personal representative except that no petition under this section may be entertained until the time for presenting claims which arose prior to the death of the decedent has expired. The petition may request the court to determine testacy, if not previously determined, to consider the final account or compel or approve an accounting and distribution, to construe any will or determine heirs and adjudicate the final settlement and distribution of the estate. After notice to all interested persons and hearing the court may enter an order or orders, on appropriate conditions, determining the persons entitled to distribution of the estate, and, as circumstances require, approving settlement and directing or approving distribution of the estate and discharging the personal representative from further claim or demand of any interested person.

(2) In such petition for complete settlement of the estate, the petitioner may apply for a decree. Upon the hearing, if in the best interests of interested persons, the court may issue its decree which shall determine the persons entitled to the estate and assign the same to them in lieu of ordering the assignment by the personal representative. The decree shall name the heirs and distributees, state their relationship to the decedent, describe the property, and state the proportions or part thereof to which each is entitled. In the estate of a testate decedent, no heirs shall be named in the decree unless all heirs be ascertained.

(3) In solvent estates, the hearing may be waived by written consent to the proposed account and decree of distribution or order of distribution by all heirs or distributees, and the court may then enter its order allowing the account and issue its decree or order of distribution.

(4) Where a decree or order for distribution is issued, the personal representative shall not be discharged until all property is paid or transferred to the persons entitled to the property, and the personal representative has otherwise fully discharged the duties of a personal representative. If an order assessing estate tax or request for documents is filed with the court by the commissioner of revenue, no discharge shall be issued until the assessment is paid or the request is complied with. If no order assessing estate tax or request for documents is filed, the court shall have the power to settle and distribute the estate and discharge the personal representative without regard to tax obligations.

(b) If one or more heirs or devisees were omitted as parties in, or were not given notice of, a previous formal testacy proceeding, the court, on proper petition for an order of complete settlement of the estate under this section, and after notice to the omitted or unnotified persons and other interested parties determined to be interested on the assumption that the previous order concerning testacy is conclusive as to those given notice of the earlier proceeding, may determine testacy as it affects the omitted persons and confirm or alter the previous order of testacy as it affects all interested persons as appropriate in the light of the new proofs. In the absence of objection by an omitted or unnotified person, evidence received in the original testacy proceeding shall constitute prima facie proof of due execution of any will previously admitted to probate, or of the fact that the decedent left no valid will if the prior proceedings determined this fact.

Laws 1974, c. 442, art. 3, § 524.3–1001. Amended by Laws 1975, c. 347, § 66, eff. Jan. 1, 1976; Laws 1979, c. 303, art. 3, § 34; Laws 1980, c. 439, § 31; Laws 1986, c. 444; Laws 1990, c. 480, art. 2, § 17, eff. Aug. 1, 1990; Laws 1995, c. 130, § 16.

Historical and Statutory Notes

Laws 1980, c. 439, which made technical adjustments and clarified certain provisions relating to estate tax, was effective for estates of decedents dying after December 31, 1979.

Laws 1995, c. 130, § 22, provides in part that chapter 130 is effective January 1, 1996.

524.3–1002. Formal proceedings terminating testate administration; order construing will without adjudicating testacy

A personal representative administering an estate under an informally probated will or any devisee under an informally probated will may petition for an order of settlement of the estate which will not adjudicate the testacy status of the decedent. The personal representative may petition at any time, and a devisee may petition after one year, from the appointment of the original personal representative, except that no petition under this section may be entertained until the time for presenting claims which arose prior to the death of the decedent has expired. The petition may request the court to consider the final account or compel or approve an accounting and distribution, to construe the will and adjudicate final settlement and distribution of the estate. After notice to all devisees and the personal representative and hearing, the court may enter an order or orders, on appropriate conditions, determining the persons entitled to distribution of the estate under the will, and, as circumstances require, approving settlement and directing or approving distribution of the estate and discharging the personal representative from further claim or demand of any devisee who is a party to the proceeding and those the devisee represents. If it appears that a part of the estate is intestate, the proceedings shall be dismissed or amendments made to meet the provisions of section 524.3–1001.

Laws 1974, c. 442, art. 3, § 524.3–1002, eff. Jan. 1, 1976. Amended by Laws 1986, c. 444.

524.3–1003. Closing estates; by sworn statement of personal representative

(a) Unless prohibited by order of the court and except for estates being administered in supervised administration proceedings, a personal representative may close an estate by filing with the court no earlier than four months after the date of original appointment of a general personal representative for the estate, a statement stating that the filer, or a prior personal representative whom the filer has succeeded, has or have:

(1) published notice to creditors and that the first publication occurred more than four months prior to the date of filing of the statement;

(2) fully administered the estate of the decedent by making payment, settlement or other disposition of all claims which were presented, expenses of administration and estate and other taxes, except as specified in the statement, and that the assets of the estate have been inventoried and distributed to the persons entitled. If any claims, expenses or taxes remain undischarged, the statement shall state in detail other arrangements which have been made to accommodate outstanding liabilities; and

(3) prior to filing the statement, sent a copy thereof to all distributees of the estate and to all creditors or other known claimants whose claims are neither

paid nor barred and has furnished a full account in writing of the personal representative's administration to the distributees whose interests are affected thereby.

(b) If no proceedings involving the personal representative are pending in the court one year after the closing statement is filed, the appointment of the personal representative terminates. Letters of appointment remain in full force until one year after the filing of the closing statement at which time the authority of the personal representative shall terminate.

Laws 1974, c. 442, art. 3, § 524.3–1003, eff. Jan. 1, 1976. Amended by Laws 1976, c. 161, § 11, eff. April 4, 1976; Laws 1978, c. 525, § 16, eff. March 24, 1978; Laws 1980, c. 439, § 32; Laws 1984, c. 438, § 1; Laws 1986, c. 444.

Historical and Statutory Notes

Laws 1980, c. 439, § 32, which made technical adjustments and clarified certain provisions relating to estate tax, was effective for estates of decedents dying after December 31, 1979.

524.3–1004. Liability of distributees to claimants

After assets of an estate have been distributed and subject to section 524.3–1006, an undischarged claim not barred may be prosecuted in a proceeding against one or more distributees. If a personal representative closes an estate without giving notice as required under section 524.3–801, paragraph (d), notwithstanding any other law to the contrary, claims arising under sections 246.53, 256B.15, 256D.16, and 261.04 shall be undischarged and unbarred claims. The governmental entities entitled to file claims under those sections shall be entitled to prosecute their claims against distributees as provided for in this section, and the limitations in section 524.3–1006 shall not apply. No distributee shall be liable to claimants for amounts in excess of the value of the distributee's distribution as of the time of distribution. As between distributees, each shall bear the cost of satisfaction of unbarred claims as if the claim had been satisfied in the course of administration. Any distributee who shall have failed to notify other distributees of the demand made by the claimant in sufficient time to permit them to join in any proceeding in which the claim was asserted against the first distributee loses the right of contribution against other distributees.

Laws 1974, c. 442, art. 3, § 524.3–1004, eff. Jan. 1, 1976. Amended by Laws 1986, c. 444; Laws 1997, c. 217, art. 2, § 17.

524.3–1005. Limitations on proceedings against personal representative

Unless previously barred by adjudication and except as provided in the closing statement, the rights of successors and of creditors whose claims have not otherwise been barred against the personal representative for breach of fiduciary duty are barred unless a proceeding to assert the same is commenced within six months after the filing of the closing statement. The rights thus barred do not include rights to recover from a personal representative for fraud, misrepresentation, or inadequate disclosure related to the settlement of the decedent's estate.

Laws 1974, c. 442, art. 3, § 524.3–1005, eff. Jan. 1, 1976.

524.3–1006. Limitations on actions and proceedings against distributees

Unless previously adjudicated in a formal testacy proceeding or in a proceeding settling the accounts of a personal representative or otherwise barred, the claim of any claimant to recover from a distributee who is liable to pay the claim, and the right of any heir or devisee, or of a successor personal representative acting in their behalf, to recover property improperly distributed or the value thereof from any distributee is forever barred at the later of (1) three years after the decedent's death; or (2) one year after the time of distribution thereof. This section does not bar an action to recover property or value received as the result of fraud.

Laws 1974, c. 442, art. 3, § 524.3–1006, eff. Jan. 1, 1976.

524.3–1007. Certificate discharging liens securing fiduciary performance

After the appointment has terminated, the personal representative, the personal representative's sureties, or any successor of either, upon the filing of an application showing, so far as is known by the applicant, that no action concerning the estate is pending in any court, is entitled to receive a certificate from the registrar that the personal representative appears to have fully administered the estate in question. The certificate evidences discharge of any lien on any property given to secure the obligation of the personal representative in lieu of bond or any surety, but does not preclude action against the personal representative or the surety.

Laws 1974, c. 442, art. 3, § 524.3–1007, eff. Jan. 1, 1976. Amended by Laws 1976, c. 161, § 12, eff. April 4, 1976; Laws 1986, c. 444.

524.3–1008. Subsequent administration

If property of the estate is omitted or discovered after an estate has been settled and the personal representative discharged or after one year after a closing statement has been filed, the court upon petition or the registrar upon application of any interested person and upon notice as it directs may appoint the same or a successor personal representative to administer the subsequently discovered estate. If a new appointment is made, unless the court or registrar orders otherwise, the provisions of this chapter apply as appropriate; but no claim previously barred may be asserted in the subsequent administration.

Laws 1974, c. 442, art. 3, § 524.3–1008. Amended by Laws 1975, c. 347, § 67, eff. Jan. 1, 1976; Laws 1995, c. 130, § 17.

Historical and Statutory Notes

Laws 1995, c. 130, § 22, provides in part that chapter 130 is effective January 1, 1996, and that §§ 1, 14, 17, 18, 19, and 20 (amending, inter alia, this section) apply to all decedents' estates, whenever the decedent died.

PART 11

COMPROMISE OF CONTROVERSIES

524.3–1101. Effect of approval of agreements involving trusts, inalienable interests, or interests of third persons

A compromise of any controversy as to admission to probate of any instrument offered for formal probate as the will of a decedent, the construction, validity, or effect of any probated will, the rights or interests in the estate of the decedent, of any successor, or the administration of the estate, if approved in a formal proceeding in the court for that purpose, is binding on all the parties thereto including those unborn, unascertained or who could not be located. An approved compromise is binding even though it may affect a trust or an inalienable interest.

Laws 1974, c. 442, art. 3, § 524.3–1101. Amended by Laws 1975, c. 347, § 68, eff. Jan. 1, 1976.

524.3–1102. Procedure for securing court approval of compromise

The procedure for securing court approval of a compromise is as follows:

(1) The terms of the compromise shall be set forth in an agreement in writing which shall be executed by all competent persons and parents acting for any minor child having beneficial interests or having claims which will or may be affected by the compromise. Execution is not required by any person whose identity cannot be ascertained or whose whereabouts is unknown and cannot reasonably be ascertained.

(2) Any interested person, including the personal representative or a trustee, then may submit the agreement to the court for its approval and for execution by the personal representative, the trustee of every affected testamentary trust, and other fiduciaries and representatives.

(3) After notice to all interested persons or their representatives, including the personal representative of the estate and all affected trustees of trusts, the court, if it finds that the contest or controversy is in good faith and that the effect of the agreement upon the interests of persons represented by fiduciaries or other representatives is just and reasonable, shall make an order approving the agreement and directing all fiduciaries under its supervision to execute the agreement. Minor children represented only by their parents may be bound only if their parents join with other competent persons in execution of the compromise. Upon the making of the order and the execution of the agreement, all further disposition of the estate is in accordance with the terms of the agreement.

Laws 1974, c. 442, art. 3, § 524.3–1102, eff. Jan. 1, 1976.

491

PART 12

COLLECTION OF PERSONAL PROPERTY BY AFFIDAVIT AND SUMMARY ADMINISTRATION PROCEDURE FOR SMALL ESTATES

524.3–1201.   Collection of personal property by affidavit

(a) Thirty days after the death of a decedent, (i) any person indebted to the decedent, (ii) any person having possession of tangible personal property or an instrument evidencing a debt, obligation, stock, or chose in action belonging to the decedent, or (iii) any safe deposit company, as defined in section 55.01, controlling the right of access to decedent's safe deposit box shall make payment of the indebtedness or deliver the tangible personal property or an instrument evidencing a debt, obligation, stock, or chose in action or deliver the entire contents of the safe deposit box to a person claiming to be the successor of the decedent, or a state or county agency with a claim authorized by section 256B.15, upon being presented a certified death record of the decedent and an affidavit, in duplicate, made by or on behalf of the successor stating that:

(1) the value of the entire probate estate, determined as of the date of death, wherever located, including specifically any contents of a safe deposit box, less liens and encumbrances, does not exceed $20,000;

(2) 30 days have elapsed since the death of the decedent or, in the event the property to be delivered is the contents of a safe deposit box, 30 days have elapsed since the filing of an inventory of the contents of the box pursuant to section 55.10, paragraph (h);

(3) no application or petition for the appointment of a personal representative is pending or has been granted in any jurisdiction;

(4) if presented, by a state or county agency with a claim authorized by section 256B.15, to a financial institution with a multiple-party account in which the decedent had an interest at the time of death, the amount of the affiant's claim and a good faith estimate of the extent to which the decedent was the source of funds or beneficial owner of the account; and

(5) the claiming successor is entitled to payment or delivery of the property.

(b) A transfer agent of any security shall change the registered ownership on the books of a corporation from the decedent to the successor or successors upon the presentation of an affidavit as provided in subsection (a).

(c) The claiming successor or state or county agency shall disburse the proceeds collected under this section to any person with a superior claim under section 524.2–403 or 524.3–805.

(d) A motor vehicle registrar shall issue a new certificate of title in the name of the successor upon the presentation of an affidavit as provided in subsection (a).

(e) The person controlling access to decedent's safe deposit box need not open the box or deliver the contents of the box if:

(1) the person has received notice of a written or oral objection from any person or has reason to believe that there would be an objection; or

(2) the lessee's key or combination is not available.

Laws 1974, c. 442, art. 3, § 524.3–1201, eff. Jan. 1, 1976. Amended by Laws 1976, c. 161, § 13, eff. April 4, 1976; Laws 1977, c. 159, § 1; Laws 1978, c. 741, § 9; Laws 1984, c. 655, art. 1, § 74; Laws 1987, c. 403, art. 2, § 151; Laws 1991, c. 11, § 1; Laws 1992, c. 461, art. 1, § 2, eff. June 1, 1992; Laws 1995, c. 130, § 18; Laws 1997, c. 217, art. 2, § 18; Laws 1997, 3rd Sp., c. 3, § 13; Laws 2001, 1st Sp., c. 9, art. 15, § 32; Laws 2002, c. 347, § 3.

Historical and Statutory Notes

Laws 2002, c. 379, art. 1, § 113, provides:

"2001 First Special Session Senate File No. 4, as passed by the senate and the house of representatives on Friday, June 29, 2001, and subsequently published as Laws 2001, First Special Session chapter 9, is reenacted. Its provisions are effective on the dates originally provided in the bill."

Laws 1995, c. 130, § 22, provides in part that chapter 130 is effective January 1, 1996, and that §§ 1, 14, 17, 18, 19, and 20 (amending, inter alia, this section) apply to all decedents' estates, whenever the decedent died.

524.3–1202. Effect of affidavit

The person paying, delivering, transferring, or issuing personal property or the evidence thereof pursuant to an affidavit meeting the requirements of section 524.3–1201 is discharged and released to the same extent as if the person dealt with a personal representative of the decedent. The person is not required to see to the application of the personal property or evidence thereof or to inquire into the truth of any statement in the affidavit. In particular, the person delivering the contents of a safe deposit box is not required to inquire into the value of the contents of the box and is authorized to rely solely upon the representation in the affidavit concerning the value of the entire probate estate. If any person to whom an affidavit is delivered refuses to pay, deliver, transfer, or issue any personal property or evidence thereof, it may be recovered or its payment, delivery, transfer, or issuance compelled upon proof of their right in a proceeding brought for the purpose by or on behalf of the persons entitled thereto. Any person to whom payment, delivery, transfer or issuance is made is answerable and accountable therefor to any personal representative of the estate or to any other person having a superior right.

Laws 1974, c. 442, art. 3, § 524.3–1202, eff. Jan. 1, 1976. Amended by Laws 1978, c. 741, § 10; Laws 1985, 1st Sp., c. 14, art. 13, § 13, eff. June 29, 1985; Laws 1986, c. 444; Laws 1995, c. 130, § 19.

Historical and Statutory Notes

Laws 1995, c. 130, § 22, provides in part that chapter 130 is effective January 1, 1996, and that §§ 1, 14, 17, 18, 19, and 20 apply to all decedents' estates, whenever the decedent died.

524.3–1203. Summary proceedings

Subdivision 1. Petition and payment. Upon petition of an interested person, the court, with or without notice, may determine that the decedent had no estate, or that the property has been destroyed, abandoned, lost, or rendered valueless, and that no recovery has been had nor can be had for it, or if there is no property except property recovered for death by wrongful act, property that is exempt from all debts and charges in the probate court, or property that may be appropriated for the payment of the property selection as provided in section 524.2–403, the allowances to the spouse and children mentioned in section 524.2–404, and the expenses and claims provided in section 524.3–805, paragraph (a), clauses (1) to (6), inclusive, the personal representative by order of the court may pay the estate in the order named. The court may then, with or without notice, summarily determine the heirs, legatees, and devisees in its final decree or order of distribution assigning to them their share or part of the property with which the personal representative is charged.

Subd. 2. Final decree or order. If upon hearing of a petition for summary assignment or distribution, for special administration, or for any administration, or for the probate of a will, the court determines that there is no need for the appointment of a representative and that the administration should be closed summarily for the reason that all of the property in the estate is exempt from all debts and charges in the probate court, a final decree or order of distribution may be entered, with or without notice, assigning that property to the persons entitled to it under the terms of the will, or if there is no will, under the law of intestate succession in force at the time of the decedent's death.

Subd. 3. Summary distribution. Summary distribution may be made under this section in any proceeding of any real, personal, or other property in kind in reimbursement or payment of the property selection as provided in section 524.2–403, the allowances to the spouse and children mentioned in section 524.2–404, and the expenses and claims provided in section 524.3–805, paragraph (a), clauses (1) to (6), inclusive, in the order named, if the court is satisfied as to the propriety of the distribution and as to the valuation, based upon appraisal in the case of real estate other than homestead, of the property being assigned to exhaust the assets of the estate.

Subd. 4. Personal representative. Summary proceedings may be had with or without the appointment of a personal representative. In all summary proceedings in which no personal representative is appointed, the court may require the petitioner to file a corporate surety bond in an amount fixed and approved by the court. The condition of the bond must be that the petitioner has made a full, true, and correct disclosure of all the facts related in the petition and will perform the terms of the decree or order of distribution issued pursuant to the petition. Any interested person suffering damages as a result of misrepresentation or negligence of the petitioner in stating facts in the petition pursuant to which an improper decree or order of distribution is issued, or the terms of the decree or order of distribution are not performed by the petitioner as required, has a cause of action against the petitioner and the surety to recover those damages in the court in which the proceeding took place. That court has jurisdiction of the cause of action.

Subd. 5. Exhaustion of estate. In any summary, special, or other administration in which it appears that the estate will not be exhausted in payment of the priority items enumerated in subdivisions 1 to 4, the estate may nevertheless be summarily closed without further notice, and the property assigned to the proper persons, if the gross probate estate, exclusive of any exempt homestead as defined in section 524.2–402, and any exempt property as defined in section 524.2–403, does not exceed the value of $100,000. If the closing and distribution of assets is made pursuant to the terms of a will, no decree shall issue until a hearing has been held for formal probate of the will as provided in sections 524.3–401 to 524.3–413.

No summary closing of an estate shall be made to any distributee under this subdivision, unless a showing is made by the personal representative or the petitioner, that all property selected by and allowances to the spouse and children as provided in section 524.2–403 and the expenses and claims provided in section 524.3–805 have been paid, and provided, further, that a bond shall be filed by the personal representative or the petitioner, conditioned upon the fact that all such obligations have been paid and that all the facts shown on the petition are true, with sufficient surety approved by the court in an amount as may be fixed by the court to cover potential improper distributions. If a personal representative is appointed, the representative's bond shall be sufficient for such purpose unless an additional bond is ordered, and the sureties on the bond shall have the same obligations and liabilities as provided for sureties on a distribution bond.

In the event that an improper distribution or disbursement is made in a summary closing, in that not all of said obligations have been paid or that other facts as shown by the personal representative or the petitioner, are not true, resulting in damage to any party, the court may vacate its summary decree or closing order, and the petitioner or the personal representative, together with the surety, shall be liable for damages to any party determined to be injured thereby as herein provided. The personal representative, petitioner, or the surety, may seek reimbursement for damages so paid or incurred from any distributee or recipient of assets under summary decree or order, who shall be required to make a contribution to cover such damages upon a pro rata basis or as may be equitable to the extent of assets so received. The court is hereby granted complete and plenary jurisdiction of any and all such proceedings and may enter such orders and judgments as may be required to effectuate the purposes of this subdivision.

Any judgment rendered for damages or the recovery of assets in such proceedings shall be upon petition and only after hearing held thereon on 14 days' notice of hearing and a copy of petition served personally upon the personal representative and the surety and upon any distributee or recipient of assets where applicable. Any action for the recovery of money or damages under this subdivision is subject to the time and other limitations imposed by section 525.02.

Amended by Laws 1995, c. 130, § 20; Laws 2000, c. 362, § 3.

Historical and Statutory Notes

Derivation:
St.1994, § 525.51.
Laws 1986, c. 444.
Laws 1975, c. 347, § 110.
Laws 1973, c. 644, § 1.
Laws 1973, c. 306, § 1.
Laws 1971, c. 497, § 6.
Laws 1969, c. 1009, § 1.
Laws 1967, c. 465, § 1.
St.Supp.1940, § 8992–125.
Laws 1937, c. 435, § 16.

Laws 1935, c. 72, § 125.
Laws 1995, c. 130, § 22, provides in part that chapter 130 is effective January 1, 1996, and that §§ 1, 14, 17, 18, 19, and 20 (amending, inter alia, this section) apply to all decedents' estates, whenever the decedent died.

Former section: St.1994, § 524.3–1203, which related to summary administrative procedures in small estates, was deleted by Laws 1995, c. 130, § 20. It was derived from Laws 1975, c. 347, § 69; Laws 1974, c. 442, art. 3, § 524.3–1203.

524.3–1204. Small estates; closing by sworn statement of personal representative

(a) Unless prohibited by order of the court and except for estates being administered by supervised personal representatives, a personal representative may close an estate administered under the summary procedures of section 524.3–1203 by filing with the court, at any time after disbursement and distribution of the estate, a statement stating that:

(1) to the best knowledge of the personal representative, the entire estate, less liens and encumbrances, did not exceed an exempt homestead as provided for in section 524.2–402, the allowances provided for in sections 524.2–403 and 524.2–404, costs and expenses of administration, reasonable funeral expenses, and reasonable, necessary medical and hospital expenses of the last illness of the decedent;

(2) the personal representative has fully administered the estate by disbursing and distributing it to the persons entitled thereto; and

(3) the personal representative has sent a copy of the closing statement to all distributees of the estate and to all creditors or other known claimants whose claims are neither paid nor barred and has furnished a full account in writing of the personal representative's administration to the distributees whose interests are affected.

(b) If no actions or proceedings involving the personal representative are pending in the court one year after the closing statement is filed, the appointment of the personal representative terminates.

(c) A closing statement filed under this section has the same effect as one filed under section 524.3–1003.

Laws 1974, c. 442, art. 3, § 524.3–1204. Amended by Laws 1975, c. 347, § 70, eff. Jan. 1, 1976; Laws 1976, c. 161, § 14, eff. April 4, 1976; Laws 1986, c. 444; Laws 1996, c. 305, art. 1, § 114.

ARTICLE 4

FOREIGN PERSONAL REPRESENTATIVES; ANCILLARY ADMINISTRATION

PART 1

DEFINITIONS

524.4–101. Definitions

In this article

(1) "Local administration" means administration by a personal representative appointed in this state pursuant to appointment proceedings described in article 3.[1]

(2) "Local personal representative" includes any personal representative appointed in this state pursuant to appointment proceedings described in article 3 and excludes foreign personal representatives who acquire the power of a local personal representative pursuant to section 524.4–205.

(3) "Resident creditor" means a person domiciled in, or doing business in this state, who is, or could be, a claimant against an estate of a nonresident decedent.

Laws 1974, c. 442, art. 4, § 524.4–101, eff. Jan. 1, 1976.

[1] Section 524.3–101 et seq.

PART 2

POWERS OF FOREIGN PERSONAL REPRESENTATIVES

524.4–201. Payment of debt and delivery of property to domiciliary foreign personal representative without local administration

At any time after the expiration of 60 days from the death of a nonresident decedent, any person indebted to the estate of the nonresident decedent or having possession or control of an instrument evidencing a debt, obligation, stock or chose in action belonging to the estate of the nonresident decedent may pay the debt, deliver the instrument evidencing the debt, obligation, stock or chose in action, to the domiciliary foreign personal representative of the nonresident decedent upon being presented with proof of appointment and an affidavit made by or on behalf of the representative stating:

(1) the date of the death of the nonresident decedent,

(2) that no local administration, or application or petition therefor, is pending in this state,

(3) that the domiciliary foreign personal representative is entitled to payment or delivery.

Laws 1974, c. 442, art. 4, § 524.4–201. Amended by Laws 1975, c. 347, § 71, eff. Jan. 1, 1976; Laws 1986, c. 444.

497

524.4–202. Payment or delivery discharges

Payment or delivery made in good faith on the basis of the proof of authority and affidavit releases the debtor or person having possession of the instrument evidencing the debt, obligation, stock or chose in action to the same extent as if payment or delivery had been made to a local personal representative.

Laws 1974, c. 442, art. 4, § 524.4–202. Amended by Laws 1975, c. 347, § 72, eff. Jan. 1, 1976.

524.4–203. Resident creditor notice

Payment or delivery under section 524.4–201 may not be made if a resident creditor of the nonresident decedent has notified the debtor of the nonresident decedent or the person having possession of the instrument evidencing the debt, obligation, stock or chose in action belonging to the nonresident decedent that the debt should not be paid nor such instrument delivered to the domiciliary foreign personal representative.

Laws 1974, c. 442, art. 4, § 524.4–203. Amended by Laws 1975, c. 347, § 73, eff. Jan. 1, 1976.

524.4–204. Proof of authority—bond

If no local administration or application or petition therefor is pending in this state, a domiciliary foreign personal representative may file the following with a court in this state in a county in which property belonging to the decedent is located:

(1) a certified or authenticated copy of the appointment and of any official bond given, and

(2) notice of an intention to exercise as to assets in this state all powers of a local personal representative and to maintain actions and proceedings in this state in accordance with section 524.4–205.

When a domiciliary foreign personal representative files a certified or authenticated copy of the appointment and of any official bond and a notice in accordance with the preceding sentence, the court administrator shall forthwith publish, at the expense of the estate, a notice once a week for two consecutive weeks in a legal newspaper in the county, giving the name and address of the domiciliary foreign personal representative and stating an intention to exercise as to assets in this state all powers of a local personal representative and to maintain actions and proceedings in this state in accordance with section 524.4–205.

Laws 1974, c. 442, art. 4, § 524.4–204. Amended by Laws 1975, c. 347, § 74, eff. Jan. 1, 1976; Laws 1986, c. 444; Laws 1986, 1st Sp., c. 3, art. 1, § 82.

524.4–205. Powers

At any time after the expiration of 60 days from a domiciliary foreign personal representative's filing in accordance with section 524.4–204 such domiciliary foreign personal representative may exercise as to assets in this state all powers of a local personal representative and may maintain actions and proceedings in this state subject to any conditions imposed upon nonresident parties generally. The power of a domiciliary foreign personal representative under this section shall not be exercised if a resident creditor of the nonresident decedent has filed a written objection thereto within 60 days from the domiciliary foreign personal representative's filing in accordance with section 524.4–204.

Laws 1974, c. 442, art. 4, § 524.4–205. Amended by Laws 1975, c. 347, § 75, eff. Jan. 1, 1976.

524.4–206. Power of representatives in transition

The power of a domiciliary foreign personal representative under section 524.4–201 or 524.4–205 shall be exercised only if there is no administration or application therefor pending in this state. Any application or petition for local administration of the estate terminates the power of the foreign personal representative to act under sections 524.4–201 and 524.4–205, but the local court may allow the foreign personal representative to exercise limited powers to preserve the estate. No assets which have been removed from this state by the foreign personal representative through exercise of powers under section 524.4–201 or 524.4–205 shall be subject to subsequent local administration. No person who, before receiving actual notice of a pending local administration, has changed position in reliance upon the powers of a foreign personal representative or who is a distributee from the foreign personal representative shall be prejudiced by reason of the application or petition for, or grant of, local administration. The local personal representative is subject to all rights in others and all duties and obligations which have accrued by virtue of the exercise of the powers by the foreign personal representative and may be substituted for the foreign personal representative in any action or proceedings in this state.

Laws 1974, c. 442, art. 4, § 524.4–206. Amended by Laws 1975, c. 347, § 76, eff. Jan. 1, 1976; Laws 1986, c. 444.

524.4–207. Provisions governing ancillary and other local administrations

In respect to a nonresident decedent, the provisions of article 3 of this chapter [1] govern (1) proceedings, if any, in a court of this state for probate of the will, appointment, removal, supervision, and discharge of the local personal representative, and any other order concerning the estate; and (2) the status, powers, duties and liabilities of any local personal representative and the rights of claimants, purchasers, distributees and others in regard to a local administration.

Laws 1974, c. 442, art. 4, § 524.4–207, eff. Jan. 1, 1976.
  [1] Section 524.3–301 et seq.

PART 3

JURISDICTION OVER FOREIGN REPRESENTATIVES

524.4–301. Jurisdiction by act of foreign personal representative

A foreign personal representative submits personally to the jurisdiction of the courts of this state in any proceeding relating to the estate by (1) filing certified or authenticated copies of the appointment as provided in section 524.4–204, (2) receiving payment of money or taking delivery of property under section 524.4–201, or (3) doing any act as a personal representative in this state which would have given the state jurisdiction over the personal representative as an individual. Jurisdiction under clause (2) is limited to the money or value of personal property collected.

Laws 1974, c. 442, art. 4, § 524.4–301. Amended by Laws 1975, c. 347, § 77, eff. Jan. 1, 1976; Laws 1986, c. 444.

524.4–302. Jurisdiction by act of decedent

In addition to jurisdiction conferred by section 524.4–301, a foreign personal representative is subject to the jurisdiction of the courts of this state to the same extent that the decedent was subject to jurisdiction immediately prior to death.

Laws 1974, c. 442, art. 4, § 524.4–302, eff. Jan. 1, 1976. Amended by Laws 1986, c. 444.

524.4–303. Service on foreign and nonresident personal representatives

(a) Service of process may be made upon a foreign personal representative and a nonresident personal representative appointed in this state by registered or certified mail, addressed to the last reasonably ascertainable address, requesting a return receipt signed by addressee only. Notice by ordinary first class mail is sufficient if registered or certified mail service to the addressee is unavailable. Service may be made upon a foreign personal representative or a nonresident personal representative appointed in this state in the manner in which service could have been made under other laws of this state on either the foreign personal representative, the nonresident personal representative appointed in this state, or the decedent immediately prior to death.

(b) If service is made upon a foreign personal representative or a nonresident personal representative appointed in this state as provided in subsection (a), the person served shall be allowed at least 30 days within which to appear or respond.

Laws 1974, c. 442, art. 4, § 524.4–303. Amended by Laws 1975, c. 347, § 78, eff. Jan. 1, 1976; Laws 1986, c. 444.

PART 4

JUDGMENTS AND PERSONAL REPRESENTATIVE

524.4–401. Effect of adjudication for or against personal representative

An adjudication rendered in any jurisdiction in favor of or against any personal representative of the estate is as binding on the local personal representative as if the local personal representative were a party to the adjudication.

Laws 1974, c. 442, art. 4, § 524.4–401, eff. Jan. 1, 1976. Amended by Laws 1986, c. 444.

ARTICLE 5

PROTECTION OF PERSONS UNDER DISABILITY AND THEIR PROPERTY

PART 1

GENERAL PROVISIONS

524.5–101. Short title

Sections 524.5–101 to 524.5–502 may be cited as the Uniform Guardianship and Protective Proceedings Act.

Laws 2003, c. 12, art. 1, § 1.

UNIFORM GUARDIANSHIP AND PROTECTIVE PROCEEDINGS ACT (1997)

Table of Jurisdictions Wherein Act Has Been Adopted

For text of Uniform Act, and variation notes and annotation materials for adopting jurisdictions, see Uniform Laws Annotated, Master Edition, Volume 8A.

Jurisdiction	Laws	Effective Date	Statutory Citation
Colorado	2000, c. 368	7–1–2001	West's C.R.S.A. §§ 15–14–101 to 15–14–433.
Minnesota	2003, c. 12	4–11–2003 *	M.S.A. §§ 524.5–101 to 524.5–502.

* Date of approval.

Historical and Statutory Notes

Laws 2003, c. 12, art. 2, § 9, provided:

"(a) Articles 1 and 2 apply to each guardianship or conservatorship proceeding and each appointment of guardian or conservator commenced on or after the effective date of articles 1 and 2. Except as otherwise provided in this section, articles 1 and 2 apply to each guardianship or conservatorship approved by the court prior to the effective date of articles 1 and 2, and to any guardianship or conservatorship proceeding pending in court on the effective date of articles 1 and 2, unless the court finds for good cause or in the interests of judicial economy that the proceeding should be completed under the provisions of Minnesota Statutes, chapter 525, as it existed prior to the effective date of articles 1 and 2.

"(b) A guardian or conservator who is not discharged prior to the effective date of articles 1 and 2 shall continue to hold the appointment but shall have only the powers specified in the order of appointment and in Minnesota Statutes, chapter 525, as it existed prior to the effective date of articles 1 and 2. Each guardian or conservator holding an appointment on the effective date of articles 1 and 2 shall continue to be bound by the duties imposed by the order of appointment; by Minnesota Statutes, chapter 525, as it existed prior to the effective date of articles 1 and 2; and by article 1, section 50; and shall be bound by any additional duties imposed by articles 1 and 2 starting on the first day of the next month starting after the effective date of articles 1 and 2 or on the next anniversary date of the appointment, whichever occurs later.

"(c) Any act done prior to the effective date of articles 1 and 2 in any proceeding and any right accrued under Minnesota Statutes, chapter 525, prior to the effective date of articles 1 and 2 shall not be impaired by articles 1 and 2. If a right is acquired, extinguished, or barred upon the expiration of a prescribed period of time which has commenced to run in accordance with the provisions of any statute before the effective date of articles 1 and 2, the provisions of the prior statute shall remain in force with respect to that right notwithstanding the statute's amendment or repeal by articles 1 and 2.

"(d) An order of the court or letters of guardianship or conservatorship issued by the court prior to the effective date of articles 1 and 2 shall remain in full force and effect in accordance with its terms and conditions and in accordance with the provisions of prior law until the court modifies the order or letters in accordance with the provisions of articles 1 and 2. Upon request for a certified copy of an order or letters which remains in full force and effect under this paragraph, the court administrator shall certify that the order or letters remains in full force and effect pursuant to this paragraph.

"(e) The court, without hearing or notice to any person, may issue new letters of guardianship or conservatorship under articles 1 and 2 to replace similar letters issued prior to the effective date of articles 1 and 2. The new letters shall be effective under articles 1 and 2 with the same force and effect as the prior letters and shall remain in full force and effect until modified by the court in accordance with the provisions of articles 1 and 2.

"(f) A power of attorney executed in accordance with Minnesota Statutes, section 524.5–505, prior to the effective date of articles 1 and 2, or any surety bond, deed, or other instrument, report, or other undertaking executed in accordance with Minnesota Statutes, chapter 525, prior to the effective date of articles 1 and 2, shall remain in full force and effect for all purposes in accordance with its terms and conditions and the provisions of the applicable statutes under which the power of attorney, surety bond, deed, or other instrument, report, or other undertaking was executed, until the power of attorney, surety bond, deed, or other instrument, report, or other undertaking expires according to its terms or pursuant to the statutes governing its execution, or is modified, terminated, or superseded by a new power of attorney, surety bond, deed, or other instrument, report, or other undertaking executed in accordance with the provisions of articles 1 and 2."

524.5–102. Definitions

Subdivision 1. Scope. As used in sections 524.5–101 to 524.5–502, the terms defined in this section have the meanings given them.

Subd. 2. Claim. "Claim," with respect to a protected person, includes a claim against an individual, whether arising in contract, tort, or otherwise, and a claim against an estate which arises at or after the appointment of a conservator, including expenses of administration.

Subd. 3. Conservator. "Conservator" means a person who is appointed by a court to manage the estate of a protected person and includes a limited conservator.

Subd. 4. Court. "Court" means the district court.

Subd. 5. Guardian. "Guardian" means a person who has qualified as a guardian of a minor or incapacitated person pursuant to appointment by a parent or spouse, or by the court, and includes a limited, emergency, or temporary substitute guardian but not a guardian ad litem.

Subd. 6. Incapacitated person. "Incapacitated person" means an individual who, for reasons other than being a minor, is impaired to the extent of lacking sufficient understanding or capacity to make or communicate responsible personal decisions, and who has demonstrated deficits in behavior which evidence an inability to meet personal needs for medical care, nutrition, clothing, shelter, or safety, even with appropriate technological assistance.

Subd. 7. Interested person. "Interested person" includes:

(i) the ward, protected person, or respondent;

(ii) a nominated guardian or conservator, or the duly appointed guardian or conservator;

(iii) legal representative;

(iv) the spouse, parent, adult children and siblings, or if none of such persons is living or can be located, the next of kin of the ward, protected person, or respondent;

(v) an adult person who has lived with a ward, protected person, or respondent for a period of more than six months;

(vi) an attorney for the ward or protected person;

(vii) a governmental agency paying or to which an application has been made for benefits for the respondent, ward, or protected person, including the county social services agency for the person's county of residence and the county where the proceeding is venued;

(viii) a health care agent or proxy appointed pursuant to a health care directive as defined in section 145C.01, a living will under chapter 145B, or other similar document executed in another state and enforceable under the laws of this state; and

(ix) any other person designated by the court.

Subd. 8. Legal representative. "Legal representative" includes a representative payee, a guardian or conservator acting for a respondent in this state or elsewhere, or a trustee or custodian of a trust or custodianship of which the respondent is a beneficiary.

Subd. 9. Letters. "Letters" includes letters of guardianship and letters of conservatorship.

Subd. 10. Minor. "Minor" means an unemancipated individual who has not attained 18 years of age.

Subd. 11. Next of kin. "Next of kin" shall be determined by the court.

Subd. 12. Parent. "Parent" means a parent whose parental rights have not been terminated.

Subd. 13. Person. "Person" means an individual, corporation, business trust, estate, trust, partnership, limited liability company, association, joint venture, government, governmental subdivision, agency, or instrumentality, or any other legal or commercial entity.

Subd. 14. Protected person. "Protected person" means a minor or other individual for whom a conservator has been appointed or other protective order has been made.

Subd. 15. Respondent. "Respondent" means an individual for whom the appointment of a guardian or conservator or other protective order is sought.

Subd. 16. State. "State" means a state of the United States, the District of Columbia, Puerto Rico, the United States Virgin Islands, or a territory or insular possession subject to the jurisdiction of the United States.

Subd. 17. Ward. "Ward" means an individual for whom a guardian has been appointed.

Laws 2003, c. 12, art. 1, § 2.

Historical and Statutory Notes

Laws 2003, c. 12, art. 2, § 9, provided:

"(a) Articles 1 and 2 apply to each guardianship or conservatorship proceeding and each appointment of guardian or conservator commenced on or after the effective date of articles 1 and 2. Except as otherwise provided in this section, articles 1 and 2 apply to each guardianship or conservatorship approved by the court prior to the effective date of articles 1 and 2, and to any guardianship or conservatorship proceeding pending in court on the effective date of articles 1 and 2, unless the court finds for good cause or in the interests of judicial economy that the proceeding should be completed under the provisions of Minnesota Statutes, chapter 525, as it existed prior to the effective date of articles 1 and 2.

"(b) A guardian or conservator who is not discharged prior to the effective date of articles 1 and 2 shall continue to hold the appointment but shall have only the powers specified in the order of appointment and in Minnesota Statutes, chapter 525, as it existed prior to the effective date of articles 1 and 2. Each guardian or conservator holding an appointment on the effective date of articles 1 and 2 shall continue to be bound by the duties imposed by the

order of appointment; by Minnesota Statutes, chapter 525, as it existed prior to the effective date of articles 1 and 2; and by article 1, section 50; and shall be bound by any additional duties imposed by articles 1 and 2 starting on the first day of the next month starting after the effective date of articles 1 and 2 or on the next anniversary date of the appointment, whichever occurs later.

"(c) Any act done prior to the effective date of articles 1 and 2 in any proceeding and any right accrued under Minnesota Statutes, chapter 525, prior to the effective date of articles 1 and 2 shall not be impaired by articles 1 and 2. If a right is acquired, extinguished, or barred upon the expiration of a prescribed period of time which has commenced to run in accordance with the provisions of any statute before the effective date of articles 1 and 2, the provisions of the prior statute shall remain in force with respect to that right notwithstanding the statute's amendment or repeal by articles 1 and 2.

"(d) An order of the court or letters of guardianship or conservatorship issued by the court prior to the effective date of articles 1 and 2 shall remain in full force and effect in accordance with its terms and conditions and in

accordance with the provisions of prior law until the court modifies the order or letters in accordance with the provisions of articles 1 and 2. Upon request for a certified copy of an order or letters which remains in full force and effect under this paragraph, the court administrator shall certify that the order or letters remains in full force and effect pursuant to this paragraph.

"(e) The court, without hearing or notice to any person, may issue new letters of guardianship or conservatorship under articles 1 and 2 to replace similar letters issued prior to the effective date of articles 1 and 2. The new letters shall be effective under articles 1 and 2 with the same force and effect as the prior letters and shall remain in full force and effect until modified by the court in accordance with the provisions of articles 1 and 2.

"(f) A power of attorney executed in accordance with Minnesota Statutes, section 524.5–505, prior to the effective date of articles 1 and 2, or any surety bond, deed, or other instrument, report, or other undertaking executed in accordance with Minnesota Statutes, chapter 525, prior to the effective date of articles 1 and 2, shall remain in full force and effect for all purposes in accordance with its terms and conditions and the provisions of the applicable statutes under which the power of attorney, surety bond, deed, or other instrument, report, or other undertaking was executed, until the power of attorney, surety bond, deed, or other instrument, report, or other undertaking expires according to its terms or pursuant to the statutes governing its execution, or is modified, terminated, or superseded by a new power of attorney, surety bond, deed, or other instrument, report, or other undertaking executed in accordance with the provisions of articles 1 and 2."

§ 524.5–103. Supplemental general principles of law applicable

Unless displaced by the particular provisions of this article, the principles of law and equity supplement its provisions.

Laws 2003, c. 12, art. 1, § 3.

Historical and Statutory Notes

Laws 2003, c. 12, art. 2, § 9, provided:

"(a) Articles 1 and 2 apply to each guardianship or conservatorship proceeding and each appointment of guardian or conservator commenced on or after the effective date of articles 1 and 2. Except as otherwise provided in this section, articles 1 and 2 apply to each guardianship or conservatorship approved by the court prior to the effective date of articles 1 and 2, and to any guardianship or conservatorship proceeding pending in court on the effective date of articles 1 and 2, unless the court finds for good cause or in the interests of judicial economy that the proceeding should be completed under the provisions of Minnesota Statutes, chapter 525, as it existed prior to the effective date of articles 1 and 2.

"(b) A guardian or conservator who is not discharged prior to the effective date of articles 1 and 2 shall continue to hold the appointment but shall have only the powers specified in the order of appointment and in Minnesota Statutes, chapter 525, as it existed prior to the effective date of articles 1 and 2. Each guardian or conservator holding an appointment on the effective date of articles 1 and 2 shall continue to be bound by the duties imposed by the order of appointment; by Minnesota Statutes, chapter 525, as it existed prior to the effective date of articles 1 and 2; and by article 1, section 50; and shall be bound by any additional duties imposed by articles 1 and 2 starting on the first day of the next month starting after effective date of articles 1 and 2 or on the next anniversary date of the appointment, whichever occurs later.

"(c) Any act done prior to the effective date of articles 1 and 2 in any proceeding and any right accrued under Minnesota Statutes, chapter 525, prior to the effective date of articles 1 and 2 shall not be impaired by articles 1 and 2. If a right is acquired, extinguished, or barred upon the expiration of a prescribed period of time which has commenced to run in accordance with the provisions of any statute before the effective date of articles 1 and 2, the provisions of the prior statute shall remain in force with respect to that right notwithstanding the statute's amendment or repeal by articles 1 and 2.

"(d) An order of the court or letters of guardianship or conservatorship issued by the court prior to the effective date of articles 1 and 2 shall remain in full force and effect in accordance with its terms and conditions and in accordance with the provisions of prior law until the court modifies the order or letters in accordance with the provisions of articles 1 and 2. Upon request for a certified copy of an order

or letters which remains in full force and effect under this paragraph, the court administrator shall certify that the order or letters remains in full force and effect pursuant to this paragraph.

"(e) The court, without hearing or notice to any person, may issue new letters of guardianship or conservatorship under articles 1 and 2 to replace similar letters issued prior to the effective date of articles 1 and 2. The new letters shall be effective under articles 1 and 2 with the same force and effect as the prior letters and shall remain in full force and effect until modified by the court in accordance with the provisions of articles 1 and 2.

"(f) A power of attorney executed in accordance with Minnesota Statutes, section 524.5–505, prior to the effective date of articles 1 and 2, or any surety bond, deed, or other

instrument, report, or other undertaking executed in accordance with Minnesota Statutes, chapter 525, prior to the effective date of articles 1 and 2, shall remain in full force and effect for all purposes in accordance with its terms and conditions and the provisions of the applicable statutes under which the power of attorney, surety bond, deed, or other instrument, report, or other undertaking was executed, until the power of attorney, surety bond, deed, or other instrument, report, or other undertaking expires according to its terms or pursuant to the statutes governing its execution, or is modified, terminated, or superseded by a new power of attorney, surety bond, deed, or other instrument, report, or other undertaking executed in accordance with the provisions of articles 1 and 2."

524.5–104. Facility of transfer

(a) A person required to transfer money or personal property to a minor may do so, as to an amount or value not exceeding $5,000 per year or a different amount that is approved by the court, by transferring it to:

(1) a person who has the care and custody of the minor and with whom the minor resides;

(2) a guardian of the minor;

(3) a custodian under the Uniform Transfers To Minors Act or custodial trustee under the Uniform Custodial Trust Act; or

(4) a financial institution as a deposit in an interest-bearing account or certificate in the sole name of the minor and giving notice of the deposit to the minor.

(b) This section does not apply if the person making payment or delivery knows that a conservator has been appointed or that a proceeding for appointment of a conservator of the minor is pending.

(c) A person who transfers money or property in compliance with this section is not responsible for its proper application.

(d) A guardian or other person who receives money or property for a minor under paragraph (a), clause (1) or (2), may only apply it to the support, care, education, health, and welfare of the minor, and may not derive a personal financial benefit except for reimbursement for necessary expenses. Any excess must be preserved for the future support, care, education, health, and welfare of the minor and any balance must be transferred to the minor upon emancipation or attaining majority.

Laws 2003, c. 12, art. 1, § 4. Amended by Laws 2004, c. 146, art. 2, § 1.

Historical and Statutory Notes

Laws 2003, c. 12, art. 2, § 9, provided:

"(a) Articles 1 and 2 apply to each guardianship or conservatorship proceeding and each appointment of guardian or conservator commenced on or after the effective date of articles 1 and 2. Except as otherwise provided in this section, articles 1 and 2 apply to each guardianship or conservatorship approved by the court prior to the effective date of articles 1 and 2, and to any guardianship or conservatorship proceeding pending in court on the effective date of articles 1 and 2, unless the court finds for good cause or in the interests of judicial economy that the proceeding should be completed under the provisions of Minnesota Statutes, chapter 525, as it existed prior to the effective date of articles 1 and 2.

"(b) A guardian or conservator who is not discharged prior to the effective date of articles 1 and 2 shall continue to hold the appointment but shall have only the powers specified in the order of appointment and in Minnesota Statutes, chapter 525, as it existed prior to the effective date of articles 1 and 2. Each guardian or conservator holding an appointment on the effective date of articles 1 and 2 shall continue to be bound by the duties imposed by the order of appointment; by Minnesota Statutes, chapter 525, as it existed prior to the effective date of articles 1 and 2; and by article 1, section 50; and shall be bound by any additional duties imposed by articles 1 and 2 starting on the first day of the next month starting after the effective date of articles 1 and 2 or on the next anniversary date of the appointment, whichever occurs later.

"(c) Any act done prior to the effective date of articles 1 and 2 in any proceeding and any right accrued under Minnesota Statutes, chapter 525, prior to the effective date of articles 1 and 2 shall not be impaired by articles 1 and 2. If a right is acquired, extinguished, or barred upon the expiration of a prescribed period of time which has commenced to run in accordance with the provisions of any statute before the effective date of articles 1 and 2, the provisions of the prior statute shall remain in force with respect to that right notwithstanding the statute's amendment or repeal by articles 1 and 2.

"(d) An order of the court or letters of guardianship or conservatorship issued by the court prior to the effective date of articles 1 and 2 shall remain in full force and effect in accordance with its terms and conditions and in accordance with the provisions of prior law until the court modifies the order or letters in accordance with the provisions of articles 1 and 2. Upon request for a certified copy of an order or letters which remains in full force and effect under this paragraph, the court administrator shall certify that the order or letters remains in full force and effect pursuant to this paragraph.

"(e) The court, without hearing or notice to any person, may issue new letters of guardianship or conservatorship under articles 1 and 2 to replace similar letters issued prior to the effective date of articles 1 and 2. The new letters shall be effective under articles 1 and 2 with the same force and effect as the prior letters and shall remain in full force and effect until modified by the court in accordance with the provisions of articles 1 and 2.

"(f) A power of attorney executed in accordance with Minnesota Statutes, section 524.5–505, prior to the effective date of articles 1 and 2, or any surety bond, deed, or other instrument, report, or other undertaking executed in accordance with Minnesota Statutes, chapter 525, prior to the effective date of articles 1 and 2, shall remain in full force and effect for all purposes in accordance with its terms and conditions and the provisions of the applicable statutes under which the power of attorney, surety bond, deed, or other instrument, report, or other undertaking was executed, until the power of attorney, surety bond, deed, or other instrument, report, or other undertaking expires according to its terms or pursuant to the statutes governing its execution, or is modified, terminated, or superseded by a new power of attorney, surety bond, deed, or other instrument, report, or other undertaking executed in accordance with the provisions of articles 1 and 2."

524.5–106. Subject–matter jurisdiction

This article applies to, and the court has jurisdiction over, guardianship and related proceedings for individuals domiciled or present in this state, protective proceedings for individuals domiciled in or having property located in this state, and property coming into the control of a guardian or conservator who is subject to the laws of this state. This article does not apply to any matters or proceedings arising under or governed by chapters 252A, 259, and 260C. Notwithstanding anything else to the contrary, chapters 252A, 259, and 260C exclusively govern the rights, duties, and powers of social service agencies, the commissioner of human services, licensed child placing agencies, and parties with respect to all matters and proceedings arising under those chapters.

Laws 2003, c. 12, art. 1, § 5.

Historical and Statutory Notes

Laws 2003, c. 12, art. 2, § 9, provided:

"(a) Articles 1 and 2 apply to each guardianship or conservatorship proceeding and each appointment of guardian or conservator commenced on or after the effective date of articles 1 and 2. Except as otherwise provided in this section, articles 1 and 2 apply to each guardianship or conservatorship approved by the court prior to the effective date of articles 1 and 2, and to any guardianship or conservatorship proceeding pending in court on the effective date of articles 1 and 2, unless the court finds for good cause or in the interests of judicial economy that the proceeding should be completed under the provisions of Minnesota Statutes, chapter 525, as it existed prior to the effective date of articles 1 and 2.

"(b) A guardian or conservator who is not discharged prior to the effective date of articles 1 and 2 shall continue to hold the appointment but shall have only the powers specified in the order of appointment and in Minnesota Statutes, chapter 525, as it existed prior to the effective date of articles 1 and 2. Each guardian or conservator holding an appointment on the effective date of articles 1 and 2 shall continue to be bound by the duties imposed by the order of appointment; by Minnesota Statutes, chapter 525, as it existed prior to the effective date of articles 1 and 2; and by article 1, section 50; and shall be bound by any additional duties imposed by articles 1 and 2 starting on the first day of the next month starting after the effective date of articles 1 and 2 or on the next anniversary date of the appointment, whichever occurs later.

"(c) Any act done prior to the effective date of articles 1 and 2 in any proceeding and any right accrued under Minnesota Statutes, chapter 525, prior to the effective date of articles 1 and 2 shall not be impaired by articles 1 and 2. If a right is acquired, extinguished, or barred upon the expiration of a prescribed period of time which has commenced to run in accordance with the provisions of any statute before the effective date of articles 1 and 2, the provisions of the prior statute shall remain in force with

respect to that right notwithstanding the statute's amendment or repeal by articles 1 and 2.

"(d) An order of the court or letters of guardianship or conservatorship issued by the court prior to the effective date of articles 1 and 2 shall remain in full force and effect in accordance with its terms and conditions and in accordance with the provisions of prior law until the court modifies the order or letters in accordance with the provisions of articles 1 and 2. Upon request for a certified copy of an order or letters which remains in full force and effect under this paragraph, the court administrator shall certify that the order or letters remains in full force and effect pursuant to this paragraph.

"(e) The court, without hearing or notice to any person, may issue new letters of guardianship or conservatorship under articles 1 and 2 to replace similar letters issued prior to the effective date of articles 1 and 2. The new letters shall be effective under articles 1 and 2 with the same force and effect as the prior letters and shall remain in full force and effect until modified by the court in accordance with the provisions of articles 1 and 2.

"(f) A power of attorney executed in accordance with Minnesota Statutes, section 524.5–505, prior to the effective date of articles 1 and 2, or any surety bond, deed, or other instrument, report, or other undertaking executed in accordance with Minnesota Statutes, chapter 525, prior to the effective date of articles 1 and 2, shall remain in full force and effect for all purposes in accordance with its terms and conditions and the provisions of the applicable statutes under which the power of attorney, surety bond, deed, or other instrument, report, or other undertaking was executed, until the power of attorney, surety bond, deed, or other instrument, report, or other undertaking expires according to its terms or pursuant to the statutes governing its execution, or is modified, terminated, or superseded by a new power of attorney, surety bond, deed, or other instrument, report, or other undertaking executed in accordance with the provisions of articles 1 and 2."

524.5–107.   Transfer of jurisdiction

(a) Following the appointment of a guardian or conservator or entry of another protective order, the court making the appointment or entering the order may transfer the proceeding to a court in another county in this state or to another state if the court is satisfied that a transfer will serve the best interest of the ward or protected person.

(b) A guardian, conservator, or like fiduciary appointed in another state may petition the court for appointment as a guardian or conservator in this state if the state has jurisdiction. The appointment may be made upon proof of appointment in the other state and presentation of a certified copy of the portion of the court record in the other state specified by the court in this state. Notice of hearing on the petition, together with a copy of the petition, must be given to the ward or protected person, if the ward or protected person has attained 14 years of age, and to the persons who would be entitled to notice if the regular procedures for appointment of a guardian or conservator under this article were applicable. The court shall make the appointment in this state unless it concludes that the appointment would not be in the best interest of the ward or protected person. Upon the filing of an acceptance of office and any required bond, the court shall issue appropriate letters of guardianship or conservatorship. Within 14 days after an appointment, the guardian or conservator shall send or deliver a copy of the order of appointment to the ward or protected person, if the ward or protected person has attained 14 years of age, and to all persons given notice of the hearing on the petition.

Laws 2003, c. 12, art. 1, § 6.

Historical and Statutory Notes

Laws 2003, c. 12, art. 2, § 9, provided:

"(a) Articles 1 and 2 apply to each guardianship or conservatorship proceeding and each appointment of guardian or conservator commenced on or after the effective date of articles 1 and 2. Except as otherwise provided in this section, articles 1 and 2 apply to each guardianship or conservatorship approved by the court prior to the effective date of articles 1 and 2, and to any guardianship or conservatorship proceeding pending in court on the effective date of articles 1 and 2, unless the court finds for good cause or in the interests of judicial economy that the proceeding should be completed under the provisions of Minnesota Statutes, chapter 525, as it existed prior to the effective date of articles 1 and 2.

"(b) A guardian or conservator who is not discharged prior to the effective date of articles 1 and 2 shall continue to hold the appointment but shall have only the powers specified in the order of appointment and in Minnesota Statutes, chapter 525, as it existed prior to the

effective date of articles 1 and 2. Each guardian or conservator holding an appointment on the effective date of articles 1 and 2 shall continue to be bound by the duties imposed by the order of appointment; by Minnesota Statutes, chapter 525, as it existed prior to the effective date of articles 1 and 2; and by article 1, section 50; and shall be bound by any additional duties imposed by articles 1 and 2 starting on the first day of the next month starting after the effective date of articles 1 and 2 or on the next anniversary date of the appointment, whichever occurs later.

"(c) Any act done prior to the effective date of articles 1 and 2 in any proceeding and any right accrued under Minnesota Statutes, chapter 525, prior to the effective date of articles 1 and 2 shall not be impaired by articles 1 and 2. If a right is acquired, extinguished, or barred upon the expiration of a prescribed period of time which has commenced to run in accordance with the provisions of any statute before the effective date of articles 1 and 2, the provisions of the prior statute shall remain in force with respect to that right notwithstanding the statute's amendment or repeal by articles 1 and 2.

"(d) An order of the court or letters of guardianship or conservatorship issued by the court prior to the effective date of articles 1 and 2 shall remain in full force and effect in accordance with its terms and conditions and in accordance with the provisions of prior law until the court modifies the order or letters in accordance with the provisions of articles 1 and 2. Upon request for a certified copy of an order or letters which remains in full force and effect under this paragraph, the court administrator shall certify that the order or letters remains in full force and effect pursuant to this paragraph.

"(e) The court, without hearing or notice to any person, may issue new letters of guardianship or conservatorship under articles 1 and 2 to replace similar letters issued prior to the effective date of articles 1 and 2. The new letters shall be effective under articles 1 and 2 with the same force and effect as the prior letters and shall remain in full force and effect

until modified by the court in accordance with the provisions of articles 1 and 2.

"(f) A power of attorney executed in accordance with Minnesota Statutes, section 524.5–505, prior to the effective date of articles 1 and 2, or any surety bond, deed, or other instrument, report, or other undertaking executed in accordance with Minnesota Statutes, chapter 525, prior to the effective date of articles 1 and 2, shall remain in full force and effect for all purposes in accordance with its terms and conditions and the provisions of the applicable statutes under which the power of attorney, surety bond, deed, or other instrument, report, or other undertaking was executed, until the power of attorney, surety bond, deed, or other instrument, report, or other undertaking expires according to its terms or pursuant to the statutes governing its execution, or is modified, terminated, or superseded by a new power of attorney, surety bond, deed, or other instrument, report, or other undertaking executed in accordance with the provisions of articles 1 and 2."

524.5–108. Venue

(a) Venue for a guardianship proceeding for a minor is in the county of this state in which the minor resides or is present at the time the proceeding is commenced.

(b) Venue for a guardianship proceeding for an incapacitated person is in the county of this state in which the respondent resides and, if the respondent has been admitted to an institution by order of a court of competent jurisdiction, in the county in which that court is located. Venue for the appointment of an emergency or a temporary guardian of an incapacitated person is also in the county in which the respondent is present.

(c) Venue for a protective proceeding is in the county of this state in which the respondent resides, whether or not a guardian has been appointed in another place or, if the respondent does not reside in this state, in any county of this state in which property of the respondent is located.

(d) If a proceeding under this article is brought in more than one county in this state, the court of the county in which the proceeding is first brought has the exclusive right to proceed unless that court determines that venue is properly in another court or that the interests of justice otherwise require that the proceeding be transferred.

(e) If it is in the best interest of the ward or protected person, the venue may be transferred to another county. Upon the filing of a petition by any interested person, or upon the court's own motion, the court shall fix a time and place for the hearing on the transfer. Notice must be given to interested persons, the district court of the county to which venue is proposed to be transferred, and any other party the court designates. Upon proof that a transfer of venue is in the best interest of the ward or protected person or the ward or protected person's estate, and upon settlement and allowance of the conservator's accounts, if any, to the time of the hearing, the court shall transmit the entire file to the court of the other county, where all subsequent proceedings must be held.

Laws 2003, c. 12, art. 1, § 7.

Historical and Statutory Notes

Laws 2003, c. 12, art. 2, § 9, provided:

"(a) Articles 1 and 2 apply to each guardianship or conservatorship proceeding and each appointment of guardian or conservator commenced on or after the effective date of articles 1 and 2. Except as otherwise provided in this section, articles 1 and 2 apply to each guardianship or conservatorship approved by the court prior to the effective date of articles 1 and 2, and to any guardianship or conservatorship proceeding pending in court on the effective date of articles 1 and 2, unless the court finds for good cause or in the interests of judicial economy that the proceeding should be completed under the provisions of Minnesota Statutes, chapter 525, as it existed prior to the effective date of articles 1 and 2.

"(b) A guardian or conservator who is not discharged prior to the effective date of articles 1 and 2 shall continue to hold the appointment but shall have only the powers specified in the order of appointment and in Minnesota Statutes, chapter 525, as it existed prior to the effective date of articles 1 and 2. Each guardian or conservator holding an appointment on the effective date of articles 1 and 2 shall continue to be bound by the duties imposed by the order of appointment; by Minnesota Statutes, chapter 525, as it existed prior to the effective date of articles 1 and 2; and by article 1, section 50; and shall be bound by any additional duties imposed by articles 1 and 2 starting on the first day of the next month starting after the effective date of articles 1 and 2 or on the next anniversary date of the appointment, whichever occurs later.

"(c) Any act done prior to the effective date of articles 1 and 2 in any proceeding and any right accrued under Minnesota Statutes, chapter 525, prior to the effective date of articles 1 and 2 shall not be impaired by articles 1 and 2. If a right is acquired, extinguished, or barred upon the expiration of a prescribed period of time which has commenced to run in accordance with the provisions of any statute before the effective date of articles 1 and 2, the provisions of the prior statute shall remain in force with respect to that right notwithstanding the statute's amendment or repeal by articles 1 and 2.

"(d) An order of the court or letters of guardianship or conservatorship issued by the court prior to the effective date of articles 1 and 2 shall remain in full force and effect in accordance with its terms and conditions and in accordance with the provisions of prior law until the court modifies the order or letters in accordance with the provisions of articles 1 and 2. Upon request for a certified copy of an order or letters which remains in full force and effect under this paragraph, the court administrator shall certify that the order or letters remains in full force and effect pursuant to this paragraph.

"(e) The court, without hearing or notice to any person, may issue new letters of guardianship or conservatorship under articles 1 and 2 to replace similar letters issued prior to the effective date of articles 1 and 2. The new letters shall be effective under articles 1 and 2 with the same force and effect as the prior letters and shall remain in full force and effect until modified by the court in accordance with the provisions of articles 1 and 2.

"(f) A power of attorney executed in accordance with Minnesota Statutes, section 524.5–505, prior to the effective date of articles 1 and 2, or any surety bond, deed, or other instrument, report, or other undertaking executed in accordance with Minnesota Statutes, chapter 525, prior to the effective date of articles 1 and 2, shall remain in full force and effect for all purposes in accordance with its terms and conditions and the provisions of the applicable statutes under which the power of attorney, surety bond, deed, or other instrument, report, or other undertaking was executed, until the power of attorney, surety bond, deed, or other instrument, report, or other undertaking expires according to its terms or pursuant to the statutes governing its execution, or is modified, terminated, or superseded by a new power of attorney, surety bond, deed, or other instrument, report, or other undertaking executed in accordance with the provisions of articles 1 and 2."

524.5–109. Practice in court

(a) Except as otherwise provided in this article, the rules of civil procedure, including the rules concerning appellate review, govern proceedings under this article.

(b) If guardianship and protective proceedings as to the same individual are commenced or pending in the same court, the proceedings may be consolidated.

Laws 2003, c. 12, art. 1, § 8.

Historical and Statutory Notes

Laws 2003, c. 12, art. 2, § 9, provided:

"(a) Articles 1 and 2 apply to each guardianship or conservatorship proceeding and each appointment of guardian or conservator commenced on or after the effective date of articles 1 and 2. Except as otherwise provided in this section, articles 1 and 2 apply to each guardianship or conservatorship approved by the court prior to the effective date of articles 1 and 2, and to any guardianship or conservatorship proceeding pending in court on the effective date of articles 1 and 2, unless the court finds for good cause or in the interests of judicial economy that the proceeding should be completed under the provisions of Minnesota Statutes, chapter 525, as it existed prior to the effective date of articles 1 and 2.

"(b) A guardian or conservator who is not discharged prior to the effective date of articles 1 and 2 shall continue to hold the appointment but shall have only the powers specified in the order of appointment and in Minnesota Statutes, chapter 525, as it existed prior to the effective date of articles 1 and 2. Each guardian or conservator holding an appointment on the effective date of articles 1 and 2 shall continue to be bound by the duties imposed by the order of appointment; by Minnesota Statutes, chapter 525, as it existed prior to the effective date of articles 1 and 2; and by article 1, section 50; and shall be bound by any additional duties imposed by articles 1 and 2 starting on the first day of the next month starting after the effective date of articles 1 and 2 or on the next anniversary date of the appointment, whichever occurs later.

"(c) Any act done prior to the effective date of articles 1 and 2 in any proceeding and any right accrued under Minnesota Statutes, chapter 525, prior to the effective date of articles 1 and 2 shall not be impaired by articles 1 and 2. If a right is acquired, extinguished, or barred upon the expiration of a prescribed period of time which has commenced to run in accordance with the provisions of any statute before the effective date of articles 1 and 2, the provisions of the prior statute shall remain in force with respect to that right notwithstanding the statute's amendment or repeal by articles 1 and 2.

"(d) An order of the court or letters of guardianship or conservatorship issued by the court prior to the effective date of articles 1 and 2 shall remain in full force and effect in accordance with its terms and conditions and in accordance with the provisions of prior law until the court modifies the order or letters in accordance with the provisions of articles 1 and 2. Upon request for a certified copy of an order or letters which remains in full force and effect under this paragraph, the court administrator shall certify that the order or letters remains in full force and effect pursuant to this paragraph.

"(e) The court, without hearing or notice to any person, may issue new letters of guardianship or conservatorship under articles 1 and 2 to replace similar letters issued prior to the effective date of articles 1 and 2. The new letters shall be effective under articles 1 and 2 with the same force and effect as the prior letters and shall remain in full force and effect until modified by the court in accordance with the provisions of articles 1 and 2.

"(f) A power of attorney executed in accordance with Minnesota Statutes, section 524.5–505, prior to the effective date of articles 1 and 2, or any surety bond, deed, or other instrument, report, or other undertaking executed in accordance with Minnesota Statutes, chapter 525, prior to the effective date of articles 1 and 2, shall remain in full force and effect for all purposes in accordance with its terms and conditions and the provisions of the applicable statutes under which the power of attorney, surety bond, deed, or other instrument, report, or other undertaking was executed, until the power of attorney, surety bond, deed, or other instrument, report, or other undertaking expires according to its terms or pursuant to the statutes governing its execution, or is modified, terminated, or superseded by a new power of attorney, surety bond, deed, or other instru-

ment, report, or other undertaking executed in accordance with the provisions of articles 1 and 2."

524.5–110. Letters of office

The court shall issue appropriate letters of guardianship upon the guardian's filing of an acceptance of office. The court shall issue appropriate letters of conservatorship upon the conservator's filing of an acceptance of office and any required bond. Letters of guardianship must indicate whether the guardian was appointed by the court, a parent, or the spouse. Any limitation on the powers of a guardian or conservator or of the assets subject to a conservatorship must be endorsed on the guardian's or conservator's letters.

Laws 2003, c. 12, art. 1, § 9.

Historical and Statutory Notes

Laws 2003, c. 12, art. 2, § 9, provided:

"(a) Articles 1 and 2 apply to each guardianship or conservatorship proceeding and each appointment of guardian or conservator commenced on or after the effective date of articles 1 and 2. Except as otherwise provided in this section, articles 1 and 2 apply to each guardianship or conservatorship approved by the court prior to the effective date of articles 1 and 2, and to any guardianship or conservatorship proceeding pending in court on the effective date of articles 1 and 2, unless the court finds for good cause or in the interests of judicial economy that the proceeding should be completed under the provisions of Minnesota Statutes, chapter 525, as it existed prior to the effective date of articles 1 and 2.

"(b) A guardian or conservator who is not discharged prior to the effective date of articles 1 and 2 shall continue to hold the appointment but shall have only the powers specified in the order of appointment and in Minnesota Statutes, chapter 525, as it existed prior to the effective date of articles 1 and 2. Each guardian or conservator holding an appointment on the effective date of articles 1 and 2 shall continue to be bound by the duties imposed by the order of appointment; by Minnesota Statutes, chapter 525, as it existed prior to the effective date of articles 1 and 2; and by article 1, section 50; and shall be bound by any additional duties imposed by articles 1 and 2 starting on the first day of the next month starting after the effective date of articles 1 and 2 or on the next anniversary date of the appointment, whichever occurs later.

"(c) Any act done prior to the effective date of articles 1 and 2 in any proceeding and any right accrued under Minnesota Statutes, chapter 525,

prior to the effective date of articles 1 and 2 shall not be impaired by articles 1 and 2. If a right is acquired, extinguished, or barred upon the expiration of a prescribed period of time which has commenced to run in accordance with the provisions of any statute before the effective date of articles 1 and 2, the provisions of the prior statute shall remain in force with respect to that right notwithstanding the statute's amendment or repeal by articles 1 and 2.

"(d) An order of the court or letters of guardianship or conservatorship issued by the court prior to the effective date of articles 1 and 2 shall remain in full force and effect in accordance with its terms and conditions and in accordance with the provisions of prior law until the court modifies the order or letters in accordance with the provisions of articles 1 and 2. Upon request for a certified copy of an order or letters which remains in full force and effect under this paragraph, the court administrator shall certify that the order or letters remains in full force and effect pursuant to this paragraph.

"(e) The court, without hearing or notice to any person, may issue new letters of guardianship or conservatorship under articles 1 and 2 to replace similar letters issued prior to the effective date of articles 1 and 2. The new letters shall be effective under articles 1 and 2 with the same force and effect as the prior letters and shall remain in full force and effect until modified by the court in accordance with the provisions of articles 1 and 2.

"(f) A power of attorney executed in accordance with Minnesota Statutes, section 524.5–505, prior to the effective date of articles 1 and 2, or any surety bond, deed, or other instrument, report, or other undertaking executed in accordance with Minnesota Statutes, chapter 525, prior to the effective date of articles 1 and 2, shall remain in full force and effect for all purposes in accordance with its terms and conditions and the provisions of the applicable statutes under which the power of attorney, surety bond, deed, or other instrument, report, or other undertaking was executed, until the power of attorney, surety bond, deed, or other instrument, report, or other undertaking expires according to its terms or pursuant to the statutes governing its execution, or is modified, terminated, or superseded by a new power of attorney, surety bond, deed, or other instrument, report, or other undertaking executed in accordance with the provisions of articles 1 and 2."

524.5–111. Effect of acceptance of appointment

By accepting appointment as guardian or conservator, a guardian or conservator submits personally to the jurisdiction of the court in any proceeding relating to the guardianship or conservatorship. The petitioner shall send or deliver notice of any proceeding to the guardian or conservator at the guardian's or conservator's address shown in the court records and at any other address then known to the petitioner.

Laws 2003, c. 12, art. 1, § 10.

Historical and Statutory Notes

Laws 2003, c. 12, art. 2, § 9, provided:

"(a) Articles 1 and 2 apply to each guardianship or conservatorship proceeding and each appointment of guardian or conservator commenced on or after the effective date of articles 1 and 2. Except as otherwise provided in this section, articles 1 and 2 apply to each guardianship or conservatorship approved by the court prior to the effective date of articles 1 and 2, and to any guardianship or conservatorship proceeding pending in court on the effective date of articles 1 and 2, unless the court finds for good cause or in the interests of judicial economy that the proceeding should be completed under the provisions of Minnesota Statutes, chapter 525, as it existed prior to the effective date of articles 1 and 2.

"(b) A guardian or conservator who is not discharged prior to the effective date of articles 1 and 2 shall continue to hold the appointment but shall have only the powers specified in the order of appointment and in Minnesota Statutes, chapter 525, as it existed prior to the effective date of articles 1 and 2. Each guardian or conservator holding an appointment on the effective date of articles 1 and 2 shall continue to be bound by the duties imposed by the order of appointment; by Minnesota Statutes, chapter 525, as it existed prior to the effective date of articles 1 and 2; and by article 1, section 50; and shall be bound by any additional duties imposed by articles 1 and 2 starting on the first day of the next month starting after the effective date of articles 1 and 2 or on the next anniversary date of the appointment, whichever occurs later.

"(c) Any act done prior to the effective date of articles 1 and 2 in any proceeding and any right accrued under Minnesota Statutes, chapter 525, prior to the effective date of articles 1 and 2 shall not be impaired by articles 1 and 2. If a right is acquired, extinguished, or barred upon the expiration of a prescribed period of time which has commenced to run in accordance with the provisions of any statute before the effective date of articles 1 and 2, the provisions of the prior statute shall remain in force with respect to that right notwithstanding the statute's amendment or repeal by articles 1 and 2.

"(d) An order of the court or letters of guardianship or conservatorship issued by the court prior to the effective date of articles 1 and 2 shall remain in full force and effect in accordance with its terms and conditions and in accordance with the provisions of prior law until the court modifies the order or letters in accordance with the provisions of articles 1 and 2. Upon request for a certified copy of an order or letters which remains in full force and effect under this paragraph, the court administrator shall certify that the order or letters remains in full force and effect pursuant to this paragraph.

"(e) The court, without hearing or notice to any person, may issue new letters of guardianship or conservatorship under articles 1 and 2 to replace similar letters issued prior to the effective date of articles 1 and 2. The new letters shall be effective under articles 1 and 2 with the same force and effect as the prior letters and shall remain in full force and effect until modified by the court in accordance with the provisions of articles 1 and 2.

"(f) A power of attorney executed in accordance with Minnesota Statutes, section 524.5–505, prior to the effective date of articles 1 and 2, or any surety bond, deed, or other instrument, report, or other undertaking executed in accordance with Minnesota Statutes, chapter 525, prior to the effective date of articles 1 and 2, shall remain in full force and effect for all purposes in accordance with its terms and conditions and the provisions of the applicable statutes under which the power of attorney, surety bond, deed, or other instrument, report, or other undertaking was executed, until the power of attorney, surety bond, deed, or other instrument, report, or other undertaking expires according to its terms or pursuant to the statutes governing its execution, or is modified, terminated, or superseded by a new power of attorney, surety bond, deed, or other instrument, report, or other undertaking executed in accordance with the provisions of articles 1 and 2."

524.5–112. Termination of or change in guardian's or conservator's appointment

(a) The appointment of a guardian or conservator terminates upon the death, resignation, or removal of the guardian or conservator or upon termination of the guardianship or conservatorship. A resignation of a guardian or conservator is effective when approved by the court. A parental or spousal appointment as guardian under an informally probated will terminates if the will is later denied probate in a formal proceeding. Termination of the appointment of a guardian or conservator does not affect the liability of either for previous acts or the obligation to account for money and other assets of the ward or protected person.

(b) A ward, protected person, or interested person may petition for removal of a guardian or conservator on the ground that removal would be in the best interest of the ward or protected person or for other good cause. A guardian or conservator may petition for permission to resign. A petition for removal or permission to resign may include a request for appointment of a successor guardian or conservator.

(c) The court may appoint an additional guardian or conservator at any time, to serve immediately or upon some other designated event, and may appoint a successor guardian or conservator in the event of a vacancy or make the appointment prior to a vacancy, to serve when a vacancy occurs. An additional or successor guardian or conservator may file an acceptance of appointment at any time after the appointment, but in no case later than 30 days after the occurrence of the vacancy or other designated event. The additional or successor guardian or conservator becomes eligible to act on the occurrence of the vacancy or designated event, or the filing of the acceptance of appointment, whichever occurs last. A successor guardian or conservator succeeds to the predecessor's powers, and a successor conservator succeeds to the predecessor's title to the protected person's assets.

Laws 2003, c. 12, art. 1, § 11.

Historical and Statutory Notes

Laws 2003, c. 12, art. 2, § 9, provided:

"(a) Articles 1 and 2 apply to each guardianship or conservatorship proceeding and each appointment of guardian or conservator commenced on or after the effective date of articles 1 and 2. Except as otherwise provided in this

section, articles 1 and 2 apply to each guardianship or conservatorship approved by the court prior to the effective date of articles 1 and 2, and to any guardianship or conservatorship proceeding pending in court on the effective date of articles 1 and 2, unless the court finds for good cause or in the interests of judicial economy that the proceeding should be completed under the provisions of Minnesota Statutes, chapter 525, as it existed prior to the effective date of articles 1 and 2.

"(b) A guardian or conservator who is not discharged prior to the effective date of articles 1 and 2 shall continue to hold the appointment but shall have only the powers specified in the order of appointment and in Minnesota Statutes, chapter 525, as it existed prior to the effective date of articles 1 and 2. Each guardian or conservator holding an appointment on the effective date of articles 1 and 2 shall continue to be bound by the duties imposed by the order of appointment; by Minnesota Statutes, chapter 525, as it existed prior to the effective date of articles 1 and 2; and by article 1, section 50; and shall be bound by any additional duties imposed by articles 1 and 2 starting on the first day of the next month starting after the effective date of articles 1 and 2 or on the next anniversary date of the appointment, whichever occurs later.

"(c) Any act done prior to the effective date of articles 1 and 2 in any proceeding and any right accrued under Minnesota Statutes, chapter 525, prior to the effective date of articles 1 and 2 shall not be impaired by articles 1 and 2. If a right is acquired, extinguished, or barred upon the expiration of a prescribed period of time which has commenced to run in accordance with the provisions of any statute before the effective date of articles 1 and 2, the provisions of the prior statute shall remain in force with respect to that right notwithstanding the statute's amendment or repeal by articles 1 and 2.

"(d) An order of the court or letters of guardianship or conservatorship issued by the court prior to the effective date of articles 1 and 2 shall remain in full force and effect in accordance with its terms and conditions and in accordance with the provisions of prior law until the court modifies the order or letters in accordance with the provisions of articles 1 and 2. Upon request for a certified copy of an order or letters which remains in full force and effect under this paragraph, the court administrator shall certify that the order or letters remains in full force and effect pursuant to this paragraph.

"(e) The court, without hearing or notice to any person, may issue new letters of guardianship or conservatorship under articles 1 and 2 to replace similar letters issued prior to the effective date of articles 1 and 2. The new letters shall be effective under articles 1 and 2 with the same force and effect as the prior letters and shall remain in full force and effect until modified by the court in accordance with the provisions of articles 1 and 2.

"(f) A power of attorney executed in accordance with Minnesota Statutes, section 524.5–505, prior to the effective date of articles 1 and 2, or any surety bond, deed, or other instrument, report, or other undertaking executed in accordance with Minnesota Statutes, chapter 525, prior to the effective date of articles 1 and 2, shall remain in full force and effect for all purposes in accordance with its terms and conditions and the provisions of the applicable statutes under which the power of attorney, surety bond, deed, or other instrument, report, or other undertaking was executed, until the power of attorney, surety bond, deed, or other instrument, report, or other undertaking expires according to its terms or pursuant to the statutes governing its execution, or is modified, terminated, or superseded by a new power of attorney, surety bond, deed, or other instrument, report, or other undertaking executed in accordance with the provisions of articles 1 and 2."

524.5–113. Notice

(a) Except for notice for which specific requirements are otherwise provided in this article or as otherwise ordered by the court for good cause, notice of a hearing on a petition is required for all petitions in the manner prescribed by this section. The petitioner shall give notice of the time and place of the hearing to all interested persons. Notice must be given by mail postmarked at least 14 days before the hearing.

(b) Proof of notice must be made before or at the hearing and filed in the proceeding.

(c) A notice under this article must be given in plain language.

(d) If a patient of a state hospital, regional center, or any state-operated service has a guardianship or conservatorship established, modified, or terminated, the head of the state hospital, regional center, or state-operated service shall be notified. The notice shall require the institution to advise the court of the existence, if known, of a health care directive as defined in section 145C.01, executed by the proposed ward, incapacitated person, or protected person, a living will executed under chapter 145B, or any other similar document executed in another state and enforceable under the laws of this state. If a ward, incapacitated person, or protected person is under the guardianship or conservatorship of the commissioner of human services as developmentally disabled or dependent and neglected or is under the temporary custody of the commissioner of human services, the court shall notify the commissioner of human services if the public guardianship or conservatorship is established, modified, or terminated.

(e) If a conservator is required to file a bond pursuant to section 524.5–415, notice of any proceeding must be sent or delivered to the surety at the address shown in the court records at the place where the bond is filed and to any other address then known to the petitioner.

Laws 2003, c. 12, art. 1, § 12. Amended by Laws 2005, c. 56, § 1.

Historical and Statutory Notes

Laws 2003, c. 12, art. 2, § 9, provided:

"(a) Articles 1 and 2 apply to each guardianship or conservatorship proceeding and each appointment of guardian or conservator commenced on or after the effective date of articles 1 and 2. Except as otherwise provided in this section, articles 1 and 2 apply to each guardianship or conservatorship approved by the court prior to the effective date of articles 1 and 2, and to any guardianship or conservatorship proceeding pending in court on the effective date of articles 1 and 2, unless the court finds for good cause or in the interests of judicial economy that the proceeding should be completed under the provisions of Minnesota Statutes, chapter 525, as it existed prior to the effective date of articles 1 and 2.

"(b) A guardian or conservator who is not discharged prior to the effective date of articles 1 and 2 shall continue to hold the appointment but shall have only the powers specified in the order of appointment and in Minnesota Statutes, chapter 525, as it existed prior to the effective date of articles 1 and 2. Each guardian or conservator holding an appointment on the effective date of articles 1 and 2 shall continue to be bound by the duties imposed by the order of appointment; by Minnesota Statutes, chapter 525, as it existed prior to the effective date of articles 1 and 2; and by article 1, section 50; and shall be bound by any additional duties imposed by articles 1 and 2 starting on the first day of the next month starting after the effective date of articles 1 and 2 or on the next anniversary date of the appointment, whichever occurs later.

"(c) Any act done prior to the effective date of articles 1 and 2 in any proceeding and any right accrued under Minnesota Statutes, chapter 525, prior to the effective date of articles 1 and 2 shall not be impaired by articles 1 and 2. If a right is acquired, extinguished, or barred upon the expiration of a prescribed period of time which has commenced to run in accordance with the provisions of any statute before the effective date of articles 1 and 2, the provisions of the prior statute shall remain in force with respect to that right notwithstanding the statute's amendment or repeal by articles 1 and 2.

"(d) An order of the court or letters of guardianship or conservatorship issued by the court prior to the effective date of articles 1 and 2 shall remain in full force and effect in accordance with its terms and conditions and in accordance with the provisions of prior law until the court modifies the order or letters in accordance with the provisions of articles 1 and 2. Upon request for a certified copy of an order or letters which remains in full force and effect under this paragraph, the court administrator shall certify that the order or letters remains in full force and effect pursuant to this paragraph.

"(e) The court, without hearing or notice to any person, may issue new letters of guardianship or conservatorship under articles 1 and 2 to replace similar letters issued prior to the effective date of articles 1 and 2. The new letters shall be effective under articles 1 and 2 with the same force and effect as the prior letters and shall remain in full force and effect until modified by the court in accordance with the provisions of articles 1 and 2.

"(f) A power of attorney executed in accordance with Minnesota Statutes, section 524.5-505, prior to the effective date of articles 1 and 2, or any surety bond, deed, or other instrument, report, or other undertaking executed in accordance with Minnesota Statutes,

chapter 525, prior to the effective date of articles 1 and 2, shall remain in full force and effect for all purposes in accordance with its terms and conditions and the provisions of the applicable statutes under which the power of attorney, surety bond, deed, or other instrument, report, or other undertaking was executed, until the power of attorney, surety bond, deed, or other instrument, report, or other undertaking expires according to its terms or pursuant to the statutes governing its execution, or is modified, terminated, or superseded by a new power of attorney, surety bond, deed, or other instrument, report, or other undertaking executed in accordance with the provisions of articles 1 and 2."

524.5-114. Waiver of notice

A person may waive notice by a writing signed by the person or the person's attorney and filed in the proceeding. However, a respondent, ward, or protected person may not waive notice.

Laws 2003, c. 12, art. 1, § 13.

Historical and Statutory Notes

Laws 2003, c. 12, art. 2, § 9, provided:

"(a) Articles 1 and 2 apply to each guardianship or conservatorship proceeding and each appointment of guardian or conservator commenced on or after the effective date of articles 1 and 2. Except as otherwise provided in this section, articles 1 and 2 apply to each guardianship or conservatorship approved by the court prior to the effective date of articles 1 and 2, and to any guardianship or conservatorship proceeding pending in court on the effective date of articles 1 and 2, unless the court finds for good cause or in the interests of judicial economy that the proceeding should be completed under the provisions of Minnesota Statutes, chapter 525, as it existed prior to the effective date of articles 1 and 2.

"(b) A guardian or conservator who is not discharged prior to the effective date of articles 1 and 2 shall continue to hold the appointment but shall have only the powers specified in the order of appointment and in Minnesota Statutes, chapter 525, as it existed prior to the effective date of articles 1 and 2. Each guardian or conservator holding an appointment on the effective date of articles 1 and 2 shall continue to be bound by the duties imposed by the order of appointment; by Minnesota Statutes, chapter 525, as it existed prior to the effective date of articles 1 and 2; and by article 1, section 50; and shall be bound by any additional duties imposed by articles 1 and 2 starting on

the first day of the next month starting after the effective date of articles 1 and 2 or on the next anniversary date of the appointment, whichever occurs later.

"(c) Any act done prior to the effective date of articles 1 and 2 in any proceeding and any right accrued under Minnesota Statutes, chapter 525, prior to the effective date of articles 1 and 2 shall not be impaired by articles 1 and 2. If a right is acquired, extinguished, or barred upon the expiration of a prescribed period of time which has commenced to run in accordance with the provisions of any statute before the effective date of articles 1 and 2, the provisions of the prior statute shall remain in force with respect to that right notwithstanding the statute's amendment or repeal by articles 1 and 2.

"(d) An order of the court or letters of guardianship or conservatorship issued by the court prior to the effective date of articles 1 and 2 shall remain in full force and effect in accordance with its terms and conditions and in accordance with the provisions of prior law until the court modifies the order or letters in accordance with the provisions of articles 1 and 2. Upon request for a certified copy of an order or letters which remains in full force and effect under this paragraph, the court administrator shall certify that the order or letters remains in full force and effect pursuant to this paragraph.

"(e) The court, without hearing or notice to any person, may issue new letters of guardianship or conservatorship under articles 1 and 2 to replace similar letters issued prior to the effective date of articles 1 and 2. The new letters shall be effective under articles 1 and 2 with the same force and effect as the prior letters and shall remain in full force and effect until modified by the court in accordance with the provisions of articles 1 and 2.

"(f) A power of attorney executed in accordance with Minnesota Statutes, section 524.5–505, prior to the effective date of articles 1 and 2, or any surety bond, deed, or other instrument, report, or other undertaking executed in accordance with Minnesota Statutes, chapter 525, prior to the effective date of arti-

cles 1 and 2, shall remain in full force and effect for all purposes in accordance with its terms and conditions and the provisions of the applicable statutes under which the power of attorney, surety bond, deed, or other instrument, report, or other undertaking was executed, until the power of attorney, surety bond, deed, or other instrument, report, or other undertaking expires according to its terms or pursuant to the statutes governing its execution, or is modified, terminated, or superseded by a new power of attorney, surety bond, deed, or other instrument, report, or other undertaking executed in accordance with the provisions of articles 1 and 2."

§ 524.5–115. Guardian ad litem

At any stage of a proceeding, a court may appoint a guardian ad litem if the court determines that representation of the interest otherwise would be inadequate. If not precluded by a conflict of interest, a guardian ad litem may be appointed to represent several individuals or interests. The court shall state on the record the duties of the guardian ad litem and its reasons for the appointment.

Laws 2003, c. 12, art. 1, § 14.

Historical and Statutory Notes

Laws 2003, c. 12, art. 2, § 9, provided:

"(a) Articles 1 and 2 apply to each guardianship or conservatorship proceeding and each appointment of guardian or conservator commenced on or after the effective date of articles 1 and 2. Except as otherwise provided in this section, articles 1 and 2 apply to each guardianship or conservatorship approved by the court prior to the effective date of articles 1 and 2, and to any guardianship or conservatorship proceeding pending in court on the effective date of articles 1 and 2, unless the court finds for good cause or in the interests of judicial economy that the proceeding should be completed under the provisions of Minnesota Statutes, chapter 525, as it existed prior to the effective date of articles 1 and 2.

"(b) A guardian or conservator who is not discharged prior to the effective date of articles 1 and 2 shall continue to hold the appointment but shall have only the powers specified in the order of appointment and in Minnesota Statutes, chapter 525, as it existed prior to the effective date of articles 1 and 2. Each guardian or conservator holding an appointment on the effective date of articles 1 and 2 shall continue to be bound by the duties imposed by the order of appointment; by Minnesota Statutes, chapter 525, as it existed prior to the effective

date of articles 1 and 2; and by article 1, section 50; and shall be bound by any additional duties imposed by articles 1 and 2 starting on the first day of the next month starting after the effective date of articles 1 and 2 or on the next anniversary date of the appointment, whichever occurs later.

"(c) Any act done prior to the effective date of articles 1 and 2 in any proceeding and any right accrued under Minnesota Statutes, chapter 525, prior to the effective date of articles 1 and 2 shall not be impaired by articles 1 and 2. If a right is acquired, extinguished, or barred upon the expiration of a prescribed period of time which has commenced to run in accordance with the provisions of any statute before the effective date of articles 1 and 2, the provisions of the prior statute shall remain in force with respect to that right notwithstanding the statute's amendment or repeal by articles 1 and 2.

"(d) An order of the court or letters of guardianship or conservatorship issued by the court prior to the effective date of articles 1 and 2 shall remain in full force and effect in accordance with its terms and conditions and in accordance with the provisions of prior law until the court modifies the order or letters in accordance with the provisions of articles 1 and 2. Upon request for a certified copy of an order

or letters which remains in full force and effect under this paragraph, the court administrator shall certify that the order or letters remains in full force and effect pursuant to this paragraph.

"(e) The court, without hearing or notice to any person, may issue new letters of guardianship or conservatorship under articles 1 and 2 to replace similar letters issued prior to the effective date of articles 1 and 2. The new letters shall be effective under articles 1 and 2 with the same force and effect as the prior letters and shall remain in full force and effect until modified by the court in accordance with the provisions of articles 1 and 2.

"(f) A power of attorney executed in accordance with Minnesota Statutes, section 524.5–505, prior to the effective date of articles 1 and 2, or any surety bond, deed, or other instrument, report, or other undertaking executed in accordance with Minnesota Statutes, chapter 525, prior to the effective date of articles 1 and 2, shall remain in full force and effect for all purposes in accordance with its terms and conditions and the provisions of the applicable statutes under which the power of attorney, surety bond, deed, or other instrument, report, or other undertaking was executed, until the power of attorney, surety bond, deed, or other instrument, report, or other undertaking expires according to its terms or pursuant to the statutes governing its execution, or is modified, terminated, or superseded by a new power of attorney, surety bond, deed, or other instrument, report, or other undertaking executed in accordance with the provisions of articles 1 and 2."

524.5–117. Multiple appointments or nominations

If a respondent or other person makes more than one written appointment or nomination of a guardian or a conservator, the most recent controls.

Laws 2003, c. 12, art. 1, § 15.

Historical and Statutory Notes

Laws 2003, c. 12, art. 2, § 9, provided:

"(a) Articles 1 and 2 apply to each guardianship or conservatorship proceeding and each appointment of guardian or conservator commenced on or after the effective date of articles 1 and 2. Except as otherwise provided in this section, articles 1 and 2 apply to each guardianship or conservatorship approved by the court prior to the effective date of articles 1 and 2, and to any guardianship or conservatorship proceeding pending in court on the effective date of articles 1 and 2, unless the court finds for good cause or in the interests of judicial economy that the proceeding should be completed under the provisions of Minnesota Statutes, chapter 525, as it existed prior to the effective date of articles 1 and 2.

"(b) A guardian or conservator who is not discharged prior to the effective date of articles 1 and 2 shall continue to hold the appointment but shall have only the powers specified in the order of appointment and in Minnesota Statutes, chapter 525, as it existed prior to the effective date of articles 1 and 2. Each guardian or conservator holding an appointment on the effective date of articles 1 and 2 shall continue to be bound by the duties imposed by the order of appointment; by Minnesota Statutes, chapter 525, as it existed prior to the effective date of articles 1 and 2; and by article 1, section 50; and shall be bound by any additional duties imposed by articles 1 and 2 starting on the first day of the next month starting after the effective date of articles 1 and 2 or on the next anniversary date of the appointment, whichever occurs later.

"(c) Any act done prior to the effective date of articles 1 and 2 in any proceeding and any right accrued under Minnesota Statutes, chapter 525, prior to the effective date of articles 1 and 2 shall not be impaired by articles 1 and 2. If a right is acquired, extinguished, or barred upon the expiration of a prescribed period of time which has commenced to run in accordance with the provisions of any statute before the effective date of articles 1 and 2, the provisions of the prior statute shall remain in force with respect to that right notwithstanding the statute's amendment or repeal by articles 1 and 2.

"(d) An order of the court or letters of guardianship or conservatorship issued by the court prior to the effective date of articles 1 and 2 shall remain in full force and effect in accordance with its terms and conditions and in accordance with the provisions of prior law until the court modifies the order or letters in accordance with the provisions of articles 1 and 2. Upon request for a certified copy of an order or letters which remains in full force and effect under this paragraph, the court administrator shall certify that the order or letters remains in full force and effect pursuant to this paragraph.

"(e) The court, without hearing or notice to any person, may issue new letters of guardianship or conservatorship under articles 1 and 2 to replace similar letters issued prior to the effective date of articles 1 and 2. The new letters shall be effective under articles 1 and 2 with the same force and effect as the prior letters and shall remain in full force and effect until modified by the court in accordance with the provisions of articles 1 and 2.

"(f) A power of attorney executed in accordance with Minnesota Statutes, section 524.5–505, prior to the effective date of articles 1 and 2, or any surety bond, deed, or other instrument, report, or other undertaking executed in accordance with Minnesota Statutes, chapter 525, prior to the effective date of articles 1 and 2, shall remain in full force and effect for all purposes in accordance with its terms and conditions and the provisions of the applicable statutes under which the power of attorney, surety bond, deed, or other instrument, report, or other undertaking was executed, until the power of attorney, surety bond, deed, or other instrument, report, or other undertaking expires according to its terms or pursuant to the statutes governing its execution, or is modified, terminated, or superseded by a new power of attorney, surety bond, deed, or other instrument, report, or other undertaking executed in accordance with the provisions of articles 1 and 2."

524.5–118. Background study

Subdivision 1. When required; exception. (a) The court shall require a background study under this section:

(1) before the appointment of a guardian or conservator, unless a background study has been done on the person under this section within the previous five years; and

(2) once every five years after the appointment, if the person continues to serve as a guardian or conservator.

(b) The background study must include criminal history data from the Bureau of Criminal Apprehension, other criminal history data held by the commissioner of human services, and data regarding whether the person has been a perpetrator of substantiated maltreatment of a vulnerable adult and a minor.

(c) The court shall request a search of the National Criminal Records Repository if the proposed guardian or conservator has not resided in Minnesota for the previous five years or if the Bureau of Criminal Apprehension information received from the commissioner of human services under subdivision 2, paragraph (b), indicates that the subject is a multistate offender or that the individual's multistate offender status is undetermined.

(d) If the guardian or conservator is not an individual, the background study must be done on all individuals currently employed by the proposed guardian or conservator who will be responsible for exercising powers and duties under the guardianship or conservatorship.

(e) If the court determines that it would be in the best interests of the ward or protected person to appoint a guardian or conservator before the background study can be completed, the court may make the appointment pending the results of the study.

(f) The fee for conducting a background study for appointment of a professional guardian or conservator must be paid by the guardian or conservator. In other cases, the fee must be paid as follows:

(1) if the matter is proceeding in forma pauperis, the fee is an expense for purposes of section 524.5–502, paragraph (a);

(2) if there is an estate of the ward or protected person, the fee must be paid from the estate; or

(3) in the case of a guardianship or conservatorship of the person that is not proceeding in forma pauperis, the court may order that the fee be paid by the guardian or conservator or by the court.

(g) The requirements of this subdivision do not apply if the guardian or conservator is:

(1) a state agency or county;

(2) a parent or guardian of a proposed ward or protected person who has a developmental disability, if the parent or guardian has raised the proposed ward or protected person in the family home until the time the petition is filed, unless counsel appointed for the proposed ward or protected person under section 524.5–205, paragraph (d); 524.5–304, paragraph (b); 524.5–405, paragraph (a); or 524.5–406, paragraph (b), recommends a background study; or

(3) a bank with trust powers, bank and trust company, or trust company, organized under the laws of any state or of the United States and which is regulated by the commissioner of commerce or a federal regulator.

Subd. 2. Procedure; criminal history and maltreatment records background check. (a) The court shall request the commissioner of human services to complete a background study under section 245C.32. The request must be accompanied by the applicable fee and the signed consent of the subject of the study authorizing the release of the data obtained to the court. If the court is requesting a search of the National Criminal Records Repository, the request must be accompanied by a set of classifiable fingerprints of the subject of the study. The fingerprints must be recorded on a fingerprint card provided by the commissioner of human services.

(b) The commissioner of human services shall provide the court with information from the Bureau of Criminal Apprehension's criminal justice information system, other criminal history data held by the commissioner of human services, and data regarding substantiated maltreatment of vulnerable adults under section 626.557 and substantiated maltreatment of minors under section 626.556 within 15 working days of receipt of a request. If the subject of the study has been the perpetrator of substantiated maltreatment of a vulnerable adult or minor, the response must include a copy of the public portion of the investigation memorandum under section 626.557, subdivision 12b, or the public portion of the investigation memorandum under section 626.556, subdivision 10f. If the court did not request a search of the National Criminal Records Repository and information from the Bureau of Criminal Apprehension indicates that the subject is a multistate offender or that multistate offender status is undetermined, the response must include this information. The commissioner shall provide the court with information from the National

Criminal Records Repository within three working days of the commissioner's receipt of the data.

(c) Notwithstanding section 626.557, subdivision 12b, or 626.556, subdivision 10f, if the commissioner of human services or a county lead agency has information that a person on whom a background study was previously done under this section has been determined to be a perpetrator of maltreatment of a vulnerable adult or minor, the commissioner or the county may provide this information to the court that requested the background study. The commissioner may also provide the court with additional criminal history or substantiated maltreatment information that becomes available after the background study is done.

Subd. 3. Form. The commissioner of human services shall develop a form to be used for requesting a background study under this section, which must include:

(1) a notification to the subject of the study that the court will request the commissioner to perform a background study under this section;

(2) a notification to the subject of the rights in subdivision 4; and

(3) a signed consent to conduct the background study.

Subd. 4. Rights. The court shall notify the subject of a background study that the subject has the following rights:

(1) the right to be informed that the court will request a background study on the subject for the purpose of determining whether the person's appointment or continued appointment is in the best interests of the ward or protected person;

(2) the right to be informed of the results of the study and to obtain from the court a copy of the results; and

(3) the right to challenge the accuracy and completeness of information contained in the results under section 13.04, subdivision 4, except to the extent precluded by section 256.045, subdivision 3.

Laws 2003, c. 12, art. 1, § 16. Amended by Laws 2004, c. 146, art. 2, § 2; Laws 2005, c. 56, § 1.

Historical and Statutory Notes

Laws 2003, c. 12, art. 2, § 9, provided:

"(a) Articles 1 and 2 apply to each guardianship or conservatorship proceeding and each appointment of guardian or conservator commenced on or after the effective date of articles 1 and 2. Except as otherwise provided in this section, articles 1 and 2 apply to each guardianship or conservatorship approved by the court prior to the effective date of articles 1 and 2, and to any guardianship or conservatorship proceeding pending in court on the effective date of articles 1 and 2, unless the court finds for good cause or in the interests of judicial economy that the proceeding should be completed under the provisions of Minnesota Statutes, chapter 525, as it existed prior to the effective date of articles 1 and 2.

"(b) A guardian or conservator who is not discharged prior to the effective date of articles 1 and 2 shall continue to hold the appointment but shall have only the powers specified in the order of appointment and in Minnesota Statutes, chapter 525, as it existed prior to the effective date of articles 1 and 2. Each guardian or conservator holding an appointment on the effective date of articles 1 and 2 shall con-

tinue to be bound by the duties imposed by the order of appointment; by Minnesota Statutes, chapter 525, as it existed prior to the effective date of articles 1 and 2; and by article 1, section 50; and shall be bound by any additional duties imposed by articles 1 and 2 starting on the first day of the next month starting after the effective date of articles 1 and 2 or on the next anniversary date of the appointment, whichever occurs later.

"(c) Any act done prior to the effective date of articles 1 and 2 in any proceeding and any right accrued under Minnesota Statutes, chapter 525, prior to the effective date of articles 1 and 2 shall not be impaired by articles 1 and 2. If a right is acquired, extinguished, or barred upon the expiration of a prescribed period of time which has commenced to run in accordance with the provisions of any statute before the effective date of articles 1 and 2, the provisions of the prior statute shall remain in force with respect to that right notwithstanding the statute's amendment or repeal by articles 1 and 2.

"(d) An order of the court or letters of guardianship or conservatorship issued by the court prior to the effective date of articles 1 and 2 shall remain in full force and effect in accordance with its terms and conditions and in accordance with the provisions of prior law until the court modifies the order or letters in accordance with the provisions of articles 1 and 2. Upon request for a certified copy of an order or letters which remains in full force and effect under this paragraph, the court administrator

shall certify that the order or letters remains in full force and effect pursuant to this paragraph.

"(e) The court, without hearing or notice to any person, may issue new letters of guardianship or conservatorship under articles 1 and 2 to replace similar letters issued prior to the effective date of articles 1 and 2. The new letters shall be effective under articles 1 and 2 with the same force and effect as the prior letters and shall remain in full force and effect until modified by the court in accordance with the provisions of articles 1 and 2.

"(f) A power of attorney executed in accordance with Minnesota Statutes, section 524.5–505, prior to the effective date of articles 1 and 2, or any surety bond, deed, or other instrument, report, or other undertaking executed in accordance with Minnesota Statutes, chapter 525, prior to the effective date of articles 1 and 2, shall remain in full force and effect for all purposes in accordance with its terms and conditions and the provisions of the applicable statutes under which the power of attorney, surety bond, deed, or other instrument, report, or other undertaking was executed, until the power of attorney, surety bond, deed, or other instrument, report, or other undertaking expires according to its terms or pursuant to the statutes governing its execution, or is modified, terminated, or superseded by a new power of attorney, surety bond, deed, or other instrument, report, or other undertaking executed in accordance with the provisions of articles 1 and 2."

PART 2

GUARDIAN OF MINOR

524.5–201. Appointment and status of guardian

A person becomes a guardian of a minor by parental appointment, by designation of a standby guardian pursuant to chapter 257B, or upon appointment by the court. The guardianship continues until terminated, without regard to the location of the guardian or minor ward.

Laws 2003, c. 12, art. 1, § 17.

Historical and Statutory Notes

Laws 2003, c. 12, art. 2, § 9, provided:

"(a) Articles 1 and 2 apply to each guardianship or conservatorship proceeding and each appointment of guardian or conservator commenced on or after the effective date of articles 1 and 2. Except as otherwise provided in this

section, articles 1 and 2 apply to each guardianship or conservatorship approved by the court prior to the effective date of articles 1 and 2, and to any guardianship or conservatorship proceeding pending in court on the effective date of articles 1 and 2, unless the court finds for good cause or in the interests of judicial economy that the proceeding should be completed under the provisions of Minnesota Statutes, chapter 525, as it existed prior to the effective date of articles 1 and 2.

"(b) A guardian or conservator who is not discharged prior to the effective date of articles 1 and 2 shall continue to hold the appointment but shall have only the powers specified in the order of appointment and in Minnesota Statutes, chapter 525, as it existed prior to the effective date of articles 1 and 2. Each guardian or conservator holding an appointment on the effective date of articles 1 and 2 shall continue to be bound by the duties imposed by the order of appointment; by Minnesota Statutes, chapter 525, as it existed prior to the effective date of articles 1 and 2; and by article 1, section 50; and shall be bound by any additional duties imposed by articles 1 and 2 starting on the first day of the next month starting after the effective date of articles 1 and 2 or on the next anniversary date of the appointment, whichever occurs later.

"(c) Any act done prior to the effective date of articles 1 and 2 in any proceeding and any right accrued under Minnesota Statutes, chapter 525, prior to the effective date of articles 1 and 2 shall not be impaired by articles 1 and 2. If a right is acquired, extinguished, or barred upon the expiration of a prescribed period of time which has commenced to run in accordance with the provisions of any statute before the effective date of articles 1 and 2, the provisions of the prior statute shall remain in force with respect to that right notwithstanding the statute's amendment or repeal by articles 1 and 2.

"(d) An order of the court or letters of guardianship or conservatorship issued by the court prior to the effective date of articles 1 and 2 shall remain in full force and effect in accordance with its terms and conditions and in

accordance with the provisions of prior law until the court modifies the order or letters in accordance with the provisions of articles 1 and 2. Upon request for a certified copy of an order or letters which remains in full force and effect under this paragraph, the court administrator shall certify that the order or letters remains in full force and effect pursuant to this paragraph.

"(e) The court, without hearing or notice to any person, may issue new letters of guardianship or conservatorship under articles 1 and 2 to replace similar letters issued prior to the effective date of articles 1 and 2. The new letters shall be effective under articles 1 and 2 with the same force and effect as the prior letters and shall remain in full force and effect until modified by the court in accordance with the provisions of articles 1 and 2.

"(f) A power of attorney executed in accordance with Minnesota Statutes, section 524.5–505, prior to the effective date of articles 1 and 2, or any surety bond, deed, or other instrument, report, or other undertaking executed in accordance with Minnesota Statutes, chapter 525, prior to the effective date of articles 1 and 2, shall remain in full force and effect for all purposes in accordance with its terms and conditions and the provisions of the applicable statutes under which the power of attorney, surety bond, deed, or other instrument, report, or other undertaking was executed, until the power of attorney, surety bond, deed, or other instrument, report, or other undertaking expires according to its terms or pursuant to the statutes governing its execution, or is modified, terminated, or superseded by a new power of attorney, surety bond, deed, or other instrument, report, or other undertaking executed in accordance with the provisions of articles 1 and 2."

524.5–202. Parental appointment of guardian

(a) A guardian may be appointed by will, by designation of a standby guardian pursuant to chapter 257B, or by other signed writing executed in the same manner as a health care directive under chapter 145C by a parent for any minor child the parent has or may have in the future. The appointment may specify the desired limitations on the powers to be given to the guardian. The appointing parent may revoke or amend the appointment prior to court confirmation.

(b) Upon petition of an appointing parent and a finding that the appointing parent will likely become unable to care for the child within two years or less, and after notice as provided in section 524.5–205, paragraph (b), the court, before the appointment becomes effective, may confirm the parent's selection of a guardian and terminate the rights of others to object.

(c) Subject to section 524.5–203, the appointment of a guardian becomes effective upon the appointing parent's death, an adjudication that the parent is an incapacitated person, or a written determination by a physician who has examined the parent that the parent is no longer able to care for the child, whichever occurs first.

(d) The guardian becomes eligible to act upon the filing of an acceptance of appointment, which must be filed within 30 days following the effective date of the guardian's appointment. The guardian shall:

(1) file the acceptance of appointment and a copy of the will with the court of the county in which the will was or could be probated or, in the case of another appointing instrument, file the acceptance of appointment and the appointing instrument with the court of the county in which the minor resides or is present; and

(2) give written notice of the acceptance of appointment to the appointing parent, if living, the minor, if the minor has attained 14 years of age, and a person other than the parent having care and custody of the minor.

(e) Unless the appointment was previously confirmed by the court, the notice given under paragraph (d), clause (2), must include a statement of the right of those notified to terminate the appointment by filing a written objection in the court as provided in section 524.5–203.

(f) Unless the appointment was previously confirmed by the court, within 30 days after filing the notice and the appointing instrument, a guardian shall petition the court for confirmation of the appointment, giving notice in the manner provided in section 524.5–205, paragraph (b).

(g) The appointment of a guardian by a parent does not supersede the parental rights of either parent. If both parents are dead or have been adjudged incapacitated persons, an appointment by the last parent who dies or was adjudged incapacitated has priority. An appointment by a parent which is effected by filing the guardian's acceptance under a will probated in the state of the testator's domicile is effective in this state.

(h) The powers of a guardian who timely complies with the requirements of paragraphs (d) and (e) relate back to give acts by the guardian which are of benefit to the minor and occurred on or after the date the appointment became effective the same effect as those that occurred after the filing of the acceptance of the appointment.

(i) The authority of a guardian appointed under this section terminates upon the first to occur of the appointment of a guardian by the court or the giving of written notice to the guardian of the filing of an objection pursuant to section 524.5–203.

Laws 2003, c. 12, art. 1, § 18.

Historical and Statutory Notes

Laws 2003, c. 12, art. 2, § 9, provided:

"(a) Articles 1 and 2 apply to each guardianship or conservatorship proceeding and each appointment of guardian or conservator commenced on or after the effective date of articles 1 and 2. Except as otherwise provided in this section, articles 1 and 2 apply to each guardianship or conservatorship approved by the court prior to the effective date of articles 1 and 2, and to any guardianship or conservatorship proceeding pending in court on the effective date of articles 1 and 2, unless the court finds for good cause or in the interests of judicial economy that the proceeding should be completed under the provisions of Minnesota Statutes, chapter 525, as it existed prior to the effective date of articles 1 and 2.

"(b) A guardian or conservator who is not discharged prior to the effective date of articles 1 and 2 shall continue to hold the appointment but shall have only the powers specified in the order of appointment and in Minnesota Statutes, chapter 525, as it existed prior to the effective date of articles 1 and 2. Each guardian or conservator holding an appointment on the effective date of articles 1 and 2 shall continue to be bound by the duties imposed by the order of appointment; by Minnesota Statutes, chapter 525, as it existed prior to the effective date of articles 1 and 2; and by article 1, section 50; and shall be bound by any additional duties imposed by articles 1 and 2 starting on the first day of the next month starting after the effective date of articles 1 and 2 or on the next anniversary date of the appointment, whichever occurs later.

"(c) Any act done prior to the effective date of articles 1 and 2 in any proceeding and any right accrued under Minnesota Statutes, chapter 525, prior to the effective date of articles 1 and 2 shall not be impaired by articles 1 and 2. If a right is acquired, extinguished, or barred upon the expiration of a prescribed period of time which has commenced to run in accordance with the provisions of any statute before the effective date of articles 1 and 2, the provisions of the prior statute shall remain in force with respect to that right notwithstanding the statute's amendment or repeal by articles 1 and 2.

"(d) An order of the court or letters of guardianship or conservatorship issued by the court prior to the effective date of articles 1 and 2 shall remain in full force and effect in accordance with its terms and conditions and in accordance with the provisions of prior law until the court modifies the order or letters in accordance with the provisions of articles 1 and 2. Upon request for a certified copy of an order or letters which remains in full force and effect under this paragraph, the court administrator shall certify that the order or letters remains in full force and effect pursuant to this paragraph.

"(e) The court, without hearing or notice to any person, may issue new letters of guardianship or conservatorship under articles 1 and 2 to replace similar letters issued prior to the effective date of articles 1 and 2. The new letters shall be effective under articles 1 and 2 with the same force and effect as the prior letters and shall remain in full force and effect until modified by the court in accordance with the provisions of articles 1 and 2.

"(f) A power of attorney executed in accordance with Minnesota Statutes, section 524.5–505, prior to the effective date of articles 1 and 2, or any surety bond, deed, or other instrument, report, or other undertaking executed in accordance with Minnesota Statutes, chapter 525, prior to the effective date of articles 1 and 2, shall remain in full force and effect for all purposes in accordance with its terms and conditions and the provisions of the applicable statutes under which the power of attorney, surety bond, deed, or other instrument, report, or other undertaking was executed, until the power of attorney, surety bond, deed, or other instrument, report, or other undertaking expires according to its terms or pursuant to the statutes governing its execution, or is modified, terminated, or superseded by a new power of attorney, surety bond, deed, or other instrument, report, or other undertaking executed in accordance with the provisions of articles 1 and 2."

524.5–203. Objection by minor or others to parental appointment

Until the court has confirmed an appointee under section 524.5–202, a minor who is the subject of an appointment by a parent and who has attained 14 years of age, the other parent, or a person other than a parent or guardian having custody or care of the minor may prevent or terminate the appointment at any time by filing in the court in which the appointing instrument is filed a written objection and by giving notice of the objection to the guardian and any other persons entitled to notice of the acceptance of the appointment. An objection may be withdrawn, and if withdrawn is of no effect. An objection does not preclude an appointment of the appointee by the court. The court may treat the filing of an objection as a petition for the appointment of an emergency or a temporary guardian under section 524.5–204, and proceed accordingly.

Laws 2003, c. 12, art. 1, § 19.

Historical and Statutory Notes

Laws 2003, c. 12, art. 2, § 9, provided:

"(a) Articles 1 and 2 apply to each guardianship or conservatorship proceeding and each appointment of guardian or conservator commenced on or after the effective date of articles 1 and 2. Except as otherwise provided in this section, articles 1 and 2 apply to each guardianship or conservatorship approved by the court prior to the effective date of articles 1 and 2, and to any guardianship or conservatorship proceeding pending in court on the effective date of articles 1 and 2, unless the court finds for good cause or in the interests of judicial economy that the proceeding should be completed under the provisions of Minnesota Statutes, chapter 525, as it existed prior to the effective date of articles 1 and 2.

"(b) A guardian or conservator who is not discharged prior to the effective date of articles 1 and 2 shall continue to hold the appointment but shall have only the powers specified in the order of appointment and in Minnesota Statutes, chapter 525, as it existed prior to the effective date of articles 1 and 2. Each guardian or conservator holding an appointment on the effective date of articles 1 and 2 shall continue to be bound by the duties imposed by the order of appointment; by Minnesota Statutes, chapter 525, as it existed prior to the effective date of articles 1 and 2; and by article 1, section 50; and shall be bound by any additional duties imposed by articles 1 and 2 starting on the first day of the next month starting after the effective date of articles 1 and 2 or on the next anniversary date of the appointment, whichever occurs later.

"(c) Any act done prior to the effective date of articles 1 and 2 in any proceeding and any right accrued under Minnesota Statutes, chapter 525, prior to the effective date of articles 1 and 2 shall not be impaired by articles 1 and 2. If a right is acquired, extinguished, or barred upon the expiration of a prescribed period of time which has commenced to run in accordance with the provisions of any statute before the effective date of articles 1 and 2, the provisions of the prior statute shall remain in force with respect to that right notwithstanding the statute's amendment or repeal by articles 1 and 2.

"(d) An order of the court or letters of guardianship or conservatorship issued by the court prior to the effective date of articles 1 and 2 shall remain in full force and effect in accordance with its terms and conditions and in accordance with the provisions of prior law until the court modifies the order or letters in accordance with the provisions of articles 1 and 2. Upon request for a certified copy of an order or letters which remains in full force and effect under this paragraph, the court administrator shall certify that the order or letters remains in full force and effect pursuant to this paragraph.

"(e) The court, without hearing or notice to any person, may issue new letters of guardianship or conservatorship under articles 1 and 2 to replace similar letters issued prior to the effective date of articles 1 and 2. The new letters shall be effective under articles 1 and 2 with the same force and effect as the prior letters and shall remain in full force and effect until modified by the court in accordance with the provisions of articles 1 and 2.

"(f) A power of attorney executed in accordance with Minnesota Statutes, section 524.5–505, prior to the effective date of articles 1 and 2, or any surety bond, deed, or other instrument, report, or other undertaking executed in accordance with Minnesota Statutes, chapter 525, prior to the effective date of articles 1 and 2, shall remain in full force and effect for all purposes in accordance with its terms and conditions and the provisions of the applicable statutes under which the power of attorney, surety bond, deed, or other instrument, report, or other undertaking was executed, until the power of attorney, surety bond, deed, or other instrument, report, or other undertaking expires according to its terms or pursuant to the statutes governing its execution, or is modified, terminated, or superseded by a new power of attorney, surety bond, deed, or other instrument, report, or other undertaking executed in accordance with the provisions of articles 1 and 2."

524.5–204. Judicial appointment of guardian: conditions for appointment

(a) The court may appoint a guardian for a minor if the court finds the appointment is in the minor's best interest, and:

(i) both parents are deceased; or

(ii) all parental rights have been terminated by court order.

If a guardian is appointed by a parent pursuant to section 524.5–202 and the appointment has not been prevented or terminated under section 524.5–203, that appointee has priority for appointment. However, the court may proceed with another appointment upon a finding that the appointee under section 524.5–202 has failed to accept the appointment within 30 days after notice of the guardianship proceeding.

(b) If necessary and on petition or motion and whether or not the conditions of paragraph (a) have been established, the court may appoint a temporary guardian for a minor upon a showing that an immediate need exists and that the appointment would be in the best interest of the minor. Notice must be given to the parents and to a minor who has attained 14 years of age. Except as otherwise ordered by the court, the temporary guardian has the authority of an unlimited guardian, but the duration of the temporary guardianship may not exceed six months. Within five days after the appointment, the temporary guardian shall send or deliver a copy of the order to all individuals who would be entitled to notice of hearing under section 524.5–205.

(c) If the court finds that following the procedures of this article will likely result in substantial harm to a minor's health or safety and that no other person appears to have authority to act in the circumstances, the court, on appropriate petition, may appoint an emergency guardian for the minor. The duration of the guardian's authority may not exceed 30 days and the guardian may exercise only the powers specified in the order. Reasonable notice of the time and place of a hearing on the petition for appointment of an emergency guardian must be given to the minor, if the minor has attained 14 years of age, to each living parent of the minor, and a person having care or custody of the minor, if other than a parent. The court may dispense with the notice if it finds from affidavit or other sworn testimony that the minor will be substantially harmed before a hearing can be held on the petition. If the guardian is appointed without notice, notice of the appointment must be given within 48 hours after the appointment and a hearing on the appropriateness of the appointment held within five days after the appointment.

Laws 2003, c. 12, art. 1, § 20.

Historical and Statutory Notes

Laws 2003, c. 12, art. 2, § 9, provided:

"(a) Articles 1 and 2 apply to each guardianship or conservatorship proceeding and each appointment of guardian or conservator commenced on or after the effective date of articles 1 and 2. Except as otherwise provided in this section, articles 1 and 2 apply to each guardianship or conservatorship approved by the court prior to the effective date of articles 1 and 2, and to any guardianship or conservatorship proceeding pending in court on the effective date of articles 1 and 2, unless the court finds for good cause or in the interests of judicial economy that the proceeding should be completed under the provisions of Minnesota Statutes, chapter 525, as it existed prior to the effective date of articles 1 and 2.

"(b) A guardian or conservator who is not discharged prior to the effective date of articles 1 and 2 shall continue to hold the appointment but shall have only the powers specified in the order of appointment and in Minnesota Statutes, chapter 525, as it existed prior to the effective date of articles 1 and 2. Each guardian or conservator holding an appointment on the effective date of articles 1 and 2 shall continue to be bound by the duties imposed by the order of appointment; by Minnesota Statutes, chapter 525, as it existed prior to the effective date of articles 1 and 2; and by article 1, section 50; and shall be bound by any additional duties imposed by articles 1 and 2 starting on the first day of the next month starting after the effective date of articles 1 and 2 or on the next anniversary date of the appointment, whichever occurs later.

"(c) Any act done prior to the effective date of articles 1 and 2 in any proceeding and any right accrued under Minnesota Statutes, chapter 525, prior to the effective date of articles 1 and 2 shall not be impaired by articles 1 and 2. If a right is acquired, extinguished, or barred upon the expiration of a prescribed period of time which has commenced to run in accordance with the provisions of any statute before the effective date of articles 1 and 2, the provisions of the prior statute shall remain in force with respect to that right notwithstanding the statute's amendment or repeal by articles 1 and 2.

"(d) An order of the court or letters of guardianship or conservatorship issued by the court prior to the effective date of articles 1 and 2 shall remain in full force and effect in accordance with its terms and conditions and in accordance with the provisions of prior law until the court modifies the order or letters in accordance with the provisions of articles 1 and 2. Upon request for a certified copy of an order or letters which remains in full force and effect under this paragraph, the court administrator shall certify that the order or letters remains in full force and effect pursuant to this paragraph.

"(e) The court, without hearing or notice to any person, may issue new letters of guardianship or conservatorship under articles 1 and 2 to replace similar letters issued prior to the effective date of articles 1 and 2. The new letters shall be effective under articles 1 and 2 with the same force and effect as the prior letters and shall remain in full force and effect until modified by the court in accordance with the provisions of articles 1 and 2.

"(f) A power of attorney executed in accordance with Minnesota Statutes, section 524.5–505, prior to the effective date of articles 1 and 2, or any surety bond, deed, or other instrument, report, or other undertaking executed in accordance with Minnesota Statutes, chapter 525, prior to the effective date of articles 1 and 2, shall remain in full force and effect for all purposes in accordance with its terms and conditions and the provisions of the applicable statutes under which the power of attorney, surety bond, deed, or other instrument, report, or other undertaking was executed, until the power of attorney, surety bond, deed, or other instrument, report, or other undertaking expires according to its terms or pursuant to the statutes governing its execution, or is modified, terminated, or superseded by a new power of attorney, surety bond, deed, or other instrument, report, or other undertaking executed in accordance with the provisions of articles 1 and 2."

524.5–205. Judicial appointment of guardian: procedure

(a) A person interested in the welfare of a minor may petition for appointment of a guardian.

(b) After a petition is filed, the court shall set a date for hearing, and the petitioner shall give notice of the time and place for hearing the petition, together with a copy of the petition, to:

(1) the minor, if the minor has attained 14 years of age and is not the petitioner;

(2) any person alleged to have had the primary care and custody of the minor during the 60 days before the filing of the petition;

(3) each living parent of the minor or, if there is none, the adult nearest in kinship that can be found;

(4) any person nominated as guardian by the minor if the minor has attained 14 years of age;

(5) any appointee of a parent whose appointment has not been prevented or terminated under section 524.5–203; and

(6) any guardian or conservator currently acting for the minor in this state or elsewhere.

(c) The court, upon hearing, shall make the appointment if it finds that a qualified person seeks appointment, venue is proper, the required notices have been given, the conditions of section 524.5–204, paragraph (a), have been met, and the best interest of the minor will be served by the appointment. In other cases, the court may dismiss the proceeding or make any other disposition of the matter that will serve the best interest of the minor.

(d) If the court determines at any stage of the proceeding, before or after appointment, that the interests of the minor are or may be inadequately represented, it may appoint a lawyer to represent the minor, giving consideration to the choice of the minor if the minor has attained 14 years of age, provided that such appointment shall expire upon the expiration of the appeal time for the order appointing guardian or the order dismissing a petition or upon such other time or event as the court may direct.

(e) Within 14 days after an appointment, a guardian shall send or deliver to the minor ward, and counsel if represented at the hearing, a copy of the order of appointment accompanied by a notice which advises the minor ward of the right to appeal the guardianship appointment in the time and manner provided by the Rules of Appellate Procedure.

Laws 2003, c. 12, art. 1, § 21.

Historical and Statutory Notes

Laws 2003, c. 12, art. 2, § 9, provided:

"(a) Articles 1 and 2 apply to each guardianship or conservatorship proceeding and each appointment of guardian or conservator commenced on or after the effective date of articles 1 and 2. Except as otherwise provided in this section, articles 1 and 2 apply to each guardianship or conservatorship approved by the court prior to the effective date of articles 1 and 2, and to any guardianship or conservatorship proceeding pending in court on the effective date of articles 1 and 2, unless the court finds for good cause or in the interests of judicial economy that the proceeding should be completed under the provisions of Minnesota Statutes, chapter 525, as it existed prior to the effective date of articles 1 and 2.

"(b) A guardian or conservator who is not discharged prior to the effective date of articles 1 and 2 shall continue to hold the appointment but shall have only the powers specified in the order of appointment and in Minnesota Statutes, chapter 525, as it existed prior to the effective date of articles 1 and 2. Each guardian or conservator holding an appointment on the effective date of articles 1 and 2 shall continue to be bound by the duties imposed by the order of appointment; by Minnesota Statutes, chapter 525, as it existed prior to the effective date of articles 1 and 2; and by article 1, section 50; and shall be bound by any additional duties imposed by articles 1 and 2 starting on the first day of the next month starting after the effective date of articles 1 and 2 or on the next anniversary date of the appointment, whichever occurs later.

"(c) Any act done prior to the effective date of articles 1 and 2 in any proceeding and any right accrued under Minnesota Statutes, chapter 525, prior to the effective date of articles 1 and 2 shall not be impaired by articles 1 and 2. If a right is acquired, extinguished, or barred upon the expiration of a prescribed period of time which has commenced to run in accordance with the provisions of any statute before the effective date of articles 1 and 2, the provisions of the prior statute shall remain in force with respect to that right notwithstanding the statute's amendment or repeal by articles 1 and 2.

"(d) An order of the court or letters of guardianship or conservatorship issued by the court prior to the effective date of articles 1 and 2 shall remain in full force and effect in accordance with its terms and conditions and in accordance with the provisions of prior law until the court modifies the order or letters in accordance with the provisions of articles 1 and 2. Upon request for a certified copy of an order or letters which remains in full force and effect under this paragraph, the court administrator shall certify that the order or letters remains in full force and effect pursuant to this paragraph.

"(e) The court, without hearing or notice to any person, may issue new letters of guardianship or conservatorship under articles 1 and 2 to replace similar letters issued prior to the effective date of articles 1 and 2. The new letters shall be effective under articles 1 and 2 with the same force and effect as the prior letters and shall remain in full force and effect until modified by the court in accordance with the provisions of articles 1 and 2.

"(f) A power of attorney executed in accordance with Minnesota Statutes, section 524.5-505, prior to the effective date of articles 1 and 2, or any surety bond, deed, or other instrument, report, or other undertaking executed in accordance with Minnesota Statutes, chapter 525, prior to the effective date of articles 1 and 2, shall remain in full force and effect for all purposes in accordance with its terms and conditions and the provisions of the applicable statutes under which the power of attorney, surety bond, deed, or other instrument, report, or other undertaking was executed, until the power of attorney, surety bond, deed, or other instrument, report, or other undertaking expires according to its terms or pursuant to the statutes governing its execution, or is modified, terminated, or superseded by a new power of attorney, surety bond, deed, or other instrument, report, or other undertaking executed in accordance with the provisions of articles 1 and 2."

524.5–206. Judicial appointment of guardian: priority of minor's nominee, limited guardianship

(a) The court shall appoint as guardian a person whose appointment will be in the best interest of the minor. The court shall appoint a person nominated by the minor, if the minor has attained 14 years of age, unless the court finds the appointment will be contrary to the best interest of the minor.

(b) In the interest of developing self-reliance of a ward or for other good cause, the court, at the time of appointment or later, on its own motion or on motion of the minor ward or other interested person, may limit the powers of a guardian otherwise granted by this article and thereby create a limited guardianship. Following the same procedure, additional powers may be granted or existing powers may be withdrawn.

Laws 2003, c. 12, art. 1, § 22.

Historical and Statutory Notes

Laws 2003, c. 12, art. 2, § 9, provided:

"(a) Articles 1 and 2 apply to each guardianship or conservatorship proceeding and each appointment of guardian or conservator commenced on or after the effective date of articles 1 and 2. Except as otherwise provided in this section, articles 1 and 2 apply to each guardianship or conservatorship approved by the court prior to the effective date of articles 1 and 2, and to any guardianship or conservatorship proceeding pending in court on the effective date of articles 1 and 2, unless the court finds for good cause or in the interests of judicial economy that the proceeding should be completed under the provisions of Minnesota Statutes, chapter 525, as it existed prior to the effective date of articles 1 and 2.

"(b) A guardian or conservator who is not discharged prior to the effective date of articles 1 and 2 shall continue to hold the appointment but shall have only the powers specified in the order of appointment and in Minnesota Statutes, chapter 525, as it existed prior to the effective date of articles 1 and 2. Each guardian or conservator holding an appointment on the effective date of articles 1 and 2 shall continue to be bound by the duties imposed by the order of appointment; by Minnesota Statutes, chapter 525, as it existed prior to the effective date of articles 1 and 2; and by article 1, section 50; and shall be bound by any additional duties imposed by articles 1 and 2 starting on the first day of the next month starting after the effective date of articles 1 and 2 or on the next anniversary date of the appointment, whichever occurs later.

"(c) Any act done prior to the effective date of articles 1 and 2 in any proceeding and any right accrued under Minnesota Statutes, chapter 525, prior to the effective date of articles 1 and 2 shall not be impaired by articles 1 and 2. If a right is acquired, extinguished, or barred upon the expiration of a prescribed period of time which has commenced to run in accordance with the provisions of any statute before the effective date of articles 1 and 2, the provisions of the prior statute shall remain in force with respect to that right notwithstanding the statute's amendment or repeal by articles 1 and 2.

"(d) An order of the court or letters of guardianship or conservatorship issued by the court prior to the effective date of articles 1 and 2 shall remain in full force and effect in accordance with its terms and conditions and in accordance with the provisions of prior law

until the court modifies the order or letters in accordance with the provisions of articles 1 and 2. Upon request for a certified copy of an order or letters which remains in full force and effect under this paragraph, the court administrator shall certify that the order or letters remains in full force and effect pursuant to this paragraph.

"(e) The court, without hearing or notice to any person, may issue new letters of guardianship or conservatorship under articles 1 and 2 to replace similar letters issued prior to the effective date of articles 1 and 2. The new letters shall be effective under articles 1 and 2 with the same force and effect as the prior letters and shall remain in full force and effect until modified by the court in accordance with the provisions of articles 1 and 2.

"(f) A power of attorney executed in accordance with Minnesota Statutes, section 524.5–505, prior to the effective date of articles 1 and 2, or any surety bond, deed, or other instrument, report, or other undertaking executed in accordance with Minnesota Statutes, chapter 525, prior to the effective date of articles 1 and 2, shall remain in full force and effect for all purposes in accordance with its terms and conditions and the provisions of the applicable statutes under which the power of attorney, surety bond, deed, or other instrument, report, or other undertaking was executed, until the power of attorney, surety bond, deed, or other instrument, report, or other undertaking expires according to its terms or pursuant to the statutes governing its execution, or is modified, terminated, or superseded by a new power of attorney, surety bond, deed, or other instrument, report, or other undertaking executed in accordance with the provisions of articles 1 and 2."

524.5–207. Powers and duties of guardian

Subdivision 1. General statement. A guardian of a minor has the powers and responsibilities of a parent who has not been deprived of custody of the minor and unemancipated child, except that a guardian is not legally obligated to provide from the guardian's own funds for the ward.

Subd. 2. Particular duties. In particular, and without qualifying subdivision 1, a guardian has the duties and powers in this subdivision.

(a) The guardian must take reasonable care of the ward's personal effects and commence protective proceedings if necessary to protect other property of the ward.

(b) The guardian may receive money payable for the support of the ward to the ward's parent, guardian, or custodian under the terms of any statutory benefit or insurance system, or any private contract, devise, trust, conservatorship, or custodianship and also may receive money or property of the ward paid or delivered by virtue of section 524.5–104. Any sums received must be applied to the ward's current needs for support, care, and education.

The guardian must exercise due care to conserve any excess for the ward's future needs unless a conservator has been appointed for the estate of the ward, in which case the excess must be paid at least annually to the conservator. Money received by the guardian under this paragraph must not be used for compensation for the guardian's services except as approved by court order or as determined by a duly appointed conservator other than the guardian.

A guardian may institute proceedings to compel the performance by any person of a duty to support the ward or to pay sums for the welfare of the ward.

(c) The guardian is empowered to facilitate the ward's education, social, or other activities and to authorize medical or other professional care, treatment, or advice. A ward who is less than 16 years of age may be admitted to a treatment facility as an informal patient according to section 253B.04 but may not be committed to any state institution except pursuant to chapter 253B. No guardian may give consent for psychosurgery, electroshock, sterilization, or experimental treatment of any kind unless the procedure is first approved by the order of the court, after a hearing as prescribed by section 524.5–313, paragraph (c), clause (4). A guardian is not liable by reason of consent for injury to the ward resulting from the negligence or acts of third persons unless it would have been illegal for a parent to have consented, or unless the guardian fails to comply with the requirements of this section which provide that a court order is necessary for commitment and for certain types of medical procedures. A guardian may consent to the marriage or adoption of the ward.

(d) A guardian must report the condition of the ward and of the ward's estate which has been subject to the guardian's possession or control, as ordered by the court on its own motion or on petition of any interested person and as required by court rule.

(e) If there is no acting conservator of the estate for the ward, the guardian has the power to apply on behalf of the ward for any assistance, services, or benefits available to the ward through any unit of government.

Laws 2003, c. 12, art. 1, § 23.

Historical and Statutory Notes

Laws 2003, c. 12, art. 2, § 9, provided:

"(a) Articles 1 and 2 apply to each guardianship or conservatorship proceeding and each appointment of guardian or conservator commenced on or after the effective date of articles 1 and 2. Except as otherwise provided in this section, articles 1 and 2 apply to each guardianship or conservatorship approved by the court prior to the effective date of articles 1 and 2, and to any guardianship or conservatorship proceeding pending in court on the effective date of articles 1 and 2, unless the court finds for good cause or in the interests of judicial economy that the proceeding should be completed under the provisions of Minnesota Statutes, chapter 525, as it existed prior to the effective date of articles 1 and 2.

"(b) A guardian or conservator who is not discharged prior to the effective date of articles 1 and 2 shall continue to hold the appointment but shall have only the powers specified in the order of appointment and in Minnesota Statutes, chapter 525, as it existed prior to the effective date of articles 1 and 2. Each guardian or conservator holding an appointment on the effective date of articles 1 and 2 shall continue to be bound by the duties imposed by the order of appointment; by Minnesota Statutes, chapter 525, as it existed prior to the effective date of articles 1 and 2; and by article 1, section 50; and shall be bound by any additional duties imposed by articles 1 and 2 starting on the first day of the next month starting after the effective date of articles 1 and 2 or on the next anniversary date of the appointment, whichever occurs later.

"(c) Any act done prior to the effective date of articles 1 and 2 in any proceeding and any right accrued under Minnesota Statutes, chapter 525, prior to the effective date of articles 1 and 2 shall not be impaired by articles 1 and 2. If a right is acquired, extinguished, or barred upon the expiration of a prescribed period of time which has commenced to run in accordance with the provisions of any statute before the effective date of articles 1 and 2, the provisions of the prior statute shall remain in force with respect to that right notwithstanding the statute's amendment or repeal by articles 1 and 2.

"(d) An order of the court or letters of guardianship or conservatorship issued by the court prior to the effective date of articles 1 and 2 shall remain in full force and effect in accordance with its terms and conditions and in accordance with the provisions of prior law until the court modifies the order or letters in accordance with the provisions of articles 1 and

2. Upon request for a certified copy of an order or letters which remains in full force and effect under this paragraph, the court administrator shall certify that the order or letters remains in full force and effect pursuant to this paragraph.

"(e) The court, without hearing or notice to any person, may issue new letters of guardianship or conservatorship under articles 1 and 2 to replace similar letters issued prior to the effective date of articles 1 and 2. The new letters shall be effective under articles 1 and 2 with the same force and effect as the prior letters and shall remain in full force and effect until modified by the court in accordance with the provisions of articles 1 and 2.

"(f) A power of attorney executed in accordance with Minnesota Statutes, section 524.5–505, prior to the effective date of articles 1 and 2, or any surety bond, deed, or other instrument, report, or other undertaking executed in accordance with Minnesota Statutes, chapter 525, prior to the effective date of articles 1 and 2, shall remain in full force and effect for all purposes in accordance with its terms and conditions and the provisions of the applicable statutes under which the power of attorney, surety bond, deed, or other instrument, report, or other undertaking was executed, until the power of attorney, surety bond, deed, or other instrument, report, or other undertaking expires according to its terms or pursuant to the statutes governing its execution, or is modified, terminated, or superseded by a new power of attorney, surety bond, deed, or other instrument, report, or other undertaking executed in accordance with the provisions of articles 1 and 2."

524.5–209. Rights and immunities of guardian

(a) A guardian of a minor ward is entitled to reasonable compensation for services as guardian and to reimbursement for expenditures made on behalf of the ward, in a manner consistent with section 524.5–502.

(b) A guardian of a minor ward is not liable to a third person for acts of the ward solely by reason of the relationship. A guardian of a minor ward is not liable for injury to the ward resulting from the negligence or act of a third person providing medical or other care, treatment, or service for the ward except to the extent that a parent would be liable under the circumstances.

(c) A guardian of a minor ward may not initiate the commitment of a ward to an institution except in accordance with section 524.5–207.

Laws 2003, c. 12, art. 1, § 24.

Historical and Statutory Notes

Laws 2003, c. 12, art. 2, § 9, provided:

"(a) Articles 1 and 2 apply to each guardianship or conservatorship proceeding and each appointment of guardian or conservator commenced on or after the effective date of articles 1 and 2. Except as otherwise provided in this section, articles 1 and 2 apply to each guardianship or conservatorship approved by the court prior to the effective date of articles 1 and 2, and to any guardianship or conservatorship proceeding pending in court on the effective date of articles 1 and 2, unless the court finds for good cause or in the interests of judicial economy that the proceeding should be completed under the provisions of Minnesota Statutes, chapter 525, as it existed prior to the effective date of articles 1 and 2.

"(b) A guardian or conservator who is not discharged prior to the effective date of articles 1 and 2 shall continue to hold the appointment but shall have only the powers specified in the order of appointment and in Minnesota Statutes, chapter 525, as it existed prior to the effective date of articles 1 and 2. Each guardian or conservator holding an appointment on the effective date of articles 1 and 2 shall continue to be bound by the duties imposed by the order of appointment; by Minnesota Statutes, chapter 525, as it existed prior to the effective date of articles 1 and 2; and by article 1, section 50; and shall be bound by any additional duties imposed by articles 1 and 2 starting on the first day of the next month starting after the effective date of articles 1 and 2 or on the next anniversary date of the appointment, whichever occurs later.

"(c) Any act done prior to the effective date of articles 1 and 2 in any proceeding and any right accrued under Minnesota Statutes, chapter 525, prior to the effective date of articles 1 and 2 shall not be impaired by articles 1 and 2. If a right is acquired, extinguished, or barred upon the expiration of a prescribed period of time which has commenced to run in accordance with the provisions of any statute before the effective date of articles 1 and 2, the provisions of the prior statute shall remain in force with respect to that right notwithstanding the statute's amendment or repeal by articles 1 and 2.

"(d) An order of the court or letters of guardianship or conservatorship issued by the court prior to the effective date of articles 1 and 2 shall remain in full force and effect in accordance with its terms and conditions and in accordance with the provisions of prior law until the court modifies the order or letters in accordance with the provisions of articles 1 and 2. Upon request for a certified copy of an order or letters which remains in full force and effect under this paragraph, the court administrator shall certify that the order or letters remains in full force and effect pursuant to this paragraph.

"(e) The court, without hearing or notice to any person, may issue new letters of guardianship or conservatorship under articles 1 and 2 to replace similar letters issued prior to the effective date of articles 1 and 2. The new letters shall be effective under articles 1 and 2 with the same force and effect as the prior letters and shall remain in full force and effect until modified by the court in accordance with the provisions of articles 1 and 2.

"(f) A power of attorney executed in accordance with Minnesota Statutes, section 524.5–505, prior to the effective date of articles 1 and 2, or any surety bond, deed, or other instrument, report, or other undertaking executed in accordance with Minnesota Statutes, chapter 525, prior to the effective date of articles 1 and 2, shall remain in full force and effect for all purposes in accordance with its terms and conditions and the provisions of the applicable statutes under which the power of attorney, surety bond, deed, or other instrument, report, or other undertaking was executed, until the power of attorney, surety bond, deed, or other instrument, report, or other undertaking expires according to its terms or pursuant to the statutes governing its execution, or is modified, terminated, or superseded by a new power of attorney, surety bond, deed, or other instrument, report, or other undertaking executed in accordance with the provisions of articles 1 and 2."

524.5–210. Termination of guardianship; other proceedings after appointment

(a) A guardianship of a minor terminates upon the minor's death, adoption, emancipation, attainment of majority, or as ordered by the court.

(b) A ward or an interested person may petition for any order that is in the best interest of the ward. The petitioner shall give notice of the hearing on the petition to interested persons pursuant to section 524.5–113 and to any other person as ordered by the court, except notice is not required for the ward if the ward has not attained 14 years of age and is not the petitioner.

Laws 2003, c. 12, art. 1, § 25.

Historical and Statutory Notes

Laws 2003, c. 12, art. 2, § 9, provided:

"(a) Articles 1 and 2 apply to each guardianship or conservatorship proceeding and each appointment of guardian or conservator commenced on or after the effective date of articles 1 and 2. Except as otherwise provided in this section, articles 1 and 2 apply to each guardianship or conservatorship approved by the court prior to the effective date of articles 1 and 2, and to any guardianship or conservatorship proceeding pending in court on the effective date of articles 1 and 2, unless the court finds for good cause or in the interests of judicial economy that the proceeding should be completed under the provisions of Minnesota Statutes, chapter 525, as it existed prior to the effective date of articles 1 and 2.

"(b) A guardian or conservator who is not discharged prior to the effective date of articles 1 and 2 shall continue to hold the appointment but shall have only the powers specified in the order of appointment and in Minnesota Statutes, chapter 525, as it existed prior to the effective date of articles 1 and 2. Each guardian or conservator holding an appointment on the effective date of articles 1 and 2 shall continue to be bound by the duties imposed by the order of appointment; by Minnesota Statutes, chapter 525, as it existed prior to the effective date of articles 1 and 2; and by article 1, section 50; and shall be bound by any additional duties imposed by articles 1 and 2 starting on the first day of the next month starting after the effective date of articles 1 and 2 or on the next anniversary date of the appointment, whichever occurs later.

"(c) Any act done prior to the effective date of articles 1 and 2 in any proceeding and any right accrued under Minnesota Statutes, chapter 525, prior to the effective date of articles 1 and 2 shall not be impaired by articles 1 and 2. If a right is acquired, extinguished, or barred upon the expiration of a prescribed period of time which has commenced to run in accordance with the provisions of any statute before the effective date of articles 1 and 2, the provisions of the prior statute shall remain in force with respect to that right notwithstanding the statute's amendment or repeal by articles 1 and 2.

"(d) An order of the court or letters of guardianship or conservatorship issued by the court prior to the effective date of articles 1 and 2 shall remain in full force and effect in accordance with its terms and conditions and in accordance with the provisions of prior law until the court modifies the order or letters in accordance with the provisions of articles 1 and 2. Upon request for a certified copy of an order or letters which remains in full force and effect under this paragraph, the court administrator shall certify that the order or letters remains in full force and effect pursuant to this paragraph.

"(e) The court, without hearing or notice to any person, may issue new letters of guardianship or conservatorship under articles 1 and 2 to replace similar letters issued prior to the effective date of articles 1 and 2. The new letters shall be effective under articles 1 and 2 with the same force and effect as the prior letters and shall remain in full force and effect until modified by the court in accordance with the provisions of articles 1 and 2.

"(f) A power of attorney executed in accordance with Minnesota Statutes, section 524.5–505, prior to the effective date of articles 1 and 2, or any surety bond, deed, or other instrument, report, or other undertaking executed in accordance with Minnesota Statutes, chapter 525, prior to the effective date of articles 1 and 2, shall remain in full force and effect for all purposes in accordance with its terms and conditions and the provisions of the applicable statutes under which the power of attorney, surety bond, deed, or other instrument, report, or other undertaking was executed, until the power of attorney, surety bond, deed, or other instrument, report, or other undertaking expires according to its terms or pursuant to the statutes governing its execution, or is modified, terminated, or superseded by a new power of attorney, surety bond, deed, or other instrument, report, or other undertaking executed in accordance with the provisions of articles 1 and 2."

524.5–211. Delegation of power by parent or guardian

(a) A parent, legal custodian, or guardian of a minor or incapacitated person, by a properly executed power of attorney, may delegate to another person, for a period not exceeding one year, any powers regarding care, custody, or property of the minor or ward, except the power to consent to marriage or adoption of a minor ward.

(b) A parent who executes a delegation of powers under this section must mail or give a copy of the document to any other parent within 30 days of its execution unless:

(1) the other parent does not have parenting time or has supervised parenting time; or

(2) there is an existing order for protection under chapter 518B or a similar law of another state in effect against the other parent to protect the parent, legal custodian, or guardian executing the delegation of powers or the child.

(c) A parent, legal custodian, or guardian of a minor child may also delegate those powers by designating a standby or temporary custodian under chapter 257B.

Laws 2003, c. 12, art. 1, § 26.

Historical and Statutory Notes

Laws 2003, c. 12, art. 2, § 9, provided:

"(a) Articles 1 and 2 apply to each guardianship or conservatorship proceeding and each appointment of guardian or conservator commenced on or after the effective date of articles 1 and 2. Except as otherwise provided in this section, articles 1 and 2 apply to each guardianship or conservatorship approved by the court prior to the effective date of articles 1 and 2, and to any guardianship or conservatorship proceeding pending in court on the effective date of articles 1 and 2, unless the court finds for good cause or in the interests of judicial economy that the proceeding should be completed under the provisions of Minnesota Statutes, chapter 525, as it existed prior to the effective date of articles 1 and 2.

"(b) A guardian or conservator who is not discharged prior to the effective date of articles 1 and 2 shall continue to hold the appointment but shall have only the powers specified in the order of appointment and in Minnesota Statutes, chapter 525, as it existed prior to the effective date of articles 1 and 2. Each guardian or conservator holding an appointment on the effective date of articles 1 and 2 shall continue to be bound by the duties imposed by the order of appointment; by Minnesota Statutes, chapter 525, as it existed prior to the effective date of articles 1 and 2; and by article 1, section 50; and shall be bound by any additional duties imposed by articles 1 and 2 starting on the first day of the next month starting after the effective date of articles 1 and 2 or on the next

anniversary date of the appointment, whichever occurs later.

"(c) Any act done prior to the effective date of articles 1 and 2 in any proceeding and any right accrued under Minnesota Statutes, chapter 525, prior to the effective date of articles 1 and 2 shall not be impaired by articles 1 and 2. If a right is acquired, extinguished, or barred upon the expiration of a prescribed period of time which has commenced to run in accordance with the provisions of any statute before the effective date of articles 1 and 2, the provisions of the prior statute shall remain in force with respect to that right notwithstanding the statute's amendment or repeal by articles 1 and 2.

"(d) An order of the court or letters of guardianship or conservatorship issued by the court prior to the effective date of articles 1 and 2 shall remain in full force and effect in accordance with its terms and conditions and in accordance with the provisions of prior law until the court modifies the order or letters in accordance with the provisions of articles 1 and 2. Upon request for a certified copy of an order or letters which remains in full force and effect under this paragraph, the court administrator shall certify that the order or letters remains in full force and effect pursuant to this paragraph.

"(e) The court, without hearing or notice to any person, may issue new letters of guardianship or conservatorship under articles 1 and 2 to replace similar letters issued prior to the effective date of articles 1 and 2. The new letters shall be effective under articles 1 and 2 with the same force and effect as the prior letters and shall remain in full force and effect until modified by the court in accordance with the provisions of articles 1 and 2.

"(f) A power of attorney executed in accordance with Minnesota Statutes, section 524.5–505, prior to the effective date of articles 1 and 2, or any surety bond, deed, or other instrument, report, or other undertaking executed in accordance with Minnesota Statutes, chapter 525, prior to the effective date of articles 1 and 2, shall remain in full force and effect for all purposes in accordance with its terms

and conditions and the provisions of the applicable statutes under which the power of attorney, surety bond, deed, or other instrument, report, or other undertaking was executed, until the power of attorney, surety bond, deed, or other instrument, report, or other undertaking expires according to its terms or pursuant to the statutes governing its execution, or is modified, terminated, or superseded by a new power of attorney, surety bond, deed, or other instrument, report, or other undertaking executed in accordance with the provisions of articles 1 and 2."

PART 3

GUARDIAN OF INCAPACITATED PERSON

524.5–301. Appointment and status of guardian

A person becomes a guardian of an incapacitated person by a parental or spousal appointment or upon appointment by the court. The guardianship continues until terminated, without regard to the location of the guardian or ward.

Laws 2003, c. 12, art. 1, § 27.

Historical and Statutory Notes

Laws 2003, c. 12, art. 2, § 9, provided:

"(a) Articles 1 and 2 apply to each guardianship or conservatorship proceeding and each appointment of guardian or conservator commenced on or after the effective date of articles 1 and 2. Except as otherwise provided in this section, articles 1 and 2 apply to each guardianship or conservatorship approved by the court prior to the effective date of articles 1 and 2, and to any guardianship or conservatorship proceeding pending in court on the effective date of articles 1 and 2, unless the court finds for good cause or in the interests of judicial economy that the proceeding should be completed under the provisions of Minnesota Statutes, chapter 525, as it existed prior to the effective date of articles 1 and 2.

"(b) A guardian or conservator who is not discharged prior to the effective date of articles 1 and 2 shall continue to hold the appointment but shall have only the powers specified in the order of appointment and in Minnesota Statutes, chapter 525, as it existed prior to the effective date of articles 1 and 2. Each guardian or conservator holding an appointment on the effective date of articles 1 and 2 shall continue to be bound by the duties imposed by the order of appointment; by Minnesota Statutes,

chapter 525, as it existed prior to the effective date of articles 1 and 2; and by article 1, section 50; and shall be bound by any additional duties imposed by articles 1 and 2 starting on the first day of the next month starting after the effective date of articles 1 and 2 or on the next anniversary date of the appointment, whichever occurs later.

"(c) Any act done prior to the effective date of articles 1 and 2 in any proceeding and any right accrued under Minnesota Statutes, chapter 525, prior to the effective date of articles 1 and 2 shall not be impaired by articles 1 and 2. If a right is acquired, extinguished, or barred upon the expiration of a prescribed period of time which has commenced to run in accordance with the provisions of any statute before the effective date of articles 1 and 2, the provisions of the prior statute shall remain in force with respect to that right notwithstanding the statute's amendment or repeal by articles 1 and 2.

"(d) An order of the court or letters of guardianship or conservatorship issued by the court prior to the effective date of articles 1 and 2 shall remain in full force and effect in accordance with its terms and conditions and in accordance with the provisions of prior law until the court modifies the order or letters in

accordance with the provisions of articles 1 and 2. Upon request for a certified copy of an order or letters which remains in full force and effect under this paragraph, the court administrator shall certify that the order or letters remains in full force and effect pursuant to this paragraph.

"(e) The court, without hearing or notice to any person, may issue new letters of guardianship or conservatorship under articles 1 and 2 to replace similar letters issued prior to the effective date of articles 1 and 2. The new letters shall be effective under articles 1 and 2 with the same force and effect as the prior letters and shall remain in full force and effect until modified by the court in accordance with the provisions of articles 1 and 2.

"(f) A power of attorney executed in accordance with Minnesota Statutes, section 524.5–505, prior to the effective date of articles 1 and 2, or any surety bond, deed, or other instrument, report, or other undertaking executed in accordance with Minnesota Statutes, chapter 525, prior to the effective date of articles 1 and 2, shall remain in full force and effect for all purposes in accordance with its terms and conditions and the provisions of the applicable statutes under which the power of attorney, surety bond, deed, or other instrument, report, or other undertaking was executed, until the power of attorney, surety bond, deed, or other instrument, report, or other undertaking expires according to its terms or pursuant to the statutes governing its execution, or is modified, terminated, or superseded by a new power of attorney, surety bond, deed, or other instrument, report, or other undertaking executed in accordance with the provisions of articles 1 and 2."

524.5–302. Appointment of guardian by will or other writing

(a) A parent, by will or other signed writing executed in the same manner as a health care directive pursuant to chapter 145C, may appoint a guardian for an unmarried child who the parent believes is an incapacitated person, may specify the desired limitations on the powers to be given to the guardian, and may revoke or amend the appointment prior to court confirmation.

(b) An individual by will or other signed writing executed in the same manner as a health care directive pursuant to chapter 145C may appoint a guardian for his or her spouse who the appointing spouse believes is an incapacitated person, may specify the desired limitations on the powers to be given to the guardian, and may revoke or amend the appointment prior to court confirmation.

(c) Subject to the right of the incapacitated person, the person having custody or care of the incapacitated person if other than the appointing parent or spouse or the adult nearest in kinship to the incapacitated person to object, the guardian's appointment becomes effective upon the death of the appointing parent or spouse, the adjudication of incapacity of the appointing parent or spouse, or a written determination by a physician who has examined the appointing parent or spouse that the appointing parent or spouse is no longer able to care for the incapacitated person, whichever occurs first.

(d) Upon petition of the appointing parent or spouse, and a finding that the appointing parent or spouse will likely become unable to care for the incapacitated person within two years or less, and after notice as provided in this section, the court, before the appointment becomes effective, may confirm the appointing parent's or spouse's selection of a guardian and terminate the rights of others to object.

(e) The guardian becomes eligible to act upon the filing of an acceptance of appointment, which must be filed within 30 days following the effective date of the guardian's appointment. The guardian shall:

(1) file the notice of acceptance of appointment and a copy of the will with the court of the county in which the will was or could be probated or, in the case of another appointing instrument, file the acceptance of appointment and the appointing instrument with the court in the county in which the incapacitated person resides or is present; and

(2) give written notice of the acceptance of appointment to the appointing parent or spouse if living, the incapacitated person, a person having custody or care of the incapacitated person other than the appointing parent or spouse, and the adult nearest in kinship.

(f) Unless the appointment was previously confirmed by the court, the notice given under paragraph (e), clause (2), must include a statement of the right of those notified to terminate the appointment by filing a written objection as provided in this section.

(g) An appointment effected by filing the guardian's acceptance under a will probated in the state of the testator's domicile is effective in this state.

(h) The filing of a written objection to an appointment by the alleged incapacitated person or another interested person in the court in which the guardian's written acceptance was filed terminates the appointment. An objection may be withdrawn and, if withdrawn, is of no effect. An objection does not preclude the court from appointing the parental or spousal appointee as guardian. The court may treat the filing of an objection as a petition for the appointment of an emergency guardian under section 524.5–311 or for the appointment of a limited or unlimited guardian under section 524.5–303 and proceed accordingly.

(i) Unless the appointment was previously confirmed by the court, within 30 days after filing the notice and the appointing instrument, a guardian appointed under this section shall file a petition in the court for confirmation of the appointment, giving notice in the manner provided in section 524.5–308, and, if necessary, for an appointment as conservator.

(j) The authority of a guardian appointed under this section terminates upon the first to occur of the appointment of a guardian by the court or the giving of written notice to the guardian of the filing of an objection pursuant to paragraph (h).

(k) The appointment of a guardian under this section is not a determination of incapacity.

(*l*) The powers of a guardian who timely complies with the requirements of paragraphs (e) and (f) relate back to give acts by the guardian which are of benefit to the incapacitated person and occurred on or after the date the appointment became effective the same effect as those that occurred after the filing of the acceptance of appointment.

Laws 2003, c. 12, art. 1, § 28.

Historical and Statutory Notes

Laws 2003, c. 12, art. 2, § 9, provided:

"(a) Articles 1 and 2 apply to each guardianship or conservatorship proceeding and each appointment of guardian or conservator commenced on or after the effective date of articles 1 and 2. Except as otherwise provided in this section, articles 1 and 2 apply to each guardianship or conservatorship approved by the court prior to the effective date of articles 1 and 2, and to any guardianship or conservatorship proceeding pending in court on the effective date of articles 1 and 2, unless the court finds for good cause or in the interests of judicial economy that the proceeding should be completed under the provisions of Minnesota Statutes, chapter 525, as it existed prior to the effective date of articles 1 and 2.

"(b) A guardian or conservator who is not discharged prior to the effective date of articles 1 and 2 shall continue to hold the appointment but shall have only the powers specified in the order of appointment and in Minnesota Statutes, chapter 525, as it existed prior to the effective date of articles 1 and 2. Each guardian or conservator holding an appointment on the effective date of articles 1 and 2 shall continue to be bound by the duties imposed by the order of appointment; by Minnesota Statutes, chapter 525, as it existed prior to the effective date of articles 1 and 2; and by article 1, section 50; and shall be bound by any additional duties imposed by articles 1 and 2 starting on the first day of the next month starting after the effective date of articles 1 and 2 or on the next anniversary date of the appointment, whichever occurs later.

"(c) Any act done prior to the effective date of articles 1 and 2 in any proceeding and any right accrued under Minnesota Statutes, chapter 525, prior to the effective date of articles 1 and 2 shall not be impaired by articles 1 and 2. If a right is acquired, extinguished, or barred upon the expiration of a prescribed period of time which has commenced to run in accordance with the provisions of any statute before the effective date of articles 1 and 2, the provisions of the prior statute shall remain in force with respect to that right notwithstanding the statute's amendment or repeal by articles 1 and 2.

"(d) An order of the court or letters of guardianship or conservatorship issued by the court prior to the effective date of articles 1 and 2 shall remain in full force and effect in accordance with its terms and conditions and in accordance with the provisions of prior law until the court modifies the order or letters in accordance with the provisions of articles 1 and 2. Upon request for a certified copy of an order or letters which remains in full force and effect under this paragraph, the court administrator shall certify that the order or letters remains in full force and effect pursuant to this paragraph.

"(e) The court, without hearing or notice to any person, may issue new letters of guardianship or conservatorship under articles 1 and 2 to replace similar letters issued prior to the effective date of articles 1 and 2. The new letters shall be effective under articles 1 and 2 with the same force and effect as the prior letters and shall remain in full force and effect until modified by the court in accordance with the provisions of articles 1 and 2.

"(f) A power of attorney executed in accordance with Minnesota Statutes, section 524.5–505, prior to the effective date of articles 1 and 2, or any surety bond, deed, or other instrument, report, or other undertaking executed in accordance with Minnesota Statutes, chapter 525, prior to the effective date of articles 1 and 2, shall remain in full force and effect for all purposes in accordance with its terms and conditions and the provisions of the applicable statutes under which the power of attorney, surety bond, deed, or other instrument, report, or other undertaking was executed, until the power of attorney, surety bond, deed, or other instrument, report, or other undertaking expires according to its terms or pursuant to the statutes governing its execution, or is modified, terminated, or superseded by a new power of attorney, surety bond, deed, or other instrument, report, or other undertaking executed in accordance with the provisions of articles 1 and 2."

524.5–303. Judicial appointment of guardian: petition

(a) An individual or a person interested in the individual's welfare may petition for a determination of incapacity, in whole or in part, and for the appointment of a limited or unlimited guardian for the individual.

(b) The petition must set forth the petitioner's name, residence, current address if different, relationship to the respondent, and interest in the appointment and, to the extent known, state or contain the following with respect to the respondent and the relief requested:

(1) the respondent's name, age, principal residence, current street address, and, if different, the address of the dwelling in which it is proposed that the respondent will reside if the appointment is made;

(2) the name and address of the respondent's:

(i) spouse, or if the respondent has none, an adult with whom the respondent has resided for more than six months before the filing of the petition; and

(ii) adult children or, if the respondent has none, the respondent's parents and adult brothers and sisters, or if the respondent has none, at least one of the adults nearest in kinship to the respondent who can be found;

(3) the name of the administrative head and address of the institution where the respondent is a patient, resident, or client of any hospital, nursing home, home care agency, or other institution;

(4) the name and address of any legal representative for the respondent;

(5) the name and address of any person nominated as guardian by the respondent;

(6) the name and address of any proposed guardian and the reason why the proposed guardian should be selected;

(7) the name and address of any health care agent or proxy appointed pursuant to a health care directive as defined in section 145C.01, a living will under chapter 145B, or other similar document executed in another state and enforceable under the laws of this state;

(8) the reason why guardianship is necessary, including a brief description of the nature and extent of the respondent's alleged incapacity;

(9) if an unlimited guardianship is requested, the reason why limited guardianship is inappropriate and, if a limited guardianship is requested, the powers to be granted to the limited guardian; and

(10) a general statement of the respondent's property with an estimate of its value, including any insurance or pension, and the source and amount of any other anticipated income or receipts.

Laws 2003, c. 12, art. 1, § 29.

Historical and Statutory Notes

Laws 2003, c. 12, art. 2, § 9, provided:

"(a) Articles 1 and 2 apply to each guardianship or conservatorship proceeding and each appointment of guardian or conservator commenced on or after the effective date of articles 1 and 2. Except as otherwise provided in this section, articles 1 and 2 apply to each guardianship or conservatorship approved by the court prior to the effective date of articles 1 and 2, and to any guardianship or conservatorship proceeding pending in court on the effective date of articles 1 and 2, unless the court finds for good cause or in the interests of judicial economy that the proceeding should be completed under the provisions of Minnesota Statutes, chapter 525, as it existed prior to the effective date of articles 1 and 2.

"(b) A guardian or conservator who is not discharged prior to the effective date of articles 1 and 2 shall continue to hold the appointment but shall have only the powers specified in the order of appointment and in Minnesota Statutes, chapter 525, as it existed prior to the effective date of articles 1 and 2. Each guardian or conservator holding an appointment on the effective date of articles 1 and 2 shall continue to be bound by the duties imposed by the order of appointment; by Minnesota Statutes, chapter 525, as it existed prior to the effective date of articles 1 and 2; and by article 1, section 50; and shall be bound by any additional duties imposed by articles 1 and 2 starting on the first day of the next month starting after the effective date of articles 1 and 2 or on the next anniversary date of the appointment, whichever occurs later.

"(c) Any act done prior to the effective date of articles 1 and 2 in any proceeding and any right accrued under Minnesota Statutes, chapter 525, prior to the effective date of articles 1 and 2 shall not be impaired by articles 1 and 2. If a right is acquired, extinguished, or barred upon the expiration of a prescribed period of time which has commenced to run in accordance with the provisions of any statute before the effective date of articles 1 and 2, the provisions of the prior statute shall remain in force with respect to that right notwithstanding the statute's amendment or repeal by articles 1 and 2.

"(d) An order of the court or letters of guardianship or conservatorship issued by the court prior to the effective date of articles 1 and 2 shall remain in full force and effect in accordance with its terms and conditions and in accordance with the provisions of prior law until the court modifies the order or letters in accordance with the provisions of articles 1 and 2. Upon request for a certified copy of an order or letters which remains in full force and effect under this paragraph, the court administrator shall certify that the order or letters remains in full force and effect pursuant to this paragraph.

"(e) The court, without hearing or notice to any person, may issue new letters of guardianship or conservatorship under articles 1 and 2 to replace similar letters issued prior to the effective date of articles 1 and 2. The new letters shall be effective under articles 1 and 2 with the same force and effect as the prior letters and shall remain in full force and effect until modified by the court in accordance with the provisions of articles 1 and 2.

"(f) A power of attorney executed in accordance with Minnesota Statutes, section 524.5–505, prior to the effective date of articles 1 and 2, or any surety bond, deed, or other instrument, report, or other undertaking executed in accordance with Minnesota Statutes, chapter 525, prior to the effective date of articles 1 and 2, shall remain in full force and effect for all purposes in accordance with its terms and conditions and the provisions of the applicable statutes under which the power of attorney, surety bond, deed, or other instrument, report, or other undertaking was executed, until the power of attorney, surety bond, deed, or other instrument, report, or other undertaking expires according to its terms or pursuant to the statutes governing its execution, or is modified, terminated, or superseded by a new power of attorney, surety bond, deed, or other instrument, report, or other undertaking executed in accordance with the provisions of articles 1 and 2."

524.5–304. Judicial appointment of guardian: preliminaries to hearing

(a) Upon receipt of a petition to establish a guardianship, the court shall set a date and time for hearing the petition and may appoint a visitor. The duties and reporting requirements of the visitor are limited to the relief requested in the petition.

(b) A proposed ward has the right to be represented by counsel at any proceeding under this article. The court shall appoint counsel to represent the proposed ward for the initial proceeding held pursuant to section 524.5–307 if neither the proposed ward nor others provide counsel unless in a meeting with a visitor the proposed ward specifically waives the right to counsel. Counsel must be appointed immediately after any petition under this article is served under section 524.5–308. Counsel has the full right of subpoena. In all proceedings under this article, counsel shall:

(1) consult with the proposed ward before any hearing;

(2) be given adequate time to prepare for all hearings; and

(3) continue to represent the person throughout any proceedings under section 524.5–307, provided that such appointment shall expire upon the expiration of the appeal time for the order appointing guardian or the order dismissing a petition, or upon such other time or event as the court may direct.

The court need not appoint counsel to represent the proposed ward on a voluntary petition, and the court may remove a court-appointed attorney at any time if the court finds that the proposed ward has made a knowing and intelligent waiver of the right to counsel or has obtained private counsel.

(c) The visitor shall personally serve the notice and petition upon the respondent and shall offer to read the notice and petition to the respondent, and if so requested the visitor shall read the notice and petition to such person. The visitor shall also interview the respondent in person, and to the extent that the respondent is able to understand:

(1) explain to the respondent the substance of the petition; the nature, purpose, and effect of the proceeding; the respondent's rights at the hearing; and the general powers and duties of a guardian;

(2) determine the respondent's views about the proposed guardian, the proposed guardian's powers and duties, and the scope and duration of the proposed guardianship;

(3) inform the respondent of the right to employ and consult with a lawyer at the respondent's own expense and the right to request a court-appointed lawyer; and

(4) inform the respondent that all costs and expenses of the proceeding, including respondent's attorneys fees, will be paid from the respondent's estate.

(d) In addition to the duties in paragraph (c), the visitor shall make any other investigation the court directs.

(e) The visitor shall promptly file a report in writing with the court, which must include:

(1) recommendations regarding the appropriateness of guardianship, including whether less restrictive means of intervention are available, the type of guardianship, and, if a limited guardianship, the powers to be granted to the limited guardian;

(2) a statement as to whether the respondent approves or disapproves of the proposed guardian, and the powers and duties proposed or the scope of the guardianship; and

(3) any other matters the court directs.

(f) The county social service agency may create a screening committee to review a petition involving an indigent person. The screening committee must consist of individuals selected by the agency with knowledge of alternatives that are less restrictive than guardianship. If the agency has created a screening committee, the court shall make its decision after the screening committee has reviewed the petition. For an indigent person, the court may appoint a guardian under contract with the county to provide these services.

Laws 2003, c. 12, art. 1, § 30. Amended by Laws 2004, c. 146, art. 2, § 3.

Historical and Statutory Notes

Laws 2003, c. 12, art. 2, § 9, provided:

"(a) Articles 1 and 2 apply to each guardianship or conservatorship proceeding and each appointment of guardian or conservator commenced on or after the effective date of articles 1 and 2. Except as otherwise provided in this section, articles 1 and 2 apply to each guardianship or conservatorship approved by the court prior to the effective date of articles 1 and 2, and to any guardianship or conservatorship proceeding pending in court on the effective date of articles 1 and 2, unless the court finds for good cause or in the interests of judicial economy that the proceeding should be completed under the provisions of Minnesota Statutes, chapter 525, as it existed prior to the effective date of articles 1 and 2.

"(b) A guardian or conservator who is not discharged prior to the effective date of articles 1 and 2 shall continue to hold the appointment but shall have only the powers specified in the order of appointment and in Minnesota Statutes, chapter 525, as it existed prior to the effective date of articles 1 and 2. Each guardian or conservator holding an appointment on the effective date of articles 1 and 2 shall continue to be bound by the duties imposed by the order of appointment; by Minnesota Statutes, chapter 525, as it existed prior to the effective date of articles 1 and 2; and by article 1, section 50; and shall be bound by any additional duties imposed by articles 1 and 2 starting on the first day of the next month starting after the effective date of articles 1 and 2 or on the next anniversary date of the appointment, whichever occurs later.

"(c) Any act done prior to the effective date of articles 1 and 2 in any proceeding and any right accrued under Minnesota Statutes, chapter 525, prior to the effective date of articles 1 and 2 shall not be impaired by articles 1 and 2. If a right is acquired, extinguished, or barred upon the expiration of a prescribed period of time which has commenced to run in accordance with the provisions of any statute before the effective date of articles 1 and 2, the provisions of the prior statute shall remain in force with respect to that right notwithstanding the statute's amendment or repeal by articles 1 and 2.

"(d) An order of the court or letters of guardianship or conservatorship issued by the court prior to the effective date of articles 1 and 2 shall remain in full force and effect in accordance with its terms and conditions and in accordance with the provisions of prior law until the court modifies the order or letters in accordance with the provisions of articles 1 and 2. Upon request for a certified copy of an order or letters which remains in full force and effect under this paragraph, the court administrator shall certify that the order or letters remains in full force and effect pursuant to this paragraph.

"(e) The court, without hearing or notice to any person, may issue new letters of guardianship or conservatorship under articles 1 and 2 to replace similar letters issued prior to the effective date of articles 1 and 2. The new letters shall be effective under articles 1 and 2 with the same force and effect as the prior letters and shall remain in full force and effect until modified by the court in accordance with the provisions of articles 1 and 2.

"(f) A power of attorney executed in accordance with Minnesota Statutes, section 524.5–505, prior to the effective date of articles 1 and 2, or any surety bond, deed, or other instrument, report, or other undertaking executed in accordance with Minnesota Statutes, chapter 525, prior to the effective date of articles 1 and 2, shall remain in full force and effect for all purposes in accordance with its terms and conditions and the provisions of the applicable statutes under which the power of attorney, surety bond, deed, or other instrument, report, or other undertaking was executed, until the power of attorney, surety bond, deed, or other instrument, report, or other undertaking expires according to its terms or pursuant to the statutes governing its execution, or is modified, terminated, or superseded by a new power of attorney, surety bond, deed, or other instrument, report, or other undertaking executed in accordance with the provisions of articles 1 and 2."

524.5–307. Judicial appointment of guardian; presence and rights at hearing

(a) Unless excused by the court for good cause, the petitioner and the proposed guardian shall attend the hearing. The respondent shall attend and participate in the hearing, unless excused by the court for good cause. The petitioner and respondent may present evidence and subpoena witnesses and documents; examine witnesses, including the visitor; and otherwise participate in the hearing. The hearing may be held in a location convenient to the respondent and may be closed upon the request of the respondent and a showing of good cause.

(b) Any person may request permission to participate in the proceeding. The court may grant the request, with or without hearing, upon a showing of good cause and after determining that the best interest of the respondent will be served. The court may attach appropriate conditions to the participation.

Laws 2003, c. 12, art. 1, § 31.

Historical and Statutory Notes

Laws 2003, c. 12, art. 2, § 9, provided:

"(a) Articles 1 and 2 apply to each guardianship or conservatorship proceeding and each appointment of guardian or conservator commenced on or after the effective date of articles 1 and 2. Except as otherwise provided in this section, articles 1 and 2 apply to each guardianship or conservatorship approved by the court prior to the effective date of articles 1 and 2, and to any guardianship or conservatorship proceeding pending in court on the effective date of articles 1 and 2, unless the court finds for good cause or in the interests of judicial economy that the proceeding should be completed under the provisions of Minnesota Statutes, chapter 525, as it existed prior to the effective date of articles 1 and 2.

"(b) A guardian or conservator who is not discharged prior to the effective date of articles 1 and 2 shall continue to hold the appointment but shall have only the powers specified in the order of appointment and in Minnesota Statutes, chapter 525, as it existed prior to the effective date of articles 1 and 2. Each guardian or conservator holding an appointment on the effective date of articles 1 and 2 shall continue to be bound by the duties imposed by the order of appointment; by Minnesota Statutes, chapter 525, as it existed prior to the effective date of articles 1 and 2; and by article 1, section 50; and shall be bound by any additional duties imposed by articles 1 and 2 starting on the first day of the next month starting after the effective date of articles 1 and 2 or on the next

anniversary date of the appointment, whichever occurs later.

"(c) Any act done prior to the effective date of articles 1 and 2 in any proceeding and any right accrued under Minnesota Statutes, chapter 525, prior to the effective date of articles 1 and 2 shall not be impaired by articles 1 and 2. If a right is acquired, extinguished, or barred upon the expiration of a prescribed period of time which has commenced to run in accordance with the provisions of any statute before the effective date of articles 1 and 2, the provisions of the prior statute shall remain in force with respect to that right notwithstanding the statute's amendment or repeal by articles 1 and 2.

"(d) An order of the court or letters of guardianship or conservatorship issued by the court prior to the effective date of articles 1 and 2 shall remain in full force and effect in accordance with its terms and conditions and in accordance with the provisions of prior law until the court modifies the order or letters in accordance with the provisions of articles 1 and 2. Upon request for a certified copy of an order or letters which remains in full force and effect under this paragraph, the court administrator shall certify that the order or letters remains in full force and effect pursuant to this paragraph.

"(e) The court, without hearing or notice to any person, may issue new letters of guardianship or conservatorship under articles 1 and 2 to replace similar letters issued prior to the effective date of articles 1 and 2. The new letters shall be effective under articles 1 and 2 with the same force and effect as the prior letters and shall remain in full force and effect until modified by the court in accordance with the provisions of articles 1 and 2.

"(f) A power of attorney executed in accordance with Minnesota Statutes, section 524.5–505, prior to the effective date of articles 1 and 2, or any surety bond, deed, or other instrument, report, or other undertaking executed in accordance with Minnesota Statutes, chapter 525, prior to the effective date of articles 1 and 2, shall remain in full force and effect for all purposes in accordance with its terms

and conditions and the provisions of the applicable statutes under which the power of attorney, surety bond, deed, or other instrument, report, or other undertaking was executed, until the power of attorney, surety bond, deed, or other instrument, report, or other undertaking expires according to its terms or pursuant to the statutes governing its execution, or is modified, terminated, or superseded by a new power of attorney, surety bond, deed, or other instrument, report, or other undertaking executed in accordance with the provisions of articles 1 and 2."

524.5–308. Notice

(a) A copy of the petition and notice of the hearing on a petition for guardianship must be served personally on the respondent pursuant to section 524.5–304, paragraph (c). The notice must include a statement that the respondent must be physically present unless excused by the court; inform the respondent of the respondent's rights at the hearing; and include a description of the nature, purpose, and consequences of an appointment. A failure to serve the respondent with a notice substantially complying with this paragraph precludes the court from granting the petition.

(b) In a proceeding to establish a guardianship, notice of the hearing shall also be given to the persons listed in the petition. Failure to give notice under this paragraph does not preclude the appointment of a guardian or the making of a protective order.

(c) Notice of the hearing on a petition for an order after appointment of a guardian shall be given to interested persons pursuant to section 524.5–113 and to any other person as ordered by the court, except notice to the ward is not required if the ward has not attained 14 years of age and is not the petitioner.

(d) The guardian shall give notice of the filing of the guardian's report, together with a copy of the report, to the ward, the court, and any other person the court directs. The notice must be sent or delivered within 14 days after the filing of the report.

Laws 2003, c. 12, art. 1, § 32. Amended by Laws 2004, c. 146, art. 2, § 4.

Historical and Statutory Notes

Laws 2003, c. 12, art. 2, § 9, provided:

"(a) Articles 1 and 2 apply to each guardianship or conservatorship proceeding and each appointment of guardian or conservator commenced on or after the effective date of articles 1 and 2. Except as otherwise provided in this section, articles 1 and 2 apply to each guardianship or conservatorship approved by the court prior to the effective date of articles 1 and 2, and to any guardianship or conservatorship proceeding pending in court on the effective

date of articles 1 and 2, unless the court finds for good cause or in the interests of judicial economy that the proceeding should be completed under the provisions of Minnesota Statutes, chapter 525, as it existed prior to the effective date of articles 1 and 2.

"(b) A guardian or conservator who is not discharged prior to the effective date of articles 1 and 2 shall continue to hold the appointment but shall have only the powers specified in the order of appointment and in Minnesota Statutes, chapter 525, as it existed prior to the effective date of articles 1 and 2. Each guardian or conservator holding an appointment on the effective date of articles 1 and 2 shall continue to be bound by the duties imposed by the order of appointment; by Minnesota Statutes, chapter 525, as it existed prior to the effective date of articles 1 and 2; and by article 1, section 50; and shall be bound by any additional duties imposed by articles 1 and 2 starting on the first day of the next month starting after the effective date of articles 1 and 2 or on the next anniversary date of the appointment, whichever occurs later.

"(c) Any act done prior to the effective date of articles 1 and 2 in any proceeding and any right accrued under Minnesota Statutes, chapter 525, prior to the effective date of articles 1 and 2 shall not be impaired by articles 1 and 2. If a right is acquired, extinguished, or barred upon the expiration of a prescribed period of time which has commenced to run in accordance with the provisions of any statute before the effective date of articles 1 and 2, the provisions of the prior statute shall remain in force with respect to that right notwithstanding the statute's amendment or repeal by articles 1 and 2.

"(d) An order of the court or letters of guardianship or conservatorship issued by the court prior to the effective date of articles 1 and 2 shall remain in full force and effect in accordance with its terms and conditions and in accordance with the provisions of prior law until the court modifies the order or letters in accordance with the provisions of articles 1 and 2. Upon request for a certified copy of an order or letters which remains in full force and effect under this paragraph, the court administrator shall certify that the order or letters remains in full force and effect pursuant to this paragraph.

"(e) The court, without hearing or notice to any person, may issue new letters of guardianship or conservatorship under articles 1 and 2 to replace similar letters issued prior to the effective date of articles 1 and 2. The new letters shall be effective under articles 1 and 2 with the same force and effect as the prior letters and shall remain in full force and effect until modified by the court in accordance with the provisions of articles 1 and 2.

"(f) A power of attorney executed in accordance with Minnesota Statutes, section 524.5–505, prior to the effective date of articles 1 and 2, or any surety bond, deed, or other instrument, report, or other undertaking executed in accordance with Minnesota Statutes, chapter 525, prior to the effective date of articles 1 and 2, shall remain in full force and effect for all purposes in accordance with its terms and conditions and the provisions of the applicable statutes under which the power of attorney, surety bond, deed, or other instrument, report, or other undertaking was executed, until the power of attorney, surety bond, deed, or other instrument, report, or other undertaking expires according to its terms or pursuant to the statutes governing its execution, or is modified, terminated, or superseded by a new power of attorney, surety bond, deed, or other instrument, report, or other undertaking executed in accordance with the provisions of articles 1 and 2."

524.5–309. Who may be guardian: priorities

(a) Subject to paragraph (c), the court, in appointing a guardian, shall consider persons otherwise qualified in the following order of priority:

(1) a guardian, other than a temporary or emergency guardian, currently acting for the respondent in this state or elsewhere;

(2) an agent appointed by the respondent under a health care directive pursuant to chapter 145C;

(3) the spouse of the respondent or a person nominated by will or other signed writing executed in the same manner as a health care directive pursuant to chapter 145C of a deceased spouse;

(4) an adult child of the respondent;

(5) a parent of the respondent, or an individual nominated by will or other signed writing executed in the same manner as a health care directive pursuant to chapter 145C of a deceased parent; and

(6) an adult with whom the respondent has resided for more than six months before the filing of the petition.

(b) The court, acting in the best interest of the respondent, may decline to appoint a person having priority and appoint a person having a lower priority or no priority. With respect to persons having equal priority, the court shall select the one it considers best qualified.

(c) Any individual or agency which provides residence, custodial care, medical care, employment training or other care or services for which they receive a fee may not be appointed as guardian unless related to the respondent by blood, marriage, or adoption.

Laws 2003, c. 12, art. 1, § 33.

Historical and Statutory Notes

Laws 2003, c. 12, art. 2, § 9, provided:

"(a) Articles 1 and 2 apply to each guardianship or conservatorship proceeding and each appointment of guardian or conservator commenced on or after the effective date of articles 1 and 2. Except as otherwise provided in this section, articles 1 and 2 apply to each guardianship or conservatorship approved by the court prior to the effective date of articles 1 and 2, and to any guardianship or conservatorship proceeding pending in court on the effective date of articles 1 and 2, unless the court finds for good cause or in the interests of judicial economy that the proceeding should be completed under the provisions of Minnesota Statutes, chapter 525, as it existed prior to the effective date of articles 1 and 2.

"(b) A guardian or conservator who is not discharged prior to the effective date of articles 1 and 2 shall continue to hold the appointment but shall have only the powers specified in the order of appointment and in Minnesota Statutes, chapter 525, as it existed prior to the effective date of articles 1 and 2. Each guardian or conservator holding an appointment on the effective date of articles 1 and 2 shall continue to be bound by the duties imposed by the order of appointment; by Minnesota Statutes, chapter 525, as it existed prior to the effective date of articles 1 and 2; and by article 1, section 50; and shall be bound by any additional duties imposed by articles 1 and 2 starting on the first day of the next month starting after the effective date of articles 1 and 2 or on the next anniversary date of the appointment, whichever occurs later.

"(c) Any act done prior to the effective date of articles 1 and 2 in any proceeding and any right accrued under Minnesota Statutes, chapter 525, prior to the effective date of articles 1 and 2 shall not be impaired by articles 1 and 2. If a

right is acquired, extinguished, or barred upon the expiration of a prescribed period of time which has commenced to run in accordance with the provisions of any statute before the effective date of articles 1 and 2, the provisions of the prior statute shall remain in force with respect to that right notwithstanding the statute's amendment or repeal by articles 1 and 2.

"(d) An order of the court or letters of guardianship or conservatorship issued by the court prior to the effective date of articles 1 and 2 shall remain in full force and effect in accordance with its terms and conditions and in accordance with the provisions of prior law until the court modifies the order or letters in accordance with the provisions of articles 1 and 2. Upon request for a certified copy of an order or letters which remains in full force and effect under this paragraph, the court administrator shall certify that the order or letters remains in full force and effect pursuant to this paragraph.

"(e) The court, without hearing or notice to any person, may issue new letters of guardianship or conservatorship under articles 1 and 2 to replace similar letters issued prior to the effective date of articles 1 and 2. The new letters shall be effective under articles 1 and 2 with the same force and effect as the prior letters and shall remain in full force and effect until modified by the court in accordance with the provisions of articles 1 and 2.

"(f) A power of attorney executed in accordance with Minnesota Statutes, section 524.5–505, prior to the effective date of articles 1 and 2, or any surety bond, deed, or other instrument, report, or other undertaking executed in accordance with Minnesota Statutes, chapter 525, prior to the effective date of articles 1 and 2, shall remain in full force and effect for all purposes in accordance with its terms and conditions and the provisions of the applicable statutes under which the power of attorney, surety bond, deed, or other instrument, report, or other undertaking was executed, until the power of attorney, surety bond, deed, or other instrument, report, or other undertaking expires according to its terms or pursuant to the statutes governing its execution, or is modified, terminated, or superseded by a new power of attorney, surety bond, deed, or other instrument, report, or other undertaking executed in accordance with the provisions of articles 1 and 2."

524.5–310. Findings; order of appointment

(a) The court may appoint a limited or unlimited guardian for a respondent only if it finds by clear and convincing evidence that:

(1) the respondent is an incapacitated person; and

(2) the respondent's identified needs cannot be met by less restrictive means, including use of appropriate technological assistance.

(b) Alternatively, the court, with appropriate findings, may treat the petition as one for a protective order under section 524.5–401, enter any other appropriate order, or dismiss the proceeding.

(c) The court shall grant to a guardian only those powers necessitated by the ward's limitations and demonstrated needs and, whenever feasible, make appointive and other orders that will encourage the development of the ward's maximum self-reliance and independence. Any power not specifically granted to the guardian, following a written finding by the court of a demonstrated need for that power, is retained by the ward.

(d) Within 14 days after an appointment, a guardian shall send or deliver to the ward, and counsel if represented at the hearing, a copy of the order of appointment accompanied by a notice which advises the ward of the right to appeal the guardianship appointment in the time and manner provided by the Rules of Appellate Procedure.

(e) Each year, within 30 days after the anniversary date of an appointment, a guardian shall send or deliver to the ward a notice of the right to request termination or modification of the guardianship and notice of the status of the ward's right to vote.

Laws 2003, c. 12, art. 1, § 34. Amended by Laws 2005, c. 156, art. 6, § 67.

Historical and Statutory Notes

Laws 2003, c. 12, art. 2, § 9, provided:

"(a) Articles 1 and 2 apply to each guardianship or conservatorship proceeding and each appointment of guardian or conservator commenced on or after the effective date of articles 1 and 2. Except as otherwise provided in this section, articles 1 and 2 apply to each guardianship or conservatorship approved by the court prior to the effective date of articles 1 and 2, and to any guardianship or conservatorship proceeding pending in court on the effective date of articles 1 and 2, unless the court finds for good cause or in the interests of judicial economy that the proceeding should be completed under the provisions of Minnesota Statutes, chapter 525, as it existed prior to the effective date of articles 1 and 2.

"(b) A guardian or conservator who is not discharged prior to the effective date of articles 1 and 2 shall continue to hold the appointment but shall have only the powers specified in the order of appointment and in Minnesota Statutes, chapter 525, as it existed prior to the effective date of articles 1 and 2. Each guardian or conservator holding an appointment on the effective date of articles 1 and 2 shall con-

tinue to be bound by the duties imposed by the order of appointment; by Minnesota Statutes, chapter 525, as it existed prior to the effective date of articles 1 and 2; and by article 1, section 50; and shall be bound by any additional duties imposed by articles 1 and 2 starting on the first day of the next month starting after the effective date of articles 1 and 2 or on the next anniversary date of the appointment, whichever occurs later.

"(c) Any act done prior to the effective date of articles 1 and 2 in any proceeding and any right accrued under Minnesota Statutes, chapter 525, prior to the effective date of articles 1 and 2 shall not be impaired by articles 1 and 2. If a right is acquired, extinguished, or barred upon the expiration of a prescribed period of time which has commenced to run in accordance with the provisions of any statute before the effective date of articles 1 and 2, the provisions of the prior statute shall remain in force with respect to that right notwithstanding the statute's amendment or repeal by articles 1 and 2.

"(d) An order of the court or letters of guardianship or conservatorship issued by the court prior to the effective date of articles 1 and 2 shall remain in full force and effect in accordance with its terms and conditions and in accordance with the provisions of prior law until the court modifies the order or letters in accordance with the provisions of articles 1 and 2. Upon request for a certified copy of an order or letters which remains in full force and effect under this paragraph, the court administrator

shall certify that the order or letters remains in full force and effect pursuant to this paragraph.

"(e) The court, without hearing or notice to any person, may issue new letters of guardianship or conservatorship under articles 1 and 2 to replace similar letters issued prior to the effective date of articles 1 and 2. The new letters shall be effective under articles 1 and 2 with the same force and effect as the prior letters and shall remain in full force and effect until modified by the court in accordance with the provisions of articles 1 and 2.

"(f) A power of attorney executed in accordance with Minnesota Statutes, section 524.5–505, prior to the effective date of articles 1 and 2, or any surety bond, deed, or other instrument, report, or other undertaking executed in accordance with Minnesota Statutes, chapter 525, prior to the effective date of articles 1 and 2, shall remain in full force and effect for all purposes in accordance with its terms and conditions and the provisions of the applicable statutes under which the power of attorney, surety bond, deed, or other instrument, report, or other undertaking was executed, until the power of attorney, surety bond, deed, or other instrument, report, or other undertaking expires according to its terms or pursuant to the statutes governing its execution, or is modified, terminated, or superseded by a new power of attorney, surety bond, deed, or other instrument, report, or other undertaking executed in accordance with the provisions of articles 1 and 2."

524.5–311. Emergency guardian

(a) If the court finds that compliance with the procedures of this article will likely result in substantial harm to the respondent's health, safety, or welfare, and that no other person appears to have authority and willingness to act in the circumstances, the court, on petition by a person interested in the respondent's welfare, may appoint an emergency guardian whose authority may not exceed 60 days and who may exercise only the powers specified in the order. A county that is acting under section 626.557, subdivision 10, by petitioning for appointment of an emergency guardian on behalf of a vulnerable adult may be granted authority to act for a period not to exceed 90 days. Immediately upon receipt of the petition for an emergency guardianship, the court shall appoint a lawyer to represent the respondent in the proceeding. Except as otherwise provided in paragraph (b), reasonable notice of the time and place of a hearing on the petition must be given to the respondent and any other persons as the court directs.

(b) An emergency guardian may be appointed without notice to the respondent and the respondent's lawyer only if the court finds from affidavit or other sworn testimony that the respondent will be substantially harmed before a hearing on the appointment can be held. If the court appoints an emergency guardian without notice to the respondent, the respondent must be given notice of the appointment within 48 hours after the appointment. The court shall hold a hearing on the appropriateness of the appointment within five days after the appointment.

(c) Appointment of an emergency guardian, with or without notice, is not a determination of the respondent's incapacity.

(d) The court may remove an emergency guardian at any time. An emergency guardian shall make any report the court requires. In other respects, the provisions of this article concerning guardians apply to an emergency guardian.

Laws 2003, c. 12, art. 1, § 35.

Historical and Statutory Notes

Laws 2003, c. 12, art. 2, § 9, provided:

"(a) Articles 1 and 2 apply to each guardianship or conservatorship proceeding and each appointment of guardian or conservator commenced on or after the effective date of articles 1 and 2. Except as otherwise provided in this section, articles 1 and 2 apply to each guardianship or conservatorship approved by the court prior to the effective date of articles 1 and 2, and to any guardianship or conservatorship proceeding pending in court on the effective date of articles 1 and 2, unless the court finds for good cause or in the interests of judicial economy that the proceeding should be completed under the provisions of Minnesota Statutes, chapter 525, as it existed prior to the effective date of articles 1 and 2.

"(b) A guardian or conservator who is not discharged prior to the effective date of articles 1 and 2 shall continue to hold the appointment but shall have only the powers specified in the order of appointment and in Minnesota Statutes, chapter 525, as it existed prior to the effective date of articles 1 and 2. Each guardian or conservator holding an appointment on the effective date of articles 1 and 2 shall continue to be bound by the duties imposed by the order of appointment; by Minnesota Statutes, chapter 525, as it existed prior to the effective date of articles 1 and 2; and by article 1, section 50; and shall be bound by any additional duties imposed by articles 1 and 2 starting on the first day of the next month starting after the effective date of articles 1 and 2 or on the next anniversary date of the appointment, whichever occurs later.

"(c) Any act done prior to the effective date of articles 1 and 2 in any proceeding and any right accrued under Minnesota Statutes, chapter 525, prior to the effective date of articles 1 and 2 shall not be impaired by articles 1 and 2. If a right is acquired, extinguished, or barred upon the expiration of a prescribed period of time which has commenced to run in accordance with the provisions of any statute before the effective date of articles 1 and 2, the provisions of the prior statute shall remain in force with respect to that right notwithstanding the statute's amendment or repeal by articles 1 and 2.

"(d) An order of the court or letters of guardianship or conservatorship issued by the court prior to the effective date of articles 1 and 2 shall remain in full force and effect in accordance with its terms and conditions and in accordance with the provisions of prior law until the court modifies the order or letters in accordance with the provisions of articles 1 and 2. Upon request for a certified copy of an order or letters which remains in full force and effect under this paragraph, the court administrator shall certify that the order or letters remains in full force and effect pursuant to this paragraph.

"(e) The court, without hearing or notice to any person, may issue new letters of guardianship or conservatorship under articles 1 and 2 to replace similar letters issued prior to the effective date of articles 1 and 2. The new letters shall be effective under articles 1 and 2 with the same force and effect as the prior letters and shall remain in full force and effect until modified by the court in accordance with the provisions of articles 1 and 2.

"(f) A power of attorney executed in accordance with Minnesota Statutes, section 524.5–505, prior to the effective date of articles 1 and 2, or any surety bond, deed, or other instrument, report, or other undertaking executed in accordance with Minnesota Statutes, chapter 525, prior to the effective date of articles 1 and 2, shall remain in full force and effect for all purposes in accordance with its terms and conditions and the provisions of the applicable statutes under which the power of attorney, surety bond, deed, or other instrument, report, or other undertaking was executed, until the power of attorney, surety bond, deed, or other instrument, report, or other undertaking expires according to its terms or pursuant to the statutes governing its execution, or is modified, terminated, or superseded by a new power of attorney, surety bond, deed, or other instrument, report, or other undertaking executed in accordance with the provisions of articles 1 and 2."

524.5–312. Temporary substitute guardian

(a) If the court finds that a guardian is not effectively performing the guardian's duties and that the welfare of the ward requires immediate action, it may appoint a temporary substitute guardian for the ward for a specified period not exceeding six months. Except as otherwise ordered by the court, a temporary substitute guardian so appointed has the powers set forth in the previous order of appointment. The authority of any unlimited or limited guardian previously appointed by the court is suspended as long as a temporary substitute guardian has authority. If an appointment is made without previous notice to the ward or the affected guardian, within five days after the appointment, the court shall inform the ward or guardian of the appointment.

(b) The court may remove a temporary substitute guardian at any time. A temporary substitute guardian shall make any report the court requires. In other respects, the provisions of this article concerning guardians apply to a temporary substitute guardian.

Laws 2003, c. 12, art. 1, § 36.

Historical and Statutory Notes

Laws 2003, c. 12, art. 2, § 9, provided:

"(a) Articles 1 and 2 apply to each guardianship or conservatorship proceeding and each appointment of guardian or conservator commenced on or after the effective date of articles 1 and 2. Except as otherwise provided in this section, articles 1 and 2 apply to each guardianship or conservatorship approved by the court prior to the effective date of articles 1 and 2, and to any guardianship or conservatorship proceeding pending in court on the effective date of articles 1 and 2, unless the court finds for good cause or in the interests of judicial economy that the proceeding should be completed under the provisions of Minnesota Statutes, chapter 525, as it existed prior to the effective date of articles 1 and 2.

"(b) A guardian or conservator who is not discharged prior to the effective date of articles 1 and 2 shall continue to hold the appointment but shall have only the powers specified in the order of appointment and in Minnesota Statutes, chapter 525, as it existed prior to the effective date of articles 1 and 2. Each guardian or conservator holding an appointment on the effective date of articles 1 and 2 shall continue to be bound by the duties imposed by the order of appointment; by Minnesota Statutes, chapter 525, as it existed prior to the effective date of articles 1 and 2; and by article 1, section 50; and shall be bound by any additional duties imposed by articles 1 and 2 starting on the first day of the next month starting after the effective date of articles 1 and 2 or on the next anniversary date of the appointment, whichever occurs later.

"(c) Any act done prior to the effective date of articles 1 and 2 in any proceeding and any right accrued under Minnesota Statutes, chapter 525, prior to the effective date of articles 1 and 2 shall not be impaired by articles 1 and 2. If a right is acquired, extinguished, or barred upon the expiration of a prescribed period of time which has commenced to run in accordance with the provisions of any statute before the effective date of articles 1 and 2, the provisions of the prior statute shall remain in force with respect to that right notwithstanding the statute's amendment or repeal by articles 1 and 2.

"(d) An order of the court or letters of guardianship or conservatorship issued by the court prior to the effective date of articles 1 and 2 shall remain in full force and effect in accordance with its terms and conditions and in

accordance with the provisions of prior law until the court modifies the order or letters in accordance with the provisions of articles 1 and 2. Upon request for a certified copy of an order or letters which remains in full force and effect under this paragraph, the court administrator shall certify that the order or letters remains in full force and effect pursuant to this paragraph.

"(e) The court, without hearing or notice to any person, may issue new letters of guardianship or conservatorship under articles 1 and 2 to replace similar letters issued prior to the effective date of articles 1 and 2. The new letters shall be effective under articles 1 and 2 with the same force and effect as the prior letters and shall remain in full force and effect until modified by the court in accordance with the provisions of articles 1 and 2.

"(f) A power of attorney executed in accordance with Minnesota Statutes, section 524.5–505, prior to the effective date of articles 1 and 2, or any surety bond, deed, or other instrument, report, or other undertaking executed in accordance with Minnesota Statutes, chapter 525, prior to the effective date of articles 1 and 2, shall remain in full force and effect for all purposes in accordance with its terms and conditions and the provisions of the applicable statutes under which the power of attorney, surety bond, deed, or other instrument, report, or other undertaking was executed, until the power of attorney, surety bond, deed, or other instrument, report, or other undertaking expires according to its terms or pursuant to the statutes governing its execution, or is modified, terminated, or superseded by a new power of attorney, surety bond, deed, or other instrument, report, or other undertaking executed in accordance with the provisions of articles 1 and 2."

524.5–313. Powers and duties of guardian

(a) A guardian shall be subject to the control and direction of the court at all times and in all things.

(b) The court shall grant to a guardian only those powers necessary to provide for the demonstrated needs of the ward.

(c) The court may appoint a guardian if it determines that all the powers and duties listed in this section are needed to provide for the needs of the incapacitated person. The court may also appoint a guardian if it determines that a guardian is needed to provide for the needs of the incapacitated person through the exercise of some, but not all, of the powers and duties listed in this section. The duties and powers of a guardian or those which the court may grant to a guardian include, but are not limited to:

(1) the power to have custody of the ward and the power to establish a place of abode within or outside the state, except as otherwise provided in this clause. The ward or any interested person may petition the court to prevent or to initiate a change in abode. A ward may not be admitted to a regional treatment center by the guardian except:

(i) after a hearing under chapter 253B;

(ii) for outpatient services; or

(iii) for the purpose of receiving temporary care for a specific period of time not to exceed 90 days in any calendar year;

(2) the duty to provide for the ward's care, comfort, and maintenance needs, including food, clothing, shelter, health care, social and recreational requirements, and, whenever appropriate, training, education, and habilitation or rehabilitation. The guardian has no duty to pay for these requirements out of personal funds. Whenever possible and appropriate, the guardian should meet these requirements through governmental benefits or services to which the

ward is entitled, rather than from the ward's estate. Failure to satisfy the needs and requirements of this clause shall be grounds for removal of a private guardian, but the guardian shall have no personal or monetary liability;

(3) the duty to take reasonable care of the ward's clothing, furniture, vehicles, and other personal effects, and, if other property requires protection, the power to seek appointment of a conservator of the estate. The guardian must give notice by mail to interested persons prior to the disposition of the ward's clothing, furniture, vehicles, or other personal effects. The notice must inform the person of the right to object to the disposition of the property within ten days of the date of mailing and to petition the court for a review of the guardian's proposed actions. Notice of the objection must be served by mail or personal service on the guardian and the ward unless the ward is the objector. The guardian served with notice of an objection to the disposition of the property may not dispose of the property unless the court approves the disposition after a hearing;

(4) (i) the power to give any necessary consent to enable the ward to receive necessary medical or other professional care, counsel, treatment, or service, except that no guardian may give consent for psychosurgery, electroshock, sterilization, or experimental treatment of any kind unless the procedure is first approved by order of the court as provided in this clause. The guardian shall not consent to any medical care for the ward which violates the known conscientious, religious, or moral belief of the ward;

(ii) a guardian who believes a procedure described in item (i) requiring prior court approval to be necessary for the proper care of the ward, shall petition the court for an order and, in the case of a public guardianship under chapter 252A, obtain the written recommendation of the commissioner of human services. The court shall fix the time and place for the hearing and shall give notice to the ward in such manner as specified in section 524.5–308 and to interested persons. The court shall appoint an attorney to represent the ward who is not represented by counsel, provided that such appointment shall expire upon the expiration of the appeal time for the order issued by the court under this section or the order dismissing a petition, or upon such other time or event as the court may direct. In every case the court shall determine if the procedure is in the best interest of the ward. In making its determination, the court shall consider a written medical report which specifically considers the medical risks of the procedure, whether alternative, less restrictive methods of treatment could be used to protect the best interest of the ward, and any recommendation of the commissioner of human services for a public ward. The standard of proof is that of clear and convincing evidence;

(iii) in the case of a petition for sterilization of a developmentally disabled ward, the court shall appoint a licensed physician, a psychologist who is qualified in the diagnosis and treatment of developmental disability, and a social worker who is familiar with the ward's social history and adjustment or the case manager for the ward to examine or evaluate the ward and to provide written reports to the court. The reports shall indicate why sterilization is being proposed, whether sterilization is necessary and is the least intrusive method for alleviating the problem presented, and whether it is in the best interest of the ward. The medical report shall specifically consider the medical risks of sterilization, the consequences of not performing the sterilization, and whether alternative methods of contraception could be used to protect the best interest of the ward;

(iv) any ward whose right to consent to a sterilization has not been restricted under this section or section 252A.101 may be sterilized only if the ward consents in writing or there is a sworn acknowledgment by an interested person of a nonwritten consent by the ward. The consent must certify that the ward has received a full explanation from a physician or registered nurse of the nature and irreversible consequences of the sterilization;

(v) a guardian or the public guardian's designee who acts within the scope of authority conferred by letters of guardianship under section 252A.101, subdivision 7, and according to the standards established in this chapter or in chapter 252A shall not be civilly or criminally liable for the provision of any necessary medical care, including, but not limited to, the administration of psychotropic medication or the implementation of aversive and deprivation procedures to which the guardian or the public guardian's designee has consented;

(5) in the event there is no duly appointed conservator of the ward's estate, the guardian shall have the power to approve or withhold approval of any contract, except for necessities, which the ward may make or wish to make;

(6) the duty and power to exercise supervisory authority over the ward in a manner which limits civil rights and restricts personal freedom only to the extent necessary to provide needed care and services;

(7) if there is no acting conservator of the estate for the ward, the guardian has the power to apply on behalf of the ward for any assistance, services, or benefits available to the ward through any unit of government;

(8) unless otherwise ordered by the court, the ward retains the right to vote.

Laws 2003, c. 12, art. 1, § 37. Amended by Laws 2005, c. 56, § 1.

Historical and Statutory Notes

Laws 2003, c. 12, art. 2, § 9, provided:

"(a) Articles 1 and 2 apply to each guardianship or conservatorship proceeding and each appointment of guardian or conservator commenced on or after the effective date of articles 1 and 2. Except as otherwise provided in this section, articles 1 and 2 apply to each guardianship or conservatorship approved by the court prior to the effective date of articles 1 and 2, and to any guardianship or conservatorship proceeding pending in court on the effective date of articles 1 and 2, unless the court finds for good cause or in the interests of judicial economy that the proceeding should be completed under the provisions of Minnesota Statutes, chapter 525, as it existed prior to the effective date of articles 1 and 2.

"(b) A guardian or conservator who is not discharged prior to the effective date of articles 1 and 2 shall continue to hold the appointment but shall have only the powers specified in the order of appointment and in Minnesota Statutes, chapter 525, as it existed prior to the effective date of articles 1 and 2. Each guardian or conservator holding an appointment on the effective date of articles 1 and 2 shall con-

tinue to be bound by the duties imposed by the order of appointment; by Minnesota Statutes, chapter 525, as it existed prior to the effective date of articles 1 and 2; and by article 1, section 50; and shall be bound by any additional duties imposed by articles 1 and 2 starting on the first day of the next month starting after the effective date of articles 1 and 2 or on the next anniversary date of the appointment, whichever occurs later.

"(c) Any act done prior to the effective date of articles 1 and 2 in any proceeding and any right accrued under Minnesota Statutes, chapter 525, prior to the effective date of articles 1 and 2 shall not be impaired by articles 1 and 2. If a right is acquired, extinguished, or barred upon the expiration of a prescribed period of time which has commenced to run in accordance with the provisions of any statute before the effective date of articles 1 and 2, the provisions of the prior statute shall remain in force with respect to that right notwithstanding the statute's amendment or repeal by articles 1 and 2.

"(d) An order of the court or letters of guardianship or conservatorship issued by the court prior to the effective date of articles 1 and 2 shall remain in full force and effect in accordance with its terms and conditions and in accordance with the provisions of prior law until the court modifies the order or letters in accordance with the provisions of articles 1 and 2. Upon request for a certified copy of an order or letters which remains in full force and effect under this paragraph, the court administrator

shall certify that the order or letters remains in full force and effect pursuant to this paragraph.

"(e) The court, without hearing or notice to any person, may issue new letters of guardianship or conservatorship under articles 1 and 2 to replace similar letters issued prior to the effective date of articles 1 and 2. The new letters shall be effective under articles 1 and 2 with the same force and effect as the prior letters and shall remain in full force and effect until modified by the court in accordance with the provisions of articles 1 and 2.

"(f) A power of attorney executed in accordance with Minnesota Statutes, section 524.5–505, prior to the effective date of articles 1 and 2, or any surety bond, deed, or other instrument, report, or other undertaking executed in accordance with Minnesota Statutes, chapter 525, prior to the effective date of articles 1 and 2, shall remain in full force and effect for all purposes in accordance with its terms and conditions and the provisions of the applicable statutes under which the power of attorney, surety bond, deed, or other instrument, report, or other undertaking was executed, until the power of attorney, surety bond, deed, or other instrument, report, or other undertaking expires according to its terms or pursuant to the statutes governing its execution, or is modified, terminated, or superseded by a new power of attorney, surety bond, deed, or other instrument, report, or other undertaking executed in accordance with the provisions of articles 1 and 2."

524.5–315. Rights and immunities of guardian; limitations

(a) A guardian is entitled to reasonable compensation for services as guardian and to reimbursement for expenditures made on behalf of the ward, in a manner consistent with section 524.5–502.

(b) A guardian is not liable to a third person for acts of the ward solely by reason of the relationship. A guardian who exercises reasonable care in choosing a third person providing medical or other care, treatment, or service for the ward is not liable for injury to the ward resulting from the wrongful conduct of the third person.

(c) A guardian, without authorization of the court, may revoke the appointment of an agent of a health care directive of which the ward is the principal, but the guardian may not, absent a court order, revoke the health care directive itself. If a health care directive is in effect, absent an order of the court to the contrary, a health care decision of the guardian takes precedence over that of an agent.

(d) A guardian may not initiate the commitment of a ward to an institution except in accordance with section 524.5–313.

Laws 2003, c. 12, art. 1, § 38.

Historical and Statutory Notes

Laws 2003, c. 12, art. 2, § 9, provided:

"(a) Articles 1 and 2 apply to each guardianship or conservatorship proceeding and each appointment of guardian or conservator commenced on or after the effective date of articles 1 and 2. Except as otherwise provided in this section, articles 1 and 2 apply to each guardianship or conservatorship approved by the court prior to the effective date of articles 1 and 2, and to any guardianship or conservatorship proceeding pending in court on the effective date of articles 1 and 2, unless the court finds for good cause or in the interests of judicial economy that the proceeding should be completed under the provisions of Minnesota Statutes, chapter 525, as it existed prior to the effective date of articles 1 and 2.

"(b) A guardian or conservator who is not discharged prior to the effective date of articles 1 and 2 shall continue to hold the appointment but shall have only the powers specified in the order of appointment and in Minnesota Statutes, chapter 525, as it existed prior to the effective date of articles 1 and 2. Each guardian or conservator holding an appointment on the effective date of articles 1 and 2 shall continue to be bound by the duties imposed by the order of appointment; by Minnesota Statutes, chapter 525, as it existed prior to the effective date of articles 1 and 2; and by article 1, section 50; and shall be bound by any additional duties imposed by articles 1 and 2 starting on the first day of the next month starting after the effective date of articles 1 and 2 or on the next anniversary date of the appointment, whichever occurs later.

"(c) Any act done prior to the effective date of articles 1 and 2 in any proceeding and any right accrued under Minnesota Statutes, chapter 525, prior to the effective date of articles 1 and 2 shall not be impaired by articles 1 and 2. If a right is acquired, extinguished, or barred upon the expiration of a prescribed period of time which has commenced to run in accordance with the provisions of any statute before the effective date of articles 1 and 2, the provisions of the prior statute shall remain in force with respect to that right notwithstanding the statute's amendment or repeal by articles 1 and 2.

"(d) An order of the court or letters of guardianship or conservatorship issued by the court prior to the effective date of articles 1 and 2 shall remain in full force and effect in accordance with its terms and conditions and in accordance with the provisions of prior law until the court modifies the order or letters in accordance with the provisions of articles 1 and 2. Upon request for a certified copy of an order or letters which remains in full force and effect under this paragraph, the court administrator shall certify that the order or letters remains in full force and effect pursuant to this paragraph.

"(e) The court, without hearing or notice to any person, may issue new letters of guardianship or conservatorship under articles 1 and 2 to replace similar letters issued prior to the effective date of articles 1 and 2. The new letters shall be effective under articles 1 and 2 with the same force and effect as the prior letters and shall remain in full force and effect until modified by the court in accordance with the provisions of articles 1 and 2.

"(f) A power of attorney executed in accordance with Minnesota Statutes, section 524.5–505, prior to the effective date of articles 1 and 2, or any surety bond, deed, or other instrument, report, or other undertaking executed in accordance with Minnesota Statutes, chapter 525, prior to the effective date of articles 1 and 2, shall remain in full force and effect for all purposes in accordance with its terms and conditions and the provisions of the applicable statutes under which the power of attorney, surety bond, deed, or other instrument, report, or other undertaking was executed, until the power of attorney, surety bond, deed, or other instrument, report, or other undertaking expires according to its terms or pursuant to the statutes governing its execution, or is modified, terminated, or superseded by a new power of attorney, surety bond, deed, or other instrument, report, or other undertaking executed in accordance with the provisions of articles 1 and 2."

524.5–316. Reports; monitoring of guardianship

(a) A guardian shall report to the court in writing on the condition of the ward at least annually and whenever ordered by the court. A report must state or contain:

(1) the current mental, physical, and social condition of the ward;

(2) the living arrangements for all addresses of the ward during the reporting period;

(3) the medical, educational, vocational, and other services provided to the ward and the guardian's opinion as to the adequacy of the ward's care; and

(4) a recommendation as to the need for continued guardianship and any recommended changes in the scope of the guardianship.

(b) The court may appoint a visitor to review a report, interview the ward or guardian, and make any other investigation the court directs.

(c) The court shall establish a system for monitoring guardianships, including the filing and review of annual reports.

Laws 2003, c. 12, art. 1, § 39.

Historical and Statutory Notes

Laws 2003, c. 12, art. 2, § 9, provided:

"(a) Articles 1 and 2 apply to each guardianship or conservatorship proceeding and each appointment of guardian or conservator commenced on or after the effective date of articles 1 and 2. Except as otherwise provided in this section, articles 1 and 2 apply to each guardianship or conservatorship approved by the court prior to the effective date of articles 1 and 2, and to any guardianship or conservatorship proceeding pending in court on the effective date of articles 1 and 2, unless the court finds for good cause or in the interests of judicial economy that the proceeding should be completed under the provisions of Minnesota Statutes, chapter 525, as it existed prior to the effective date of articles 1 and 2.

"(b) A guardian or conservator who is not discharged prior to the effective date of articles 1 and 2 shall continue to hold the appointment but shall have only the powers specified in the order of appointment and in Minnesota Statutes, chapter 525, as it existed prior to the effective date of articles 1 and 2. Each guardian or conservator holding an appointment on the effective date of articles 1 and 2 shall continue to be bound by the duties imposed by the order of appointment; by Minnesota Statutes, chapter 525, as it existed prior to the effective date of articles 1 and 2; and by article 1, section 50; and shall be bound by any additional duties imposed by articles 1 and 2 starting on the first day of the next month starting after the effective date of articles 1 and 2 or on the next anniversary date of the appointment, whichever occurs later.

"(c) Any act done prior to the effective date of articles 1 and 2 in any proceeding and any right accrued under Minnesota Statutes, chapter 525, prior to the effective date of articles 1 and 2 shall not be impaired by articles 1 and 2. If a right is acquired, extinguished, or barred upon the expiration of a prescribed period of time

which has commenced to run in accordance with the provisions of any statute before the effective date of articles 1 and 2, the provisions of the prior statute shall remain in force with respect to that right notwithstanding the statute's amendment or repeal by articles 1 and 2.

"(d) An order of the court or letters of guardianship or conservatorship issued by the court prior to the effective date of articles 1 and 2 shall remain in full force and effect in accordance with its terms and conditions and in accordance with the provisions of prior law until the court modifies the order or letters in accordance with the provisions of articles 1 and 2. Upon request for a certified copy of an order or letters which remains in full force and effect under this paragraph, the court administrator shall certify that the order or letters remains in full force and effect pursuant to this paragraph.

"(e) The court, without hearing or notice to any person, may issue new letters of guardianship or conservatorship under articles 1 and 2 to replace similar letters issued prior to the effective date of articles 1 and 2. The new letters shall be effective under articles 1 and 2 with the same force and effect as the prior letters and shall remain in full force and effect until modified by the court in accordance with the provisions of articles 1 and 2.

"(f) A power of attorney executed in accordance with Minnesota Statutes, section 524.5–505, prior to the effective date of articles 1 and 2, or any surety bond, deed, or other instrument, report, or other undertaking executed in accordance with Minnesota Statutes, chapter 525, prior to the effective date of articles 1 and 2, shall remain in full force and effect for all purposes in accordance with its terms and conditions and the provisions of the applicable statutes under which the power of attorney, surety bond, deed, or other instrument, report, or other undertaking was executed, until the power of attorney, surety bond, deed, or other instrument, report, or other undertaking expires according to its terms or pursuant to the statutes governing its execution, or is modified, terminated, or superseded by a new power of attorney, surety bond, deed, or other instrument, report, or other undertaking executed in accordance with the provisions of articles 1 and 2."

524.5–317. Termination or modification of guardianship

(a) A guardianship terminates upon the death of the ward or upon order of the court.

(b) On petition of any person interested in the ward's welfare the court may terminate a guardianship if the ward no longer needs the assistance or protection of a guardian. The court may modify the type of appointment or powers granted to the guardian if the extent of protection or assistance previously granted is currently excessive or insufficient or the ward's capacity to provide for support, care, education, health, and welfare has so changed as to warrant that action.

(c) Except as otherwise ordered by the court for good cause, the court, before terminating a guardianship, shall follow the same procedures to safeguard the rights of the ward as apply to a petition for guardianship. Upon presentation by the petitioner of evidence establishing a prima facie case for termination, the court shall order the termination and discharge the guardian unless it is proven that continuation of the guardianship is in the best interest of the ward.

Laws 2003, c. 12, art. 1, § 40.

Historical and Statutory Notes

Laws 2003, c. 12, art. 2, § 9, provided:

"(a) Articles 1 and 2 apply to each guardianship or conservatorship proceeding and each appointment of guardian or conservator commenced on or after the effective date of articles 1 and 2. Except as otherwise provided in this section, articles 1 and 2 apply to each guardianship or conservatorship approved by the court prior to the effective date of articles 1 and 2, and to any guardianship or conservatorship proceeding pending in court on the effective date of articles 1 and 2, unless the court finds for good cause or in the interests of judicial economy that the proceeding should be completed under the provisions of Minnesota Statutes, chapter 525, as it existed prior to the effective date of articles 1 and 2.

"(b) A guardian or conservator who is not discharged prior to the effective date of articles 1 and 2 shall continue to hold the appointment but shall have only the powers specified in the order of appointment and in Minnesota Statutes, chapter 525, as it existed prior to the effective date of articles 1 and 2. Each guardian or conservator holding an appointment on the effective date of articles 1 and 2 shall continue to be bound by the duties imposed by the order of appointment; by Minnesota Statutes, chapter 525, as it existed prior to the effective date of articles 1 and 2; and by article 1, section 50; and shall be bound by any additional duties imposed by articles 1 and 2 starting on the first day of the next month starting after the effective date of articles 1 and 2 or on the next anniversary date of the appointment, whichever occurs later.

"(c) Any act done prior to the effective date of articles 1 and 2 in any proceeding and any right accrued under Minnesota Statutes, chapter 525, prior to the effective date of articles 1 and 2 shall not be impaired by articles 1 and 2. If a right is acquired, extinguished, or barred upon the expiration of a prescribed period of time which has commenced to run in accordance with the provisions of any statute before the effective date of articles 1 and 2, the provisions of the prior statute shall remain in force with respect to that right notwithstanding the statute's amendment or repeal by articles 1 and 2.

"(d) An order of the court or letters of guardianship or conservatorship issued by the court prior to the effective date of articles 1 and 2 shall remain in full force and effect in accordance with its terms and conditions and in

accordance with the provisions of prior law until the court modifies the order or letters in accordance with the provisions of articles 1 and 2. Upon request for a certified copy of an order or letters which remains in full force and effect under this paragraph, the court administrator shall certify that the order or letters remains in full force and effect pursuant to this paragraph.

"(e) The court, without hearing or notice to any person, may issue new letters of guardianship or conservatorship under articles 1 and 2 to replace similar letters issued prior to the effective date of articles 1 and 2. The new letters shall be effective under articles 1 and 2 with the same force and effect as the prior letters and shall remain in full force and effect until modified by the court in accordance with the provisions of articles 1 and 2.

"(f) A power of attorney executed in accordance with Minnesota Statutes, section 524.5–505, prior to the effective date of articles 1 and 2, or any surety bond, deed, or other instrument, report, or other undertaking executed in accordance with Minnesota Statutes, chapter 525, prior to the effective date of articles 1 and 2, shall remain in full force and effect for all purposes in accordance with its terms and conditions and the provisions of the applicable statutes under which the power of attorney, surety bond, deed, or other instrument, report, or other undertaking was executed, until the power of attorney, surety bond, deed, or other instrument, report, or other undertaking expires according to its terms or pursuant to the statutes governing its execution, or is modified, terminated, or superseded by a new power of attorney, surety bond, deed, or other instrument, report, or other undertaking executed in accordance with the provisions of articles 1 and 2."

PART 4

PROTECTION OF PROPERTY OF PROTECTED PERSON

524.5–401. Protective proceeding

Upon petition and after notice and hearing, the court may appoint a limited or unlimited conservator or make any other protective order provided in this part in relation to the estate and affairs of:

(1) a minor, if the court determines that the minor owns money or property requiring management or protection that cannot otherwise be provided or has or may have business affairs that may be jeopardized or prevented because of the minor's age, or that money is needed for support and education and that protection is necessary or desirable to obtain or provide money; and

(2) any individual, including a minor, if the court determines that, for reasons other than age:

(i) by clear and convincing evidence, the individual is unable to manage property and business affairs because of an impairment in the ability to receive and evaluate information or make decisions, even with the use of appropriate technological assistance, or because the individual is missing, detained, or unable to return to the United States; and

(ii) by a preponderance of evidence, the individual has property that will be wasted or dissipated unless management is provided or money is needed for the support, care, education, health, and welfare of the individual or of individuals who are entitled to the individual's support and that protection is necessary or desirable to obtain or provide money.

Laws 2003, c. 12, art. 1, § 41.

Historical and Statutory Notes

Laws 2003, c. 12, art. 2, § 9, provided:

"(a) Articles 1 and 2 apply to each guardianship or conservatorship proceeding and each appointment of guardian or conservator commenced on or after the effective date of articles 1 and 2. Except as otherwise provided in this section, articles 1 and 2 apply to each guardianship or conservatorship approved by the court prior to the effective date of articles 1 and 2, and to any guardianship or conservatorship proceeding pending in court on the effective date of articles 1 and 2, unless the court finds for good cause or in the interests of judicial economy that the proceeding should be completed under the provisions of Minnesota Statutes, chapter 525, as it existed prior to the effective date of articles 1 and 2.

"(b) A guardian or conservator who is not discharged prior to the effective date of articles 1 and 2 shall continue to hold the appointment but shall have only the powers specified in the order of appointment and in Minnesota Statutes, chapter 525, as it existed prior to the effective date of articles 1 and 2. Each guardian or conservator holding an appointment on the effective date of articles 1 and 2 shall continue to be bound by the duties imposed by the order of appointment; by Minnesota Statutes, chapter 525, as it existed prior to the effective date of articles 1 and 2; and by article 1, section 50; and shall be bound by any additional duties imposed by articles 1 and 2 starting on the first day of the next month starting after the effective date of articles 1 and 2 or on the next anniversary date of the appointment, whichever occurs later.

"(c) Any act done prior to the effective date of articles 1 and 2 in any proceeding and any right accrued under Minnesota Statutes, chapter 525, prior to the effective date of articles 1 and 2 shall not be impaired by articles 1 and 2. If a right is acquired, extinguished, or barred upon the expiration of a prescribed period of time which has commenced to run in accordance with the provisions of any statute before the effective date of articles 1 and 2, the provisions of the prior statute shall remain in force with respect to that right notwithstanding the statute's amendment or repeal by articles 1 and 2.

"(d) An order of the court or letters of guardianship or conservatorship issued by the court prior to the effective date of articles 1 and 2 shall remain in full force and effect in accordance with its terms and conditions and in accordance with the provisions of prior law until the court modifies the order or letters in accordance with the provisions of articles 1 and 2. Upon request for a certified copy of an order or letters which remains in full force and effect under this paragraph, the court administrator shall certify that the order or letters remains in full force and effect pursuant to this paragraph.

"(e) The court, without hearing or notice to any person, may issue new letters of guardianship or conservatorship under articles 1 and 2 to replace similar letters issued prior to the effective date of articles 1 and 2. The new letters shall be effective under articles 1 and 2 with the same force and effect as the prior letters and shall remain in full force and effect until modified by the court in accordance with the provisions of articles 1 and 2.

"(f) A power of attorney executed in accordance with Minnesota Statutes, section 524.5–505, prior to the effective date of articles 1 and 2, or any surety bond, deed, or other instrument, report, or other undertaking executed in accordance with Minnesota Statutes, chapter 525, prior to the effective date of articles 1 and 2, shall remain in full force and effect for all purposes in accordance with its terms and conditions and the provisions of the applicable statutes under which the power of attorney, surety bond, deed, or other instrument, report, or other undertaking was executed, until the power of attorney, surety bond, deed, or other instrument, report, or other undertaking expires according to its terms or pursuant to the statutes governing its execution, or is modified, terminated, or superseded by a new power of attorney, surety bond, deed, or other instrument, report, or other undertaking executed in accordance with the provisions of articles 1 and 2."

524.5–402. Jurisdiction over business affairs of protected person

After the service of notice in a proceeding seeking a conservatorship or other protective order and until termination of the proceeding, the court in which the petition is filed has:

(1) exclusive jurisdiction to determine the need for a conservatorship or other protective order;

(2) exclusive jurisdiction to determine how the estate of the protected person which is subject to the laws of this state must be managed, expended, or distributed to or for the use of the protected person, individuals who are in fact dependent upon the protected person, or other claimants; and

(3) concurrent jurisdiction to determine the validity of claims against the person or estate of the protected person and questions of title concerning assets of the estate.

Laws 2003, c. 12, art. 1, § 42.

Historical and Statutory Notes

Laws 2003, c. 12, art. 2, § 9, provided:

"(a) Articles 1 and 2 apply to each guardianship or conservatorship proceeding and each appointment of guardian or conservator commenced on or after the effective date of articles 1 and 2. Except as otherwise provided in this section, articles 1 and 2 apply to each guardianship or conservatorship approved by the court prior to the effective date of articles 1 and 2, and to any guardianship or conservatorship proceeding pending in court on the effective date of articles 1 and 2, unless the court finds for good cause or in the interests of judicial economy that the proceeding should be completed under the provisions of Minnesota Statutes, chapter 525, as it existed prior to the effective date of articles 1 and 2.

"(b) A guardian or conservator who is not discharged prior to the effective date of articles 1 and 2 shall continue to hold the appointment but shall have only the powers specified in the order of appointment and in Minnesota Statutes, chapter 525, as it existed prior to the effective date of articles 1 and 2. Each guardian or conservator holding an appointment on the effective date of articles 1 and 2 shall continue to be bound by the duties imposed by the order of appointment; by Minnesota Statutes, chapter 525, as it existed prior to the effective date of articles 1 and 2; and by article 1, section 50; and shall be bound by any additional duties imposed by articles 1 and 2 starting on the first day of the next month starting after the effective date of articles 1 and 2 or on the next anniversary date of the appointment, whichever occurs later.

"(c) Any act done prior to the effective date of articles 1 and 2 in any proceeding and any right accrued under Minnesota Statutes, chapter 525, prior to the effective date of articles 1 and 2 shall not be impaired by articles 1 and 2. If a right is acquired, extinguished, or barred upon the expiration of a prescribed period of time which has commenced to run in accordance with the provisions of any statute before the effective date of articles 1 and 2, the provisions of the prior statute shall remain in force with respect to that right notwithstanding the statute's amendment or repeal by articles 1 and 2.

"(d) An order of the court or letters of guardianship or conservatorship issued by the court prior to the effective date of articles 1 and 2 shall remain in full force and effect in accordance with its terms and conditions and in accordance with the provisions of prior law until the court modifies the order or letters in accordance with the provisions of articles 1 and 2. Upon request for a certified copy of an order or letters which remains in full force and effect under this paragraph, the court administrator shall certify that the order or letters remains in full force and effect pursuant to this paragraph.

"(e) The court, without hearing or notice to any person, may issue new letters of guardianship or conservatorship under articles 1 and 2 to replace similar letters issued prior to the effective date of articles 1 and 2. The new letters shall be effective under articles 1 and 2 with the same force and effect as the prior letters and shall remain in full force and effect until modified by the court in accordance with the provisions of articles 1 and 2.

"(f) A power of attorney executed in accordance with Minnesota Statutes, section 524.5–505, prior to the effective date of articles 1 and 2, or any surety bond, deed, or other instrument, report, or other undertaking executed in accordance with Minnesota Statutes, chapter 525, prior to the effective date of articles 1 and 2, shall remain in full force and effect for all purposes in accordance with its terms and conditions and the provisions of the applicable statutes under which the power of attorney, surety bond, deed, or other instrument, report, or other undertaking was executed, until the power of attorney, surety bond, deed, or other instrument, report, or other undertaking expires according to its terms or pursuant to the statutes governing its execution, or is modified, terminated, or superseded by a new power of

attorney, surety bond, deed, or other instru-   accordance with the provisions of articles 1 and
ment, report, or other undertaking executed in   2."

524.5–403. Original petition for appointment or protective order

(a) The following may petition for the appointment of a conservator or for any other appropriate protective order:

(1) the person to be protected;

(2) an individual interested in the estate, affairs, or welfare of the person to be protected; or

(3) a person who would be adversely affected by lack of effective management of the property and business affairs of the person to be protected.

(b) The petition must set forth the petitioner's name, residence, current address if different, relationship to the respondent, and interest in the appointment or other protective order, and, to the extent known, state or contain the following with respect to the respondent and the relief requested:

(1) the respondent's name, age, principal residence, current street address, and, if different, the address of the dwelling where it is proposed that the respondent will reside if the appointment is made;

(2) if the petition alleges impairment in the respondent's ability to receive and evaluate information, a brief description of the nature and extent of the respondent's alleged impairment;

(3) if the petition alleges that the respondent is missing, detained, or unable to return to the United States, a statement of the relevant circumstances, including the time and nature of the disappearance or detention and a description of any search or inquiry concerning the respondent's whereabouts;

(4) the name and address of the respondent's:

(i) spouse, or if the respondent has none, an adult with whom the respondent has resided for more than six months before the filing of the petition; and

(ii) adult children or, if the respondent has none, the respondent's parents and adult brothers and sisters or, if the respondent has none, at least one of the adults nearest in kinship to the respondent who can be found;

(5) the name of the administrative head and address of the institution where the respondent is a patient, resident, or client of any hospital, nursing home, home care agency, or other institution;

(6) the name and address of any legal representative for the respondent;

(7) the name and address of any health care agent or proxy appointed pursuant to a health care directive as defined in section 145C.01, a living will under chapter 145B, or other similar document executed in another state and enforceable under the laws of this state;

(8) a general statement of the respondent's property with an estimate of its value, including any insurance or pension, and the source and amount of other anticipated income or receipts; and

(9) the reason why a conservatorship or other protective order is in the best interest of the respondent.

(c) If a conservatorship is requested, the petition must also set forth to the extent known:

(1) the name and address of any proposed conservator and the reason why the proposed conservator should be selected;

(2) the name and address of any person nominated as conservator by the respondent if the respondent has attained 14 years of age; and

(3) the type of conservatorship requested and, if an unlimited conservatorship, the reason why limited conservatorship is inappropriate or, if a limited conservatorship, the property to be placed under the conservator's control and any limitation on the conservator's powers and duties.

Laws 2003, c. 12, art. 1, § 43.

Historical and Statutory Notes

Laws 2003, c. 12, art. 2, § 9, provided:

"(a) Articles 1 and 2 apply to each guardianship or conservatorship proceeding and each appointment of guardian or conservator commenced on or after the effective date of articles 1 and 2. Except as otherwise provided in this section, articles 1 and 2 apply to each guardianship or conservatorship approved by the court prior to the effective date of articles 1 and 2, and to any guardianship or conservatorship proceeding pending in court on the effective date of articles 1 and 2, unless the court finds for good cause or in the interests of judicial economy that the proceeding should be completed under the provisions of Minnesota Statutes, chapter 525, as it existed prior to the effective date of articles 1 and 2.

"(b) A guardian or conservator who is not discharged prior to the effective date of articles 1 and 2 shall continue to hold the appointment but shall have only the powers specified in the order of appointment and in Minnesota Statutes, chapter 525, as it existed prior to the effective date of articles 1 and 2. Each guardian or conservator holding an appointment on the effective date of articles 1 and 2 shall continue to be bound by the duties imposed by the order of appointment; by Minnesota Statutes, chapter 525, as it existed prior to the effective date of articles 1 and 2; and by article 1, section 50; and shall be bound by any additional duties imposed by articles 1 and 2 starting on the first day of the next month starting after the

effective date of articles 1 and 2 or on the next anniversary date of the appointment, whichever occurs later.

"(c) Any act done prior to the effective date of articles 1 and 2 in any proceeding and any right accrued under Minnesota Statutes, chapter 525, prior to the effective date of articles 1 and 2 shall not be impaired by articles 1 and 2. If a right is acquired, extinguished, or barred upon the expiration of a prescribed period of time which has commenced to run in accordance with the provisions of any statute before the effective date of articles 1 and 2, the provisions of the prior statute shall remain in force with respect to that right notwithstanding the statute's amendment or repeal by articles 1 and 2.

"(d) An order of the court or letters of guardianship or conservatorship issued by the court prior to the effective date of articles 1 and 2 shall remain in full force and effect in accordance with its terms and conditions and in accordance with the provisions of prior law until the court modifies the order or letters in accordance with the provisions of articles 1 and 2. Upon request for a certified copy of an order or letters which remains in full force and effect under this paragraph, the court administrator shall certify that the order or letters remains in full force and effect pursuant to this paragraph.

"(e) The court, without hearing or notice to any person, may issue new letters of guardianship or conservatorship under articles 1 and 2 to replace similar letters issued prior to the

566

effective date of articles 1 and 2. The new letters shall be effective under articles 1 and 2 with the same force and effect as the prior letters and shall remain in full force and effect until modified by the court in accordance with the provisions of articles 1 and 2.

"(f) A power of attorney executed in accordance with Minnesota Statutes, section 524.5–505, prior to the effective date of articles 1 and 2, or any surety bond, deed, or other instrument, report, or other undertaking executed in accordance with Minnesota Statutes, chapter 525, prior to the effective date of articles 1 and 2, shall remain in full force and effect

for all purposes in accordance with its terms and conditions and the provisions of the applicable statutes under which the power of attorney, surety bond, deed, or other instrument, report, or other undertaking was executed, until the power of attorney, surety bond, deed, or other instrument, report, or other undertaking expires according to its terms or pursuant to the statutes governing its execution, or is modified, terminated, or superseded by a new power of attorney, surety bond, deed, or other instrument, report, or other undertaking executed in accordance with the provisions of articles 1 and 2."

524.5–404. Notice

(a) A copy of the petition and the notice of hearing on a petition for conservatorship or other protective order must be served personally on the respondent pursuant to section 524.5–406, paragraph (c), but if the respondent's location is unknown or personal service cannot be made, service on the respondent must be made by substituted service or publication. The notice must include a statement that the respondent must be physically present unless excused by the court, inform the respondent of the respondent's rights at the hearing, and, if the appointment of a conservator is requested, include a description of the nature, purpose, and consequences of an appointment. A failure to serve the respondent with a notice substantially complying with this paragraph precludes the court from granting the petition.

(b) In a proceeding to establish a conservatorship or for another protective order, notice of the hearing shall also be given to the persons listed in the petition. Failure to give notice under this paragraph does not preclude the appointment of a conservator or the making of another protective order.

(c) Notice of the hearing on a petition for an order after appointment of a conservator or making of another protective order, shall be given to interested persons pursuant to section 524.5–113 and to any other person as ordered by the court, except notice to the protected person is not required if the protected person has not attained 14 years of age and is not missing, detained, or unable to return to the United States.

(d) The conservator shall give notice of the filing of the conservator's inventory, together with a copy of the inventory, to the protected person and any other person the court directs. The notice must be sent or delivered within 14 days after the filing of the inventory.

Laws 2003, c. 12, art. 1, § 44.

Historical and Statutory Notes

Laws 2003, c. 12, art. 2, § 9, provided:

"(a) Articles 1 and 2 apply to each guardianship or conservatorship proceeding and each

appointment of guardian or conservator commenced on or after the effective date of articles 1 and 2. Except as otherwise provided in this

section, articles 1 and 2 apply to each guardianship or conservatorship approved by the court prior to the effective date of articles 1 and 2, and to any guardianship or conservatorship proceeding pending in court on the effective date of articles 1 and 2, unless the court finds for good cause or in the interests of judicial economy that the proceeding should be completed under the provisions of Minnesota Statutes, chapter 525, as it existed prior to the effective date of articles 1 and 2.

"(b) A guardian or conservator who is not discharged prior to the effective date of articles 1 and 2 shall continue to hold the appointment but shall have only the powers specified in the order of appointment and in Minnesota Statutes, chapter 525, as it existed prior to the effective date of articles 1 and 2. Each guardian or conservator holding an appointment on the effective date of articles 1 and 2 shall continue to be bound by the duties imposed by the order of appointment; by Minnesota Statutes, chapter 525, as it existed prior to the effective date of articles 1 and 2; and by article 1, section 50; and shall be bound by any additional duties imposed by articles 1 and 2 starting on the first day of the next month starting after the effective date of articles 1 and 2 or on the next anniversary date of the appointment, whichever occurs later.

"(c) Any act done prior to the effective date of articles 1 and 2 in any proceeding and any right accrued under Minnesota Statutes, chapter 525, prior to the effective date of articles 1 and 2 shall not be impaired by articles 1 and 2. If a right is acquired, extinguished, or barred upon the expiration of a prescribed period of time which has commenced to run in accordance with the provisions of any statute before the effective date of articles 1 and 2, the provisions of the prior statute shall remain in force with respect to that right notwithstanding the statute's amendment or repeal by articles 1 and 2.

"(d) An order of the court or letters of guardianship or conservatorship issued by the court prior to the effective date of articles 1 and 2 shall remain in full force and effect in accordance with its terms and conditions and in accordance with the provisions of prior law until the court modifies the order or letters in accordance with the provisions of articles 1 and 2. Upon request for a certified copy of an order or letters which remains in full force and effect under this paragraph, the court administrator shall certify that the order or letters remains in full force and effect pursuant to this paragraph.

"(e) The court, without hearing or notice to any person, may issue new letters of guardianship or conservatorship under articles 1 and 2 to replace similar letters issued prior to the effective date of articles 1 and 2. The new letters shall be effective under articles 1 and 2 with the same force and effect as the prior letters and shall remain in full force and effect until modified by the court in accordance with the provisions of articles 1 and 2.

"(f) A power of attorney executed in accordance with Minnesota Statutes, section 524.5–505, prior to the effective date of articles 1 and 2, or any surety bond, deed, or other instrument, report, or other undertaking executed in accordance with Minnesota Statutes, chapter 525, prior to the effective date of articles 1 and 2, shall remain in full force and effect for all purposes in accordance with its terms and conditions and the provisions of the applicable statutes under which the power of attorney, surety bond, deed, or other instrument, report, or other undertaking was executed, until the power of attorney, surety bond, deed, or other instrument, report, or other undertaking expires according to its terms or pursuant to the statutes governing its execution, or is modified, terminated, or superseded by a new power of attorney, surety bond, deed, or other instrument, report, or other undertaking executed in accordance with the provisions of articles 1 and 2."

524.5–405. Original petition: minors; preliminaries to hearing

(a) Upon the filing of a petition to establish a conservatorship or for another protective order for the reason that the respondent is a minor, the court shall set a date for hearing. If the court determines at any stage of the proceeding that the interests of the minor are or may be inadequately represented, it may appoint a lawyer to represent the minor, giving consideration to the choice of the minor if the minor has attained 14 years of age.

(b) While a petition to establish a conservatorship or for another protective order is pending, after preliminary hearing and without notice to others, the court may make orders to preserve and apply the property of the minor as may be required for the support of the minor or individuals who are in fact dependent upon the minor, and may appoint an agent to assist in that task.

Laws 2003, c. 12, art. 1, § 45.

Historical and Statutory Notes

Laws 2003, c. 12, art. 2, § 9, provided:

"(a) Articles 1 and 2 apply to each guardianship or conservatorship proceeding and each appointment of guardian or conservator commenced on or after the effective date of articles 1 and 2. Except as otherwise provided in this section, articles 1 and 2 apply to each guardianship or conservatorship approved by the court prior to the effective date of articles 1 and 2, and to any guardianship or conservatorship proceeding pending in court on the effective date of articles 1 and 2, unless the court finds for good cause or in the interests of judicial economy that the proceeding should be completed under the provisions of Minnesota Statutes, chapter 525, as it existed prior to the effective date of articles 1 and 2.

"(b) A guardian or conservator who is not discharged prior to the effective date of articles 1 and 2 shall continue to hold the appointment but shall have only the powers specified in the order of appointment and in Minnesota Statutes, chapter 525, as it existed prior to the effective date of articles 1 and 2. Each guardian or conservator holding an appointment on the effective date of articles 1 and 2 shall continue to be bound by the duties imposed by the order of appointment; by Minnesota Statutes, chapter 525, as it existed prior to the effective date of articles 1 and 2; and by article 1, section 50; and shall be bound by any additional duties imposed by articles 1 and 2 starting on the first day of the next month starting after the effective date of articles 1 and 2 or on the next anniversary date of the appointment, whichever occurs later.

"(c) Any act done prior to the effective date of articles 1 and 2 in any proceeding and any right accrued under Minnesota Statutes, chapter 525, prior to the effective date of articles 1 and 2 shall not be impaired by articles 1 and 2. If a right is acquired, extinguished, or barred upon the expiration of a prescribed period of time which has commenced to run in accordance with the provisions of any statute before the effective date of articles 1 and 2, the provisions of the prior statute shall remain in force with

respect to that right notwithstanding the statute's amendment or repeal by articles 1 and 2.

"(d) An order of the court or letters of guardianship or conservatorship issued by the court prior to the effective date of articles 1 and 2 shall remain in full force and effect in accordance with its terms and conditions and in accordance with the provisions of prior law until the court modifies the order or letters in accordance with the provisions of articles 1 and 2. Upon request for a certified copy of an order or letters which remains in full force and effect under this paragraph, the court administrator shall certify that the order or letters remains in full force and effect pursuant to this paragraph.

"(e) The court, without hearing or notice to any person, may issue new letters of guardianship or conservatorship under articles 1 and 2 to replace similar letters issued prior to the effective date of articles 1 and 2. The new letters shall be effective under articles 1 and 2 with the same force and effect as the prior letters and shall remain in full force and effect until modified by the court in accordance with the provisions of articles 1 and 2.

"(f) A power of attorney executed in accordance with Minnesota Statutes, section 524.5–505, prior to the effective date of articles 1 and 2, or any surety bond, deed, or other instrument, report, or other undertaking executed in accordance with Minnesota Statutes, chapter 525, prior to the effective date of articles 1 and 2, shall remain in full force and effect for all purposes in accordance with its terms and conditions and the provisions of the applicable statutes under which the power of attorney, surety bond, deed, or other instrument, report, or other undertaking was executed, until the power of attorney, surety bond, deed, or other instrument, report, or other undertaking expires according to its terms or pursuant to the statutes governing its execution, or is modified, terminated, or superseded by a new power of attorney, surety bond, deed, or other instrument, report, or other undertaking executed in accordance with the provisions of articles 1 and 2."

524.5–406. Original petition: persons under disability; preliminaries to hearing

(a) Upon the filing of a petition for a conservatorship or other protective order for a respondent for reasons other than being a minor, the court shall set a date for hearing and the court may appoint a visitor. The duties and reporting requirements of the visitor are limited to the relief requested in the petition.

(b) A respondent has the right to be represented by counsel at any proceeding under this article. The court shall appoint counsel to represent the respondent for the initial proceeding held pursuant to section 524.5–408 if neither the respondent nor others provide counsel, unless in a meeting with a visitor, the proposed respondent specifically waives the right to counsel. Counsel must be appointed immediately after any petition under this part is served pursuant to section 524.5–404. Counsel has the full right of subpoena. In all proceedings under this part, counsel shall:

(1) consult with the respondent before any hearing;

(2) be given adequate time to prepare for all hearings; and

(3) continue to represent the respondent throughout any proceedings under section 524.5–408, provided that such appointment shall expire upon the expiration of the appeal time for the order appointing conservator or the order dismissing a petition, or upon such other time or event as the court may direct.

The court need not appoint counsel to represent the respondent on a voluntary petition, and the court may remove a court-appointed attorney at any time if the court finds that the respondent has made a knowing and intelligent waiver of the right to counsel or has obtained private counsel.

(c) The visitor shall personally serve the notice and petition upon the respondent and shall offer to read the notice and petition to the respondent, and if so requested, the visitor shall read the notice and petition to such person. The visitor shall also interview the respondent in person, and to the extent that the respondent is able to understand:

(1) explain to the respondent the substance of the petition and the nature, purpose, and effect of the proceeding;

(2) if the appointment of a conservator is requested, inform the respondent of the general powers and duties of a conservator and determine the respondent's views regarding the proposed conservator, the proposed conservator's powers and duties, and the scope and duration of the proposed conservatorship;

(3) inform the respondent of the respondent's rights, including the right to employ and consult with a lawyer at the respondent's own expense, and the right to request a court-appointed lawyer; and

(4) inform the respondent that all costs and expenses of the proceeding, including respondent's attorney fees, will be paid from the respondent's estate.

(d) In addition to the duties set out in paragraph (c), the visitor shall make any other investigations the court directs.

(e) The visitor shall promptly file a report with the court which must include:

(1) recommendations regarding the appropriateness of a conservatorship, including whether less restrictive means of intervention are available, the type of conservatorship, and, if a limited conservatorship, the powers and duties to be granted the limited conservator, and the assets over which the conservator should be granted authority;

(2) a statement as to whether the respondent approves or disapproves of the proposed conservator, and the powers and duties proposed or the scope of the conservatorship; and

(3) any other matters the court directs.

(f) While a petition to establish a conservatorship or for another protective order is pending, after preliminary hearing and without notice to others, the court may make orders to preserve and apply the property of the respondent as may be required for the support of the respondent or individuals who are in fact dependent upon the respondent, and may appoint an agent to assist in that task.

Laws 2003, c. 12, art. 1, § 46. Amended by Laws 2004, c. 146, art. 2, § 5.

Historical and Statutory Notes

Laws 2003, c. 12, art. 2, § 9, provided:

"(a) Articles 1 and 2 apply to each guardianship or conservatorship proceeding and each appointment of guardian or conservator commenced on or after the effective date of articles 1 and 2. Except as otherwise provided in this section, articles 1 and 2 apply to each guardianship or conservatorship approved by the court prior to the effective date of articles 1 and 2, and to any guardianship or conservatorship proceeding pending in court on the effective date of articles 1 and 2, unless the court finds for good cause or in the interests of judicial economy that the proceeding should be completed under the provisions of Minnesota Statutes, chapter 525, as it existed prior to the effective date of articles 1 and 2.

"(b) A guardian or conservator who is not discharged prior to the effective date of articles 1 and 2 shall continue to hold the appointment but shall have only the powers specified in the order of appointment and in Minnesota Statutes, chapter 525, as it existed prior to the effective date of articles 1 and 2. Each guardian or conservator holding an appointment on the effective date of articles 1 and 2 shall continue to be bound by the duties imposed by the order of appointment; by Minnesota Statutes, chapter 525, as it existed prior to the effective date of articles 1 and 2; and by article 1, section 50; and shall be bound by any additional duties imposed by articles 1 and 2 starting on the first day of the next month starting after the effective date of articles 1 and 2 or on the next

anniversary date of the appointment, whichever occurs later.

"(c) Any act done prior to the effective date of articles 1 and 2 in any proceeding and any right accrued under Minnesota Statutes, chapter 525, prior to the effective date of articles 1 and 2 shall not be impaired by articles 1 and 2. If a right is acquired, extinguished, or barred upon the expiration of a prescribed period of time which has commenced to run in accordance with the provisions of any statute before the effective date of articles 1 and 2, the provisions of the prior statute shall remain in force with respect to that right notwithstanding the statute's amendment or repeal by articles 1 and 2.

"(d) An order of the court or letters of guardianship or conservatorship issued by the court prior to the effective date of articles 1 and 2 shall remain in full force and effect in accordance with its terms and conditions and in accordance with the provisions of prior law until the court modifies the order or letters in accordance with the provisions of articles 1 and 2. Upon request for a certified copy of an order or letters which remains in full force and effect under this paragraph, the court administrator shall certify that the order or letters remains in full force and effect pursuant to this paragraph.

"(e) The court, without hearing or notice to any person, may issue new letters of guardianship or conservatorship under articles 1 and 2 to replace similar letters issued prior to the effective date of articles 1 and 2. The new letters shall be effective under articles 1 and 2 with the same force and effect as the prior letters and shall remain in full force and effect until modified by the court in accordance with the provisions of articles 1 and 2.

"(f) A power of attorney executed in accordance with Minnesota Statutes, section 524.5–505, prior to the effective date of articles 1 and 2, or any surety bond, deed, or other instrument, report, or other undertaking executed in accordance with Minnesota Statutes, chapter 525, prior to the effective date of articles 1 and 2, shall remain in full force and effect for all purposes in accordance with its terms and conditions and the provisions of the applicable statutes under which the power of attorney, surety bond, deed, or other instrument, report, or other undertaking was executed, until the power of attorney, surety bond, deed, or other instrument, report, or other undertaking expires according to its terms or pursuant to the statutes governing its execution, or is modified, terminated, or superseded by a new power of attorney, surety bond, deed, or other instrument, report, or other undertaking executed in accordance with the provisions of articles 1 and 2."

524.5–408. Original petition: procedure at hearing

(a) Unless excused by the court for good cause, the petitioner and the proposed conservator shall attend the hearing. The respondent shall attend and participate in the hearing unless excused by the court for good cause. The petitioner and respondent may present evidence and subpoena witnesses and documents, examine witnesses, including the visitor, and otherwise participate in the hearing. The hearing may be held in a location convenient to the respondent and may be closed upon request of the respondent and a showing of good cause.

(b) Any person may request permission to participate in the proceeding. The court may grant the request, with or without hearing, upon a showing of good cause and after determining that the best interest of the respondent will be served. The court may attach appropriate conditions to the participation.

Laws 2003, c. 12, art. 1, § 47. Amended by Laws 2004, c. 146, art. 2, § 6.

Historical and Statutory Notes

Laws 2003, c. 12, art. 2, § 9, provided:

"(a) Articles 1 and 2 apply to each guardianship or conservatorship proceeding and each appointment of guardian or conservator commenced on or after the effective date of articles 1 and 2. Except as otherwise provided in this section, articles 1 and 2 apply to each guardianship or conservatorship approved by the court prior to the effective date of articles 1 and 2, and to any guardianship or conservatorship proceeding pending in court on the effective date of articles 1 and 2, unless the court finds for good cause or in the interests of judicial economy that the proceeding should be completed under the provisions of Minnesota Statutes, chapter 525, as it existed prior to the effective date of articles 1 and 2.

"(b) A guardian or conservator who is not discharged prior to the effective date of articles 1 and 2 shall continue to hold the appointment but shall have only the powers specified in the order of appointment and in Minnesota Statutes, chapter 525, as it existed prior to the effective date of articles 1 and 2. Each guardian or conservator holding an appointment on the effective date of articles 1 and 2 shall continue to be bound by the duties imposed by the order of appointment; by Minnesota Statutes, chapter 525, as it existed prior to the effective date of articles 1 and 2; and by article 1, section 50; and shall be bound by any additional duties imposed by articles 1 and 2 starting on the first day of the next month starting after the effective date of articles 1 and 2 or on the next anniversary date of the appointment, whichever occurs later.

"(c) Any act done prior to the effective date of articles 1 and 2 in any proceeding and any right accrued under Minnesota Statutes, chapter 525, prior to the effective date of articles 1 and 2 shall not be impaired by articles 1 and 2. If a right is acquired, extinguished, or barred upon the expiration of a prescribed period of time which has commenced to run in accordance with the provisions of any statute before the effective date of articles 1 and 2, the provisions of the prior statute shall remain in force with respect to that right notwithstanding the statute's amendment or repeal by articles 1 and 2.

"(d) An order of the court or letters of guardianship or conservatorship issued by the court prior to the effective date of articles 1 and 2 shall remain in full force and effect in accordance with its terms and conditions and in accordance with the provisions of prior law until the court modifies the order or letters in accordance with the provisions of articles 1 and 2. Upon request for a certified copy of an order or letters which remains in full force and effect under this paragraph, the court administrator shall certify that the order or letters remains in full force and effect pursuant to this paragraph.

"(e) The court, without hearing or notice to any person, may issue new letters of guardianship or conservatorship under articles 1 and 2 to replace similar letters issued prior to the effective date of articles 1 and 2. The new letters shall be effective under articles 1 and 2 with the same force and effect as the prior letters and shall remain in full force and effect

until modified by the court in accordance with the provisions of articles 1 and 2.

"(f) A power of attorney executed in accordance with Minnesota Statutes, section 524.5–505, prior to the effective date of articles 1 and 2, or any surety bond, deed, or other instrument, report, or other undertaking executed in accordance with Minnesota Statutes, chapter 525, prior to the effective date of articles 1 and 2, shall remain in full force and effect for all purposes in accordance with its terms and conditions and the provisions of the applicable statutes under which the power of attorney, surety bond, deed, or other instrument, report, or other undertaking was executed, until the power of attorney, surety bond, deed, or other instrument, report, or other undertaking expires according to its terms or pursuant to the statutes governing its execution, or is modified, terminated, or superseded by a new power of attorney, surety bond, deed, or other instrument, report, or other undertaking executed in accordance with the provisions of articles 1 and 2."

524.5–409. Findings; order of appointment

(a) The court may appoint a limited or unlimited conservator for a respondent only if it finds that:

(1) by clear and convincing evidence, the individual is unable to manage property and business affairs because of an impairment in the ability to receive and evaluate information or make decisions, even with the use of appropriate technological assistance, or because the individual is missing, detained, or unable to return to the United States;

(2) by a preponderance of evidence, the individual has property that will be wasted or dissipated unless management is provided or money is needed for the support, care, education, health, and welfare of the individual or of individuals who are entitled to the individual's support and that protection is necessary or desirable to obtain or provide money; and

(3) the respondent's identified needs cannot be met by less restrictive means, including use of appropriate technological assistance.

(b) Alternatively, the court, with appropriate findings, may enter any other appropriate order, or dismiss the proceeding.

(c) The court, whenever feasible, shall grant to a conservator only those powers necessitated by the protected person's limitations and demonstrated needs and make appointive and other orders that will encourage the development of the protected person's maximum self-reliance and independence.

(d) Within 14 days after an appointment, the conservator shall send or deliver to the protected person, if the protected person has attained 14 years of age and is not missing, detained, or unable to return to the United States, and counsel if represented at the hearing, a copy of the order of appointment accompanied by a notice which advises the protected person of the right to appeal the conservatorship appointment in the time and manner provided by the Rules of Appellate Procedure.

(e) Each year, within 30 days after the anniversary date of an appointment, a conservator shall send or deliver to the protected person a notice of the right to request termination or modification of the conservatorship.

(f) The appointment of a conservator or the entry of another protective order is not a determination of incapacity of the protected person.

Laws 2003, c. 12, art. 1, § 48.

Historical and Statutory Notes

Laws 2003, c. 12, art. 2, § 9, provided:

"(a) Articles 1 and 2 apply to each guardianship or conservatorship proceeding and each appointment of guardian or conservator commenced on or after the effective date of articles 1 and 2. Except as otherwise provided in this section, articles 1 and 2 apply to each guardianship or conservatorship approved by the court prior to the effective date of articles 1 and 2, and to any guardianship or conservatorship proceeding pending in court on the effective date of articles 1 and 2, unless the court finds for good cause or in the interests of judicial economy that the proceeding should be completed under the provisions of Minnesota Statutes, chapter 525, as it existed prior to the effective date of articles 1 and 2.

"(b) A guardian or conservator who is not discharged prior to the effective date of articles 1 and 2 shall continue to hold the appointment but shall have only the powers specified in the order of appointment and in Minnesota Statutes, chapter 525, as it existed prior to the effective date of articles 1 and 2. Each guardian or conservator holding an appointment on the effective date of articles 1 and 2 shall continue to be bound by the duties imposed by the order of appointment; by Minnesota Statutes, chapter 525, as it existed prior to the effective date of articles 1 and 2; and by article 1, section 50; and shall be bound by any additional duties imposed by articles 1 and 2 starting on the first day of the next month starting after the effective date of articles 1 and 2 or on the next anniversary date of the appointment, whichever occurs later.

"(c) Any act done prior to the effective date of articles 1 and 2 in any proceeding and any right accrued under Minnesota Statutes, chapter 525, prior to the effective date of articles 1 and 2 shall not be impaired by articles 1 and 2. If a right is acquired, extinguished, or barred upon the expiration of a prescribed period of time which has commenced to run in accordance with the provisions of any statute before the effective date of articles 1 and 2, the provisions of the prior statute shall remain in force with respect to that right notwithstanding the statute's amendment or repeal by articles 1 and 2.

"(d) An order of the court or letters of guardianship or conservatorship issued by the court prior to the effective date of articles 1 and 2 shall remain in full force and effect in accordance with its terms and conditions and in accordance with the provisions of prior law until the court modifies the order or letters in accordance with the provisions of articles 1 and 2. Upon request for a certified copy of an order or letters which remains in full force and effect under this paragraph, the court administrator shall certify that the order or letters remains in full force and effect pursuant to this paragraph.

"(e) The court, without hearing or notice to any person, may issue new letters of guardianship or conservatorship under articles 1 and 2 to replace similar letters issued prior to the effective date of articles 1 and 2. The new letters shall be effective under articles 1 and 2 with the same force and effect as the prior letters and shall remain in full force and effect until modified by the court in accordance with the provisions of articles 1 and 2.

"(f) A power of attorney executed in accordance with Minnesota Statutes, section 524.5–505, prior to the effective date of articles 1 and 2, or any surety bond, deed, or other instrument, report, or other undertaking executed in accordance with Minnesota Statutes, chapter 525, prior to the effective date of articles 1 and 2, shall remain in full force and effect for all purposes in accordance with its terms and conditions and the provisions of the applicable statutes under which the power of attorney, surety bond, deed, or other instrument, report, or other undertaking was executed, until the power of attorney, surety bond, deed, or other instrument, report, or other undertaking expires according to its terms or pursuant to the statutes governing its execution, or is modified, terminated, or superseded by a new power of attorney, surety bond, deed, or other instrument, report, or other undertaking executed in accordance with the provisions of articles 1 and 2."

524.5–410. Powers of court

(a) After hearing and upon determining that a basis for a conservatorship or other protective order exists, the court has the following powers, which may be exercised directly or through a conservator:

(1) with respect to a minor for reasons of age, all the powers over the estate and business affairs of the minor which may be necessary for the best interest of the minor and members of the minor's immediate family; and

(2) with respect to an adult, or to a minor for reasons other than age, for the benefit of the protected person and individuals who are in fact dependent on the protected person for support, all the powers over the estate and business affairs of the protected person which the protected person could exercise if an adult, present, and not under conservatorship or other protective order.

(b) Subject to the provisions of section 524.5–110 relating to letters of office, the court may at any time limit the powers of a conservator otherwise conferred and may remove or modify any limitation.

Laws 2003, c. 12, art. 1, § 49.

Historical and Statutory Notes

Laws 2003, c. 12, art. 2, § 9, provided:

"(a) Articles 1 and 2 apply to each guardianship or conservatorship proceeding and each appointment of guardian or conservator commenced on or after the effective date of articles 1 and 2. Except as otherwise provided in this section, articles 1 and 2 apply to each guardianship or conservatorship approved by the court prior to the effective date of articles 1 and 2, and to any guardianship or conservatorship proceeding pending in court on the effective date of articles 1 and 2, unless the court finds for good cause or in the interests of judicial economy that the proceeding should be completed under the provisions of Minnesota Statutes, chapter 525, as it existed prior to the effective date of articles 1 and 2.

"(b) A guardian or conservator who is not discharged prior to the effective date of articles 1 and 2 shall continue to hold the appointment but shall have only the powers specified in the order of appointment and in Minnesota Statutes, chapter 525, as it existed prior to the effective date of articles 1 and 2. Each guardian or conservator holding an appointment on the effective date of articles 1 and 2 shall continue to be bound by the duties imposed by the order of appointment; by Minnesota Statutes, chapter 525, as it existed prior to the effective date of articles 1 and 2; and by article 1, section 50; and shall be bound by any additional duties imposed by articles 1 and 2 starting on the first day of the next month starting after the effective date of articles 1 and 2 or on the next anniversary date of the appointment, whichever occurs later.

"(c) Any act done prior to the effective date of articles 1 and 2 in any proceeding and any right accrued under Minnesota Statutes, chapter 525, prior to the effective date of articles 1 and 2 shall not be impaired by articles 1 and 2. If a right is acquired, extinguished, or barred upon the expiration of a prescribed period of time which has commenced to run in accordance with the provisions of any statute before the effective date of articles 1 and 2, the provisions of the prior statute shall remain in force with respect to that right notwithstanding the statute's amendment or repeal by articles 1 and 2.

"(d) An order of the court or letters of guardianship or conservatorship issued by the court prior to the effective date of articles 1 and 2 shall remain in full force and effect in accordance with its terms and conditions and in

accordance with the provisions of prior law until the court modifies the order or letters in accordance with the provisions of articles 1 and 2. Upon request for a certified copy of an order or letters which remains in full force and effect under this paragraph, the court administrator shall certify that the order or letters remains in full force and effect pursuant to this paragraph.

"(e) The court, without hearing or notice to any person, may issue new letters of guardianship or conservatorship under articles 1 and 2 to replace similar letters issued prior to the effective date of articles 1 and 2. The new letters shall be effective under articles 1 and 2 with the same force and effect as the prior letters and shall remain in full force and effect until modified by the court in accordance with the provisions of articles 1 and 2.

"(f) A power of attorney executed in accordance with Minnesota Statutes, section 524.5–505, prior to the effective date of articles 1 and 2, or any surety bond, deed, or other instrument, report, or other undertaking executed in accordance with Minnesota Statutes, chapter 525, prior to the effective date of articles 1 and 2, shall remain in full force and effect for all purposes in accordance with its terms and conditions and the provisions of the applicable statutes under which the power of attorney, surety bond, deed, or other instrument, report, or other undertaking was executed, until the power of attorney, surety bond, deed, or other instrument, report, or other undertaking expires according to its terms or pursuant to the statutes governing its execution, or is modified, terminated, or superseded by a new power of attorney, surety bond, deed, or other instrument, report, or other undertaking executed in accordance with the provisions of articles 1 and 2."

524.5–411. Required court approval

(a) After notice to affected persons as provided in this section, and after hearing, and upon express authorization of the court, a conservator may:

(1) make gifts;

(2) convey, release, or disclaim contingent and expectant interests in property, including marital property rights and any right of survivorship incident to joint tenancy or tenancy by the entireties;

(3) exercise or release a power of appointment;

(4) create a revocable or irrevocable trust of property of the estate, whether or not the trust extends beyond the duration of the conservatorship, or to revoke or amend a trust revocable by the protected person;

(5) subject to the terms of the plan document, contract, or agreement, exercise rights to elect options and change beneficiaries under insurance policies and annuities or surrender the policies and annuities for their cash value, and any change pursuant to this clause, shall invalidate the existing elections and beneficiary designations;

(6) exercise any right to exempt property and an elective share in the estate of the protected person's deceased spouse and to renounce or disclaim any interest by testate or intestate succession or by transfer inter vivos;

(7) subject to the terms of the plan document, contract, or agreement, exercise rights to elect options and change beneficiaries under any qualified or nonqualified retirement plan including, but not limited to, defined benefit plans, defined contribution plans, plans governed by sections 401(k), 403, 408, or 457 of the Internal Revenue Code [1] and the regulations thereto, and the right to exercise the options provided a plan participant or beneficiary under section 401 and related provisions of the Internal Revenue Code and the regulations

thereto, and any change pursuant to this clause, shall invalidate the existing elections and beneficiary designations;

(8) exercise the power to create, terminate, or alter the beneficial interests and beneficiaries of, a payable on death (POD) account, a transfer on death (TOD) security registration or account, or joint tenancy interests with rights of survivorship; and

(9) make, amend, or revoke the protected person's will.

(b) Notice of any hearing pursuant to this section shall not be given pursuant to section 524.5–113. Notice of any hearing under this section shall be given to all affected persons, in plain language, and shall provide the time and place of the hearing and be given by mail postmarked at least 14 days before the hearing. Proof of notice must be made before or at the hearing and filed in the proceeding. For purposes of this section, notice to "affected persons":

(1) shall always include (i) the protected person, (ii) the duly appointed conservator, (iii) the protected person's heirs–at–law, (iv) any state agency or county social services agency paying benefits to or for the benefit of the protected person, (v) any state agency to which an application for benefits has been submitted and any state or county agency that has prepared an asset assessment or could prepare an asset assessment under section 256B.059, subdivision 2, for the protected person or spouse, and (vi) subject to the limitations of paragraph (c), all beneficiaries of the protected person's existing will or revocable trust;

(2) shall also include, subject to the limitations of paragraph (c), any person who has a beneficial vested or contingent interest that may be affected by the exercise of the power under this section; and

(3) shall also include any other persons designated by the court.

(c) For purposes of this section, when giving notice, or for purposes of giving consent or approval, or objecting with regard to any proceedings under this section, the sole holder or all coholders of a presently exercisable or testamentary general power of appointment, power of revocation, or unlimited power of withdrawal, under an existing will or trust, are deemed to represent and act for beneficiaries to the extent that their interests as objects, takers in default, or otherwise, are subject to the power.

(d) A conservator, in making, amending, or revoking the protected person's will, shall comply with sections 524.2–501 to 524.2–517 acting on behalf of the protected person.

(e) The court, in exercising or in approving a conservator's exercise of the powers listed in paragraph (a), shall consider primarily the decision that the protected person would have made, to the extent that the decision can be ascertained. The court shall also consider:

(1) the financial needs of the protected person and the needs of individuals who are dependent on the protected person for support and the interests of creditors;

(2) possible effect on income, estate, gift, inheritance, or other tax liabilities;

(3) eligibility for governmental assistance with the goal of avoiding reliance on such programs;

(4) the protected person's previous pattern of giving or level of support;

(5) the existing estate plan;

(6) the protected person's life expectancy and the probability that the conservatorship will terminate before the protected person's death;

(7) whether the protected person's needs can be met from the person's remaining assets after any transfer is made, taking into account the effect of any transfer on eligibility for medical assistance long-term care services; and

(8) any other factors the court considers relevant.

(f) If an affected person, as defined in this article, is a minor or an incapacitated person as defined by this article and has no guardian or conservator within the state, or if an affected person is unborn, unascertained, or a person whose identity or address is unknown to the petitioner, the court shall represent that person, unless the court, upon the application of the guardian, conservator, or any other affected person, appoints a guardian ad litem to represent the affected person.

(g) Notwithstanding the power granted to the conservator by the court under this section, the conservator owes no duty to any person other than the protected person. The conservator shall not be held liable for the exercise or the failure to exercise, or the decision to exercise or the decision to decline to exercise, the powers granted by this section. The conservator, however, may be held liable to the protected person's estate for gross negligence related to the implementation of any action approved by the court under this section.

(h) The Uniform Guardianship and Protective Proceedings Act does not repeal section 524.2–215 as it applies to wards, protected persons, or respondents, expressly or by implication. If there is a conflict between the act and section 524.2–215, section 524.2–215 controls and the guardian or conservator shall exercise the rights of the ward, protected person, or respondent under section 524.2–215 without the need for any court order.

Laws 2003, c. 12, art. 1, § 50.

[1] All text references to Internal Revenue Code sections are to Title 26 of U.S.C.A.

Historical and Statutory Notes

Laws 2003, c. 12, art. 2, § 9, provided:

"(a) Articles 1 and 2 apply to each guardianship or conservatorship proceeding and each appointment of guardian or conservator commenced on or after the effective date of articles 1 and 2. Except as otherwise provided in this section, articles 1 and 2 apply to each guardianship or conservatorship approved by the court prior to the effective date of articles 1 and 2, and to any guardianship or conservatorship proceeding pending in court on the effective date of articles 1 and 2, unless the court finds for good cause or in the interests of judicial economy that the proceeding should be completed under the provisions of Minnesota Statutes, chapter 525, as it existed prior to the effective date of articles 1 and 2.

"(b) A guardian or conservator who is not discharged prior to the effective date of articles 1 and 2 shall continue to hold the appointment but shall have only the powers specified in the order of appointment and in Minnesota Statutes, chapter 525, as it existed prior to the effective date of articles 1 and 2. Each guardian or conservator holding an appointment on the effective date of articles 1 and 2 shall continue to be bound by the duties imposed by the order of appointment; by Minnesota Statutes, chapter 525, as it existed prior to the effective date of articles 1 and 2; and by article 1, section 50; and shall be bound by any additional duties imposed by articles 1 and 2 starting on the first day of the next month starting after the effective date of articles 1 and 2 or on the next anniversary date of the appointment, whichever occurs later.

"(c) Any act done prior to the effective date of articles 1 and 2 in any proceeding and any right accrued under Minnesota Statutes, chapter 525, prior to the effective date of articles 1 and 2 shall not be impaired by articles 1 and 2. If a right is acquired, extinguished, or barred upon the expiration of a prescribed period of time which has commenced to run in accordance with the provisions of any statute before the effective date of articles 1 and 2, the provisions of the prior statute shall remain in force with respect to that right notwithstanding the statute's amendment or repeal by articles 1 and 2.

"(d) An order of the court or letters of guardianship or conservatorship issued by the court prior to the effective date of articles 1 and 2 shall remain in full force and effect in accordance with its terms and conditions and in accordance with the provisions of prior law until the court modifies the order or letters in accordance with the provisions of articles 1 and 2. Upon request for a certified copy of an order or letters which remains in full force and effect under this paragraph, the court administrator shall certify that the order or letters remains in full force and effect pursuant to this paragraph.

"(e) The court, without hearing or notice to any person, may issue new letters of guardianship or conservatorship under articles 1 and 2 to replace similar letters issued prior to the effective date of articles 1 and 2. The new letters shall be effective under articles 1 and 2 with the same force and effect as the prior letters and shall remain in full force and effect until modified by the court in accordance with the provisions of articles 1 and 2.

"(f) A power of attorney executed in accordance with Minnesota Statutes, section 524.5–505, prior to the effective date of articles 1 and 2, or any surety bond, deed, or other instrument, report, or other undertaking executed in accordance with Minnesota Statutes, chapter 525, prior to the effective date of articles 1 and 2, shall remain in full force and effect for all purposes in accordance with its terms and conditions and the provisions of the applicable statutes under which the power of attorney, surety bond, deed, or other instrument, report, or other undertaking was executed, until the power of attorney, surety bond, deed, or other instrument, report, or other undertaking expires according to its terms or pursuant to the statutes governing its execution, or is modified, terminated, or superseded by a new power of attorney, surety bond, deed, or other instrument, report, or other undertaking executed in accordance with the provisions of articles 1 and 2."

524.5–412. Protective arrangements and single transactions

(a) If a basis is established for a protective order with respect to an individual, the court, without appointing a conservator, may:

(1) authorize, direct, or ratify any transaction necessary or desirable to achieve any arrangement for security, service, or care meeting the foreseeable needs of the protected person, including:

(i) subject to the procedural and notice requirements of section 524.5–418, the sale, mortgage, lease, or other transfer of property;

(ii) purchase of an annuity;

(iii) making a contract for lifetime care, a deposit contract, or a contract for training and education; or

(iv) addition to or establishment of a suitable trust, including a trust created under the Uniform Custodial Trust Act; and

(2) authorize, direct, or ratify any other contract, trust, will, or transaction relating to the protected person's property and business affairs, including a settlement of a claim, upon determining that it is in the best interest of the protected person.

(b) In deciding whether to approve a protective arrangement or other transaction under this section, the court shall consider the factors listed in section 524.5–411, paragraph (e).

(c) The court may appoint an agent to assist in the accomplishment of any protective arrangement or other transaction authorized under this section. The agent has the authority conferred by the order and shall serve until discharged by order after report to the court; provided, however, that if a conservator is appointed, only the conservator has the power to sign all real estate deeds.

Laws 2003, c. 12, art. 1, § 51.

Historical and Statutory Notes

Laws 2003, c. 12, art. 2, § 9, provided:

"(a) Articles 1 and 2 apply to each guardianship or conservatorship proceeding and each appointment of guardian or conservator commenced on or after the effective date of articles 1 and 2. Except as otherwise provided in this section, articles 1 and 2 apply to each guardianship or conservatorship approved by the court prior to the effective date of articles 1 and 2, and to any guardianship or conservatorship proceeding pending in court on the effective date of articles 1 and 2, unless the court finds for good cause or in the interests of judicial economy that the proceeding should be completed under the provisions of Minnesota Statutes, chapter 525, as it existed prior to the effective date of articles 1 and 2.

"(b) A guardian or conservator who is not discharged prior to the effective date of articles 1 and 2 shall continue to hold the appointment but shall have only the powers specified in the order of appointment and in Minnesota Statutes, chapter 525, as it existed prior to the effective date of articles 1 and 2. Each guardian or conservator holding an appointment on the effective date of articles 1 and 2 shall continue to be bound by the duties imposed by the order of appointment; by Minnesota Statutes, chapter 525, as it existed prior to the effective date of articles 1 and 2; and by article 1, section 50; and shall be bound by any additional duties imposed by articles 1 and 2 starting on

the first day of the next month starting after the effective date of articles 1 and 2 or on the next anniversary date of the appointment, whichever occurs later.

"(c) Any act done prior to the effective date of articles 1 and 2 in any proceeding and any right accrued under Minnesota Statutes, chapter 525, prior to the effective date of articles 1 and 2 shall not be impaired by articles 1 and 2. If a right is acquired, extinguished, or barred upon the expiration of a prescribed period of time which has commenced to run in accordance with the provisions of any statute before the effective date of articles 1 and 2, the provisions of the prior statute shall remain in force with respect to that right notwithstanding the statute's amendment or repeal by articles 1 and 2.

"(d) An order of the court or letters of guardianship or conservatorship issued by the court prior to the effective date of articles 1 and 2 shall remain in full force and effect in accordance with its terms and conditions and in accordance with the provisions of prior law until the court modifies the order or letters in accordance with the provisions of articles 1 and 2. Upon request for a certified copy of an order or letters which remains in full force and effect under this paragraph, the court administrator shall certify that the order or letters remains in full force and effect pursuant to this paragraph.

"(e) The court, without hearing or notice to any person, may issue new letters of guardianship or conservatorship under articles 1 and 2 to replace similar letters issued prior to the effective date of articles 1 and 2. The new letters shall be effective under articles 1 and 2 with the same force and effect as the prior letters and shall remain in full force and effect until modified by the court in accordance with the provisions of articles 1 and 2.

"(f) A power of attorney executed in accordance with Minnesota Statutes, section 524.5–505, prior to the effective date of articles 1 and 2, or any surety bond, deed, or other instrument, report, or other undertaking executed in accordance with Minnesota Statutes, chapter 525, prior to the effective date of articles 1 and 2, shall remain in full force and effect for all purposes in accordance with its terms and conditions and the provisions of the applicable statutes under which the power of attorney, surety bond, deed, or other instrument, report, or other undertaking was executed, until the power of attorney, surety bond, deed, or other instrument, report, or other undertaking expires according to its terms or pursuant to the statutes governing its execution, or is modified, terminated, or superseded by a new power of attorney, surety bond, deed, or other instrument, report, or other undertaking executed in accordance with the provisions of articles 1 and 2."

524.5–413. Who may be conservator; priorities

(a) Except as otherwise provided in paragraph (d), the court, in appointing a conservator, shall consider persons otherwise qualified in the following order of priority:

(1) a conservator, guardian of the estate, or other like fiduciary appointed or recognized by an appropriate court of any other jurisdiction in which the protected person resides;

(2) a person nominated as conservator by the respondent, including the respondent's most recent nomination made in a durable power of attorney, if the respondent has attained 14 years of age and at the time of the nomination had sufficient capacity to express a preference;

(3) an agent appointed by the respondent to manage the respondent's property under a durable power of attorney;

(4) the spouse of the respondent;

(5) an adult child of the respondent;

(6) a parent of the respondent; and

(7) an adult with whom the respondent has resided for more than six months before the filing of the petition.

(b) A person having priority under paragraph (a), clause (1), (4), (5), or (6), may designate in writing a substitute to serve instead and thereby transfer the priority to the substitute.

(c) The court, acting in the best interest of the protected person, may decline to appoint a person having priority and appoint a person having a lower priority or no priority. With respect to persons having equal priority, the court shall select the one it considers best qualified.

(d) Any individual or agency which provides residence, custodial care, medical care, employment training, or other care or services for which they receive a fee may not be appointed as conservator unless related to the respondent by blood, marriage, or adoption.

Laws 2003, c. 12, art. 1, § 52.

Historical and Statutory Notes

Laws 2003, c. 12, art. 2, § 9, provided:

"(a) Articles 1 and 2 apply to each guardianship or conservatorship proceeding and each appointment of guardian or conservator commenced on or after the effective date of articles 1 and 2. Except as otherwise provided in this section, articles 1 and 2 apply to each guardianship or conservatorship approved by the court prior to the effective date of articles 1 and 2, and to any guardianship or conservatorship proceeding pending in court on the effective date of articles 1 and 2, unless the court finds for good cause or in the interests of judicial economy that the proceeding should be completed under the provisions of Minnesota Statutes, chapter 525, as it existed prior to the effective date of articles 1 and 2.

"(b) A guardian or conservator who is not discharged prior to the effective date of articles 1 and 2 shall continue to hold the appointment but shall have only the powers specified in the order of appointment and in Minnesota Statutes, chapter 525, as it existed prior to the effective date of articles 1 and 2. Each guardian or conservator holding an appointment on the effective date of articles 1 and 2 shall continue to be bound by the duties imposed by the order of appointment; by Minnesota Statutes, chapter 525, as it existed prior to the effective date of articles 1 and 2; and by article 1, section 50; and shall be bound by any additional duties imposed by articles 1 and 2 starting on the first day of the next month starting after the effective date of articles 1 and 2 or on the next anniversary date of the appointment, whichever occurs later.

"(c) Any act done prior to the effective date of articles 1 and 2 in any proceeding and any right accrued under Minnesota Statutes, chapter 525, prior to the effective date of articles 1 and 2 shall not be impaired by articles 1 and 2. If a right is acquired, extinguished, or barred upon the expiration of a prescribed period of time which has commenced to run in accordance with the provisions of any statute before the effective date of articles 1 and 2, the provisions of the prior statute shall remain in force with

respect to that right notwithstanding the statute's amendment or repeal by articles 1 and 2.

"(d) An order of the court or letters of guardianship or conservatorship issued by the court prior to the effective date of articles 1 and 2 shall remain in full force and effect in accordance with its terms and conditions and in accordance with the provisions of prior law until the court modifies the order or letters in accordance with the provisions of articles 1 and 2. Upon request for a certified copy of an order or letters which remains in full force and effect under this paragraph, the court administrator shall certify that the order or letters remains in full force and effect pursuant to this paragraph.

"(e) The court, without hearing or notice to any person, may issue new letters of guardianship or conservatorship under articles 1 and 2 to replace similar letters issued prior to the effective date of articles 1 and 2. The new letters shall be effective under articles 1 and 2 with the same force and effect as the prior letters and shall remain in full force and effect until modified by the court in accordance with the provisions of articles 1 and 2.

"(f) A power of attorney executed in accordance with Minnesota Statutes, section 524.5–505, prior to the effective date of articles 1 and 2, or any surety bond, deed, or other instrument, report, or other undertaking executed in accordance with Minnesota Statutes, chapter 525, prior to the effective date of articles 1 and 2, shall remain in full force and effect for all purposes in accordance with its terms and conditions and the provisions of the applicable statutes under which the power of attorney, surety bond, deed, or other instrument, report, or other undertaking was executed, until the power of attorney, surety bond, deed, or other instrument, report, or other undertaking expires according to its terms or pursuant to the statutes governing its execution, or is modified, terminated, or superseded by a new power of attorney, surety bond, deed, or other instrument, report, or other undertaking executed in accordance with the provisions of articles 1 and 2."

524.5–414. Petition for order subsequent to appointment

(a) A protected person or an interested person may file a petition in the appointing court for an order:

(1) requiring bond or collateral or additional bond or collateral, or reducing bond;

(2) requiring an accounting for the administration of the protected person's estate;

(3) directing distribution;

(4) removing the conservator and appointing a temporary or successor conservator;

(5) modifying the type of appointment or powers granted to the conservator if the extent of protection or management previously granted is currently excessive or insufficient or the protected person's ability to manage the estate and business affairs has so changed as to warrant the action; or

(6) granting other appropriate relief.

(b) A conservator may petition the appointing court for instructions concerning fiduciary responsibility.

(c) On notice and hearing the petition, the court may give appropriate instructions and make any appropriate order.

(d) The court may, at its own discretion, waive the notice or hearing requirements for the relief requested in a petition filed under this section.

Laws 2003, c. 12, art. 1, § 53.

Historical and Statutory Notes

Laws 2003, c. 12, art. 2, § 9, provided:

"(a) Articles 1 and 2 apply to each guardianship or conservatorship proceeding and each appointment of guardian or conservator commenced on or after the effective date of articles 1 and 2. Except as otherwise provided in this section, articles 1 and 2 apply to each guardianship or conservatorship approved by the court prior to the effective date of articles 1 and 2, and to any guardianship or conservatorship proceeding pending in court on the effective date of articles 1 and 2, unless the court finds for good cause or in the interests of judicial economy that the proceeding should be completed under the provisions of Minnesota Statutes, chapter 525, as it existed prior to the effective date of articles 1 and 2.

"(b) A guardian or conservator who is not discharged prior to the effective date of articles 1 and 2 shall continue to hold the appointment but shall have only the powers specified in the order of appointment and in Minnesota Statutes, chapter 525, as it existed prior to the effective date of articles 1 and 2. Each guardian or conservator holding an appointment on the effective date of articles 1 and 2 shall continue to be bound by the duties imposed by the order of appointment; by Minnesota Statutes,

chapter 525, as it existed prior to the effective date of articles 1 and 2; and by article 1, section 50; and shall be bound by any additional duties imposed by articles 1 and 2 starting on the first day of the next month starting after the effective date of articles 1 and 2 or on the next anniversary date of the appointment, whichever occurs later.

"(c) Any act done prior to the effective date of articles 1 and 2 in any proceeding and any right accrued under Minnesota Statutes, chapter 525, prior to the effective date of articles 1 and 2 shall not be impaired by articles 1 and 2. If a right is acquired, extinguished, or barred upon the expiration of a prescribed period of time which has commenced to run in accordance with the provisions of any statute before the effective date of articles 1 and 2, the provisions of the prior statute shall remain in force with respect to that right notwithstanding the statute's amendment or repeal by articles 1 and 2.

"(d) An order of the court or letters of guardianship or conservatorship issued by the court prior to the effective date of articles 1 and 2 shall remain in full force and effect in accordance with its terms and conditions and in accordance with the provisions of prior law until the court modifies the order or letters in

accordance with the provisions of articles 1 and 2. Upon request for a certified copy of an order or letters which remains in full force and effect under this paragraph, the court administrator shall certify that the order or letters remains in full force and effect pursuant to this paragraph.

"(e) The court, without hearing or notice to any person, may issue new letters of guardianship or conservatorship under articles 1 and 2 to replace similar letters issued prior to the effective date of articles 1 and 2. The new letters shall be effective under articles 1 and 2 with the same force and effect as the prior letters and shall remain in full force and effect until modified by the court in accordance with the provisions of articles 1 and 2.

"(f) A power of attorney executed in accordance with Minnesota Statutes, section 524.5–505, prior to the effective date of articles

1 and 2, or any surety bond, deed, or other instrument, report, or other undertaking executed in accordance with Minnesota Statutes, chapter 525, prior to the effective date of articles 1 and 2, shall remain in full force and effect for all purposes in accordance with its terms and conditions and the provisions of the applicable statutes under which the power of attorney, surety bond, deed, or other instrument, report, or other undertaking was executed, until the power of attorney, surety bond, deed, or other instrument, report, or other undertaking expires according to its terms or pursuant to the statutes governing its execution, or is modified, terminated, or superseded by a new power of attorney, surety bond, deed, or other instrument, report, or other undertaking executed in accordance with the provisions of articles 1 and 2."

524.5–415. Bond

The court may require a conservator to furnish a bond conditioned upon faithful discharge of all duties of the conservatorship according to law, with sureties as it may specify.

Laws 2003, c. 12, art. 1, § 54.

Historical and Statutory Notes

Laws 2003, c. 12, art. 2, § 9, provided:

"(a) Articles 1 and 2 apply to each guardianship or conservatorship proceeding and each appointment of guardian or conservator commenced on or after the effective date of articles 1 and 2. Except as otherwise provided in this section, articles 1 and 2 apply to each guardianship or conservatorship approved by the court prior to the effective date of articles 1 and 2, and to any guardianship or conservatorship proceeding pending in court on the effective date of articles 1 and 2, unless the court finds for good cause or in the interests of judicial economy that the proceeding should be completed under the provisions of Minnesota Statutes, chapter 525, as it existed prior to the effective date of articles 1 and 2.

"(b) A guardian or conservator who is not discharged prior to the effective date of articles 1 and 2 shall continue to hold the appointment but shall have only the powers specified in the order of appointment and in Minnesota Statutes, chapter 525, as it existed prior to the effective date of articles 1 and 2. Each guardian or conservator holding an appointment on the effective date of articles 1 and 2 shall continue to be bound by the duties imposed by the order of appointment; by Minnesota Statutes, chapter 525, as it existed prior to the effective

date of articles 1 and 2; and by article 1, section 50; and shall be bound by any additional duties imposed by articles 1 and 2 starting on the first day of the next month starting after the effective date of articles 1 and 2 or on the next anniversary date of the appointment, whichever occurs later.

"(c) Any act done prior to the effective date of articles 1 and 2 in any proceeding and any right accrued under Minnesota Statutes, chapter 525, prior to the effective date of articles 1 and 2 shall not be impaired by articles 1 and 2. If a right is acquired, extinguished, or barred upon the expiration of a prescribed period of time which has commenced to run in accordance with the provisions of any statute before the effective date of articles 1 and 2, the provisions of the prior statute shall remain in force with respect to that right notwithstanding the statute's amendment or repeal by articles 1 and 2.

"(d) An order of the court or letters of guardianship or conservatorship issued by the court prior to the effective date of articles 1 and 2 shall remain in full force and effect in accordance with its terms and conditions and in accordance with the provisions of prior law until the court modifies the order or letters in accordance with the provisions of articles 1 and 2. Upon request for a certified copy of an order

or letters which remains in full force and effect under this paragraph, the court administrator shall certify that the order or letters remains in full force and effect pursuant to this paragraph.

"(e) The court, without hearing or notice to any person, may issue new letters of guardianship or conservatorship under articles 1 and 2 to replace similar letters issued prior to the effective date of articles 1 and 2. The new letters shall be effective under articles 1 and 2 with the same force and effect as the prior letters and shall remain in full force and effect until modified by the court in accordance with the provisions of articles 1 and 2.

"(f) A power of attorney executed in accordance with Minnesota Statutes, section 524.5–505, prior to the effective date of articles 1 and 2, or any surety bond, deed, or other instrument, report, or other undertaking executed in accordance with Minnesota Statutes, chapter 525, prior to the effective date of articles 1 and 2, shall remain in full force and effect for all purposes in accordance with its terms and conditions and the provisions of the applicable statutes under which the power of attorney, surety bond, deed, or other instrument, report, or other undertaking was executed, until the power of attorney, surety bond, deed, or other instrument, report, or other undertaking expires according to its terms or pursuant to the statutes governing its execution, or is modified, terminated, or superseded by a new power of attorney, surety bond, deed, or other instrument, report, or other undertaking executed in accordance with the provisions of articles 1 and 2."

524.5–416. Terms and requirements of bond

(a) The following rules apply to any bond required:

(1) Except as otherwise provided by the terms of the bond, sureties and the conservator are jointly and severally liable.

(2) By executing the bond of a conservator, a surety submits to the jurisdiction of the court that issued letters to the primary obligor in any proceeding pertaining to the fiduciary duties of the conservator in which the surety is named as a party. Notice of any proceeding must be sent or delivered to the surety at the address shown in the court records at the place where the bond is filed and to any other address then known to the petitioner.

(3) On petition of a successor conservator or any interested person, a proceeding may be brought against a surety for breach of the obligation of the bond of the conservator.

(4) The bond of the conservator may be proceeded against until liability under the bond is exhausted.

(b) A proceeding may not be brought against a surety on any matter as to which an action or proceeding against the primary obligor is barred.

Laws 2003, c. 12, art. 1, § 55.

Historical and Statutory Notes

Laws 2003, c. 12, art. 2, § 9, provided:

"(a) Articles 1 and 2 apply to each guardianship or conservatorship proceeding and each appointment of guardian or conservator commenced on or after the effective date of articles 1 and 2. Except as otherwise provided in this section, articles 1 and 2 apply to each guardianship or conservatorship approved by the court prior to the effective date of articles 1 and 2, and to any guardianship or conservatorship proceeding pending in court on the effective date of articles 1 and 2, unless the court finds for good cause or in the interests of judicial economy that the proceeding should be completed under the provisions of Minnesota Statutes, chapter 525, as it existed prior to the effective date of articles 1 and 2.

"(b) A guardian or conservator who is not discharged prior to the effective date of articles 1 and 2 shall continue to hold the appointment but shall have only the powers specified in the order of appointment and in Minnesota Statutes, chapter 525, as it existed prior to the effective date of articles 1 and 2. Each guardian or conservator holding an appointment on the effective date of articles 1 and 2 shall continue to be bound by the duties imposed by the order of appointment; by Minnesota Statutes, chapter 525, as it existed prior to the effective date of articles 1 and 2; and by article 1, section 50; and shall be bound by any additional duties imposed by articles 1 and 2 starting on the first day of the next month starting after the effective date of articles 1 and 2 or on the next anniversary date of the appointment, whichever occurs later.

"(c) Any act done prior to the effective date of articles 1 and 2 in any proceeding and any right accrued under Minnesota Statutes, chapter 525, prior to the effective date of articles 1 and 2 shall not be impaired by articles 1 and 2. If a right is acquired, extinguished, or barred upon the expiration of a prescribed period of time which has commenced to run in accordance with the provisions of any statute before the effective date of articles 1 and 2, the provisions of the prior statute shall remain in force with respect to that right notwithstanding the statute's amendment or repeal by articles 1 and 2.

"(d) An order of the court or letters of guardianship or conservatorship issued by the court prior to the effective date of articles 1 and 2 shall remain in full force and effect in accordance with its terms and conditions and in accordance with the provisions of prior law until the court modifies the order or letters in accordance with the provisions of articles 1 and

2. Upon request for a certified copy of an order or letters which remains in full force and effect under this paragraph, the court administrator shall certify that the order or letters remains in full force and effect pursuant to this paragraph.

"(e) The court, without hearing or notice to any person, may issue new letters of guardianship or conservatorship under articles 1 and 2 to replace similar letters issued prior to the effective date of articles 1 and 2. The new letters shall be effective under articles 1 and 2 with the same force and effect as the prior letters and shall remain in full force and effect until modified by the court in accordance with the provisions of articles 1 and 2.

"(f) A power of attorney executed in accordance with Minnesota Statutes, section 524.5–505, prior to the effective date of articles 1 and 2, or any surety bond, deed, or other instrument, report, or other undertaking executed in accordance with Minnesota Statutes, chapter 525, prior to the effective date of articles 1 and 2, shall remain in full force and effect for all purposes in accordance with its terms and conditions and the provisions of the applicable statutes under which the power of attorney, surety bond, deed, or other instrument, report, or other undertaking was executed, until the power of attorney, surety bond, deed, or other instrument, report, or other undertaking expires according to its terms or pursuant to the statutes governing its execution, or is modified, terminated, or superseded by a new power of attorney, surety bond, deed, or other instrument, report, or other undertaking executed in accordance with the provisions of articles 1 and 2."

524.5–417. General powers and duties of conservator

(a) A conservator shall be subject to the control and direction of the court at all times and in all things.

(b) The court shall grant to a conservator only those powers necessary to provide for the demonstrated needs of the protected person.

(c) The court may appoint a conservator if it determines that all the powers and duties listed in this section are needed to provide for the needs of the protected person. The court may also appoint a conservator if it determines that a conservator is necessary to provide for the needs of the protected person through the exercise of some, but not all, of the powers and duties listed in this section. The duties and powers of a conservator include, but are not limited to:

(1) the duty to pay the reasonable charges for the support, maintenance, and education of the protected person in a manner suitable to the protected person's station in life and the value of the estate. Nothing herein contained shall release parents from obligations imposed by law for the support, mainte-

nance, and education of their children. The conservator has no duty to pay for these requirements out of personal funds. Wherever possible and appropriate, the conservator should meet these requirements through governmental benefits or services to which the protected person is entitled, rather than from the protected person's estate. Failure to satisfy the needs and requirements of this section shall be grounds for removal, but the conservator shall have no personal or monetary liability;

(2) the duty to pay out of the protected person's estate all lawful debts of the protected person and the reasonable charges incurred for the support, mainte- nance, and education of the protected person's spouse and dependent children and, upon order of the court, pay such sum as the court may fix as reasonable for the support of any person unable to earn a livelihood who is legally entitled to support from the protected person;

(3) the duty to possess and manage the estate, collect all debts and claims in favor of the protected person, or, with the approval of the court, compromise them, institute suit on behalf of the protected person and represent the protected person in any court proceedings, and invest all funds not currently needed for the debts and charges named in clauses (1) and (2) and the management of the estate, in accordance with the provisions of sections 48A.07, subdivision 6, 501B.151, and 524.5–423, or as otherwise ordered by the court. The standard of a fiduciary shall be applicable to all investments by a conserva- tor. A conservator shall also have the power to purchase certain contracts of insurance as provided in section 50.14, subdivision 14, clause (b);

(4) where a protected person has inherited an undivided interest in real estate, the court, on a showing that it is for the best interest of the protected person, may authorize an exchange or sale of the protected person's interest or a purchase by the protected person of any interest other heirs may have in the real estate, subject to the procedures and notice requirements of section 524.5–418;

(5) the power to approve or withhold approval of any contract, except for necessities, which the protected person may make or wish to make; and

(6) the power to apply on behalf of the protected person for any assistance, services, or benefits available to the protected person through any unit of government.

(d) The conservator shall have the power to revoke, suspend, or terminate all or any part of a durable power of attorney of which the protected person is the principal with the same power the principal would have if the principal were not incapacitated. If a durable power of attorney is in effect, a decision of the conservator takes precedence over that of an attorney–in–fact.

(e) Transaction set aside. If a protected person has made a financial trans- action or gift or entered into a contract during the two-year period before establishment of the conservatorship, the conservator may petition for court review of the transaction, gift, or contract. If the court finds that the protected person was incapacitated or subject to duress, coercion, or undue influence when the transaction, gift, or contract was made, the court may declare the transaction, gift, or contract void except as against a bona fide transferee for value and order reimbursement or other appropriate relief. This paragraph does not affect any other right or remedy that may be available to the protected person with respect to the transaction, gift, or contract.

(f) After the filing of the petition, a certificate of the district court certified to that fact may be filed for record with the Minnesota secretary of state in the same manner as provided in section 336.9–501. The certificate shall state that a petition is pending and the name and address of the person for whom a conservator is sought. If a conservator is appointed on the petition, and if the conservatorship order removes or restricts the right of the protected person to transfer property or to contract, then all contracts except for necessaries, and all transfers of personal property, tangible or intangible, including, but not limited to, cash or securities transfers at banks, brokerage houses, or other financial institutions, or transfers of cash or securities, made by the protected person after the filing and before the termination of the conservatorship shall be voidable.

Laws 2003, c. 12, art. 1, § 56. Amended by Laws 2004, c. 146, art. 2, § 7; Laws 2005, c. 91, § 1.

Historical and Statutory Notes

Laws 2003, c. 12, art. 2, § 9, provided:

"(a) Articles 1 and 2 apply to each guardianship or conservatorship proceeding and each appointment of guardian or conservator commenced on or after the effective date of articles 1 and 2. Except as otherwise provided in this section, articles 1 and 2 apply to each guardianship or conservatorship approved by the court prior to the effective date of articles 1 and 2, and to any guardianship or conservatorship proceeding pending in court on the effective date of articles 1 and 2, unless the court finds for good cause or in the interests of judicial economy that the proceeding should be completed under the provisions of Minnesota Statutes, chapter 525, as it existed prior to the effective date of articles 1 and 2.

"(b) A guardian or conservator who is not discharged prior to the effective date of articles 1 and 2 shall continue to hold the appointment but shall have only the powers specified in the order of appointment and in Minnesota Statutes, chapter 525, as it existed prior to the effective date of articles 1 and 2. Each guardian or conservator holding an appointment on the effective date of articles 1 and 2 shall continue to be bound by the duties imposed by the order of appointment; by Minnesota Statutes, chapter 525, as it existed prior to the effective date of articles 1 and 2; and by article 1,

section 50; and shall be bound by any additional duties imposed by articles 1 and 2 starting on the first day of the next month starting after the effective date of articles 1 and 2 or on the next anniversary date of the appointment, whichever occurs later.

"(c) Any act done prior to the effective date of articles 1 and 2 in any proceeding and any right accrued under Minnesota Statutes, chapter 525, prior to the effective date of articles 1 and 2 shall not be impaired by articles 1 and 2. If a right is acquired, extinguished, or barred upon the expiration of a prescribed period of time which has commenced to run in accordance with the provisions of any statute before the effective date of articles 1 and 2, the provisions of the prior statute shall remain in force with respect to that right notwithstanding the statute's amendment or repeal by articles 1 and 2.

"(d) An order of the court or letters of guardianship or conservatorship issued by the court prior to the effective date of articles 1 and 2 shall remain in full force and effect in accordance with its terms and conditions and in accordance with the provisions of prior law until the court modifies the order or letters in accordance with the provisions of articles 1 and 2. Upon request for a certified copy of an order or letters which remains in full force and effect under this paragraph, the court administrator shall certify that the order or letters remains in full force and effect pursuant to this paragraph.

"(e) The court, without hearing or notice to any person, may issue new letters of guardianship or conservatorship under articles 1 and 2 to replace similar letters issued prior to the effective date of articles 1 and 2. The new letters shall be effective under articles 1 and 2 with the same force and effect as the prior letters and shall remain in full force and effect until modified by the court in accordance with the provisions of articles 1 and 2.

"(f) A power of attorney executed in accordance with Minnesota Statutes, section 524.5–505, prior to the effective date of articles 1 and 2, or any surety bond, deed, or other instrument, report, or other undertaking execut-ed in accordance with Minnesota Statutes, chapter 525, prior to the effective date of articles 1 and 2, shall remain in full force and effect for all purposes in accordance with its terms and conditions and the provisions of the applicable statutes under which the power of attorney, surety bond, deed, or other instrument, report, or other undertaking was executed, until the power of attorney, surety bond, deed, or other instrument, report, or other undertaking expires according to its terms or pursuant to the statutes governing its execution, or is modified, terminated, or superseded by a new power of attorney, surety bond, deed, or other instrument, report, or other undertaking executed in accordance with the provisions of articles 1 and 2."

524.5–418. General powers and duties of conservator with respect to real property

This section is applicable only to conservatorships and not to decedents' estates. As used in this section, the word "mortgage" includes an extension of an existing mortgage, subject to the provisions of this section, and the word "lease" means a lease for one or more years, unless the context indicates otherwise. The conservator shall have the following powers and duties with respect to conservatorship real property.

(a) The court may direct a sale, mortgage, or lease of any real estate of a protected person when the personal property is insufficient to pay debts and other charges against the estate, or to provide for the support, maintenance, and education of the protected person, a spouse, and dependent children, or when it shall determine the sale, mortgage, or lease to be for the best interest of the protected person. The homestead of a protected person shall not be sold, mortgaged, or leased unless the written consent of the spouse has been filed.

(b) A conservator may file a petition to sell, mortgage, or lease alleging briefly the facts constituting the reasons for the application and describing the real estate involved therein. The petition may include all the real estate of the protected person or any part or parts thereof. It may apply for different authority as to separate parcels. It may apply in the alternative for authority to sell, mortgage, or lease.

(1) Upon the filing of such petition, the court shall fix the time and place for the hearing thereof. Notice of the hearing shall be given to interested persons and shall state briefly the nature of the application made by the petition. If publication of notice is required by the court, published notice shall be given by publication once a week for two consecutive weeks in a legal newspaper designated by the petitioner in the county wherein the proceedings are pending, or, if no such designation be made, in any legal newspaper in the county, or, if the city of the protected person's residence is situated in more than one county, in any legal newspaper in the city. The first publication shall be had within

two weeks after the date of the order fixing the time and place for the hearing. Proof of publication and mailing shall be filed before the hearing. No defect in any notice or in the publication or service thereof shall invalidate any proceedings.

(2) Upon the hearing, the court shall have full power to direct the sale, mortgage, or lease of all the real estate described in the petition, or to direct the sale, mortgage, or lease of any one or more parcels thereof, provided that any such direction shall be within the terms of the application made by the petition. The order shall describe the real estate to be sold, mortgaged, or leased, and may designate the sequence in which the several parcels shall be sold, mortgaged, or leased. If the order be for a sale, it shall direct whether the real estate shall be sold at private sale or public auction. An order to mortgage shall fix the maximum amount of the principal and the maximum rate of interest and shall direct the purpose for which the proceeds shall be used. An order for sale, mortgage, or lease shall remain in force until terminated by the court, but no private sale shall be made after one year from the date of the order unless the real estate shall have been reappraised under order of the court within six months preceding the sale.

(3) The court may order a sale of real estate for cash, part cash, and a purchase-money mortgage of not more than 50 percent of the purchase price, or on contract for deed. The initial payment under a sale on contract shall not be less than ten percent of the total purchase price, and the unpaid purchase price shall bear interest at a rate of not less than four percent per annum and shall be payable in reasonable monthly, quarterly, semiannual, or annual payments, and the final installment shall become due and payable not later than ten years from the date of the contract. Such contract shall provide for conveyance by conservator's or quit claim deed, which deed shall be executed and delivered upon full performance of the contract without further order of the court. In the event of termination of the interest of the purchaser and assigns in such contract, the real estate may be resold under the original order and a reappraisal within six months preceding the sale. A sale of the vendor's interest in real estate sold by the conservator on contract may be made under order of the court, with or without notice, upon an appraisal of such interest within six months preceding the sale; no such sale shall be made for less than its value as fixed by such appraisal.

(4) If a sale at public auction is ordered, two weeks' published notice of the time and place of sale shall be given. Proof of publication shall be filed before the confirmation of the sale. Such publication and sale may be made in the county where the real estate is situated or in the county of the proceedings. If the parcels to be sold are contiguous and lie in more than one county, notice may be given and the sale may be made in either of such counties or in the county of the proceedings. The conservator may adjourn the sale from time to time, if for the best interests of the estate and the persons concerned, but not exceeding six months in all. Every adjournment shall be announced publicly at

the time and place fixed for the sale and, if for more than one day, further notice thereof shall be given as the court may direct.

(5) If a private sale be ordered, the real estate shall be reappraised by two or more disinterested persons under order of the court unless a prior appraisal of the real estate has been made by two or more disinterested persons not more than six months before the sale, which reappraisal shall be filed before the confirmation of the sale. No real estate shall be sold at private sale for less than its value as fixed by such appraisal.

(6) If the bond is insufficient, before confirmation of a sale or lease, or before execution of a mortgage, the conservator shall file an additional bond in such amount as the court may require.

(7) Upon making a sale or lease, the conservator shall file a report thereof. Upon proof of compliance with the terms of the order, the court may confirm the sale or lease and order the conservator to execute and deliver the proper instrument.

(c) When a protected person is entitled under contract of purchase to any interest in real estate, such interest may be sold for the same reasons and in the same manner as other real estate of a protected person. Before confirmation, the court may require the filing of a bond conditioned to save the estate harmless. Upon confirmation, the conservator shall assign the contract and convey by conservator's or quit claim deed.

(d) When the estate of a protected person is liable for any charge, mortgage, lien, or other encumbrance upon the real estate therein, the court may refuse to confirm the sale or lease until after the filing of a bond in such amount as the court may direct conditioned to save the estate harmless.

(e) When any real estate of a protected person is desired by any person, firm, association, corporation, or governmental agency having the power of eminent domain, the conservator may agree, in writing, upon the compensation to be made for the taking, injuring, damaging, or destroying thereof, subject to the approval of the court. When the agreement has been made, the conservator shall file a petition, of which the agreement shall be a part, setting forth the facts relative to the transaction.

(1) The court, with notice to interested persons, shall hear, determine, and act upon the petition. If publication of notice is required by the court, published notice shall be given by publication once a week for two consecutive weeks in a legal newspaper designated by the petitioner in the county wherein the proceedings are pending, or, if no such designation be made, in any legal newspaper in the county, or, if the city of the protected person's residence is situated in more than one county, in any legal newspaper in the city. The first publication shall be within two weeks after the date of the order fixing the time and place for the hearing. Proof of publication and mailing shall be filed before the hearing. No defect in any notice or in the publication or service thereof shall invalidate any proceedings.

(2) If the court approves the agreement, the conservator, upon payment of the agreed compensation, shall convey the real estate sought to be acquired and execute any release which may be authorized.

(f) When it is for the best interests of the estate of a protected person, real estate may be platted by the conservator under such conditions and upon such notice as the court may order.

(g) When any protected person is legally bound to make a conveyance or lease, the court, without further notice, may direct the conservator to make the conveyance or lease to the person entitled thereto. The petition may be made by any person claiming to be entitled to the conveyance or lease, or by the conservator, or by any interested person or person claiming an interest in the real estate or contract, and shall show the description of the land and the facts upon which the claim for conveyance or lease is based. Upon proof of the petition, the court may order the conservator to execute and deliver an instrument of conveyance or lease upon performance of the contract.

(h) A conservator without order of the court may make an extension of an existing mortgage for a period of five years or less, if the extension agreement contains the same prepayment privileges and the rate of interest does not exceed the lowest rate in the mortgage extended.

(i) No conservator shall be liable personally on any mortgage note or by reason of the covenants in any instrument or conveyance executed in the capacity of conservator.

(j) No sale, mortgage, lease, or conveyance by a conservator shall be subject to collateral attack on account of any irregularity in the proceedings if the court which ordered the same had jurisdiction of the estate.

(k) No proceeding to have declared invalid the sale, mortgage, lease, or conveyance by a conservator shall be maintained by any person claiming under or through the protected person unless such proceeding is begun within five years immediately succeeding the date of such sale, mortgage, lease, or conveyance; provided, however, that in case of real estate sold by a conservator, no action for its recovery shall be maintained by or under the protected person unless it is begun within five years after the termination of the protective proceedings and that, in cases of fraud, minors, and others under legal disability to sue when the right of action first accrues may begin such action at any time within five years after the disability is removed.

(l) After the filing of the petition, a certificate of the district court certified to that fact may be filed for record in the office of the county recorder for abstract property, or with the registrar of titles for registered property, of any county in which any real estate owned by the proposed protected person is situated and, if the protected person is a resident of this state, in the county of residence. The certificate shall state that a petition is pending and the name and address of the person for whom a conservator is sought. If a conservator is appointed on the petition, and if the conservatorship order removes or restricts the right of the protected person to transfer property or to contract, then all contracts and all transfers of real property made by the protected person after the filing and before the termination of the conservatorship shall be void.

Laws 2003, c. 12, art. 1, § 57.

Historical and Statutory Notes

Laws 2003, c. 12, art. 2, § 9, provided:

"(a) Articles 1 and 2 apply to each guardianship or conservatorship proceeding and each appointment of guardian or conservator commenced on or after the effective date of articles 1 and 2. Except as otherwise provided in this section, articles 1 and 2 apply to each guardianship or conservatorship approved by the court prior to the effective date of articles 1 and 2, and to any guardianship or conservatorship proceeding pending in court on the effective date of articles 1 and 2, unless the court finds for good cause or in the interests of judicial economy that the proceeding should be completed under the provisions of Minnesota Statutes, chapter 525, as it existed prior to the effective date of articles 1 and 2.

"(b) A guardian or conservator who is not discharged prior to the effective date of articles 1 and 2 shall continue to hold the appointment but shall have only the powers specified in the order of appointment and in Minnesota Statutes, chapter 525, as it existed prior to the effective date of articles 1 and 2. Each guardian or conservator holding an appointment on the effective date of articles 1 and 2 shall continue to be bound by the duties imposed by the order of appointment; by Minnesota Statutes, chapter 525, as it existed prior to the effective date of articles 1 and 2; and by article 1, section 50; and shall be bound by any additional duties imposed by articles 1 and 2 starting on the first day of the next month starting after the effective date of articles 1 and 2 or on the next anniversary date of the appointment, whichever occurs later.

"(c) Any act done prior to the effective date of articles 1 and 2 in any proceeding and any right accrued under Minnesota Statutes, chapter 525, prior to the effective date of articles 1 and 2 shall not be impaired by articles 1 and 2. If a right is acquired, extinguished, or barred upon the expiration of a prescribed period of time which has commenced to run in accordance with the provisions of any statute before the effective date of articles 1 and 2, the provisions of the prior statute shall remain in force with

respect to that right notwithstanding the statute's amendment or repeal by articles 1 and 2.

"(d) An order of the court or letters of guardianship or conservatorship issued by the court prior to the effective date of articles 1 and 2 shall remain in full force and effect in accordance with its terms and conditions and in accordance with the provisions of prior law until the court modifies the order or letters in accordance with the provisions of articles 1 and 2. Upon request for a certified copy of an order or letters which remains in full force and effect under this paragraph, the court administrator shall certify that the order or letters remains in full force and effect pursuant to this paragraph.

"(e) The court, without hearing or notice to any person, may issue new letters of guardianship or conservatorship under articles 1 and 2 to replace similar letters issued prior to the effective date of articles 1 and 2. The new letters shall be effective under articles 1 and 2 with the same force and effect as the prior letters and shall remain in full force and effect until modified by the court in accordance with the provisions of articles 1 and 2.

"(f) A power of attorney executed in accordance with Minnesota Statutes, section 524.5–505, prior to the effective date of articles 1 and 2, or any surety bond, deed, or other instrument, report, or other undertaking executed in accordance with Minnesota Statutes, chapter 525, prior to the effective date of articles 1 and 2, shall remain in full force and effect for all purposes in accordance with its terms and conditions and the provisions of the applicable statutes under which the power of attorney, surety bond, deed, or other instrument, report, or other undertaking was executed, until the power of attorney, surety bond, deed, or other instrument, report, or other undertaking expires according to its terms or pursuant to the statutes governing its execution, or is modified, terminated, or superseded by a new power of attorney, surety bond, deed, or other instrument, report, or other undertaking executed in accordance with the provisions of articles 1 and 2."

524.5–419. Inventory; records

(a) Within 60 days after appointment, a conservator shall prepare and file with the appointing court a detailed inventory of the estate subject to the conservatorship, together with an oath or affirmation that the inventory is believed to be complete and accurate as far as information permits.

(b) A conservator shall keep records of the administration of the estate and make them available for examination on reasonable request of the court, ward, protected person, or any attorney representing such persons.

Laws 2003, c. 12, art. 1, § 58.

Historical and Statutory Notes

Laws 2003, c. 12, art. 2, § 9, provided:

"(a) Articles 1 and 2 apply to each guardianship or conservatorship proceeding and each appointment of guardian or conservator commenced on or after the effective date of articles 1 and 2. Except as otherwise provided in this section, articles 1 and 2 apply to each guardianship or conservatorship approved by the court prior to the effective date of articles 1 and 2, and to any guardianship or conservatorship proceeding pending in court on the effective date of articles 1 and 2, unless the court finds for good cause or in the interests of judicial economy that the proceeding should be completed under the provisions of Minnesota Statutes, chapter 525, as it existed prior to the effective date of articles 1 and 2.

"(b) A guardian or conservator who is not discharged prior to the effective date of articles 1 and 2 shall continue to hold the appointment but shall have only the powers specified in the order of appointment and in Minnesota Statutes, chapter 525, as it existed prior to the effective date of articles 1 and 2. Each guardian or conservator holding an appointment on the effective date of articles 1 and 2 shall continue to be bound by the duties imposed by the order of appointment; by Minnesota Statutes, chapter 525, as it existed prior to the effective date of articles 1 and 2; and by article 1, section 50; and shall be bound by any additional duties imposed by articles 1 and 2 starting on the first day of the next month starting after the effective date of articles 1 and 2 or on the next anniversary date of the appointment, whichever occurs later.

"(c) Any act done prior to the effective date of articles 1 and 2 in any proceeding and any right accrued under Minnesota Statutes, chapter 525, prior to the effective date of articles 1 and 2 shall not be impaired by articles 1 and 2. If a right is acquired, extinguished, or barred upon the expiration of a prescribed period of time which has commenced to run in accordance with the provisions of any statute before the effective date of articles 1 and 2, the provisions of the prior statute shall remain in force with

respect to that right notwithstanding the statute's amendment or repeal by articles 1 and 2.

"(d) An order of the court or letters of guardianship or conservatorship issued by the court prior to the effective date of articles 1 and 2 shall remain in full force and effect in accordance with its terms and conditions and in accordance with the provisions of prior law until the court modifies the order or letters in accordance with the provisions of articles 1 and 2. Upon request for a certified copy of an order or letters which remains in full force and effect under this paragraph, the court administrator shall certify that the order or letters remains in full force and effect pursuant to this paragraph.

"(e) The court, without hearing or notice to any person, may issue new letters of guardianship or conservatorship under articles 1 and 2 to replace similar letters issued prior to the effective date of articles 1 and 2. The new letters shall be effective under articles 1 and 2 with the same force and effect as the prior letters and shall remain in full force and effect until modified by the court in accordance with the provisions of articles 1 and 2.

"(f) A power of attorney executed in accordance with Minnesota Statutes, section 524.5–505, prior to the effective date of articles 1 and 2, or any surety bond, deed, or other instrument, report, or other undertaking executed in accordance with Minnesota Statutes, chapter 525, prior to the effective date of articles 1 and 2, shall remain in full force and effect for all purposes in accordance with its terms and conditions and the provisions of the applicable statutes under which the power of attorney, surety bond, deed, or other instrument, report, or other undertaking was executed, until the power of attorney, surety bond, deed, or other instrument, report, or other undertaking expires according to its terms or pursuant to the statutes governing its execution, or is modified, terminated, or superseded by a new power of attorney, surety bond, deed, or other instrument, report, or other undertaking executed in accordance with the provisions of articles 1 and 2."

524.5–420. Reports; appointment of visitor; monitoring

(a) A conservator shall report to the court for administration of the estate annually unless the court otherwise directs, upon resignation or removal, upon termination of the conservatorship, and at other times as the court directs. An order, after notice and hearing, allowing an intermediate report of a conservator adjudicates liabilities concerning the matters adequately disclosed in the accounting. An order, after notice and hearing, allowing a final report adjudicates all previously unsettled liabilities relating to the conservatorship.

(b) A report must state or contain a listing of the assets of the estate under the conservator's control and a listing of the receipts, disbursements, and distributions during the reporting period.

(c) The court may appoint a visitor to review a report or plan, interview the protected person or conservator, and make any other investigation the court directs. In connection with a report, the court may order a conservator to submit the assets of the estate to an appropriate examination to be made in a manner the court directs.

(d) The court shall establish a system for monitoring of conservatorships, including the filing and review of conservators' reports and plans.

Laws 2003, c. 12, art. 1, § 59.

Historical and Statutory Notes

Laws 2003, c. 12, art. 2, § 9, provided:

"(a) Articles 1 and 2 apply to each guardianship or conservatorship proceeding and each appointment of guardian or conservator commenced on or after the effective date of articles 1 and 2. Except as otherwise provided in this section, articles 1 and 2 apply to each guardianship or conservatorship approved by the court prior to the effective date of articles 1 and 2, and to any guardianship or conservatorship proceeding pending in court on the effective date of articles 1 and 2, unless the court finds for good cause or in the interests of judicial economy that the proceeding should be completed under the provisions of Minnesota Statutes, chapter 525, as it existed prior to the effective date of articles 1 and 2.

"(b) A guardian or conservator who is not discharged prior to the effective date of articles 1 and 2 shall continue to hold the appointment but shall have only the powers specified in the order of appointment and in Minnesota Statutes, chapter 525, as it existed prior to the effective date of articles 1 and 2. Each guardian or conservator holding an appointment on the effective date of articles 1 and 2 shall continue to be bound by the duties imposed by the order of appointment; by Minnesota Statutes, chapter 525, as it existed prior to the effective

date of articles 1 and 2; and by article 1, section 50; and shall be bound by any additional duties imposed by articles 1 and 2 starting on the first day of the next month starting after the effective date of articles 1 and 2 or on the next anniversary date of the appointment, whichever occurs later.

"(c) Any act done prior to the effective date of articles 1 and 2 in any proceeding and any right accrued under Minnesota Statutes, chapter 525, prior to the effective date of articles 1 and 2 shall not be impaired by articles 1 and 2. If a right is acquired, extinguished, or barred upon the expiration of a prescribed period of time which has commenced to run in accordance with the provisions of any statute before the effective date of articles 1 and 2, the provisions of the prior statute shall remain in force with respect to that right notwithstanding the statute's amendment or repeal by articles 1 and 2.

"(d) An order of the court or letters of guardianship or conservatorship issued by the court prior to the effective date of articles 1 and 2 shall remain in full force and effect in accordance with its terms and conditions and in accordance with the provisions of prior law until the court modifies the order or letters in accordance with the provisions of articles 1 and 2. Upon request for a certified copy of an order

or letters which remains in full force and effect under this paragraph, the court administrator shall certify that the order or letters remains in full force and effect pursuant to this paragraph.

"(e) The court, without hearing or notice to any person, may issue new letters of guardianship or conservatorship under articles 1 and 2 to replace similar letters issued prior to the effective date of articles 1 and 2. The new letters shall be effective under articles 1 and 2 with the same force and effect as the prior letters and shall remain in full force and effect until modified by the court in accordance with the provisions of articles 1 and 2.

"(f) A power of attorney executed in accordance with Minnesota Statutes, section 524.5–505, prior to the effective date of articles 1 and 2, or any surety bond, deed, or other

instrument, report, or other undertaking executed in accordance with Minnesota Statutes, chapter 525, prior to the effective date of articles 1 and 2, shall remain in full force and effect for all purposes in accordance with its terms and conditions and the provisions of the applicable statutes under which the power of attorney, surety bond, deed, or other instrument, report, or other undertaking was executed, until the power of attorney, surety bond, deed, or other instrument, report, or other undertaking expires according to its terms or pursuant to the statutes governing its execution, or is modified, terminated, or superseded by a new power of attorney, surety bond, deed, or other instrument, report, or other undertaking executed in accordance with the provisions of articles 1 and 2."

524.5–421. Title after appointment

(a) The appointment of a conservator does not vest title of the protected person's property in the conservator.

(b) Letters of conservatorship are evidence of the conservator's power to act on behalf of the protected person. An order terminating a conservatorship terminates the conservator's powers to act on behalf of the protected person.

(c) Subject to the requirements of general statutes governing the filing or recordation of documents of title to land or other property, letters of conservatorship and orders terminating conservatorships may be filed or recorded to give notice of title as between the conservator and the protected person.

Laws 2003, c. 12, art. 1, § 60.

Historical and Statutory Notes

Laws 2003, c. 12, art. 2, § 9, provided:

"(a) Articles 1 and 2 apply to each guardianship or conservatorship proceeding and each appointment of guardian or conservator commenced on or after the effective date of articles 1 and 2. Except as otherwise provided in this section, articles 1 and 2 apply to each guardianship or conservatorship approved by the court prior to the effective date of articles 1 and 2, and to any guardianship or conservatorship proceeding pending in court on the effective date of articles 1 and 2, unless the court finds for good cause or in the interests of judicial economy that the proceeding should be completed under the provisions of Minnesota Statutes, chapter 525, as it existed prior to the effective date of articles 1 and 2.

"(b) A guardian or conservator who is not discharged prior to the effective date of articles 1 and 2 shall continue to hold the appointment but shall have only the powers specified in the

order of appointment and in Minnesota Statutes, chapter 525, as it existed prior to the effective date of articles 1 and 2. Each guardian or conservator holding an appointment on the effective date of articles 1 and 2 shall continue to be bound by the duties imposed by the order of appointment; by Minnesota Statutes, chapter 525, as it existed prior to the effective date of articles 1 and 2; and by article 1, section 50; and shall be bound by any additional duties imposed by articles 1 and 2 starting on the first day of the next month starting after the effective date of articles 1 and 2 or on the next anniversary date of the appointment, whichever occurs later.

"(c) Any act done prior to the effective date of articles 1 and 2 in any proceeding and any right accrued under Minnesota Statutes, chapter 525, prior to the effective date of articles 1 and 2 shall not be impaired by articles 1 and 2. If a right is acquired, extinguished, or barred upon the expiration of a prescribed period of time which has commenced to run in accordance with the provisions of any statute before the effective date of articles 1 and 2, the provisions of the prior statute shall remain in force with respect to that right notwithstanding the statute's amendment or repeal by articles 1 and 2.

"(d) An order of the court or letters of guardianship or conservatorship issued by the court prior to the effective date of articles 1 and 2 shall remain in full force and effect in accordance with its terms and conditions and in accordance with the provisions of prior law until the court modifies the order or letters in accordance with the provisions of articles 1 and 2. Upon request for a certified copy of an order or letters which remains in full force and effect under this paragraph, the court administrator shall certify that the order or letters remains in full force and effect pursuant to this paragraph.

"(e) The court, without hearing or notice to any person, may issue new letters of guardianship or conservatorship under articles 1 and 2 to replace similar letters issued prior to the effective date of articles 1 and 2. The new letters shall be effective under articles 1 and 2 with the same force and effect as the prior letters and shall remain in full force and effect until modified by the court in accordance with the provisions of articles 1 and 2.

"(f) A power of attorney executed in accordance with Minnesota Statutes, section 524.5–505, prior to the effective date of articles 1 and 2, or any surety bond, deed, or other instrument, report, or other undertaking executed in accordance with Minnesota Statutes, chapter 525, prior to the effective date of articles 1 and 2, shall remain in full force and effect for all purposes in accordance with its terms and conditions and the provisions of the applicable statutes under which the power of attorney, surety bond, deed, or other instrument, report, or other undertaking was executed, until the power of attorney, surety bond, deed, or other instrument, report, or other undertaking expires according to its terms or pursuant to the statutes governing its execution, or is modified, terminated, or superseded by a new power of attorney, surety bond, deed, or other instrument, report, or other undertaking executed in accordance with the provisions of articles 1 and 2."

524.5–422. Protected person's interest nonalienable

(a) Except as otherwise provided in paragraphs (c) and (d), the interest of a protected person in property is not transferable or assignable by the protected person. An attempted transfer or assignment by the protected person, although ineffective to affect property rights, may give rise to a claim against the protected person for restitution or damages which, subject to presentation and allowance, may be satisfied as provided in section 524.5–429.

(b) Upon appointment of a conservator, property vested in a protected person is not subject to levy, garnishment, or similar process for claims against the protected person unless allowed pursuant to section 524.5–429.

(c) A person without knowledge of the conservatorship who in good faith and for security or substantially equivalent value receives delivery from a protected person of tangible personal property of a type normally transferred by delivery of possession is protected as if the protected person or transferee had valid title.

(d) A third party who deals with the protected person with respect to property subject to a conservatorship is entitled to any protection provided in other law.

(e) Nothing in this section or in this article shall prevent the imposition, enforcement, or collection of a lien under sections 514.980 to 514.985.

Laws 2003, c. 12, art. 1, § 61.

<h3 style="text-align:center">Historical and Statutory Notes</h3>

Laws 2003, c. 12, art. 2, § 9, provided:

"(a) Articles 1 and 2 apply to each guardianship or conservatorship proceeding and each appointment of guardian or conservator commenced on or after the effective date of articles 1 and 2. Except as otherwise provided in this section, articles 1 and 2 apply to each guardianship or conservatorship approved by the court prior to the effective date of articles 1 and 2, and to any guardianship or conservatorship proceeding pending in court on the effective date of articles 1 and 2, unless the court finds for good cause or in the interests of judicial economy that the proceeding should be completed under the provisions of Minnesota Statutes, chapter 525, as it existed prior to the effective date of articles 1 and 2.

"(b) A guardian or conservator who is not discharged prior to the effective date of articles 1 and 2 shall continue to hold the appointment but shall have only the powers specified in the order of appointment and in Minnesota Statutes, chapter 525, as it existed prior to the effective date of articles 1 and 2. Each guardian or conservator holding an appointment on the effective date of articles 1 and 2 shall continue to be bound by the duties imposed by the order of appointment; by Minnesota Statutes, chapter 525, as it existed prior to the effective date of articles 1 and 2; and by article 1, section 50; and shall be bound by any additional duties imposed by articles 1 and 2 starting on the first day of the next month starting after the effective date of articles 1 and 2 or on the next anniversary date of the appointment, whichever occurs later.

"(c) Any act done prior to the effective date of articles 1 and 2 in any proceeding and any right accrued under Minnesota Statutes, chapter 525, prior to the effective date of articles 1 and 2 shall not be impaired by articles 1 and 2. If a right is acquired, extinguished, or barred upon the expiration of a prescribed period of time which has commenced to run in accordance with the provisions of any statute before the effective date of articles 1 and 2, the provisions of the prior statute shall remain in force with

respect to that right notwithstanding the statute's amendment or repeal by articles 1 and 2.

"(d) An order of the court or letters of guardianship or conservatorship issued by the court prior to the effective date of articles 1 and 2 shall remain in full force and effect in accordance with its terms and conditions and in accordance with the provisions of prior law until the court modifies the order or letters in accordance with the provisions of articles 1 and 2. Upon request for a certified copy of an order or letters which remains in full force and effect under this paragraph, the court administrator shall certify that the order or letters remains in full force and effect pursuant to this paragraph.

"(e) The court, without hearing or notice to any person, may issue new letters of guardianship or conservatorship under articles 1 and 2 to replace similar letters issued prior to the effective date of articles 1 and 2. The new letters shall be effective under articles 1 and 2 with the same force and effect as the prior letters and shall remain in full force and effect until modified by the court in accordance with the provisions of articles 1 and 2.

"(f) A power of attorney executed in accordance with Minnesota Statutes, section 524.5–505, prior to the effective date of articles 1 and 2, or any surety bond, deed, or other instrument, report, or other undertaking executed in accordance with Minnesota Statutes, chapter 525, prior to the effective date of articles 1 and 2, shall remain in full force and effect for all purposes in accordance with its terms and conditions and the provisions of the applicable statutes under which the power of attorney, surety bond, deed, or other instrument, report, or other undertaking was executed, until the power of attorney, surety bond, deed, or other instrument, report, or other undertaking expires according to its terms or pursuant to the statutes governing its execution, or is modified, terminated, or superseded by a new power of attorney, surety bond, deed, or other instrument, report, or other undertaking executed in accordance with the provisions of articles 1 and 2."

524.5–423. Sale, encumbrance, or other transaction involving conflict of interest

Any transaction involving the conservatorship estate which is affected by a conflict between the conservator's fiduciary and personal interests is voidable unless the transaction is expressly authorized by the court after notice to interested persons. A transaction affected by a conflict between personal and fiduciary interests includes any sale, encumbrance, or other transaction involving the conservatorship estate entered into by the conservator, the spouse, descendant, agent, or lawyer of a conservator, or corporation or other enterprise in which the conservator has a beneficial interest. Notwithstanding a conflict between the conservator's fiduciary and personal interests, if the protected person is a parent, child, or sibling of the conservator, the court has discretion to allow a transaction of beneficial interest to the conservator, as long as the conservator can prove that this transaction is primarily in the best interest of the protected person.

Laws 2003, c. 12, art. 1, § 62. Amended by Laws 2005, c. 91, § 2.

Historical and Statutory Notes

Laws 2003, c. 12, art. 2, § 9, provided:

"(a) Articles 1 and 2 apply to each guardianship or conservatorship proceeding and each appointment of guardian or conservator commenced on or after the effective date of articles 1 and 2. Except as otherwise provided in this section, articles 1 and 2 apply to each guardianship or conservatorship approved by the court prior to the effective date of articles 1 and 2, and to any guardianship or conservatorship proceeding pending in court on the effective date of articles 1 and 2, unless the court finds for good cause or in the interests of judicial economy that the proceeding should be completed under the provisions of Minnesota Statutes, chapter 525, as it existed prior to the effective date of articles 1 and 2.

"(b) A guardian or conservator who is not discharged prior to the effective date of articles 1 and 2 shall continue to hold the appointment but shall have only the powers specified in the order of appointment and in Minnesota Statutes, chapter 525, as it existed prior to the effective date of articles 1 and 2. Each guardian or conservator holding an appointment on the effective date of articles 1 and 2 shall continue to be bound by the duties imposed by the order of appointment; by Minnesota Statutes, chapter 525, as it existed prior to the effective date of articles 1 and 2; and by article 1, section 50; and shall be bound by any additional duties imposed by articles 1 and 2 starting on the first day of the next month starting after the effective date of articles 1 and 2 or on the next anniversary date of the appointment, whichever occurs later.

"(c) Any act done prior to the effective date of articles 1 and 2 in any proceeding and any right accrued under Minnesota Statutes, chapter 525, prior to the effective date of articles 1 and 2 shall not be impaired by articles 1 and 2. If a right is acquired, extinguished, or barred upon the expiration of a prescribed period of time which has commenced to run in accordance with the provisions of any statute before the effective date of articles 1 and 2, the provisions of the prior statute shall remain in force with respect to that right notwithstanding the statute's amendment or repeal by articles 1 and 2.

"(d) An order of the court or letters of guardianship or conservatorship issued by the court prior to the effective date of articles 1 and 2 shall remain in full force and effect in accordance with its terms and conditions and in accordance with the provisions of prior law until the court modifies the order or letters in accordance with the provisions of articles 1 and 2. Upon request for a certified copy of an order or letters which remains in full force and effect under this paragraph, the court administrator shall certify that the order or letters remains in full force and effect pursuant to this paragraph.

"(e) The court, without hearing or notice to any person, may issue new letters of guardianship or conservatorship under articles 1 and 2 to replace similar letters issued prior to the effective date of articles 1 and 2. The new letters shall be effective under articles 1 and 2 with the same force and effect as the prior letters and shall remain in full force and effect until modified by the court in accordance with the provisions of articles 1 and 2.

"(f) A power of attorney executed in accordance with Minnesota Statutes, section 524.5–505, prior to the effective date of articles 1 and 2, or any surety bond, deed, or other instrument, report, or other undertaking executed in accordance with Minnesota Statutes, chapter 525, prior to the effective date of articles 1 and 2, shall remain in full force and effect for all purposes in accordance with its terms and conditions and the provisions of the applicable statutes under which the power of attorney, surety bond, deed, or other instrument, report, or other undertaking was executed, until the power of attorney, surety bond, deed, or other instrument, report, or other undertaking expires according to its terms or pursuant to the statutes governing its execution, or is modified, terminated, or superseded by a new power of attorney, surety bond, deed, or other instrument, report, or other undertaking executed in accordance with the provisions of articles 1 and 2."

Laws 2005, c. 91, § 2, amending this section, also provided that the amendment was effective July 1, 2005, and included all proceedings open or pending on that date.

524.5–424. Protection of person dealing with conservator

(a) A person who assists or deals with a conservator in good faith and for value in any transaction other than one requiring a court order under section 524.5–410 or 524.5–411 is protected as though the conservator properly exercised the power. The fact that a person knowingly deals with a conservator does not alone require the person to inquire into the existence of a power or the propriety of its exercise, but restrictions on powers of conservators which are endorsed on letters as provided in section 524.5–110 are effective as to other persons. A person need not see to the proper application of assets of the estate paid or delivered to a conservator.

(b) Protection provided by this section extends to any procedural irregularity or jurisdictional defect that occurred in proceedings leading to the issuance of letters and is not a substitute for protection provided to persons assisting or dealing with a conservator by comparable provisions in other law relating to commercial transactions or to simplifying transfers of securities by fiduciaries.

Laws 2003, c. 12, art. 1, § 63.

Historical and Statutory Notes

Laws 2003, c. 12, art. 2, § 9, provided:

"(a) Articles 1 and 2 apply to each guardianship or conservatorship proceeding and each appointment of guardian or conservator commenced on or after the effective date of articles 1 and 2. Except as otherwise provided in this section, articles 1 and 2 apply to each guardianship or conservatorship approved by the court prior to the effective date of articles 1 and 2, and to any guardianship or conservatorship proceeding pending in court on the effective date of articles 1 and 2, unless the court finds for good cause or in the interests of judicial economy that the proceeding should be completed under the provisions of Minnesota Statutes, chapter 525, as it existed prior to the effective date of articles 1 and 2.

"(b) A guardian or conservator who is not discharged prior to the effective date of articles 1 and 2 shall continue to hold the appointment but shall have only the powers specified in the order of appointment and in Minnesota Statutes, chapter 525, as it existed prior to the effective date of articles 1 and 2. Each guardian or conservator holding an appointment on the effective date of articles 1 and 2 shall continue to be bound by the duties imposed by the order of appointment; by Minnesota Statutes, chapter 525, as it existed prior to the effective date of articles 1 and 2; and by article 1, section 50; and shall be bound by any additional duties imposed by articles 1 and 2 starting on the first day of the next month starting after the effective date of articles 1 and 2 or on the next anniversary date of the appointment, whichever occurs later.

"(c) Any act done prior to the effective date of articles 1 and 2 in any proceeding and any right accrued under Minnesota Statutes, chapter 525, prior to the effective date of articles 1 and 2 shall not be impaired by articles 1 and 2. If a right is acquired, extinguished, or barred upon the expiration of a prescribed period of time which has commenced to run in accordance with the provisions of any statute before the effective date of articles 1 and 2, the provisions of the prior statute shall remain in force with respect to that right notwithstanding the statute's amendment or repeal by articles 1 and 2.

"(d) An order of the court or letters of guardianship or conservatorship issued by the court prior to the effective date of articles 1 and 2 shall remain in full force and effect in accordance with its terms and conditions and in

accordance with the provisions of prior law until the court modifies the order or letters in accordance with the provisions of articles 1 and 2. Upon request for a certified copy of an order or letters which remains in full force and effect under this paragraph, the court administrator shall certify that the order or letters remains in full force and effect pursuant to this paragraph.

"(e) The court, without hearing or notice to any person, may issue new letters of guardianship or conservatorship under articles 1 and 2 to replace similar letters issued prior to the effective date of articles 1 and 2. The new letters shall be effective under articles 1 and 2 with the same force and effect as the prior letters and shall remain in full force and effect until modified by the court in accordance with the provisions of articles 1 and 2.

"(f) A power of attorney executed in accordance with Minnesota Statutes, section 524.5–505, prior to the effective date of articles 1 and 2, or any surety bond, deed, or other instrument, report, or other undertaking executed in accordance with Minnesota Statutes, chapter 525, prior to the effective date of articles 1 and 2, shall remain in full force and effect for all purposes in accordance with its terms and conditions and the provisions of the applicable statutes under which the power of attorney, surety bond, deed, or other instrument, report, or other undertaking was executed, until the power of attorney, surety bond, deed, or other instrument, report, or other undertaking expires according to its terms or pursuant to the statutes governing its execution, or is modified, terminated, or superseded by a new power of attorney, surety bond, deed, or other instrument, report, or other undertaking executed in accordance with the provisions of articles 1 and 2."

524.5–426. Delegation

(a) A conservator may not delegate to an agent or another conservator the entire administration of the estate, but a conservator may otherwise delegate the performance of functions that a prudent person of comparable skills may delegate under similar circumstances.

(b) The conservator shall exercise reasonable care, skill, and caution in:

(1) selecting an agent;

(2) establishing the scope and terms of a delegation, consistent with the purposes and terms of the conservatorship;

(3) periodically reviewing an agent's overall performance and compliance with the terms of the delegation; and

(4) redressing an action or decision of an agent which would constitute a breach of fiduciary duty if performed by the conservator.

(c) A conservator who complies with paragraphs (a) and (b) is not liable to the protected person or to the estate for the decisions or actions of the agent to whom a function was delegated.

(d) In performing a delegated function, an agent shall exercise reasonable care to comply with the terms of the delegation.

(e) By accepting a delegation from a conservator subject to the laws of this state, an agent submits to the jurisdiction of the courts of this state.

Laws 2003, c. 12, art. 1, § 64.

Historical and Statutory Notes

Laws 2003, c. 12, art. 2, § 9, provided:

"(a) Articles 1 and 2 apply to each guardianship or conservatorship proceeding and each appointment of guardian or conservator commenced on or after the effective date of articles 1 and 2. Except as otherwise provided in this

section, articles 1 and 2 apply to each guardianship or conservatorship approved by the court prior to the effective date of articles 1 and 2, and to any guardianship or conservatorship proceeding pending in court on the effective date of articles 1 and 2, unless the court finds for good cause or in the interests of judicial economy that the proceeding should be completed under the provisions of Minnesota Statutes, chapter 525, as it existed prior to the effective date of articles 1 and 2.

"(b) A guardian or conservator who is not discharged prior to the effective date of articles 1 and 2 shall continue to hold the appointment but shall have only the powers specified in the order of appointment and in Minnesota Statutes, chapter 525, as it existed prior to the effective date of articles 1 and 2. Each guardian or conservator holding an appointment on the effective date of articles 1 and 2 shall continue to be bound by the duties imposed by the order of appointment; by Minnesota Statutes, chapter 525, as it existed prior to the effective date of articles 1 and 2; and by article 1, section 50; and shall be bound by any additional duties imposed by articles 1 and 2 starting on the first day of the next month starting after the effective date of articles 1 and 2 or on the next anniversary date of the appointment, whichever occurs later.

"(c) Any act done prior to the effective date of articles 1 and 2 in any proceeding and any right accrued under Minnesota Statutes, chapter 525, prior to the effective date of articles 1 and 2 shall not be impaired by articles 1 and 2. If a right is acquired, extinguished, or barred upon the expiration of a prescribed period of time which has commenced to run in accordance with the provisions of any statute before the effective date of articles 1 and 2, the provisions of the prior statute shall remain in force with respect to that right notwithstanding the statute's amendment or repeal by articles 1 and 2.

"(d) An order of the court or letters of guardianship or conservatorship issued by the court prior to the effective date of articles 1 and 2 shall remain in full force and effect in accordance with its terms and conditions and in accordance with the provisions of prior law until the court modifies the order or letters in accordance with the provisions of articles 1 and 2. Upon request for a certified copy of an order or letters which remains in full force and effect under this paragraph, the court administrator shall certify that the order or letters remains in full force and effect pursuant to this paragraph.

"(e) The court, without hearing or notice to any person, may issue new letters of guardianship or conservatorship under articles 1 and 2 to replace similar letters issued prior to the effective date of articles 1 and 2. The new letters shall be effective under articles 1 and 2 with the same force and effect as the prior letters and shall remain in full force and effect until modified by the court in accordance with the provisions of articles 1 and 2.

"(f) A power of attorney executed in accordance with Minnesota Statutes, section 524.5–505, prior to the effective date of articles 1 and 2, or any surety bond, deed, or other instrument, report, or other undertaking executed in accordance with Minnesota Statutes, chapter 525, prior to the effective date of articles 1 and 2, shall remain in full force and effect for all purposes in accordance with its terms and conditions and the provisions of the applicable statutes under which the power of attorney, surety bond, deed, or other instrument, report, or other undertaking was executed, until the power of attorney, surety bond, deed, or other instrument, report, or other undertaking expires according to its terms or pursuant to the statutes governing its execution, or is modified, terminated, or superseded by a new power of attorney, surety bond, deed, or other instrument, report, or other undertaking executed in accordance with the provisions of articles 1 and 2."

524.5–427. Principles of distribution by conservator

(a) Unless otherwise specified in the order of appointment and endorsed on the letters of appointment, a conservator may expend or distribute income or principal of the estate of the protected person without further court authorization or confirmation for the support, care, education, health, and welfare of the protected person and individuals who are in fact dependent on the protected person, including the payment of child or spousal support, in accordance with paragraphs (b) to (e).

(b) The conservator shall consider recommendations relating to the appropriate standard of support, care, education, health, and welfare for the protected person or an individual who is in fact dependent on the protected person made by a guardian, if any, and, if the protected person is a minor, the conservator shall consider recommendations made by a parent.

(c) The conservator may not be surcharged for money paid to persons furnishing support, care, education, or benefit to the protected person or an individual who is in fact dependent on the protected person pursuant to the recommendations of a parent or guardian of the protected person unless the conservator knows that the parent or guardian derives personal financial benefit therefrom, including relief from any personal duty of support, or the recommendations are not in the best interest of the protected person.

(d) In making distributions under this section, the conservator shall consider:

(1) the size of the estate, the estimated duration of the conservatorship, and the likelihood that the protected person, at some future time, may be fully self-sufficient and able to manage business affairs and the estate;

(2) the accustomed standard of living of the protected person and individuals who are in fact dependent on the protected person; and

(3) other money or sources used for the support of the protected person.

(e) Money expended under this section may be paid by the conservator to any person, including the protected person, to reimburse for expenditures that the conservator might have made or in advance for services to be rendered to the protected person if it is reasonable to expect the services will be performed and advance payments are customary or reasonably necessary under the circumstances.

Laws 2003, c. 12, art. 1, § 65.

Historical and Statutory Notes

Laws 2003, c. 12, art. 2, § 9, provided:

"(a) Articles 1 and 2 apply to each guardianship or conservatorship proceeding and each appointment of guardian or conservator commenced on or after the effective date of articles 1 and 2. Except as otherwise provided in this section, articles 1 and 2 apply to each guardianship or conservatorship approved by the court prior to the effective date of articles 1 and 2, and to any guardianship or conservatorship proceeding pending in court on the effective date of articles 1 and 2, unless the court finds for good cause or in the interests of judicial economy that the proceeding should be completed under the provisions of Minnesota Statutes, chapter 525, as it existed prior to the effective date of articles 1 and 2.

"(b) A guardian or conservator who is not discharged prior to the effective date of articles 1 and 2 shall continue to hold the appointment but shall have only the powers specified in the order of appointment and in Minnesota Stat-

utes, chapter 525, as it existed prior to the effective date of articles 1 and 2. Each guardian or conservator holding an appointment on the effective date of articles 1 and 2 shall continue to be bound by the duties imposed by the order of appointment; by Minnesota Statutes, chapter 525, as it existed prior to the effective date of articles 1 and 2; and by article 1, section 50; and shall be bound by any additional duties imposed by articles 1 and 2 starting on the first day of the next month starting after the effective date of articles 1 and 2 or on the next anniversary date of the appointment, whichever occurs later.

"(c) Any act done prior to the effective date of articles 1 and 2 in any proceeding and any right accrued under Minnesota Statutes, chapter 525, prior to the effective date of articles 1 and 2 shall not be impaired by articles 1 and 2. If a right is acquired, extinguished, or barred upon the expiration of a prescribed period of time which has commenced to run in accordance with the provisions of any statute before the effective date of articles 1 and 2, the provisions of the prior statute shall remain in force with respect to that right notwithstanding the statute's amendment or repeal by articles 1 and 2.

"(d) An order of the court or letters of guardianship or conservatorship issued by the court prior to the effective date of articles 1 and 2 shall remain in full force and effect in accordance with its terms and conditions and in accordance with the provisions of prior law until the court modifies the order or letters in accordance with the provisions of articles 1 and 2. Upon request for a certified copy of an order or letters which remains in full force and effect under this paragraph, the court administrator shall certify that the order or letters remains in full force and effect pursuant to this paragraph.

"(e) The court, without hearing or notice to any person, may issue new letters of guardianship or conservatorship under articles 1 and 2 to replace similar letters issued prior to the effective date of articles 1 and 2. The new letters shall be effective under articles 1 and 2 with the same force and effect as the prior

letters and shall remain in full force and effect until modified by the court in accordance with the provisions of articles 1 and 2.

"(f) A power of attorney executed in accordance with Minnesota Statutes, section 524.5–505, prior to the effective date of articles 1 and 2, or any surety bond, deed, or other instrument, report, or other undertaking executed in accordance with Minnesota Statutes, chapter 525, prior to the effective date of articles 1 and 2, shall remain in full force and effect for all purposes in accordance with its terms and conditions and the provisions of the applicable statutes under which the power of attorney, surety bond, deed, or other instrument, report, or other undertaking was executed, until the power of attorney, surety bond, deed, or other instrument, report, or other undertaking expires according to its terms or pursuant to the statutes governing its execution, or is modified, terminated, or superseded by a new power of attorney, surety bond, deed, or other instrument, report, or other undertaking executed in accordance with the provisions of articles 1 and 2."

524.5–428. Death of protected person

(a) If a protected person dies, the conservator shall deliver to the court for safekeeping any will of the deceased protected person which may have come into the conservator's possession, inform the personal representative named in the will of the delivery, and retain the estate for delivery to a duly appointed personal representative of the decedent or other persons entitled thereto.

(b) If a personal representative has not been appointed within 90 days after the death of a protected person and an application or petition for appointment is not before the court, the conservator may apply or petition for appointment as personal representative in order to administer and distribute the decedent's estate.

Laws 2003, c. 12, art. 1, § 66.

Historical and Statutory Notes

Laws 2003, c. 12, art. 2, § 9, provided:

"(a) Articles 1 and 2 apply to each guardianship or conservatorship proceeding and each appointment of guardian or conservator commenced on or after the effective date of articles 1 and 2. Except as otherwise provided in this section, articles 1 and 2 apply to each guardianship or conservatorship approved by the court prior to the effective date of articles 1 and 2, and to any guardianship or conservatorship proceeding pending in court on the effective date of articles 1 and 2, unless the court finds for good cause or in the interests of judicial

economy that the proceeding should be completed under the provisions of Minnesota Statutes, chapter 525, as it existed prior to the effective date of articles 1 and 2.

"(b) A guardian or conservator who is not discharged prior to the effective date of articles 1 and 2 shall continue to hold the appointment but shall have only the powers specified in the order of appointment and in Minnesota Statutes, chapter 525, as it existed prior to the effective date of articles 1 and 2. Each guardian or conservator holding an appointment on the effective date of articles 1 and 2 shall con-

tinue to be bound by the duties imposed by the order of appointment; by Minnesota Statutes, chapter 525, as it existed prior to the effective date of articles 1 and 2; and by article 1, section 50; and shall be bound by any additional duties imposed by articles 1 and 2 starting on the first day of the next month starting after the effective date of articles 1 and 2 or on the next anniversary date of the appointment, whichever occurs later.

"(c) Any act done prior to the effective date of articles 1 and 2 in any proceeding and any right accrued under Minnesota Statutes, chapter 525, prior to the effective date of articles 1 and 2 shall not be impaired by articles 1 and 2. If a right is acquired, extinguished, or barred upon the expiration of a prescribed period of time which has commenced to run in accordance with the provisions of any statute before the effective date of articles 1 and 2, the provisions of the prior statute shall remain in force with respect to that right notwithstanding the statute's amendment or repeal by articles 1 and 2.

"(d) An order of the court or letters of guardianship or conservatorship issued by the court prior to the effective date of articles 1 and 2 shall remain in full force and effect in accordance with its terms and conditions and in accordance with the provisions of prior law until the court modifies the order or letters in accordance with the provisions of articles 1 and 2. Upon request for a certified copy of an order or letters which remains in full force and effect under this paragraph, the court administrator

shall certify that the order or letters remains in full force and effect pursuant to this paragraph.

"(e) The court, without hearing or notice to any person, may issue new letters of guardianship or conservatorship under articles 1 and 2 to replace similar letters issued prior to the effective date of articles 1 and 2. The new letters shall be effective under articles 1 and 2 with the same force and effect as the prior letters and shall remain in full force and effect until modified by the court in accordance with the provisions of articles 1 and 2.

"(f) A power of attorney executed in accordance with Minnesota Statutes, section 524.5–505, prior to the effective date of articles 1 and 2, or any surety bond, deed, or other instrument, report, or other undertaking executed in accordance with Minnesota Statutes, chapter 525, prior to the effective date of articles 1 and 2, shall remain in full force and effect for all purposes in accordance with its terms and conditions and the provisions of the applicable statutes under which the power of attorney, surety bond, deed, or other instrument, report, or other undertaking was executed, until the power of attorney, surety bond, deed, or other instrument, report, or other undertaking expires according to its terms or pursuant to the statutes governing its execution, or is modified, terminated, or superseded by a new power of attorney, surety bond, deed, or other instrument, report, or other undertaking executed in accordance with the provisions of articles 1 and 2."

524.5–429. Claims against protected person

(a) A conservator may pay, or secure by encumbering assets of the estate, claims against the estate or against the protected person arising before or during the conservatorship upon their presentation and allowance in accordance with the priorities stated in paragraph (d). A claimant may present a claim by:

(1) sending or delivering to the conservator a written statement of the claim, indicating its basis, the name and address of the claimant, and the amount claimed; or

(2) filing a written statement of the claim, in the form prescribed by rule, with the clerk of court and sending or delivering a copy of the statement to the conservator.

(b) A claim is deemed presented on receipt of the written statement of claim by the conservator or the filing of the claim with the court, whichever occurs first. A presented claim is allowed if it is not disallowed by written statement sent or delivered by the conservator to the claimant within 60 days after its presentation. The conservator before payment may change an allowance to a disallowance in whole or in part, but not after allowance by a court order or judgment or an order directing payment of the claim. The presentation of a claim tolls the running of any statute of limitations relating to the claim until 30 days after its disallowance.

(c) A claimant whose claim has not been paid may petition the court for determination of the claim at any time before it is barred by a statute of limitations and, upon due proof, procure an order for its allowance, payment, or security by encumbering assets of the estate. If a proceeding is pending against a protected person at the time of appointment of a conservator or is initiated against the protected person thereafter, the moving party shall give to the conservator notice of any proceeding that could result in creating a claim against the estate.

(d) If it appears that the estate is likely to be exhausted before all existing claims are paid, the conservator shall distribute the estate in money or in kind in payment of claims in the following order:

(1) costs and expenses of administration;

(2) claims of the federal or state government having priority under other law;

(3) reasonable and necessary medical, hospital, or nursing home expenses of the protected person, including compensation of persons attending the ward, protected person, or respondent;

(4) claims incurred by the conservator for support, care, education, health, and welfare previously provided to the protected person or individuals who are in fact dependent on the protected person;

(5) claims arising before the conservatorship; and

(6) all other claims.

(e) Preference may not be given in the payment of a claim over any other claim of the same class, and a claim due and payable may not be preferred over a claim not due.

(f) If assets of the conservatorship are adequate to meet all existing claims, the court, acting in the best interest of the protected person, may order the conservator to give a mortgage or other security on the conservatorship estate to secure payment at some future date of any or all claims.

Laws 2003, c. 12, art. 1, § 67.

Historical and Statutory Notes

Laws 2003, c. 12, art. 2, § 9, provided:

"(a) Articles 1 and 2 apply to each guardianship or conservatorship proceeding and each appointment of guardian or conservator commenced on or after the effective date of articles 1 and 2. Except as otherwise provided in this section, articles 1 and 2 apply to each guardianship or conservatorship approved by the court prior to the effective date of articles 1 and 2, and to any guardianship or conservatorship proceeding pending in court on the effective date of articles 1 and 2, unless the court finds for good cause or in the interests of judicial economy that the proceeding should be completed under the provisions of Minnesota Statutes, chapter 525, as it existed prior to the effective date of articles 1 and 2.

"(b) A guardian or conservator who is not discharged prior to the effective date of articles 1 and 2 shall continue to hold the appointment but shall have only the powers specified in the order of appointment and in Minnesota Statutes, chapter 525, as it existed prior to the effective date of articles 1 and 2. Each guardian or conservator holding an appointment on the effective date of articles 1 and 2 shall continue to be bound by the duties imposed by the order of appointment; by Minnesota Statutes, chapter 525, as it existed prior to the effective date of articles 1 and 2; and by article 1, section 50; and shall be bound by any additional duties imposed by articles 1 and 2 starting on the first day of the next month starting after the effective date of articles 1 and 2 or on the next anniversary date of the appointment, whichever occurs later.

"(c) Any act done prior to the effective date of articles 1 and 2 in any proceeding and any right accrued under Minnesota Statutes, chapter 525, prior to the effective date of articles 1 and 2 shall not be impaired by articles 1 and 2. If a right is acquired, extinguished, or barred upon the expiration of a prescribed period of time which has commenced to run in accordance with the provisions of any statute before the effective date of articles 1 and 2, the provisions of the prior statute shall remain in force with respect to that right notwithstanding the statute's amendment or repeal by articles 1 and 2.

"(d) An order of the court or letters of guardianship or conservatorship issued by the court prior to the effective date of articles 1 and 2 shall remain in full force and effect in accordance with its terms and conditions and in accordance with the provisions of prior law

until the court modifies the order or letters in accordance with the provisions of articles 1 and 2. Upon request for a certified copy of an order or letters which remains in full force and effect under this paragraph, the court administrator shall certify that the order or letters remains in full force and effect pursuant to this paragraph.

"(e) The court, without hearing or notice to any person, may issue new letters of guardianship or conservatorship under articles 1 and 2 to replace similar letters issued prior to the effective date of articles 1 and 2. The new letters shall be effective under articles 1 and 2 with the same force and effect as the prior letters and shall remain in full force and effect until modified by the court in accordance with the provisions of articles 1 and 2.

"(f) A power of attorney executed in accordance with Minnesota Statutes, section 524.5–505, prior to the effective date of articles 1 and 2, or any surety bond, deed, or other instrument, report, or other undertaking executed in accordance with Minnesota Statutes, chapter 525, prior to the effective date of articles 1 and 2, shall remain in full force and effect for all purposes in accordance with its terms and conditions and the provisions of the applicable statutes under which the power of attorney, surety bond, deed, or other instrument, report, or other undertaking was executed, until the power of attorney, surety bond, deed, or other instrument, report, or other undertaking expires according to its terms or pursuant to the statutes governing its execution, or is modified, terminated, or superseded by a new power of attorney, surety bond, deed, or other instrument, report, or other undertaking executed in accordance with the provisions of articles 1 and 2."

524.5–430. Personal liability of conservator

(a) Except as otherwise agreed, a conservator is not personally liable on a contract properly entered into in a fiduciary capacity in the course of administration of the estate unless the conservator fails to reveal in the contract the representative capacity and identify the estate.

(b) A conservator is personally liable for obligations arising from ownership or control of property of the estate or for other acts or omissions occurring in the course of administration of the estate only if personally at fault.

(c) Claims based on contracts entered into by a conservator in a fiduciary capacity, obligations arising from ownership or control of the estate, and claims based on torts committed in the course of administration of the estate may be asserted against the estate by proceeding against the conservator in a fiduciary capacity, whether or not the conservator is personally liable therefor.

(d) A question of liability between the estate and the conservator personally may be determined in a proceeding for accounting, surcharge, or indemnification, or in another appropriate proceeding or action.

(e) A conservator is not personally liable for any environmental condition on or injury resulting from any environmental condition on land solely by reason of being appointed conservator.

Laws 2003, c. 12, art. 1, § 68.

Historical and Statutory Notes

Laws 2003, c. 12, art. 2, § 9, provided:

"(a) Articles 1 and 2 apply to each guardianship or conservatorship proceeding and each appointment of guardian or conservator commenced on or after the effective date of articles 1 and 2. Except as otherwise provided in this section, articles 1 and 2 apply to each guardianship or conservatorship approved by the court prior to the effective date of articles 1 and 2, and to any guardianship or conservatorship proceeding pending in court on the effective date of articles 1 and 2, unless the court finds for good cause or in the interests of judicial economy that the proceeding should be completed under the provisions of Minnesota Statutes, chapter 525, as it existed prior to the effective date of articles 1 and 2.

"(b) A guardian or conservator who is not discharged prior to the effective date of articles 1 and 2 shall continue to hold the appointment but shall have only the powers specified in the order of appointment and in Minnesota Statutes, chapter 525, as it existed prior to the effective date of articles 1 and 2. Each guardian or conservator holding an appointment on the effective date of articles 1 and 2 shall continue to be bound by the duties imposed by the order of appointment; by Minnesota Statutes, chapter 525, as it existed prior to the effective date of articles 1 and 2; and by article 1, section 50; and shall be bound by any additional duties imposed by articles 1 and 2 starting on the first day of the next month starting after the effective date of articles 1 and 2 or on the next anniversary date of the appointment, whichever occurs later.

"(c) Any act done prior to the effective date of articles 1 and 2 in any proceeding and any right accrued under Minnesota Statutes, chapter 525, prior to the effective date of articles 1 and 2 shall not be impaired by articles 1 and 2. If a right is acquired, extinguished, or barred upon the expiration of a prescribed period of time which has commenced to run in accordance with the provisions of any statute before the effective date of articles 1 and 2, the provisions of the prior statute shall remain in force with respect to that right notwithstanding the statute's amendment or repeal by articles 1 and 2.

"(d) An order of the court or letters of guardianship or conservatorship issued by the court prior to the effective date of articles 1 and 2 shall remain in full force and effect in accordance with its terms and conditions and in accordance with the provisions of prior law until the court modifies the order or letters in accordance with the provisions of articles 1 and 2. Upon request for a certified copy of an order or letters which remains in full force and effect under this paragraph, the court administrator shall certify that the order or letters remains in full force and effect pursuant to this paragraph.

"(e) The court, without hearing or notice to any person, may issue new letters of guardianship or conservatorship under articles 1 and 2 to replace similar letters issued prior to the effective date of articles 1 and 2. The new letters shall be effective under articles 1 and 2 with the same force and effect as the prior letters and shall remain in full force and effect until modified by the court in accordance with the provisions of articles 1 and 2.

"(f) A power of attorney executed in accordance with Minnesota Statutes, section 524.5–505, prior to the effective date of articles 1 and 2, or any surety bond, deed, or other instrument, report, or other undertaking executed in accordance with Minnesota Statutes, chapter 525, prior to the effective date of articles 1 and 2, shall remain in full force and effect for all purposes in accordance with its terms and conditions and the provisions of the applicable statutes under which the power of attorney, surety bond, deed, or other instrument, report, or other undertaking was executed, until the power of attorney, surety bond, deed, or other instrument, report, or other undertaking expires according to its terms or pursuant to the statutes governing its execution, or is modified, terminated, or superseded by a new power of attorney, surety bond, deed, or other instrument, report, or other undertaking executed in accordance with the provisions of articles 1 and 2."

524.5–431. Termination of proceedings

(a) A conservatorship terminates upon the death of the protected person or upon order of the court. Unless created for reasons other than that the protected person is a minor, a conservatorship created for a minor also terminates when the protected person attains majority or is emancipated.

(b) Upon the death of a protected person, the conservator shall conclude the administration of the estate by distribution of probate property to the personal representative of the protected person's estate. The conservator shall distribute nonprobate property to the successor in interest. The conservator shall file a final report and petition for discharge no later than 30 days after distribution, and notice of hearing for allowance of said report shall be given to interested persons and to the personal representative of the protected person's estate.

(c) On petition of any person interested in the protected person's welfare, the court may terminate the conservatorship if the protected person no longer needs the assistance or protection of a conservator. Termination of the conservatorship does not affect a conservator's liability for previous acts or the obligation to account for funds and assets of the protected person.

(d) Except as otherwise ordered by the court for good cause, before terminating a conservatorship, the court shall follow the same procedures to safeguard the rights of the protected person that apply to a petition for conservatorship. Upon the establishment of a prima facie case for termination, the court shall order termination unless it is proved that continuation of the conservatorship is in the best interest of the protected person.

(e) Upon termination of a conservatorship, whether or not formally distributed by the conservator, title to assets of the estate remains vested in the formerly protected person or passes to the person's successors subject to administration, including claims of creditors and allowances of surviving spouse and dependent children, and subject to the rights of others resulting from abatement, retainer, advancement, and ademption. The order of termination must provide for expenses of administration and direct the conservator to execute appropriate instruments to evidence the transfer of title or confirm a distribution previously made and to file a final report and a petition for discharge upon approval of the final report.

(f) The court shall enter a final order of discharge upon the approval of the final report and satisfaction by the conservator of any other conditions placed by the court on the conservator's discharge.

Laws 2003, c. 12, art. 1, § 69.

Historical and Statutory Notes

Laws 2003, c. 12, art. 2, § 9, provided:

"(a) Articles 1 and 2 apply to each guardianship or conservatorship proceeding and each appointment of guardian or conservator commenced on or after the effective date of articles 1 and 2. Except as otherwise provided in this section, articles 1 and 2 apply to each guardianship or conservatorship approved by the court prior to the effective date of articles 1 and 2, and to any guardianship or conservatorship proceeding pending in court on the effective date of articles 1 and 2, unless the court finds for good cause or in the interests of judicial economy that the proceeding should be completed under the provisions of Minnesota Statutes, chapter 525, as it existed prior to the effective date of articles 1 and 2.

"(b) A guardian or conservator who is not discharged prior to the effective date of articles 1 and 2 shall continue to hold the appointment but shall have only the powers specified in the order of appointment and in Minnesota Statutes, chapter 525, as it existed prior to the effective date of articles 1 and 2. Each guardian or conservator holding an appointment on the effective date of articles 1 and 2 shall continue to be bound by the duties imposed by the order of appointment; by Minnesota Statutes, chapter 525, as it existed prior to the effective date of articles 1 and 2; and by article 1, section 50; and shall be bound by any additional duties imposed by articles 1 and 2 starting on the first day of the next month starting after the effective date of articles 1 and 2 or on the next anniversary date of the appointment, whichever occurs later.

"(c) Any act done prior to the effective date of articles 1 and 2 in any proceeding and any right accrued under Minnesota Statutes, chapter 525, prior to the effective date of articles 1 and 2 shall not be impaired by articles 1 and 2. If a right is acquired, extinguished, or barred upon the expiration of a prescribed period of time which has commenced to run in accordance with the provisions of any statute before the effective date of articles 1 and 2, the provisions of the prior statute shall remain in force with respect to that right notwithstanding the statute's amendment or repeal by articles 1 and 2.

"(d) An order of the court or letters of guardianship or conservatorship issued by the court prior to the effective date of articles 1 and 2 shall remain in full force and effect in accordance with its terms and conditions and in accordance with the provisions of prior law until the court modifies the order or letters in accordance with the provisions of articles 1 and 2. Upon request for a certified copy of an order or letters which remains in full force and effect under this paragraph, the court administrator shall certify that the order or letters remains in full force and effect pursuant to this paragraph.

"(e) The court, without hearing or notice to any person, may issue new letters of guardianship or conservatorship under articles 1 and 2 to replace similar letters issued prior to the effective date of articles 1 and 2. The new letters shall be effective under articles 1 and 2 with the same force and effect as the prior letters and shall remain in full force and effect until modified by the court in accordance with the provisions of articles 1 and 2.

"(f) A power of attorney executed in accordance with Minnesota Statutes, section 524.5–505, prior to the effective date of articles 1 and 2, or any surety bond, deed, or other instrument, report, or other undertaking executed in accordance with Minnesota Statutes, chapter 525, prior to the effective date of articles 1 and 2, shall remain in full force and effect for all purposes in accordance with its terms and conditions and the provisions of the applicable statutes under which the power of attorney, surety bond, deed, or other instrument, report, or other undertaking was executed, until the power of attorney, surety bond, deed, or other instrument, report, or other undertaking expires according to its terms or pursuant to the statutes governing its execution, or is modified, terminated, or superseded by a new power of attorney, surety bond, deed, or other instrument, report, or other undertaking executed in accordance with the provisions of articles 1 and 2."

524.5–432. Payment of debt and delivery of property to foreign conservator without local proceeding

(a) A person who is indebted to or has the possession of tangible or intangible property of a protected person may pay the debt or deliver the property to a foreign conservator, guardian of the estate, or other court-appointed fiduciary of the state of residence of the protected person. Payment or delivery may be made only upon proof of appointment and presentation of an affidavit made by or on behalf of the fiduciary stating that a protective proceeding relating to the protected person is not pending in this state and the foreign fiduciary is entitled to payment or to receive delivery.

(b) Payment or delivery in accordance with paragraph (a) discharges the debtor or possessor, absent knowledge of any protective proceeding pending in this state.

Laws 2003, c. 12, art. 1, § 70.

Historical and Statutory Notes

Laws 2003, c. 12, art. 2, § 9, provided:

"(a) Articles 1 and 2 apply to each guardianship or conservatorship proceeding and each appointment of guardian or conservator commenced on or after the effective date of articles 1 and 2. Except as otherwise provided in this section, articles 1 and 2 apply to each guardianship or conservatorship approved by the court prior to the effective date of articles 1 and 2, and to any guardianship or conservatorship proceeding pending in court on the effective date of articles 1 and 2, unless the court finds for good cause or in the interests of judicial economy that the proceeding should be completed under the provisions of Minnesota Statutes, chapter 525, as it existed prior to the effective date of articles 1 and 2.

"(b) A guardian or conservator who is not discharged prior to the effective date of articles 1 and 2 shall continue to hold the appointment but shall have only the powers specified in the order of appointment and in Minnesota Statutes, chapter 525, as it existed prior to the effective date of articles 1 and 2. Each guardian or conservator holding an appointment on the effective date of articles 1 and 2 shall continue to be bound by the duties imposed by the order of appointment; by Minnesota Statutes, chapter 525, as it existed prior to the effective date of articles 1 and 2; and by article 1, section 50; and shall be bound by any additional duties imposed by articles 1 and 2 starting on the first day of the next month starting after the effective date of articles 1 and 2 or on the next anniversary date of the appointment, whichever occurs later.

"(c) Any act done prior to the effective date of articles 1 and 2 in any proceeding and any right accrued under Minnesota Statutes, chapter 525, prior to the effective date of articles 1 and 2 shall not be impaired by articles 1 and 2. If a right is acquired, extinguished, or barred upon the expiration of a prescribed period of time which has commenced to run in accordance with the provisions of any statute before the effective date of articles 1 and 2, the provisions of the prior statute shall remain in force with respect to that right notwithstanding the statute's amendment or repeal by articles 1 and 2.

"(d) An order of the court or letters of guardianship or conservatorship issued by the court prior to the effective date of articles 1 and 2 shall remain in full force and effect in accordance with its terms and conditions and in accordance with the provisions of prior law until the court modifies the order or letters in accordance with the provisions of articles 1 and 2. Upon request for a certified copy of an order or letters which remains in full force and effect under this paragraph, the court administrator shall certify that the order or letters remains in full force and effect pursuant to this paragraph.

"(e) The court, without hearing or notice to any person, may issue new letters of guardianship or conservatorship under articles 1 and 2 to replace similar letters issued prior to the effective date of articles 1 and 2. The new letters shall be effective under articles 1 and 2 with the same force and effect as the prior letters and shall remain in full force and effect until modified by the court in accordance with the provisions of articles 1 and 2.

"(f) A power of attorney executed in accordance with Minnesota Statutes, section 524.5–505, prior to the effective date of articles 1 and 2, or any surety bond, deed, or other instrument, report, or other undertaking executed in accordance with Minnesota Statutes, chapter 525, prior to the effective date of articles 1 and 2, shall remain in full force and effect for all purposes in accordance with its terms and conditions and the provisions of the applicable statutes under which the power of attorney, surety bond, deed, or other instrument, report, or other undertaking was executed, until the power of attorney, surety bond, deed, or other instrument, report, or other undertaking expires according to its terms or pursuant to the statutes governing its execution, or is modified, terminated, or superseded by a new power of attorney, surety bond, deed, or other instrument, report, or other undertaking executed in

accordance with the provisions of articles 1 and 2."

524.5–433.   Foreign conservator: proof of authority; bond; powers

If a conservator has not been appointed in this state and a petition in a protective proceeding is not pending in this state, a conservator appointed in the state in which the protected person resides may file in a court of this state, in a county in which property belonging to the protected person is located, authenticated copies of letters of appointment and of any bond. Thereafter, the conservator may exercise all powers of a conservator appointed in this state as to property in this state and may maintain actions and proceedings in this state subject to any conditions otherwise imposed upon nonresident parties.

Laws 2003, c. 12, art. 1, § 71.

Historical and Statutory Notes

Laws 2003, c. 12, art. 2, § 9, provided:

"(a) Articles 1 and 2 apply to each guardianship or conservatorship proceeding and each appointment of guardian or conservator commenced on or after the effective date of articles 1 and 2. Except as otherwise provided in this section, articles 1 and 2 apply to each guardianship or conservatorship approved by the court prior to the effective date of articles 1 and 2, and to any guardianship or conservatorship proceeding pending in court on the effective date of articles 1 and 2, unless the court finds for good cause or in the interests of judicial economy that the proceeding should be completed under the provisions of Minnesota Statutes, chapter 525, as it existed prior to the effective date of articles 1 and 2.

"(b) A guardian or conservator who is not discharged prior to the effective date of articles 1 and 2 shall continue to hold the appointment but shall have only the powers specified in the order of appointment and in Minnesota Statutes, chapter 525, as it existed prior to the effective date of articles 1 and 2. Each guardian or conservator holding an appointment on the effective date of articles 1 and 2 shall continue to be bound by the duties imposed by the order of appointment; by Minnesota Statutes, chapter 525, as it existed prior to the effective date of articles 1 and 2; and by article 1, section 50; and shall be bound by any additional duties imposed by articles 1 and 2 starting on the first day of the next month starting after the effective date of articles 1 and 2 or on the next anniversary date of the appointment, whichever occurs later.

"(c) Any act done prior to the effective date of articles 1 and 2 in any proceeding and any right accrued under Minnesota Statutes, chapter 525,

prior to the effective date of articles 1 and 2 shall not be impaired by articles 1 and 2. If a right is acquired, extinguished, or barred upon the expiration of a prescribed period of time which has commenced to run in accordance with the provisions of any statute before the effective date of articles 1 and 2, the provisions of the prior statute shall remain in force with respect to that right notwithstanding the statute's amendment or repeal by articles 1 and 2.

"(d) An order of the court or letters of guardianship or conservatorship issued by the court prior to the effective date of articles 1 and 2 shall remain in full force and effect in accordance with its terms and conditions and in accordance with the provisions of prior law until the court modifies the order or letters in accordance with the provisions of articles 1 and 2. Upon request for a certified copy of an order or letters which remains in full force and effect under this paragraph, the court administrator shall certify that the order or letters remains in full force and effect pursuant to this paragraph.

"(e) The court, without hearing or notice to any person, may issue new letters of guardianship or conservatorship under articles 1 and 2 to replace similar letters issued prior to the effective date of articles 1 and 2. The new letters shall be effective under articles 1 and 2 with the same force and effect as the prior letters and shall remain in full force and effect until modified by the court in accordance with the provisions of articles 1 and 2.

"(f) A power of attorney executed in accordance with Minnesota Statutes, section 524.5–505, prior to the effective date of articles 1 and 2, or any surety bond, deed, or other instrument, report, or other undertaking executed in accordance with Minnesota Statutes, chapter 525, prior to the effective date of articles 1 and 2, shall remain in full force and effect for all purposes in accordance with its terms and conditions and the provisions of the applicable statutes under which the power of attorney, surety bond, deed, or other instrument, report, or other undertaking was executed, until the power of attorney, surety bond, deed, or other instrument, report, or other undertaking expires according to its terms or pursuant to the statutes governing its execution, or is modified, terminated, or superseded by a new power of attorney, surety bond, deed, or other instrument, report, or other undertaking executed in accordance with the provisions of articles 1 and 2."

PART 5

MISCELLANEOUS PROVISIONS

524.5–501. Guardianship, conservatorship; workers' compensation proceedings

(a) When a matter is referred under section 176.092, subdivision 3, the court shall determine whether the employee or dependent is a minor or an incapacitated person, shall appoint a guardian or conservator if the employee or dependent is a minor or an incapacitated person, and shall return the matter to the source of referral.

(b) The court shall oversee the use of monetary benefits paid to a conservator as provided in this article or under rule 145 of the General Rules of Practice for the district courts. There is a rebuttable presumption that a settlement or award approved by the commissioner of the Department of Labor and Industry or a compensation judge is reasonable and fair to the employee or dependent.

(c) Subject to the approval of the court, the insurer or self–insured employer shall pay the costs and guardian, conservator, and attorney fees of the employee or dependent associated with the appointment of a guardian or conservator and as required under section 176.092.

Laws 2003, c. 12, art. 1, § 72.

Historical and Statutory Notes

Laws 2003, c. 12, art. 2, § 9, provided:

"(a) Articles 1 and 2 apply to each guardianship or conservatorship proceeding and each appointment of guardian or conservator commenced on or after the effective date of articles 1 and 2. Except as otherwise provided in this section, articles 1 and 2 apply to each guardianship or conservatorship approved by the court prior to the effective date of articles 1 and 2, and to any guardianship or conservatorship proceeding pending in court on the effective date of articles 1 and 2, unless the court finds for good cause or in the interests of judicial economy that the proceeding should be completed under the provisions of Minnesota Statutes, chapter 525, as it existed prior to the effective date of articles 1 and 2.

"(b) A guardian or conservator who is not discharged prior to the effective date of articles 1 and 2 shall continue to hold the appointment but shall have only the powers specified in the order of appointment and in Minnesota Statutes, chapter 525, as it existed prior to the effective date of articles 1 and 2. Each guardian or conservator holding an appointment on the effective date of articles 1 and 2 shall continue to be bound by the duties imposed by the order of appointment; by Minnesota Statutes, chapter 525, as it existed prior to the effective date of articles 1 and 2; and by article 1, section 50; and shall be bound by any additional duties imposed by articles 1 and 2 starting on the first day of the next month starting after the effective date of articles 1 and 2 or on the next anniversary date of the appointment, whichever occurs later.

"(c) Any act done prior to the effective date of articles 1 and 2 in any proceeding and any right accrued under Minnesota Statutes, chapter 525, prior to the effective date of articles 1 and 2 shall not be impaired by articles 1 and 2. If a right is acquired, extinguished, or barred upon the expiration of a prescribed period of time which has commenced to run in accordance with the provisions of any statute before the effective date of articles 1 and 2, the provisions of the prior statute shall remain in force with respect to that right notwithstanding the statute's amendment or repeal by articles 1 and 2.

"(d) An order of the court or letters of guardianship or conservatorship issued by the court prior to the effective date of articles 1 and 2 shall remain in full force and effect in accordance with its terms and conditions and in accordance with the provisions of prior law until the court modifies the order or letters in accordance with the provisions of articles 1 and 2. Upon request for a certified copy of an order or letters which remains in full force and effect under this paragraph, the court administrator shall certify that the order or letters remains in full force and effect pursuant to this paragraph.

"(e) The court, without hearing or notice to any person, may issue new letters of guardian-

ship or conservatorship under articles 1 and 2 to replace similar letters issued prior to the effective date of articles 1 and 2. The new letters shall be effective under articles 1 and 2 with the same force and effect as the prior letters and shall remain in full force and effect until modified by the court in accordance with the provisions of articles 1 and 2.

"(f) A power of attorney executed in accordance with Minnesota Statutes, section 524.5–505, prior to the effective date of articles 1 and 2, or any surety bond, deed, or other instrument, report, or other undertaking executed in accordance with Minnesota Statutes, chapter 525, prior to the effective date of articles 1 and 2, shall remain in full force and effect for all purposes in accordance with its terms and conditions and the provisions of the applicable statutes under which the power of attorney, surety bond, deed, or other instrument, report, or other undertaking was executed, until the power of attorney, surety bond, deed, or other instrument, report, or other undertaking expires according to its terms or pursuant to the statutes governing its execution, or is modified, terminated, or superseded by a new power of attorney, surety bond, deed, or other instrument, report, or other undertaking executed in accordance with the provisions of articles 1 and 2."

524.5–502. Compensation and expenses

(a) The court may authorize a proceeding under this article to proceed in forma pauperis, as provided in chapter 563.

(b) In proceedings under this article, a lawyer or health professional rendering necessary services with regard to the appointment of a guardian or conservator, the administration of the protected person's estate or personal affairs, or the restoration of that person's capacity or termination of the protective proceeding shall be entitled to compensation from the protected person's estate or from the county having jurisdiction over the proceedings if the ward or protected person is indigent. When the court determines that other necessary services have been provided for the benefit of the ward or protected person by a lawyer or health professional, the court may order fees to be paid from the estate of the protected person or from the county having jurisdiction over the proceedings if the ward or protected person is indigent. If, however, the court determines that a petitioner, guardian, or conservator has not acted in good faith, the court shall order some or all of the fees or costs incurred in the proceedings to be borne by the petitioner, guardian, or conservator not acting in good faith. In determining compensation for a guardian or conservator of an indigent person, the court shall consider a fee schedule recommended by the Board of County Commissioners. The fee schedule may also include a maximum compensation based on the living arrangements of the ward or protected person. If these services are provided by a public or private agency, the county may contract on a fee-for-service basis with that agency.

(c) When the court determines that a guardian or conservator has rendered necessary services or has incurred necessary expenses for the benefit of the ward or protected person, the court may order reimbursement or compensation to be paid from the estate of the protected person or from the county having jurisdiction over the guardianship or protective proceeding if the ward or protected person is indigent. The court may not deny an award of fees solely because the ward or protected person is a recipient of medical assistance. In determining compensation for a guardian or conservator of an indigent person, the court shall consider a fee schedule recommended by the Board of County Commissioners. The fee schedule may also include a maximum compensation based on the living arrangements of the ward or protected person. If these services are provided by a public or private agency, the county may contract on a fee-for-service basis with that agency.

(d) The court shall order reimbursement or compensation if the guardian or conservator requests payment and the guardian or conservator was nominated by the court or by the county adult protection unit because no suitable relative or other person was available to provide guardianship or protective proceeding services necessary to prevent maltreatment of a vulnerable adult, as defined in section 626.5572, subdivision 15. In determining compensation for a guardian or conservator of an indigent person, the court shall consider a fee schedule recommended by the Board of County Commissioners. The fee schedule may also include a maximum compensation based on the living arrangements of the ward or protected person. If these services are provided by a public or private agency, the county may contract on a fee-for-service basis with that agency.

(e) When a county employee serves as a guardian or conservator as part of employment duties, the court shall order compensation if the guardian or conservator performs necessary services that are not compensated by the county. The court may order reimbursement to the county from the protected person's estate for compensation paid by the county for services rendered by a guardian or conservator who is a county employee but only if the county shows that after a diligent effort it was unable to arrange for an independent guardian or conservator.

Laws 2003, c. 12, art. 1, § 73.

Historical and Statutory Notes

Laws 2003, c. 12, art. 2, § 9, provided:

"(a) Articles 1 and 2 apply to each guardianship or conservatorship proceeding and each appointment of guardian or conservator commenced on or after the effective date of articles 1 and 2. Except as otherwise provided in this section, articles 1 and 2 apply to each guardianship or conservatorship approved by the court prior to the effective date of articles 1 and 2, and to any guardianship or conservatorship proceeding pending in court on the effective date of articles 1 and 2, unless the court finds for good cause or in the interests of judicial economy that the proceeding should be completed under the provisions of Minnesota Statutes, chapter 525, as it existed prior to the effective date of articles 1 and 2.

"(b) A guardian or conservator who is not discharged prior to the effective date of articles 1 and 2 shall continue to hold the appointment but shall have only the powers specified in the order of appointment and in Minnesota Statutes, chapter 525, as it existed prior to the effective date of articles 1 and 2. Each guardian or conservator holding an appointment on the effective date of articles 1 and 2 shall continue to be bound by the duties imposed by the order of appointment; by Minnesota Statutes, chapter 525, as it existed prior to the effective date of articles 1 and 2; and by article 1, section 50; and shall be bound by any additional duties imposed by articles 1 and 2 starting on the first day of the next month starting after the effective date of articles 1 and 2 or on the next anniversary date of the appointment, whichever occurs later.

"(c) Any act done prior to the effective date of articles 1 and 2 in any proceeding and any right accrued under Minnesota Statutes, chapter 525, prior to the effective date of articles 1 and 2 shall not be impaired by articles 1 and 2. If a right is acquired, extinguished, or barred upon the expiration of a prescribed period of time which has commenced to run in accordance with the provisions of any statute before the effective date of articles 1 and 2, the provisions of the prior statute shall remain in force with respect to that right notwithstanding the statute's amendment or repeal by articles 1 and 2.

"(d) An order of the court or letters of guardianship or conservatorship issued by the court prior to the effective date of articles 1 and 2 shall remain in full force and effect in accordance with its terms and conditions and in accordance with the provisions of prior law until the court modifies the order or letters in accordance with the provisions of articles 1 and 2. Upon request for a certified copy of an order or letters which remains in full force and effect under this paragraph, the court administrator shall certify that the order or letters remains in full force and effect pursuant to this paragraph.

"(e) The court, without hearing or notice to any person, may issue new letters of guardianship or conservatorship under articles 1 and 2 to replace similar letters issued prior to the effective date of articles 1 and 2. The new letters shall be effective under articles 1 and 2 with the same force and effect as the prior letters and shall remain in full force and effect until modified by the court in accordance with the provisions of articles 1 and 2.

"(f) A power of attorney executed in accordance with Minnesota Statutes, section 524.5–505, prior to the effective date of articles 1 and 2, or any surety bond, deed, or other instrument, report, or other undertaking executed in accordance with Minnesota Statutes, chapter 525, prior to the effective date of articles 1 and 2, shall remain in full force and effect for all purposes in accordance with its terms and conditions and the provisions of the applicable statutes under which the power of attorney, surety bond, deed, or other instrument, report, or other undertaking was executed, until the power of attorney, surety bond, deed, or other instrument, report, or other undertaking expires according to its terms or pursuant to the statutes governing its execution, or is modified, terminated, or superseded by a new power of attorney, surety bond, deed, or other instrument, report, or other undertaking executed in accordance with the provisions of articles 1 and 2."

524.5–505.   Repealed by Laws 2003, c. 12, art. 2, § 8

Historical and Statutory Notes

The repealed section, which related to the delegation by a parent or guardian of the powers regarding the care, custody, or property of a minor or ward, was derived from:

Laws 2000, c. 458, § 7.

Laws 2000, c. 404, § 12.

Laws 1997, c. 65, § 5.

Laws 1996, c. 455, art. 6, § 15.

Laws 1986, c. 444.

Laws 1982, c. 472, § 7.

Laws 2003, c. 12, art. 2, § 9, provided:

"(a) Articles 1 and 2 apply to each guardianship or conservatorship proceeding and each appointment of guardian or conservator commenced on or after the effective date of articles 1 and 2. Except as otherwise provided in this section, articles 1 and 2 apply to each guardianship or conservatorship approved by the court prior to the effective date of articles 1 and 2, and to any guardianship or conservatorship proceeding pending in court on the effective date of articles 1 and 2, unless the court finds for good cause or in the interests of judicial economy that the proceeding should be completed under the provisions of Minnesota Statutes, chapter 525, as it existed prior to the effective date of articles 1 and 2.

"(b) A guardian or conservator who is not discharged prior to the effective date of articles 1 and 2 shall continue to hold the appointment but shall have only the powers specified in the order of appointment and in Minnesota Statutes, chapter 525, as it existed prior to the effective date of articles 1 and 2. Each guardian or conservator holding an appointment on the effective date of articles 1 and 2 shall continue to be bound by the duties imposed by the order of appointment; by Minnesota Statutes, chapter 525, as it existed prior to the effective date of articles 1 and 2; and by article 1, section 50; and shall be bound by any additional duties imposed by articles 1 and 2 starting on the first day of the next month starting after the effective date of articles 1 and 2 or on the next anniversary date of the appointment, whichever occurs later.

"(c) Any act done prior to the effective date of articles 1 and 2 in any proceeding and any right accrued under Minnesota Statutes, chapter 525, prior to the effective date of articles 1 and 2 shall not be impaired by articles 1 and 2. If a right is acquired, extinguished, or barred upon the expiration of a prescribed period of time which has commenced to run in accordance with the provisions of any statute before the effective date of articles 1 and 2, the provisions of the prior statute shall remain in force with respect to that right notwithstanding the statute's amendment or repeal by articles 1 and 2.

"(d) An order of the court or letters of guardianship or conservatorship issued by the court prior to the effective date of articles 1 and 2 shall remain in full force and effect in accordance with its terms and conditions and in accordance with the provisions of prior law until the court modifies the order or letters in accordance with the provisions of articles 1 and 2. Upon request for a certified copy of an order or letters which remains in full force and effect under this paragraph, the court administrator shall certify that the order or letters remains in full force and effect pursuant to this paragraph.

"(e) The court, without hearing or notice to any person, may issue new letters of guardianship or conservatorship under articles 1 and 2 to replace similar letters issued prior to the effective date of articles 1 and 2. The new letters shall be effective under articles 1 and 2 with the same force and effect as the prior

letters and shall remain in full force and effect until modified by the court in accordance with the provisions of articles 1 and 2.

"(f) A power of attorney executed in accordance with Minnesota Statutes, section 524.5–505, prior to the effective date of articles 1 and 2, or any surety bond, deed, or other instrument, report, or other undertaking executed in accordance with Minnesota Statutes, chapter 525, prior to the effective date of articles 1 and 2, shall remain in full force and effect for all purposes in accordance with its terms and conditions and the provisions of the applicable statutes under which the power of attorney, surety bond, deed, or other instrument, report, or other undertaking was executed, until the power of attorney, surety bond, deed, or other instrument, report, or other undertaking expires according to its terms or pursuant to the statutes governing its execution, or is modified, terminated, or superseded by a new power of attorney, surety bond, deed, or other instrument, report, or other undertaking executed in accordance with the provisions of articles 1 and 2."

Prior to repeal, § 524.5–505 read:

"**524.5–505. Delegation of powers by parent or guardian**

"(a) A parent or a guardian of a minor or incapacitated person, by a properly executed power of attorney, may delegate to another person, for a period not exceeding six months, any powers regarding care, custody, or property of the minor or ward, except the power to consent to marriage or adoption of a minor ward.

"(b) A parent who executes a delegation of powers under this section must mail or give a copy of the document to any other parent within 30 days of its execution unless:

"(1) the other parent does not have visitation rights or has supervised visitation rights; or

"(2) there is an existing order for protection under chapter 518B or a similar law of another state in effect against the other parent to protect the parent executing the delegation of powers or the child.

"(c) A parent of a minor child may also delegate those powers by designating a standby or temporary custodian under chapter 257B."

ARTICLE 6

NONPROBATE TRANSFERS ON DEATH (1989)

PART 1

PROVISIONS RELATING TO EFFECT OF DEATH

Minnesota in 1974 did not enact Part 1 of Article 6 of the Uniform Probate Code consisting of section 6–101, which related to nonprobate transfers on death.

PART 2

MINNESOTA MULTIPARTY ACCOUNTS ACT

524.6–201. Definitions

Subdivision 1. Scope. As used in sections 524.6–201 to 524.6–214, the terms defined in this section have the meanings given them.

Subd. 2. Account. "Account" means a contract of deposit of funds between a depositor and a financial institution, and includes a checking account, savings account, certificate of deposit, share account and other like arrangement.

Subd. 3. Financial institution. "Financial institution" means any organization authorized to do business under state or federal laws relating to financial institutions, including, without limitation, banks and trust companies, savings banks, savings associations, and credit unions.

Subd. 4. Joint account. "Joint account" means an account so designated, and any account payable on request to one or more of two or more parties and to the survivor of them.

Subd. 5. Multiple-party account. A "multiple-party account" means a joint account or a P.O.D. account. It does not include accounts established for deposit of funds of a partnership, joint venture, or other association for business purposes, or accounts controlled by one or more persons as the duly authorized agent or trustee for a person, corporation, unincorporated association, charitable or civic organization or a regular fiduciary or trust account where the relationship is established other than by deposit agreement.

Subd. 6. Net contribution. "Net contribution" of a party to a joint account as of any given time is the sum of all deposits thereto made by or for the party, less all withdrawals made by or for the party which have not been paid to or applied to the use of any other party, plus a pro rata share of any interest or dividends included in the current balance. The term includes any proceeds of deposit life insurance added to the account by reason of the death of the party whose net contribution is in question.

Subd. 7. Party. "Party" means a person who, by the terms of the account, has a present right, subject to request, to payment from a multiple-party account. A P.O.D. payee is a party only after the account becomes payable by reason of the payee surviving the original party. Unless the context otherwise requires, it includes a guardian, conservator, personal representative, or assignee, including an attaching creditor, of a party. It also includes a person identified as a trustee of an account for another whether or not a beneficiary is named, but it does not include any named beneficiary unless the beneficiary has a present right of withdrawal.

Subd. 8. Payment. "Payment" of sums on deposit includes withdrawal, payment on check or other directive of a party, and any pledge of sums on deposit by a party and any setoff, or reduction or other disposition of all or part of an account pursuant to a pledge.

Subd. 9. Proof of death. "Proof of death" includes (a) a certified or authenticated copy of a death record purporting to be issued by an official or agency of the place where the death purportedly occurred which shall be prima facie proof of the fact, place, date and time of death and the identity of the decedent, (b) a certified or authenticated copy of any record or report of any governmental agency, domestic or foreign, that a person is dead which shall be prima facie evidence of the fact, place, date and time of death and the identity of the decedent.

Subd. 10. P.O.D. account. "P.O.D. account" means an account payable on request to one or more parties and on the death of the parties to one or more P.O.D. payees. The term also means an account in the name of one or more parties as trustee for one or more beneficiaries where the relationship is established by the form of the account and the deposit agreement with the financial institution and there is no subject of the trust other than the sums on deposit in the account. A P.O.D. account does not include a trust account established under a testamentary trust or inter vivos trust, or a fiduciary account arising from a fiduciary relationship such as attorney-client.

Subd. 11. P.O.D. payee. "P.O.D. payee" means a person designated on a P.O.D. account as one to whom the account is payable on request after the death of one or more persons.

Subd. 12. Request. "Request" means a proper request for withdrawals, or a check or order for payment, which complies with all conditions of the account, including special requirements concerning necessary signatures and regulations of the financial institution; but if the financial institution conditions withdrawal or payment on advance notice, for purposes of this part the request for withdrawal or payment is treated as immediately effective and a notice of intent to withdraw is treated as a request for withdrawal.

Subd. 13. Sums on deposit. "Sums on deposit" means the balance payable on a multiple-party account including interest, dividends and, in addition, any deposit life insurance proceeds added to the account by reason of the death of a party.

Subd. 14. Withdrawal. "Withdrawal" includes payment to a third person pursuant to check or other directive of a party.

Amended by Laws 1995, c. 202, art. 1, § 25, eff. May 25, 1995; Laws 2001, 1st Sp., c. 9, art. 15, § 32.

Historical and Statutory Notes

Laws 2002, c. 379, art. 1, § 113, provides:

"2001 First Special Session Senate File No. 4, as passed by the senate and the house of representatives on Friday, June 29, 2001, and subsequently published as Laws 2001, First Special Session chapter 9, is reenacted. Its provisions are effective on the dates originally provided in the bill."

Derivation:

Laws 1994, c. 472, § 63.

St.1992, § 528.02.

Laws 1987, c. 384, art. 2, § 1.

Laws 1986, c. 444.

Laws 1985, c. 292, §§ 9 to 11, 22.

Laws 1973, c. 619, § 2.

524.6–202. Ownership as between parties, and others; protection of financial institutions

The provisions of sections 524.6–203 to 524.6–205 concerning beneficial ownership as between parties, or as between parties and P.O.D. payees or beneficiaries of multiple-party accounts, are relevant only to controversies between these persons and their creditors and other successors, and have no bearing on the power of withdrawal of these persons as determined by the terms of account contracts. The provisions of sections 524.6–208 to 524.6–212 govern the liability of financial institutions who make payments pursuant thereto, and their setoff rights.

Derivation:

Laws 1994, c. 472, § 63.

St.1992, § 528.03.

Laws 1973, c. 619, § 3.

524.6–203. Ownership during lifetime

(a) A joint account belongs, during the lifetime of all parties, to the parties in proportion to the net contributions by each to the sums on deposit, unless there is clear and convincing evidence of a different intent.

(b) A P.O.D. account belongs to the original purchasing or depositing party during the party's lifetime and not to the P.O.D. payee or payees; if two or more parties are named as original parties, during their lifetimes, rights as between them are governed by clause (a).

Derivation:

Laws 1994, c. 472, § 63.

St.1992, § 528.04.

Laws 1985, c. 292, § 12.

Laws 1973, c. 619, § 4.

524.6–204. Right of survivorship

(a) Sums remaining on deposit at the death of a party to a joint account belong to the surviving party or parties as against the estate of the decedent unless there is clear and convincing evidence of a different intention, or there is a different disposition made by a valid will as herein provided, specifically referring to such account. If there are two or more surviving parties, their respective ownerships during lifetime shall be in proportion to their previous ownership interests under section 524.6–203 augmented by an equal share for each survivor of any interest the decedent may have owned in the account immediately before death; and the right of survivorship continues between the surviving parties. The interest so determined is also the interest disposable by will.

(b) If the account is a P.O.D. account, on the death of the original party or of the survivor of two or more original parties, any sums remaining on deposit belong to the P.O.D. payees if surviving, or to the survivor of them if one or more die before the surviving original party; if two or more P.O.D. payees survive, there is no right of survivorship in event of death of a P.O.D. payee thereafter unless the terms of the account or deposit agreement expressly provide for survivorship between them.

(c) In other cases, the death of any party to a multiple-party account has no effect on beneficial ownership of the account other than to transfer the rights of the decedent as part of the estate.

(d) A right of survivorship arising from the express terms of the account, or under this section, or under a P.O.D. payee designation, may be changed by specific reference by will, but the terms of such will shall not be binding upon any financial institution unless it has been given a notice in writing of a claim thereunder, in which event the deposit shall remain undisbursed until an order has been made by the probate court adjudicating the decedent's interest disposable by will.

Derivation:
Laws 1994, c. 472, § 63.
St.1992, § 528.05.

Laws 1985, c. 292, § 13.
Laws 1973, c. 619, § 5.

524.6–205. Effect of a written notice to financial institution

The provisions of section 524.6–204 as to rights of survivorship are determined by the form of the account at the death of a party. This form may be altered by written order given by a party to the financial institution to change the form of the account or to stop or vary payment under the terms of the account. The order or request must be signed by a party and received by the financial institution during the party's lifetime.

Derivation:
Laws 1994, c. 472, § 63.
St.1992, § 528.06.

Laws 1985, c. 292, § 14.
Laws 1973, c. 619, § 6.

524.6–206. Accounts and transfers nontestamentary

Any transfers resulting from the application of section 524.6–204 are effective by reason of the account contracts involved and this statute, and are not to be considered as subject to probate except as to the transfers expressly changed by will, as provided for by section 524.6–204, clause (d).

Derivation:
Laws 1994, c. 472, § 63.
St.1992, § 528.07.

Laws 1985, c. 292, § 15.
Laws 1973, c. 619, § 7.

524.6–207. Rights of creditors

No multiple-party account will be effective against an estate of a deceased party to transfer to a survivor sums needed to pay debts, taxes, and expenses of administration, including statutory allowances to the surviving spouse, minor children and dependent children or against the state or a county agency with a claim authorized by section 256B.15, if other assets of the estate are insufficient, to the extent the deceased party is the source of the funds or beneficial owner. A surviving party or P.O.D. payee who receives payment from a multiple-party account after the death of a deceased party shall be liable to account to the deceased party's personal representative or the state or a county agency with a claim authorized by section 256B.15 for amounts the decedent owned beneficially immediately before death to the extent necessary to discharge any such claims and charges remaining unpaid after the application of the assets of the decedent's estate. No proceeding to assert this liability shall be commenced by the personal representative unless the personal representative has received a written demand by a surviving spouse, a creditor or one acting for a minor dependent child of the decedent, and no proceeding shall be commenced later than two years following the death of the decedent. Sums recovered by the personal representative shall be administered as part of the decedent's estate. This section shall not affect the right of a financial institution to make payment on multiple-party accounts according to the terms thereof, or make it liable to the estate of a deceased party unless, before payment, the institution has been served with process in a proceeding by the personal representative or the state or a county agency with a claim authorized by section 256B.15, or has been presented by the state or a county agency with a claim authorized by section 256B.15 with an affidavit pursuant to section 524.3–1201. Upon being presented with such an affidavit, the financial institution shall make payment of the multiple-party account to the affiant in an amount equal to the lesser of the claim stated in the affidavit or the extent to which the affidavit identifies the decedent as the source of funds or beneficial owner of the account.

Amended by Laws 1995, c. 207, art. 2, § 35; Laws 1997, c. 217, art. 2, § 19.

Derivation:
Laws 1994, c. 472, § 63.
St.1992, § 528.08.

Laws 1985, c. 292, § 16.
Laws 1973, c. 619, § 8.

524.6–208. Financial institution protection; payment on signature of one party

Financial institutions may enter into multiple-party accounts to the same extent that they may enter into single-party accounts. Any multiple-party account may be paid, on request, to any one or more of the parties. A financial institution shall not be required to inquire as to the source of funds received for deposit to a multiple-party account, or to inquire as to the proposed application of any sum withdrawn from an account.

A minor may be a party to a joint account.

Derivation:
Laws 1994, c. 472, § 63.
St.1992, § 528.09.

Laws 1985, c. 292, § 17.
Laws 1973, c. 619, § 9.

524.6–209. Financial institution protection; payment after death or disability; joint account

Any sums in a joint account may be paid, on request, to any party without regard to whether any other party is incapacitated or deceased at the time the payment is demanded; but payment may not be made to the personal representative or heirs of a deceased party unless proofs of death are presented to the financial institution showing that the decedent was the last surviving party or unless there is no right of survivorship under section 524.6–204, or unless a will provides other distribution; in which case the procedure set forth in section 524.6–204, clause (d), shall be followed. A minor may be a party to a joint account.

Derivation:
Laws 1994, c. 472, § 63.
St.1992, § 528.10.

Laws 1985, c. 292, § 18.
Laws 1973, c. 619, § 10.

524.6–210. Financial institution protection; payment of P.O.D. account

Any P.O.D. account may be paid, on request, to any original party to the account. Payment of the interest of a P.O.D. payee may be made, on request, to the P.O.D. payee or to the personal representative or heirs of a deceased P.O.D. payee upon presentation to the financial institution of proof of death showing that the P.O.D. payee survived all persons named as original parties. Payment may be made to the personal representative or heirs of a deceased original party if proof of death is presented to the financial institution showing that the original party was the survivor of all other persons named on the account either as an original party or as P.O.D. payee.

Derivation:
Laws 1994, c. 472, § 63.
St.1992, § 528.11.

Laws 1985, c. 292, § 19.
Laws 1973, c. 619, § 11.

524.6–211. Financial institution protection; discharge

Payment made pursuant to sections 524.6–208 to 524.6–210 discharges the financial institution from all claims for amounts so paid whether or not the payment is consistent with the beneficial ownership of the account as between parties, P.O.D. payees, or beneficiaries by will or otherwise, or their successors. The protection here given does not extend to payments made after a financial institution has received written notice from any person entitled to request payment to the effect that withdrawals in accordance with the terms of the account should not be permitted. Unless the notice is withdrawn by the person giving it, the successor of any deceased party and all other parties entitled to payment must concur in any demand for withdrawal if the financial institution is to be protected under this section. No other notice or any other information shown to have been available to a financial institution shall affect its right to the protection provided here. The protection here provided shall not affect the rights of parties in disputes between themselves or their successors concerning the beneficial ownership of funds in, or withdrawn from, multiple-party accounts.

Derivation:
Laws 1994, c. 472, § 63.
St.1992, § 528.13.

Laws 1985, c. 292, § 20.
Laws 1973, c. 619, § 13.

524.6–212. Financial institution protection; setoff

Without qualifying any other statutory right to setoff or lien and subject to any contractual provision, if a party to a multiple-party account is indebted to a financial institution, the financial institution has a right to setoff against the account in which the party has or had immediately before death a present right of withdrawal. The amount of the account subject to setoff is that proportion to which the debtor is, or was immediately before death, beneficially entitled, and in the absence of proof of net contributions, to an equal share with all parties having present rights of withdrawal.

Derivation:
Laws 1994, c. 472, § 63.
St.1992, § 528.14.

Laws 1986, c. 444.
Laws 1973, c. 619, § 14.

524.6–213. Forms

Subdivision 1. Survivorship account. Deposits made using a form of account containing the following language signed by the depositor shall be conclusive evidence of the intent of the depositor, in the absence of fraud or misrepresentation, subject, nevertheless, to other disposition made by will as provided in section 524.6–204, clause (d), to establish a survivorship account:

(a) "I (we) direct that the balance remaining in this account shall be PAYABLE ON DEATH (of the survivor of us) to:

....
....
                    Signed: ....
                                     ....

Dated: ...."

624

(b) "I (we) intend and agree that the balance in this account, upon the death of any party to this account, shall belong to the surviving party, or if there are two or more surviving parties, they shall take as JOINT TENANTS.

Signed: ....
....

Dated: ....,"

Subd. 2. Account subject to power of attorney with no survivorship rights. Where no rights of survivorship are intended and the account is one to be established for convenience only between a depositor and an agent, the following language is recommended for use, and when so used, the account shall be construed as a matter of law to be an account subject to a power of attorney with no survivorship rights, the form to read as follows:

"I .... (grantor of power), hereby constitute and appoint
....
.... (grantee of power), as my attorney-in-fact, to deposit or withdraw funds held in .... (name of bank), in account No.
....

Signed: ....

Dated:

Acknowledgment: In the presence of .... (an authorized person), ... (name of financial institution)."

The power so granted is subject to the provisions of sections 508.72, 508A.72, and 523.01 to 523.24.

Derivation:

Laws 1994, c. 472, § 63.

St.1993 Supp., § 528.15.

Laws 1993, c. 13, art. 2, § 1.

Laws 1986, 1st Sp., c. 3, art. 1, § 63.

Laws 1985, c. 292, § 21.

Laws 1984, c. 603, § 28.

Laws 1973, c. 619, § 15.

524.6–214. Citation

Sections 524.6–201 to 524.6–214 may be cited as the "Minnesota Multiparty Accounts Act."

Derivation:
Laws 1994, c. 472, § 63.
St.1992, § 528.01.

Laws 1987, c. 384, art. 2, § 1.

Laws 1973, c. 619, § 1.

PART 3

UNIFORM TOD SECURITY REGISTRATION ACT

524.6–301. Definitions

In sections 524.6–301 to 524.6–311:

(1) "Beneficiary form" means a registration of a security which indicates the present owner of the security and the intention of the owner regarding the person who will become the owner of the security upon the death of the owner.

(2) "Register," including its derivatives, means to issue a certificate showing the ownership of a certificated security or, in the case of an uncertificated security, to initiate or transfer an account showing ownership of securities.

(3) "Registering entity" means a person who originates or transfers a security title by registration, and includes a broker maintaining security accounts for customers and a transfer agent or other person acting for or as an issuer of securities.

(4) "Security" means a share, participation, or other interest in property, in a business, or in an obligation of an enterprise or other issuer, and includes a certificated security, an uncertificated security, and a security account.

(5) "Security account" means (i) a reinvestment account associated with a security, a securities account with a broker, a cash balance in a brokerage account, cash, cash equivalents, interest, earnings, or dividends earned or declared on a security in an account, a reinvestment account, or a brokerage account, whether or not credited to the account before the owner's death, (ii) an investment management or custody account with a trust company or a trust division of a bank with trust powers, including the securities in the account, a cash balance in the account, and cash, cash equivalents, interest, earnings, or dividends earned or declared on a security in the account, whether or not credited to the account before the owner's death, or (iii) a cash balance or other property held for or due to the owner of a security as a replacement for or product of an account security, whether or not credited to the account before the owner's death.

Laws 1992, c. 461, art. 2, § 1, eff. June 1, 1992. Amended by Laws 2001, c. 15, § 12.

UNIFORM NONPROBATE TRANSFERS ON DEATH ACT

Table of Jurisdictions Wherein Act Has Been Adopted

For text of Uniform Act, and variation notes and annotation materials for adopting jurisdictions, see Uniform Laws Annotated, Master Edition, Volume 8B.

Jurisdiction	Laws	Effective Date	Statutory Citation
Alabama [3]	1997, Nos. 97–644, 97–703	Part 2 3–1–1998; Part 3 8–1–1997	Code 1975, §§ 5–24–1 to 5–24–34, 8–6–140 to 8–6–151.

Jurisdiction	Laws	Effective Date	Statutory Citation
Alaska	1996, c. 75	1–1–1997	AS 13.06.050, 13.33.101 to 13.33.310.
Arizona	1994, c. 290	After 12–31–1994	A.R.S. §§ 14–6101 to 14–6311.
Arkansas [2]	1993, No. 114	8–13–1993	A.C.A. §§ 28–14–101 to 28–14–112.
California [1]	1998, c. 242	1–1–1999	West's Ann.Cal. Probate Code, §§ 5000 to 5003, 5500 to 5512.
Colorado	1990, S.B. 90–91	7–1–1990	West's C.R.S.A. §§ 15–10–201, 15–15–101 to 15–15–311.
Connecticut [2]	1997, No. 97–42	5–14–1997 *	C.G.S.A. §§ 45a–468 to 45a–468m.
Delaware [2]	70 Del. Laws, c. 394	6–26–1996	12 Del. C. §§ 801 to 812.
District of Columbia ...	2001, D.C. Law 13–292	4–27–2001	D.C. Official Code, 2001 Ed. §§ 19–601.01 to 19–603.11.
Florida [3]	1994, c. 94–216	1–1–1995	West's F.S.A. §§ 655.82, 711.50 to 711.512.
Georgia [2]	1999, Act 392	7–1–1999	O.C.G.A. §§ 53–5–60 to 53–5–71.
Hawaii [2]	1998, c. 63	4–29–1998	HRS §§ 539–1 to 539–12.
Idaho [2]	1996, c. 303	7–1–1996	I.C. §§ 15–6–301 to 15–6–312.
Illinois [2]	1994, P.A. 88–577	1–1–1995	S.H.A. 815 ILCS 10/0.01 to 10/10.
Indiana [2]	2002, P.L. 2–2002	7–1–2002	West's A.I.C. 32–17–9–1 to 32–17–9–15.
Iowa [2]	1997, c. 178	7–1–1997	I.C.A. §§ 633.800 to 633.811.
Kansas [2]	1994, c. 44	7–1–1994	K.S.A. 17–49a01 to 17–49a12.
Kentucky [2]	1998, c. 407	8–1–1998	KRS 292.6501 to 292.6512.
Maine [2]	1997, c. 627	3–27–1998 *	18–A M.R.S.A. §§ 6–301 to 6–312.
Maryland [2]	1994, c. 644	10–1–1994	Code, Estates and Trusts, §§ 16–101 to 16–112.
Massachusetts [2]	1998, c. 377	11–5–1998*	M.G.L.A. c. 201E, §§ 101 to 402.
Michigan [1]	1998, P.A. 386	4–1–2000	M.C.L.A. §§ 700.6101 to 700.6310.
Minnesota [2]	1992, c. 461	6–1–1992	M.S.A. §§ 524.6–301 to 524.6–311.
Mississippi [2]	1997, c. 413	3–24–1997	Code 1972, §§ 91–21–1 to 91–21–25.
Montana	1993, c. 494	10–1–1993	MCA §§ 72–1–103, 72–6–111 to 72–6–311.
Nebraska	1993, LB 250	5–6–1993*	R.R.S 1943, §§ 30–2209, 30–2715 to 30–2746.
Nevada [2]	1997, c. 115	10–1–1997	N.R.S. 111.480 to 111.650.
New Hampshire [2]	1997, c. 231	1–1–1998	RSA 563–C:1 to 563–C:12.
New Jersey [2]	1995, c. 130	6–22–1995*	N.J.S.A. 3B:30–1 to 3B:30–12.
New Mexico	1992, c. 66	7–1–1992	NMSA 1978, §§ 45–1–201, 45–6–101 to 45–6–311.
New York [2]	2005, c. 325	1–1–2006	McKinney's EPTL 13–4.1 to 13–4.12.
North Carolina [2]	2005, c. 411	10–1–2005	G.S. §§ 41–40 to 41–51.
North Dakota	1991, c. 351	7–1–1991	NDCC 30.1–01–06, 30.1–31–01 to 30.1–31–30.
Ohio [2]	1993, H.B. 62	10–1–1993	R.C. §§ 1709.01 to 1709.11.
Oklahoma [2]	1994, c. 208	9–1–1994	71 Okl.St.Ann. §§ 901 to 913.
Oregon [2]	1991, c. 306	6–19–1991*	ORS 59.535 to 59.585.
Pennsylvania [2]	1996, P.L. 1118	12–18–1996*	20 Pa.C.S.A. §§ 6401 to 6413.
Rhode Island [2]	1998, c. 98–260	7–9–1998	Gen. Laws 1956, §§ 7–11.1–1 to 7–11.1–12.
South Carolina [2]	1997, No. 102	6–13–1997	Code 1976, §§ 35–6–10 to 35–6–100.
South Dakota [2]	1995, c. 168	Registrations of securities in beneficiary form by decedents dy-	SDCL 29A–6–301 to 29A–6–311.

Jurisdiction	Laws	Effective Date	Statutory Citation
		ing on or after 7–1–1996	
Tennessee [2]	1995, c. 471	7–1–1995	T.C.A. §§ 35–12–101 to 35–12–113.
Utah [2]	1995, c. 9	5–1–1995	U.C.A. 1953, 75–6–301 to 75–6–313.
Vermont [2]	1999, Act 23	5–17–1999*	9 V.S.A. §§ 4351 to 4360.
Virginia [2]	1994, c. 422		Code 1950, §§ 64.1–206.1 to 64.1–206.8.
Washington [2]	1993, c. 287	7–25–1993	West's RCWA 21.35.005 to 21.35.901.
West Virginia [2]	1994, c. 62	3–10–1994*	Code, 36–10–1 to 36–10–12.
Wisconsin [1]	1989, Act 331	5–11–1990	W.S.A. 705.20 to 705.30.
Wyoming [2]	1993, c. 171	7–1–1993	Wyo.Stat.Ann. §§ 2–16–101 to 2–16–112.

* Date of approval.

[1] Adopted only Parts 1 and 3 of the Act.

[2] Adopted only Part 3 of the Act.

[3] Adopted only Parts 2 and 3 of the Act.

UNIFORM TOD SECURITY REGISTRATION ACT

Table of Jurisdictions Wherein Act Has Been Adopted

For text of Uniform Act, and variation notes and annotation materials for adopting jurisdictions, see Uniform Laws Annotated, Master Edition, Volume 8B.

Jurisdiction	Laws	Effective Date	Statutory Citation
Alabama	1997, No. 97–703	8–1–1997	Code 1975, §§ 8–6–140 to 8–6–151.
Alaska	1996, c. 75	1–1–1997	AS 13.06.050, 13.33.301 to 13.33.310.
Arizona	1994, c. 290	After 12–31–1994	A.R.S. §§ 14–6301 to 14–6311.
Arkansas	1993, No. 114	8–13–1993	A.C.A. §§ 28–14–101 to 28–14–112.
California	1998, c. 242	1–1–1999	West's Ann.Cal. Probate Code, §§ 5500 to 5512.
Colorado	1990, S.B. 90–91	7–1–1990	West's C.R.S.A. §§ 15–10–201, 15–15–301 to 15–15–311.
Connecticut	1997, No. 97–42	5–14–1997 *	C.G.S.A. §§ 45a–468 to 45a–468m.
Delaware	70 Del. Laws, c. 394	6–26–1996	12 Del. C. §§ 801 to 812.
District of Columbia ...	2001, D.C. Law 13–292	4–27–2001	D.C. Official Code, 2001 Ed. §§ 19–603.01 to 19–603.11.
Florida	1994, c. 94–216	1–1–1995	West's F.S.A. §§ 711.50 to 711.512.
Georgia	1999, Act 392	7–1–1999	O.C.G.A. §§ 53–5–60 to 53–5–71.
Hawaii	1998, c. 63	4–29–1998	HRS §§ 539–1 to 539–12.
Idaho	1996, c. 303	7–1–1996	I.C. §§ 15–6–301 to 15–6–312.
Illinois	1994, P.A. 88–577	1–1–1995	S.H.A. 815 ILCS 10/0.01 to 10/12.
Indiana	2002, P.L. 2–2002	7–1–2002	West's A.I.C. 32–17–9–1 to 32–17–9–15.
Iowa	1997, c. 178	7–1–1997	I.C.A. §§ 633.800 to 633.811.
Kansas	1994, c. 44	7–1–1994	K.S.A. 17–49a01 to 17–49a12.
Kentucky	1998, c. 407	8–1–1998	KRS 292.6501 to 292.6512.
Maine	1997, c. 627	3–27–1998 *	18–A M.R.S.A. §§ 6–301 to 6–312.
Maryland	1994, c. 644	10–1–1994	Code, Estates and Trusts, §§ 16–101 to 16–112.
Massachusetts	1998, c. 377	11–5–1998 *	M.G.L.A. c. 201E, §§ 101 to 402.

Jurisdiction	Laws	Effective Date	Statutory Citation
Michigan	1998, P.A. 386	4–1–2000	M.C.L.A. §§ 700.6301 to 700.6310.
Minnesota	1992, c. 461	6–1–1992	M.S.A. §§ 524.6–301 to 524.6–311.
Mississippi	1997, c. 413	3–24–1997	Code 1972, §§ 91–21–1 to 91–21–25.
Montana	1993, c. 494	10–1–1993	MCA §§ 72–1–103, 72–6–301 to 72–6–311.
Nebraska	1993, LB 250	5–6–1993*	R.R.S. 1943, §§ 30–2209, 30–2734 to 30–2746.
Nevada	1997, c. 115	10–1–1997	N.R.S. 111.480 to 111.650.
New Hampshire	1997, c. 231	1–1–1998	RSA 563–C:1 to 563–C:12.
New Jersey	1995, c. 130	6–22–1995*	N.J.S.A. 3B:30–1 to 3B:30–12.
New Mexico	1992, c. 66	7–1–1992	NMSA 1978, §§ 45–1–201, 45–6–301 to 45–6–311.
New York	2005, c. 325	1–1–2006	McKinney's EPTL 13–4.1 to 13–4.12.
North Carolina	2005, c. 411	10–1–2005	G.S. §§ 41–40 to 41–51.
North Dakota	1991, c. 351	7–1–1991	NDCC 30.1–01–06, 30.1–31–21 to 30.1–31–30.
Ohio	1993, H.B. 62	10–1–1993	R.C. §§ 1709.01 to 1709.11.
Oklahoma	1994, c. 208	9–1–1994	71 Okl.St.Ann. §§ 901 to 913.
Oregon	1991, c. 306	6–19–1991 *	ORS 59.535 to 59.585.
Pennsylvania	1996, P.L. 1118	12–18–1996 *	20 Pa.C.S.A. §§ 6401 to 6413.
Rhode Island	1998, c. 98–260	7–9–1998	Gen. Laws 1956, §§ 7–11.1–1 to 7–11.1–12.
South Carolina	1997, No. 102	6–13–1997	Code 1976, §§ 35–6–10 to 35–6–100.
South Dakota	1995, c. 168	Registrations of securities in beneficiary form by decedents dying on or after 7–1–1996.	SDCL 29A–6–301 to 29A–6–311.
Tennessee	1995, c. 471	7–1–1995	T.C.A. §§ 35–12–101 to 35–12–113.
Utah	1995, c. 9	5–1–1995	U.C.A. 1953, 75–6–301 to 75–6–313.
Vermont	1999, P.A. 23	5–17–1999 *	9 V.S.A. §§ 4351 to 4360.
Virginia	1994, c. 422		Code 1950, §§ 64.1–206.1 to 64.1–206.8.
Washington	1993, c. 287	7–25–1993	West's RCWA 21.35.005 to 21.35.901.
West Virginia	1994, c. 62	3–10–1994*	Code, 36–10–1 to 36–10–12.
Wisconsin	1989, Act 331	5–11–1990	W.S.A. 705.21 to 705.30.
Wyoming	1993, c. 171	7–1–1993	Wyo.Stat.Ann. §§ 2–16–101 to 2–16–112.

* Date of approval.

524.6–302. Registration in beneficiary form; sole or joint tenancy ownership

Only individuals whose registration of a security shows sole ownership by one individual or multiple ownership by two or more with right of survivorship, rather than as tenants in common, may obtain registration in beneficiary form. Multiple owners of a security registered in beneficiary form hold as joint tenants with right of survivorship, as tenants by the entireties, or as owners of community property held in survivorship form, and not as tenants in common.

Laws 1992, c. 461, art. 2, § 2, eff. June 1, 1992.

524.6–303. Registration in beneficiary form; applicable law

A security may be registered in beneficiary form if the form is authorized by this or a similar statute of the state of organization of the issuer or registering entity, the location of the registering entity's principal office, the office of its transfer agent or its office making the registration, or by this or a similar statute of the law of the state listed as the owner's address at the time of registration. A registration governed by the law of a jurisdiction in which this or similar legislation is not in force or was not in force when a registration in beneficiary form was made is nevertheless presumed to be valid and authorized as a matter of contract law.

Laws 1992, c. 461, art. 2, § 3, eff. June 1, 1992.

524.6–304. Origination of registration in beneficiary form

A security, whether evidenced by certificate or account, is registered in beneficiary form when the registration includes a designation of a beneficiary to take the ownership at the death of the owner or the deaths of all multiple owners.

Laws 1992, c. 461, art. 2, § 4, eff. June 1, 1992.

524.6–305. Form of registration in beneficiary form

Registration in beneficiary form may be shown by the words "transfer on death" or the abbreviation "TOD," or by the words "pay on death" or the abbreviation "POD," after the name of the registered owner and before the name of a beneficiary.

Laws 1992, c. 461, art. 2, § 5, eff. June 1, 1992.

524.6–306. Effect of registration in beneficiary form

The designation of a TOD beneficiary on a registration in beneficiary form has no effect on ownership until the owner's death. A registration of a security in beneficiary form may be canceled or changed at any time by the sole owner or all then surviving owners without the consent of the beneficiary.

Laws 1992, c. 461, art. 2, § 6, eff. June 1, 1992.

524.6–307. Death of owner; creditors

Subdivision 1. Ownership on death of owner. On death of a sole owner or the last to die of all multiple owners, ownership of securities registered in beneficiary form passes to the beneficiary or beneficiaries who survive all owners. On proof of death of all owners and compliance with any applicable requirements of the registering entity, a security registered in beneficiary form may be reregistered in the name of the beneficiary or beneficiaries who survive the death of all owners. Until division of the security after the death of all owners, multiple beneficiaries surviving the death of all owners hold their interests as tenants in common. If no beneficiary survives the death of all owners, the security belongs to the estate of the deceased sole owner or the estate of the last to die of all multiple owners.

Subd. 2. Rights of creditors. A registration in beneficiary form is not effective against an estate of a deceased sole owner or a deceased last to die of multiple owners to transfer to a beneficiary or beneficiaries sums needed to pay debts, taxes, and expenses of administration, including statutory allowances to the surviving spouse, minor children, and dependent children, if other assets of the estate are insufficient. A TOD beneficiary in whose name a security is registered after the death of the owner is liable to account to the deceased owner's personal representative for securities so registered or their proceeds to the extent necessary to discharge such claims and charges remaining unpaid after the application of the assets of the decedent's estate. A proceeding to assert this liability may not be commenced unless the personal representative has received a written demand by a surviving spouse, a creditor, or one acting for a minor dependent child of the decedent, and a proceeding may not be commenced later than two years following the death of the decedent. A beneficiary against whom the proceeding is brought may elect to transfer to the personal representative the security registered in the name of the beneficiary after the death of the deceased owner if the beneficiary still owns the security, or the net proceeds received by the beneficiary upon disposition of the security by the beneficiary, and that transfer fully discharges the beneficiary from all liability under this subdivision. Amounts or securities recovered by the personal representative must be administered as part of the deceased owner's estate.

This subdivision does not affect the right of a registering entity to register a security in the name of the beneficiary, or make a registering entity liable to the estate of a deceased owner, except for a reregistration after a registering entity has received written notice from any claimant to an interest in the security objecting to implementation of a registration in beneficiary form.

Laws 1992, c. 461, art. 2, §§ 7, 8, eff. June 1, 1992.

524.6–308. Protection of registering entity

(a) A registering entity is not required to offer or to accept a request for security registration in beneficiary form. If a registration in beneficiary form is offered by a registering entity, the owner requesting registration in beneficiary form assents to the protections given to the registering entity by sections 524.6–301 to 524.6–311.

(b) By accepting a request for registration of a security in beneficiary form, the registering entity agrees that the registration will be implemented on death of the deceased owner as provided in sections 524.6–301 to 524.6–311.

(c) A registering entity is discharged from all claims to a security by the estate, creditors, heirs, or devisees of a deceased owner if it registers a transfer of the security in accordance with section 524.6–307 and does so in good faith reliance (i) on the registration, (ii) on sections 524.6–301 to 524.6–311, and (iii) on information provided to it by affidavit of the personal representative of the deceased owner, or by the surviving beneficiary or by the surviving beneficiary's representatives, or other information available to the registering entity.

The protections of sections 524.6–301 to 524.6–311 do not extend to a reregistration or payment made after a registering entity has received written notice from any claimant to any interest in the security objecting to implementation of a registration in beneficiary form. No other notice or other information available to the registering entity affects its right to protection under sections 524.6–301 to 524.6–311.

(d) The protection provided by sections 524.6–301 to 524.6–311 to the registering entity of a security does not affect the rights of beneficiaries in disputes between themselves and other claimants to ownership of the security transferred or its value or proceeds.

Laws 1992, c. 461, art. 2, § 9, eff. June 1, 1992.

524.6–309. Nontestamentary transfer; revocation of designation

Subdivision 1. Nontestamentary transfer on death. (a) A transfer on death resulting from a registration in beneficiary form is effective by reason of the contract regarding the registration between the owner and the registering entity and sections 524.6–301 to 524.6–311 and is not testamentary.

(b) Sections 524.6–301 to 524.6–311 do not limit the rights of creditors of security owners against beneficiaries and other transferees under other laws of this state.

Subd. 2. Revocation of beneficiary designation by will. A registration in beneficiary form may be canceled by specific reference to the security or the securities account in the will of the sole owner or the last to die of multiple owners, but the terms of the revocation are not binding on the registering entity unless it has received written notice from any claimant to an interest in the security objecting to implementation of a registration in beneficiary form prior to the registering entity reregistering the security. If the beneficiary designation is canceled, the security belongs to the estate of the deceased sole owner or the estate or the last to die of all multiple owners.

Laws 1992, c. 461, art. 2, §§ 10, 11, eff. June 1, 1992.

524.6–310. Terms, conditions, and forms for registration

(a) A registering entity offering to accept registrations in beneficiary form may establish the terms and conditions under which it will receive requests (i) for registrations in beneficiary form, and (ii) for implementation of registrations in beneficiary form, including requests for cancellation of previously registered TOD beneficiary designations and requests for reregistration to effect a change of beneficiary. The terms and conditions so established may provide for proving death, avoiding or resolving any problems concerning fractional shares, designating primary and contingent beneficiaries, and substituting a named beneficiary's descendants to take in the place of the named beneficiary in the event of the beneficiary's death. Substitution may be indicated by appending to the name of the primary beneficiary the letters LDPS, standing for "lineal descendants per stirpes." This designation substitutes a deceased beneficiary's descendants who survive the owner for a beneficiary who fails to so survive, the descendants to be identified and to share in accordance with the law of the beneficiary's domicile at the owner's death governing inheritance by descendants of an intestate. Other forms of identifying beneficiaries who are to take on one or more contingencies, and rules for providing proofs and assurances needed to satisfy reasonable concerns by registering entities regarding conditions and identities relevant to accurate implementation of registrations in beneficiary form, may be contained in a registering entity's terms and conditions.

(b) The following are illustrations of registrations in beneficiary form which a registering entity may authorize:

(1) Sole owner-sole beneficiary: John S. Brown TOD (or POD) John S. Brown Jr.

(2) Multiple owners-sole beneficiary: John S. Brown Mary B. Brown JT TEN TOD John S. Brown Jr.

(3) Multiple owners-primary and secondary (substituted) beneficiaries: John S. Brown Mary B. Brown JT TEN TOD John S. Brown Jr. SUB BENE Peter Q. Brown *or* John S. Brown Mary B. Brown JT TEN TOD John S. Brown Jr. LDPS.

Laws 1992, c. 461, art. 2, § 12, eff. June 1, 1992.

524.6–311. Application

Sections 524.6–301 to 524.6–311 apply to registrations of securities in beneficiary form made before, on, or after June 1, 1992, by decedents dying on or after June 1, 1992.

Laws 1992, c. 461, art. 2, § 13, eff. June 1, 1992.

ARTICLE 8

EFFECTIVE DATE AND REPEALER

524.8–101. Provisions for transition

Except as provided elsewhere in this chapter, on the effective date of this chapter:

(1) the chapter applies to any wills of decedents dying thereafter;

(2) the chapter applies to any proceedings in court then pending or thereafter commenced regardless of the time of the death of decedent except to the extent that in the opinion of the court the former procedure should be made applicable in a particular case in the interest of justice or because of infeasibility of application of the procedure of this chapter;

(3) every personal representative including a person administering an estate of a minor or incompetent holding an appointment on that date, continues to hold the appointment but has only the powers conferred by this chapter and is subject to the duties imposed with respect to any act occurring or done thereafter;

(4) an act done before the effective date in any proceeding and any accrued right is not impaired by this chapter. If a right is acquired, extinguished or barred upon the expiration of a prescribed period of time which has commenced to run by the provisions of any statute before the effective date, the provisions shall remain in force with respect to that right;

(5) any rule of construction or presumption provided in this chapter applies to instruments executed and multiple party accounts opened before the effective date unless there is a clear indication of a contrary intent.

Laws 1974, c. 442, art. 8, § 524.8–101. Amended by Laws 1975, c. 347, § 80, eff. Jan. 1, 1976.

524.8–102. Specific repealer

Minnesota Statutes, 1973 Supplement, Sections 525.331, 525.481, 525.482, 525.485, 525.501, and 525.80, are repealed. Minnesota Statutes 1971, Sections 525.222, 525.23, 525.231, 525.24, 525.241, 525.243, 525.244, 525.25, 525.251, 525.252, 525.273, 525.28, 525.281, 525.282, 525.29, 525.291, 525.292, 525.30, 525.301, 525.302, 525.303, 525.304, 525.31, 525.311, 525.312, 525.314, 525.315, 525.316, 525.32,[1] 525.321,[1] 525.322,[1] 525.323,[1] 525.324,[1] 525.34, 525.35, 525.36, 525.37, 525.38, 525.40, 525.401, 525.47, 525.486, 525.49, 525.50, 525.502, 525.503, 525.504, 525.52, 525.805, 525.81, 525.82, 525.89, and 525.91, are repealed.

Laws 1974, c. 442, art. 8, § 524.8–102, eff. Jan. 1, 1976.

[1] Repeal of this section effective August 1, 1974, notwithstanding section 524.8–101. See § 524.8–103.

524.8–103. Early effective date

Notwithstanding section 524.8–101, the provisions of Laws 1974, chapter 442 relating to bonds found at sections 524.3–603 to 524.3–606 and Laws 1974, chapter 442, article 9, and that portion of section 524.8–102 which repeals Minnesota Statutes 1971, sections 525.32 to 525.324, are effective August 1, 1974.

Laws 1974, c. 442, art. 8, § 524.8–103, eff. Jan. 1, 1976.

Chapter 525

PROBATE PROCEEDINGS

POWERS OF COURT

PERSONNEL

INTESTATE SUCCESSION

WILLS

PROBATE PROCEEDINGS

For complete statutory history see Minnesota Statutes Annotated.

POWERS OF COURT

525.01.   Renumbered 487.01 in St.1971

525.0105.   Repealed by Laws 1971, c. 951, § 44

525.011 to 525.03.   Repealed by Laws 2006, c. 260, art. 5, § 54, eff. July 1, 2006

525.031.   Fees for copies

The fees for copies of all documents shall be the same as the fee established for such copies on civil proceedings under section 357.021, subdivision 2.

Amended by Laws 1967, c. 128, § 1, eff. April 1, 1967; Laws 1986, c. 442, § 13.

525.033.   Fees for filing petitions

The district court shall collect a fee as established by section 357.021, subdivision 2, clause (1), for filing a petition to commence a proceeding under this chapter and chapter 524. The fee for copies of all documents in probate proceedings must be the same as the fee established for certified copies in civil proceedings under section 357.021, subdivision 2. Fees collected under this section and section 525.031 must be forwarded to the commissioner of finance for deposit in the state treasury and credited to the general fund.

Laws 1978, c. 730, § 3. Amended by Laws 1986, c. 442, § 14; Laws 1987, c. 11, § 1; Laws 1989, c. 335, art. 3, § 35, eff. July 1, 1990; Laws 1995, c. 189, § 8; Laws 1996, c. 277, § 1; Laws 2003, c. 112, art. 2, § 50, par. (b).

Historical and Statutory Notes

Laws 1989, c. 335, art. 3, § 58, subd. 2, as amended by Laws 1989, c. 356, § 67, and Laws 1989 1st Sp., c. 1, art. 5, § 48, provides:

"(a) Except as provided in paragraph (b) and subdivision 3, in all judicial districts except the eighth, sections 6, 8, 13, 15, 22, 23, 30, 31, 32, 33, 34, 35, 36, 37, 38, and 56, are effective July 1, 1990.

"(b) For all judicial districts, section 6 is effective July 1, 1989, with respect to the increase in fees under section 7. For all judicial districts, sections 7 and 11 are effective July 1, 1989.

"(c) Except as otherwise provided in this section, section 6 is effective for counties in the eighth judicial district on January 1, 1990."

PERSONNEL

525.04. Repealed by Laws 1981, 1st Sp., c. 4, art. 3, § 8, eff. June 7, 1981

525.041. Written decision shall be filed within 90 days; mandatory

The decision of every issue of law or fact shall be in writing and shall be filed within 90 days after submission unless prevented by illness or casualty.

Upon the filing of any appealable order, judgment, or decree, except in uncontested matters or where the final decision was announced at the hearing, the court shall give notice by mail of such filing to each party, or the attorney, who appeared of record at the hearing.

Amended by Laws 1967, c. 317, § 1, eff. May 6, 1967; Laws 1986, c. 444.

525.05. Judge or referee; grounds for disqualification

The following shall be grounds for disqualification of any judge or referee from acting in any matter: (1) That the judge or the judge's spouse or any of either of their kin nearer than first cousin is interested as representative, heir, devisee, legatee, ward, or creditor in the estate involved therein; (2) that it involves the validity or interpretation of a will drawn or witnessed by the judge; (3) that the judge may be a necessary witness in the matter; (4) that it involves a property right in respect to which the judge has been engaged or is engaged as an attorney; or (5) that the judge was engaged in a joint enterprise for profit with the decedent at the time of death or that the judge is then engaged in a joint enterprise for profit with any person interested in the matter as representative, heir, devisee, legatee, ward, or creditor. When grounds for disqualification exist, the judge may, and upon proper petition of any person interested in the estate must, request another judge or a judge who has retired to act in the judge's stead in the matter.

Amended by Laws 1961, c. 6, § 1; Laws 1981, c. 31, § 12; Laws 1986, c. 444; Laws 1995, c. 189, § 8; Laws 1996, c. 277, § 1; Laws 2006, c. 271, art. 11, § 47, eff. July 1, 2006.

525.051 to 525.09. Repealed by Laws 2006, c. 260, art. 5, § 54, eff. July 1, 2006

525.091. Destruction and reproduction of probate records

Subdivision 1. Original documents. The court administrator of any county upon order of the judge exercising probate jurisdiction may destroy all the original documents in any probate proceeding of record in the office five years after the file in such proceeding has been closed provided the original or a Minnesota state archives commission approved photographic, photostatic, microphotographic, microfilmed, or similarly reproduced copy of the original of the following enumerated documents in the proceeding are on file in the office.

Enumerated original documents:

(a) In estates, the jurisdictional petition and proof of publication of the notice of hearing thereof; will and certificate of probate; letters; inventory and appraisal; orders directing and confirming sale, mortgage, lease, or for conveyance of real estate; order setting apart statutory selection; receipts for federal estate taxes and state estate taxes; orders of distribution and general protection; decrees of distribution; federal estate tax closing letter, consent to discharge by commissioner of revenue and order discharging representative; and any amendment of the listed documents.

When an estate is deemed closed as provided in clause (d) of this subdivision, the enumerated documents shall include all claims of creditors.

(b) In guardianships or conservatorships, the jurisdictional petition and order for hearing thereof with proof of service; letters; orders directing and confirming sale, mortgage, lease or for conveyance of real estate; order for restoration to capacity and order discharging guardian; and any amendment of the listed documents.

(c) In mental, inebriety, and indigent matters, the jurisdictional petition; report of examination; warrant of commitment; notice of discharge from institution, or notice of death and order for restoration to capacity; and any amendment of the listed documents.

(d) Except for the enumerated documents described in this subdivision, the court administrator may destroy all other original documents in any probate proceeding without retaining any reproduction of the document. For the purpose of this subdivision, a proceeding is deemed closed if no document has been filed in the proceeding for a period of 15 years, except in the cases of wills filed for safekeeping and those containing wills of decedents not adjudicated upon.

Subd. 2. Repealed by Laws 2008, c. 277, art. 1, § 98, subd. 11, eff. July 1, 2008.

Subd. 3. Effect of copies. A photographic, photostatic, microphotographic, microfilmed, or similarly reproduced record is of the same force and effect as the original and may be used as the original document or book of record in all proceedings.

Subd. 4. Exception. This section does not apply to the court of any county until the county board of the county adopts a resolution authorizing the destruction of probate records pursuant to the provisions of this section. When the county board has complied with this subdivision, section 525.092 and any act amendatory thereof shall no longer apply to the probate court of that county.

Laws 1965, c. 883, § 1. Amended by Laws 1971, c. 484, § 1, eff. May 26, 1971; Laws 1973, c. 582, § 3; Laws 1975, c. 347, §§ 85 to 87, eff. Jan. 1, 1976; Laws 1979, c. 303, art. 3, §§ 35, 36; Laws 1986, c. 444; Laws 1986, 1st Sp., c. 3, art. 1, § 82; Laws 1995, c. 189, § 8; Laws 1996, c. 277, § 1.

525.092. Court administrator may destroy certain papers

Subdivision 1. Certain vouchers and receipts. The court administrator of the district court is hereby authorized to destroy all vouchers or receipts filed in estates and guardianship proceedings of record in the office after such estates or guardianships have been closed for a period of 25 years, or more, except receipts for any federal or state taxes.

Subd. 2. Certain guardianships excepted. The provisions of this section shall not apply to guardianships of incompetent or insane persons, nor to guardianships of minors until one year after the minor has become 18 years old.

Laws 1947, c. 117, §§ 1, 2. Amended by Laws 1949, c. 409, § 1; Laws 1951, c. 21, § 1; Laws 1973, c. 725, § 75, eff. June 1, 1973; Laws 1986, c. 444; Laws 1986, 1st Sp., c. 3, art. 1, § 82; Laws 1995, c. 189, § 8; Laws 1996, c. 277, § 1.

525.093. Repealed by Laws 1965, c. 883, § 2

525.094. Repealed by Laws 1965, c. 883, § 2

525.095. Court administrator may issue orders under direction of the court

The judge may authorize the court administrator or any deputy court administrator to issue orders for hearing petitions for general administration, for the probate of any will, for determination of descent, for sale, lease, mortgage, or conveyance of real estate, for the settlement and allowance of any account, for partial or final distribution, for commitment, orders limiting the time to file claims and fixing the time and place for the hearing thereon, and to issue notice of the entry of any order. The issuance of any such order or notice by the court administrator or deputy court administrator shall be prima facie evidence of authority to issue it.

Amended by Laws 1986, c. 444; Laws 1986, 1st Sp., c. 3, art. 1, § 82.

525.10. Referee; appointment; bond; office abolished

Subdivision 1. Office abolished. The office of referee is abolished. No vacancy in the office of referee shall be filled, nor new office created.

Subd. 2. Incumbents. Persons holding the office of referee on June 30, 1980, in the Second and August 15, 1980, in the Fourth Judicial District may continue to serve at the pleasure of the chief judge of the district under the terms and conditions of their appointment. All referees are subject to the administrative authority and assignment power of the chief judge of the district as provided in section 484.69, subdivision 3, and are not limited to assignment to probate court. All referees are subject to the provisions of section 484.70. Part time referees holding office in the Second Judicial District pursuant to this subdivision shall cease to hold office on July 31, 1984.

Subd. 3. Referees. Each referee in probate court shall be an attorney at law duly admitted in this state. The appointment shall be in writing and filed in the court. The referee has the power to take acknowledgments and administer oaths.

Amended by Laws 1957, c. 212, § 1; Laws 1973, c. 524, § 14; Laws 1974, c. 165, § 1; Laws 1974, c. 387, § 1; Laws 1976, c. 181, § 2; Laws 1981, c. 272, § 6.

525.101. Compensation of referee

Such referee shall receive from the county as compensation $3,600 per annum in counties having more than 500,000 inhabitants, payable from the general funds of the county not otherwise appropriated, at the same time and in the same manner and subject to the provisions of law applicable to the compensation of the judge. The county shall furnish a suitable office in the courthouse or in some other suitable place or places designated by the judge. The judge may assign to the referee from the court's clerks and employees such clerical help as may be necessary to properly discharge the duties.

Amended by Laws 1957, c. 212, § 2; Laws 1971, c. 471, § 1, eff. May 22, 1971; Laws 1986, c. 444.

525.102. Reference

After such appointment the judge by order may refer to the referee any matter, cause, or proceeding pending in such court. In all matters so referred the referee shall find the facts and report the findings to the judge. In all matters referred and reported the referee may append the referee's signature to the order or decree of the court; and whenever this signature shall be so appended, it shall constitute conclusive evidence that the matter was referred, heard, and reported in the manner required by law and the order of the court therein, provided that the failure of the referee to append the referee's signature to any such order or decree shall not affect its validity.

Amended by Laws 1986, c. 444.

525.103. Delivery of books and records

When the term of office of such referee expires or is terminated, the referee shall deliver to the successor or to the judge all books and papers in the referee's possession relating to the office. Upon failure to do so within five days after demand by the successor or the judge, the referee shall be guilty of a gross misdemeanor.

Amended by Laws 1986, c. 444.

525.11. Reporter; appointment and duties

The judge may appoint a competent stenographer as reporter and secretary in all matters pertaining to official duties to hold office during the judge's pleasure. Such reporter shall make a complete record of all testimony given and all proceedings had before the court upon the trial of issue of fact except that in commitment proceedings a tape recording of the proceedings may be kept in lieu of a stenographic record. The reporter shall inscribe all questions in the exact language thereof, all answers thereto precisely as given by the witness or sworn interpreter, all objections made and the grounds thereof as stated by counsel, all rulings thereon, all exceptions taken, all admissions made, all oral stipulations, and all oral motions and orders. When directed by the judge, the reporter shall make a record of any matter or proceeding and without charge shall read to or transcribe for such judge any record made or any tape recording made in a commitment proceeding. Upon completion of every trial or proceeding, such reporter shall file the stenographic record or tape recording in the manner directed by the judge. Upon request of any person and payment of fees by such person, the reporter shall furnish a transcript. The reporter may take acknowledgments, administer oaths, and certify copies of the stenographic record or transcript of either such record or tape recording made in a commitment proceeding.

Amended by Laws 1974, c. 482, § 8; Laws 1986, c. 444.

525.111. Compensation; transcript fees

Where the salary of the reporter is not provided for by law, compensation shall be paid by the representative as an expense of administration or guardianship, or by the party or parties presenting or contesting the proceedings reported, as the court may determine. In addition to the salary fixed by law or compensation fixed by the court, the reporter shall receive for transcripts furnished such fees as may be fixed by the court not exceeding those allowed by law to the district court reporters of the same county.

Amended by Laws 1986, c. 444.

525.112. Court reporters for Hennepin county court

The county judge or judge of probate of any county now having or which may hereafter have 400,000 inhabitants, or over, may appoint a competent stenographer as court reporter and secretary, who shall be paid a salary of $3,000 per annum; and, in addition to this salary, the court reporter may also be paid such fees for transcripts of evidence made in relation to probate hearings, as the judge of probate shall fix and allow, and appoint two additional clerks who shall be competent stenographers, who shall each be paid a salary of $1,200 per annum.

Amended by Laws 1975, c. 347, § 88, eff. Jan. 1, 1976.

525.113. Additional employees

The reporter and clerk mentioned in section 525.112 shall be employed and appointed in addition to the court administrator, deputy court administrators, and employees now provided by law, to hold office during the pleasure of the judge of probate and shall perform the duties imposed by law and such judge, and their salary shall be paid from the county funds in the same manner as prescribed for the payment of other employees of such court.

Amended by Laws 1986, 1st Sp., c. 3, art. 1, § 82.

525.12. Auditor; appointment

The court may appoint an auditor in any matter involving an annual, partial, or final account, or the amount due on a claim or an offset thereto. Such appointment may be made with or without notice and on the court's own motion or upon the petition of the personal representative or of any person interested in the estate or guardianship.

Amended by Laws 1975, c. 347, § 89, eff. Jan. 1, 1976.

525.121. Powers

The auditor shall have the same power as the court to set hearings, grant adjournments, compel the attendance of witnesses or the production of books, papers, and documents, and to hear all proper evidence relating to such matter. The auditor shall report findings of fact to the court.

Amended by Laws 1986, c. 444.

525.122. Compensation of auditor

The auditor shall be allowed such reasonable fees, disbursements, and expenses as may be determined by the court and shall be paid by the personal representative as expenses of administration, guardianship or conservatorship or by the person applying for such audit as the court may determine.

Amended by Laws 1975, c. 347, § 90, eff. Jan. 1, 1976.

INTESTATE SUCCESSION

525.13. Estate

As used in sections 525.13 to 525.161, the word "estate" includes every right and interest of a decedent in property, real or personal, except such as are terminated or otherwise extinguished by the death.

Amended by Laws 1985, c. 250, § 24; Laws 1986, c. 444.

Historical and Statutory Notes

Laws 1985, c. 250, § 28, provides that this amendment is effective for estates of decedents dying after December 31, 1986.

Continuing Effect. For continuing effect of prior law for wills or instruments executed on or before December 31, 1986, see § 524.2–114 as quoted in the Historical and Statutory Notes under § 524.2–115.

525.14. Descent of cemetery lot

Subject to the right of interment of the decedent therein, a cemetery lot or burial plot, unless disposed of as provided in section 306.29, shall descend free of all debts as follows:

(1) to the decedent's surviving spouse, a life estate with right of interment of the spouse therein, and remainder over to the person who would be entitled to the fee if there were no spouse, provided, however, if no person entitled to the remainder of the fee survives, then the entire fee to the surviving spouse with right of interment therein;

(2) if there is no surviving spouse, then to the decedent's eldest surviving child;

(3) if there is no surviving child, then to the decedent's youngest surviving sibling;

(4) if there is no surviving spouse, child or sibling of the decedent, then, if not sold during administration of decedent's estate, to the cemetery association or private cemetery in trust as a burial lot for the decedent and such of the decedent's relatives as the governing body thereof shall deem proper.

The cemetery association or private cemetery, or, with its consent, any person to whom the lot shall descend may grant and convey the lot to any of the decedent's parents, siblings or descendants.

A crypt or group of crypts or burial vaults owned by one person in a public or community mausoleum shall be deemed a cemetery lot.

Grave markers, monuments, memorials and all structures lawfully installed or erected on any cemetery lot or burial plot shall be deemed to be a part of and shall descend with the lot or plot.

Amended by Laws 1969, c. 852, § 1, eff. May 29, 1969; Laws 1981, c. 25, § 1.

Historical and Statutory Notes

Laws 1981, c. 25, § 2, read:

"This act is effective for estates of decedents dying after the date of final enactment [Governor signed bill April 13, 1981]."

525.145. Repealed by Laws 1995, c. 130, § 21, eff. Jan. 1, 1996

Historical and Statutory Notes

See, now, M.S.A. § 524.2–402.

525.15. Allowances to spouse

When any person dies, testate or intestate,

(1) The surviving spouse shall be allowed from the personal property of which the decedent was possessed or to which the decedent was entitled at the time of death, the wearing apparel, and, as selected, furniture and household goods not exceeding $6,000 in value, and other personal property not exceeding $3,000 in value, subject to an award of property with sentimental value to the decedent's children under section 525.152;

(2) When, except for one automobile, all of the personal estate of the decedent is allowed to the surviving spouse by clause (1), the surviving spouse shall also be allowed the automobile;

(3) If there be no surviving spouse, the minor children shall receive the property specified in clause (1) as selected in their behalf;

(4) During administration, but not exceeding 18 months, unless an extension shall have been granted by the court, or, if the estate be insolvent, not exceeding 12 months, the spouse or children, or both, constituting the family of the decedent shall be allowed reasonable maintenance;

(5) In the administration of an estate of a nonresident decedent, the allowances received in the domiciliary administration shall be deducted from the allowances under this section.

Amended by Laws 1947, c. 45, § 1; Laws 1955, c. 189, § 1; Laws 1975, c. 347, § 91, eff. Jan. 1, 1976; Laws 1981, c. 103, § 1; Laws 1986, c. 444; Laws 1988, c. 417, § 1, eff. Aug. 1, 1988.

Repeal

This section is repealed by Laws 1994, c. 472, § 64, effective January 1, 1996, applicable to the rights of successors of decedents dying on or after January 1, 1996, and to any wills of decedents dying on or after January 1, 1996.

Historical and Statutory Notes

Laws 1981, c. 103, § 2, provides that this act is effective for estates of decedents dying after July 31, 1981.

Laws 1988, c. 417, § 4 provides that this act is effective August 1, 1988 and applies to estates of decedents dying on or after that date.

Laws 1994, c. 472, § 65, provides:

"(a) This act takes effect on January 1, 1996.

"(b) Except as provided elsewhere in this act:

"(1) this act applies to the rights of successors of decedents dying on or after its effective date and to any wills of decedents dying on or after its effective date;

"(2) if, before the effective date of this act, a right is either acquired, extinguished, waived, or barred upon the expiration of a prescribed period of time which commenced to run by the provisions of any statute before the effective date, the provisions of this act neither revoke, revive, restore, nor remove the bar of such right; and

"(3) any rule of construction or presumption provided in this act applies to instruments executed and multiple party accounts opened before the effective date of this act unless there is a clear indication of contrary intent."

Continuing Effect. For continuing effect of law relating to wills or other instruments executed before January 1, 1996, see § 524.2–115.

See, now, M.S.A. §§ 524.2–403 and 524.2–404.

525.151. Allowance selection and maintenance payment

The surviving spouse, and conservators or guardians of the minor children, may select the property of the estate allowed to them under section 525.15, clauses (1), (2) and (3), subject to an award of property with sentimental value to the decedent's children under section 525.152. The personal representative may make these selections if the surviving spouse or the conservators or guardians of the minor children are unable or fail to do so within a reasonable time or if there are no conservators or guardians of the minor children. The personal representative may execute an instrument or deed of distribution to establish the ownership of the property, provided that any notice required under section 525.152, subdivision 3, has been given and eligible children have failed to request an award of property with sentimental value or the court has denied the request. The personal representative may determine maintenance in periodic installments not exceeding $500 per month for one year, if the estate is insolvent or 18 months if the estate is solvent, and may disburse funds of the estate in payment of such maintenance. The personal representative or any interested person aggrieved by any selection, determination, payment, proposed payment, or failure to act under this section may petition the court for appropriate relief. Relief may include provision for a family allowance larger or smaller than that which the personal representative determined or could have determined.

Laws 1975, c. 347, § 92, eff. Jan. 1, 1976. Amended by Laws 1986, c. 444; Laws 1988, c. 417, § 2, eff. Aug. 1, 1988; Laws 1989, c. 219, § 1.

Repeal

This section is repealed by Laws 1994, c. 472, § 64, effective January 1, 1996, applicable to the rights of successors of decedents dying on or after January 1, 1996, and to any wills of decedents dying on or after January 1, 1996.

Historical and Statutory Notes

Laws 1988, c. 417, § 4 provides that this amendment is effective August 1, 1988, and applies to estates of decedents dying on or after that date.

Laws 1994, c. 472, § 65, provides:

"(a) This act takes effect on January 1, 1996.

"(b) Except as provided elsewhere in this act:

"(1) this act applies to the rights of successors of decedents dying on or after its effective date and to any wills of decedents dying on or after its effective date;

"(2) if, before the effective date of this act, a right is either acquired, extinguished, waived, or barred upon the expiration of a prescribed period of time which commenced to run by the provisions of any statute before the effective date, the provisions of this act neither revoke, revive, restore, nor remove the bar of such right; and

"(3) any rule of construction or presumption provided in this act applies to instruments executed and multiple party accounts opened before the effective date of this act unless there is a clear indication of contrary intent."

Continuing Effect. For continuing effect of law relating to wills or other instruments executed before January 1, 1996, see § 524.2–115.

See, now, M.S.A. §§ 524.2–404.

525.152. Award of property with sentimental value to children

Subdivision 1. Definitions. (a) "Eligible child" means a child of the decedent who:

(1) is not the child of the surviving spouse, if any;

(2) if there is no surviving spouse, is not a minor, and has a different parent than minor children of the decedent; and

(3) if the decedent dies testate, is a devisee under the decedent's will.

(b) "Sentimental value" means significant emotional or nostalgic value arising out of the relationship of an individual with the decedent or arising out of the relationship of the eligible child with the individual who is the nondecedent parent of the eligible child.

Subd. 2. Ineligible property. The following property is not eligible for an award under this section:

(1) real property;

(2) personal property that is the subject of a specific devise under the decedent's will where the will was executed before August 1, 1989, and where the devise specifically identifies the particular item of property, unless the property is selected under section 524.2–403;

(3) personal property that is the subject of a specific devise under a separate writing under section 524.2–513, unless the property is selected under section 524.2–403; and

(4) personal property disposed of by a premarital agreement.

Subd. 3. Notice to eligible children; petition. At the time of an allowance selection under section 524.2–403, the person making the selection shall serve personally or by mail a written itemized notice of the property selected to every eligible child of the decedent. This requirement does not apply if an award of property with sentimental value already has been made under this section. Within 30 days of receipt of the notice of selection, an eligible child may petition the court to award property with sentimental value contained in the notice, or other property with sentimental value that belonged to the decedent, to the eligible child.

Subd. 4. Court decision. The court shall award property with sentimental value to an eligible child if it finds that the property's sentimental value to the child outweighs its sentimental value to the person entitled to the allowance selection. If more than one eligible child petitions the court for an award of the same property, the court shall award the property to the child for whom the property has the greatest sentimental value. In awarding property with sentimental value to an eligible child, the court shall give weight to the following factors:

(1) the relationship of the eligible child to the acquisition and use of the property;

(2) whether the property was acquired prior to the decedent's marriage to the surviving spouse or prior to the birth of minor children who are entitled to an allowance selection; and

(3) whether the property belonged to the individual who is the nondecedent parent of the eligible child.

Subd. 5. Payment to estate. (a) As a condition of an award of sentimental property under this section, the court shall order that the eligible child pay the value of the property to the estate or that the value of the property be deducted from the eligible child's share of the estate. The surviving spouse or minor children may make an additional allowance selection in place of property with sentimental value awarded to an eligible child.

(b) If the court awards property under subdivision 4, the court shall appoint an appraiser who shall determine the value of the property. The value of the property is its appraised value as of the date of the decedent's death without reference to its sentimental value to the eligible child or any other person.

Laws 1988, c. 417, § 3, eff. Aug. 1, 1988. Amended by Laws 1989, c. 219, § 2; Laws 1997, c. 7, art. 1, §§ 166 to 168.

Historical and Statutory Notes

Laws 1988, c. 417, § 4, provides that this section is effective August 1, 1988, and applies to estates of decedents dying on or after that date.

525.16. Repealed by Laws 1985, c. 250, § 27

Historical and Statutory Notes

Effective Date and Continuing Effect. Laws 1985, c. 250, § 28, provides that the repeal of § 525.16 by Laws 1985, c. 250, § 27, is effective for estates of decedents dying after December 31, 1986. For continuing effect of this section for wills or other instruments executed on or before December 31, 1986, see § 524.2–114 as quoted in the Historical and Statutory Notes under § 524.2–115.

525.161. No surviving spouse or kindred, notices to attorney general

When it appears from the petition or application for administration of the estate, or otherwise, in a proceeding in the court that the intestate left surviving no spouse or kindred, the court shall give notice of such fact and notice of all subsequent proceedings in such estate to the attorney general forthwith; and the attorney general shall protect the interests of the state during the course of administration. The residue which escheats to the state shall be transmitted to the attorney general. All moneys, stocks, bonds, notes, mortgages and other securities, and all other personal property so escheated shall then be given into the custody of the commissioner of finance who shall immediately credit the moneys received to the general fund. The commissioner of finance shall hold such stocks, bonds, notes, mortgages and other securities, and all other personal property, subject to such investment, sale or other disposition as the State Board of Investment may direct pursuant to section 11A.04, clause (9). The attorney general shall immediately report to the State Executive Council all real property received in the individual escheat, and any sale or disposition of such real estate shall be made in accordance with sections 16B.281 to 16B.287.

Laws 1955, c. 194, § 1. Amended by Laws 1957, c. 861, § 1; Laws 1969, c. 399, § 1; Laws 1973, c. 492, § 14; Laws 1975, c. 347, § 93, eff. Jan. 1, 1976; Laws 1980, c. 607, art. 14, § 46, eff. April 24, 1980; Laws 2003, c. 112, art. 2, § 48, eff. May 28, 2003; Laws 2004, c. 262, art. 1, § 39, eff. Aug. 1, 2004.

525.17 to 525.173. Repealed by Laws 1985, c. 250, § 27

Historical and Statutory Notes

Effective Date and Continuing Effect. Laws 1985, c. 250, § 28, provides that the repeal of §§ 525.17 to 525.173 by Laws 1985, c. 250, § 27, is effective for estates of decedents dying after December 31, 1986. For continuing effect of these sections for wills or other instruments executed on or before December 31, 1986, see § 524.2–114 as quoted in the Historical and Statutory Notes under § 524.2–115.

WILLS

525.18 to 525.191. Repealed by Laws 1975, c. 347, § 144, eff. Jan. 1, 1976

525.20 to 525.202. Repealed by Laws 1985, c. 250, § 27

Historical and Statutory Notes

Effective Date and Continuing Effect. Laws 1985, c. 250, § 28, provides that the repeal of §§ 525.20 to 525.202 by Laws 1985, c. 250, § 27, is effective for estates of decedents dying after December 31, 1986. For continuing effect of these sections for wills or other instruments executed on or before December 31, 1986, see § 524.2–114 as quoted in the Historical and Statutory Notes under § 524.2–115.

525.203. Repealed by Laws 1975, c. 347, § 144, eff. Jan. 1, 1976

525.21. Quantity of estate devised

Every devise of real estate shall convey all the estate of the testator therein subject to liens and encumbrances thereon unless a different intention appears from the will.

525.211. Repealed by Laws 1975, c. 347, § 144, eff. Jan. 1, 1976

525.212 to 525.216. Repealed by Laws 1985, c. 250, § 27

Historical and Statutory Notes

Effective Date and Continuing Effect. Laws 1985, c. 250, § 28, provides that the repeal of §§ 525.212 to 525.216 by Laws 1985, c. 250, § 27, is effective for estates of decedents dying after December 31, 1986. For continuing effect of these sections for wills or other instruments executed on or before December 31, 1986, see § 524.2–114 as quoted in the Historical and Statutory Notes under § 524.2–115.

525.22.   Deposit of wills

A will in writing enclosed in a sealed wrapper upon which is endorsed the name and address of the testator, the day when, and the person by whom it is delivered, may be deposited in the probate court of the county where the testator resides. The court shall give a certificate of its deposit and shall retain such will. The court administrator shall receive a fee, as provided in section 357.021, subdivision 2, for each will deposited. During the testator's lifetime, such will shall be delivered only to the testator or upon the testator's written order witnessed by at least two subscribing witnesses and duly acknowledged. After the testator's death, the court shall open the will publicly and retain the same. Notice shall be given to the executor named therein and to such other persons as the court may designate. If the proper venue is in another court, the will shall be transmitted to such court; but before such transmission a true copy thereof shall be made by and retained in the court in which the will was deposited.

Amended by Laws 1986, c. 444; Laws 1990, c. 544, § 2.

Repeal

This section is repealed by Laws 1994, c. 472, § 64, effective January 1, 1996, applicable to the rights of successors of decedents dying on or after January 1, 1996, and to any wills of decedents dying on or after January 1, 1996.

Historical and Statutory Notes

Laws 1994, c. 472, § 65, provides:

"(a) This act takes effect on January 1, 1996.

"(b) Except as provided elsewhere in this act:

"(1) this act applies to the rights of successors of decedents dying on or after its effective date and to any wills of decedents dying on or after its effective date;

"(2) if, before the effective date of this act, a right is either acquired, extinguished, waived, or barred upon the expiration of a prescribed period of time which commenced to run by the provisions of any statute before the effective date, the provisions of this act neither revoke, revive, restore, nor remove the bar of such right; and

"(3) any rule of construction or presumption provided in this act applies to instruments executed and multiple party accounts opened before the effective date of this act unless there is a clear indication of contrary intent."

Continuing Effect. For continuing effect of law relating to wills or other instruments executed before January 1, 1996, see § 524.2–115.

See, now, M.S.A. § 524.2–515.

525.221.   Duty of custodian

After the death of a testator, the person having custody of the will shall deliver it to the court which has jurisdiction thereof. Every person who neglects to deliver a will after being duly ordered to do so shall be guilty of contempt of court.

Amended by Laws 1986, c. 444.

Repeal

This section is repealed by Laws 1994, c. 472, § 64, effective January 1, 1996, applicable to the rights of successors of decedents dying on or after January 1, 1996, and to any wills of decedents dying on or after January 1, 1996.

Historical and Statutory Notes

Laws 1994, c. 472, § 65, provides:

"(a) This act takes effect on January 1, 1996.

"(b) Except as provided elsewhere in this act:

"(1) this act applies to the rights of successors of decedents dying on or after its effective date and to any wills of decedents dying on or after its effective date;

"(2) if, before the effective date of this act, a right is either acquired, extinguished, waived, or barred upon the expiration of a prescribed period of time which commenced to run by the provisions of any statute before the effective date, the provisions of this act neither revoke, revive, restore, nor remove the bar of such right; and

"(3) any rule of construction or presumption provided in this act applies to instruments executed and multiple party accounts opened before the effective date of this act unless there is a clear indication of contrary intent."

Continuing Effect. For continuing effect of law relating to wills or other instruments executed before January 1, 1996, see § 524.2–115.

See, now, M.S.A. § 524.2–516.

525.222. Repealed by Laws 1974, c. 442, art. 8, § 524.8–102, eff. Jan. 1, 1976

525.2221. Wills not affected

Notwithstanding any other provision of law to the contrary, the provisions of any will executed prior to June 1, 1973 relating to ones "minority" or "majority" or other related terms shall be governed by the definitions of such terms existing at the time of the execution of the will.

Laws 1973, c. 725, § 86, eff. June 1, 1973.

UNIFORM TESTAMENTARY ADDITIONS TO TRUSTS ACT

525.223. Uniform testamentary additions to trusts act

Subdivision 1. Testamentary additions to trusts. A devise, the validity of which is determinable by the law of this state, may be made by a will to the trustee or trustees of a trust established or to be established by the testator or by the testator and some other person or persons or by some other person or persons, including a funded or unfunded life insurance trust, although the trustor has reserved any or all rights of ownership of the insurance contracts, if the trust is identified in the testator's will and its terms are set forth in a written instrument, other than a will, executed before or concurrently with the execution of the testator's will or in the valid last will of a person who has predeceased the testator, regardless of the existence, size, or character of the corpus of the trust. The devise shall not be invalid because the trust is amendable or revocable, or both, or because the trust was amended after the execution of the will or after the death of the testator. Unless the testator's will provides otherwise, the property so devised (a) shall not be deemed to be held under a testamentary trust of the testator but shall become a part of the trust to which it is given and (b) shall be administered and disposed of in accordance with the provisions of the instrument or will setting forth the terms of the trust, including any amendments thereto made before the death of the testator, regardless of whether made before or after the execution of the testator's will, and, if the testator's will so provides, including any amendments to the trust made after the death of the testator. A revocation or termination of the trust before the death of the testator shall cause the devise to lapse.

Subd. 2. Effect on prior wills. This section shall not invalidate any devise made by a will executed prior to the effective date of Laws 1963, Chapter 13.

Subd. 3. Uniformity of Interpretation. This section shall be so construed as to effectuate its general purpose to make uniform the law of those states which enact it.

Subd. 4. Short title. This section is the uniform testamentary additions to trusts act.

Subd. 5. Effective date. This section shall take effect upon final enactment, and shall apply to all wills and trusts heretofore or hereafter executed.

Laws 1963, c. 13, §§ 1–5. Amended by Laws 1975, c. 347, §§ 97, 98, eff. Jan. 1, 1976.

Repeal

This section is repealed by Laws 1994, c. 472, § 64, effective January 1, 1996, applicable to the rights of successors of decedents dying on or after January 1, 1996, and to any wills of decedents dying on or after January 1, 1996.

Historical and Statutory Notes

Laws 1994, c. 472, § 65, provides:

"(a) This act takes effect on January 1, 1996.

"(b) Except as provided elsewhere in this act:

"(1) this act applies to the rights of successors of decedents dying on or after its effective date and to any wills of decedents dying on or after its effective date;

"(2) if, before the effective date of this act, a right is either acquired, extinguished, waived, or barred upon the expiration of a prescribed period of time which commenced to run by the provisions of any statute before the effective date, the provisions of this act neither revoke, revive, restore, nor remove the bar of such right; and

"(3) any rule of construction or presumption provided in this act applies to instruments executed and multiple party accounts opened before the effective date of this act unless there is a clear indication of contrary intent."

Continuing Effect. For continuing effect of law relating to wills or other instruments executed before January 1, 1996, see § 524.2–115.

See, now, M.S.A. § 524.2–511.

PROBATE OF WILLS

525.23, 525.231. Repealed by Laws 1974, c. 442, art. 8, § 524.8–102, eff. Jan. 1, 1976

525.24. Repealed by Laws 1974, c. 442, art. 8, § 524.8–102, eff. Jan. 1, 1976

525.241. Repealed by Laws 1974, c. 442, art. 8, § 524.8–102, eff. Jan. 1, 1976

525.242. Secondary evidence

If no subscribing witness competent to testify resides in the state at the time appointed for proving the will, the court may admit the testimony of other witnesses to prove the capacity of the testator and the execution of the will, and as evidence of such execution may admit proof of the handwriting of the testator and of the subscribing witnesses.

525.243 to 525.252. Repealed by Laws 1974, c. 442, art. 8, § 524.8–102, eff. Jan. 1, 1976

525.253. Sale of devised property

Subdivision 1. General rule. Unless a contrary intent appears from the will, an agreement made by a testator for the sale or transfer of real property disposed of by the will previously made, does not revoke or adeem such disposal; but all the right, title, and interest of the decedent in such property and in said agreement shall pass, according to the terms of the will. Such an agreement shall be enforceable and subject to the same remedies for specific performance or otherwise against the devisees as exists against a decedent's successors if the same passed by succession.

Subd. 2. Applicability. This section shall be applicable to estates of decedents dying after June 5, 1969.

Laws 1969, c. 944, §§ 1, 2, eff. June 5, 1969. Amended by Laws 1975, c. 347, § 99, eff. Jan. 1, 1976.

525.26 to 525.262. Repealed by Laws 1975, c. 347, § 144, eff. Jan. 1, 1976

525.27 to 525.272. Repealed by Laws 1975, c. 347, § 144, eff. Jan. 1, 1976

525.273. Repealed by Laws 1974, c. 442, art. 8, § 524.8–102, eff. Jan. 1, 1976

525.28 to 525.292. Repealed by Laws 1974, c. 442, art. 8, § 524.8–102, eff. Jan. 1, 1976

525.30 to 525.304. Repealed by Laws 1974, c. 442, art. 8, § 524.8–102, eff. Jan. 1, 1976

DETERMINATION OF DESCENT

525.31. Essentials

Whenever any person has been dead for more than three years and has left real or personal property, or any interest therein, and no will or authenticated copy of a will probated outside this state in accordance with the laws in force in the place where probated has been probated nor proceedings had in this state, any interested person or assignee or successor of an interested person may petition the court of the county of the decedent's residence or of the county wherein such real or personal property, or any part thereof, is situated to determine the descent of such property and to assign such property to the persons entitled thereto.

Laws 1975, c. 347, § 100, eff. Jan. 1, 1976. Amended by Laws 1976, c. 161, § 15, eff. April 4, 1976.

525.311. Contents of petition

Such petition shall show so far as known to the petitioner:

(1) The name of the decedent, the place of residence, the date and place of death, the age and address at such date, and whether the decedent died testate or intestate;

(2) The names, ages, and addresses of heirs, personal representatives, and devisees;

(3) That no will or authenticated copy of a will probated outside of this state in accordance with the laws in force in the place where probated has been probated nor proceedings had in this state;

(4) A description of the real or personal property, or interest therein and if a homestead, designated as such, the interest therein of the decedent, the value thereof at the date of death, and the interest therein of the petitioner;

(5) If the decedent left a will which has not been probated in this state, such will or authenticated copy of a will probated outside of this state in accordance

with the laws in force in the place where probated shall be filed and the petition shall contain a prayer for its probate.

(6) That the devisee or successors and assigns possess the property devised in accordance with the will, any heir or a successor and assigns possess such property which passes to such heir under the laws of intestate succession in force at the decedent's death, or such property was not possessed or claimed by anyone by virtue of the decedent's title during the time period for testacy proceedings.

(7) In any such proceeding wherein it appears that the property affected descends through several decedents under circumstances qualifying for a descent proceeding under this section in each case, the court in its discretion may consolidate the proceedings into one and may accept the filing of one petition for the several decedents where no interests are prejudiced thereby. The notice and other requirements of this section and sections 525.31 and 525.312 shall be complied with, and the matter shall be then adjudicated under one title combining the names of the several decedents and making appropriate findings for each decedent and determining heirship.

Laws 1975, c. 347, § 100, eff. Jan. 1, 1976. Amended by Laws 1986, c. 444.

525.312. Decree of descent

Upon the filing of such petition, the court shall fix the time and place for the hearing thereof, notice of which shall be given pursuant to section 524.1–401. Notice of the hearing, in the form prescribed by court rule, shall also be given under direction of the court administrator by publication once a week for two consecutive weeks in a legal newspaper in the county where the hearing is to be held, the last publication of which is to be at least ten days before the time set for hearing. Upon proof of the petition and of the will if there be one; or upon proof of the petition and of an authenticated copy of a will duly proved and allowed outside of this state in accordance with the laws in force in the place where proved, if there be one; and if a clearance for medical assistance claims is on file in the proceeding and any medical assistance claims are paid or satisfied, the court shall allow the same and enter its decree of descent assigning the real or personal property, or any interest therein, to the persons entitled thereto pursuant to the will or such authenticated copy, if there be one, otherwise pursuant to the laws of intestate succession in force at the time of the decedent's death. The decree of descent shall operate to assign the property free and clear of any and all claims for medical assistance arising under section 525.313 without regard to the final disposition of those claims. The court may appoint two or more disinterested persons to appraise the property.

Laws 1975, c. 347, § 100, eff. Jan. 1, 1976. Amended by Laws 1977, c. 207, § 1; Laws 1979, c. 303, art. 3, § 37; Laws 1986, 1st Sp., c. 3, art. 1, § 82; Laws 2000, c. 400, § 7.

525.313. Clearance for medical assistance claims

(a) The court shall not enter a decree of descent until the petitioner has filed a clearance for medical assistance claims under this section, and until any medical assistance claims filed under this section have been paid, settled, or otherwise finally disposed of.

(b) After filing the petition, the petitioner or the petitioner's attorney shall apply to the county agency in the county in which the petition is pending for a clearance of medical assistance claims. The application must state the decedent's name, date of birth, and Social Security number; the name, date of birth, and Social Security number of any predeceased spouse of the decedent; the names and addresses of the devisees and heirs; and the name, address, and telephone number of the petitioner or the attorney making the application on behalf of the petitioner, and include a copy of the notice of hearing.

(c) The county agency shall determine whether the decedent or any of the decedent's predeceased spouses received medical assistance under chapter 256B or general assistance medical care under chapter 256D giving rise to a claim under section 256B.15. If there are no claims, the county agency shall issue the petitioner a clearance for medical assistance claims stating no medical assistance claims exist. If there is a claim, the county agency shall issue the petitioner a clearance for medical assistance claims stating that a claim exists and the total amount of the claim. The county agency shall mail the completed clearance for medical assistance claims to the applicant within 15 working days after receiving the application without cost to the applicant or others.

(d) The petitioner or attorney shall file the certificate in the proceedings for the decree of descent as soon as practicable after it is received. Notwithstanding any rule or law to the contrary, if a medical assistance claim appears in a clearance for medical assistance claims, then:

(1) the claim shall be a claim against the decedent's property which is the subject of the petition. The county agency issuing the certificate shall be the claimant. The filing of the clearance for medical assistance claims in the proceeding for a decree of descent constitutes presentation of the claim;

(2) the claim shall be an unbarred and undischarged claim and shall be payable, in whole or in part, from the decedent's property which is the subject of the petition, including the net sale proceeds from any sale of property free and clear of the claim under this section;

(3) the claim may be allowed, denied, appealed, and bear interest as provided for claims in estates under chapter 524; and

(4) the county agency may collect, compromise, or otherwise settle the claim with the estate, the petitioner, or the assignees of the property on whatever terms and conditions are deemed appropriate.

(e) Any of the decedent's devisees, heirs, successors, assigns, or their successors and assigns, may apply for a partial decree of descent to facilitate the good faith sale of their interest in any real or personal property described in the petition free and clear of any medical assistance claim any time before the entry of a decree of descent under section 525.312. The applicant must prove an interest in the property as provided under section 525.312. The court may enter a partial decree of descent any time after it could hear and decide the petition for a decree of descent. A partial decree of descent shall assign the interests in the real and personal property described in the application to the parties entitled to the property free and clear of any and all medical assistance claims. The net sale proceeds from the sale shall be:

(1) substituted in the estate according to this section for the property sold;

(2) paid over to and held by the petitioner pending the entry of a decree of descent;

(3) used for payment of medical assistance claims; and

(4) distributed according to the decree of descent after any medical assistance claims are paid.

(f) The clearance for medical assistance claims must:

(1) include the case name, case number, and district court in which the proceeding for a decree of descent is pending;

(2) include the name, date of birth, and Social Security number of the decedent and any of the decedent's predeceased spouses;

(3) state whether there are medical assistance claims against the decedent, or a predeceased spouse, and the total amount of each claim; and

(4) include the name, address, and telephone number of the county agency giving the clearance for medical assistance claims. The certificate shall be signed by the director of the county agency or the director's designee. The signature of the director or the director's designee does not require an acknowledgment.

(g) All recoveries under this section are recoveries under section 256B.15.

(h) For purposes of this section and chapter 256B, all property identified in the petition and all subsequent amendments to the petition shall constitute an estate.

(i) No clearance for medical assistance claims is required under this section and section 525.312 in an action for a decree of descent proceeding in which all of the following apply to the decedent whose property is the subject of the proceeding:

(1) the decedent's estate was previously probated in this state;

(2) the previous probate was not a special administration or summary proceeding; and

(3) the decedent's property, which is the subject of the petition for a decree of descent, was omitted from the previous probate.

Laws 2000, c. 400, § 8. Amended by Laws 2002, c. 347, § 4.

Historical and Statutory Notes

Laws 2002, c. 347, § 5, provides that § 4 (amending this section) applies to proceedings for a decree of descent commenced after July 31, 2002.

525.314 to 525.316. Repealed by Laws 1974, c. 442, art. 8, § 524.8–102, eff. Jan. 1, 1976

525.32 to 525.324. Repealed by Laws 1974, c. 442, art. 8, § 524.8–102, eff. Aug. 1, 1974

525.33. Repealed by Laws 1975, c. 347, § 144, eff. Jan. 1, 1976

525.331. Repealed by Laws 1974, c. 442, art. 8, § 524.8–102, eff. Jan. 1, 1976

PROPERTY DISPOSITION

525.34 to 525.36. Repealed by Laws 1974, c. 442, art. 8, § 524.8–102, eff. Jan. 1, 1976

525.37. Foreclosure of mortgages

The guardian or conservator shall have the same right to foreclose a mortgage, lien, or pledge or collect the debt secured thereby as the ward or conservatee would have had, if competent, and may complete any such proceeding commenced by such ward or conservatee.

Laws 1975, c. 347, § 101, eff. Jan. 1, 1976. Amended by Laws 1986, c. 444.

525.38. Realty acquired

When a foreclosure sale or a sale on execution for the recovery of a debt due the estate is had or redemption is made the personal representative shall receive the money paid and execute the necessary satisfaction or release. If bid in by the personal representative or if bid in by the decedent or ward and the redemption period expired during the administration of the estate or guardianship or conservatorship without redemption, the real estate shall be treated as personal property. If not so sold, mortgaged, or leased, the real estate or, if so sold, mortgaged, or leased, the proceeds shall be assigned or distributed to the same persons and in the same proportions as if it had been part of the personal estate of the decedent, unless otherwise provided in the will.

Laws 1975, c. 347, § 102, eff. Jan. 1, 1976.

525.39.   Repealed by Laws 1975, c. 347, § 144, eff. Jan. 1, 1976

525.391.   Property fraudulently conveyed

When the property available for the payment of debts is insufficient to pay the same in full, the representative may recover any property which the decedent may have disposed of with intent to defraud creditors, or by conveyance or transfer which for any reason is void as to them.   Upon the application of any creditor and upon making the payment of or providing security for the expenses thereof as directed by the court, the representative shall prosecute all actions necessary to recover the property.

Amended by Laws 1986, c. 444.

525.392.   Property converted

If any person embezzles, alienates, or converts to personal use any of the personal estate of a decedent or ward before the appointment of a representative, such person shall be liable for double the value of the property so embezzled, alienated, or converted.

Amended by Laws 1986, c. 444.

525.393.   Disposal by coroner

When personal property of a decedent has come into the custody of any coroner and has not been surrendered as hereinafter provided and no will has been admitted to probate or no administration has been had within three months after the decedent's death, the coroner, after the expiration of said time, shall file in the court an inventory of all such property and a fingerprint of each finger of each hand of the decedent.   Wearing apparel and such other property as the coroner determines to be of nominal value, may be surrendered by the coroner to the spouse or to any blood relative of the decedent.   If no will is admitted to probate nor administration had within six months after death, the coroner shall sell the same at public auction upon such notice and in such manner as the court may direct.   The coroner shall be allowed reasonable expenses for the care and sale of the property, and shall deposit the net proceeds of such sale with the county treasurer in the name of the decedent, if known.   The treasurer shall give the coroner duplicate receipts therefor, one of which the coroner shall file with the county auditor and the other in the court. If a representative shall qualify within six years from the time of such deposit, the treasurer shall pay the same to such representative.

Amended by Laws 1975, c. 347, § 103, eff. Jan. 1, 1976; Laws 1986, c. 444.

525.40, 525.401.   Repealed by Laws 1974, c. 442, art. 8, § 524.8–102, eff. Jan. 1, 1976

525.41 to 525.46.   Repealed by Laws 1975, c. 347, § 144, eff. Jan. 1, 1976

ACCOUNTING, DISTRIBUTION

525.47.   Repealed by Laws 1974, c. 442, art. 8, § 524.8–102, eff. Jan. 1, 1976

525.475.   Dormant estate; removal of representative or attorney

(1) In a supervised administration under sections 524.3–501 to 524.3–505:

(a) If an order of complete settlement of the estate or a decree, as provided in section 524.3–1001, is not entered within 18 months after appointment of the personal representative, the court shall order the personal representative and the attorney to show good cause why an order of complete settlement of the estate or a decree has not been entered.

(b) If good cause is not shown the court shall order the removal of the personal representative, instruct the personal representative to dismiss the attorney and employ another attorney, if necessary, to complete the administration of the estate, or shall order such other or further relief as may be appropriate.   In addition, the court may refer a record of the proceeding to the state Board of Professional Responsibility.   If removal of the personal representative is ordered, the court shall also direct by order the disposition of the assets remaining in the name of, or under the control of, the personal representative being removed.

(c) If good cause is shown, the court shall order that the time for administration of the estate be extended for an additional period not to exceed one year. If an order of complete settlement of the estate or a decree, as provided in section 524.3–1001, is not entered within such extended period, the court shall again order the personal representative and the attorney to show cause why an order of complete settlement or a decree has not been entered.   If good cause is not shown, the provisions of paragraph (b) of this section shall be applicable. If good cause is shown, the court shall order that the time for administration of the estate be again extended for an additional period not to exceed one year and the provisions of this paragraph (c) of this section shall be applicable to such additional extension.

(2) In an administration other than a supervised administration under sections 524.3–501 to 524.3–505:

(a) Upon the petition of an interested person and upon showing of probable cause for relief, the court shall order the personal representative and the attorney to show cause why the estate has not been closed pursuant to the provisions of sections 524.3–1001 to 524.3–1003.

(b) If good cause is not shown, the court shall order the removal of the personal representative, instruct the personal representative to dismiss the attorney and employ another attorney, if necessary, to complete the administration of the estate or shall order such other or further relief as may be appropriate. In addition, the court may refer a record of the proceeding to the state Board of Professional Responsibility. If removal of the personal representative is ordered, the court shall also direct by order the disposition of the assets remaining in the name of, or under the control of, the personal representative being removed.

(c) If good cause is shown, the court shall enter an order so finding. An interested party may thereafter again petition the court for an order directing the personal representative and the attorney to show cause why the estate has not been closed pursuant to the provisions of sections 524.3–1001 to 524.3–1003.

(3) An attorney dismissed pursuant to this section and who is seeking attorney fees for services rendered to the estate has the burden of affirmatively proving that the estate has benefited from the services and that the benefits warrant the payment of the requested fee.

Laws 1975, c. 347, § 104, eff. Jan. 1, 1976. Amended by Laws 1986, c. 444.

525.48. Final account, attorney fees and representative fees

Any full or final account to distributees shall include a statement of attorney fees and representative fees. This statement shall include the total fees charged to date and estimated future fees to be charged.

Amended by Laws 1974, c. 442, art. 9, § 2, eff. Aug. 1, 1974; Laws 1975, c. 347, § 105, eff. Jan. 1, 1976.

Historical and Statutory Notes

Laws 1975, c. 347, § 145, provides: "Except as provided in Minnesota Statutes 1974, Section 524.8–103, this act and Laws 1974, Chapter 442 are effective on January 1, 1976."

525.481. Repealed by Laws 1974, c. 442, art. 8, § 524.8–102, eff. Jan. 1, 1976

525.482. Repealed by Laws 1974, c. 442, art. 8, § 524.8–102, eff. Jan. 1, 1976

525.483. Recording decree

A certified copy of any decree of distribution may be filed for record in the office of the county recorder of any county. It shall not be necessary to pay real estate taxes in order to record such certified copy, but the same shall be first presented to the county auditor for entry upon the transfer record and shall have noted thereon "Transfer entered" over that person's official signature. Upon request, the court shall furnish a certified copy of any decree of distribution, omitting the description of any property except that specified in the request, but indicating omissions by the words "other property omitted." Such copy and its record shall have the same force and effect as to property therein described as though the entire decree had been so certified and recorded.

Amended by Laws 1976, c. 181, § 2; Laws 1986, c. 444.

525.484. Property of deceased persons to be transferred to representatives of foreign countries in certain cases

Whenever any person who is entitled to any property in an estate is a citizen of and a resident in any foreign country with the government of which the United States maintains diplomatic relations, the personal representative of the estate may deliver or pay such property to an accredited diplomatic or consular representative of the government of such foreign country for delivery or payment to such person, or, if such property has been deposited with the county treasurer pursuant to section 524.3–914, the court upon application as therein provided shall grant its order authorizing and directing the county auditor to issue a warrant to the county treasurer to pay such money or deliver such property to such accredited diplomatic or consular representative, and the personal representative of such estate or the county treasurer shall be discharged from that person's trust and all further liability thereunder upon filing the receipt of such diplomatic or consular representative for such property with such court, provided that such diplomatic or consular representative has been licensed by proper federal authority to receive such property of the nationals of such country, where such license is required.

This section shall not apply where such citizen of and resident in any such foreign country has appeared in person or by duly authorized representative other than such diplomatic or consular representative.

Amended by Laws 1975, c. 347, § 106, eff. Jan. 1, 1976; Laws 1986, c. 444.

525.485. Repealed by Laws 1974, c. 442, art. 8, § 524.8–102, eff. Jan. 1, 1976

525.486. Termination of trusts; distribution

In any administration of an estate in probate, wherein the decedent died testate and has established a testamentary trust, and it appears to the court that the operative events have occurred whereby said trust is terminated prior to distribution in whole or in part, the court shall have jurisdiction in its discretion to adjudge and determine that said trust be terminated in whole or in part without further proceedings in any other court of general jurisdiction and may make its decree or order of distribution accordingly to the extent that the trust is no longer operative.

Laws 1975, c. 347, § 107, eff. Jan. 1, 1976.

525.49.   Repealed by Laws 1974, c. 442, art. 8, § 524.8–102, eff. Jan. 1, 1976

525.491.   Attorney's lien

When any attorney at law has been retained to appear for any heir or devisee, such attorney may perfect a lien upon the client's interest in the estate for compensation for such services as may have been rendered respecting such interest, by serving upon the personal representative before distribution is made, a notice of intent to claim a lien for agreed compensation, or the reasonable value of services. The perfecting of such a lien, as herein provided, shall have the same effect as the perfecting of a lien as provided in section 481.13, and such lien may be enforced and the amount thereupon determined in the manner therein provided.

Laws 1961, c. 265, § 2. Amended by Laws 1975, c. 347, § 108, eff. Jan. 1, 1976; Laws 1986, c. 444.

525.50.   Repealed by Laws 1974, c. 442, art. 8, § 524.8–102, eff. Jan. 1, 1976

525.501.   Repealed by Laws 1974, c. 442, art. 8, § 524.8–102, eff. Jan. 1, 1976

525.502, 525.503.   Repealed by Laws 1974, c. 442, art. 8, § 524.8–102, eff. Jan. 1, 1976

525.504.   Repealed by Laws 1981, c. 313, § 26, eff. Oct. 1, 1981

525.51.   Repealed by Laws 1995, c. 130, § 21, eff. Jan. 1, 1996.

Historical and Statutory Notes

See, now, M.S.A. § 524.3–1203, including note regarding the applicability to all decedents' estates, whenever the decedent died, of the amendment of § 524.3–1203 by Laws 1995, c. 130, § 20.

525.515.   Basis for attorney's fees

(a) Notwithstanding any law to the contrary, an attorney performing services for the estate at the instance of the personal representative, guardian or conservator shall have such compensation therefor out of the estate as shall be just and reasonable. This section shall apply to all probate proceedings.

(b) In determining what is a fair and reasonable attorney's fee effect shall be given to a prior agreement in writing by a testator concerning attorney fees. Where there is no prior agreement in writing with the testator consideration shall be given to the following factors in determining what is a fair and reasonable attorney's fee:

(1) the time and labor required;

(2) the experience and knowledge of the attorney;

(3) the complexity and novelty of problems involved;

(4) the extent of the responsibilities assumed and the results obtained; and

(5) the sufficiency of assets properly available to pay for the services;

(c) An interested person who desires that the court review attorney fees shall seek review of attorney fees in the manner provided in section 524.3–721. In determining the reasonableness of the attorney fees, consideration shall be given to all the factors listed in clause (b) and the value of the estate shall not be the controlling factor.

Laws 1971, c. 497, § 8, eff. May 26, 1971. Amended by Laws 1971, Ex.Sess., c. 48, § 50; Laws 1974, c. 442, art. 9, § 3, eff. Aug. 1, 1974; Laws 1975, c. 347, § 111, eff. Jan. 1, 1976.

Historical and Statutory Notes

Laws 1971, Ex.Sess., c. 32, § 27, provides that "the provisions of Laws 1971, chapter 497, section 8 [coded as this section], apply to a proceeding under Minnesota Statutes 1969, Section 525.51."

Laws 1971, Ex.Sess., c. 32, was the state employees pay raise bill. Laws 1971, Ex.Sess.,

c. 32, § 34, provides: "Except as otherwise provided herein, this act is effective as of October 31, 1971, except that all salary provisions made in this act shall be effective the beginning of the first pay period following November 12, 1971."

525.52.   Repealed by Laws 1974, c. 442, art. 8, § 524.8–102, eff. Jan. 1, 1976

525.521 to 525.527.   Repealed by Laws 1975, c. 347, § 144, eff. Jan. 1, 1976

525.528.   Federal estate tax; marital deduction

Whenever the decedent leaves a surviving spouse or by law the spouse is presumed to have survived and the representative of the decedent's estate, and the decedent's trustee or any other fiduciary is permitted or required to exercise a discretion, even though stated as sole, absolute or uncontrolled, to select assets in kind at values other than their values at the date or dates of distribution thereof, including values to be determined in the discretion of the representative, trustee or other fiduciary and even though such discretion is stated as sole, absolute or uncontrolled, to satisfy a bequest or transfer within the meaning of the marital deduction provisions of section 2056 of the United States Internal Revenue Code [1] or such cognate provisions of federal law as may hereafter be applicable, such representative, trustee or other fiduciary shall be subject to the general fiduciary obligation of fairness and pursuant thereto shall select assets fairly representative of appreciation or depreciation in the value of all property available on the date or dates of distribution for selection and distribution in satisfaction of such bequest or transfer, unless other language of the will or trust instrument expressly refers to this section and states that it shall not be applicable. This section shall apply to the estates of decedents dying after May 26, 1965, to trusts created after May 26, 1965, and to trusts, whenever created, which are revocable after May 26, 1965.

Laws 1965, c. 765, § 1.

[1] 26 U.S.C.A. § 2056.

ADVANCEMENTS

525.53, 525.531. Repealed by Laws 1975, c. 347, § 144, eff. Jan. 1, 1976

525.532. Disclaimer of interests passing by will, intestate succession or under certain powers of appointment

Subdivision 1. Definitions. As used in this section, unless otherwise clearly required by the context:

(a) "Beneficiary" means and includes any person entitled, but for that person's disclaimer, to take an interest: by intestate succession; by devise; by legacy or bequest; by succession to a disclaimed interest by will, intestate succession or through the exercise or nonexercise of a testamentary power of appointment; by virtue of a renunciation and election to take against a will; as beneficiary of a testamentary trust; pursuant to the exercise or nonexercise of a testamentary power of appointment; as donee of a power of appointment created by testamentary instrument; or otherwise under a testamentary instrument;

(b) "Interest" means and includes the whole of any property, real or personal, legal or equitable, or any fractional part, share or particular portion or specific assets thereof or any estate in any such property or power to appoint, consume, apply or expend property or any other right, power, privilege or immunity relating thereto;

(c) "Disclaimer" means a written instrument which declines, refuses, releases, renounces or disclaims an interest which would otherwise be succeeded to by a beneficiary, which instrument defines the nature and extent of the interest disclaimed thereby and which must be signed, witnessed and acknowledged by the disclaimant in the manner provided for deeds of real estate.

Subd. 2. Right to disclaim. A beneficiary may disclaim any interest in whole or in part, or with reference to specific parts, shares or assets thereof, by filing a disclaimer in court in the manner hereinafter provided. A guardian, executor, administrator or other personal representative of the estate of a minor, incompetent or deceased beneficiary, if that person deems it in the best interests of those interested in the estate of such beneficiary and of those who take the beneficiary's interest by virtue of the disclaimer and not detrimental to the best interests of the beneficiary, with or without an order of the probate court, may execute and file a disclaimer on behalf of the beneficiary within the time and in the manner in which the beneficiary could disclaim if living, of legal age and competent. A beneficiary likewise may execute and file a disclaimer by agent or attorney so empowered.

Subd. 3. Filing deadline. Such disclaimer shall be filed at any time after the creation of the interest, but in all events within nine months after the death of the person by whom the interest was created or from whom it would have been received, or, if the disclaimant is not finally ascertained as a beneficiary or the interest has not become indefeasibly fixed both in quality and quantity as of the death of such person, then such disclaimer shall be filed not later than nine months after the event which would cause the disclaimant so to become finally ascertained and the interest to become indefeasibly fixed both in quality and quantity.

Subd. 4. Effectiveness; procedures. Such disclaimer shall be effective upon being filed in the court in which the estate of the person by whom the interest was created or from whom it would have been received is, or has been, administered or, if no probate administration has been commenced, then in the court where it would be pending if commenced. A copy of the disclaimer shall be delivered or mailed to the personal representative, trustee or other person having legal title to, or possession of, the property in which the interest disclaimed exists, and no such representative, trustee or person shall be liable for any otherwise proper distribution or other disposition made without actual notice of the disclaimer. If an interest in or relating to real estate is disclaimed, the original of the disclaimer, or a copy of the disclaimer certified as true and complete by the court administrator of the court wherein the same has been filed, shall be filed in the office of the county recorder or the registrar of titles, as hereinafter provided, in the county or counties where the real estate is situated and shall constitute notice to all persons only from and after the time of such filing. If title to such real estate has not been registered under the provisions of chapter 508, such disclaimer or certified copy shall be filed with the county recorder. If title to such real estate has been registered under the provisions of chapter 508, such disclaimer or certified copy shall be filed with the registrar of titles.

Subd. 5. Descent of disclaimed property. Unless the person by whom the interest was created or from whom it would have been received has otherwise provided by will or other appropriate instrument with reference to the possibility of a disclaimer by the beneficiary, the property in which the interest disclaimed existed shall descend, be distributed or otherwise be disposed of in the same manner as if the disclaimant had died immediately preceding the death or other event which causes the disclaimant to become finally ascertained as a beneficiary and the interest to become indefeasibly fixed both in quality and quantity, and, in any case, the disclaimer shall relate for all purposes to such date, whether filed before or after such death or other event. However, one disclaiming an interest in a nonresiduary gift, devise or bequest shall not be excluded, unless the disclaimer so provides, from sharing in a gift, devise or bequest of the residue even though, through lapse, such residue includes the assets disclaimed. An interest of any nature in or to the estate of an intestate may be declined, refused or disclaimed as herein provided without ever vesting in the disclaimant.

Subd. 6. Limitation. The right to disclaim otherwise conferred by this section shall be barred if the beneficiary is insolvent at the time of the event giving rise to the right to disclaim. Any voluntary assignment or transfer of, or contract to assign or transfer, an interest in real or personal property, or written waiver of the right to disclaim the succession to an interest in real or personal property, by any beneficiary, or any sale or other disposition of an interest in real or personal property pursuant to judicial process, made before the beneficiary has filed a disclaimer, as herein provided, bars the right otherwise hereby conferred on such beneficiary to disclaim as to such interest.

Subd. 7. Spendthrift and similar provisions. The right to disclaim granted by this section shall exist irrespective of any limitation imposed on the interest of the disclaimant in the nature of an express or implied spendthrift provision or similar restriction. A disclaimer, when filed as provided in this section, or a written waiver of the right to disclaim, shall be binding upon the disclaimant or beneficiary so waiving and all parties thereafter claiming by, through or under that person, except that a beneficiary so waiving may thereafter transfer, assign or release the interest if such is not prohibited by an express or implied spendthrift provision. If an interest in real estate is disclaimed and the disclaimer is duly filed in accordance with the provisions of subdivision 4, the spouse of the disclaimant, if such spouse has consented to the disclaimer in writing, shall thereupon be automatically debarred from any spouse's statutory or common law right or estate by curtesy or in dower or otherwise in such real estate to which such spouse, except for such disclaimer, would have been entitled.

Subd. 8. Rights under other law. This section shall not abridge the right of any person, apart from this section, under any existing or future statute or rule of law, to disclaim any interest or to assign, convey, release, renounce or otherwise dispose of any interest.

Subd. 9. Interests existing on May 22, 1965. Any interest which exists on May 22, 1965 but which has not then become indefeasibly fixed both in quality and quantity, or the taker of which has not then become finally ascertained, may be disclaimed after May 22, 1965, in the manner provided herein.

Laws 1965, c. 552, § 1. Amended by Laws 1975, c. 347, §§ 112, 113, eff. Jan. 1, 1976; Laws 1976, c. 181, § 2; Laws 1980, c. 439, § 33; Laws 1986, c. 444; Laws 1986, 1st Sp., c. 3, art. 1, § 82.

UNIFORM DISCLAIMER OF TRANSFERS BY WILL, INTESTACY OR APPOINTMENT ACT

Table of Jurisdictions Wherein Act Has Been Adopted

For text of Uniform Act, and variation notes and annotation materials for adopting jurisdictions, see Uniform Laws Annotated, Master Addition Volume 8A.

Jurisdiction	Laws	Effective Date	Statutory Citation
Delaware	63 Del.Laws [1982], c. 448	7–23–1982[1]	12 Del.C. §§ 601 to 608.
Florida	1974, c. 74–106	7–1–1975	West's F.S.A. § 732.801.

Jurisdiction	Laws	Effective Date	Statutory Citation
Idaho	1971, c. 111	7–1–1972	I.C. § 15–2–801.
Illinois[2]	1975, P.A. 79–328	1–1–1976	S.H.A. 755 ILCS 5/2–7.
Kansas	1968, c. 367	7–1–1968	K.S.A. 59–2291 to 59–2294.
Kentucky	1974, c. 329	6–21–1974	KRS 394.610 to 394.680.
Maine	1975, c. 311	5–21–1975[1]	18–A M.R.S.A. § 2–801.
Minnesota	1965, c. 552		M.S.A. § 525.532.
Nebraska	1974, L.B.354	1–1–1977	R.R.S. 1943, § 30–2352.
New Jersey	1979, c. 484	2–28–1980	N.J.S.A. 3A:25–39 to 3A:25–50.
North Carolina . . .	1975, c. 371	10–1–1975	G.S. §§ 31B–1 to 31B–7.
Oregon	1975, c. 480	1–1–1976	ORS 112.650 to 112.667.

[1] Date of approval.

[2] See General Statutory Note, ante.

525.539 to 525.61. Repealed by Laws 2003, c. 12, art. 2, § 8

Historical and Statutory Notes

The repealed sections, which related to guardianships and conservatorships, were derived from:

Laws 2003, c. 12, art. 2, § 9, provided:

"(a) Articles 1 and 2 apply to each guardianship or conservatorship proceeding and each appointment of guardian or conservator commenced on or after the effective date of articles 1 and 2. Except as otherwise provided in this section, articles 1 and 2 apply to each guardianship or conservatorship approved by the court prior to the effective date of articles 1 and 2, and to any guardianship or conservatorship proceeding pending in court on the effective date of articles 1 and 2, unless the court finds for good cause or in the interests of judicial economy that the proceeding should be completed under the provisions of Minnesota Statutes, chapter 525, as it existed prior to the effective date of articles 1 and 2.

"(b) A guardian or conservator who is not discharged prior to the effective date of articles 1 and 2 shall continue to hold the appointment but shall have only the powers specified in the order of appointment and in Minnesota Statutes, chapter 525, as it existed prior to the effective date of articles 1 and 2. Each guardian or conservator holding an appointment on the effective date of articles 1 and 2 shall continue to be bound by the duties imposed by the order of appointment; by Minnesota Statutes, chapter 525, as it existed prior to the effective date of articles 1 and 2; and by article 1, section 50; and shall be bound by any additional duties imposed by articles 1 and 2 starting on the first day of the next month starting after the effective date of articles 1 and 2 or on the next

anniversary date of the appointment, whichever occurs later.

"(c) Any act done prior to the effective date of articles 1 and 2 in any proceeding and any right accrued under Minnesota Statutes, chapter 525, prior to the effective date of articles 1 and 2 shall not be impaired by articles 1 and 2. If a right is acquired, extinguished, or barred upon the expiration of a prescribed period of time which has commenced to run in accordance with the provisions of any statute before the effective date of articles 1 and 2, the provisions of the prior statute shall remain in force with respect to that right notwithstanding the statute's amendment or repeal by articles 1 and 2.

"(d) An order of the court or letters of guardianship or conservatorship issued by the court prior to the effective date of articles 1 and 2 shall remain in full force and effect in accordance with its terms and conditions and in accordance with the provisions of prior law until the court modifies the order or letters in accordance with the provisions of articles 1 and 2. Upon request for a certified copy of an order or letters which remains in full force and effect under this paragraph, the court administrator shall certify that the order or letters remains in full force and effect pursuant to this paragraph.

"(e) The court, without hearing or notice to any person, may issue new letters of guardianship or conservatorship under articles 1 and 2 to replace similar letters issued prior to the effective date of articles 1 and 2. The new letters shall be effective under articles 1 and 2 with the same force and effect as the prior letters and shall remain in full force and effect until modified by the court in accordance with the provisions of articles 1 and 2.

"(f) A power of attorney executed in accordance with Minnesota Statutes, section 524.5–505, prior to the effective date of articles 1 and 2, or any surety bond, deed, or other instrument, report, or other undertaking executed in accordance with Minnesota Statutes, chapter 525, prior to the effective date of articles 1 and 2, shall remain in full force and effect for all purposes in accordance with its terms and conditions and the provisions of the applicable statutes under which the power of attorney, surety bond, deed, or other instrument, report, or other undertaking was executed, until the power of attorney, surety bond, deed, or other instrument, report, or other undertaking expires according to its terms or pursuant to the statutes governing its execution, or is modified, terminated, or superseded by a new power of attorney, surety bond, deed, or other instrument, report, or other undertaking executed in accordance with the provisions of articles 1 and 2."

Prior to repeal, §§ 525.539 to 525.61 read:

"**525.539. Definitions**

"Subdivision 1. Scope. For the purposes of sections 525.54 to 525.5515; 525.56; 525.57 to 525.581; 525.583 to 525.61; 525.62; 525.63; 525.67; and 525.69, the following terms shall have the meanings given them.

"Subd. 2. Guardian. 'Guardian' means a person or entity who is appointed by the court to exercise all of the powers and duties designated in section 525.56 for the care of an incapacitated person or that person's estate, or both.

"Subd. 3. Conservator. 'Conservator' means a person appointed by the court to exercise some, but not all, of the powers designated in section 525.56 for the care of an incapacitated person or that person's estate, or both.

"Subd. 4. Ward. 'Ward' means an incapacitated person for whom the court has appointed a guardian.

"Subd. 5. Conservatee. 'Conservatee' means an incapacitated person for whom the court has appointed a conservator.

"Subd. 6. Visitor. 'Visitor' means a person who is trained in law, health care, or social work and is an officer, employee, or special appointee of the court with no personal interest in the proceedings.

"Subd. 7. Best interests of the ward or conservatee. 'Best interests of the ward or conservatee' means all relevant factors to be considered or evaluated by the court in nominating a guardian or conservator, including but not limited to:

"(1) the reasonable preference of the ward or conservatee, if the court determines the ward or conservatee has sufficient capacity to express a preference;

"(2) the interaction between the proposed guardian or conservator and the ward or conservatee; and

"(3) the interest and commitment of the proposed guardian or conservator in promoting the welfare of the ward or conservatee and the proposed guardian's or conservator's ability to maintain a current understanding of the ward's or conservatee's physical and mental status and needs. In the case of a ward or a conservatorship of the person, welfare includes:

"(i) food, clothing, shelter, and appropriate medical care;

"(ii) social, emotional, religious, and recreational requirements; and

"(iii) training, education, and rehabilitation.

"Kinship is not a conclusive factor in determining the best interests of the ward or conservatee but should be considered to the extent that it is relevant to the other factors contained in this subdivision.

"Subd. 8. Professional guardian or conservator. 'Professional guardian or conservator' means a person who acts as a guardian or conservator at the same time for two or more wards or conservatees who are not related to the guardian or conservator by blood or marriage.

"**525.54. Adults subject to guardianship and conservatorship**

"Subdivision 1. Adults subject to guardianship and conservatorship. Upon petition as provided in this chapter, the court, if satisfied of the need therefor, may appoint one or more persons suitable and competent to discharge the trust as guardians of the person or estate or of both or as conservators of the person or the estate or of both, of any incapacitated person. The county human services agency may create a screening committee to review a petition involving an indigent person. The screening committee must be made up of individuals selected by the agency with knowledge of the availability of alternatives that are less restrictive than guardianships or conservatorships. If the agency has created a screening committee, the court shall make its decision after the screening committee has reviewed the petition. For indigent persons, the court may appoint a guardian or conservator under contract with the county to provide these services.

"Subd. 2. Guardianship or conservatorship of the person. 'Incapacitated person' means, in the case of guardianship or conservatorship of the person, any adult person who is impaired to the extent of lacking sufficient understanding or capacity to make or communicate responsible personal decisions, and who has demonstrated deficits in behavior which evidence an inability to meet personal needs for medical care, nutrition, clothing, shelter, or safety.

"Subd. 3. Guardianship or conservatorship of the estate. Appointment of a guardian or conservator may be made in relation to the estate and financial affairs of an adult person: (a) voluntarily, upon the person's petition or consent in writing if the court is satisfied of the need thereof; (b) involuntarily, upon the court's determination that (1) the person is unable to manage the person's property and affairs effectively because the person is an incapacitated person, and (2) the person has property which will be dissipated unless proper management is provided, or that funds are needed for the support, care and welfare of the person or those entitled to be supported by the person, and (3) a guardian or conservator is necessary to adequately protect the person's estate or financial affairs; or (c) involuntarily, upon the court's determination that an indigent incapacitated person is institutionalized and has a demonstrated need for guardianship or conservatorship services beyond financial services available through the institution as required by chapter 144A and sections 256B.35 and 256B.36, or through the county human services agency, to the extent the agency provides these services. The need for a guardian or conservator may not be based solely on the fact that the ward or conservatee is a recipient of medical assistance or is institutionalized. 'Incapacitated person' means, in the case of guardianship or conservatorship of the estate of an adult, any adult person who is impaired to the extent that the person lacks sufficient understanding or capacity to make or communicate responsible decisions concerning the person's estate or financial affairs, and who has demonstrated deficits in behavior which evidence an inability to manage the estate, or who is unable to manage the estate or financial affairs effectively by reason of detention by a foreign power or disappearance.

"Subd. 4. Voting. The appointment of a conservator shall not deprive the conservatee of the right to vote, unless the right is restricted by court order.

"Subd. 5. Competency. Appointment of a guardian is evidence of the incompetency of the incapacitated person. Appointment of a conservator is not evidence of incompetency.

"Subd. 6. Authority to appoint guardian. Nothing contained in this section shall diminish the power of the court to appoint a guardian to serve or protect the interest of any person under disability in any proceedings therein.

"Subd. 7. Certain protective arrangements. If it is established in a proper proceeding under section 525.551 that a basis exists for the appointment of a guardian or conservator, the court, instead of appointing a guardian or conservator, may (a) authorize, direct or ratify any transaction necessary or desirable to achieve any security, service, or care arrangement meeting the foreseeable needs of the protected person. Protective arrangements include, but are not limited to: payment, delivery, deposit or retention of funds or property; sale, mortgage, lease or other transfer of property; entry into an annuity contract, a contract for life care, a deposit contract or a contract for training and education; or addition to or establishment of a suitable trust; or (b) authorize, direct or ratify any contract, trust or other transaction relating to the protected person's financial affairs or involving the protected person's estate if the court determines that the transaction is in the best interests of the protected person.

"Before approving a protective arrangement or other transaction under this subdivision, the court shall consider the interests of creditors and dependents of the protected person and, in view of the disability, whether the protected person needs the continuing protection of a guardian or conservator. The court may appoint a special conservator with or without bond to assist in the accomplishment of any protective arrangement or other transaction authorized under this subdivision, who shall have the authority conferred by the order and serve until discharged by order after making a report to the court of all matters done pursuant to the order of appointment.

"525.541. Petitioners

"Any person may petition for the appointment of a guardian or conservator or for a protective order for any person believed to be subject to guardianship or conservatorship. The petition of an adult person for the appointment of a guardian or conservator of that person or that person's estate shall have priority over the petition of any other person.

"525.542. Contents of petition

"Subdivision 1. Information. The petition shall show (1) the name and address of the person for whom a guardian or conservator, is sought, (2) the date of birth, (3) the names and addresses of living parents, children, brothers and sisters, or in the event that none of these persons are living, the names and addresses of nearest kindred, (4) if married, the name and address of the spouse, (5) the grounds for the guardianship or conservatorship, with a statement that the proposed ward or conservatee may demand a written bill of particulars, (6) if conservatorship is requested, the powers the petitioner believes are necessary in order for a conservator to protect and supervise the proposed conservatee's person or property, (7) the probable value and general character of real and personal property and the probable amount of debts, (8) the names, ages, addresses, and occupations of the proposed guardians or conservators.

"Subd. 2. Bill of particulars. A bill of particulars may be requested from the petitioner by the proposed ward or conservatee, and when so requested shall be delivered to the proposed ward or conservatee within ten days or prior to the hearing, whichever is sooner. The bill of particulars shall be in writing and shall include specific factual information which the petitioner believes supports the need for appointment of a guardian or conservator, such as mental and physical condition, financial transactions, personal actions, or actual occurrences which are claimed to demonstrate the proposed ward's or conservatee's inability to manage the estate, or to provide for personal needs for food, clothing, shelter or health care.

"**525.543. Lis pendens**

"After the filing of the petition, a certificate of the district court certified to that fact may be filed for record in the office of the county recorder of any county in which any real estate owned by the proposed ward or conservatee is situated and if a resident of this state, in the county of residence. The certificate shall state that a petition is pending and the name and address of the person for whom a guardian or conservator is sought. If a guardian or conservator is appointed on the petition, and, in the case of a conservatorship, if the conservatorship order removes or restricts the right of the conservatee to transfer property or to contract, then all contracts except for necessaries, and all transfers of real or personal property made by the ward or conservatee after the filing and before the termination of the guardianship or conservatorship shall be void.

"**525.544. Nomination or appointment of guardian or conservator**

"Subdivision 1. By proposed ward or conservatee. (a) In the petition or in a written instrument executed before or after the petition is filed, the proposed ward or conservatee may, if acting with sufficient capacity to form an intelligent preference, nominate a conservator

or guardian or give instructions to the conservator or guardian.

"(b) The written instrument must either:

"(1) be executed and attested in the same manner as a will; or

"(2) be signed by the proposed ward or conservatee, or in the proposed ward's or conservatee's name by some other individual in the presence of and at the direction of the proposed ward or conservatee, and acknowledged by the proposed ward or conservatee before a notary public who is not the nominated conservator or guardian.

"(c) The court shall appoint the person so nominated as conservator or guardian and shall charge the person with the instructions, unless the court finds that the appointment of the nominee or the instructions are not in the best interests of the proposed ward or conservatee.

"Subd. 2. Other cases. If the proposed ward or conservatee lacks capacity or fails to nominate a conservator or guardian, the court may appoint a qualified person after review by a screening committee as provided in section 525.54, subdivision 1, if any, if the court finds that the person's appointment is in the best interests of the proposed ward or conservatee. A proposed guardian or conservator need not reside in this state if the proposed guardian or conservator is able to maintain a current understanding of the ward's or conservatee's physical and mental status and needs. If the proposed ward or conservatee lacks capacity or fails to give instructions, the court may give the guardian or conservator powers as required in accordance with section 525.56. If the proposed ward or conservatee is indigent, the court may appoint a guardian or conservator under contract with the county, or a public or private agency under contract with the county, to provide these services.

"**525.545. Background study**

"Subdivision 1. When required; exception. (a) The court shall require a background study under this section:

"(1) before the appointment of a guardian or conservator, unless a background study has been done on the person under this section within the previous five years; and

"(2) once every five years after the appointment, if the person continues to serve as a guardian or conservator.

"(b) The background study must include criminal history data from the bureau of criminal apprehension and data regarding whether the person has been a perpetrator of substantiated maltreatment of a vulnerable adult.

"(c) The court shall request a search of the National Criminal Records Repository if the proposed guardian or conservator has not resided in Minnesota for the previous five years or if the bureau of criminal apprehension information received from the commissioner of human services under subdivision 2, paragraph (b), indicates that the subject is a multistate offender or that the individual's multistate offender status is undetermined.

"(d) If the guardian or conservator is not an individual, the background study must be done on all individuals currently employed by the proposed guardian or conservator who will be responsible for exercising powers and duties under the guardianship or conservatorship.

"(e) If the court determines that it would be in the best interests of the ward or conservatee to appoint a guardian or conservator before the background study can be completed, the court may make the appointment pending the results of the study.

"(f) The fee for conducting a background study for appointment of a professional guardian or conservator must be paid by the guardian or conservator. In other cases, the fee must be paid as follows:

"(1) if the matter is proceeding in forma pauperis, the fee is an expense for purposes of section 563.01;

"(2) if there is an estate of the ward or conservatee, the fee must be paid from the estate; or

"(3) in the case of a guardianship or conservatorship of the person that is not proceeding in forma pauperis, the court may order that the fee be paid by the guardian or conservator or by the court.

"(g) The requirements of this subdivision do not apply if the guardian or conservator is:

"(1) a state agency or county;

"(2) a parent or guardian of a proposed ward or conservatee who has mental retardation or a related condition, if the parent or guardian has raised the proposed ward or conservatee in the family home until the time the petition is filed, unless counsel appointed for the proposed ward or conservatee under section 525.5501 recommends a background study; or

"(3) a bank with trust powers, bank and trust company, or trust company, organized under the laws of any state or of the United States and which is regulated by the commissioner of commerce or a federal regulator.

"Subd. 2. Procedure; criminal history and maltreatment records background check. (a) The court shall request the commissioner of human services to complete a background study under section 245A.041. The request must be accompanied by the applicable fee and the signed consent of the subject of the study authorizing the release of the data obtained to the court. If the court is requesting a search of the National Criminal Records Repository, the request must be accompanied by a set of classifiable fingerprints of the subject of the study. The fingerprints must be recorded on a fingerprint card provided by the commissioner of human services.

"(b) The commissioner of human services shall provide the court with information from the bureau of criminal apprehension's criminal justice information system and data regarding substantiated maltreatment of vulnerable adults under section 626.557 within 15 working days of receipt of a request. If the subject of the study has been the perpetrator of substantiated maltreatment of a vulnerable adult, the response must include a copy of the public portion of the investigation memorandum under section 626.557, subdivision 12b. If the court did not request a search of the National Criminal Records Repository and information from the bureau of criminal apprehension indicates that the subject is a multistate offender or that multistate offender status is undetermined, the response must include this information. The commissioner shall provide the court with information from the National Criminal Records Repository within three working days of the commissioner's receipt of the data.

"(c) Notwithstanding section 626.557, subdivision 12b, if the commissioner of human services or a county lead agency has information that a person on whom a background study was previously done under this section has been determined to be a perpetrator of maltreatment of a vulnerable adult, the commissioner or the county may provide this information to the court that requested the background study. The commissioner may also provide the court with additional criminal history information that becomes available after the background study is done.

"Subd. 3. Form. The commissioner of human services shall develop a form to be used for requesting a background study under this section, which must include:

"(1) a notification to the subject of the study that the court will request the commissioner to perform a background study under this section;

"(2) a notification to the subject of the rights in subdivision 4; and

"(3) a signed consent to conduct the background study.

"Subd. 4. Rights. The court shall notify the subject of a background study that the subject has the following rights:

"(1) the right to be informed that the court will request a background study on the subject for the purpose of determining whether the person's appointment or continued appointment is in the best interests of the ward or conservatee;

"(2) the right to be informed of the results of the study and to obtain from the court a copy of the results; and

"(3) the right to challenge the accuracy and completeness of information contained in the results under section 13.04, subdivision 4, except to the extent precluded by section 256.045, subdivision 3.

"525.55. Notice of hearing

"Subdivision 1. Time of notice; to whom given. In all cases, upon the filing of the petition the court shall fix the time and place for the hearing and shall order that notice be given of the hearing. At least 14 days prior to the hearing, personal service of the notice shall be made upon the proposed ward or conservatee. Notice by mail postmarked at least 14 days before the hearing shall also be served on:

"(1) the spouse, parents, adult children, brothers and sisters;

"(2) a health care agent or proxy appointed pursuant to a health care directive as defined in section 145C.01, a living will under chapter 145B, or other similar document executed in another state and enforceable under the laws of this state; and

"(3) if none of those in clause (1) or (2) are alive or can be located, on the nearest kindred as determined by the court, and on any other persons the court may direct.

"If the person is a patient, resident, or client of any hospital, nursing home, home care agency, or other institution, notice by mail shall also be given to the administrative head of the institution. If the person is a nonresident or if after diligent search cannot be found in this state, notice shall be given in the manner and to those persons as the court may determine.

"Subd. 2. Form; service. The notice shall be written in language which can be easily understood. Included with the notice shall be a copy of the petition. The notice shall contain information regarding the nature, purpose and legal effects of the guardianship or conservatorship proceedings on the proposed ward or conservatee. The notice shall state that the person may be adjudged incapable of self care for person or property, and by reason thereof, a guardian or conservator may be appointed, and that the adjudication may transfer to the appointed guardian or conservator certain rights, including the right to manage and control property, to enter into contracts and to determine residence. The notice shall further contain information regarding the rights of the proposed ward or conservatee in the proceeding, including the right to attend the hearing, to be represented by an attorney, to oppose the proceeding, and to present evidence. The notice shall state that if the proposed ward or conservatee wishes to exercise the right to be represented by an attorney, that person must either obtain counsel of choice, or ask the court to appoint an attorney to represent that person, and that the county shall pay a reasonable attorney's fee if that person is indigent. The procedure for requesting a court appointed attorney shall be described in the notice. If the proposed ward or conservatee is a patient, resident, or client of any hospital, nursing home, home care agency, or other institution, the notice must further require the institution to advise the court of the existence, if known, of a health care directive, as defined in section 145C.01; executed by the proposed ward or conservatee, a living will executed under chapter 145B, or any other similar document executed in another state and enforceable under the laws of this state.

"The process server shall inquire whether the proposed ward or conservatee desires the notice and petition to be read to that person, and shall read the notice and petition if requested to do so. In place of a process server, the court may appoint a visitor to deliver the notice and petition and explain them to the proposed ward or conservatee.

"Subd. 3. Defective notice or service. A defect in the service of notice or process, other than personal service upon the proposed ward or conservatee within the time allowed and the form prescribed in subdivisions 1 and 2, shall not invalidate any guardianship or conservatorship proceedings.

"525.5501. Right to counsel

"Subdivision 1. General. A proposed ward or conservatee has the right to be represented by counsel at any proceeding under this chapter. The court shall appoint counsel to represent the proposed ward or conservatee for the initial proceeding held pursuant to section 525.551 if neither the proposed ward or conservatee nor others provide counsel unless in a meeting with a visitor the proposed ward or conservatee specifically waives the right to counsel. Counsel must be appointed immediately after any petition under this chapter is served under section 525.55.

"Counsel has the full right of subpoena. In all proceedings under this chapter, counsel shall:

"(1) consult with the proposed ward or proposed conservatee before any hearing;

"(2) be given adequate time to prepare for all hearings; and

"(3) continue to represent the person throughout any proceedings under section 525.551 unless released as counsel by the court.

"The court need not appoint counsel to represent the proposed ward or conservatee on a voluntary petition and the court may remove a court-appointed attorney at any time if the court finds that the proposed ward or conservatee has made a knowing and intelligent waiver of the right to counsel or has obtained private counsel.

"Subd. 2. Filing fee surcharge. A person who pays a filing fee for a petition or application under this chapter and chapter 524 shall pay a surcharge of $20, in addition to the filing fee and other surcharges imposed by law. The court administrator shall transmit the surcharge to the county treasurer for deposit in the county treasury.

"Subd. 3. Payment of counsel. A proposed ward or conservatee shall pay the costs of counsel out of assets of, or available to, the ward or conservatee. If the proposed ward or conservatee is indigent, the costs of counsel shall be paid by the county from amounts deposited in the county treasury under subdivision 2.

"Subd. 4. Exclusion. This section does not apply in the counties that make up the eighth judicial district.

"525.551. Hearing; appointment; bond; prosecution; notice

"Subdivision 1. Attendance at hearing. If the proposed ward or conservatee is within the state, that person shall be present at the hearing unless in a meeting with a visitor that person specifically waives the right to appear in person or is not able to attend by reason of medical condition as evidenced by a written statement from a licensed physician. The written statement shall be evidence only of the proposed ward's or conservatee's medical inability to attend the hearing, and shall not be considered in determining the issue of incapacity. The written statement must also inform the court of the physician's knowledge, if any, of the existence of a health care directive, as defined in section 145C.01, executed by the proposed ward or conservatee, a living will executed under chapter 145B, or any other similar document executed in another state and enforceable under the laws of this state. In any instance in which a proposed ward or conservatee is absent from the hearing, the court shall specify in its findings of fact the reason for nonattendance.

"If a visitor delivered the notice and petition pursuant to section 525.55 and the proposed ward or conservatee has waived the right to attend the hearing, the visitor may testify as to the notice and any waiver of the right to appear in person, and as to other matters which may assist the court in determining the need for a guardian or conservator and the extent of the power to be granted.

"Subd. 2. Interchangeability of petition. If the circumstances warrant, the court may treat a petition for guardianship as a petition for conservatorship.

"Subd. 3. Conduct of hearing; proof. The proposed ward or conservatee has the right to summon and cross-examine witnesses. The rules of evidence apply. In the proceedings, there is a legal presumption of capacity and the burden of proof is on the petitioner. The standard of proof is that of clear and convincing evidence.

"Subd. 4. Record of proceedings. In all proceedings the court shall take and preserve an accurate stenographic record or tape recording of the proceedings.

"Subd. 5. Findings. In all cases the court shall make specific written findings of fact, state separately its conclusions of law, and direct the entry of an appropriate judgment or order.

"If upon completion of the hearing and consideration of the record the court finds: (a) that the requirements for the voluntary appointment of a conservator or guardian have been met, or (b)(1) that the proposed ward or conservatee is incapacitated as defined in section 525.54; and (2) in need of the supervision and protection of a guardian or conservator; and (3) that no appropriate alternatives to the guardianship or conservatorship exist which are less restrictive of the person's civil rights and liberties, such as those set forth in section 525.54, subdivision 7, it shall enter its order or judgment granting all of the powers set out in section 525.56, subdivision 3, in the case of a guardian of the person, and section 525.56, subdivision 4, in the case of a guardian of the estate, or specifying the powers of the conservator pursuant to section 525.56. The court shall make a finding that appointment of the person chosen as guardian or conservator is in the best interests of the ward or conservatee. Except as provided in section 525.544, subdivision 1, if more than one person has petitioned the court to serve as guardian or conservator, or if the petition is contested, the court shall make a finding that the person to be appointed as guardian or conservator is the most suitable and best qualified person among those who are available before making the appointment. The court's finding as to the best available guardian must specifically address the reasons for the court's determination that the appointment of that person is in the best interests of the ward or conservatee. The court must also clarify the respective legal authorities of a guardian or conservator appointed under this chapter and any existing health care agent or proxy appointed under a health care directive as defined in section 145C.01, a living will under chapter 145B, or other similar document executed in another state and enforceable under the laws of this state.

"The court may enumerate in its findings which legal rights the proposed ward or conservatee is incapable of exercising.

"Subd. 6. Bond. Upon the filing of a bond by the guardian or conservator of an estate in an amount the court may direct and an oath according to law, or upon the filing of an acceptance of the trust pursuant to section 48A.08, subdivision 4, letters of guardianship or conservatorship shall issue. If there is no personal property, the court may waive the filing of a bond, but if the guardian or conservator receives or becomes entitled to any property of the ward or conservatee the guardian or conservator shall immediately file a report thereof and a bond in an amount the court may direct. In case of breach of a condition of the bond an action thereon may be prosecuted by leave of the court by any interested person or by the court on its own motion.

"Subd. 7. Notification. If a patient of a state hospital, regional center, or any state-operated service has a guardianship or conservatorship established, modified, or terminated, the head of the state hospital, regional center, or state-operated service shall be notified. If a ward or conservatee is under the guardianship or conservatorship of the commissioner of human services as mentally retarded or dependent and neglected or is under the temporary custody of the commissioner of human services, the court shall notify the commissioner of human services if the public guardianship or conservatorship is established, modified, or terminated.

"525.5515. Letters of guardianship or conservatorship

"Subdivision 1. Copy of order to ward or conservatee. A copy of the order appointing the guardian or conservator shall be served by mail upon the ward or conservatee and that person's counsel, if that person was represented at the hearing. The order shall be accompanied by a notice which advises the ward or conservatee of the right to appeal the guardianship or conservatorship appointment within 30 days.

"Subd. 2. Contents of letters. Letters of guardianship or conservatorship shall issue to the guardian or conservator. They shall contain: (a) the name, address and telephone number of the guardian or conservator; (b) the name, address and telephone number of the ward or conservatee; (c) whether it is of the estate or of the person or both; and (d) the legal limitations, if any, imposed by the court on the guardian or conservator.

"525.552. Reduction of bond

"Any conservator or guardian may deposit money belonging to the conservatee or ward, in a bank or trust company or in a savings association and make the money subject to withdrawal only upon order of the court. Upon such deposit, the court may reduce or waive bond.

"525.56. Guardian's or conservator's powers and duties

"Subdivision 1. Court's direction and control. A guardian or conservator shall be subject to the control and direction of the court at all times and in all things.

"Subd. 2. Only necessary powers. The court shall grant to a guardian or conservator only those powers necessary to provide for the demonstrated needs of the ward or conservatee.

"Subd. 3. Specific powers and duties, guardian or conservator of person. The court may appoint a guardian of the person if it determines that all the powers and duties listed in this subdivision are needed to provide for the needs of the incapacitated person. The court may appoint a conservator of the person if it determines that a conservator is needed to provide for the needs of the incapacitated person through the exercise of some, but not all, of the powers and duties listed in this subdivision. The duties and powers of a guardian or those which the court may grant to a conservator of the person include, but are not limited to:

"(1) The power to have custody of the ward or conservatee and the power to establish a place of abode within or without the state, except as otherwise provided in this clause. The ward or conservatee or any person interested in the ward's or conservatee's welfare may petition the court to prevent or to initiate a change in abode. A ward or conservatee may not be admitted to a regional treatment center by the guardian or conservator except (1) after a hearing pursuant to chapter 253B; (2) for outpatient services; or (3) for the purpose of receiving temporary care for a specific period of time not to exceed 90 days in any calendar year.

"(2) The duty to provide for the ward's or conservatee's care, comfort and maintenance needs, including food, clothing, shelter, health care, social and recreational requirements, and, whenever appropriate, training, education, and habilitation or rehabilitation. The guardian or conservator has no duty to pay for these requirements out of personal funds. Whenever possible and appropriate, the guardian or conservator should meet these requirements through governmental benefits or services to which the ward or conservatee is entitled, rather than from the ward's or conservatee's estate. Failure to satisfy the needs and requirements of this clause shall be grounds for removal of a private guardian or conservator, but the guardian or conservator shall have no personal or monetary liability.

"(3) The duty to take reasonable care of the ward's or conservatee's clothing, furniture, vehicles, and other personal effects, and, if other property requires protection, the power to seek appointment of a guardian or conservator of the estate. The guardian or conservator must give notice in the manner required and to those persons specified in section 525.55 prior to the disposition of the ward's or conservatee's clothing, furniture, vehicles, or other personal effects. The notice must inform the person of the right to object to the disposition of the property within ten days and to petition the court for a review of the guardian's or conservator's proposed actions. Notice of the objection must be served by mail or personal service on the guardian or conservator and the ward or conservatee unless the ward or conservatee be the objector. The guardian or conservator served with notice of an objection to the disposition of the property may not dispose of the property unless the court approves the disposition after a hearing.

"(4)(a) The power to give any necessary consent to enable the ward or conservatee to receive necessary medical or other professional care, counsel, treatment or service, except that no guardian or conservator may give consent for psychosurgery, electroshock, sterilization, or experimental treatment of any kind unless the procedure is first approved by order of the court as provided in this clause. The guardian or conservator shall not consent to any medical care for the ward or conservatee which violates the known conscientious, religious, or moral belief of the ward or conservatee.

"(b) A guardian or conservator who believes a procedure described in clause (4)(a) requiring prior court approval to be necessary for the proper care of the ward or conservatee shall petition the court for an order and, in the case of a public guardianship or conservatorship under chapter 252A, obtain the written recommendation of the commissioner of human services. The court shall fix the time and place for the hearing and shall give notice to the ward or conservatee and to the other persons specified in section 525.55, subdivision 1. The notice shall comply with the requirements of, and be served in the manner provided in section 525.55, subdivision 2. The court shall appoint an attorney to represent the ward or conservatee who is not represented by counsel. In every case the court shall determine if the procedure is in the best interests of the ward or conservatee. In making its determination, the court shall consider a written medical report which specifically considers the medical risks of the procedure, whether alternative, less restrictive methods of treatment could be used to protect the best interests of the ward or conservatee, and any recommendation of the commissioner of human services for a public ward or conservatee. The standard of proof is that of clear and convincing evidence.

"(c) In the case of a petition for sterilization of a mentally retarded ward or conservatee, the court shall appoint a licensed physician, a psychologist who is qualified in the diagnosis and treatment of mental retardation, and a social worker who is familiar with the ward's or conservatee's social history and adjustment or the case manager for the ward or conservatee to examine or evaluate the ward or conservatee and to provide written reports to the court. The reports shall indicate why sterilization is being proposed, whether sterilization is necessary and is the least intrusive method for alleviating the problem presented, and whether it is in the best interests of the ward or conservatee. The medical report shall specifically consider the medical risks of sterilization, the consequences of not performing the sterilization, and whether alternative methods of contraception could be used to protect the best interests of the ward or conservatee.

"(d) Any conservatee whose right to consent to a sterilization has not been restricted under this section or section 252A.101, may be sterilized only if the conservatee consents in writing or there is a sworn acknowledgment by an interested person of a nonwritten consent by the conservatee. The consent must certify that the conservatee has received a full explanation from a physician or registered nurse of the nature and irreversible consequences of the sterilization operation.

"(e) A guardian or conservator or the public guardian's designee who acts within the scope of authority conferred by letters of guardianship under section 252A.101, subdivision 7, and according to the standards established in this chapter or in chapter 252A shall not be civilly or criminally liable for the provision of any necessary medical care, including but not limited to, the administration of psychotropic medication or the implementation of aversive and deprivation procedures to which the guardian or conservator or the public guardian's designee has consented.

"(5) The power to approve or withhold approval of any contract, except for necessities, which the ward or conservatee may make or wish to make.

"(6) The duty and power to exercise supervisory authority over the ward or conservatee in a manner which limits civil rights and restricts personal freedom only to the extent necessary to provide needed care and services.

"Subd. 4. Duties of guardian or conservator of the estate. The court may appoint a guardian of the estate if it determines that all the powers and duties listed in this subdivision are needed to provide for the needs of the incapacitated person. The court may appoint a conservator of the estate if it determines that a conservator is necessary to provide for the needs of the incapacitated person through the exercise of some, but not all, of the powers and duties listed in this subdivision. The duties and powers of a guardian or those which the court may grant to a conservator include, but are not limited to:

"(1) The duty to pay the reasonable charges for the support, maintenance, and education of the ward or conservatee in a manner suitable to the ward's or conservatee's station in life and the value of the estate. Nothing herein contained shall release parents from obligations imposed by law for the support, maintenance, and education of their children. The guardian or conservator has no duty to pay for these requirements out of personal funds. Wherever possible and appropriate, the guardian or conservator should meet these requirements through governmental benefits or services to which the ward or conservatee is entitled, rather than from the ward's or conservatee's estate. Failure to satisfy the needs and requirements of this clause shall be grounds for removal, but the guardian or conservator shall have no personal or monetary liability;

"(2) The duty to pay out of the ward's or conservatee's estate all just and lawful debts of the ward or conservatee and the reasonable charges incurred for the support, maintenance, and education of the ward's or conservatee's spouse and dependent children and, upon order of the court, pay such sum as the court may fix as reasonable for the support of any person

unable to earn a livelihood who is legally entitled to support from the ward or conservatee;

"(3) The duty to possess and manage the estate, collect all debts and claims in favor of the ward or conservatee, or, with the approval of the court, compromise them, institute suit on behalf of the ward or conservatee and represent the ward or conservatee in any court proceedings, and invest all funds not currently needed for the debts and charges named in clauses (1) and (2) and the management of the estate, in accordance with the provisions of sections 48A.07, subdivision 6, and 501B.151, or as otherwise ordered by the court. The standard of a fiduciary shall be applicable to all investments by a guardian or conservator. A guardian or conservator shall also have the power to purchase certain contracts of insurance as provided in section 50.14, subdivision 14, clause (b);

"(4) Where a ward or conservatee has inherited an undivided interest in real estate, the court, on a showing that it is for the best interest of the ward or conservatee, may authorize an exchange or sale of the ward's or conservatee's interest or a purchase by the ward or conservatee of any interest other heirs may have in the real estate.

"Subd. 5. Transaction set aside. If a ward or conservatee has made a financial transaction or gift or entered into a contract during the two-year period before establishment of the guardianship or conservatorship, the guardian or conservator may petition for court review of the transaction, gift, or contract. If the court finds that the ward or conservatee was incompetent or subject to duress, coercion, or undue influence when the transaction, gift, or contract was made, the court may declare the transaction, gift, or contract void except as against a bona fide transferee for value and order reimbursement or other appropriate relief. This subdivision does not affect any other right or remedy that may be available to the ward or conservatee with respect to the transaction, gift, or contract.

"525.561. Contents of inventory

"Within one month after appointment, unless a longer time has been granted by the court, every guardian or conservator shall make and exhibit to the court a verified inventory of all the estate of the ward or conservatee which shall have come to the guardian's or conservator's possession or knowledge. Such property shall be classified therein as follows: (1) real estate, with plat or survey description, and if a homestead, designated as such, (2) furniture and household goods, (3) wearing apparel, (4) corporation stocks described by certificate numbers, (5) mortgages, bonds, notes, and other written evidence of debt, described by name of debtor, recording data, or other identification, (6) all other personal property accurately identified. All encumbrances, liens, and other charges on any item shall be stated. The guardian or conservator shall set forth in the inventory the fair market value of all assets listed therein. If appraisers are appointed by the court, the value of assets other than those assets specified in section 525.562, subdivision 1, clause (b) shall be determined by the court appointed appraisers. Such value shall be the value at the date of appointment of the guardian or conservator. Such inventory shall show the net value of each item after deducting all encumbrances, liens and charges and the total net value of each class of items and of all classes.

"525.562. Appraisal

"Subdivision 1. Inventory without appraisal. For the usual purposes of administration, the inventory filed by the guardian or conservator pursuant to section 525.561 shall be sufficient without any appraisal of assets by court appointed appraisers in the following instances:

"(a) Where no sale of assets is to be made, and then an appraisal shall be had only as to assets which are to be sold and which are not included in clause (b) below.

"(b) As to the following assets:

"(1) Cash or deposits in any financial institution;

"(2) Securities, bonds or other obligations of the United States government or agency thereof; and

"(3) Securities listed on the New York Stock Exchange or the American Stock Exchange, and such other securities markets as may be designated by a rule of court, if the market value thereof can be readily ascertained.

"Subd. 2. Appointment of appraisers; duties. In all other instances, and in all instances enumerated under clauses (a) and (b) above where an appraisal is necessary for some special administrative purpose, the court shall appoint two or more disinterested and qualified appraisers who shall appraise the assets required to be appraised and shall set down in figures after each item after deducting the encumbrances, liens and charges, the net value thereof and show the total amount of each class, and of all classes, and forthwith deliver such inventory and appraisal certified by them, to the guardian, or conservator, who shall immediately file the same. Such assets shall be appraised at the fair market value thereof as of the date of the appointment of the guardian or conservator or time of sale of assets as circumstances may require as directed by the court.

"Subd. 3. Appraisal fees, disbursements, and expenses. The appraisers shall be allowed such reasonable fees, necessary disbursements and expenses as may be fixed by the court, and be paid by the guardian or conservator as expenses of guardianship or conservatorship. In fixing the fee so allowed, the court shall not give any consideration to items not requiring appraisal by this section, even though such assets be included with other appraisable assets in an inventory and appraisal filed pursuant hereto.

"525.57. Transfer of venue

"When it is for the best interest of the ward or conservatee or the estate the venue may be transferred to another county. Upon the filing of a petition by any person interested in the ward or conservatee or in the estate the court shall fix the time and place for the hearing thereof, and shall give notice to the persons and in the manner required by section 525.55. Upon proof that a transfer of venue is for the best interest of the ward or conservatee or the estate, and upon the settlement and allowance of the guardian's or conservator's accounts to the time of the hearing, the court shall transmit the entire file to the court of the other county where all subsequent proceedings shall be held.

"525.58. Filing of accounts; filing of affidavit

"Subdivision 1. Annual account. Except where expressly waived or modified by the court, every guardian or conservator of the estate annually shall file with the court within 30 days of the anniversary date of the guardian's or conservator's appointment a verified account covering the period from the date of appointment or the last account. The guardian or conservator of the estate shall give a copy of the annual account to the ward or conservatee except where expressly waived by the court after a finding that the ward or conservatee is so incapacitated as to be unable to understand the account or there is a serious likelihood of harm to the ward or conservatee. The court or its designee shall annually review the court file to insure that the account has been filed and that the account contains the information required by this section. If an account has not been filed or if the account does not contain the information required by this section the court shall order the guardian or conservator to file an appropriate account. The examination and acceptance shall not constitute an adjudication or determination of the merits of the account filed nor shall it constitute the court's approval of the account. At the termination of the guardianship or conservatorship, or upon the guardian's or conservator's removal or resignation, the guardian or conservator or the surety, or in the event of death or disability, the guardian's or conservator's representative or surety shall file a verified final account with a petition for the settlement and allowance thereof. Every account shall show in detail all property received and disbursed, the property on hand, the present address of the ward or conservatee and of the guardian or conservator, and unless the guardian or conservator be a corporation, the amount of the bond, the names and addresses of all sureties thereon, that each unincorporated surety is a resident of this state, is not under disability, and is worth the amount in which the surety justified.

"Subd. 2. Notice of right to petition for restoration of capacity. Except where expressly waived by the court after a finding that the ward or conservatee is so incapacitated as to be unable to understand any notice, or there is a serious likelihood of harm to the ward or conservatee, every guardian or conservator shall annually give notice to the ward or conservatee of the right to petition for restoration to capacity, discharge of guardian or conservator, or modification of the orders of guardianship or conservatorship. A waiver shall not be effective for more than two years without a redetermination by the court. The notice shall describe the procedure for preparing and filing such a petition. Notice shall also inform the ward or conservatee that after a petition is filed the court will hold a hearing on the matter and that the ward or conservatee has the right to be present and to be represented by counsel at the hearing. The form of the notice shall be approved or supplied by the court.

"Subd. 3. Affidavit. Except where expressly waived by the court as provided in subdivision 2, every guardian or conservator shall file annually with the court an affidavit of having given the notice required by subdivision 2 to the ward or conservatee and every guardian or conservator of an estate shall file an affidavit stating that a copy of the annual account has been given to the ward or conservatee.

"Subd. 4. Annual report of the guardian of the person. Except where expressly waived by the court, every guardian or conservator of the person shall annually file a report under oath with the court within 30 days of the anniversary date of the appointment of the guardian or conservator. The report shall contain the guardian's or conservator's good faith evaluation of the following information for the preceding year:

"(a) changes in the medical condition of the ward or conservatee;

"(b) changes in the living conditions of the ward or conservatee;

"(c) changes in the mental and emotional condition of the ward or conservatee;

"(d) a listing of hospitalizations of the ward or conservatee; and

"(e) if the ward or conservatee is institutionalized, an evaluation of the care and treatment received by the ward or conservatee, and if the ward or conservatee is indigent, a review of the continued need for guardian or conservator services beyond those provided by the institution or the county human services agency. The court shall request the assistance of the county human services agency to assist in making this need determination. If a continued need for guardian or conservator services exists, the county may contract for these services with other public or private agencies.

"The court or its designee shall annually review the court file to insure that the report has been filed and that the report contains the information required by this subdivision. If a report has not been filed or if the report does not contain the information required by this subdivision, the court shall order the guardian or conservator to file an appropriate report.

"525.581. Notice of hearing on account

"The court on its own motion may, or upon the petition of the guardian, conservator, ward, conservatee, or any person interested in the ward or conservatee or the ward's or conservatee's estate shall, fix the time and place for the hearing on any account, notice of which shall be given to the ward or conservatee and to other persons as the court may direct. Wherever any funds have been received from the veterans' administration, notice by mail shall be given to the regional office having charge thereof.

"525.582. Adjudication on account

"(a) Unless otherwise ordered, the guardian or conservator shall, and other persons may, be examined on the hearing. If the account be correct, it shall be settled and allowed; if incorrect, it shall be corrected and then settled and allowed. The order of settlement and allowance shall show the amount of the personal property remaining. Upon settlement of the final account, and upon delivery of the property on hand to the person entitled thereto, the court shall discharge the guardian or conservator and the sureties. Any person for whom a guardian or conservator has been appointed and who has become of age or has been restored to capacity may show to the court that the person has settled with the guardian or conservator and may petition for the guardian's or conservator's discharge without further hearing. Upon such petition, the court may discharge the guardian or conservator and the sureties.

"(b) If, after hearing on notice as the court may require to the guardian, conservator and any surety, there is determined to be mismanagement, a shortage of funds, or other misconduct for which the guardian, conservator or a surety is liable, the court shall settle the account and enter judgment against the guardian, conservator or any surety as may be appropriate. The judgment may be filed, docketed and enforced in the same manner as any other judgment. This remedy is in addition to any other remedy available for breach of any condition of the bond.

"(c) The resignation of a guardian or conservator shall not take effect until the court examines and allows the final account and makes an order accepting the resignation.

"(d) If a guardian or conservator becomes unsuitable, incapacitated or disabled, or violates the trust or fails to perform any duty imposed by law or the lawful order of the court, the court upon petition or the court's own motion may remove the guardian or conservator after notice.

"**525.583. Allowance and wages of conservatee; limited accountability of conservator**

"The court, upon its own motion or upon petition of the conservator or conservatee, may authorize or direct the conservator to pay to the conservatee out of the conservatorship estate a reasonable allowance for the personal use of the conservatee in the amount the court may determine to be for the best interests of the conservatee. Unless otherwise ordered by the court, if the conservatee shall at any time during the continuance of the conservatorship be employed, the wages or salary for employment shall not be a part of the conservatorship estate and the wages and salaries shall be paid to, and be subject to the control of, the conservatee to the same extent as if the conservatorship did not exist. The conservator shall not be accountable for the allowances or wages and salary.

"**525.59. Succeeding guardian or conservator**

"If a guardian or conservator dies, resigns, or is removed, the court may appoint a successor with at least 14 days prior notice to the ward or conservatee, a spouse, parents, adult children and siblings, and to other persons as the court may direct. A ward or conservatee having capacity to do so may nominate a person to serve as successor or may give instructions to the succeeding guardian or conservator or may do both. The court shall appoint the person so nominated and shall charge the appointee with the instructions, unless the court finds that the appointment of the nominee or the instructions

or both are not in the best interests of the ward or conservatee."

"**525.591. Special guardian or conservator**

"Subdivision 1. Petition. A person may file a verified petition for a special guardian or conservator. The petition must contain:

"(1) all of the information required in section 525.542;

"(2) the reasons that the petitioner believes the proposed ward or conservatee is in need of a special guardian or conservator; and

"(3) the reasons why the regular procedure for obtaining guardianship or conservatorship is not appropriate.

"Subd. 2. Hearing on application; notice. Upon receipt of a petition under this section, the court shall order a hearing to be held no later than 14 days from the date of the order and no sooner than 48 hours from the date of the order. Personal service notifying the proposed conservatee or ward of the scheduled hearing must be made immediately after receipt of a hearing date and at least 48 hours before the scheduled hearing date. Notice must be given in language which can be easily understood and must contain the information required by section 525.55, subdivision 2, regarding the purpose of the hearing and the rights of the proposed ward or conservatee. A copy of the petition must be served with the notice.

"Subd. 2a. Emergency appointment. (a) The court may waive the notice and hearing requirements in subdivision 2 upon a showing that immediate and reasonably foreseeable and irreparable harm to the person or the person's estate will result from a 48–hour delay. The court must make findings of fact in its order that support such a showing. Only under those circumstances may the court appoint a special guardian or conservator without notice. Notice of an appointment must be personally served on the proposed ward or conservatee.

"(b) An appointment without notice or hearing under paragraph (a) expires seven days after the court's order unless the petitioner has scheduled a hearing under subdivision 2, in which case the special conservatorship or special guardianship remains in effect until the hearing.

"Subd. 2b. Adults; showing required. Only upon a clear showing of necessity may a court appoint any special guardian or special conservator of an adult person, as designated in section 525.54, whether or not a petition for general guardianship or conservatorship has been filed. In its order, the court must make specific findings of fact establishing the necessity of the appointment of the special guardian or conservator.

"Subd. 3. No appeal. There shall be no appeal from any order appointing or refusing to appoint a special guardian or conservator.

"Subd. 4. Limited powers. The court shall grant to a special guardian or conservator only those powers necessary to provide for the demonstrated needs of the ward or conservatee as provided for in the powers enumerated and specified in section 525.56.

"Subd. 5. Inventory and appraisal. Within 14 days after appointment, a special guardian or conservator of the estate shall file an inventory and appraisal of the personal property according to the requirements of sections 525.561 and 525.562. The court shall specify in its order the duration of the special guardianship or conservatorship. Except as otherwise provided in this section, the appointment of a special guardian or conservator may not exceed 30 days in duration. A county that is acting under section 626.557, subdivision 10, by petitioning for appointment of a special guardian or conservator on behalf of a vulnerable adult is not subject to this 30–day limit.

"Subd. 6. Duration limits; exceptions. If a petition is filed requesting appointment of a general guardian or conservator for a person for whom a special guardian or conservator has been appointed, but a final hearing on the petition cannot be held after proper notice within 30 days of the appointment of the special guardian or conservator because the petition becomes contested, a hearing date is not available within the time limit or other good cause exists, the appointment of the special guardian or conservator may be extended as provided in this subdivision. The court, on its own motion or upon request of the petitioner or the special guardian or conservator, may extend the appointment to the date of the hearing on the petition. At that time, if the court finds that grounds for appointment of the special guardian or conservator still exist, the court may further extend the appointment to the date of a final decision on the petition. If a special guardian or conservator is appointed for the sole purpose of representing the ward or conservatee in litigation or any other legal proceeding, other than the pending guardianship or conservatorship proceedings, the court may specify that the appointment will last until the litigation or proceeding is finally concluded.

"Subd. 7. Final accounting. The power of a special guardian or conservator ends and the special guardian or conservator must prepare a final accounting when one of the following events first occurs:

"(1) the time specified for the special guardianship or conservatorship in the court order has expired; or

"(2) a general guardian or conservator has been appointed for the ward or conservatee.

"If a special guardian or conservator has been appointed to protect the ward's or conservatee's interest in any matter wherein the interest of the general guardian or conservator appears to conflict with that of the ward or conservatee, or to protect the ward's or conservatee's interest upon suspension of an order of removal of a general guardian or conservator by appeal, the power of the special guardian or conservator shall not cease until terminated by the court."

"525.60. Termination

"Subdivision 1. The guardianship or conservatorship of an adult ward or conservatee shall terminate upon death or upon the ward's or conservatee's restoration to capacity. When there is no further need for any guardianship or conservatorship, the court may terminate the same upon notice as it may direct. Termination does not affect a guardian's or conservator's liability for prior acts, nor the obligation to account for funds and assets of the ward or conservatee."

"525.61. Restoration to capacity; modification of guardianship or conservatorship

"Subdivision 1. General. Any adult person who is under guardianship or conservatorship or the guardian or conservator, or any other person may petition the court in which the person was so adjudicated to be restored to capacity or to have a guardianship transferred to a conservatorship or to modify the guardianship or conservatorship. Upon the filing of the petition, the court shall fix the time and place for the hearing thereof, notice of which shall be given to the ward or conservatee, guardian or conservator, and to those other persons and in a manner provided in section 525.55.

"Subd. 2. Restoration to capacity. To obtain an order of restoration to capacity the petitioner must prove by a preponderance of the evidence that the ward or conservatee is no longer incapacitated as defined in section 525.54, and is able to make provisions for personal care or self-management of property. If a ward or conservatee has the functional ability to care for self or for property, or to make provisions for personal care or the care of property, the fact of impairment to some extent by a mental condition shall not preclude restoration to capacity. In any proceedings for restoration, the court may appoint one person duly licensed by a health related licensing board and one

accredited social worker with expertise in eval-
uating persons who have the disabilities similar
to those found to be the reason for the ward's or
conservatee's incapacity, to assist in the determination of mental condition and functional
ability to care for self or property. The court
shall allow and order paid to each health professional and social worker a reasonable sum
for services. Upon the order, the county auditor shall issue a warrant on the county treasurer
for the payment thereof.

"Subd. 3. Appointment of new guardian or
conservator. Upon a motion to remove a
guardian or conservator and appoint a new
guardian or conservator, the court shall consider whether the existing guardian or conservator
has performed the applicable duties and wheth-

er the continued appointment of the guardian or
conservator is in the best interests of the ward
or conservatee. The court shall appoint a new
guardian or conservator if it finds that:

"(1) the existing guardian or conservator has
failed to perform the duties associated with the
guardianship or conservatorship or to provide
for the best interests of the ward or conservatee;
and

"(2) the best interests of the ward or conservatee will be better served by the appointment
of a new guardian or conservator.

"The court's decision must include the specific findings required by section 525.551, subdivision 5."

525.611 to 525.614.   Repealed by Laws 1980, c. 493, § 40, eff. Aug. 1, 1981

Historical and Statutory Notes

Laws 1981, 2nd Sp., c. 6, § 1, provides:

"Laws 1980, Chapter 493 and Laws 1981,
Chapter 313, are effective October 1, 1981."

525.615 to 525.62.   Repealed by Laws 2003, c. 12, art. 2, § 8

Historical and Statutory Notes

Laws 2003, c. 12, art. 2, § 9, provided:

"(a) Articles 1 and 2 apply to each guardianship or conservatorship proceeding and each
appointment of guardian or conservator commenced on or after the effective date of articles
1 and 2. Except as otherwise provided in this
section, articles 1 and 2 apply to each guardianship or conservatorship approved by the court
prior to the effective date of articles 1 and 2,
and to any guardianship or conservatorship
proceeding pending in court on the effective
date of articles 1 and 2, unless the court finds
for good cause or in the interests of judicial
economy that the proceeding should be completed under the provisions of Minnesota Statutes, chapter 525, as it existed prior to the
effective date of articles 1 and 2.

"(b) A guardian or conservator who is not
discharged prior to the effective date of articles
1 and 2 shall continue to hold the appointment
but shall have only the powers specified in the
order of appointment and in Minnesota Statutes, chapter 525, as it existed prior to the
effective date of articles 1 and 2. Each guardian or conservator holding an appointment on
the effective date of articles 1 and 2 shall continue to be bound by the duties imposed by the
order of appointment; by Minnesota Statutes,

chapter 525, as it existed prior to the effective
date of articles 1 and 2; and by article 1,
section 50; and shall be bound by any additional duties imposed by articles 1 and 2 starting on
the first day of the next month starting after the
effective date of articles 1 and 2 or on the next
anniversary date of the appointment, whichever
occurs later.

"(c) Any act done prior to the effective date of
articles 1 and 2 in any proceeding and any right
accrued under Minnesota Statutes, chapter 525,
prior to the effective date of articles 1 and 2
shall not be impaired by articles 1 and 2. If a
right is acquired, extinguished, or barred upon
the expiration of a prescribed period of time
which has commenced to run in accordance
with the provisions of any statute before the
effective date of articles 1 and 2, the provisions
of the prior statute shall remain in force with
respect to that right notwithstanding the statute's amendment or repeal by articles 1 and 2.

"(d) An order of the court or letters of guardianship or conservatorship issued by the court
prior to the effective date of articles 1 and 2
shall remain in full force and effect in accordance with its terms and conditions and in
accordance with the provisions of prior law
until the court modifies the order or letters in

accordance with the provisions of articles 1 and 2. Upon request for a certified copy of an order or letters which remains in full force and effect under this paragraph, the court administrator shall certify that the order or letters remains in full force and effect pursuant to this paragraph.

"(e) The court, without hearing or notice to any person, may issue new letters of guardianship or conservatorship under articles 1 and 2 to replace similar letters issued prior to the effective date of articles 1 and 2. The new letters shall be effective under articles 1 and 2 with the same force and effect as the prior letters and shall remain in full force and effect until modified by the court in accordance with the provisions of articles 1 and 2.

"(f) A power of attorney executed in accordance with Minnesota Statutes, section 524.5–505, prior to the effective date of articles 1 and 2, or any surety bond, deed, or other instrument, report, or other undertaking executed in accordance with Minnesota Statutes, chapter 525, prior to the effective date of articles 1 and 2, shall remain in full force and effect for all purposes in accordance with its terms and conditions and the provisions of the applicable statutes under which the power of attorney, surety bond, deed, or other instrument, report, or other undertaking was executed, until the power of attorney, surety bond, deed, or other instrument, report, or other undertaking expires according to its terms or pursuant to the statutes governing its execution, or is modified, terminated, or superseded by a new power of attorney, surety bond, deed, or other instrument, report, or other undertaking executed in accordance with the provisions of articles 1 and 2."

Prior to repeal, §§ 525.615 to 525.62 read:

"**525.615. Status of guardian of minor; general**

"A person becomes a guardian of a minor by acceptance of a testamentary appointment or upon appointment by the court. The guardianship status continues until terminated, without regard to the location from time to time of the guardian and minor ward.

"**525.6155. Testamentary appointment of guardian of minor**

"The parent of a minor may appoint by will a guardian of an unmarried minor. Subject to the right of the minor under section 525.616, a testamentary appointment becomes effective upon filing the guardian's acceptance in the court in which the will is probated, if before acceptance, both parents are dead or the surviving parent is adjudged incapacitated. If both parents are dead, an effective appointment by

the parent who died later has priority. This state recognizes a testamentary appointment effected by filing the guardian's acceptance under a will probated in another state which is the testator's domicile. Upon acceptance of appointment, written notice of acceptance must be given within five days by the guardian to the minor, to the person having the minor's care, to the minor's adult siblings, grandparents, aunts and uncles. Notice shall state that any person interested in the welfare of the minor, or the minor, if 14 or more years of age, may file with the court a written objection to the appointment in accordance with section 525.616.

"**525.616. Objection by minor of 14 or older or interested adult to testamentary appointment**

"A minor of 14 or more years or any adult interested in the minor's welfare may prevent an appointment of the minor's testamentary guardian from becoming effective, or may cause a previously accepted appointment to terminate, by filing with the court in which the will is probated a written objection to the appointment before it is accepted or within 30 days after its acceptance. An objection may be withdrawn. An objection does not preclude appointment by the court in a proper proceeding of the testamentary nominee, or any other suitable person.

"**525.6165. Court appointment of guardian of minor; conditions for appointment**

"The court may appoint a guardian for an unmarried minor if all parental rights of custody have been terminated or suspended by prior court order. A guardian appointed by will as provided in section 525.6155 whose appointment has not been prevented or nullified under section 525.616 has priority over any guardian who may be appointed by the court but the court may proceed with an appointment upon a finding that the testamentary guardian has failed to accept the testamentary appointment within 30 days after notice of the guardianship proceeding.

"**525.617. Court appointment of guardian of minor; venue**

"The venue for guardianship proceedings for a minor is in the place where the minor resides or is present.

"**525.6175. Court appointment of guardian of minor; qualification; priority of minor's nominee**

"The court may appoint as guardian any person whose appointment would be in the best interests of the minor. The court shall appoint a person nominated by the minor, if the minor is 14 years of age or older, unless the court finds the appointment contrary to the best interests of the minor.

"525.618. Court appointment of guardian of minor; procedure

"Subdivision 1. Time of notice; to whom. Notice of the time and place of hearing of a petition for the appointment of a guardian of a minor shall be given by the petitioner in the following manner and to the following persons:

"(a) The minor, if 14 or more years of age, by personal service at least 14 days prior to the date of hearing;

"(b) The person who has had the principal care and custody of the minor during the 60 days preceding the date of the petition by personal service, at least 14 days prior to the date of hearing;

"(c) Any living parent of the minor residing in Minnesota by personal service, at least 14 days prior to the date of hearing;

"(d) Any living parent of the minor residing outside of Minnesota, and any adult brothers and sisters of the minor, service by mail, at least 14 days prior to the date of hearing; and

"(e) To any other persons that the court may direct.

"Subd. 2. Required findings. Upon hearing, if the court finds that a qualified person seeks appointment, venue is proper, the required notices have been given, the requirements of section 525.6165 have been met, and the welfare and best interests of the minor will be served by the requested appointment, it shall make the appointment. In other cases the court may dismiss the proceedings, or make any other disposition of the matter that will best serve the interests of the minor.

"Subd. 3. Temporary guardian. If necessary, the court may appoint a temporary guardian, with the status of an ordinary guardian of a minor, but the authority of a temporary guardian shall not last longer than six months.

"Subd. 4. Attorney for minor. If, at any time in the proceeding, the court determines that the interests of the minor are or may be inadequately represented, it may appoint an attorney to represent the minor, giving consideration to the preference of the minor if the minor is 14 years of age or older.

"Subd. 5. Copy of order to ward or conservatee. A copy of an order appointing a guardian or conservator of a minor shall be served by mail upon the ward or conservatee and counsel, if represented at the hearing. The order shall be accompanied by a notice which advises the ward or conservatee of the right to appeal the

guardianship or conservatorship appointment within 30 days.

"Subd. 6. Contents of letters. Letters of guardianship or conservatorship shall issue to the guardian or conservator. They shall contain: (a) the name, address, and telephone number of the guardian or conservator; (b) the name, address, and telephone number of the ward or conservatee; (c) whether it is a guardianship or conservatorship or both; and (d) the legal limitations, if any, imposed by the court on the guardian or conservator.

"525.6185. Consent to service by acceptance of appointment; notice

"By accepting a testamentary or court appointment as guardian, a guardian submits personally to the jurisdiction of the court in any proceeding relating to the guardianship that may be instituted by any interested person. Notice of any proceeding shall be given by mail or personal service upon the guardian at least 14 days prior to the date of the hearing.

"525.619. Powers and duties of guardian of minor

"A guardian of a minor has the powers and responsibilities of a parent who has not been deprived of custody of the minor and unemancipated child, except that a guardian is not legally obligated to provide from the guardian's own funds for the ward. In particular, and without qualifying the foregoing, a guardian:

"(a) must take reasonable care of the ward's personal effects and commence protective proceedings if necessary to protect other property of the ward.

"(b) may receive money payable for the support of the ward to the ward's parent, guardian or custodian under the terms of any statutory benefit or insurance system, or any private contract, devise, trust, conservatorship or custodianship and also may receive money or property of the ward paid or delivered by virtue of section 525.6196. Any sums so received shall be applied to the ward's current needs for support, care and education. The guardian must exercise due care to conserve any excess for the ward's future needs unless a conservator has been appointed for the estate of the ward, in which case the excess shall be paid over at least annually to the conservator. Sums so received by the guardian are not to be used for compensation for the guardian's services except as approved by order of court or as determined by a duly appointed conservator other than the guardian. A guardian may institute proceedings to compel the performance by any person of a duty to support the ward or to pay sums for the welfare of the ward.

"(c) The guardian is empowered to facilitate the ward's education, social, or other activities and to authorize medical or other professional care, treatment or advice. A ward who is less than 16 years of age may be admitted to a treatment facility as an informal patient according to section 253B.04 but may not be committed to any state institution except pursuant to chapter 253B. No guardian may give consent for psychosurgery, electroshock, sterilization or experimental treatment of any kind unless the procedure is first approved by the order of the court, after a hearing as prescribed by section 525.56, subdivision 3.

"A guardian is not liable by reason of consent for injury to the ward resulting from the negligence or acts of third persons unless it would have been illegal for a parent to have consented, or unless the guardian fails to comply with the requirements of this section which provide that a court order is necessary for commitment and for certain types of medical procedures. A guardian may consent to the marriage or adoption of the ward.

"(d) A guardian must report the condition of the ward and of the ward's estate which has been subject to the guardian's possession or control, as ordered by the court on its own motion or on petition of any person interested in the minor's welfare and as required by court rule.

"525.6192. Termination of appointment of guardian; general

"A guardian's authority and responsibility terminates upon the death, resignation or removal of the guardian or upon the minor's death, adoption, marriage or attainment of majority, but termination does not affect the guardian's liability for prior acts, nor the obligation to account for funds and assets of the ward. A guardian may be discharged without notice or hearing on petition and acceptance of the guardian's accounts by the ward after the ward marries or attains majority, or, in the case of the ward's death, by the personal representative of the ward's estate. In other cases the court may discharge the guardian upon approval of the guardian's accounts after notice and a hearing. Resignation of a guardian does not terminate the guardianship until it has been approved by the court. A testamentary appointment under an informally probated will terminates if the will is later denied probate in a formal proceeding.

"525.6194. Proceedings subsequent to appointment; venue

"(a) The court where the ward resides has concurrent jurisdiction with the court which appointed the guardian, or in which acceptance of a testamentary appointment was filed, over resignation, removal, accounting and other proceedings relating to the guardianship.

"(b) If the court located where the ward resides is not the court in which acceptance of appointment is filed, the court in which proceedings subsequent to appointment are commenced shall in all appropriate cases notify the other court, in this or another state, and after consultation with that court determine whether to retain jurisdiction or transfer the proceedings to the other court, whichever is in the best interests of the ward. A copy of any order accepting a resignation or removing a guardian shall be sent to the court in which acceptance of appointment is filed.

"525.6195. Resignation or removal proceedings

"(a) Any person interested in the welfare of a ward, or the ward, if 14 or more years of age, may petition for removal of a guardian on the ground that removal would be in the best interests of the ward. A guardian may petition for permission to resign. A petition for removal or for permission to resign may, but need not, include a request for appointment of a successor guardian.

"(b) After notice and hearing on a petition for removal or for permission to resign, the court may terminate the guardianship and make any further order that may be appropriate.

"(c) If, at any time in the proceeding, the court determines that the interests of the ward are, or may be, inadequately represented, it may appoint an attorney to represent the minor, giving consideration to the preference of the minor if the minor is 14 or more years of age.

"525.6196. Facility of payment or delivery

"Any person other than a personal representative subject to section 524.3–915, clause (b), who is under a duty to pay or deliver money or personal property to a minor may perform this duty, in amounts not exceeding $5,000 per annum, by paying or delivering the money or property to, (1) the minor, if 16 years of age or married; (2) any person having the care and custody of the minor with whom the minor resides; (3) a guardian of the minor; or (4) a financial institution incident to a deposit in a federally insured savings account in the sole name of the minor and giving notice of the deposit to the minor. This section does not apply if the person making payment or delivery has actual knowledge that a conservator has been appointed or proceedings for appointment of a conservator of the estate of the minor are pending. The persons, other than the minor or any financial institution under clause (4), receiving money or property for a minor, are obligated to apply the money to the support and education of the minor, but may not pay themselves except by way of reimbursement for out-of-pocket expenses for goods and services necessary for the minor's support. Any excess sums shall be preserved for future support of the minor. Any balance not so used and any property received for the minor must be turned over to the minor on attaining majority. Persons who pay or deliver in accordance with provisions of this section are not responsible for the proper application of it.

"525.6197. Discharge of guardian or conservator; property of a minor

"When a minor receives or is entitled to personal property, the court may order a guardian or conservator to make payment of up to $2,000 of the property to the parent or parents, custodian, or the person, corporation, or institution with whom the minor child is, for the benefit, support, maintenance, and education of the minor or may direct the investment of the whole or any part of that amount in a savings account, savings certificate, or certificate of deposit in a bank, savings bank, or savings association in the name of the minor. When so invested the savings account passbook, savings certificate, certificate of deposit, or other acknowledgment of receipt of the deposit by the depository is to be kept as provided by the court. The depository shall be instructed not to allow the investment to be withdrawn, except by order of the court. The court may authorize the use of any part or all of that amount to purchase United States government savings bonds in the minor's name. The bonds shall be kept as provided by the court and retained until the minor reaches majority unless otherwise authorized by an order of the court.

"525.6198. Protective proceedings; appointment of conservator of estate of minor

"Upon petition and after notice and hearing in accordance with the provisions of section 525.618 the court may appoint a conservator or make other protective order for cause as follows:

"(1) Appointment of a conservator or other protective order may be made in relation to the estate and affairs of a minor if the court determines that a minor owns money or property that requires management or protection which cannot otherwise be provided, has or may have business affairs which may be jeopardized or prevented by minority, or that funds are needed for support and education and that protection is necessary or desirable to obtain or provide funds.

"(2) The court may grant to the conservator of the estate of a minor any or all of the powers and duties enumerated in section 525.56, subdivision 4, and the conservator shall be subject to the requirements of sections 525.58, subdivision 1, 525.581 and 525.582 regarding an inventory and accounting, except that the court may waive the requirement that the annual account be served on the ward. The conservator shall file a bond with the court in such amount as the court may direct.

"525.6199. Guardianship, conservatorship; workers' compensation proceedings

"Subdivision 1. Referral. When a matter is referred under section 176.092, subdivision 3, the court shall determine whether the employee or dependent is a minor or an incapacitated person, shall appoint a guardian or conservator if the employee or dependent is a minor or an incapacitated person, and shall return the matter to the source of referral.

"Subd. 2. Court oversight. The court shall oversee the use of monetary benefits paid to a guardian or conservator as provided in this chapter or under rule 145 of the general rules of practice for the district courts. There is a rebuttable presumption that a settlement or award approved by the commissioner of the department of labor and industry or a compensation judge is reasonable and fair to the employee or dependent.

"Subd. 3. Costs. Subject to the approval of the court, the insurer or self-insured employer shall pay the costs and a reasonable attorney fee of the employee or dependent associated with the appointment of a guardian or conservator required under section 176.092.

"525.62. Mortgage and lease

"Sections 525.62 to 525.702 shall be applicable only to guardianships and conservatorships and not to decedents' estates. As used in sections 525.62 to 525.702, the word 'mortgage' includes an extension of an existing mortgage, subject to the provisions of section 525.691, and the word 'lease' means a lease for one or more years, unless the context indicates otherwise."

525.621. Repealed by Laws 1980, c. 493, § 40, eff. Oct. 1, 1981

Historical and Statutory Notes

Laws 1981, 2nd Sp., c. 6, § 1, provides:

"Laws 1980, Chapter 493 and Laws 1981, Chapter 313, are effective October 1, 1981."

525.63 to 525.692. Repealed by Laws 2003, c. 12, art. 2, § 8

Historical and Statutory Notes

See, now, generally, M.S.A. § 524.5–101 et seq.

Laws 2003, c. 12, art. 2, § 9, provided:

"(a) Articles 1 and 2 apply to each guardianship or conservatorship proceeding and each appointment of guardian or conservator commenced on or after the effective date of articles 1 and 2. Except as otherwise provided in this section, articles 1 and 2 apply to each guardianship or conservatorship approved by the court prior to the effective date of articles 1 and 2, and to any guardianship or conservatorship proceeding pending in court on the effective date of articles 1 and 2, unless the court finds for good cause or in the interests of judicial economy that the proceeding should be completed under the provisions of Minnesota Statutes, chapter 525, as it existed prior to the effective date of articles 1 and 2.

"(b) A guardian or conservator who is not discharged prior to the effective date of articles 1 and 2 shall continue to hold the appointment but shall have only the powers specified in the order of appointment and in Minnesota Statutes, chapter 525, as it existed prior to the effective date of articles 1 and 2. Each guardian or conservator holding an appointment on the effective date of articles 1 and 2 shall continue to be bound by the duties imposed by the order of appointment; by Minnesota Statutes, chapter 525, as it existed prior to the effective date of articles 1 and 2; and by article 1, section 50; and shall be bound by any additional duties imposed by articles 1 and 2 starting on the first day of the next month starting after the effective date of articles 1 and 2 or on the next anniversary date of the appointment, whichever occurs later.

"(c) Any act done prior to the effective date of articles 1 and 2 in any proceeding and any right accrued under Minnesota Statutes, chapter 525, prior to the effective date of articles 1 and 2 shall not be impaired by articles 1 and 2. If a right is acquired, extinguished, or barred upon the expiration of a prescribed period of time which has commenced to run in accordance with the provisions of any statute before the effective date of articles 1 and 2, the provisions of the prior statute shall remain in force with respect to that right notwithstanding the statute's amendment or repeal by articles 1 and 2.

"(d) An order of the court or letters of guardianship or conservatorship issued by the court prior to the effective date of articles 1 and 2 shall remain in full force and effect in accordance with its terms and conditions and in accordance with the provisions of prior law until the court modifies the order or letters in accordance with the provisions of articles 1 and 2. Upon request for a certified copy of an order or letters which remains in full force and effect under this paragraph, the court administrator shall certify that the order or letters remains in full force and effect pursuant to this paragraph.

"(e) The court, without hearing or notice to any person, may issue new letters of guardianship or conservatorship under articles 1 and 2 to replace similar letters issued prior to the effective date of articles 1 and 2. The new letters shall be effective under articles 1 and 2 with the same force and effect as the prior letters and shall remain in full force and effect until modified by the court in accordance with the provisions of articles 1 and 2.

"(f) A power of attorney executed in accordance with Minnesota Statutes, section 524.5–505, prior to the effective date of articles 1 and 2, or any surety bond, deed, or other instrument, report, or other undertaking executed in accordance with Minnesota Statutes, chapter 525, prior to the effective date of articles 1 and 2, shall remain in full force and effect for all purposes in accordance with its terms and conditions and the provisions of the applicable statutes under which the power of attorney, surety bond, deed, or other instrument, report, or other undertaking was executed, until the power of attorney, surety bond, deed, or other instrument, report, or other undertaking expires according to its terms or pursuant to the statutes governing its execution, or is modified, terminated, or superseded by a new power of attorney, surety bond, deed, or other instrument, report, or other undertaking executed in accordance with the provisions of articles 1 and 2."

Prior to repeal, §§ 525.63 to 525.692 read:

"525.63. Reasons for sale, mortgage, lease

"The court may direct a sale, mortgage, or lease of any real estate of a ward or conservatee when the personal property is insufficient to pay debts and other charges against the estate, or to provide for the support, maintenance, and education of the ward or conservatee, a spouse, and dependent children, or when it shall determine the sale, mortgage, or lease to be for the best interest of the ward or conservatee.

"The homestead of a ward or conservatee shall not be sold, mortgaged, or leased unless the written consent of the spouse has been filed.

"525.64. Petition, notice, hearing

"A guardian or conservator may file a petition to sell, mortgage, or lease alleging briefly the facts constituting the reasons for the application and describing the real estate involved therein. The petition may include all the real estate of the ward or conservatee or any part or parts thereof. It may apply for different authority as to separate parcels. It may apply in the alternative for authority to sell, mortgage, or lease. Upon the filing of such petition, the court shall fix the time and place for the hearing thereof. Notice of the hearing shall state briefly the nature of the application made by the petition and shall be given pursuant to section 525.83 except that no publication is required unless otherwise ordered. Upon the hearing, the court shall have full power to direct the sale, mortgage, or lease of all the real estate described in the petition, or to direct the sale, mortgage, or lease of any one or more parcels thereof, provided that any such direction shall be within the terms of the application made by the petition.

"525.641. Order for sale, mortgage, lease

"The order shall describe the real estate to be sold, mortgaged, or leased, and may designate the sequence in which the several parcels shall be sold, mortgaged, or leased. If the order be for a sale, it shall direct whether the real estate shall be sold at private sale or public auction. An order to mortgage shall fix the maximum amount of the principal and the maximum rate of interest and shall direct the purpose for which the proceeds shall be used. An order for sale, mortgage, or lease shall remain in force until terminated by the court, but no private sale shall be made after one year from the date of the order unless the real estate shall have been reappraised under order of the court within three months preceding the sale.

"525.642. Terms of sale

"The court may order a sale of real estate for cash, part cash and a purchase-money mortgage of not more than 50 percent of the purchase price, or on contract for deed. The initial payment under a sale on contract shall be not less than ten percent of the total purchase price, and the unpaid purchase price shall bear interest at a rate of not less than four percent per annum and shall be payable in reasonable monthly, quarterly, semiannual, or annual payments, and the final installment shall become due and payable not later than ten years from the date of the contract. Such contract shall provide for conveyance by quitclaim deed, which deed shall be executed and delivered upon full performance of the contract without further order of the court. In the event of termination of the interest of the purchaser and assigns in such contract, the real estate may be resold under the original order and a reappraisal within three months preceding the sale. A sale of the vendor's interest in real estate sold by the guardian or conservator on contract may be made under order of the court, with or without notice, upon an appraisal of such interest within three months preceding the sale; no such sale shall be made for less than its value as fixed by such appraisal.

"525.65. Public sale

"If a sale at public auction be ordered, three weeks' published notice of the time and place of sale shall be given. Proof of publication shall be filed before the confirmation of the sale. Such publication and sale may be made in the county where the real estate is situated or in the county of the proceedings. If the parcels to be sold are contiguous and lie in more than one county, notice may be given and the sale may be made in either of such counties or in the county of the proceedings. The guardian or conservator may adjourn the sale from time to time, if for the best interests of the estate and the persons concerned, but not exceeding three months in all. Every adjournment shall be announced publicly at the time and place fixed for the sale and, if for more than one day, further notice thereof shall be given as the court may direct.

"525.651. Private sale

"If a private sale be ordered, the real estate shall be reappraised by two or more disinterested persons under order of the court unless a prior appraisal of the real estate has been made by two or more disinterested persons not more than three months before the sale, which reappraisal shall be filed before the confirmation of the sale. No real estate shall be sold at private sale for less than its value as fixed by such appraisal.

"525.652. Additional bond

"If the existing bond be insufficient, before confirmation of a sale or lease, or before execution of a mortgage, the guardian or conservator shall file an additional bond in such amount as the court may require.

"525.66. Sale of contract interest

"When a ward or conservatee is entitled under contract of purchase to any interest in real estate, such interest may be sold for the same reasons and in the same manner as other real estate of a ward or conservatee. Before confirmation, the court may require the filing of a bond conditioned to save the estate harmless. Upon confirmation, the guardian or conservator shall assign the contract and convey by quitclaim deed.

"525.661. Sale subject to charge

"When the estate of a ward or conservatee is liable for any charge, mortgage, lien, or other encumbrance upon the real estate therein, the court may refuse to confirm the sale or lease until after the filing of a bond in such amount as the court may direct conditioned to save the estate harmless.

"525.662. Confirmation

"Upon making a sale or lease, the guardian or conservator shall file a report thereof. Upon proof of compliance with the terms of the order, the court may confirm the sale or lease and order the guardian or conservator to execute and deliver the proper instrument.

"525.67. Agreement and sale for public purpose

"When any real estate of a ward or conservatee is desired by any person, firm, association, corporation, or governmental agency having the power of eminent domain, the guardian or conservator may agree, in writing, upon the compensation to be made for the taking, injuring, damaging, or destroying thereof, subject to the approval of the court. When the agreement has been made, the guardian or conservator shall file a petition, of which the agreement shall be a part, setting forth the facts relative to the transaction. The court, with notice as provided in section 525.83, except that no publication is required unless it is ordered by the court, shall hear, determine, and act upon the petition. If the court approves the agreement, the guardian or conservator, upon payment of the agreed compensation, shall convey the real estate sought to be acquired and execute any release which may be authorized.

"525.68. Platting

"When it is for the best interests of the estate of a ward or conservatee, real estate may be platted by the guardian or conservator under such conditions and upon such notice as the court may order.

"525.69. Conveyance of vendor's title

"When any ward or conservatee is legally bound to make a conveyance or lease, the court, without further notice, may direct the guardian or conservator to make the conveyance or lease to the person entitled thereto. The petition may be made by any person claiming to be entitled to the conveyance or lease, or by the guardian or conservator, or by any person interested in the estate or claiming an interest in the real estate or contract, and shall show the description of the land and the facts upon which the claim for conveyance or lease is based. Upon proof of the petition, the court may order the guardian or conservator to execute and deliver an instrument of conveyance or lease upon performance of the contract.

"525.691. Mortgage extension

"A guardian or conservator without order of the court may make an extension of an existing mortgage for a period of five years or less, if the extension agreement contains the same prepayment privileges and the rate of interest does not exceed the lowest rate in the mortgage extended.

"525.692. Liability on mortgage note

"No guardian or conservator shall be liable personally on any mortgage note or by reason of the covenants in any instrument or conveyance executed in the capacity of guardian or conservator."

525.693. Repealed by Laws 1975, c. 347, § 144, eff. Jan. 1, 1976

525.70. Repealed by Laws 2003, c. 12, art. 2, § 8

Historical and Statutory Notes

Laws 2003, c. 12, art. 2, § 9, provided:

"(a) Articles 1 and 2 apply to each guardianship or conservatorship proceeding and each appointment of guardian or conservator commenced on or after the effective date of articles 1 and 2. Except as otherwise provided in this section, articles 1 and 2 apply to each guardianship or conservatorship approved by the court prior to the effective date of articles 1 and 2, and to any guardianship or conservatorship proceeding pending in court on the effective date of articles 1 and 2, unless the court finds for good cause or in the interests of judicial economy that the proceeding should be completed under the provisions of Minnesota Statutes, chapter 525, as it existed prior to the effective date of articles 1 and 2.

"(b) A guardian or conservator who is not discharged prior to the effective date of articles 1 and 2 shall continue to hold the appointment but shall have only the powers specified in the order of appointment and in Minnesota Statutes, chapter 525, as it existed prior to the effective date of articles 1 and 2. Each guardian or conservator holding an appointment on the effective date of articles 1 and 2 shall continue to be bound by the duties imposed by the order of appointment; by Minnesota Statutes, chapter 525, as it existed prior to the effective date of articles 1 and 2; and by article 1, section 50; and shall be bound by any additional duties imposed by articles 1 and 2 starting on the first day of the next month starting after the effective date of articles 1 and 2 or on the next anniversary date of the appointment, whichever occurs later.

"(c) Any act done prior to the effective date of articles 1 and 2 in any proceeding and any right accrued under Minnesota Statutes, chapter 525, prior to the effective date of articles 1 and 2 shall not be impaired by articles 1 and 2. If a right is acquired, extinguished, or barred upon the expiration of a prescribed period of time which has commenced to run in accordance with the provisions of any statute before the effective date of articles 1 and 2, the provisions of the prior statute shall remain in force with respect to that right notwithstanding the statute's amendment or repeal by articles 1 and 2.

"(d) An order of the court or letters of guardianship or conservatorship issued by the court prior to the effective date of articles 1 and 2 shall remain in full force and effect in accordance with its terms and conditions and in accordance with the provisions of prior law

until the court modifies the order or letters in accordance with the provisions of articles 1 and 2. Upon request for a certified copy of an order or letters which remains in full force and effect under this paragraph, the court administrator shall certify that the order or letters remains in full force and effect pursuant to this paragraph.

"(e) The court, without hearing or notice to any person, may issue new letters of guardianship or conservatorship under articles 1 and 2 to replace similar letters issued prior to the effective date of articles 1 and 2. The new letters shall be effective under articles 1 and 2 with the same force and effect as the prior letters and shall remain in full force and effect until modified by the court in accordance with the provisions of articles 1 and 2.

"(f) A power of attorney executed in accordance with Minnesota Statutes, section 524.5–505, prior to the effective date of articles 1 and 2, or any surety bond, deed, or other instrument, report, or other undertaking executed in accordance with Minnesota Statutes, chapter 525, prior to the effective date of articles 1 and 2, shall remain in full force and effect for all purposes in accordance with its terms and conditions and the provisions of the applicable statutes under which the power of attorney, surety bond, deed, or other instrument, report, or other undertaking was executed, until the power of attorney, surety bond, deed, or other instrument, report, or other undertaking expires according to its terms or pursuant to the statutes governing its execution, or is modified, terminated, or superseded by a new power of attorney, surety bond, deed, or other instrument, report, or other undertaking executed in accordance with the provisions of articles 1 and 2."

Prior to repeal, § 525.70 read:

"**525.70. Validity of proceedings**

"No sale, mortgage, lease, or conveyance by a guardian or conservator shall be subject to collateral attack on account of any irregularity in the proceedings if the court which ordered the same had jurisdiction of the estate."

525.701.   Repealed by Laws 1975, c. 347, § 144, eff. Jan. 1, 1976

525.702 to 525.705.   Repealed by Laws 2003, c. 12, art. 2, § 8

Historical and Statutory Notes

Laws 2003, c. 12, art. 2, § 9, provided:

"(a) Articles 1 and 2 apply to each guardianship or conservatorship proceeding and each appointment of guardian or conservator com-

menced on or after the effective date of articles 1 and 2. Except as otherwise provided in this section, articles 1 and 2 apply to each guardianship or conservatorship approved by the court prior to the effective date of articles 1 and 2, and to any guardianship or conservatorship proceeding pending in court on the effective date of articles 1 and 2, unless the court finds for good cause or in the interests of judicial economy that the proceeding should be completed under the provisions of Minnesota Statutes, chapter 525, as it existed prior to the effective date of articles 1 and 2.

"(b) A guardian or conservator who is not discharged prior to the effective date of articles 1 and 2 shall continue to hold the appointment but shall have only the powers specified in the order of appointment and in Minnesota Statutes, chapter 525, as it existed prior to the effective date of articles 1 and 2. Each guardian or conservator holding an appointment on the effective date of articles 1 and 2 shall continue to be bound by the duties imposed by the order of appointment; by Minnesota Statutes, chapter 525, as it existed prior to the effective date of articles 1 and 2; and by article 1, section 50; and shall be bound by any additional duties imposed by articles 1 and 2 starting on the first day of the next month starting after the effective date of articles 1 and 2 or on the next anniversary date of the appointment, whichever occurs later.

"(c) Any act done prior to the effective date of articles 1 and 2 in any proceeding and any right accrued under Minnesota Statutes, chapter 525, prior to the effective date of articles 1 and 2 shall not be impaired by articles 1 and 2. If a right is acquired, extinguished, or barred upon the expiration of a prescribed period of time which has commenced to run in accordance with the provisions of any statute before the effective date of articles 1 and 2, the provisions of the prior statute shall remain in force with respect to that right notwithstanding the statute's amendment or repeal by articles 1 and 2.

"(d) An order of the court or letters of guardianship or conservatorship issued by the court prior to the effective date of articles 1 and 2 shall remain in full force and effect in accordance with its terms and conditions and in accordance with the provisions of prior law until the court modifies the order or letters in accordance with the provisions of articles 1 and 2. Upon request for a certified copy of an order or letters which remains in full force and effect under this paragraph, the court administrator shall certify that the order or letters remains in full force and effect pursuant to this paragraph.

"(e) The court, without hearing or notice to any person, may issue new letters of guardianship or conservatorship under articles 1 and 2 to replace similar letters issued prior to the effective date of articles 1 and 2. The new letters shall be effective under articles 1 and 2 with the same force and effect as the prior letters and shall remain in full force and effect until modified by the court in accordance with the provisions of articles 1 and 2.

"(f) A power of attorney executed in accordance with Minnesota Statutes, section 524.5–505, prior to the effective date of articles 1 and 2, or any surety bond, deed, or other instrument, report, or other undertaking executed in accordance with Minnesota Statutes, chapter 525, prior to the effective date of articles 1 and 2, shall remain in full force and effect for all purposes in accordance with its terms and conditions and the provisions of the applicable statutes under which the power of attorney, surety bond, deed, or other instrument, report, or other undertaking was executed, until the power of attorney, surety bond, deed, or other instrument, report, or other undertaking expires according to its terms or pursuant to the statutes governing its execution, or is modified, terminated, or superseded by a new power of attorney, surety bond, deed, or other instrument, report, or other undertaking executed in accordance with the provisions of articles 1 and 2."

Prior to repeal, §§ 525.702 to 525.705 read:

"**525.702. Limitation of action**

"No proceeding to have declared invalid the sale, mortgage, lease, or conveyance by a guardian or conservator shall be maintained by any person claiming under or through the ward or conservatee unless such proceeding is begun within five years immediately succeeding the date of such sale, mortgage, lease, or conveyance, provided, that in case of real estate sold by a guardian or conservator, no action for its recovery shall be maintained by or under the ward or conservatee unless it is begun within five years next after the termination of the guardianship or conservatorship; and that, in cases of fraud, minors and others under legal disability to sue when the right of action first accrues may begin such action at any time within five years after the disability is removed.

"**525.703. Costs**

"Subdivision 1. In forma pauperis. The court may authorize a proceeding under sections 525.54 to 525.702 to proceed in forma pauperis, as provided in chapter 563.

"Subd. 2. Lawyer or health professional. In proceedings under sections 525.54 to 525.702 a lawyer or health professional rendering necessary services with regard to the appointment of a guardian or conservator, the administration of the ward's or conservatee's estate or personal affairs or the restoration of that person's capacity, shall be entitled to reasonable compensation from the estate of the ward or conservatee or from the county having jurisdiction over the proceedings if the ward or conservatee is indigent. When the court determines that other necessary services have been provided for the benefit of the ward or conservatee by a lawyer or health professional, the court may order reasonable fees to be paid from the estate of the ward or conservatee or from the county having jurisdiction over the proceedings if the ward or conservatee is indigent. If, however, the court determines that a petitioner, guardian or conservator has not acted in good faith, the court shall order some or all of the fees or costs incurred in the proceedings to be borne by the petitioner, guardian, or conservator not acting in good faith. In determining reasonable compensation for a guardian or conservator of an indigent person, the court shall consider a fee schedule recommended by the board of county commissioners. The fee schedule may also include a maximum compensation based on the living arrangements of the ward or conservatee. If these services are provided by a public or private agency, the county may contract on a fee for service basis with that agency.

"Subd. 3. Guardian or conservator. (a) When the court determines that a guardian or conservator of the person or the estate has rendered necessary services or has incurred necessary expenses for the benefit of the ward or conservatee, the court may order reimbursement or reasonable compensation to be paid from the estate of the ward or conservatee or from the county having jurisdiction over the guardianship or conservatorship if the ward or conservatee is indigent. The court may not deny an award of fees solely because the ward or conservatee is a recipient of medical assistance. In determining reasonable compensation for a guardian or conservator of an indigent person, the court shall consider a fee schedule recommended by the board of county commissioners. The fee schedule may also include a maximum compensation based on the

living arrangements of the ward or conservatee. If these services are provided by a public or private agency, the county may contract on a fee for service basis with that agency.

"(b) The court shall order reimbursement or reasonable compensation if the guardian or conservator requests payment and the guardian or conservator was nominated by the court or by the county adult protection unit because no suitable relative or other person was available to provide guardianship or conservatorship services necessary to prevent maltreatment of a vulnerable adult, as defined in section 626.5572, subdivision 15. In determining reasonable compensation for a guardian or conservator of an indigent person, the court shall consider a fee schedule recommended by the board of county commissioners. The fee schedule may also include a maximum compensation based on the living arrangements of the ward or conservatee. If these services are provided by a public or private agency, the county may contract on a fee for service basis with that agency.

"(c) When a county employee serves as a guardian or conservator as part of employment duties, the court shall order reasonable compensation if the guardian or conservator performs necessary services that are not compensated by the county. The court may order reimbursement to the county from the ward's or conservatee's estate for reasonable compensation paid by the county for services rendered by a guardian or conservator who is a county employee but only if the county shows that after a diligent effort it was unable to arrange for an independent guardian or conservator.

"525.705. Preexisting guardianships and conservatorships

"All guardians and conservators serving prior to August 1, 1981, shall have all powers and duties of section 525.56, subdivision 3, as to the person and section 525.56, subdivision 4, as to the estate, unless restricted by any existing court order, until those powers or duties are restricted or changed by court order."

APPEALS

525.71. Appealable orders

(a) Appeals to the Court of Appeals may be taken from any of the following orders, judgments, and decrees issued by a judge of the court under this chapter or chapter 524:

(1) an order admitting, or refusing to admit, a will to probate;

(2) an order appointing, or refusing to appoint, or removing, or refusing to remove, a representative other than a special administrator, temporary or emergency guardian, agent, or conservator;

(3) an order authorizing, or refusing to authorize, the sale, mortgage, or lease of real estate, or confirming, or refusing to confirm, the sale or lease of real estate;

(4) an order directing, or refusing to direct, a conveyance or lease of real estate under contract;

(5) an order permitting, or refusing to permit, the filing of a claim, or allowing or disallowing a claim or counterclaim, in whole or in part, when the amount in controversy exceeds $100;

(6) an order setting apart, or refusing to set apart, property, or making, or refusing to make, an allowance for the spouse or children;

(7) an order determining, or refusing to determine, venue; an order transferring, or refusing to transfer, venue;

(8) an order directing, or refusing to direct, the payment of a bequest or distributive share when the amount in controversy exceeds $100;

(9) an order allowing, or refusing to allow, an account of a representative or any part of it when the amount in controversy exceeds $100;

(10) an order adjudging a person in contempt;

(11) an order vacating, or refusing to vacate, a previous appealable order, judgment, or decree alleged to have been procured by fraud or misrepresentation, or through surprise or excusable inadvertence or neglect;

(12) a judgment or decree of partial or final distribution or an order determining or confirming distribution or any order of general protection;

(13) an order entered pursuant to section 576.142;

(14) an order granting or denying restoration to capacity;

(15) an order made directing, or refusing to direct, the payment of representative's fees or attorneys' fees, and in such case the representative and the attorney shall each be deemed an aggrieved party and entitled to appeal;

(16) an order, judgment, or decree relating to or affecting estate taxes or refusing to amend, modify, or vacate such an order, judgment, or decree; and

(17) an order extending the time for the settlement of the estate beyond five years from the date of the appointment of the representative.

(b) Appeals to the Court of Appeals may also be taken from any other properly appealable order pursuant to the Rules of Civil Appellate Procedure.

(c) An order appointing, refusing to appoint, removing, or refusing to remove a temporary or emergency guardian under sections 524.5–204, paragraphs (b) and (c), 524.5–311, and 524.5–312, or temporary or emergency conservator or agent under sections 524.5–406, paragraph (f), and 524.5–412, or a special administrator under section 524.3–614, is not an appealable order under this section or the Rules of Civil Appellate Procedure.

Amended by Laws 1963, c. 740, § 24; Laws 1974, c. 447, § 4; Laws 1975, c. 347, § 135, eff. Jan. 1, 1976; Laws 1979, c. 303, art. 3, § 38; Laws 1983, c. 247, § 186, eff. Aug. 1, 1983; Laws 2004, c. 146, art. 2, § 8.

525.711. Repealed by Laws 1983, c. 247, § 219, eff. Aug. 1, 1983

525.712. Requisites

The appeal may be taken under the Rules of Appellate Procedure by any person aggrieved after service by any party of written notice of the filing of the order, judgment, or decree appealed from, or if no written notice is served, within six months after the filing of the order, judgment, or decree. Except as provided in this section, the appeal shall be perfected and determined upon the record as provided in the Rules of Appellate Procedure.

Amended by Laws 1953, c. 476, § 1; Laws 1980, c. 344, § 1; Laws 1987, c. 346, § 17; Laws 1996, c. 305, art. 1, § 116; Laws 2000, c. 362, § 4.

525.713. Repealed by Laws 1980, c. 344, § 2

525.714. Suspension by appeal

The appeal shall suspend the operation of the order, judgment, or decree appealed from until the appeal is determined or the Court of Appeals orders otherwise. The Court of Appeals may require the appellant to give additional bond for the payment of damages which may be awarded against the appellant in consequence of the suspension, on the appellant's failure to obtain a reversal of the order, judgment, or decree appealed from. Nothing herein contained shall prevent the probate court from appointing special representatives nor prevent special representatives from continuing to act as such.

Amended by Laws 1983, c. 247, § 187, eff. Aug. 1, 1983; Laws 1986, c. 444; Laws 1995, c. 189, § 8; Laws 1996, c. 277, § 1.

525.72. Repealed by Laws 1980, c. 344, § 2

525.73. Affirmance; reversal

When the appellant fails to prosecute the appeal, or the order, judgment, or decree appealed from or reviewed is sustained, judgment shall be entered in the Court of Appeals affirming the decision of the court. Upon the filing in the court of a certified transcript of the judgment, the court shall proceed as if no appeal had been taken. If the order, judgment, or decree reviewed is reversed or modified, the Court of Appeals shall remand the case to the court with directions to proceed in conformity with its decision. Upon the filing in the court of a certified transcript of the judgment, it shall proceed as directed by the Court of Appeals.

Amended by Laws 1983, c. 247, § 188, eff. Aug. 1, 1983; Laws 1986, c. 444; Laws 1995, c. 189, § 8; Laws 1996, c. 277, § 1.

525.731. Judgment; execution

The party prevailing on the appeal shall be entitled to costs and disbursements to be taxed as in a civil action. If judgment be rendered against the estate, they shall be an adjudicated claim against it. If judgment be rendered against an appellant other than the state, the Veterans' Administration, or representative appealing on behalf of the estate, judgment shall be entered against the appellant and the sureties on the appeal bond and execution may issue thereon.

Amended by Laws 1986, c. 444.

525.74. Repealed by Laws 1982, c. 501, § 26, eff. Aug. 1, 1983; Laws 1983, c. 247, § 219, eff. Aug. 1, 1983

525.749 to 525.79. Repealed by Laws 1967, c. 638, § 22, eff. Jan. 1, 1968

GENERAL PROVISIONS

525.80. Representative

As used in this chapter, the word "representative," unless the context otherwise indicates, includes personal representatives as that term is defined in chapter 524, guardians, and conservators.

Laws 1975, c. 347, § 136, eff. Jan. 1, 1976.

Historical and Statutory Notes

St.1971, § 525.80, as amended by Laws 1971, c. 725, § 76, was repealed by Laws 1947, c. 442, art. 8, § 524.8–102, effective January 1, 1976. Prior to the effective date of the repealer a new but similar section was enacted as § 525.80 by Laws 1975, c. 347, § 136. Prior to repeal § 525.80 read:

"As used in this chapter, the word "representative," unless the context otherwise indicates, includes executors, general administrators, special administrators, administrators with the will annexed, administrators de bonis non, general guardians, and special guardians. Commencing with June 1, 1973, the word "minor" means a person under the age of 18 years."

525.805. Repealed by Laws 1974, c. 442, art. 8, § 524.8–102, eff. Jan. 1, 1976

525.81, 525.82. Repealed by Laws 1974, c. 442, art. 8, § 524.8–102, eff. Jan. 1, 1976

525.83. Notice

When notice of hearing is required by any provision of this chapter by reference to this section, the notice shall be given once a week for three consecutive weeks in a legal newspaper designated by the petitioner in the county wherein the proceedings are pending; or, if no such designation be made, in any legal newspaper in the county; or, if the city of the decedent's residence is situated in more than one county, in any legal newspaper in the city. The first publication shall be had within two weeks after the date of the order fixing the time and place for the hearing.

At least 14 days prior to the date fixed for hearing the petitioner, the petitioner's attorney or agent, shall in guardianship or conservatorship mail a copy of the notice to the ward or conservatee, and other persons as the court may direct and in decedents' estates shall mail a copy of the notice to each heir, devisee, and legatee whose name and address are known.

Proof of publication and mailing shall be filed before the hearing. No defect in any notice nor in the publication or service thereof shall invalidate any proceedings.

Amended by Laws 1957, c. 30, § 1; Laws 1971, c. 497, § 7, eff. May 26, 1971; Laws 1973, c. 123, art. 5, § 7; Laws 1973, c. 404, § 1; Laws 1975, c. 347, § 137, eff. Jan. 1, 1976; Laws 1980, c. 493, § 25, eff. Aug. 1, 1981; Laws 1986, c. 444.

Historical and Statutory Notes

Laws 1981, 2nd Sp., c. 6, § 1, provides:

"Laws 1980, Chapter 493 and Laws 1981, Chapter 313, are effective October 1, 1981."

525.831. Notice to attorney general of devises for charitable purposes

Whenever a will provides for a devise for a charitable purpose, as defined in section 501B.35, subdivision 2, the personal representative shall provide the attorney general with the notices or documents, if any, required by section 501B.41, subdivision 5.

Laws 1978, c. 601, § 28, eff. March 29, 1978. Amended by Laws 1989, c. 340, art. 2, § 5, eff. Jan. 1, 1990.

525.84. Erroneous escheat

When any property has escheated to the state because the decedent left surviving no spouse nor kindred or because of the failure of a devisee or legatee to receive under a will admitted to probate, or when application is made to prove a will disposing of property escheated to the state, upon the petition of the representative or any person interested in the estate and upon 20 days' notice to the attorney general and to such other persons as the court may direct, the court may admit the will to probate as provided by law, or make its determination of heirship and enter its order assigning the escheated property to the persons entitled thereto.

Amended by Laws 1975, c. 347, § 138, eff. Jan. 1, 1976.

525.841. Escheat returned

In all such cases the commissioner of finance shall be furnished with a certified copy of the court's order assigning the escheated property to the persons entitled thereto, and upon notification of payment of the estate tax, the commissioner of finance shall draw a warrant or execute a proper conveyance to the persons designated in such order. In the event any escheated property has been sold pursuant to sections 11A.04, clause (9), and 11A.10, subdivision 2, or 16B.281 to 16B.287, then the warrant shall be for the appraised value as established during the administration of the decedent's estate. There is hereby annually appropriated from any moneys in the state treasury not otherwise appropriated an amount sufficient to make payment to all such designated persons. No interest shall be allowed on any amount paid to such persons.

Amended by Laws 1957, c. 861, § 8; Laws 1973, c. 492, § 14; Laws 1975, c. 347, § 139, eff. Jan. 1, 1976; Laws 1979, c. 303, art. 3, § 40; Laws 1980, c. 607, art. 14, § 46, eff. April 24, 1980; Laws 1986, c. 444; Laws 2003, c. 112, art. 2, § 49, eff. May 28, 2003; Laws 2004, c. 262, art. 1, § 40, eff. Aug. 1, 2004.

525.85. Disclosure proceedings

Upon the filing of a petition by the representative or any person interested in the estate, alleging that any person has concealed, converted, embezzled, or disposed of any property belonging to the estate of a decedent or that any person has possession or knowledge of any will or codicil of such decedent, or of any instruments in writing relating to such property, the court, upon such notice as it may direct may order such person to appear before it for disclosure. Refusal to appear or submit to examination, or failure to obey any lawful order based thereon shall constitute contempt of court.

525.86, 525.87. Repealed by Laws 1975, c. 347, § 144, eff. Jan. 1, 1976

525.88. State patents

Where patents for public lands have been or may be issued, in pursuance of any law of this state, to a person who has died before the date of such patent, the title to the land designated therein shall inure to and become vested in the heirs, devisees, or assignees of such deceased patentees as if the patent had been issued to the deceased person during life.

525.881.   Federal patents

When any person holding a homestead or tree claim entry under the laws of the United States has died before making final proof and final proof has afterwards been made by the heirs, devisees, or representatives, and a patent has been granted to the "heirs" or "devisees," the district court of the county in which the real estate so patented is situated, may determine who are such heirs or devisees, and may determine their respective shares in such homestead or tree claim. The provisions of the Code of Civil Procedure relating to the determination of adverse claims to real estate in so far as the same may be applicable, shall pertain to and govern the procedure in the action provided for in this section.

Amended by Laws 1986, c. 444.

525.89.   Repealed by Laws 1974, c. 442, art. 8, § 524.8–102, eff. Jan. 1, 1976

525.90.   Renumbered 524.2–702 in St.1994

525.91.   Letters, contents

All letters issued by the courts to representatives of estates of deceased persons shall state the date of death of the deceased.

Laws 1975, c. 347, § 140, eff. Jan. 1, 1976.

Historical and Statutory Notes

St.1971, § 525.91 was repealed by Laws 1974, c. 442, art. 8, § 524.8–102, effective January 1, 1976. A similar provision was enacted by Laws 1975, c. 347, § 140, effective January 1, 1976, and coded as § 525.91.

UNIFORM ANATOMICAL GIFT ACT

UNIFORM ANATOMICAL GIFT ACT (1987)

Table of Jurisdictions Wherein Act Has Been Adopted

For text of Uniform Act, and variation notes and annotation materials for adopting jurisdictions, see Uniform Laws Annotated, Master Edition, Volume 8A.

Jurisdiction	Laws	Effective Date	Statutory Citation
Alabama[3]	2003, c. 347	1–1–2004	Code 1975, §§ 22–19–50 to 22–19–59.7.
Arizona	1996, c. 333	5–1–1996	A.R.S. §§ 36–841 to 36–850.
Arkansas	1989, No. 436	3–9–1989	A.C.A. §§ 20–17–601 to 20–17–618.
California	1988, c. 1095	1–1–1989	West's Ann.Cal. Health & Safety Code, §§ 7150 to 7157.
Connecticut	P.A. 88–318	7–1–1988	C.G.S.A. §§ 19a–279a to 19a–280a.
Hawaii	1988, c. 267	6–13–1988	HRS §§ 327–1 to 327–14.
Idaho	1989, c. 237		I.C. §§ 39–3401 to 39–3418.
Indiana[1]	1969, c. 166	3–13–1969*	West's A.I.C. 29–2–16–1 to 29–2–16–17.
Iowa	1995, S.F.117	7–1–1995	I.C.A. §§ 142C.1 to 142C.18.
Minnesota	1991, c. 202	8–1–1991	M.S.A. §§ 525.921 to 525.9224

Jurisdiction	Laws	Effective Date	Statutory Citation
Montana	1989, c. 540	10–1–1989	MCA 72–17–101 to 72–17–312.
Nevada.............	1989, c. 200	10–31–1989	NRS 451.500 to 451.590.
New Hampshire	1997, c. 336	1–1–1998	RSA 291–A:1 to 291–A:16.
New Mexico	1995, c. 116	7–1–1995	NMSA 1978 §§ 24–6A–1 to 24–6A–15.
North Dakota	1989, c. 303	7–12–1989	NDCC 23–06.2–01 to 23–06.2–12.
Oregon	1995, c. 717	9–9–1995	ORS 97.950 to 97.968.
Rhode Island	1989, c. 268	7–1–1989	Gen.Laws 1956, §§ 23–18.6–1 to 23–18.6–15.
Tennessee[2]	1969, c. 35	3–25–1969	T.C.A. §§ 68–30–101 to 68–30–116.
Utah................	1990, c. 131	4–23–1990	U.C.A.1953, 26–28–1 to 26–28–12.
Vermont.............	1989, No. 273	6–21–1990	18 V.S.A. §§ 5238 to 5248.
Virgin Islands	2000, No. 6354	6–30–2000*	19 V.I.C. §§ 401 to 415.
Virginia	1990, c. 959		Code 1950, §§ 32.1–289 to 32.1–297.1.
Washington	1993, c. 228	7–25–1993	West's RCWA 68.50.500 to 68.50.640, 68.50.901 to 68.50.904.
West Virginia	2000, c. 9	6–9–2000	Code, §§ 16–19–1 to 16–19–14.
Wisconsin	1989, Act 298	5–8–1990	W.S.A. 157.06.

* Date of approval.

[1] The Indiana act, as amended by P.L.126–1995 and 135–1995, without reference to each other, retains the basic format and many of the provisions of the Uniform Anatomical Gift Act of 1968, but now also contains many of the major provisions of the Uniform Anatomical Gift Act of (1987). Accordingly, the citation of the Indiana act is set forth in the tables for both the 1968 and 1987 acts.

[2] The Tennessee act, as amended by L.2001, c. 404, effective July 1, 2001, retains the basic format and many of the provisions of the Uniform Anatomical Gift Act of 1968, but now also contains many of the major provisions of the Uniform Anatomical Gift Act of (1987). Accordingly, the citation of the Tennessee act is set forth in the tables for both the 1968 and 1987 acts.

[3] Alabama enacted the Uniform Anatomical Gift Act (1987) effective January 1, 2004, without repealing the Uniform Anatomical Gift Act (1968). Accordingly, Alabama is set forth in the tables for both of these acts.

525.921 to 525.9219. Repealed by Laws 2007, c. 120, art. 1, § 26, eff. April 1, 2008

525.922. Repealed by Laws 1991, c. 202, § 42

525.9221 to 525.9224. Repealed by Laws 2007, c. 120, art. 1, § 26, eff. April 1, 2008

525.923 to 525.929. Repealed by Laws 1991, c. 202, § 42

525.93. Repealed by Laws 1991, c. 202, § 42

525.94. Repealed by Laws 1991, c. 202, § 42

525.95. Fiduciary powers, suspension during war service

Subdivision 1. Definitions. The definitions in this subdivision apply to this section.

(a) "War service" includes the following, during a period when the United States is engaged in war or other major military engagement with a foreign nation:

(1) active membership in the military forces of the United States or any of its allies;

(2) acceptance for membership in the military forces of the United States or any of its allies and awaiting induction into that service;

(3) participation in work abroad in connection with a governmental agency of the United States or any of its allies, with the Red Cross, or with a similar service;

(4) internment by an enemy or absence from the United States and inability to return; and

(5) service arising out of or in connection with the war or other major military engagement, which in the opinion of the court prevents the fiduciary from giving the proper attention to duties.

(b) "Fiduciary" refers to a trustee of a testamentary trust or of an express trust, a guardian of a person or conservator of a person's estate, an executor of a will, an administrator of the estate of the decedent, a custodian under the Minnesota Uniform Transfers to Minors Act, or an advisor or consultant in a testamentary or express trust.

Subd. 2. Powers of fiduciary may be suspended; petition. A fiduciary who contemplates entering war service, a fiduciary who is engaged in war service, a cofiduciary, or an interested person may petition the proper court having jurisdiction in matters of that nature for the suspension of the powers and duties of the fiduciary during the period of war service and until the further order of the court, and may petition for the reinstatement of the fiduciary upon the fiduciary's return.

Subd. 3. Notice of hearing. Notice of the hearing on a petition under subdivision 2 must be given to persons and in the manner the court directs.

Subd. 4. Hearing; order. After a hearing on a petition under subdivision 2 or in the case of an executor, administrator, or guardian on the court's own motion, the court may:

(1) order the suspension of the powers and duties of the fiduciary who is in war service for the period of the war service and until the further order of the court;

(2) appoint a successor fiduciary to serve for the period of suspension of the powers and duties of the fiduciary and until the further order of the court, if upon suspension of powers and duties, there is no fiduciary to exercise the powers and duties of the fiduciary who is in war service, or if in the opinion of the court the appointment of a cofiduciary is advisable;

(3) decree that the ownership and title to the trust property vests in the successor fiduciary or cofiduciary, as the case may be, and that the duties, powers, and discretions, or those of the powers and discretions that are not personal to the fiduciary, may be exercised by the cofiduciary or successor fiduciary;

701

(4) make other orders the court considers advisable with respect to the trust estate or its administration, and authorize a reasonable compensation to the successor fiduciary; or

(5) reserve jurisdiction for the entry of further orders and for the reinstatement of the fiduciary.

Upon petition, the court shall order the reinstatement of the fiduciary when the fiduciary's war service has terminated if it appears that the trust is not fully executed or administration of the estate is not completed.

Subd. 5. Responsibility of fiduciary. The fiduciary has no responsibility for the acts and doings of the cofiduciary or successor fiduciary during the period of the suspension of the fiduciary's powers and duties, but is not relieved of responsibility for the fiduciary's own acts or doings in the administration of the trust fund or estate. A successor fiduciary appointed under this section is not responsible for the acts of the predecessor fiduciary.

Laws 1989, c. 340, art. 1, § 75. Amended by Laws 2005, c. 10, art. 4, § 24.

Historical and Statutory Notes

Laws 1989, c. 340, art. 1, § 76 provides:

"Except as required by section 645.35 or as otherwise provided in sections 47 [section 501B.55], 60 [section 501B.71], 62 [section 501B.73], 70 [section 501B.86], subdivision 9, and 72 [section 501B.88], this article is effective January 1, 1990, and applies to trusts, property interests, and powers of appointment whenever created to the extent permitted under the United States Constitution and the Minnesota Constitution."

Chapter 525A

ANATOMICAL GIFTS

For complete statutory history see Minnesota Statutes Annotated

525A.01. Short title

This chapter may be cited as the "Darlene Luther Revised Uniform Anatomical Gift Act."

Laws 2007, c. 120, art. 1, § 1, eff. April 1, 2008.

REVISED ANATOMICAL GIFT (2006)

Table of Jurisdictions Wherein Act Has Been Adopted

For text of Uniform Act, and variation notes and annotation materials for adopting jurisdictions, see Uniform Laws Annotated, Master Edition, Volume 8A.

Jurisdiction	Laws	Effective Date	Statutory Citation
Arizona	2007, c. 281	7–2–2007 *	A.R.S. §§ 36–841 to 36–863.
Arkansas	2007, c. 839	4–3–2007	A.C.A. §§ 20–17–1201 to 20–17–1227.
California	2007, c. 629	1–1–2008	West's Ann.Cal. Health & Safety Code, §§ 7150 to 7151.40.
Colorado	2007, c. 207	7–1–2007	West's C.R.S.A. §§ 12–34–101 to 12–34–125.
Idaho	2007, c. 30	7–1–2007	I.C. §§ 39–3401 to 39–3425.
Indiana	2007, c. 147	7–1–2007	West's A.I.C. 29–2–16.1–1 to 29–2–16.1–21.
Iowa	2007, S.F.509	4–5–2007 *	I.C.A. §§ 142C.1 to 142C.18.
Kansas	2007, c. 127	7–1–2007	K.S.A. 65–3220 to 65–3244.
Minnesota	2007, c. 120	4–1–2008	M.S.A. §§ 525A.01 to 525A.25
Montana	2007, c. 345	10–1–2007	MCA 72–17–101 to 72–17–312.
Nevada	2007, c. 232	5–31–2007 *	N.R.S. 451.500 to 451.598.
New Mexico	2007, c. 323	7–1–2007	NMSA 1978 §§ 24–6B–1 to 24–6B–25.
North Carolina ...	2007, S.L. 2007–538	10–1–2007	G.S. §§ 130A–412.3 to 130A–412.33.
North Dakota	2007, c. 237	4–9–2007 *	NDCC 23–06.6–01 to 23–06.6–23.
Oregon	2007, c. 681	1–1–2008	ORS 97.951 to 97.982.
Rhode Island.....	2007, c. 476	7–6–2007	Gen.Laws 1956, §§ 23–18.6.1–1 to 23–18.6.1–25.
South Dakota	2007, c. 197	7–1–2007	SDCL 34–26–48 to 34–26–72.
Tennessee	2007, c. 428	7–1–2007	T.C.A. §§ 68–30–101 to 68–30–120.
Utah	2007, c. 60	7–1–2007	U.C.A.1953, 26–28–101 to 26–28–125.
Virginia	2007, cc. 92 and 907	1	Code 1950, §§ 32.1–291.1 to 32.1–291.25.

* Date of approval.

[1] Virginia L.2007, c. 92, was approved February 23, 2007, and L.2007, c. 907, was approved April 4, 2007.

525A.02. Definitions

Subdivision 1. Scope. The definitions in this section apply to this chapter.

Subd. 2. Adult. "Adult" means an individual who is at least 18 years of age.

Subd. 3. Agent. "Agent" means an individual who is:

(1) a health care agent, as defined in section 145C.01, subdivision 2; or

(2) expressly authorized to make an anatomical gift on the principal's behalf by any other record signed by the principal.

Subd. 4. Anatomical gift. "Anatomical gift" means a donation of all or part of a human body to take effect after the donor's death for the purpose of transplantation, therapy, research, or education.

Subd. 5. Decedent. "Decedent" means a deceased individual whose body or part is or may be the source of an anatomical gift. The term includes a stillborn infant or an embryo or fetus that has died of natural causes in utero.

Subd. 6. Disinterested witness. "Disinterested witness" means a witness other than the spouse, child, parent, sibling, grandchild, grandparent, or guardian of the individual who makes, amends, revokes, or refuses to make an anatomical gift, or another adult who exhibited special care and concern for the individual. The term does not include a person to which an anatomical gift could pass under section 525A.11.

Subd. 7. Document of gift. "Document of gift" means a donor card or other record used to make an anatomical gift. The term includes a statement or symbol on a driver's license, identification card, or donor registry.

Subd. 8. Donor. "Donor" means an individual whose body or part is the subject of an anatomical gift.

Subd. 9. Donor registry. "Donor registry" means a database that contains records of anatomical gifts and amendments to or revocations of anatomical gifts.

Subd. 10. Driver's license. "Driver's license" means a license or permit issued under chapter 171 to operate a vehicle, whether or not conditions are attached to the license or permit.

Subd. 11. Eye bank. "Eye bank" means a person that is licensed, accredited, or regulated under federal or state law to engage in the recovery, screening, testing, processing, storage, or distribution of human eyes or portions of human eyes.

Subd. 12. Guardian. "Guardian" means a person appointed by a court to make decisions regarding the support, care, education, health, or welfare of an individual. The term does not include a guardian ad litem.

Subd. 13. Hospital. "Hospital" means a facility licensed as a hospital under the law of any state or a facility operated as a hospital by the United States, a state, or a subdivision of a state.

Subd. 14. Identification card. "Identification card" means a Minnesota identification card issued under chapter 171.

Subd. 15. Know. "Know" means to have actual knowledge.

Subd. 16. Medical examiner. "Medical examiner" includes coroner.

Subd. 17. Minor. "Minor" means an individual who is under 18 years of age.

Subd. 18. Organ procurement organization. "Organ procurement organization" means a person designated by the secretary of the United States Department of Health and Human Services as an organ procurement organization.

Subd. 19. Parent. "Parent" means a parent whose parental rights have not been terminated.

Subd. 20. Part. "Part" means an organ, an eye, or tissue of a human being. The term does not include the whole body.

Subd. 21. Person. "Person" means an individual, corporation, business trust, estate, trust, partnership, limited liability company, association, joint venture, public corporation, government or governmental subdivision, agency, or instrumentality, or any other legal or commercial entity.

Subd. 22. Physician. "Physician" means an individual authorized to practice medicine or osteopathy under the law of any state.

Subd. 23. Procurement organization. "Procurement organization" means an eye bank, organ procurement organization, or tissue bank.

Subd. 24. Prospective donor. "Prospective donor" means an individual who is dead or near death and has been determined by a procurement organization to have a part that could be medically suitable for transplantation, therapy, research, or education. The term does not include an individual who has made a refusal.

Subd. 25. Reasonably available. "Reasonably available" means able to be contacted by a procurement organization without undue effort and willing and able to act in a timely manner consistent with existing medical criteria necessary for the making of an anatomical gift.

Subd. 26. Recipient. "Recipient" means an individual into whose body a decedent's part has been or is intended to be transplanted.

Subd. 27. Record. "Record" means information that is inscribed on a tangible medium or that is stored in an electronic or other medium and is retrievable in perceivable form.

Subd. 28. Refusal. "Refusal" means a record created under section 525A.07 that expressly states an intent to bar other persons from making an anatomical gift of an individual's body or part.

Subd. 29. Sign. "Sign" means, with the present intent to authenticate or adopt a record:

(1) to execute or adopt a tangible symbol; or

(2) to attach to or logically associate with the record an electronic symbol, sound, or process.

Subd. 30. State. "State" means a state of the United States, the District of Columbia, Puerto Rico, the United States Virgin Islands, or any territory or insular possession subject to the jurisdiction of the United States.

Subd. 31. Technician. "Technician" means an individual determined to be qualified to remove or process parts by an appropriate organization that is licensed, accredited, or regulated under federal or state law. The term includes an enucleator.

Subd. 32. Tissue. "Tissue" means a portion of the human body other than an organ or an eye. The term does not include blood unless the blood is donated for the purpose of research or education.

Subd. 33. Tissue bank. "Tissue bank" means a person that is licensed, accredited, or regulated under federal or state law to engage in the recovery, screening, testing, processing, storage, or distribution of tissue.

706

Subd. 34. Transplant hospital. "Transplant hospital" means a hospital that furnishes organ transplants and other medical and surgical specialty services required for the care of transplant patients.

Laws 2007, c. 120, art. 1, § 2, eff. April 1, 2008.

525A.03. Applicability

This chapter applies to an anatomical gift or amendment to, revocation of, or refusal to make an anatomical gift, whenever made.

Laws 2007, c. 120, art. 1, § 3, eff. April 1, 2008.

525A.04. Who may make anatomical gift before donor's death

Subject to section 525A.08, an anatomical gift of a donor's body or part may be made during the life of the donor for the purpose of transplantation, therapy, research, or education in the manner provided in section 525A.05 by:

(1) an adult donor;

(2) a minor donor, if the minor is:

(i) emancipated; or

(ii) authorized under state law to apply for a driver's license because the donor is at least 16 years of age;

(3) an agent of the donor, unless the health care directive, as defined in section 145C.01, subdivision 5a, or other record prohibits the agent from making an anatomical gift;

(4) a parent of the donor, if the donor is an unemancipated minor; or

(5) the donor's guardian.

Laws 2007, c. 120, art. 1, § 4, eff. April 1, 2008.

525A.05. Manner of making anatomical gift before donor's death

(a) A donor may make an anatomical gift:

(1) by authorizing a statement or symbol indicating that the donor has made an anatomical gift to be imprinted on the donor's driver's license or identification card;

(2) in a will;

(3) during a terminal illness or injury of the donor, by any form of communication addressed to at least two adults, at least one of whom is a disinterested witness; or

(4) as provided in paragraph (b).

(b) A donor or other person authorized to make an anatomical gift under section 525A.04 may make a gift by a donor card or other record signed by the donor or other person making the gift or by authorizing that a statement or symbol indicating that the donor has made an anatomical gift be included on a donor registry. If the donor or other person is physically unable to sign a record, the record may be signed by another individual at the direction of the donor or other person and must:

(1) be witnessed by at least two adults, at least one of whom is a disinterested witness, who have signed at the request of the donor or the other person; and

(2) state that it has been signed and witnessed as provided in clause (1).

(c) Revocation, suspension, expiration, or cancellation of a driver's license or identification card upon which an anatomical gift is indicated does not invalidate the gift.

(d) An anatomical gift made by will takes effect upon the donor's death whether or not the will is probated. Invalidation of the will after the donor's death does not invalidate the gift.

(e) The making of an anatomical gift does not authorize or direct a denial of health care.

Laws 2007, c. 120, art. 1, § 5, eff. April 1, 2008.

525A.06. Amending or revoking anatomical gift before donor's death

(a) Subject to section 525A.08, a donor or other person authorized to make an anatomical gift under section 525A.04 may amend or revoke an anatomical gift by:

(1) a record signed by:

(i) the donor;

(ii) the other person; or

(iii) subject to paragraph (b), another individual acting at the direction of the donor or the other person if the donor or other person is physically unable to sign; or

(2) a later-executed document of gift that amends or revokes a previous anatomical gift or portion of an anatomical gift, either expressly or by inconsistency.

(b) A record signed pursuant to paragraph (a), clause (1), item (iii), must:

(1) be witnessed by at least two adults, at least one of whom is a disinterested witness, who have signed at the request of the donor or the other person; and

(2) state that it has been signed and witnessed as provided in clause (1).

(c) Subject to section 525A.08, a donor or other person authorized to make an anatomical gift under section 525A.04 may revoke an anatomical gift by the destruction or cancellation of the document of gift, or the portion of the document of gift used to make the gift, with the intent to revoke the gift.

(d) A donor may amend or revoke an anatomical gift that was not made in a will by any form of communication during a terminal illness or injury addressed to at least two adults, at least one of whom is a disinterested witness.

(e) A donor who makes an anatomical gift in a will may amend or revoke the gift in the manner provided for amendment or revocation of wills or as provided in paragraph (a).

Laws 2007, c. 120, art. 1, § 6, eff. April 1, 2008.

525A.07. Refusal to make anatomical gift; effect of refusal

(a) An individual may refuse to make an anatomical gift of the individual's body or part by:

(1) a record signed by:

(i) the individual; or

(ii) subject to paragraph (b), another individual acting at the direction of the individual if the individual is physically unable to sign;

(2) the individual's will, whether or not the will is admitted to probate or invalidated after the individual's death; or

(3) any form of communication made by the individual during the individual's terminal illness or injury addressed to at least two adults, at least one of whom is a disinterested witness.

(b) A record signed pursuant to paragraph (a), clause (1), item (ii), must:

(1) be witnessed by at least two adults, at least one of whom is a disinterested witness, who have signed at the request of the individual; and

(2) state that it has been signed and witnessed as provided in clause (1).

(c) An individual who has made a refusal may amend or revoke the refusal:

(1) in the manner provided in paragraph (a) for making a refusal;

(2) by subsequently making an anatomical gift pursuant to section 525A.05 that is inconsistent with the refusal; or

(3) by destroying or canceling the record evidencing the refusal, or the portion of the record used to make the refusal, with the intent to revoke the refusal.

(d) Except as otherwise provided in section 525A.08, paragraph (h), in the absence of an express, contrary indication by the individual set forth in the refusal, an individual's unrevoked refusal to make an anatomical gift of the individual's body or part bars all other persons from making an anatomical gift of the individual's body or part.

Laws 2007, c. 120, art. 1, § 7, eff. April 1, 2008.

525A.08. Preclusive effect of anatomical gift, amendment, or revocation

(a) Except as otherwise provided in paragraph (g) and subject to paragraph (f), in the absence of an express, contrary indication by the donor, a person other than the donor is barred from making, amending, or revoking an anatomical gift of a donor's body or part if the donor made an anatomical gift of the donor's body or part under section 525A.05 or an amendment to an anatomical gift of the donor's body or part under section 525A.06. An anatomical gift made in a will, a designation on a driver's license or identification card, or a health care directive under chapter 145C, and not revoked, establishes the intent of the person making the designation and may not be overridden by any other person.

(b) A donor's revocation of an anatomical gift of the donor's body or part under section 525A.06 is not a refusal and does not bar another person specified in section 525A.04 or 525A.09 from making an anatomical gift of the donor's body or part under section 525A.05 or 525A.10.

(c) If a person other than the donor makes an unrevoked anatomical gift of the donor's body or part under section 525A.05 or an amendment to an anatomical gift of the donor's body or part under section 525A.06, another person may not make, amend, or revoke the gift of the donor's body or part under section 525A.10.

(d) A revocation of an anatomical gift of a donor's body or part under section 525A.06 by a person other than the donor does not bar another person specified in section 525A.09 from making an anatomical gift of the body or part under section 525A.05 or 525A.10.

(e) In the absence of an express, contrary indication by the donor or other person authorized to make an anatomical gift under section 525A.04, an anatomical gift of a part is neither a refusal to give another part nor a limitation on the making of an anatomical gift of another part at a later time by the donor or another person.

(f) In the absence of an express, contrary indication by the donor or other person authorized to make an anatomical gift under section 525A.04, an anatomical gift of a part for one or more of the purposes set forth in section 525A.04 is not a limitation on the making of an anatomical gift of the part for any of the other purposes by the donor or any other person under section 525A.05 or 525A.10.

(g) If a donor who is an unemancipated minor dies, a parent of the donor who is reasonably available may revoke or amend an anatomical gift of the donor's body or part.

(h) If an unemancipated minor who signed a refusal dies, a parent of the minor who is reasonably available may revoke the minor's refusal.

Laws 2007, c. 120, art. 1, § 8, eff. April 1, 2008.

525A.09. Who may make anatomical gift of decedent's body or part

(a) Subject to paragraphs (b) and (c) and unless barred by section 525A. 07 or 525A.08, an anatomical gift of a decedent's body or part for the purpose of transplantation, therapy, research, or education may be made by any member of the following classes of persons who is reasonably available, in the order of priority listed:

(1) an agent of the decedent at the time of death who could have made an anatomical gift under section 525A.04, clause (2), immediately before the decedent's death;

(2) the spouse of the decedent;

(3) adult children of the decedent;

(4) parents of the decedent;

(5) adult siblings of the decedent;

(6) adult grandchildren of the decedent;

(7) grandparents of the decedent;

(8) the persons who were acting as the guardians of the person of the decedent at the time of death;

(9) an adult who exhibited special care and concern for the decedent; and

(10) any other person having lawful authority to dispose of the decedent's body.

(b) If there is more than one member of a class listed in paragraph (a), clause (1), (3), (4), (5), (6), (7), or (9), entitled to make an anatomical gift, an anatomical gift may be made by a member of the class unless that member or a person to which the gift may pass under section 525A. 11 knows of an objection by another member of the class. If an objection is known, the gift may be made only by a majority of the members of the class who are reasonably available.

(c) A person may not make an anatomical gift if, at the time of the decedent's death, a person in a prior class under paragraph (a) is reasonably available to make or to object to the making of an anatomical gift.

Laws 2007, c. 120, art. 1, § 9, eff. April 1, 2008.

525A.10. Manner of making, amending, or revoking anatomical gift of decedent's body or part

(a) A person authorized to make an anatomical gift under section 525A.09 may make an anatomical gift by a document of gift signed by the person making the gift or by that person's oral communication that is electronically recorded or is contemporaneously reduced to a record and signed by the individual receiving the oral communication.

(b) Subject to paragraph (c), an anatomical gift by a person authorized under section 525A.09 may be amended or revoked orally or in a record by any member of a prior class who is reasonably available. If more than one member of the prior class is reasonably available, the gift made by a person authorized under section 525A.09 may be:

(1) amended only if a majority of the reasonably available members agree to the amending of the gift; or

(2) revoked only if a majority of the reasonably available members agree to the revoking of the gift or if they are equally divided as to whether to revoke the gift.

(c) A revocation under paragraph (b) is effective only if, before an incision has been made to remove a part from the donor's body or before invasive procedures have begun to prepare the recipient, the procurement organization, transplant hospital, or physician or technician knows of the revocation.

Laws 2007, c. 120, art. 1, § 10, eff. April 1, 2008.

525A.11. Persons that may receive anatomical gift; purpose of anatomical gift

(a) An anatomical gift may be made to the following persons named in the document of gift:

(1) a hospital; accredited medical school, dental school, college, or university; organ procurement organization; or nonprofit organization in medical education or research, for research or education;

(2) subject to paragraph (b), an individual designated by the person making the anatomical gift if the individual is the recipient of the part; and

(3) an eye bank or tissue bank.

(b) If an anatomical gift to an individual under paragraph (a), clause (2), cannot be transplanted into the individual, the part passes in accordance with paragraph (g) in the absence of an express, contrary indication by the person making the anatomical gift.

(c) If an anatomical gift of one or more specific parts or of all parts is made in a document of gift that does not name a person described in paragraph (a) but identifies the purpose for which an anatomical gift may be used, the following rules apply:

(1) if the part is an eye and the gift is for the purpose of transplantation or therapy, the gift passes to the appropriate eye bank;

(2) if the part is tissue and the gift is for the purpose of transplantation or therapy, the gift passes to the appropriate tissue bank;

(3) if the part is an organ and the gift is for the purpose of transplantation or therapy, the gift passes to the appropriate organ procurement organization as custodian of the organ; and

(4) if the part is an organ, an eye, or tissue and the gift is for the purpose of research or education, the gift passes to the appropriate procurement organization.

(d) For the purpose of paragraph (c), if there is more than one purpose of an anatomical gift set forth in the document of gift but the purposes are not set forth in any priority, the gift must be used for transplantation or therapy, if suitable. If the gift cannot be used for transplantation or therapy, the gift may be used for research or education.

(e) If an anatomical gift of one or more specific parts is made in a document of gift that does not name a person described in paragraph (a) and does not identify the purpose of the gift, the gift may be used only for transplantation or therapy, and the gift passes in accordance with paragraph (g).

(f) If a document of gift specifies only a general intent to make an anatomical gift by words such as "donor," "organ donor," or "body donor," or by a symbol or statement of similar import, the gift may be used only for transplantation or therapy, and the gift passes in accordance with paragraph (g).

(g) For purposes of paragraphs (b), (e), and (f), the following rules apply:

(1) if the part is an eye, the gift passes to the appropriate eye bank;

(2) if the part is tissue, the gift passes to the appropriate tissue bank; and

(3) if the part is an organ, the gift passes to the appropriate organ procurement organization as custodian of the organ.

(h) An anatomical gift of an organ for transplantation or therapy, other than an anatomical gift under paragraph (a), clause (2), passes to the organ procurement organization as custodian of the organ.

(i) If an anatomical gift does not pass pursuant to paragraphs (a) to (h) or the decedent's body or part is not used for transplantation, therapy, research, or education, custody of the body or part passes to the person under obligation to dispose of the body or part.

(j) A person may not accept an anatomical gift if the person knows that the gift was not effectively made under section 525A.05 or 525A.10 or if the person knows that the decedent made a refusal under section 525A.07 that was not revoked. For purposes of this paragraph, if a person knows that an anatomical gift was made on a document of gift, the person is deemed to know of any amendment or revocation of the gift or any refusal to make an anatomical gift on the same document of gift.

(k) Except as otherwise provided in paragraph (a), clause (2), nothing in this chapter affects the allocation of organs for transplantation or therapy.

Laws 2007, c. 120, art. 1, § 11, eff. April 1, 2008.

525A.12. Search and notification

(a) The following persons shall make a reasonable search of an individual who the person reasonably believes is dead or near death for a document of gift or other information identifying the individual as a donor or as an individual who made a refusal:

(1) a law enforcement officer, firefighter, paramedic, or other emergency rescuer finding the individual; and

(2) if no other source of the information is immediately available, a hospital, as soon as practical after the individual's arrival at the hospital.

(b) If a document of gift or a refusal to make an anatomical gift is located by the search required by paragraph (a), clause (1), and the individual or deceased individual to whom it relates is taken to a hospital, the person responsible for conducting the search shall send the document of gift or refusal to the hospital. If a body is transferred to the custody of the medical examiner, the first responder must notify the first responder's dispatcher. A dispatcher notified under this section must notify the state's federally designated organ procurement organization and inform the organization of the deceased's name, donor status, and location.

(c) A person is not subject to criminal or civil liability for failing to discharge the duties imposed by this section.

Laws 2007, c. 120, art. 1, § 12, eff. April 1, 2008.

525A.13. Delivery of document of gift not required; right to examine

(a) A document of gift need not be delivered during the donor's lifetime to be effective.

(b) Upon or after an individual's death, a person in possession of a document of gift or a refusal to make an anatomical gift with respect to the individual shall allow examination and copying of the document of gift or refusal by a person authorized to make or object to the making of an anatomical gift with respect to the individual or by a person to which the gift could pass under section 525A.11.

Laws 2007, c. 120, art. 1, § 13, eff. April 1, 2008.

525A.14. Rights and duties of procurement organization and others

(a) When a hospital refers an individual at or near death to a procurement organization, the organization shall make a reasonable search of the records of the Department of Public Safety and any donor registry that it knows exists for the geographical area in which the individual resides to ascertain whether the individual has made an anatomical gift.

(b) A procurement organization must be allowed reasonable access to information in the records of the Department of Public Safety to ascertain whether an individual at or near death is a donor.

(c) When a hospital refers an individual at or near death to a procurement organization, the organization may conduct any reasonable examination necessary to ensure the medical suitability of a part that is or could be the subject of an anatomical gift for transplantation, therapy, research, or education from a donor or a prospective donor. During the examination period, measures necessary to ensure the medical suitability of the part may not be withdrawn unless the hospital or procurement organization knows that the individual expressed a contrary intent.

(d) Unless prohibited by law other than this chapter, at any time after a donor's death, the person to which a part passes under section 525A.11 may conduct any reasonable examination necessary to ensure the medical suitability of the body or part for its intended purpose.

(e) Unless prohibited by law other than this chapter, an examination under paragraph (c) or (d) may include an examination of all medical and dental records of the donor or prospective donor.

(f) Upon the death of a minor who was a donor or had signed a refusal, unless a procurement organization knows the minor is emancipated, the procurement organization shall conduct a reasonable search for the parents of the minor and provide the parents with an opportunity to revoke or amend the anatomical gift or revoke the refusal.

(g) Upon referral by a hospital under paragraph (a), a procurement organization shall make a reasonable search for any person listed in section 525A.09 having priority to make an anatomical gift on behalf of a prospective donor. If a procurement organization receives information that an anatomical gift to any other person was made, amended, or revoked, it shall promptly advise the other person of all relevant information.

(h) Subject to sections 525A.11, paragraph (i), and 525A.23, the rights of the person to which a part passes under section 525A.11 are superior to the rights of all others with respect to the part. The person may accept or reject an anatomical gift in whole or in part. Subject to the terms of the document of gift and this chapter, a person that accepts an anatomical gift of an entire body may allow embalming, burial, or cremation, and use of remains in a funeral service. If the gift is of a part, the person to which the part passes under section 525A.11, upon the death of the donor and before embalming, burial, or cremation, shall cause the part to be removed without unnecessary mutilation.

(i) Neither the physician who attends the decedent at death nor the physician who determines the time of the decedent's death may participate in the procedures for removing or transplanting a part from the decedent.

(j) A physician or technician may remove a donated part from the body of a donor that the physician or technician is qualified to remove.

Laws 2007, c. 120, art. 1, § 14, eff. April 1, 2008.

525A.15. Coordination of procurement and use

Each hospital in this state shall enter into agreements or affiliations with procurement organizations for coordination of procurement and use of anatomical gifts.

Laws 2007, c. 120, art. 1, § 15, eff. April 1, 2008.

525A.16. Sale or purchase of parts prohibited; felony

(a) Except as otherwise provided in paragraph (b), a person that for valuable consideration, knowingly purchases or sells a part for transplantation or therapy if removal of a part from an individual is intended to occur after the individual's death, commits a felony and upon conviction is subject to a fine not exceeding $10,000 or imprisonment not exceeding five years, or both.

(b) A person may charge a reasonable amount for the removal, processing, preservation, quality control, storage, transportation, implantation, or disposal of a part.

Laws 2007, c. 120, art. 1, § 16, eff. April 1, 2008.

525A.17. Prohibited acts; felony

A person that, in order to obtain a financial gain, intentionally falsifies, forges, conceals, defaces, or obliterates a document of gift, an amendment or revocation of a document of gift, or a refusal commits a felony and upon conviction is subject to a fine not exceeding $10,000 or imprisonment not exceeding five years, or both.

Laws 2007, c. 120, art. 1, § 17, eff. April 1, 2008.

525A.18. Immunity

(a) A person that acts in accordance with this chapter or with the applicable anatomical gift law of another state, or attempts in good faith to do so, is not liable for the act in a civil action, criminal prosecution, or administrative proceeding.

(b) Neither the person making an anatomical gift nor the donor's estate is liable for any injury or damage that results from the making or use of the gift.

(c) In determining whether an anatomical gift has been made, amended, or revoked under this chapter, a person may rely upon representations of an individual listed in section 525A.09, paragraph (a), clause (2), (3), (4), (5), (6), (7), or (8), relating to the individual's relationship to the donor or prospective donor unless the person knows that the representation is untrue.

(d) An anatomical gift under this chapter is not a sale of goods as that term is defined in section 336.2-105, paragraph (1), or the sale of a product.

Laws 2007, c. 120, art. 1, § 18, eff. April 1, 2008.

525A.19. Law governing validity; choice of law as to execution of document of gift; presumption of validity

(a) A document of gift is valid if executed in accordance with:

(1) this chapter;

(2) the laws of the state or country where it was executed; or

(3) the laws of the state or country where the person making the anatomical gift was domiciled, has a place of residence, or was a national at the time the document of gift was executed.

(b) If a document of gift is valid under this section, the law of this state governs the interpretation of the document of gift.

(c) A person may presume that a document of gift or amendment of an anatomical gift is valid unless that person knows that it was not validly executed or was revoked.

Laws 2007, c. 120, art. 1, § 19, eff. April 1, 2008.

525A.20. Donor registry

(a) The Department of Public Safety shall provide donor information to an organ procurement organization or eye bank that administers any donor registry that this state establishes, contracts for, or recognizes for the purpose of transferring to the donor registry all relevant information regarding a donor's making, amendment to, or revocation of an anatomical gift.

(b) A donor registry must:

(1) allow a donor or other person authorized under section 525A.04 to include on the donor registry a statement or symbol that the donor has made, amended, or revoked an anatomical gift;

(2) be accessible to a procurement organization to allow it to obtain relevant information on the donor registry to determine, at or near death of the donor or a prospective donor, whether the donor or prospective donor has made, amended, or revoked an anatomical gift; and

(3) be accessible, for purposes of clauses (1) and (2), seven days a week on a 24-hour basis.

(c) Personally identifiable information on a donor registry about a donor or prospective donor may not be used or disclosed without the express consent of the donor, prospective donor, or person that made the anatomical gift for any purpose other than to determine, at or near death of the donor or prospective donor, whether the donor or prospective donor has made, amended, or revoked an anatomical gift.

(d) This section does not prohibit any person from creating or maintaining a donor registry that is not established by or under contract with the state. Any such registry must comply with paragraphs (b) and (c).

Laws 2007, c. 120, art. 1, § 20, eff. April 1, 2008.

525A.21. Effect of anatomical gift on health care directive

(a) In this section, "health care directive" has the meaning given in section 145C.01, subdivision 5a.

(b) If a prospective donor has a health care directive and the terms of the declaration or directive and the express or implied terms of a potential anatomical gift are in conflict with regard to the administration of measures necessary to ensure the medical suitability of a part for transplantation or therapy, the prospective donor's attending physician and the prospective donor shall confer to resolve the conflict. If the prospective donor is incapable of resolving the conflict, an agent acting under the prospective donor's declaration or directive or, if there is none or the agent is not reasonably available, another person authorized by a law other than this chapter to make health care decisions on behalf of the prospective donor, shall act for the donor to resolve the conflict. The conflict must be resolved as expeditiously as possible. Information relevant to the resolution of the conflict may be obtained from the appropriate procurement organization and any other person authorized to make an anatomical gift for the prospective donor under section 525A.09. Before resolution of the conflict, measures necessary to ensure the medical suitability of the part may not be withheld or withdrawn from the prospective donor if withholding or withdrawing the measures is not contraindicated by appropriate end-of-life care.

Laws 2007, c. 120, art. 1, § 21, eff. April 1, 2008.

525A.22. Cooperation between medical examiner and procurement organization

(a) A medical examiner shall cooperate with procurement organizations to maximize the opportunity to recover anatomical gifts for the purpose of transplantation, therapy, research, or education.

(b) If a medical examiner receives notice from a procurement organization that an anatomical gift might be available or was made with respect to a decedent whose body is under the jurisdiction of the medical examiner and a postmortem examination is going to be performed, unless the medical examiner denies recovery in accordance with section 525A.23, the medical examiner or designee shall conduct a postmortem examination of the body or the part in a manner and within a period compatible with its preservation for the purposes of the gift.

(c) A part may not be removed from the body of a decedent under the jurisdiction of a medical examiner for transplantation, therapy, research, or education unless the part is the subject of an anatomical gift. The body of a decedent under the jurisdiction of the medical examiner may not be delivered to a person for research or education unless the body is the subject of an anatomical gift. This paragraph does not preclude a medical examiner from performing the medicolegal investigation upon the body or parts of a decedent under the jurisdiction of the medical examiner.

Laws 2007, c. 120, art. 1, § 22, eff. April 1, 2008.

525A.23. Facilitation of anatomical gift from decedent whose body is under jurisdiction of medical examiner

(a) Upon request of a procurement organization, a medical examiner shall release to the procurement organization the name, contact information, and available medical and social history of a decedent whose body is under the jurisdiction of the medical examiner. If the decedent's body or part is medically suitable for transplantation, therapy, research, or education, the medical examiner shall release postmortem examination results to the procurement organization. The procurement organization may make a subsequent disclosure of the postmortem examination results or other information received from the medical examiner only if relevant to transplantation or therapy.

(b) The medical examiner may conduct a medicolegal examination by reviewing all medical records, laboratory test results, x-rays, other diagnostic results, and other information that any person possesses about a donor or prospective donor whose body is under the jurisdiction of the medical examiner which the medical examiner determines may be relevant to the investigation.

(c) A person that has any information requested by a medical examiner pursuant to paragraph (b) shall provide that information as expeditiously as possible to allow the medical examiner to conduct the medicolegal investigation within a period compatible with the preservation of parts for the purpose of transplantation, therapy, research, or education.

(d) If an anatomical gift has been or might be made of a part of a decedent whose body is under the jurisdiction of the medical examiner and a postmortem examination is not required, or the medical examiner determines that a postmortem examination is required but that the recovery of the part that is the subject of an anatomical gift will not interfere with the examination, the medical examiner and procurement organization shall cooperate in the timely removal of the part from the decedent for the purpose of transplantation, therapy, research, or education.

(e) If an anatomical gift of a part from the decedent under the jurisdiction of the medical examiner has been or might be made, but the medical examiner initially believes that the recovery of the part could interfere with the postmortem investigation into the decedent's cause or manner of death, the medical examiner shall consult with the procurement organization or physician or technician designated by the procurement organization about the proposed recovery. After consultation, the medical examiner may allow the recovery.

(f) Following the consultation under paragraph (e), in the absence of mutually agreed-upon protocols to resolve conflict between the medical examiner and the procurement organization, if the medical examiner intends to deny recovery of an organ for transplantation, the medical examiner or designee, at the request of the procurement organization, shall attend the removal procedure for the part before making a final determination not to allow the procurement organization to recover the part. During the removal procedure, the medical examiner or designee may allow recovery by the procurement organization to proceed, or, if the medical examiner or designee reasonably believes that the part may be involved in determining the decedent's cause or manner of death, deny recovery by the procurement organization.

(g) If the medical examiner or designee denies recovery under paragraph (f), the medical examiner or designee shall:

(1) explain in a record the specific reasons for not allowing recovery of the part;

(2) include the specific reasons in the records of the medical examiner; and

(3) provide a record with the specific reasons to the procurement organization.

(h) If the medical examiner or designee allows recovery of a part under paragraph (d), (e), or (f), the procurement organization, upon request, shall cause the physician or technician who removes the part to provide the medical examiner with a record describing the condition of the part, a biopsy, a photograph, and any other information and observations that would assist in the postmortem examination.

(i) If a medical examiner or designee is required to be present at a removal procedure under paragraph (f), upon request the procurement organization requesting the recovery of the part shall reimburse the medical examiner or designee for the additional costs incurred in complying with paragraph (f).

Laws 2007, c. 120, art. 1, § 23, eff. April 1, 2008.

525A.24. Relation to Electronic Signatures in Global and National Commerce Act

This chapter modifies, limits, and supersedes the Electronic Signatures in Global and National Commerce Act, United States Code, title 15, section 7001 et seq., but does not modify, limit, or supersede section 101(a) of that act, United States Code, title 15, section 7001, or authorize electronic delivery of any of the notices described in section 103(b) of that act, United States Code, title 15, section 7003(b).

Laws 2007, c. 120, art. 1, § 24, eff. April 1, 2008.

525A.25. Anatomical gift; relation to Uniform Commercial Code

The provision or use of any part of a human body, including blood, blood components, bone marrow, or solid organs from living donors, for the purpose of injection, transfusion, or transplantation in the human body is the rendition of a health care service by each person participating in the provision or use and is not a sale of goods, as that term is defined in section 336.2-105, paragraph (1), or a sale of a product.

Laws 2007, c. 120, art. 1, § 25, eff. April 1, 2008.

Chapter 527

UNIFORM TRANSFERS TO MINORS ACT

For complete statutory history see Minnesota Statutes Annotated.

527.01 to 527.11. **Repealed by Laws 1985, c. 221, § 25, eff. Jan. 1, 1986**

527.21. **Definitions**

For purposes of this chapter:

(1) "Adult" means an individual who has attained the age of 21 years, notwithstanding any law to the contrary.

(2) "Benefit plan" means an employer's plan for the benefit of an employee or partner.

(3) "Broker" means a person lawfully engaged in the business of effecting transactions in securities or commodities for the person's own account or for the account of others.

(4) "Conservator" means a person appointed or qualified by a court to act as general, limited, or temporary guardian of a minor's property or a person legally authorized to perform substantially the same functions.

(5) "Court" means a court that exercises probate jurisdiction.

(6) "Custodial property" means (i) any interest in property transferred to a custodian under this chapter and (ii) the income from and proceeds of that interest in property.

(7) "Custodian" means a person so designated under section 527.29 or a successor or substitute custodian designated under section 527.38.

(8) "Financial institution" means a bank, trust company, savings institution, or credit union, chartered and supervised under state or federal law.

(9) "Legal representative" means an individual's personal representative or conservator.

(10) "Member of the minor's family" means the minor's parent, stepparent, spouse, grandparent, brother, sister, uncle, or aunt, whether of the whole or half blood or by adoption.

(11) "Minor" means an individual who has not attained the age of 21 years, notwithstanding any law to the contrary.

(12) "Person" means an individual, corporation, organization, or other legal entity.

(13) "Personal representative" means an executor, administrator, successor personal representative, or special administrator of a decedent's estate or a person legally authorized to perform substantially the same functions.

(14) "State" includes any state of the United States, the District of Columbia, the Commonwealth of Puerto Rico, and any territory or possession subject to the legislative authority of the United States.

(15) "Street name or nominee name" means registration used by a broker or financial institution for holding securities when not registered in the name of the beneficial owner.

(16) "Transfer" means a transaction that creates custodial property under section 527.29.

(17) "Transferor" means a person who makes a transfer under this chapter.

(18) "Trust company" means a financial institution, corporation, or other legal entity, authorized to exercise general trust powers.

Laws 1985, c. 221, § 1, eff. Jan. 1, 1986. Amended by Laws 1985, 1st Sp., c. 13, § 364, eff. Jan. 1, 1986.

UNIFORM TRANSFERS TO MINORS ACT
Table of Jurisdictions Wherein Act Has Been Adopted
For text of Uniform Act, and variation notes and annotation materials for adopting jurisdictions, see Uniform Laws Annotated, Master Edition, Volume 8C.

Jurisdiction	Laws	Effective Date	Statutory Citation
Alabama	1986, No. 86–453	10–1–1986	Code 1975, §§ 35–5A–1 to 35–5A–24.
Alaska	1990, c. 11	1–1–1991	AS 13.46.010 to 13.46.999.
Arizona	1988, c. 81	5–16–1988 *	A.R.S. §§ 14–7651 to 14–7671.
Arkansas	1985, No. 476	3–21–1985	A.C.A. §§ 9–26–201 to 9–26–227.
California	1984, c. 243	6–24–1984 *	West's Ann.Cal.Prob.Code, §§ 3900 to 3925.
Colorado	1984, p. 383	7–1–1984	West's C.R.S.A. §§ 11–50–101 to 11–50–126.
Connecticut	1995, P.A. 95–117	10–1–1995	C.G.S.A. §§ 45a–557 to 45a–560b.
Delaware	70 Del. Laws, c. 393	6–26–1996	12 Del. C. §§4501 to 4523.
District of Columbia	1986, D.C. Law 6–87	3–12–1986	D.C. Official Code, 2001 Ed. §§ 21–301 to 21–324.
Florida	1985, c. 85–95	10–1–1985	West's F.S.A. §§ 710.101 to 710.126.
Georgia	1990, p. 667	7–1–1990	O.C.G.A. §§ 44–5–110 to 44–5–134.
Hawaii	1985, No. 91	7–1–1985	HRS §§ 553A–1 to 553A–24.
Idaho	1984, c. 152	7–1–1984	I.C. §§ 68–801 to 68–825.
Illinois	1985, P.A. 84–915	7–1–1986	S.H.A. 760 ILCS 20/1 to 20/24.
Indiana	1989, P.L. 267–1989	5–4–1989 *	West's A.I.C. 30–2–8.5–1 to 30–2–8.5–40.
Iowa	1986, H.F. 2381	4–7–1986 *	I.C.A. §§ 565B.1 to 565B.25.
Kansas	1985, c. 143	4–4–1985 *	K.S.A. 38–1701 to 38–1726.
Kentucky	1986, c. 182	3–28–1986 *	KRS 385.012 to 385.252.
Louisiana	1987, No. 469	1–1–1988	LSA–R.S. 9:751 to 9:773.
Maine	1987, c. 734	4–19–1988 *	33 M.R.S.A. §§ 1651 to 1674.
Maryland	1989, c. 638	7–1–1989	Code, Estates and Trusts, §§ 13–301 to 13–324.
Massachusetts	1986, c. 362	1–30–1987	M.G.L.A. c. 201A, §§ 1 to 24.
Michigan	1998, P.A. 433	12–30–1998	M.C.L.A. §§ 554.521 to 554.552.
Minnesota	1985, c. 221	1–1–1986	M.S.A. §§ 527.21 to 527.44.
Mississippi	1994, c. 416	1–1–1995	Code 1972, §§ 91–20–1 to 91–20–49.
Missouri	1985, S.B. 35, 17, 18, 84, 206, 259, 278	7–30–1985 *	V.A.M.S. §§ 404.005 to 404.094.
Montana	1985, c. 102		MCA 72–26–501 to 72–26–803.
Nebraska	1992, LB 907	2–28–1992 *	R.R.S.1943, §§ 43–2701 to 43–2724.
Nevada	1985, c. 51	3–28–1985 *	N.R.S. 167.010 to 167.100.
New Hampshire	1985, No. 197:1	7–30–1985	RSA 463–A:1 to 463–A:26.
New Jersey [1]	1987, c. 18	7–1–1987	N.J.S.A. 46:38A–1 to 46:38A–57.
New Mexico	1989, c. 357	7–1–1989	NMSA 1978, §§ 46–7–11 to 46–7–34.
New York	1996, c. 304	7–10–1996	McKinney's EPTL, 7–6.1 to 7–6.26.
North Carolina	1987, c. 563	10–1–1987	G.S. §§ 33A–1 to 33A–24.
North Dakota	1985, c. 508		NDCC 47–24.1–01 to 47–24.1–22.
Ohio	2006, H.B. 416	1–1–2007	R.C. §§ 5814.01 to 5814.09.
Oklahoma	1986, c. 261	11–1–1986	58 Okl.St.Ann. §§ 1201 to 1225.
Oregon	1985, c. 665	1–1–1986	ORS 126.805 to 126.886.
Pennsylvania	1992, Act 152	12–16–1992	20 Pa.C.S.A., §§ 5301 to 5321.
Rhode Island	1985, c. 389	6–28–1985	Gen.Laws 1956, §§ 18–7–1 to 18–7–26.
South Dakota	SL 1986, c. 409		SDCL 55–10A–1 to 55–10A–26.
Tennessee	1992, c. 664	10–1–1992	T.C.A. §§ 35–7–101 to 35–7–126.

Jurisdiction	Laws	Effective Date	Statutory Citation
Texas	1995, c. 1043	9–1–1995	V.T.C.A. Property Code, §§ 141.001 to 141.025.
Utah...............	1990, c. 272	7–1–1990	U.C.A.1953, 75–5a–101 to 75–5a–123.
Virgin Islands	2001, No. 6423	8–2–2001 *	15 V.I.C. §§ 1251a to 1251x.
Virginia	1988, c. 516		Code 1950, §§ 31–37 to 31–59.
Washington	1991, c. 193	7–1–1991	West's RCWA 11.114.010 to 11.114.904.
West Virginia	1986, c. 169	7–1–1986	Code 36–7–1 to 36–7–24.
Wisconsin	1987–89, c. 191	4–8–1988	W.S.A. 54.854 to 54.898.
Wyoming	1987, c. 201	5–22–1987	Wyo.Stat.Ann. §§ 34–13–114 to 34–13–137.

* Date of approval.

[1] Repealed Gifts to Minors Act of 1966, effective July 1, 2007. Transfers to Minors Act adopted, effective July 1, 1987. See General Statutory Note, post.

527.22. Scope and jurisdiction

(a) This chapter applies to a transfer that refers to this chapter in the designation under section 527.29, paragraph (a), by which the transfer is made, if at the time of the transfer, the transferor, the minor, or the custodian is a resident of this state or the custodial property is located in this state. The custodianship so created remains subject to this chapter despite a subsequent change in residence of a transferor, the minor, or the custodian, or the removal of custodial property from this state.

(b) A person designated as custodian under this chapter is subject to personal jurisdiction in this state with respect to any matter relating to the custodianship.

(c) A transfer that purports to be made and which is valid under the Uniform Transfers to Minors Act, the Uniform Gifts to Minors Act, or a substantially similar act, of another state is governed by the law of the designated state and may be executed and is enforceable in this state if at the time of the transfer, the transferor, the minor, or the custodian is a resident of the designated state or the custodial property is located in the designated state.

Laws 1985, c. 221, § 2, eff. Jan. 1, 1986.

527.23. Nomination of custodian

(a) A person having the right to designate the recipient of property transferable upon the occurrence of a future event may revocably nominate a custodian to receive the property for a minor beneficiary upon the occurrence of the event by naming the custodian followed in substance by the words: "as custodian for .... (name of minor) under the Minnesota Uniform Transfers to Minors Act." The nomination may name one or more persons as substitute custodians to whom the property must be transferred, in the order named, if the first nominated custodian dies before the transfer or is unable, declines, or is ineligible to serve. The nomination may be made in a will, a trust, a deed, an instrument exercising a power of appointment, or in a writing designating a

725

beneficiary of contractual rights which is registered with or delivered to the payor, issuer, or other obligor of the contractual rights.

(b) A custodian nominated under this section must be a person to whom a transfer of property of that kind may be made under section 527.29, paragraph (a).

(c) The nomination of a custodian under this section does not create custodial property until the nominating instrument becomes irrevocable or a transfer to the nominated custodian is completed under section 527.29. Unless the nomination of a custodian has been revoked, upon the occurrence of the future event the custodianship becomes effective and the custodian shall enforce a transfer of the custodial property pursuant to section 527.29.

Laws 1985, c. 221, § 3, eff. Jan. 1, 1986.

527.24. Transfer by gift or exercise of power of appointment

A person may make a transfer by irrevocable gift to, or the irrevocable exercise of a power of appointment in favor of, a custodian for the benefit of a minor pursuant to section 527.29.

Laws 1985, c. 221, § 4, eff. Jan. 1, 1986.

527.25. Transfer authorized by will or trust

(a) A personal representative or trustee may make an irrevocable transfer pursuant to section 527.29 to a custodian for the benefit of a minor as authorized in the governing will or trust.

(b) If the testator or settlor has nominated a custodian under section 527.23 to receive the custodial property, the transfer must be made to that person.

(c) If the testator or settlor has not nominated a custodian under section 527.23, or all persons so nominated as custodian die before the transfer or are unable, decline, or are ineligible to serve, the personal representative or the trustee, as the case may be, shall designate the custodian from among those eligible to serve as custodian for property of that kind under section 527.29, paragraph (a).

Laws 1985, c. 221, § 5, eff. Jan. 1, 1986.

527.26. Other transfer by fiduciary

(a) Subject to paragraph (c), a personal representative or trustee may make an irrevocable transfer to another adult or trust company as custodian for the benefit of a minor pursuant to section 527.29, in the absence of a will or under a will or trust that does not contain an authorization to do so.

(b) Subject to paragraph (c), a conservator may make an irrevocable transfer to another adult or trust company as custodian for the benefit of the minor pursuant to section 527.29.

(c) A transfer under paragraph (a) or (b) may be made only if (i) the personal representative, trustee, or conservator considers the transfer to be in the best interest of the minor, (ii) the transfer is not prohibited by or inconsistent with provisions of the applicable will, trust agreement, or other governing instrument, and (iii) the transfer is authorized by the court if it exceeds $10,000 in value.

Laws 1985, c. 221, § 6, eff. Jan. 1, 1986.

527.27. Transfer by obligor

(a) Subject to paragraphs (b) and (c), a person not subject to section 527.25 or 527.26 who holds property of or owes a liquidated debt to a minor not having a conservator may make an irrevocable transfer to a custodian for the benefit of the minor pursuant to section 527.29.

(b) If a person having the right to do so under section 527.23 has nominated a custodian under that section to receive the custodial property, the transfer must be made to that person.

(c) If no custodian has been nominated under section 527.23, or all persons so nominated as custodian die before the transfer or are unable, decline, or are ineligible to serve, a transfer under this section may be made to an adult member of the minor's family or to a trust company unless the property exceeds $10,000 in value.

Laws 1985, c. 221, § 7, eff. Jan. 1, 1986.

527.28. Receipt for custodial property

A written acknowledgment of delivery by a custodian constitutes a sufficient receipt and discharge for custodial property transferred to the custodian pursuant to this chapter.

Laws 1985, c. 221, § 8, eff. Jan. 1, 1986.

527.29. Manner of creating custodial property and effecting transfer; designation of initial custodian; control

(a) Custodial property is created and a transfer is made whenever:

(1) an uncertificated security or a certificated security in registered form is either:

(i) registered in the name of the transferor, an adult other than the transferor, or a trust company, followed in substance by the words: "as custodian for .... (name of minor) under the Minnesota Uniform Transfers to Minors Act"; or

(ii) delivered if in certificated form, or any document necessary for the transfer of an uncertificated security is delivered, together with any necessary endorsement to an adult other than the transferor or to a trust company as custodian, accompanied by an instrument in substantially the form set forth in paragraph (b);

(2) money is paid or delivered, or a security held in the name of a broker, financial institution, or its nominee is transferred, to a broker or financial institution for credit to an account in the name of the transferor, an adult other than the transferor, or a trust company, followed in substance by the words: "as custodian for .... (name of minor) under the Minnesota Uniform Transfers to Minors Act";

(3) the ownership of a life or endowment insurance policy or annuity contract is either:

(i) registered with the issuer in the name of the transferor, an adult other than the transferor, or a trust company, followed in substance by the words: "as custodian for .... (name of minor) under the Minnesota Uniform Transfers to Minors Act"; or

(ii) assigned in a writing delivered to an adult other than the transferor or to a trust company whose name in the assignment is followed in substance by the words: "as custodian for .... (name of minor) under the Minnesota Uniform Transfers to Minors Act";

(4) an irrevocable exercise of a power of appointment or an irrevocable present right to future payment under a contract is the subject of a written notification delivered to the payor, issuer, or other obligor that the right is transferred to the transferor, an adult other than the transferor, or a trust company, whose name in the notification is followed in substance by the words: "as custodian for .... (name of minor) under the Minnesota Uniform Transfers to Minors Act";

(5) an interest in real property is recorded in the name of the transferor, an adult other than the transferor, or a trust company, followed in substance by the words: "as custodian for .... (name of minor) under the Minnesota Uniform Transfers to Minors Act";

(6) a certificate of title issued by a department or agency of a state or of the United States which evidences title to tangible personal property is either:

(i) issued in the name of the transferor, an adult other than the transferor, or a trust company, followed in substance by the words: "as custodian for .... (name of minor) under the Minnesota Uniform Transfers to Minors Act"; or

(ii) delivered to an adult other than the transferor or to a trust company, endorsed to that person followed in substance by the words: "as custodian for .... (name of minor) under the Minnesota Uniform Transfers to Minors Act"; or

(7) an interest in any property not described in clauses (1) to (6) is transferred to an adult other than the transferor or to a trust company by a written instrument in substantially the form set forth in paragraph (b).

(b) An instrument in the following form satisfies the requirements of paragraph (a), clauses (1)(ii) and (7):

"TRANSFER UNDER THE MINNESOTA UNIFORM
TRANSFERS TO MINORS ACT

I, ... (name of transferor or name and representative capacity if a fiduciary) hereby transfer to .... (name of custodian), as custodian for .... (name of minor) under the Minnesota Uniform Transfers to Minors Act, the following: (insert a description of the custodial property sufficient to identify it).

Dated: ....

....

(Signature)

.... (name of custodian) acknowledges receipt of the property described above as custodian for the minor named above under the Minnesota Uniform Transfers to Minors Act.

Dated: ....

....

(Signature of Custodian)"

(c) A transferor shall place the custodian in control of the custodial property as soon as practicable.

Laws 1985, c. 221, § 9, eff. Jan. 1, 1986. Amended by Laws 1987, c. 142, § 1.

527.30. Single custodianship

A transfer may be made only for one minor, and only one person may be the custodian. All custodial property held under this chapter by the same custodian for the benefit of the same minor constitutes a single custodianship.

Laws 1985, c. 221, § 10, eff. Jan. 1, 1986.

527.31. Validity and effect of transfer

(a) The validity of a transfer made in a manner prescribed in this chapter is not affected by:

(1) failure of the transferor to comply with section 527.29, paragraph (c) concerning possession and control;

(2) designation of an ineligible custodian, except designation of the transferor in the case of property for which the transferor is ineligible to serve as custodian under section 527.29, paragraph (a); or

(3) death or incapacity of a person nominated under section 527.23 or designated under section 527.29 as custodian or the disclaimer of the office by that person.

(b) A transfer made pursuant to section 527.29 is irrevocable, and the custodial property is indefeasibly vested in the minor, but the custodian has all the rights, powers, duties, and authority provided in this chapter, and neither the minor nor the minor's legal representative has any right, power, duty, or authority with respect to the custodial property except as provided in this chapter.

(c) By making a transfer, the transferor incorporates in the disposition all the provisions of this chapter and grants to the custodian, and to any third person dealing with a person designated as custodian, the respective powers, rights, and immunities provided in this chapter.

Laws 1985, c. 221, § 11, eff. Jan. 1, 1986.

527.32. Care of custodial property

(a) A custodian shall:

(1) take control of custodial property;

(2) register or record title to custodial property if appropriate; and

(3) collect, hold, manage, invest, and reinvest custodial property.

(b) In dealing with custodial property, a custodian shall observe the standard of care that would be observed by a prudent person dealing with property of another and is not limited by any other statute restricting investments by fiduciaries. If a custodian has a special skill or expertise or is named custodian on the basis of representations of a special skill or expertise, the custodian shall use that skill or expertise. However, a custodian, in the custodian's discretion and without liability to the minor or the minor's estate, may retain any custodial property received from a transferor.

(c) A custodian may invest in or pay premiums on life insurance or endowment policies on (i) the life of the minor only if the minor or the minor's estate is the sole beneficiary, or (ii) the life of another person in whom the minor has an insurable interest only to the extent that the minor, the minor's estate, or the custodian in the capacity of custodian, is the irrevocable beneficiary.

(d) A custodian at all times shall keep custodial property separate and distinct from all other property in a manner sufficient to identify it clearly as custodial property of the minor. Custodial property consisting of certificated securities may be held on deposit at a stock brokerage firm or financial institution registered in a street name or nominee name. Custodial property consisting of an undivided interest is so identified if the minor's interest is held as a tenant in common and is fixed. Custodial property subject to recordation is so identified if it is recorded, and custodial property subject to registration is so identified if it is either registered, or held in an account designated, in the name of the custodian, followed in substance by the words: "as a custodian for .... (name of minor) under the Minnesota Uniform Transfers to Minors Act."

(e) A custodian shall keep records of all transactions with respect to custodial property, including information necessary for the preparation of the minor's tax returns, and shall make them available for inspection at reasonable intervals by a parent or legal representative of the minor or by the minor if the minor has attained the age of 14 years.

Laws 1985, c. 221, § 12, eff. Jan. 1, 1986. Amended by Laws 1985, 1st Sp., c. 13, § 365, eff. Jan. 1, 1986.

527.33. Powers of custodian

(a) A custodian, acting in a custodial capacity, has all the rights, powers, and authority over custodial property that unmarried adult owners have over their own property, but a custodian may exercise those rights, powers, and authority in that capacity only.

(b) This section does not relieve a custodian from liability for breach of section 527.32.

Laws 1985, c. 221, § 13, eff. Jan. 1, 1986.

527.34. Use of custodial property

(a) A custodian may deliver or pay to the minor or expend for the minor's benefit so much of the custodial property as the custodian considers advisable for the use and benefit of the minor, without court order and without regard to (i) the duty or ability of the custodian personally or of any other person to support the minor, or (ii) any other income or property of the minor which may be applicable or available for that purpose.

(b) On petition of an interested person or the minor if the minor has attained the age of 14 years, the court may order the custodian to deliver or pay to the minor or expend for the minor's benefit so much of the custodial property as the court considers advisable for the use and benefit of the minor.

(c) A delivery, payment, or expenditure under this section is in addition to, not in substitution for, and does not affect any obligation of a person to support the minor.

Laws 1985, c. 221, § 14, eff. Jan. 1, 1986.

527.35. Custodian's expenses, compensation, and bond

(a) A custodian is entitled to reimbursement from custodial property for reasonable expenses incurred in the performance of the custodian's duties.

(b) Except for one who is a transferor under section 527.24, a custodian has a noncumulative election during each calendar year to charge reasonable compensation for services performed during that year.

(c) Except as provided in section 527.38, paragraph (f), a custodian need not give a bond.

Laws 1985, c. 221, § 15, eff. Jan. 1, 1986.

527.36. Exemption of third person from liability

A third person in good faith and without court order may act on the instructions of or otherwise deal with any person purporting to make a transfer or purporting to act in the capacity of a custodian and, in the absence of knowledge, is not responsible for determining:

(1) the validity of the purported custodian's designation;

(2) the propriety of, or the authority under this chapter for, any act of the purported custodian;

(3) the validity or propriety under this chapter of any instrument or instructions executed or given either by the person purporting to make a transfer or by the purported custodian; or

(4) the propriety of the application of any property of the minor delivered to the purported custodian.

Laws 1985, c. 221, § 16, eff. Jan. 1, 1986.

527.37. Liability to third persons

(a) A claim based on (i) a contract entered into by a custodian acting in a custodial capacity, (ii) an obligation arising from the ownership or control of custodial property, or (iii) a tort committed during the custodianship, may be asserted against the custodial property by proceeding against the custodian in the custodial capacity, whether or not the custodian or the minor is personally liable therefor.

(b) A custodian is not personally liable:

(1) on a contract properly entered into in the custodial capacity unless the custodian fails to reveal that capacity and to identify the custodianship in the contract; or

(2) for an obligation arising from control of custodial property or for a tort committed during the custodianship unless the custodian is personally at fault.

(c) A minor is not personally liable for an obligation arising from ownership of custodial property or for a tort committed during the custodianship unless the minor is personally at fault.

Laws 1985, c. 221, § 17, eff. Jan. 1, 1986.

527.38. **Renunciation, resignation, death, or removal of custodian; designation of successor custodian**

(a) A person nominated under section 527.23 or designated under section 527.29 as custodian may decline to serve by delivering a valid disclaimer to the person who made the nomination or to the transferor or the transferor's legal representative. If the event giving rise to a transfer has not occurred and no substitute custodian able, willing, and eligible to serve was nominated under section 527.23, the person who made the nomination may nominate a substitute custodian under section 527.23; otherwise the transferor or the transferor's legal representative shall designate a substitute custodian at the time of the transfer, in either case from among the persons eligible to serve as custodian for that kind of property under section 527.29, paragraph (a). The custodian so designated has the rights of a successor custodian.

(b) A custodian at any time may designate a trust company or an adult other than a transferor under section 527.24 as successor custodian by executing and dating an instrument of designation before a subscribing witness other than the successor. If the instrument of designation does not contain or is not accompanied by the resignation of the custodian, the designation of the successor does not take effect until the custodian resigns, dies, becomes incapacitated, or is removed.

(c) A custodian may resign at any time by delivering written notice to the minor if the minor has attained the age of 14 years and to the successor custodian and by delivering the custodial property to the successor custodian.

(d) If a custodian is ineligible, dies, or becomes incapacitated without having effectively designated a successor and the minor has attained the age of 14 years, the minor may designate as successor custodian, in the manner prescribed in paragraph (b), an adult member of the minor's family, a conservator of the minor, or a trust company. If the minor has not attained the age of 14 years or fails to act within 60 days after the ineligibility, death, or incapacity, the conservator of the minor becomes successor custodian. If the minor has no conservator or the conservator declines to act, the transferor, the legal representative of the transferor or of the custodian, an adult member of the minor's family, or any other interested person may petition the court to designate a successor custodian.

(e) A custodian who declines to serve under paragraph (a) or resigns under paragraph (c), or the legal representative of a deceased or incapacitated custodian, as soon as practicable, shall put the custodial property and records in the possession and control of the successor custodian. The successor custodian by action may enforce the obligation to deliver custodial property and records and becomes responsible for each item as received.

(f) A transferor, the legal representative of a transferor, an adult member of the minor's family, a guardian of the minor, the conservator of the minor's estate, or the minor if the minor has attained the age of 14 years may petition the court to remove the custodian for cause and to designate a successor custodian other than a transferor under section 527.24 or to require the custodian to give appropriate bond.

Laws 1985, c. 221, § 18, eff. Jan. 1, 1986. Amended by Laws 2005, c. 10, art. 4, § 25.

527.39. Accounting by and determination of liability of custodian

(a) A minor who has attained the age of 14 years, the minor's guardian or legal representative, an adult member of the minor's family, a transferor, or a transferor's legal representative may petition the court (i) for an accounting by the custodian or the custodian's legal representative; or (ii) for a determination of responsibility, as between the custodial property and the custodian personally, for claims against the custodial property unless the responsibility has been adjudicated in an action under section 527.37 to which the minor or the minor's legal representative was a party.

(b) A successor custodian may petition the court for an accounting by the predecessor custodian.

(c) The court, in a proceeding under this chapter or in any other proceeding, may require or permit the custodian or the custodian's legal representative to account.

(d) If a custodian is removed under section 527.38, paragraph (f), the court shall require an accounting and order delivery of the custodial property and records to the successor custodian and the execution of all instruments required for transfer of the custodial property.

Laws 1985, c. 221, § 19, eff. Jan. 1, 1986. Amended by Laws 2005, c. 10, art. 4, § 26.

527.40. Termination of custodianship

The custodian shall transfer in an appropriate manner the custodial property to the minor or to the minor's estate upon the earlier of:

(1) the minor's attainment of 21 years of age with respect to custodial property transferred under section 527.24 or 527.25;

(2) the minor's attainment of age 18 with respect to custodial property transferred under section 527.26 or 527.27; or

(3) the minor's death.

Laws 1985, c. 221, § 20, eff. Jan. 1, 1986.

527.405. Conveyance by custodian

Subdivision 1. Affidavit of custodian. In support of a real property transaction where an interest in real property is held in a custodianship, a custodian shall furnish to the grantee or other party to the transaction an affidavit attesting that:

(1) the custodian has not resigned or been removed prior to executing the conveyance; and

(2) the custodianship has not terminated, or if the custodianship has terminated that the conveyance is to the minor or to the personal representative of the minor's estate.

Subd. 2. Form of affidavit. An affidavit under this section must be substantially in the following form:

AFFIDAVIT OF CUSTODIAN

State of Minnesota
County of ....
.........., being first duly sworn on oath says, that:
1. Affiant was appointed or designated as custodian in the document dated .... and filed for record .... as Document No. ...., (or in book .... of page ....) in the office of the (County Recorder) (Registrar of Titles) of ...... County, Minnesota (being the document which originally conveyed the real estate to the custodian).
2. Affiant is the grantor custodian for the minor in the document dated ...., conveying to .... an interest in the real property in .... County, Minnesota, legally described as:
(insert legal description here)
3. The name of the minor is ....
4. The custodianship (check one) .... has not terminated prior to the date of the document described in paragraph 2 above (or) .... has terminated and the conveyance is to the minor or to the personal representative of the minor's estate.
5. Affiant's address is: ....
6. Affiant has not resigned and does not have actual knowledge of affiant's removal as custodian.
Affiant knows the matters herein stated are true and makes this affidavit for the purpose of inducing the passing of title to the real property.
....
Affiant
Subscribed and sworn to before me this day of ......, 20....
....
Notary Public
This instrument was drafted by ....

Subd. 3. Effect of affidavit. An affidavit by a custodian under this section is conclusive proof that the custodian has not resigned or been removed as custodian prior to executing the conveyance and that the custodianship has not terminated, or that if the custodianship has terminated, the conveyance is to the minor or to the personal representative of the minor's estate. However, the affidavit is not conclusive as to a party dealing directly with the custodian who has actual knowledge that the custodian has resigned or been removed or that the custodianship has terminated and the conveyance is not to the minor or the personal representative of the minor's estate.

Laws 2002, c. 403, § 5.

527.41. Applicability

Sections 527.21 to 527.40 apply to a transfer within the scope of section 527.22 made after January 1, 1986, if:

(1) the transfer purports to have been made under Minnesota Statutes 1984, sections 527.01 to 527.11; or

(2) the instrument by which the transfer purports to have been made uses in substance the designation "as custodian under the Uniform Gifts to Minors Act" or "as custodian under the Uniform Transfers to Minors Act" of any other state, and the application of sections 527.21 to 527.40 is necessary to validate the transfer.

Laws 1985, c. 221, § 21, eff. Jan. 1, 1986. Amended by Laws 1986, 1st Sp., c. 3, art. 1, § 60.

527.42. Effect on existing custodianships

(a) Any transfer of custodial property as now defined in sections 527.21 to 527.40 made before January 1, 1986, is validated notwithstanding that there was no specific authority in Minnesota Statutes 1984, sections 527.01 to 527.11 for the coverage of custodial property of that kind or for a transfer from that source at the time the transfer was made.

(b) Sections 527.21 to 527.40 apply to all transfers made before January 1, 1986, in a manner and form prescribed in Minnesota Statutes 1984, sections 527.01 to 527.11, except insofar as the application impairs constitutionally vested rights or extends the duration of custodianships in existence before January 1, 1986.

(c) Sections 527.21 and 527.40 with respect to the age of a minor for whom custodial property is held under those sections do not apply to custodial property held in a custodianship that terminated because of the minor's attainment of the age of 18 after May 31, 1973, and before January 1, 1986.

Laws 1985, c. 221, § 22, eff. Jan. 1, 1986. Amended by Laws 1986, 1st Sp., c. 3, art. 1, § 61.

527.43. Savings provision

To the extent that sections 527.21 to 527.40, by virtue of section 527.42, paragraph (b), do not apply to transfers made in a manner prescribed in Minnesota Statutes 1984, sections 527.01 to 527.11 or to the powers, duties, and immunities conferred by transfers in that manner upon custodians and persons dealing with custodians, the repeal of Minnesota Statutes 1984, sections 527.01 to 527.11 does not affect those transfers or those powers, duties, and immunities.

Laws 1985, c. 221, § 23, eff. Jan. 1, 1986. Amended by Laws 1986, 1st Sp., c. 3, art. 1, § 62.

527.44. Short title

This chapter may be cited as the "Minnesota Uniform Transfers to Minors Act."

Laws 1985, c. 221, § 24, eff. Jan. 1, 1986.

Chapter 529

UNIFORM CUSTODIAL TRUST ACT

For complete statutory history see Minnesota Statutes Annotated.

529.001.   Renumbered 15.001 in St.2008

529.01.   Definitions

As used in sections 529.01 to 529.19:

(1) "Adult" means an individual who is at least 18 years of age.

(2) "Beneficiary" means an individual for whom property has been transferred to or held under a declaration of trust by a custodial trustee for the individual's use and benefit under sections 529.01 to 529.19.

(3) "Conservator" means a person appointed or qualified by a court to manage the estate of an individual or a person legally authorized to perform substantially the same functions.

(4) "Court" means the district court of this state.

(5) "Custodial trust property" means an interest in property transferred to or held under a declaration of trust by a custodial trustee under sections 529.01 to 529.19 and the income from and proceeds of that interest.

(6) "Custodial trustee" means a person designated as trustee of a custodial trust under sections 529.01 to 529.19 or a substitute or successor to the person designated.

(7) "Guardian" means a person appointed or qualified by a court as a guardian of an individual, including a limited guardian, but not a person who is only a guardian ad litem.

(8) "Holder of the beneficiary's power of attorney" means a person who is a holder of the beneficiary's unrevoked power of attorney if the document creating the power of attorney grants powers similar or identical to those defined as "beneficiary transactions" in section 523.24, subdivision 7.

(9) "Incapacitated" means lacking the ability to manage property and business affairs effectively by reason of mental illness, developmental disability, physical illness or disability, chronic use of drugs, chronic intoxication, confinement, detention by a foreign power, disappearance, minority, or other disabling cause.

(10) "Legal representative" means a personal representative or conservator.

(11) "Member of the beneficiary's family" means a beneficiary's spouse, descendant, stepchild, parent, stepparent, grandparent, brother, sister, uncle, or aunt, whether of the whole or half blood or by adoption.

(12) "Person" means an individual, corporation, business trust, estate, trust, partnership, joint venture, association, or any other legal or commercial entity.

(13) "Personal representative" means an executor, administrator, or special administrator of a decedent's estate, a person legally authorized to perform substantially the same functions, or a successor to any of them.

(14) "State" means a state, territory, or possession of the United States, the District of Columbia, or the commonwealth of Puerto Rico.

(15) "Transferor" means a person who creates a custodial trust by transfer or declaration.

(16) "Trust company" means a financial institution, corporation, or other legal entity, authorized to exercise general trust powers.

Laws 1990, c. 476, § 1. Amended by Laws 2005, c. 56, § 1.

UNIFORM CUSTODIAL TRUST ACT

Table of Jurisdictions Wherein Act Has Been Adopted

For text of Uniform Act, and variation notes and annotation materials for adopting jurisdictions, see Uniform Laws Annotated, Master Edition, Volume 7A, Pt. I.

Jurisdiction	Laws	Effective Date	Statutory Citation
Alaska	1994, c. 10	7–5–1994	A.S. 13.60.010 to 13.60.990.
Arizona	2002, c. 220	8–22–2002	A.R.S. §§ 14–9101 to 14–9119.

Jurisdiction	Laws	Effective Date	Statutory Citation
Arkansas	1991, Act No. 273	7–15–1991	A.C.A. §§ 28–72–401 to 28–72–422.
Colorado	1999, c. 295	8–4–1999	West's C.R.S.A. §§ 15–1.5–101 to 15–1.5–122.
District of Columbia . . .	2002, D.C. Law 14–177	7–23–2002	D.C. Official Code, 2001 Ed. §§ 19–1101 to 19–1120.
Hawaii	1989, Act 76	5–8–1989	HRS §§ 554B–1 to 554B–22.
Idaho	1989, c. 230		I.C. §§ 68–1301 to 68–1322.
Indiana	2003, c. 3	7–1–2003	West's A.I.C. §§ 30–2–8.6–1 to 30–2–8.6–39.
Louisiana	1995, Act 655	1–1–1998	L.S.A.–R.S. §§ 9:2260.1 to 9:2260.21.
Massachusetts	1993, c. 434	1–12–1994*	M.G.L.A. c. 203B, §§ 1 to 19.
Minnesota	1990, c. 476	4–19–1990*	M.S.A. §§ 529.01 to 529.19.
Missouri	1986, S.B. No. 651		V.A.M.S. §§ 404.400 to 404.650.
Nebraska	1997, LB 51	9–13–1997	R.R.S. 1943, §§ 30–3501 to 30–3522.
Nevada	2007, c. 103	5–22–2007*	N.R.S. 166A.010 to 166A.360.
New Mexico	1992, c. 66	7–1–1992	NMSA 1978 §§ 45–7–501 to 45–7–522.
North Carolina	1995, c. 486	10–1–1995	G.S. §§33B–1 to 33B–22.
Rhode Island	1988, c. 623		Gen.Laws 1956, §§ 18–13–1 to 18–13–22.
Virginia	1990, c. 264		Code 1950, §§ 55–34.1 to 55–34.19.
Wisconsin	1991, Act 246	5–12–1992	W.S.A. 54.950 to 54.988.

  * Date of approval

529.02. Custodial trust; general

(a) A person may create a custodial trust of property by a written transfer of the property to another person, evidenced by registration or by other instrument of transfer, executed in any lawful manner, naming as beneficiary, an individual who may be the transferor, in which the transferee is designated, in substance, as custodial trustee under the Minnesota Uniform Custodial Trust Act.

(b) A person may create a custodial trust of property by a written declaration, evidenced by registration of the property or by other instrument of declaration executed in any lawful manner, describing the property and naming as beneficiary an individual other than the declarant, in which the declarant as title holder is designated, in substance, as custodial trustee under the Minnesota Uniform Custodial Trust Act. A registration or other declaration of trust for the sole benefit of the declarant is not a custodial trust under sections 529.01 to 529.19.

(c) Title to custodial trust property is in the custodial trustee and the beneficial interest is in the beneficiary.

(d) Except as provided in subsection (e), a transferor may not terminate a custodial trust.

(e) The beneficiary, if not incapacitated, or the holder of the beneficiary's power of attorney, may terminate a custodial trust by delivering to the custodial trustee a writing signed by the beneficiary or holder of the beneficiary's power of attorney declaring the termination. If not previously terminated, the custodial trust terminates on the death of the beneficiary.

(f) Any person may augment existing custodial trust property by the addition of other property pursuant to sections 529.01 to 529.19.

(g) The transferor may designate, or authorize the designation of, a successor custodial trustee in the trust instrument.

(h) Sections 529.01 to 529.19 do not displace or restrict other means of creating trusts. A trust whose terms do not conform to sections 529.01 to 529.19 may be enforceable according to its terms under other law.

Laws 1990, c. 476, § 2.

529.03. Custodial trustee for future payment or transfer

(a) A person having the right to designate the recipient of property payable or transferable upon a future event may create a custodial trust upon the occurrence of the future event by designating in writing the recipient, followed in substance by: "as custodial trustee for .... (name of beneficiary) under the Minnesota Uniform Custodial Trust Act."

(b) Persons may be designated as substitute or successor custodial trustees to whom the property must be paid or transferred in the order named if the first designated custodial trustee is unable or unwilling to serve.

(c) A designation under this section may be made in a will, a trust, a deed, a multiple-party account, an insurance policy, an instrument exercising a power of appointment, or a writing designating a beneficiary of contractual rights. Otherwise, to be effective, the designation must be registered with or delivered to the fiduciary, payor, issuer, or obligor of the future right.

Laws 1990, c. 476, § 3.

529.04. Form and effect of receipt and acceptance by custodial trustee, jurisdiction

(a) Obligations of a custodial trustee, including the obligation to follow directions of the beneficiary, arise under sections 529.01 to 529.19 upon the custodial trustee's acceptance, express or implied, of the custodial trust property.

(b) The custodial trustee's acceptance may be evidenced by a writing stating in substance:

CUSTODIAL TRUSTEE'S RECEIPT AND ACCEPTANCE

I, ... (name of custodial trustee) acknowledge receipt of the custodial trust property described below or in the attached instrument and accept the custodial trust as custodial trustee for .... (name of beneficiary) under the Minnesota Uniform Custodial Trust Act. I undertake to administer and distribute the custodial trust property pursuant to the Minnesota Uniform Custodial Trust Act. My obligations as custodial trustee are subject to the directions of the beneficiary unless the beneficiary is designated as, is, or becomes incapacitated. The custodial trust property consists of ....

Dated: ....

....

(signature of custodial trustee)

(c) Upon accepting custodial trust property, a person designated as custodial trustee under sections 529.01 to 529.19 is subject to personal jurisdiction of the court with respect to any matter relating to the custodial trust.

Laws 1990, c. 476, § 4.

529.05. Multiple beneficiaries; separate custodial trusts; survivorship

(a) Beneficial interests in a custodial trust created for multiple beneficiaries are deemed to be separate custodial trusts of equal undivided interests for each beneficiary. Except in a transfer or declaration for use and benefit of husband and wife, for whom survivorship is presumed, a right of survivorship does not exist unless the instrument creating the custodial trust specifically provides for survivorship or survivorship is required as to community or marital property.

(b) Custodial trust property held under sections 529.01 to 529.19 by the same custodial trustee for the use and benefit of the same beneficiary may be administered as a single custodial trust.

(c) A custodial trustee of custodial trust property held for more than one beneficiary shall separately account to each beneficiary pursuant to sections 529.06 and 529.14 for the administration of the custodial trust.

Laws 1990, c. 476, § 5.

529.06. General duties of custodial trustee

(a) If appropriate, a custodial trustee shall register or record the instrument vesting title to custodial trust property.

(b) If the beneficiary is not incapacitated, a custodial trustee shall follow the directions of the beneficiary in the management, control, investment, or retention of the custodial trust property. In the absence of effective contrary direction by the beneficiary while not incapacitated, the custodial trustee shall observe the standard of care set forth in section 501B.151. However, a custodial trustee, in the custodial trustee's discretion, may retain any custodial trust property received from the transferor.

(c) Subject to subsection (b), a custodial trustee shall take control of and collect, hold, manage, invest, and reinvest custodial trust property.

(d) A custodial trustee at all times shall keep custodial trust property of which the custodial trustee has control, separate from all other property in a manner sufficient to identify it clearly as custodial trust property of the beneficiary. Custodial trust property, the title to which is subject to recordation, is so identified if an appropriate instrument so identifying the property is recorded, and custodial trust property subject to registration is so identified if it is registered, or held in an account in the name of the custodial trustee, designated in substance: "as custodial trustee for........ (name of beneficiary) under the Minnesota Uniform Custodial Trust Act."

(e) A custodial trustee shall keep records of all transactions with respect to custodial trust property, including information necessary for the preparation of tax returns, and shall make the records and information available at reasonable times to the beneficiary or legal representative of the beneficiary.

Laws 1990, c. 476, § 6. Amended by Laws 1996, c. 314, § 7.

Historical and Statutory Notes

Laws 1996, c. 314, § 9, provides in part that § 7 (amending this section) is effective January 1, 1997.

529.07. General powers of custodial trustee

(a) A custodial trustee, acting in a fiduciary capacity, has all the rights and powers over custodial trust property which an unmarried adult owner has over individually owned property, but a custodial trustee may exercise those rights and powers in a fiduciary capacity only.

(b) This section does not relieve a custodial trustee from liability for a violation of section 529.06.

Laws 1990, c. 476, § 7.

529.08. Use of custodial trust property

(a) A custodial trustee shall pay to the beneficiary or expend for the beneficiary's use and benefit so much or all of the custodial trust property as the beneficiary while not incapacitated may direct from time to time.

(b) If the beneficiary is incapacitated, the custodial trustee shall expend so much or all of the custodial trust property as the custodial trustee considers advisable for the use and benefit of the beneficiary and individuals who were supported by the beneficiary when the beneficiary became incapacitated, or who are legally entitled to support by the beneficiary. Expenditures may be made in the manner, when, and to the extent that the custodial trustee determines suitable and proper, without court order and without regard to other support, income, or property of the beneficiary.

(c) A custodial trustee may establish checking, savings, or other similar accounts of reasonable amounts under which either the custodial trustee or the beneficiary may withdraw funds from, draw checks against, or use a debit or credit card to make payments from the accounts. Funds withdrawn from, checks written against, or payments made from the account by the beneficiary are distributions of custodial trust property by the custodial trustee to the beneficiary.

Laws 1990, c. 476, § 8.   Amended by Laws 2008, c. 201, § 1, eff. Aug. 1, 2008.

529.09. Determination of incapacity; effect

(a) The custodial trustee shall administer the custodial trust as for an incapacitated beneficiary if (i) the transferor has so directed in the instrument creating the custodial trust, or (ii) the custodial trustee has determined that the beneficiary is incapacitated.

(b) A custodial trustee may determine that the beneficiary is incapacitated in reliance upon (i) previous direction or authority given by the beneficiary while not incapacitated, including direction or authority pursuant to a durable power of attorney, (ii) the certificate of the beneficiary's physician, or (iii) other persuasive evidence.

(c) If a custodial trustee for an incapacitated beneficiary reasonably concludes that the beneficiary's incapacity has ceased, or that circumstances concerning the beneficiary's ability to manage property and business affairs have changed since the creation of a custodial trust directing administration as for an incapacitated beneficiary, the custodial trustee must administer the trust as for a beneficiary who is not incapacitated.

(d) On petition of the beneficiary, the custodial trustee, or other person interested in the custodial trust property or the welfare of the beneficiary, the court shall determine whether the beneficiary is incapacitated.

(e) Absent determination of incapacity of the beneficiary under subsection (b) or (d), a custodial trustee who has reason to believe that the beneficiary is incapacitated shall administer the custodial trust in accordance with the provisions of sections 529.01 to 529.19 applicable to an incapacitated beneficiary.

(f) Incapacity of a beneficiary does not terminate (i) the custodial trust, (ii) any designation of a successor custodial trustee, (iii) rights or powers of the custodial trustee, or (iv) any immunities of third persons acting on instructions of the custodial trustee.

Laws 1990, c. 476, § 9.

529.10. Exemption of third person from liability

A third person in good faith and without a court order may act on instructions of, or otherwise deal with, a person purporting to make a transfer as, or purporting to act in the capacity of, a custodial trustee.   In the absence of knowledge to the contrary, the third person is not responsible for determining:

(1) the validity of the purported custodial trustee's designation;

(2) the propriety of, or the authority under sections 529.01 to 529.19 for, any action of the purported custodial trustee;

(3) the validity or propriety of an instrument executed or instruction given pursuant to sections 529.01 to 529.19 either by the person purporting to make a transfer or declaration or by the purported custodial trustee; or

(4) the propriety of the application of property vested in the purported custodial trustee.

Laws 1990, c. 476, § 10.

529.11. Liability to third person

(a) A claim based on a contract entered into by a custodial trustee acting in a fiduciary capacity, an obligation arising from the ownership or control of custodial trust property, or a tort committed in the course of administering the custodial trust, may be asserted by a third person against the custodial trust property by proceeding against the custodial trustee in a fiduciary capacity, whether or not the custodial trustee or the beneficiary is personally liable.

(b) A custodial trustee is not personally liable to a third person:

(1) on a contract properly entered into in a fiduciary capacity unless the custodial trustee fails to reveal that capacity or to identify the custodial trust in the contract; or

(2) for an obligation arising from control of custodial trust property or for a tort committed in the course of the administration of the custodial trust unless the custodial trustee is personally at fault.

(c) A beneficiary is not personally liable to a third person for an obligation arising from beneficial ownership of custodial trust property or for a tort committed in the course of administration of the custodial trust unless the beneficiary is personally in possession of the custodial trust property giving rise to the liability or is personally at fault.

(d) Subsections (b) and (c) do not preclude actions or proceedings to establish liability of the custodial trustee or beneficiary to the extent the person sued is protected as the insured by liability insurance.

Laws 1990, c. 476, § 11.

529.12. Declination, resignation, incapacity, death, or removal of custodial trustee; designation of successor custodial trustee

(a) Before accepting the custodial trust property, a person designated as custodial trustee may decline to serve by notifying the person who made the designation, the transferor, or the transferor's legal representative. If an event giving rise to a transfer has not occurred, the substitute custodial trustee designated under section 529.03 becomes the custodial trustee, or, if a substitute custodial trustee has not been designated, the person who made the designation may designate a substitute custodial trustee pursuant to section 529.03. In other cases, the transferor or the transferor's legal representative may designate a substitute custodial trustee.

(b) A custodial trustee who has accepted the custodial trust property may resign by (i) delivering written notice to a successor custodial trustee, if any, the beneficiary and, if the beneficiary is incapacitated, to the beneficiary's conservator, if any, and (ii) transferring or registering, or recording an appropriate instrument relating to, the custodial trust property, in the name of, and delivering the records to, the successor custodial trustee identified under subsection (c).

(c) If a custodial trustee or successor custodial trustee is ineligible, resigns, dies, or becomes incapacitated, the successor designated under section 529.02, subsection (g), or 529.03 becomes custodial trustee. If there is no effective provision for a successor, the beneficiary, if not incapacitated, or the holder of the beneficiary's power of attorney, may designate a successor custodial trustee.

(d) If a successor custodial trustee is not designated pursuant to subsection (c), the transferor, the legal representative of the transferor or of the custodial trustee, an adult member of the beneficiary's family, the conservator of the beneficiary, a person interested in the custodial trust property, or a person interested in the welfare of the beneficiary, may petition the court to designate a successor custodial trustee in accordance with the procedures set forth in sections 501B.16 to 501B.25.

(e) A custodial trustee who declines to serve or resigns, or the legal representative of a deceased or incapacitated custodial trustee, as soon as practicable, shall put the custodial trust property and records in the possession and control of the successor custodial trustee. The successor custodial trustee may enforce the obligation to deliver custodial trust property and records and becomes responsible for each item as received.

(f) A beneficiary, the beneficiary's conservator, an adult member of the beneficiary's family, a guardian of the beneficiary, a person interested in the custodial trust property, or a person interested in the welfare of the beneficiary, may petition the court to remove the custodial trustee for cause and designate a successor custodial trustee, to require the custodial trustee to furnish a bond or other security for the faithful performance of fiduciary duties, or for other appropriate relief.

Laws 1990, c. 476, § 12. Amended by Laws 2005, c. 10, art. 4, § 27.

529.13. Expenses, compensation, and bond of custodial trustee

Except as otherwise provided in the instrument creating the custodial trust, in an agreement with the beneficiary, or by court order, a custodial trustee:

(1) is entitled to reimbursement from custodial trust property for reasonable expenses incurred in the performance of fiduciary services;

(2) has a noncumulative election, to be made no later than six months after the end of each calendar year, to charge a reasonable compensation for fiduciary services performed during that year; and

(3) need not furnish a bond or other security for the faithful performance of fiduciary duties.

Laws 1990, c. 476, § 13.

529.14. Reporting and accounting by custodial trustee; determination of liability of custodial trustee

(a) Upon the acceptance of custodial trust property, the custodial trustee shall provide a written statement describing the custodial trust property and shall thereafter provide a written statement of the administration of the custodial trust property (i) once each year, (ii) upon request at reasonable times by the beneficiary or the beneficiary's legal representative, (iii) upon resignation or removal of the custodial trustee, and (iv) upon termination of the custodial trust. The statements must be provided to the beneficiary or to the beneficiary's legal representative, if any. Upon termination of the beneficiary's interest, the custodial trustee shall furnish a current statement to the person to whom the custodial trust property is to be delivered.

(b) A beneficiary, the beneficiary's legal representative, an adult member of the beneficiary's family, a person interested in the custodial trust property, or a person interested in the welfare of the beneficiary may petition the court for an accounting by the custodial trustee or the custodial trustee's legal representative.

(c) A successor custodial trustee may petition the court for an accounting by a predecessor custodial trustee.

(d) In an action or proceeding under sections 529.01 to 529.19 or in any other proceeding, the court may require or permit the custodial trustee or the custodial trustee's legal representative to account. The custodial trustee or the custodial trustee's legal representative may petition the court for approval of final accounts.

(e) If a custodial trustee is removed, the court shall require an accounting and order delivery of the custodial trust property and records to the successor custodial trustee and the execution of all instruments required for transfer of the custodial trust property.

(f) On petition of the custodial trustee or any person who could petition for an accounting, the court, after notice to interested persons, may issue instructions to the custodial trustee or review the propriety of the acts of a custodial trustee or the reasonableness of compensation determined by the custodial trustee for the services of the custodial trustee or others.

(g) All proceedings described in this section shall be conducted in accordance with the procedures set forth in sections 501B.16 to 501B.25.

Laws 1990, c. 476, § 14.

529.15. Limitations of action against custodial trustee

(a) Except as provided in subsection (c), unless previously barred by adjudication, consent, or limitation, a claim for relief against a custodial trustee for accounting or breach of duty is barred as to a beneficiary, a person to whom custodial trust property is to be paid or delivered, or the legal representative of an incapacitated or deceased beneficiary or payee:

(1) who has received a final account or statement fully disclosing the matter unless an action or proceeding to assert the claim is commenced within two years after receipt of the final account or statement; or

(2) who has not received a final account or statement fully disclosing the matter unless an action or proceeding to assert the claim is commenced within three years after the termination of the custodial trust.

(b) Except as provided in subsection (c), a claim for relief to recover from a custodial trustee for fraud, misrepresentation, or concealment related to the final settlement of the custodial trust or concealment of the existence of the custodial trust, is barred unless an action or proceeding to assert the claim is commenced within five years after the termination of the custodial trust.

(c) A claim for relief is not barred by this section if the claimant:

(1) is a minor, until the earlier of two years after the claimant becomes an adult or dies;

(2) is an incapacitated adult, until the earliest of two years after (i) the appointment of a conservator, (ii) the removal of the incapacity, or (iii) the death of the claimant; or

(3) was an adult, now deceased, who was not incapacitated, until two years after the claimant's death.

Laws 1990, c. 476, § 15.

529.16. Distribution on termination

(a) Upon termination of a custodial trust, the custodial trustee shall transfer the unexpended custodial trust property:

(1) to the beneficiary, if not incapacitated or deceased;

(2) to the holder of the beneficiary's power of attorney;

(3) to the conservator or other recipient designated by the court for an incapacitated beneficiary; or

(4) upon the beneficiary's death, in the following order:

(i) to the survivor of multiple beneficiaries if survivorship is provided for pursuant to section 529.05;

(ii) as designated in the instrument creating the custodial trust; or

(iii) to the estate of the deceased beneficiary.

(b) If, when the custodial trust would otherwise terminate, the distributee is incapacitated, the custodial trust continues for the use and benefit of the distributee as beneficiary until the incapacity is removed or the custodial trust is otherwise terminated.

(c) Death of a beneficiary does not terminate the power of the custodial trustee to discharge obligations of the custodial trustee or beneficiary incurred before the termination of the custodial trust.

Laws 1990, c. 476, § 16. Amended by Laws 1991, c. 199, art. 1, § 80.

529.17. Methods and forms for creating custodial trusts

(a) If a transaction, including a declaration with respect to or a transfer of specific property, otherwise satisfies applicable law, the criteria of section 529.02 are satisfied by:

(1) the execution and either delivery to the custodial trustee or recording of an instrument in substantially the following form:

TRANSFER UNDER THE MINNESOTA UNIFORM CUSTODIAL TRUST ACT

I, ... (name of transferor or name and representative capacity if a fiduciary), transfer to .... (name of trustee other than transferor), as custodial trustee for .... (name of beneficiary) as beneficiary and .... as distributee on termination of the trust in absence of direction by the beneficiary under the Minnesota Uniform Custodial Trust Act, the following: (insert a description of the custodial trust property legally sufficient to identify and transfer each item of property).

Dated: ....

....

(Signature); or

(2) the execution and the recording or giving notice of its execution to the beneficiary of an instrument in substantially the following form:

DECLARATION OF TRUST UNDER THE MINNESOTA
UNIFORM CUSTODIAL TRUST ACT

I, ... (name of owner of property), declare that henceforth I hold as custodial trustee for .... (name of beneficiary other than transferor) as beneficiary and .... as distributee on termination of the trust in absence of direction by the beneficiary under the Minnesota Uniform Custodial Trust Act, the following: (insert a description of the custodial trust property legally sufficient to identify and transfer each item of property).

Dated: ....

....

(Signature)

(b) Customary methods of transferring or evidencing ownership of property may be used to create a custodial trust, including any of the following:

(1) registration of a security in the name of a trust company, an adult other than the transferor, or the transferor if the beneficiary is other than the transferor, designated in substance "as custodial trustee for .... (name of beneficiary) under the Minnesota Uniform Custodial Trust Act";

(2) delivery of a certificated security, or a document necessary for the transfer of an uncertificated security, together with any necessary endorsement, to an adult other than the transferor or to a trust company as custodial trustee, accompanied by an instrument in substantially the form prescribed in subsection (a)(1);

(3) payment of money or transfer of a security held in the name of a broker or a financial institution or its nominee to a broker or financial institution for credit to an account in the name of a trust company, an adult other than the transferor, or the transferor if the beneficiary is other than the transferor, designated in substance; "as custodial trustee for .... (name of beneficiary) under the Minnesota Uniform Custodial Trust Act";

(4) registration of ownership of a life or endowment insurance policy or annuity contract with the issuer in the name of a trust company, an adult other than the transferor, or the transferor if the beneficiary is other than the transferor, designated in substance: "as custodial trustee for .... (name of beneficiary) under the Minnesota Uniform Custodial Trust Act";

(5) delivery of a written assignment to an adult other than the transferor or to a trust company whose name in the assignment is designated in substance by the words: "as custodial trustee for .... (name of beneficiary) under the Minnesota Uniform Custodial Trust Act";

(6) irrevocable exercise of a power of appointment, pursuant to its terms, in favor of a trust company, an adult other than the donee of the power, or the donee who holds the power if the beneficiary is other than the donee, whose name in the appointment is designated in substance: "as custodial trustee for .... (name of beneficiary) under the Minnesota Uniform Custodial Trust Act";

(7) delivery of a written notification or assignment of a right to future payment under a contract to an obligor which transfers the right under the contract to a trust company, an adult other than the transferor, or the transferor if the beneficiary is other than the transferor, whose name in the notification or assignment is designated in substance: "as custodial trustee for .... (name of beneficiary) under the Minnesota Custodial Trust Act";

(8) execution, delivery, and recordation of a conveyance of an interest in real property in the name of a trust company, an adult other than the transferor, or the transferor if the beneficiary is other than the transferor, designated in substance: "as custodial trustee for .... (name of beneficiary) under the Minnesota Uniform Custodial Trust Act";

(9) issuance of a certificate of title by an agency of a state or of the United States which evidences title to tangible personal property:

(i) issued in the name of a trust company, an adult other than the transferor, or the transferor if the beneficiary is other than the transferor, designated in substance: "as custodial trustee for . . . . (name of beneficiary) under the Minnesota Uniform Custodial Trust Act"; or

(ii) delivered to a trust company or an adult other than the transferor or endorsed by the transferor to that person designated in substance: "as custodial trustee for . . . . (name of beneficiary) under the Minnesota Uniform Custodial Trust Act"; or

(10) execution and delivery of an instrument of gift to a trust company or an adult other than the transferor, designated in substance: "as custodial trustee for . . . . (name of beneficiary) under the Minnesota Uniform Custodial Trust Act."

Laws 1990, c. 476, § 17.

529.18. Applicable law

(a) Sections 529.01 to 529.19 apply to a transfer or declaration creating a custodial trust that refers to sections 529.01 to 529.19 if, at the time of the transfer or declaration, the transferor, beneficiary, or custodial trustee is a resident of or has its principal place of business in this state or custodial trust property is located in this state. The custodial trust remains subject to sections 529.01 to 529.19 despite a later change in residence or principal place of business of the transferor, beneficiary, or custodial trustee, or removal of the custodial trust property from this state.

(b) A transfer made pursuant to an act of another state substantially similar to sections 529.01 to 529.19 is governed by the law of that state and may be enforced in this state.

Laws 1990, c. 476, § 18.

529.19. Short title

Sections 529.01 to 529.19 may be cited as the "Minnesota Uniform Custodial Trust Act."

Laws 1990, c. 476, § 19.

Chapter 573

PERSONAL REPRESENTATIVES, HEIRS; ACTIONS

For complete statutory history see Minnesota Statutes Annotated.

573.01. Survival of causes

A cause of action arising out of an injury to the person dies with the person of the party in whose favor it exists, except as provided in section 573.02. All other causes of action by one against another, whether arising on contract or not, survive to the personal representatives of the former and against those of the latter.

Amended by Laws 1967, c. 158, § 1, eff. April 13, 1967; Laws 1983, c. 243, § 4, eff. June 2, 1983; Laws 1983, c. 347, § 1, eff. June 15, 1983.

Historical and Statutory Notes

Laws 1983, c. 347, § 4, provides, in part, that the amendment to this section is effective on June 15, 1983 and "applies to all causes of action arising on or after that date".

573.02. Action for death by wrongful act; survival of actions

Subdivision 1. Death action. When death is caused by the wrongful act or omission of any person or corporation, the trustee appointed as provided in subdivision 3 may maintain an action therefor if the decedent might have maintained an action, had the decedent lived, for an injury caused by the wrongful act or omission. An action to recover damages for a death caused by the alleged professional negligence of a physician, surgeon, dentist, hospital or sanitarium, or an employee of a physician, surgeon, dentist, hospital or sanitarium shall be commenced within three years of the date of death, but in no event shall be commenced beyond the time set forth in section 541.076. An action to recover damages for a death caused by an intentional act constituting murder may be commenced at any time after the death of the decedent. Any other action under this section may be commenced within three years after the date of death provided that the action must be commenced within six years after the act or omission. The recovery in the action is the amount the jury deems fair and just in reference to the pecuniary loss resulting from the death, and shall be for the exclusive benefit of the surviving spouse and next of kin, proportionate to the pecuniary loss severally suffered by the death. The court then determines the proportionate pecuniary loss of the persons entitled to the recovery and orders distribution accordingly. Funeral expenses and any demand for the support of the decedent allowed by the court having jurisdiction of the action, are first deducted and paid. Punitive damages may be awarded as provided in section 549.20.

If an action for the injury was commenced by the decedent and not finally determined while living, it may be continued by the trustee for recovery of damages for the exclusive benefit of the surviving spouse and next of kin, proportionate to the pecuniary loss severally suffered by the death. The court on motion shall make an order allowing the continuance and directing pleadings to be made and issues framed as in actions begun under this section.

Subd. 2. Injury action. When injury is caused to a person by the wrongful act or omission of any person or corporation and the person thereafter dies from a cause unrelated to those injuries, the trustee appointed in subdivision 3 may maintain an action for special damages arising out of such injury if the decedent might have maintained an action therefor had the decedent lived.

Subd. 3. Trustee for action. Upon written petition by the surviving spouse or one of the next of kin, the court having jurisdiction of an action falling within the provisions of subdivisions 1 or 2, shall appoint a suitable and competent person as trustee to commence or continue such action and obtain recovery of damages therein. The trustee, before commencing duties shall file a consent and oath. Before receiving any money, the trustee shall file a bond as security therefor in such form and with such sureties as the court may require.

Subd. 4. Applicability. This section shall not apply to any death or cause of action arising prior to its enactment, nor to any action or proceeding now pending in any court of the state of Minnesota, except, notwithstanding section 645.21, this section shall apply to any death or cause of action arising prior to its enactment which resulted from an intentional act constituting murder, and to any such action or proceeding now pending in any court of the state of

Minnesota with respect to issues on which a final judgment has not been entered.

Amended by Laws 1951, c. 697, § 1; Laws 1955, c. 407, § 1; Laws 1957, c. 712, § 1; Laws 1965, c. 837, § 1, eff. May 27, 1965; Laws 1967, c. 158, § 2, eff. April 13, 1967; Laws 1971, c. 43, § 1, eff. March 12, 1971; Laws 1973, c. 717, § 30, eff. Jan. 1, 1974; Laws 1978, c. 593, § 1; Laws 1983, c. 347, §§ 2, 3, eff. June 15, 1983; Laws 1986, c. 444; Laws 2002, c. 403, § 6, eff. Aug. 1, 1999.

Rules of Civil Procedure

Section 573.02 was excepted from the Rules of Civil Procedure governing the procedure in the district courts in all suits of a civil nature, insofar as it was inconsistent or in conflict with the procedure and practice provided by the Rules. See Rules Civ.Proc., Rule 81.01, and Rules Civ.Proc., Appendix A.

Historical and Statutory Notes

Laws 2002, c. 403, § 6, amending subd. 1, also provides in part that the amendment is effective retroactive to August 1, 1999.

Laws 1978, c. 593, § 2, provided that this act is effective for deaths occurring on or after the effective date of this act. Laws 1978, c. 593 did not contain appropriation items or a specific effective date. See § 645.02 for method of determining the effective date.

573.03. Default judgment; judgment not lien upon real estate

When a judgment is taken against an executor or administrator upon failure to answer it shall not be deemed evidence of assets in hand unless the complaint alleged assets and was personally served on the executor or administrator. No judgment against any executor or administrator shall bind, or in any way affect, the real property which belonged to the decedent, nor shall the same be liable upon execution issued upon such judgment.

Amended by Laws 1986, c. 444.

573.04. Executor's wrong, to whom liable

No person shall be liable to an action, as executor of a wrong committed by that person, for having taken, received, or interfered with the property of a deceased person, but shall be responsible to the executor, or general or special administrator, of such decedent for the value of all property so taken or received and for all damages caused by the person's acts to the estate.

Amended by Laws 1986, c. 444.

573.05. Action by foreign executor

Any foreign executor or administrator may commence and prosecute an action in this state, in a representative capacity, in the same manner and under the same restrictions as in case of a resident. Before commencing such action the foreigner shall file an authenticated copy of appointment as executor or administrator with the district court of the county in which such action is to be commenced.

Amended by Laws 1986, c. 444; Laws 1995, c. 189, § 8; Laws 1996, c. 277, § 1.

573.06. Next of kin; liability for debts; contribution

The next of kin of a deceased person are liable to an action by a creditor of the estate, to recover the distributive shares received by them out of such estate, or so much thereof as shall be necessary to satisfy the deceased person's debt, which action may be against all or against any one or more of them. The plaintiff may recover the value of all assets received by all the defendants, if necessary to satisfy the plaintiff's demand, and the plaintiff's recovery shall be apportioned among the defendants in proportion to the value of the assets received by each without deduction on account of there being other relatives who have received assets. Any one against whom such recovery has been had may maintain an action for contribution against all or any other relatives of the decedent to whom assets have been paid, and may recover of each defendant such proportionate share of the amount paid by plaintiff as the value of assets received by each bears to the value of all the assets distributed to all the relatives.

Amended by Laws 1986, c. 444.

573.07. Legatees; when liable

Legatees are liable to an action by a creditor of the testator to recover the value of legacies received by them. Such action may be brought against all or any one or more of the legatees. The plaintiff cannot recover without showing:

(1) that no assets were delivered by the executor or administrator to the heirs or next of kin; or

(2) that the value of the assets so delivered has been recovered by another creditor; or

(3) that such assets are not sufficient to satisfy the demands of the plaintiff, in which case the plaintiff can recover only the deficiency.

The whole amount which the plaintiff can recover shall be apportioned among all the legatees, in proportion to the amount of their legacies, respectively, and each legatee's proportion only can be recovered of each legatee.

Amended by Laws 1986, c. 444.

573.08. Costs; judgment, when discharged

If an action be brought against several next of kin jointly, or several legatees jointly, for assets delivered to them, and a recovery be had against them, the costs shall be apportioned among the several defendants in proportion to the amount of the damages recovered against each. In either case, the payment or satisfaction of the judgment recovered against any one of the defendants shall discharge that defendant and that defendant's property from such judgment.

Amended by Laws 1986, c. 444.

573.09. Heirs and devisees; when liable

Heirs and devisees are liable to an action by a creditor of a deceased person to recover a debt, to the extent of the value of any real property inherited by or devised to them. If such action be against the heirs, all heirs who are liable shall be made parties thereto. The heirs shall not be liable for the debt unless it shall appear that the personal assets were not sufficient to discharge it, or that, after due proceedings before the district court, the creditor is unable to collect the debt from the personal representatives of the decedent, or from the next of kin or a legatee; and if the personal assets were sufficient to pay a part of the debt, or in case a part thereof has been collected, as hereinbefore mentioned, the heirs of such deceased person are liable for the residue. Nothing in this section shall affect the liability of heirs for a debt of their ancestors, where, by will, such debt was expressly charged exclusively on the real property descended such heirs, or directed to be paid out of the real property so descended, before resorting to the personal property.

Amended by Laws 1986, c. 444; Laws 1995, c. 189, § 8; Laws 1996, c. 277, § 1.

573.10. Apportionment of liability; contribution

When the heirs, devisees, or legatees have received real or personal estate, and are liable by law for any debts, such liability shall be in proportion to the estate they have, respectively, received, and a creditor may recover the creditor's claim against a part or all of them to the amount of such liability. If, by the testator's will, any part of the testator's estate, or any devisees or legatees, are made exclusively liable for the debt, the devisees or legatees shall contribute among themselves accordingly.

Amended by Laws 1986, c. 444.

573.11. New parties; issues; apportionment

If all the persons liable for the payment of any such debt shall not be included as defendants, the action shall not thereby be dismissed or barred; but the court may order any other parties brought in, and allow such amendments as may be necessary, on such terms as it may prescribe. If more than one person is liable, and the creditor shall bring action against all or any of them, and those liable shall dispute the debt, or the amount claimed, the court may order an issue to be framed, and direct the amount to be ascertained by a jury, and shall determine how much each is liable to pay.

573.12. Estate of deceased heirs, when liable

If any of the heirs, devisees, or legatees die without having paid a just share of the debts, the estate shall be liable therefor as for a personal debt, to the extent of liability if living.

Amended by Laws 1986, c. 444.

573.13. Contribution among heirs

When any heir, devisee, or legatee pays more than a proportional share of such debt, the other persons liable shall be holden and compelled to contribute their just proportion of the same.

Amended by Laws 1986, c. 444.

573.14. Priority among debts

When the next of kin, legatees, heirs, and devisees are liable for the debts of their ancestor, or testator, they shall give preference in the payment of the same, and be liable therefor, in the following order:

(1) debts entitled to a preference under the laws of the United States;

(2) judgments against the ancestor or testator, according to the priority thereof, respectively;

(3) debts due to other creditors.

573.15. No preference between debts of same class

No preference shall be given by any next of kin, legatee, heir, or devisee to one debt over another of the same class, except one specified in section 573.14, clause (2); nor shall a debt due and payable be entitled to a preference over one not due; nor shall the commencement of an action against any next of kin, legatee, heir, or devisee, for the recovery of a debt, entitle it to preference over others of the same class.

573.16. Defenses; other debts outstanding or paid

The next of kin, legatees, heirs, and devisees may show, in their defense, that there are unsatisfied debts of a prior class, or others of the same class as the debt in action; and if it shall appear that the value of the personal property delivered, or of the real estate descended or devised, to them does not exceed the debts of a prior class, judgment shall be rendered in their favor. If the value of such property exceeds the amount of debts which are entitled to preference over the debt in action, judgment shall be rendered against them only for such a sum as bears a just proportion to the other debts of the same class. If a debt of a class prior to the one in action, or of the same class, is paid by any next of kin, legatees, heirs, or devisees, they may prove such payment, and the amount thereof shall be treated, in ascertaining the amount to be recovered, as if it were unpaid.

573.17. Real property descended; lien of judgment

If it appears that the real property so descended was not alienated by the heir at the time of the commencement of the action, the court shall order that plaintiff's debt, or the proportion thereof which the plaintiff is entitled to recover, be levied upon such real estate, and not otherwise; and every judgment rendered in such action has preference as a lien on such real estate, to any judgment obtained against such heir for a personal debt.

Amended by Laws 1986, c. 444.

573.18. Personal liability; alienation before suit

If it appears in the action that before the commencement thereof the heir has aliened the real property descended to that heir, or any part thereof, that heir shall be personally liable for the value of that aliened; and judgment may be rendered therefor, and execution awarded, as in actions for personal debts. No real property aliened in good faith by an heir, before action commenced against the heir, shall be liable to execution or in any manner affected by a judgment against the heir.

Amended by Laws 1986, c. 444.

573.19. Heirs and devisees; limit of recovery

In actions brought against several heirs or several devisees jointly, the amount of plaintiff's recovery shall be apportioned among all the heirs of the ancestor, or all the devisees of the testator, in proportion to the value of the real property descended or devised, and such proportion only can be recovered of each.

573.20. Devisees, when liable; limitations

Devisees made liable to creditors of their testator by the provisions of this chapter shall not be held liable unless it shall appear that the testator's personal assets and the real property descended to the testator's heirs were insufficient to discharge the debt, or that after due proceedings before the district court the creditor has been unable to recover the debt, or any part thereof, from the personal representative of the testator, or next of kin, legatees, or heirs. In either of these cases, the amount of the deficiency of the personal assets, and of the real property descended to satisfy the debt of the plaintiff, and the amount which the plaintiff may have failed to recover from the personal representative, next of kin, legatees, and heirs of the testator, may be recovered of the devisees, to the extent of the real property devised to them, respectively. Nothing in this section shall affect the liability of the devisees for a debt of their testator which was charged by will exclusively upon the real property devised, or made payable exclusively by such devisees, or out of the real property devised before resorting to the personal property or to any other real property descended or devised.

Amended by Laws 1986, c. 444; Laws 1995, c. 189, § 8; Laws 1996, c. 277, § 1.

573.21. Devisees; application

The provisions of this chapter with regard to heirs, and to proceedings by and against them, and to judgments and executions against them, are applicable to actions and proceedings against devisees, and they must in like manner be jointly sued.

Chapter 576

RECEIVERS, PROPERTY OF ABSENTEES

For complete statutory history see Minnesota Statutes Annotated.

576.01. Receivers, when authorized

Subdivision 1. Appointment. A receiver may be appointed in the following cases:

(1) before judgment, on the application of any party to the action who shall show an apparent right to property which is the subject of such action and is in the possession of an adverse party, and the property, or its rents and profits, are in danger of loss or material impairment, except in cases wherein judgment upon failure to answer may be had without application to the district court;

(2) by the judgment, or after judgment, to carry the same into effect, or to preserve the property pending an appeal, or when an execution has been returned unsatisfied and the judgment debtor refuses to apply property in satisfaction of the judgment;

(3) in the cases provided by law, when a corporation is dissolved, or is insolvent or in imminent danger of insolvency, or has forfeited its corporate

760

rights; and, in like cases, of the property within this state of foreign corporations;

(4) in such other cases as are now provided by law, or are in accordance with the existing practice, except as otherwise prescribed in this section.

Subd. 2. Mortgage appointments. A receiver shall be appointed in the following case:

After the first publication of notice of sale for the foreclosure of a mortgage pursuant to chapter 580, or with the commencement of an action to foreclose a mortgage pursuant to chapter 581, and during the period of redemption, if the mortgage being foreclosed secured an original principal amount of $100,000 or more or is a lien upon residential real estate containing more than four dwelling units and was not a lien upon property which was entirely homesteaded, residential real estate containing four or less dwelling units where at least one unit is homesteaded, or agricultural property, the foreclosing mortgagee or the purchaser at foreclosure sale may at any time bring an action in the district court of the county in which the mortgaged premises or any part thereof is located for the appointment of a receiver; provided, however, if the foreclosure is by action under chapter 581, a separate action need not be filed. Pending trial of the action on the merits, the court may make a temporary appointment of a receiver following the procedures applicable to temporary injunctions under the Rules of Civil Procedure. If the motion for temporary appointment of a receiver is denied, the trial of the action on the merits shall be held as early as practicable, but not to exceed 30 days after the motion for temporary appointment of a receiver is heard. The court shall appoint a receiver upon a showing that the mortgagor has breached a covenant contained in the mortgage relating to any of the following:

(1) application of tenant security deposits as required by section 504B.178;

(2) payment when due of prior or current real estate taxes or special assessments with respect to the mortgaged premises, or the periodic escrow for the payment of the taxes or special assessments;

(3) payment when due of premiums for insurance of the type required by the mortgage, or the periodic escrow for the payment of the premiums;

(4) keeping of the covenants required of a landlord or licensor pursuant to section 504B.161, subdivision 1.

The receiver shall be an experienced property manager. The court shall determine the amount of the bond to be posted by the receiver.

The receiver shall collect the rents, profits and all other income of any kind, manage the mortgaged premises so to prevent waste, execute leases within or beyond the period of the receivership if approved by the court, pay the expenses listed in clauses (1), (2), and (3) in the priority as numbered, pay all expenses for normal maintenance of the mortgaged premises and perform the terms of any assignment of rents which complies with section 559.17, subdivision 2.

Reasonable fees to the receiver shall be paid prior thereto. The receiver shall file periodic accountings as the court determines are necessary and a final accounting at the time of discharge.

The purchaser at foreclosure sale shall have the right, at any time and without limitation as provided in section 582.03, to advance money to the receiver to pay any or all of the expenses which the receiver should otherwise pay if cash were available from the mortgaged premises. Sums so advanced, with interest, shall be a part of the sum required to be paid to redeem from the sale. The sums shall be proved by the affidavit of the purchaser, an agent or attorney, stating the expenses and describing the mortgaged premises. The affidavit must be recorded with the county recorder or the registrar of titles, and a copy thereof shall be furnished to the sheriff and the receiver at least ten days before the expiration of the period of redemption.

Any sums collected which remain in the possession of the receiver at termination of the receivership shall, in the event the termination of the receivership is due to the reinstatement of the mortgage debt or redemption of the mortgaged premises by the mortgagor, be paid to the mortgagor; and in the event termination of the receivership occurs at the end of the period of redemption without redemption by the mortgagor or any other party entitled to redeem, interest accrued upon the sale price pursuant to section 580.23 or section 581.10 shall be paid to the purchaser at foreclosure sale. Any net sum remaining shall be paid to the mortgagor, except if the receiver was enforcing an assignment of rents which complies with section 559.17, subdivision 2, in which case any net sum remaining shall be paid pursuant to the terms of the assignment.

This subdivision shall apply to all mortgages executed on or after August 1, 1977, and to amendments or modifications of such mortgages, and to amendments or modifications made on or after August 1, 1977, to mortgages executed before August 1, 1977, if the amendment or modification is duly recorded and is for the principal purpose of curing a default.

Amended by Laws 1974, c. 447, § 5; Laws 1977, c. 202, § 1; Laws 1986, c. 444; Laws 1992, c. 376, art. 2, § 2; Laws 1999, c. 199, art. 2, § 32, eff. July 1, 1999; Laws 2005, c. 4, § 141.

576.011.　Definitions

Subdivision 1. Generally. For the purpose of Laws 1974, chapter 447, sections 6 to 16 the terms defined in this section have the meanings given them.

Subd. 2. Court. "Court" means the court having probate jurisdiction for the county where an absentee last resided.

Subd. 3. Person. "Person in interest" means the absentee, heirs, any person who would have an interest in the absentee's estate had the absentee died intestate at any time between the commencement of the absence and the date set for any proceeding prescribed by section 576.142, any person who would have an interest under the absentee's will or purported will, an insurer or surety of the absentee, an owner of any reversionary, remainder, joint or contractual interest which might be affected by the death of the absentee, creditor of the absentee, and any other person whom the court finds is properly in interest.

Laws 1974, c. 447, § 6. Amended by Laws 1986, c. 444; Laws 1995, c. 189, § 8; Laws 1996, c. 277, § 1.

576.02. Repealed by Laws 1974, c. 394, § 12

576.04. Absentees; possession, management, and disposition of property

If a person entitled to or having an interest in property within or without the jurisdiction of the state has disappeared or absconded from the place within or without the state where last known to be, and has no agent in the state, and it is not known where the person is, or if such person, having a spouse or minor child or children dependent to any extent upon the person for support, has thus disappeared, or absconded without making sufficient provision for such support, and it is not known where the person is, or, if it is known that the person is without the state, any one who would under the law of the state be entitled to administer upon the estate of such absentee if deceased, or if no one is known to be so entitled, some person deemed suitable by the court, or such spouse, or some one in such spouse's or minors' behalf, may file a petition, under oath, in the court for the county where any such property is situated or found, stating the name, age, occupation, and last known residence or address of such absentee, the date and circumstances of the disappearance or absconding, and the names and residences of other persons, whether members of such absentee's family or otherwise, of whom inquiry may be made, whether or not such absentee is a citizen of the United States, and if not, of what country the absentee is a citizen or native, and containing a schedule of the property, real and personal, so far as known, and its location within or without the state, and a schedule of contractual or property rights contingent upon the absentee's death, and praying that real and personal property may be taken possession of and a receiver thereof appointed under this chapter. No proceedings shall be commenced under the provisions of sections 576.04 to 576.16, except upon good cause shown until at least three months after the date on which it is alleged in such petition that such person so disappeared or absconded.

Amended by Laws 1947, c. 165, § 1; Laws 1974, c. 447, § 7; Laws 1986, c. 444; Laws 1995, c. 189, § 8; Laws 1996, c. 277, § 1.

576.05. Warrant; sheriff to take possession of property; fees and costs

The court may thereupon issue a warrant directed to the sheriff or a deputy, which may run throughout the state, commanding the officer to take possession of the property named in the schedule and hold it subject to the order of the court and make return of the warrant as soon as may be, with the officer's doings thereon and with a schedule of the property so taken. The officer shall post a copy of the warrant upon each parcel of land named in the schedule and cause so much of the warrant as relates to land to be recorded in the office of the county recorder for the county where the land is located. The officer shall receive such fees for serving the warrant as the court allows, but not more than those established by law for similar service upon a writ of attachment. If the petition is dismissed, the fees and the cost of publishing and serving the notice hereinafter provided shall be paid by the petitioner; if a receiver is appointed, they shall be paid by the receiver and allowed in the receiver's account.

Amended by Laws 1976, c. 181, § 2; Laws 1986, c. 444.

576.06. Notice of seizure; appointment of receiver; disposition of property

Upon the return of such warrant, the court may issue a notice reciting the substance of the petition, warrant, and officer's return, which shall be addressed to such absentee and to all persons who claim an interest in such property, and to all whom it may concern, citing them to appear at a time and place named and show cause why a receiver of the property named in the officer's schedule should not be appointed and the property held and disposed of under sections 576.04 to 576.16.

576.07. Publication of notice

The return day of the notice shall be not less than 30, nor more than 60, days after its date. The court shall order the notice to be published once in each of three successive weeks in one or more newspapers within the state, and to be posted in two or more conspicuous places in the county within the state where the absentee last resided or was known to have been either temporarily or permanently, and upon each parcel of land named in the officer's schedule, and a copy to be mailed to the last known address of such absentee. In all cases where the absentee is not a citizen of the United States, a copy of the notice shall be ordered by the court to be served within such time, by mail, on the consular representative of the foreign country of which the absentee is a citizen, if there be one in this state, otherwise on the secretary of state, who shall forward the same to the chief diplomatic representatives of such country at Washington. The court may order other and further notice to be given within or without the state.

576.08. Hearing by court; dismissal of proceeding; appointment and bond of receiver

The absentee, or any person who claims an interest in any of the property, may appear and show cause why the prayer of the petition should not be granted. The court may, after hearing, dismiss the petition and order the property in possession of the officer to be returned to the person entitled thereto, or it may appoint a receiver of the property which is in the possession of the officer and named in the schedule. If a receiver is appointed, the court shall find and record the date of the disappearance or absconding of the absentee; and the receiver shall give a bond to the state in the sum and with the conditions the court orders, to be approved by the court. In the appointment of the receiver the court shall give preference to the spouse of the absentee, if the spouse is competent and suitable.

Amended by Laws 1981, c. 31, § 18; Laws 1986, c. 444.

576.09. Possession of property by receiver

After the approval of the bond the court may order the sheriff or a deputy to transfer and deliver to such receiver the possession of the property under the warrant, and the receiver shall file in the office of the court administrator a schedule of the property received.

Amended by Laws 1986, c. 444; Laws 1986, 1st Sp., c. 3, art. 1, § 82.

576.10. Additional property; receiver to take possession

The receiver, after filing a petition, may be authorized and directed to take possession of any additional property, including a business concern, within or without the state which belongs to such absentee and to demand and collect all debts due the absentee from any person within or without the state and hold the same as if it had been transferred and delivered to the receiver by the officer. The receiver, after filing a petition, may also be authorized and directed to exercise any rights under a life insurance policy or an annuity contract which the absentee could have exercised, including, but not limited to, the right to borrow against it, surrender it for its cash surrender value, or continue it in force by payment of premiums.

Amended by Laws 1947, c. 165, § 2; Laws 1974, c. 447, § 8; Laws 1986, c. 444.

576.11. Where no corporeal property; receiver; bond

If the absentee has left no corporeal property within or without the state, but there are debts and obligations due or owing to the absentee from persons within or without the state, a petition may be filed, as provided in section 576.04, stating the nature and amount of such debts and obligations, so far as known, and praying that a receiver thereof may be appointed. The court may thereupon issue a notice, as above provided, without issuing a warrant, and may, upon the return of the notice and after a hearing, dismiss the petition or appoint a receiver and authorize and direct the receiver to demand and collect the debts and obligations specified in the petition. The receiver shall give bond, as provided in section 576.08, and hold the proceeds of such debts and obligations and all property received, and distribute the same as provided in sections 576.12 to 576.16. The receiver may be further authorized and directed as provided in section 576.10.

Amended by Laws 1947, c. 165, § 3; Laws 1986, c. 444.

576.12.   Care of property; lease; sale; control of business

Subdivision 1.   Order for care of property. The court may make orders for the care, custody, leasing, and investing of all property and its proceeds in the possession of the receiver. If any of the property consists of assets subject to likely rapid decline in value or live animals or is perishable or cannot be kept without a great or disproportionate expense, the court may, after the return of the warrant, order such property to be sold at public or private sale. After the appointment of a receiver, upon the receiver's petition and after notice, the court may order all or part of the property, including the rights of the absentee in land, to be sold at public or private sale to supply money for payments authorized by sections 576.04 to 576.16, to preserve value, or for reinvestment approved by the court.

Subd. 2.   Absentee business. The court may make orders for the management of an absentee's business in possession of the receiver. The court may authorize the receiver or person designated by the receiver to operate the business in conformance with sound business practice. Upon the receiver's petition and after notice, the court may authorize the sale of the business to supply money for payments authorized by sections 576.04 to 576.16, to preserve value, or for reinvestment approved by the court.

Amended by Laws 1974, c. 447, § 9; Laws 1986, c. 444.

576.121.   Advance life insurance payments to absentee's beneficiary

If the beneficiary under an insurance policy on the life of an absentee is the absentee's spouse, child, or other person dependent upon the absentee for support and advance payments under the policy are necessary to support and maintain the beneficiary, the beneficiary shall be entitled to advance payments as the court determines under section 576.122. "Beneficiary" under this section includes an heir at law of the person whose life is insured if the policy is payable to the insured's estate.

Laws 1979, c. 54, § 1. Amended by Laws 1986, c. 444.

576.122.   Hearing by court; determination of right to advance life insurance payments

Subdivision 1.   Petition for hearing. A petition may be filed requesting a hearing to determine entitlement to advance payment under an insurance policy on the life of an absentee. The petition shall contain the beneficiary's name, address, relationship to absentee, and the grounds justifying advance payment.

Subd. 2.   Notification of hearing. Upon the filing of the petition, the court by certified mail shall notify the insurer who issued the policy of the date, time and place of the hearing. The insurer may appear at the hearing as a party in interest.

Subd. 3. Evidentiary burden. The petitioner has the burden to show by a fair preponderance of the evidence that:

(a) the absentee is missing, and there is reason to believe, dead;

(b) the beneficiary is a spouse, child, or other person dependent upon the absentee for support and maintenance; and

(c) the beneficiary has no source of income sufficient for support and maintenance at an adequate level.

Subd. 4. Advance payments. The court shall order periodic advance payments in appropriate amounts taking into consideration the needs of the beneficiary, the likelihood of the absentee's death, the amount payable under the policy, the possibility of the beneficiary providing the insurer with security for any reimbursement that may be required under section 576.123, subdivision 2 and any other relevant factors.

Payment made by the insurer under a court order shall discharge it from any liability to any party for the amounts paid.

Laws 1979, c. 54, § 2. Amended by Laws 1986, c. 444.

576.123. Reappearance of absentee

Subdivision 1. Insurance payments; reduction. If an absentee is declared dead after advance insurance payments have been made pursuant to section 576.122, the amount payable under the policy shall be reduced by the total amount of payments made under section 576.122.

Subd. 2. Reimbursement of insurer. If an absentee is found to be living after advance insurance payments have been made to a beneficiary pursuant to section 576.122, the absentee and beneficiary shall reimburse the insurer the amount of the payments made.

If the insurer is unable to obtain full reimbursement, the amount payable under the policy shall be reduced to the extent necessary to allow full reimbursement. Failure of the absentee and beneficiary to reimburse the insurer upon demand for payment sent by the insurer by certified mail to the last known address of the absentee and beneficiary shall be sufficient to show the insurer's inability to obtain reimbursement.

Laws 1979, c. 54, § 3.

576.13. Use of proceeds

The court may order the property or its proceeds acquired by mortgages, lease, or sale to be applied in payment of charges incurred or that may be incurred in the support and maintenance of the absentee's spouse and minor child or children, and to the discharge of such debts and claims for maintenance, as defined in section 518.003, subdivision 3a, as may be proved against the absentee.

Amended by Laws 1978, c. 772, § 62; Laws 2005, c. 164, § 29, eff. June 4, 2005; Laws 2005, 1st Sp., c. 7, § 28, eff. July 26, 2005.

Historical and Statutory Notes

Laws 2005, c. 164, § 29, as amended by Laws 2005, 1st Sp., c. 7, § 28, provided:

"The revisor of statutes shall create in the first edition of Minnesota Statutes published after June 30, 2006, a new chapter which shall be comprised of the provisions of Minnesota Statutes, chapter 518, that relate to the provision of support for children. The transferred provisions shall be arranged as follows:

"(1) definitions;

"(2) computations of basic support and the related calculations, adjustments, and guidelines that may affect the computations;

"(3) child care support;

"(4) medical support;

"(5) ability to pay and self-support reserves;

"(6) deviation factors; and

"(7) collection, administrative, and other matters.

"The new chapter shall be edited by the revisor in accordance with usual editorial practices as provided by Minnesota Statutes, section 3C.10. If the revisor determines that additional changes are necessary to assure the clarity and utility of the new chapter, the revisor shall draft and propose appropriate legislation to the legislature."

Laws 2005, c. 164, § 32, provided:

"Except as otherwise provided, this act is effective January 1, 2007, and applies to orders adopted or modified after that date. Sections 1 to 3 of this act are effective July 1, 2005."

576.14. Claims; adjustment by receiver

The court may authorize the receiver to adjust by arbitration or compromise any demand in favor of or against the estate of the absentee. The court may authorize the receiver to pay all taxes for which the absentee is liable and all taxes assessed on the absentee's property.

Amended by Laws 1974, c. 447, § 10; Laws 1986, c. 444.

576.141. Presumption of death from absence

An absentee who is missing for a continuous period of four years, during which, after diligent search, the absentee has not been seen or heard of or from, and whose absence is not satisfactorily explained, shall be presumed, in any action or proceeding involving the property of the person, contractual or property rights contingent upon the absentee's death or the administration of the absentee's estate, to have died four years after the date the unexplained absence commenced. If the person was exposed to a specific peril of death, that fact may be a sufficient basis for determining that the absentee died less than four years after the date the absence commenced.

Laws 1974, c. 447, § 11. Amended by Laws 1986, c. 444.

Minnesota Rules of Evidence

Presumptions in civil actions, see Rule 301.

576.142. Hearing by court; determination of death of an absentee

Subdivision 1. Request hearing. A person in interest may request a hearing in the following circumstances:

(1) if an absentee is absent from the domicile without being in communication after being exposed to a specific peril and a diligent search has been made; or

(2) if an absentee has been absent from the domicile for a period of four consecutive years or more without being in communication and a diligent search has been made; or

(3) if unforeseeable or changing circumstances necessitate court authorization for action in respect to the management or disposition of the absentee's business or property.

Subd. 2. Petition. The person requesting the hearing shall file a petition stating name, address, relationship to the absentee, and the specific grounds for the hearing requested.

Subd. 3. Notification. Upon the filing of the petition, the court shall notify all proper persons in interest of the date, time and place of the hearing.

Subd. 4. Service of notice. The notice shall in all cases be served as follows:

(1) by publication in the county in which the petition is filed once in each of three successive weeks, in a newspaper designated by the court; and

(2) upon all persons in interest by ordinary mail.

Subd. 5. Order; death of absentee. The court, if satisfied by the evidence adduced at a hearing in support of a petition alleging the absentee is missing after being exposed to a specific peril or that an absentee has been absent for four or more consecutive years, shall enter an order establishing as a matter of law the death of the absentee and the date thereof. The court shall order the distribution of the absentee's property to the persons and in the manner prescribed in chapters 524 and 525.

Subd. 6. Hearing. Upon a hearing brought pursuant to subdivision 1, clause (c), the court shall have full power to make orders appropriate to conserve the absentee's property or business or to protect the rights of the persons in interest.

Laws 1974, c. 447, § 12. Amended by Laws 1975, c. 347, § 142, eff. Jan. 1, 1976; Laws 1986, c. 444.

576.143. Degree of burden of proof

The burden of proof is on the party bringing the action to declare the absentee dead. If there is a showing that the absentee was exposed to a specific peril at the time of disappearance the burden of proof shall be by a fair preponderance of the evidence. If the absentee was in no unusual danger or peril at the time of disappearance, the burden of proof shall be by clear and convincing evidence.

Laws 1974, c. 447, § 13. Amended by Laws 1986, c. 444.

Minnesota Rules of Evidence

Presumptions in civil actions, burden of going forward and burden of proof, see Rule 301.

576.144. Dissolution of marriage

If the court finds the absentee dead in accordance with section 576.142, the absentee's marriage is dissolved. The court shall enter the conclusion of law dissolving the marriage on the order which establishes the death of the absentee as a matter of law.

Laws 1974, c. 447, § 14. Amended by Laws 1986, c. 444.

576.15. Compensation of receiver; title of absentee lost after four years

The receiver shall be allowed such compensation and disbursements as the court orders, to be paid out of the property or proceeds. If, within four years after the date of the disappearance or absconding, as found and recorded by the court, the absentee appears, and has not been declared dead under section 576.142, or an administrator, executor, assignee in insolvency, or trustee in bankruptcy of the absentee is appointed, the receiver shall account for, deliver, and pay over to the absentee the remainder of the property. If the absentee does not appear and claim the property within four years, all the absentee's right, title, and interest in the property, real or personal, or the proceeds thereof, shall cease, and no action shall be brought by the absentee on account thereof.

If the absentee is declared dead pursuant to section 576.142 and appears before the expiration of four years, the absentee shall have no right, title and interest in the property, real or personal, or the proceeds thereof.

Amended by Laws 1974, c. 447, § 15; Laws 1986, c. 444.

576.16. Property distribution; time limitation

If the receiver is not appointed within three years after the date found by the court under section 576.08, the time limited for accounting for, or fixed for distributing, the property or its proceeds, or for barring actions relative thereto, shall be one year after the date of the appointment of the receiver instead of the four years provided in sections 576.14 and 576.15.

The provisions of sections 576.04 to 576.16 shall not be construed as exclusive, but as providing additional and cumulative remedies.

Amended by Laws 1974, c. 447, § 16; Laws 1975, c. 347, § 143, eff. Jan. 1, 1976.

GENERAL RULES OF PRACTICE FOR THE DISTRICT COURTS

TITLE V. PROBATE RULES

TITLE V. PROBATE RULES

RULE 401. APPLICABILITY OF RULES

Rules 401 through 416 apply to all Probate proceedings.

Adopted Sept. 5, 1991, eff. Jan. 1, 1992.

RULE 402. DEFINITIONS

(a) Formal Proceedings. A formal proceeding is a hearing conducted before the court with notice to interested persons. Formal proceedings seek a judicial determination.

Current with amendments received through November 1, 2007.
For later amendments see Westlaw®
772

(b) Informal Proceedings. An informal proceeding is conducted by the judge, the registrar, or the person or persons designated by the judge for probate of a will or appointment of a personal representative. Informal proceedings seek an administrative determination and not a judicial determination and are granted without prior notice and hearing.

(c) Supervised Administration. Supervised administration is a single, continuous, in rem proceeding commenced by a formal proceeding.

(d) Code. The code is the Uniform Probate Code as adopted by the State of Minnesota.

Adopted Sept. 5, 1991, eff. Jan. 1, 1992.

RULE 403. DOCUMENTS

(a) Preparation of Original Documents. It shall be the responsibility of lawyers and others appearing before the court or registrar to prepare for review and execution appropriate orders, decrees, statements, applications, petitions, notices and related documents, complete and properly drafted, to address the subject matter and relief requested.

(b) Official Forms. The official forms adopted by the Minnesota District Judges' Association or promulgated by the Commissioner of Commerce shall be used.

(c) Documents and Files. The court shall make its files and records available for inspection and copying.

No file, or any part thereof, shall be taken from the custody of the court, except the original court order required to be displayed to an individual or entity when the order is served. A document or exhibit which has been filed or submitted in any proceeding can thereafter be withdrawn only with the permission of the court. Any document which is written in a language other than English shall be accompanied by a verified translation into the English language.

(d) Verification of Filed Documents. Every document filed with the court must be verified as required by the code, except a written statement of claim filed with the court administrator by a creditor or a pleading signed by the lawyer for a party in accordance with the Minnesota Rules of Civil Procedure.

Adopted Sept. 5, 1991, eff. Jan. 1, 1992.

RULE 404. NOTICE IN FORMAL PROCEEDINGS

(a) General Notice Requirements. In all formal proceedings notice of a hearing on any petition shall be given as provided in the code after the court issues the order for hearing. Where mailed notice is required, proof of mailing the notice of hearing shall be filed with the court administrator before any formal order will issue. Mailed notice shall be given to any interested person as defined by the code or to the person's lawyer. Where notice by personal

Current with amendments received through November 1, 2007.
For later amendments see Westlaw®
773

service or publication is required by the code, proof of personal service or publication shall be filed with the court administrator before the formal order will issue.

(b) Notice of Proceedings for Determination of Testacy and Appointment of Personal Representative. In proceedings which adjudicate testacy, notice of the hearing on the petition shall be given after the court administrator issues the order for hearing. Proof of publication of the order for hearing, in accordance with the code, shall be filed with the court administrator before the order will issue. In proceedings for the formal appointment of a personal representative, the same notice requirements shall pertain except notice by publication shall not be required if testacy has been previously determined. Where creditors claims are to be barred, the published notice shall include notice to creditors.

Mailed notice shall be given to all known heirs-at-law, all devisees under any will submitted for formal probate and all interested persons as defined by the code or ordered by the court and shall include in appropriate cases the attorney general, foreign consul and lawyers representing the interested persons.

Mailed notice shall be given to the surviving spouse of the following rights:

(1) The right to receive the decedent's wearing apparel, furniture and household goods and other personal property as provided in the code or by law.

(2) The right to receive maintenance payments during administration of the estate as provided in the code or by law.

(3) The right to take an elective share of one-third of the augmented estate as provided in the code and the homestead as provided in the code or by law.

(c) Waiver of Notice in Formal Proceedings. Except in proceedings governed by subdivision (b) of this rule, an interested person may waive notice of any formal proceeding in accordance with the code. The written waiver shall evidence the person's consent to the order sought in the proceeding.

Adopted Sept. 5, 1991, eff. Jan. 1, 1992.

RULE 405. INTERIM ORDERS

(a) Interim Orders Available From Court Only. The court has no power to intervene in any unsupervised administration unless a formal petition invoking the court's authority is filed by an interested person.

The court or registrar does not have authority to issue ex parte interim orders in unsupervised proceedings except that the registrar may issue the certificate of discharge provided for in the code.

In supervised administration, the court may issue ex parte orders only for strong and compelling reasons.

(b) [Rule 405 adopted without a paragraph (b).]

Adopted Sept. 5, 1991, eff. Jan. 1, 1992.

Current with amendments received through November 1, 2007.
For later amendments see Westlaw®
774

RULE 406. UNCONTESTED FORMAL PROCEEDINGS

(a) Uncontested Formal Proceedings; Hearings and Proof. The court shall call the calendar in open court for all hearings set for a designated time. If a petition in a formal proceeding is unopposed, the court will enter in the record the fact that there was no appearance in opposition to the petition and that no objection has been filed with the court. Thereupon, the court shall:

(1) Make its determination after conducting a hearing in open court, requiring appearance of petitioner and testimony or other proof of the matters necessary to support the order sought; or

(2) Make its determination on the strength of the pleadings without requiring the appearance of petitioner or of petitioner's lawyer and without requiring testimony or proof other than the verified pleadings; or

(3) Make its determination based on such combination of (1) and (2) above as the court in its discretion deems proper.

In any uncontested formal proceeding, the court shall determine that (i) the time required for any notice has expired; (ii) any required notice has been given; (iii) the court has jurisdiction of the subject matter; (iv) venue is proper; and (v) the proceeding was commenced within the time limitations prescribed by the code as a prerequisite to determining other issues presented to the court for determination in the proceeding. The court shall be satisfied that the pleadings and any other proof presented support the order sought in any uncontested formal proceeding.

(b) [Rule 406 adopted without a paragraph (b).]

Adopted Sept. 5, 1991, eff. Jan. 1, 1992.

RULE 407. APPOINTMENT

(a) Nomination and Renunciation. When two or more persons have equal or higher priority to appointment as personal representative, those who do not renounce must concur in writing in nominating another to act for them, or in applying for appointment. In formal appointment proceedings, concurrence by persons who have equal or higher priority is presumed after notice has been given unless a written objection is filed.

(b) Nonresident Personal Representatives. The court or registrar may appoint a nonresident personal representative.

Adopted Sept. 5, 1991, eff. Jan. 1, 1992.

RULE 408. INFORMAL PROCEEDINGS

(a) Contents of the Application. Application for informal probate or appointment proceedings shall contain information required by the code and the approximate value of the following categories of assets:

Probate Assets
    Homestead $_____

Current with amendments received through November 1, 2007.
For later amendments see Westlaw®
775

Other Real Estate	$_____
Cash	$_____
Securities	$_____
Other	$_____
Non–Probate Assets	
Joint Tenancy	$_____
Insurance	$_____
Other	$_____
Approximate Indebtedness	$_____

In all estate proceedings, whether testate or intestate, the application must contain a statement that specifically eliminates all heirs or devisees other than those listed in the application.

Probate Committee Comment

Original Advisory Committee Comment—Not kept current.

Examples

(These are not intended to be exhaustive)

The statements will necessarily vary, depending upon who survives the decedent, and must close out any class affected:

(1) Where only the spouse survives, the application should state "That decedent left no surviving issue, natural or adopted, legitimate or illegitimate."

(2) Where only children survive, the application should state "That the decedent left surviving no spouse; no children, natural or adopted, legitimate or illegitimate, other than herein named; and no issue of any deceased children."

(3) Where the spouse and children survive, the application should state "That the decedent left surviving no children, natural or adopted, legitimate or illegitimate, other than herein named and no issue of any deceased children."

(4) Where only brothers or sisters of decedent survive, the application should state "That the decedent left surviving no spouse; issue; parents; brothers or sisters other than herein named; and no issue of deceased brothers or sisters."

(5) Where only first cousins survive, the application should state "That the decedent left surviving no spouse; issue; parents; brothers or sisters or issue thereof, grandparents; aunts or uncles; and no first cousins other than herein named."

(6) In all cases, the application should state either:

(a) That all the heirs-at-law survived the decedent for 120 hours or more; or

(b) That all the heirs-at-law survived the decedent for 120 hours or more except the following: (name or names).

(7) In all cases where a spouse and children survive, the application should state either:

(a) That all of the issue of the decedent are also issue of the surviving spouse; or

(b) That one or more of the issue of the decedent are not also issue of the surviving spouse.

(b) Will Testimony. The registrar shall not require any affidavit or testimony with respect to execution of a will prior to informal probate if it is a self-proved will or appears to have been validly executed.

Current with amendments received through November 1, 2007.
For later amendments see Westlaw®
776

Probate Committee Comment

Original Advisory Committee Comment—Not kept current.

Applicants for informal probate of a will which is not self-proved are encouraged to preserve evidence concerning the execution of the will if a formal testacy proceeding may later be required or desired.

(c) Appearances. The applicant is required to appear before the registrar unless represented by counsel. The registrar may also waive appearance by counsel.

(d) Informal Proceedings: Notice of Informal Probate of Will and Informal Appointment of Personal Representative. In informal proceedings, notice of appointment of a personal representative shall be given after the registrar issues the order appointing the personal representative. Proof of placement for publication shall be filed with the court administrator before letters will issue. Where mailed notice is required, an affidavit of mailing of the order appointing the personal representative shall be filed with the court administrator before letters will issue. If the informal proceedings include the informal probate of a will, the notice shall include notice of the issuance of the statement of informal probate of the will. Where creditors claims are to be barred, the published notice shall include notice to creditors.

Mailed notice shall be given to all known heirs-at-law, all devisees under any will submitted for informal probate and all interested persons as defined by the code and shall include in appropriate cases the attorney general, foreign consul and lawyers representing interested persons.

Mailed notice shall be given to the surviving spouse of the following rights:

(1) The right to receive the decedent's wearing apparel, furniture and household goods and other personal property as provided in the code or by law.

(2) The right to receive maintenance payments during administration of the estate as provided in the code or by law.

(3) The right to take an elective share of one-third of the augmented estate as provided in the code and the homestead as provided in the code or by law.

Adopted Sept. 5, 1991, eff. Jan. 1, 1992.

RULE 409. FORMAL TESTACY AND APPOINTMENT PROCEEDINGS

(a) Contents of Petition. A petition in formal testacy and appointment proceedings shall contain the information required by the code and the information concerning the approximate value of assets required by Minn. Gen. R. Prac. 408(a). In all estate proceedings, whether testate or intestate, the petition must contain an allegation that specifically eliminates all heirs or devisees other than as listed in the petition.

(b) Conversion to Supervised Administration. Any estate which has been commenced as an informal proceeding or as an unsupervised formal proceeding may be converted at any time to a supervised administration upon petition.

Current with amendments received through November 1, 2007.
For later amendments see Westlaw®
777

The court shall enter an order for hearing on said petition. Notice of hearing shall be given in accordance with Minn. Gen. R. Prac. 404(a). If testacy has not been adjudicated in a prior formal proceeding, notice of hearing must meet the specific notice requirements for formal testacy proceedings provided by Minn. Gen. R. Prac. 404(b) including notice by publication.

Adopted Sept. 5, 1991, eff. Jan. 1, 1992.

RULE 410. TRANSFER OF REAL ESTATE

(a) Transfers of Real Estate in Supervised and Unsupervised Administration; Transfer by Personal Representative of Real Property for Value; Documents Required. A personal representative shall provide a transferee of real property for value with the following documents:

(1) A certified copy of unrestricted letters (30 days must have elapsed since date of issuance of letters to an informally appointed personal representative);

(2) A certified copy of the will; and

(3) A personal representative's deed or other instrument transferring any interest in real property which shall contain the marital status of the decedent and the consent of spouse, if any.

(b) Distribution of Real Property; Documents Required. A personal representative shall provide a distributee of real property with the following documents:

(1) When distribution is made by decree, a certified copy of the decree of distribution assigning any interest in real property to the distributee.

(2) When distribution is made by deed from a personal representative in unsupervised administration:

(i) A certified copy of unrestricted letters (30 days must have elapsed since date of issuance of letters to an informally appointed personal representative);

(ii) A certified copy of the will; and

(iii) A personal representative's deed of distribution of any interest in real property to the distributee which shall contain the marital status of the decedent and consent of spouse, if any.

(3) When distribution is made by deed from the personal representative in supervised administration:

(i) A certified copy of unrestricted letters;

(ii) A certified copy of an order of distribution which authorizes the distribution of any interest in real property to the distributee;

(iii) A certified copy of the will; and

(iv) A personal representative's deed of distribution of any interest in real property to the distributee.

Adopted Sept. 5, 1991, eff. Jan. 1, 1992.

Current with amendments received through November 1, 2007.
For later amendments see Westlaw®
778

RULE 411. CLOSING ESTATES

(a) Notice of Formal Proceedings for Complete Settlement Under Minn. Stat. § 524.3–1001. If testacy has been adjudicated in a prior formal proceeding, notice of hearing on a petition for complete settlement under Minn. Stat. § 524.3–1001 must meet the requirements of Minn. Gen. R. Prac. 404(a), but notice by publication specifically provided for in Minn. Stat. § 524.3–403 is not required. If testacy has not been adjudicated in a prior formal proceeding, notice of hearing on a petition for complete settlement under Minn. Stat. § 524.3–1001, must meet the specific notice requirements for formal testacy proceedings provided in Minn. Stat. § 524.3–403, including notice by publication.

(b) Notice of Formal Proceedings for Settlement of Estate Under Minn. Stat. § 524.3–1002. If an estate is administered under an informally probated will and there has been no adjudication of testacy in a prior formal proceeding, the court may make a final determination of rights between the devisees under the will and against the personal representative under Minn. Stat. § 524.3–1002, if no part of the estate is intestate. The court will not adjudicate the testacy status of the decedent. Notice of hearing on a petition must meet the requirements of Minn. Stat. § 524.1–401. Notice by publication specifically provided for in Minn. Stat. § 524.3–403 is not required.

Adopted Sept. 5, 1991, eff. Jan. 1, 1992.

RULE 412. FEES, VOUCHERS, AND TAX RETURNS

(a) Fees. The court may require documentation or it may appoint counsel to determine the reasonableness of the fees charged by the lawyer and the personal representative. The court may order the fees of the appointed counsel to be paid out of the estate.

(b) Vouchers. Unless otherwise ordered by the court, vouchers for final and interim accounts need not be filed.

(c) Tax Returns. Unless ordered by the court, copies of the United States Estate Tax closing letter and the Minnesota notification of audit results need not be filed.

Adopted Sept. 5, 1991, eff. Jan. 1, 1992.

RULE 413. SUBSEQUENT PROCEEDINGS

(a) Authority of Personal Representative During One Year Period After Filing Closing Statement. For one year from the date of filing the closing statement authorized by the code, the personal representative shall have full and complete authority to execute further transfers of property; to complete transactions; to complete distributions; to correct misdescriptions or improper identification of assets; or to transfer or distribute omitted property. During this period, the personal representative shall ascertain any matters of unfin-

Current with amendments received through November 1, 2007.
For later amendments see Westlaw®
779

ished administration which must be completed prior to the termination of the representative's authority.

(b) Authority of Personal Representative to Transfer or Distribute Omitted Property During One Year Period After Filing Closing Statement. In the case of omitted property discovered after the filing of the closing statement authorized by the code, but before termination of the personal representative's authority, the personal representative must, as required by the code, file a supplementary inventory with the court and mail a copy to any surviving spouse, other distributees, and other interested persons, including creditors whose claims are unpaid and not barred. Proof of service by mail must be filed with the court prior to any transfer of the omitted property by the personal representative.

(c) Notice of Proceedings for Subsequent Administration After Termination of Personal Representative's Authority. Appointment of a personal representative in subsequent administration may only be secured in formal proceeding. If testacy has been adjudicated in a formal proceeding, notice of hearing must meet the requirements of Minn. Gen. R. Prac. 404(a), but the notice by publication specifically provided for in Minn. Stat. § 524.3–403 is not required. If testacy has not been adjudicated previously and only appointment of a personal representative is sought, notice of hearing must meet the specific notice requirements for formal testacy proceedings provided in Minn. Stat. § 524.3–403, but notice by publication is not required. In the case of subsequent administration involving omitted property, the personal representative must comply with the inventory, mailing and filing requirements of Minn. Gen. R. Prac. 413(b).

(d) Proof Required for Formal Settlement or Distribution in Subsequent Administration. During a subsequent administration, when an order of settlement of the estate and decree or order of distribution is sought, the court must be satisfied with the pleadings and any other proof (including accounting for all assets, disbursements, and distributions made during the prior administration) before issuing its order.

Adopted Sept. 5, 1991, eff. Jan. 1, 1992.

RULE 414. FIDUCIARIES

If the lawyer for the estate, a partner, associate or employee is the personal representative of the estate, except where one of them is a family member of the decedent, the administration shall be supervised. In such a case, both the lawyer for the estate and the personal representative must keep separate time records and differentiate the charges for their duties in each capacity. The lawyer should only serve as fiduciary at the unsolicited suggestion of the client and the lawyer must realize that there are legal, ethical and practical problems that must be overcome in order to perform the duties of a fiduciary and lawyer.

Adopted Sept. 5, 1991, eff. Jan. 1, 1992.

Current with amendments received through November 1, 2007.
For later amendments see Westlaw®
780

RULE 415. REGISTRAR

(a) **Authority.** The functions of the registrar may be performed either by a judge of the court or by a person designated by the court in a written order filed and recorded in the office of the court, subject to the following:

(1) Each judge of the court may at any time perform the functions of registrar regardless of whether the court has designated other persons to perform those functions.

(2) The functions and powers of the registrar are limited to the acts and orders specified by the code and these rules.

(3) Any person designated registrar by the court shall be subject to the authority granted by and the continuing direction of the court.

(4) The registrar is not empowered to intervene or issue orders resolving conflicts related to the administration of the estate.

(b) **Registrar Has No Continuing Authority.** The registrar does not have any continuing authority over an estate after the informal probate is granted or denied and shall not require the filing of any additional documents other than are required by the code (law) and these rules.

Adopted Sept. 5, 1991, eff. Jan. 1, 1992.

RULE 416. GUARDIANSHIPS AND CONSERVATORSHIPS

(a) **Responsibility of Lawyer.** Upon the appointment of a conservator or guardian of the estate, the appointee shall nominate a lawyer of record for that conservatorship or guardianship, or shall advise the court that he or she shall act pro se. The named lawyer shall be the lawyer of record until terminated by the conservator or guardian, or, with the consent of the court, by withdrawal of the lawyer. If the lawyer is terminated by the conservator or guardian, written notice of substitution or pro se representation shall be given to the court (by the conservator or guardian, or by the lawyer who has received oral or written notice of termination), and until such notice, the former lawyer shall be recognized.

(b) **Visitors in Guardianship and Conservatorship Proceedings.** A visitor, as defined by law, may be appointed in every general guardianship or conservatorship proceeding.

Every visitor shall have training and experience in law, health care or social work, as the case may be, depending upon the circumstances of the proposed ward or conservatee.

The visitor shall be an officer of the court and shall be disinterested in the guardianship or conservatorship proceedings. If the court at any time determines that the visitor, or the firm or agency by which he or she is employed, has or had, at the time of hearing, a conflict of interest, the court shall immediately appoint a new visitor and may, if necessary, require a hearing de novo.

Current with amendments received through November 1, 2007.
For later amendments see Westlaw®
781

The visitor shall, (a) without outside interferences, meet with the proposed ward or conservatee, either once or more than once as the visitor deems necessary, (b) observe his or her appearance, lucidity and surroundings, (c) serve, read aloud, if requested, and explain the petition and notice of hearing, (d) assist, if requested, in obtaining a private or court appointed lawyer, (e) advise the proposed ward or conservatee that a report will be filed at least five (5) days before the hearing and that the report is available to the proposed ward or conservatee or the ward's or conservatee's lawyer, (f) prepare a written report to the court setting forth all matters the visitor deems relevant in determining the need for a guardian or conservator, including recommendations concerning appointment and limitation of powers, (g) file the original report with the court and, (h) serve a copy upon the petitioner or petitioner's lawyer at least five (5) days prior to the hearing, (i) appear, testify and submit to cross examination at the hearing concerning his or her observations and recommendations, unless such appearance is excused by the court.

(c) **Voluntary Petition.** If an adult voluntarily petitions or consents to the appointment of a guardian or conservator of the estate as set forth in the law, then it is not necessary for such adult to be an "incapacitated person" as defined by the law.

(d) **Amount of Bond.** The court may, at any time, require the filing of a bond in such amount as the court deems necessary and the court, either on request of an interested party, or on its own motion, may increase or decrease the amount of the bond. The court, in requiring a bond, if any, or in determining the amount thereof, shall take into account not only the nature and value of the assets, but also the qualifications of the guardian or conservator.

(e) **Effect of Allowance of Accounts.** The filing, examination and acceptance of an annual account, without notice of hearing, shall not constitute a determination or adjudication on the merits of the account, nor does it constitute the court's approval of the account.

(f) **Required Periodic Settlement of Accounts.** No order settling and allowing an annual or final account shall be issued by the court except on a hearing with notice to interested parties. A hearing for the settlement and allowance of an annual or final account may be ordered upon the request of the court or any interested party. A hearing shall be held for such purpose in each guardianship or conservatorship of the estate at least once every five years upon notice as set forth in the law, and the rules pursuant thereto. However, in estates of the value of $20,000 or less, the five year hearing requirement may be waived by the court in its discretion. Such five year hearings shall be held within 150 days after the end of the accounting period of each fifth annual unallowed account and the court administrator shall notify such guardian or conservator, the guardian's or conservator's lawyer and the court if the hearing is not held within the 150 day period.

(g) **Notice of Hearing on Account.** Notice of time and place for hearing on the petition for final settlement and allowance of any account shall be given to

Current with amendments received through November 1, 2007.
For later amendments see Westlaw®
782

the ward or conservatee, to the guardian or conservator if such person was not the petitioner for settlement of the accounts, to the spouse, adult children and such other interested persons as the court may direct. Whenever any funds have been received by the estate from the Veterans Administration during the period of accounting, notice by mail shall be given to the regional office. The notice may be served in person or by depositing a copy in the U.S. mail to the last known address of the person or entity being served. When a ward or conservatee is restored to capacity, that person is the only interested person. When a ward or conservatee dies, the personal representative of the estate is the only interested person.

   (h) Appearance on Petition for Adjudication of Accounts. When a verified annual or final account is filed in accord with the law and an adjudication is sought, and notice given as required by the law or waived as provided below, and the court determines that the account should be allowed, the account may be allowed upon the pleadings without appearance of the guardian or conservator. If the ward, conservatee or any interested person shall object to the account, or demand the appearance of the guardian or conservator for hearing on the account, at any time up to and including the date set for the hearing, the court will continue the hearing, if necessary, to a later date and require the appearance of the guardian/conservator for examination. Notice of hearing may be waived with the consent of all interested persons.

   (i) Successor Guardian; Notice to Ward or Conservatee. The notice required by law shall include the right of the ward or conservatee to nominate and instruct the successor.

Adopted Sept. 5, 1991, eff. Jan. 1, 1992.

RULE 417.   TRUSTEES—ACCOUNTING—PETITION FOR APPOINTMENT

Rule 417.01.   Petition for Confirmation of Trustee

   Except in those cases in which a trust company or national banking association having trust powers is the trustee or one of the trustees, the petition for confirmation of the appointment of the trustee or trustees shall include an inventory, including a description of the assets of the trust known to the petitioners and an estimate by them of the market value of such assets at the date of the petition. The petition shall also set forth the relationship, if any, of the trustee or trustees to the beneficiaries of the trust.

Amended Nov. 13, 1992, eff. Jan. 1, 1993.

Rule 417.02.   Annual Account

   Every trustee subject to the continuing supervision of the district court shall file an annual account, duly verified, of the trusteeship with the court administrator within 60 days after the end of each accounting year. Such accounts

Current with amendments received through November 1, 2007.
For later amendments see Westlaw®
783

may be submitted on form 417.02 appended to these rules, and shall contain the following:

(a) Statements of the total inventory or carrying value and of the total fair market value of the assets of the trust principal as of the beginning of the accounting period. In cases where a previous account has been rendered, the totals used in these statements shall be the same as those used for the end of the last preceding accounting period.

(b) A complete itemized inventory of the assets of the trust principal as of the end of the accounting period, showing both the inventory or carrying value of each asset and also the fair market value thereof as of such end of the accounting period, unless, because such value is not readily ascertainable or for other sufficient reason, this provision cannot reasonably be complied with. Where the fair market value of any item at the end of the accounting period is not used, a notation of such fact and the reason therefor shall be indicated on the account.

(c) An itemized statement of all income transactions during the period of such account.

(d) A summary statement of all income transactions during the period of such account, including the totals of distributions of income to beneficiaries and the totals of trustees' fees and attorneys' fees charged to income.

(e) An itemized statement of all principal transactions during the period of such account.

(f) A reconciliation of all principal transactions during the period of such account, including the totals of distributions of principal to beneficiaries and the totals of trustees' fees and attorneys' fees charged to principal as well as the totals of liquidations and reinvestments of principal cash.

(g) A list of all assets that realized a net income less than one per cent of the inventory value or acquisition cost, and an explanation of the amount of net income realized and the reasons for retaining the assets.

Amended Nov. 13, 1992, eff. Jan. 1, 1993. Amended Dec. 14, 1995, eff. Jan. 1, 1996.

Rule 417.03. Taxes

Final accounts shall also disclose the state of the property of the trust estate as to unpaid or delinquent taxes and such taxes shall be paid by the trustee to the extent that the funds in the trust permit, over and beyond the cost and expenses of the trust administration, except where a special showing is made by the trustee that it is in the best interests of the trust and is lawful for the unpaid or delinquent taxes not to be paid.

Amended Nov. 13, 1992, eff. Jan. 1, 1993.

Current with amendments received through November 1, 2007.
For later amendments see Westlaw®
784

Rule 417.04. Service on Beneficiaries

There shall also be filed with the court administrator proof of mailing of such account to the last addresses known to the trustee of, or of the service of such account upon, such of the following beneficiaries or their natural or legal guardians as are known to, or reasonably ascertainable by, the trustee:

(a) Beneficiaries entitled to receive income or principal at the date of the accounting; and

(b) Beneficiaries who, were the trust terminated at the date of the accounting, would be entitled to share in distributions of income or principal.

Amended Nov. 13, 1992, eff. Jan. 1, 1993.

Rule 417.05. Court Administrator Records; Notice

The court administrator shall keep a list of trusteeships and notify each trustee and the court when any such annual account has not been filed within 120 days from the end of the accounting year.

Amended Nov. 13, 1992, eff. Jan. 1, 1993.

Rule 417.06. Hearing

Hearings upon annual accounts may be ordered upon the request of any interested party. A hearing shall be held on such annual accounts at least once every five years by mailing, at least 15 days before the date of the hearing, a copy of the order for hearing to those beneficiaries of the trust who are known to or reasonably ascertainable by the petitioner, to any other person requesting notice, or as ordered by the court. In trusts of the value of $20,000 or less, the five year hearing requirement may be waived by the court in its discretion. Any hearing on an account may be ex parte if each party in interest then in being shall execute waiver of notice in writing which shall be filed with the court administrator, but no account shall be finally allowed except upon a hearing on the record in open court. Such five year hearings shall be held within 150 days after the end of the accounting period of each fifth annual unallowed account, and the court administrator shall notify each trustee and the Court if the hearing is not held within such 150 day period.

Amended Nov. 13, 1992, eff. Jan. 1, 1993.

RULE 418. DEPOSIT OF WILLS

(a) Deposit by Testator. Any testator may deposit his or her will with the court administrator in any county subject to the following rules. Wills shall be placed in a sealed envelope with the name, address, and birth date of the testator placed on the outside. The administrator shall give a receipt to the person depositing the will.

(b) Withdrawal by Testator or Agent. Any will may be withdrawn by the testator in person upon presentation of identification and signing an appropriate receipt. A testator's attorney or other agent may withdraw the will by

Current with amendments received through November 1, 2007.
For later amendments see Westlaw®
785

presenting a written authorization signed by the testator and two witnesses with the testator's signature notarized.

(c) Examination by Guardian or Conservator. A guardian or conservator of the testator may review the will upon presentation of identification bearing the photograph of the person seeking review and a copy of valid letters of guardianship or conservatorship. If the guardianship or conservatorship proceedings are venued in a county other than that where the will is filed, the required copy of the letters shall be certified by the issuing court within 30 days of the request to review the will. The will may only be examined by the guardian or conservator in the presence of the court administrator or deputy administrator, who shall reseal it after the review is completed and shall endorse on the resealed envelope the date it was opened, by whom it was opened and that the original was placed back in the envelope.

(d) Copies. No copies of the original will shall be made during the testator's lifetime.

Adopted Oct. 10, 1996.

Advisory Committee Comment—1996 Amendment

This rule is new and is intended to provide a standard mechanism for handling wills deposited with the court for safekeeping. Minn.Stat. § 524.2–515, became effective in 1996 to permit deposit of any will by the testator. This rule is intended to provide uniform and orderly rules for deposit and withdrawal of wills that are deposited pursuant to this statute.

Historical Notes

The order of the Minnesota Supreme Court [CX-89-1863] dated October 10, 1996, provides in part that these amendments are effective July 1, 1997, except that rules 119 and 418 are effective January 1, 1997, that these amendments shall apply to all actions pending on the effective dates and to those filed thereafter, and that "(t)he inclusion of Advisory Committee comments is made for convenience and does not reflect court approval of the comments made therein".

Current with amendments received through November 1, 2007.
For later amendments see Westlaw®
786

APPENDIX OF FORMS
FOR
TITLE V.   PROBATE RULES

FORM 417.02.   TRUSTEE'S ACCOUNTING

State of Minnesota		District Court
COUNTY	JUDICIAL DISTRICT CASE NO.	

Case Type: _____

In the Matter of the Trust Created under Article
_____ of the Last Will of _____.

ALTERNATIVE FOR INTER VIVOS TRUSTS:
In the Matter of the Trust Created under
Agreement By and Between _____,
Settlor, and _____ and _____,
Trustees, dated _____.

**TRUSTEE'S
ANNUAL
ACCOUNT**

	Principal	Income
Assets on Hand as of _____ (Schedule 1)	$	$
Increases to Assets:		
Interest (Schedule 2)	$ 0.00	$
Dividends (Schedule 3)	$ 0.00	$
Capital gains distributions (Schedule 4)	$	$ 0.00
Gains on sales and other dispositions (Schedule 5)	$	$ 0.00
Return of capital (Schedule 6)	$	$ 0.00
Other increases (Schedule 7)	$	$
Decreases to Assets:		
Losses on sales and other dispositions (Schedule 8)	($)	($ .00)
Administration expenses (Schedule 9)	($)	($)
Taxes (Schedule 10)	($)	($)
Trustee fees	($)	($)
Attorney fees	($)	($)
Other decreases (Schedule 11)	($)	($)
Balance Before Distributions	$	$

Form 417.02

Distributions to Beneficiaries (Schedule 12)		($)	($)
Principal and Income Balances		$ 0.00	$ 0.00

Total Assets on Hand as of _____ $ _____
(Income plus principal) (Schedule 13)

Assets which realized a net income of less than 1% of their inventory values or acquisition costs are listed on Schedule 14.

[NAME OF TRUST]
ASSETS ON HAND
[Beginning DATE]
Schedule 1

	Market Value as of [DATE]	Values at Cost or Basis Principal	Values at Cost or Basis Income
Cash or Cash Equivalents			
Checking account	$	$	$
Savings account	$	$	$
Money market account	$	$	$
Stocks and Bonds			
Stocks	$	$	$ 0.00
Corporate bonds	$	$	$ 0.00
Municipal bonds	$	$	$ 0.00
Real Estate	$	$	$ 0.00
Real Estate	$	$	$ 0.00
Other Assets			$
Life insurance policies			
(cash value)	$	$	$
Other assets	$	$	$
Total Assets on Hand as of			
[Date] _____.	0.00	0.00	0.00

Note: This schedule reflects assets on hand at the beginning of the period. Identify each asset thoroughly. Provide the name of the bank and account number for each account holding cash or cash equivalents. Provide the number of shares or par value of each security. Provide the address of each parcel of real estate.

[NAME OF TRUST]
INTEREST
Schedule 2

	Income
Checking account(s)	
1.	$

	Income
2.	$

Savings account(s)
1.	$
2.	$

Corporate bonds
1.	$
2.	$
3.	$

Municipal bonds
1.	$
2.	$
3.	$

Other interest
1.	$
2.	$
3.	$

Total Interest	$ 0.00

Identify each interest-producing asset. List each bank account by name and account number. Identify each bond or other asset that pays interest.

[NAME OF TRUST]
DIVIDENDS
Schedule 3

Stocks	Income
1	$
2	$
3	$
4	$
5	$
6	$
7	$
8	$
9	$
10	$
11	$
12	$
13	$
14	$
15	$

Total Dividends	0.00

Identify each security that paid dividends.

Form 417.02

[NAME OF TRUST]
CAPITAL GAINS DISTRIBUTIONS
Schedule 4

	Principal
Capital gains distributions:	
1	$
2	$
3	$
4	$
5	$
6	$
7	$
8	$
9	$
10	$
11	$
12	$
13	$
14	$
Total Capital Gains Distributions	0.00

Identify each security that paid a capital gains distribution.

[NAME OF TRUST]
GAINS ON SALES AND OTHER DISPOSITIONS
Schedule 5

Principal

Sale of _____ shares of _____:
  Proceeds received $
  Less cost or basis   ($) $ 0.00

Sale of _____ shares of _____:
  Proceeds received $
  Less cost or basis   ($) $ 0.00

Sale of _____ shares of _____:
  Proceeds received $
  Less cost or basis   ($) $ 0.00

Sale of _____ shares of _____:
  Proceeds received $
  Less cost or basis   ($) $ 0.00

Sale of _____ shares of _____:
  Proceeds received $
  Less cost or basis   ($) $ 0.00

Sale of _____ shares of _____:
  Proceeds received $

			Principal
Less cost or basis	($	)	$ 0.00

Sale of _____ shares of _____:
Proceeds received	$		
Less cost or basis	($	)	$ 0.00

Sale of _____ shares of _____:
Proceeds received	$		
Less cost or basis	($	)	$ 0.00

Sale of _____ shares of _____:
Proceeds received	$		
Less cost or basis	($	)	$ 0.00

Total Gains			$ 0.00

[NAME OF TRUST]
RETURN OF CAPITAL
Schedule 6

Return of capital:	Principal
1.	$
2.	$
3.	$
4.	$
5.	$
6.	$
7.	$
8.	$
9.	$
10.	$
11.	$
12.	$
13.	$
14.	$

Total Return of Capital	0.00

Identify each security that paid a return of capital.

[NAME OF TRUST]
OTHER INCREASES
Schedule 7

Securities added to trust by Settlor	Principal	Income
		$ 0.00
1	$	$
2	$	$
3	$	$

Form 417.02

	Principal	Income
4	$	$
5	$	$
6	$	$
7	$	$
8	$	$
9	$	$
Income transferred to principal	$	$ 0.00

Other increases:

	Principal	Income
1	$	$
2	$	$
3	$	$
4	$	$
5	$	$
6	$	$
7	$	$
8	$	$
9	$	$
Total Other Increases	0.00	0.00

[NAME OF TRUST]
LOSSES ON SALES AND OTHER DISPOSITIONS
Schedule 8

Principal

Sale of _____ shares of _____:
Proceeds received $
Less cost or basis   ($) $ 0.00

Sale of _____ shares of _____:
Proceeds received $
Less cost or basis   ($) $ 0.00

Sale of _____ shares of _____:
Proceeds received $
Less cost or basis   ($) $ 0.00

Sale of _____ shares of _____:
Proceeds received $
Less cost or basis   ($) $ 0.00

Sale of _____ shares of _____:
Proceeds received $
Less cost or basis   ($) $ 0.00

Sale of _____ shares of _____:
Proceeds received $
Less cost or basis   ($) $ 0.00

Sale of _____ shares of _____:
Proceeds received $

	Principal
Less cost or basis	($_____) $ 0.00

Sale of _____ shares of _____:
Proceeds received $____
Less cost or basis ($_____) $ 0.00

Sale of _____ shares of _____:
Proceeds received $____
Less cost or basis ($_____) $ 0.00

Total Losses $ 0.00

[NAME OF TRUST]
ADMINISTRATIVE EXPENSES
Schedule 9

	Principal	Income
Bank account fees	$	$
Check charges	$	$
Broker annual fees	$	$
Photocopies	$	$
Postage	$	$
Maintenance of real estate (schedule attached)	$	$
Other (schedule attached)	$	$

Total Administrative Expenses	$ 0.00	$ 0.00

[NAME OF TRUST]
TAXES
Schedule 10

	Principal	Income
Foreign dividend tax	$ 0.00	$
U.S. fiduciary income tax	$	$
Minnesota fiduciary income tax	$	$

793

Form 417.02

	Principal	Income
Total taxes	$ 0.00	$ 0.00

Note: The portion of fiduciary income tax allocated to capital gains is charged against principal. The portion of foreign dividend tax is allocated to income.

[NAME OF TRUST]
OTHER DECREASES
Schedule 11

	Principal	Income
Income transferred to principal	$	$ 0.00

Other decreases:

	Principal	Income
1.	$	$
2.	$	$
3.	$	$
4.	$	$
5.	$	$
6.	$	$
7.	$	$
8.	$	$
9.	$	$
10.	$	$
Total Other decreases	0.00	0.00

[NAME OF TRUST]
DISTRIBUTIONS TO BENEFICIARIES
Schedule 12

	Principal	Income
Name of each beneficiary and date and description of distribution:		
1.	$	$
2.	$	$
3.	$	$
4.	$	$
5.	$	$
6.	$	$
7.	$	$
8.	$	$
9.	$	$
10.	$	$
11.	$	$
12.	$	$
13.	$	$
14.	$	$
15.	$	$
Total Distributions to Beneficiaries	0.00	0.00

[NAME OF TRUST]
ASSETS ON HAND
[ending DATE]
Schedule 13

	Market Value as of [DATE]	Values at Cost or Basis Principal	Values at Cost or Basis Income
Cash or Cash Equivalents			
Checking account	$	$	$
Savings account	$	$	$
Money market account	$	$	$
Stocks and Bonds			
Stocks	$	$	$ 0.00
Corporate bonds	$	$	$ 0.00
Municipal bonds	$	$	$ 0.00
Real Estate	$	$	$ 0.00
Other Assets			$
Life insurance policies (cash value)	$	$	$
Other assets	$	$	$
Total Assets on Hand as of [Date]____.	0.00	$.	$.

Note: This schedule reflects assets on hand at the end of the accounting period. Identify each asset thoroughly. Provide the name of the bank and account number for

795

Form 417.02

each account holding cash or cash equivalents. Provide the number of shares or par value of each security. Provide the address of each parcel of real estate.

[NAME OF TRUST]
ASSETS WHICH REALIZED A NET INCOME OF
LESS THAN 1% OF THEIR INVENTORY
VALUES OR ACQUISITION COSTS
Schedule 14

Description of Asset	Amount of Net Income Realized	Income as Percentage of Cost/Basis
1. Reason why this asset should be retained:	$	%
2. Reason why this asset should be retained:	$	%
3. Reason why this asset should be retained:	$	%
4. Reason why this asset should be retained:	$	%
5. Reason why this asset should be retained:	$	%

Under penalties of perjury, we have read this Annual Account and we know or believe its contents are true and correct.

_____   _____
Trustee   Date
Address:

_____   _____
Trustee   Date
Address:

796

Notarial Stamp or Seal (or Other Title or Rank)	Signed and sworn to (or affirmed) before me on (date)_____ by_____ and_____ Trustees.
	_____ Signature of Notary Public or Other Official

Amended Nov. 13, 1992, eff. Jan. 1, 1993; Dec. 14, 1995, eff. Jan. 1, 1996.

*

INDEX

ACKNOWLEDGMENTS

AGRICULTURAL PRODUCTS
Job Opportunity Building Zones, generally, this index
Warehouse Receipts, generally, this index

AGRICULTURE
Corporate farming, **500.24**
Corporations, family farm, **500.24**
Declaratory judgment, rental value, continuation of leases after death of life tenant, **500.25**
Definitions, corporate farming, **500.24**
Family farm defined, **500.24**
Farm tenancy, definitions, life estates, **500.25**
Fines and penalties, corporate farm reports, late filing, **500.24**
Income Tax—State, this index
Investigations, aliens, ownership of land, **500.221**
Job Opportunity Building Zones, generally, this index
Lands. Agricultural Lands, generally, this index
Leases,
  Continuation of leases after death of life tenant, **500.25**
  Corporate farming, conservation practices, **500.24**
Life estates, death of life tenant, continuation of lease, **500.25**
Limited liability companies, farming, **500.24**
Notice, offer, sales or leases, **500.245**
Partnerships, family farm, **500.24**
Pension or investment funds, corporate farming, **500.24**
Real estate. Agricultural Lands, generally, this index
Subpoenas, aliens, land ownership, **500.221**

AIDERS AND ABETTORS
Accomplices and Accessories, generally, this index

AIR FORCE
Military Forces, generally, this index

ALCOHOL
Alcoholic Beverages, generally, this index

ALCOHOLIC BEVERAGES
Fines and penalties,
  Reports, sales, **289A.60**
  Sales, reports, **289A.60**
Reports, sales, fines and penalties, **289A.60**
Sales, reports, fines and penalties, **289A.60**

ALCOHOLICS AND INTOXICATED PERSONS
Probate courts, records, destruction and reproduction, **525.091**
Records and recordation, probate courts, destruction and reproduction, **525.091**

ALIENATION OF PROPERTY
Expectant estates, **500.16**
  Defeat or bar by alienation, **500.15**

ALIENATION OF PROPERTY—Cont'd
Ground lease providing for construction of building, **500.21**
Guardian and ward, double damages, **525.392**
Heir, personal liability for alienation before suit, **573.18**
Probate proceedings, double damages, **525.392**
Suspension, power of alienation,
  Accumulation of rents and profits, **500.17**
  Instrument executing power, **502.73**

ALIENS
Agricultural lands, restriction on acquisition, **500.221**
Corporations, agricultural land, restrictions on acquisition, **500.221**
Crimes and offenses, agricultural lands, **500.221**
Fines and penalties, agricultural lands, **500.221**
Forests, ownership, **500.221**
Income tax—state, real estate holdings, information returns, **289A.12**
Intestate succession, **524.2–111, 524.2–112**
Lumber and timber, ownership, **500.221**
Real estate, restrictions on acquisitions, **500.221**
Timber and lumber, ownership, **500.221**

ALTERATION OF INSTRUMENTS
Forgery, generally, this index

ALTERNATIVE DISPUTE RESOLUTION
Arbitration and Award, generally, this index

AMBULANCES
Health Maintenance Organizations, generally, this index

ANATOMICAL GIFTS
Guardian and ward, health care directive, **145C.05**
Health care directive, **145C.05**
Living wills,
  Forms, **145B.04**
  Health care directive, **145C.05**

ANCILLARY ADMINISTRATION
Probate Proceedings, this index

ANNUALIZED INCOME INSTALLMENT
Definitions, corporate income tax, **289A.26**

ANNUITIES
Conservators and conservatorships,
  Powers and duties, **524.5–411**
  Protective orders, **524.5–412**
Insurance, this index

ANNULMENT
Marriage, this index

APARTMENT BUILDINGS
Condominiums, generally, this index
Landlord and Tenant, generally, this index
Townhouses, generally, this index

APPEAL AND REVIEW
  See, also, Certiorari, this index

CERTIFICATES

COMMERCIAL

CONSERVATORS

CONSERVATORS

CONSERVATORS AND CONSERVATORSHIPS
   —Cont'd
Reports,
   Administration, **524.5–420**
   Assets, **524.5–420**
   Visitors, **524.5–406**
Representation, affected persons, **524.5–411**
Reproduction of records, **525.091**
Residence, jurisdiction, **524.5–106**
Resignation, **524.5–112**
   Custodial property, **527.38**
Restitution, assignments, **524.5–422**
Retirement and pensions, powers and duties,
   524.5–411
Review,
   Appointment, notice, **524.5–409**
   Rules and regulations, **524.5–109**
Rules and regulations,
   Appeal and review, **524.5–109**
   Civil procedure, **524.5–109**
Salaries. Compensation and salaries, generally,
   ante
Sales,
   Protective orders, **524.5–412**
   Real estate, **524.5–418**
   Wills, **524.2–606**
Securities, voidable transfers, **524.5–417**
Security, protective orders, **524.5–412**
Service of process,
   Petitions, hearings, **524.5–404**
   Visitors, **524.5–406**
Services, protective orders, **524.5–412**
Settlement, powers and duties, **524.5–417**
Signatures, wills, **524.2–502**
Single custodianship, children and minors,
   527.30
Social services, powers and duties, **524.5–417**
Standard of care, children and minors, custodi-
   al property, **527.32**
Standards, distributions, **524.5–427**
Statute of limitations,
   Claims, **524.5–429**
   Real estate, **524.5–418**
Successor custodian, children and minors, gifts,
   527.38
Successors, appointment, **524.5–112**
Support, powers and duties, **524.5–417**
Surcharges, **524.5–427**
Sureties and suretyship,
   Actions and proceedings, **524.5–416**
   Jurisdiction, **524.5–416**
Surviving spouses, medical assistance,
   524.2–215
Temporary conservators, orders, **524.5–414**
Termination, **524.5–431**
   Appointment, **524.5–112**
   Notice, **524.5–409**
   Orders, **524.5–421**
   Title to property, **524.5–431**
Termination of conservatorship, custodianship,
   527.40
Third parties, good faith, **524.5–424**

CONSERVATORS AND CONSERVATORSHIPS
   —Cont'd
Title to property,
   Appointment, **524.5–421**
   Concurrent jurisdiction, **524.5–402**
   Notice, **524.5–421**
   Termination, **524.5–431**
Transfer on death accounts, powers and duties,
   524.5–411
Transfers,
   Conflict of interest, **524.5–104**
   Foreign states, **524.5–107**
   Jurisdiction, **524.5–107**
   Money, **524.5–104**
   Personal property, **524.5–104**
   Priorities and preferences, **524.5–413**
   Venue, **524.5–108**
Transfers to minors, **527.21 et seq.**
Trusts and trustees,
   Custodial, **529.01 et seq.**
   Custodial trusts, **529.01 et seq.**
   Powers and duties, **524.5–411**
   Protective orders, **524.5–412**
   Real estate, disposition, **501B.47 et seq.**
Undue influence, void transactions, **524.5–417**
Uniform Probate Code, waiver of notice,
   524.1–402
Validity, children and minors, gifts, **527.31**
Venue, **524.5–108**
Visitors, appointment, **524.5–406, 524.5–420**
Voidable transactions, conflict of interest,
   524.5–423
Wages. Compensation and salaries, generally,
   ante
Waiver,
   Attorneys, **524.5–406**
   Notice, **524.5–114**
Waste, appointment, **524.5–401**
Wills,
   Powers and duties, **524.5–411**
   Protective orders, **524.5–412**
   Sales, **524.2–606**
   Signatures, **524.2–502**
Workers compensation, appointment,
   524.5–501

CONSOLIDATION
Merger and Consolidation, generally, this index

CONSTRUCTION
Job Opportunity Building Zones, generally, this
   index

CONSTRUCTION OF LAW
Statutes, this index

CONSTRUCTION OF WILLS
Wills, this index

CONSULS
Probate Proceedings, this index

CONSUMER CREDIT
Credit, generally, this index

CONTAINERS

CONTAINERS
Safe Deposit Companies and Boxes, generally, this index

CONTEMPORANEOUS WRITINGS
Intestate succession, advancements, **524.2–109**

CONTEMPT
Wills,
Delivery, **525.221**
Duty of custodian of will, **524.2–516**

CONTEST OF WILLS
Probate Proceedings, this index

CONTINGENT REMAINDERS
Conditional limitations, **500.11**
Effect, **500.15**
Posthumous birth defeating estate dependent on contingency of death without issue, **500.14**
Premature termination of precedent estate, **500.15**

CONTRACTORS
Income Tax—State, this index

CONTRACTS
Actions and proceedings, survival, **573.01**
Attorney fees, flags, **500.215**
Conservators and Conservatorships, this index
Custodial trusts,
Liability to third persons, **529.11**
Trustee for future payment or transfer, designation, **529.03**
Deeds and Conveyances, generally, this index
Flags, restrictive covenants, **500.215**
Guardian and ward, powers and duties, **524.5–313**
Leases, generally, this index
Power of attorney, statutory short form, **523.23, 523.24**
Presumption of death, absence for continuous periods, **576.141 et seq.**
Probate Proceedings, this index
Restrictive covenants, flags, **500.215**
Safe Deposit Companies and Boxes, this index
Sales, generally, this index
State flag, restrictive covenants, **500.215**
Statutory short form power of attorney, **523.23, 523.24**
Survival of actions, **573.01**
Trusts and Trustees, this index
United States flag, restrictive covenants, **500.215**
Wills, **524.2–514**

CONTRACTS FOR DEED
Conservators and conservatorships, **524.5–418**

CONTRIBUTIONS
Gifts, generally, this index
Heirs, devisees or legatees, payment of debt of deceased, **573.13**
Probate Proceedings, this index

CONVALESCENT HOMES
Nursing Homes, generally, this index

CONVERSION
Conservators and conservatorships, disclosure proceedings, **525.85**
Guardian and ward,
Disclosure proceedings, **525.85**
Double damages, **525.392**
Probate Proceedings, this index

CONVEYANCES
Deeds and Conveyances, generally, this index

CONVICTION OF CRIME
Crimes and Offenses, this index

COOPERATIVE APARTMENTS
Condominiums, generally, this index

COOPERATIVE ASSOCIATIONS
Investment Companies, generally, this index

COOPERATIVE BANKS
Savings Associations, generally, this index

COPYRIGHTS
Trusts and trustees, allocation of income and principal, **501B.69**

CORONERS
Decedents property, disposal by, **525.393**
Fingerprints and fingerprinting, filing in probate court, **525.393**
Probate proceedings, disposal of property in custody, **525.393**

CORPORATE FARMING
Generally, **500.24 et seq.**

CORPORATE INCOME TAX
Abusive tax shelters, promotion, penalty, **289A.60**
Accomplices and accessories, understatement of liability, fines and penalties, **289A.60**
Additional assessments, interest, **289A.55**
Annual returns, **289A.08**
Assessments, **289A.35**
Early assessment, request for, **289A.38**
Excess of amount reported on return, **289A.37**
Reportable transactions, **289A.38**
Audits and auditors, **289A.35**
Bad debts,
Certified service provider, **289A.50**
Refunds, **289A.50**
Bankruptcy, suspension of time, collection, **289A.41**
Certified service provider, bad debts, **289A.50**
Composite returns, **289A.08, 289A.60**
Credit, bad debts, **289A.50**
Criminal penalties, **289A.63**
Disclosure,
Reportable transactions, **289A.38**
Tax shelters, **289A.121**
Early assessment, request for, **289A.38**

CORPORATE

CRIMES AND OFFENSES—Cont'd
Husband and Wife, generally, this index
Income Tax—State, this index
Living wills, **145B.105**
Murder. Homicide, generally, this index
Oaths and Affirmations, generally, this index
Penalties. Fines and Penalties, generally, this index
Principal and accessory. Accomplices and Accessories, generally, this index
Probate Courts, this index
Referee in probate, failure to deliver books and papers to successor, **525.103**
Safe deposit companies and boxes, **55.04**
License law violations, **55.08**
Sales and Use Tax, this index
Second and subsequent offenses,
Agricultural lands, foreign ownership, registration, **500.221**
Foreign ownership, agricultural land, registration, **500.221**
Taxation, this index
Trial, generally, this index

CRIMINAL CODE
Crimes and Offenses, generally, this index

CRIMINAL HISTORY RECORD INFORMATION
Conservators and conservatorships, **524.5–118**
Guardian and ward, **524.5–118**

CRIMINAL PROCEDURE
Crimes and Offenses, generally, this index

CRIPPLED PERSONS
Handicapped Persons, generally, this index

CRYPTS
Descent, **525.14**

CULTIVATION OF LAND
Agriculture, generally, this index

CURATORS
Fiduciaries, generally, this index

CURRENT BENEFICIARY
Definitions, corporate farming, **500.24**

CUSTODIAL PROPERTY
Definitions, transfers to minors, **527.21**

CUSTODIAL TRUST ACT
Generally, **529.01 et seq.**

CUSTODIAL TRUST PROPERTY
Definitions, **529.01**

CUSTODIAL TRUSTEE
Definitions, custodial trusts, **529.01**

CUSTODIAN BANK
Fiduciaries, securities transfers, central depository, **520.32**

CUSTODIANS
Children and Minors, this index
Definitions, transfers to minors, **527.21**
Forms, real estate, affidavits, **501B.571**
Personal property, certificates and certification, **501B.561**
Real estate,
Affidavits, **501B.571**
Certificates and certification, **501B.561**
Securities, deposit with federal reserve bank, **520.33**
Transfers to minors, **527.21 et seq.**

CUSTODY
Children and Minors, this index

DAMAGES
Agricultural lands, properties purchased by former owners, **500.245**
Apportionment, wrongful death, **573.02**
Beneficiaries, wrongful death action, **573.02**
Bond of trustee, wrongful death action, **573.02**
Causes of action, survival,
Homicide, **573.02**
Wrongful death, **573.01, 573.02**
Children and Minors, this index
Conservators and conservatorships, **524.5–430**
Assignments, **524.5–422**
Corporations, wrongful death, **573.02**
Death, this index
Homicide, limitation of actions, **573.02**
Husband and wife, wrongful death, **573.02**
Limitation of actions, wrongful death, **573.02**
Next of kin, wrongful death, **573.02**
Parties, wrongful death action, **573.02**
Personal representatives, improper exercise of power, **524.3–712**
Power of Attorney, this index
Probate Proceedings, this index
Punitive damages, wrongful death, **573.02**
Special damages, survival of action for injuries unrelated to death, **573.02**
Treble damages, power of attorney, false affidavits, **523.22**
Trustees, wrongful death action, **573.02**
Wills, duty of custodian of will, **524.2–516**
Wrongful death actions, **573.02**

DE MINIMIS
Definitions, corporate farming, **500.24**

DEAD BODIES
Cemeteries and Dead Bodies, generally, this index

DEATH
Absence and absentees,
Degree of burden of proof, **576.143**
Determination of death, court hearing, **576.142**
Dissolution of marriage, **576.144**
Presumption of death,
Continuous absence, **576.141 et seq.**
Probate proceedings, **524.1–107**

DEATH

EMPLOYERS

ESTATE

FEDERAL

FINANCIAL

FINANCIAL CORPORATIONS—Cont'd
Powers and duties, children and minors, custodial property, **527.33**
Powers of appointment, children and minors, gifts, **527.24**
Privileges and immunities, custodial property, **527.36, 527.37**
Receipts, children and minors, custodial property, **527.28**
Records and recordation, children and minors, custodial property, **527.32**
Removal, custodial property, **527.38**
Renunciation, custodial property, **527.38**
Resignation, custodial property, **527.38**
Savings Associations, generally, this index
Savings Banks, generally, this index
Single custodianship, children and minors, **527.30**
Standard of care, children and minors, custodial property, **527.32**
Successor custodian, children and minors, gifts, **527.38**
Termination, custodianship, **527.40**
Transfers to minors, **527.21 et seq.**
Trust Companies, generally, this index
Validity, children and minors, gifts, **527.31**

FINANCIAL INSTITUTIONS
Financial Corporations, generally, this index

FINANCIAL INTEREST
Conflict of Interest, generally, this index

FINANCIAL REPORTS
Financial Statements and Reports, generally, this index

FINANCIAL STATEMENTS AND REPORTS
Power of attorney, statutory short form, **523.23, 523.24**
Statutory short form power of attorney, **523.23, 523.24**

FINES AND PENALTIES
Adult health care, living wills, **145B.105**
Agricultural Lands, this index
Alcoholic Beverages, this index
Aliens, agricultural lands, registration, **500.221**
Corporate Income Tax, this index
Corporations, this index
County Treasurers, generally, this index
Estate Taxes, this index
Foreign ownership, agricultural lands, registration, **500.221**
Health care directive, **145C.13**
Income Tax—State, this index
Job opportunity building zones, reports, **289A.12**
Living wills, **145B.105**
Mines and Minerals, this index
Power of attorney, statutory short form, **523.23, 523.24**
Probate Proceedings, this index
Sales and Use Tax, this index

FINES AND PENALTIES—Cont'd
Statutory short form power of attorney, **523.23, 523.24**
Tax Delinquencies, this index
Tax Return Preparers, this index
Taxation, this index

FINGERPRINTS AND FINGERPRINTING
Conservators and conservatorships, criminal history record information, **524.5–118**
Guardian and ward, criminal history record information, **524.5–118**
Probate proceedings, decedent in custody of coroner, filing, **525.393**

FIREPROOF
Safe deposit companies, fireproof vault required, **55.07**

FIRES AND FIRE PROTECTION
Safe deposit companies and boxes, **55.07**

FISH AND GAME
Income Tax—State, this index

FLAGS
Attorney fees, restrictive covenants, **500.215**
Restrictive covenants, state flag, **500.215**
State flag, restrictive covenants, **500.215**

FOOD
Guardian and ward, powers and duties, **524.5–313**

FORECLOSURE
Conservators and conservatorships, **525.37**
Guardian and ward, **525.37**
Probate Proceedings, this index
Receivers and receivership, appointments, **576.01**

FOREIGN BORN PERSONS
Probate, notice of hearing, consul or diplomatic representative, **524.3–403**

FOREIGN CONSERVATORS
Conservators and conservatorships,
Payment, **524.5–432**
Powers and duties, **524.5–433**

FOREIGN CORPORATIONS
Agricultural lands, acquisition, foreign countries, **500.221**
Forests, acquisition, **500.221**
Lumber and timber, acquisition, **500.221**
Real estate, agricultural, acquisition, foreign countries, **500.221**
Receivers, grounds for appointment, **576.01**
Restrictions on acquisitions, **500.221**
Timber and lumber, acquisition, **500.221**
Title to real property, acquisition, foreign countries, **500.221**

FOREIGN COUNTRIES
Agricultural lands, acquisition, **500.221**
Conflict of Laws, generally, this index

FUTURE

FUTURE ESTATES
Accumulations, rents and profits, **500.17**
Agricultural life estates, termination, **500.25**
Alienation by owner of precedent estate as defeating future estate, **500.15**
Alternative future estates, **500.14**
Conservators and conservatorships, powers and duties, **524.5–411**
Contingent estate, **500.12**
    Probability, **500.14**
Death,
    Contingent estates, **500.14**
    Without issue, posthumous birth, effect, **500.14**
Definitions, **500.10**
Destruction of precedent estate by act of owner, **500.15**
Division of estates in expectancy, **500.08**
Failure of heirs or issue, **500.14**
Posthumous birth defeating, **500.14**
Posthumous child entitled to, **500.14**
Probability or improbability of contingency, **500.14**
Remainders, generally, this index
Rents and profits, **500.17**
Rule against perpetuities, **501A.01 et seq.**
Time,
    Commencement of expectant estate, **500.18**
    Vesting, **500.14**
Two or more estates, **500.14**
Vested estates, **500.12**

FUTURE INTERESTS
Future Estates, generally, this index

GARNISHMENT
Conservators and conservatorships, **524.5–422**
Power of attorney, statutory short form, **523.23, 523.24**
Statutory short form power of attorney, **523.23, 523.24**

GENERAL PROPERTY TAX
Taxation, generally, this index

GENERAL SALES TAX LAW
Sales and Use Tax, generally, this index

GENERATION SKIPPING TRANSFER TAX
Apportionment, **524.3–916**

GIFTED LAND
Definitions, corporate farming, **500.24**

GIFTS
Anatomical Gifts, generally, this index
Children and Minors, this index
Class gifts, rule against perpetuities, **501A.03**
Conservators and Conservatorships, this index
Farm lands, ownership by pension or investment fund, **500.24**
Infants. Children and Minors, this index
Insurance, this index
Irrevocable gifts, transfers to minors, **527.24**

GIFTS—Cont'd
Power of attorney, statutory short form, **523.23, 523.24**
Statutory short form power of attorney, **523.23, 523.24**
Transfers to minors, **527.21 et seq.**
Trusts and Trustees, this index
Wills, class gifts, **524.2–705, 524.2–708**

GIRLS
Children and Minors, generally, this index

GOLD
Mines and Minerals, generally, this index

GOOD FAITH
Custodial trusts, exemption of third person from liability, **529.10**
Health care directive, **145C.10**
Power of attorney, **523.21**
Probate Proceedings, this index
Purchasers. Bona Fide Purchasers, generally, this index
Securities, this index

GOODS, WARES AND MERCHANDISE
Household Goods and Furniture, generally, this index
Sales, generally, this index

GOVERNMENTAL BOARDS
Boards and Commissions, generally, this index

GRANDCHILDREN AND GRANDPARENTS
Intestate succession, **524.2–103**

GRANDFATHER RIGHTS
Living wills, **145B.15, 145B.17**

GRANTS
Deeds and Conveyances, generally, this index

GRAPHITE
Mines and Minerals, generally, this index

GRATUITIES
Gifts, generally, this index

GRAVE MARKERS
Cemetery lots, descent, **525.14**

GRAVES
Cemeteries and Dead Bodies, generally, this index

GRAVEYARDS
Cemeteries and Dead Bodies, generally, this index

GROSS INCOME
Income Tax—State, this index

GROSS MISDEMEANORS
Crimes and Offenses, generally, this index

GROSS NEGLIGENCE
Conservators and conservatorships, **524.5–411**

GUARDIAN

GUARDIAN

HEALTH CARE
Definitions, living wills, **145C.01**

HEALTH CARE AGENT
Definitions, living wills, **145C.01**

HEALTH CARE AND TREATMENT
Medical Care and Treatment, generally, this index

HEALTH CARE DECISIONS
Definitions, living wills, **145B.02**

HEALTH CARE DIRECTIVE
Generally, **145C.01 et seq.**
Conservators and conservatorships, notice, **524.5–113**
Definitions, living wills, **145C.01**
Guardian and Ward, this index

HEALTH CARE FACILITIES
Adult health care,
    Health care directive, **145C.01 et seq.**
    Living wills, **145B.01 et seq.**
Agents, health care directive, **145C.01 et seq.**
Definitions, living wills, **145B.02**
Directives, health care directive, **145C.01 et seq.**
Durable power of attorney, health care directive, **145C.01 et seq.**
Health care directive, **145C.01 et seq.**
Hospitals, generally, this index
Instructions, health care directive, **145C.01 et seq.**
Life sustaining health care, health care directive, **145C.15**
Living wills, **145B.01 et seq.**
    Health care directive, **145C.01 et seq.**
Nursing Homes, generally, this index
Power of attorney, health care directive, **145C.01 et seq.**
Privileges and immunities, health care directive, **145C.11**
Visitation, health care directive, **145C.07**

HEALTH CARE INSTITUTIONS
Health Care Facilities, generally, this index

HEALTH CARE INSTRUCTION
Definitions, living wills, **145C.01**

HEALTH CARE POWER OF ATTORNEY
Definitions, living wills, **145C.01**

HEALTH CARE PROVIDERS
Agents and agency, health care directive, **145C.01 et seq.**
Conservators and conservatorships, compensation and salaries, **524.5–502**
Definitions, living wills, **145B.02**
Directives, health care directive, **145C.01 et seq.**
Durable power of attorney, health care directive, **145C.01 et seq.**
Guardian and ward, compensation and salaries, **524.5–502**
Health care directive, **145C.01 et seq.**

HEALTH CARE PROVIDERS—Cont'd
Instructions, health care directive, **145C.01 et seq.**
Life sustaining health care, health care directive, **145C.15**
Power of attorney, health care directive, **145C.01 et seq.**
Privileges and immunities, health care directive, **145C.11**

HEALTH MAINTENANCE ACT
Health Maintenance Organizations, generally, this index

HEALTH MAINTENANCE ORGANIZATIONS
Adult health care,
    Health care directive, **145C.01 et seq.**
    Living wills, **145B.01 et seq.**
Definitions, living wills, **145B.02**
Health care directive, **145C.01 et seq.**
Life sustaining health care, health care directive, **145C.15**
Living wills, **145B.01 et seq.**
    Health care directive, **145C.01 et seq.**
Privileges and immunities, health care directive, **145C.11**

HEALTH PLAN COMPANY
Health Care Providers, generally, this index

HEIRS
Alienation of real property descended, personal liability in respect of, **573.18**
Definitions, Uniform Probate Code, **524.1–201**
Estate limited on death without heirs, **500.14**
Intestate Succession, generally, this index
Personal liability for debts of deceased, **573.18**
Probate Proceedings, this index

HOLDER OF THE BENEFICIARYS POWER OF ATTORNEY
Definitions, custodial trusts, **529.01**

HOME CARE SERVICES
Adult health care, health care directive, **145C.01 et seq.**
Health care directive, **145C.01 et seq.**
Life sustaining health care, health care directive, **145C.15**
Living wills, **145B.01 et seq.**
    Health care directive, **145C.01 et seq.**
Privileges and immunities, health care directive, **145C.11**

HOME COMPANIES
Investment Companies, generally, this index

HOME MANAGEMENT SERVICES
Home Care Services, generally, this index

HOMEOWNERS ASSOCIATIONS
Restrictive covenants, flags, **500.215**

HOMES FOR CHILDREN
Adoption, generally, this index

HOMES

HOMES FOR THE AGED
Nursing Homes, generally, this index

HOMESTEAD
Deeds and conveyances, spouses, **500.19**
Intestate Succession, this index
Probate Proceedings, this index
Property Tax Refunds, generally, this index
Taxation. Property Tax Refunds, generally, this index
Wills, **524.2–402**

HOMESTEAD ASSOCIATIONS
Savings Associations, generally, this index

HOMICIDE
Damages, limitation of actions, **573.02**
Life insurance, murder committed by beneficiary, **524.2–803**
Probate proceedings, killer disinherited, **524.2–803**
Wills, killer disinherited, **524.2–803**
Wrongful death, limitation of actions, **573.02**

HORIZONTAL PROPERTY
Condominiums, generally, this index

HOSPICES
Health care directive, **145C.01 et seq.**

HOSPITALIZATION
Hospitals, generally, this index

HOSPITALS
Adult health care,
  Health care directive, **145C.01 et seq.**
  Living wills, **145B.01 et seq.**
Agents, health care directive, **145C.01 et seq.**
Commencement of action, death by professional negligence, **573.02**
Death, professional negligence, commencement of action, **573.02**
Directives, health care directive, **145C.01 et seq.**
Health care directive, **145C.01 et seq.**
Health Maintenance Organizations, generally, this index
Instructions, health care directive, **145C.01 et seq.**
Life sustaining health care, health care directive, **145C.15**
Living wills, **145B.01 et seq.**
  Health care directive, **145C.01 et seq.**
Maltreatment of patients, death by professional negligence, commencement of action, **573.02**
Mental institutions. Mentally Ill Persons, generally, this index
Power of attorney, health care directive, **145C.01 et seq.**
Privileges and immunities, health care directive, **145C.11**
Probate proceedings, claims against estate, last illness, **524.3–805**
Professional negligence, death by, commencement of action, **573.02**

HOSPITALS—Cont'd
Sanatoriums, generally, this index
Wrongful death actions, **573.02**

HOUSEHOLD GOODS AND FURNITURE
Guardian and ward, powers and duties, **524.5–313**
Intestate succession, allowances to spouse, **525.15**
Probate proceedings, spousal allowances, **525.15**

HOUSES OF WORSHIP
Religious Corporations and Associations, generally, this index

HOUSING
Condominiums, generally, this index
Guardian and ward,
  Powers and duties, **524.5–313**
  Reports, **524.5–316**
Mortgages, generally, this index
Property Tax Refunds, generally, this index
Rentals. Landlord and Tenant, generally, this index
Townhouses, generally, this index

HUMAN SERVICES
Social Services, generally, this index

HUSBAND AND WIFE
  See, also, Marriage, generally, this index
Actions and proceedings, Dram Shop Act, wrongful death, **573.02**
Cemetery lot, descent to surviving spouse, **525.14**
Deeds and conveyances, homestead, **500.19**
Dissolution of marriage. Marriage, this index
Intestate Succession, this index
Legal separation. Marriage, this index
Marriage, generally, this index
Probate Proceedings, this index
Wrongful death actions, **573.02**

HYDRATION
Living wills, **145B.12**
  Reasonable medical practice, **145B.13**

ILLNESS
Intestate succession, last illness, intestate estate, **524.2–101**
Mentally Ill Persons, generally, this index

IMPRISONMENT
Crimes and Offenses, generally, this index
Fines and Penalties, generally, this index

INCAPACITATED
Definitions, custodial trusts, **529.01**

INCAPACITATED PERSONS
Definitions, guardianships and conservatorships, **524.5–102**

INCOME

INCOME

INDEMNITY

INCOME TAX—STATE—Cont'd
Returns—Cont'd
  Small business corporations, filing requirement, **289A.09**
  Social Security benefits, federal officials, copies, **289A.12**
  Social security number, supplying, **289A.12**
  Statements to payees, **289A.12**
  Voter registration form, **289A.08**
S corporations,
  Delinquent taxes, fines and penalties, **289A.60**
  Distributions, trusts and trustees, **501B.64**
  Due date, returns, **289A.18**
  Electronic payment, **289A.20**
  Estimated tax, withholding, **289A.20**
  Extensions for filing, **289A.19**
  Fines and penalties, **289A.60**
  Payment, due date, **289A.20**
  Returns, **289A.09, 289A.12**
    Extensions for filing, **289A.19**
  Tax identification number, fines and penalties, **289A.60**
  Tax liability, **289A.31**
  Trusts and trustees, distributions, **501B.64**
  Withholding, estimated tax, **289A.20**
Sales or exchanges, direct sales, returns, **289A.12**
Schools and School Districts, this index
Securities, dividends, investment companies, exempt interest dividends, returns, **289A.12**
Separate returns of spouses, **289A.08**
Shares and shareholders, dividends, investment companies, exempt interest dividends, returns, **289A.12**
Shelters, tax shelters, **289A.121**
Signatures,
  Electronic transactions, withholding, **289A.09**
  Returns, **289A.08**
    Partnerships or S corporations, **289A.12**
  Withholding, electronic transactions, **289A.09**
Small business corporations. S corporations, generally, ante
Social security, federal officials required to file returns, copies, **289A.12**
Social security numbers,
  Failure to furnish or incorrect, fines and penalties, **289A.60**
  Supplying to return preparer, **289A.12**
State, returns, **289A.12**
Statutory short form power of attorney, **523.23, 523.24**
Stock and stockholders, dividends, investment companies, exempt interest dividends, returns, **289A.12**
Substantial understatement of liability, penalty, **289A.60**
Support, delinquency, withholding from return, **289A.50**
Tax assessments. Assessments, generally, ante
Tax credits. Credits, generally, ante
Tax Return Preparers, generally, this index
Tax returns. Returns, generally, ante
Tax shelters, **289A.121**

INCOME TAX—STATE—Cont'd
Tax shelters—Cont'd
  Fines and penalties, **289A.60**
Time,
  Assessment and collection of tax, **289A.38**
  Extension of time, generally, ante
  Payment of tax, estimated tax, **289A.25**
Transferees of property, liability for tax, **289A.31**
Trusts and trustees. Estates and trusts, generally, ante
Underpayment, estimated tax, **289A.25**
Understatement of liability, fines and penalties, reportable transactions, **289A.60**
Unemployment insurance, returns, **289A.12**
United States. Income Tax—Federal, generally, this index
Use taxes, information, **289A.08**
Venue, criminal prosecutions, **289A.63**
Voter registration forms, insertion on return, **289A.08**
Withholding,
  Depository, **289A.20**
  Electronic payment, **289A.20**
  Electronic transactions, **289A.09**
  Entertainers, ante
  Estates and trusts, estimated tax, **289A.20**
  Estimated tax, **289A.20**
  Excessive, refund, **289A.50**
  Federal annuities, request, **289A.09**
  Federal tax changes, reports, **289A.38**
  Fines and penalties, **289A.60**
  Partnerships, ante
  Payment, due date, **289A.20**
  Personal liability, payment, **289A.31**
  Refunds, interest, **289A.56**
  S corporations, estimated tax, **289A.20**
  Signatures, electronic transactions, **289A.09**
Worthless debts. Bad debts, generally, ante

INCOMPETENTS
Developmentally Disabled Persons, generally, this index
Mentally Ill Persons, generally, this index

INCUMBRANCES
Liens and Incumbrances, generally, this index

INDEBTEDNESS
Bad Debts, generally, this index
Bankruptcy, generally, this index
Conservators and conservatorships, **525.37**
  Powers and duties, **524.5–417**
Debtors and Creditors, generally, this index
Guardian and ward, **525.37**
Loans, generally, this index
Probate Proceedings, this index

INDEMNITY AND INDEMNIFICATION
Probate proceedings, liability as between estates and personal representatives, **524.3–808**

I–47

INDIGENT

INDIGENT PERSONS
Conservators and conservatorships, compensation and salaries, **524.5–502**
Disclaimer of interest, testamentary instruments, **525.532**
General assistance medical care. Social Services, this index
Guardian and ward, compensation and salaries, **524.5–502**
Medical assistance. Social Services, this index
Old age assistance. Social Services, generally, this index
Poorhouses and poor farms. Social Services, generally, this index
Social Services, generally, this index

INDIVIDUAL RETIREMENT ACCOUNTS
Endowment contracts, returns by issuers, **289A.12**
Income Tax—State, this index

INDORSEMENTS
Endorsements, generally, this index

INDUSTRIAL LOAN AND THRIFT COMPANIES
Power of attorney, statutory short form, **523.23, 523.24**
Safe deposit companies and boxes, **55.06**
Statutory short form power of attorney, **523.23, 523.24**

INDUSTRY
Labor and Employment, generally, this index

INFANTS
Children and Minors, generally, this index

INFERENCES
Presumptions. Evidence, this index

INFIRMARIES
Health Care Facilities, generally, this index

INFORMAL PROBATE AND APPOINTMENT PROCEEDINGS
Probate Proceedings, this index

INFORMATION RETURNS
Income Tax—State, this index

INHERITANCE
Intestate Succession, generally, this index

INHERITANCE, ESTATE OF
Generally, **500.01, 500.02, 500.05**
Fee simple estate, **500.02**

INHERITANCE AND TRANSFER TAXES
Estate Tax—Federal, generally, this index
Estate Taxes, generally, this index

INJUNCTIONS
Agricultural lands, foreign ownership, **500.221**
Aliens, agricultural land, acquisition, **500.221**
Corporate farming, **500.24**
  Aliens, **500.221**

INJUNCTIONS—Cont'd
Probate proceedings, personal representatives, **524.3–607**
Safe deposit companies, violation of law, **55.06**
Solar easements, **500.30**
Tax return preparers, property tax refund, **289A.60**

INSANE PERSONS
Mentally Ill Persons, generally, this index

INSOLVENCY
  See, also, Bankruptcy, generally, this index
Bankruptcy, generally, this index
Corporations, this index
Disclaimer of interest, testamentary instruments, **525.532**
Power of attorney, statutory short form, **523.23, 523.24**
Statutory short form power of attorney, **523.23, 523.24**

INSPECTION AND INSPECTORS
Banks and Banking, this index
Children and minors, custodial property, records and recordation, **527.32**
Credit Unions, this index

INSTRUCTIONS AND INSTRUCTORS
Education, generally, this index

INSURANCE
Accident and health insurance,
  Group insurance. Health Maintenance Organizations, generally, this index
  Health care directive, **145C.12**
  Health Maintenance Organizations, generally, this index
Adult health care, living wills, effect, life insurance or annuity, **145B.11**
Annuities,
  Absentees property, receiver to take possession, **576.10**
  Gifts, children and minors, **527.21 et seq.**
  Income Tax—State, this index
  Intestate succession, augmented estate, **524.2–202**
  Receivers and receivership, possession, **576.10**
  Transfers, children and minors, **527.21 et seq.**
  Trusts and trustees, allocation of principal and income, **501B.69**
Banks and banking, children and minors, custodial property, **527.29**
Beneficiaries,
  Life insurance, post
  Murder of insured, **524.2–803**
Children and minors,
  Life insurance, post
  Transfers, **527.21 et seq.**
Compensation and salaries. Workers Compensation, generally, this index
Conservators and conservatorships, powers and duties, **524.5–411**

INTERESTED

INTERESTED PERSONS
Definitions,
  Guardianships and conservatorships,
    524.5–102
  Settlement of disputes respecting domicile of
    decedent for death tax purposes, **291.41**
  Uniform Probate Code, **524.1–201**
Probate Proceedings, this index

INTERNAL REVENUE CODE
Definitions,
  Estate taxes, **291.005, 291.03**
  Tax returns, **289A.02**
Income Tax—Federal, generally, this index

INTERNATIONAL WILLS
Wills, this index

INTERPRETATION OF STATUTES
Statutes, generally, this index

INTERSTATE ARBITRATION OF DEATH TAXES ACT
Generally, **291.41 et seq.**

INTERSTATE COMPROMISE OF DEATH TAXES ACT
Generally, **291.41 et seq.**

INTESTACY, WILLS AND DONATIVE TRANSFERS ACT
Generally, **524.2–101 et seq.**

INTESTATE SUCCESSION
  Generally, **524.2–101 et seq., 525.13 et seq.**
Absentees, determination of death, court hearing, **576.142**
Acknowledgments, advancements, **524.2–109**
Actions and proceedings, personal representative, obtaining property, **524.2–205**
Adopted children, **524.2–114**
Advancements, **524.2–109**
After acquired property, sentimental value, award to children of prior marriage, **525.152**
Afterborn heirs, **524.2–108**
Agricultural land, aliens, **500.221**
Alienage, **524.2–111**
Aliens, **524.2–111, 524.2–112**
  Agricultural land, **500.221**
Allowances to spouse, **524.2–206**
Annuities, augmented estate, **524.2–202**
Application of law, instruments referencing intestacy laws, **524.2–115**
Appraisal and appraisers,
  Determination of descent, **525.312**
  Sentimental property, **525.152**
Attorney general, notice to of no surviving spouse or kindred, **525.161**
Augmented estate, **524.2–203**
  Definitions, **524.2–202**
  Trusts and trustees, **524.2–202**
Brothers and sisters, shares, **524.2–103**
Cemetery lot, **525.14**

INTESTATE SUCCESSION—Cont'd
Children and minors,
  Adopted, **524.2–114**
  Children of prior marriage, sentimental property, award, **525.152**
  Illegitimate children, **524.2–114**
  Sentimental value property, awards, **525.15**
    Children of prior marriage, property, award, **525.152**
  Shares, **524.2–103**
Civil law, computation, degree of kindred, **524.2–107**
Community property, augmented estate, **524.2–202**
Computation,
  Augmented estate, **524.2–202**
  Degree of kindred, **524.2–107**
Conception, afterborn heirs, **524.2–108**
Conservators and conservatorships, powers and duties, **524.5–411**
Contemporaneous writings, advancements, **524.2–109**
Contracts, elective shares and other rights, waiver, **524.2–204**
Credit life insurance, augmented estate, **524.2–202**
Death, simultaneous death, **524.2–702**
Debts, **524.2–101**
  Decedents, **524.2–110**
Deeds and conveyances, transfer on death deeds, **524.2–702**
Definitions,
  Augmented estate, **524.2–202**
  Estate, **525.13**
  Sentimental value, children, **525.152**
Degree of kindred, **524.2–107**
Determination of descent, **525.31 et seq.**
Disability compensation, augmented estate, **524.2–202**
Disclaimer of interest, **525.532**
  Devolution of estate, **524.3–101**
Elective shares, surviving spouse, **524.2–201 et seq.**
Erroneous escheat, **525.84, 525.841**
Escheat, **524.2–105**
  Erroneous, **525.84, 525.841**
Estate Tax—Federal, generally, this index
Estate Taxes, generally, this index
Exempt property, **524.2–403**
  Survival, heirs, **524.2–104**
  Surviving spouse, waiver, **524.2–204**
Expenses and expenditures, **524.2–101**
  Augmented estate, **524.2–202**
Family allowance, **525.15, 525.151**
  Augmented estates, **524.2–202**
  Waiver, surviving spouse, **524.2–204**
Federal patents, **525.881**
Funeral expenses, **524.2–101**
  Augmented estate, **524.2–202**
Furniture, allowances to spouse, **525.15**
General assistance medical care, claims, clearance, **525.313**

INTESTATE

JOINT TENANTS—Cont'd
Deeds and conveyances, conveyances into joint tenancy, **500.19**
Dissolution of marriage, severance, **500.19**
Grants and devises to two or more persons creating estates in common and not in joint tenancy, **500.19**
Homicide, killers interest severed, **524.2–803**
Intestate succession, simultaneous death, **524.2–702**
Multiparty accounts, **524.6–201 et seq.**
Nature and properties of estate, **500.19**
Nonprobate transfers on death, **524.6–201 et seq.**
Partition, generally, this index
Probate proceedings, simultaneous death, **524.2–702**
Safe deposit boxes, liability of company permitting access to box, **55.10**
Savings accounts, nonprobate transfers on death, **524.6–201 et seq.**
Severance, real estate, **500.19**
Straw man transaction, abolishment, **500.19**
Survivorship, nonprobate transfers on death, **524.6–201 et seq.**
Unities, real estate, abolishment, **500.19**

JOINT VENTURES
Custodial trusts, **529.01 et seq.**

JUDGES
County Courts, this index
Probate Courts, this index

JUDGMENTS AND DECREES
Attachment, generally, this index
Confession of Judgment, generally, this index
Deficiency judgments, probate proceedings, secured creditors, **524.3–104**
Entry of judgment. Supersedeas or Stay, generally, this index
Homicide convictions, effect on intestate succession, wills, **524.2–803**
Income Tax—State, this index
Intestate Succession, this index
Joint tenancy, severance, **500.19**
Probate Proceedings, this index
Receivers and receiverships, appointment to carry into effect, **576.01**
Satisfaction of Judgments, generally, this index
Supersedeas or Stay, generally, this index

JURISDICTION
Children and Minors, this index
Conservators and Conservatorships, this index
Corporations, fiduciaries, securities transfers, **520.28**
Custodial trusts, **529.04**
Custodian, transfers to minors, **527.22**
District Courts, this index
Fiduciaries, securities transfers, **520.28**
Guardian and Ward, this index
Probate Proceedings, this index
Transfers to minors, **527.22**

JURISDICTION—Cont'd
Trusts and Trustees, this index
Venue, generally, this index

JURY
See, also, Trial, generally, this index
Advisory jury, probate proceedings, **524.1–306**
Constitutional guaranty of jury trial, probate proceedings, **524.1–306**
Discretion of court, probate proceedings, **524.1–306**
Probate proceedings, **524.1–306**
Uniform Probate Code, **524.1–306**
Waiver of jury trial, probate proceedings, **524.1–306**

JUVENILE COURTS
Adoption, generally, this index

JUVENILE DELINQUENTS AND DEPENDENTS
Adoption, generally, this index

KINDRED
Relatives, generally, this index

LABOR AND EMPLOYMENT
Compensation and Salaries, generally, this index
Income tax—state, withholding deposits, electronic payment, **289A.20**
Job Opportunity Building Zones, generally, this index
Pensions. Retirement and Pensions, generally, this index
Power of attorney, statutory short form, **523.23, 523.24**
Retirement and Pensions, generally, this index
Salaries. Compensation and Salaries, generally, this index
Statutory short form power of attorney, **523.23, 523.24**
Wages. Compensation and Salaries, generally, this index
Workers Compensation, generally, this index

LABOR RELATIONS ACT
Labor and Employment, generally, this index

LAND
Real Estate, generally, this index

LAND CLASSIFICATION
Classification. Real Estate, this index

LAND PATENTS
Death of patentee before issuance of patent, persons in whom title vests, **525.88**
Heirs and devisees, determination of respective shares, **525.881**
Issuance, death of patentee, title, **525.88**
Title, vesting, death before issuance, **525.88**

LANDLORD AND TENANT
Attorney fees, flags, **500.215**
Flags, restrictive covenants, **500.215**
Property Tax Refunds, generally, this index

I–53

LIENS AND INCUMBRANCES—Cont'd
Wills, conveyance subject to liens and incumbrances, **525.21**

LIFE ESTATES
Agriculture, continuation of leases after death of life tenant, **500.25**
Chattels real, estate for life of another, **500.05**
Classification, **500.01**
Creation in a term of years, **500.11**
Farm tenancy, definitions, **500.25**
Freehold estates, **500.05**

LIFE INSURANCE
Insurance, this index

LIMITATION OF ACTIONS
Agricultural lands, right of first refusal, **500.24**
Conditions subsequent, enforcement of breach, **500.20**
Conservators and conservatorships,
  Claims, **524.5–429**
  Real estate, **524.5–418**
Corporate farming, enforcement of restrictions, **500.24**
Custodial trustees, **529.15**
Damages, this index
Death, this index
Distribution of estates. Probate Proceedings, this index
Elective share, spouse, **524.2–205, 524.2–211**
Estate Taxes, this index
Income Tax—State, this index
Intestate succession, elective share, spouse, **524.2–205, 524.2–211**
Personal representatives. Probate Proceedings, this index
Probate Proceedings, this index
Receivers and receiverships, accounting and distribution of property, absence and absentees, **576.15, 576.16**
Sales and Use Tax, this index
Wrongful death, murder, **573.02**

LIMITED GUARDIANSHIP
Guardian and ward, best interests of the child, **524.5–206**

LIMITED LIABILITY COMPANIES
Agricultural lands, farming and ownership, **500.24**
Farming, agricultural lands, **500.24**
Trusts and trustees, distributions, **501B.64**

LIMITED LIABILITY PARTNERSHIPS
Trusts and trustees, distributions, **501B.64**

LIMITED PARTNERSHIPS
Partnerships, this index

LIQUIDATION
Power of attorney, statutory short form, **523.23, 523.24**
Probate Proceedings, this index

LIQUIDATION—Cont'd
Statutory short form power of attorney, **523.23, 523.24**

LIQUOR
Alcoholic Beverages, generally, this index

LIS PENDENS
Agricultural lands,
  Foreign ownership, divestment, notice, **500.221**
  Right of first refusal, **500.24**

LITIGATION COSTS
Attorney Fees, generally, this index

LIVING WILLS
  Generally, **145B.01 et seq.**
Aged persons, **145B.01 et seq.**
  Health care directive, **145C.01 et seq.**
Anatomical gifts,
  Forms, **145B.04**
  Health care directive, **145C.05**
Application of law, **145B.011**
Conservators and Conservatorships, this index
Guardian and Ward, this index
Health care directive, **145C.01 et seq.**
Hospitals, this index

LOAN COMPANIES
Industrial Loan and Thrift Companies, generally, this index

LOANS
Mortgages, generally, this index
Pawnbrokers, generally, this index
Power of attorney, statutory short form, **523.23, 523.24**
Probate proceedings, **524.3–715**
Safe deposit companies and boxes, valuable personal property, storage, **55.02**
Statutory short form power of attorney, **523.23, 523.24**
Trusts and trustees, powers and duties, **501B.81**

LOGS AND LOGGING
Timber and Lumber, generally, this index

LONG TERM CARE
Nursing Homes, generally, this index

LORD CAMPBELLS ACT
Generally, **573.02**

LOST OR DESTROYED DOCUMENTS
Wills, petition for formal probate, **524.3–402**

LOTS
Cemeteries and Dead Bodies, this index

LUMBER
Timber and Lumber, generally, this index

MACHINERY AND EQUIPMENT
Sales and use tax. Capital Equipment, this index

MAIL

MAIL AND MAILING
Certified or registered mail. Probate Proceedings, this index
Conservators and conservatorships,
  Hearings, notice, **524.5–411**
  Notice, **524.5–113, 525.83**
Guardian and ward, notice, **524.5–113, 525.83**
Notice. Probate Proceedings, this index
Probate Proceedings, this index

MAINTENANCE AND REPAIRS
Buildings and Building Regulations, this index

MALPRACTICE
Wrongful death actions, **573.02**

MANAGEMENT
Managers and Management, generally, this index

MANAGERS AND MANAGEMENT
Power of attorney, statutory short form, **523.23, 523.24**
Receivers, absentees business in possession of receiver, **576.12**
Statutory short form power of attorney, **523.23, 523.24**

MANGANESE
Mines and Minerals, generally, this index

MANUFACTURED HOMES AND MANUFAC-TURED HOME PARKS
Property Tax Refunds, generally, this index

MAPS AND PLATS
See, also, Subdivisions, generally, this index
Power of attorney, statutory short form, **523.23, 523.24**
Probate proceedings, vacation, powers of personal representatives, **524.3–715**
Statutory short form power of attorney, **523.23, 523.24**
Vacations, personal representatives, **524.3–715**

MARINES
Military Forces, generally, this index

MARITAL DEDUCTION
Federal estate tax, selection of asset, **525.528**

MARRIAGE
Accident and health insurance. Insurance, this index
Actions and proceedings,
  Dissolution of marriage, generally, post
  Legal separation, post
Annulment,
  Adult health care, living wills, effect, proxy designation, **145B.09**
  Conservators and conservatorships, former spouse, revocation, **524.2–804**
  Guardian and ward, former spouse, revocation, **524.2–804**
  Health care directive, **145C.09**

MARRIAGE—Cont'd
Annulment—Cont'd
  Living wills, effect, proxy designation, **145B.09**
  Power of appointment, former spouse, **524.2–804**
  Probate proceedings, effect of annulment, **524.2–802**
  Third parties, wills, **524.2–804**
  Trusts, **501B.90**
  Wills,
    Former spouse, **524.2–804**
    Revocation, **524.2–804**
Children and minors. Support, generally, this index
Custody. Children and Minors, this index
Death, dissolution of marriage, absentees, **576.144**
Decree of separation, probate proceedings, effect, **524.2–802**
Definitions, elective share, surviving spouse, **524.2–201**
Dissolution of marriage,
  Absentees, presumed dead, **576.144**
  Adult health care, living wills, effect, proxy designation, **145B.09**
  Conservators and conservatorships, former spouse, revocation, **524.2–804**
  Custody. Children and Minors, this index
  Guardian and ward, former spouse, revocation, **524.2–804**
  Health care directive, **145C.09**
  Income Tax—State, this index
  Joint tenants, severance, **500.19**
  Living wills, effect, proxy designation, **145B.09**
  Maintenance,
    Absentees, proceeds of property used to discharge claim for, **576.13**
    Income tax—state, withholding, **289A.50**
    Property sale or mortgage, proceeds, **576.13**
    Refunds, income taxes, withholding, **289A.50**
    Withholding income tax refunds, **289A.50**
  Power of appointment, former spouse, **524.2–804**
  Power of attorney,
    Durable power, termination, **523.08**
    Nondurable power, termination, **523.09**
  Probate proceedings, effect, **524.2–802**
  Support, generally, this index
  Third parties, wills, **524.2–804**
  Trusts, **501B.90**
  Wills,
    Former spouse, **524.2–804**
    Revocation, **524.2–804**
Divorce. Dissolution of marriage, generally, ante
Federal estate tax, marital deduction, selection of assets, **525.528**
Guardian and Ward, this index

MENTALLY

MENTALLY ILL PERSONS—Cont'd
Probate courts—Cont'd
Records, destruction and reproduction,
525.091
Probate proceedings, distribution of estates,
524.3–915
Records and recordation, probate courts, destruction and reproduction, **525.091**
Social Services, generally, this index
Termination,
Durable power of attorney, **523.08**
Power of attorney, incompetency of a principal, **523.09**

MENTALLY RETARDED PERSONS
Developmentally Disabled Persons, generally,
this index

MERCY KILLING
Durable power of attorney for health care,
145C.14
Health care directive, **145C.14**
Living wills, practices not condoned, **145B.14**

MERGER AND CONSOLIDATION
Conservators and conservatorships, actions and
proceedings, **524.5–109**
Corporations, this index
Guardian and ward, actions and proceedings,
524.5–109
Power of attorney, statutory short form, **523.23,
523.24**
Statutory short form power of attorney, **523.23,
523.24**

MICROFILMING
Probate court records, **525.091**

MICROPHOTOGRAPHING
Probate court records, **525.091**

MILITARY CODE
Military Forces, generally, this index
National guard. Military Forces, this index

MILITARY FORCES
Income Tax—State, this index
Militia, generally, this index
National guard, income tax, time extensions,
289A.39
Power of attorney, statutory short form, **523.23,
523.24**
Reserve forces, income tax—state, time extensions, **289A.39**
Statutory short form power of attorney, **523.23,
523.24**

MILITARY SERVICE
Military Forces, generally, this index

MILITIA
Power of attorney, statutory short form, **523.23,
523.24**
Statutory short form power of attorney, **523.23,
523.24**

MINES AND MINERALS
Delinquent taxes, fines and penalties, **289A.60**
Electronic transactions, income tax—state,
withholding, **289A.09**
Exploration, lease or arrangement, personal
representatives, **524.3–715**
Fines and penalties,
Late payments, **289A.19**
Occupation tax on mining, post
Taxation, **289A.60**
Income, trust principal and income, disposition,
501B.67
Income tax—state,
Electronic transactions, withholding, **289A.09**
Withholding, electronic transactions, **289A.09**
Interest, late payments, **289A.19**
Late payments,
Fines and penalties, **289A.19**
Interest, **289A.19**
Leases,
Exploration, personal representatives,
524.3–715
Personal representatives, **524.3–715**
Net proceeds tax,
Early audits, requests, **289A.38**
Fines and penalties,
Late payments, **289A.19**
Understatement of liability, **289A.60**
Interest, late payments, **289A.19**
Late payments, **289A.19**
Overpayments, **289A.56**
Payment, **289A.20**
Late payments, **289A.19**
Liability, **289A.31**
Returns, **289A.01 et seq., 289A.20**
Due date, **289A.18**
Filing, extensions, **289A.19**
Understatement of liability, penalty, **289A.60**
Occupation tax on mining, **289A.01 et seq.**
Assessment and taxation of ore, **289A.35**
Audits and auditors, **289A.35**
Early audits, requests, **289A.38**
Fines and penalties,
Late payments, **289A.19**
Understatement of liability, **289A.60**
Interest, late payments, **289A.19**
Late payments, **289A.19**
Overpayments, **289A.56**
Payment,
Due date, **289A.20**
Late payments, **289A.19**
Liability, **289A.31**
Returns,
Due date, **289A.18**
Filing, extensions, **289A.19**
Payment,
Fines and penalties, **289A.19**
Late payments, **289A.19**
Occupation tax on mining, ante
Personal representatives, lease or arrangement,
524.3–715
Pooling agreement, personal representatives,
524.3–715

MINES AND MINERALS—Cont'd
Probate proceedings, lease or arrangement, **524.3–715**
Taxation,
    Fines and penalties, **289A.60**
    Net proceeds tax, generally, ante
    Occupation tax on mining, generally, ante
Trusts and trustees, development, powers and duties, **501B.81**
Unitization agreement, personal representatives, **524.3–715**

MINING
Mines and Minerals, generally, this index

MINING COMPANY
Definitions, tax returns, **289A.02**

MINNESOTA, STATE OF
State, generally, this index

MINNESOTA GROSS ESTATE
Definitions, estate taxes, **291.005**

MINNESOTA STATUTES
Statutes, generally, this index

MINORS
Children and Minors, generally, this index

MISDEMEANORS
Crimes and Offenses, generally, this index

MISSING PERSONS
Absence and Absentees, generally, this index

MONEY
Conservators and conservatorships, transfers, **524.5–104**
Guardian and ward,
    Accounts and accounting, **524.5–207**
    Transfers, **524.5–104**
Probate Proceedings, this index

MONITORS
Conservators and conservatorships, reports, **524.5–420**
Guardian and ward, **524.5–316**

MONUMENTS AND MEMORIALS
Cemeteries and dead bodies, descent, **525.14**

MORTGAGES
Conservators and Conservatorships, this index
Definitions,
    Conservators and conservatorships, **524.5–418**
    Uniform Probate Code, **524.1–201**
Escrows and Escrow Agents, generally, this index
Joint tenancies, application of law, **500.19**
Power of attorney, statutory short form, **523.23, 523.24**
Power of sale, security, **502.77**
Probate Proceedings, this index

MORTGAGES—Cont'd
Receivers and receiverships, appointments, **576.01**
Statutory short form power of attorney, **523.23, 523.24**
Trusts and trustees, **501B.46 et seq.**
    Powers and duties, **501B.81**

MOSQUES
Religious Corporations and Associations, generally, this index

MOTHER AND CHILD
Children and Minors, generally, this index

MOTIONS
Probate proceedings, supervised administration, **524.3–501**
Supervised administration of estates, **524.3–501**

MOTOR CARRIERS
Bills of Lading, generally, this index
Sales and use tax, interstate commerce, refunds, interest, **289A.56**

MOTOR VEHICLES
Guardian and ward, powers and duties, **524.5–313**
Intestate Succession, this index
Probate proceedings, spousal allowance, **525.15**
Surviving spouse of decedent, allowance, **525.15**

MULTIPARTY ACCOUNTS
Custodial trustee for future payment or transfer, designation, **529.03**
Nonprobate transfers on death, **524.6–201 et seq.**

MULTIPLE DWELLINGS
Condominiums, generally, this index
Townhouses, generally, this index

MUNICIPALITIES
Indigent Persons, generally, this index
Ordinances, generally, this index
Poor persons. Indigent Persons, generally, this index

MURDER
Homicide, generally, this index

MUTUAL SAVINGS BANKS
Savings Associations, generally, this index

NATIONAL GUARD
Military Forces, this index

NATURAL DEATH
Health care directive, **145C.01 et seq.**
Living wills, **145B.01 et seq.**

NATURAL RESOURCES
Income from, disposition, **501B.67**
Probate proceedings, leases, exploration or removal, **524.3–715**

NATURAL

NOTICE—Cont'd
Job opportunity building zones, reports, **289A.12**
Personal representatives. Probate Proceedings, this index
Power of attorney,
Revocation, **523.11**
Signatures, evidence, nontermination, **523.18**
Probate Proceedings, this index
Safe Deposit Companies and Boxes, this index
Sales, this index
Sales and Use Tax, this index
Savings Banks, this index
Trust Companies, this index
Trusts and Trustees, this index
Wills, this index

NURSES AND NURSING
Adult health care, health care directive, **145C.01 et seq.**
Health care directive, **145C.01 et seq.**
Home Care Services, generally, this index
Life sustaining health care, health care directive, **145C.15**
Living wills, **145B.01 et seq.**
Health care directive, **145C.01 et seq.**
Privileges and immunities, health care directive, **145C.11**

NURSING HOMES
Adult health care,
Health care directive, **145C.01 et seq.**
Living wills, **145B.01 et seq.**
Directives, health care directive, **145C.01 et seq.**
Health care directive, **145C.01 et seq.**
Instructions, health care directive, **145C.01 et seq.**
Life sustaining health care, health care directive, **145C.15**
Living wills, **145B.01 et seq.**
Health care directive, **145C.01 et seq.**
Privileges and immunities, health care directive, **145C.11**
Probate proceedings, claims against estate, **524.3–805**

NUTRITION
Health care directive, **145C.15**
Living wills, **145B.12**
Reasonable medical practice, **145B.13**

NUTRITIONAL SERVICES
Home Care Services, generally, this index

OATHS AND AFFIRMATIONS
Conservators and conservatorships, inventory, **524.5–419**
Informal probate and appointment proceedings. Probate Proceedings, this index
Probate court reporter, **525.11**
Probate Proceedings, this index
Reference and referees, probate, power to administer oath, **525.10**
Trust Companies, this index

OBLIGATIONS
Probate Proceedings, this index

OCCUPATION TAX ON MINING
Mines and Minerals, this index

OCCUPATIONAL THERAPY AND THERAPISTS
Home Care Services, generally, this index

OFFENSES
Crimes and Offenses, generally, this index

OFFICIAL BONDS
Bonds (Officers and Fiduciaries), generally, this index

OFFICIAL OATHS
Oaths and Affirmations, generally, this index

OIL AND GAS
Leases, definitions, Uniform Probate Code, **524.1–201**
Trusts and trustees, exploration and removal, **501B.81**

OLD AGE
Aged Persons, generally, this index

OLD AGE ASSISTANCE
Social Services, generally, this index

OMITTED PROPERTY
Probate Proceedings, this index

OPEN PITS
Mines and Minerals, generally, this index

OPINION AND EXPERT TESTIMONY
Witnesses, this index

ORDERS
Absent insured, advance life insurance payments to beneficiaries, **576.122**
Bank Deposits and Collections, this index
Conservators and Conservatorships, this index
Fiduciaries, war service, suspension of powers, **525.95**
Formal testacy and appointment proceedings. Probate Proceedings, this index
Guardian and Ward, this index
Income Tax—State, this index
Informal probate and appointment proceedings. Probate Proceedings, this index
Joint tenancy, severance, **500.19**
Judgments and Decrees, generally, this index
Life insurance, proceeds, absent insured, advance payments to beneficiaries, **576.122**
Personal representatives. Probate Proceedings, this index
Probate Proceedings, this index
Receivers and receivership, absentees, life insurance payments, **576.122**
Safe deposit companies, liability for permitting access to box, **55.10**
Show cause orders, receivers, absentees, **576.06**

ORDERS

PERSONS

PAYMENT—Cont'd
Life insurance. Insurance, this index
Mines and Minerals, this index
Power of attorney, statutory short form, **523.23, 523.24**
Probate Proceedings, this index
Sales and Use Tax, this index
Savings Banks, this index
Statutory short form power of attorney, **523.23, 523.24**
Trust Companies, this index
Trusts and Trustees, this index

PEACE OFFICERS
Arrest, generally, this index

PECUNIARY INTEREST
Conflict of Interest, generally, this index

PENALTIES
Fines and Penalties, generally, this index

PENDENCY OF ACTIONS
Probate Proceedings, this index
Supervised administration of estates, stay of informal application, **524.3–503**
Wrongful death caused by murder, limitation of actions, **573.02**

PENSIONS AND RETIREMENT
Retirement and Pensions, generally, this index

PER CAPITA AT EACH GENERATION
Wills, construction, **524.2–709**

PER STIRPES
Construction of wills, **524.2–709**

PERISHABLE PROPERTY
Receivers for absentees, sale of, **576.12**

PERJURY
Probate proceedings, documents filed, **524.1–310**

PERMANENT TOTAL DISABILITY
Handicapped Persons, generally, this index

PERPETUITIES
Generally, **501A.01 et seq.**
Application of law, prospective application, **501A.05**
Charities, exclusion, **501A.04**
Class gifts, reformations to bring within rule, **501A.03**
Common law rule of perpetuities, supersession, **501A.06**
Exclusions, **501A.04**
Fiduciaries, application of law, **501A.04**
Nondonative transfer, application of law, **501A.04**
Nonvested property interests, validity, **501A.01**
Power of appointment, **501A.02**
Prospective application, **501A.05**
Reformation, **501A.03**

PERPETUITIES—Cont'd
Retirement and pensions, trusts and powers of appointment, exclusion, **501A.04**
State, exclusions, **501A.04**
Trusts and trustees, **501B.09**
Discretionary power to distribute principal, exclusion, **501A.04**
Survivors death, **501A.01**

PERSON WITH A DISABILITY
Definitions, supplemental needs trusts, public assistance, eligibility, **501B.89**

PERSONAL CARE SERVICES
Home Care Services, generally, this index

PERSONAL INJURIES
Survival of actions, **573.01**
Workers Compensation, generally, this index
Wrongful death actions, **573.02**

PERSONAL PROPERTY
Bailment, generally, this index
Certificates and certification, custodians, **501B.561**
Children and minors, property transfers, **527.21 et seq.**
Conservators and conservatorships,
Transfers, **524.5–104**
Voidable transfers, **524.5–417**
Custodians, certificates and certification, **501B.561**
Estate Tax—Federal, generally, this index
Estate Taxes, generally, this index
Executions, generally, this index
Gifts, children and minors, **527.21 et seq.**
Guardian and Ward, this index
Intestate Succession, this index
Power of attorney, statutory short form, **523.23, 523.24**
Sales, generally, this index
Sales and Use Tax, generally, this index
Statutory short form power of attorney, **523.23, 523.24**
Taxation. Sales and Use Tax, generally, this index
Transfers to minors, **527.21 et seq.**

PERSONAL PROPERTY TAXATION
Assessments. Tax Assessments, generally, this index

PERSONAL REPRESENTATIVES
Definitions,
Estate taxes, **291.005**
Transfers to minors, **527.21**
Probate Proceedings, this index

PERSONAL SERVICES
Income Tax—State, this index

PERSONS
Definitions,
Custodial trusts, **529.01**
Fiduciaries, **520.01**

I–63

PERSONS

POWER

PRIORITIES

PROBATE

PROBATE

PROBATE

PROBATE

PROBATE PROCEEDINGS—Cont'd
Formal testacy and appointment proceedings
—Cont'd
Orders of court—Cont'd
Modification, **524.3–413**
Petition, **524.3–410, 524.3–412**
More than one instrument probated,
524.3–410
Finality of orders, **524.3–412**
Partial intestacy, **524.3–411**
Finality of order, **524.3–412**
Petitions, formal orders, **524.3–107**
Request, **524.3–401, 524.3–402**
Uncontested cases, **524.3–405**
Vacation, **524.3–412, 524.3–413**
Earlier testacy proceeding, **524.3–703**
Petition, **524.3–410, 524.3–412**
Partial intestacy, **524.3–411**
Pending proceedings,
Application for informal probate or infor-
mal appointment, **524.3–401**
Distribution of assets, **524.3–703**
Petitions, **524.3–105, 524.3–401, 524.3–402**
Appointment of different personal represen-
tative, **524.3–401**
Commencement of proceeding, **524.3–401**
Confirmation of previous informal appoint-
ment, **524.3–401**
Determine testacy, **524.3–1001**
Final order entered, **524.3–410**
Effect of order, **524.3–412**
Formal orders, **524.3–107**
Lost, destroyed or unavailable will,
524.3–402
Modification of orders, **524.3–412**
Orders for determination, **524.3–105**
Probate of another will, **524.3–412**
Request for relief, **524.3–107**
Set aside informal probate, **524.3–401**
Time, vacation of order, **524.3–412**
Vacate or modify previous order, **524.3–410**
Vacation of orders, **524.3–412**
Place of hearing, **524.3–403**
Pleadings, **524.1–403**
Objection to probate, **524.3–404**
Order for probate, uncontested cases,
524.3–405
Power of amendment, orders, **524.1–403**
Power of appointment, orders, **524.1–403**
Power of revocation, orders, **524.1–403**
Presumption, signature to contested will,
524.3–406
Prior appointment,
Commencement of proceedings, **524.3–108**
Stay of powers, **524.3–414**
Priority for appointment, **524.3–203**
Property, omission, **524.3–413**
Publication, notice, **524.3–403**
Hearing, death of alleged decedent, doubt,
524.3–403
Petition for modification or vacation of or-
der and probate of another will,
524.3–412

PROBATE PROCEEDINGS—Cont'd
Formal testacy and appointment proceedings
—Cont'd
Rebuttal, contested cases, **524.3–406**
Request for appointment of personal repre-
sentative, **524.3–401**
Revocation, burden of proof, **524.3–407**
Rules of court, **Rule 401 et seq., foll. 576.16**
Self proving will, **524.3–406**
Signature to will, contested cases, **524.3–406**
Special administrator, **524.3–108**
Appointed, **524.3–614**
State of testacy, determination, **524.3–409**
Stay of proceedings, **524.3–409, 524.3–414**
Conflicting claims as to domicile,
524.3–202
Supervised administration, joining, **524.3–502**
Time,
Commencement of proceedings, **524.3–108**
Hearing, **524.3–403**
Required for notice expired, **524.3–409**
Two or more instruments offered for pro-
bate, **524.3–410**
Orders of court, **524.3–412**
Two or more instruments offered for probate,
524.3–410
Unavailable will, petition, **524.3–402**
Uncontested cases, **524.3–405**
Undue influence, burden of proof, **524.3–407**
Unrevoked wills formally probated, **524.3–409**
Vacation of orders, **524.3–412**
Earlier testacy proceedings, **524.3–703**
Valid wills, formally probated, **524.3–409**
Validity of will, final order of foreign court,
524.3–408
Venue, **524.3–201**
Burden of proof, contested cases,
524.3–407
Proper venue, finding, **524.3–409**
Will, lost or destroyed, notice, **524.3–403**
Fraud, **524.1–106**
Acknowledgment or affidavit, **524.3–406**
Burden of proof, **524.3–407**
Execution of will, **524.3–406**
Formal testacy and appointment proceedings,
ante
Limitation of actions, **524.3–1006**
Closing estates, **524.3–1005**
Fraudulent transfers, **525.391**
Funeral expenses,
Claims against estate, **524.3–805**
Payment, **524.3–715**
Funerals, executor following instructions,
524.3–701
Furniture, spousal allowance, **525.15**
Future claims against estate, **524.3–810**
Future interests, distributions, **524.2–711**
General assistance medical care, claims, clear-
ance, **525.313**
General devises, distribution, **524.3–902**
General pecuniary devise, interest, **524.3–904**
General power of appointment, acting for bene-
ficiaries, **524.1–108**

PROBATE

PROBATE

PROBATE

PROBATE PROCEEDINGS—Cont'd
Letters of administration,
  Personal representatives, post
  Revenue commissioner, **291.21**
Levies against estate, **524.3–812**
Liens and incumbrances, **573.17**
  Abandonment of property, **524.3–715**
  Attorneys liens, **525.491**
  Claims against estates, real estate, **573.17**
  Decedents net probate estate, elective share, spouse, **524.2–204**
  Encumbered assets, claims against estate, **524.3–814**
  Foreclosure, guardians or conservators, **525.37**
  Inventory, **524.3–706**
  Personal representatives, post
  Small estates, summary administration, **524.3–1203, 524.3–1204**
  Transferred property subject to prior liens, **524.3–710**
Life insurance, homicide, killer disinherited, **524.2–803**
Life sustaining health care, health care directive, **145C.15**
Limitation of actions, **524.3–109**
  Claims against decedents estates, **524.3–801 et seq., 524.3–1006**
  Closing estates, **524.3–1005**
  Decedents action, **524.3–109**
  Distribution in kind, liability, **524.3–909**
  Distribution of estates, ante
  Fraud, **524.1–106, 524.3–1006**
    Closing estates, **524.3–1005**
  Informal probate and appointment proceedings, ante
  Multiple party accounts, **524.6–207**
  Nonprobate transfers on death, **524.6–207**
  Personal representatives, post
  Recovery of distributions, unclaimed assets, **524.3–914**
Limitations,
  Commencement of proceedings, determination, **524.3–409**
    Orders of court, **524.3–412**
  Contest of informal probate, **524.3–108**
  Powers and rights, **524.3–101**
    Personal representatives, **524.3–714**
Liquidation, corporation or business enterprise, **524.3–715**
Litigation for benefit of estate compensation of attorney, **524.3–720**
Living persons, governmental records or reports, evidence, **524.1–107**
Living wills, **145B.01 et seq.**
  Health care directive, **145C.01 et seq.**
Loans, personal representatives, borrowing money, **524.3–715**
Location of assets, aiding determination, **524.3–201**
Loss resulting from breach of fiduciary duty, **524.3–712**
Lost will, petition for formal probate, **524.3–402**

PROBATE PROCEEDINGS—Cont'd
Mail and mailing,
  Death of alleged decedent, notice of hearing, address of decedent, **524.3–403**
  Demand for notice of order or filing, **524.3–204**
  Informal appointment proceedings, notice requirements, **524.3–310**
  Informal probate, notice requirements, **524.3–306**
  Inventory, **524.3–706**
  Notice, post
Maintenance of spouse and children, allowance, **525.15, 525.151**
Management of assets, **524.3–715**
  Special administrators, **524.3–616**
Management of property, **524.3–709**
Marriage,
  Dissolution, annulment or separation, effect, **524.2–802**
  Elective share, surviving spouse, **524.2–201**
  Personal representatives, dissolution of marriage, former spouse, **524.2–804**
Mechanics liens, jurisdiction of foreclosure, **524.3–105**
Medical assistance, claims against estates, **524.3–805, 525.312, 525.313**
Medical expenses,
  Last illness, claims against estate, **524.3–805**
  Small estates, summary administration, **524.3–1203, 524.3–1204**
Mentally ill persons, probate judge, distribution, conservator or guardian, **524.3–915**
Merger, corporation or business enterprise, **524.3–715**
Minerals, lease for exploration or removal, **524.3–715**
Minors. Children and minors, generally, ante
Misrepresentation. Fraud, generally, ante
Missing persons. Absence and absentees, generally, ante
Mistake,
  Burden of proof, **524.3–407**
  Omitted or incorrectly described property, formal testacy proceedings, **524.3–413**
Money, transactions, **524.3–715**
Mortgages, **524.3–715**
  Decedents net probate estate, elective share, spouse, **524.2–204**
  Foreclosure,
    Guardians or conservators, **525.37**
    Recovery of indebtedness, **525.38**
  Personal representatives, post
Motions, supervised administration, **524.3–501**
Motor vehicles,
  Allowances to spouse, **525.15**
  Certificate of title, new, **524.3–1201**
Multiparty accounts,
  Collection by affidavit, **524.3–1201**
  Limitation of actions, **524.6–207**
  Nonprobate transfers on death, **524.6–201 et seq.**
Murder, killer disinherited, **524.2–803**

PROBATE

I–82

PROBATE

PROBATE PROCEEDINGS—Cont'd
Orders—Cont'd
 Foreign countries, transfer of property to diplomatic or consular representatives, **525.484**
 Formal testacy and appointment proceedings, ante
 Informal probate and appointment proceedings, ante
 Interested persons bound by orders, **524.3–106**
 Interim orders, proceedings affecting devolution and administration, **524.3–105**
 Issuance, **525.095**
 Nonresident decedent, **524.4–207**
 Notice, demand, **524.3–204**
 Partial intestacy, **524.3–411**
  Finality of order, **524.3–412**
 Personal representatives, post
 Restraining orders, **524.3–607**
 Special administrators, appointment, **524.3–614**
 Supervised administration of estates, post
 Transfer of property, **524.3–711**
Partial decrees, medical assistance, claims, clearance, **525.313**
Partial distributions, **524.3–105**
 Supervised administration, interim order, **524.3–505**
Partial intestacy, **524.3–411**
Parties, claims against estates, **573.11**
 Joinder, heirs, **573.21**
Partition,
 Assets, **524.3–715**
 Distribution, **524.3–911**
Party walls, disposition, **524.3–715**
Patents, public lands, **525.88, 525.881**
Payment,
 Calls, assessments, securities, **524.3–715**
 Claims and taxes, closing estate, **524.3–1003**
  Proper application, **524.3–714**
 Foreign personal representatives, **524.4–202, 524.4–203**
 Order, small estates, **524.3–1203**
 Successors, indebtedness, **524.3–1201, 524.3–1202**
 Unsecured debts, recovery of property transferred, **524.3–710**
Payors and third parties, protection, elective share, spouses, **524.2–214**
Pendency of actions,
 Application of law, **524.8–101**
 Distribution of assets, **524.3–703**
 No proceedings pending, certificate of administration, **524.3–1007**
 Supervised administration pending stay of informal application, **524.3–503**
Perjury, documents filed, **524.1–310**
Person under legal disability, distribution of estates, **524.3–915**
Personal representatives, **524.3–601 et seq.**
 Accountability of person receiving personal property, **524.3–1202**

PROBATE PROCEEDINGS—Cont'd
Personal representatives—Cont'd
 Accounts and accounting, generally, ante
 Acting personal representatives, restraining order, **524.3–401**
 Actions and proceedings,
  Bond of representative, **524.3–606**
  Standing to sue, **524.3–703**
 Adverse or pecuniary interest, **524.3–713**
 Age, renunciation of right, **524.3–203**
 Agent, conflict of interest, **524.3–713**
 Ambassadors and consuls, notice of hearings, mailing, **525.83**
 Ancillary personal representative, appointment, **524.3–611**
 Annulment, former spouse, **524.2–804**
 Appointment, **524.3–103**
  Acceptance, **524.3–103**
   Jurisdiction of court, **524.3–602**
   Statement, **524.3–601**
  Ancillary personal representative, **524.3–611**
  Application for appointment,
   Formal proceeding, **524.3–414**
   Informal appointment, **524.3–307**
  Application not made, delivery of personal property to successor, **524.3–1201**
  Authority to distribute intestate asset, **524.3–703**
  Bond not filed, **524.3–605**
  Coexecutors, exercise of powers, **524.3–718**
  Combining proceedings, **524.3–107**
  Commencement of proceedings, **524.3–104**
  Continuing to hold appointment, **524.8–101**
  Defects in notice, validity of appointment, **524.1–401**
  Foreign counties, **524.3–303**
  Informal probate and appointment proceedings, generally, ante
  Misrepresentation, removal from office, **524.3–611**
  Nonresident decedent, **524.4–207**
  Petition not made, delivery of property to successor, **524.3–1201**
  Priority, **524.3–203**
  Qualifications, formal proceeding, **524.3–414**
  Request, formal testacy proceeding, **524.3–401**
  Special administrators, **524.3–614 et seq.**
  Stay of informal appointment proceedings, **524.3–414**
  Subsequently discovered estate, **524.3–1008**
  Subsequently probated will, **524.3–612**
  Succeeding other personal representative, **524.3–301**
  Successor personal representatives, **524.3–613**
   Bond not filed, **524.3–605**
  Validity of appointment, affected by defects in notice or publication, **524.1–401**
 Appraisal and appraisers, generally, ante

I–83

PROBATE

PROBATE

PROBATE

PROBATE

PROBATE PROCEEDINGS—Cont'd
Unclaimed assets, **524.3–914**
Undue influence, burden of proof, **524.3–407**
Uniform Estate Tax Apportionment Act, **524.3–916**
Uniform Nonprobate Transfers on Death Act, **524.6–201 et seq.**
Uniform Simultaneous Death Act, **524.2–702**
Uniform Transfer on Death Security Registration Act, **524.6–301 et seq.**
Unincorporated business, continuing, **524.3–715**
Unitization agreement, minerals or natural resources, **524.3–715**
Unliquidated claims, **524.3–810**
Unrevoked wills,
    Formally probated, **524.3–409**
    Not probated, evidence of devise, **524.3–102**
Unsecured debts, payment, recovery of transferred property, **524.3–710**
Vacations, plats, **524.3–715**
Valid wills, formally probated, **524.3–409**
Validity of will, final order of foreign court, **524.3–408**
Value of estates,
    Adjusting differences, **524.3–715**
    Affidavit of successor, collection of personal property, **524.3–1201**
    Appraiser, **524.3–707**
    Distribution in kind, **524.3–906**
    Elective shares, surviving spouse, **524.2–207, 524.2–208**
    Small estates, summary administration, statement, **524.3–1204**
    Supplementary inventory or appraisement, **524.3–708**
Value of property distributed, distribution in kind, liability, **524.3–909**
Valueless property, abandonment, **524.3–715**
Ventures, continuing, **524.3–715**
Venue, **524.1–303, 524.3–201**
    Burden of proof, contested cases, **524.3–407**
    Formal testacy and appointment proceedings, ante
    Informal probate and appointment proceedings, ante
    Proper venue, determination, **524.3–409**
Verdict, advisory, **524.1–306**
Verification, documents filed, **524.1–310**
Voidable transfer of property, adverse or pecuniary interest, **524.3–713**
Voting stocks or securities, **524.3–715**
Waiver,
    Bond of personal representative, demand after, **524.3–605**
    Distribution in kind, objections, **524.3–906**
    Elective share, spouse, **524.2–213**
    Hearing, petition settling estate, **524.3–1001**
    Notice, **524.1–402, 524.3–204**
    Trial by jury, **524.1–306**
Warrants for payment of money, foreign countries, transfer of property to diplomatic or consular representatives, **525.484**
Wearing apparel, allowances to spouse, **525.15**

PROBATE PROCEEDINGS—Cont'd
Widows and widowers. Surviving spouses, generally, ante
Wrongful death actions, **524.3–105**

PROCEEDINGS
Actions and Proceedings, generally, this index

PROCESS
Attachment, generally, this index
Conservators and conservatorships, service of process, petitions, hearings, **524.5–404**
Executions, generally, this index
Foreign personal representatives, **524.4–303**
Injunctions, generally, this index
Nonresident personal representatives, service, **524.4–303**
Notice, generally, this index
Personal representatives. Probate Proceedings, this index
Power of attorney, statutory short form, **523.23, 523.24**
Probate Proceedings, this index
Registered mail, foreign personal representatives, service, **524.4–303**
Service of process, conservators and conservatorships, petitions, hearings, **524.5–404**
Statutory short form power of attorney, **523.23, 523.24**

PROFESSIONAL SERVICES
Attorneys, generally, this index
Physicians and Surgeons, generally, this index

PROFESSIONS AND OCCUPATIONS
Accountants, generally, this index
Attorneys, generally, this index
Nurses and Nursing, generally, this index

PROFITS
Accumulation, future interest, **500.17**
Trusts and Trustees, this index

PROMISSORY NOTES
Negotiable Instruments, generally, this index

PROMOTION
Tax shelters, abusive, penalties, **289A.60**

PROOF
Evidence, generally, this index

PROOF OF DEATH
Definitions, nonprobate transfers, **524.6–201**

PROOF OF DEATH ACCOUNTS
Nonprobate transfers on death, **524.6–201 et seq.**

PROPERTY
Attachment, generally, this index
Children and minors, transfers to minors, **527.21 et seq.**
Custodian, transfers to minors, **527.21 et seq.**
Definitions,
    Elective share, surviving spouse, **524.2–201**

PROPERTY

PROPERTY—Cont'd
Definitions—Cont'd
 Uniform Probate Code, **524.1–201**
Estate Tax—Federal, generally, this index
Estate Taxes, generally, this index
Perpetuities, generally, this index
Personal Property, generally, this index
Real Estate, generally, this index
Rule against perpetuities. Perpetuities, generally, this index
Taxation. Sales and Use Tax, generally, this index
Trusts and Trustees, this index

PROPERTY TAX REFUND RETURN PREPARERS
Tax Return Preparers, generally, this index

PROPERTY TAX REFUNDS
Amended returns, federal changes, **289A.38**
Claims, time, **289A.40**
Disallowance, fraudulent claims, **289A.60**
Federal changes, amended returns, **289A.38**
Fines and penalties, fraudulent claims, **289A.60**
Frivolous returns, fines and penalties, **289A.60**
Late claim filing, disallowance of claim, **289A.60**
Manufactured homes or manufactured home parks, claims, **289A.60**
Return preparers. Tax Return Preparers, generally, this index
Returns, amended returns, federal changes, **289A.38**
Tax Return Preparers, generally, this index
Time, claims, **289A.40**

PROSECUTION
Crimes and Offenses, generally, this index

PROTECTED PERSONS
Definitions, guardianships and conservatorships, **524.5–102**

PROTECTIVE PROCEEDINGS FOR MINORS AND DISABLED PERSONS
Probate Proceedings, this index

PROTEST
Negotiable Instruments, this index

PROXIES
Adult health care, living wills, **145B.06**
 Medical information, access, **145B.08**
Health care, living wills, adults, **145B.06**
 Medical information, access, **145B.08**
Living wills, **145B.04, 145B.06**
 Medical information, access, **145B.08**
Probate proceedings, **524.3–715**
Shares and shareholders, probate proceedings, **524.3–715**

PRUDENT INVESTOR ACT
Generally, **501B.151**

PSYCHIATRISTS AND PSYCHIATRY
Mentally Ill Persons, generally, this index

PSYCHOPATHIC PERSONALITIES
Mentally Ill Persons, generally, this index

PSYCHOTIC PERSONALITIES
Mentally Ill Persons, generally, this index

PUBLIC ACCOUNTANTS
Accountants, generally, this index

PUBLIC BUILDINGS
Buildings and Building Regulations, generally, this index

PUBLIC BURIAL GROUNDS
Cemeteries and Dead Bodies, generally, this index

PUBLIC CEMETERIES
Cemeteries and Dead Bodies, generally, this index

PUBLIC CORPORATIONS
Cemeteries and Dead Bodies, generally, this index
Retirement and Pensions, generally, this index

PUBLIC DOMAIN
Public Lands, generally, this index

PUBLIC EXAMINER
Accountants, generally, this index

PUBLIC GROUNDS
Public Lands, generally, this index

PUBLIC LANDS
Claims, tree claims, determination of heirs or devisees, **525.881**
Death of patentee before issuance of patent, determination of heirs or devisees, **525.881**
Homesteads, determination of heirs or devisees, **525.881**
Intestate succession, state patents, **525.88**
Land Patents, generally, this index
Mines and Minerals, generally, this index
Patents. Land Patents, generally, this index
Probate proceedings, state patents, **525.88**
Title to property,
 Listing of title in heirs, **525.88**
 Vesting in heirs, **525.88**
Tree claims, determination of heirs or devisees, **525.881**

PUBLIC POLICY
Corporate farming, **500.24**

PUBLIC PROPERTY
Public Lands, generally, this index

PUBLIC RECORDS
Records and Recordation, generally, this index

PUBLIC WELFARE
Social Services, generally, this index

RECEIVERS

REFUNDS
Corporate Income Tax, this index
Estate Taxes, this index
Income Tax—State, this index
Sales and Use Tax, this index
Taxation, bad debts, **289A.50**

REGISTERED NURSES
Nurses and Nursing, generally, this index

REGISTERING ENTITY
Definitions, transfer on death security registration, **524.6–301**

REGISTERS
Definitions, transfer on death security registration, **524.6–301**

REGISTRARS
Definitions, Uniform Probate Code, **524.1–201**
Probate Proceedings, this index

REGISTRATION
Agricultural land, foreign ownership, **500.221**
Custodial trusts, **529.06**
Foreign ownership, agricultural lands, **500.221**
Sales and Use Tax, this index
Securities, this index
Transfer on death security registration, **524.6–301 et seq.**
Vital Statistics, this index

REGISTRATION OF VOTERS
Elections, this index

REGISTRY
Registration, generally, this index

REGISTRY SYSTEM
International wills, **524.2–1010**

REGULATED INVESTMENT COMPANY
Definitions, exempt free dividends, income tax returns, **289A.12**
Trusts, principal and income, **501B.64**

REHABILITATION
Guardian and ward, powers and duties, **524.5–313**

RELATIVES
Conservators and conservatorships,
Compensation and salaries, **524.5–413**
Conflict of interest, **524.5–423**
Costs, actions for assets, **573.08**
Power of attorney, statutory short form, **523.23, 523.24**
Statutory short form power of attorney, **523.23, 523.24**

RELEASE
Definitions, power of appointment over property held in trust, **502.79**
Power of appointment held in trust, **502.79**
Power of attorney, statutory short form, **523.23, 523.24**

RELEASE—Cont'd
Probate proceedings, recovery of indebtedness, **525.38**
Statutory short form power of attorney, **523.23, 523.24**

RELIEF
Indigent Persons, generally, this index
Social Services, generally, this index

RELIGIOUS CORPORATIONS AND ASSOCIATIONS
Charitable Trusts, generally, this index
Power of attorney, statutory short form, **523.23, 523.24**
Statutory short form power of attorney, **523.23, 523.24**

RELIGIOUS FARM
Definitions, corporate farming, **500.24**

RELIGIOUS SOCIETIES
Religious Corporations and Associations, generally, this index

REMAINDERPERSON
Definitions, trusts, **501B.59**

REMAINDERS
Generally, **500.10, 500.11**
Agriculture, continuation of leases after death of life tenant, **500.25**
Contingent Remainders, generally, this index
Definitions, **500.11**
Limited on life estate created in term of years, **500.11**
Posthumous child,
Defeating remainder contingent of death without issue, **500.14**
Remainderman, **500.14**
Time of vesting, **500.11**
Transfer, **500.11**
Transferability, **500.16**
Vesting by purchase, **500.14**

REMARRIAGE
Marriage, this index

RENTAL HOUSING
Landlord and Tenant, generally, this index

RENTS
Credits. Property Tax Refunds, generally, this index
Life estate, termination, **500.25**
Property Tax Refunds, generally, this index
Receivers and receivership, appointments, **576.01**
Safe Deposit Companies and Boxes, generally, this index
Taxation. Property Tax Refunds, generally, this index
Trusts and Trustees, this index

SAFE

SAFE DEPOSIT COMPANIES AND BOXES
—Cont'd

Loss, limitation of liability, **55.12**

Negligence, limitation of liability, **55.12**

Notice,
> Death of tenant, liability for permitting access to box, **55.10**
> Forfeitures, **55.06**
> Intention to revoke license for violation of law, **55.095**

Order of court, liability for permitting access to box, **55.10**

Place of business, unlawful to engage in business in any place other than that designated in license, **55.04**

Power of attorney, statutory short form, **523.23, 523.24**

Powers, **55.02**

Presumption of dealing with tenant in individual and not in representative capacity, **55.11**

Probate proceedings, collection of assets, **524.3–1201, 524.3–1202**

Savings associations, **55.06**

Savings Banks, this index

Statutory short form power of attorney, **523.23, 523.24**

Stipulations, limitation of liability, **55.12**

Supervision and control by commissioner of banks, **55.095**

Taking possession by commissioner for violation of law, **55.095**

Trust companies, **55.06, 55.095**
> Application of law relating to safe deposit companies, **55.15**
> License and bond requirement, **55.06**

Trust relationship of tenant, company not charged with notice of, **55.11**

Valuable personal property defined, **55.01**

Wills, death of tenant, access, **55.10**

Writing, application for license, **55.04**

SAFETY DEPOSIT COMPANIES AND BOXES

Safe Deposit Companies and Boxes, generally, this index

SAILORS

Military Forces, generally, this index

SALARIES

Compensation and Salaries, generally, this index

SALES

Alcoholic Beverages, this index

Banks and Banking, this index

Bona Fide Purchasers, generally, this index

Conservators and Conservatorships, this index

Coroners sale of decedents property, **525.393**

Estate taxes, payment, **291.16**

Notice, decedents property by coroner, **525.393**

Personal representatives. Probate Proceedings, this index

Power of attorney, statutory short form, **523.23, 523.24**

SALES—Cont'd

Probate Proceedings, this index

Receivers, Absentees property, assets subject to likely rapid decline in value, **576.12**

Securities, generally, this index

Statutory short form power of attorney, **523.23, 523.24**

Subdivisions, generally, this index

Taxation. Sales and Use Tax, generally, this index

Trustees Powers Act, **501B.79 et seq.**

Trusts and Trustees, this index

Wills, this index

SALES AND USE TAX

Accelerated payment, **289A.60**

Accomplices and accessories, understatement of liability, fines and penalties, **289A.60**

Advertisements, this index

Assessments, **289A.35**
> Excess of amount reported on return, **289A.37**
> Reportable transactions, **289A.38**
> Time, **289A.38, 289A.40**

Audits and auditors, **289A.35**

Bad debts,
> Certified service provider, **289A.50**
> Refunds, **289A.50**

Bankruptcy, suspension of time, collection, **289A.41**

Capital Equipment, this index

Certificates and certification. Exemptions, post

Certified service provider, bad debts, **289A.50**

Collection,
> Criminal penalties, **289A.63**
> Notice, refunds, **289A.50**
> Time, **289A.38, 289A.40**

Consolidated returns, fines and penalties, **289A.60**

Credit, bad debts, **289A.50**

Crimes and offenses, penalties, **289A.63**

Decedents estates, liability, **289A.31**

Delinquencies, fines and penalties, **289A.60**

Disclosure,
> Reportable transactions, **289A.38**
> Tax shelters, **289A.121**

Due date, payment, **289A.20**

Electronic payment, **289A.20**

Errors, **289A.37**

Estates of decedents, personal liability, **289A.31**

Evidence, presumptions, validity of assessment, **289A.37**

Exemptions,
> Certificates and certification, fines and penalties, **289A.60**
> Transactions, refunds, **289A.50**

Extension of time,
> Consent, **289A.42**
> Filing returns, **289A.19**
> Interest, **289A.55**

Failure to file return, time for assessment, **289A.38**

False or fraudulent return, time for assessment, **289A.38**

SATISFACTION

SELF

STATE

TAX

TRANSFER

TRANSFER OF PROPERTY
Probate Proceedings, this index

TRANSFER ON DEATH SECURITY REGISTRA-TION ACT
Generally, **524.6–301 et seq.**

TRANSFER TAXES
Estate Tax—Federal, generally, this index
Estate Taxes, generally, this index

TRANSFEROR
Definitions,
    Custodial trusts, **529.01**
    Transfers to minors, **527.21**

TRANSFERS TO MINORS ACT
Generally, **527.21 et seq.**

TREATIES
Agricultural lands, aliens, acquisition, **500.221**

TREBLE DAMAGES
Damages, this index

TREES
Timber and Lumber, generally, this index

TRIAL
    See, also, Jury, generally, this index
Appearance, generally, this index
Bias of jurors. Jury, generally, this index
Evidence, generally, this index
Judgments and Decrees, generally, this index
Jurisdiction, generally, this index
Place of trial. Venue, generally, this index
Pleadings, generally, this index
Process, generally, this index
Supersedeas or Stay, generally, this index
Third Parties, generally, this index
Venue, generally, this index
Verdicts,
    Advisory verdict, probate proceedings,
        524.1–306
    Probate proceedings, advisory verdict,
        524.1–306
    Uniform Probate Code, advisory verdict,
        524.1–306
Waiver of jury trial. Jury, this index
Witnesses, generally, this index

TROVER
Conversion, generally, this index

TRUST COMPANIES
    See, also, Banks and Banking, generally, this
        index
Accounts and accounting,
    Custodial liability, **527.39**
    Multiparty accounts, **524.6–201 et seq.**
    Nonprobate transfers on death, **524.6–201 et seq.**
Acknowledgments, children and minors, custo-
    dial property, **527.28**
Application of law, custodial property, **527.41 et seq.**

TRUST COMPANIES—Cont'd
Appointments, custodians, transfers to minors,
    527.23
Bonds (officers and fiduciaries), custodial prop-
    erty, **527.38**
Care, children and minors, custodial property,
    527.32
Certificates and certification, fiduciaries, securi-
    ty transfers, central depository, **520.32**
Certificates of deposit, nonprobate transfers on
    death, **524.6–201 et seq.**
Children and minors, transfer of property,
    527.21 et seq.
Commingling funds, children and minors, cus-
    todial property, **527.32**
Compensation and salaries, children and mi-
    nors, custodial property, **527.35**
Custodial trusts, **529.01 et seq.**
Custodian, fiduciaries, security transfers, cen-
    tral depository, **520.32**
Death,
    Custodial property, **527.38**
    Nonprobate transfers on death, **524.6–201 et seq.**
Definitions,
    Custodial trusts, **529.01**
    Transfers to minors, **527.21**
Deposits, nonprobate transfers on death,
    524.6–201 et seq.
Discharge, nonprobate transfers on death,
    524.6–211
Disclaimer, custodial property, **527.38**
Domicile and residence, children and minors,
    gifts, **527.22**
Expenses and expenditures, children and mi-
    nors, custodial property, **527.35**
Fiduciaries,
    Custodial trusts, **529.01 et seq.**
    Securities transfers, central depository,
        520.32
Forms, children and minors, gifts, **527.29**
Inspections and inspectors, children and mi-
    nors, custodial property, **527.32**
Insurance, this index
Investment Companies, generally, this index
Jurisdiction, children and minors, gifts, **527.22**
Managing agent, fiduciaries, securities trans-
    fers, central depository, **520.32**
Nominations, custodians, transfers to minors,
    527.23
Notice, commissioner of intention to conduct
    safe deposit company business, **55.15**
Oaths and affirmations, **527.23**
Payment, children and minors, custodial prop-
    erty, **527.34**
Power of attorney, statutory short form, **523.23, 523.24**
Powers and duties, children and minors, custo-
    dial property, **527.33**
Powers of appointment, children and minors,
    gifts, **527.24**
Privileges and immunities, custodial property,
    527.36, 527.37

TRUST COMPANIES—Cont'd
Receipts, children and minors, custodial property, **527.28**
Receiving valuable personal property for safe keeping, license and bond, **55.06**
Records and recordation,
 Children and minors, custodial property, **527.32**
 Fiduciaries, securities transfers, central depository, **520.32**
Removal, custodial property, **527.38**
Resignation, custodial property, **527.38**
Safe Deposit Companies and Boxes, this index
Securities,
 Fiduciaries, central depository, **520.32**
 Fiduciary capacity, federal reserve banks, deposits, **520.33**
Single custodianship, children and minors, **527.30**
Standard of care, children and minors, custodial property, **527.32**
Statutory short form power of attorney, **523.23, 523.24**
Successor custodian, children and minors, gifts, **527.38**
Survivorship, nonprobate transfers on death, **524.6–201 et seq.**
Termination, custodianship, **527.40**
Transfers, property, children and minors, **527.21 et seq.**
Validity, children and minors, gifts, **527.31**

TRUST DEEDS
Mortgages, generally, this index

TRUSTEES
Trusts and Trustees, generally, this index

TRUSTEES POWERS ACT
Generally, **501B.79 et seq.**

TRUSTS AND TRUSTEES
Generally, **501B.01 et seq.**
Accounts and accounting, **501B.23**
 Compromise and settlement, **501B.154**
 Custodial liability, **527.39**
 Custodial trusts, **529.14**
  Multiple beneficiaries, **529.05**
 Sole proprietorships, **501B.665**
Accumulation of rents and profits, **500.17**
Acknowledgments, children and minors, custodial property, **527.28**
Actions and proceedings,
 Charitable trusts, enforcement, **501B.41**
 Combined proceedings, **501B.53**
 Death, **573.02**
 Powers and duties, **501B.81**
Actual notice, certificate of trust, **501B.56**
Additional trustees, appointment, **501B.14**
Additions to assets, **501B.81**
Adjustment, **501B.705**
Administration, **501B.60**
 Charitable trusts, **501B.31**
 Delegation of powers and duties, **501B.152**

TRUSTS AND TRUSTEES—Cont'd
Administration—Cont'd
 Principal and Income Act, **501B.59 et seq.**
 Private foundations, **501B.32 et seq.**
 Prudent investor rule, **501B.151**
 Split interest trusts, **501B.32 et seq.**
Advances, powers and duties, **501B.81**
Affidavits, real property transactions, trustee, **501B.57**
Age of majority, application of law, **501B.88**
Agents, designation, **501B.152**
Agreements. Contracts, generally, post
Agricultural lands, foreign ownership, **500.221**
Alienation of property. Disposition of property, generally, post
Aliens, agricultural lands, acquisition, **500.221**
Allocation of income and principal, property subject to depletion, **501B.69**
Amendment, certificate of trust, **501B.56**
Annuities, allocation of principal and income, **501B.69**
Annulment of marriage, **501B.90**
Appeal and review,
 Orders regarding administration of trust, **501B.16, 501B.21**
 Prudent Investor Act, **501B.151**
Application of law,
 Age of majority, **501B.88**
 Certificate of trust, **501B.56**
 Custodial property, **527.41 et seq.**
 Custodial trusts, **529.18**
 Principal and Income Act, **501B.72, 501B.73**
 Prohibition, exercise of certain powers by trustee, **501B.14**
Appointment,
 Custodians, transfers to minors, **527.23**
 Guardian, minor or incompetent, **501B.19**
 Successor trustees, **501B.08**
 Trustees, confirmation, **501B.22**
Apportionment,
 Estate taxes, **524.3–916**
 Generation skipping transfer tax, **524.3–916**
 Income, **501B.59 et seq.**
Ascertainment, principal and income, **501B.59 et seq.**
Assets,
 Prudent Investor Act, **501B.151**
 Retention, **501B.81**
Attorney fees, charges against income and principal, **501B.71**
Attorney general, charitable trusts,
 Representation, **501B.31**
 Supervision, **501B.22**
Bank deposits and collections, disclaimer of interest, **501B.86 et seq.**
Beneficiary,
 Nonmerger of trusts, trustee as beneficiary, **501B.13**
 Representation, charitable trusts, attorney general, **501B.31**
 Trustee as beneficiary, distributions, **501B.14**
Bequests, determination of, charitable trusts, **501B.31**

TRUSTS

TRUSTS

TRUSTS